Computer Networks: An Open Source Approach

Computer Networks: An Open Source Approach

Ying-Dar Lin
National Chiao Tung University

Ren-Hung Hwang
National Chung Cheng University

Fred Baker
Cisco Systems, Inc.

The McGraw·Hill Companies

COMPUTER NETWORKS: AN OPEN SOURCE APPROACH

Published by McGraw-Hill, a business unit of The McGraw-Hill Companies, Inc., 1221 Avenue of the Americas, New York, NY 10020.

Some ancillaries, including electronic and print components, may not be available to customers outside the United States.

This book is printed on acid-free paper.

1 2 3 4 5 6 7 8 9 0 DOC/DOC 1 0 9 8 7 6 5 4 3 2 1

ISBN 978-0-07-337624-0
MHID 0-07-337624-8

Vice President & Editor-in-Chief: *Marty Lange*
Vice President EDP/Central Publishing Services: *Kimberly Meriwether David*
Global Publisher: *Raghothaman Srinivasan*
Senior Marketing Manager: *Curt Reynolds*
Development Editor: *Lorraine K. Buczek*
Senior Project Manager: *Jane Mohr*
Design Coordinator: *Brenda A. Rolwes*
Cover Designer: *Studio Montage, St. Louis, Missouri*
Cover Image: *The illustration "Packet Factory" was drafted by Ying-Dar Lin and then drawn by his 12-year-old daughter, Melissa Hou-Yun Lin. It mimics routing and forwarding at the control plane (up to the 3rd floor) and the data plane (up to the 2nd floor), respectively.*
Buyer: *Susan K. Culbertson*
Media Project Manager: *Balaji Sundararaman*
Compositor: *Glyph International*
Typeface: *10/12 Times LT Std*
Printer: *R. R. Donnelley*

All credits appearing on page or at the end of the book are considered to be an extension of the copyright page.

Library of Congress Cataloging-in-Publication Data

Lin, Ying–Dar.
Computer networks : an open source approach / Ying-Dar Lin, Ren-Hung Hwang, Fred Baker.
p. cm.
Includes bibliographical references and index.
ISBN-13: 978-0-07-337624-0 (alk. paper)
ISBN-10: 0-07-337624-8 (alk. paper)
1. Computer networks—Management. 2. Computer networks—Computer programs. 3. Open source software. I. Hwang, Ren-Hung. II. Baker, Fred, 1952- III. Title.
TK5105.5.L55 2011
004.6—dc22

2010047921

www.mhhe.com

Dedication

Dedicated to Our Sweet Families .... 3 wives and 8 children.

About the Authors

Ying-Dar Lin is Professor of Computer Science at National Chiao Tung University (NCTU) in Taiwan. He received his Ph.D. in Computer Science from UCLA in 1993. He spent his sabbatical year as a visiting scholar at Cisco Systems in San Jose in 2007–2008. Since 2002, he has been the founder and director of Network Benchmarking Lab (NBL, www.nbl.org.tw), which reviews network products with real traffic. He also cofounded L7 Networks Inc. in 2002, which was later acquired by D-Link Corp. His research interests include design, analysis, implementation, and benchmarking of network protocols and algorithms, quality of services, network security, deep packet inspection, P2P networking, and embedded hardware/software co-design. His work on "multi-hop cellular" has been cited over 500 times. He is currently on the editorial boards of *IEEE Communications Magazine, IEEE Communications Surveys and Tutorials, IEEE Communications Letters, Computer Communications,* and *Computer Networks.*

Ren-Hung Hwang is Research Distinguished Professor of Computer Science as well as director of Ching-Jiang Learning Center at National Chung Cheng University in Taiwan. He received his Ph.D. in Computer Science from the University of Massachusetts, Amherst, in 1993. He has published more than 150 international journal and conference papers in the computer networking area. His research interests include ubiquitous computing, P2P networking, next-generation wireless networks, and e-Learning. He was the program chair of the 10th International Symposium on Pervasive Systems, Algorithms, and Networks (I-SPAN) held in KaoHsiung, Taiwan, 2009. He is currently on the editorial board of the *Journal of Information Science and Engineering*. He received the Outstanding Teaching Award from National Chung Cheng University in 2002 and several Outstanding Communication and Network Courseware Design Awards from the Ministry of Education, Taiwan from 1998 to 2001. He currently also serves as a committee member of the IP Committee of TWNIC and the Criteria and Procedures Committee of the Institute of Engineering Education Taiwan (IEET).

Fred Baker has been active in the networking and communications industry since the late 1970s, working successively for CDC, Vitalink, and ACC. He is currently a Fellow at Cisco Systems. He was IETF chair from 1996 to 2001. He has chaired a number of IETF working groups, including Bridge MIB, DS1/DS3 MIB, ISDN MIB, PPP Extensions, IEPREP, and IPv6 Operations, and served on the Internet Architecture Board from 1996 to 2002. He has coauthored or edited around 40 RFCs and contributed to others. The subjects covered include network management, OSPF and RIPv2 routing, quality of service (using both the Integrated Services and

Differentiated Services models), lawful interception, precedence-based services on the Internet, and others. In addition, he has served as a member of the Board of Trustees of the Internet Society 2002–2008, having served as its chair from 2002 through 2006. He is also a former member of the Technical Advisory Council of the Federal Communications Commission. He currently co-chairs the IPv6 Operations Working Group in the IETF, and is a member of the Internet Engineering Task Force Administrative Oversight Committee.

Brief Contents

Contents

Chapter **4**

Internet Protocol Layer 223

Chapter 6

Application Layer 417

Preface

TRENDS IN NETWORKING COURSES

Technologies in computer networks have gone through many generations of evolution; many failed or faded away, some prevailed, and some are emerging today. The Internet technologies driven by TCP/IP currently dominate. Thus, a clear trend in organizing the content of courses in computer networks is to center around TCP/IP, adding *some* lower-layer link technologies and *many* upper-layer applications, while eliminating details about the faded technologies, and perhaps explaining why they faded away.

Textbooks on computer networking have also gone through several iterations of evolution, from traditional, and sometimes dry, protocol descriptions to the application-driven, top-down approach and the system-aspect approach. One trend is to explain more of the *why*, in addition to the *how,* for protocol behaviors so that readers can better appreciate various protocol designs. The evolution, however, shall continue.

GAP BETWEEN DESIGN AND IMPLEMENTATION

Another less clear trend is to add practical flavors to the protocol descriptions. Readers of other textbooks might not know *where* and *how* the protocol designs could be implemented. The net result is that when they do their research in the graduate schools they tend to simulate their designs for performance evaluation, instead of real implementation with real benchmarking. When they join the industry, they need to start from scratch to learn the implementation environment, skills, and issues. Apparently there is a *gap* between *knowledge* and *skills* for students trained by these textbooks. This gap could be bridged with *live running codes* easily accessible from the *open source* community.

AN OPEN SOURCE APPROACH

Almost all protocols in use today have implementations in the Linux operating system and in many open source packages. The Linux and open source communities have grown, and their applications predominate in the networking world. However, the abundant resources available there are *not yet leveraged* by the regular textbooks in computer science, and more specifically in computer networks. We envision a trend in textbooks for several courses that could leverage open source resources to narrow the gap between domain knowledge and hands-on skills. These courses include Operating Systems (with Linux kernel implementations as examples of process management, memory management, file system management, I/O management, etc.), Computer Organizations (with verilog codes in www.opencores.org as examples of processors, memory units, I/O device controllers, etc.), Algorithms (with GNU libraries as examples of classical algorithms), and Computer Networks (with open source codes as examples of protocol implementations). This text might prove to be an early example of this trend.

Our open source approach bridges the gap by *interleaving* the descriptions of protocol behaviors with vivid sample implementations extracted from open source packages. These examples are explicitly numbered with, say, Open Source Implementation 3.4. The source sites from which complete live examples can be downloaded are referred to in the text, so students can access them on the Internet easily. For example, immediately after explaining the concept of longest prefix matching in routing table lookup, we illustrate how the routing table is organized (as an ordered array of hash tables according to prefix lengths) and how this matching is implemented (as the *first* matching, since the matching process starts from the hash table with the longest prefixes) in the Linux kernel. This enables instructors to lecture on the design of routing table lookup and its implementation, and give sound hands-on projects to, for example, profile the bottleneck of routing table lookup or modify hash table implementation. We argue that this interleaving approach is better than a *separating* approach with a *second* course or text. It benefits the *average* students most because it ties together design and implementation, and the majority of students would not need a second course. With other textbooks, instructors, teaching assistants, and students have to make an extra effort to bridge this gap that has long been ignored, or in most cases, simply left untouched.

The protocol descriptions in this text are interleaved with 56 representative open source implementations, ranging from the Verilog or VHDL code of codec, modem, CRC32, CSMA/CD, and crypto, to the C code of adaptor driver, PPP daemon and driver, longest prefix matching, IP/TCP/UDP checksum, NAT, RIP/OSPF/BGP routing daemons, TCP slow-start and congestion avoidance, socket, popular packages supporting DNS, FTP, SMTP, POP3, SNMP, HTTP, SIP, streaming, P2P, to QoS features such as traffic shaper and scheduler, and security features such as firewall, VPN, and intrusion detection. This system-awareness is further fortified by *hands-on exercises* right at the end of each open source implementation and at the end of each chapter, where readers are asked to *run, search, trace, profile,* or *modify* the source codes of particular *kernel* code segments, *drivers,* or *daemons.* Students equipped with such system-awareness and hands-on skills, in addition to their protocol domain knowledge, can be expected to do more sound research works in academia and solid development works in industry.

WHY IS MORE IMPORTANT THAN *HOW*

This text was written with the idea that it is more important to understand *why* a protocol is designed a certain way than it is to know *how* it works. Many key concepts and underlying principles are illustrated before we explain how the mechanisms or protocols work. They include statelessness, control plane and data plane, routing and switching, collision and broadcast domains, scalability of bridging, classless and classful routing, address translation and configuration, forwarding versus routing, window flow control, RTT estimation, well-known ports and dynamic ports, iterative and concurrent servers, ASCII application protocol messages, variable-length versus fixed-field protocol messages, transparent proxy, and many others.

Misunderstandings are as important as understandings, and they deserve special treatment to identify them. We arrange each chapter to start with general issues to raise fundamental questions. We have added sidebars about Principles in Action, Historical Evolution, and Performance Matters. We end with unnumbered sections on Common Pitfalls (for common misunderstandings in the reader community), Further Readings, FAQs on big questions for readers to preview and review, and a set of hands-on and written exercises.

PREPARING THE AUDIENCE WITH SKILLS

Whether the instructors or students are familiar with Linux systems should not play a critical factor in adopting this textbook. The Linux-related hands-on skills are covered in Appendices B, C, and D. Three appendices equip readers with enough hands-on skills, including Linux kernel overview (with a tutorial on source code tracing), development tools (`vim`, `gcc`, `make`, `gdb`, `ddd`, `kgdb`, `cscope`, `cvs/svn`, `gprof/kernprof`, `busybox`, `buildroot`), and network utilities (`host`, `arp`, `ifconfig`, `ping`, `traceroute`, `tcpdump`, `wireshark`, `netstat`, `ttcp`, `webbench`, `ns`, `nist-net`, `nessus`). Appendix A also has a section introducing readers to open source resources. There is also a section on "A Packet's Life" in Chapter 1 to vividly illustrate the book's roadmap.

Lowering the barrier of adopting open source implementations is considered. Instead of code listing and explanation, it is structured into Overview, Block Diagram when needed, Data Structures, Algorithm Implementation, and Exercises. This provides for ease of adoption for both students and instructors.

PEDAGOGICAL FEATURES AND SUPPLEMENTS

Textbooks usually have a rich set of features to help readers and class support materials to help instructors. We offer a set of features and a set of class support materials, summarized as follows:

1. Fifty-six explicitly numbered Open Source Implementations for key protocols and mechanisms.
2. Four appendices on Who's Who in Internet and open source communities, Linux kernel overview, development tools, and network utilities.
3. Logically reasoned *why, where,* and *how* of protocol designs and implementations.
4. Motivating general issues at the beginning of each chapter with big questions to answer.
5. "A Packet's Life" from the server and router perspectives to illustrate the book's roadmap and show how to trace packet flows in codes.

6. "Common Pitfalls" illustrated at the end of each chapter, identifying common misunderstandings.
7. Hands-on Linux-based exercises in addition to written exercises.
8. Sixty-nine sidebars about historical evolution, principles, in action, and performance matters.
9. End-of-chapter FAQs to help readers identify key questions to answer and review after reading each chapter.
10. Class support materials, including PowerPoint lecture slides, solutions manual, and the text images in PowerPoint are available at the textbook Web site: www.mhhe.com/lin.

AUDIENCE AND COURSE ROADMAP

The book is intended to be a textbook in Computer Networks for senior undergraduates or first-year graduate students in computer science or electrical engineering. It could also be used by professional engineers in the data communication industry. For the undergraduate course, we recommend instructors cover only Chapters 1 through 6. For the graduate course, all chapters should be covered. For instructors who lecture both undergraduate and graduate courses, two other possible differentiations are heavier hands-on assignments and additional reading assignments in the graduate course. In either undergraduate or graduate courses, instructors could assign students to study the appendices in the first few weeks to get familiar with Linux and its development and utility tools. That familiarity could be checked by either a hands-on test or a hands-on assignment. Throughout the course, both written and hands-on exercises can be assigned to reinforce knowledge and skills.

The chapters are organized as follows:

- Chapter 1 offers background on the requirements and principles of networking, and then presents the Internet solutions to meet the requirements given the underlying principles. Design philosophies of the Internet, such as statelessness, connectionlessness, and the end-to-end argument are illustrated. Throughout the process, we raise key concepts, including connectivity, scalability, resource sharing, data and control planes, packet and circuit switching, latency, throughput, bandwidth, load, loss, jitter, standards and interoperability, routing and switching. Next we take Linux as an implementation of the Internet solutions to illustrate where and how the Internet architecture and its protocols are implemented into chips, drivers, kernel, and daemons. The chapter ends with a book roadmap and the interesting description of "A Packet's Life."
- Chapter 2 gives a concise treatment of the physical layer. It first offers conceptual background on analog and digital signals, wired and wireless media, coding, modulation, and multiplexing. Then it covers classical techniques and standards on coding, modulation, and multiplexing. Two open source implementations illustrate the hardware implementation of Ethernet PHY using 8B/10B encoding and WLAN PHY using OFDM.

- Chapter 3 introduces three dominant links: PPP, Ethernet, and WLAN. Bluetooth and WiMAX are also described. LAN interconnection through layer-2 bridging is then introduced. At the end, we detail the adaptor drivers that transmit and receive packets to and from the network interface card. Ten open source implementations, including hardware design of CRC32 and Ethernet MAC, are presented.
- Chapter 4 discusses the data plane and control plane of the IP layer. The data plane discussion includes IP forwarding process, routing table lookup, checksum, fragmentation, NAT, and the controversial IPv6, while the control plane discussion covers address management, error reporting, unicast routing, and multicast routing. Both routing protocols and algorithms are detailed. Twelve open source implementations are interleaved to illustrate how these designs are implemented.
- Chapter 5 moves up to the transport layer to cover the end-to-end, or host-to-host, issues. Both UDP and TCP are detailed, especially the design philosophies, behaviors, and versions of TCP. Then RTP for real-time multimedia traffic is introduced. A unique section follows to illustrate socket design and implementation where packets are copied between the kernel space and the user space. Ten open source implementations are presented.
- Chapter 6 covers both traditional applications, including DNS, Mail, FTP, Web, and SNMP, and new applications, including VoIP, streaming, and P2P applications. Eight open source packages that implement these eight applications are discussed.
- Chapter 7 touches on the advanced topic of QoS, where various traffic control modules such as policer, shaper, scheduler, dropper, and admission control are presented. Though the IntServ and DiffServ standard frameworks have not been widely deployed, many of these traffic control modules are embedded in products that are used every day. Hence they deserve a chapter. Six open source implementations are presented.
- Chapter 8 looks into network security issues ranging from access security (guarded by TCP/IP firewall and application firewall), data security (guarded by VPN), and system security (guarded by intrusion detection and antivirus). Both algorithms (table lookup, encryption, authentication, deep packet inspection) and standards (3DES, MD5, IPsec) are covered. Eight open source implementations are added.

ACKNOWLEDGMENTS

The draft of this text has gone through much evolution and revision. Throughout the process, many people have directly or indirectly contributed. First, many lab members and colleagues at National Chiao Tung University, National Chung Cheng University, and Cisco Systems, Inc., have contributed ideas, examples, and code explanations to this book. In particular, we would like to thank Po-Ching Lin, Shih-Chiang Weafon Tsao, Yi-Neng Lin, Huan-Yun Wei, Ben-Jye Chang, Shun-Lee Stanley Chang, Yuan-Cheng Lai, Jui-Tsun Jason Hung, Shau-Yu Jason Cheng,

Chia-Yu Ku, Hsiao-Feng Francis Lu, and Frank Lin. Without their inputs, we would not have been able to embed many interesting and original ideas into this book. We also thank the National Science Council (NSC) in Taiwan, the Industrial Technology Research Institute (ITRI), D-Link Corporation, Realtek Semiconductor Corporation, ZyXEL Corporation, Cisco Systems, Inc., and Intel Corporation for supporting our networking research in the past few years.

Next, we wish to thank the following who reviewed drafts of all or parts of the manuscript: Emmanuel Agu, Worcester Polytechnic University; Tricha Anjali, Illinois Institute of Technology; Ladislau Boloni, University of Central Florida; Charles Colbourn, Arizona State University; XiaoJiang Du, Temple University; Jiang Guo, California State University, Los Angeles; Robert Kerbs, California State Polytechnic University, Pomona; Fang Liu, The University of Texas-Pan American; Oge Marques, Florida Atlantic University; Mitchell Neilsen, Kansas State University; Mahasweta Sarkar, San Diego State University; Edwin Sloan, Hillsborough Community College; Ioannis Viniotis, North Carolina State University; Bin Wang, Wright State University; Daniel Zappala, Brigham Young University. Thanks also to Chih-Chiang Wang, National Kaohsiung University of Applied Sciences, who polished the manuscript grammatically.

Finally, we would like to thank the folks at McGraw-Hill who coached us through the editorial and production phases. A special thanks should go to our Global Publisher, Raghu Srinivasan, our Developmental Editor, Lorraine Buczek, our production Project Manager, Jane Mohr, and Project Manager, Deepti Narwat. They have been very supportive coaches throughout this endeavor.

McGraw-Hill Digital Offerings Include

McGraw-Hill Create™

Craft your teaching resources to match the way you teach! With McGraw-Hill Create™, www.mcgrawhillcreate.com, you can easily rearrange chapters, combine material from other content sources, and quickly upload content you have written like your course syllabus or teaching notes. Find the content you need in Create by searching through thousands of leading McGraw-Hill textbooks. Arrange your book to fit your teaching style. Create even allows you to personalize your book's appearance by selecting the cover and adding your name, school, and course information. Order a Create book and you'll receive a complimentary print review copy in 3–5 business days or a complimentary electronic review copy (eComp) via email in minutes. Go to www.mcgrawhillcreate.com today and register to experience how McGraw-Hill Create™ empowers you to teach *your* students *your* way.

McGraw-Hill Higher Education and Blackboard have teamed up.

Blackboard, the Web-based course-management system, has partnered with McGraw-Hill to better allow students and faculty to use online materials and activities to complement face-to-face teaching. Blackboard features exciting social learning and teaching tools that foster more logical, visually impactful and active learning opportunities for students. You'll transform your closed-door classrooms into communities where students remain connected to their educational experience 24 hours a day.

This partnership allows you and your students access to McGraw-Hill's Create™ right from within your Blackboard course—all with one single sign-on. McGraw-Hill and Blackboard can now offer you easy access to industry leading technology and content, whether your campus hosts it, or we do. Be sure to ask your local McGraw-Hill representative for details.

Electronic Textbook Options

This text is offered through CourseSmart for both instructors and students. CourseSmart is an online resource where students can purchase the complete text online at almost half the cost of a traditional text. Purchasing the eTextbook allows students to take advantage of CourseSmart's web tools for learning, which include full text search, notes and highlighting, and email tools for sharing notes between classmates. To learn more about CourseSmart options, contact your sales representative or visit www.CourseSmart.com.

Chapter 1

Fundamentals

Computer networking or *data communications* is a set of disciplines concerned with communication between computer systems or devices. It has its *requirements* and underlying *principles*. Since the first node of ARPANET (Advanced Research Project Agency Network, later renamed Internet) was established in 1969, the store-and-forward *packet switching* technologies formed the Internet architecture, which is *a* solution to meeting the requirements and underlying principles of data communications. This solution converged with the TCP/IP protocol suite in 1983 and continued to evolve thereafter.

The Internet, or the TCP/IP protocol suite, is just one possible solution that happens to be the dominant one. There are other solutions that also meet the requirements and satisfy the underlying principles of data communications. For example, X.25 and Open System Interconnection (OSI) were also developed in the 1970s but were eventually replaced by TCP/IP. Asynchronous Transfer Mode (ATM), once popular in the 1990s, has compatibility difficulties with TCP/IP and thus faded away. Multi-Protocol Label Switching (MPLS) survived because it was designed from the beginning to be complementary to TCP/IP.

Similarly, there are many implementations of the Internet solution on all sorts of computer systems or devices. Among them, the open-source implementations share the same *open* and *bottom-up* spirit as the Internet architecture, offering the public practical accessibility to the software's source code. In the bottom-up approach, volunteers contribute their designs or implementations while seeking support and consensus from the developer community, in contrast to the top-down approach driven by the authority. Being open-source and freely available, these implementations serve as solid *running* examples of how various networking mechanisms work in specific details.

In this chapter, we intend to acquaint readers with computer network fundamentals used throughout this text. Section 1.1 identifies key requirements for data communications by giving definitions of a computer network in terms of *connectivity, scalability,* and *resource sharing*. It also introduces the concept of packet switching. In Section 1.2, the underlying principles governing data communications are identified. Performance measures such as *bandwidth, offered load, throughput, latency, latency variation,* and *loss* are defined first. We then explain the design issues in *protocols* and *algorithms* used for processing *control packets* and *data packets*. As the Internet is one possible solution to computer networking, Section 1.3 describes the Internet's version of solutions to connectivity, scalability, and resource sharing as well as its control- and data-packet processing. Section 1.4 discusses how the open-source implementations further realize the Internet solution in running systems, especially in Linux. We show why and how various protocol and algorithm modules are implemented into the *kernel, drivers, daemons,* and *controllers* of a computer system. We plot the *roadmap* for this book in Section 1.5 by showing *a packet's life* traversing through various modules in a Web server and in an intermediate interconnection device. This section also lays a foundation for understanding the open-source implementations described in subsequent chapters. Contributors to the designs and open-source implementations of the Internet solution, along with other short-lived networking technologies, are reviewed in Appendix A as the supplementary materials to this chapter.

After reading this chapter, you should be able to explain (1) *why* the Internet solution was designed in the way it is, and (2) *how* this open solution was implemented in real systems.

1.1 REQUIREMENTS FOR COMPUTER NETWORKING

The set of requirements for computer networking can be translated into a set of *objectives* that must be met when designing, implementing, and operating a computer network. Over the years, this set did change gradually, but its core requirements remain the same: "connecting an ever increasing number of users and applications through various shared media and devices such that they can communicate with each other." This sentence indicates three requirements for data communications and the relevant issues to be addressed: (1) *connectivity:* who and how to connect, (2) *scalability:* how many to connect, and (3) *resource sharing:* how to utilize the connectivity. This section presents these core requirements and discusses generic solutions to meeting these requirements in most computer networks (not just the Internet).

1.1.1 Connectivity: Node, Link, Path

A computer network, from the aspect of connectivity, can be viewed as "a *connected graph* constructed from a set of *nodes* and *links,* where any pair of nodes can reach each other through a *path* consisting of a sequence of concatenated nodes and links." We need connectivity between human users to exchange messages or engage in conversation, between application programs to maintain the network operations, or between users and application programs to access data or services. Various media and devices can be used to establish connectivity between nodes, with the device being *hub, switch, router,* or *gateway* and the media being *wired* or *wireless*.

Node: Host or Intermediary

A node in a computer network can be either a *host computer* or an *intermediary interconnection device*. The former is an *end*-point computer that *hosts* users and applications, while the latter serves as an *intermediate* point with more than one link interface to interconnect host computers or other intermediaries. Devices such as hubs, switches, routers, and gateways are common examples of intermediaries. Unlike a computer-based host, an intermediary might be equipped with specially designed CPU-offloading hardware to boost the processing speed or to reduce the hardware and processing costs. As the link or wire speed increases, *wire-speed* processing requires either faster CPU or special hardware, e.g., application specific integrated circuit (ASIC), to offload the CPU.

Link: Point-to-Point or Broadcast

A link in a computer network is called *point-to-point* if it connects exactly *two* nodes with one on each end, or *broadcast* if it connects more than two attached nodes. The key difference is that nodes attached to a broadcast link need to *contend* for the right to transmit. Nodes communicating over a point-to-point link usually transmit as they wish if it is a *full-duplex* link; take turns to transmit if it is a *half-duplex* link; or utilize two links to transmit, one for each direction, if it is a *simplex* link. That is, a full-duplex link and a half-duplex link support simultaneous bidirectional and one-at-a-time bidirectional, respectively, while a simplex link supports unidirectional communication only.

The physical appearance of a link can be *wired* or *wireless,* be it point-to-point or broadcast. Usually links in local area networks (LANs), wired or wireless, are of broadcast type, while links in wide area networks (WANs) are point-to-point. This is because the multiple access methods used in broadcast links are usually more efficient over short distances, as we shall see in Chapter 3. However, exceptions do exist. For example, the satellite-based ALOHA system uses broadcast-type links for WANs. Ethernet, originally designed as broadcast links for LANs, has evolved into point-to-point in both LANs and WANs.

Wired or Wireless

For wired links, common media include twisted pairs, coaxial cables, and fiber optics. A twisted pair has two copper lines twisted together for better immunity to noise; they are widely used as the access lines in the plain old telephone system (POTS) and LANs such as Ethernet. A Category-5 (Cat-5) twisted pair, with a thicker gauge than the twisted pair for in-home POTS wiring, can carry 10 Mbps over a distance of several kilometers to 1 Gbps or higher over 100 meters or so. Coaxial cables separate a thicker copper line from a thinner nested copper wire with plastic shield, and are suitable for long-haul transmissions such as cable TV distribution of over 100 6-MHz TV channels for an area spanning 40 km wide. Through cable modems, some channels each can be digitized at the rate of 30 Mbps for data, voice, or video services. Fiber optics has large capacity and it can carry signals for much longer distances. Fiber optic cables are used mostly for backbone networks (Gbps to Tbps) and sometimes for local networks (100 Mbps to 10 Gbps).

For wireless links, there are radio ($10^4 \sim 10^8$ Hz), microwave ($10^8 \sim 10^{11}$ Hz), infrared ($10^{11} \sim 10^{14}$ Hz), and beyond (ultra-velvet, X ray, Gamma ray) in the increasing order of their transmission frequency. A low-frequency (below several GHz) wireless link is usually a broadcast one, which is *omnidirectional,* while a high-frequency (over tens of GHz) wireless link could be point-to-point, which is more directional. As wireless data communication is still in its booming stage, the prevailing systems include wireless LANs (54 Mbps to 600 Mbps data transfer rate within a 100-m radius), general packet radio service (GPRS) (128 kbps within a few km), 3G (3rd Generation, 384 kbps to several Mbps within a few km), and Bluetooth (several Mbps within 10 m), all operating within 800 MHz to 2 GHz microwave spectrum.

Historical Evolution: Link Standards

There are many link standards for data communications nowadays. We may classify links into the following categories: *local*, *last-mile*, and *leased lines*. Table 1.1 lists the names and data rates of these link standards. The local links are deployed for use in local area networks, where Category-5 (Cat-5)–based Ethernet and 2.4 GHz wireless LANs are two dominant technologies. The former is faster and has dedicated transmission channels over the Cat-5 twisted-pair wire, but the latter is simple to set up and has higher mobility.

TABLE 1.1 Popular Wired and Wireless Link Technologies

	Wired	Wireless
Local	Cat-5 twisted-pair Ethernet (10 Mbps ~ 1 Gbps)	2.4 GHz band WLAN (2 ~ 54 Mbps ~ 600 Mbps)
Last-mile	POTS (28.8 ~ 56 kbps) ISDN (64 ~ 128 kbps) ADSL (16 kbps ~ 55.2 Mbps) CATV (30 Mbps) FTTB (10 Mbps ~)	GPRS (128 kbps) 3G (384 kbps ~ several Mbps) WiMAX (40 Mbps)
Leased-line	T1 (1.544 Mbps) T3 (44.736 Mbps) OC-1 (51.840 Mbps) OC-3 (155.250 Mbps) OC-12 (622.080 Mbps) OC-24 (1.244160 Gbps) OC-48 (2.488320 Gbps) OC-192 (9.953280 Gbps) OC-768 (39.813120 Gbps)	

The so-called last-mile or first-mile links span the "first mile" from a home or a mobile user to an Internet service provider (ISP). Among the items in this category, asymmetric digital subscriber line (ADSL), cable TV (CATV), and fiber-to-the-block (FTTB) are the most popular wired link technologies, and 3G and WiMAX (Worldwide Interoperability for Microwave Access) are the most popular wireless technologies for the present. POTS and Integrated Service Digital Network (ISDN) are outdated technologies.

For wired technology, FTTB is faster than the others, but also more expensive. ADSL leverages traditional telephone lines, and its transfer rate degrades with increasing distance to the ISP. CATV leverages TV coaxial cables; it has less limitation in distance, but the bandwidth is shared with the TV programs' signals. If you need site-to-site connectivity that does not go through the public shared network, you can lease a dedicated line from a *carrier*. In North America, for example, leased line services from carriers include copper-based Digital Signal 1 (DS1, T1) and DS3 (T3), and various optical STS-x (synchronous transport signal, OC-x [optical carrier]) links. The latter option, though expensive, is becoming more popular since it can meet the increasing demand for bandwidth.

Path: Routed or Switched?

Any attempt to connect two remote nodes must first find a path, a sequence of concatenated intermediate links and nodes, between them. A path can be either *routed* or *switched*. When node *A* wants to send messages to node *B*, the messages are routed if they are transferred through non-preestablished and independently selected paths, perhaps through different paths. By routing, the destination address of the message is *matched* against a "routing" table to find the output link for the destination. This matching process usually requires several *table-lookup operations*, each of which costs one *memory access* and one *address comparison*. On the other hand, a switched path requires the intermediate nodes to establish the path and record the *state* information of this path in a "switching" table before a message can be sent. Messages to be sent are then attached with an *index number* which points to some specific state information stored in the "switching" table. Switching a message then becomes easy indexing into the table with just one memory access. Thus, switching is much faster than routing but at the cost of setup overhead.

We can view a routed path as a *stateless* or *connectionless* concatenation of intermediate links and nodes, a switched path as a *stateful* or *connection-oriented* concatenation. ATM has all its connections switched; that is, before the data begins to flow, a connection along a path between the source and the destination has to be established and memorized at all the intermediate nodes on the path. The Internet, in contrast, is stateless and connectionless, and Section 1.3 shall discuss the philosophy behind its connectionless design.

Historical Evolution: ATM Faded

ATM once was the presumed backbone switching technology for data communications. Unlike the Internet architecture, ATM adopted the concept of *stateful switching* from POTS: Its switches keep connection-oriented state information to decide how connections should be switched. Because ATM came up in the early 1990s, it had to find a way to coexist with the Internet architecture, the most dominant networking technology at that time. However, integrating connection-oriented switching with a connectionless routing technology creates lots of overhead. The integration of these two could take the form of internetworking the ATM domain with the Internet domain, or of a layered hybrid that uses ATM to carry the Internet packets. Both require finding existing ATM connections or establishing but later tearing down new ATM connections after sending out just a few packets. Moreover, the layered-hybrid approach brutally wrecks the stateless nature of the Internet architecture. Quickly or slowly, ATM is meant to be gone.

1.1.2 Scalability: Number of Nodes

Being able to connect 10 nodes is totally different from being able to connect millions of nodes. Since what could work on a small group does not necessarily work on a huge group, we need a *scalable* method to achieve the connectivity. Thus, a computer network, from the aspect of scalability, must offer "a scalable platform to a *large* number of nodes so that each node *knows* how to reach any other node."

Hierarchy of Nodes

One straightforward method to connect a huge number of nodes is to organize them into many groups, each consisting of a small number of nodes. If the number of groups is very large, we can further cluster these groups into a number of *supergroups,* which, if necessary, can be further clustered into *"super-supergroups."* This recursive clustering method creates a manageable tree-like hierarchical structure, where each group (or supergroup, "super-supergroup," etc.) connects with only a small number of other groups. If such clustering is not applied, the interconnection network for a huge number of nodes may look like a chaotic mesh. Figure 1.1

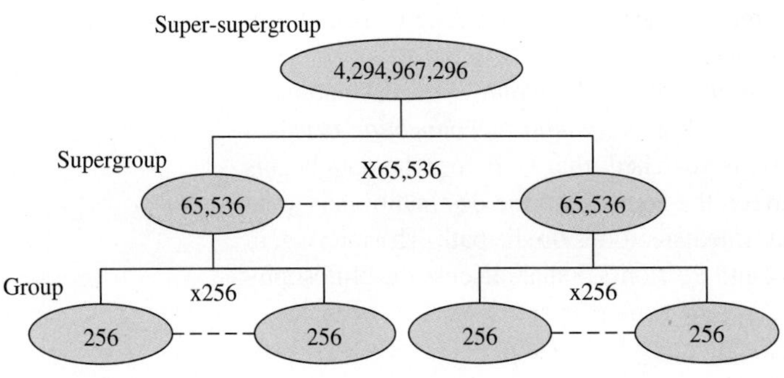

FIGURE 1.1 Hierarchy of nodes: grouping of billions of nodes in a three-level hierarchy.

illustrates how 4 billion nodes could be organized and connected into a simple three-level hierarchy, with 256 branches at the bottom and middle levels and 65,536 branches at the top level. As we shall see in Section 1.3, the Internet uses a similar clustering method where group and supergroup are termed subnet and domain, respectively.

LAN, MAN, WAN

It would be natural to form a bottom-level group with the nodes which reside within a small geographical area, say of several square kilometers. The network that connects the small bottom-level group is called a local area network (LAN). For a group of size 256, it would require at least 256 (for a ring-shaped network) and at most 32,640 point-to-point links (for a fully connected mesh) to establish the connectivity. Since it would be tedious to manage this many links in a small area, broadcast links thus come to play the dominant role here. By attaching all 256 nodes to a single broadcast link (with a bus, ring, or star topology), we can easily achieve and manage their connectivity. The application of a single broadcast link can be extended to a geographically larger network, say metropolitan area network (MAN), to connect remote nodes or even LANs. MANs usually have a *ring* topology so as to construct *dual buses* for fault tolerance to a link failure.

However, such a broadcast ring arrangement has put limitations on the degree of fault tolerance and on the number of nodes or LANs a network could support. Point-to-point links fit in naturally for unlimited, wide area connectivity. A wide area network (WAN) usually has a *mesh* topology due to the randomness in the locations of geographically dispersed network sites. A tree topology is inefficient in WAN's case because in a tree network, all traffic has to ascend toward the root and at some branch descend to the destination node. If the traffic volume between two leaf nodes is huge, a tree network might need an additional point-to-point link to connect them directly, which then creates a loop in the topology and turns the tree into a mesh.

In Figure 1.1, a bottom-level group by default is a LAN implemented as a *hub* or a *switch* connecting less than 256 hosts. A middle-level supergroup could be a campus or enterprise network with less than 256 LANs interconnected by *routers* into a tree or meshed structure. At the top level, there could be tens of thousands of supergroups connected by point-to-point links as a meshed WAN.

1.1.3 Resource Sharing

With scalable connectivity established, we now address how to share this connectivity, i.e., the capacities of links and nodes, with network users. Again, we can define a computer network, from the aspect of resource sharing, as "a *shared* platform where *capacities* of nodes and links are used to transfer *communication messages* between nodes." This is where data communications and the traditional voice communications differ most from each other.

Packet Switching vs. Circuit Switching

In POTS, a *circuit* between the caller and the callee has to be found and *switched* first before a voice conversation can begin. During the whole course of the conversation, the 64-kbps circuit has to be maintained between the conversing parties, even if both remain silent all the time. This kind of *dedicated* resource allocation is called *circuit switching,* which provides stable resource supplies and thus can sustain high quality in a *continuous* data stream such as video or audio signals. However, circuit switching is not suitable for data communications where interactive or file-transfer applications pump data whenever they want but remain idle most of the time. Apparently, allocating a dedicated circuit for such bursty traffic is very inefficient.

A more relaxed and efficient practice of resource sharing is to have all traffic compete for the right of way. However, with this practice, congestion resulting from bursty data traffic thus becomes inevitable. So how do we handle such traffic congestion? We *queue* it up! Putting *buffer* space at nodes can absorb most congestion caused by temporary data bursts, but if congestion persists for a long period of time, loss eventually will happen due to buffer overflow. This mode of *store-and-forward* resource sharing is called *packet switching* or *datagram switching,* where messages in data traffic are chopped into *packets* or *datagrams,* stored at the buffer queue of each intermediate node on the path, and forwarded along the path toward their destination.

POTS exercises circuit switching, whereas the Internet and ATM exercise packet switching. As explained in Section 1.1.1, ATM's paths are "switched" while the Internet's paths are "routed." It thus might confuse readers that the Internet has "routed" paths in the packet "switching" network. Unfortunately, this community does not differentiate these networking technologies by name. To be precise, the Internet runs packet routing while ATM and POTS run packet switching and circuit switching, respectively. In some sense, ATM imitates circuit switching with connection setup for better communication quality.

Packetization

To send out a message, some header information must be attached to the message to form a *packet* so that the network knows how to handle it. The message itself is then called the *payload* of the packet. The header information usually contains the source and destination addresses and many other fields to control the packet delivery process. But how large can packets and payload be? It depends on the underlying link technologies. As we shall see in Section 2.4, a link has its limit on the packet length, which could cause the sending node to fragment its message into smaller pieces and attach a header to each piece for transmission over the link, as illustrated in Figure 1.2. The packet headers would tell the intermediate nodes and the destination node how to deliver and how to reassemble the packets. With the header, each packet can be processed either totally independently or semi-independently when traversing through the network.

It is the *protocol* that defines and standardizes the header fields. By definition, a protocol is a set of standard rules for data representation, signaling, and error

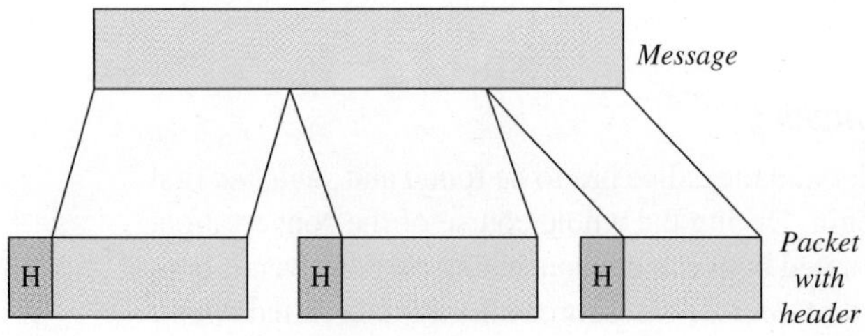

FIGURE 1.2 Packetization: fragmenting a message into packets with added headers.

detection required to send information over a communication channel. These standard rules define the header fields of protocol messages and how the receiving side should react upon receiving the protocol messages. As we shall see in Section 1.3, a message fragment might have been *encapsulated* with several layers of headers, each of which describes a set of protocol parameters and is added in front of its preceding header.

Queuing

As mentioned previously, network nodes allocate buffer queues to absorb the congestion caused by the bursty data traffic. Therefore, when a packet arrives at a node, it joins a buffer queue with other packet arrivals, waiting to be processed by the processor in the node. Once the packet moves to the front of the queue, it gets served by the processor, which figures out how to process the packet according to the header fields. If the node processor decides to forward it to another data-transfer port, the packet then joins another buffer queue waiting to be transmitted by the transmitter of that port. When a packet is being transmitted over a link, it takes some time to propagate the packet's data from one side to the other side of the link, be it point-to-point or broadcast. If the packet traverses through a path with 10 nodes and hence 10 links, this process will be repeated 10 times.

Figure 1.3 illustrates the queuing process at a node and the node's out-link, which can be modeled as a *queuing system* with a *queue* and a *server*. The server in a node is usually a processor or a set of ASICs whose service time depends on the clock rate of the nodal modules (e.g., CPU, memory, ASIC). On the other hand, the service time in a link is actually the sum of (1) the *transmission time,* which depends on how fast the transceiver (transmitter and receiver) can pump the data and how large the packet is, and (2) the *propagation time,* which depends on how long the transmitted signal has to propagate. The former stage at the node has only one server to process the packets, and the time the packet spends in this stage can be reduced by using faster transceivers. However, the latter stage at the link has a number of *parallel servers* (which is equivalent to the maximum number of allowed outstanding packets in the link), and the time consumed here *cannot* be reduced regardless of the adopted technologies. Signals propagate through any links at a speed around 2×10^8 m/sec. In conclusion, nodal processing time and transmission time, including their queuing times, can be further reduced as the technologies evolve, but the propagation time would remain fixed since its value is bounded by the speed of light.

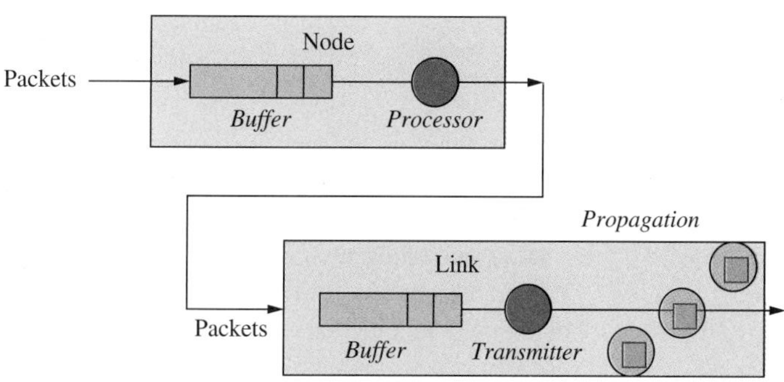

FIGURE 1.3 Queuing at a node and a link.

Principle in Action: Datacom vs. Telecom

Here is a good place to reemphasize the major differences between *datacom*, i.e., data communications or computer networking, and *telecom*, i.e., telecommunications, to finalize our discussions on the requirements for computer networking. Among connectivity, scalability, and resource sharing, they do not differ much from each other in scalability, but the main differences lie in the type of connectivity they employ and the way they share resources. The traditional telecom establishes only one type of connectivity between two communication parties, supporting one single application (telephony). On the other hand, there exists a wide spectrum of applications in datacom, which demands various types of connectivity. The connectivity may be set between two clients (e.g. telephony), between a client and a server process (e.g. file download or streaming), between two server processes (e.g., mail relay or content update), or even among a group of individuals or processes. Each application might have a unique traffic profile, either bursty or continuous. Unlike homogeneous and usually continuous telecom traffic, which is carried by the circuit-switching technology at high efficiency, datacom traffic requires packet switching to utilize resource sharing. However, compared to the *buffer-less* circuit switching where the call-blocking or call-dropping probability is the only major concern, packet switching introduces more complex performance issues. As we shall see in the next section, datacom needs to control buffer overflow or loss, throughput, latency, and latency variation.

1.2 UNDERLYING PRINCIPLES

As the underlying technology of data communications, packet switching has laid down the principles for data communications to follow. We can divide the set of principles into three categories: *performance,* which governs the quality of services of packet switching, *operations,* which details the types of mechanisms needed for packet handling, and *interoperability,* which defines what should be put into standard protocols and algorithms, and what should *not.*

1.2.1 Performance Measures

In this subsection, we provide fundamental background so that you can appreciate the rules of the packet switching game. This background is important when analyzing the behavior of a whole system or a specific protocol entity. To design and implement a system or protocol without knowing, *beforehand or afterward,* its performance measures under the common or extreme operational scenarios is not an acceptable practice in this area. Performance results of a system come either from mathematical analysis or system simulations *before* the real system is implemented, or from experiments on a test bed *after* the system has been implemented.

How a system performs, as perceived by a user, depends on three things: (1) the hardware *capacity* of the system, (2) the *offered load* or input traffic to this system, and (3) the internal *mechanisms* or *algorithms* built into this system to handle the offered load. A system with a high capacity but poorly designed mechanisms would not scale well when handling a heavy offered load, though it might perform fairly well with a light offered load. Nevertheless, a system with excellent designs but a small capacity should not be put at a point with heavy traffic volume. The hardware capacity is often called *bandwidth,* a common term in the networking area, be it a node, link, path, or even a network as a whole. The offered load of a system may vary, from light load, normal operational load, to extremely heavy load (say wire-speed stress load). There should be a close match between bandwidth and offered load, if the system is to stay in a *stable* operation while allowing the designed internal mechanisms to play the tricks to gain more performance. For packet switching, *throughput* (the output traffic as compared to the offered load of input traffic) appears to be the performance measure that concerns us most, though other measures such as *latency* (often called *delay*), *latency variation* (often called *jitter*), and *loss* are also important.

Bandwidth, Offered Load, and Throughput

The term "bandwidth" comes from the study of electromagnetic radiation, and originally refers to the width of a band of frequencies used to carry data. However, in computer networking the term is normally used to describe the maximum amount of data that can be handled by a system, be it a node, link, path, or network, in a certain period of time. For example, an ASIC might be able to encrypt 100 million bytes per second (MBps), a transceiver might be able to transmit 10 million bits per second (Mbps), and an end-to-end path consisting of five 100 Mbps nodes and five 10 Mbps links might be able to handle up to 10 Mbps given no other interfering traffic along the path.

One may think of the bandwidth of a link as the number of bits transmitted and *contained* in the distance propagated by the signal in one second. Since the speed of light in a medium is fixed at around 2×10^8 m/sec, higher bandwidth means more bits contained in 2×10^8 m. For a transcontinental link of 6000 miles (9600 km, with a propagation delay of 9600 km/(2×10^8 m) = 48 ms) with a bandwidth of 10 Gbps, the maximum number of bits contained in the link is thus 9600 km/(2×10^8 m) $\times$ 10 Gbps = 480 Mbits. Similarly, the "width" of a transmitted bit propagating on a link varies according to the link bandwidth, too. As shown in Figure 1.4, the bit width

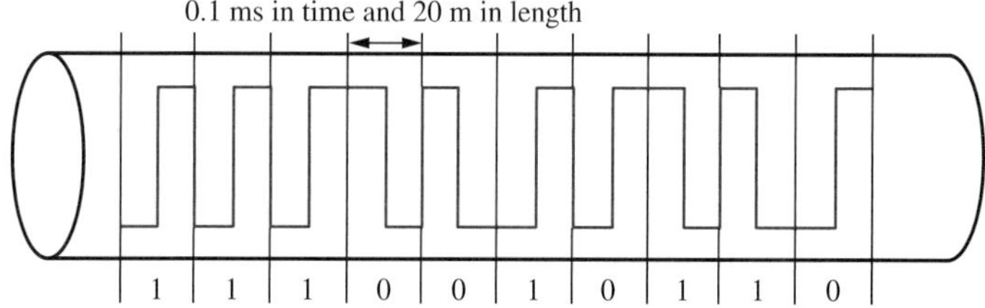

FIGURE 1.4 Bit width in time and length for a 10-Mbps link where the transmitted data are encoded by the widely used Manchester code.

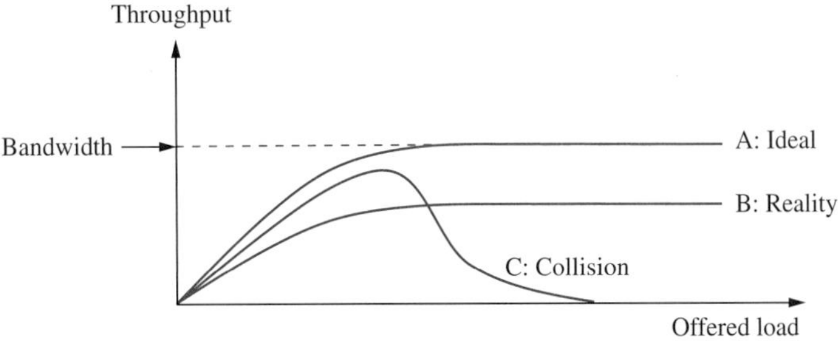

FIGURE 1.5 Bandwidth, offered load, and throughput.

in a 10-Mbps link is $1/(10 \times 10^6) = 0.1$ μs *in time,* or 0.1 μs $\times 2 \times 10^8$ m/sec = 20 m, *in length*. The signal wave of one bit actually occupies 20 meters in the link.

The offered load or input traffic can be *normalized* with respect to the bandwidth and used to indicate the *utilization* or how busy the system is. For a 10-Mbps link, an offered load of 5 Mbps means a normalized load of 0.5, meaning the link would be 50% busy on the average. It is possible for the normalized load to exceed 1, though it would put the system in an unstable state. The throughput or output traffic may or may not be the same as the offered load, as shown in Figure 1.5. Ideally, they should be the same before the offered load reaches the bandwidth (see curve A). Beyond that, the throughput converges to the bandwidth. But in reality, the throughput might be lower than the offered load (see curve B) due to buffer overflow (in a node or link) or collisions (in a broadcast link) even before the offered load reaches the bandwidth. In links with uncontrolled collisions, the throughput may drop down to zero as the offered load continues to increase, as plotted by curve C in Figure 1.5. With careful design, we might prevent that from happening by having the throughput converge to a value lower than the bandwidth.

Latency: Node, Link, Path

In addition to throughput, latency is another key measure we care about. *Queuing theory,* first developed by Agner Krarup Erlang in 1909 and 1917, tells us if both packet inter-arrival time and packet service time are *exponentially distributed* and the former is larger than the latter, plus infinite buffer size, the mean latency is the inverse of the difference between bandwidth and offered load, i.e.,

$$T = 1/(\mu - \lambda),$$

where μ is bandwidth, λ is offered load, and T is mean latency. Though in reality exponential distribution does not hold for real network traffic, this equation gives us a basic relationship between bandwidth, offered load, and latency. From the equation, latency will be halved if both bandwidth and offered load are doubled, which means larger systems usually have lower latency. In other words, resources should *not* be split into smaller pieces, from the latency point of view. Again, if a system is split into two equally small systems to handle equally divided offered load, the latency for both smaller systems would be doubled.

The latency for a packet is actually the sum of queuing time and service time. The latter is relatively insensitive to the offered load, but the former is quite sensitive to the offered load. The service time at a node is usually the CPU time spent in

Principle in Action: Little's Result

For a node, one interesting question is how many packets are contained in a node if we can measure its offered load and latency. The theorem developed by John Little in 1961 answered this: If the throughput equals the offered load, which means no loss, the mean *occupancy* (the mean number of packets in the node) equals the mean throughput multiplied by the mean latency. That is,

$$N = \lambda \times T$$

where λ is mean offered load, T is mean latency, and N is mean occupancy. Little's result is powerful because it does not have to assume the distribution of these variables. One useful application of this result is to estimate the buffer size of a black-box node. Suppose we can measure the maximum no-loss throughput of a node and its latency under such throughput; the occupancy obtained by multiplying them is approximately the minimum required buffer size inside the node. In Figure 1.6, the estimation of occupancy holds provided no loss happens.

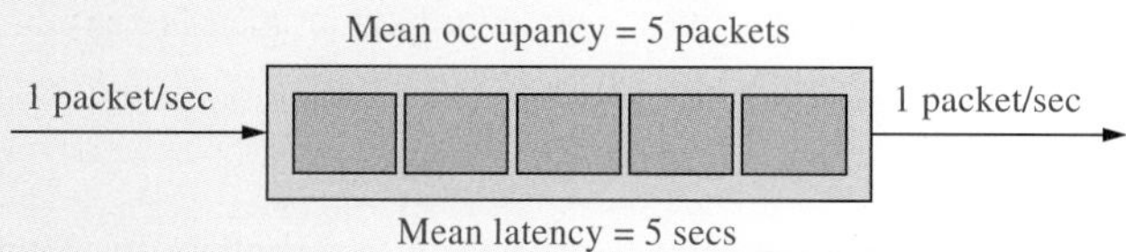

FIGURE 1.6 Little's result: How many packets in the box?

processing a packet. On the other hand, the service time at a link consists of transmission time and propagation time. That is, at a node,

$$latency = queuing + processing.$$

But at a link,

$$latency = queuing + transmission + propagation.$$

Similar to Little's result for a node, the *bandwidth delay product* (BDP) for a link tells how many bits are contained in a pipe in transit. Figure 1.7 compares the number of bits contained in a long, fat pipe (link) to the number in a short, thin pipe. The delay here, denoted by *L,* is the propagation time instead of transmission or

FIGURE 1.7 Bandwidth delay product: long, fat pipe vs. short, thin pipe.

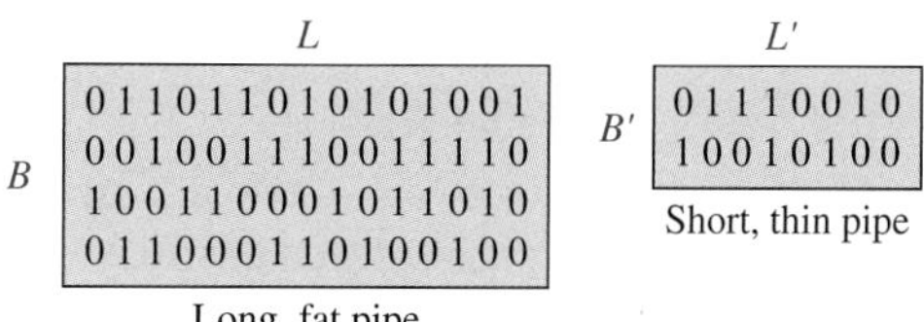

queuing time, and is determined by the length of the link. BDP is an important factor for designing traffic control mechanisms. Links or paths with a large BDP should exercise a more preventive control mechanism instead of a reactive one since it would be too late to react to congestion.

Jitter or Latency Variation

Some applications in data communications, packet voice, for example, need not only small but also consistent latency. Some other applications, video and audio streaming, for example, may tolerate very high latency and can even *absorb latency variation* or *jitter* to some extent. Because the streaming server pumps *one-way* continuous traffic to clients, the perceived playout quality would be good provided the playout buffer at clients would not underflow—that is, get empty—or overflow. Such clients use a playout buffer to absorb the jitter by delaying the playout times of *all* packets to some *aligned* timeline. For example, if the jitter is 2 seconds, the client automatically delays the playout time of all packets to the packet playout timestamps plus 2 seconds. Thus, a buffer that can queue packets for 2 seconds must be in place. Though the latency is prolonged, the jitter is absorbed or reduced. For packet voice, such jitter elimination cannot be adopted completely because of the interactivity required between two peers. Here you cannot sacrifice latency too much for jitter elimination. Nevertheless, jitter is not an important measure at all for noncontinuous traffic.

Loss

The last but not the least performance measure is the packet loss probability. There are two primary reasons for packet loss: *congestion* and *error*. Data communication systems are prone to congestion. When congestion occurs at a link or a node, packets queue up at buffers in order to absorb the congestion. But if congestion persists, buffers start to overflow. Suppose a node has three links with equal bandwidth. When wire-speed traffic is incoming from both link 1 and link 2 heading to link 3, the node would have at least 50% packet loss. For such *rate mismatch,* buffering cannot play any trick here; some sorts of control mechanisms must be used instead. Buffering works only for short-term congestion.

Errors that happen at links or nodes also contribute to packet loss. Though many wired links now have good transmission quality with very low bit error rate, most wireless links still have high bit error rates due to interference and signal degradation. A single bit error or multiple bit errors could render the whole packet useless and hence dropped. Transmission is not the only source of errors; *memory errors* at nodes may also account for a significant percentage, especially when the memory module has been on for years. When packets queue in nodal buffers, bit errors may hit the buffer memory so that the bytes *read out* are not the same as the bytes *written in.*

1.2.2 Operations at Control Plane

Control Plane vs. Data Plane

Operating a packet-switching network involves handling two kinds of packets: *control* and *data*. The control packets carry the messages meant for directing nodes on how to transfer data packets, while the data packets enclose the messages that users or applications actually want to transfer. The set of operations for handling control packets is called the *control plane,* while the one for data packets is called the *data plane*. Though there are some other operations for management purposes that are hence called the management plane, here we merge them into the control plane for simplicity. The key difference between the control plane and the data plane is that the former usually happens in *background* with longer timescales, say hundreds of milliseconds *(ms)* to tens of seconds, while the latter occurs in *foreground* with shorter timescales and more real-time, say microseconds *(μs)* to nanoseconds *(ns)*. The control plane often requires more complex computation per operation in order to decide, for example, how to route traffic and how to allocate resources so as to optimize resource sharing and utilization. On the other hand, the data plane has to process and forward packets on the fly so as to optimize throughput, latency, and loss. This subsection identifies what mechanisms should be in place for the control plane while leaving the data plane to the next subsection. Their design considerations are also raised here.

Again, the mission of the control plane in data communications is to provide good instructions for the data plane to carry data packets. As shown in Figure 1.8, to achieve that, the control plane of intermediary equipment needs to figure out where to route packets (to which links or ports), which usually requires exchange of control packets and complex route computation. In addition, the control plane may also need to deal with miscellaneous issues such as error reporting, system configuration and management, and resource allocation. Whether this mission is done well usually does not directly affect the performance measures as much as what the data plane is capable of. Instead, the control plane concerns more whether the resources have been utilized efficiently, fairly, and optimally. We now look at what mechanisms might be put into the control plane.

Routing

Most literatures do not differentiate *routing* and *forwarding*. Here we define routing as finding where to send packets and forwarding as sending packets. Routing is thus to *compute* the routes and *store* them in tables which are *looked up* when forwarding packets. Routing is usually done in the background periodically, so as to maintain and update the *forwarding tables*. (Note that many literatures refer to forwarding tables as routing tables. We use both terms in this text to mean the same thing.) It would be too late to compute the route when a packet arrives and needs to be

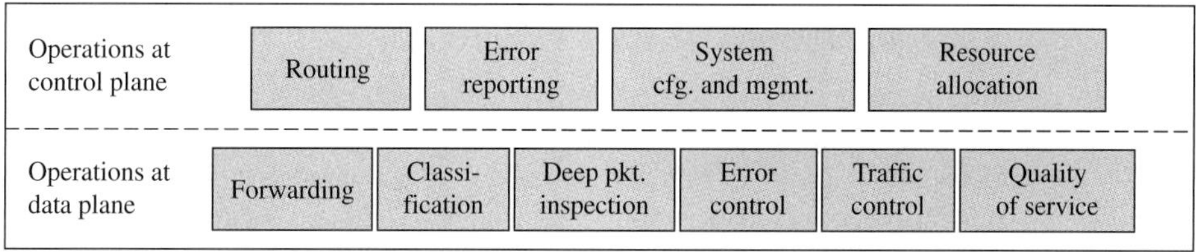

FIGURE 1.8 Some operations at the control plane and the data plane in an intermediary.

forwarded right away. There would be time only for table lookup, but not for running a route computation algorithm.

Routing as route computation is not as simple as one might think at first glance. There are many questions to be answered before you come to design a routing algorithm.

Should the route be determined *hop-by-hop* at each intermediate router or computed at the source host, i.e. *source-routed?*

What is the *granularity* of the routing decision: *per destination, per source-destination, per flow,* or even *per packet* in the extreme?

For a given granularity, do we choose *single-path* routing or *multiple-path* routing?

Is the route computation based on *global* or *partial* information of the network?

How to distribute the global or partial information? By *broadcasting* among all routers or *exchanging* between neighboring routers?

What is the optimal path by definition? Is it the *shortest,* the *widest,* or the *most robust* one?

Should the router support only one-to-one forwarding or one-to-many forwarding, that is, *unicasting* or *multicasting?*

All these must be carefully thought out first. We underline those design choices that are made by the Internet, but a different set of choices would be possible for other network architectures. We do not plan to elaborate here how these choices really work in the Internet. Here we merely raise the design issues of routing protocols and algorithms, while leaving the details to Chapter 4.

Traffic and Bandwidth Allocation

It is possible to consider routing from an even more performance-oriented perspective. If traffic volume and bandwidth resources could be measured and manipulated, we would be able to allocate a certain traffic volume and direct it through paths with certain allocated bandwidth. Allocating or assigning traffic has another label similar to routing, namely *traffic engineering*. Both *bandwidth allocation* and traffic engineering usually have specific optimization objectives, such as minimizing the averaged end-to-end latency and optimal load balancing, given a set of system constraints to satisfy. Because such an optimization problem needs very complex computation, which might not be finished in real time, and also because only a few systems are capable of adjusting bandwidth allocation on the fly, traffic and bandwidth allocation are usually done off-line at the *management plane* or during the network planning stage.

1.2.3 Operations at Data Plane

Unlike the operations at the control plane, which may apply only to the control packets in the timescale of hundreds of milliseconds to tens of seconds, things at the data plane apply to *all* packets and proceed in microseconds or less. Forwarding packets appears to be the primary job at the data plane since a packet arriving to an interface port or link could be forwarded to another port. In fact, forwarding might be just one of the *services* offered at the data plane. Other services might be packet filtering, encryption, or even content filtering. All these services require *classifying* packets by checking several fields, mostly in the header but maybe even in the payload, against the rules maintained by the control plane or preconfigured by administrators. Once matched, the matching rules tell what services the packet should receive and how to apply those services.

Forwarding itself cannot guarantee the healthy functioning of a network. In addition to forwarding and other value-added services already mentioned, *error control* and *traffic control* are two other basic per-packet operations at the data plane; the former is to ensure the packet is transmitted intact without bit errors, while the latter is to avoid congestion and maintain good throughput performance. Without these two basic operations, forwarding alone would turn the network into congestion-prone, erroneous chaos. Here we take a closer look at these operations listed in Figure 1.8.

Forwarding

Depending on how routing at the control plane is determined, packet forwarding involves examining one or several header fields in a packet. It may just take the destination address field to look up the forwarding table, or it may take more fields in doing so. Decisions made in routing directly determine how forwarding can be done, including which header field to examine, which entry in the forwarding table to match, etc. It appears that how this game (forwarding) can be played is already settled by another game (routing) decided somewhere else, but in fact there is still much room for players here. Probably the most important question to answer for packet forwarding is how fast you need to forward packets. Suppose that a router node has four links, each of 10 Gbps capacity, and also that the packet size is small and fixed at 64 bytes. The maximum number of aggregated packets per second (pps) at the router would be $4 \times 10\text{ G}/(64 \times 8) = 78{,}125{,}000$, which means this router would need to forward 78,125,000 pps (merely 12.8 *ns* per packet) if *wire-speed forwarding* is desired. This certainly poses challenges in designing the forwarding mechanism.

How to implement the *data structure* of the forwarding table and the *lookup* and *update* algorithms on this data structure are open to the designers. These designs determine whether a node is capable of wire-speed forwarding. In some circumstances, specific ASIC might be needed to offload this job from CPU so as to achieve a forwarding speed of millions of packets per second. While *speed* certainly is the goal of this game, *size* also matters. The data structure to store the forwarding table might be constrained. For 80,000 forwarding entries each of 2 to 3 bytes, one might try to store them into a tree or a hash table with no more than hundreds of kilobytes (KB) or in flat index tables of hundreds of megabytes (MB). An immediate observation is that there is a tradeoff between *time complexity* and *space complexity* in the forwarding-table implementation.

Classification

As mentioned previously, many services need packet classification operations, a matching process that takes one or several fields in the packet header to match against a set of rules. A rule has two parts: *condition* and *action,* specifying under what condition on the field(s) the action should be applied to the matching packet. Since each service has its own set of fields to examine against its own set of rules, a *classifier* and its associated rules, or *classification database,* would be needed for a specific service. For the forwarding service, the forwarding table is its classification database.

A question similar to how fast you need to forward packets is how fast you need to classify packets. The speed here depends on two things: the number of fields (from one to several) and the number of rules (from several to tens of thousands), and both numbers directly affect the classifier's throughput *scalability*. Thus, designing a multi-field classification algorithm that can scale well with the number of fields and the number of rules is the goal. A design is less scalable if it has high throughput when the two numbers are small but much dropped throughput when either one is relatively large. Similar to forwarding, one may resort to ASIC hardware designs to achieve high throughput of packet classification.

Deep Packet Inspection

Both forwarding and classification examine packet header fields. But there are things, often malicious, hidden deep in the packet *payload*. For example, intrusions and viruses reside deep in the application headers and payloads, respectively. Knowledge about these contents is usually abstracted into a database of *signatures,* which is used to match against the payload of incoming packets. This matching process is called *deep packet inspection* (DPI) since it looks deep into the payload. Because the signatures are usually expressed in simple character strings or regular expressions, *string matching* is the key operation in DPI.

Again, how fast you can perform string matching is the major concern. This, compared to the one-dimensional forwarding and two-dimensional classification, is a *three-dimensional* problem where the *number* of signatures, the *length* of signatures, and the *size* of character set of the signature strings are the parameters. It would be even more challenging to design an algorithm that scales both *up* and *down* well in this large *problem space*. After all, it is an open design issue that also requires ASIC hardware solutions for high throughput.

Error Control

As discussed in Subsection 1.2.1, bit errors may hit packets. The errors might occur during packet transmission or when packets are stored in memory. Two fundamental questions need to be answered: (1) *detect* or *correct?* (2) *hop-by-hop* or *end-to-end?* The first question concerns how the receiver of a packet in error detects and handles the error. Two approaches exist: The receiver may detect the error by the extra redundant bits and notify the sender to retransmit, or it may detect and correct the error directly if the extra redundant bits can indicate the exact bits that are in error. The latter approach would require more redundant bits, and hence produce higher overhead. Whether to do error correction depends on the type of traffic being carried. For real-time traffic, notifying the sender to retransmit is not an appealing approach. It is then feasible to simply drop packets in error without further actions if the application can tolerate a small percentage of loss; otherwise, error correction should be exercised.

The second question is all about *where* the error might occur: link or node? If bit errors only occur at links, error control can be placed at each link's receiver to detect or also correct the errors. By doing so, a path would be error-free because all links can recover errors. However, if packets stored at nodes suffer from memory errors, bit errors would be carried over undetected because the transmitting side and the receiving side of a link only watch for the transmission errors on this link. In other words, the *concatenated* hop-by-hop (link-by-link) error control is not enough, and an end-to-end error control is necessary as well. One might ask: Why not remove the hop-by-hop error control and keep only the end-to-end error control? From the error control's point of view, it is fine to do that. The problem is the time needed to recover the error: Removing the hop-by-hop error control would prolong the error recovery process. Doing so may even create difficulty in recovering errors if the links' bit error rate is too high because the probability of having an end-to-end error recovery succeed is the *product* of the probability of each link along the path succeeding in error recovery. This is actually the end-to-end argument to be detailed in Section 1.3.

Traffic Control

Another per-packet operation at the data plane is *regulating* the pumping process of a packet stream. Pumping packets too quickly may overflow the intermediate routers or the destination node, resulting in many retransmissions that intensify the congestion. Pumping too slowly may underflow their buffers, leading to low utilization of the bandwidth resources. Traffic control is a generic term for any mechanism for avoiding or resolving congestion, but congestion itself could be quite complicated. It could be an end-to-end (between a source and a destination on a path), hop-by-hop (between a sender and a receiver on a link), or hot-spot (a bottleneck node or link) phenomenon. *Flow control* is a kind of traffic control that maneuvers the sender-receiver synchronization to prevent a faster sender from overrunning a slower receiver. The sender and the receiver could be connected by a link or a path, so flow control could be either hop-by-hop or end-to-end.

As another kind of traffic control, *congestion control* deals with the more complicated bottleneck congestion caused by a set of traffic sources. A bottleneck, either a node or a link, could have many packet flows passing through, each contributing partially to the congestion. Asking the sources to slow down or stop is an obvious resolution. However, there are details to work out. Who should slow down and by how much? What is the *policy* behind the process? We can have all or some sources reduce the transmission rate by the same or different amounts, but it should be the underlying policy to decide these. *Fairness* appears to be a sound policy, but how to define fairness and how to enforce the fairness policy in an efficient manner are design choices which vary from one network architecture to another.

Quality of Service

The network may work just fine with flow control and congestion control to maintain *satisfactory* operations. But there could be more stringent requirements that explicitly specify the *traffic parameters* such as rate and burst length and their expected *performance measures* such as latency and loss; that is, explicit *quality of service (QoS)*. This has posed a great challenge to packet switching for decades! Various traffic control modules, such as *policer, shaper,* and *scheduler,* might be placed at the entry points or the core of a network to regulate traffic to meet the QoS objectives. Though several solution architectures have been proposed, none of them have been deployed in operational networks at large. Chapter 7 addresses these developments in detail. Nevertheless, many traffic control modules have been embedded into various devices as *partial* QoS solutions.

1.2.4 Interoperability

Standard vs. Implementation-Dependent

There are two possible ways for various devices to talk with each other. One is to buy all devices from only one vendor. The other is to define *standard protocols* between devices so that as long as vendors follow these protocols, we can *interoperate* devices bought from different vendors. This kind of interoperability is a must, especially when we do not want to be bound to specific vendors after we buy the first batch of devices from them. On the other hand, vendors who dominate the market might wish to put some *proprietary protocols,* which are defined by vendors themselves instead of standard organizations, into their devices in order to bind their customers. But if this is not carefully done, their market share might slip silently.

Then what should be defined as standards and what should not? Interoperability serves as the criterion. For the packet handling process, some parts need to be standardized while the rest might be left for vendors to decide. The parts that need standardization are the ones that affect interoperability of devices from *different* vendors. The formats of *protocol messages* certainly need to be standardized. However, many internal mechanisms (e.g., the data structure of a table and its lookup and update algorithms) that do not affect the interoperability with other devices are *implementation-dependent* (vendor-specific), and it is often these vendor-specific designs that make a difference in the resultant performance. This subsection points out where standard and implementation-dependent designs could play a part.

Standard Protocols and Algorithms

Protocols by default should be standardized, though some proprietary protocols do exist. Such proprietary protocols may become *de facto* standards if they dominate the market. When defining a *protocol specification* besides the architectural framework, two interfaces need to be defined: *peer interface* and *service interface*. The peer interface formats the protocol messages to be exchanged between systems supporting that protocol, while the service interface defines the function calls for other modules on the same node machine to access the services offered by a module. A protocol may have several types of messages, each with its own header format. A header contains several fields of fixed or variable lengths. Of course, both the *syntax* (format) and *semantics* (interpretation) of each header field are standardized. A sender encodes information for the protocol handshake into the *header* of a protocol message, and appends data, if any, as the *payload* of this protocol message.

Control protocols place control data in the header of protocol messages for the operation of the control plane. On the other hand, *data protocols* put all kinds of data, either user data or control data, in the payload of their protocol messages. Their headers information only tells how the packets should be forwarded.

In addition to the syntax and semantics of protocol messages, some algorithms at the control and the data plane should be standardized, too. For example, routing algorithms at the control plane must be agreed upon by all participating routers if they are to reach a *consistent* view of the shortest path. If two neighboring routers, say *A* and *B,* use different routing algorithms to compute their shortest path to destination *X,* it is possible that *A* would point to *B* as the next hop of the shortest path to *X,* and vice versa for *B,* which results in packets destined for *X* looping between *A* and *B* once these packets arrive at *A* or *B*. Error detection or correction algorithms at the data plane are similar examples. If the sender and the receiver used different algorithms for data *encoding* and *decoding,* respectively, things would not work at all.

Implementation-Dependent Design

Unlike a protocol specification, there exists much flexibility in a *protocol implementation*. Not every part of an algorithms at the control and the data plane needs to be standardized. For example, realizing a routing algorithm, e.g., Dijkstra's, requires a data structure to store the network topology and an algorithm on that data structure to find the shortest paths to all destinations, but the implementation does not need to be standardized. One may design a more efficient method to compute than the one stated in a textbook. Another example is the table lookup algorithm in packet forwarding. It is always an interesting challenge to design a data structure to store a large number of entries and to design its lookup and update algorithms so that they can beat the best current design in terms of speed and size.

Layered Protocols

Actually, the interoperability issue occurs not only between two systems but also between two protocols. One single protocol is not enough to drive a system. In fact, it is a *protocol stack* that drives the whole system. A protocol stack consists of a *layered* set of protocols, where each layer covers parts of data communication mechanisms and provides services to the upper layers. It is a natural evolution to *abstract* a complex system into *modular* entities, i.e., layered protocols here, such that the lower layers hide the details from and provide services to their upper layers.

As two systems need to use the same protocol to communicate, protocols at different layers also need a service interface such as *send* and *recv* to exchange data within one system. When a common interface is used between these two protocols, the system has more flexibility to replace any protocols in the protocol stack when needed. For example, when two remote-end hosts *X* and *Y* have a protocol stack of *A-B-C,* where *A* is the upper layer and *C* is the protocol for a specific link, it should be possible for *X* to replace *C* with *D,* say the protocol for a more reliable link, while still keeping its *A* and *B* unchanged to interoperate with the corresponding *A* and *B* in *Y*. However, since *X* runs *C* and *Y* runs *D* on two separate links, there should be an intermediary device, say *Z,* between *X* and *Y* to bridge them together.

1.3 THE INTERNET ARCHITECTURE

Given the principle constraints of packet switching, the Internet has its solutions to achieving the three requirements of data communications, namely connectivity, scalability, and resource sharing as identified in Section 1.1. All the solutions picked for the Internet architecture have philosophical justification. Nevertheless, there exist other data communication architectures, such as the faded Asynchronous Transfer Mode (ATM) and the emerging Multi-Protocol Label Switching (MPLS). They all have something in common and something unique, compared to the Internet architecture; of course, they also have a set of philosophies to justify their architectural design choices. Whether a particular solution prevails often depends on (1) who comes first, and (2) who best satisfies the three requirements. The Internet apparently came first back in 1969 and has met the requirements satisfactorily, though consistently under pressure to undergo fundamental changes.

This section reveals key solutions adopted in the Internet architecture. To resolve connectivity in addition to stateless routing, the *end-to-end argument* serves as a key philosophy in defining *where* a mechanism should be placed, or what should be done *inside* and *outside* the network. Under the guidance of this argument the protocol layers are defined; then the concepts of *subnet* and *domain* emerged to support the needed scalability. As the trickiest issue in packet switching, resource sharing has been resolved by a *common best-effort carrier* service, Internet Protocol (IP), plus two *end-to-end services:* Transmission Control Protocol (TCP) and User Datagram Protocol (UDP). TCP offers end-to-end congestion control to share bandwidth *politely* and a reliable *loss-free* service, while UDP offers a plain uncontrolled and unreliable service.

1.3.1 Solutions to Connectivity

Two disjoint end points are connected through a path with nodes and links. To decide how to establish and maintain this end-to-end connectivity in the Internet, one must make three decisions: (1) *routed or switched connectivity,* (2) *end-to-end* or *hop-by-hop* mechanisms to maintain the correctness (reliable and orderly delivery of packets) of this connectivity, and (3) how to *organize the tasks* in establishing and maintaining this connectivity. For the Internet it was decided to *route* this connectivity, maintain its correctness at the *end-to-end* level, and organize the tasks into four *protocol layers.*

Routing: Stateless and Connectionless

Although switching is faster than routing, as discussed in Subsection 1.1.1, it requires the switching devices to memorize the *state* information, i.e., the mapping of (input port, incoming virtual circuit number) to (output port, outgoing virtual circuit number) in the *virtual circuit table,* of all passing connections. Unlike the continuous voice traffic in telecom, data traffic is usually *bursty*. It would be inefficient, in terms of *memory usage,* to keep the state information of a connection which is *long-lived but bursty,* since the state information is kept in memory for a long time but used only occasionally. Similarly, it is inefficient, in terms of *initial time delay,* to establish the state information for a *short-lived* connection, which costs large overhead for just a few packets. In short, switching is less efficient than routing for data communications in terms of space and time overhead.

However, routing does not win in all aspects. As introduced in Subsection 1.1.1, routing in the Internet takes the full destination address of a packet to match against the entries in the forwarding table (sometimes called routing table), which requires the matching process to traverse a large data structure and hence costs several memory accesses and match instructions. Switching, on the other hand, takes the virtual

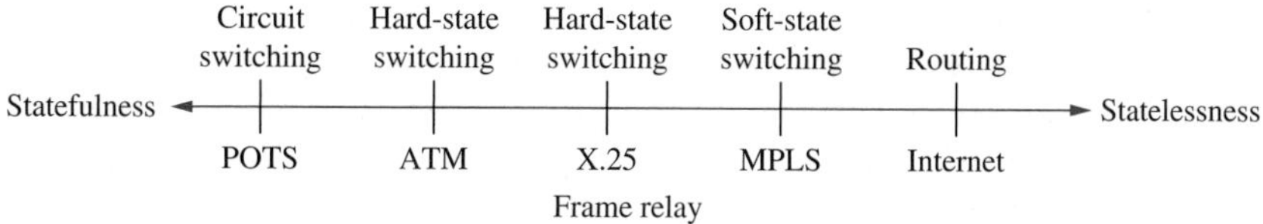

FIGURE 1.9 The spectrum of statefulness.

circuit number of a packet to index into the virtual circuit table, and hence requires only *one* memory access.

Many network architectures, including ATM, X.25, Frame Relay, and MPLS, have adopted switching. They can be viewed as the data communication solutions from the telecommunication industry, with their common root from POTS, which is of course a switching system. Figure 1.9 puts all these architectures onto the

Principle in Action: Constantly Challenged Statelessness

One would say that the most unique choice made by the Internet architecture is *stateless routing*. The decision in its very beginning has led it to a *stateless connectionless* network where all packets are routed independently without establishing paths in the intermediate routers in advance. Stateless means that routers do not keep any state information to track the packet streams passing through. With the simplicity of stateless routing (along with other key design choices to be touched on in this section), the Internet scales pretty well and offers flexible connectivity and economical resource sharing to all applications in data communications.

Actually, whether the Internet should remain purely stateless raises a lot of controversy. In fact, many new demands, especially those on quality of service (QoS) and multicasting, have drawn many proposals that would put statefulness elements into the Internet architecture, as we shall see in Chapter 4 and Chapter 7, respectively. QoS and multicasting are not the only two that call for infrastructural changes. As another pressing demand, *wire-speed forwarding,* due to the rapid increase in link bandwidth, calls for packet switching instead of routing. MPLS aims to speed up the Internet by switching more packets but routing less. As stated before, switching is faster than routing because the former just needs simple *indexing* into the *virtual circuit table,* while the latter requires much more complex *matching* during table lookup. Unlike ATM, which is *hard-state switching,* MPLS is *soft-state switching,* meaning that it can turn back to stateless routing if the switching entry for a packet stream expires or does not exist. Whether MPLS can be massively deployed onto the original Internet architecture is still under research, but the new demands, QoS for guaranteed performance, multicasting for group communications or distributions, and wire-speed forwarding for much faster infrastructure, will not quit until they can be satisfied.

spectrum of statefulness, where the state means not only the table entries memorized in nodes but also link bandwidth reserved for streams of flows or connections. POTS is purely circuit switching with both kinds of states previously mentioned, while the rest are packet switching. Among the latter group, the Internet and MPLS are routing and "soft-state" switching, respectively, and the others are "hard-state" switching. ATM is more stateful than X.25 and Frame Relay because it provides bandwidth allocation to individual connections.

The End-to-End Argument

To provide reliable and orderly delivery of packets from sources to destinations, error and traffic control should be exercised on a hop-by-hop basis or an end-to-end basis, i.e., for all links or only at end hosts. The *hop-by-hop argument* says that if the transmissions on all links are reliable and orderly, the reliability and order will be guaranteed for the end-to-end transmissions. However, this argument is true only when nodes are error free. Because a path consists of nodes and links, guaranteeing the correctness of link operations does not cover the correctness of node operations and hence that of the end-to-end delivery along the path. Error and traffic control mechanisms are still needed at the end hosts to guard against the nodal errors. The end-to-end argument, which says do not put it in a lower layer unless it can be completely done there, thus wins here. Though some hop-by-hop error and traffic control still can be put at links, they are merely for *performance optimization* to detect and recover the error earlier. The end-to-end mechanisms still serve as the primary guards to guarantee the correctness of the connectivity.

The end-to-end argument has also pushed complexity toward the network *edge* and kept the network core simple enough to scale well. Processing of application-aware services should be done only at the end hosts, *outside* instead of *inside* the network, while leaving one single carrier service inside the network. We shall see this in the solutions to resource sharing.

The Four-Layer Protocol Stack

Abstraction in designing a complex data communication system leads to layered protocols where lower layers hide the details from the upper layers. But how many layers are needed and what exactly to put in each layer? The four-layer Internet architecture is sometimes called the TCP/IP architecture after its two important protocols, which represent two layers. The bottom layer is the link layer, which may consist of many protocols for various links. A link layer protocol is *hardware dependent* and implemented by a combination of hardware (adaptor card) and software (adaptor driver). Based on the link layer, the IP layer consists of one single protocol (IP) to provide the *host-to-host connectivity* (end-to-end connectivity vs. hop-by-hop connectivity in the data link layer) through stateless routing. The third layer is the transport layer, which contains two protocols (TCP and UDP). TCP and UDP provide the process-to-process connectivity needed for the top application layer. The transport layer hides the details of the underlying network topology behind a *virtual link* or *channel* abstraction for the communicating processes at the application layer. The application layer has a protocol for each client–server or peer-to-peer application.

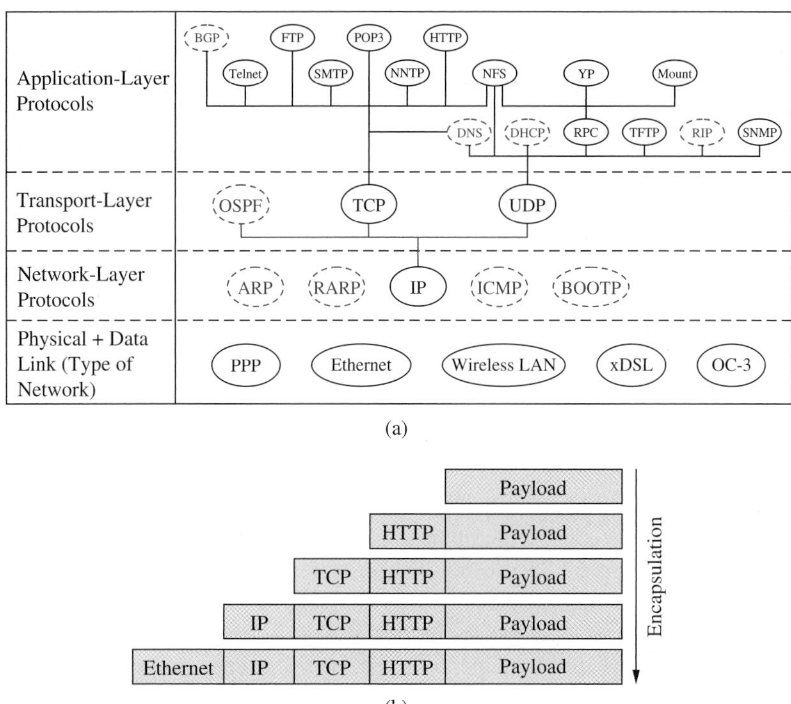

FIGURE 1.10 (a) Internet Protocol stack: commonly used protocols. (b) Packet encapsulation.

Figure 1.10(a) shows the Internet Protocol stack with commonly used protocols. The protocols marked with dotted circles are control plane protocols, while the rest are data plane protocols. It is important to note that TCP, UDP, and IP serve as the core protocols to support a lot of application protocols while overriding many possible links. We shall cover the details of important protocols in Figure 1.10(a) in later chapters. An example hierarchy in this four-layer protocol stack is HTTP-TCP-IP-Ethernet, with a data payload encapsulated by the HTTP header, the TCP header, the IP header, and then the Ethernet header when transmitted, and the other way around when received, as shown in Figure 1.10(b).

1.3.2 Solutions to Scalability

How to cluster a large number of nodes determines how scalable a system can be. Addressing these nodes is then the key issue. Figure 1.1 illustrates a way to organize four billion nodes in a three-level hierarchy. But how do we address and organize these nodes? For the Internet to scale to four billion hosts as a design objective, three fundamental design problems must be answered: (1) how many levels of hierarchy, (2) how many entities in each hierarchy, and (3) how to manage this hierarchy. If the grouping of nodes has just one level and the size of a group is 256, the number of groups would be 16,777,216, which is too large for the interconnection routers to handle. These routers have to be aware of such a large number of groups. As Figure 1.1 suggests, if another level is added and the size of a supergroup is also 256, the number of groups within a supergroup and the number of supergroups would be 256 and 65,536, respectively. The 256 is a manageable size for a network operator, which is an organization or an ISP, while 65,536 is an acceptable size for core routers. Thus, the Internet adopts a three-level hierarchy with *subnet* as its lowest level and *autonomous system* (AS) as its middle level, while leaving many ASs at the top level.

Subnet

The Internet uses a subnet to denote nodes in a physical network with a *contiguous address block*. A physical network consists of a link, either point-to-point or broadcast, and the nodes attached to it. A subnet on a broadcast link forms a LAN, which is a broadcast domain. That is, packets destined for a host on a LAN can be transmitted by any host or router on this LAN and received by the destined host in one hop automatically. However, packets transmitted between subnets or LANs need hop-by-hop forwarding by routers. A subnet on a point-to-point link usually forms a WAN link between two routers. Figure 1.11 illustrates subnets defined by *netmask* and *prefix,* which are formally discussed in Chapter 4.

The size of a subnet on a point-to-point link is fixed at two nodes. The size of a subnet on a broadcast link usually depends on performance and administration policy. However, putting too many hosts on one subnet would result in serious contention. Meanwhile, the administration policy usually prefers a fixed size for all subnets in its management domain. A subnet of size 256 is a common setting.

Autonomous System (AS)

Nodes on the Internet are grouped to form a number of subnets interconnected by routers. Today the Internet has over 50 million hosts and millions of routers. If the average size of a subnet is 50, the number of subnets would be one million, which means routers would have too many subnet entries to memorize and look up.

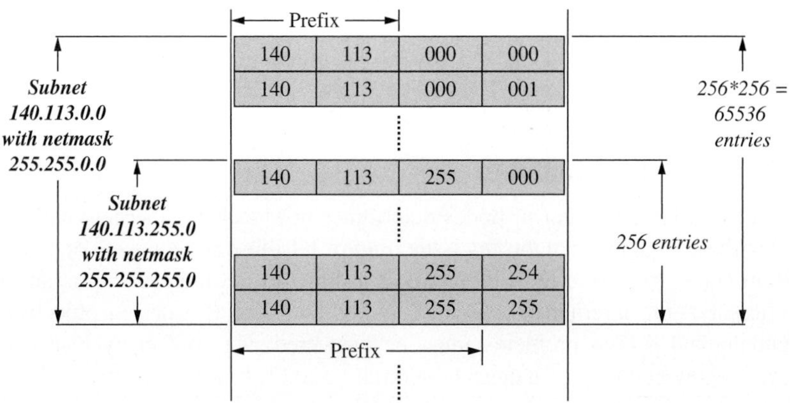

FIGURE 1.11 Subnet, netmask, prefix: segmented contiguous address blocks.

Apparently, another level of hierarchy is needed on top of subnet. An autonomous system (AS, sometimes called a *domain*) is composed of subnets and their interconnection routers administered by an organization. A router inside an AS knows all the intra-AS routers and subnets in the AS, plus one or several inter-AS routers in charge of routing between ASs. A packet destined to a host in the same AS will be forwarded by intra-AS routers. Things get more complicated if a packet is destined to a host in another AS. It will be first forwarded by several intra-AS routers to one of the inter-AS routers of the local AS, then forwarded by inter-AS routers to the destination AS, and finally forwarded by intra-AS routers of that destination AS to the destination host.

With subnets and ASs, either intra-AS or inter-AS packet forwarding can be carried out in a scalable way without too much burden at intra-AS and inter-AS routers. If the average number of subnets within an AS is 50, the number of ASs would be 20,000, which is an affordable number for inter-AS routers to handle. AS not only solves the scalability issue but also retains the administration authority for network operators. Routing and other operations inside an AS can be separated and hidden from the outside world.

Figure 1.12 illustrates the AS at National Chiao Tung University where, under the same AS, each department is assigned multiple subnets. The entire Internet has tens of thousands of such domains.

1.3.3 Solutions to Resource Sharing

Data communications has a large variety of applications in comparison to telecommunications, which is primarily used for telephony only. It is then important to decide whether the Internet architecture should have multiple types of connectivity, one for each type of application.

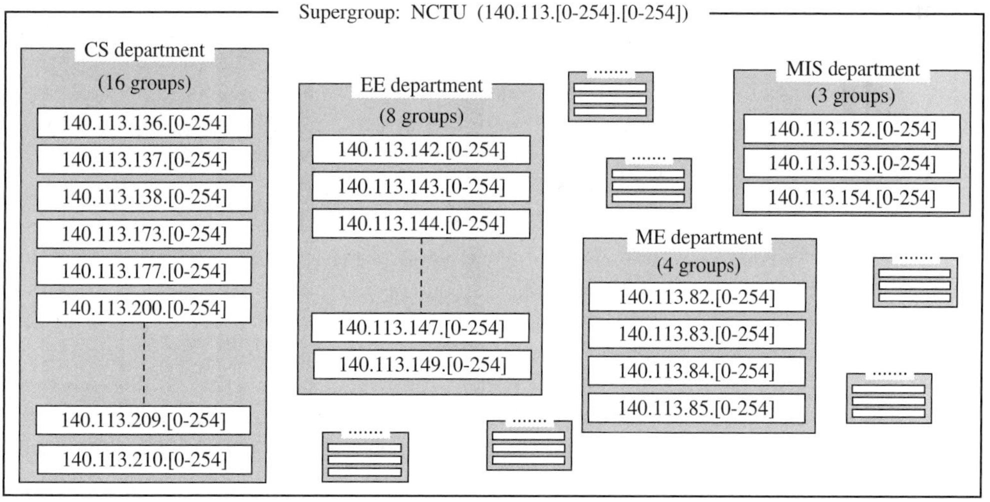

FIGURE 1.12 An example domain, AS, or supergroup: NCTU.

The variety of applications is not the only issue. Congestion due to packet switching presents an even tougher challenge. Some sorts of congestion control and flow control should be imposed to avoid the buffer overflow in the network and at the receivers. Derived from the end-to-end argument, it is believed that traffic control should be exercised mainly on the *sources* instead of on intermediate routers.

In summary, three questions have been answered by the Internet architecture in deciding ways of resource sharing: (1) whether to differentiate the treatment of traffic from different applications, (2) what the resource sharing policy is, and (3) where to put traffic control mechanisms to enforce the policy. The Internet offers a common best-effort service inside the network while using end-to-end congestion and flow control to practice the fairness policy in bandwidth sharing.

Common Best-Effort Service: IP

The applications could be categorized into at least three types: *interactive*, *file transfer,* and *real-time*. Interactive applications generate small amounts of traffic but require timely responses. On the other hand, file transfer applications pump voluminous traffic but can tolerate higher latency. Real-time applications have both continuous traffic volume and low latency requirements. If the decision is to have a type of connectivity to support each application category, the routers inside the Internet would be type-aware so as to treat packets differently. However, the Internet offers one single type of connectivity service, namely the best-effort IP service. All IP packets are treated equally in sharing the limited resources.

As a *carrier* service at the core of the Internet, IP has the most *native* form of packet switching. It is native because, in addition to forwarding, it does not have value-added services except a simple checksum for error detection; it has no traffic control built in, and it is unreliable in terms of throughput, latency, jitter, and loss. That is, it cannot guarantee how fast packets can be delivered, when the packets would reach their destinations, and even whether they can reach their destinations at all. In-order delivery of a sequence of packets cannot be guaranteed, either; the order of arrivals of a packet stream to the destination might not be the same as the order of departures from the source. Nevertheless, it drops a packet if the checksum is invalid, and leaves the error recovery, if any, to the end-to-end protocols. If an application needs error recovery or traffic control, it has to depend on a specific end-to-end protocol for these value-added services.

End-to-End Congestion Control and Error Recovery: TCP

TCP is a *polite* end-to-end protocol that regulates the *outstanding bits* of a packet flow from a source so that all flows can share the resources *fairly*. By asking all sources to be polite and responsive to congestion, the chance to run into congestion and the time to recover from congestion are reduced. TCP is also a *reliable* end-to-end protocol that runs error recovery. It is reliable in terms of *loss;* that is, packet loss due to error or congestion is recovered by the TCP protocol. However, it is still unreliable in terms of other performance measures such as throughput, latency, and jitter. For packet switching to guarantee these performance measures would require additional, and usually stateful, mechanisms to be imposed *inside* the network. Though solutions do exist, none of them have been largely deployed. The no-loss guarantee from TCP is sufficient for most applications in data communications.

There are also many applications that do not need the no-loss guarantee. For example, the packet voice or video streaming applications can tolerate a *small* percentage of loss while still maintaining playout quality. In fact, the prolonged end-to-end retransmissions for error recovery are not acceptable for such real-time applications. Some other applications, such as network management, may have their own error control built into their clients and servers, and thus do not rely on error control in the underlying end-to-end transport service. For these applications, UDP serves as an alternative. UDP is another end-to-end protocol, though it is quite *primitive,* with only a simple checksum for error detection, but no error recovery or traffic control. In Figure 1.10(a), we can see the applications riding over TCP and UDP, respectively.

To avoid congestion and share bandwidth fairly, an interesting philosophy is embedded into TCP: The number of *outstanding bits* from each flow should be approximately the same; that is, the traffic contributed to the Internet should be the same for all active TCP flows. The number of outstanding bits is in fact the bandwidth delay product (BDP). For this BDP to be the same, if a TCP flow travels a longer path with higher delay, its bandwidth or transmission rate should be smaller. TCP flows do not have explicit transmission rates. Instead, they use *window size* to control the BDP (the number of outstanding bits). Consider a link with many TCP flows passing through, where the number of hops or the end-to-end delay for these flows might be different. To achieve the same BDP, their transmission rates would be different. A transcontinental TCP flow surely would have a lower transmission rate than a local TCP flow, even if the bandwidth is abundant and there is no congestion.

In addition to the fairness policy, TCP needs to *adjust* its window-based control to reflect the current network and receiver conditions. First, the rate should be *bounded* to the capability of the receiver. Second, the rate should be decreased when the network starts to congest and increased when the congestion subsides. But how fast should TCP decrease and increase its rate or window size? *Additive Increase and Multiplicative Decrease (AIMD)* appears to be a good choice that eats up bandwidth *slowly* but responds to congestion *quickly*. Many performance issues and considerations require further clarification and are addressed in Chapter 5.

1.3.4 Control-Plane and Data-Plane Operations

With decisions in resolving connectivity, scalability, and resource sharing, there are still many details to work out in order for the Internet to operate as expected. They include routing and error reporting at the control plane, forwarding, error control, and traffic control at the data plane.

Control-Plane Operations

In Subsection 1.2.2, we raised the issues involved in designing a routing protocol and its algorithm. The choices made can be summarized as follows: precomputed in background, hop-by-hop, per-destination-prefix (subnet or AS) granularity, partial or global network state information for intra-AS routing, partial network state information for inter-AS routing, and mostly single shortest path. There are rationales behind these choices. On-demand source routing would be appropriate when the network topology is quite dynamic, otherwise, precomputed hop-by-hop routing at each router would fit. With a scalable hierarchy of subnets and ASs, the granularity for intra-AS and inter-AS routing is thus per-subnet and per-AS, respectively.

As discussed in Subsection 1.3.2, within an AS where the number of subnets is small, tens to hundreds, either partial or global network state information can be collected easily. However, the number of ASs worldwide could be tens of thousands, so collecting up-to-date global network state information would be difficult. Global network state information contains the entire network topology, and is constructed by *link states* broadcast from *all* routers. On the other hand, partial network state information contains the next hop and the distance to a destination subnet or AS, and is constructed by *distance vectors* exchanged between *neighboring* routers. Finally, the single shortest path instead of multiple paths is a choice for simplicity. Having multiple paths to a given destination subnet or AS would have better resource utilization and load balancing, but also complicates the designs in routing and forwarding. With more than one entry for a given destination in the forwarding table, maintaining the entries in the control plane and choosing which entry to go in the data plane are nontrivial. Routing Information Protocol (RIP), which relies on partial network state information, and Open Shortest Path First (OSPF), which relies on global network state information, are two common intra-AS routing protocols, while Border Gateway Protocol (BGP), which relies on partial network state information, dominates in inter-AS routing.

There are some other works at the control plane. Multicast routing, error reporting, and host configuration need to be addressed. Multicast routing is more complicated than unicast routing. Though many solutions exist, we leave the discussions to Chapter 4. Error reporting is to report to the source when an error occurs in handling a packet at a router or the destination. It can also be used to probe the network. Internet Control Message Protocol (ICMP) is the protocol for error reporting. The host configuration protocol, Dynamic Host Configuration Protocol (DHCP), is an effort to automate the configuration task to achieve plug-in-play. Though fully *automatic configuration* of the whole network is still not possible today, DHCP frees administrators from having to manually configure the IP address and other parameters of all host machines. Router configuration, however, has to be done manually.

Data-Plane Operations

Forwarding a packet is actually a table lookup process, taking the destination IP address in the packet to match against the IP prefix in table entries. For intra-AS and inter-AS forwarding, the granularity of table entries is per-subnet and per-AS, respectively. The IP prefix for a subnet or an AS may be of any length from 2 to 32. The entry with matched prefix contains the next-hop information for forwarding the packet. However, it is possible to have more than one matched prefix if an address block is allocated to two subnets or ASs. For example, if the address block of 140.113 is split into two parts, 140.113.23 and the rest, and assigned to two ASs, the inter-AS forwarding table will contain two entries with prefix 140.113 and 140.113.23. When a packet destined to 140.113.23.52 is received, it will match both entries. By default, the one with the *longest prefix matching* is followed.

Following the end-to-end argument discussed in Subsection 1.3.1, error control in the Internet is put into the end-to-end TCP and UDP. Checksum in TCP and UDP checks against errors in the whole packet, though it can only detect a single bit error. If an error is detected, a UDP receiver just drops and ignores the packet, but a TCP receiver acknowledges the TCP sender to ask for retransmission. Checksum in IP just protects the packet header to avoid errors in protocol processing; it does not protect the packet payload. If an error is detected at a node, the node drops the packet and sends back an ICMP packet to the source. How the source handles it is implementation dependent. For the purpose of efficiency, many underlying links also put error control at the link layer, but such error control is independent of what has been done at TCP, UDP, and IP.

The purposes of traffic control are to avoid and resolve congestion, as well as to fairly share the bandwidth resources. TCP provides a fairly satisfactory solution, as discussed in Subsection 1.3.3. UDP, on the other hand, is a wild rider that sends packets as it wishes. Although TCP traffic still dominates today in terms of traffic volume, streaming and VoIP applications may someday push UDP traffic to surpass TCP's. TCP traffic would suffer when mixed with UDP traffic. This calls for another round of research to control UDP traffic by the end-to-end congestion and flow control similar to TCP's. In short, a UDP flow should be *TCP-friendly* so that its impact on the coexisting TCP flows is the same as the impact of a TCP flow on the other coexisting TCP flows.

Principle in Action: Flavors of the Internet Architecture

This is the right place to re-emphasize the "flavors" possessed by the Internet. To solve connectivity and resource sharing issues, the Internet embraces the end-to-end argument to an extreme that pushes the complexity toward the edge device while keeping the core network stateless. The core runs unreliable stateless routing, while the edge takes care of correctness and healthiness by error control and congestion control, respectively. A simple three-level hierarchy with subnets and domains is enough to scale the Internet up to billions of nodes. Extra mechanisms then need to comply with these flavors. OSI, ATM, QoS by IntServ/DiffServ, and IP multicast were all counter-examples that failed to replace or even coexist with the Internet. They all need a stateful core that keeps entries for pass-by connections. MPLS, which switches more packets and routes fewer packets, also faces the same difficulty. Though its flexible, soft-state switching allows MPLS to better comply with stateless routing, and thus to easily deploy on a small scale, say an ISP, Internet-wide adoption of MPLS is still challenging.

1.4 OPEN SOURCE IMPLEMENTATIONS

The Internet architecture presents an integrated set of solutions to meet the requirements and principles of data communications, and this set of solutions is an open standard. Open source implementations of the Internet architecture push the same spirit of openness one step further. This section addresses the *why* and the *how* of open source implementations of the Internet architecture. We first compare the practices of open and closed implementations. Then we illustrate the software architecture in a Linux system, be it a host or a router. This architecture is then deconstructed into several parts: *kernel, drivers, daemons,* and *controllers,* with each part briefly reviewed.

We leave more implementation overview and two sets of useful tools to three appendices. Appendix B examines the source tree of the Linux kernel and summarizes its networking codes. Common development and utility tools are collectively presented in Appendix C and Appendix D, respectively. Readers are encouraged to browse these appendices before doing the hands-on exercises in this text. In addition, nontechnical aspects of open source, including the history, licensing models, and resources, are reviewed in Section A.2 of Appendix A.

1.4.1 Open vs. Closed

Vendors: System, IC, Hardware, and Software

Before describing ways to implement the Internet architecture, we should identify the major components in a system and the involved vendors. For either a host or a router, a system consists of software, hardware, and IC components. On a host, the Internet architecture is mostly implemented in software and partially in ICs. Among the protocol stack, TCP, UDP, and IP are implemented in the operating system, while the application protocols and the link protocols are implemented in application programs and the ICs on the interface card, respectively. The implementation in a router is similar except that parts of the protocol implementation might be shifted from software to ICs if the CPU cannot deliver the desired wire-speed processing.

A *system vendor* may develop and integrate all these three types of components internally, or outsource some of them to the *component vendors* of software, hardware, or ICs. For example, a router system vendor may design, implement, and manufacture the hardware with onboard chips from one or several IC vendors, while licensing and modifying the software from a software vendor.

From Proprietary, Third-Party, to Open Source

There exist three ways to implement the Internet architecture into a system which is either a host or a router. They are (1) *proprietary closed,* (2) *third-party closed,* and (3) *open source*. A large system vendor can afford to maintain a large team of hundreds of engineers to design and implement the *proprietary closed* software and ICs. The result is a closed system whose intellectual property is owned solely by the vendor. For small system vendors, maintaining such a large team is too costly. Thus, they would rather resort to the *third-party* solutions provided by software or IC vendors who transfer their implementations to system vendors and charge them a licensing fee and per-copy royalty (for software) or a purchase price (for ICs).

The open source implementations of software and ICs offer the third way of implementing a system. Without having to maintain a large team internally or be bound to specific component vendors, a system vendor can leverage the existing abundant software resources while a system or IC vendor could utilize increasing IC resources. They in turn could contribute back to this open source community.

Openness: Interface or Implementation?

When we address openness, it is important to point out what is being open. Is it *interface or implementation?* By open source, we mean open implementation. The Internet architecture is an open interface, while Linux is an open implementation of this open interface. In fact, one of the criteria for a protocol to become a part of the Internet architecture is to have *running code* that is stable and openly available. Here open interface and open implementation proceed hand-in-hand. On the other hand, the Structured Network Architecture (SNA) of IBM was a closed interface and had a closed implementation, while Microsoft Windows is a closed implementation of the open Internet architecture. SNA has disappeared, but Windows still stands firmly. For *interoperability* of systems from different vendors, the open interface is a must, but not necessary the open implementation. Open implementations, however, have many virtues. A popular open source package has world wide *contributors,* which leads to fast *patches,* to fix bugs or enhance functions, and often better *code quality*.

1.4.2 Software Architecture in Linux Systems

When converting an architecture into a real system, it is important to identify *where* to implement *what*. Several key decisions must be made: Where to implement the control-plane and data-plane operations? What should be implemented into the hardware, ICs, or software? If implemented into software, which part of the software architecture should it be? To decide these for a Linux-based system, one should understand its software architecture first.

The Process Model

Like any other UNIX-like or modern operating systems, a Linux system has *user space* and *kernel space* programs. Kernel space programs provide services to user space programs. A *process* is an *incarnation* of a user space or kernel space program which can be scheduled to run on a CPU. Kernel space processes reside in the kernel memory space to *manage* the operations of the system so as to provide services to user space processes, though they do *not* provide services directly. User space processes reside in the user memory space and can run in the *foreground* as application *clients* or the *background* as application *servers*. Within the kernel space, there are some programs, called device drivers, to execute some I/O operations on peripheral devices. A driver is hardware dependent and must be aware of the peripheral hardware in order to control it.

When a user space process needs a specific service (e.g., sending or receiving a packet) from the kernel space programs, it issues a *system call,* which generates a *software interrupt* in the kernel space. The process then switches to the kernel space to execute kernel space programs to carry out the requested service. Once done, the process returns to the user space to run its user space program. Note that the services are provided by kernel space *programs* (not the kernel space *processes* that administer the system as mentioned above), which are executed by user space processes when they switch into the kernel space. System calls serve as the application program interface (API) between the user space and the kernel space. *Socket* is a *subset* of system calls that are dedicated to *networking* purposes. Subsection 1.4.4 has more on socket.

Where to Implement What?

Given the above process model, several observations can be applied to decide where to implement what. Since kernel space programs provide fundamental services to user space programs, *application-independent* programs should be implemented as kernel space programs while leaving application clients and servers to user space programs. Within the kernel space, *hardware-dependent* processing should be implemented as device drivers, while the rest reside in the core operating system. Following these guidelines, where to implement what in Linux systems becomes obvious. All application protocols are implemented into the user space clients and servers, while TCP, UDP, and IP are implemented into the Linux kernel. Various hardware-dependent link layers are implemented as drivers and hardware. Depending on what has been put into the hardware, either a simple onboard circuit or an ASIC, the driver for a link can be a link layer protocol handler or a pure "packet reader and writer." For links where *timing* is important in guaranteeing the correct link protocol operation, the link layer protocol should be done by an ASIC without CPU involvement. Otherwise, the hardware for the link can be a simple transceiver while leaving the protocol processing to the driver program for the link.

With forwarding in IP, error control mostly in TCP and some in IP and UDP, and traffic control in TCP, but all implemented into the Linux kernel, one question remains: Where should we put the control-plane operations of the Internet? They include routing in RIP, OSPF, and BGP, error reporting in ICMP, host configuration in DHCP, etc. Since ICMP is simple and application-independent, it is placed right into the kernel as a companion protocol of IP. Though application-independent, RIP, OSPF, BGP, and DHCP are complicated (especially the former three, which need to run complex route computation algorithms) but for processing of control packets only. Thus, they are put into the user space programs, which run as *daemon* processes in background persistently. One can see that all unicast and multicast routing protocols are implemented into daemons. Another reason for not putting them into the kernel is because there are so many of them. But implementing them as daemons creates another problem. Routing daemons need to update forwarding tables, which are looked up by the IP forwarding program residing in the kernel. The resolution is for the routing daemon to write the data structures inside the kernel through the socket API between the user space and the kernel space.

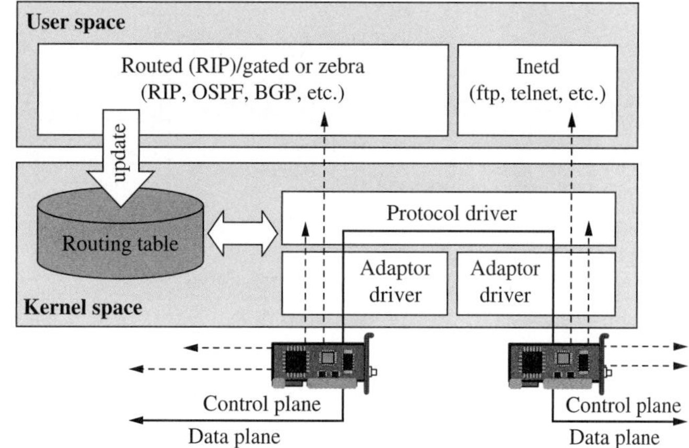

FIGURE 1.13 Software architecture in Linux systems: router.

Inside a Router and a Host

Following are two examples to show readers what common operations are implemented in network nodes and where they are placed. Figure 1.13 illustrates the common operations of a router. The routing protocols (RIP, OSPF, BGP, etc.) are implemented in daemon programs (*routed, gated,* or *zebra* for advanced routing protocols), which update the routing table (also called the forwarding table) inside the kernel for the *"protocol driver"* to look up. The protocol driver consists of IP, ICMP, TCP, and UDP and calls the adaptor drivers to send and receive packets. Another daemon, *inetd* (the super network daemon), invokes various programs for network-related services. As the arrowed lines show, packets at the control plane are processed in the protocol driver by ICMP or up in the daemons by RIP, OSPF, BGP, etc. However, packets at the data plane are to be forwarded at the IP layer in the protocol driver.

Similarly, Figure 1.14 shows the operations of a server host machine. The servers of various application protocols (e.g., Web, mail) are implemented in daemon programs (e.g., *apache, qmail, net-snmp,* etc.). The obvious difference between a

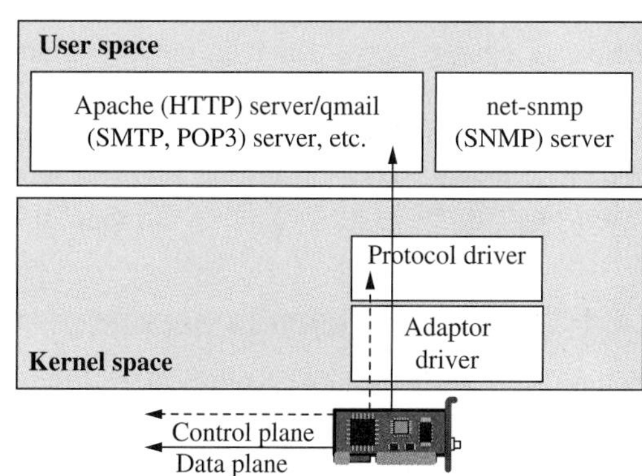

FIGURE 1.14 Software architecture in Linux systems: server host.

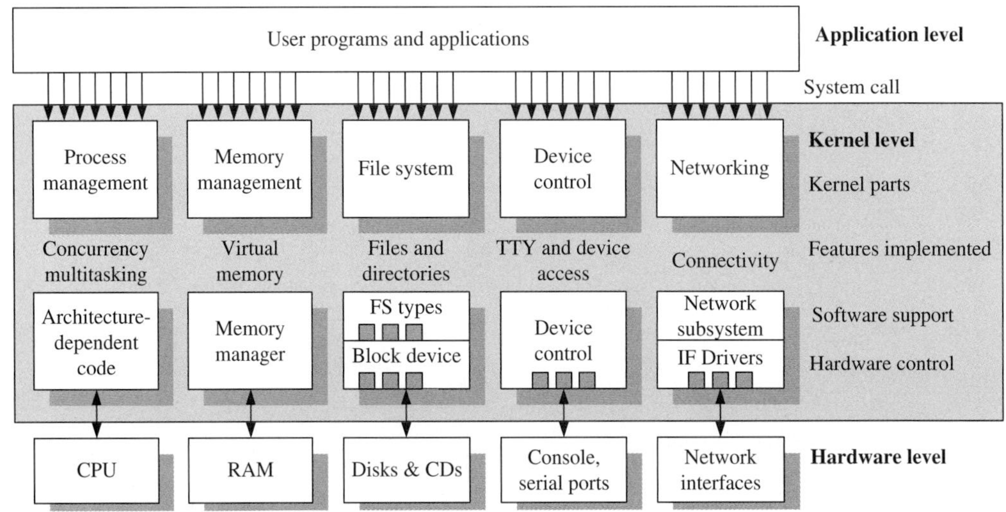

FIGURE 1.15 Kernel components.

host and a router is that there is no packet forwarding in a host, and hence it needs only one link interface or adaptor card. For this host, most packets are data-plane packets that go up to and down from the daemon servers. The only control-plane protocol might be ICMP for error reporting.

1.4.3 Linux Kernel

Having positioned the protocol entities into daemons, Linux kernel, drivers, and ICs, let us examine the *internals* of these components. We do not intend to cover them in great detail. Instead, we just touch on the key features of each component.

Figure 1.15 displays the key components inside the Linux kernel. There are five major components: process management, memory management, file system, device control, and networking, just like any UNIX-like operating system. We do not plan to elaborate on what each component is for.

Each component has two layers: hardware-independent and hardware-dependent. The hardware-dependent part is in fact the drivers for disks, consoles, and adaptor cards, or CPU architecture-dependent codes and virtual memory managers for various CPU architectures. Among these components, networking is the focus of our concern. Appendix B describes the *source tree* of the Linux kernel, especially the networking part.

1.4.4 Clients and Daemon Servers

On top of the kernel, user space processes run their user space programs, although they occasionally invoke system calls and switch into the kernel to receive services. For networking services, the socket APIs provide a set of system calls for a

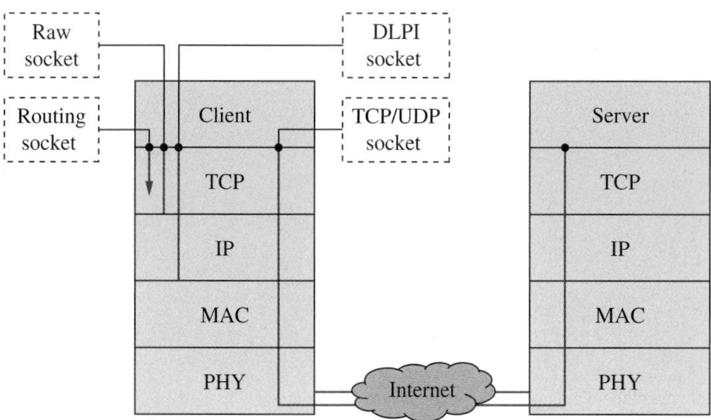

FIGURE 1.16 Clients and daemon servers: four socket APIs.

user-space process to communicate with another remote user-space process (through TCP or UDP sockets), generate its own IP packets (through raw socket), listen to an interface card directly (through the Data Link Provider Interface socket), or talk to the kernel of the same machine (through the routing socket). These sockets are illustrated in Figure 1.16. For each system call in a specific socket API, the Linux kernel implements this system call by a set of kernel space functions.

These sockets are used in different applications. For example, the Apache server, along with many other servers, uses the TCP socket. The zebra routing daemon utilizes the routing socket to update the forwarding table inside the kernel, while using the UDP socket, the raw socket, and the TCP socket to send and receive RIP, OSPF, and BGP protocol messages, respectively. The protocol stack in Figure 1.10(a) indicates the socket APIs they choose. RIP, OSPF, and BGP are on top of UDP, IP, and TCP, respectively.

1.4.5 Interface Drivers

A device driver is a set of dynamically linked functions called by the kernel. It is essential to know that the driver operations are triggered by *hardware interrupts*. A device generates a hardware interrupt when it has finished an I/O operation or detected an event that needs to be handled. This interrupt must be handled by a driver that *understands* this device, but all interrupts are first handled by the kernel. How does the kernel know which driver to choose to handle this hardware interrupt? The driver for that device should have itself *registered* to the kernel as an interrupt service routine to handle a specific numbered hardware interrupt. However, parts of the driver are not inside the interrupt service routine. The parts that are called by the kernel but not due to interrupt handling are not in the interrupt service routine. Figure 1.17 shows the driver for a network interface card. The packet receiver and parts of the packet transmitter are registered as the interrupt service routine for the interface card. They are called by the kernel due

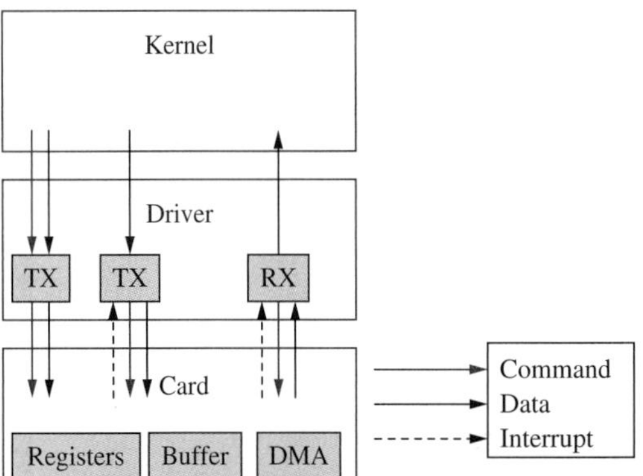

FIGURE 1.17 Interrupt-driven interface drivers: in and out.

to hardware interrupts from the interface card. Parts of the transmitter are not registered in the interrupt service routine because it is called when the kernel has packets to transmit.

In addition to transmitting and receiving packets, the driver may do some processing of the link layer protocol. Though some parts of the link layer protocol could be implemented into the ASICs in the interface card, there may still be some protocol processing inside the driver, as we shall see in Chapter 3.

1.4.6 Device Controllers

As described in Subsection 1.4.5, the driver stands behind the kernel to handle the interrupt generated by a device. Also, the driver needs to configure the device in the initialization phase or when the kernel wants to change some configuration. Then how can a driver talk with a device? In fact, inside the device there is a device controller, which usually is an integrated circuit (IC) chip responsible for communicating with the driver. The controller provides a set of *registers* for the driver to *read* and *write*. By writing or reading these registers, the driver can issue *commands* to or read *status* from the device. Besides, based on the type of CPU architecture, there are two different methods to access these registers. Some CPUs provide a set of special I/O commands, e.g., *in* and *out,* for the driver to talk with the device while some reserve a range of memory addresses for the driver to issue I/O commands like memory access, i.e., memory-mapped I/O.

The device controller is indeed the core of a device. It constantly monitors the device and immediately responds to the events from the outside environment or the driver. For example, the controller in a network adapter may run a MAC protocol to transmit a packet once it senses the driver has written a *transmit* command into its command register. It may repeatedly try to retransmit should a collision occur. In the meantime, it would monitor the network line to detect an incoming packet, receive it into the adapter memory, check its correctness based on the MAC header, and then trigger an interrupt to ask the corresponding driver to move the packet into the host memory.

1.5 BOOK ROADMAP: A PACKET'S LIFE

We have gone through the journey that introduces the why and the how regarding the Internet architecture and its open source implementations. But not enough details have been touched on so far. The subsequent chapters look into detailed why and how in each layer of the protocol stack, and we address two pressing issues on the Internet: QoS and security. Before proceeding to these chapters, it is both instructive and entertaining to see how a packet might be stored and processed inside an end host or an intermediary device. This section also provides you with the background to understand the open source implementations covered in this text.

1.5.1 Packet Data Structure: `sk_buff`

For the packet encapsulation mentioned in Section 1.3, cooperation among multiple network *layers* (or *modules*) is needed to wrap data into a packet or unwrap data from a packet. To avoid frequent data copying between these modules, a common data structure is used to store and describe a packet, and thus each module can pass or access the packet simply by a *memory pointer*. In Linux, such a data structure is named `sk_buff`, which is defined in file `skbuff.h`.

An `sk_buff` structure is used to store one packet and its related information, e.g., length, type, or any data that are exchanged along with the packet between the network modules. As shown in Figure 1.18, the structure includes many pointer variables, most of which point to an additional *fixed-size* memory space where the packet is actually stored. A field name with a prefix "+" represents an offset based on the field `head`. The variables `next` and `prev` would link the structure with the previous and next `sk_buff` so that packets in a node are maintained in a *doubly linked list*. The variables `dev` and `sk` indicate the network device and the socket,

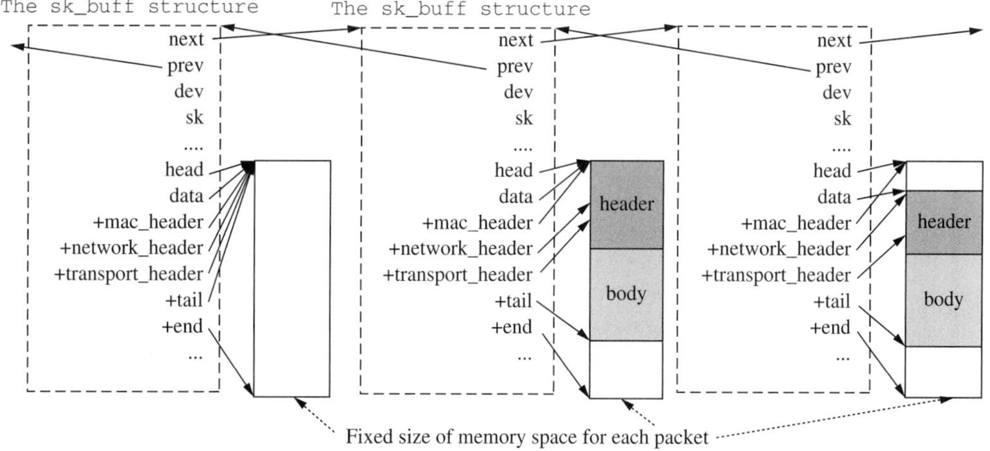

FIGURE 1.18 The doubly linked list of the `sk_buff` structure and some important fields in each `sk_buff`.

respectively, which the packet is received from or going to be transmitted to. The variables `transport_header`, `network_header` and `mac_header` contain the *offset* of the header positions of layers 4, 3, and 2, respectively, in the packet stored from the position pointed by the `head` variable.

Besides the data structure, a set of routines are provided for the network modules to allocate or free `sk_buff` and modify the data in `sk_buff`. When a packet is received from a network device, the routine `alloc_skb()` is called to allocate a buffer for the packet. As shown in the leftmost `sk_buff` of Figure 1.18, at first since no packet is stored in the allocated space, all pointers to the packet space have the same value as the variable `head`. When an incoming packet arrives to the allocated space, which may look like the middle `sk_buff` in Figure 1.18, the routine `skb_put()` would be called to move the pointer *tail* toward the end and the three header pointers to their corresponding positions. Next, the routine `skb_pull()` would be called to move down the pointer *data* every time when a protocol module removes its header and passes the packet to the *upper-layer protocol*. The packet in the upper-layer protocol may look like the rightmost `sk_buff` in Figure 1.18. Finally, after a packet is handled, the routine `kfree_skb()` is called to return the memory space of the `sk_buff`.

In the next two subsections, we shall deconstruct a *packet's life* in a Web server and in a gateway (or a router) into several stages and associate these stages with our subsequent chapters. This serves as a roadmap of this book.

1.5.2 A Packet's Life in a Web Server

Four packet flows often seen in a Web server are plotted in Figure 1.19. In general, when an Internet client wants to fetch a page from a Web server, the client sends out a packet indicating the destination Web server and the requested page. Next, the packet is forwarded by a sequence of routers to the Web server. After it is received by the network interface card (NIC) of the server, its journey in the server begins as plotted by path *A*. First, the NIC will decode the signal into data, which is a process covered in ***Chapter 2***. The NIC then alerts the adapter driver to move the packet into the memory space which was allocated from the `sk_buff` pool by the driver in advance. By reading ***Chapter 3***, readers can further learn the protocols and mechanisms operated in NIC and the adapter driver.

Once the packet is stored in an `sk_buff`, the adaptor driver calls and passes a pointer to the `sk_buff` of the packet to the IP module's reception function. The reception function then checks the validity of the packet and hooks the packet on the IP *prerouting* table for security check. The table is one of the important structures used by `netfilter`, the firewall module embedded in the Linux kernel. The structures and operations in the IP module will be detailed in ***Chapter 4,*** with the *security operations* left to ***Chapter 8.*** Next, the packet is pushed into the TCP module by `netfilter`, and ***Chapter 5*** will describe how to draw the user data out of the packet in an `sk_buff`, do error control, and pass it to the application program, which herein is the Web server. Since the Web server is a user space program, the data, which is the payload of the packet, has to be duplicated from the kernel memory to the user memory. Meanwhile, based on the header of the

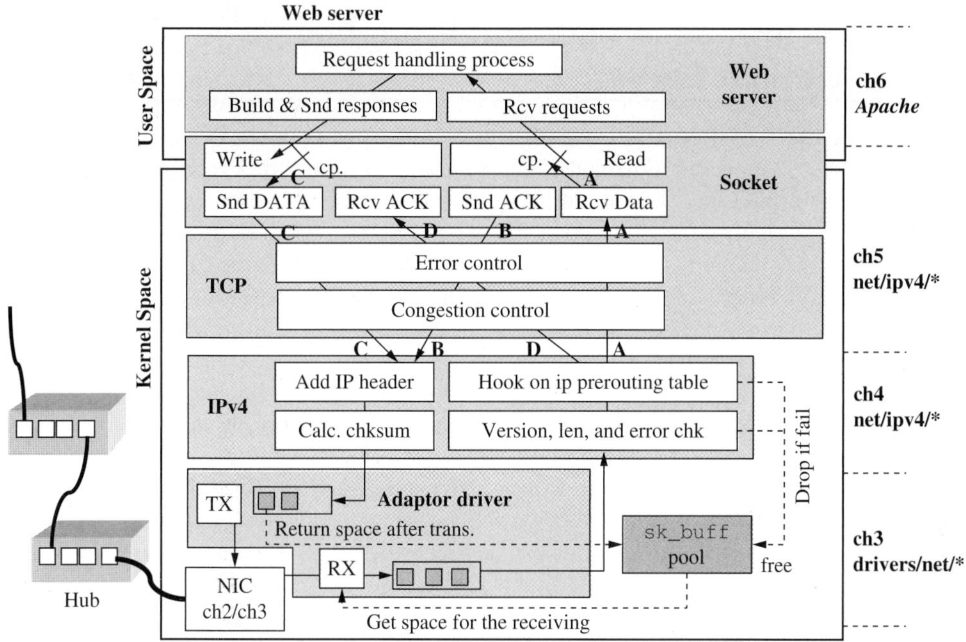

FIGURE 1.19 Life of four packets in a Web server.

received packet, the TCP module builds the ACK packet, which is then transmitted along path *B*. The ACK passes down through the TCP module, IP module, adaptor driver, NIC, and network path, and arrives at the client side. Thus, the client side is assured that the request for the desired Web page has been successfully delivered to the Web server.

In the meantime, the Web server, covered in ***Chapter 6,*** processes the request in its *socket* data structure, which was duplicated from the TCP module, generates the response and sends it via the socket interface. The response passes through the TCP and IP modules as indicated by path *C,* being encapsulated with the protocol headers and maybe fragmented into multiple packets when leaving the IP module for transmission through the Internet. Finally, the space allocated to the packet will be released back to the `sk_buff` pool. Later when the Internet client receives the response, its TCP module sends back a TCP ACK to the TCP module of the Web server, which goes through path *D* to confirm that the response has been successfully delivered to the Internet client.

1.5.3 A Packet's Life in a Gateway

Since the goal of a router or a gateway is to forward or to filter packets in the Internet or between the Internet and an intranet, it has at least two network adaptors as shown

Performance Matters: From Socket to Driver within a Server

Figure 1.20 illustrates the packet processing time within a PC server with an Intel 82566DM-2 Ethernet adaptor and a 2.0 GHz CPU. The layer interfaces within the Linux kernel are instrumented with the function `rdtscll()` (or the assembly command `RDTSC` on x86 machines), which reads the `TSC` (Time-Stamp Counter in units of CPU ticks or cycles) to measure the CPU time eclipse in each layer. For a 2.0 GHz CPU, a cycle equals 0.5 ns. The tests are repeated to obtain the average consumed CPU time of each protocol layer, where the test results with significantly larger time eclipse than the average consumed CPU time are not counted to exclude the effect of context switching and interrupt handling. Unless otherwise specified, all sidebars of Performance Matters in this text adopt this method. One could use `do_gettimeofday()` and `printk()`, or simply rely on the profiling tool `gprof/kernprof` introduced in Appendix C for time measurement, but they would be accurate only to the μs scale.

The consumed CPU time can be deconstructed into two parts. The first part, RX, describes the time measured from receiving a packet by the device driver in the link layer, processing the packet in the IP and transport layers, and delivering it to the user space. The second part, TX, depicts the time spent in each protocol layer in the kernel space to process an outgoing packet coming from the user-space server program. The total time is 34.18 μs, which is the round-trip time within a server excluding the request and response handling in the server program. In both parts, the transport layer accounts for the highest percentage of time. Apparently, it consumes a lot of time in copying data between the user and kernel space. Here, the link layer consumes the least time for both RX and TX. However, one must know that the time spent in the link layer heavily depends on the performance of the device driver and the underlying hardware. In some cases, as we shall see in the next subsection, it consumes as much time as the IP layer.

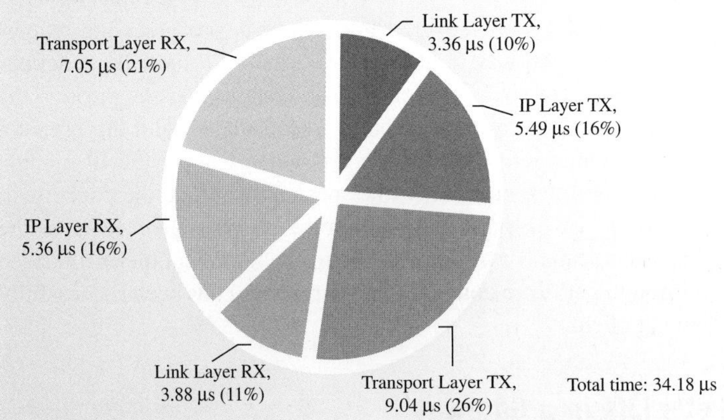

FIGURE 1.20 CPU time from socket to driver within a server.

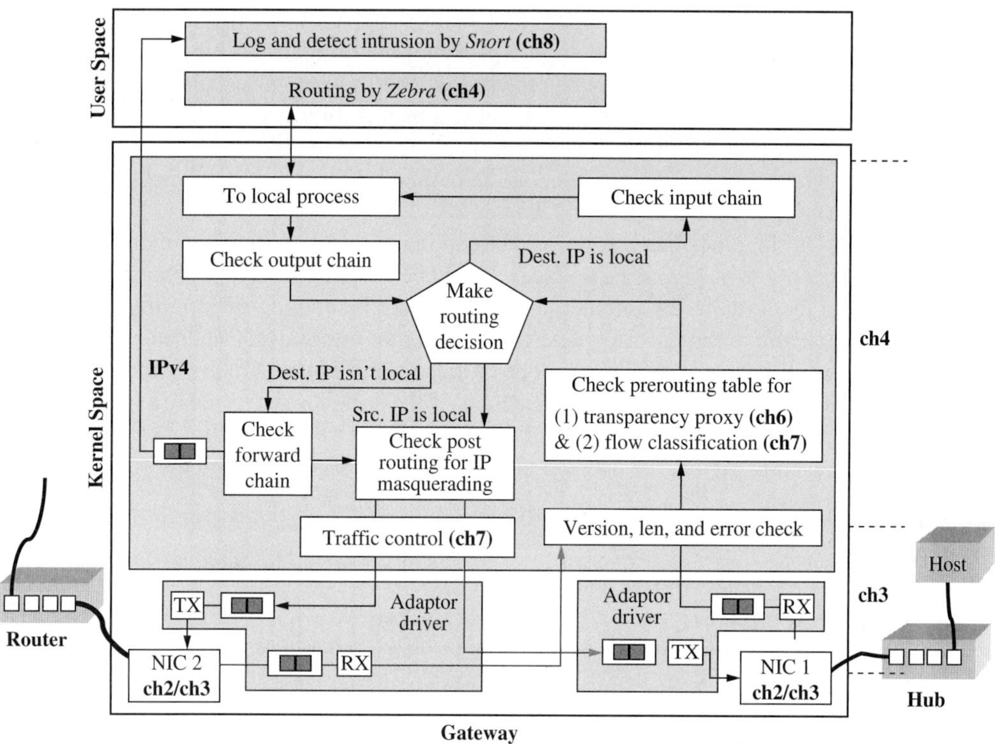

FIGURE 1.21 A packet's life in a geteway.

in Figure 1.21. Note that an intranet is a private network securely sharing any part of an organization's resources with its employees. Also, the routing and filtering modules need to determine which adaptor to forward a packet to and whether a packet should be discarded for the security of the intranet, respectively. The basic operations, such as `sk_buff` handling, error control, and interaction between modules, remain the same as the ones in a server. A router or a gateway usually has no TCP or upper-layer modules except some daemons for routing and security functions, but it would have forwarding, firewall, and QoS functions turned *on* in the kernel, as we can see in Figure 1.21.

Upon receiving a packet from the intranet, as indicated on the right hand side of Figure 1.21, the gateway may first verify its correctness and then check the *pre-routing* table to determine whether to forward the packet into the Internet. For example, if the functionality of transparency proxy is enabled in the gateway, then a packet of a URL request, instead of being sent to the actual website, may be redirected to a local Web proxy to seek the cached pages, as a *proxy* addressed in ***Chapter 6.*** Then it makes its forwarding or routing decision by checking the *forward chain,* i.e., forwarding table or routing table, with a remote destination IP address; this process is illustrated in ***Chapter 4.*** Because of security considerations and lack of IP address, a gateway might provides the *network address translation*

(NAT) function of having a public IP address shared by all hosts in the intranet. For NAT function, when the outgoing packets pass through the *post-routing* module, their source addresses may be replaced, which is commonly called *IP masquerading,* also covered in ***Chapter 4.*** Finally, a packet might be attached to a tag in the *pre-routing* module to distinguish the packet's service class and priority in forwarding with bandwidth reservation on the output link, which is managed by the *traffic control* module introduced in ***Chapter 7.***

On the other hand, for a packet coming from the Internet as indicated on the lefthand side of Figure 1.21, since it would be checked to see if it contained malware from the hosts in the Internet, the packet could be *duplicated* from the normal *forward chain* to the intrusion detection module for log analysis and detection. `SNORT` is such a software module. It will be introduced in ***Chapter 8*** along with several other modules that offer the security functions. If the packet is addressed to a local process, say a routing daemon covered in ***Chapter 4,*** it goes through the *input chain* and up to the daemon. Again, the daemon may send its packets out through the *output chain.*

Performance Matters: From Input Port to Output Port within a Router

Unlike the case in a server, packets usually do not need to go through the transport layer within a router or gateway. As depicted in Figure 1.21, the network adaptor first raises an interrupt when a packet arrives. The device driver in the link layer triggers DMA transferring to move the packet from the adaptor buffer to the kernel memory. Then the packet is passed to the IP layer, which checks the routing table and forwards the packet to the appropriate outgoing adaptor. Again, the device driver of the outgoing adaptor utilizes DMA transferring to copy the packet from the kernel memory to the adaptor buffer, and then asks the adaptor to transmit it. Throughout the process, the transport layer and above are untouched. Some control-plane packets, however, might go up to the transport and application layers. Figure 1.22 shows the CPU time spent in processing a packet within a router. Here the DMA time is one exception. It is actually the time eclipse instead of the consumed CPU time. All other times are consumed CPU times. The PC-based router has an Intel Pro/100 Ethernet adaptor and a 1.1 GHz CPU.

Due to the lower-speed CPU, the time of the IP layer RX here is higher than the result shown in Figure 1.20. Furthermore, when compared with Figure 1.20, both of the RX and TX times spent in the link layer increase significantly because the performance of the Intel Pro/100 Ethernet adaptor, a 100 Mb adaptor, is lower than that of the Intel 82566DM-2 Ethernet adaptor, a gigabit adaptor. Another noticeable difference between the router and server cases is the time for transmitting a packet through the IP layer, i.e., IP layer TX. Although both cases walk through a similar path in the IP layer TX, the information carried by `sk_buff` is different. Within a router, the `sk_buff` contains ready-to-send information except for the source MAC address, which needs to be changed.

However, within a server, the IP layer has to prepend the whole Ethernet header to `sk_buff` before sending it to the link layer, which causes the processing time of the IP layer TX within a server to be higher than the one within a router. Finally, although with lower-speed hardware, the total packet processing time, i.e., 29.14 μs, is still less than the time within a server with high-end hardware as shown in Figure 1.20.

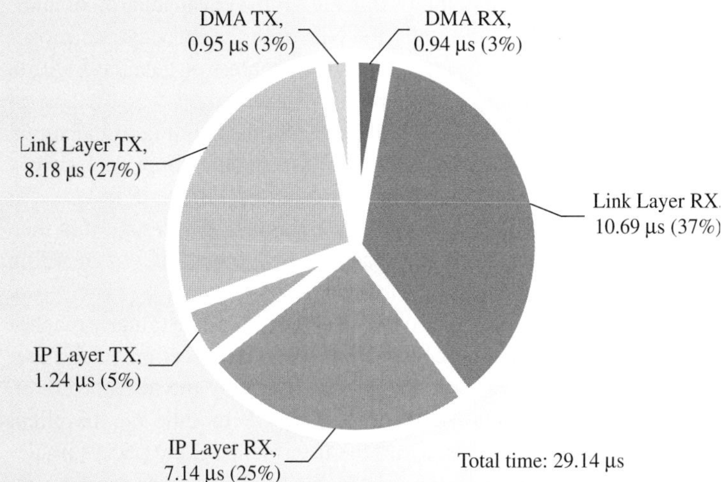

FIGURE 1.22 CPU time from input to output within a router.

Principle in Action: A Packet's Life in the Internet

It is indeed entertaining to examine a packet's life in a Web server and in a router or gateway. Now let us tell the whole story from a packet's birth at a client, through its routing along several routers, and finally its arrival to the Web server. Described in ***Chapter 6,*** the client program first calls the "`socket`" function for the kernel to prepare a set of socket data structures, and then calls the "`connect`" function to ask the kernel TCP module to establish a TCP connection with the Web server side's TCP module by the three-way handshake as detailed in ***Chapter 5.*** Normally there will be three packets (SYN, SYN-ACK, ACK) sent between the two corresponding TCP modules. That is, before the HTTP request can be sent there are already three packets exchanged. They follow procedures similar to those of the HTTP request at the client, routers or gateways, and the server, except that they terminate at the TCP module and do not go up to the client and server programs.

Continued

After the TCP connection is set up between the client and the server, the client program gives *birth* to the life of an HTTP request in its user memory space and calls the "`write`" function to send the request to the kernel. The interrupted kernel then copies the HTTP request from the user space into its socket data structures, including the `sk_buff`, to store the HTTP request message. The "`write`" function in the client program returns at this point. The kernel TCP module then takes care of the rest by encapsulating the HTTP request with a TCP header and passing it down to the IP module for the encapsulation of an IP header, then the adaptor driver, and finally the NIC with the link-layer encapsulation. This packet then traverses through a series of routers or gateways within each, going through the procedure described in Subsection 1.5.3. That is, at each router or gateway, its reception at a NIC triggers the decoding of the signal into data (detailed in ***Chapter 2***), and interrupts the adaptor driver (detailed in ***Chapter 3***), which copies it into an `sk_buff` and passes it to the IP module for forwarding through the normal forward chain (detailed in ***Chapter 4***). It is then handled by the adaptor driver again, which passes it to another NIC for encoding and transmission (detailed in ***Chapter 2***).

Forwarded by several routers, the encapsulated HTTP request finally reaches its server. It then goes through the procedure described in Subsection 1.5.2. After passing through a NIC, being copied into an `sk_buff` by the adaptor driver, checked by the IP module, acknowledged by the TCP module on the client side, and copied by the socket interface into the user memory, the packet finally reaches the server program. Lying in the user memory of the server program, its lifetime is *terminated* after the server parses the HTTP request message and prepares the HTTP response. The server program then repeats the same procedure to send the HTTP response back to the client program. The response also triggers a TCP acknowledgment from the client TCP module to the server's. If this is the end of the HTTP session, normally four packets (FIN, ACK, FIN, ACK) will be sent to terminate the TCP connection. There will be at least 3 (TCP connection setup) + 1 (HTTP request) + 1 (ACK to the request) + 1 (HTTP response if it is short enough to fit into a packet) + 1 (ACK to the response) + 4 (TCP connection tear-down) = 11 packets exchanged in completing an HTTP session.

1.6 SUMMARY

We started from the three requirements or objectives, i.e., connectivity, scalability, and resource sharing, that must be satisfied in building computer networks. Then we explained the principles or constraints on performance, operations, and interoperability that limit the solution space that we could explore. Next the Internet solutions were presented along with their Linux-based open source implementations. Finally we laid out this book's roadmap by illustrating a packet's life within a Web server and a router. In this chapter, we introduced many concepts and terminologies that will be used throughout this book. Among them, switching, routing, stateless, soft-state, best-effort, data plane, and control plane are important for readers to comprehend.

The single biggest design decision made in the Internet evolution is the end-to-end argument. It pushes the complexity of error and traffic control to end hosts, while keeping the core network simple. The core is so simple that it runs stateless routing instead of stateful switching and offers only best effort, unreliable IP services. The end-to-end transport layer at hosts then runs reliable connection-oriented TCP with error and traffic control, or unreliable connectionless UDP without much control. It is the *polite* TCP running flow and congestion control that keeps the Internet *healthy* and *fair* in the resource sharing community. Another big decision is structuring the Internet into a three-level hierarchy with domains and subnets of contiguous IP address blocks. It solves the scalability issue by breaking the routing problem into intra-domain problems and inter-domain problems. The problem size of the former is usually less than 256, while the size of the latter is at the scale of 65,536; both sizes are manageable but require different schemes to scale.

The Evolving Hourglass

Today the Internet has a *single* IP technology at the network layer and several at the transport layer, but it rides on *many* types of links and offers *huge* application services. This *hourglass-shaped* protocol stack continues to evolve with many innovations to come. The middle layers remain quite stable but face the pressure to transit from IPv4 to IPv6 and limit the impolite UDP traffic, as we shall describe in Chapter 4 and Chapter 5, respectively. Meanwhile, its statelessness has been challenged constantly, as we have explained. The lower layers have converged to one or several technologies in each market segment, though the *last-mile wireless* remains an unsettled battlefield. We have much to see in Chapter 2 and Chapter 3. At the top, traditional client-server applications continue to evolve slowly, but the new peer-to-peer (P2P) applications emerge at a fast pace, as we shall see in Chapter 6.

In the late 1990s and early 2000s, it was hoped that the Internet could be re-engineered to provide quality of service (QoS) to *guarantee* latency, throughput, or loss rate. But all proposals required *adding* some statefulness into the core network, which conflicted with its original stateless nature and thus failed. Today many QoS technologies are applied only at the link level but not at the end-to-end level. Chapter 7 has more to say on that. In addition to *wireless* and *P2P, security* probably is the hottest pressing issue. From the early concerns of controlling "who can access what" and protecting "private data on the public Internet," the attention has been shifted to protecting systems from intrusions, viruses, and spam. Chapter 8 has a comprehensive coverage on them.

COMMON PITFALLS

Transmission Delay vs. Propagation Delay

These two are obviously different. But surprisingly, some readers might not be able to differentiate between them after the first reading if we did not compare them. Transmission delay represents the total time needed by a device to fully push a packet into a network link. The delay depends on the length of the packet (packet size) and the bandwidth of the link. For example, for a packet with length 250 bytes, i.e., 2000 bits, its transmission time in a host with 1 Gbps link is 2000 (bits)/10^9 (bits/sec) = 2 μs.

Propagation delay represents the total time for a packet to pass through a link. It depends on the rate and the distance the signal travels. Since the packet is transmitted in electrons, the traveling rate is a fraction of light speed and is only affected by the transmission media. For example, for a packet passing through an intercontinental submarine cable with length 1000 km, its propagation delay is 100 km/ ($2*10^8$ m/sec) = 50 μs.

Throughput vs. Utilization

The same thing happens to these two terms. Throughput is used to describe how much data, usually in bits or bytes, are transmitted or handled by a device over a unit of time, usually a second. For example, we measure the amount of data via the outgoing link in 1 minute and get $75*10^6$ bytes, then we can calculate the average throughput as $75*10^6$

(bytes)/60 (sec) = $1.25*10^6$ Bps. That is, there is data of $1.25*10^6$ bytes passing through the link per second on average. Throughput could be normalized by the capacity of the system, which renders a value between 0 and 1.

On the other hand, the utilization means what percentage of the bandwidth in a link is used or the percentage of the time a device is busy. By following the same example above and assuming that the bandwidth of the link is $100*10^6$ bps, then the utilization of the link would be $1.25*10^6$ Bps/$100*10^6$ bps = 10%.

Layer 2, 3, 4, 7 Switches

It is common to hear layer-2 to layer-7 switches, but why do we need so many kinds of switches? The basic operating principle for a switch is relying on the *tag* of a packet to select a port. Such a principle could be used to build the switches for different layers, which rely on different protocols to get the tag. For example, a layer-2 switch may learn and *memorize* where an adaptor is by observing the *source* MAC address of incoming packets from a port, and then switch packets with that destination MAC address to the port later on. Thus, MAC address is used as the tag in a layer-2 switch.

Similarly, IP address, flow id, and URL may be used as the tag in the switch of layer-3, layer-4, and layer-7, respectively. A layer-3 IP switch, which is in fact the MPLS technology, simplifies the tag to a number and asks the upstream switch to label future packets with this number for fast *indexing* into the tag table. Such an IP switch would run faster than the traditional IP router. A layer-4 switch uses the five-tuple flow id (source IP address, destination IP address, source port number, destination port number, protocol id) as the tag, and switches packets of the same flow to the same output port. This *persistent switching* is important for e-commerce applications where throughout the transaction the user is switched to the same server machine. A layer-7 Web switch goes one step further to use the application header information, such as URL or Web page cookie, as the tag for persistent switching. Doing so could allow an e-commerce transaction to last even longer across many connections or flows. It is interesting to note that there is no layer-5 or layer-6 simply because people like to call the application layer layer-7 instead of layer-5 due to the 7-layer OSI model.

Baseband vs. Broadband

Some readers confuse broadband with large bandwidth and baseband with little bandwidth. In fact, these two terms barely convey any meaning about the amount of bandwidth. In baseband transmissions, the digital signal of the data is directly transmitted via the link. It is the original *square shape* of the signal that is transmitted. It is easy to send or receive such a signal. However, a link can carry one such signal at a time. Such a square-shaped signal decays easily and cannot sustain for a long distance; thus baseband is used mostly for LANs.

In broadband transmissions, the digital signal of the data is mixed with an *analog carrier* signal adjusted to a special frequency. In this way, not only can the resulting signal travel a long distance and have the digital signal recovered at the receiver, the link also could transport multiple digital signals in parallel by mixing each digital signal with an analog carrier of a *different* frequency. However, a more complex transceiver is needed. Broadband is used mostly for WANs.

Modem vs. Codec

Some readers might think we can use a codec *reversely* as a modem or vice versa, but in fact we cannot. A modem is a device to transform digital data into analog signals for transmission and vice versa. The former is called *modulation*, while the latter is *demodulation*. The goal is to enhance the capability of *noise tolerance* for the *long-distance* transmission. The most popular example is Internet access from your home PC via ADSL modem or cable modem.

A codec is a device to transform analog data into digital signals and vice versa. Its goal is to leverage the *error recovery* capability of digital signals. The popular example is when you speak on a cellular phone your analog voice is digitalized first at the phone, then modulated into analog signal also at the phone for long-distance transmission to the base station and beyond. The digital signal can be recovered easily at each transmission hop, and thus, after demodulated at the receiver side, renders the original analog voice.

FURTHER READINGS

Other Textbooks

Searching on scholar.google.com finds us six important textbooks on computer networks. These textbooks are listed here and ordered by the number of times they are cited.

- A. S. Tanenbaum, *Computer Networks,* 4th edition, Prentice Hall, 2002.
- D. Bertsekas and R. Gallager, *Data Networks,* 2nd edition, Prentice Hall, 1992.
- W. Stallings, *Data and Computer Communications,* 8th edition, Prentice Hall, 2006.
- J. F. Kurose and K. W. Ross, *Computer Networking: A Top-Down Approach,* 3rd edition, Addison-Wesley, 2003.
- L. L. Peterson and B. S. Davie, *Computer Networks: A System Approach,* 4th edition, Elsevier, 2007.
- D. E. Comer, *Internetworking with TCP/IP, Volume I: Principles, Protocols, and Architecture,* 4th edition, Prentice Hall, 2000.

The Tanenbaum book is a traditional one with a bit of everything and story-telling descriptions. It has more how than why. The one by Bertsekas and Gallager focuses solely on performance modeling and analysis, and should be used for the second course. The Stallings book is encyclopedically flat structured, with more emphasis on lower layers. Kurose and Ross feature a top-down order in presenting layered protocols, with much heavier treatments on upper layers. Peterson and Davie address more system implementation issues, but mostly without running examples. The Comer book focuses only on the TCP/IP protocol stack, and leaves example codes to the second volume.

The Internet Architecture

The first three of the following readings discuss the general philosophies driving the design of the Internet architecture. They serve as good references if readers are interested in tracking down the stories. The Ethernet article serves as the classic reference for the origin of Ethernet. Though Ethernet is not a part of the Internet architecture, we still include it here because it is the dominating wired infrastructure that *carries* the Internet architecture. The next three are critical Request for Comments (RFCs) that build the *foundation* of the Internet architecture. The next one is the RFC that started the decade-long effort to re-engineer the Internet for QoS guarantee. At the end are two important research works on congestion control, which maintains the *healthiness* of the Internet. The website of the Internet Engineering Task Force (IETF) has all RFCs defining the Internet along with many other resources.

- J. Saltzer, D. Reed, and D. Clark, "End-to-End Arguments in System Design," *ACM Transactions on Computer Systems,* Vol 2, No. 4, pp. 277–288, Nov. 1984.
- D. Clark, "The Design Philosophy of the DARPA Internet Protocols," *ACM SIGCOMM,* pp. 106–114, Aug. 1988.
- K. Hafner and M. Lyon, *Where Wizards Stay up Late: The Origins of the Internet,* Simon & Schuster, 1996.
- R. M. Metcalfe and D. R. Boggs, "Ethernet: Distributed Packet Switching for Local Computer Networks," *Communications of the ACM,* Vol. 19, Issue 7, pp. 395–404, July 1976.
- J. Postel, "Internet Protocol," RFC 791, Sept. 1981.
- J. Postel, "Transmission Control Protocol," RFC 793, Sept. 1981.
- M. Allman, V. Paxson, W. Stevens, "TCP Congestion Control," RFC 2581, Apr. 1999.
- R. Braden, D. Clark, S. Shenker, "Integrated Services in the Internet Architecture: An Overview," RFC 1633, June 1994.
- V. Jacobson and M. J. Karels, "Congestion Avoidance and Control," *ACM Computer Communication Review: Proceedings of the SIGCOMM,* Aug. 1988.
- S. Floyd and K. Fall, "Promoting the Use of End-to-End Congestion Control in the Internet," *IEEE/ACM Transactions on Networking,* Vol. 7, Issue 4, Aug. 1999.
- Internet Engineering Task Force, www.ietf.org.

Open Source Development

The first two of the following are the first open source *project* and the first *article* on open source, respectively. The third one is the extended book version of the first article on open source. The next two are an overview of the open source development with the first on the technical aspects and the second on how a project effort is organized. FreshMeat.net is the hub to download from a huge library of open source packages, while SourceForge.net hosts many open source projects. Even the hardware could be open source. OpenCores.org is the hub for open source hardware components.

- R. Stallman, The GNU project, http://www.gnu.org.
- E. S. Raymond, "The Cathedral and the Bazaar," May 1997, http://www.tuxedo.org/~esr/writings/cathedral-bazaar/cathedral-bazaar.
- E. S. Raymond, *The Cathedral and the Bazaar: Musings on Linux and Open Source by an Accidental Revolutionary,* O'Reilly & Associates, Jan. 2001.
- M. W. Wu and Y. D. Lin, "Open Source Software Development: an Overview," *IEEE Computer,* June 2001.
- K. R. Lakhani and E. Von Hippel, "How Open Source Software Works: 'Free' User-to-User Assistance," *Research Policy,* Vol. 32, Issue 6, pp. 923-943, June 2003.

- Freshmeat, freshmeat.net.
- SourceForge, sourceforge.net.
- OpenCores, opencores.org.

Performance Modeling and Analysis

The first two of the following entries are the first work in Danish on queuing theory by Agner Krarup Erlang in 1909 and 1917, while the third entry is the classic paper often called the Little's result, published in 1961. The Kleinrock books in 1975/1976 are the classic and first pieces that applied queuing theory to modeling computer and communications systems. The Leon-Garcia book is a text for the first course on random processes, which serve as the foundation for queuing systems modeling. The final three are additional or newer texts on performance analysis.

- A. K. Erlang, "The Theory of Probabilities and Telephone Conversations," *Nyt Tidsskrift for Matematik B,* Vol. 20, 1909.
- A. K. Erlang, "Solutions of Some Problems in the Theory of Probabilities of Significance in Automatic Telephone Exchanges," *Elektrotkeknikeren,* Vol. 13, 1917.
- J. D. C. Little, "A Proof of the Queueing Formula L = λW," *Operations Research,* Vol. 9, pp. 383-387, 1961.
- L. Kleinrock, *Queueing Systems, Volume 1: Theory,* John Wiley and Sons, 1975.
- L. Kleinrock, *Queueing Systems, Volume 2: Applications,* John Wiley and Sons, 1976.
- A. Leon-Garcia, *Probability, Statistics, and Random Processes for Electrical Engineering,* 3rd edition, Prentice Hall, 2008.
- R. Jain, *The Art of Computer Systems Performance Analysis: Techniques for Experimental Design, Measurement, Simulation and Modeling,* John Wiley and Sons, 1991.
- T. G. Robertazzi, *Computer Networks and Systems: Queueing Theory and Performance Evaluation,* 3rd edition, Springer-Verlag, 2000.
- L. Lipsky, *Queuing Theory: A Linear Algebraic Approach,* 2nd edition, Springer, 2008.

FREQUENTLY ASKED QUESTIONS

1. How does Internet scale to billions of hosts? (Describe what structure and levels are used to organize the hosts, and calculate the numbers of entities at each level.)
   Answer:
   Three-level hierarchy where 256 hosts could be grouped into a subnet and 256 subnets could be grouped into a domain, which could result in 65,536 domains with four billion hosts.
2. Routing vs. switching: stateful or stateless, connection-oriented or connectionless, matching or indexing? (Associate these features with routing and switching.)
   Answer:
   Routing: stateless, connectionless, matching.
   Switching: stateful, connection-oriented, indexing.
3. What may increase or decrease the latency inside the Internet? (What are the factors that might increase or decrease the latency of queuing, transmission, processing, and propagation, respectively?)
   Answer:
   Queuing: traffic load, network bandwidth or CPU capacity
   Transmission: network bandwidth.
   Processing: CPU capacity.
   Propagation: length of links/paths.
4. What do Little's result and bandwidth-delay product tell us? (Hints: The former is about a node, while the latter is about a link or path.)
   Answer:
   Little's result: In a node, the mean number of packets is the product of the mean packet arrival rate and the mean delay/latency, i.e., the mean number in the box equals mean rate multiplied by mean delay.
   Bandwidth-delay product: the maximum number of outstanding bits in transit in a link/path.
5. What does the end-to-end argument say about networking?
   Answer:
   If a problem cannot be fully resolved at a lower layer (or at routers), resolve it at an upper layer (or at end hosts). This pushes the complexity from core routers to end hosts.
6. According to the end-to-end argument, at which single layer should we put error control for the Internet? But then why do we put it in many layers including link, IP, and transport layers?
   Answer:
   At the end-to-end transport layer because both link and nodal errors could be detected and corrected

there, i.e., the link layer can only handle the link errors but not nodal errors. But for the purpose of efficiency, error control is also put into the link and IP layers to handle errors earlier.

7. What types of mechanisms should be put into the control plane and data plane, respectively? (Specify their type of packets, purpose, granularity of processing time, and example operation.)
   Answer:
   Control plane: control packets, maintain the normal operations of data plane, usually seconds, routing.
   Data plane: data packets, transfer packets correctly, usually in microseconds, forwarding.
8. What are standard and implementation-dependent components in a router? (Specify their types of components and example.)
   Answer:
   Standard: protocol message formats and algorithms that affect interoperability between routers; routing protocol such as RIP.
   Implementation-dependent: internal data structures and algorithms that do not affect interoperability; routing table and its lookup algorithm.
9. What's inside a Linux distribution? (Specify what types of files you would find in a distribution and how they are organized.)
   Answer:
   Types of files: documents, configuration files, log files, binary object files, image files, source programs of the kernel and application packages.
   Organization: into directories.
10. When do we implement a mechanism of a network device into ASIC, driver, kernel, and daemon, respectively? (Specify their guidelines and examples.)
   Answer:
   ASIC: usually PHY/MAC and sometimes accelerators of IP/TCP/UDP and upper layers; Ethernet/WLAN PHY/MAC and crypto accelerator.
   Driver: usually interface between MAC and IP and sometimes some link layers; Ethernet/WLAN driver and PPP driver.
   Kernel: usually IP/TCP/UDP layers; NAT and TCP/IP firewall.
   Daemon: application clients, servers, or peers; Web client, server, and proxy.

EXERCISES

Hands-On Exercises

1. Visit freshmeat.net, sourceforge.net, and opencores.org, then summarize and compare what they have.
2. Install a newest Linux distribution, and summarize: (1) its installation process and (2) things inside a Linux distribution.
3. First read Appendix B, then look up the programs under `/src`, `/usr/src`, or other directories where the source files reside, depending on the version of the Linux distribution being used; summarize and categorize what's inside that directory.
4. Follow the instructions in Appendix C to debug an application program and the Linux kernel using `gdb` and `kgdb`. Also use `gprof` and `kprof` to profile an application program and the Linux kernel, respectively. Give a report on how you do these and what you have found in debugging and profiling.
5. Try out the tools `host`, `arp`, `ping`, `traceroute`, `tcpdump`, and `netstat` described in Appendix D to explore and summarize your network environment.
6. Trace the Linux kernel code to find:
   - **a.** Which function calls `alloc_skb()` to allocate `sk_buff` for the request and the response, respectively, in Figure 1.19.
   - **b.** Which function calls `kfree_skb()` to release `sk_buff` for the request and the response, respectively, in Figure 1.19.
   - **c.** Which function calls `alloc_skb()` to allocate `sk_buff` in Figure 1.21.
   - **d.** Which function calls `kfree_skb()` to release `sk_buff` in Figure 1.21.
   - **e.** How you trace these dynamically or statically.
7. Find an RFC with a status of `"Standard"` (STD).
   - **a.** Read it and summarize how a protocol is described in an RFC.
   - **b.** Search in the source tree of Linux or a Linux distribution to find an open source implementation. Describe how the protocol is implemented in the code you find.

c. If you are to develop an open source implementation from scratch, how would you implement yours from that RFC?

Written Exercises

1. Consider a transcontinental link of 5000 miles with a bandwidth of 40 Gbps. Assume the propagation speed is 2×10^8 m/sec.
   a. What is the width of one bit in time and in length, respectively?
   b. How many bits can be contained in the link at most?
   c. What is the transmission time of a packet of 1500 bytes?
   d. What is the propagation time through this link?
2. A stream of packets travel along a path with 10 links and nodes in the Internet. Each link is 100 km long and of 45 Mbps capacity, and has a propagation speed of 2×10^8 m/sec. Assume no flow control, no other traffic along the path, and the source pumps packets at wire speed.
   a. What is the number of bits contained in each link?
   b. If the average latency through each node is 5 ms, what is the average number of bits contained in each node?
   c. How many bits on the average are contained in the path?
3. Suppose a 1 Gbps link has exponential packet interarrival time and service time. We like to apply the queuing theory and Little's result to calculate mean latency and occupancy.
   a. If the mean arrival rate is 500 Mbps, what are the mean latency, queuing time, and occupancy?
   b. If the link bandwidth and mean arrival rate are increased by an order of magnitude to 10 Gbps and 5 Gbps, respectively, what are the mean latency, queuing time, and occupancy?
4. If 30% of packets have a size of 64 bytes, 50% of packet have a size of 1500 bytes, and the rest have a size uniformly distributed between 64 and 1500 bytes, what is the maximum number of aggregated packets per second (pps) at a router with 12 links each of 10 Gbps?
5. Suppose there are 3,000,000 new phone call arrivals per minute to the switched telephone system worldwide, with each call lasting for 5 minutes on average, and there are 6 hops (i.e. 6 links and 6 nodes) on average between the callers and callees. How many memory entries are occupied on average to support the switched connectivity worldwide?
6. In a clustering of 4,294,967,296 nodes, if we still want to keep the three-level hierarchy like the one in Figure 1.1 but like to have the *same* number of group members, groups, and supergroups at the group, supergroup, and "super-supergroup" levels, respectively, what is that number approximately?
7. If, due to the shortage of IP addresses, we *halve* the size at the group and the supergroup levels in Figure 1.1, with at most 128 group members for a group and 128 groups for a supergroup, how many supergroups can we allow?
8. Compare the differences in the requirements and principles for data communications and tele(voice)-communications. Name the three most important differences and explain.
9. Why is the Internet designed as a routed instead of a switched network? If it were designed as a switched network, what layers and mechanisms would need to be changed?
10. Here we compare the overhead of routing packets and switching packets. Why is the time complexity of routing higher than switching, while the space complexity of switching is higher than routing?
11. If a new routing protocol is to be supported in routers, what should be defined as standard and what should be left as implementation-dependent design?
12. Content networking demands the Internet itself become more application-aware, i.e., knowing who is accessing what data and talking to whom, which would disrupt the original end-to-end argument. What changes may be brought into the network to support content networking?
13. ATM (asynchronous transfer mode) and MPLS (multi-protocol label switching) do not have stateless core networks. What states do they keep? What is the main difference in the way they keep these states?
14. ATM (asynchronous transfer mode) is an alternative technology for data communications. Why does it have high overhead when interoperating with IP to carry IP packets?
15. MPLS (multi-protocol label switching) is a standard for IP switching that aims to switch most but route few IP packets. What is the barrier to its deployment? How can we reduce the effect of this barrier?
16. When supporting a protocol, we may put the protocol entity into the kernel or a daemon process. What are the considerations here? That is, when will you put it into the kernel and a daemon, respectively?

17. In Figure 1.13, why do we put the routing task as a daemon in the user space while keeping the routing table lookup in the kernel? Why not put both in the user space or the kernel?
18. When you write a driver for a network adaptor, which parts should be written into an interrupt service routine? Which parts should not?
19. When you implement a data link protocol, which parts will you implement into the hardware and the driver, respectively?
20. We need to understand how the hardware works along with its driver.
    a. What is the interface between the driver of a network adaptor and the controller of the network adaptor?
    b. How does the driver ask the controller to send a packet and how does the controller report it has completed the job?
    c. How does the controller report to the driver when a packet has arrived at the network adaptor?
21. `Linux`, `apache`, `sendmail`, `GNU C library`, `bind`, `freeS/wan`, and `snort` are popular open source packages. Search on the Internet to find out the license model for each of them, and summarize the differences between these license models.
22. When you type in a URL at your browser, you get the corresponding homepage within seconds. Briefly describe what happened at your host, the intermediate routers, and the related server, respectively. Read Section 1.5.2 before writing your answers so that your answer is precise, but do not assume you are running on Linux systems.

2

Chapter

Physical Layer

The physical (PHY) layer is the *bottommost* layer of the OSI model or the TCP/IP model in computer networks, and it is the only layer that interacts with transmission media. A transmission *medium* is a material substance that can propagate energy waves called *signals* from a sender to a receiver; moreover, the free space can also be considered a transmission medium for electromagnetic waves. The transmission media can only carry signals instead of data, but the information source from the link layer is of digital data. Thus the physical layer must *convert* the digital data into an appropriate signal waveform. In modern digital communications, such conversion is a two-step process. It first applies *information coding* to the digital data for data compression and protection and then *modulates* the coded data into signals that are appropriate for transmission over the communication medium. It should be noted that in analog communication only the latter process of modulation is used.

To enable high-speed transmissions, the physical layer needs to decide which coding or modulation technique to use based on the properties of the medium. A wired medium is *more reliable;* thus the physical layer focuses solely on improving its throughput and utilization. In contrast, a wireless medium is less reliable and exposed to the public; thus the physical layer has to cope with noise and interference and prevent the data from being corrupted. Techniques to deal with a medium full of noise, interference, and even multipath fading are then required in addition to improving the throughput and utilization.

Multiple *channels* could exist on a medium. A channel between a transmitter and a receiver can be *physical* or *logical*. In wired networks, a physical channel is a transmission path traversing through cables, while in wireless networks a physical channel is a *band* of frequencies in the *spectra of electromagnetic waves*. A logical channel is a *sub-channel* where the transmission medium is partitioned by various division methods such as *time*-division, *frequency*-division, *code*-division, or *spatial*-division. Thus, another kind of technique called *multiplexing* is needed to better utilize a medium.

In this chapter, the fundamental conversion techniques are presented. In Section 2.1, we first address the differences between analog data/signals and digital data/signals. Next we illustrate the transmission and reception flows, the data/signal conversion through coding and modulation, multiplexing for better utilization, and factors that impair signals. Section 2.2 characterizes the transmission media in two categories: wired and wireless. Various techniques of *line coding* (or called *digital baseband modulation*) are presented in Section 2.3, to achieve better sender-receiver clock *synchronization*. Classical techniques such as non-return-to-zero (NRZ),

Manchester, alternate mark inversion (AMI), multilevel transmission (MLT-3), and 4B/5B are introduced. An open source implementation of the 8B/10B encoder is presented.

Digital modulation techniques are covered in Section 2.4, including amplitude-shift keying (ASK), frequency-shift keying (FSK), phase-shift keying (PSK), and quadrature amplitude modulation (QAM). The modulation is to transfer a digital bit stream over an analog *passband* channel where an analog carrier signal is modulated by the digital bit stream. In other words, the coded data is converted into a passband signal, a real (or complex) continuous-time waveform, for digital transmission. The resulting signal is a real continuous-time waveform contained within a limited bandwidth centered at the frequency of the carrier. Next we introduce the basic *multiplexing* techniques, including time-division multiplexing (TDM), frequency-division multiplexing (FDM), and wavelength-division multiplexing (WDM).

Advanced topics are left to Section 2.5, including *spread spectrum,* code division multiple access (CDMA), orthogonal frequency-division multiplexing (OFDM), and multiple-input and multiple-output (MIMO). The goals of spread spectrum include antijamming, anti-interference, multiple accesses, and privacy protection. These are achieved by *spreading* the source bits into a sequence of *chips* with higher *chip rate* and lower *power density*. Direct sequence spread spectrum (DSSS), frequency hopping spread spectrum (FHSS), and CDMA are three explained examples. OFDM is a digital communication technique that makes use of *multiple carriers*. MIMO communication represents a new communication medium where *multiple antennas* are used at both the transmitter and receiver ends. MIMO can improve the reliability and throughput of communication by introducing spatial multiplexing and spatial diversity. Finally, we discuss an open source implementation of the IEEE 802.11a transmitter using OFDM.

2.1 GENERAL ISSUES

The physical layer sends out signals over and receives signals from the transmission media. Several issues must be addressed to generate a signal that can be transmitted and received through a specific medium with high channel throughput and utilization. First, data from the link layer must be converted into digital signals or analog signals for digital transmission. We first differentiate analog data/signals from digital data/signals. Next, the transmission and reception flows undergo several conversions in the physical layer. These two flows need to be illustrated. The third issue is the need for coding and modulation. To further improve the channel utilization, we need techniques such as multiplexing and multiple accesses to enable multiple users to access the same channel. This is our fourth issue. Finally, in response to channel impairments, especially in the wireless media, several *compensation* measures are needed.

2.1.1 Data and Signal: Analog or Digital

Data and signals can be either analog or digital. In computers, data are commonly of digital type, and analog data such as voice and video are usually converted into digital values for storage and communication. This is because analog data represented in the form of analog signals are easily affected by noise. Digital data and signals can be regenerated by regenerative repeaters and protected from corruption by error-correcting codes, so they are more robust to noise. Therefore, analog data are often converted to digital data in the form of a bit stream. Later, they are transformed into signals for transmission. Thus, digital data are used in computer networks to represent analog sources such as images, voices, audio, and video.

In computer networks, bit streams, or messages, move from one machine to another across network connections through the transmission media. The transmission media convey the energy of signals along a physical path, either cables for electrical signals, fibers for optical signals, or free space for electromagnetic signals. In general, analog signals could travel farther and are more sustainable than digital signals. The physical layer plays the role of converting digital data into either digital or analog signals suitable for specific transmission media. Here we identify the differences between data and signals, and between analog and digital.

Analog Data and Signal

An analog signal is a continuous-time signal that contains analog information generated by an analog source, such as a sound or an image. It is often of continuous value. An example of analog communication is the vocal-auditory communications system. Analog signals can be *sampled* and *quantized* into digital signals for storage and communication.

Digital Data and Signal

Digital data take on discrete values such as the zeros and ones in computers. They can be transformed into digital signals and transmitted directly for a short distance. Alternatively, they can modulate *carriers* (i.e., periodic analog signals) so that modulated signals can be transmitted over a long distance. Most textbooks treat modulated signals as digital signals because they consider digital modulation schemes a form of digital transmission or data transmission, even though the modulation is a form of digital-to-analog conversion. A digital signal can be derived from an analog signal by sampling at discrete times and by *quantizing* into *discrete values*. In other words, a sampled analog signal becomes a discrete-time signal which can be further quantized into a digital signal. If a waveform has only *two* levels to represent binary states "0" and "1," it is a binary digital signal that represents a bit stream. Here we define several terms more formally.

Sampling is a process that picks up samples at discrete times from a continuous-time (or continuous-space in image processing) signal. Each sampled value is held constant within the sampling period. For instance, a continuous-time signal $x(t)$, where t is a variable defined on the entire real line of continuous time, can be sampled into a discrete-time signal whose sampled values at the sample time instants can be represented by a numeric sequence or a discrete-time function $x[n]$, where n is a discrete variable taking values from the set of integers to represent the discrete time. A sampled signal is a discrete-time signal with continuous values.

Quantization is a process for mapping a range of values to a discrete *finite* set of numbers or values. Such a mapping process is usually performed by the use of analog-to-digital converters (ADC). A quantized signal can be of continuous time but with discrete values. Quantization introduces *quantization error,* or quantization noise.

Reconstruction is an *interpolation* process that recovers the original continuous-time signal from the sampled discrete-time signal. To perfectly reconstruct the original signal from a sequence of samples, it suffices to sample at a rate that is equal to or higher than *twice* the highest frequency of the original signal. This sufficient condition is a result of the *Nyquist-Shannon sampling theorem.*

Principle in Action: Nyquist Theorem vs. Shannon Theorem

A communication channel is a connection between a sender and a receiver where information is conveyed over a path with a transmission medium such as a cable, fiber, or a spectrum of radio frequencies. The channel can be noiseless or noisy. If the channel is considered noiseless, its maximum data rate is subject to the Nyquist theorem; if noisy, the maximum data rate is subject to the Shannon theorem.

What is the sampling rate for a signal to be accurately reconstructed, and what is the maximum data rate when information is transmitted over a noiseless channel? These problems were proposed by Harry Nyquist in 1924, and they were resolved later by the Nyquist sampling theorem and maximum data rate he derived. As Nyquist sampling theorem asserts, to uniquely reconstruct a signal without aliasing, a system must sample at least twice as fast as the bandwidth of the signal. For instance, if a limited bandwidth signal has a maximum frequency f_{max}, the sampling rate f_s must be greater than $2 \times f_{max}$. The Nyquist theorem shows that the maximum data rate of a noiseless channel with bandwidth B(Hz) is $2 \times B \log_2 L$ if L states are used by a signal encoding method to represent symbols. For example, if a noiseless phone line of 3 kHz and one-bit signal encoding (two states) is used, what is the maximum data rate when a voice is delivered over the phone line? According to the Nyquist theorem, the maximum data rate is $2 \times 3k \times \log_2 2$ kbps, or 6 kbps.

In practice, channels are not noiseless but have many unwanted noises, such as thermal noise, inter-modulation noise, crosstalk noise, and impulse noise. A new theorem of maximum data rate for noisy channels is necessary. In 1948, Claude Elwood Shannon proposed "A Mathematical Theory of Communication" and "Communication in the Presence of Noise" for calculating the maximum data rate of a noisy channel. The Shannon theorem states that if a signal with a signal-to-noise ratio (SNR) S/N is transmitted over a noisy channel of bandwidth B(Hz), the maximum data rate is $B \times \log_2 2(1 + S/N)$. The Shannon theorem is also called Shannon's limit. This limit is irrelevant to the encoding method, but it is related to SNR. Again, considering a noisy phone line of 3 kHz, what is the maximum data rate if the SNR is 30 dB? According to the Shannon's limit, the maximum data rate is $3k \times \log_2 2 \times (1 + 1000)$ kbps, or about 32.9 kbps.

Periodic and Aperiodic Signals

As mentioned previously, a signal can be either analog or digital. If it is continuous-time and continuous-value, then it is an analog signal. If it is discrete-time and discrete-value, it is a digital signal. Besides such differentiation, signals can also be classified into either *periodic* or *aperiodic*. A periodic signal is one that repeats itself after a certain amount of time, while an aperiodic signal does not. Both analog and digital signals can be either periodic or aperiodic. For example, a sound signal of a human voice is an aperiodic analog signal; a digital clock signal is a periodic digital signal. Other than the *time-domain* characterization of signals, an alternative approach can be made in the *frequency-domain* based on the *Fourier theory*. A signal is said to be periodic if it has a line spectrum consisting of possibly *infinite discrete* frequencies. A line spectrum is a spectrum in which energy is concentrated at particular wavelengths. On the other hand, a signal is said to be aperiodic if it has a *continuous* spectrum with possibly *infinite* support. Furthermore, a signal is said to be *band-limited* if it has *finite* support; say it is properly contained in the frequency band from *f1* to *f2*. Figure 2.1 shows the spectra of analog signals. In Figure 2.1(a), *discrete* frequencies *100 kHz and 400 kHz* are used to represent two periodic analog signals with different amplitudes. In Figure 2.1(b), an aperiodic band-limited analog signal is shown.

The spectra of digital signals are depicted in Figure 2.2. According to the Fourier theory, a periodic digital signal has a line spectrum that is obtained by multiplying the *sinc* spectrum by a periodic line spectrum consisting of a *discrete* frequency pulse train. The aperiodic digital signal has a continuous spectrum that is obtained by multiplying the sinc spectrum by a periodic continuous spectrum ranging from zero to infinite. The Fourier theory also says that a digital signal can be represented by a weighted *combination* of *sinusoidal,* sine and cosine, signals with *different* frequencies, amplitudes, and phases. Combining Figure 2.1 and Figure 2.2 we can conclude that

- if a signal is periodic, then its spectrum is discrete; if aperiodic, then the spectrum is continuous;
- if a signal is analog, then its spectrum is aperiodic; if digital, then the spectrum is a periodic spectrum multiplied by the sinc function.

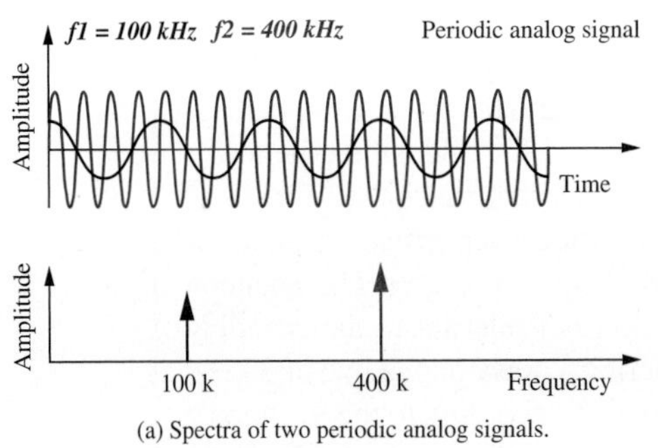

(a) Spectra of two periodic analog signals.

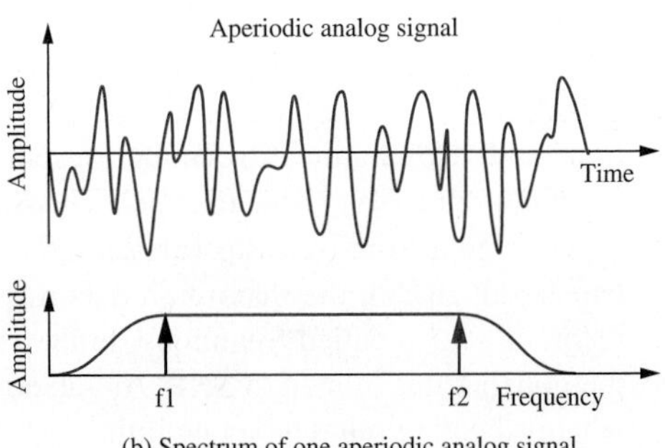

(b) Spectrum of one aperiodic analog signal.

FIGURE 2.1 Spectra of analog signals.

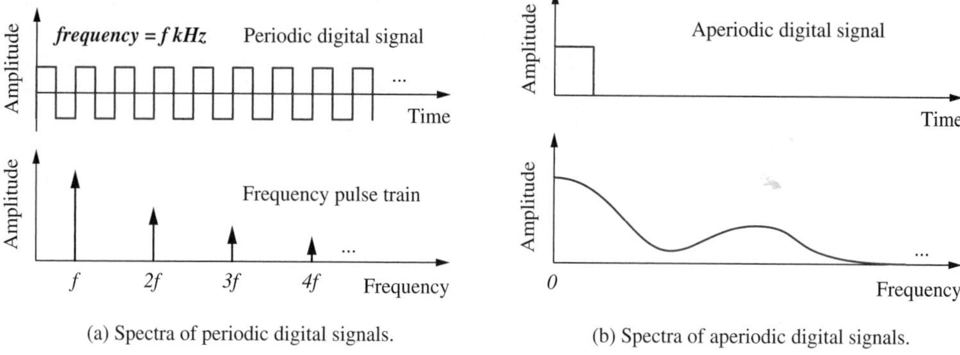

FIGURE 2.2 Spectra of digital signals.

In digital communications, *periodic analog* signals or *aperiodic digital* signals are frequently used because periodic analog signals demand less bandwidth and aperiodic digital signals can represent various values for digital data, as illustrated in Figure 2.1(a) and Figure 2.2(b). In the rest of this chapter, without explicit indication, a digital signal implies an *aperiodic digital* signal for a data stream, a *clock* signal means a *periodic digital* signal, a *carrier* refers to a *periodic analog* signal, and a *modulated* signal indicates an *aperiodic analog* signal.

2.1.2 Transmission and Reception Flows

Having explained the properties of analog and digital signals and distinguishing the aspects of periodic and aperiodic signals, we now illustrate a simplified transmission and reception flow over a physical layer in Figure 2.3. Message symbols from an information source are first compressed by source coding and are then *coded* into channel symbols by channel coding. A *symbol* is a binary tuple of certain length. Message symbols are a sequence of data streams from an information source. Channel

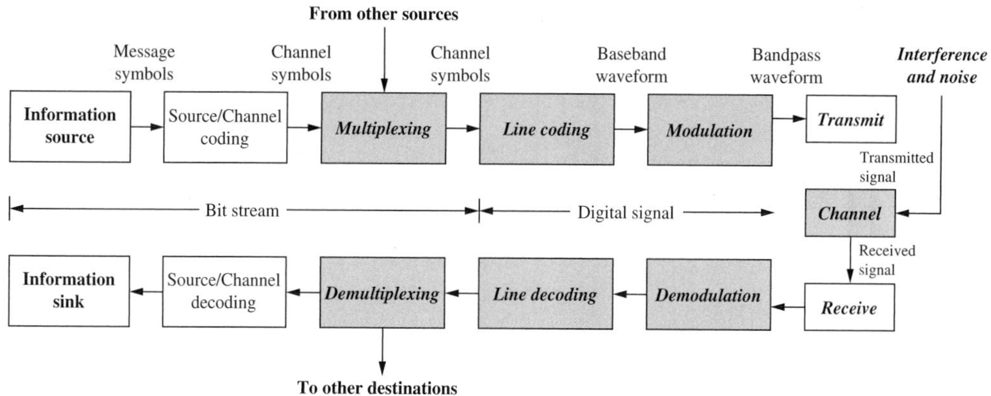

FIGURE 2.3 The transmission and reception flow of a digital communications system.

symbols represent the data stream that has been processed by source coding and channel coding, and may be multiplexed with the symbols from other sources. The combined channel symbols are then processed by line coding (or digital baseband modulation) into a baseband waveform. Now the baseband signal can be directly transmitted to a receiver via wired networks such as cables, or it can be further modulated with carriers by digital modulation and transmitted over wireless networks. The modulated signal is a *bandpass* waveform, a passband signal coming from digital modulation and used for digital transmission. (Many textbooks consider it a digital signal, rather than an analog signal, if the modulated signal is carrying digital data instead of analog data.) Finally, the transmitter in the digital communications system converts the bandpass waveform (still a baseband signal) to a transmitted signal, i.e., an RF (radio frequency) signal. The transmitted signal, together with interference and noise, is sent over a channel.

Multiplexing divides resources into multiple channels to improve channel utilization by sharing transmission facilities whose combined capacity is larger than the requirements of a data flow. It merges other data flows of digital streams, or digital signals such as the passband signals. Hence multiplexing could take place at different places. Multiplexing can create logical channels in frequency, time, code, or space by frequency-division multiplexing (FDM), time-division multiplexing (TDM), code-division multiplexing (CDM), or space-division multiplexing (SDM). The schemes of multiplexing differ in how they divide a physical channel into multiple channels or logical channels. FDM is analog technology, while TDM and CDM are digital technology. Thus, the location of TDM or CDM can be at the multiplexing/demultiplexing modules shown in Figure 2.3, and the occurrence of FDM is *after* the passband modulation where other signals are merged to share the channel. A communication system can build multiple channels by, say, TDM, and one of these channels can be accessed by a group of users using a specific multiple access scheme such as carrier sense multiple access (CSMA). Note that multiplexing schemes are provided at the physical layer, while multiple access techniques are determined at the link layer.

Baseband or Broadband

The baseband waveform in Figure 2.3 is a digital signal that can travel directly on a baseband channel without further conversion into analog signals. This is called *baseband* transmission, where the passband modulation is bypassed. If the channel is a *broadband* channel, the digital signals require a modulation different from the simple line coding. Broadband refers to data transmission over a frequency band that is much higher than that of the digital signal so that multiple data streams can be sent at the same time and multiple signals can share the same medium.

As mentioned before, an aperiodic digital signal has a spectrum that is obtained by multiplying a periodic continuous spectrum by a sinc function. The amplitude of the spectrum is decreasing and approaching zero at high frequencies. Thus the spectrum at high frequencies can be *ignored*. Messages transmitted in baseband or broadband depend on the properties of transmission media and channels:

- If a physical channel is a *low-pass* wideband channel, digital signals can be transmitted over the channel directly. The received signal has only a minor distortion due to the loss of high frequencies and can be recovered at the receiver. Such baseband transmission handles aperiodic digital signals as shown in Figure 2.2(b), whose high-frequency components have low amplitudes and could be ignored.

- If a physical channel has a limited bandwidth that does *not* start from zero, the channel is a *bandpass* channel. Messages transmitted over the bandpass channel need a carrier to carry the messages, and a modulated signal of passband waveform (called a passband signal) is transmitted over the channel. The frequencies of passband signals are *centered* at the frequency of the carrier. This is broadband transmission. Broadband transmission carries data across a bandpass channel where a digital baseband signal must be converted into a passband signal by modulation. In digital transmission, the passband signal is considered a digital signal, but its waveform is the form of an *aperiodic* analog signal whose spectrum occupies a limited bandwidth, as shown in Figure 2.1(b).

2.1.3 Transmission: Line Coding and Digital Modulation

In the world of communications, a physical layer exploits a variety of coding and modulation techniques to convert data into signals so that messages can be carried over a physical channel and signals can travel through transmission media. In computer networks, the techniques of line coding and digital modulation are emphasized. The former converts a bit stream into a digital signal for baseband channels, while the latter transfers a digital baseband signal into a passband signal for bandpass channels. Either line coding or digital modulation is for the same purpose of digital transmission, or data transmission, but they require different conversions.

Synchronization, Baseline Wandering, and DC Components

Line coding, also known as *digital baseband modulation,* uses *discrete-time discrete-value* signals, i.e., square waves or digital signals, characterized only by *amplitude* and *timing* to transmit 0's and 1's. However, in a data stream, a long sequence of the same bit value without changing the signal value may cause the loss of *synchronization* at the receiver's clock and drift from the baseline.

Self-synchronization can be used to calibrate the receiver's clock for synchronizing bit intervals at the transmitter and at the receiver. Baseline is used for determining the values of the received signal for digital data. A *baseline wandering,* or drift, makes it harder for a decoder to determine the digital values of a received signal. Meanwhile, some coding techniques such as non-return-to-zero (NRZ) may still introduce the direct current (DC) components. This makes the digital signal have a nonzero frequency component at 0 Hz, i.e., a *DC component* or DC bias.

Applying such coding to a long sequence of the same bit value not only risks synchronization, but also yields a digital signal having a constant voltage without phase change. Compared to a signal of a DC-balanced waveform (without DC components), a signal with DC components consumes more power. Moreover, there are some types of channels that cannot transmit a DC voltage or current. To transmit digital signals over such channels, a scheme of line coding without DC components is required.

In summary, the major goals of line coding are preventing *baseline wandering,* eliminating *DC components,* activating *self-synchronization,* providing *error detection* and *correction,* and enhancing the signal's immunity to *noise* and *interference.*

Amplitude, Frequency, Phase, and Code

Digital modulation uses *continuous-* or *discrete-time continuous-value* signals, or analog signals, characterized by *amplitude, frequency, phase,* or *code,* to represent a bit stream from an information source. It transforms a digital bit stream into a passband signal for long-distance transmission over a bandpass channel with a limited bandwidth centered at the carrier frequency. For example, conveying a message over a wireless channel requires the process of line coding and digital modulation so that a message can be carried by a carrier and its modulated signal can travel through the free space over a bandpass channel. With the use of amplitude, frequency, phase, code, and their combinations, a wide range of digital modulation techniques could be developed. Complicated modulation techniques generally aim to transmit at a high data rate when the channel is low-bandwidth and noisy.

Furthermore, line coding or digital modulation could be optimized to *adapt* to the characteristics of any given medium. For example, in wireless communications, *link adaptation,* or *adaptive coding and modulation* (ACM), is the technique that matches the methods of coding and modulation and the parameters of communication protocols to the channel conditions.

2.1.4 Transmission Impairments

Transmission media are not perfect. Signals received are not exactly the same as those transmitted. Several factors might impair the transmission reliability of the media, such as *attenuation, fading, distortion, interference,* or *noise*. These transmission impairments and their compensation measures are addressed here.

Attenuation: Attenuation is the gradual loss in intensity of flux such as radio waves or electrical signals. Attenuation affects the propagation of waves and signals. When a signal travels through a medium, it loses some of its *energy* because of the resistance of the transmission medium. For example, as the electromagnetic waves are absorbed by water particles or are scattered in wireless communications, the intensity of electromagnetic radiation is attenuated. Thus, low-noise amplifiers are required at both transmitter and receiver ends to amplify the signal so that the original message can be detected and recovered after certain processing. Amplification is a means of countering the attenuation impairment.

Fading: In wireless communications, a modulated waveform traveling over a certain medium could experience fading. Fading is a time-varying deviation of attenuation since it varies with time, geographical position, or radio frequency. There are two types of fading: *multipath fading* if caused by multipath propagation and *shadow fading* if shadowed by obstacles. A channel experiencing fading is called a fading channel.

Distortion: The *shape* of a received signal may not be exactly the same as the original one. This distortion impairment commonly occurs to composite signals. After propagation, the shape of a composite signal is distorted because the composite signal is composed of signals of different frequencies which encounter different propagation delays. This yields different phase shifts and hence distorts the signal shape. A digital signal is commonly represented by a *composite analog* signal that is composed of several periodic analog signals. Therefore, digital signals are often distorted after transmission and cannot travel far. To compensate for this impairment, one would use the waveform of analog signals that are suitable for long-distance transmission.

Interference: Interference is typically distinguished from noise. It is anything that disrupts a signal that travels over a channel. It usually adds *unwanted* signals to the *desired* signal. Several famous interference examples include co-channel interference (CCI), also known as crosstalk, inter-symbol interference (ISI), and intercarrier interference (ICI).

Noise: Noise is a random fluctuation of an analog signal. Electronic noise happens to all electronic circuits. Thermal noise, or Nyquist noise, is an electronic noise generated by the thermal agitation of charge carriers. It is often *white;* that is, the power spectral density is nearly *uniform* throughout the frequency spectrum. Other kinds of noise are induced noise, impulse noise, and quantization noise. Noise affects the ability of receivers to recover the transmitted data. Induced noise comes from sources such as appliances. Impulse noise is derived from power lines or lightning, while quantization noise is introduced from quantization errors. *Signal-to-noise ratio* (SNR), defined as the ratio of the average of signal power to the average of noise power, is a measure that *limits* the theoretical bit rate. To compensate for the impact of noise on the transmitted data, we may either *raise* the signal power or *lower* the transmission bit rate. Another resort is using modulation techniques that are more robust against noise.

Because the intensity of signals fades during propagation, the physical layer commonly converts a bit stream or digital waveform to a modulated passband signal, and sends the signal through a physical channel. These conversion techniques, coding and modulation, would mitigate these impairments on communication systems. At the receiver, signals are detected, demodulated, and decoded and the original data are recovered. In other words, a digital communication system needs the capability of conveying messages through a noisy channel, filtering out noise, and recovering signals from propagation fading.

Historical Evolution: Software Defined Radio

In traditional wireless systems, signals are typically processed by hardware, such as ASIC chips, rather than software. Because the hardware technology of general-purpose processors had advanced to a new level that made signal processing in real time possible, software defined radio (SDR), or software radio, emerged. The concept of software radio was first proposed by J. Mitola in 1991.

Continued

It dramatically increases the flexibility of radio systems by making them able to adapt to multiple wireless standards at a lower cost than traditional systems.

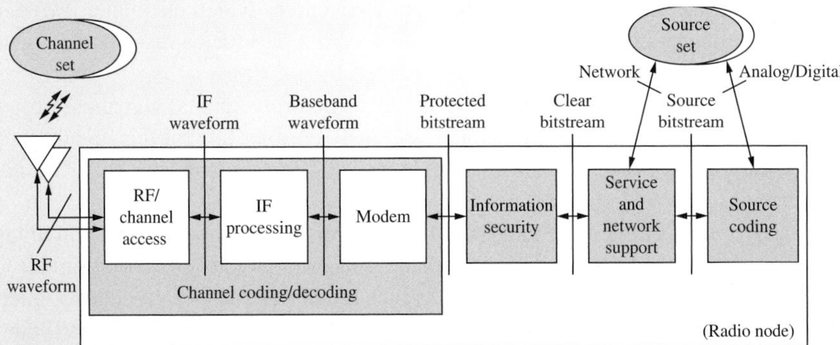

FIGURE 2.4 A functional model for a signal flow in a wireless communications system.

The signal processing flows in the traditional and SDR communications systems are the same. The difference is *where* the signal is *digitized* and then processed by *software*. Figure 2.4 illustrates a radio node that can perform various wireless standards via a series of radio functions. Compared to Figure 2.3, Figure 2.4 expands to include the units of IF (intermediate frequency) processing and RF (radio frequency) channel access that are used to manipulate the RF waveform and IF waveform, respectively. RF, ranging from 3 kHz to 300 GHz, is a collective oscillation of carriers while IF, ranging from 10 to 100 MHz, is generated by mixing the RF and local oscillator (LO) frequency to a *lower* frequency for easier processing.

In a wireless communications system, digital signals at the transmitter are first modulated into bandpass waveforms (still in the range of baseband frequency), then *up-converted* into IF and RF waveforms for transmission over a radio channel. At the receiver, received RF waveforms are first processed by the RF/channel access module, then converted into IF waveforms and *down-converted* into baseband waveforms that are further demodulated and decoded into bit streams. In SDR, the signal digitization could take place at the RF, IF, *or* baseband waveforms, which is called RF digitization, IF digitization, or baseband digitization. RF digitization is an ideal place for an SDR to *fully* process the rest of radio functions in software. However, it is difficult for a software radio to implement the RF digitization because of the hardware limitation of a *high-speed* wideband ADC (analog-to-digital converter) and the computing capacity of the general-purpose processor. In addition, baseband digitization is not considered a software radio system because there is no gain for this and it is the same as the digitization of a traditional communications system. As a result, *IF digitization* is the best choice for SDR digitization.

Several public software radio projects, such as SpeakEasy, Joint Tactical Radio System (JTRS), and GNU Radio, have been developed for software radio systems. The GNU Radio project, started in 2001 by Eric Blossom, is devoted to building a radio system with minimal hardware demands. GNU Radio is an open source development toolkit that provides a library of signal processing blocks in C++ and the glue in Python for building software radios. GRC (GNU Radio Companion), a GUI tool, allows users to interconnect signal processing blocks in a manner similar to Labview or Simulink, while building a radio system. GRC can facilitate the study of GNU Radio and drastically reduce the learning curve. USRP (Universal Software Radio Peripheral), developed by Matt Ettus, is now the most popular hardware platform for GNU Radio.

2.2 MEDIUM

Transmission media are used by the physical layer to convey signals between senders and receivers. They are the free space for wireless media, and the metallic and fiber-optic cables for wired media. Since the techniques of coding and modulation we might adopt partially depend on the type of transmission media, we first examine the characteristics of these transmission media. Another factor that affects which technique to choose is the operating *quality* of the media, which heavily depends on the *distance* and the environmental *impairments*.

2.2.1 Wired Medium

Common wired media for metallic and fiber-optic cables include *twisted pairs, coaxial cables,* and *optical fibers.* A signal, electrical or optical, that travels through these media is directional and limited by the properties of physical media.

Twisted Pair

Twisted pairs consist of two copper conductors twisted together to prevent electromagnetic *interferences* from the externals and *crosstalk* between the pairs. A twisted-pair cable may be *shielded* or not. A shielded cable is called shielded twisted pair (STP) and an unshielded cable is called unshielded twisted pair (UTP). The structures of STP and UTP are shown in Figure 2.5(a) and (b). STP has an additional metal shield to provide extra protection from electromagnetic interferences, but UTP is more common due to its lower cost. As the technology has advanced, UTP has

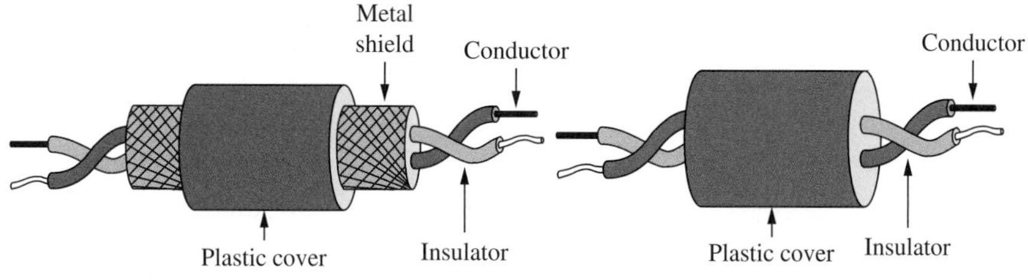

(a) Shielded twisted pair, STP.

(b) Unshielded twisted pair, UTP.

FIGURE 2.5 Twisted pair cable.

TABLE 2.1 Specifications of Common Twisted Pair Cables

Specifications	Description
Category 1/2	For traditional phone lines; not specified in TIA/EIA
Category 3	Transmission characteristics specified up to 16 MHz
Category 4	Transmission characteristics specified up to 20 MHz
Category 5(e)	Transmission characteristics specified up to 100 MHz
Category 6(a)	Transmission characteristics specified up to 250 MHz (Cat-6) and 500 MHz (Cat-6a)
Category 7	Transmission characteristics specified up to 600 MHz

been good enough for practical use. Twisted pairs are categorized according to the maximum allowed signal frequency. Table 2.1 summarizes the common specifications in the ANSI EIA/TIA Standard 568 (American National Standards Institute, Electronic Industries Association, Telecommunications Industry Association). The higher category means the pair of copper conductors have more twists per inch and can sustain higher signal frequency and hence higher bit rate. The length limitation depends on the target bit rate; the shorter the cable, the higher the bit rate.

To transmit at a higher bit rate, one could either use a cable that supports a higher frequency or design a more complicated coding or modulation scheme to encode more bits in the same time period. Although designing a complicated *codec* or *modem* to transmit data in a low-frequency signal is possible, the *circuitry cost* may be too high to make this design practical. As the cable cost is lowered in these years, it is more economical to transmit over a better cable than to rely on complicated coding or modulation schemes. For example, although the Ethernet technology for transmitting 100 Mbps over Category 3/4 does exist, it is rarely found in practice. Almost all existing 100 Mbps Ethernet interfaces are 100BASE-T running over the Category 5 cable.

Coaxial Cable

A coaxial cable consists of an inner conductor surrounded by an insulating layer, a braided outer conductor, then another insulating layer, and a plastic jacket, as shown in Figure 2.6. The cables are common for many applications, such as cable TV networks and broadband Internet access using cable modems. It was also once a popular medium for Ethernet, but it has been replaced by twisted pairs and fibers.

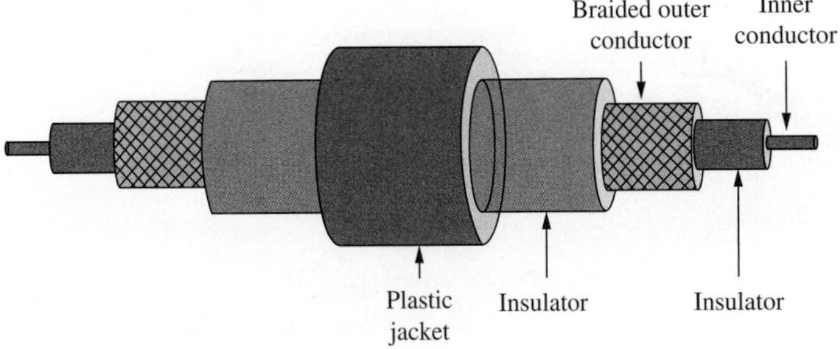

FIGURE 2.6 Coaxial cable.

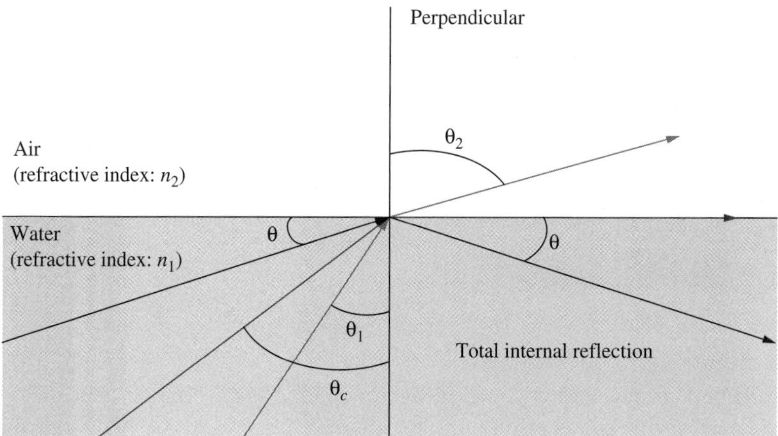

FIGURE 2.7 Refraction of light and total internal reflection.

Different types of coaxial cables have different inner and outer parameters, which in turn affect the transmission characteristics such as impedance. The most popular type is RG-6, which has a diameter of 0.0403 inches and can operate at around 3 GHz.

Optical Fiber

Light can travel from one transparent medium into another, but the direction of the light changes. This is called *refraction* of light. How much the direction changes depends on the *refractive index* of the medium, the ratio of the speed of light in a vacuum to that in the medium. This relationship of the refraction phenomenon, Snell's law, was derived by Willebrord Snell. Snell's law states $n_1 \sin \theta_1 = n_2 \sin \theta_2$, as shown in Figure 2.7. When the light is traveling from a medium with a higher refractive index to another with a lower refractive index, the light could be refracted at 90º, a refractive angle. Now the incident angle is at a *critical angle,* or θ_c, as shown in Figure 2.7. If a light hits the interface of these two media at an incident angle larger than θ_c, it will not go into the second medium but will be reflected back into the first medium. This is known as the *total internal reflection*. Applications of optical fiber are based on the principle of the total internal reflection.

FIGURE 2.8 Optical fiber.

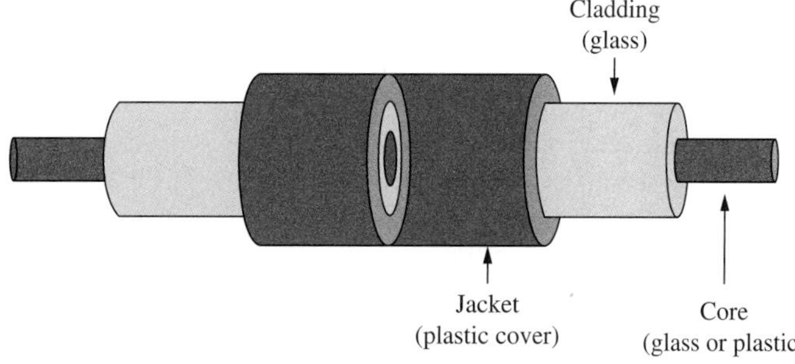

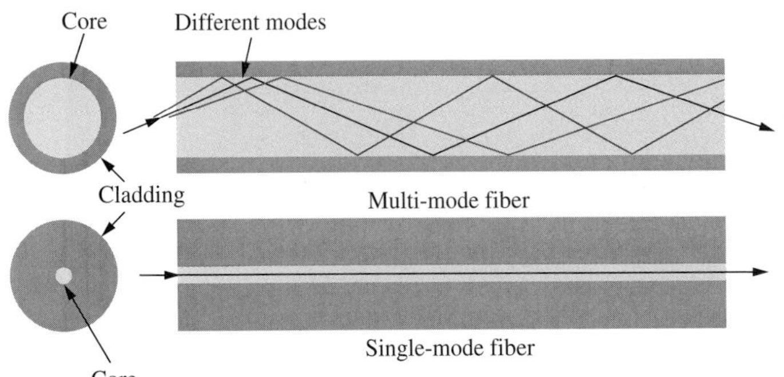

FIGURE 2.9 Single-mode and multi-mode fibers.

Optical fibers propagate the signal in light along the inner core of cables. The light can be kept inside the core due to total internal reflection. The light sources can be light emitting diode (LED) or laser. The structure of optical fiber is shown in Figure 2.8, where a thin glass or plastic core is surrounded by a cladding glass with a different density, and then a jacket. The medium of cladding has a *low* refractive index, and the medium of core has a *high* refractive index.

The distinct patterns of light guided through an optical fiber are called *modes*. If a fiber carries the light by more than one mode at a specific wavelength, it is called a *multi-mode* fiber. Some fiber may have a very thin core that allows only one mode to be carried. This is called *single-mode* fiber. Figure 2.9 shows the two main categories of optical fibers, multi-mode and single-mode. Multi-mode fibers have a thicker core (typically larger than 50 micrometers) where the light travels by reflection, instead of in a straight line. Despite having the less expensive transmitter and receiver, the multi-mode fiber also introduces higher modal *dispersion* due to the diversity in propagation velocity of the light signal. The dispersion limits the bandwidth and the communication distance of the multi-mode fiber. Single-mode fibers have a much thinner core (typically less than 10 micrometers) to force light signals to travel in a straight line. It allows longer and faster transmission but at a higher manufacturing cost.

Optical fibers have advantages over copper wires because of their low attenuation and invulnerability to external electromagnetic interferences. They are also harder to tap than copper cables. Thus they are often used in *high-speed* and *long-distance* transmission. They are mostly deployed as backbones rather than for personal use due to the high deployment cost.

2.2.2 Wireless Medium

The wireless medium is the free space that allows electromagnetic waves to travel without using any physical cables. The electromagnetic waves are broadcast in the free space and received by any receiving antenna that is within the reach of these waves.

Propagation Methods

Three methods of propagating electromagnetic waves are *ground* propagation, *sky* propagation, and *line-of-sight* propagation. The ground propagation is used by low-frequency waves or signals that travel around the lower part of the atmosphere. Applications of ground propagation are radio navigation or radio beacons. The higher-frequency waves travel up to the ionosphere and reflect down to the earth via sky propagation. AM (amplitude modulation) radio, FM (frequency modulation) radio, cellular phones, WLANs, VHF (very high frequency) TV, UHF (ultra high frequency) TV, and citizens band belong to this application. In line-of-sight propagation, high-frequency waves are transmitted from the source to the destination directly. Satellite communications are applications that adopt the method of line-of-sight propagation. The name *line-of-sight* implies that the sender and the receiver need to see each other in a straight line. But it is true only for very high-frequency waves which are very *unidirectional.* Many of the signals in this category could travel with *refraction* and *diffraction,* in addition to straight-line propagation and *reflection.* Refraction is the change in traveling speed, and hence direction, when the waves enter another medium at an angle. Diffraction means the bending of waves around obstacles and the spreading out of waves past small openings.

Transmission Waves: Radio, Microwave, Infrared

The electromagnetic waves used for transmissions are classified into three categories: radio, microwave, and infrared. Radio ranges from about 3 kHz to 1 GHz. The range covers VLF (very low frequency, 3 ~ 30 KHz), LF (low frequency, 30 ~ 300 kHz), MF (middle frequency, 300 kHz ~ 3 MHz), HF (high frequency, 3 ~ 30 MHz), VHF (very high frequency, 30 MHz ~ 300 MHz), and part of UHF (ultra high frequency 300 MHz ~ 3 GHz). Radio waves usually use *omni-directional* antennas that send and receive signals from *all* directions via the ground or sky propagation. The disadvantage of using omni-directional antennas is that signals are susceptible to interference from other users nearby who are using the same frequency. The benefit is that signals can be sent by one antenna but received by many receivers. It is suitable for multicasting or broadcasting. Moreover, radio waves that propagate through the sky can travel a long distance. This is why radio waves are selected for long-distance broadcast. Applications are FM radio and AM radio, television broadcasting, and paging.

Microwaves typically range from 1 GHz to 300 GHz, covering part of UHF (ultra high frequency 300 MHz ~ 3 GHz), SHF (super high frequency, 3 ~ 30 GHz), and EHF (extremely high frequency, 30 ~ 300 GHz). However, most applications usually fall in the range of 1 GHz to 40 GHz. For instance, the global positioning system (GPS) transmits signals at about 1.2 GHz to 1.6 GHz, IEEE802.11 uses 2.4 GHz and 5 GHz, and WiMAX works between 2 and 11 GHz. Microwaves of higher frequencies use directional antennas to send and receive signals, if the transmitting and receiving antennas can be aligned for *line-of-sight* propagation. This type of directional antenna is a horn that can send out microwaves in parallel beams, employing the curved shape of the horn. The directional receiving antenna is a parabolic dish that can catch a wide range of parallel beams at a common point for collecting these signals. The collected signals are then conveyed to the receiver through a conducted line.

Similar to radio waves, microwave transmission needs available bands in the spectrum allocated from regulatory authorities. Fortunately, the ISM (industrial, scientific, and medical) bands are available for *unlicensed* operations. A common example that uses the ISM bands is the microwave oven operating in the 2.4 GHz band. Cordless phones, WLANs, and many short-range wireless devices also operate in the ISM bands, as the bands are license free. Because multiple wireless devices sharing the ISM bands usually operate at the same time, avoiding interferences among these devices is necessary. *Spread spectrum,* which *spreads* the signal power over a wider spectrum, is one of the technologies used in WLANs to avoid interference. Because a signal spread over a *wider* spectrum may not be affected by *narrow*-band interference, the receiver thus has a better chance to recover the spread signal accurately. Spread spectrum is introduced in Section 2.5.

Infrared waves range from 300 GHz to 400 THz for short-range transmissions. Because of the properties of high frequencies, infrared waves *cannot* penetrate walls; hence they can be used in one room without interfering with devices in other rooms. Some devices such as wireless keyboards, mice, laptops, and printers use infrared waves to transmit data via line-of-sight propagation.

Mobility

The most obvious advantage of wireless communication over wired communication is *mobility*. Unlike wired connections using cables for transmissions, wireless connections use the wireless spectrum. Most wireless systems use the microwave spectrum, especially 800 MHz to 2 GHz, to balance between *omni-directionality* and a *high bit rate*. A higher spectrum could offer a higher bit rate, but then it would become more directional and lose mobility.

2.3 INFORMATION CODING AND BASEBAND TRANSMISSION

In computer networking and information processing, a code is a scheme for converting information from one form or representation to another, and coding is a process that converts an information source into symbols, while decoding reverses the process. In the transmission and reception flows in Section 2.1, the information source in computer networks is processed by *source coding, channel coding,* and *line coding* before transmission or further modulation. Source coding and channel coding are in the field of *information and coding theory,* but line coding belongs to the field of digital baseband modulation.

Source coding intends to compress and reduce the demand of storage space and therefore improve the efficiency of data transmission over channels, especially for storing or conveying image, audio, video, and speech. Source coding usually occurs at the application layer. Channel coding typically adds extra bits to the original data so that the data become more robust to impairments introduced by the channel. It is performed at both the link layer and the physical layer. Line coding not only converts digital data into digital signals but also deals with the issues of baseline wandering, loss of synchronization, and DC components, as discussed in Section 2.1. This section describes source and channel coding and presents various line coding schemes.

2.3.1 Source and Channel Coding

Source Coding

Source coding is designed to form efficient descriptions of information sources so that the required storage or bandwidth resources can be reduced. It has become a fundamental subsystem in communications, and it uses techniques from *digital signal processing* (DSP) and *integrated circuits* (IC). Several compression algorithms and standards exist for source coding in the areas of images, audio, video, and speech. Some applications for source compression are as follows:

Image compression: Without compression, image sources are too heavy to be stored and conveyed over channels. Joint Photographic Experts Group (JPEG) and Motion Picture Experts Group (MPEG) are two popular schemes for image compression.

Audio compression: Popular techniques for audio compression include compact disc (CD), digital versatile disc (DVD), digital audio broadcasting (DAB), and Motion Picture Experts Group audio layer 3 (MP3).

Speech compression: Speech compression is usually applied to telephony, especially to cellular telephony. G.72x and G.711 are example standards.

Channel Coding

Channel coding is used to protect digital data through a noisy transmission medium or over an imperfect storage medium that may cause errors while transferring or retrieving data. The transmitter in a communication system usually adds redundant bits to a message, according to a predetermined algorithm. The receiver can detect and correct the errors caused by noise, fading, or interferences. The performance of any channel code is limited by the Shannon's channel coding theorem, which states that it is possible to transmit digital data nearly *error-free over a noisy channel* as long as the transmission rate is set below some quantity, known as the channel capacity. More formally stated, for any infinitesimal $\varepsilon > 0$ and any data rate less than the channel capacity, there exists a scheme of encoding and decoding that ensures that the error probability for a *sufficiently long* code is less than ε. Conversely, the Shannon's channel coding theorem also states that transmitting at a rate above the channel capacity is bound to have an error probability bounded away from 0.

For an error correcting system, two schemes are usually used for a receiver to correct errors. One is automatic repeat-request (ARQ), the other is forward error correction (FEC). Unlike ARQ, FEC can correct errors without asking the transmitter to retransmit original data. *Bit interleaving* is another scheme used in digital communications against *burst errors,* though it increases latency. It permutes the coded bits of a data stream such that only a limited number of consecutive coded bits are affected by burst errors during transmission.

Error correcting codes can be classified as *block codes* and *convolutional codes.* Convolutional codes are processed bit-by-bit with arbitrary-length bit streams, while block codes are manipulated block-by-block with fixed-size blocks of bit streams. Common examples of block code include *Hamming codes and Reed-Solomon codes.* Turbo codes, a very powerful error correction technique developed in 1993, are derived from the convolutional codes with a predetermined interleaver.

Hamming codes were discovered in 1950 and remain in use in applications such as error correction in memory devices. Reed-Solomon codes are used for a wide variety of applications. For instance, CD, DVD, Blu-ray disc, digital subscriber line (DSL), Worldwide Interoperability for Microwave Access (WiMAX), digital video broadcasting (DVB), Advanced Television Systems Committee (ATSC), and redundant array of independent disk (RAID) systems are applications that use Reed-Solomon codes. Convolutional codes usually are applied to the applications in digital radio, mobile, and satellite communications. Turbo codes can approach the channel capacity or the Shannon limit. Turbo codes are widely used in the 3G mobile standards, the long term evolution (LTE) project, and the IEEE 802.16 WiMAX standard.

2.3.2 Line Coding

Line coding is a process that applies pulse modulation to a binary symbol, and a pulse-code modulation (PCM) waveform is generated. PCM waveforms are known as *line codes*. Pulse modulation employs a regular sequence of pulses to represent a corresponding sequence of information-carrying quantities. There are four basic forms of pulse modulation: pulse-amplitude modulation (PAM), pulse-code modulation (PCM), pulse-width modulation (PWM) or pulse-duration modulation (PDM), and pulse-position modulation (PPM). Unlike PAM, PWM, and PPM, PCM uses a sequence of two distinct amplitudes to represent a *quantized* sample or a corresponding bit stream, so PCM becomes the favorite pulse modulation for modern digital communications. This is because detecting and deciding the values of data from a *two-state* sequence is simpler than accurately measuring the amplitude, the duration, and the position of a pulse at a receiver in PAM, PWM, and PPM, respectively. All line coding schemes described here belong to PCM.

Self-Synchronization

Data stored in computer networks are sequences of bits in digital forms. These sequences need to be converted to digital signals for transmission over a physical channel. As mentioned earlier in Section 2.1, line coding converts digital data into digital signals for communicating over a baseband channel. If the communication is performed over a bandpass or a broadband channel, a different scheme for converting the data into passband signals will be used. Figure 2.10 illustrates a line coding scheme where digital data is sent from a transmitter to a receiver.

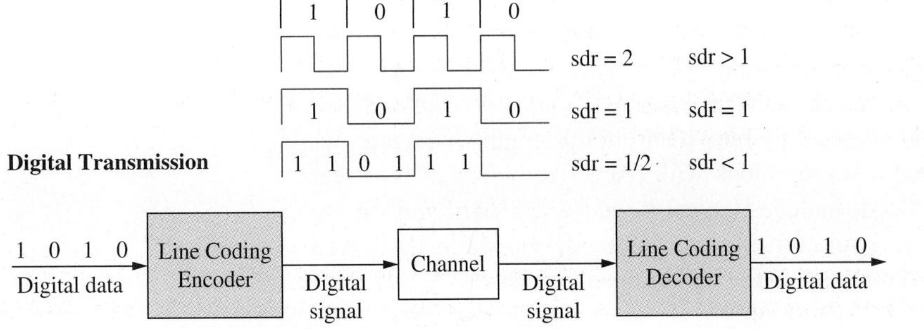

FIGURE 2.10 Line coding and signal-to-data ratio.

At a receiver, the line decoder's bit *intervals* must exactly match the line encoder's bit intervals at the corresponding transmitter. Any minor variation or offset of bit intervals may result in a misinterpretation of the signals. To guarantee that a receiver will correctly decode the received signals into a sequence of bits the same as that from the transmitter, it is important to synchronize the receiver clock with the transmitter clock. If a line encoding scheme embeds bit interval information in a digital signal, the received signal can help the receiver synchronize its clock with the transmitter clock, and its line decoder can retrieve exactly the digital data from the digital signal. This is the technique of self-synchronization. Some line coding schemes provide self-synchronization, while others don't.

Signal-to-Data Ratio (sdr)

In Figure 2.10, the signal-to-data ratio (sdr) (analogous to the term SNR) is a ratio of the number of signal elements to the number of data elements. *Data rate* is the number of data elements sent in one second, also called *bit rate* (in bps), while *signal rate* is the number of signal elements sent in one second, also called *baud rate, pulse rate,* or *modulation rate*. The relation between signal rate and data rate can be expressed as $S = c \times N \times sdr$, where S is the signal rate, c is the case factor, and N is the data rate. The case factor c is specified for the worst case, the best case, or the average case. Under the average case, the value of c is assumed to be 1/2. The smaller the signal rate is, the less bandwidth a channel requires. Hence it is seen from this discussion that if $sdr > 1$, the signal may contain self-synchronization information, and the required channel bandwidth increases.

In Section 2.1, we mentioned that an aperiodic digital signal has an infinite range of continuous spectra. However, most of the high-frequency spectra are small in amplitude and can be ignored. Hence, an effective limited bandwidth can be used for digital signals, rather than the bandwidth with infinite range. Bandwidth is often defined as a range of frequencies in Hertz for transmission channels. Therefore, we assume that the bandwidth in Hertz (frequency) is proportional to baud rate (signal rate), while bandwidth in bits per second (bps) is proportional to bit rate (data rate).

Line Coding Schemes

The terminologies in line coding are briefly expressed here. In a binary waveform, "1" is called *"mark"* or *"HI,"* and "0" is called *"space"* or *"LO."* In *unipolar* signaling, "1" represents a finite voltage of V volts, and "0" means zero voltage. In *polar* signaling, "1" has a finite voltage of V volts, and "0" has $-V$ voltage. Last, in *bipolar* signaling, "1" is a finite voltage of V or $-V$ volts, and "0" is zero voltage. Line coding schemes can be classified into several categories, as listed in Table 2.2. In addition to the above three categories, there are the types *multilevel* and *multitransition*. Because unipolar signals are DC-unbalanced and demand more power for transmission than polar signals, they are normally not in use today. The waveforms of line coding schemes are depicted in Figure 2.11. The required bandwidth for each coding scheme is illustrated in Figure 2.12. Next we give detailed descriptions of these schemes with these two figures. Two advanced coding schemes, run length limited (RLL) and block coding, are also presented.

TABLE 2.2 Categories of Line Coding

Category of Line Coding	Line Coding
Unipolar	NRZ
Polar	NRZ, RZ, Manchester, differential Manchester
Bipolar	AMI, Pseudoternery
Multilevel	2B1Q, 8B6T
Multitransition	MLT3

Unipolar Non-Return-to-Zero (NRZ) Without Self-Synchronization

With this scheme, bit 1 is defined as a positive voltage, and bit 0 as a zero voltage. Because the signal does not return to zero at the *middle* of the bit, the scheme is called non-return-to-zero. The required power of unipolar NRZ is twice that of polar NRZ.

Polar Non-Return-to-Zero (NRZ) Without Self-Synchronization

This scheme of coding defines a positive level for 1 and another negative level for 0. There are several variants of polar NRZ, including polar non-return-to-zero level (polar NRZ-L), polar non-return-to-zero inverted (polar NRZI), and polar non-return-to-zero space (polar NRZS).

Polar Non-Return-to-Zero Level (NRZ-L): The scheme defines a positive level for 1 and another negative level for 0. If a long sequence of bits (either bit 1's or bit 0's) without change occurs, the bit interval information could be lost. This scheme requires the extra support of clock synchronization between the transmitter and the receiver.

Polar Non-Return-to-Zero Space (NRZ-S): The "1" denotes no change in the signal level and "0" denotes a transition in the signal level. High-level Data Link

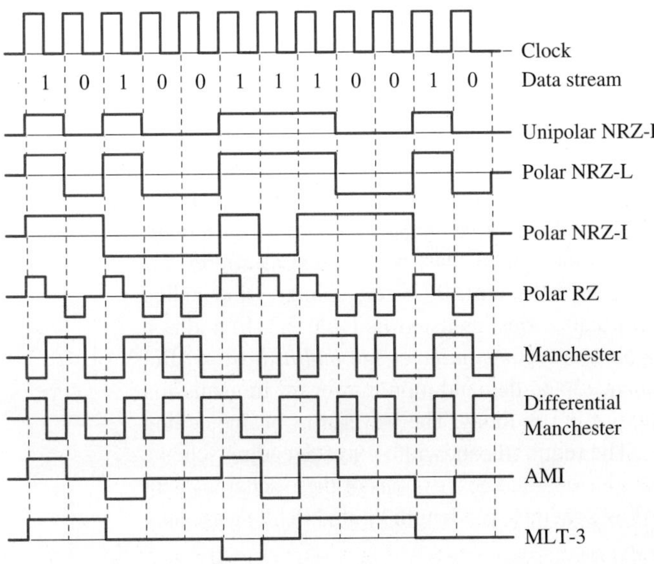

FIGURE 2.11 The waveforms of line coding schemes.

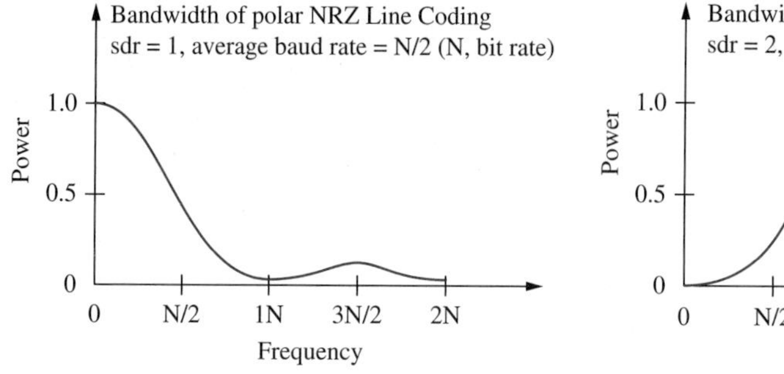

(a) The bandwidth of polar NRZ-L and polar NRZ-I.

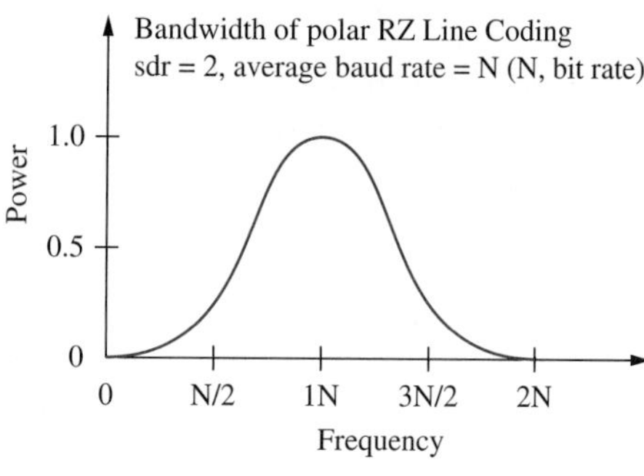

(b) The bandwidth of polar RZ.

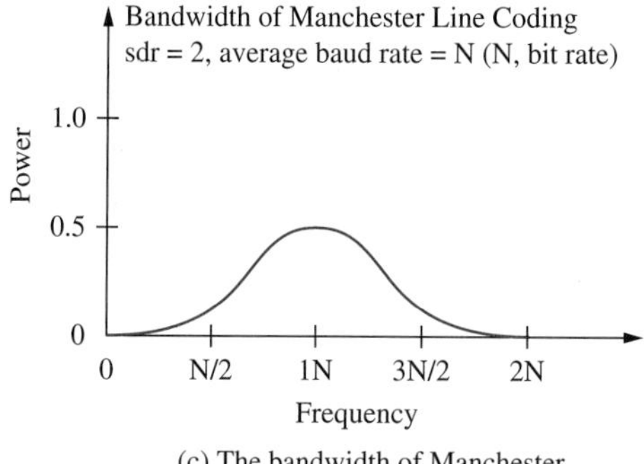

(c) The bandwidth of Manchester.

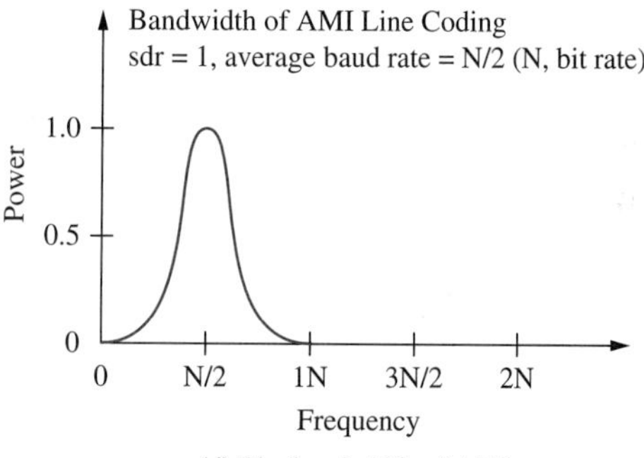

(d) The bandwidth of AMI.

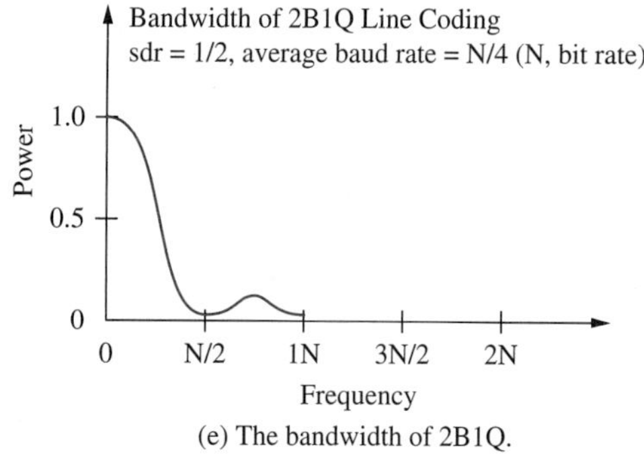

(e) The bandwidth of 2B1Q.

FIGURE 2.12 The bandwidth of line coding.

Control (HDLC) and Universal Serial Bus (USB) use this scheme, but *stuffing* bit 0's in a long sequence of bit 1's. Because the stuffed bit 0's can invoke transitions, a long "no change" can be avoided and clock synchronization can be achieved.

Polar Non-Return-to-Zero Inverted (NRZ-I): Contrary to NRZ-S, here bit "1" means a transition, and bit "0" means no transition. Given a bit, transitions occur at the leading edges of clocks. Similarly, a long sequence of bit 0's without transitions destroys the property of synchronization. Block coding discussed in the previous subsection can be applied to this scheme before polar NRZ-I coding to reduce the loss of synchronization. RLL, to be further discussed later, can also be used to combine with NRZ-I.

Both problems of baseline wandering and synchronization in polar NRZ-L are *twice* as severe as in polar NRZ-S and polar NRZ-I, because in polar NRZ-L both bit "1" and bit "0" may yield a long sequence of bits without change and therefore cause a skewed average signal power and loss of synchronization, while in polar NRZ-S and polar NRZ-I, only one type of bit, either bit "1" or bit "0," will generate a long sequence of bits without change. All polar NRZ schemes have no self-clocking and no rest condition, which is at the signal level zero; hence an additional synchronization mechanism is required to prevent bit slip. For instance, disk and tape use the RLL coding with polar NRZ-I, and USB uses bit stuffing with polar NRZ-S. The scheme of polar NRZ is very simple and cheap. The 1000BASE-X Ethernet still uses polar NRZ because its corresponding block coding 8B/10B provides sufficient synchronization for high-speed transmission in Ethernet.

The sdr of polar NRZ is 1, so the average signal rate (baud rate) $S = c \times N \times sdr = 1/2 \times N \times 1 = N/2$. If the bandwidth is proportional to the baud rate, the bandwidth of polar NRZ can be expressed in Figure 2.12(a). Because a high power density is around frequency 0 and most energy is distributed in the range from frequency 0 to $N/2$, it means that the DC components carry a lot of power, and that the power is *not* evenly distributed between the two sides of signal frequency $N/2$. Polar NRZ consumes more power than other schemes with nearly zero DC components.

Polar Return-to-Zero (RZ) with Self-Synchronization

The binary signal could be encoded by polar return-to-zero (polar RZ) coding as shown in Figure 2.8. The pulse representing bit "1" or bit "0" *always* returns to a neutral or rest condition, which is denoted as zero, at the halfway point of the current bit. The benefit of this coding is that signals are self-clocking for synchronization, but at a cost of using *doubled* bandwidth, compared to polar NRZ. The bandwidth of polar RZ is shown in Figure 2.12(b). Here the average baud rate of polar RZ coding is N, the same as bit rate, and sdr is 2. The power intensity is evenly distributed on two sides of the baud rate N where DC components carry very little power close to zero. However, using *three* levels of voltage increases the complexity of coding and decoding devices. Hence the Manchester and differential Manchester schemes have better performance than polar RZ. Polar RZ is no longer in use.

Polar Manchester and Differential Manchester with Self-Synchronization

The Manchester coding represents "1" by low-to-high transition and "0" by high-to-low transition, where each transition happens at the *middle* of a period of bit "1" or "0." This scheme is a combination of polar RZ and polar NRZ-L. It guarantees *self-clocking* by introducing a signal transition at each data bit. Again, this doubles the signal frequency, so Manchester coding asks for twice the bandwidth that polar NRZ requires. Hence, Manchester coding is not adopted for higher transmission rates such as the 100 Mbps Ethernet. However, in the lower-speed version of IEEE 802.3 (Ethernet) and IEEE 802.4 (token bus), such as 10BASE-T, Manchester is used for its advantage of self-clocking.

The differential Manchester is a variant of the Manchester but outperforms the latter. In the differential Manchester, a "1" requires the *first half* of the signal to be the same as the previous one, and "0" to be the opposite of the previous, where a transition always occurs at the midpoint of the signal. Such a scheme results in *one* transition with "1" and *two* transitions with "0." It is a combination of polar RZ and polar NRZ-I. Because *detecting* the transition of a signal is more reliable than *comparing* the amplitude of a signal to a fixed threshold, the differential Manchester encoding has better error performance than the Manchester coding. IEEE 802.5 (token ring LAN) employs the differential Manchester.

Neither Manchester nor differential Manchester have the baseline wandering and DC components problems, but they have to double the signal rate when compared to polar NRZ. Their sdr (2) and average signal rate *N* are the same as those of polar RZ. The bandwidth is shown as in Figure 2.12(c).

Bipolar Alternate Mark Inversion (AMI) and Pseudoternary Without Self-Synchronization

In the AMI coding, a "0" or "space" is encoded into a zero volt and a "1" or "mark" is encoded into an *alternate* positive or negative volt, as shown in Figure 2.11. The pseudoternary is a variation of AMI where bit "1" is represented with zero volt, and bit "0" is encoded into a positive or negative volt. By alternating the voltage of the same bit value, DC is balanced. This scheme might lose synchronization if data contain a long sequence of 0's in AMI or 1's in pseudoternary. To compensate for this, the AMI encoder adds a "1" as bit 8 after *seven* consecutive zeros. By this bit-stuffing, which is similar to that used in polar NRZ-S, the overall line code is longer than the source code by less than 1% on average. This coding is used for long-distance communications by T-carriers. Two advantages of this scheme are zero DC-components and better error detection. Its bandwidth is shown in Figure 2.12(d). The sdr and signal rate are the same as those of polar NRZ. Unlike polar NRZ, AMI has no DC components problems even if there is a long sequence of bit "1" or bit "0," and its power intensity concentrates around the signal rate *N/2* instead of zero.

To avoid adding extra bits, a variant of AMI called modified AMI using *scrambling* is used by T-carriers and E-carriers. It does not increase the number of bits in the original data. We look at two scrambling schemes: bipolar with 8-zero substitution (B8ZS) and high-density bipolar 3-zero (HDB3). The B8ZS coding *replaces* 8 consecutive 0's with 000VB0VB, where V denotes a *violation* bit that is a nonzero bit that breaks the AMI coding rule and B is another nonzero bit that follows the AMI coding rule. The HDB3 coding uses either 000V or B00V to replace four consecutive 0's, depending on the number of nonzero bits after the last replacement. If odd, it uses 000V; if even, it uses B00V. The intention of this rule is to keep an even number of nonzero bits after each replacement.

Multilevel Coding: m Binary, n Levels (mBnL)

The purpose of multilevel coding schemes is to reduce the signal rate or channel bandwidth by using multiple levels in signaling to represent digital data. The notation mBnL is used to express the scheme of coding. The letter B means binary data; L means

TABLE 2.3 The Mapping Table for 2B1Q Coding

Dibit (2 bits)	00	01	10	11
If previous signal level positive next signal level =	+1	+3	–1	–3
If previous signal level negative next signal level =	–1	–3	+1	+3

the number of levels in signaling; m is the length of the binary data pattern, and n is the length of the signal pattern. If L = 2, B (binary) is used, instead of L. Similarly, if L = 3, T (ternary) is used; if L = 4, Q (quaternary) is used. Therefore, we may see some types of multilevel coding schemes such as 2B1Q, 4B3T, and 8B6T.

According to the notation mBnL, we can have 2^m patterns of binary data, and L^n patterns of signals. If $2^m = L^n$, all the signal patterns are used to represent the data patterns. If $2^m < L^n$, there exist more signals patterns than data patterns. These extra signal patterns can be used to prevent baseline wandering and to provide synchronization and error detection. If $2^m > L^n$, the number of signal patterns is not enough to present the data patterns; hence it is impossible to completely encode all the binary data. Here we discuss three typical schemes.

Two-binary, one-quaternary (2B1Q): Two-bit data are mapped into a signal element where the signal has four levels, as shown in Table 2.3; thus sdr equals 1/2. The average baud rate is calculated as $c \times N \times sdr = \frac{1}{2} \times N \times 1/2 = N/4$, i.e., one-fourth of the bit rate. The bandwidth of 2B1Q is shown in Figure 2.12(e). Compared to NRZ, 2B1Q requires only one-half of the bandwidth used in NRZ. In other words, 2B1Q carries twice the data rate that NRZ does under the same baud rate. However, the devices using 2B1Q are more complex than those of NRZ because 2B1Q uses four levels to represent four data patterns. To *differentiate* the four levels, more complex circuits are required in the devices. There are no redundant signal patterns for this coding because $2^m = 2^2 = L^n = 4^1$. The physical layer of Integrated Services Digital Network (ISDN) uses this coding scheme.

4B3T and 8B6T: The line coding 4B3T is used in the ISDN Basic Rate Interface (BRI), and it represents four bits with three pulses. 8B6T is used by the 100BASE-4T cable. Because 8B means data patterns and 6T means signal patterns, many redundant signal patterns can be used for DC balancing, synchronization, and error detection. Because sdr is 6/8, the average baud rate becomes *3N/8,* i.e., $c \times N \times sdr = 1/2 \times N \times 6/8 = 3N/8$.

Multilevel Transmission 3 Levels (MLT-3) Without Self-Synchronization

Both polar NRZ-I and differential Manchester are two-level transmission coding that encodes the binary data based on the change of consecutive bit values. The MLT-3 uses three levels to encode binary data. To encode bit "1," it uses three levels, +1, 0, –1, and four transitions from level +1, 0, –1, 0, to +1 in turns as a cycle. Level +1 denotes a positive physical level, and level –1 denotes a negative one. To encode bit "0," the level remains unchanged as the previous bit. Because MLT-3 uses *four transitions* to complete a full cycle, or four data elements are converted into one signal element (signal pattern), the sdr is analogous to 1/4. According to $S = c \times N \times sdr$, under the worse case of $c = 1$, the baud rate becomes $S = c \times N \times sdr = 1 \times N \times 1/4 = N/4$; the baud rate is only *one-fourth* of the data rate. This feature makes MLT-3 suitable for transmission over copper cables at a lower frequency. 100BASE-TX adopts MLT-3 because the copper cable can support only 31.25 MHz for the baud rate, but the data rate is up to 125 Mbps.

Run Length Limited (RLL)

RLL limits the length of repeated bits to avoid a long, consecutive bit stream without transitions. Run length is the number of bits with unchanged values. If polar NRZ-I is appended to RLL to encode the source data, where a "1" represents a transition and a "0" no transition, the run length becomes the count of 0's. RLL uses two parameters—*d* for the minimum zero-bit run length, and *k* for the maximum zero-bit run length. Therefore, the notation of RLL is *(d, k)* RLL. The simplest form of RLL is (0,1) RLL. The industry standards of RLL for some hard disks are (2,7) RLL and (1,7) RLL. Their encoding tables are given in Table 2.4. Table 2.4(c), (1,7) RLL, maps two bits of data onto three bits. A pair of bits *(x, y)* is converted based on the rule, (NOT *x*, *x* AND *y*, NOT *y*), except that the sequence of four bits *(x*, 0, 0, *y)* is converted into (NOT *x*, *x* AND *y*, NOT *y*, 0, 0, 0).

Block Coding

Block coding, also known as channel coding, is a kind of error detecting/correcting technique that maps an input sequence to another sequence with longer length for a better error performance. The degree of improvement in error performance by using channel coding can be measured by the notion of coding gain, which is the ratio of the SNRs of the uncoded and the coded data required for the same error performance. The redundant bits introduced by block coding can be used for *synchronization* and *error detection* and can therefore simplify the subsequent line coding. Usually block coding is performed before line coding. A block code, when used as an error detection code, can detect transmission *errors* at the receiver and drop the erroneous

TABLE 2.4 Examples of RLL Coding

(a) (0,1) RLL		(b) (2,7) RLL		(c) (1,7) RLL	
Data	**(0,1) RLL**	**Data**	**(2, 7) RLL**	**Data**	**(1, 7) RLL**
0	10	11	1000	00 00	101 000
1	11	10	0100	00 01	100 000
		000	000100	10 00	001 000
		010	100100	10 01	010 000
		011	001000	00	101
		0011	00001000	01	100
		0010	00100100	10	001
				11	010

frames. Block coding can be represented by *mB/nB* where an *m*-bit stream is encoded into an *n*-bit codeword. There are commonly three steps in block coding: partition, encoding, and concatenation. For example, a bit stream is partitioned into *m*-bit segments which are encoded into *n*-bit codewords. Finally these *n*-bit codewords are concatenated to form a new bit stream.

Block codes are generally decoded by hard-decision algorithms and have been widely used in many communication systems. Two kinds of block codes, four binary/five binary (4B/5B) and eight binary/ten binary (8B/10B), are explored here.

The 4B/5B block coding transforms each block of four bits into five bits. The coding of 4B/5B maps a set of four bits into a set of five bits as shown in Table 2.5, where the 5-bit codeword has at most *one* leading zero and at most *two* trailing zeros. If any 5-bit codeword is concatenated with any other 5-bit codeword, the resulting binary tuple will have at most three consecutive 0's. A long sequence of bit 0's can never happen after the 4B/5B encoder. Moreover, the 5-bit word patterns from valid

TABLE 2.5 4B/5B Encoding Table

Name	4B	5B	Description
0	0000	11110	hex data 0
1	0001	01001	hex data 1
2	0010	10100	hex data 2
3	0011	10101	hex data 3
4	0100	01010	hex data 4
5	0101	01011	hex data 5
6	0110	01110	hex data 6
7	0111	01111	hex data 7
8	1000	10010	hex data 8
9	1001	10011	hex data 9
A	1010	10110	hex data A
B	1011	10111	hex data B
C	1100	11010	hex data C
D	1101	11011	hex data D
E	1110	11100	hex data E
F	1111	11101	hex data F
Q	n/a	00000	Quiet (signal lost)
I	n/a	11111	Idle
J	n/a	11000	Start #1
K	n/a	10001	Start #2
T	n/a	01101	End
R	n/a	00111	Reset
S	n/a	11001	Set
H	n/a	00100	Halt

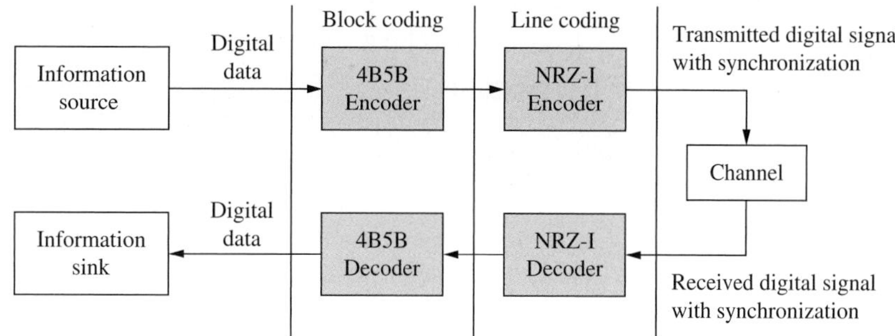

FIGURE 2.13 The architecture of combing 4B/5B coding and NRZ-I coding.

data words can be chosen intelligently to balance the numbers of 1's and 0's in the signal and to guarantee a sufficient number of transitions in the line coding. Because the data space is expanded from 16 4-bit words to 32 5-bit codewords, 16 extra codewords are available for additional purposes, such as control words that represent the start and the end of a frame. Some words can be reserved intentionally for error detection. Because no valid data words can be transformed into these reserved words, a transmission error can be detected if a reserved word is present at the receiver.

The 4B/5B coding is commonly used with polar NRZ-I coding, as shown in the architecture in Figure 2.13. Extra bit "1" yields an extra transition for synchronization. The predefined encoding table converts four bits to five bits with at least *two* transitions per block of bits. After applying the 4B/5B block coding, the bit rate of the output increases by 25 percent. The 4-bit codewords transmitting at a 100 Mbps bit rate now require 125 Mbps to send the new 5-bit codewords. The technique of 4B/5B avoids the NRZ-I synchronization problem, but it still leaves the DC components problem unresolved. The fundamental frequency is only one-fourth of the digital data rate, thus at least four bits are required to generate a complete cycle. The output signal can be easily carried by a CAT-5 cable.

More complex block coding methods such as 8B/10B and 64B/66B are commonly applied to high-speed transmissions. These complex coding techniques can balance the numbers of 0's and 1's transmitted on the line by tallying where there are more 0's or 1's and choosing the proper coding on the fly, depending on which bit is transmitted more frequently. Since the 10-bit codeword has an imbalance of at most one additional one or zero, the tally contains only one bit called the running disparity (RD). Each transmission of a codeword updates RD, where RD+ denotes the case when there are more 1's than 0's, and RD– denotes the opposite. Moreover, a wider code space also allows a higher degree of error detection in the physical layer.

Before concluding this section we remark that the 8B/10B and 64B/66B codes introduced earlier are among the simplest in error detecting/correcting codes and are mainly used in wired short-distance communication where the communication channel is more reliable and less noisy. For channels that are highly noisy, such as those in wireless communications, a much more powerful code with longer length is often required. The code length can go up to thousands or tens of thousands in such applications. Furthermore, compared to the *hard-decision* algorithm used in the decoding of the 8B/10B code, a much more complicated *soft-decision* algorithm that operates on the probabilistic domain is often used to decode such long codes.

Open Source Implementation 2.1: 8B/10B Encoder

Overview

8B/10B has been widely adopted as the line coding by a variety of high-speed data communication standards, including PCI Express, IEEE 1394b, serial ATA, DVI/HDMI, and Gigabit Ethernet. It maps 8-bit symbols to 10-bit symbols with bounded disparity, which provides two important properties. One is the DC-balance property, i.e., the same number of 0's and 1's for a given data stream, to avoid a charge being built up in certain media. Another property is the maximum run-length, i.e., maximum numbers of contiguous 0's or 1's, which gives enough state changes for clock synchronization. An open source example is available from the OpenCores website at http://opencores.org, which presents the implementations of 8B/10B encoder and decoder in the VHDL codes, where 8B/10B encoder is composed of a 5B/6B encoder and a 3B/4B encoder.

Block Diagram

Figure 2.14 illustrates the architecture of the OPENCORE 8B/10B encoder. It accepts an 8-bit parallel raw (unencoded) data byte consisting of bits *H, G, F, E, D, C, B, A*. *A* is the least significant bit. There is also an input bit, *K*, to indicate that the character input should be encoded as one of the 12 allowable control characters.

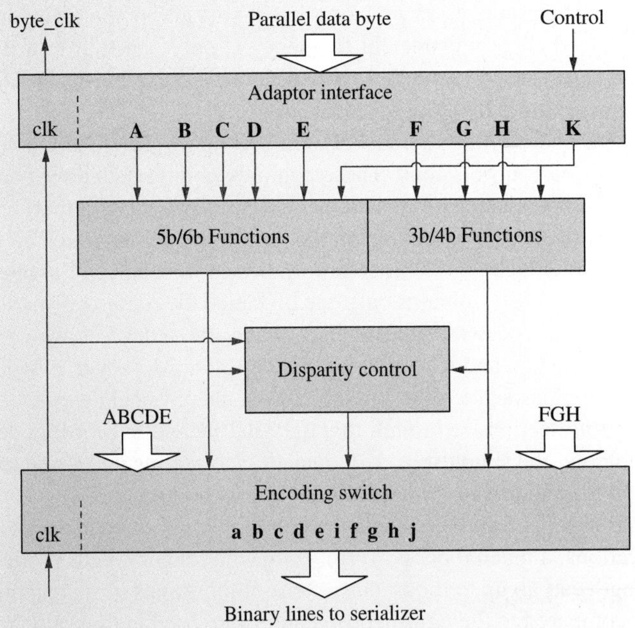

FIGURE 2.14 Block diagram of 8B/10B encoder.

The code maps an 8-bit parallel data input to a 10-bit output with two encoders. One is the 5B/6B encoder, which maps the five input bits (*A, B, C, D*, and *E*) into a 6-bit group (*a, b, c, d, e*, and *i*), and the other is 3B/4B encoder, which maps the remaining three bits (*F, G*, and *H*) into a 4-bit group (*f, g, h*, and *j*).

In order to reduce the number of input patterns, the function modules group several input bits into classes. For example, each 5-bit codeword can be classified into four classes (L04, L13, L22, and L40) according to the first four bits (*A, B, C*, and *D*). The disparity control generates control signals to the encoding switch to indicate the choice of positive or negative disparity encoding. The encoding switch reuses the classification results and outputs the encoded bits at each clock.

Data Structures

The data structures of 8B/10B encoder are mainly the 8 input bits and 10 output bits. All of the inputs and outputs are synchronized to the *clk* as follows: (1) *K, H, G* and *F* are latched internally on the falling edge of the *clk*. (2) *j, h, g*, and *f* are updated on the falling edge of the *clk*. (3) *E, D, C, B*, and *A* are latched internally on the rising edge of the *clk*. (4) *i, e, d, c, b*, and *a* are updated on the rising edge of the *clk*.

Algorithm Implementations

In the OPENCORE 8B/10B project, the VHDL implementation of 8B/10B encoder is in 8b10_enc.vhd, and enc_8b10b_TB.vhd is the testbench file for the encoder. Figure 2.15 shows the code segment of the 5B/6B function module, which is a combinational logic of several NOT, AND, and OR gates. The other modules are also constructed from these simple logic gates, and the entire implementation of 8B/10B encoder does not require any complex arithmetic operations, such as addition and multiplication. Because the descriptions of the entire 8B/10B encoder codes would be too verbose, we refer the readers to 8b10_enc.vhd for the relevant details in the computation of each bit.

```
    L40 <= AI and BI and CI and DI ;                  -- 1,1,1,1
    -- Four 0's
    L04 <= not AI and not BI and not CI and not DI ;
    -- 0,0,0,0
    -- One 1 and three 0's

L13 <= (not AI and not BI and not CI and DI)      -- 0,0,0,1
    or (not AI and not BI and CI and not DI)      -- 0,0,1,0
    or (not AI and BI and not CI and not DI)      -- 0,1,0,0
    or (AI and not BI and not CI and not DI);     -- 1,0,0,0
-- Three 1's and one 0

L31 <= (AI and BI and CI and not DI)              -- 1,1,1,0
    or (AI and BI and not CI and DI)              -- 1,1,0,1
```

Continued

```
    or (AI and not BI and CI and DI)              -- 1,0,1,1
    or (not AI and BI and CI and DI) ;            -- 0,1,1,1
-- Two 1's and two 0's

L22 <= (not AI and not BI and CI and DI)          -- 0,0,1,1
    or (not AI and BI and CI and not DI)          -- 0,1,1,0
    or (AI and BI and not CI and not DI)          -- 1,1,0,0
    or (AI and not BI and not CI and DI)          -- 1,0,0,1
    or (not AI and BI and not CI and DI)          -- 0,1,0,1
    or (AI and not BI and CI and not DI) ;        -- 1,0,1,0
```

FIGURE 2.15 The code segment of the 5B/6B function.

Exercises

Find the code segment in 8b10_enc.vhd related to the 3B/4B coding switch in Figure 2.14 and show which line of code controls the output timing, i.e., falling or rising edge of the *clk* signal.

2.4 DIGITAL MODULATION AND MULTIPLEXING

In telecommunications and computer networks, digital modulation is required to convert a digital bit stream to a bandpass waveform for traveling over an analog bandpass channel. The bandpass waveform, a passband signal, is derived from a sinusoidal analog carrier modulated by the amplitude, the phase, or the frequency of a digital bit stream. The process is called digital *passband* modulation, or simply digital modulation, in contrast to the digital baseband modulation or line coding. Either the modulated signals or the original digital signals could be further multiplexed onto a physical channel to better utilize the channel. We first introduce the fundamental digital modulation schemes, including amplitude-shift keying (ASK), phase-shift keying (PSK), frequency-shift keying (FSK), and the hybrid quadrature amplitude modulation (QAM). Then we present two basic multiplexing schemes: time-division multiplexing (TDM) and frequency-division multiplexing (FDM). We leave code-division multiplexing (CDM) and several other advanced techniques to Section 2.5.

2.4.1 Passband Modulation

Passband modulation is a two-step process. It first converts the digital signal to a baseband complex-valued signal according to the modulation scheme used, such as ASK, PSK, FSK, or QAM. These baseband waveforms are then multiplied by a complex-valued sinusoidal carrier signal with much higher carrier frequency. After removing the imaginary component, the resulting real-valued passband signal is then ready for transmission. The former is usually called a *digital modulation,* while the latter is done by frequency mixing. The digital modulation is emphasized here and shown in Figure 2.16. Unlike the line coding for baseband transmission described

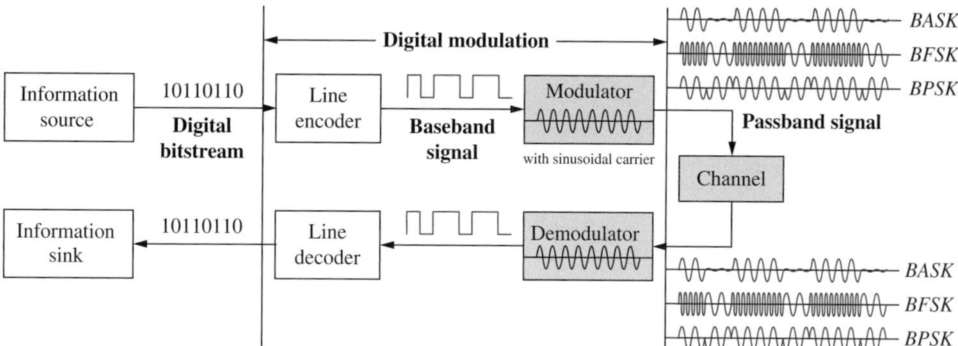

FIGURE 2.16 Digital modulation.

in Section 2.3, the signal rate S is equal to $N \times 1/r$. The case factor is not considered here. The value of r is the number of data elements that an analog signal can carry, and N is the data rate. S is the digital signal rate before modulation.

In digital communications, baseband digital signals are commonly carried by *sinusoidal carriers* of higher frequency for transmissions over higher-frequency channels. What is a sinusoidal carrier, and how can a carrier carry the messages? In bandpass communication, a sender must generate a high-frequency signal, called a carrier, to carry data signals. A receiver is tuned to the frequency of the carrier to receive the "carrier-carried" data signals from the sender. Any aspects of the carrier or the changes of the aspects in amplitude, frequency, and phase can be used to represent digital data. The technique using digital data to modify one or more aspects of carriers is called *modulation* or *shift keying*. They are classified into amplitude-shift keying (ASK), frequency-shift keying (FSK), and phase-shift keying (PSK). A hybrid technique including both amplitude and phase aspects exists and is called quadrature amplitude modulation (QAM). QAM is more efficient than ASK, FSK, and PSK since it utilizes more aspects. In addition, the change of the aspects of a carrier, such as the change of phases, is used in differential PSK (DPSK).

Constellation Diagram

The constellation diagram is a tool that defines a mapping from digital data patterns to the signal constellation points. The constellation points in the diagram are used to define the amplitude and phase of a signal element. The diagram is employed in all digital modulations. Figure 2.17 is an example of a constellation diagram for 4-PSK using two carriers; one along the real axis is an *in-phase* axis, and the other along the imaginary axis is a *quadrature* axis. In this figure four constellation points can be used to define four distinct signal elements to map into *four* data patterns of *two* bits.

Four basic modulations in digital modulation—ASK, FSK, PSK, and DPSK—are illustrated in Figure 2.18. Next we introduce each of them and QAM.

Amplitude-Shift Keying (ASK)

The technique of amplitude-shift keying (ASK) uses different levels of amplitude of carriers to represent digital data. Usually two levels of amplitude are used in

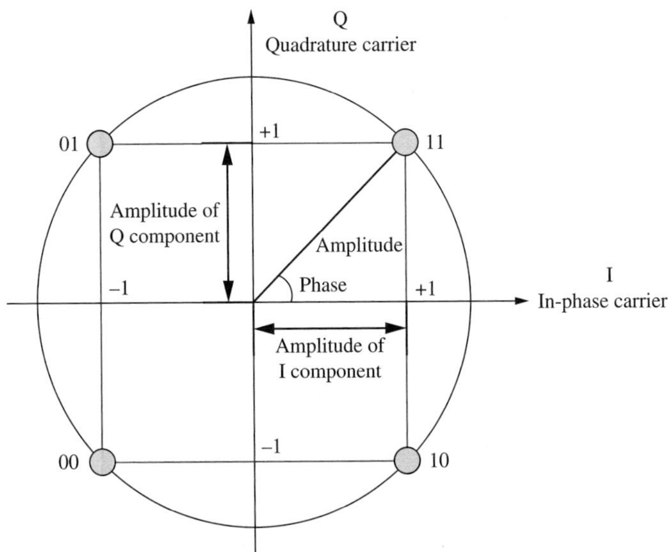

FIGURE 2.17 A constellation diagram: constellation points with two bits: b_0b_1.

ASK, one for bit "1" and the other for "0," while the frequency and phase of the carrier do not change during modulation. ASK with two levels of amplitude is called binary ASK (BASK), or on-off keying (OOK). Its constellation diagram is shown in Figure 2.19(a). Only one carrier, the in-phase carrier, is used, and zero voltage denotes bit "0," while a positive voltage denotes bit "1." Its modulated waveform is illustrated in Figure 2.18 where a unipolar NRZ line encoder is used to encode the digital data and generate the digital signal to modulate a carrier. According to BASK, the value r is 1 and $S = N \times 1/r = N$. The signal rate S is equal to the data rate N. If the bandwidth of the signal is proportional to the signal rate, we may obtain the bandwidth $BW = (1 + d)S$, where d is a factor between 0 and 1, depending on the modulation

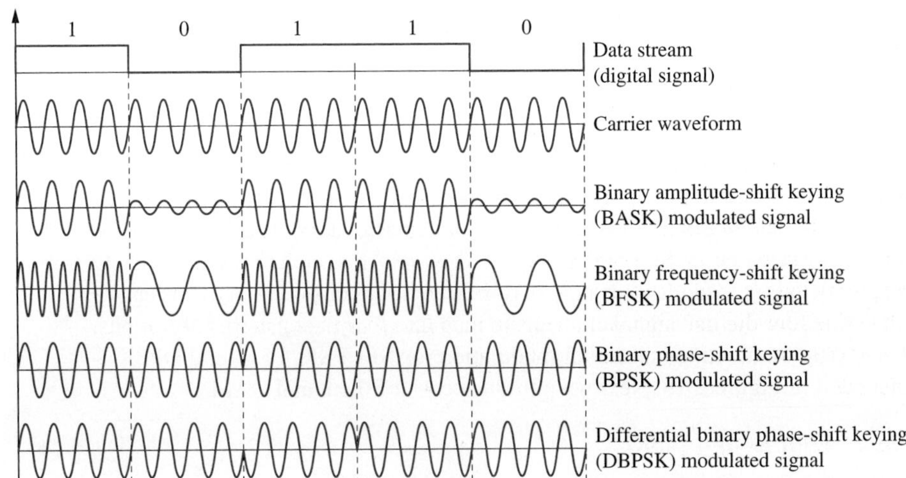

FIGURE 2.18 The waveforms of four basic digital modulations.

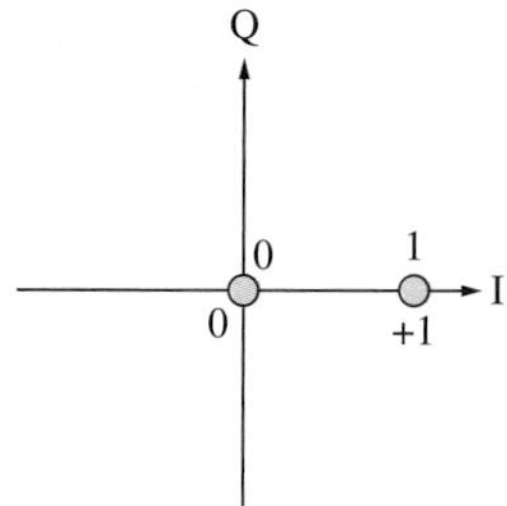

(a) The constellation of ASK (OOK): b_0.

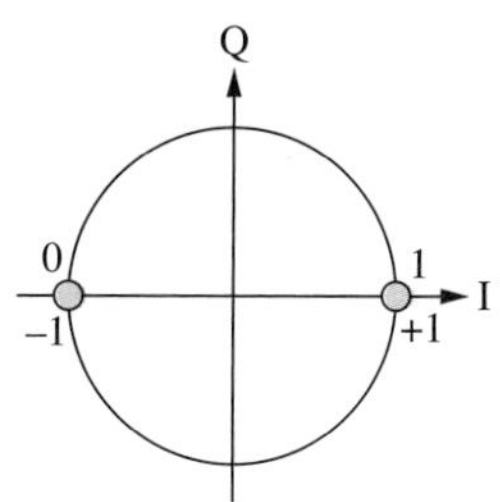

(b) The constellation of 2-PSK (BPSK): b_0.

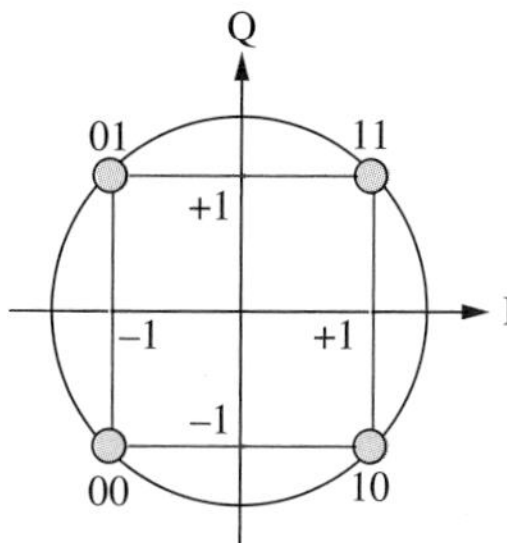

(c) The constellation of 4-PSK (QPSK): b_0b_1.

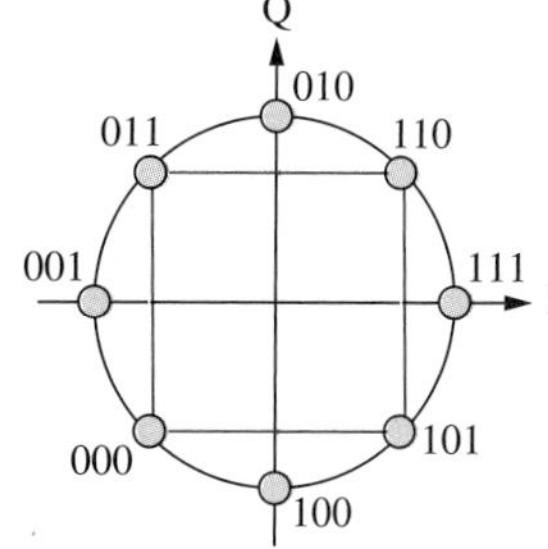

(d) The constellation of 8-PSK: $b_0b_1b_2$.

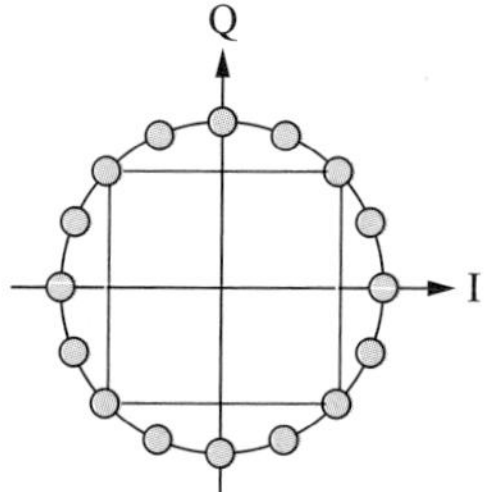

(e) The constellation of 16-PSK: $b_0b_1b_2b_3$.

FIGURE 2.19 The constellation diagrams of ASK and PSK.

and filtering process. Though the carrier is a sinusoidal signal, the modulated signal of ASK is an aperiodic analog signal. According to Figure 2.1(b), the bandwidth is a finite range of frequencies around the carrier frequency, as shown in Figure 2.20(a). The mechanism for implementing ASK is shown in Figure 2.20(b). For a simplified implementation, a multiplier multiplies the baseband waveform, an output of unipolar NRZ, by the carrier from a local oscillator to obtain a modulated signal. Such multiplication is called frequency mixing, which is the second step of passband modulation.

Frequency-Shift Keying (FSK)

The technique of frequency-shift keying (FSK) uses the carrier frequencies to represent digital data. In other words, the carrier frequencies are changed to represent the

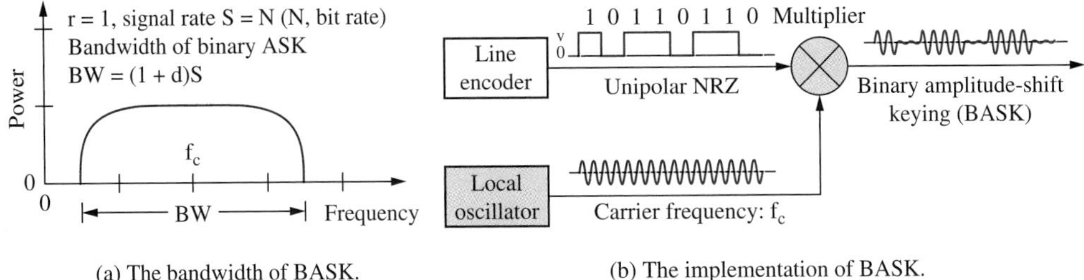

(a) The bandwidth of BASK. (b) The implementation of BASK.

FIGURE 2.20 The bandwidth and implementation of BASK.

value of a digital signal. The simplest FSK scheme uses "1" as mark frequency and "0" as space frequency. Figure 2.18 shows the waveform of binary frequency-shift keying (BFSK), compared with other shift keying techniques. Figure 2.21(a) shows the spectrum of BFSK where two distinct frequencies, f_1 and f_2, are used to represent "0" and "1," respectively.

In BFSK, the ratio of the number of bit elements to the number of signal elements is 1, i.e., $r = 1$, and the signal rate S is $N \times 1/r = N \times 1/1 = N$. If the technique of BFSK is considered a combination of *two* BASK schemes with different frequencies, the bandwidth for each frequency is $S(1 + d)$. The difference between two center frequencies is $2\Delta f$. The difference must be greater than the *sum* of a half bandwidth centered at frequency f_1 and a half bandwidth centered at frequency f_2, i.e., $S(1 + d)$. Because d is a factor between 0 and 1, in the worst case $d = 1$, then $2\Delta f \geq 2S$, i.e., $\Delta f \geq S$. This guarantees that the spectra of the two signals do *not* overlap, so the signals do not interfere with each other in the frequency domain. The total bandwidth of the modulated signal of BFSK is $BW = S(1 + d) + 2\Delta f$, as shown in Figure 2.21(a).

A simplified implementation scheme for BFSK is shown in Figure 2.21(b) where a voltage-controlled oscillator (VCO) is used to change the frequency of the carrier. The input to the FSK mechanism is a unipolar NRZ signal that is mapped into the input voltage to the voltage-controlled oscillator. The FSK and its variants, minimum shift keying (MSK) and audio FSK (AFSK), are applied to the GSM mobile phone standard and caller ID to convey messages.

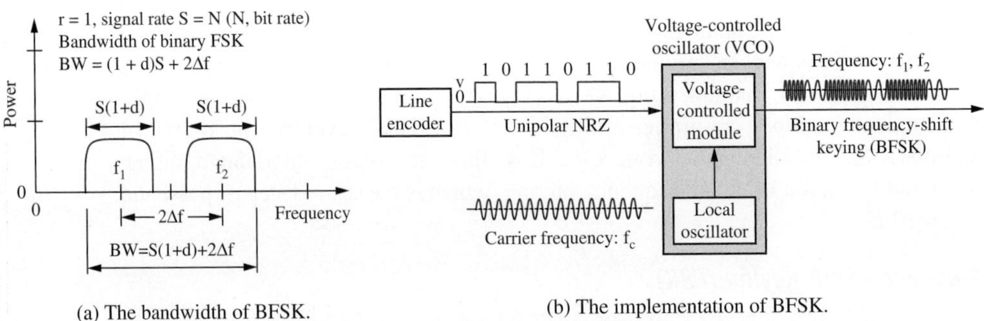

(a) The bandwidth of BFSK. (b) The implementation of BFSK.

FIGURE 2.21 The bandwidth and implementation of BFSK.

Phase-Shift Keying (PSK)

The technique of phase-shift keying (PSK) encodes an equal number of bits into a symbol by modulating the phases of a carrier. In other words, the phase of a carrier is used to represent digital data. In the keying, the amplitude and frequency of the carrier remain the same. A receiver can retrieve the digital signal from the received signals by mapping a finite number of phases to a finite number of bit patterns.

The constellation diagrams for m-PSK, such as 2-PSK, 4-PSK, 8PSK, and 16-PSK, are shown in Figure 2.19, which places constellation points uniformly around a circle. Only phase differences appear on these PSK constellation diagrams. According to the figures, we find BPSK uses only one carrier, the in-phase carrier, while the rest of m-PSKs use two carriers, both in-phase carrier and quadrature carrier. This arrangement can help PSK achieve a maximum phase separation and avoid interference. The number of the constellation points is a power of 2 because digital data are commonly delivered in binary bits.

Binary phase-shift keying (BPSK): BPSK is the simplest PSK that uses only one carrier, the in-phase carrier. As shown in the constellation diagram in Figure 2.19(b), two different phases represent the binary data; the phase of 0° for bit "1" and the phase of 180° for bit "0." A polar NRZ line encoder is used to facilitate the implementation of BPSK, as shown in Figure 2.22(b). The positive voltage of the polar NRZ signal does not change the phase of the carrier, while the negative voltage of the polar NRZ digital signal converts the phase of the carrier to 180° out of phase. The technique of BPSK is more immune to noise than BASK because the amplitude of signals is more easily degraded by noise than the phase of signals. Moreover, BPSK merely uses one frequency while BFSK uses two frequencies. Thus BPSK outperforms BFSK. The bandwidth of BPSK is the same as that of BASK but less than that of BFSK, as shown in Figure 2.22(a).

Quadrature phase-shift keying (QPSK): QPSK is a modulation using two carriers, an in-phase carrier and a quadrature carrier, to carry two sequences of digital data. Figure 2.23 illustrates a simplified implementation for QPSK. It can be analogous to two distinct BPSK modulations with a 90° phase difference. In the figure, a bit stream 11000110 is first *split* into two substreams evenly. Each of them is processed by a polar NRZ-L line encoder to generate a modulating signal. One modulates the in-phase carrier to an I-signal (in-phase signal); the other modulates the quadrature carrier to a Q-signal (quadrature signal). Combining the I-signal and Q-signal yields a QPSK signal. Each signal element may have one of the four phases, 45°, 135°, –45°, and –135°. Consequently, a binary bit stream 11000110 is transformed into a QPSK signal. The waveforms, I-signal, Q-signal,

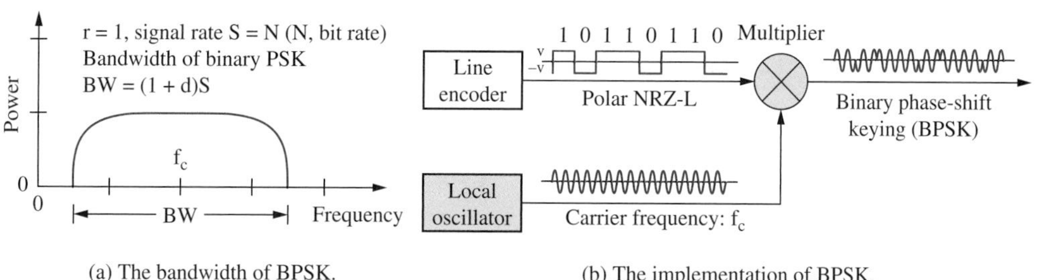

(a) The bandwidth of BPSK.

(b) The implementation of BPSK.

FIGURE 2.22 The bandwidth and implementation of BPSK.

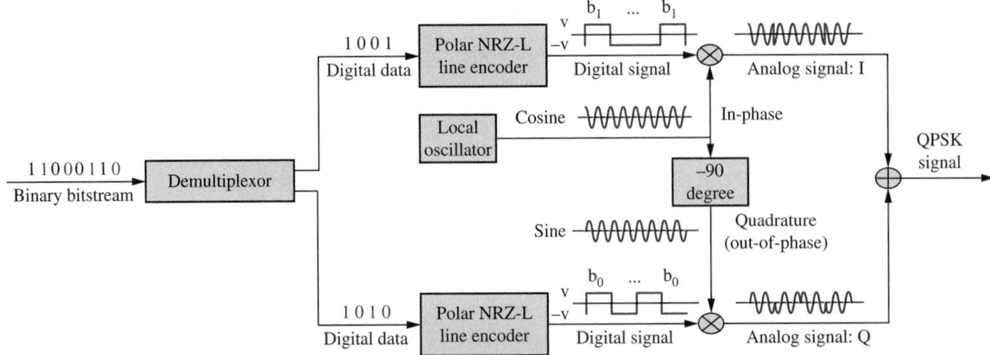

FIGURE 2.23 A simplified implementation of QPSK.

and QPSK-signal are shown in Figure 2.24. The amplitude on the real axis modulates a cosine wave carrier into an I-signal while the amplitude on the imaginary axis modulates a sine wave carrier into a Q-signal. A QPSK signal received at a receiver is then processed through matched filters, samplers, decision devices, and multiplexer to recover the original data. QPSK encodes two data elements (two bits) into one signal element. This enables the technique to process data at double the rate that BPSK does. The phase delay inherently occurs at the received QPSK signal, so the clock at the receiver must synchronize to that at the transmitter. Moreover, this so-called *Doppler shift* can cause offset in the relative frequency. The phase delay and frequency offset induced by channels must be compensated by precisely tuning the sinusoidal functions at the receiver. A cable system standard, Data Over Cable Service Interface Specification (DOCSIS), specifies QPSK or 16-QAM for upstream modulation.

Differential phase-shift keying (DPSK): DPSK is a variant of PSK. Bit patterns here are mapped to the changes of signal phases. This scheme significantly simplifies

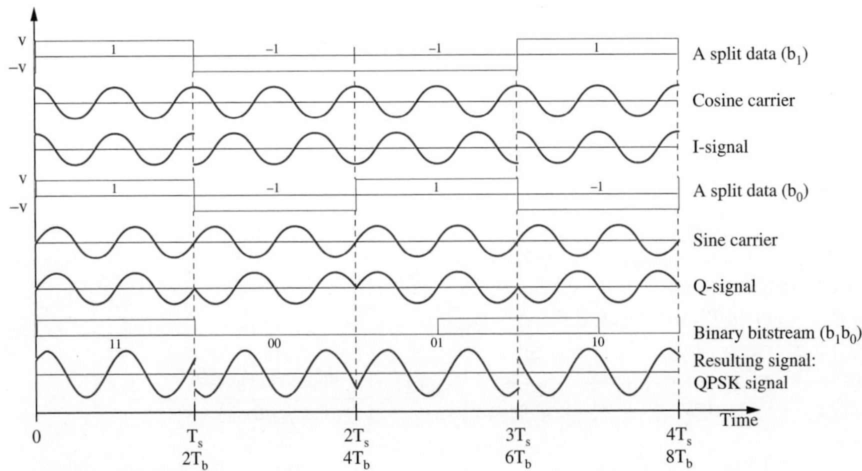

FIGURE 2.24 The I, Q, and QPSK waveforms.

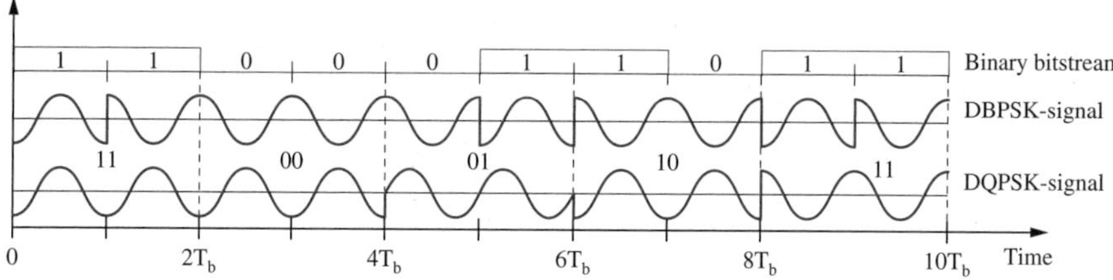

FIGURE 2.25 Signals of DBPSK and DQPSK.

the complexity of the modulation and demodulation devices. The waveforms of differential binary phase-shift keying (DBPSK) and DQPSK are shown in Figure 2.25.

In the DBPSK modulation, if the phase of a signal is changed, the following signal represents bit 1; otherwise it is 0. In the DQPSK modulation, the following two bits are based on the change of the signal phase. Without changing the phase, the pair of bits is 00. If the change of the signal phase is $\pi/4$, the following two bits are 01. If $-\pi/4$, the pair of bits is 10. If the phase change is π, then the pair of bits is 11. Because the demodulator of DPSK does not need a reference signal, the design of a modem is simplified at a cost of higher error probabilities. However, the drawback can be removed by increasing the SNR a little bit. Therefore, DPSK is widely used in the Wi-Fi wireless communication standards.

Quadrature Amplitude Modulation (QAM)

The quadrature amplitude modulation (QAM) changes a carrier's amplitude as well as phase to form the waveforms of different signal elements. QAM uses levels of amplitude, in-phase carrier, and quadrature carrier, so it is a combination of ASK and PSK. A higher transmission rate can be achieved using QAM than ASK and PSK due to more than one aspect used to represent multiple bits in a signal. For instance, *two* levels of amplitude and *two* difference phases can be used to represent 2-bit patterns for *four* combinations. A combination represents a symbol. Hence, a symbol of 2^N combinations can carry N-bit data at a time. QAM needs at least two amplitudes and two phases.

Like QPSK, QAM uses two sinusoidal carriers that are out of phase by 90°. QAM employs two types of constellation diagrams: *circular* and *rectangular*. Figure 2.26 shows several circular constellation diagrams, where the diagram of 4-QAM is the same as that of QPSK. Figure 2.27 shows the rectangular constellation diagrams, such as 4-QAM, 8-QAM, and 16-QAM. In Figure 2.28, a 64-QAM rectangular constellation represents 64 combinations of different amplitudes and phases. This modulation can transmit six bits per symbol. However, increasing the number of combinations makes the *circuitry* for encoding and decoding more complicated, and it is getting harder to tell the *difference* between the combinations when so many combinations are packed in a symbol. Because the modulated signal is prone to error, a transmission using this modulation requires extra error detection techniques.

On the QAM transmitter, a data stream is split into *two* substreams. Each substream is processed by an ASK modulator. The output on the I-channel is multiplied by a cosine function, and that on the Q-channel is multiplied by a sine function. The resulting QAM signal is obtained by adding the I-signal and Q-signal. The QAM

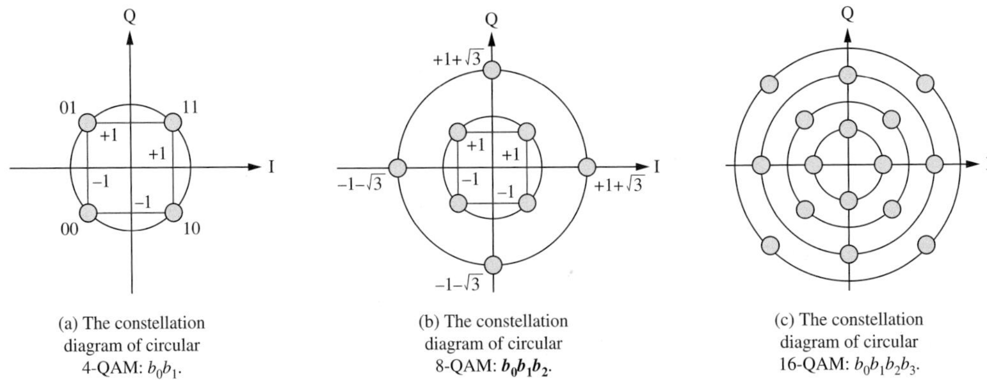

(a) The constellation diagram of circular 4-QAM: b_0b_1.

(b) The constellation diagram of circular 8-QAM: $b_0b_1b_2$.

(c) The constellation diagram of circular 16-QAM: $b_0b_1b_2b_3$.

FIGURE 2.26 The circular constellation diagrams.

receiver reverses the process to retrieve the original data. DOCSIS employs 64-QAM or 256-QAM for downstream modulation, while using QPSK or 16-QAM for upstream modulation. Furthermore, the newer DOCSIS 2.0 and 3.0 also use 32-QAM, 64-QAM, and 128-QAM for *upstream* modulation.

2.4.2 Multiplexing

A physical channel in a transmission medium may provide bandwidth greater than required for a data stream. To efficiently utilize the capacity of the channel, several

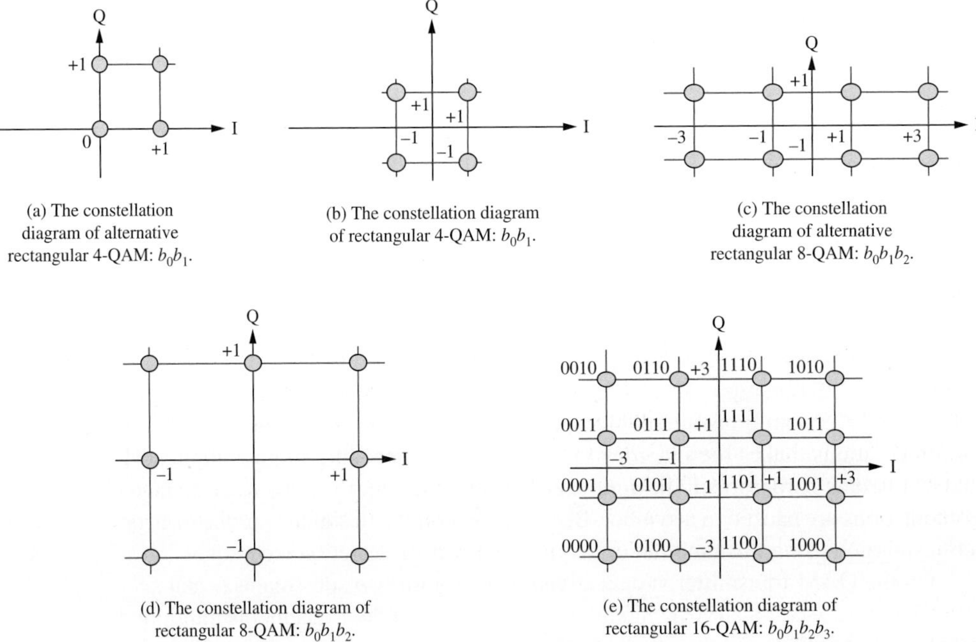

(a) The constellation diagram of alternative rectangular 4-QAM: b_0b_1.

(b) The constellation diagram of rectangular 4-QAM: b_0b_1.

(c) The constellation diagram of alternative rectangular 8-QAM: $b_0b_1b_2$.

(d) The constellation diagram of rectangular 8-QAM: $b_0b_1b_2$.

(e) The constellation diagram of rectangular 16-QAM: $b_0b_1b_2b_3$.

FIGURE 2.27 The rectangular constellation diagrams.

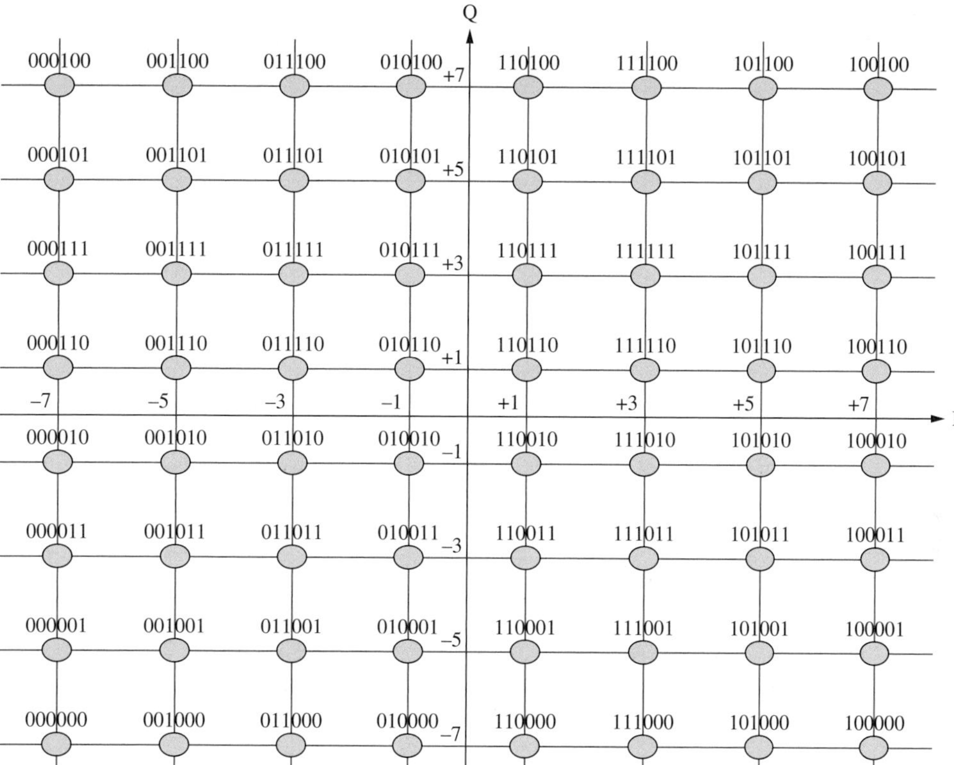

FIGURE 2.28 The constellation of rectangular 64-QAM: $b_0 b_1 b_2 b_3 b_4 b_5$.

channel access schemes are applied. Using channel access methods, multiple transceivers can share a transmission medium. There are three types of channel access methods: circuit-mode, packet-mode, and duplexing. Multiplexing is one of the circuit-mode methods used in the physical layer. The channel access methods in the link layer are packet-mode methods that are based on multiple access protocols in the media access control (MAC) sublayer. The duplexing methods are used to separate the uplink and downlink channels. The methods of packet-mode and duplexing are skipped here.

A multiplexing system with multiplexer (MUX) and demultiplexer (DEMUX) is shown in Figure 2.29. This figure shows the data streams from multiple data sources multiplexed and transmitted over a shared physical channel. The multiplexing techniques include TDM, FDM, wavelength-division multiplexing (WDM), code division multiple access (CDMA), and spatial multiplexing (SM). Table 2.6 shows channel access and their corresponding multiplexing methods. We introduce the basic ones here while leaving CDMA to Section 2.5.1.

Time-Division Multiplexing (TDM)

TDM is a technique to combine multiple digital signals from low-rate channels into a high-rate channel shared alternately in time slots. A simplified scheme of TDM is

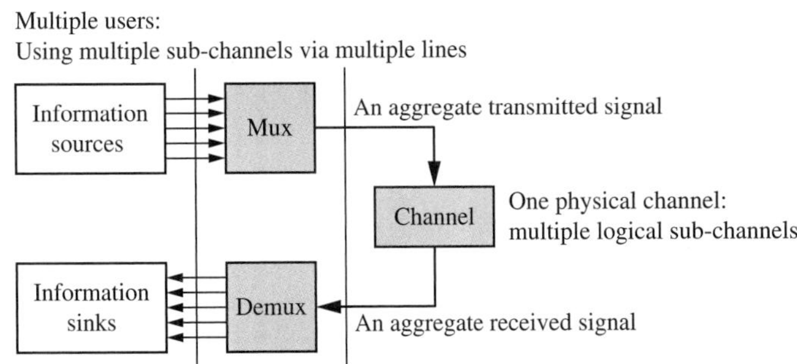

FIGURE 2.29 A physical channel used for multiple users via multiple sub-channels.

shown in Figure 2.30, where data streams from different sources are *interleaved* in a stream of time slots.

TDM divides a time domain into several recurrent time slots of certain time length. Each time slot is considered part of a sub-channel or logical channel. Each sub-channel is used to transmit a data stream. The interleaved time slots require synchronization at a demultiplexer. It can be implemented by adding one or more synchronization bits at the beginning of each transmitted frame. This is called *synchronous* TDM, compared to *statistical* TDM, which can dynamically allocate time slots to sub-channels without assigning time slots to empty input lines. If the input data rates are different, several techniques can be used, such as multilevel multiplexing, multi-slot allocation, and pulse stuffing (or bit stuffing, bit padding). The telephony industry uses T lines to implement the digital signal service. T lines are categorized from T1 to T4 with different service data rates.

TABLE 2.6 The Mapping of Channel Access Scheme and Multiplexing

Multiplexing	Channel Access Scheme	Applications
FDM (frequency-division multiplexing)	FDMA (frequency division multiple access)	1G cell phone
WDM (wavelength-division multiplexing)	WDMA (wave-length division multiple access)	fiber-optical
TDM (time-division multiplexing)	TDMA (time division multiple access)	GSM telephone
SS (spread spectrum)	CDMA (code division multiple access)	3G cell phone
DSSS (direct sequence SS)	DS-CDMA (direct sequence CDMA)	802.11b/g/n
FHSS (frequency hopping SS)	FH-CDMA (frequency hopping CDMA)	Bluetooth
SM (spatial multiplexing)	SDMA (space division multiple access)	802.11n, LTE, WiMAX
STC (space time coding)	STMA (space time multiple access)	802.11n, LTE, WiMAX

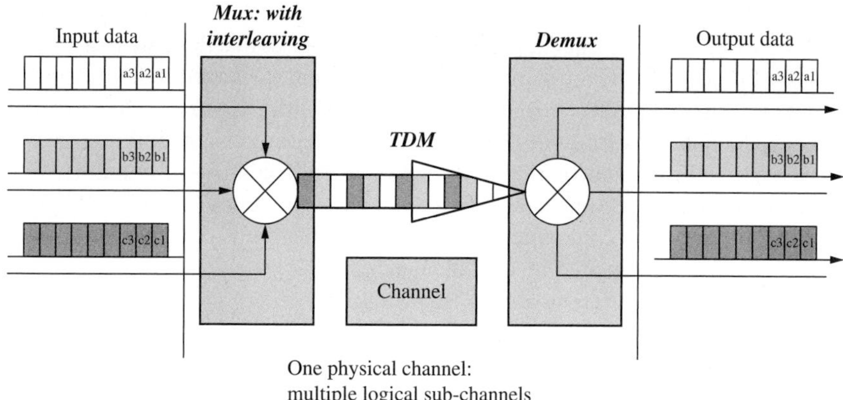

FIGURE 2.30 The process of time-division multiplexing (TDM).

TDM can be extended to the time-division multiple access (TDMA) scheme. The TDMA policy at the link layer is enforced through TDM at the physical layer that actually does the job. The GSM telephone system is one of its applications.

Frequency-Division Multiplexing (FDM)

FDM divides a frequency domain into several non-overlapping frequency ranges, each becoming a sub-channel used by a sub-carrier. Figure 2.31 shows the process of FDM. At a transmitter, the multiplexing process combines all waveforms derived from data streams, where a sub-channel uses a sub-carrier, and results in a *composite* signal that is transmitted over a physical channel. At the receiver, several bandpass filters are used to extract messages for sub-channels from a received composite signal. FDM is only applied to analog signals. A digital signal can be converted into an analog signal by modulation, and then FDM can be applied. The radio broadcasting of AM and FM signals are two typical applications using FDM. For example, the bandwidth from 530 kHz to 1700 kHz is assigned to AM radio. This is the bandwidth of a physical channel medium and is shared by several radio stations.

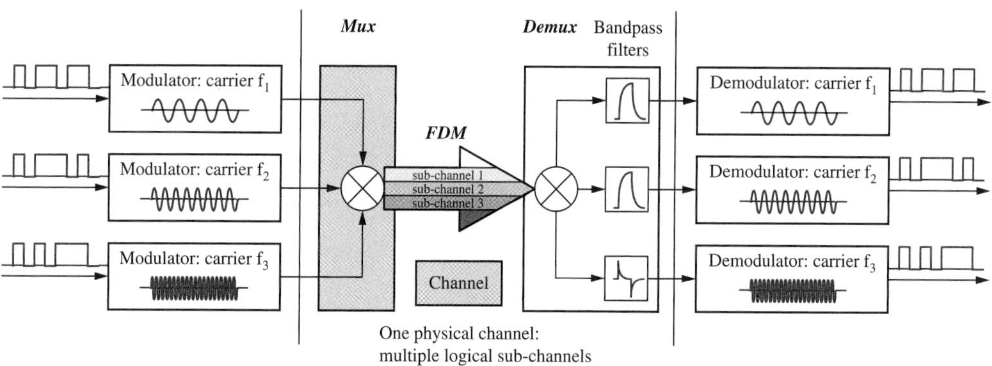

FIGURE 2.31 The process of frequency-division multiplexing (FDM).

Frequency-division multiple access (FDMA) is an access method extended from FDM. Orthogonal frequency-division multiple access (OFDMA) is a variant of FDMA based on orthogonal frequency-division multiplexing (OFDM). Single-carrier FDMA (SC-FDMA) is another variant of FDMA based on single-carrier frequency domain equalization (SC-FDE). Wavelength-division multiple access (WDMA) is also a variant of FDMA based on wavelength-division multiplexing (WDM). WDM is in fact equivalent to frequency-division multiplexing, but WDM is often used in fiber-optic communications where wavelength is the common term to describe the carrier modulated by optical signals. WDM uses different wavelengths of laser light to carry different signals, and each wavelength is specified as a sub-channel in a single optical fiber. Because the data rate of the optical fibers is much higher than that of twisted pair cables, WDM is normally used to aggregate the data from multiple users. SONET (Synchronous Optical Networking) is an application using WDM.

2.5 ADVANCED TOPICS

Several advanced topics in digital modulation are described in this section. Readers with little electrical engineering background could skip this section at the first-time reading. More tutorials and comprehensive treatments can be found in the texts for data or digital communications. For communications requiring reliable and secure transmission, such as military and wireless applications, the *spread spectrum* techniques are often considered since signals after spreading are noise-like in the frequency spectrum and hard to detect and interfere with. Direct sequence spread spectrum (DSSS) and frequency hopping spread spectrum (FHSS) are two typical schemes. As an advanced multiplexing or multiple access scheme, code division multiple access (CDMA) exercises the concept of spread spectrum for multiple sources to represent data by *orthogonal* or *statistical uncorrelated* codes and spread data over the entire channel.

In comparison with single-carrier modulation, a multicarrier system performs modulations over several separate carrier signals to improve the *bandwidth utilization* and cope with the *multipath fading*. With the implementation of Fast Fourier Transform (FFT), multicarrier modulation such as the orthogonal frequency-division multiplexing (OFDM) has been widely used in many communication systems today. Recently, multiple-input multiple-output (MIMO) systems having multiple transmitting antennas at the transmitter side and multiple receiving antennas at the receiver side become very popular since they offer the great performance gains in terms of throughput and reliability.

Table 2.7 shows a comparison of the existing IEEE 802.11 WLAN standards that use the techniques of spread spectrum, CCK, and OFDM.

2.5.1 Spread Spectrum

The spectrum of a data stream could be spread over a wider frequency band. Spreading could provide extra redundancy to reduce the vulnerability of wireless

TABLE 2.7 The Modulation Techniques Used in IEEE 802.11 WLAN Standards

	802.11a	802.11b	802.11g	802.11n
Bandwidth	580 MHz	83.5 MHz	83.5 MHz	83.5 MHz/ 580 MHz
Operating frequency	5 GHz	2.4 GHz	2.4 GHz	2.4 GHz/5 GHz
Number of non-overlapping channels	24	3	3	3/24
Number of spatial streams	1	1	1	1, 2, 3, or 4
Date rate per channel	6–54 Mbps	1–11 Mbps	1–54 Mbps	1–600 Mbps
Modulation scheme	OFDM	DSSS, CCK	DSSS, CCK, OFDM	DSSS, CCK, OFDM,
Sub-carrier modulation scheme	BPSK, QPSK, 16 QAM, 64 QAM	n/a	BPSK, QPSK, 16 QAM, 64 QAM	BPSK, QPSK, 16 QAM, 64 QAM

communications from eavesdropping, jamming, and noise. Data streams in spread spectrum (SS) are carried by a specific *pseudo-noise* (PN) sequence. This is accomplished when the data stream modulates the PN sequence. A PN sequence is composed of *repetitive* occurrences of a PN code represented by a sequence of *chips*. Combining a PN sequence and an input data stream, a *spreading sequence* of the data stream is formed. A chip itself is a bit. Compared with data bits, chips are just the bit sequence out of the PN code generator. Therefore, a chip is typically a rectangular pulse of +1 or −1 amplitude. The energy of the resulting spread signal is distributed over a *wider* bandwidth than the signal of a data stream. The redundancy, like the redundancy in error correction codes, can enhance data recovery at receivers when signals are impaired.

Pseudo-Noise (PN) Code and Sequence

A PN sequence, also known as a pseudo-random numerical (PRN) sequence, is not a real random sequence, but is generated with a deterministic pattern. The sequence is repetitive where a PN code repeatedly occurs in the sequence. Similar to a bit that is an atomic element in a data stream, a chip is an atomic element in a PN code. Chip rate is the number of chips processed per second. In Figure 2.32, the PN code is an 11-bit Barker code of 11 chips. It repeatedly occurs to form the PN sequence. A spread sequence is generated by modulating the PN sequence with a data stream using the *XOR* operator. The chip rate in Figure 2.32 is 11 times the data rate. The chip rate of the spread sequence is the same as that of the PN sequence, but much higher than that of the data stream. This explains why transmitting a spread sequence demands larger bandwidth than the data stream.

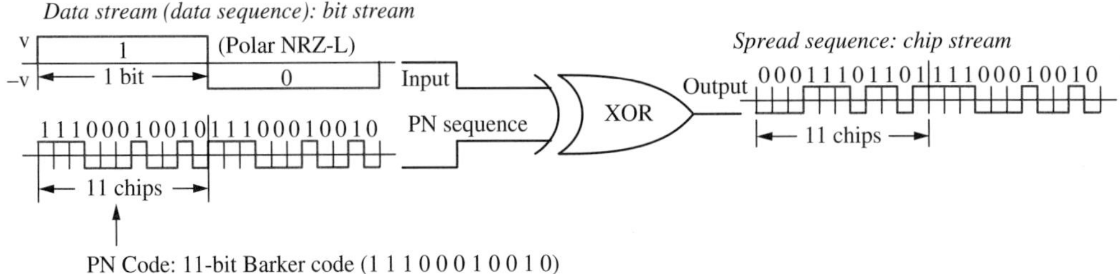

FIGURE 2.32 A data stream spread by a PN sequence.

Figure 2.33 shows the *broadened* bandwidth with spread energy of the transmitted signal from the spread sequence. A measure, *process gain* (PG), for the spreading process is defined by the ratio of chip rate (C) to data rate (R). The chip rate is always higher than the bit rate. Moreover, the rate of PN code determines the bandwidth of the transmitted spread waveform. Process gain is used to measure the performance advantage of spread spectrum against narrowband interference. It can be viewed as the signal-to-*jammer (interference)* power ratio at the receiver after despreading. Assuming the data rate is constant, then the larger the chip rate, the higher the PG. This means the spread spectrum occupies a larger bandwidth. If PG is large enough, the spread waveform can travel over a noisy channel with its power *smaller* than that of noise, while the data stream can still be recovered at the receiver. How do we calculate the process gain? For instance, if an 11-bit Barker code is used as the PN code, the process gain is calculated as $\log_{10} \frac{C}{R} dB = 10 \log_{10} \frac{11}{1} dB = 10.414\ dB$ (chips/bit). Here *dB* stands for decibel. It is a logarithmic unit expressing the magnitude of a physical quantity, such as the chip rate, relative to a specified reference level, such as the data rate.

The PN sequence plays a key role while spreading a data stream; its type and length determine the capability of a spread spectrum system. A good selection of a PN sequence can help a matched filter to efficiently *reject* the multipath signals that are *delayed* by more than one chip time. We will see a similar practice in CDMA later where PN codes are also used at receivers to *despread* the received signals.

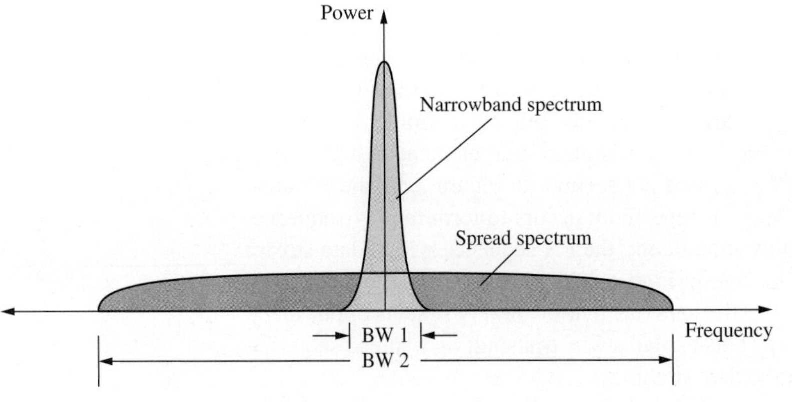

FIGURE 2.33 A comparison between a spread spectrum and a narrowband spectrum.

TABLE 2.8 Barker Codes and Willard Codes

Code Length (N)	Barker Codes	Willard Codes
2	10 or 11	n/a
3	110	110
4	1101 or 1110	1100
5	11101	11010
7	1110010	1110100
11	11100010010	11101101000
13	1111100110101	1111100101000

Barker Codes, Willard Codes, and Complementary Code Keying (CCK)

The IEEE 802.11 standard uses the 11-bit Barker code at a chip rate of 11 chips/data symbol as a PN code. Barker codes have good correlation properties. Willard codes are obtained by computer simulation and optimization, and may provide better performance than Barker codes. A list of Barker codes and Willard codes is shown in Table 2.8. A long PN sequence can be constructed cyclically by Barker codes or Willard codes. The technique of DSSS uses 11-bit and 13-bit Barker codes. The IEEE 802.11b standard uses an 11-bit Barker code cyclically to spread data streams at 1 Mbps or 2 Mbps.

The high-speed extension of the IEEE 802.11 standard employs CCK as the modulation scheme to encode data at 5.5 or 11 Mbps in the 2.4 GHz band. Unlike the Barker code, a CCK sequence can totally eliminate *side lobes*. In the frequency spectrum, a side lobe is any lobe but the desired *major* lobe. Moreover, CCK codewords can effectively reject noise and multipath interference with a special mathematical property, which is skipped here.

A Spread Spectrum System

Figure 2.34 shows a spread spectrum system where spread signals travel through a noisy channel with narrowband/wideband interference and multiple paths. In the

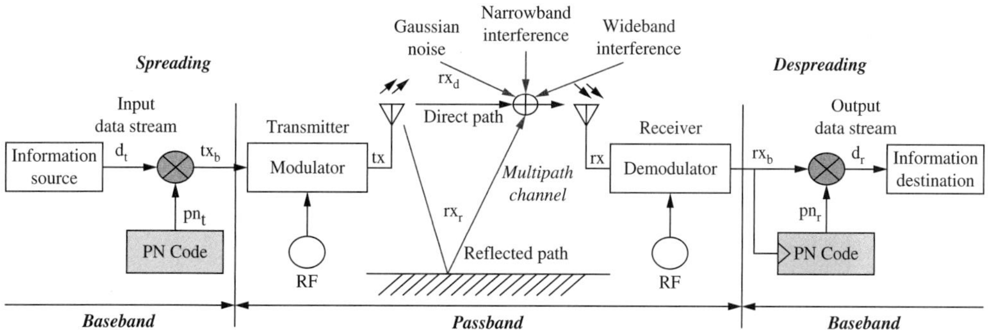

FIGURE 2.34 A spread spectrum system over a noisy channel.

spread spectrum system, an input data stream d_t with a bit rate R_b is spread by the PN sequence pn_t of a chip rate R_c. A spread chip stream tx_b is obtained. The baseband bandwidth R_b of the input data stream is spread to a wider range of R_c. A bandwidth expansion factor *SF* or processing gain G_p is obtained by R_c/R_b. Followed by passband modulations, tx_b becomes *tx* for transmission. At the receiver, a spread spectrum signal *rx* is received by the antenna and then demodulated. The demodulated signal rx_b is then despread by a PN sequence pn_r using *autocorrelation* and *crosscorrelation*. The autocorrelation of two *correlated* sequences, say the PN sequences from the desired data signal and its multipath signal, would be close to 1, while the crosscorrelation of two *uncorrelated* sequences, say the PN sequences from a desired data signal and an interference signal, would be close to 0. An output data stream d_r is obtained after despreading. If the PN code of pn_r is equal to that of pn_t, then the PN sequence pn_r is synchronized to pn_t. Input data stream d_t can be recovered as output data stream d_r because the autocorrelation of pn_t and pn_r is discernible, i.e., close to 1.

On the other hand, an input data stream cannot be recovered at the receiver if the crosscorrelation of pn_t and pn_r is small, unrecognizable, and noise–like, i.e., close to 0. Without the knowledge of the PN code used in the transmitter, the receiver treats the spread spectrum signal as white noise-like signals. Accordingly, the privacy of communication holds between two parties if the PN code is not revealed to third parties.

Like multiplexing, spread spectrum could combine several data sources with different PN sequences for transmissions, but it requires a *larger* bandwidth for transmission. The privacy and anti-jamming is improved. Spread signals are noise-like, which enables the signals to be blended into the background of jamming waveforms and travel over the channel without being detected or eavesdropped. It is particularly designed for wireless communications whose transmission media are exposed to the public and the transmission signals are easily intercepted.

In wireless communications, there are multiple propagation paths from atmospheric reflection or refraction, or reflections from ground, building, or other objects. These multipath signals, say rx_r in Figure 2.34, may fluctuate the received signal from the *direct path,* say rx_d in Figure 2.34. The signal from each path has its own attenuation and time delay. The receiver must *separate* the signal of the direct path from the signals of other paths as well as interferences and noise. If multipath signals are delayed more than a chip time, they become *uncorrelated* to the desired signal with autocorrelation far from 1 and crosscorrelation close to 0. In other words, the PN sequence from the *indirect paths* is no longer synchronized to the PN sequence from the direct path. Therefore this *multipath fading* in a spread spectrum system does not cause a significant impact and can be effectively filtered.

Direct Sequence Spread Spectrum (DSSS)

As seen in Figure 2.34, a spread spectrum system is usually followed by a passband modulator such as BPSK, M-ary PSK (MPSK, M is greater than 2), and QAM. Figure 2.35(a) shows a scenario where a DSSS system is followed by an M-ary PSK modulator. Because the MPSK modulator has in-phase and quadrature components, the system requires *two* spreading processes. The input data are *split* into two data

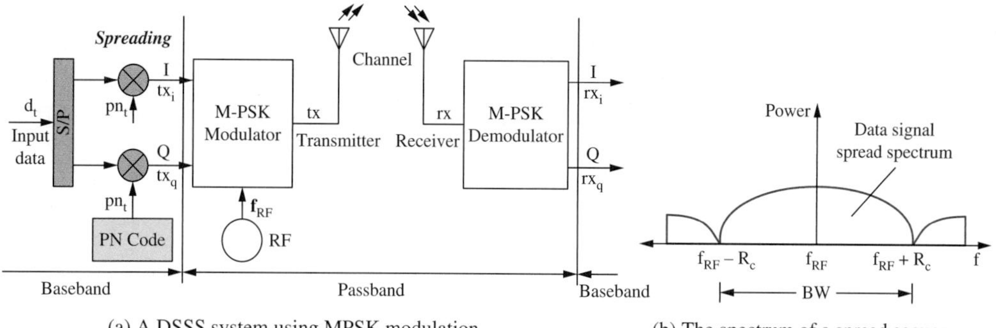

(a) A DSSS system using MPSK modulation.

(b) The spectrum of a spread sequence.

FIGURE 2.35 A DSSS and the spectrum of a spread sequence.

substreams, each spread by a PN sequence; one is for the in-phase component, the other for the quadrature component. DSSS substitutes each bit of a data stream with a PN code or its complement. The spectrum of the transmitted signal is determined by the chip rate R_c in Figure 2.35(b), of the spread stream, rather than the bit rate R_b of the data stream.

Impact of Interference and Noise on DSSS

Suppose a DSSS system is influenced by interference signal i. At a receiver, a received signal is a composite signal including interference signals and noise. The composite signal is despread by a PN sequence to recover the data stream from the transmitter. How the spread spectrum technique can mitigate the impact of interference and noise is explained here.

- If i is a narrowband interference, which means i is a signal from another data stream. After despreading, the resulting sequence from the narrowband interference becomes a spread sequence with a *flattened* spectrum and much lower power density than the spectrum of the desired data stream. It can be filtered out using a low-pass filter. Therefore, spread spectrum can rule out the narrowband interference, but conventional narrowband techniques cannot.
- If i is a wideband interference as a spread sequence from another user but using a different PN sequence. After despreading, the resulting sequence from the wideband interference is flattened again because the wideband interference uses a different PN sequence, and then the dot product of this crosscorrelation is significantly small and noise-like, compared to the wideband signal using the same PN code. The flattened interference can be easily filtered out by a low-pass filter. This demonstrates that spread spectrum can remove wideband interference.
- If i is a noise, the resulting sequence from the noise is still a noise-like spread sequence at the chip rate and has a low power density. The spectrum of a flattened Gaussian noise can also be filtered out by a low-pass filter. The signals of the spread spectrum system are more immune to noise, which is significant when signals travel over a noisy channel.

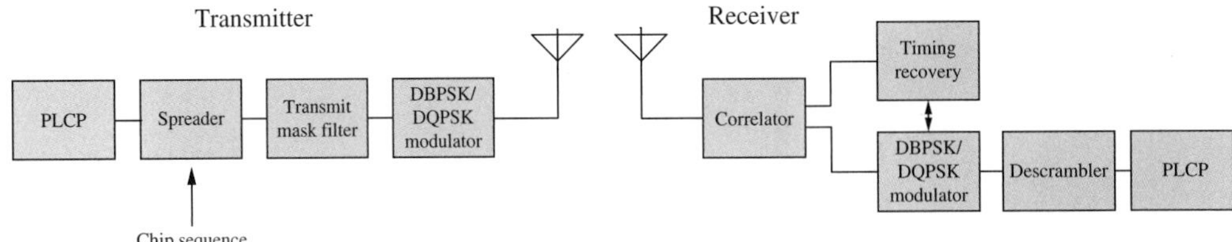

FIGURE 2.36 DSSS transceiver.

IEEE 802.11 is commonly allowed to use 11 channels from 2.412 to 2.462 GHz, each 5 MHz wide. Channel 1 is centered at 2.412 GHz. IEEE 802.11 applies the DSSS modulation at 1 and 2 Mbps, while IEEE 802.11b uses the CCK modulation at 5.5 and 11 Mbps. IEEE 802.11g supports the extended rate PHY (ERP). The ERP-DSSS, ERP-CCK, and ERP-OFDM modulations are used for backward compatibility. The physical layer of DSSS in WLAN includes two sublayers: PLCP (Physical Layer Convergence Procedure) and PMD (Physical Medium Dependent) sublayers. The PLCP is mainly for framing. The PMD sublayer is shown in Figure 2.36, where the spreader is located in this sublayer.

Frequency Hopping Spread Spectrum (FHSS)

FHSS divides a bandwidth into N sub-channels such that a transmitted signal *hops* among these sub-channels. The transmitted signal dwells in each sub-channel for a period of time, called *dwell time*. In Figure 2.37(a), a PN code generator produces a PN sequence pn_t mapped into *frequency words,* which represent a frequency hopping sequence in a table. These frequency words are fed into a frequency synthesizer in turn to generate N carriers with different frequencies, as shown in Figure 2.37(b). The transmitter hops among these N carriers in order. In Figure 2.37, the FHSS system combines the M-FSK modulator and FH modulator for modulation and frequency hopping, respectively. The transmitter and the receiver of FHSS use the same hop pattern. During each hop, the bandwidth of the transmitted signal is the same as that of the output signal of M-FSK. The signal dwelling in an FHSS sub-channel is a narrowband signal.

FHSS uses a pool of carriers of different frequencies for source signals. One carrier is used at a time, thus the messages can be transmitted by different carriers. If there are n carriers in this pool, the required bandwidth is n times the bandwidth used by a single carrier, plus several guard bands. Unlike DSSS, which spreads source codes by the PN sequence, FHSS *selects* a frequency from a mapping table derived from the PN code. The required bandwidth can be shared by multiple users only if different frequencies are used at each hop. The concept of sharing bandwidth among different frequencies is analogous to the technique of frequency-division multiplexing (FDM). A PN code generator repeatedly produces bit patterns for a frequency synthesizer. These patterns can be used to select carriers to carry the input message within a hopping period. It is possible that more than one user can pick the same sub-channel to transmit, which results in *jamming*. When a symbol is repeatedly transmitted in several hops, the receiver still can recover the symbol if it is not jammed in the majority of hops.

FIGURE 2.37 An FHSS system and the spectrum of sub-channels.

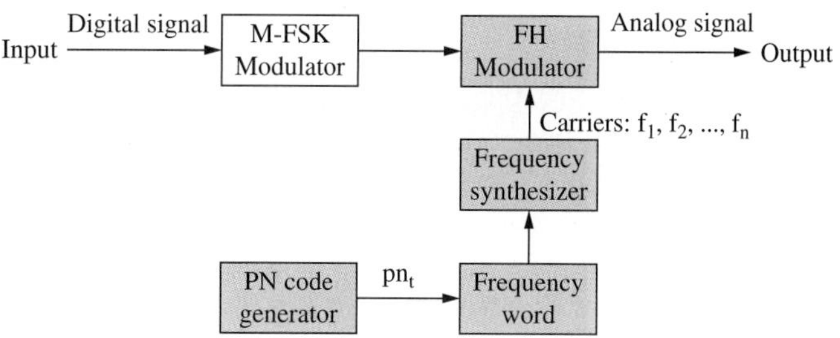

(a) FHSS with a PN code generator to select carrier hopping frequencies.

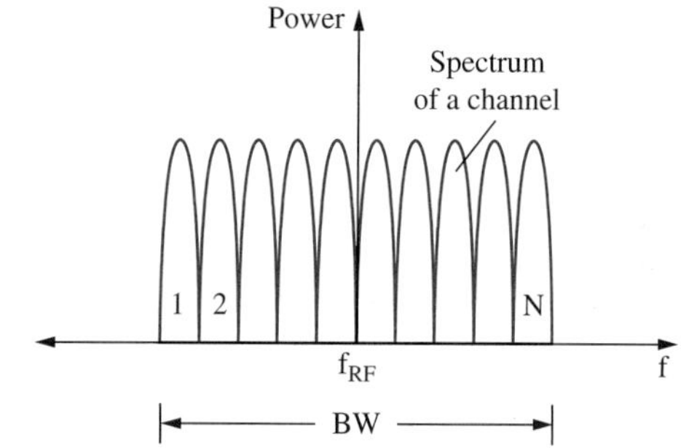

(b) The spectrum of an FHSS channel consisting of N sub-channels.

If the hopping period is short, it is difficult for an eavesdropper who hops to intercept the signals without the knowledge of the PN code. It is also difficult for an intruder without knowledge about the PN code to jam the traffic by hopping different frequencies in the sequence as a user does. FHSS is used in Bluetooth and the original IEEE 802.11. However, when it comes to *fast hopping* under high-speed transmission in short intervals, *synchronization* between the transmitter and the receiver becomes difficult. Therefore, it is not used in IEEE 802.11 a/b/g/n.

Code Division Multiple Access (CDMA)

Code division multiplexing (CDM) allows signals from several independent sources to travel over a channel at the same time and on the same frequency band simultaneously. CDM is a spread spectrum technique, and it is used by the multiple access technology of code division multiple access (CDMA). Thus CDMA is a spread spectrum multiple access (SSMA) technique. Unlike TDMA and FDMA, CDMA does not divide a physical channel into multiple sub-channels in time or frequency. Each user in a CDMA system occupies the *entire* bandwidth of a physical channel at the same time while using an individual orthogonal code or a PN code. Indeed, CDMA multiplexes different users by a set of orthogonal codes or PN codes. Several variants of CDMA have their own multiplexing methods, such as direct sequence CDMA (DS-CDMA), based on DSSS, and frequency hopping CDMA (FH-CDMA), based on FHSS.

CDMA can also be categorized as *synchronous CDMA* and *asynchronous CDMA*. Synchronous CDMA uses orthogonal codes, while asynchronous CDMA uses PN codes. Orthogonal codes are *vectors* with strictly zero pair-wise *inner-product,* while the PN codes are statistical and have pair-wise autocorrelation close to 1 if closely correlated and pair-wise crosscorrelation close to 0 if uncorrelated. Both of them use the gain of spread spectrum for receivers to identify the desired signal against other unwanted signals. If a desired user's signal is not correlated with other users' signals, the inner-product is zero in synchronous CDMA and the crosscorrelation in asynchronous CDMA approaches zero. Similar to the resolution to multipath interference in the generic spread spectrum, a desired signal would have zero inner-product or low autocorrelation with a signal modulated with the *same* orthogonal code or PN code if *shifted* more than a chip time. Again, this property helps to remove multipath interference.

Synchronous CDMA

In synchronous CDMA, orthogonal codes are mapped to a set of vectors mutually orthogonal with zero inner-product. Orthogonal codes are assigned to users for spreading the user data spectrum. The codes can be obtained from the orthogonal variable spreading factor (OVSF) code tree as shown in Figure 2.38. These codes are pair-wise orthogonal.

The OVSF code tree is based on Hadamard matrix, a square matrix that has +1 or −1 entries, and whose rows are mutually orthogonal. Each code, or *chip code,* is assigned to an individual user to denote a bit of a data stream. For example, if an orthogonal code is (1, −1, 1, −1), the code vector can be represented as $\boldsymbol{v}$ = 1, −1, 1, −1. If $\boldsymbol{v}$ denotes bit 0 and $-\boldsymbol{v}$ denotes bit 1, a data stream of "10110" can be represented as ($-\boldsymbol{v}$, $\boldsymbol{v}$, $-\boldsymbol{v}$, $-\boldsymbol{v}$, $\boldsymbol{v}$). The data stream is spread as (−(1, −1, 1, −1), (1, −1, 1, −1), −(1, −1, 1, −1), −(1, −1, 1, −1), (1, −1, 1, −1)), and finally becomes (−1, 1, −1, 1, −1, 1, −1, 1, −1, 1, −1, 1, −1, 1, −1, 1, 1, −1, 1, −1). The process is implemented by the *XOR* operator, as illustrated in Figure 2.39. A data signal has a pulse duration T_b, while an orthogonal code signal has T_c. In other words, the bandwidth of the data signal is $1/T_b$, and the bandwidth of the orthogonal code is $1/T_c$. A spreading factor, or processing gain, is a bandwidth ratio of orthogonal signal to data signal, T_b/T_c, which limits the upper bound of the total number of users.

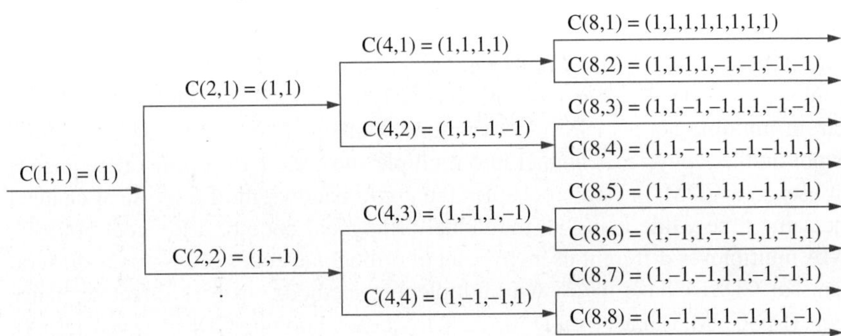

FIGURE 2.38 The OVSF code tree for synchronous CDMA.

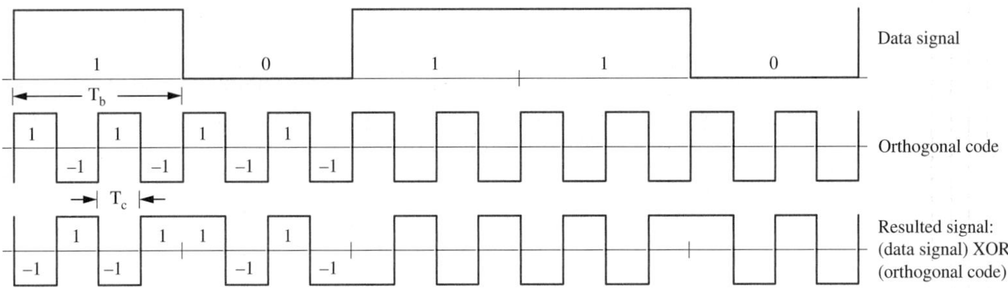

FIGURE 2.39 Spreading a data signal using one orthogonal code for one sub-channel.

Asynchronous CDMA

Asynchronous CDMA exploits PN codes. As in the generic spread spectrum, a PN code is a binary sequence with randomness that is reproduced with a deterministic behavior at a receiver. PN codes are used in asynchronous CDMA for spreading and despreading users' signals as the orthogonal codes in synchronous CDMA. They are *statistically* nearly uncorrelated. Unlike the synchronous CDMA, the signals of other users do appear as noise to and slightly interfere with the desired signal. That is, signals with different PN codes become a wideband noise to the desired signal with a specific PN code. Even though a signal received has the same specified PN code as the intended signal, it also appears as a noise to the desired signal if it is received within a time offset.

While synchronous CDMA, TDMA, and FDMA can utterly reject other signals due to code orthogonality, time slots, and frequency channels, respectively, asynchronous CDMA can only partially reject unwanted signals. If the unwanted signals are much stronger than the desired signal, the desired signal will be severely affected. Thus a power control scheme is required to manage the transmitted power at each station. Despite this disadvantage, asynchronous CDMA has the following advantages.

1. Asynchronous CDMA use the spectrum more efficiently than TDMA and FDMA. Each time slot in TDMA requires a *guard time* to synchronize the transmission time of all users. Each channel in FDMA demands a *guard band* to prevent interference from adjacent channels. Both guard time and guard band waste the usage of spectrum.
2. Asynchronous CDMA can allocate PN-code to active users *flexibly* without a strict limit on the number of users, while synchronous CDMA, TDMA, and FDMA can only allocate their resources to a *fixed* number of simultaneous users, depending on the fixed number of orthogonal codes, time slots, and frequency bands. This is due to the low-, but nonzero-crosscorrelation nature of the PN codes and the operations of autocorrelation and crosscorrelation. In the high-traffic bursts of telephony and data communications, asynchronous CDMA is more efficient in allocating PN codes to *more* users. However, the number of users in asynchronous CDMA is still limited by the bit error rate because the signal-to-interference ratio (SIR) varies inversely with the number of the users.

3. As with synchronous CDMA using orthogonal codes, asynchronous CDMA provides a significant level of privacy based on the anti-jamming capabilities of the PN sequences. The use of pseudo-random codes endows a spread spectrum signal with noise-like properties. Without the knowledge of a specified PN sequence, the receiver of asynchronous CDMA cannot decode the message.

Advantages of CDMA

Here we summarize the advantages of CDMA using spread spectrum. The technology of CDMA can effectively reduce multipath fading and narrowband interference because the CDMA signal is a spread spectrum signal that occupies a wide range of bandwidth. Only a small portion of the signal is affected by narrowband interference and multipath fading. The interfered-with portion could be *removed* by filtering, while the lost data could be *recovered* by the use of error correction techniques. Multipath interference can also be *rejected* by CDMA because the delayed signals from multipath become nearly uncorrelated with the desired signal, even though both of them have the same PN code.

CDMA can *reuse* the same frequency because channels are separated by various orthogonal codes or PN codes, while FDMA and TDMA cannot. The ability to reuse frequencies among adjacent cells in a cellular system enables CDMA to use the technique of *soft handoff*. Soft handoff is a feature whereby a cellular phone can connect with several cells simultaneously during a call. The cellular phone maintains a list of power measurement of adjacent cells to decide whether to request a soft handover. Soft handoff allows a mobile station to hold a better signal strength and quality.

2.5.2 Single-Carrier vs. Multiple-Carrier

Multiple-carrier modulation (MCM) *splits* a data stream into multiple data substreams; each modulates a corresponding carrier for a narrowband sub-channel. The modulated signals could be further multiplexed by frequency-division multiplexing (FDM). This is called *multicarrier* transmission. A composite signal produced by MCM is a broadband signal that is more immune to multipath fading and intersymbol interference. If sub-channels are multiplexed by code division multiplexing (CDM) instead, we call it *multi-code* transmission. Only orthogonal frequency division multiplexing (OFDM) for multiple carriers is discussed here.

Orthogonal Frequency-Division Multiplexing (OFDM)

The main feature of OFDM is the orthogonality of sub-carriers that allows data to simultaneously travel over sub-channels constituted by these orthogonal sub-carriers in a *tight* frequency space without interference from each other. OFDM combines the techniques of multiplexing, modulation, and multiple carriers to build a communications system. OFDM is simply implemented by an inversed fast Fourier transform paired with a fast Fourier transform (IFFT/FFT). Unlike conventional FDM where each data stream occupies only a sub-channel with a specific carrier, OFDM splits a data stream to use multiple sub-channels at the same time. The benefit of using

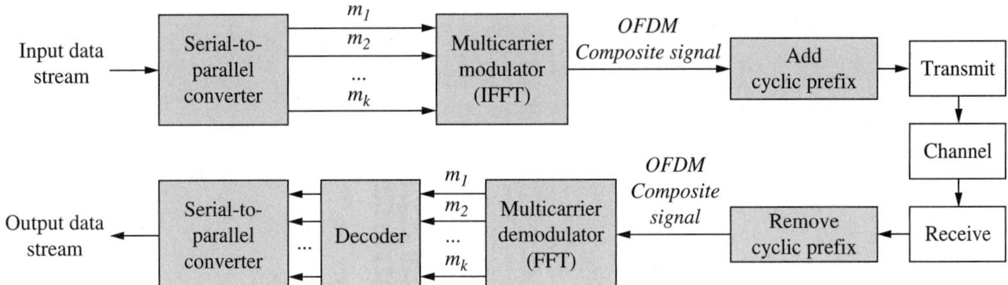

FIGURE 2.40 A multicarrier OFDM system.

multiple carriers is if one sub-channel fails, the data stream still can be recovered at the receiver because only a portion of data is impaired by, for example, a burst error.

A block diagram of an OFDM system is shown in Figure 2.40. IFFT performs the function of multicarrier modulator to produce OFDM composite signals. A cyclic prefix is added to the OFDM signal as a guard interval to avoid inter-symbol interference (ISI), and removed at the receiver. A symbol is a state of the channel that persists for a fixed period of time. It can be encoded by one or several bits. Therefore, a sequence of symbols or the transitions between symbols can represent data. The demodulator at the receiver is implemented by FFT.

An OFDM System with IFFT and FFT

The multicarrier modulator is commonly implemented by an IFFT process, as depicted in Figure 2.41. To generate an OFDM signal, IFFT combines signals from orthogonal carriers modulated by individual data substreams. IFFT has a counterpart FFT. Either a time-domain signal or a frequency-domain signal can be processed by FFT or IFFT. If a signal is processed by a pair of IFFT and FFT, the output is the same as the original one. This is how the mechanism of OFDM is implemented by a pair of IFFT and FFT. In Figure 2.41, IFFT converts frequency-domain signals to a time-domain signal, while FFT does the reverse. Here the time-domain input bits of IFFT are considered frequency amplitudes in the frequency domain; the output composite signal of IFFT is a time-domain-like signal. IFFT and FFT are mathematical concepts; both are linear processes and completely reversible.

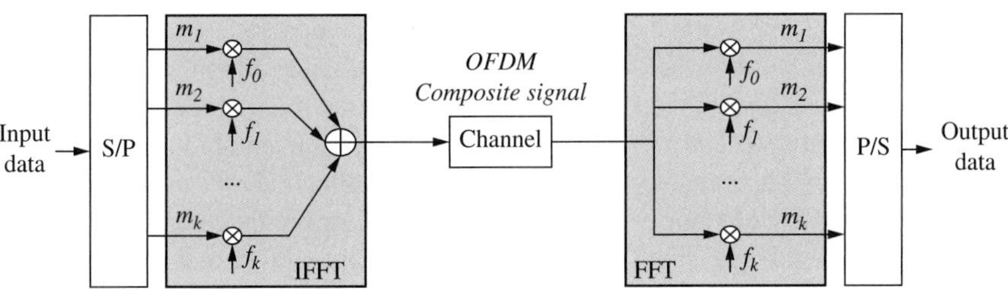

FIGURE 2.41 A functional diagram of IFFT and FFT.

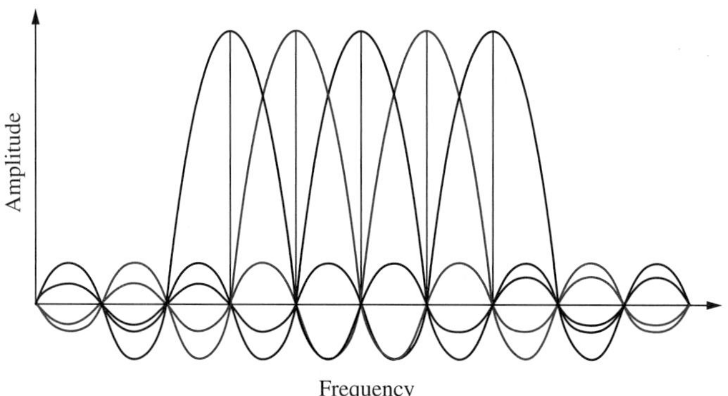

FIGURE 2.42 The orthogonality diagram of OFDM.

Orthogonality

The orthogonality of signals in the frequency domain is shown in Figure 2.42. Two signals that *cross over* at the point of *zero amplitude* are orthogonal to each other. Each frequency is assigned a sub-carrier or sub-channel and can be applied with a typical modulation scheme such as QAM or QPSK.

Using a cyclic prefix as a guard interval between symbols simplifies the direct convolution of the transmitted signals and the multipath channel response to a circular convolution, which is equivalent to a direct multiplication after taking the FFT operation, and thereby eliminates the ISI. However, OFDM requires accurate frequency synchronization between transmitter and receiver because any shift of frequencies destroys the orthogonality of the sub-carriers and causes inter-carrier interference (ICI) or crosstalk between sub-carriers.

Multipath Fading

In wireless communications, multipath propagation is a phenomenon that a transmitted signal reaches the receiver antenna through different paths at different times. Because reflectors surround a transmitter and a receiver, the transmitted signal is reflected and reaches the receiver from multiple paths. Multipath signals may cause different levels of constructive or destructive interference, phase shift, delay, and attenuation. Strong destructive interference refers to a deep fade that makes the signal-to-noise ratio drop suddenly and causes the communication between the two parties to fail. The multipath signals can be regarded as a direct convolution of the transmitted signals and the multipath channel response. Though such an effect can be removed or mitigated by channel equalization at the receiver, by modulating the signal at the frequency domain, and by the use of a cyclic prefix, the direct convolution is simplified to a circular convolution, and in turn it becomes a direct multiplication in the frequency domain, after taking the FFT operation at the receiver. Hence, OFDM removes completely the need of complicated equalization at the receiving end and simplifies the receiver design. In case a deep fade to specific sub-carriers occurs, the received signal can still be recovered by coding skills with error correction code.

Applications of OFDM

The applications of OFDM are ADSL and VDSL broadband access, Power Line Communication (PLC), DVB-C2, wireless LANs in IEEE 802.11a/g/n, the digital audio systems such as DAB and DAB+, the terrestrial digital TV system, and WiMAX in IEEE 802.16e. OFDM was designed for a bit stream to be transmitted over a communication channel with a sequence of OFDM symbols, but it can also be used with multiple access by time, frequency, or code. Orthogonal frequency-division multiple access (OFDMA) assigns different sub-channels to different users to achieve FDMA.

2.5.3 Multiple Inputs, Multiple Outputs (MIMO)

A multiple input and multiple output (MIMO) system basically consists of antenna *arrays* and *adaptive* signal processing units at senders and receivers. The system exploits several *diversity* schemes for data communications. The diversity schemes, such as time diversity, frequency diversity, spatial diversity, and multiuser diversity, endow the signals with an ability to combat against fading. Time diversity demands a signal be transferred at different time instants, while frequency diversity requires a signal be conveyed by multiple frequency channels. The spatial diversity allows a signal to be sent from multiple transmit antennas and/or be received by multiple receive antennas. Multiuser diversity is implemented by opportunistic user scheduling that selects the best users based on the channel information. MIMO takes advantage of these diversity schemes to enhance system reliability.

MIMO is applied to both wired and wireless systems. For example, gigabit DSL (digital subscriber line) is a wired application. Here we focus on the MIMO wireless transmission systems using antenna arrays. The antenna arrays provide *spatial diversity* by using multiple transmit and receive antennas to improve the quality and reliability, such as bit error rate (BER), of a wireless link. The link with antenna arrays offers multiple propagation paths for signals to pass through. Multipath signals with different propagation delays and fades to the receiver then create *space-divided* channels. MIMO turns the disadvantage of multipath propagation in conventional wireless systems into an advantage, especially to those systems without line-of-sight transmission. The user's data rate is also increased when MIMO exploits multipath propagation.

In spatial division multiplexing (SDM), also known as *spatial multiplexing* (SM), multiple bit streams are transmitted via different antennas in parallel. Space division multiple access (SDMA) is a channel access method that can create spatial pipes in parallel via spatial multiplexing and diversity. SDMA uses the *smart* antenna technology, which evolved from MIMO, and the knowledge of the spatial location of mobile stations to perform the radiation pattern at the base station where the transmission and reception are adaptive to each user to obtain the highest gain. On the contrary, in the conventional cellular systems, the base station has no knowledge of the locations of mobile stations, so the signals are sent in all directions. This could waste the transmission power and cause interference with the adjacent cells using the same frequency.

Categories of MIMO Systems

MIMO can be categorized based on the usage of *channel knowledge* or the *number of users*. Based on the awareness of channel knowledge, the types of MIMO can be classified into three groups: *precoding, spatial multiplexing* (SM), and *diversity coding*. The method of precoding requires the channel state information (CSI), yet the method of diversity coding does not. Spatial multiplexing can either use or not use the channel knowledge.

The channel-aware precoding exploits feedback information about channel states to arrange the beamforming or spatial processing at a transmitter. Beamforming is a signal processing technique, or a spatial filter, that combines a set of radio signals from a group of small *nondirectional* antennas to simulate a larger *directional* antenna. This simulated directional antenna is steered to determine the direction of a transmitted signal. This precoding method can increase the signal gain and reduce the multipath fading. The SM technique requires the knowledge of the configuration of antennas for a high-rate signal stream to be split into several lower-rate substreams transmitted at different antennas using the same frequency channel. The method of diversity coding demands no channel knowledge. A signal is coded at a transmitter by space-time coding to exploit independent fadings in the multi-antenna links. There is no beamforming or array gain for a MIMO system using the diversity coding technique.

If a MIMO system is classified based on the number of users, the types of MIMO are single-user MIMO (SU-MIMO) and multi-user MIMO (MU-MIMO). SU-MIMO is a point-to-point communication where link throughput and reliability are major concerns, with the space-time codes and stream-multiplexed transmission. Multiple antennas expand the degrees of freedom for signal processing and detection. Thus, SU-MIMO boosts the performance of the physical layer.

However, the MU-MIMO system emphasizes system throughput. MIMO applies to both the physical layer and the link layer. In link layers, multi-access protocols in the spatial dimension greatly increase the performance benefits of antenna arrays in MIMO, such as a greater per-user rate or channel reliability. MIMO demands multi-user information to design user scheduling to increase the system throughput. Therefore MU-MIMO combines coding and modulation in the physical layer with resource allocation and user scheduling in the link layer. An optimal user scheduling depends on the selection of precoding and channel state feedback technique. This leads to a *cross-layer* design issue for wireless communications using MU-MIMO.

A MU-MIMO System

We now briefly describe the architecture of a MU-MIMO system using the precoding technique, as shown in Figure 2.43 with the wireless broadcast channels built with antenna arrays. In this figure, a base station (BS) with multiple transmit antennas sends messages to mobile stations (MSs). Each mobile station, equipped with an antenna array of M_r antennas, has a reception entity to process multiple substreams in parallel. The reception entity first employs minimum mean-squared-error filtering (MMSE) and successive interference cancellation (SIC) to each substream. The module MMSE-SIC has two aspects—interference nulling and interference

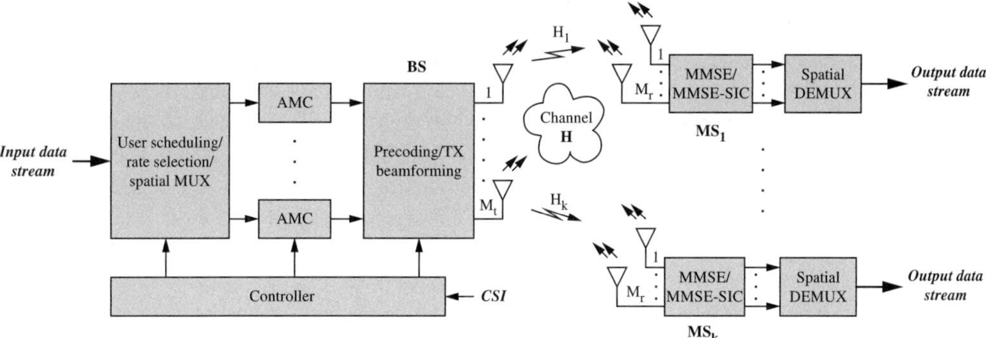

FIGURE 2.43 A multiuser MIMO system.

canceling, either removing or subtracting the interference from those already detected substreams. Then those substreams are merged by spatial demultiplexing. Finally, we obtain the output data stream at the receiver.

Because this architecture is a MU-MIMO system that requires channel information for multiuser scheduling, the BS uses a controller to collect channel state information feedback from receivers. This information includes channel direction information (CDI) and channel quality information (CQI). CDI determines the direction of *beamforming,* and CQI adjusts the transmitted power for each beam. The controller uses the information at the base station to perform space-time processing such as multiuser scheduling, power and modulation adaptation such as AMC (adaptive coding and modulation, or *link adaptation*), and beamforming. The controller controls AMC to select the type of coding, modulation, and the protocol parameters. The selections of AMC are based on the radio link condition such as path loss, interference, and sensitivity of the receiver to increase the efficiency of use of antennas for higher throughput. In brief, the base station combines the information of CSI feedback signaling for beamforming to obtain an optimal transmit pattern while transmitting messages. The functions of AMC and precoding aim to maximize the link throughput and minimize the error rate.

A MU-MIMO system exploits user diversity for user scheduling. An effective user scheduling provides several advantages in space and time domains, such as spatial beamforming, uplink feedback signaling, and advanced receivers. It can be combined with the modified SIC reception; for instance, all transmit antennas can be allocated to the best users based on SIC or minimum mean squared error (MMSE).

In conclusion, a MIMO system sends out multiple data streams in parallel via multiple antennas to improve reliability and spectral efficiency, while the space-time block coding (STBC) may help achieve full transmit diversity. Beamforming can improve link reliability by rejecting interference and combining beams linearly. Transmit and receive diversity can reduce the fluctuation of fading to obtain the diversity gain. Spatial multiplexing uses the multiplexing gain by sending out different data signals at various transmit antennas at the same time.

Applications of MIMO

EDGE (Enhanced Data rates for GSM Evolution) and HSDPA (high-speed downlink packet access) are MIMO systems that use a rate adaptation algorithm to manage the coding and modulation scheme according to the quality of the radio channel. The standard of 3GPP WCDMA/HSDPA uses MU-MIMO with user scheduling. IEEE 802.11n-2009 improves network throughput to a maximum of 600 Mbps by adding multiple-input multiple-output (MIMO) with four spatial streams at each of the 40 MHz channels. Furthermore, IEEE 802.11n exercises frame aggregation at the link layer.

Open Source Implementation 2.2: IEEE 802.11a Transmitter with OFDM

Overview

802.11a is an IEEE standard for wireless communication. The standard employs the OFDM modulation scheme, which is widely used in many other wireless communication systems, including WiMAX and LTE. An open source example is available from the OpenCores website at http://opencores.org, which presents an implementation of 802.11a transmitter in the language of Bluespec System Verilog (BSV). We first give an overview of the modules and the processing flow in this OFDM transmitter, and then look at the operations of the convolutional encoder.

Block Diagram

Figure 2.44 illustrates the architecture of the OpenCores 802.11a transmitter, which mainly consists of controller, scrambler, convolutional encoder, interleaver, mapper, inverse fast Fourier transform (IFFT), and cyclic extender. They are described as follows:

- Controller: The controller receives packets from the MAC layer as a stream of data (PHY payload) and creates header fields for each data packet.

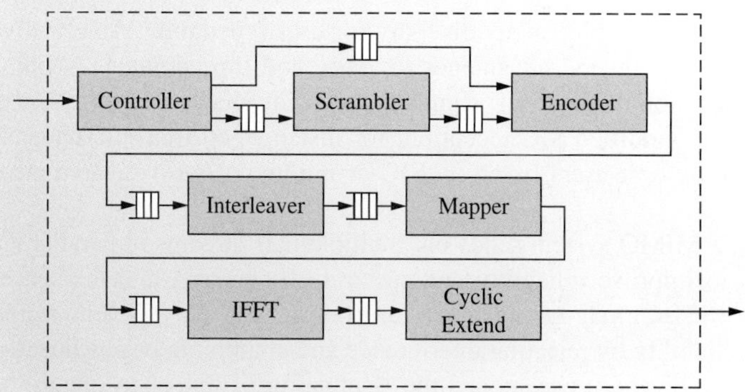

FIGURE 2.44 Block diagram of 802.11a transmitter.

- Scrambler: The scrambler XORs each data packet with a pseudorandom pattern of bits.
- Convolutional Encoder: The convolutional encoder generates two bits of output for every input bit it receives.
- Interleaver: The interleaver reorders the bits in a single packet. It operates on the OFDM symbols in block sizes of 48, 96, or 192 bits, depending on which rate is being used.
- Mapper: The mapper also operates at the OFDM symbol level. It translates the interleaved data into the 64 complex numbers that are the modulation values for different frequency "tones."
- IFFT: The IFFT maps the complex modulation values to each sub-carrier and performs a 64-point inverse fast Fourier transform to translate them into the time domain.
- Cyclic Extender: The cyclic extender extends the IFFT-ed symbol by appending the beginning and end of the message to the full message body.

The design of the OpenCores 802.11a transmitter only implements the lowest three data rates ({6, 12, 24} Mb/s) of the 802.11a specification. At these rates the puncturer does no operation on the data, so we omit it from our discussion.

Data Structures and Algorithm Implementations

The top module, called Transmitter.bsv, handles the transmission flow. The flow starts with Controller.bsv, which first creates a packet header (the signal field with length 24 bits in the PHY packet format) and then gets the data stream (data field in PHY packet format) from the MAC layer. Therefore, the controller has two FIFO outputs; one is the *toC* consisting of one 24-bit element (control element), and another is *toS*, which includes several 24-bit elements, depending on MAC layer data length (data elements). The data elements of *toS* then input to Scrambler.bsv and are XORed with a pseudorandom pattern of bits. Meanwhile, the control element of *toC* is passed to Convolutional.bsv and encoded at the 1/2 coding rate.

At the next cycle, the scramble data elements start to encode, still at the 1/2 coding rate since the supporting data rates are only 6, 12, and 24 Mb/s. Convolutional.bsv encodes the 24-bit input element to a FIFO element of 48 coded bits (1/2 coding rate). Interleaver.bsv gets coded bits from the FIFO queue and operates on the OFDM symbols, in block sizes of 48, 96, or 192 bits, depending on which rate is being used. It reorders the bits in a single packet.

Assuming each block only operates on one packet at a time, this means that at the fastest rate we can expect to output only once every four cycles, where a block size of 192 bits needs four input-encoded bit streams. Mapper.bsv translates the interleaved bits (48 bits) directly into the 64 complex data (frequency "tones"). IFFT.bsv performs a 64-point inverse fast Fourier transform, which translates the complex frequency data into the time-domain data (IFFT-ed symbol with 64 complex data). The OpenCores 802.11a transmitter provides

Continued

several implementations of IFFT and proposes a combinational design based on a four-point butterfly. Finally, CyclicExtender.bsv creates a full transmission message with the structure of the last 16 complex data of the input IFFT-ed symbol following the IFFT-ed symbol.

```
Bit#(n6) history; // Bit#(n6) means bit vector with
length (n+6)
if(input_rate == RNone) // for new entry of the same
packet at next cycle
     history = {input_data, histVal};
else
     history = {input_data, 6'b0}; // for an new packet

Bit#(nn) rev_output_data = 0;
Bit#(1) shared = 0;
Bit#(6) newHistVal = histVal;

for(Integer i = 0; i < valueOf(n); i = i + 1)
begin // encoding
      shared = input_data[i]^history[i + 4]^history[i +
      3]^history[i + 0];
      rev_output_data[(2*i)+0] = shared^history[i +
      1];//output data A
      rev_output_data[(2*i)+1] = shared^history[i +
      5];//output data B
         // save the delay register status for next new
         entry
         // only last update will be saved
      newHistVal = {input_data[i], newHistVal[5:1]};
end
      // enqueue encoded bit stream
RateData#(nn) retval = RateData{
      rate: input_rate,
      data: reverseBits(rev_output_data)};

outputQ.enq(retval);

// setup for next cycle
histVal <= newHistVal;
```

FIGURE 2.45 A segment of codes in Convolutional.bsv.

To avoid the verbosity, we just explain a segment of BSV codes in Figure 2.45 that programs the key of the convolutional encoder in detail.

Figure 2.46 shows a circuit of the convolutional encoder, which can be described concisely as one bit per cycle with a shift register and a few OR gates. *History* represents a bit stream consisting of input bits and the bits of all delay registers (T_b) in the shift register. For each *for* loop iteration, two output encoded bits are generated from the OR operations of the current input bit and the delay register bits. The encoded bits are saved as a bit stream stored in *rev_output_data*. The values of each delay register *newHistVal* will be saved for the next 24-bit input bit stream of the same packet. For a new packet, the value of each delay register is reset to zero.

Exercises

Calculate the output bits and states when one encodes these bits using the convolutional encoder in Figure 2.46. Summarize in Table 2.9 how the state and output values change with each iteration.

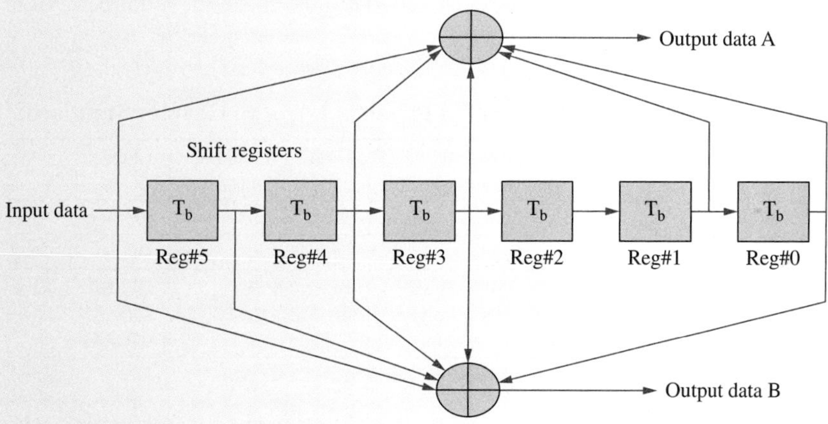

FIGURE 2.46 The circuit of the convolutional encoder defined in 802.11a.

TABLE 2.9 The Output Bits and States of the Convolutional Encoder

Iteration	1	2	3	4	5	6	7	8	9	10
Input bit	0	1	1	0	1	1	0	0	0	0
Shift Regs[543210]	**000000**									
Output[A,B]										

Historical Evolution: Cellular Standards

Cellular standards have evolved from 1G, 2G, and 3G to 4G. The properties of their physical layers are shown in Table 2.10. In 1G, data signals are delivered in analog; for instance, the standard of AMPS or TACS. In 2G the transmission of data signals becomes digital; the GSM standard is the prevailing one. The 3G standards provide high-speed IP data networks for multimedia and *spread spectrum* transmission, including CDMA2000 and LTE (long-term evolution). Now, the 4G standards must support the features of all-IP switched networks, mobile ultra-broadband access, multicarrier transmission (OFDM), and MIMO, or called antenna array or smart antenna. The standards of LTE-advanced and WiMAX-m (IEEE802.16m) are two of the proposals for 4G. Moreover, some people believe that the converged solution supporting multiple protocols can also be considered 4G. Therefore software radio and cognitive radio are taken into account as 4G technologies. The *OFDM* technology, rather than *CDMA*, is adopted in 4G because of its simplicity in modulation and multiplexing; it can fulfill the speed requirement of gigabit, specified in the 4G standard. Turbo codes are used in 4G to minimize the required SNR at the reception side.

TABLE 2.10 Properties of the Physical Layer of Cellular Standards

Cellular standards	AMPS	GSM 850/900/ 1800/1900	UMTS (WCDMA, 3GPP FDD/TDD)	LTE
Generation	1G	2G	3G	Pre-4G
Radio signal	Analog	Digital	Digital	Digital
Modulation	FSK	GMSK/8PSK (EDGE only)	BPSK/QPSK/ 8PSK/16QAM	QPSK/ 16QAM/ 64QAM
Multiple access	FDMA	TDMA/FDMA	CDMA/TDMA	DL: OFDMAUL: SC-FDMA
Duplex (uplink/ downlink)	n/a	FDD	FDD/TDD	FDD+TDD (FDD focus)
Channel bandwidth	30 kHz	200 kHz	5 MHz	1.25/2.5/5/ 10/15/20 MHz
Number of channels	333/666/832 channels	124/124/374/ 299 (8 users per channel)	Depends on services	>200 users per cell (for 5 MHz spectrum)
Peak data rate	Signaling rate = 10 kbps	14.4 kbps 53.6 kbps (GPRS) 384 kbps (EDGE)	144 kbps (mobile)/ 384 kbps (pedestrian)/ 2 Mbps (indoors)/ 10 Mbps (HSDPA)	DL:100 MbpsUL: 50 Mbps (for 20 MHz spectrum)

Historical Evolution: LTE-Advanced vs. IEEE 802.16m

The LTE standard is a pre-4G technology, but it does not fully comply with IMT-advanced requirements. Hence, the LTE-advanced standard, an evolution of LTE, should meet or exceed the requirements of IMT-advanced. LTE-advanced is backward compatible with LTE; it has several technical features, such as coordinated multiple point transmission and reception, support of wider bandwidth, spatial-division multiplexing (SDM), and relaying functionality. The relaying functionality enhances the coverage of high data rates, group mobility, and temporary network deployment, and provides coverage in new areas. LTE-advanced also employs band aggregation of spectra in 20 MHz chunks to obtain the bandwidth for a logical channel. This can lead to a total of 100 MHz (5 chunks) transmission in each direction, downlink or uplink. The enhanced peak data rate of ITE-advanced that supports advanced services is 100 Mbps for high mobility, or 1 Gbps for low mobility. Unlike WiMAX, LTE-advanced applies SC-FDMA to uplink (UL). Both use OFDMA in downlink (DL). Accordingly, LTE-advanced technology is more energy efficient than WiMAX.

WiMAX is a standard developed by IEEE 802.16, and its evolved standard, WiMAX-m, is an alternative to LTE-advanced. WiMAX-m is an amendment to IEEE Standard 802.16e under the PAR P802.16m. Both WiMAX-m and LTE-advanced are equipped with several "magic bullet" technologies—*OFDM*, *MIMO*, and *smart antennas*. These technologies enable all-IP networks. Both LTE-advanced and WiMAX-m support all-IP packet-switched networks, mobile ultra-broadband access, and multicarrier transmission.

The properties of physical layers for the standards of mobile WiMAX (IEEE802.16e), WiMAX-m (IEEE802.16m), 3GPP-LTE, and LTE-advanced are listed in Table 2.11. The peak data rate of WiMAX-m is expected to be over 350 Mbps for downlink, while for LTE-advanced, it is 1 Gbps. The coverage of WiMAX-m and LTE-advanced are almost the same in cell size; for instance, the optimized cell size is from 1 km to 5 km. When the cell size is 30 km, the performance is reasonable. The system should still function with acceptable performance if the cell size is up to 100 km. The mobility of WiMAX-m and that of LTE-advanced are similar, about 350 km/h up to 500 km/h. With WiMAX-m, the spectral efficiency for downlink is more than 17.5 bps/Hz, while for uplink, more than 10 bps/Hz. LTE-advanced has a higher requirement in spectral efficiency, which is 30 bps/Hz for downlink and 15 bps/Hz for uplink. Both WiMAX-m and LTE-advanced use MIMO techniques to improve space utilization. The legacy of WiMAX is IEEE802.16e, while the legacies of LTE-advanced are GSM, GPRS, EGPRS, UMTS, HSPA, and LTE.

Continued

TABLE 2.11 The Properties of the Physical Layer for the Standards of Mobile WiMAX, WiMAX-m, LTE, and LTE-Advanced

Feature	Mobile WiMAX(3G) (IEEE802.16e)	WiMAX-m(4G) (IEEE 802.16m)	3GPP-LTE (pre-4G) (E-UTRAN)	LTE-advanced (4G)
Multiple access	WirelessMAN-OFDMA	WirelessMAN-OFDMA	DL: OFDMA UL: SC-FDMA	DL: OFDMA UL: SC-FDMA
Peak data rate (TX × RX)	DL: 64 Mbps (2 × 2) UL: 28 Mbps (2×2 collaborative MIMO) (10 MHz)	DL: > 350 Mbps (4 × 4) UL: > 200 Mbps (2 × 4) (20 MHz)	DL: 100 Mbps UL: 50Mbps	DL: 1 Gbps UL: 500 Mbps
Channel bandwidth	1.25/5/10/20 MHz	5/10/20 MHz and more (scalable bandwidths)	1.25–20 MHz	Band aggregation (chunks, each 20 MHz)
Coverage (cell radius, cell size)	2–7 km	Up to 5 km (optimized) 5–30 km (graceful degradation in spectral efficiency) 30–100 km (system should be functional)	1–5 km (typical) up to 100 km	5 km (optimal) 30 km (reasonable performance), up to 100 km (acceptable performance)
Mobility	Up to 60 ~ 120 km/h	120–350 km/h,up to 500 km/h	Up to 250 km/h	350 km/h, up to 500 km/h
Spectral efficiency (bps/Hz) (TX × RX)	DL: 6.4 (peak) UL: 2.8 (peak)	DL: >17.5 (peak) UL: > 10 (peak)	5 bps/Hz	DL: 30 (8 × 8) UL: 15 (4 × 4)
MIMO (TX×RX) (antenna techniques)	DL: 2 × 2 UL: 1 × N (Collaborative SM)	DL: 2 × 2 or 2 × 4 or 4 × 2 or 4 × 4 UL: 1 × 2 or 1 × 4 or 2 × 2 or 2 × 4	2 × 2	DL: 2 × 2 or 4 × 2 or 4 × 4 or 8 × 8 UL: 1 × 2 or 2 × 4
Legacy	IEEE802.16a ~ d	IEEE802.16e	GSM/GPRS/ EGPRS/ UMTS/ HSPA	GSM/GPRS/ EGPRS/ UMTS/HSPA/ LTE

2.6 SUMMARY

In this chapter we have learned the attributes of the physical layer and technologies used in this layer, mostly coding and modulation schemes. Popular line coding schemes, including NRZ, RZ, Manchester, AMI, mBnL, MLT, and RLL, and block coding schemes such as 4B/5B and 8B/10B, have been illustrated, where self-synchronization plays the dominant role. We have learned the basic modulation schemes, including ASK, PSK, and FSK, the hybrid QAM, and the advanced ones, including spread spectrum (DSSS, FHSS, CDMA), multi-carrier OFDM, and MIMO. The challenge of delivering more bits under a given bandwidth and SNR has been driving the innovations. We also covered the basic multiplexing schemes, such as TDM, FDM, and WDM. In summary, which schemes to use depends on the properties of the transmission medium, channel condition, and the target bit rate. For wired links, QAM, WDM, and OFDM are considered advanced. For vulnerable wireless links, OFDM, MIMO, and smart antenna are now the preferred choices for advanced systems.

For simplicity, the physical layer does not discriminate frames from the link layer. Therefore, the frames from the link layer are converted to raw bit streams and delivered to the physical layer for further processing. The raw bit streams are manipulated by line coding and modulation into signals, so the signals can travel over a physical channel with a specific transmission medium. At the receiver, the signals experience a reverse process and are converted into bit streams for delimiting by a mechanism, *framing,* at the link layer. Framing is discussed in Chapter 3.

A physical channel can be shared by multiple users if the channel capacity is more than what is required. Multiplexing technologies such as FDM, WDM, TDM, SS, DSSS, FHSS, OFDM, SM, or STC are used in the physical layer to enable multiple users to access a shared physical channel. Correspondingly, to access a shared channel, the link layer must provide an arbitration mechanism to optimize usage of and access to the channel. The channel access schemes implemented in the link layer include FDMA, WDMA, TDMA, CDMA, DS-CDMA, FH-CDMA, OFDMA, SDMA, and STMA.

Signals traveling over a channel are subject to distortion, interference, noise, and other signals, especially over a wireless communication channel. Because errors are likely to happen during the transmission, the receiver must be able to detect them. To fix this problem, the link layer may drop, correct, or ask to retransmit a corrupted frame. Therefore, error control functions such as checksum and cyclic redundancy check (CRC) are used at the link layer. To access a channel, the link layer must check the availability of the physical channel to determine if it is idle/free or busy. This is the packet-mode channel access method. For instance, CSMA/CD (carrier sense multiple access with collision detection) is suitable for a wired channel, while CSMA/CA (carrier sense multiple access with collision avoidance) is for a wireless channel. These are covered in Chapter 3.

COMMON PITFALLS

Data Rate, Baud Rate, and Symbol Rate

Data rate, also called bit rate (bitrate), is defined as the number of bits that are delivered or processed per unit of time. The unit of data rate is bit/sec or bps. The gross bitrate, raw bitrate, line rate, or data signaling rate is the total number of bits transferred per second over a communication link, including data and protocol overhead. In digital communications, a symbol can represent one or several bits of data. Symbol rate, or baud rate, is the number of symbols that change the states per second under a digital modulated signal or a line code. The unit of symbol rate is symbols/sec, or baud. The maximum baud rate in a baseband channel is called the Nyquist rate, which is a half of the channel bandwidth.

Bandwidth in Computing and Signal Processing

Bandwidth in computing indicates the data rate, also called network bandwidth. The unit is in bps. Bandwidth in signal processing may refer to baseband bandwidth or passband bandwidth, depending on the context. The baseband bandwidth is the upper cutoff frequency of a baseband signal. The passband bandwidth refers to the difference between the upper and lower cutoff frequencies of a passband signal. Bandwidth in signal processing is typically measured in hertz.

Narrowband, Wideband, Broadband, and Ultraband

Narrowband: In wireless communications, narrowband implies that a channel is sufficiently narrow where the frequency response on this channel can be considered flat, i.e., the values of the frequency response are similar. Frequency response is a measure of system output spectra in response to input signals on a channel. In an audio channel, narrowband indicates that sounds only occupy a narrow range of frequencies.

Wideband: In communications, wideband is used to describe a wide range of frequencies in a spectrum. It is the opposite of narrowband. When a channel has a high data rate, it is required to use a wideband bandwidth.

Broadband: In telecommunications, broadband refers to a signaling method that handles a relatively wide range of *frequencies,* which can be divided into channels. In data communications, it means multiple pieces of data are sent *simultaneously* to increase the effective rate of transmission.

Ultraband or ultra-wide band: This is a radio technology used at very *low* energy for short-range, high-bandwidth communications using a large portion of the radio spectrum.

FURTHER READINGS

PHY

Few popular texts for computer networks have a dedicated chapter on the physical layer, and none of them could fully cover all topics. Readers interested in more details need to look into the texts for data communications. The Proakis book is a comprehensive treatment on digital communications. It presents communication theory for graduate-level courses. The one by Sklar is another good text that covers many types of digital communications while combining both theories and applications. As the book title implies, Forouzan and Fegan tries to balance the treatment of communications at the physical and link layers and networking at the upper layers. It gives electrical engineering students more computer science flavors than other texts. Similarly, throughout this chapter, we try to give computer science students more electrical engineering flavors and some open source tastes. The Web site ComplextoReal.com managed by Charan Langton provides a collection of online tutorials on various topics in analog and digital communications. The articles "Certain Topics in Telegraph Transmission Theory" by Harry Nyquist and "A Mathematical Theory of Communication" and "Communication in the Presence of Noise" by Claud Elwood Shannon are the foundation of modern digital communications.

- J. G. Proakis, *Digital Communications,* McGraw-Hill, 2007.
- B. Forouzan and S. Fegan, *Data Communications and Networking,* McGraw-Hill, 2003.
- C. Langton, "Intuitive Guide to Principles of Communications," http://www.complextoreal.com/tutorial.htm
- B. Sklar, *Digital Communications,* 2nd edition, Prentice-Hall, 2001.
- H. Nyquist, "Certain Factors Affecting Telegraph Speed," *Bell System Technical Journal,* 1924, and "Certain Topics in Telegraph Transmission Theory," *Transactions of the American Institute of Electrical Engineers,* Vol. 47, pp. 617–644, 1928.
- H. Nyquist, "Certain Topics in Telegraph Transmission Theory," *Proceedings of the IEEE,* Vol. 90, No. 2, pp. 280–305, 2002. (Reprinted from *Transactions of the AIEE,* February, pp. 617–644, 1928.)
- C. E. Shannon, "A Mathematical Theory of Communication," *Bell System Technical Journal,* Vol. 27, pp. 379–423, pp.623–656, July & October 1948.
- C. E. Shannon, "Communication in the Presence of Noise," *Proceedings of the IEEE,* Vol. 86, No. 2, 1998. (Reprinted from *Proceedings of the IRE,* Vol. 37, No. 1, pp. 10–21, 1949.)

Spread Spectrum

Lamarr and Antheil co-invented the early form of the spread spectrum communication technology. In June 1941, they submitted the idea of a "secret communication system" patented as the U.S. Patent 2292387. This is the birth of spread spectrum in the form of frequency-hopping spread spectrum. For further study on the theory of spread spectrum, readers are referred to the book by Torrieri. The report by Nayerlaan introduces the fundamental concepts and applications of spread spectrum.

- H. Lamarr and G. Antheil, "Secret Communication System," U.S. Patent 2,292,387, Aug. 1942.
- D. Torrieri, *Principles of Spread-Spectrum Communication Systems,* Springer, 2004.
- J. D. Nayerlaan, "Spread Spectrum Applications," Oct. 1999, http://sss-mag.com/sstopics.html.

OFDM

Following spread spectrum, OFDM has evolved long enough to converge into some books. The following books address the design issues of OFDM systems. Li and Stuber provide comprehensive discussions on theories and practices of OFDM. The book by Chiueh and Tsai gives a concise yet comprehensive background on digital communications before addressing the design of OFDM receivers. Hardware design issues for physical IC implementations are also addressed. The Hanzo and Munster book is an in-depth treatment of OFDM, MIMO-OFDM, and MC-CDMA.

- T. Chiueh and P. Tsai, *OFDM Baseband Receiver Design for Wireless Communications,* Wiley, 2007.
- L. Hanzo, M. Münster, B. J. Choi, and T. Keller, *OFDM and MC-CDMA for Broadband Multi-User Communications, WLANs and Broadcasting,* Wiley-IEEE Press, 2003.
- G. Li and G. Stuber, *Orthogonal Frequency Division Multiplexing for Wireless Communications,* Springer, 2006.

MIMO

MIMO is still a young subject. The Oestges book offers insights into space-time division for MIMO channels. It associates propagation, channel modeling, signal processing, and space-time coding. Kim's paper is a multiuser MIMO system for WCDMA/HSDPA using user scheduling, spatial beamforming, and feedback signaling control systems. Gesbert's papers discuss multiuser MIMO and other theories about MIMO systems.

- C. Oestges and B. Clerckx, *MIMO Wireless Communications: From Real-World Propagation to Space-Time Code Design,* Computers—Academic Press, 2007.
- D. Gesbert and J. Akhtar, "Breaking the Barriers of Shannon Capacity: An Overview of MIMO Wireless Systems," *Telenor's Journal: Telektronikk,* pp. 53–64, 2002.
- D. Gesbert, M. Kountouris, R. Heath, C. Chae, and T. Salzer, "From Single User to Multiuser Communications: Shifting the MIMO Paradigm," *IEEE Signal Processing Magazine,* Vol. 24, No. 5, pp. 36–46, 2007.
- D. Gesbert, M. Shafi, D. Shiu, P. Smith, A. Naguib, et al., "From Theory to Practice: An Overview of MIMO Space-Time Coded Wireless Systems," *IEEE Journal on Selected Areas in Communications,* Vol. 21, No. 3, pp. 281–302, Apr. 2003.
- S. Kim, H. Kim, C. Park, and K. Lee, "On the Performance of Multiuser MIMO Systems in WCDMA/HSDPA: Beamforming, Feedback and User Diversity," *IEICE Transactions on Communications,* Vol. E89-B, No. 8, pp. 2161–2169, 2006.

Development Environments

In computer networks, messages are sent from one node to another through a link where signals are processed in the physical layer. Actually, some signal processing can be handled either in hardware or in software. Software-defined radio proposed in Mitola's paper deals with some signal-processing steps, such as modulation and demodulation, by radio functions in software in a general-purpose processor. The GNU Radio Project provides the open source solutions along that track.

Though parts of signal processing can be implemented in software, a communications system still needs a hardware platform to transfer signals. The components on the hardware platform may include AD/DA converter, power amplifer (PA), mixer, oscillator, phase-locked loop (PLL), and microcontroller or microprocessor. These components are either analog or digital integrated circuits. Therefore, tools for analog circuit design and digital circuit design are required to develop the hardware platform for a communication system. For instance, Matlab and Simulink can be used for system analysis, design, and simulation. Verilog (System Verilog) and VHDL can help to design and simulate digital IC. Automatic conversion tools from MatLab/Simulink models to HDL models have been developed to expedite the digital IC system design. SPICE (Simulation Program with Integrated Circuit Emphasis) and Agilent ADS (Advanced Design System) are tools for analog integrated circuit design and radio frequency IC design. Their references are listed as follows:

- J. Mitola, "Software Radio Architecture: A Mathematical Perspective," *IEEE Journal on Selected Areas in Communications,* Vol. 17, No. 4, pp. 514–538, Apr. 1999.
- GNU Radio Project: http://gnuradio.org/redmine/wiki/gnuradio
- The MathWorks: A Software Provider for Technical Computing and Model-Based Design, http://www.mathworks.com/
- VASG: Maintaining and Extending the VHDL Standard (IEEE 1076), http://www.eda.org/vasg/

- IEEE P1800: Standard for System Verilog: Unified Hardware Design, Specification and Verification Language, http://www.eda.org/sv-ieee1800/
- SPICE: A General-Purpose Open Source Analog Electronic Circuit Simulator, http://bwrc.eecs.berkeley.edu/Classes/IcBook/SPICE/
- Agilent Technologies Advanced Design System (ADS) 2009: A High-frequency/High-speed Platform for Co-design of Integrated Circuits (IC), Packages, Modules and Boards, http://www.home.agilent.com/

FREQUENTLY ASKED QUESTIONS

1. What are bit rate and baud rate?
   Answer:
   Bit rate (or data rate): The number of bits being transmitted per unit of time.
   Baud rate (or symbol rate): The number of symbols being transmitted per unit of time.
2. What is the difference between sampling theorem, Nyquist theorem, and Shannon theorem?
   Answer:
   Sampling theorem: Calculate the sampling rate under which a signal can be uniquely reconstructed.
   Nyquist theorem: Calculate the maximum data rate for a noiseless channel.
   Shannon theorem: Calculate the maximum data rate for a noisy channel.
3. In digital communications, what kinds of signals are often used, and why?
   Answer:
   In digital communications, the periodic analog signals and the aperiodic digital signals are commonly used because the former demand less bandwidth and the latter represent digital data.
4. What are the advantages of digital signals, compared with analog signals?
   Answer:
   Digital signals: more immune to noise and easier to recover when signals travel over transmission media
   Analog signals: subject to corruption by noise, interference and harder to recover completely.
5. Why is line coding needed in the physical layer?
   Answer:
   Line coding can prevent baseline wandering and the introduction of DC components, and can enable self-synchronization, provide error detection and correction, and increase signals' immunity to noise and interference.
6. What factors may impair the transmission capability of a physical layer, especially over the wireless channel?
   Answer:
   Attenuation, fading, distortion, interference, and noise.
7. What is the constellation diagram?
   Answer:
   It is a tool that defines a mapping between an analog signal and its corresponding digital data patterns.
8. What are the basic modulations in digital communications?
   Answer:
   ASK, FSK, and PSK are three basic modulations in digital communications.
   ASK: Different levels of carrier amplitude are used to represent digital data.
   FSK: Different carrier frequencies are used to represent digital data.
   PSK: The phases of a carrier, not the change of the phase, are used to represent digital data.
   QAM: A combination of ASK and PSK changes the levels of carrier amplitude and phase to form waveforms of different signal elements.
9. In digital communications, why are modulations necessary for signals that travel over high-frequency channels?
   Answer:
   If a baseband digital signal (with a lower frequency) wants to travel over a high-frequency channel, it must be carried by a sinusoidal carrier. In other words, the signal has to modulate carriers of higher frequencies so that the data signals can be conveyed via the channel.
10. Why multiplexing?
    Answer:
    When the bandwidth of a channel is more than required for a data stream, the channel can be shared by multiple users to improve the channel utilization.
11. What are the benefits of spread spectrum?
    Answer:
    Noise-like signals after spreading, hard to detect and interfere with, and extra redundancy to reduce the vulnerability of wireless communications to eavesdropping, jamming, and noise.

12. What is the main feature of OFDM? Why OFDM, not CDMA, in 4G?
 Answer:
 Main feature of OFDM: Orthogonality of sub-carriers that allows data to be transmitted at the same time over sub-channels.
 Advantages of OFDM:
 1. Combining multiplexing, modulation, and multiple carriers
 2. Higher rate than CDMA (a technique of spread spectrum)
13. Compare traditional radio systems to soft radio systems.
 Answer:
 Software radio implements radio functions for signal processing as many as possible in software, rather than the dedicated circuitry used in traditional radio systems. Moreover, the functions of modulation and demodulation in a software radio system are also performed by software programs, instead of hardware devices.
 Advantages of software radio:
 1. More flexible to different standards, especially with a reconfigurable hardware to support the signal processing at higher frequencies.
 2. Reduced cost of switching to other standards and time-to-market.

EXERCISES

Hands-On Exercises

1. Find and summarize the network-related modules in www.opencores.org into a table. In the table, compare their protocol layer, purpose, programming language, and key implemented algorithms or mechanisms.
2. Find the PHY (physical) layer modules in www.opencores.org. For each module, describe how complete the implementation is, i.e., which parts of the algorithms or mechanisms are implemented and which parts are not. Associate your discussions with the algorithms or mechanisms described in this chapter.
3. GNU Radio is a package for software radio systems. Build a GNU Radio system on your machine with the Linux operating system.
 a. Download the latest stable release of GNU Radio from http://gnuradio.org/redmine/wiki/gnuradio/Download.
 b. Read the instructions from http://gnuradio.org/redmine/wiki/gnuradio/BuildGuide. Follow these instructions and build a GNU Radio system.
 c. Install all required and dependent packages for GNU Radio, as discussed on the GNU Radio Web site.
 d. Many software radio examples reside in the folder, /usr/share/gnuradio/examples. Run the example … /gnuradio/examples/audio/dial_tone.py. This example is like a "Hello World" example in any programming languages such as C++, Java, or Python. Try to run more examples. (Hint: GNU Radio package is already collected in the Fedora repository. It is much easier for you to install this package with the tool *yum,* or *rpm.*)
4. Install the GRC (GNU Radio Companion) tool from http://www.joshknows.com/grc on your machine. GRC can facilitate the study of GNU Radio. Now exploit the GRC tool to design the following systems:
 a. a system that can filter a noisy channel, and
 b. a QAM modulator/demodulator system.
 (Hint: You may refer to "GNU Radio Testbed" written by Naveen Manicka.)

Written Exercises

1. Why is a data stream usually represented as an aperiodic digital signal? Why is a modulated signal represented as an aperiodic analog signal?
2. Compare the number of required frequencies and the size of bandwidth to represent the following signals: (a) periodic analog, (b) aperiodic analog, (c) periodic digital, and (d) aperiodic digital.
3. What is the difference between fading and attenuation?
4. What is the difference between noise and interference?
5. Explain what sdr (signal-to-data-ratio) and SNR (signal-to-noise-ratio) mean and how they can be used for evaluation.
6. Compare the capability of high-frequency signals and low-frequency signals in straight-line propagation, reflection, refraction, and diffraction.
7. Among unipolar NRZ-L, Polar NRZ-L, NRZ-I, and RZ, Manchester, differential Manchester, AMI, and MLT-3, which schemes have no issues on synchronization, baseline wandering, and DC components, respectively?

8. Draw the waveforms using the schemes of unipolar NRZ-L, Polar NRZ-L, NRZ-I, and RZ for the following data streams. Calculate the value of sdr (signal-to-data ratio) and the average baud rate.
   a. 101010101010
   b. 111111000000
   c. 111000111000
   d. 000000000000
   e. 111111111111
9. Draw the waveforms using the schemes of Manchester and differential Manchester for the following data streams. Calculate the value of sdr (signal-to-data ratio) and the average baud rate.
   a. 101010101010
   b. 111111000000
   c. 111000111000
   d. 000000000000
   e. 111111111111
10. Draw the waveforms using the scheme of MLT-3 for the following data streams. Calculate the value of sdr (signal-to-data ratio) and the average baud rate.
    a. 101010101010
    b. 111111000000
    c. 111000111000
    d. 000000000000
    e. 111111111111
11. Given a data stream of a bit rate 1 Mbps, 2 Mbps, or 54 Mbps, calculate the baud rate using the modulation of BFSK, BASK, BPSK, QPSK, 16-PSK, 4-QAM, 16-QAM, and 64-QAM.
12. Given the baud rates of 8 kBd and 64 kBd, calculate the bit rate for the modulation of BFSK, BASK, BPSK, QPSK, 16-PSK, 4-QAM, 16-QAM, and 64-QAM.
13. Given a data stream of a bit rate 56 kbps or 256 kbps, what are the chip rate and process gain if the 11-bit or 13-bit Barker code is used as the PN code to spread the data stream?
14. What are the major differences between synchronous CDMA and asynchronous CDMA?
15. Compare the PN codes and the orthogonal codes used in CDMA. Why can we support more users with PN codes than with orthogonal codes?
16. How can we tell whether two PN codes used in asynchronous CDMA are correlated or uncorrelated?
17. How can we tell whether two codes used in synchronous CDMA are orthogonal to each other?
18. Explain why spread spectrum can mitigate surrounding noise and remove interference from other adjacent users, either narrowband or wideband. Why is it able to provide a better protection for privacy?
19. In FHSS, is it possible for two transmitting stations to hop to the same sub-channel at the same time, that is, to collide? Justify your answer.
20. What are the main components used to implement the multicarrier mechanism in OFDM? How does a data stream exploit multiple carriers and travel through an OFDM channel?
21. What are the criteria for two signals to be orthogonal to each other in OFDM?
22. What are the advantages and disadvantages for a MIMO system with or without the knowledge of channel state information?
23. What are the major differences between single-user MIMO and multi-user MIMO?

Chapter 3

Link Layer

Effective and efficient data transmission over physical links from one node to another is more than simply *modulating* or *encoding* bit streams into signals. Several issues must be addressed first for successful data transmission. For example, crosstalk noise between adjacent link pairs can unexpectedly impair transmission signals and result in errors, so the link layer needs proper error control mechanisms for reliable data transmission. The transmitter might transmit at a rate *faster* than what the receiver can handle, and has to slow down if this situation happens notify the receiver where the source of the packets is. If multiple nodes share a LAN, an *arbitration* mechanism is required to determine who can transmit next. Beyond all of the above, we need to interconnect LANs—that is, we need to bridge different LANs to extend packet forwarding beyond a single LAN. Although these issues need to be addressed by a set of functions above the physical link, the link layer in the OSI architecture manages physical links for the upper-layer functions and therefore exempts the upper layers from the tedious work of controlling the physical link. The link layer greatly alleviates upper-layer protocol design and makes it virtually independent of physical transmission characteristics.

In this chapter, we present (1) functions or services provided in the link layer, (2) popular real-world link protocols, and (3) a set of selected open-source software and *hardware* implementations of link-layer technologies. Section 3.1 addresses the general issues in designing link layer functions, including *framing, addressing, error control, flow control, access control,* and *interfaces* with other layers. We illustrated the interfaces and packet flows with the network adaptor, and the upper IP layer with function calls in Linux, as a *zoom-in* of a packet's life in Section 1.5.

Given a vast variety of real-world link technologies summarized in Table 3.1, it is hardly possible to describe all of them in this chapter, so here we focus on only a few mainstream link technologies. We detail (1) Point-to-Point Protocol, or PPP for short, in Section 3.2, along with its open-source implementation, (2) a wired broadcast link protocol, Ethernet, in Section 3.3 along with its Verilog *hardware* implementation, and (3) a wireless broadcast link protocol, wireless LAN or WLAN, in Section 3.4, plus a summary on Bluetooth, and WiMAX. We select these examples due to their popularity. PPP is popular in the last-mile dial-up services or in routers carrying various network protocols over point-to-point links. Ethernet has been dominating the wired LAN technology, and is also poised to be *ubiquitous* in MANs and WANs. In contrast to desktop PCs that usually use wired links to connect to the network, users of mobile devices such as laptop computers and cellular phones prefer wireless

TABLE 3.1 Link Protocols

	PAN/LAN	MAN/WAN
Obsolete or fading away	Token Bus (802.4) Token Ring (802.5) HIPPI Fiber Channel Isochronous (802.9) Demand Priority (802.12) FDDI ATM HIPERLAN	DQDB (802.6) HDLC X.25 Frame Relay SMDS ISDN B-ISDN
Mainstream or still active	Ethernet (802.3) WLAN (802.11) Bluetooth (802.15) Fiber Channel HomeRF HomePlug	Ethernet (802.3) Point-to-Point Protocol (PPP) DOCSIS xDSL SONET Cellular (3G, LTE, WiMAX ([802.16]) Resilient Packet Ring (802.17) ATM

link technologies, i.e., WLAN, Bluetooth and WiMAX. Since multiple LANs can be interconnected by bridging, we cover this technology in Section 3.5, along with the open-source implementations of its two key components, *self-learning* and *spanning tree*. Finally, Section 3.6 illustrates the general concepts of Linux device *drivers,* and we then go into details of Ethernet driver implementation.

3.1 GENERAL ISSUES

Sandwiched between the physical link and the network layer, the link layer provides control over physical communications and services to the upper network layer. This layer performs the following major functions.

Framing: Data transmitted on a physical link are packed in units of *frames*. A frame contains two main parts: control information in the header, and the data in the payload. Control information, such as the destination address, the upper-layer protocol in use, the error detection code, and so on, are critical to frame processing. The data part handed from the upper layer is *encapsulated* with the control information into the frame. Because frames are transmitted as raw bit streams in the physical layer, the link layer service should turn frames into bit streams upon transmission, and break the bit stream into frames upon reception. Most literature uses the two terms, *packets* and *frames,* interchangeably, but we specifically refer to a *packet data unit* in the link layer as a *frame*.

Addressing: We need to specify an address when writing a letter to our friends, and we also need a phone number when making phone calls to them. Addressing in the link layer is needed for the same reason. A link-layer address, often presented in a numeric form of a certain length, specifies the identity of a host. When host *A* wants to transmit a frame to host *B*, it includes its address and host *B*'s address as the source and destination addresses in the frame's control information.

Error control and reliability: Frames transmitted over physical media are subject to errors, and the receiver must be capable of detecting these errors through a certain mechanism. Upon detecting an error, the receiver may simply drop the frame, or it may acknowledge the error occurrence and request that the transmitter retransmit the frame. For data-link technology like Ethernet, the bit error rate is extremely low, so the retransmission mechanism could be left to a high-layer protocol such as TCP for high efficiency. For wireless link technology like 802.11, the transmitter will wait for an acknowledgment from the receiver for a certain amount of time, and if no acknowledgment is received upon timeout, the transmitter will retransmit the last frame so as to ensure the retransmission could be in time.

Flow control: The transmitter may send at a rate faster than what the receiver can afford. In this case, the receiver has to discard the excess frames and make the transmitter retransmit the discarded frames, but doing so just wastes their capacity. Flow control provides a mechanism to let the receiver *slow down* the transmitter in order to avoid the receiver being overloaded with the data from the transmitter side.

Medium access control: There must be an arbitration mechanism to decide who gets to transmit next when multiple hosts want to transmit data over shared media. A good arbitration mechanism must offer fair access to the shared medium while keeping the shared medium highly utilized in case many hosts have backlogs; that is, data queued to be transmitted.

3.1.1 Framing

Since data are transmitted as raw bit streams in the physical layer, the link layer must identify the beginning and the end of each frame when receiving a bit stream. On the other hand, it must also turn frames into a raw bit stream for physical transmission. This function is called framing.

Frame Delimiting

Several methods can be used to delimit the frames. Special bit patterns or *sentinel* characters can be used to mark the frame boundary, such as the HDLC frames which will be introduced later. Some Ethernet systems use special *physical encoding* to mark frame boundaries, while others identify the boundary simply by the presence

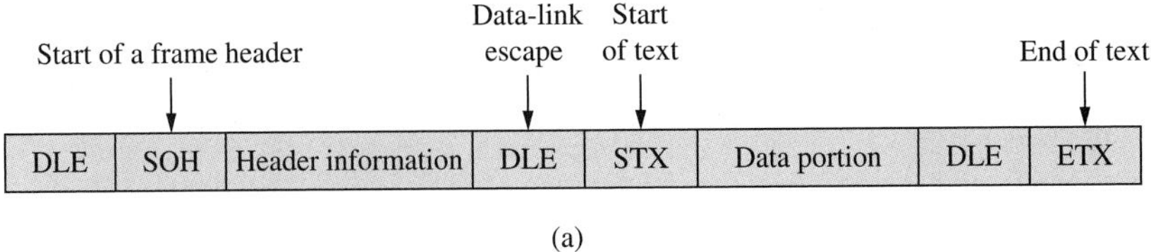

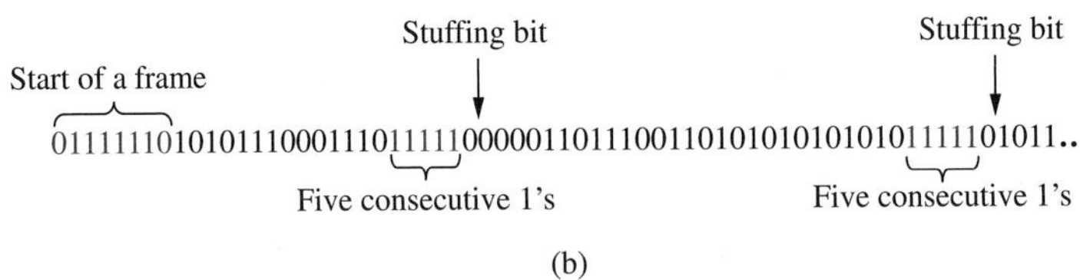

FIGURE 3.1 (a) Byte-stuffing and (b) bit-stuffing.

or absence of signal.[1] The former has been used since the birth of fast Ethernet (i.e., 100 Mbps) because it can detect the physical link status. The latter is unable to do so because it cannot tell whether the physical link is broken or whether no frames are being transmitted (no signal is on the link in both cases). It was once used in 10 Mbps Ethernet, but is no longer used with newer Ethernet technology.

A frame could be bit-oriented or byte-oriented, depending on its basic unit. A bit-oriented framing protocol can specify a special bit pattern, say 01111110 in HDLC, to mark the beginning and the end of the frame, while a byte-oriented framing protocol can specify special characters, say SOH (start of header) and STX (start of text), to mark the beginning of frame header and data. Since an ambiguity may exist when normal data characters or bits exhibit the same pattern as the special ones, a technique called *byte-* or *bit-stuffing* is used to resolve the ambiguity, as illustrated in Figure 3.1. In a byte-oriented frame, a special *escape* character, namely DLE (data link escape), precedes a special character to indicate the next character is normal data. Because DLE itself is also a special character, two consecutive DLEs represent a normal DLE character. In HDLC, a binary 0 is inserted after every sequence of *five* consecutive 1's so that the pattern 01111110 never appears in normal data. Both the transmitter and the receiver follow the same rule to resolve the ambiguity.

Ethernet takes a different framing approach. For example, 100BASE-X uses special encoding to mark the boundary; by *4B/5B* encoding, described in Chapter 2, only *16* out of *32* (= 2^5) possible codes come from actual data while the rest serve as *control codes*. These control codes are uniquely recognizable by the receiver and thus used to delimit a frame out of a bit stream. Another Ethernet system, 10BASE-T, recognizes the frame boundary simply based on the presence or absence of a signal.

[1] Ethernet uses the term "stream" to refer to physical encapsulation of a frame. Strictly speaking, special encoding or presence of signal delimit stream, not frame. However, we do not with bother the details here.

Frame Format

The frame header contains control information, and the frame data includes data of the link layer or the network layer. The latter again contains control information and data from the higher layers. Typical control information in the frame header includes the following fields:

Address: This usually indicates both the source and the destination address. A receiver knows the frame is destined for itself if the destination address in the frame header matches its own. The receiver also can respond to the source of an incoming frame by filling in the destination address of the outgoing frame with the source address of the incoming frame.

Length: This may indicate the entire frame length or merely the data length.

Type: The type of the network layer protocol is encoded in this field. The link layer protocol can read the code to determine which network layer module, say Internet Protocol (IP), to invoke to further process the data field.

Error detection code: This is the value of a mathematical *function* for the content in a frame as the input argument. The transmitter computes the function and embeds the value in the frame. Upon receiving the frame, the receiver computes the function in the same way to see if the result matches the value embedded in the frame. If not, it implies the content has been altered somewhere during transmission.

3.1.2 Addressing

An address is an identifier for distinguishing a host from others in communications. Although a *name* is easier to remember, a numerical address is a more compact representation in low-layer protocols. We leave the concept of using names as host identifiers to Chapter 5 (see *Domain Name System*).

Global or Local Address

An address can be globally unique or locally unique. A globally unique address is unique worldwide, while a locally unique address is only unique in a local site. In general, a locally unique address consumes fewer bits but requires the administrator's efforts to ensure the local uniqueness. Since a few bits of overhead in the address are trivial, globally unique addresses are preferred nowadays so that the administrator simply adds a host to the network at will, and does not need to worry about the conflict over local addresses.

Address Length

How long should an address be? A long address takes more bits to be transmitted, and is harder to remember or refer to, but a short address may not be enough to ensure global uniqueness. For a set of locally unique addresses, 8 or 16 bits should be enough, but much more is required to support globally unique addresses. A very popular addressing format in IEEE 802 is 48-bit long. We leave it as an exercise for readers to determine whether this length is sufficient for global usage.

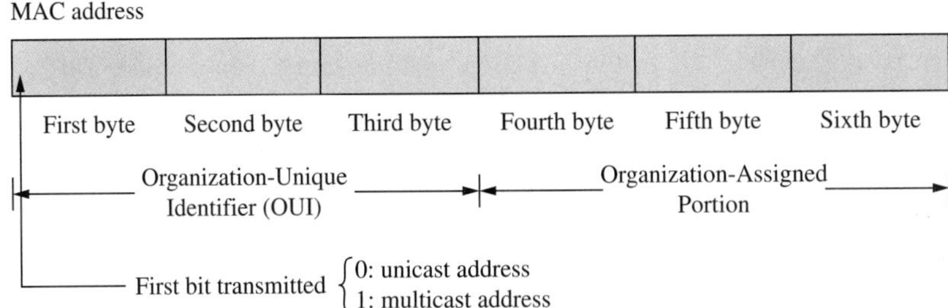

FIGURE 3.2 IEEE 802 address format.

IEEE 802 MAC Address

IEEE 802 standards provide excellent examples of the link addressing format because they are widely adopted in many link protocols, including Ethernet, Fiber Distribution Data Interface (FDDI), and wireless LAN. While IEEE 802 specifies the use of either 2-byte- or 6-byte-long addresses, most implementations adopt the 6-byte (or 48-bit) addressing format. To ensure its global uniqueness, the address is partitioned into two parts: *Organization-Unique Identifier* (OUI) and Organization-Assigned Portion, each occupying three bytes. The IEEE administers the former, so organizations can contact the IEEE to apply for an OUI,[2] and after that they are in charge of the uniqueness of their OUI's Organization-Assigned Portion. In theory, with IEEE 802 specifications, 2^{48} (around 10^{15}) addresses can be assigned, and this number is large enough to ensure global uniqueness. An IEEE 802 address is often written in *hexadecimal,* with every two digits separated by a dash or a colon, e.g., 00-32-4f-cc-30-58. Figure 3.2 illustrates IEEE 802 address format.

The first bit in transmission order is reserved to indicate whether the address is *unicast* or *multicast.*[3] A unicast address is destined for a single host, while a multicast address is destined for a group of hosts. A special case of multicast is *broadcast,* where *all* bits in the address are *1*'s. A broadcast-type frame is destined for all hosts as far as it can reach in the link layer. Note that the transmission order of *bits* in each byte in the address may be different from the order in which they are stored in memory. In Ethernet, the transmission order is *least* significant bit (LSB) first in each byte, called *little-endian.* For example, given a byte $b_7b_6...b_0$, Ethernet first transmits b_0, then b_1, b_2, and so on. In other protocols such as FDDI and Token Ring, the transmission order is *most* significant bit (MSB) first in each byte, which is called *big-endian.*

3.1.3 Error Control and Reliability

Frames are subject to errors during transmission, and the link-layer devices are supposed to detect these errors in time. As mentioned in Subsection 3.1.1, error detection code is a function of the frame content, computed by the transmitter to fill in a

[2] See http://standards.ieee.org/regauth/oui/oui.txt for information about how OUI has been assigned.

[3] The second bit can indicate whether the address is globally unique or locally unique. However, such usage is infrequent, so we ignore it here.

field of the frame. The receiver will use the same algorithm to recompute the error detection code with the received frame content to and see if both code values match. If not, an error must have occurred during transmission. In the following we illustrate two commonly used error detection functions: *checksum* and *cyclic redundancy check* (CRC).

Error Detection Code

The checksum computation simply divides the frame content into blocks of m bits and takes the m-bit *sum* of these blocks. The computation is simple, and can be easily implemented in software. In Open Source Implementation 3.1, we will introduce a piece of code that implements the checksum computation.

Another powerful technique is cyclic redundancy check, which is more complicated than checksum but easy to implement in hardware. Suppose m bits are in the frame content. The transmitter can generate a sequence of k bits as the *frame check sequence* (FCS) such that the whole frame of $m+k$ bits can be divided by a predetermined bit pattern called *generator*. The receiver divides the received frame in the same way to see if the remainder is *zero*. If the remainder is nonzero, there are errors during transmission. The following example demonstrates a trivial CRC procedure to generate the FCS.

frame content F = 11010001110 (11 bits)

generator B = 101011 (6 bits)

FCS = (5 bits)

The procedure goes as follows:

Step 1 Shift F by 2^5 and append five 0's to it, which yields 1101000111000000.

Step 2 The resulting pattern in Step 1 is divided by B. The process is as follows:

(the computation is all module-2 arithmetic)

```
                  11000001111
         ________________
101011 ) 1101000111000000
         101011
         ______________
          111110
          101011
          ______________
           101011
           101011
         ______________
                 110000
                 101011
         ______________
                  110110
                  101011
         ______________
                   111010
                   101011
         ______________
                    10001  <-- the remainder
```

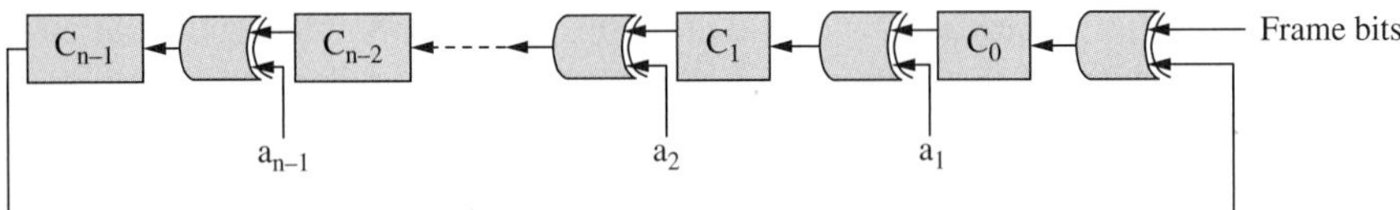

FIGURE 3.3 CRC circuit diagram.

Step 3 The remainder in this computation is appended to the original frame content, yielding 1101000111010001. The frame is then transmitted. The receiver divides the incoming frame content by the same generator to verify the frame. We leave the verification on the receiver side as an exercise.

The above description is simplified because the reasoning behind the practical CRC computation is rather mathematically complex. It has been proven that the CRC can detect many kinds of errors, including

1. single-bit error.
2. double-bit error.
3. any burst errors whose length is less than that of the FCS.

The CRC computation can be easily implemented in hardware with *exclusive-OR* gates and *shift registers*. Suppose we represent the generator with the form $a_n a_{n-1} a_{n-2} \ldots a_1 a_0$, where bits a_n and a_0 must be 1. We plot a general circuit architecture that implements the CRC computation in Figure 3.3. The frame content is shifted into this circuit bit by bit, and the final bit pattern in the shift registers is the FCS, i.e., $C_{n-1}C_{n-2}\ldots C_1C_0$. The initial values of $C_{n-1}C_{n-2}\ldots C_1C_0$ are insignificant because they will be shifted out once the computation begins. For very high-speed links, circuits of parallel CRC computation are employed to meet the high-speed requirement.

Data Reliability

But how does the receiver respond to an erroneous frame? The receiver can respond in the following ways:

1. Silently discard the incorrect incoming frame.
2. Reply with positive acknowledgment when the incoming frame is correct.
3. Reply with negative acknowledgment when the incoming frame is incorrect.

The transmitter may retransmit the received erroneous frame or simply just ignore the errors. In the latter case, higher-layer protocols, say TCP, will handle the retransmission.

Another decision to make is whether to implement data acknowledgment in the link layer. Ethernet does not use the acknowledgment mechanism because its bit error rate is quite low, so demanding an acknowledgment for each transmitted frame is overkill. The acknowledgment mechanism is therefore left to the higher-layer protocol such as TCP. For wireless links, the bit error rate is much higher than Ethernet (i.e., less reliable), so it is safer to acknowledge every transmitted frame. The use of the acknowledgment mechanism, however, is at the price of lowered throughput because the sender must wait for the acknowledgment before the next transmission. There is still a trade-off between high throughput and the capability to detect an error in time in a link-layer design.

Principle in Action: CRC or Checksum?

Checksum is used in higher-layer protocols such as TCP, UDP, and IP, while CRC is found in Ethernet and wireless LAN. There are two reasons behind this distinction. First, CRC is easily implemented in hardware, but *not* in software. Because higher-layer protocols are almost always implemented in software, using checksum for them is a natural choice. Second, CRC is mathematically proven to be robust to a number of errors in physical transmission. Since CRC has filtered out *most* transmission errors, using checksum to *double-check* unusual errors (e.g., those that happen within a network device) should be sufficient in practice.

Principle in Action: Error Correction Code

Error *detection* codes like CRC and checksum can only detect transmission error. Once an error is found, the receiver is unable to do anything but discard the frame. An alternative is *forward error correction* (FEC) using error *correction* code. By FEC, the sender side appends even *more* redundant bits to the message. The key difference between error correction and error detection is that it is possible to *infer* the bits with errors and correct them. After the erroneous bits in a frame are "corrected," the frame can be accepted without retransmission. We will not go into the mathematical details here, but rather point out a general principle: More bits to be corrected require more redundant bits to be used. A question therefore arises: Is it worthwhile to add more redundant bits for error correction?

The answer depends on the *bit error rate*, the possible *direction* of transmission, and the *importance* of data. In common data-link protocols such as Ethernet, the bit error rate is pretty low, e.g., 1 bit error every 10^{10} bits transmitted in Ethernet. Using error correction codes in this case apparently is overkill, and even for a wireless LAN, error detection is sufficient. When data are transmitted over the Internet, most errors come from packet dropping due to Internet congestion, so error correction codes still cannot help too much here.

Common applications of error correction codes are space telecommunications, data storage, and satellite broadcasting. The cost of retransmission in space telecommunications is high, so it is worthwhile to use error correction codes. Since satellite broadcasting is *one-way,* there is no acknowledgment or retransmission; thus error correction is needed. In data storage, if an error occurs, error detection helps little because the data storage is the *only* data source and the error cannot be recovered anyway. In this case, error correction codes can at least recover bit errors to a certain degree. In satellite broadcasting, since there is no way for the receiver to notify the source of bit errors, error correction is preferred.

Open Source Implementation 3.1: Checksum

Overview

Checksum computation is a common error detection code used in Internet protocols, such as IP, UDP, and TCP. Its efficiency is critical to good routing performance, as *every* packet needs the checksum computation in its network-layer header and transport-layer header. For example, the checksum field in the TCP header covers both the header and payload content in the TCP segment as well as a pseudo header of additional information such as the source and destination IP addresses. If the checksum computation in the TCP protocol stack is not implemented well, it will consume a significant number of CPU cycles in the packet forwarding process.

Block Diagram

Figure 3.4 is a block diagram that illustrates how checksum is implemented. In the beginning, the `sum` and `checksum` variables are initialized to 0 and kept updated for each batch of 16-bit word input from the covered range of octets of a packet. After the final-batch computation, the `sum's` value is folded (see following discussion) to derive the `checksum` value. The following details the Linux implementation of checksum computation.

Data Structures

The data structure of checksum computation is trivial. It contains a `sum` variable that accumulates the 16-bit words throughout the fields and payload being covered, and a `count` variable to count how many 16-bit words are left. Note that the `sum` variable is a 32-bit word to capture overflow from the accumulation. After computing the last 16-bit word, the `sum` variable is folded into a 16-bit word, and the `checksum` value is the 1's complement of the folded value.

Algorithm Implementations

For those octets to be covered in the checksum computation, the adjacent octets are first paired to form 16-bit words, and then the 1's complement sum of these pairs is computed. If there is a byte left without a pair, it is added into the checksum directly. Finally, the 1's complement of the result is filled into the checksum

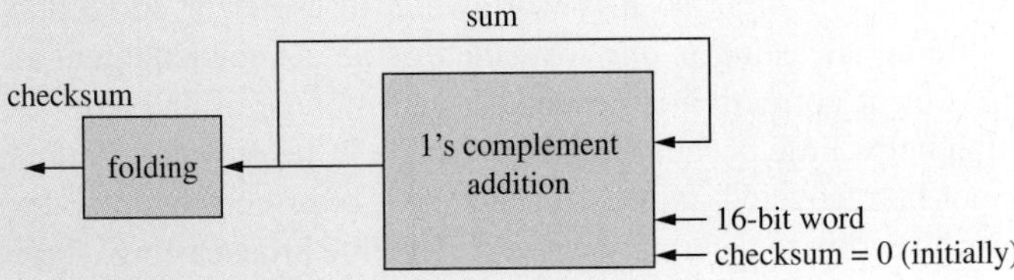

FIGURE 3.4 Block diagram of checksum computation.

field. The receiver follows the same procedure to compute over the same octets for the checksum field. If the result is all 1's, the check succeeds. Because the Linux implementation of checksum is usually written in assembly languages for efficiency, we present the C code in RFC 1071 for better readability. Open Source Implementation 4.3 in Chapter 4 explains the assembly version of IP checksum computation in the Linux kernel.

```
/* Compute Internet Checksum for "count" bytes
*        beginning at location "addr".
*/
register long sum = 0;
while( count > 1 ) {
        sum += * (unsigned short) addr++;
        count -= 2;
}
/* Add left-over byte, if any */
if( count > 0 )
        sum += * (unsigned char *) addr;
/* Fold 32-bit sum to 16 bits */
while (sum>>16)
        sum = (sum & 0xffff) + (sum >> 16);
checksum = ~sum;
```

Exercises

1. The TTL field of an IP packet is subtracted by 1 when the IP packet passes through a router, and thus the checksum value after the subtraction must be changed. Please find an efficient algorithm to recompute the new checksum value. (Hint: See RFC 1071 and 1141.)
2. Explain why the IP checksum does not cover the payload in its computation.

Open Source Implementation 3.2: Hardware CRC-32

Overview

CRC-32 is a commonly used error detection code for many MAC protocols, including Ethernet and 802.11 Wireless LAN. For high-speed computation, CRC-32 is usually implemented in hardware as part of the on-chip functions in the network interface card. As the data in batches of 4 bits are input from or output to the physical link, they are processed sequentially to derive the 32-bit CRC value. The computation result is either used to verify the correctness of a frame or appended to a frame to be transmitted.

Continued

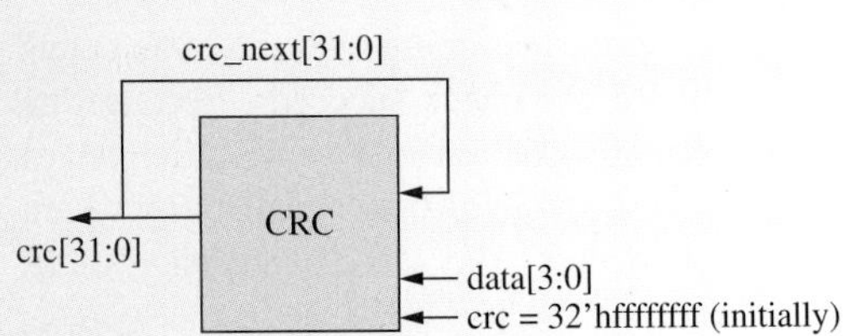

FIGURE 3.5 Block diagram of CRC-32 computation.

Block Diagram

Figure 3.5 is a block diagram that illustrates how CRC is implemented in hardware. Initially, 32 bits of 1's are assigned to the `crc` variable. When each batch of four bits is swept in, the bits update the current `crc` variable to `crc_next`, which is assigned back to `crc` for the next batch of 4-bit data. The updating process involves computation with many parameters, so we omit its details. After all data is processed, the value stored in the `crc` variable is the final result.

Data Structures

The data structure of CRC-32 computation is mainly the 32-bit `crc` variable that keeps the latest state after reading each batch of 4-bit data. The final result of CRC-32 computation is the state after reading the final batch of data.

Algorithm Implementations

An open-source implementation of CRC-32 can be found in the Ethernet MAC project on the OpenCores Web site (http://www.opencores.org). See the Verilog implementation `eth_crc.v` in the CVS repository of the project. In this implementation, the data come into the CRC module sequentially in batches of four bits. The CRC value is initialized to all 1's in the beginning. Each bit of the current CRC value comes from xor'ing the selected bits in the incoming 4-bit input and those of the CRC value from the previous round. Because of the complication in computation, we refer the readers to `eth_crc.v` for the relevant details in each bit's computation. After the data bits' computation finishes, the final CRC value is derived at the same time. The receiver follows the same procedure to compute the CRC value and check the correctness of the incoming frames.

Exercises

1. Could the algorithm in `eth_src.v` be easily implemented in software? Justify your answer.
2. Why do we use CRC-32 rather than the checksum computation in the link layer?

3.1.4 Flow Control

Flow control addresses the problem of a fast transmitter and a slow receiver. It provides a method that allows an overwhelmed receiver to tell the transmitter to slow down its transmission rate. The simplest flow-control method is *stop-and-wait,* in which the transmitter transmits one frame, waits for the acknowledgment from the receiver, and then transmits the next. This method, however, results in a very low utilization of the transmission link. Better methods are introduced as follows.

Sliding Window Protocol

More efficient flow control can be achieved by the *sliding window protocol,* in which the transmitter can transmit up to a fixed number of frames without acknowledgments. When the acknowledgments are returned from the receiver, the transmitter can move forward to transmit more frames. For the purpose of tracking which outgoing frame corresponds to which returned acknowledgment, each frame is labeled with a *sequence number*. The range of sequence numbers should be large enough to prevent the number from being used by more than one frame at the same time; otherwise, there will be ambiguity since we have no way of telling whether the sequence number represents an old or a new frame.

Figure 3.6 illustrates an example of sliding window. Suppose the *window size* of the transmitter is 9, meaning that the transmitter can transmit up to nine frames, say frame no. 1 to no. 9, without acknowledgments. Suppose the transmitter has transmitted four frames (see Figure 3.6[a]) and received an acknowledgment that the first three frames are successfully received. The window will slide forward by three frames meaning that by now eight frames (i.e., frames no. 5 to no. 12) can be transmitted without acknowledgments (See Figure 3.6[b]). The window originally covering frames no. 1 to no. 9 now covers frames no. 4 to no. 12, which in some sense acts as if the window slides along the sequence of frames. Sliding window flow control

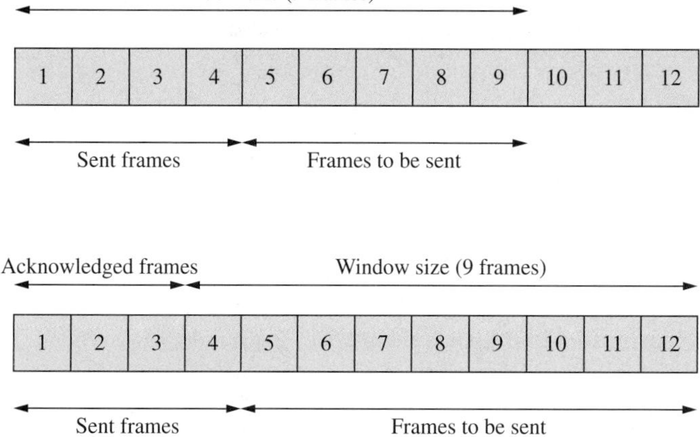

FIGURE 3.6 Sliding window over transmitted frames.

is a very important technique in Transmission Control Protocol (TCP), an excellent and most practical example that adopts the sliding window. We shall introduce its application in TCP in Chapter 4.

Other Approaches

There are more methods to implement flow control. For example, the mechanisms in Ethernet include *back pressure* and *PAUSE frame*. However, to understand these methods requires the knowledge of how these protocols operate. We leave these flow control techniques to Subsection 3.3.2.

3.1.5 Medium Access Control

Medium access control, also simply referred to as MAC, is needed when multiple nodes share a common physical medium. It includes an arbitration mechanism that every node should obey in order to share fairly and efficiently. We summarize the techniques into two categories.

Contention-Based Approach

By this approach, multiple nodes contend for the use of the shared medium. A classical example is ALOHA, in which nodes transmit data at will. If two or more nodes transmit at the same time, a *collision* occurs, and their frames in transmission will be garbled, degrading the throughput performance. A refinement is the *slotted* ALOHA, in which a node is allowed to transmit only in the beginning of its time slot. Further refinements include *carrier sense* and *collision detection*. Carrier sense means the node *senses* if there is an ongoing transmission (in a signal called a *carrier*) over the shared medium. The transmitter will *wait* politely until the shared medium is free. Collision detection *shortens* the garbled bit stream by stopping the transmission once a collision is detected.

Contention-Free Approach

The contention-based approach becomes inefficient if a collision cannot be detected in time. A complete frame might have been garbled *before* the transmission can be stopped. Two commonly seen contention-free approaches are round-robin and reservation-based. In the former, a token is circulated among nodes one after another to allow fair share of the medium, and only a node in possession of the token has the right to transmit its frame. Typical examples include Token Ring and FDDI; their mechanisms are similar despite different structures. The reservation-based approach manages to reserve a channel of the shared medium before the transmitter actually transmits the frame. A well-known example is the RTS/CTS mechanism in IEEE 802.11 WLAN. We will talk more about this mechanism in Section 3.4. Using reservation incurs a performance trade-off since the process itself induces overhead. If a frame loss is insignificant, e.g., a *short* frame, a contention-based approach may work better in this case. If only two nodes are on a point-to-point link, the access control might not be necessary at all if it is a full-duplex link. We will further discuss full-duplex operation in Section 3.2.

3.1.6 Bridging

Connecting separate LANs into an interconnected network can extend the network's communication range. An interconnection device operating in the link layer is called a *MAC bridge,* or simply *bridge,* which interconnects LANs as if their nodes were in the same LAN. The bridge knows *whether* it should forward an incoming frame and to *which* interface port. To support *plug-and-play* operation and easy administration, the bridge should automatically learn which port a destination host belongs to.

As the topology of a bridged network gets larger, network administrators may inadvertently create a *loop* within the topology. IEEE 802.1D, or the IEEE MAC bridges standard, stipulates a *spanning tree protocol (STP)* to eliminate loops in a bridged network. There are other issues such as separating LANs logically, combining multiple links into a trunk for a higher transmission rate, and specifying the priority of a frame. We shall introduce the details in Section 3.5.

3.1.7 Link-Layer Packet Flows

The link layer lies above the physical link and below the network layer. During packet transmission, it receives a packet from the network layer, encapsulates the packet with appropriate link information such as MAC addresses in the frame header and the frame check sequence in the tail, and transmits the frame over the physical link. Upon receiving a packet from the physical link, the link layer extracts the header information, verifies the frame check sequence, and passes the payload to the network layer according to the protocol information in the header. But what are the actual *packet flows* between these layers? Continued from a packet's life in Section 1.5, we illustrate the packet flows for both frame reception and transmission in Open Source Implementation 3.3.

Open Source Implementation 3.3: Link-Layer Packet Flows in Call Graphs

Overview

The packet flow of the link layer follows two paths. In the reception path, a frame is received from the physical link and then passed to the network layer. In the transmission path, a frame is received from the network layer and then passed to the physical link. Part of the interface between the link layer and the physical link is located in hardware. The Ethernet interface, for example, will be introduced in Open Source Implementation 3.5. We introduce the code in the device driver to emphasize the *software* part in frame transmission or reception.

Block Diagram

Figure 3.7 illustrates the interfaces above and below the link layer and the overall packet flows. The "Algorithms" section will explain the details of how

Continued

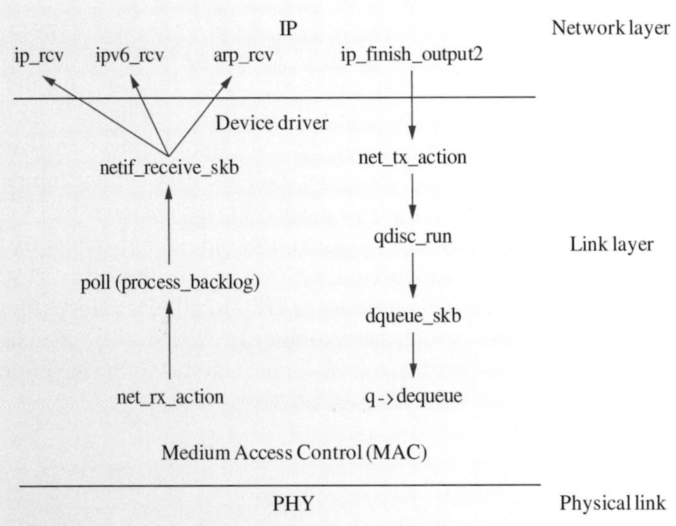

FIGURE 3.7 Link-layer packet flows.

packets flow through the functions in Figure 3.7. For the hardware interfaces between the MAC and PHY, please refer to Open Source Implementation 3.5: CSMA/CD for a typical Ethernet example.

Data Structures

The most critical data structure is the `sk_buff` structure, which represents a packet in the Linux kernel. Some fields in `sk_buff` are for bookkeeping purposes, and the others store the packet content, including the header and payload. For example, the following fields in the structure contain the header and payload information.

```
sk_buff_data_t              transport_header;
sk_buff_data_t              network_header;
sk_buff_data_t              mac_header;
unsigned char               *head,
                            *data;
```

Algorithm Implementations

Packet Flow in the Reception Path

When the network interface receives a frame, an interrupt is generated to signal the CPU to deal with the frame. The interrupt handler allocates the `sk_buff` structure with the `dev_alloc_skb()` function and copies the frame into the structure. The handler then initializes some fields in `sk_buff`, particularly the `protocol` field for use of the upper layer, and notifies the kernel about the frame arrival for further processing.

Two mechanisms can implement the notification process: (1) the old function netif_rx(), and (2) the new API net_rx_action() for handling ingress frames since kernel version 2.6. The former is purely interrupt-driven, while the latter uses a hybrid of *interrupts* and *polling* for higher efficiency. For example, when the kernel is handling a frame and another new frame has arrived, the kernel can keep handling the former frame and frames in the ingress queue until the queue is empty without being interrupted by the new arrival. According to some benchmark results, the CPU load is lower in cases of using the new API at high traffic loads, so we focus on the new API here.

The interrupt handling routine may involve one or more frames, depending on the driver's design. When the kernel is interrupted by a new frame arrival, it calls the net_rx_action() function to poll a list of interfaces from a software interrupt NET_RX_SOFTIRQ. The software interrupt is a *bottom-half* handler, which can be executed in the background to avoid occupying the CPU too long for processing the frame arrival. The polling is executed in a round-robin fashion with a maximum number of frames that are allowed to be processed. The net_rx_action() function invokes the poll() virtual function (a generic function which will in turn call the specific polling function on a device) on each device to dequeue from the ingress queue. If an interface is unable to clear out its ingress queue because the number of frames allowed to be processed or the available execution time of net_rx_action() has reached the limit, it must wait until the next poll. In this example, the default handler process_backlog() is used for the poll() function.

The poll() virtual function in turn calls netif_receive_skb() to process the frame. When net_rx_action() is invoked, the L3 protocol type has already been in the protocol field of sk_buff, set by the interrupt handler. Therefore, netif_receive_skb() knows the L3 protocol type and can copy the frame to the L3 protocol handler associated with the protocol field by calling

```
ret = pt_prev->func(skb, skb->dev, pt_prev, orig_
dev);
```

Here the function pointer func points to common L3 protocol handlers, such as ip_rcv(), ip_ipv6_rcv(), and arp_rcv(), which handle IPv4, IPv6, and ARP, respectively (to be covered in Chapter 4). Up to now, the frame reception process is complete, and the L3 protocol handler takes over the frame and decides what to do next.

Packet Flow in the Transmission Path

Packet flow in the transmission path is symmetric to that in the reception path. The function net_tx_action() is the counterpart of net_rx_action(), and it is called when some device is ready to transmit a frame from the software interrupt NET_TX_SOFTIRQ. Like net_rx_action() from NET_RX_SOFTIRQ, the bottom-half handler net_tx_action() can

Continued

manage time-consuming tasks, such as releasing the buffer space after a frame has been transmitted. The `net_tx_action()` performs two tasks: (1) ensuring the frames waiting to be sent are really sent by the `dev_queue_xmit()` function, and (2) deallocating the `sk_buff` structure after the transmission is completed. The frames in the egress queue may be scheduled for transmission following a certain *queuing discipline*. The `qdisc_run()` function selects the next frame to transmit, and calls `dequeue_skb()` to release a packet from the queue `q`. This function then calls the `dequeue()` virtual function of the associated queuing discipline on the queue `q`.

Exercises

Explain why the CPU load could be lowered by using the new `net_rx_action()` function at high traffic loads.

3.2 POINT-TO-POINT PROTOCOL

This section focuses on the *Point-to-Point Protocol (PPP),* a widely used protocol in traditional dial-up lines or ADSL to the Internet. PPP was derived from an old but widely used protocol, *High-Level Data Link Control (HDLC).* Within its operations are two protocols, *Link Control Protocol (LCP)* and *Network Control Protocol (NCP).* As Ethernet extends to homes and organizations with a bridge device such as an ADSL modem connected to the *Internet Service Provider (ISP),* there is the need for *PPP over Ethernet (PPPoE).* Figure 3.8 shows the relationship between these components.

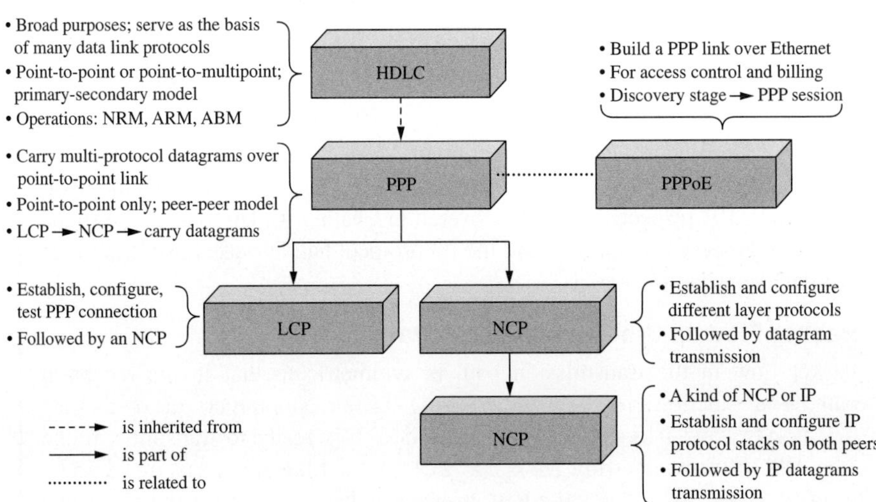

FIGURE 3.8 Relationship between PPP-related protocols.

3.2.1 High-Level Data Link Control (HDLC)

Derived from an early protocol, *Synchronous Data Link Control (SDLC) protocol* by IBM, the HDLC protocol is an ISO standard and the basis of many other link protocols. For example, the PPP uses HDLC-like framing. IEEE 802.2 *Logical Link Control* (LLC) is a modification of HDLC. CCITT (renamed ITU in 1993) modified HDLC as part of the X.25 standard, called *Link Access Procedure, Balanced* (LAP-B). Among all the variants, HDLC supports point-to-point and point-to-multipoint link, and half-duplex and full-duplex link. Next we take a look at the HDLC operation.

HDLC Operation: Medium Access Control

In HDLC, nodes are either *primary* or *secondary stations*. HDLC supports the following three transfer modes, each of which offers a way of controlling nodes to access the medium.

Normal response mode (NRM): The secondary station can only *passively* transmit data in response to the primary's *poll*. The response may consist of one or more frames. In a point-to-multipoint scenario, secondary stations must communicate through the primary.

Asynchronous response mode (ARM): The secondary station can *initiate* the data transfer without the primary's poll, but the primary is still responsible for controlling the connection.

Asynchronous balanced mode (ABM): Both parties in communication can play the role of the primary and the secondary, which means both stations have equal status. This type of station is called a *combined station*.

NRM is often used in a point-to-multipoint link such as the one between a computer and its terminals. Although ARM is rarely used, it has advantages at point-to-point links, but ABM is even better. ABM has less overhead such as that of the primary's poll, and both parties can have control over the link. ABM is especially suitable for point-to-point links.

Data Link Functions: Framing, Addressing, and Error Control

We look at the HDLC's framing, addressing, and error control issues by directly examining the frame format, and then we discuss flow control and medium access control. Figure 3.9 depicts the HDLC frame format.

Flag: The flag value is fixed at 01111110 to delimit the beginning and the end of the frame. As illustrated in Subsection 3.1.1, bit stuffing is used to avoid ambiguity between actual data and the flag value.

	Flag	Address	Control	Information	FCS	Flag
bits	8	8	8	Any	16	8

FIGURE 3.9 HDLC frame format.

Address: The address indicates the *secondary station* involved in transmission, particularly in the point-to-multipoint situation. A secondary station works under the control of the *primary station,* as mentioned in the HDLC operation.

Control: This field indicates the frame type as well as other control information such as the frame's *sequence number.* HDLC has three types of frames: *information, supervisory,* and *unnumbered.* We will look at them in more detail later.

Information: The information field can be of an arbitrary length in bits. It carries the data payload to be transmitted.

FCS: A 16-bit CRC-CCITT code is used. HDLC allows both positive and negative acknowledgments. The error control in HDLC is complex. Positive acknowledgments can indicate a successful frame or all frames up to a point, while negative acknowledgments can reject a received frame or a specified frame. We do not go into the details here. Interested readers are encouraged to read on from the list of supplementary materials in "Further Readings."

Data Link Functions: Flow Control and Error Control

Flow control in HDLC also uses a sliding-window mechanism. The transmitter keeps a counter to record the *sequence number* of the *next* frame to send. On the other side, the receiver keeps a counter to record the *expected* sequence number of the next incoming frame, and checks whether the sequence number of the received frame matches the expected one. If the sequence number is correct and the frame is not garbled, the receiver increases its counter by 1 and positively acknowledges the sender by transmitting a message containing the next expected sequence number. If the received frame is unexpected or an error with the frame is detected using the FCS field, the frame is dropped, and a negative acknowledgment asking for retransmission is sent back to the sender. Upon receiving the negative acknowledgment that indicates the frame to be retransmitted, the transmitter will do the retransmission. This approach is the error-control mechanism in HDLC.

Frame Type

These functions are achieved through various kinds of frames. An information frame, called I-frame, carries data from the upper layer and also carries some control information, including *two* three-bit fields that record its own sequence number and the acknowledged sequence number from the receiver. These sequence numbers are for flow-control and error-control purposes, as mentioned previously. A *poll/final* (P/F) is also included in the control information to indicate a poll from the primary station or the last response from the secondary station.

A supervisory frame, called an S-frame, carries control information only. As we have seen in the previous discussion of HDLC frame format, both positive and negative acknowledgments are supported for error control. Once there is an error, the transmitter can retransmit either all outstanding frames or only the erroneous frame as specified in the control information. The receiver can also send the transmitter an S-frame, asking it to temporarily halt the transmit operation.

An unnumbered frame, called a U-frame, is also used for the control purpose, but it does not carry any sequence number, so that is how the name is derived. The U-frame includes miscellaneous commands for mode settings, information transfer, and recovery, but we do not go into details here.

3.2.2 Point-to-Point Protocol (PPP)

The PPP is a standard protocol defined by IETF to carry multi-protocol packets over a point-to-point link. It is widely used for dial-up and leased-line access to the Internet. To carry multi-protocol packets, it has three main components:

1. An encapsulation method to encapsulate packets from the network layer.
2. A *Link Control Protocol* (LCP) to handle the cycle of connection setup, configuration, and teardown.
3. A *Network Control Protocol* (NCP) to configure different network-layer options.

We first look at the PPP operation and then study its functions.

PPP Operation

In a *service subscription* scenario, before entering the HDLC-like MAC operation, PPP needs to complete the login and the configuration before sending any data packets. The PPP operation follows the phase diagram in Figure 3.10. PPP first sends LCP packets to *establish* and test the connection. After the connection is set up, the peer that initiated the connection may *authenticate* itself before any network-layer packets are exchanged. Then PPP starts to send NCP packets to *configure* one or more *network* layer protocols for the communication. Once the configuration is done, the network-layer packets can be sent over the link before the connection goes to the terminate phase.

We explain each major transition in the diagram as follows:

Dead to Establish: The transition is invoked by carrier detection or network administrator configuration when a peer starts using the physical link.

Establish to Authenticate: The LCP starts to set up the connection by exchanging configuration packets between peers. All options not negotiated are set to their default values. Only options independent of the network layer are negotiated, and the options for network layer configuration are left to the NCP.

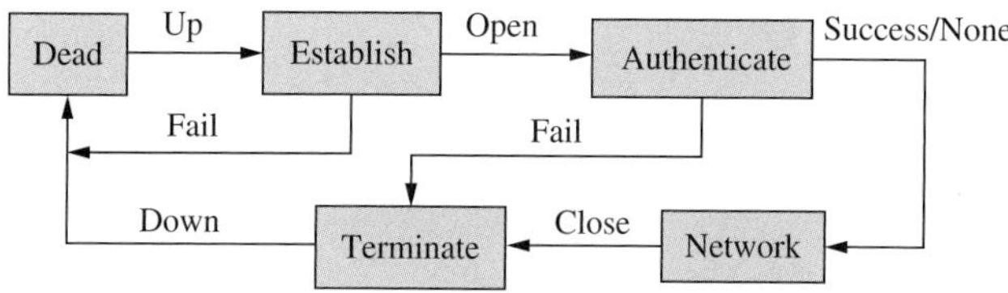

FIGURE 3.10 Phase diagram of PPP connection setup and teardown.

TABLE 3.2 The LCP Frame Types

Class	Type	Function
Configuration	Configure-request	Open a connection by giving desired changes to options
	Configure-ack	Acknowledge Configure-request
	Configure-nak	Deny Configure-request because of unacceptable options
	Configure-reject	Deny Configure-request because of unrecognizable options
Termination	Terminate-request	Request to close the connection
	Terminate-ack	Acknowledge Terminate-request
Maintenance	Code-reject	Unknown requests from the peer
	Protocol-reject	Unsupported protocol from the peer
	Echo-request	Echo back the request (for debugging)
	Echo-reply	The echo for Echo-request (for debugging)
	Discard-request	Just discard the request (for debugging)

Authenticate to Network: Authentication is optional in PPP, but if it is required in the link establishment phase, the operation will switch to the authentication phase. If the authentication fails, the connection will be terminated; otherwise, the proper NCP starts to negotiate each network layer protocol.

Network to Terminate: The termination happens in many situations, including loss of carrier, authentication failure, expiration of an idle connection, user termination, etc. The LCP is responsible for exchanging Terminate packets to close the connection, and later the PPP tells the network layer protocol to close.

There are three classes of LCP frames: Configuration, Termination, and Maintenance. A pair of Configure-request and Configure-ack frames can open a connection. The options such as the maximum receive unit or the authentication protocol are negotiable during the connection setup. Table 3.2 summarizes the other functions. The LCP frame is a special case of the PPP frame. Therefore, before we look at the LCP frame format, we first introduce the PPP frame format.

Data Link Functions: Framing, Addressing, and Error Control

The PPP frame is encapsulated in an HDLC-like format, as depicted in Figure 3.11. The flag value is exactly the same as in HDLC. It serves as the delimiter for framing.

The differences between the PPP frame and the HDLC frame are summarized as follows:

1. The address value is fixed at 11111111, which is the all-stations address in the HDLC format. Since only two peers are in a point-to-point link, there is no need to indicate an individual station address.

	Flag 01111110	Address 11111111	Control 00000011	Protocol	Information	FCS	Flag 01111110
bits	8	8	8	8 or 16	Any	16 or 32	8

FIGURE 3.11 PPP frame format.

2. The control code has the fixed value 00000011, which corresponds to an unnumbered frame in the HDLC format. This implies that by default, *no* sequence numbers and acknowledgment are used in the PPP. Interested readers are referred to RFC 1663, which defines an extension to make the PPP connection reliable.
3. A Protocol field is added to indicate which type of network layer protocol the frame is carrying, say IP or IPX. The default field length is 16 bits, but it can be reduced to 8 bits using the LCP negotiation.
4. The maximum length of the Information field, called the Maximum Receive Unit (MRU), is by default 1500 bytes. Other values for MRU are negotiable.
5. The default FCS is 16 bits long, but it can be extended to 32 bits through the LCP negotiation. The receiver drops the received frame if an error is detected within the frame. The responsibility of frame retransmission falls on the upper-layer protocols.

Data Link Functions: No Flow Control and Medium Access Control

Because PPP is full-duplex and only two stations are in a point-to-point link, *no* medium access control is needed for PPP. On the other hand, PPP does *not* provide flow control, which is left to upper-layer protocols.

LCP and NCP negotiation

The LCP frame is a PPP frame with the Protocol field value 0xc021, where 0x stands for a hexadecimal number. The negotiation information is embedded in the Information field as four main fields: *Code* to indicate the LCP type, *Identifier* to match requests and replies, *Length* to indicate the total length of the four fields, and *Data* to carry the negotiation options.

Since IP is the dominant network-layer protocol in the Internet, we are particularly interested in IP over PPP. We introduce NCP for IP— *Internet Protocol Control Protocol* (IPCP)—in Subsection 3.2.3.

3.2.3 Internet Protocol Control Protocol (IPCP)

IPCP is a member of NCP to configure IP over PPP. PPP first establishes a connection by LCP, and then uses NCP to configure the network layer protocol it carries. After the configuration, data packets can be transmitted over the link. IPCP uses a frame format similar to that of the LCP, and its frame is also a special case of the PPP frame with the Protocol field set to 0x8021. The exchange mechanism used by IPCP is the same as that used by the LCP. Through IPCP, IP modules on both peers can be enabled, configured, and disabled.

IPCP provides the configuration options: IP-Addresses, IP-Compression-Protocol, and IP-Address. The first is obsolete and is replaced by the third. The second indicates the use of Van Jacobson's *TCP/IP header compression*. The third allows the peer to provide an *IP address* to be used on the local end. After IPCP negotiation, normal IP packets can be transmitted over the PPP link by encapsulating IP packets in the PPP frame with the Protocol field value 0x0021.

Open Source Implementation 3.4: PPP Drivers

Overview

The implementation of PPP in Linux is primarily composed of two parts: the data-plane PPP driver and the control-plane PPP daemon (PPPd). A PPP driver establishes a network interface and passes packets between the serial port, the kernel networking code, and the PPP daemon. The PPP driver handles the functions in the data link layer described in previous subsections. PPPd negotiates with the peer to establish the link connection and sets up the PPP network interface. PPPd also supports authentication, so it can control which other systems may establish a PPP connection and can specify their IP addresses.

Block Diagram

A PPP driver is made of the PPP generic layer and the PPP channel driver, as shown in Figure 3.12.

Data Structures

There are asynchronous and synchronous PPP drivers in Linux (see `ppp_async.c` and `ppp_synctty.c` under the `drivers/net` directory). Their difference resides in the type of `tty` device to which a PPP channel driver is attached. When the attached `tty` device is a synchronous HDLC card, such as the FarSync T-Series cards manufactured by FarSite Communications Ltd., the synchronous PPP channel driver is used. On the other hand, when the `tty` devices are asynchronous serial lines, such as the PEB 20534 controller manufactured by Infineon Technologies AG, the asynchronous PPP channel driver is used.

The associated I/O function pointers for both drivers are defined in the `tty_ldisc_ops` structure by which the associated I/O functions can be correctly invoked. For example, the `read` field points to `ppp_asynctty_read()` for asynchronous PPP, while it points to `ppp_sync_read()` for synchronous PPP.

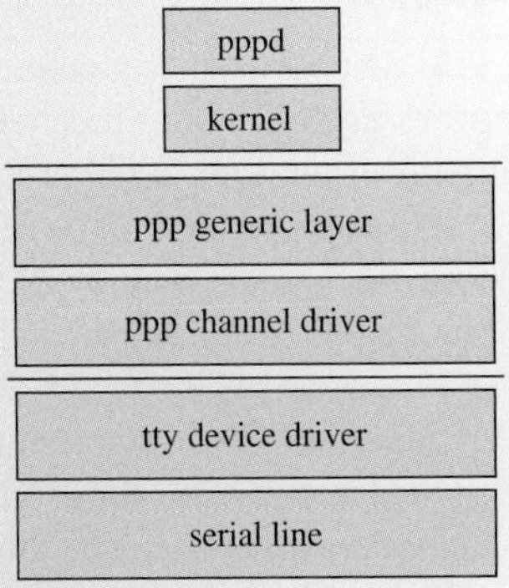

pppd	handles control-plane packets
kernel	handles data-plane packets
ppp generic layer	handles PPP network interface, /dev/ppp device, VJ compression, multilink
ppp channel driver	handles encapsulation and framing

FIGURE 3.12 PPP software architecture.

Rather than going into the details of both PPP drivers, we introduce the generic flows of packet transmission and reception below as they can better reflect the packet flow in the PPP driver.

Algorithm Implementations

Packet Transmission

A data packet to be sent is stored in the `sk_buff` structure. It is passed to `ppp_start_xmit()`, which prepends the PPP header to the packet and stores the packet in the transmit queue, namely `xq` (see the `ppp_file` structure in `ppp_generic.c`). Finally, `ppp_start_xmit()` invokes `ppp_xmit_process()`, which takes the packets out of the `xq` queue, and calls `ppp_send_frame()` for some packet processing such as header compression. After this step, `ppp_send_frame()` calls either the asynchronous PPP function, `ppp_async_send()`, or the synchronous PPP function, `ppp_sync_send()`, to send the packets through individual drivers.

Packet Reception

When either the asynchronous or synchronous driver receives an incoming packet, the packet is passed to the `ppp_input()` function of the PPP generic driver, which adds the incoming packet into the receive queue, namely `rq`. The PPPd will read the packets from the queue over the `/dev/ppp` device.

Exercises

Discuss why the PPP functions are implemented in software, while the Ethernet functions are implemented in hardware.

3.2.4 PPP over Ethernet (PPPoE)

The Need for PPPoE

As Ethernet technology becomes cheap and dominant, it is not uncommon that users set up their own Ethernet LAN at home or in the office. On the other hand, the broadband access technology, say ADSL, has become a common method to access the Internet from home or office. Multiple users on an Ethernet LAN access the Internet through the same broadband bridging devices, so service providers desire a method to have access control and billing on a *per-user* basis, similar to conventional dial-up services.

PPP has conventionally been a solution to building the point-to-point relationship between peers, but an Ethernet network involves multiple stations. The *PPP over Ethernet (PPPoE) protocol* is designed to coordinate the two conflicting philosophies. It creates a *virtual interface* on an Ethernet interface so that each individual station on a LAN can establish a PPP session with a remote PPPoE server, which is located in the ISP and known as *Access Concentrator (AC),* through common bridging devices. Each user on the LAN sees a PPP interface just like that seen in the dial-up service, but the PPP frames are encapsulated in the Ethernet frames. Through PPPoE, the user's computer obtains an IP address, and the ISP can easily associate the IP address with a specific user name and password.

PPPoE Operation

The PPPoE runs in two stages: the Discovery stage and the PPP Session stage. In the Discovery stage, the user station discovers the MAC address of the access concentrator and establishes a PPPoE session with the access concentrator; a unique PPPoE session identifier is also assigned to the session. Once the session is established, both peers enter the PPP Session stage and do exactly what a PPP session does, say LCP negotiation.

The Discovery stage proceeds in the following four steps:

1. The station to access the Internet broadcasts an Initiation frame to ask remote access concentrators to return their MAC addresses.
2. The remote access concentrators reply with their MAC addresses.
3. The original station selects one access concentrator and sends a Session-Request frame to the selected access concentrator.
4. The access concentrator generates a PPPoE session identifier and returns a Confirm frame with the session id.

The PPP Session stage runs in the same way as a normal PPP session does, as explained in Subsection 3.2.2, except only PPP frames are carried on Ethernet frames. When the LCP terminates a PPP session, the PPPoE session is torn down as well. A new PPP session requires a new PPPoE session starting from the Discovery stage.

A normal PPP termination process can terminate a PPPoE session. PPPoE allows either the initiating station or the access concentrator to send an explicit Terminate frame to close a session. Once the Terminate frame is sent or received, no further frame transmission is allowed, even for normal PPP termination frames.

3.3 ETHERNET (IEEE 802.3)

Originally proposed by Bob Metcalfe in 1973, Ethernet is a former competitor for LAN technology that eventually became the winner. In over 30 years, Ethernet has been reinvented many times to accommodate new demands, resulting in the large IEEE 802.3 standard, and the evolution continues well into the future. We introduce readers to the evolution and philosophy of Ethernet and also describe the hot topics currently under development.

3.3.1 Ethernet Evolution: A Big Picture

As the title of the standard, "Carrier sense multiple access with collision detection (CSMA/CD) access method and physical layer specification," suggests, Ethernet is most clearly distinguished from other LAN technologies, such as Token Bus and Token Ring, by its medium access method. A lab at Xerox gave birth to the technology in 1973, which was later standardized by DEC, Intel, and Xerox in 1981

1973	1980	1981	1982	1983
3 Mb/s experimental Ethernet	DIX Consortium formed	DIX Ethernet Spec ver. 1 10 Mb/s Ethernet	DIX Ethernet Spec ver. 2	IEEE 802.3 10BASE5

1997	1995	1993	1990	1985
Full-duplex Ethernet	100BASE-T	10BASE-F	10BASE-T	10BASE-2

1998	1999	2000	2002	2003
1000BASE-X	1000BASE-T	Link aggregation	10GBASE on fiber	Ethernet in the First Mile

2008	2006
40G and 100G development	10GBASE-T

FIGURE 3.13 Milestones in the development of Ethernet standards.

and known as the DIX Ethernet. Although this standard bore little resemblance to the original design at Xerox, the essence of CSMA/CD was preserved in the standard. In 1983, the IEEE 802.3 Working Group approved a standard based on the DIX Ethernet with only insignificant changes. This standard became the well-known IEEE 802.3 standard. Since Xerox relinquished the trademark name "Ethernet," the distinction between the two terms Ethernet and the IEEE 802.3 standard no longer exists when people refer to them. In fact, the IEEE 802.3 Working Group has been leading Ethernet development since its first version of the standard. Figure 3.13 illustrates the milestones in the development of Ethernet standards. It has experienced several significant revisions during the past 30 years. We list the major trends.

From low to high speed: Starting from a prototype running at 3 Mbps, Ethernet has grown up to 10 Gbps—a boost of more than 3000 times in speed. An ongoing work (IEEE 802.3ba) aiming to further boost the data rate up to 40 Gbps and 100 Gbps has started. As astonishing as that is, the technology still remains cheap, making it widely accepted around the world. Ethernet has been built into almost every motherboard of desktop computers and laptops. We are sure that Ethernet will be ubiquitous for wired connectivity.

From shared to dedicated media: The original Ethernet runs on a *bus* topology of coaxial cables. Multiple stations *share* the bus with the CSMA/CD MAC algorithm, and collisions on the Ethernet bus are common. As of the development of 10BASE-T, *dedicated* media between two devices become the majority. Dedicated media are necessary to the later development of *full-duplex* Ethernet. Full-duplex allows both stations to transmit over the dedicated media simultaneously, which in effect doubles the bandwidth!

From LAN to MAN and to WAN: Ethernet was well known as a LAN technology. Two factors helped the technology move toward the MAN and WAN markets. The first is the cost. Ethernet has low cost in implementation because of its simplicity. It takes less pain and money to build up the interoperability if the MAN and WAN are also Ethernet. The second comes from *full duplex,* which eliminates the need for CSMA/CD and thus lifts the *distance restriction* on Ethernet usage—the data can be transmitted as far as a physical link can reach.

Richer medium: The term "ether" was once thought of as the medium to propagate electromagnetic waves through space. Although Ethernet never uses ether to transmit data, it does carry messages on a variety of media: coaxial cables, twisted pairs, and optical fibers. "Ethernet is Multimedia!"—the amusing words by Rich Seifert in his book *Gigabit Ethernet* (1998) best depict the scenario. Table 3.3 lists all the 802.3 family members in terms of their speed and the media they can run on.

Not all the 802.3 members are commercially successful. For example, 100BASE-T2 has never been a commercial product. In contrast, some are so successful that almost everybody can find a *network interface card* (NIC) of 10BASE-T or 100BASE-TX behind a computer on a LAN. Most new motherboards for desktop computers come with an Ethernet interface of 100BASE-TX or 1000BASE-T nowadays. The number in the parentheses indicates the year when the IEEE approved the specification.

TABLE 3.3 The 802.3 Family

Speed \ Medium	Coaxial Cable	Twisted Pairs	Fiber
under 10 Mbps		1BASE5 (1987) 2BASE-TL (2003)	
10 Mbps	10BASE5 (1983) 10BASE2 (1985) 10BROAD36 (1985)	10BASE-T (1990) 10PASS-TS (2003)	10BASE-FL (1993) 10BASE-FP (1993) 10BASE-FB (1993)
100 Mbps		100BASE-TX (1995) 100BASE-T4 (1995) 100BASE-T2 (1997)	100BASE-FX (1995) 100BASE-LX/BX10 (2003)
1 Gbps		1000BASE-CX (1998) 1000BASE-T (1999)	1000BASE-SX (1998) 1000BASE-LX (1998) 1000BASE-LX/BX10 (2003) 1000BASE-PX10/20 (2003)
10 Gbps		10GBASE-T (2006)	10GBASE-R (2002) 10GBASE-W (2002) 10GBASE-X (2002)

The Ethernet Nomenclature

Ethernet is rich in its physical specification, as presented in Table 3.3. The notation follows the format {1/10/100/1000/10G}{BASE/BROAD/PASS}[-]phy. The first item is the speed. The second item states whether the signaling is baseband or broadband. Almost all Ethernet signaling is *baseband,* except the old 10BROAD36 and 10PASS-TS. Originally the third item represented the maximum length in units of 100 m, with no dash in between the second and the third item. It had later been changed to indicate the physical specifications such as medium type and signal encoding, with a dash connecting it to the second item.

Historical Evolution: Competitors to Ethernet

Historically, there were a number of LAN technologies such as Token Ring, Token Bus, FDDI, DQDB, and ATM LAN emulation competing with Ethernet, but Ethernet eventually stood out above others in wired LAN systems. A fundamental reason behind Ethernet's success is that Ethernet is simpler than other technologies, and simplicity means lower cost. People do not want to pay more than what is necessary, and in this regard Ethernet certainly wins.

Why is Ethernet cheaper than others? Ethernet lacks fancy functions that the other technologies can offer, such as priority, mechanisms for quality of service, and central control. Hence Ethernet does not need to handle tokens, and neither does it have the complexities of joining and leaving a ring. CSMA/CD is quite simple and can be easily implemented into hardware logic (see Open Source Implementation 3.5). Full duplex is even simpler. This advantage makes Ethernet the winner.

However, Ethernet still encounters a number of competitors for the time being. The strongest one among them is the wireless LAN. Wireless LAN has higher mobility, the characteristic that Ethernet does not possess. Wherever mobility is needed, wireless LAN wins. However, when mobility is unnecessary, e.g., using a desktop computer, Ethernet is still the choice since most motherboards have built-in Ethernet interfaces. On the other hand, Ethernet also attempts to extend itself to first-mile and WAN technologies. Given the large installation bases of existing xDSL and SONET technologies, we think it will take a long time for Ethernet to gradually replace them if the replacement eventually happens. However, for the same reason Ethernet is so popular, if the existing installations are cheap and satisfactory, the replacement may never happen.

3.3.2 The Ethernet MAC

Ethernet Framing, Addressing, and Error Control

The 802.3 MAC sublayer is the medium-independent part of Ethernet. Along with the *Logical Link Control* (LLC) sublayer specified in IEEE 802.2, they compose the data-link layer in the OSI layer model. The functions associated with the MAC sublayer

	Preamble	SFD	DA	SA	T/L	Data	FCS
bytes	7	1	6	6	2	46-1500	4

SFD: Start of Frame Delimit DA: Destination Address SA: Source Address T/L: Type length
FCS: Frame Check Sequence

FIGURE 3.14 Ethernet frame format.

include data encapsulation and media access control, and those for the LLC sublayer are intended to be common interfaces for Ethernet, Token Ring, WLAN, and so on. Linux also implements the latter part in functions like bridge configuration, since the configuration frames are specified in the LLC format (See Section 3.6). Figure 3.14 presents the untagged[4] Ethernet frame. Through the frame format, we first introduce Ethernet framing, addressing, and error control, and we leave issues of medium access control and flow control to a later discussion.

Preamble: This field synchronizes the physical signal timing on the receiver side. Its value is fixed at 1010…1010 in the transmission order,[5] 56 bits long. Note that the frame boundary may be marked by special physical encoding or by the absence of the signal, depending on what is specified in the PHY. For example, 100BASE-X Ethernet converts the first byte of the preamble, /1010/1010/, into two special code groups /J/K/ of the value /11000/10001/ using 4B/5B encoding. The 4B/5B encoding converts the normal data value 1010 (in the transmission order) to 01011 to avoid ambiguity. Similarly, 100BASE-X appends two special code groups /T/R/ of the value /01101/10001/ to mark a frame end.

SFD: This field indicates the start of the frame with the value 10101011 in the transmission order. Historically, the DIX Ethernet standard specified an 8-byte preamble with exactly the same value as the first two fields in an 802.3 frame, but they differed only in nomenclature.

DA: This field includes the 48-bit destination MAC address in the format introduced in Subsection 3.1.2.

SA: This field includes the 48-bit source MAC address.

Type/Length: This field has two meanings, for historical reasons. The DIX standard specified this field to be a code of payload protocol type, say IP, while the IEEE 802.3 standard specified this field to be the length of the *data* field[6] and left the protocol type to the LLC sublayer. The 802.3 standard later (in 1997) approved the type field, resulting in the *dual* interpretations of this field today. The way to distinguish them is simple: Because the data field is never larger than 1500 bytes, a value less than or equal to *1500* means a

[4] An Ethernet frame can carry a VLAN tag. We shall see that frame format when we cover VLAN in Section 3.5.

[5] Ethernet transmission is in Little-Endian bit ordering which is clarified in the Pitfalls and Misleading.

[6] There is a wide misconception that the length field indicates the frame size. This is not true. The frame end is marked by special physical encoding or the absence of signal. The Ethernet MAC can easily *count* how many bytes it has received in a frame.

length field and a value larger than or equal to *1536* (=0x600) means a type field. Although the purposes are different, these two interpretations can coexist due to the easy distinction mentioned above. The values in between are intentionally not defined. Most frames use this field as the type field because the dominating network layer protocol, IP, uses it as the type field.

Data: This field carries the data varying from 46 to 1500 bytes.

FCS: This field carries a 32-bit CRC code as a frame check sequence. If the receiver finds an incorrect frame, it discards the frame silently. The transmitter knows nothing about whether the frame is discarded. The responsibility of frame retransmission is left to upper-layer protocols such as TCP. This approach is quite efficient because the transmitter does not need to wait for an acknowledgment in order to start the next transmission. The error is not a big problem here because the bit error rate is assumed to be very low in the Ethernet physical layer.

The frame size is variable. We often *exclude* the first two fields and say an Ethernet frame has the minimum length of 64 (=6+6+2+46+4) bytes and the maximum length of 1518 (=6+6+2+1500+4) bytes.

Medium Access Control: Transmission and Reception Flow

We now show how a frame is transmitted and received inside the Ethernet MAC, and you shall see how CSMA/CD works in great detail. Figure 3.15 shows what role the MAC sublayer plays during the frame transmission and reception.

CSMA/CD works in a simple way, as its name implies. With a frame to transmit, CSMA/CD *senses* the cable first. If a carrier signal is sensed, i.e., the cable is busy, it continues sensing the cable until the cable becomes idle; otherwise, it waits for a small gap, and then transmits. If a *collision* is detected during transmission, CSMA/CD *jams* the cable, *aborts* the transmission, and waits for a random *back-off* time interval before retrying. Figure 3.16 presents the transmission flow, and the exact procedure following. Note that on *full-duplex* links, carrier sense and collision detection effectively disappear.

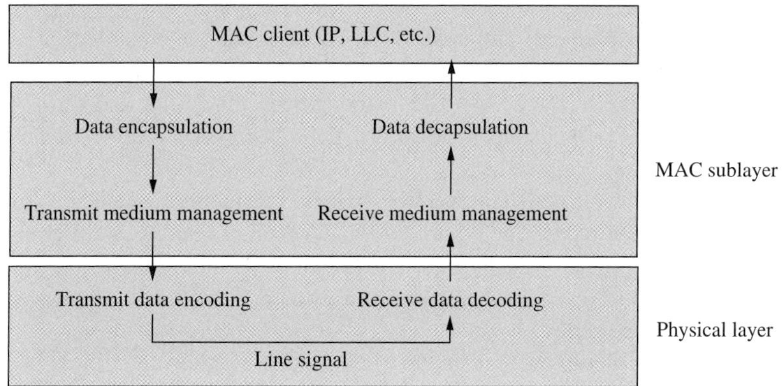

FIGURE 3.15 Frame transmission and reception in the MAC sublayer.

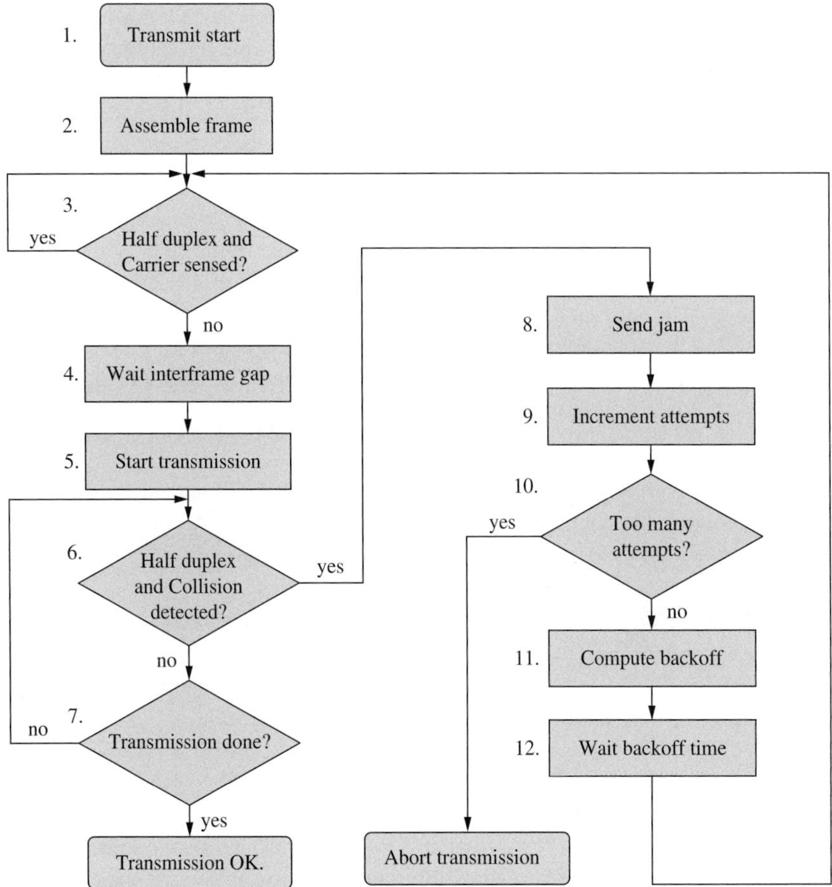

FIGURE 3.16 Frame transmission flow of CSMA/CD.

1. The MAC client (IP, LLC, etc.) asks for frame transmission.
2. The MAC sublayer prepends and appends MAC information (preamble, SFD, DA, SA, type, and FCS) to the data from the MAC client.
3. In the half-duplex mode, the CSMA/CD method senses the carrier to determine whether the transmission channel is busy. If so, the transmission is deferred until the channel is clear.
4. Wait for a period of time called *inter-frame gap* (IFG). The time length is 96 bit times for all Ethernet types. The *bit time* is the duration of one bit transmission and thus is the reciprocal of the bit rate. The IFG allows time for the receiver to do processing such as interrupts and pointer adjustment for incoming frames.
5. Start to transmit the frame.
6. In the half-duplex mode, the transmitter should keep monitoring if there is a collision during transmission. The monitoring method depends on the attached medium. Multiple transmissions on a coaxial cable result in higher absolute

voltage levels than normal. For twisted pairs, a collision is asserted by perceiving a received signal on the receive pair while transmitting the frame.

7. In case no collision is detected during transmission, the frame is transmitted until done. If a collision is detected in the half-duplex mode, proceed with steps 8–12.
8. The transmitter transmits a 32-bit-long *jam* signal to ensure that the collision is long enough that all involved stations are aware of it. The pattern of the jam signal is unspecified. Common implementations are to keep transmitting 32 more data bits or to use the circuit that generates the preamble to transmit alternating 1's and 0's.
9. Abort the current transmission and attempt to schedule another transmission!
10. The maximum number of attempts to retransmit is 16. If still not able to transmit, abort the frame.
11. On an attempt to retransmit, a back-off time interval in units of slots is chosen randomly from the range of 0 to $2^k - 1$, where $k = min(n, 10)$ and n is the number of attempts. The range grows exponentially, so the algorithm is referred to as *truncated binary exponential back-off*. The duration of a time slot is 512 bit times for 10/100 Mbps Ethernet and 4096 bit times for 1 Gbps Ethernet. We shall talk about the reason behind the choice of the time-slot duration when we discuss Gigabit Ethernet in Subsection 3.3.3.
12. Wait the back-off time interval and then attempt to retransmit.

Receiving a frame is much easier when a sequence of checks is done on the frame length (check if the frame is too short or too long), destination MAC address, FCS, and octet boundary before passing it to the MAC client. Figure 3.17 illustrates the reception flow. The procedure follows.

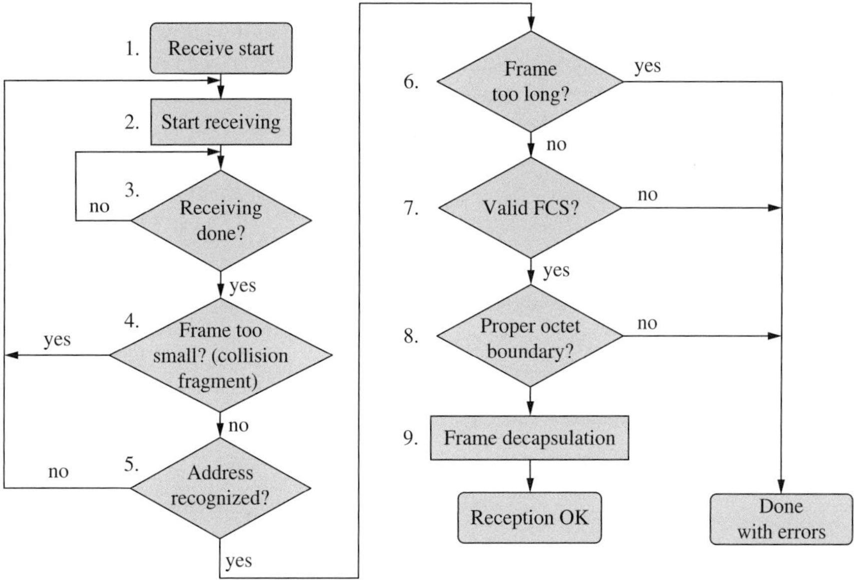

FIGURE 3.17 Frame reception flow of CSMA/CD.

1. The arrival of a frame is detected by the physical layer of the receiver.
2. The receiver decodes the received signal and passes the data, except the preamble and SFD, up to the MAC sublayer.
3. The receiving process goes on as long as the received signal continues. When the signal ceases, the incoming frame is truncated to an octet boundary.
4. If the frame is too short (shorter than 512 bits), it is treated as a collision fragment and dropped.
5. If the destination address is not for the receiver, the frame is dropped.
6. If the frame is too long, it is dropped and the error is recorded for management statistics.
7. If the frame has an incorrect FCS, it is dropped and the error is recorded.
8. If the frame size is not an integer number of octets, it is dropped and the error is recorded.
9. If everything is OK, the frame is de-capsulated and the fields are passed up to the MAC client.

Can Collision Cause Bad Performance?

The term *collision* sounds terrible! However, collision is part of the normal arbitration mechanism of CSMA/CD and not a result of system malfunction. Collision can cause a garbled frame, but it is not so bad if the transmission can be stopped when a collision is detected. Before further analyzing the wasted bit times caused by a collision, we first answer a critical question: Where can a collision occur? We answer this question with the frame transmission model in Figure 3.18.

Suppose Station A transmits a minimum frame of 64 bytes, and the propagation time before the frame's first bit arrives at station B is t. Even with carrier sense, Station B is likely to transmit anytime before t and cause a collision. Further, suppose the worst-case scenario in which Station B transmits right at time t, which results in a collision. The collision then takes another t to propagate back to station A. If Station A finishes transmitting the minimum frame before the round-trip time $2t$ expires, it has no chance to invoke collision detection and to schedule a retransmission, and thus the frame is lost. For CSMA/CD to function normally, the round-trip time should be *less*

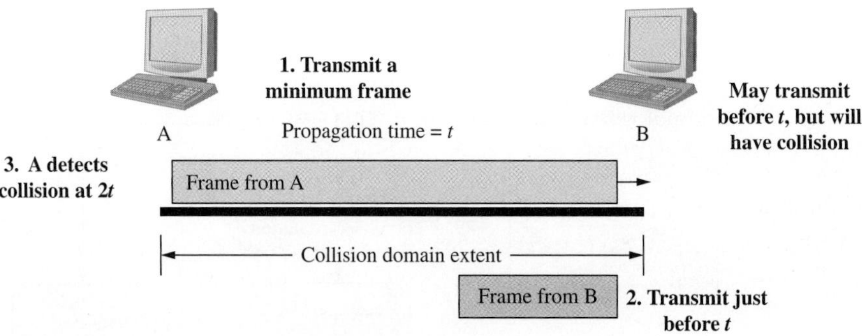

FIGURE 3.18 Collision detection with propagation delay.

than the time required to transmit a minimum frame, meaning the CSMA/CD mechanism limits the extent between two stations in a *collision domain*. This limitation complicates the half-duplex Gigabit Ethernet design, and we shall talk more about this issue when we introduce Gigabit Ethernet in Subsection 3.3.3. Because the minimum frame size is 64 bytes, it also means that a collision must occur during the first 64 bytes of a frame under the distance limitation. If more than 64 bytes have been transmitted, the chance of collision has been ruled out due to carrier sense by other stations.

If we take the 32-bit jam into consideration, the actual number of bits in a frame that have been transmitted plus the jam cannot exceed 511 bits, as described in step 4 of the frame reception flow, because 512 bits (= 64 bytes) is the minimum length of a normal frame. Otherwise, the receiver will think of these bits as a normal frame rather than a collision fragment. Therefore, the maximum number of wasted bit times is 511 + 64 (from the preamble) + 96 (from the IFG) = 671. This is only a small portion for a large frame. In addition, we must emphasize that it is the worst case. Most collisions are detected during the preamble phase because the distance between two transmitting stations is not that far. In this case, the number of wasted bit times is only 64 (from the preamble) + 32 (from the jam) + 96 (from the IFG) = 192.

Maximum Frame Rate

How many frames can a transmitter (receiver) transmit (receive) in a second? This is an interesting question, especially when you design or analyze a packet processing device, say a switch, to find out how many frames per second your device may need to process.

Frame transmission begins with a 7-byte preamble and a 1-byte SFD. For a link to reach its maximum transmission rate in frames per second, all frames to be transmitted should be kept to the minimum size, i.e., 64 bytes. Do not forget the IFG of 12 bytes (= 96 bits) between two successive frame transmissions. In total, a frame transmission occupies $(7 + 1 + 64 + 12) \times 8 = 672$ bit times. In a 100 Mbps system, the maximum number of frames that can be transmitted each second is therefore $100 \times 10^6 / 672 = 148{,}800$. This value is referred to as the *maximum frame rate* for the 100 Mbps link. If a switch has 48 interface ports, the aggregated maximum frame rate would be $148{,}800 \times 48 = 7{,}140{,}400$; that is, over 7 million.

Full-Duplex MAC

Early Ethernet used coaxial cables as the transmission medium and connected stations into a bus topology. Twisted pairs have replaced most uses of coaxial cables due to ease of management. The dominant approach is to use a twisted-pair cable connecting each station with a concentration device such as a hub or switch to form a *star* topology. For popular 10BASE-T and 100BASE-TX, a wire *pair* in a twisted-pair cable is dedicated to either transmitting or receiving.[7] A collision is thus identified by perceiving a received signal on the receive pair while transmitting on

[7] In 1000BASE-T, transmission and reception can happen simultaneously in a pair. Arbitration is still not necessary at the cost of sophisticated DSP circuits to separate the two signals.

the transmit pair. However, this is still inefficient. Since the medium is dedicated to point-to-point communication in the star topology setting, why does the new Ethernet technology need collision as an "arbitration" method?

In 1997, the IEEE 802.3x Task Force added full-duplex operation in Ethernet—that is, transmission and reception can proceed at the same time. No carrier sense or collision detection is supported in the full duplex mode because they are not needed anymore—there is no "multiple access" on a dedicated medium. Therefore, CS, MA, and CD are all gone! Interestingly, this is quite a dramatic change in Ethernet design since Ethernet was known for its CSMA/CD. Three conditions should be satisfied in order to run full-duplex Ethernet:

1. The transmission medium must be capable of transmitting and receiving on *both* ends without interference.
2. The transmission medium should be dedicated for exactly two stations, forming a *point-to-point* link.
3. *Both* stations should be able to be configured into the full-duplex mode.

The IEEE 802.3 standard explicitly rules out the possibility of running the full-duplex mode on a repeater hub because the bandwidth in the hub is shared, not dedicated. Three typical scenarios of full-duplex transmission are the station-to-station link, the station-to-switch link, and the switch-to-switch link. In any case, these links need to be dedicated point-to-point links.

Full-duplex Ethernet in effect *doubles* the bandwidth between two stations. It also lifts the *distance* limitation that resulted from the use of CSMA/CD. This is very important to *high-speed* and *wide-area* transmission, as we shall discuss in Subsection 3.3.3. Nowadays, virtually all Ethernet interfaces support full duplex. Either communication party's interface can perform *autonegotiation* to determine whether both parties support full duplex. If so, both will operate in full duplex for higher efficiency.

Ethernet Flow Control

Flow control in Ethernet depends on the duplex mode. The half-duplex mode employs a technique called *false carrier,* by which if the receiver cannot afford more incoming frames, it can transmit a carrier, say a series of 1010…10, on the shared medium until it can afford more frames. The transmitter will sense the carrier and defer its subsequent transmission. Alternatively, the congested receiver can force a collision whenever a frame transmission is detected, causing the transmitter to back off and reschedule its transmission. This technique is referred to as *force collision*. Both techniques are collectively called *back pressure*.

However, back pressure is void in the full-duplex mode because CSMA/CD is no longer in use. IEEE 802.3 specifies a PAUSE frame for flow control in the full-duplex mode. The receiver explicitly sends a PAUSE frame to the transmitter, and upon receiving the PAUSE frame, the transmitter stops transmitting immediately. The PAUSE frame carries a field, `pause_time`, to tell the transmitter how long it should halt its transmission. Since it is not easy to estimate the pause time in advance, in practice `pause_time` is set to the maximum value to stop the transmission, and another PAUSE frame with `pause_time` = 0 is sent to the transmitter to resume the transmitter's transmission when the receiver can accept more frames.

Flow control is optional in Ethernet. It can be enabled by the user or through autonegotiation. IEEE 802.3 provides an optional sublayer between MAC and LLC, namely the MAC control sublayer, which defines MAC control frames to provide real-time manipulation of MAC sublayer operation. The PAUSE frame is a kind of MAC control frame.

Open Source Implementation 3.5: CSMA/CD

Overview

CSMA/CD is part of the Ethernet MAC, and most of the Ethernet MAC is implemented in hardware. An open source Ethernet example is available from OPENCORE (www.opencores.org), which presents a *synthesizable* Verilog code. By synthesizable, we mean the Verilog code is complete enough to be compiled through a series of tools into a circuit. It provides the implementation of the layer-2 protocol according to the IEEE specifications for 10 Mbps and 100 Mbps Ethernet.

Block Diagram

Figure 3.19 illustrates the architecture of OPENCORE Ethernet Core, which mainly consists of host interface, transmit (TX) module, receive (RX) module, MAC control module, and media independent interface (MII) management module. They are described as follows:

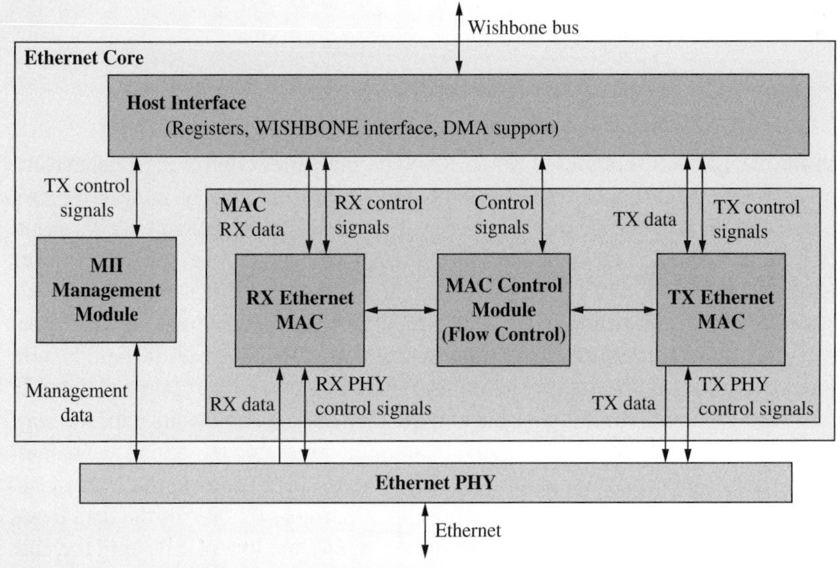

FIGURE 3.19 Architecture of Ethernet MAC core.

Continued

1. The TX and RX modules enable all transmit and receive functionalities. These modules handle preamble generation and removal. Both modules incorporate the CRC generators for error detection. In addition, the TX module conducts the random time generation used in the back-off process and monitors the `CarrierSense` and `Collision` signals to exercise the main body of CSMA/CD.
2. The MAC control module provides full-duplex flow control, which transfers the PAUSE control frames between the communicating stations. Therefore, the MAC control module supports control frame detection and generation, interfaces to TX and RX MAC, PAUSE timer, and Slot timer.
3. The MII management module implements the standard of IEEE 802.3 MII, which provides the interconnections between the Ethernet PHY and MAC layers. Through the MII interface, the processor can force Ethernet PHY to run at 10 Mbps or 100 Mbps, and configure it to perform in full- or half-duplex mode. The MII management module has the submodules for operation controller, shift registers, output control module, and clock generator.
4. The host interface is a WISHBONE (WB) bus connecting the Ethernet MAC to the processor and external memory. The WB is an interconnection specification of OPENCORE projects, and only DMA transfers are supported for data transfer so far. The host interface also has status and register modules. The status module records the statuses written to the related buffer descriptors. The register module is used for Ethernet MAC operations, and it includes configuration registers, DMA operation, and transmit status and receive status.

Data Structures and Algorithm Implementations

State Machines: TX and RX

In the TX and RX modules, TX and RX state machines control their behaviors, respectively. Figure 3.20 presents both state machines. We only describe the behaviors of the TX state machine here, since the RX state machine works similarly. The TX state machine starts from the `Defer` state, waits until the carrier is absent (i.e., the `CarrierSense` signal is false), and then enters the `IFG` state. After the inter-frame gap (IFG), the TX state machine enters the `Idle` state, waiting for a transmission request from the WB interface. If there is still no carrier present, the state machine goes to the `Preamble` state and starts a transmission; otherwise, it goes back to the `Defer` state and waits until the carrier is absent again. In the `Preamble` state, the preamble 0x5555555 and start frame delimiter 0xd are sent, and the TX state machine goes to the `Data[0]` and `Data[1]` states to transmit nibbles, i.e., in units of 4 bits, of the data byte. The nibble transmission starts from the least significant byte (LSB) until the end of the frame, and each time a byte is transmitted, the TX state machine tells the Wishbone interface to provide the next data byte to transmit.

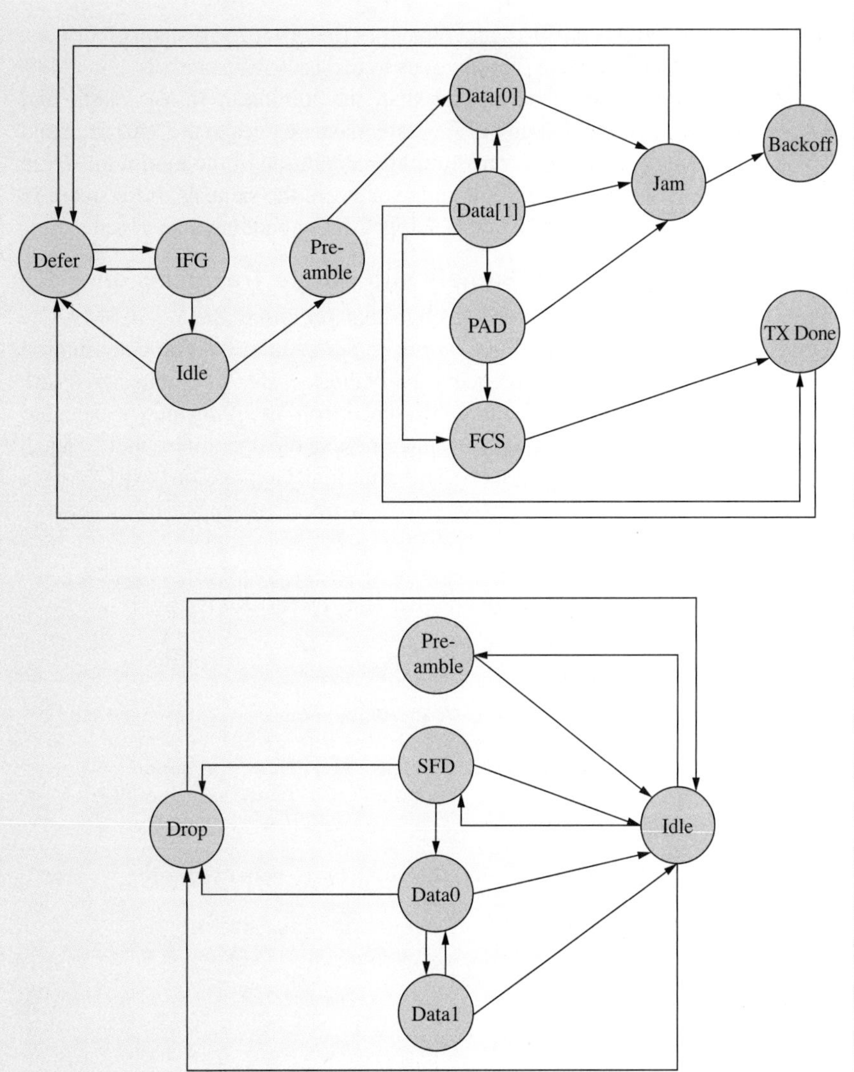

FIGURE 3.20 The TX (upper) and RX (lower) state machines.

- If a collision occurs during transmission, the TX state machine goes to the `Jam` state to send a jam signal, waits for a period of backoff time in the `Backoff` state, and then goes back to the `Defer` state for the next transmission attempt.
- When only one byte is left to be sent (no collision during transmission),
  1. If the total frame length is greater than or equal to the minimum frame length, then the TX state machine enters the `FCS` state to calculate the 32-bit CRC value from the data and append the value to the end of the

Continued

frame if CRC is enabled, and then goes to the TxDone state; otherwise, the TX state machine directly goes to the TxDone state.

2. If the frame length is shorter than the minimum frame length and padding is enabled, then the TX state machine goes to the PAD state and the data is padded with zeros until the condition of the minimum frame length is satisfied. The remaining states are the same as those stated in (1). However, the PAD state is skipped when padding is disabled.

Programming CSMA/CD Signals and Nibble Transmission

Figure 3.21 is a segment of Verilog code that *programs* the key CSMA/CD signals and nibble transmission. An *output signal* is an arithmetic combination of various *input signals,* updated once in every *clock cycle*. All output signals are updated in *parallel*, which is the key difference from the *sequentially* executed software code. The symbols ~, &, |, ^ , and = denote the operations "not," "and," "or," "xor," and "assign," respectively. The conditional expression "exp1 ? exp2 :

```
CSMA/CD Signals
assign StartDefer = StateIFG & ~Rule1 & CarrierSense & NibCnt[6:0]
<= IPGR1 & NibCnt[6:0] != IPGR2
| StateIdle & CarrierSense
| StateJam & NibCntEq7 & (NoBckof | RandomEq0 | ~ColWindow |
RetryMax)
| StateBackOff & (TxUnderRun | RandomEqByteCnt)
| StartTxDone | TooBig;
assign StartDefer = StateIdle & ~TxStartFrm & CarrierSense
              | StateBackOff & (TxUnderRun | RandomEqByteCnt);
assign StartData[1] = ~Collision & StateData[0] & ~TxUnderRun &
                    ~MaxFrame;
assign StartJam = (Collision | UnderRun) & ((StatePreamble
  & NibCntEq15)
             |(StateData[1:0]) | StatePAD | StateFCS);
assign StartBackoff = StateJam & ~RandomEq0 & ColWindow &
~RetryMax & NibCntEq7 & ~NoBckof;

Nibble transmission
always @ (StatePreamble or StateData or StateData or StateFCS or
StateJam or StateSFD or TxData or Crc or NibCnt or NibCntEq15)
begin
if(StateData[0]) MTxD_d[3:0] = TxData[3:0];    // Lower nibble
else if(StateData[1]) MTxD_d[3:0] = TxData[7:4]; // Higher nibble
else if(StateFCS) MTxD_d[3:0]={~Crc[28],~Crc[29],~Crc[30],
~Crc[31]}; // Crc
else if(StateJam)     MTxD_d[3:0] = 4'h9;      // Jam pattern
else if(StatePreamble)
if(NibCntEq15)      MTxD_d[3:0] = 4'hd;    // SFD
else       MTxD_d[3:0] = 4'h5;               // Preamble
     else      MTxD_d[3:0] = 4'h0;
end
```

FIGURE 3.21 CSMA/CD signals and nibble transmission.

exp3" has exactly the same meaning (i.e., if the result of exp1 is true, exp2 is evaluated; otherwise, exp3 is evaluated) as that in the C language.

A station in the half-duplex mode observes the activity on the PHY media. Besides the carrier due to the transmission of a frame, a collision resulting from simultaneous transmission of more than one station (denoted by the `Collision` variable) is also observed. If a collision occurs, all stations stop transmitting, set `StartJam` (entering the `Jam` state) and back off for a random time (`StartBackOff` is set) in the `Backoff` state. The state machine may go back to the `Defer` state if the carrier is present in the `Jam` state or the `Backoff` state.

The code under "nibble transmission" selects the nibble (4 bits) to be transmitted based on which state the TX machine is in. The TX state machine switches between the `Data[0]` and `Data[1]` states during little-endian transmission, so `MTxD_d`, the transmit data nibble, is loaded with `TxData[3:0]` and `TxData[7:4]` alternatively. In the `FCS` state, the CRC value is loaded nibble by nibble, as the CRC calculation is implemented with the `crc` shift register. In the `Jam` state, the arbitrary hex value of 1001 (i.e., 4′h9) is loaded as the jam signal, though the content of the jam signal is unspecified in the 802.3 standard. In the `Preamble` state, the preamble 0x5555555 and start frame delimiter 0xd are loaded in turn.

Since the TX module starts the backoff process after a collision has been detected, it waits for some duration derived from a pseudorandom, as shown in Figure 3.22. The "binary exponential" algorithm is applied to generate a random backoff time within the predefined restriction. An element `x[i]` in the array `x`

```
assign Random [0] = x[0];
assign Random [1] = (RetryCnt > 1) ? x[1] : 1'b0;
assign Random [2] = (RetryCnt > 2) ? x[2] : 1'b0;
assign Random [3] = (RetryCnt > 3) ? x[3] : 1'b0;
assign Random [4] = (RetryCnt > 4) ? x[4] : 1'b0;
assign Random [5] = (RetryCnt > 5) ? x[5] : 1'b0;
assign Random [6] = (RetryCnt > 6) ? x[6] : 1'b0;
assign Random [7] = (RetryCnt > 7) ? x[7] : 1'b0;
assign Random [8] = (RetryCnt > 8) ? x[8] : 1'b0;
assign Random [9] = (RetryCnt > 9) ? x[9] : 1'b0;
always @ (posedge MTxClk or posedge Reset)
begin
  if(Reset)
    RandomLatched <= 10'h000;
  else
   begin
     if(StateJam & StateJam _ q)
      RandomLatched <= Random;
   end
end
assign RandomEq0 = RandomLatched == 10'h0;
```

FIGURE 3.22 Backoff random generator.

Continued

is a random bit with value 0 or 1, and the array `x` can be viewed as the binary representation of a 10-bit random value (total 10 bits, as the range of the random number is from 0 to 2^k-1, where `k = min(n, 10)` and `n` is the number of retrials.) According to each statement in Figure 3.22, when `RetryCnt` is larger than `i`, `Random[i]` may be set to 1 if `x[i] = 1`; otherwise, `Random[i]` is set to 0 by assigning bit 0 (denoted by 1'b0) to it. In other words, one more high-bit in the random values is likely to be set to 1 when `RetryCnt` is increased by one, which means the range of the random values grows exponentially with the number of retrials. After the random value is derived, it will be latched into the `RandomLatched` variable if the transmission channel is jammed (judged from the `StateJam` and `StateJam_q` variables), e.g., due to collision. If the random value happens to be 0 (i.e., backoff time is 0), the `RandomEq0` variable is set and the backoff procedure will not be started (`StartBackoff` is false in the last assign statement of Figure 3.21).

Exercises

1. If the Ethernet MAC operates in the full-duplex mode (very common at present), which components in the design should be disabled?
2. Since the full-duplex mode has a simpler design than the half-duplex mode, and the former's efficiency is higher than the latter's, why do we still bother implementing half-duplex mode in the Ethernet MAC?

Historical Evolution: Power-Line Networking: HomePlug

Ethernet is a dominant technology for LANs, but it demands to deploy network cables from one node to another for wired connection. Although wireless LAN can eliminate the wires completely, the wireless signals are subject to various interferences and are less stable. A less popular but useful solution between the former two technologies, HomePlug, leverages the power lines to transmit data. Ethernet cables can be hooked up to a power-line adapter, which is then plugged into a power outlet. The other device can also do the same to finish the connection, and the data is transmitted via the power-line infrastructure. The infrastructure is commonly available in ordinary homes, so no extra lines are needed between two power outlets.

HomePlug relies on the OFDM modulation over the power lines. The HomePlug 1.0 specification allows for speeds up to 14 Mbit/s in half-duplex. A proprietary solution allows up to 85 Mbps in the turbo mode. A later specification boosts the speed to 189 Mbps. The solution could be a cheap alternative to the deployment of wires in ordinary homes or offices.

TABLE 3.4 Physical Specifications of Gigabit Ethernet

Task Forces	Specification Name	Description
IEEE 802.3z (1998)	1000BASE-CX	25 m 2-pair shielded twisted pairs (STP) with 8B/10B encoding
	1000BASE-SX	Multi-mode fiber of short-wave laser with 8B/10B encoding
	1000BASE-LX	Multi- or single-mode fiber of long-wave laser with 8B/10B encoding
IEEE 802.3ab (1999)	1000BASE-T	100 m 4-pair Category 5 (or better) unshielded twisted pairs (UTP) with 8B1Q4

3.3.3 Selected Topics in Ethernet

Gigabit Ethernet

The task of creating specifications for Gigabit Ethernet was originally divided between two task forces: 802.3z and 803.3ab. A later task force for Ethernet in the First Mile (EFM) also specified three new PHYs running at the gigabit rate. For clarity, we leave the latter part to our discussion of EFM. Table 3.4 lists only the specifications in 802.3z and 803.3ab.

A difficulty in Gigabit Ethernet design is the distance restriction of CSMA/CD, which is not a problem for 10 Mbps and 100 Mbps Ethernet. The distance is about 200 m for copper connection in 100 Mbps Ethernet, and it is enough for normal configurations. The distance is even longer for 10 Mbps Ethernet. However, Gigabit Ethernet transmits ten times faster than 100 Mbps Ethernet does, making the distance restriction ten times shorter. A restriction of about 20 m is unacceptable for many network deployments, and an objective of Gigabit Ethernet is to lift the distance restriction with the frame format (i.e., the minimum frame size) unchanged.

The IEEE 802.3 standard appends a series of *extension bits* after a frame to ensure the frame transmission time exceeds the round-trip time. These bits can be any nondata symbols in the physical layer. The technique, called *carrier extension,* in effect extends the frame length without changing the minimum frame size. Nevertheless, the resultant throughput is poor despite the technique's good intent. In contrast, full-duplex Ethernet does not need CSMA/CD at all, making this solution unnecessary. Full-duplex Ethernet's implementation is simpler than half-duplex Ethernet. The throughput is much higher, and the restriction on distance is no longer a concern. Why do we bother implementing half-duplex Gigabit Ethernet if it is unnecessary? Gigabit Ethernet switches can support full duplex, and they are cheaper than ever with the advance of ASIC technology that implements the switching function. For the deployment of Gigabit Ethernet, it is the performance rather than the cost that is of concern now. The market has proved the failure of half-duplex Gigabit Ethernet since only full-duplex Gigabit Ethernet products exist on the market nowadays.

10 Gigabit Ethernet

Just like *Moore's Law,* which states that the power of microprocessors doubles every 18 months, the speed of Ethernet has also grown exponentially since its early days. The 10 Gigabit Ethernet standard developed by the IEEE 802.3ae Task Force came out in 2002. It was later extended to operate on twisted pairs in 2006, 10GBASE-T. The 10 Gigabit Ethernet bears the following features:

Full duplex only: The IEEE 802.3 people learned a lesson from the development of Gigabit Ethernet: Only the full-duplex mode is in the 10 Gigabit Ethernet; the half-duplex mode is not even considered.

Compatibility with past standards: The frame format and the MAC operations remain unchanged, making the interoperability with existing products rather easy.

Move toward the WAN market: Since Gigabit Ethernet has moved toward the MAN market, 10 Gigabit Ethernet will go further into the WAN market. On one hand, the longest distance in the new standard is 40 km; on the other hand, a WAN PHY is defined to interface with OC-192 (OC: Optical Carrier) in the synchronous optical networking *(SONET)* infrastructure, which operates at a rate very close to 10 gigabit. The IEEE 802.3ae comes with an optional WAN PHY besides the LAN PHY. Both PHYs have the same transmission media, and thus the same transmission distance. The difference is that the WAN PHY has a *WAN Interface Sublayer* (WIS) in the *Physical Coding Sublayer* (PCS). The WIS is a framer that maps an Ethernet frame into a SONET payload, which simplifies the task of attaching Ethernet to OC-192 devices.

Table 3.5 lists the physical specifications in IEEE802.ae. The character "W" in the code names denotes a WAN PHY, which can be directly connected to an OC-192 interface. The others are for LAN only. Every physical specification except 10GBASE-LX4 uses a complex 64B/66B block coding. 10GBASE-LX4 uses

TABLE 3.5 Physical Specifications in the IEEE 802.3ae

Code Name	Wave Length	Transmission Distance (m)
10GBASE-LX4	1310 nm	300
10GBASE-SR	850 nm	300
10GBASE-LR	1310 nm	10,000
10GBASE-ER	1550 nm	10,000
10GBASE-SW	850 nm	300
10GBASE-LW	1310 nm	10,000
10GBASE-EW	1550 nm	40,000

Historical Evolution: Backbone Networking: SONET/SDH and MPLS

SONET and SDH are multiplexing protocols over optical fibers. SONET stands for *synchronous optical network*, and SDH stands for *synchronous digital hierarchy*. The former is used in the United States and Canada, and the latter is for the rest of world. The carrier level of SONET is denoted by OC-x, the line rate of which is roughly 51.8*x Mbps. Therefore, the line rate of OC-3 is roughly 155 Mbps, and that of OC-12 is roughly 622 Mbps, and so on. High-speed SONET/SDH, such as OC-192 at roughly 10 Gbps, is usually deployed in the backbone.

Due to the large infrastructure of SONET/SDH, it is difficult to replace it with Ethernet rapidly. This is why 10 Gigabit Ethernet supports the so-called WAN PHY, which can be *directly* connected to an OC-192 interface. Therefore, it is feasible to make 10 Gigabit Ethernet *coexist* with the existing SONET/SDH infrastructure.

To forward packets in such high-speed networks, multi-protocol label switching (MPLS) allows an edge router to tag packets with *labels*, and the core routers can just examine the labels for packet forwarding. This mechanism is faster than expensive IP longest prefix match in ordinary routers, as we shall see in Chapter 4.

8B/10B blocking coding, and relies on four wavelength division multiplexing (WDM) channels to achieve a 10 Gbps transmission rate. Except for the first batch of 10 gigabit specifications in IEEE 802.3ae, later specifications such as 10GBASE-CX4 and 10GBASE-T allow even *copper wires* to transmit at 10 Gbps. An extension to Ethernet Passive Optical Network (EPON) running at 10 Gbps has also been under development since 2008.

Ethernet in the First Mile

We see Ethernet dominating the wired LAN, and are seeing it taking over the WAN, but how about the interface between LAN and WAN? Given abundant bandwidth on both the LAN and WAN, you might still access Internet at home through ADSL, cable modems, and so on. The segment of the subscriber access network between LAN and WAN, also called the *first mile* or *last mile,* may become the bottleneck of an end-to-end connection. The protocol conversion due to the use of different technologies in LAN, first mile, and WAN incurs nontrivial overhead. With the popularity of subscriber access network, this potential market becomes highly noticeable to Ethernet developers.

An effort in the IEEE 802.3ah *Ethernet in the First Mile (EFM)* Task Force defined a standard for this market. If Ethernet could be everywhere in the wired networks, no protocol conversion would be needed, which also would reduce the overall overhead cost. All in all, the standard is expected to provide a cheap and fast

TABLE 3.6 Physical Specifications in the IEEE 802.3ah

Code Name	Description
100BASE-LX10	100 Mbps on a pair of optical fibers up to 10 km
100BASE-BX10	100 Mbps on an optical fiber up to 10 km
1000BASE-LX10	1000 Mbps on a pair of optical fibers up to 10 km
1000BASE-BX10	1000 Mbps on an optical fiber up to 10 km
1000BASE-PX10	1000 Mbps on passive optical network up to 10 km
1000BASE-PX20	1000 Mbps on passive optical network up to 20 km
2BASE-TL	At least 2 Mbps over SHDSL up to 2700 m
10PASS-TS	At least 10 Mbps over VDSL up to 750 m

technology to the potentially broad first-mile market. Ethernet is poised to be ubiquitous, and the goals of the standard include the following:

New topologies: The requirements for the subscriber access network include point-to-point on fiber, point-to-multipoint on fiber, and point-to-point on copper. The standard meets these requirements.

New PHYs: Table 3.6 summarizes the PHYs in IEEE 802.3ah, including the following specifications:

Point-to-point optics: The PHYs are single-mode fibers from one point to the other. They include 100BASE-LX10, 100BASE-BX10, 1000BASE-LX10, and 1000BASE-BX10, where LX denotes a pair of fibers and BX denotes a single fiber. Here 10 means the transmission distance is 10 km, which is longer than the maximum distance of 5 km in IEEE 802.3z Gigabit Ethernet.

Point-to-multipoint optics: In this topology, a single point serves multiple premises. In the branch is a passive optical splitter that is not powered, so the topology is also called passive optical network (PON). The PHYs include 1000BASE-PX10 and 1000BASE-PX20. The former can transmit 10 km, while the latter can transmit up to 20 km. Another effort to push Ethernet PON up to the 10 Gbps transmission rate is ongoing in IEEE 802.3av. Zheng and Mouftah in 2005 gave an overview of the media access control in Ethernet PON.

Point-to-point copper: The PHYs are for nonloaded, voice grade copper cables. The PHYs include 2BASE-TL and 10PASS-TS. The former is at least 2 Mbps up to 2700 m over SHDSL, and the latter is at least 10 Mbps up to 750 m over VDSL. They are more economical solutions if the optical fibers are unavailable.

Far-end operations, administration, and maintenance (OAM): Reliability is critical to the subscriber access network. For easy OAM, the standard defines new methods for remote failure indication, remote loopback, and link monitoring.

Historical Evolution: First-Mile Networking: xDSL and Cable Modem

The various *digital subscriber line* (DSL) technologies provide data transmission over the old telephone lines. Since telephone lines are ubiquitous, the DSL technologies are also very popular. The letter "x" in xDSL denotes a type in the DSL technologies, including ADSL for *asymmetric DSL,* vDSL for *very high-speed* DSL, SHDSL for *symmetric high-speed DSL,* and so on. Due to their popularity, even the point-to-point copper in the EFM leverages the technology of SHDSL and vDSL in the physical layer, while keeping Ethernet frames in the link layer.

Among the types of DSL technologies, ADSL is the most popular. ADSL provides different speeds for downstream and upstream. The downstream speed is up to 24 Mbps, and the upstream speed is up to 3.5 Mbps, depending on the distance from the ADSL modem to the local telephone office. vDSL is also popular for the application of fiber-to-the-block (FTTB), since the cost of fiber-to-the-home (FTTH) is high. The fiber can reach a street cabinet close to the homes, from which the vDSL is deployed. Since the distance of copper wires is short, the speed could be very high, up to 100 Mbps in the latest vDSL2 standard.

In contrast to xDSL, which transmits data via phone lines, cable modems are based on the data over cable service interface specification (DOCSIS), which is the standard that specifies data transmission via the cable TV system. The upstream and downstream throughput is around 30 to 40 Mbps. Although cable modems enjoy larger overall bandwidth and long distance due to their transmission media, the CATV cable, the bandwidth is *shared* among the CATV subscribers. In comparison, the xDSL users have *dedicated* bandwidth over the access network in the first mile. Both are still competing technologies.

3.4 WIRELESS LINKS

Wireless links are appealing because users are free from the distance constraints of wires, which may be inconvenient or expensive to deploy. However, wireless links feature characteristics different from wired links, imposing special requirements on the protocol design. We list these characteristics below.

Less reliability: Signals propagate in the air without any protection, making the transmission easily impaired by *interference, path loss,* or *multipath distortion*. Outside interference comes from nearby wireless signal sources. Microwave ovens and Bluetooth devices to wireless links are possible sources of noise because they all operate in the *unlicensed* ISM (industrial, scientific, and medical) band. Path loss is the *attenuation* that the signal undergoes as it propagates in the air. The attenuation is more serious than the one in the wire because the signal is distributed over the air rather than concentrated on a wired link. Multipath distortion results from *delayed* *parts* of the signal because they bounce off physical obstacles and thus travel through different paths to the receiver.

More mobility: Because there is no wire limiting the mobility of a station, the network topology of wireless networks may vary dynamically. Note that mobility and wireless are *different* concepts though they are often mentioned together. Wireless is not necessary for mobility. For example, a mobile station can be carried to a location and then plugged into a wired network. Mobility is also not necessary for wireless. For example, two high buildings can communicate with *fixed* wireless relay devices because wiring between them is too expensive. This example is quite common in network deployment.

Less power availability: Mobile stations are often battery powered, and they may sometimes be put into *sleep* mode to conserve power. If the receiver is in sleep mode, transmitters shall *buffer* the data until the receiver awakens to receive them.

Less security: All stations within the transmission range can easily eavesdrop on the data propagating in the air. Optional encryption and authentication mechanisms could keep the data secure from outside threats.

In this section, we select the IEEE 802.11 wireless LAN, Bluetooth, and WiMAX as the examples to introduce wireless links. We select these three because IEEE 802.11 undoubtedly dominates wireless local area network, Bluetooth dominates wireless personal area network, and WiMAX is promising in becoming popular in wireless metropolitan area network. Because of their dominance and importance, they can represent the technology of wireless links.

3.4.1 IEEE 802.11 Wireless LAN

WLAN Evolution

The IEEE 802.11 Working Group was established in 1990 to develop MAC and PHY specifications for wireless local area networks. The development process took so long that the first version of standards did not appear until 1997. Initially, three kinds of PHYs, infrared, *direct sequence spread spectrum (DSSS),* and *frequency-hopping spread spectrum (FHSS),* were specified to allow transmission at 1 Mbps and 2 Mbps. Spread spectrum techniques are intended to make signals robust against interference. It was later enhanced in two amendments, 802.11a and 802.11b, in 1999. IEEE 802.11b extends the DSSS system to a higher data rate at 5.5 Mbps and 11 Mbps. IEEE 802.11a specifies a new *orthogonal frequency division multiplexing (OFDM)* operating at the *5 GHz* band, as opposed to the 2.4 GHz band of previous standards. The data rate is increased significantly to 54 Mbps. However, these two standards are not compatible with each other. IEEE 802.11b products operating at 11 Mbps have been popular in the market. The 802.11g standard with OFDM also operates at 54 Mbps, and is compatible with 802.11b by using its modulation for backward compatibility. IEEE 802.11n, which could operate at 300 Mbps with MIMO-OFDM, features multiple transmitters and receivers with OFDM as described in Chapter 2.

Besides the ever-increasing speed in wireless LAN, IEEE 802.11 also enhances itself in terms of other functions. IEEE 802.11e defines a set of *QoS* functions for certain time-critical applications. IEEE 802.11*i* specifies an enhancement mechanism for *security* because the wired equivalent privacy (WEP) in the original 802.11 standard was proved to be insecure. Some standards under development are also interesting. IEEE 802.11*s* defines how devices in the ad hoc mode create a *mesh* network; IEEE 802.11*k* and IEEE 802.11*r* are for wireless *roaming*. The former provides information to find the most appropriate access point, while the latter allows connectivity of devices in motion and fast handoffs.

Building Blocks

The basic building block of an 802.11 wireless LAN is a *basic service set (BSS)*. A BSS is composed of stations capable of MAC and PHY that conform to the IEEE 802.11 standard. A standalone BSS is called an *independent BSS (IBSS),* or more often than not, is referred to as an *ad hoc network* because it is often formed without planning in advance. A minimum BSS contains only two stations. Multiple BSSs can be connected through a *distribution system (DS)*. The IEEE 802.11 standard does not mandate what the DS should be, but an Ethernet network is a commonly used DS. A DS and a BSS are connected through an *access point (AP)*. This extended network structure is called an *infrastructure*. Figure 3.23 illustrates the building blocks in wireless LAN. Figure 3.24 depicts the layering in the IEEE 802.11. The IEEE 802.11 PHYs consist of infrared, DSSS, FHSS, and OFDM, as described in Chapter 2. Above them is the MAC sublayer. We shall focus on the IEEE 802.11 MAC in this section. For issues on PHY, we encourage interested readers to refer to "Further Readings."

CSMA/CA

The IEEE 802.11 MAC allocates bandwidth with two major functions: *distributed coordination function (DCF)* and *point coordination function (PCF)*. The DCF is

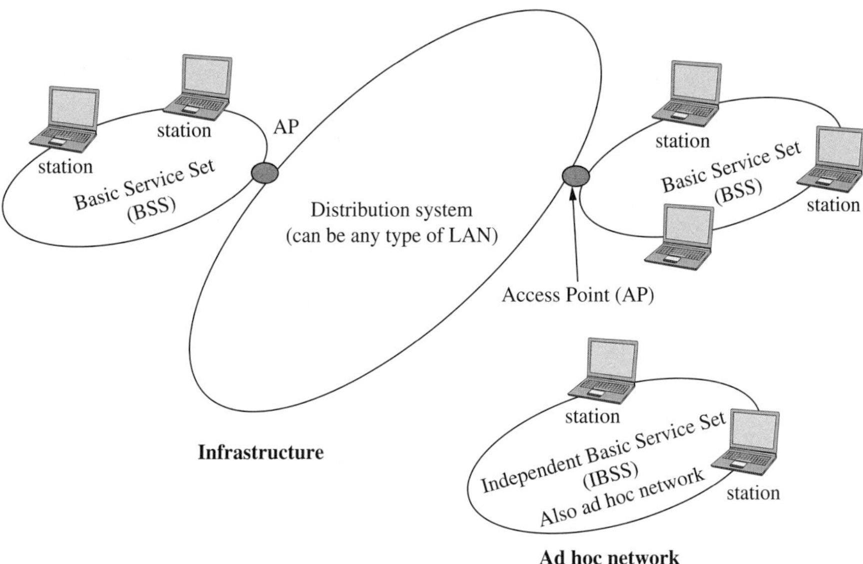

FIGURE 3.23 IEEE 802.11 building blocks in wireless LAN.

802.2 LLC				Data link layer
802.11 MAC				
FHSS	DSSS	IR	OFDM	Physical layer

FHSS: Frequency Hopping Spread Spectrum
DSSS: Direct Sequence Spread Spectrum
OFDM: Orthogonal Frequency Division Multiplexing
IR: Infrared

FIGURE 3.24 Layering in the IEEE 802.11.

mandatory in IEEE 802.11. The PCF is performed only in an infrastructure network. Both coordination functions can operate within the same BSS simultaneously.

The philosophy behind DCF is known as *carrier sense multiple access with collision avoidance (CSMA/CA)*. The most noticeable difference from the Ethernet MAC is the collision avoidance. As with CSMA/CD, a station must listen before transmitting. If a station is transmitting, other stations will be deferred until the channel is free. Once the channel is clear, the station will wait for a short period of time, known as *inter-frame space (IFS)*, which is the same as inter-frame gap (IFG) in Ethernet. During the time of last transmission, it is likely that multiple stations are waiting to transmit. If they all are allowed to transmit after IFS, it is very likely to result in a collision. To *avoid* possible collisions, the stations have to wait a random backoff time in units of *slots* before transmission. The backoff time is randomly selected from the range of `0` to `CW`. `CW` stands for

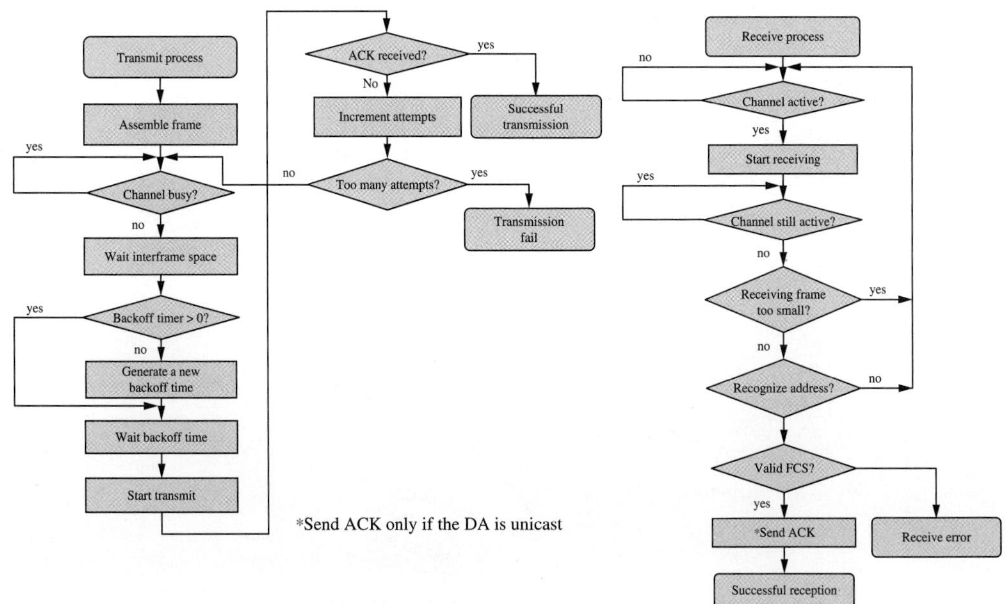

FIGURE 3.25 CSMA/CA flowchart.

Contention Window, ranging from CWmin to CWmax. CWmin, CWmax, and the slot time all depend on the PHY characteristics. Initially, CW is set to CWmin. The backoff time is decreased by one slot time if the channel is free for an IFS period; otherwise, the backoff time is fixed until the channel is free. When the backoff time finally reaches zero, the station starts to transmit. The receiver sends an acknowledgment back to the sender when a frame is received successfully. The acknowledgment is needed for the sender to judge whether the frame has collided at the receiver. Principle in Action: "Why Not CSMA/CD in WLAN?" has more on this. Figure 3.25 summarizes the CSMA/CA procedure. The receive process is similar to that of CSMA/CD except for the acknowledgment.

RTS/CTS: Clear Up First

An optional refinement to reduce the cost of collisions is an explicit RTS/CTS mechanism, as illustrated in Figure 3.27. Before transmitting a frame, the transmitter

Principle in Action: Why Not CSMA/CD in WLAN?

An obvious distinction between the IEEE 802.11 MAC and the IEEE 802.3 MAC is that *collision detection* in WLAN is difficult to implement. The cost of *full-duplex RF* (short for radio frequency) is high, and potentially hidden stations make collision detection fail. The latter is known as the *hidden terminal problem,* as illustrated in Figure 3.26. Station A and Station C cannot sense each other's presence because they are located out of each other's transmission range. If they both transmit data to Station B simultaneously, a collision will occur *at Station B* but cannot be detected by Station A and Station C. Unlike collision detection in Ethernet, which stops transmission immediately if a collision is detected, the sender has no way to find out if a frame in transmission is impaired until the transmission is completed with no acknowledgment being received at the sender. Thus, the cost of collision is significant if a *long* frame is transmitted. On the other hand, the receiver should reply with an acknowledgment if the frame is received successfully and the FCS is correct. Ethernet has no need for such an acknowledgment.

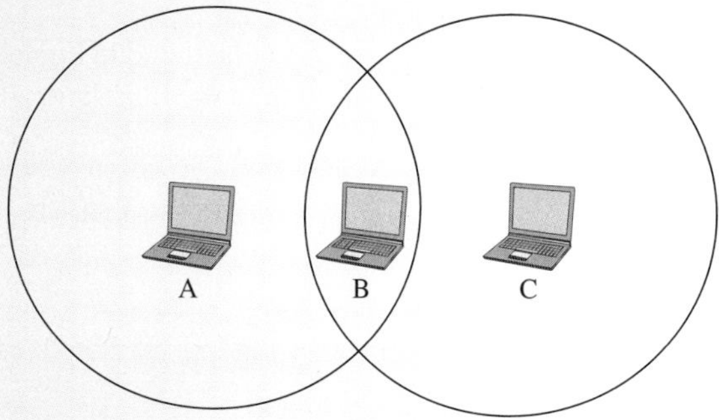

FIGURE 3.26 The hidden terminal problem.

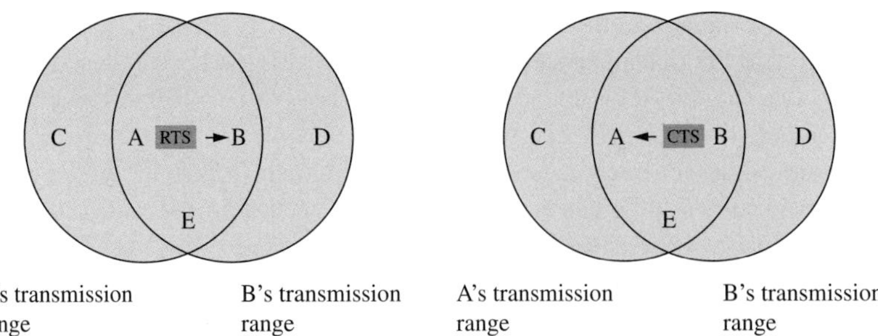

FIGURE 3.27 RTS/CTS mechanism.

(Station A) notifies the target receiver (Station B) with a *small request to send (RTS)*. The RTS is vulnerable to collision, but its cost is small. The receiver responds with a small *clear to send (CTS)* frame, which also notifies all stations (including Station A and Station D) within its transmission range. Both frames carry a duration field. The duration field in the RTS signals stations (such as Station C) around the sender (Station A) to wait as the receiver transmits the CTS back to the sender. Other stations (such as Station D) within the transmission range of the receiver (Station B) would refrain from sending in the duration specified in the CTS and do not need to perform carrier sense physically, so the frame following CTS would be free from collision at the receiver (Station B). Therefore this mechanism is also called *virtual carrier sense*. Note that collision only matters at the *receiver,* not at the *sender*. Furthermore, the RTS/CTS mechanism is only applicable to *unicast* frames. In the case of multicast and broadcast, multiple CTSs from the receivers will result in a collision. Similarly, the acknowledgment frame in reply to the transmitted frame will not be sent in this case.

Interleaved PCF and DCF

A *point coordinator (PC)* that resides in the AP exercises the PCF within each BSS. The PC periodically transmits a *beacon* frame to announce a *contention-free period (CFP)*. Every station within the BSS is aware of the beacon frame and keeps silent during the CFP. The PC has the authority to determine who can transmit, and only the station *polled* by the PC is allowed to transmit. The polling sequence is left unspecified in the standard and is *vendor specific*.

The DCF and PCF can coexist in the scenario illustrated in Figure 3.28. The CFP is in the first step and the CP is in the second step in the illustration.

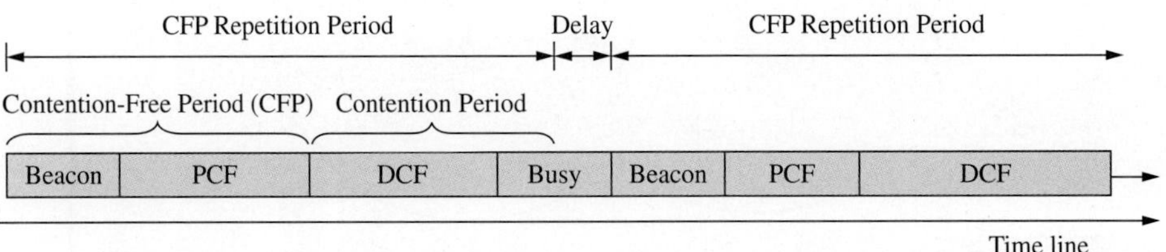

FIGURE 3.28 DCF and PCF coexistence.

General frame format

	Frame control	Duration/ ID	Address 1	Address 2	Address 3	Sequence control	Address 4	Frame body	FCS
bytes	2	2	6	6	6	2	6	0-2312	4

FIGURE 3.29 Generic IEEE 802.11 frame format.

1. The DCF can immediately follow a CFP, and the BSS enters a period called a *contention period (CP)*.
2. Afterwards, the PC transmits a beacon frame with a field called *CFP repetition period,* but a CFP repetition period is delayed if the channel happens to be busy at the end of the CP.

Figure 3.29 depicts the generic IEEE 802.11 MAC frame format. Certain frame types may contain only a subset of these fields. The four address fields can record the source address, the destination address, the transmitter address (from the access point to a wireless station in wireless bridging), and the receiver address (to the access point connected to another interface). The latter two addresses are optional, and are used in bridging with an access point. We categorize the frames into three types:

1. Control frames: RTS, CTS, ACK, etc.
2. Data frames: normal data
3. Management frames: beacon, etc.

To fully cover these types requires deep understanding of every IEEE 802.11 operation. Besides the four addresses, the frame control field specifies the frame type and some information associated with the frame. The duration/ID field specifies the expected busy period of the medium or the BSS identifier that a station belongs to. The sequence control field specifies the sequence number of a frame to avoid duplicate frames. Because the usage of the format is complex and depends on the frame type, readers can refer to the IEEE 802.11 standard for details.

Open Source Implementation 3.6: IEEE 802.11 MAC Simulation with NS-2

Overview

Unlike CSMA/CD, CSMA/CA has had no open source hardware implementation available until now. We therefore introduce an 802.11 MAC simulation with a popular open source simulator NS-2. NS-2 is a discrete event simulator for networking research, and it provides substantial support for simulating TCP, routing, and multicast protocols over wired and wireless networks. In an event-based simulator, all activities in the network are statistically generated as *events* with *timestamp,* which are scheduled to happen by the event scheduler. Many researchers use NS-2 to evaluate their protocols in the early design stage. Recently NS-2 has been widely used to simulate the behavior of 802.11 networks.

Continued

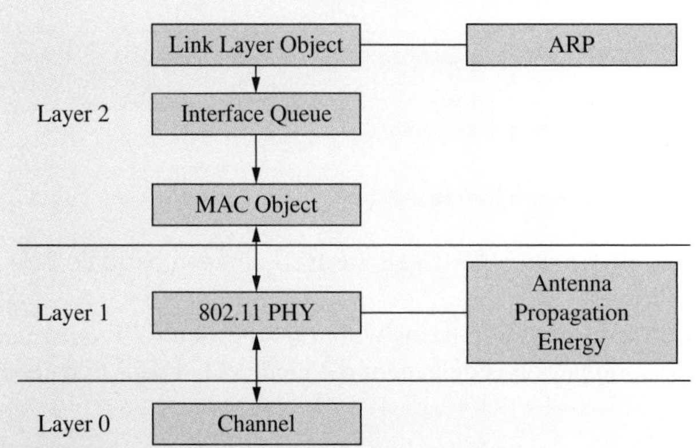

FIGURE 3.30 The architecture of NS-2 802.11 MAC and PHY.

Block Diagram

Figure 3.30 presents the architecture of NS-2 802.11 MAC and PHY, which consists of several network modules. For simplicity, they can be classified into the following three major layers:

- Layer 2 has three sublayers. The first is Link Layer Object, which is the counterpart of Logical Link Control (LLC) in a conventional LAN. Link Layer Object works together with the address resolution protocol (ARP), which will be described in Chapter 4. The second is the interface queue, which assigns the priority to routing protocol messages such as dynamic source routing protocol (DSR). The third sublayer is the 802.11 MAC layer, which handles all unicast frames for RTS/CTS/DATA/ACK and all broadcast frames for DATA. The CSMA/CA is implemented in this layer.
- Layer 1 is the 802.11 PHY, a network interface that can set the parameters based on direct sequence spread spectrum. These parameters include the type of antenna, energy model, and radio-propagation model.
- Layer 0 is the channel layer. It simulates the physical air media for wireless communication. The channel layer delivers frames from a wireless node to its neighbors within the sensing range, and duplicates frames to layer 1.

Data Structures

The most important data structures in this design are a set of timers, including transmit timer, backoff timer, receive timer, defer timer, and so on as described below. The following section will elaborate on the operation of 802.11 MAC and PHY by describing the interaction of these timers with the function calls.

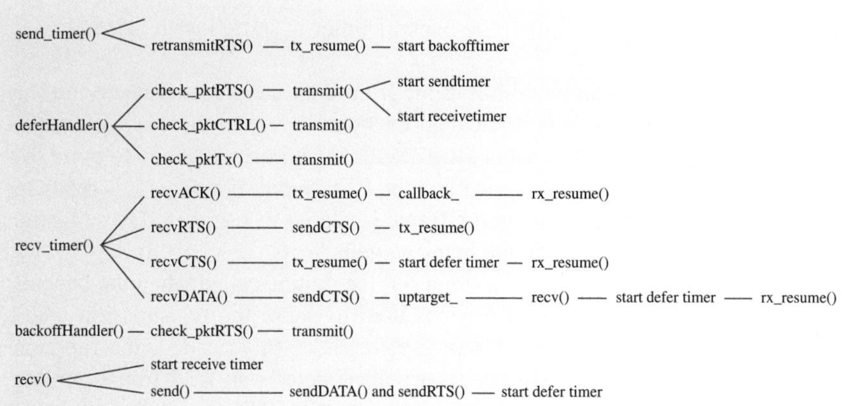

FIGURE 3.31 The NS-2 source code of 802.11 MAC.

Algorithm Implementations

NS-2 Source Code for 802.11 MAC

The 802.11 MAC is a subclass of MAC, and its related source codes are `mac-802_11.cc`, `mac-802_11.h`, `mac-timer.cc`, and `mac-timer.h`. To provide a better understanding of the NS-2 MAC source code, Figure 3.31 lists the major entry functions and depicts the calling sequences of their related functions. Since NS-2 is event-based, besides the major `recv()` function, `send_timer()`, `deferHandler()`, `recv_timer()`, and `backoff-Handler()` are also the entry points when their corresponding events are triggered. As for the reception and transmission flows of 802.11 MAC, the `recv()` function handles incoming frames from both the physical layer and the upper layer. Another `send()` function is an entry point of the transmission flow, but it is called by the `recv()` function for the outgoing frames.

Following is a detailed explanation of the major entry points.

- `send_timer()` is used to handle the acknowledgment frames from other mobile nodes and is called when the transmit timer expires. The timer expiration is interpreted differently depending on which type of frame is sent. For example, if the last frame sent is an RTS, the expiration means a CTS is not received, either because the RTS collides or because the receiving node is deferring the transmission. The MAC responds by retransmitting the RTS with the function `RetransmitRTS()`. If the last frame is a data frame, the expiration means that an ACK has not been received, and the MAC calls `RetransmitDATA()` to handle this situation. After the timer expiration is handled accordingly and a frame has been prepared for retransmission, the control returns to `tx_resume()` function. The `send_timer()` function directly calls `tx_resume()` without further retransmission when the last frame is CTS or ACK. After `tx_resume()`,

Continued

if a frame is retransmitted, the backoff timer is started with an increased contention window.

- `recv()` handles an incoming frame from both the physical layer and the upper layer, and `send()` is called by `recv()` when there is a frame to transmit. Also, `send()` calls `sendDATA()` and `sendRTS()` to build the MAC header for the data frame and the RTS frame. If `recv()` is ready to receive any frame, the incoming frame is passed to `recv_timer()` with the receive timer of the frame being started.
- `backoffHandler()` is an event service routine called when the backoff timer expires. The backoff timer is used to pause the transmission when the channel is busy. After `backoffHandler()` is called, the function `check_pktRTS()` then checks whether there is an RTS frame waiting to be sent. If there is no pending RTS frame, an RTS or a data frame will be transmitted at the timer expiration, depending on whether the RTS/CTS mechanism is enabled.
- `recv_timer()` is the receive timer handler, which checks the type and subtype of the received frames. The receive timer handler is called when the receive timer expires. The timer expiration means that a frame has been fully received and can be readily acted on. The decision of MAC `recv_timer()` is based on the received frame's type. A frame will be dropped if it is `MAC_Type_Management`. If an RTS, CTS, ACK, or DATA frame is received, the `recvRTS()`, `recvCTS()`, `recvACK()`, or `recvDATA()` will be called, respectively. After the frames are handled properly, the control is handed to `rx_resume()`.
- `deferHandler()` is also an event service routine and is called when the defer timer has expired. The defer timer represents the defer time plus a backoff time, which ensures the wireless node waits enough time before transmission to decrease the chance of collision. After the routine is called, the check function calls `check_pktRTS()`, `check_pktTx()`, and `check_pktCTRL()` to prepare a new transmission. If any of these `check_` functions return a value of zero, the `check_` functions must have succeeded in transmitting a frame, so the defer handler ends. For the RTS and control frames, the transmitting procedure may also start the receive timer and the send timer to receive an acknowledgment frame from another mobile node.

CSMA/CA Operation

The CSMA/CA operation is exercised in the `send()` function. Figure 3.32 shows the code, where `mhBackoff_.busy() == 0` means the backoff timer is not busy, `is_idle()==1` the wireless channel is idle, and `mhDefer_.busy() == 0` the defer timer is not busy. If the wireless channel is idle and both the backoff and the defer timers are not busy, the `send()` function will proceed with a defer operation; otherwise, the waiting continues without the timer reset. If it proceeds with a defer operation, the sending frame has to defer

```
void send(Packet *p, Handler *h) {
...
if(mhBackoff_.busy() == 0) {
    if(is_idle()) {
    if (mhDefer_.busy() == 0) {
        rTime = (Random::random() % cw_)*
       (phymib_.getSlotTime());
        mhDefer_.start(phymib_.getDIFS() + rTime);
    }
} else {
        mhBackoff_.start(cw_, is_idle());
    }
  }
}
```

FIGURE 3.32 CSMA/CA operation in send() function.

a DIFS time plus a random time as `phymib_.getDIFS() + rTime`. The random time is computed from `(Random::random() % cw_)*(phymib_.getSlotTime())` and in the interval from zero to `cw_` value, where `cw_`is the current contention window. If the backoff timer is not busy but the wireless channel is not idle, which means the PHY medium is detected to be busy, the node starts the backoff timer by calling `mhBackoff_.start(cw_, is_idle())`.

Simulation with Tcl Script

An NS-2 simulation can be started by a Tcl script file that defines the simulation scenario. A Tcl script contains network topology definition, wireless node configuration, node coordinates, and movement scenario and packet tracing.

Figure 3.33 depicts a simple scenario for an ad hoc network consisting of two mobile nodes, node 0 and node 1. The move area of the mobile nodes is within 500 m × 500 m. A TCP connection is also set up for the FTP service. Table 3.7 describes the detailed scenario in the *wireless.tcl* script file, which defines the example in Figure 3.33.

Exercises

1. Why is the `send()` function called from `recv()`?
2. Why should a sending frame wait for a random period of time?

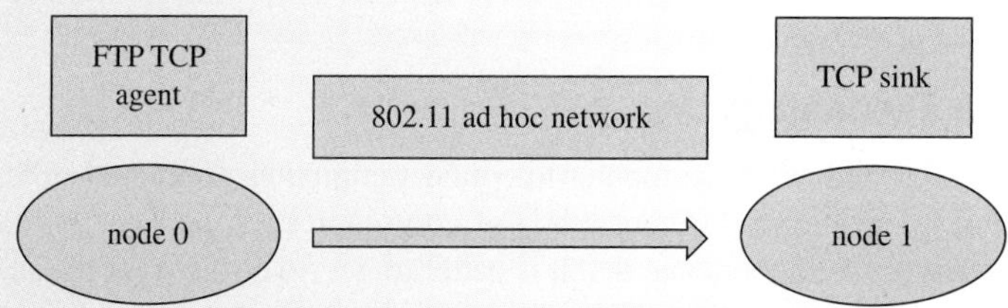

FIGURE 3.33 An NS-2 example of two mobile nodes with TCP and FTP.

Continued

TABLE 3.7 NS-2 Tcl Script for Figure 3.33

Description	Major Codes of wireless.tcl
Define options: channel type, radio-propagation model, etc.	set val(chan) Channel/WirelessChannel ;# channel type set val(prop) Propagation/TwoRayGround ;# radio-propagation model set val(netif) Phy/WirelessPhy ;# network interface type …
Create a simulation, trace, and topography	set ns_ [new Simulator] # Create a simulation object set tracefd [open simple.tr w] #Define a trace file to record all frames … set topo [new Topography] #Create a topography $topo load_flatgrid 500 500 # Set the range of topography 500m × 500m
Setup channel and configure MAC node	create-god $val(nn) # Create God set chan_1_ [new $val(chan)] # configure node $ns_ node-config -adhocRouting $val(rp) \ # Set the parameters for node-llType $val(ll) \ …
Setup parameters for 802.11 PHY	Phy/WirelessPhy set Pt_ 0.031622777 Phy/Wireless Phy set bandwidth_ 11Mb…
Disable random motion	for {set i 0} {$i < $val(nn) } {incr i} { set node_($i) [$ns_ node] $node_($i) random-motion 0 }
Setup and initialize coordinates (X,Y,Z) for two wireless nodes	$node_(0) set X_ 10.0 # Setup coordinate node 0 at (10.0, 20.0, 0.0) … $ns_ initial_node_pos $node_(0) 10 $ns_ initial_node_pos $node_(1) 10
Setup TCP and FTP flow between nodes	set tcp [new Agent/TCP/Sack1] #Create a TCP connection … $ftp attach-agent $tcp
Start the simulation	$ns_ at 1.0 "$ftp start" #at 1.0 s, start the transmission … $ns_ run

3.4.2 Bluetooth Technology

Besides plenty of cables behind our computer to connect computer peripherals, there are even more cables connecting different kinds of communication and networking devices. These cables are so cumbersome that it is better to get rid of them for the sake of convenience. Bluetooth, named after a Danish king in the tenth century, is the very technology supporting short-range (usually within 10 m) radio links to replace cables connecting electronic devices. In 1998, five major companies, Ericsson, Nokia, IBM,

Toshiba, and Intel cooperated to develop Bluetooth technology. To ensure the proliferation of Bluetooth, the development goal was to integrate many functions in a single chip to reduce the cost. A *Bluetooth Special Interest Group (Bluetooth SIG),* composed of many companies, was formed later to promote and define the new standard.

Bluetooth devices operate at the 2.4 GHz ISM band, the same as most IEEE 802.11 devices using frequency hopping. The frequency band ranges from 2.400 GHz to 2.4835 GHz, within which are 79 1 MHz channels used for *frequency hopping* to avoid interference from other signals. Below and above these channels are guard bands of 2 MHz and 2.5 MHz, respectively. An observant reader may have immediately noticed the possible interference problem when devices of IEEE 802.11 and Bluetooth operate at close range. The coexistence problem of IEEE 802.11 and Bluetooth devices is a big issue, and we shall talk more about this at the end of this subsection. Bluetooth is categorized in the domain of wireless *personal* area network (wireless PAN) for its short distance.

Master and Slaves in Piconet and Scatternet

Figure 3.34 illustrates the basic Bluetooth topologies. Like BSS in the IEEE 802.11, multiple devices sharing the same *channel* form a *piconet.* Unlike an IBSS, in which all stations are treated equally, a piconet consists of exactly one master and multiple slaves. The master has the authority to control channel access in the piconet, say, deciding the *hopping sequence*. The slaves can be either *active* or *parked,* and a master controls up to *seven* active slaves at the same time. Parked slaves do not communicate, but they still keep *synchronized* with the master and can become active as the master demands. If a master desires to communicate with more than seven slaves, it tells one or more active slaves to enter the park mode, and then invites the desired parked slaves to be active. For more devices to communicate simultaneously, multiple piconets can *overlap* with one another to form a larger *scatternet*. Figure 3.34 also illustrates two piconets forming a scatternet with a *bridge* node, which can be a slave in both piconets or the master in one piconet. The bridge node participates in both piconets in a *time-division* manner such that sometimes it belongs to one piconet and sometimes it belongs to another.

Inquiry and Paging Procedures

Bluetooth devices must be aware of each other to communicate. An *inquiry* procedure is designed for the devices in the neighborhood to *discover* each other, followed

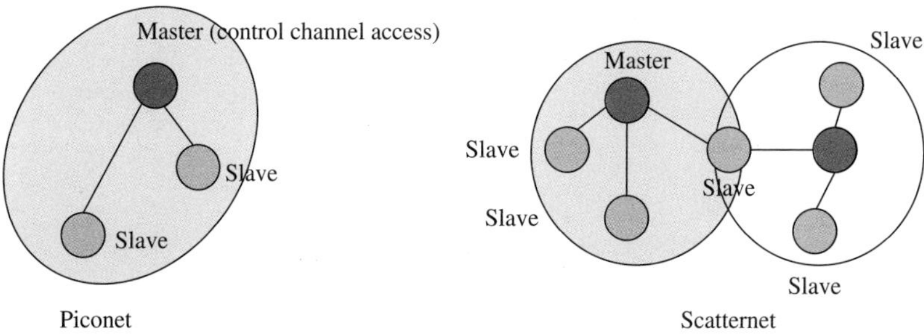

FIGURE 3.34 The Bluetooth topologies: piconet and scatternet.

by a *paging* procedure to build up a *connection*. Initially, all Bluetooth devices are by default in standby mode. A device intending to communicate will try to *broadcast* an inquiry within its coverage area. Other devices around the broadcasting one may respond to the inquiry with information about themselves, such as addresses, if they are willing to do so. Upon receiving these responses, the inquirer knows about its surrounding devices and becomes the master in the piconet, whereas other devices become the slaves in the piconet. After an inquiry, the master sends a *unicast* message to the destination device. The destination then responds with an acknowledgment, so a connection between the master and the destination device is established. A moment later, a slave can run the same paging procedure to take over the role of the master in the piconet. The details of this process are illustrated in Figure 3.35. It is worth noticing that multiple responses to an inquiry may result in a collision. Hence, the receiving devices should defer the responses for a random backoff time.

Frequency-Hopped Slots

A piconet channel is divided into time slots, each accommodating a different hopping frequency. The duration of a time slot is *625 μs,* which is the reciprocal of the hop rate *1600 hops/s*. The master/slave pair time-multiplexes the slots in the 79 1 MHz channels with the same hopping sequence, where the hopping sequence is derived from a pseudorandom sequence known to both. The other slaves are irrelevant to the communication process. At the data rate of 1 Mbps, each slot ideally can carry *625 bits* of data. However, since certain time intervals within a slot are reserved for the use of frequency hopping and stabilization, each time slot in reality can carry at most *366-bit* data information. Normally, each slot carries a Bluetooth *frame,* which has fields of 72-bit access code, 54-bit header information, and the payload of a variable length. Apparently, it is inefficient to transmit payload of only 366 – 72 – 54 = 240 bits *(30 bytes)* in a time slot that ideally could carry 625 bits. To improve the efficiency, a Bluetooth frame is allowed to occupy up to *five* consecutive time slots at the same frequency, so an overhead of only 625 – 366 = 259 bits for frequency-hopping control is consumed in the five slots.

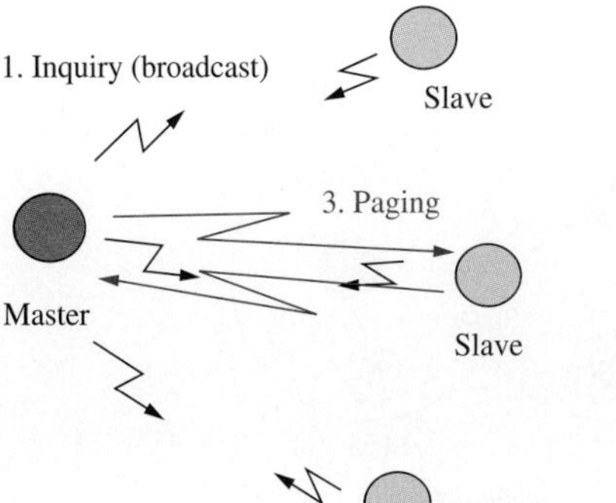

FIGURE 3.35 Inquiry and paging procedures.

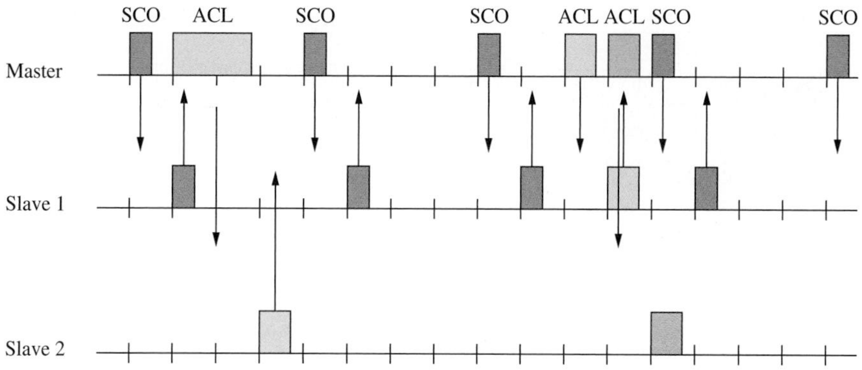

FIGURE 3.36 Time slots in the SCO link and the ACL link.

Interleaved Reserved and Allocated Slots

A Bluetooth connection has two options to use the time slots to communicate. The first is the *synchronous connection-oriented link (SCO link),* which reserves time slots regularly for time-constrained information such as voice data. For example, a telephone-grade voice has a sampling rate of 8 KHz, each sample generating one byte; in other words, a byte is generated every 0.125 ms. Because a frame can carry 30 bytes in each time slot, one slot should be reserved to carry voice data every 3.75 ms (0.125 ms × 30). Each time slot has a length of 625 μs, meaning one out of *six* (3.75 ms/625 μs) slots is reserved. The second is the *asynchronous connectionless link (ACL link),* by which time slots are allocated on demand rather than being reserved. The master is in charge of the slot allocation requested from one or multiple slaves to avoid collisions and to control the quality of service (QoS) of the link. The slave is allowed to send an ACL frame to the master when the master polls it. Similar to PCF and DCF in WLAN, SCO and ACL slots are interleaved; the major difference, however, is that ACL runs a *collision-free* polling and slot allocation. Figure 3.36 illustrates the time slots of both the SCO link and the ACL link. The frames in the SCO link are quite regular, while those in the ACL link are on demand.

Figure 3.37 depicts the protocol stack in the Bluetooth specification. Each software module's function is described on the right-hand side of the figure. The modules above the thick black line are implemented in software, and the others are implemented in hardware. The link manager protocol above the baseband and RF modules is responsible for link setup between Bluetooth units. This protocol can also deal with negotiation of packet sizes and encryption keys, and it performs the actual encryption and decryption.

The L2CAP (Logical Link Control and Adaptation Layer) module supports multiplexing, segmentation, and reassembly of packets for higher-layer protocols. It also supports QoS communication. The service discovery protocol can discover the services available on the other Bluetooth devices. The RFCOMM provides the basis for replacing serial communication via cables using Bluetooth. It can emulate the circuits of RS-232 serial ports over L2CAP. The HCI (host control interface) control provides the software interface for the host to control the Bluetooth hardware.

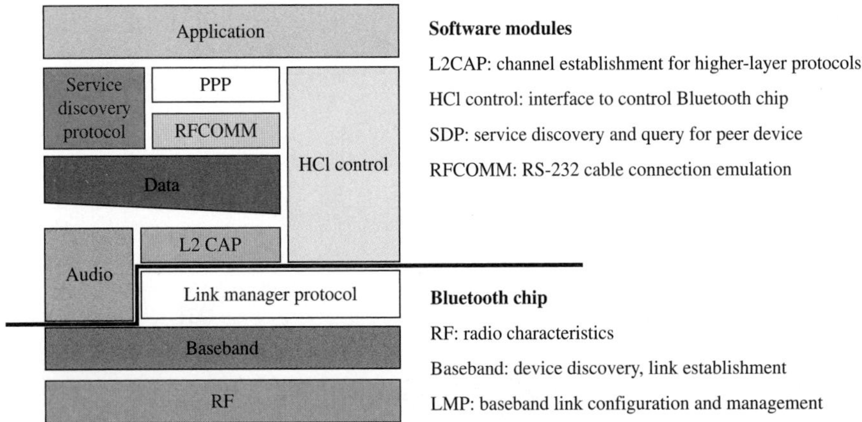

FIGURE 3.37 The Bluetooth protocol stack, where baseband and link manager protocol play the role of a MAC sublayer.

3.4.3 WiMAX Technology

The WiMAX (Worldwide Interoperability for Microwave Access) technology specified in IEEE 802.16 can support wireless communications over a long distance, up to dozens of miles. In contrast to wireless LAN in IEEE 802.11 and wireless PAN in IEEE 802.15, WiMAX is also called wireless MAN, named after its long-distance communication range. The deployment of WiMAX devices can be *fixed* or *mobile*. IEEE 802.16-2004 specifies the technology for fixed connections. The major applications of IEEE 802.16-2004 are broadband access for *"first mile,"* where wired connections such as ADSL or cable modems are costly. IEEE 802.16e-2005 specifies the technology for mobile connections, and its applications are Internet access via *mobile devices*.

MAC with Bandwidth Allocation and Scheduling

WiMAX differs from 802.11 Wireless LAN in many aspects. First, they target different applications. IEEE 802.11 is primarily developed for connections at a short range such as home or office usage, but WiMAX is developed for broadband connections over a distance of miles. Second, they use different medium access control mechanisms. IEEE 802.11 is contention-based, meaning a number of wireless devices must compete for available bandwidth. Therefore, it is less appropriate for time-sensitive applications such as VoIP unless QoS services offered by 802.11e are provided. In contrast, WiMAX uses a scheduling algorithm to allocate bandwidth among the devices. In WiMAX, a base station allocates a time slot to a device such that no other devices can use that slot. By doing so, the base station can serve a large number of subscriber stations and control the slot allocation for time-sensitive applications. In fact, its MAC resembles the cable modem standard DOCSIS since both have the uplink/downlink structure facilitating centralized bandwidth allocation and scheduling. For more details, an NS-2 module for simulation of WiMAX networks can be found at *http://www.lrc.ic.unicamp.br/wimax_ns2*.

Historical Evolution: Comparing Bluetooth and IEEE 802.11

Bluetooth and IEEE 802.11 are designed for different purposes. IEEE 802.11 intends to be a wireless LAN standard, while Bluetooth is designed for the wireless personal area network (wireless PAN, or WPAN). Table 3.8 summarizes a comparison between IEEE 802.11 and Bluetooth. The IEEE 802.15 WPAN Working Group and the Bluetooth SIG are cooperating to improve the Bluetooth standard. The IEEE 802.15 Task Group 2 focuses on addressing the coexistence problem due to possible interference, so coexistence of these two standards can be expected.

TABLE 3.8 A Comparison of Bluetooth and IEEE 802.11

	IEEE 802.11	Bluetooth
Frequency	2.4 GHz (802.11, 802.11b) 5 GHz (802.11a)	2.4 GHz
Data rate	1, 2 Mbps (802.11) 5.5, 11 Mbps (802.11b) 54 Mbps (802.11a)	1–3 Mbps (53–480 Mbps in proposal)
Range	around 100 m	Within 1–100 m, depending on the class of power
Power consumption	Higher (with 1 W, usually 30–100 mW)	Lower (1 mW–100 mW, usually about 1 mW)
PHY specification	Infrared OFDM FHSS DSSS	(Adaptive) FHSS
MAC	DCF PCF	Slot allocation
Price	Higher	Lower
Major application	Wireless LAN	Short-range connection

From OFDM to OFDMA

In the physical layer, WiMAX uses a much wider licensed spectrum from 2 GHz to 11 GHz and from 10 GHz to 66 GHz, unlike 802.11, which uses the license-free ISM band. The initial version of WiMAX operates from 10 GHz to 66 GHz. Operating at such a high frequency has the advantage of more available bandwidth, but the signal is also easily affected by *obstacles*. Therefore WiMAX needs to deploy a large number of base stations at a high cost to circumvent obstacles. A later version of WiMAX supports frequencies from 2 GHz to 11 GHz, where some bands require a license while the others are license free. Deployment also becomes easier and less expensive due to the lower frequency. To avoid WiMAX devices interfering with devices running other technologies in the same frequency range, the standard provides schemes to *dynamically* select the frequency. Moreover, WiMAX supports a *mesh* mode to enable a subscriber station to get data from another. The mesh mode can simplify the deployment of WiMAX because a subscriber station can be deployed as a relay station in a location where an obstacle to the communication between the base station and another subscriber station is located. WiMAX supports OFDM in its physical layer and a new scheme called OFDMA (orthogonal frequency division multiple access), which assigns *subcarriers* to multiple users for multiple accesses. With OFDMA, multiple users can access the channel on different subcarriers simultaneously, which is not the case for WLAN, which uses CSMA/CA for medium access.

Resources available in OFDMA in the *time* domain are managed in terms of *symbols,* while those in the *frequency* domain are in terms of *subcarriers* and further grouped into *sub-channels*. Subcarriers are units of carriers in a finer granularity than sub-channels in the logical partition of the frequency domain. The minimum frequency-time resource unit is one time slot that contains *48* data subcarriers and a duration of *two* symbols for downloading or *three* symbols for uploading in the mandatory PUSC (partial usage of sub-channels) mode. The 802.16 PHY supports time division duplex (TDD), frequency division duplex (FDD), and half-duplex FDD modes—though independent of OFDMA in concept, they all can work with OFDMA. TDD is preferred in WiMAX since it needs only one channel to support time slots and adjust unbalanced downlink/uplink loads. In contrast, the FDD needs two channels for DL and UL, respectively. The transceiver design is also easier in TDD than in FDD.

Note that WiMAX also supports mobile operation in IEEE 802.16e-2005. The standard supports handoffs and roaming at speed up to 75 mph. This operation works at a lower frequency from 2.3 GHz to 2.5 GHz to allow a mobile device to move around, even if an obstacle exists between the device and the base station. OFDMA is required for a mobile device to finely utilize the sub-channels and reduce *interference*. WiMAX for mobile applications is in competition with the popular 3G and its next generation 3GPP, but which one will win the game is still not clear to date. Although 3G already has a wide coverage around the world so far, WiMAX has a higher data rate up to 75 Mbps, and its base station can cover an area within a radius of 30 miles. Most laptop computers at present are equipped with neither WiMAX nor 3G for wireless Internet access, so this would be the first potential market for WiMAX to prevail.

IEEE 802.16e supports both *soft* and *hard* handoffs. With hard handoff, a user is stuck to one station at a time, which means the old connection must be torn down before a new connection is established. Hard handoff is simple and sufficient for data applications. With soft handoff, a new connection can be set up *before* an old connection is disconnected, so the latency from the switch is shorter. Therefore, soft handoff is more suitable for time-critical applications.

Unlike 802.11, which is intended for short-range communications, WiMAX is mainly applied to metropolitan area networks and therefore must control all data transmission to/from devices to avoid *synchronization* problems. In the next section we describe the WiMAX frame structure under TDD mode, describe the five uplink scheduling service classes whose connections fill up the frame, and detail the packet flow in the MAC of a base station.

TDD Subframe

Figure 3.38 shows the frame structure under TDD, which includes (1) UL-MAP and DL-MAP for *control* messages, and (2) downlink and uplink *data* subframes. The

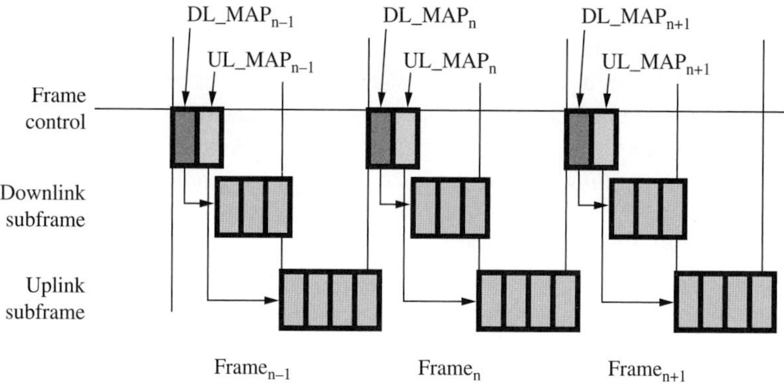

FIGURE 3.38 TDD subframe structure.

bandwidth allocation algorithm determines the scheduled time slots for the downlink and the uplink, and indicates the schedule in the UL-MAP and DL-MAP messages. All UL-MAP/DL-MAP and data subframes are composed of a number of *OFDMA slots,* in which a slot is one sub-channel by *three* OFDMA symbols in uplink and one sub-channel by *two* OFDMA symbols in downlink. This mode is named *PUSC* (partial usage of sub-channels), the mandatory mode in 802.16.

Uplink Scheduling Classes

The 802.16e-2005 currently supports five uplink scheduling classes, namely the Unsolicited Grant Service (UGS), Real-Time Polling Service (rtPS), Non-Real-Time Polling Service (nrtPS), Best Effort (BE), and the lately proposed Extended Real-Time Polling Service (ertPS). Table 3.9 summarizes the characteristics of these service classes, which are very similar to the ones in DOCSIS. Each service class defines a different data handling mechanism to carry out service differentiation. The UGS has the highest priority

TABLE 3.9 Service Classes and the Corresponding QoS Parameters

Feature		UGS	ertPS	rtPS	nrtPS	BE
Request Size		Fixed	Fixed but Changeable	Variable	Variable	Variable
Unicast Polling		N	N	Y	Y	N
Contention		N	Y	N	Y	Y
QoS Parameters	Min. rate	N	Y	Y	Y	N
	Max. rate	Y	Y	Y	Y	Y
	Latency	Y	Y	Y	N	N
	Priority	N	Y	Y	Y	Y
Application		VoIP without silence suppression, T1/E1	Video, VoIP with silence suppression	Video, VoIP with silence suppression	FTP, Web browsing	E-mail, message-based services

and reserves a *fixed* number of slots at each interval for bandwidth guarantee. rtPS, nrtPS, and BE rely on *periodic polling* to gain transmission opportunities from the base station, while ertPS reserves a *fixed* number of slots as UGS does and in the *contention* period notifies the BS of possible reservation changes. nrtPS and BE both *contend* for transmission opportunities according to their preconfigured priority if they do not get enough bandwidth from *polling*. An nrtPS service is always superior to that of BE.

Detailed Packet Flow in the MAC Layer

The complete packet flow in the uplink and downlink of a BS MAC is illustrated as follows. For the downlink processing flow, both IP and ATM packets in the network layer are transformed from/to the MAC *convergence sublayer* (CS) by en-/de-capsulating the MAC headers. According to the addresses and ports, packets are classified to the corresponding connection identifier of a *service flow,* which further determines the QoS parameters. Fragmentation and packing are then performed to form a basic MAC *protocol data unit* (PDU), whose size frequently adapts to the channel quality, followed by the allocation of resulting PDUs into queues. Once the allocation starts, the *bandwidth management unit* arranges the data burst transmissions to fill up the frame. The *MAP builder* then writes the arrangements, namely the allocation results, into the MAP messages to notify the PHY interface when sending/receiving the scheduled data in the time frame. Encryption, header checksum, and frame CRC calculations are carried out to the PDUs before they are finally sent to the PHY. The uplink processing flow is similar to that of the downlink except that the base station also receives standalone or piggybacked bandwidth requests. Among the above operations, it is obvious that the bandwidth management, and thus

Historical Evolution: Comparing 3G, LTE, and WiMAX

IEEE 802.16e-2005, also known as mobile WiMAX, is designed to support mobile applications. As mentioned in the text, WiMAX has a high data rate (75 Mbps) and long distance (30 miles), while 3G has a data rate of only around 3 Mbps. However, 3G can have its users from those who use cellular phones.

Will WiMAX eventually become a popular solution for mobile applications? It has been endorsed by several vendors. For example, Intel incorporates mobile WiMAX capabilities into its next-generation laptop Wi-Fi chips. The 3G technology is also evolving—the next-generation LTE (Long Term Evolution), developed by the Third Generation Partnership Project (www.3gpp.org), can reach 300 Mbps downstream and 100 Mbps upstream, and it can be deployed quickly given the already large infrastructure of 3G technology. The IEEE also adopts the WiMAX 2.0 in the IEEE 802.16m standard, which further boosts the data rate to 100 Mbps for mobile users and 1 Gbps for fixed applications. The competition is fierce. In the meantime, the deployment of mobile WiMAX is still not wide, due to delay in implementation and interoperability certification. Time-to-market here is a critical factor that will determine whether mobile WiMAX will succeed in the market.

the bandwidth allocation algorithm, are critical and need to be carefully designed to improve the system performance.

3.5 BRIDGING

Network administrators usually connect separate LANs into an interconnected network to extend a LAN or to improve its administration. An interconnection device operating at the link layer is called a *MAC bridge,* or simply *bridge*. It is often called a *Layer-2 switch,* Ethernet switch, or simply *switch,* and we shall see why later. A bridge interconnects LANs as if they were in the same LAN. The IEEE 802.1D standard has stipulated its operation. We shall introduce the ins and outs below.

Almost all bridges are *transparent* bridges because all stations on the interconnected LANs are unaware of their existence. The transmitting station simply encapsulates the destination MAC address into a frame and sends out the frame as if the destination were on the same LAN. The bridge automatically forwards this frame. Another category of bridges is source-routing bridges. In this category, the station should discover the route and encapsulate forwarding information in the frame to instruct the bridge how to forward. Since Ethernet dominates the LAN market, this category is seldom seen, so we introduce only the transparent bridge.

The bridge has ports to which LANs are connected. Each port operates in the *promiscuous mode,* meaning it receives *every* frame on the LAN attached to it, no matter what the destination address is. If a frame has to be forwarded to another port, the bridge will do it accordingly.

3.5.1 Self-Learning

The mystery lies in how the bridge knows *whether* it should forward an incoming frame and to *which* port it should forward. Figure 3.39 illustrates the bridge operation. A bridge keeps an address table, also called forwarding table, to store the mapping of MAC addresses to port numbers. Initially, the address table is blank, and the bridge knows nothing about the location of stations. Suppose Station 1 with MAC address 00-32-12-12-6d-aa transmits a frame to Station 2 with MAC address 00-1c-6f-12-dd-3e. Because Station 1 is connected to Port 3 of the bridge, the bridge will receive the frame from Port 3. By checking the *source* address field of the frame, the bridge *learns* the MAC address 00-32-12-12-6d-aa is located on the segment to which Port 3 is connected, and then keeps the learned fact in the address table. However, it still does not know where the destination address 00-1c-6f-12-dd-3e is located. To ensure that the destination can receive the frame, it simply broadcasts the frame to every port except the port where the frame originates. Suppose Station 2 transmits a frame to somewhere a moment later. The bridge will learn that its address comes from Port 2 and will keep this fact in the address table as well. Subsequent frames destined for Station 2 will be forwarded to Port 2 only, without broadcast. This process is called *self-learning*.

Self-learning greatly saves the bandwidth of all other segments and reduces the collision probability, if any. Of course, if Station 2 always remains silent, the bridge

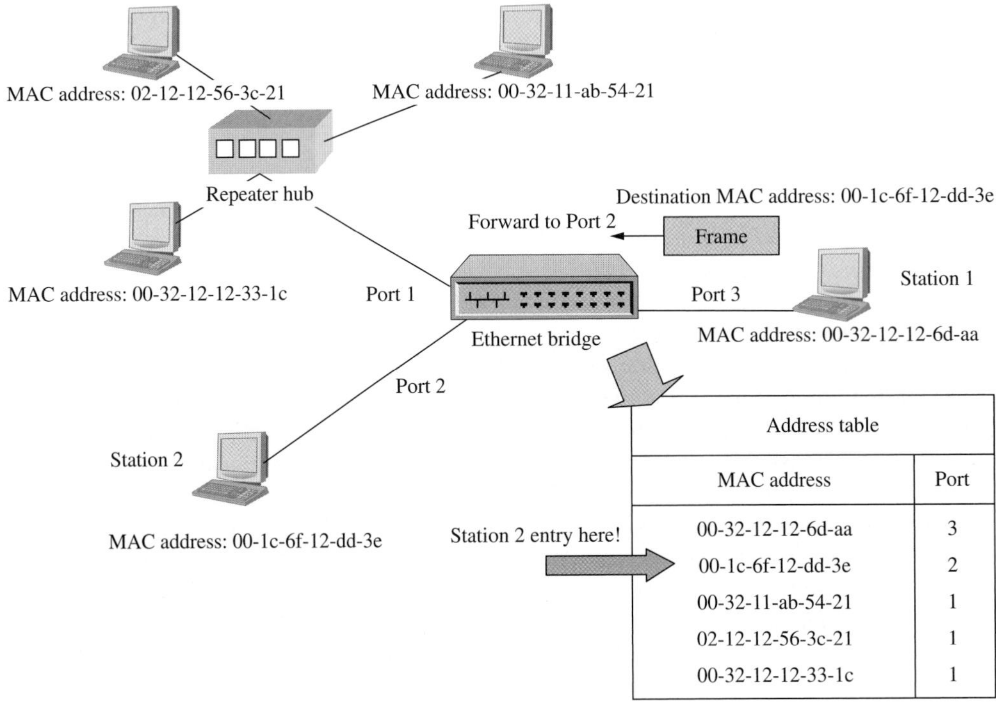

FIGURE 3.39 Bridge operation: self-learning.

will never know where it is, and every frame destined for Station 2 will be broadcast, but this situation rarely happens. A typical scenario is that Station 2 responds after receiving a frame destined for it, and the bridge can learn where Station 2 is from the response.

Sometimes a station may be relocated or removed, making its entry in the address table stale. An *aging* mechanism is applied to solve this problem. If a station has not been heard from for a given period of time, its entry will expire. Subsequent frames destined for the station will be flooded until its existence is learned again.

If the destination address is a multicast or broadcast address, the bridge will forward the frame to all ports except the source. It is wasteful to flood the frame, however. To reduce the unnecessary flooding cost, the IEEE 802.1D standard specifies a *GMRP,* short for *GARP Multicast Registration Protocol. GARP* is a subset of *Generic Attribute Registration Protocol (GARP).* When this protocol is enabled, the bridge can register the requirement from the intended receivers of multicast addresses. The registration information will propagate among bridges to identify all intended receivers. If no multicast demand is found on a given path, a *multicast pruning* is performed to cut off this path. Through this mechanism, multicast frames are forwarded only to those paths where there are intended receivers.

Note that in Figure 3.39, there is a device called a *repeater hub,* or often simply *hub*. The device is a Layer 1 device, meaning it simply restores signal amplitude and timing, and propagates signal to all ports other than the port the frame comes from,

Historical Evolution: Cut-Through vs. Store-and-Forward

Recall that the destination address (DA) field is the first in the frame except the preamble and SFD fields. Looking up the DA in the address table, the bridge can determine where to forward the frame. The bridge can start to forward the frame out of the destination port *before* the frame is received completely. This operation is called *cut-through*. On the other hand, if the bridge forwards only *after* the frame is received completely, its operation is called *store-and-forward*.

The distinction between these two approaches has its historic reason. Before 1991, a switch was called a bridge, both in the IEEE standard and in the market. Early bridges operated in a store-and-forward manner. In 1991, Kalpana Corporation marketed the first cut-through bridge under the name "switch" to differentiate its product from store-and-forward bridges and to declare lower latency due to the cut-through operation. Arguments then were raised among proponents of store-and-forward and cut-through approaches. Table 3.10 summarizes the comparisons of these two mechanisms.

TABLE 3.10 Comparisons of Store-and-Forward and Cut-Through

	Store-and-Forward	Cut-Through
Transmitting time	Transmit a frame *after* receiving completely	May transmit a frame *before* receiving completely[8]
Latency	*Slightly larger* latency	May have *slightly smaller* latency
Broadcast/Multicast	No problem with broadcast or multicast frames	Generally not possible for broadcast or multicast frames
Error checking	Can check FCS *in time*	May be *too late* to check FCS
Popularity	Mostly found in the market	Less popular in the market

but knows nothing about the frame. After all, frames are nothing more than a series of encoded bits to the physical layer.

Bridge vs. Switch

Following Kalpana's name convention, bridges are marketed under the name "switch," no matter whether their operation is store-and-forward or cut-through. The IEEE standard still uses the name "bridge" and explicitly underlines that the two terms are synonyms. Most switches provide only store-and-forward nowadays because the

[8] If the LAN of the outgoing port or the output queue is occupied by other frames, a frame still cannot be forwarded even in a cut-through switch.

Open Source Implementation 3.7: Self-Learning Bridging

Overview

A switch maintains a forwarding database to determine to which port a frame should be forwarded. The learning process of the database is automatic to minimize the efforts of management. That is why we call it self-learning. The key of self-learning is quite simple: If an incoming frame with the source MAC address *A* comes from port *n,* it means the host with MAC address *A* is reachable from port *n,* and a frame destined for *A* will be forwarded to port *n* by the switch. We will introduce the source code of the self-learning mechanism in the Linux kernel, as a Linux host can also serve as a switch (or bridge).

Block Diagram

Figure 3.40 illustrates the learning process, where the forwarding database is implemented as a hash table. If there is a hash collision, entries of the same bucket are stored in a linked list.

When a frame with source MAC address *A* enters a switch, the switch computes the hash value of *A* to locate the entry in the forwarding database, and tries to find *A* in that bucket (perhaps traversing through the linked list). If *A* has been in the database, the original entry will be deleted, meaning the corresponding port of *A* is to be updated. Finally, *A* and the port to which the frame comes will be recorded in the forwarding table.

Data Structures

The most important data structure is the forwarding database, which is defined in the `net_bridge` structure (see `br_private.h`). The hash field in the structure is the hash table, defined as follows:

```
struct hlist_head hash[BR_HASH_SIZE];
```

The entry in the list contains the association of the MAC address with the port, defined as follows. Here `mac` is the MAC address, and `dst` is the corresponding

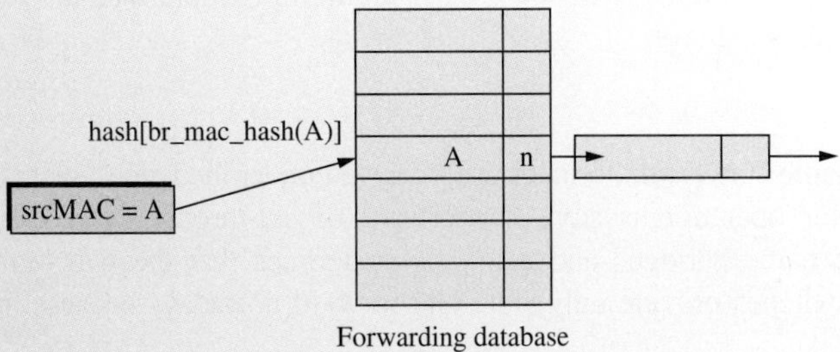

FIGURE 3.40 The self-learning process of a forwarding database.

port. Since it is possible that a host is connected to a different port, if the `ageing_timer` expires, the entry should be deleted or it will become outdated.

```
struct net_bridge_fdb_entry
{
      struct hlist_node        hlist;
struct net_bridge_port         *dst;
struct rcu_head                rcu;
atomic_t                       use_count;
unsigned long                  ageing_timer;
mac_addr                       addr;
unsigned char                  is_local;
unsigned char                  is_static;
};
```

Algorithm Implementations

Linux implements the lookup table in `net/bridge/br_fdb.c`, where `fdb` denotes the forwarding database. The lookup process takes a MAC address to identify an entry in the database, and computes the hash function of `br_mac_hash()` to identify the right hash table bucket. The following code segment in `br_fdb.c` illustrates how the table is looked up.

```
struct net_bridge_fdb_entry *_br_fdb_get(struct
net_bridge *br, const unsigned char *addr)
{
        struct hlist_node *h;
        struct net_bridge_fdb_entry *fdb;
             hlist_for_each_entry_rcu(fdb,h,
             &br->hash[br_mac_hash(addr)],hlist) {
             if (!compare_ether_addr(fdb->addr.addr,
                                              addr)) {
                   if (unlikely(has_expired(br, fdb)))
                         break;
                   return fdb;
             }
        }
        return NULL;
}
```

The macro `hlist_for_each_entry_rcu()` searches through the linked list pointed by `&br->hash[br_mac_hash(addr)]` to find the right entry in `net_bridge_fdb_entry`, which contains the port to be forwarded. Here rcu (Read-Copy-Update) is a synchronization mechanism added into the Linux kernel during the development of version 2.5 to provide mutual exclusion between threads. The lookup comes with an aging mechanism to void the search.

Continued

If an entry has expired, the search is just ignored. This mechanism keeps the database up to date if the network topology is changed.

A new entry is inserted into the forwarding database when a frame is received. This is called the self-learning mechanism in the bridge operation. The code segment is also in `br_fdb.c`, as illustrated below.

```
static int fdb_insert(struct net_bridge *br, struct
net_bridge_port *source, const unsigned char *addr)
{
       struct hlist_head *head = &br->hash[br_mac_
        hash(addr)]; struct net_bridge_fdb_entry *fdb;
       if (!is_valid_ether_addr(addr))
              return -EINVAL;
       fdb = fdb_find(head, addr);
       if (fdb) {
              if (fdb->is_local)
                     return 0;
              fdb_delete(fdb);
       }
       if (!fdb_create(head, source, addr, 1))
              return -ENOMEM;
       return 0;
}
```

The insertion begins with looking up the incoming MAC address in the forwarding database. If an entry is found, it is replaced with the new entry; otherwise, the new entry is inserted into the database.

Exercises

1. Trace the source code and find out how the aging timer works.
2. Find out how many entries are there in the `fdb` hash table of your Linux kernel source.

cut-through design has no significant benefit, as shown in Table 3.10. The term "switch" is also common on devices that make forwarding decisions based on the information from upper layers. That is why we see L3 switch, L4 switch, and L7 switch today.

3.5.2 Spanning Tree Protocol

As the topology of a bridged network becomes larger and more complex, network administrators may inadvertently create a *loop* in the topology. This situation is undesirable because frames can circulate around the loop and the address table may become unstable. For example, consider the following disaster in which two 2-port switches form a loop and a station broadcasts a frame onto the loop. Each switch will forward the broadcast frame to the other upon receiving it, making it circulate around the loop indefinitely.

To address the loop problem, IEEE 802.1D stipulates a *spanning tree protocol (STP)* to eliminate loops in a bridged network. Almost all switches support this protocol for its simplicity in implementation. Figure 3.41 is a trivial example imposed with a spanning tree, and its procedural steps are listed below.

1. Initially, each switch and port is assigned an identifier composed of a manageable *priority* value and switch address (or port number for port identifier). For simplicity, we use 1 to 6 as the identifiers in this illustration.
2. Each link is specified a cost that can be inversely proportional to the link speed. We assume all link costs are 1 here.
3. The switch with the *least* identifier serves as the *root*. The root is elected through the exchange of frames of configuration information among switches.
4. Each LAN is connected to a port of some switch in an *active* topology. The port through which the LAN transmits frames originating from the root is called the *designated port* (DP), and the switch is called the *designated bridge*. The port through which the switch receives frames from the root is called the *root port* (RP).
5. Periodically, configuration information propagates downward from the root on the *bridge protocol data unit* (BPDU) whose destination address is a *reserved* multicast address for switches, 01-80-C2-00-00-00. The BPDU frame contains information such as the root identifier, the transmitting switch identifier, the transmitting port identifier, and the cost of the path from the root.
6. Each switch may configure itself based on the information carried in the received BPDUs. The configuration rules are:
    - If the switch finds it can provide a *lower* path cost by comparing with the path cost *advertised* in BPDUs, it will attempt to be a designated bridge by transmitting BPDUs with its lower path cost.
    - In case of ambiguity, e.g., multiple choices of equal path cost, the switch or port with the least identifier is selected as the designated bridge (port).

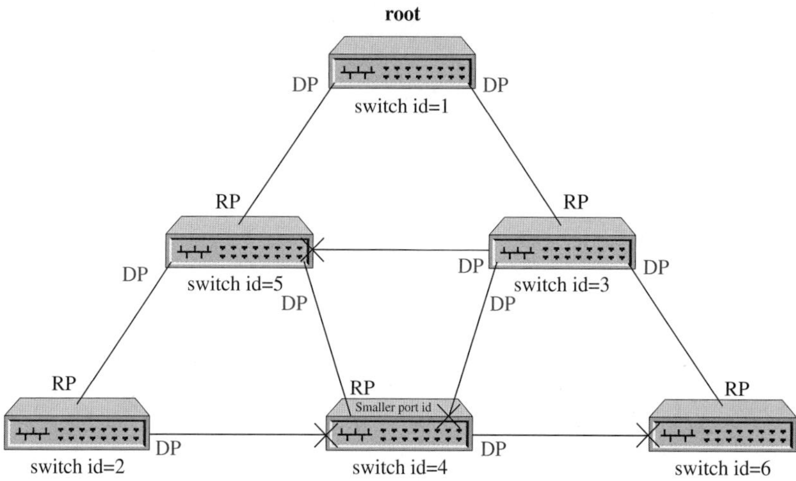

FIGURE 3.41 A bridged network with loops.

- If the switch finds it has a *lower* identifier than that of the current root, it will attempt to become the new root by transmitting BPDUs with its identifier as the root identifier.
- Note that a switch does not forward any incoming BPDUs, but may create new BPDUs to carry its new states to others.

7. All ports other than DPs and RPs are *blocked*. A blocked port is not allowed to forward or receive data frames, but it still keeps *listening* to BPDUs to see if it can be active again.

Figure 3.41 also presents the resulting spanning tree. The readers are encouraged to trace the procedure. The protocol is so effective that it dynamically updates the spanning tree according to possible topological changes.

Open Source Implementation 3.8: Spanning Tree

Overview

Spanning tree configuration is updated from information in the ingress BPDUs, as described in the text. When a bridge receives a BPDU, it first builds a structure that contains BPDU information by parsing the frame, and then updates the bridge configuration according to the BPDU information. After that, the new root is selected and the designated port is determined. The states of ports are then updated according to the new configuration.

Block Diagram

Figure 3.42 illustrates the call flow of handling BPDU frames. The flow basically follows the sequence introduced above. We will describe the details of each function call below.

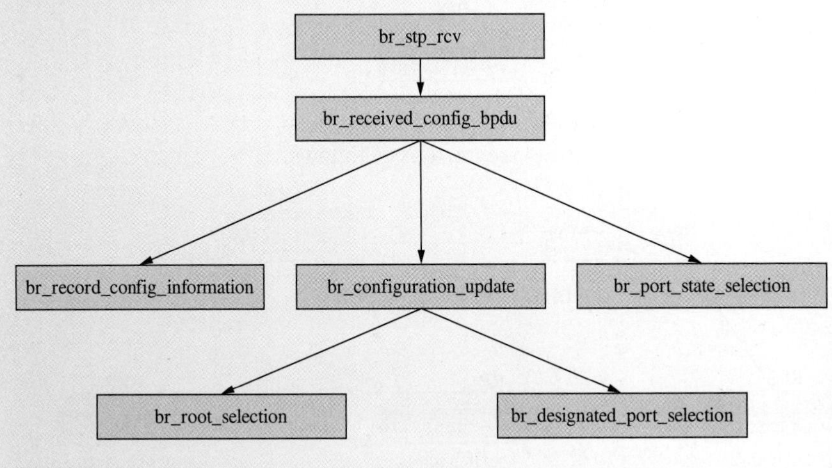

FIGURE 3.42 Call flows of handling BPDU frames.

Data Structures

The `br_config_bpdu` is the most important structure (defined in `net/bridge/br_private_stp.h`), which derives the BPDU information from the BPDU frame after parsing the frame. It contains the following fields in the structure, and these fields can be directly mapped from the protocol fields in a BPDU frame.

```
struct br_config_bpdu
{
        unsigned        topology_change:1;
        unsigned        topology_change_ack:1;
        bridge_id       root;
        int             root_path_cost;
        bridge_id       bridge_id;
        port_id         port_id;
        int             message_age;
        int             max_age;
        int             hello_time;
        int             forward_delay;
};
```

The received BPDU frame is used to update the global bridge configuration in the `net_bridge` structure (defined in `net/bridge/br_private.h`). This structure is not only for the spanning tree protocol but also for other protocols. It also contains the whole data structures needed by a bridge, say the forwarding database. Hence we do not discuss it in this section.

Algorithm Implementations

The `br_stp_rcv()` function in `br_stp_bpdu.c` (under the net/bridge directory) handles updates on spanning tree configuration. The function parses the BPDU and builds a `br_config_bpdu` structure of BPDU information. The structure and the port information are then passed to the function `br_received_config_bpdu()` in `br_stp.c`. This function first calls `br_record_config_information()` to register the BPDU information at the port, and then calls `br_configuration_update()` to update the bridge configuration. The code segment is as follows:

```
void br_received_config_bpdu(struct net_bridge_port
*p, struct br_config_bpdu *bpdu)
{
        // Skip some statements here
        if (br_supersedes_port_info(p, bpdu)) {
                br_record_config_information(p, bpdu);
                br_configuration_update(br);
        br_port_state_selection(br);
        // Skip some statements here
}
```

Continued

After the configuration is updated, the port state is also updated in `br_port_state_selection()` according to the port's assigned role. For example, a port may be blocked to avoid a loop. Note that `br_configuration_update()` may be called from more than one place. For example, the system administrator may execute a command to disable a port or change a path cost. This case will also trigger the update of bridge configuration.

The `br_configuration_update()` function simply calls two functions `br_root_selection()` and `br_designated_port_selection()` to select a new root and determine the designated port, respectively. The path cost may also be updated if the root or the designated port is changed.

Exercises

1. Briefly describe how the BPDU frame is propagated along the topology of spanning trees.
2. Study the `br_root_selection()` function to see how a new root is selected.

3.5.3 Virtual LAN

Once a device is connected to a LAN, it belongs to that LAN. That is, the deployment of LANs is completely determined by *physical* connectivity. In some applications, we need to build *logical* connectivity on top of physical deployment. For example, we may want some ports in a switch to belong to one LAN, and others to belong to another. Further, we may want to assign ports across *multiple* switches to the same LAN and all other ports to another LAN. Generally, we need flexibility in the network deployment.

Virtual LAN (VLAN) can provide for the logical configuration of LANs. Administrators can simply work with management tools without changing the physical connectivity of the underlying network topology. Additionally, with VLAN separation, ports of a switch can be assigned to different VLANs, each functioning as a physically separated switch. By doing so, we can enhance network *security* and save bandwidth because traffic, particularly multicast and broadcast traffic, can be confined within a specifically defined VLAN to which the traffic belongs. For example, a broadcast frame or a frame with an *unknown* unicast destination address will appear on *all* ports of a switch without VLAN such that not only does this frame consume bandwidth on *unintended* ports, but malicious users can monitor it as well. By dividing the ports of a switch into several VLANs, the frame will be confined within a VLAN composed of the ports the frame is intended for.

Figure 3.43 illustrates a practical example to show the usefulness of VLAN. Consider we have two IP subnets: 140.113.88.0 and 140.113.241.0, each consisting of several stations. If we want to connect these two IP subnets with a router, we may deploy the network in the manner depicted in Figure 3.43.

If we configure the switch with two VLANs instead, only *one* switch is needed. The router is connected to a port that belongs to *two* VLANs, and configured with

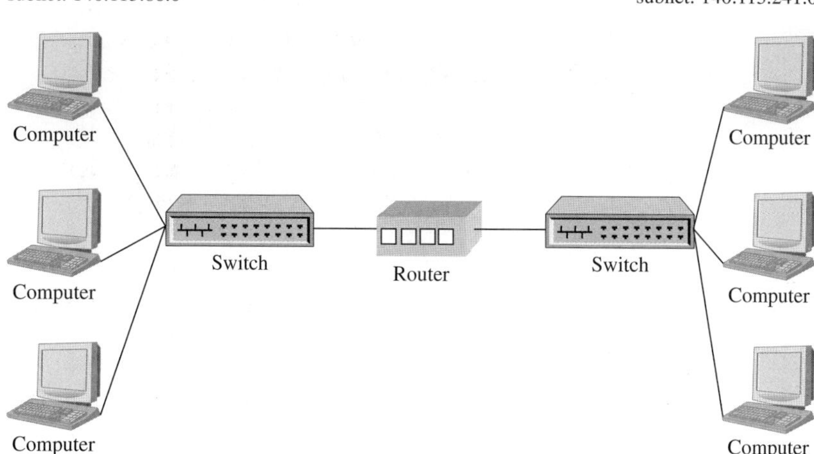

FIGURE 3.43 Two-switch deployment without VLAN.

Principle in Action: VLAN vs. Subnet

VLAN is a Layer-2 concept, which allows network administrators to configure the connectivity at Layer 2 without physically rewiring. For example, port 1 and port 2 of a switch can be configured to belong to a VLAN, while port 3 and port 4 belong to another. Although they are all in the same switch, the connectivity could be logically dissected. Hosts in the same VLAN can communicate without higher layer devices, particularly routers, and VLAN confines the range that a broadcast frame can reach (only within a VLAN).

Subnet is a Layer-3 concept. Hosts in a subnet can send packets to each other directly without the help of routers, including broadcast packets. Both terms look similar in the context of restricting the broadcast domain. What are their differences?

A subnet is configured by setting the IP addresses of the hosts with identical prefixes where the subnet mask determines the prefix length. In comparison, VLAN is configured on a switch, a Layer-2 device. The former is *logical*, while the latter is a *physical* separation. Therefore, it is possible to configure multiple subnets in the same VLAN (e.g., connecting to the same switch without separate VLANs), but logically these subnets are separated. Despite the logical separation, a Layer-2 broadcast frame (with the destination MAC address of all 1's) can still reach the entire VLAN. In this situation, it would be better to configure multiple VLANs on the switch to physically separate the broadcast domain.

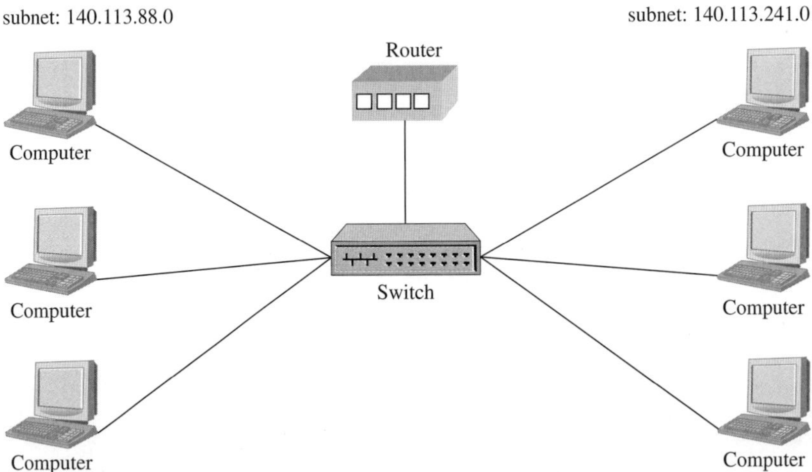

FIGURE 3.44 One-switch deployment with VLAN and one-armed router.

two IP addresses, one for each subnet. The router in this case is called the *one-armed* router, as illustrated in Figure 3.44. Nowadays, many switches, i.e., Layer-3 switches, have the ability to serve as normal routers that can forward frames based on Layer-3 information. With VLAN, administrators can arbitrarily group ports into several IP subnets, which is very convenient for network administration.

The IEEE 802.1Q standard specifies a set of protocols and algorithms to support the VLAN operation. This standard describes the architectural framework for VLAN in the aspects of configuration, distribution of configuration information, and relay. The first is self-explanatory. The second is concerned with methods that allow the distribution of VLAN membership among VLAN-aware switches. The third deals with how to classify and forward incoming frames, and the procedure to modify the frames by adding, changing, or removing *tags*. We discuss the concept of tag next.

The IEEE 802.1Q standard does not specify how stations should be associated with VLANs. The VLAN membership can be based on ports, MAC addresses, IP subnets, protocols, and applications. Each frame can be associated with a tag that bears a VLAN identifier so that the switch can quickly identify its VLAN association without complicated field classification. The tag slightly changes the frame format, however. The format of a tagged frame is depicted in Figure 3.45.[9] A VLAN identifier has *12 bits,* allowing a maximum number of *4094* (i.e., $2^{12}-2$) VLANs, given that one identifier is reserved unused and another is used to indicate a priority tag (see below).

Priority

If the load in a LAN is high, the users will perceive long latency. Some voice or video applications are time-sensitive, and their quality will be deteriorated with the long latency. Traditionally, LAN technology solves the problem with *over-provisioning*

[9] Note that the use of VLAN is not confined to Ethernet. The VLAN standard also applies to other LAN standards, say Token Ring. However, since Ethernet is the most popular, we discuss Ethernet frame here.

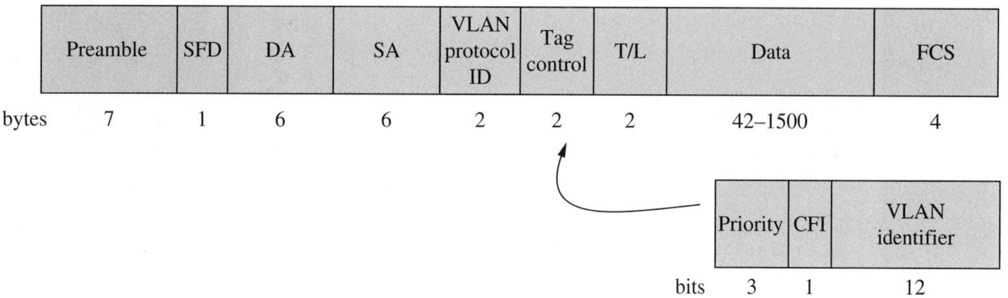

FIGURE 3.45 Format of a tagged frame.

that provides more bandwidth than needed. This solution is feasible because high bandwidth is inexpensive in wired LAN. But in the case of short-term congestion, the traffic may temporarily exceed the available bandwidth, so higher priority can be assigned to frames of critical applications to guarantee they receive better service.

Ethernet inherently does not have the priority mechanism. As of IEEE 802.1p, which was later integrated into IEEE 802.1D, a priority value can be optionally assigned to an Ethernet frame. This value is also carried in a tagged frame, as illustrated in Figure 3.45. A tagged frame has *four* more bytes added into it. They are a 2-byte type field that indicates a VLAN protocol type (the value = 0x8100) and a 2-byte tag control information field. The latter is further divided into three fields: priority, canonical format indicator (CFI), and VLAN identifier. A tagged frame does not necessarily carry VLAN information. The tag can contain only the priority of the frame. The VLAN identifier helps the switch to identify the VLAN to which the frame belongs. The CFI field looks mysterious. It is a one-bit field that indicates whether the possible MAC addresses carried in the MAC data are in canonical format. We do not go into the details of canonical form here. Interested readers are referred to clause 9.3.2 in the IEEE 802.1Q document.

Because three bits are in the priority field, the priority mechanism allows eight priority classes. Table 3.11 lists the suggested mapping of priority values to traffic

TABLE 3.11 Suggested Mapping of Priority Values and Traffic Types

Priority	Traffic Type
1	Background
2	Spare
0 (default)	Best effort
3	Excellent effort
4	Controlled load
5	< 100 ms latency and jitter
6	< 10 ms latency and jitter
7	Network control

types in the standard. A switch can classify the incoming traffic and arrange appropriate queue services to meet the user's demand based on the tag value.

Link Aggregation

The final issue we would like to introduce is *link aggregation*. Multiple links can be aggregated as if they were a pipe of larger capacity. For example, users can aggregate two gigabit links into a single two-gigabit link if a larger link capacity is desired. They do not have to buy 10-gigabit Ethernet products, since link aggregation already brings flexibility in network deployment.

Link aggregation was originally a technique of Cisco, dubbed *EtherChannel,* often referred to as port trunking, and was later standardized in the IEEE 802.3ad in 2000. The operation is not confined to links between switches; links between a switch and a station and between two stations can also be aggregated. The principle of link aggregation is simple: The transmitter *distributes* frames among aggregated links, and the receiver *collects* these frames from the aggregated links. However, some difficulties complicate the design. For example, consider the case in which several short frames follow a long frame. If the long frame is distributed to one link and the short frames are distributed to another, the receiver might receive these frames *out of order*. Although an upper layer protocol such as TCP can deal with out-of-order frames, it is inefficient to do so. The ordering of frames in a flow must be maintained in the link layer. A flow may need to be moved from one link to another for load-balancing or because of link failure. To meet these requirements, a *link aggregation control protocol* (LACP) is designed. We refer readers to clause 43 in the IEEE 802.3 standard for details.

3.6 DEVICE DRIVERS OF A NETWORK INTERFACE

3.6.1 Concepts of Device Drivers

One of the main functions of an operating system is to control I/O devices. The I/O part in the operating system can be structured in four layers, as presented in Figure 3.46. The interrupt handler can also be thought as part of the driver.

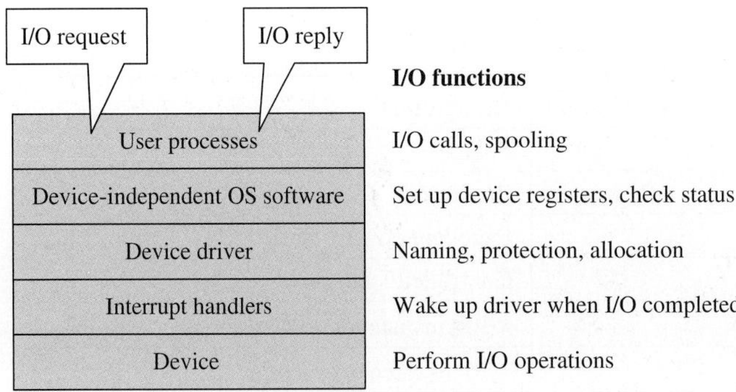

FIGURE 3.46 Structure of I/O software.

All of the device-dependent codes are embedded in the device drivers. The device drivers issue *commands* to the device *registers* and check whether they are carried out properly. Thus, the network device driver is the only part of the operating system that knows how many registers the network adaptor has and what they are used for.

The job of a device driver is to accept abstract requests from the device-independent software above it, and to handle these requests by issuing commands to device registers. After commands have been issued, either the device driver *blocks* itself until the interrupt comes in to unblock it, or the operation finishes immediately so the driver does not need to block.

3.6.2 Communicating with Hardware in a Linux Device Driver

Before a device driver can communicate with a device, it must initialize the environment. The initialization includes *probing I/O ports* for communicating with *device registers,* and *probing IRQs* for correctly installing the *interrupt handler.* We will also discuss *direct memory access* for transferring a large batch of data.

Probing I/O Ports

A hardware device typically has several registers, and they are mapped to a region of consecutive addresses for reading and writing. Reading and writing these addresses (actually, the registers) therefore can control the device. Not all I/O ports are bound to device registers. A user can dump the content in /proc/ioports to view the mapping of the addresses to the devices.

The programmer of a device can request a region in the I/O ports for a device. The request must first check whether the region has been allocated to other devices. Note that the checking must be performed with allocation in an *atomic* operation, or other devices may acquire the region after the checking and produce in an error. After acquiring a region in the I/O ports, the device driver can probe the device registers by reading or writing the ports in units of 8 bits, 16 bits, or 32 bits, depending on the register widths. These operations are performed with special functions, to be introduced later. After the operations, the driver can return the region to the system if the region is not used anymore.

Interrupt Handling

Besides constantly probing the device registers, the driver can use an *interrupt* to relinquish the CPU to other tasks during probing. An interrupt is an asynchronous event generated from the hardware to get the CPU's attention. A device driver can register a piece of code, namely the handler, to an interrupt, so that the handler is executed if the interrupt occurs. The interrupts on a system are numbered, and the mapping from the numbers to the device can be viewed from the file /proc/interrupts.

The registry of interrupt lines is similar to the acquisition of I/O ports. The driver can request for an interrupt line, use it, and release it after finishing its work. A question is which interrupt line is to be used by a device. Although the user can manually specify an interrupt line, this practice requires extra effort to figure out which interrupt line is available. A better solution is autodetection. For example, the PCI standard requires devices to declare the interrupt lines to be used in a register, so the driver can learn the interrupt line of the device by retrieving the number from the I/O ports. Not every device supports such autodetection, so an alternative is to ask the device to generate an interrupt and watch which line is active if the support is unavailable.

A problem with interrupt handling is how to perform long tasks within an interrupt handler. There is often much work to do in response to a device interrupt, but interrupt handlers need to finish quickly and not keep blocking other interrupts for too long. Linux resolves this problem by splitting the interrupt handler into two halves. The *top half* is the routine that responds to the interrupt, and it is also the handler registered with the interrupt line. The *bottom half* handles the time-consuming part, and the top half schedules its execution at a safe time, meaning the requirement of execution time is not so critical. Therefore, after the top-half handler has finished, the CPU can be released to handle other tasks. The Linux kernel has two mechanisms to implement bottom-half processing: *BH* (also called bottom half) and *tasklets*. The former is old. New Linux kernel implements tasklets since version 2.4, so we focus on the latter when introducing the bottom-half processing.

Direct Memory Access (DMA)

Direct memory access (DMA) is a hardware mechanism to efficiently transfer a large batch of data to and from main memory without the CPU's involvement. This mechanism can significantly increase the throughput of a device and relieve the processor's burden.

DMA data transfer can be triggered in two ways: (1) software asks for data from the system calls such as *read,* and (2) hardware writes data asynchronously. The former is used when a program explicitly demands data from the system call, and the latter is used when a data-acquisition device can asynchronously write the acquired data into the memory even when no process has required it yet.

The steps in the former are summarized as follows:

1. The driver allocates a DMA buffer when a process needs to read the data. The process is put to sleep for the DMA buffer to read data from the hardware.
2. The hardware writes data into the DMA buffer, and raises an interrupt after the writing ends.
3. The interrupt handler gets the data and awakens the process. Now, the process has the data.

The steps in the latter are summarized as follows:

1. The hardware raises an interrupt to announce the data arrival.
2. The interrupt handler allocates the DMA buffer and notifies the hardware to transfer.
3. The hardware writes data from the device to the buffer, and raises another interrupt when it is done.
4. The handler dispatches the new data and awakens relevant processes to handle the data.

We shall take a close look at the related functions in the following open source implementation.

Open Source Implementation 3.9: Probing I/O Ports, Interrupt Handling, and DMA

Overview

The Linux device drivers interact with the hardware through I/O port probing, interrupt handling, and DMA. I/O ports are mapped to the registers on a hardware device, so that a device driver can access the I/O ports to read or write the registers. For example, a driver can write a command into the registers, or read the status of the device. Ordinarily, when the driver assigns a task to the device for execution, it may constantly poll the status registers to know whether the task has been finished, but doing so is likely to waste CPU cycles if the task is not finished immediately. The driver can turn to the interrupt mechanism, which notifies the CPU, after which the associated interrupt handler is invoked to handle the interrupt. Therefore, the CPU does not need to be busy waiting. If there is bulk data to be transferred, the DMA can handle the transfer on behalf of the CPU. The function calls associated with these mechanisms are described next.

Function Calls

I/O Ports

Since Linux kernel version 2.4, the I/O ports have been integrated into the generic resource management. We can use the following functions in the device driver to acquire the I/O ports of a device:

```
struct resource *request_region (unsigned long start,
unsigned long n, char* name);
void release_region (unsigned long start , unsigned
long len);
```

We use `request_region()` to reserve the I/O ports, where `start` is the starting address of the I/O-port region, `n` is the number of I/O ports to be acquired, and `name` is the device name. If a nonzero value is returned, the request succeeds. The driver then should call `release_region()` to release the ports when it finishes.

After acquiring the region of I/O ports, the device driver can access the ports to control the registers on a device, which could be command or status register. Most hardware differentiates between 8-bit, 16-bit, and 32-bit ports, so a C program must call different functions to access ports of different sizes. The Linux kernel defines the following functions to access I/O ports:

```
unsigned inb (unsigned port);
void outb (unsigned char byte, unsigned port);
```

The `inb()` reads byte (8-bit) port, while the `outb()` writes byte port.

Continued

```
unsigned inw (unsigned port);
void outw (unsigned char byte, unsigned port);
```

The `inw()` reads 16-bit port, while the `outw()` writes 16-bit port.

```
unsigned inl (unsigned port);
void outl (unsigned char byte, unsigned port);
```

The `inl()` reads 32-bit port, while the `outl()` writes 32-bit port.

Besides the single-shot in and out operations, Linux supports the following string operations, which may actually be performed by a single CPU instruction or a tight loop if the CPU has no instruction for string I/O.

```
void insb (unsigned port, void *addr, unsigned long
count);
void outsb (unsigned port, void *addr, unsigned long
count);
```

The `insb()` reads `count` bytes from byte port, and stores these bytes to memory starting at the address `addr`. The `outsb()` writes `count` bytes located at memory address `addr` to byte port.

```
void insw (unsigned port, void *addr, unsigned long
count);
void outsw (unsigned port, void *addr, unsigned long
count);
```

Their operations are similar, except the port is a 16-bit port.

```
void insl (unsigned port, void *addr, unsigned long
count);
void outsl (unsigned port, void *addr, unsigned long
count);
```

Their operations are similar, except the port is a 32-bit port.

Interrupt Handling

Like the approach to acquire I/O ports, the driver uses the following functions to register (install) and release (uninstall) an interrupt handler to an interrupt line.

```
#include <linux/sched.h>;
int request_irq(unsigned int irq, irqreturn_t
(*handler) (int, void *, struct pt_regs *), unsigned
long flags, const char *dev_name ,void *dev_id);
void free_irq (unsigned int irq, void *dev_id);
```

In the former, `irq` is the interrupt line to be requested, and `handler` is the associated interrupt handler. The other parameters are: `flags` are the interrupt's attributes, `dev_name` the device name, and `dev_id` the pointer to the device's data structure. The meaning of the parameters for `free_irq()` is the same as those for `request_irq()`.

When an interrupt occurs, the interrupt handling in the Linux kernel pushes the interrupt number onto the stack, and calls `do_IRQ()` to acknowledge the interrupt. The function `do_IRQ()` will then look up the interrupt handler associated with the interrupt, and will call it through the `handle_IRQ_event()` function if there is one; otherwise, the function will return, and the CPU can continue processing any pending software interrupts. The interrupt handler is usually fast, so the other interrupts will not be blocked too long. The interrupt handler can release the CPU quickly and schedule its bottom half at a safe time.

New versions of Linux use *tasklet* for the bottom-half function. For example, if you write a function `func()` to be used as a bottom-half routine, the first step is to declare the tasklet by the macro `DECLARE_TASKLET(task,func,0)`, where `task` is the tasklet name. After the tasklet is scheduled by `tasklet_schedule(&task)`, the tasklet routine and task will be executed shortly at the system's convenience.

The following functions are useful for using tasklets:

```
DECLARE_TASKLET(name, function, data);
```

The macro declares the tasklet, where `name` is the tasklet name, `function` is the actual tasklet function to be executed, and `data` is the argument to be passed to the tasklet function.

```
tasklet_schedule(struct tasklet_struct *t);
```

The function schedules the tasklet to be executed at the system's convenience, where *t* points to the tasklet structure.

Direct Memory Access

The DMA buffer allocation is a little bit complicated due to the coherency issue with the CPU cache. The CPU should invalidate its cache mapping to the DMA buffer if the content of the buffer is changed. Therefore, the driver should be careful to make sure the CPU is aware of the DMA transfer. To relieve the programmers' efforts in this problem, Linux provides some functions for the allocation. Here we introduce a common approach to buffer allocation.

After the driver allocates the buffer (with `kmalloc()`, for example), it indicates the buffer mapping to that on the device with the following function.

```
dma_addr_t dma_map_single(struct device *dev,
void *buffer, size_t size, enum dma_data_direction
direction);
```

The `dev` argument indicates the device, `buffer` is the starting address of the buffer, `size` is the buffer size, and `direction` is the direction that the data is

Continued

moving (e.g., from the device, to the device, or bidirectional). After the transfer, the mapping is deleted with the function

```
dma_addr_t dma_unmap_single(struct device *dev,
void *buffer, size_t size, enum dma_data_direction
direction);
```

Like I/O ports and interrupts, the DMA channel should be registered before its use. The two functions for the registry and the release are

```
int request_dma(unsigned int channel, const char
*name);
void free_dma(unsigned int channel);
```

The `channel` argument is a number between 0 and `MAX_DMA_CHANNELS` (usually 8 on a PC), defined by kernel configuration. The `name` argument identifies the device.

After the registration, the driver should configure the DMA controller for proper operation. The following functions can perform the configurations:

```
void set_dma_mode(unsigned int channel, char mode);
```

The first argument is the DMA channel, and the `mode` argument could be `DMA_MODE_READ` for reading from the device, `DMA_MODE_WRITE` for writing to the device, and `DMA_MODE_CASCADE` for connecting two DMA controllers.

```
void set_dma_addr(unsigned int channel, unsigned int
addr);
```

The first argument is the DMA channel, and the `addr` argument is the address of the DMA buffer.

```
void set_dma_count(unsigned int channel, unsigned int
count);
```

The first argument is the DMA channel, and the *count* argument is the number of bytes to transfer.

Exercises

1. Explain how a tasklet is scheduled by studying the `tasklet_schedule()` function call.
2. Enumerate a case in which polling is preferable to interrupting.

A typical Linux system has a number of device drivers for its various hardware components. Among these drivers, that for network devices is the most closely related to computer networks. The Linux kernel supports a number of network interface drivers (see the drivers/net directory). We chose the driver for the ne2000 Ethernet interface as an example to introduce the design of network interface drivers.

Open Source Implementation 3.10: The Network Device Driver in Linux

Overview

This section uses a practical example to explain how the device driver is implemented to interact with a network interface. The interaction primarily includes device initialization, transmission process, and reception process. In device initialization, the driver allocates the space and initializes the important data structures of the network interface, such as the IRQ numbers and the MAC address. In the transmission and reception processes, the device driver uses interrupts for notification of process completion.

Block Diagram

The most important flows in the device driver are frame transmission and reception. We illustrate the flows in Figure 3.47 and Figure 3.48 in the "Algorithm Implementations" section below.

Data Structures

The `net_device` data structure is associated with the information about a network device. When a network interface is initialized, the space of this structure for that interface is allocated and registered. This structure is quite large, containing the fields related to configuration, statistics, device status, list management, and so on. We list several fields in the configuration associated with initialization.

`char name[IFNAMSIZ]`: the name of the device, such as `eth0`.
`unsigned int irq`: the interrupt number used by the device.

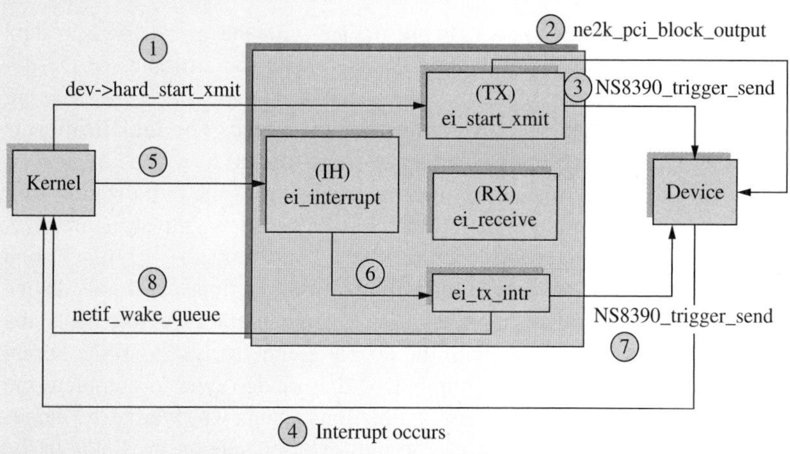

FIGURE 3.47 The sequence of executed functions during frame transmission.

Continued

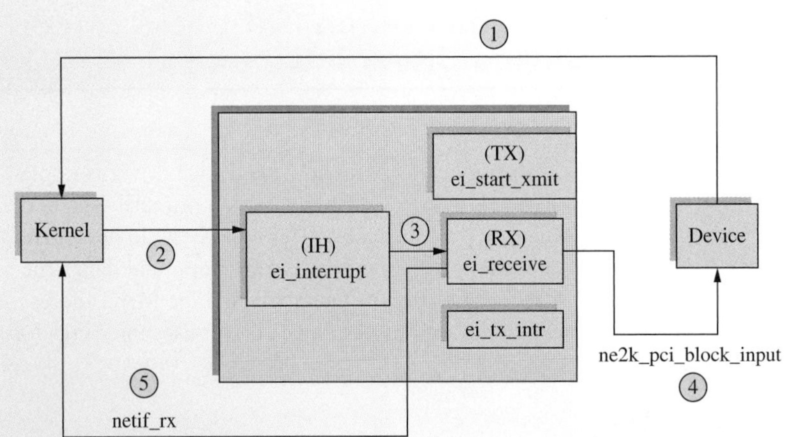

FIGURE 3.48 The sequence of executed functions during frame reception.

`unsigned short type`: the number to indicate the device type, such as Ethernet.

`unsigned char dev_addr[MAX_ADDR_LEN]`: the link layer address of the device.

`unsigned char addr_len`: the length of the link layer address, say six bytes in Ethernet.

`int promiscuity`: running in the promiscuous mode or not.

Algorithm Implementations

Device Initialization

The Linux kernel represents a network device with the `net_device` data structure, which involves the fields associated with the attributes of the device. Before the network interface can be usable, its `net_device` structure must be initialized, and the device must be registered. The initialization is performed with the `alloc_netdev()` function in `net/core/dev.c` and returns a pointer to the newly allocated structure if the initialization succeeds. Three parameters are passed to `alloc_netdev`: the structure size, the device name, and the setup routine. The `alloc_netdev()` function is generic, and can be invoked from the initialization functions of various device types. For example, `alloc_etherdev()` in net/ethernet/eth.c calls the `alloc_netdev()` function with the device name "`eth%d`", so the kernel can assign the first unassigned number of that device type to complete the name with the `dev_alloc_name()` function. That is why we see the names such as "`eth0`" in the user space. The initialization sets up the fields in the net_device data structure for IRQ, I/O memory, I/O port, MAC address, queueing discipline, and so on.

After allocating and initializing the net_device structure with alloc_netdev(), the netdev_boot_setup_check() function may check the optional boot-up configuration parameters for the network device, such as the IRQ number. After the procedure, the device is registered in the device database with the register_netdevice() function. Similarly, the function unregister_netdevice() is called when the device driver is unloaded from the kernel, and the resources occupied by the device, such as the IRQ, should also be released.

Transmission Process

Figure 3.47 presents the transmission process in the example of ne2000 Ethernet interface. When the kernel has a frame to transmit, it first calls the generic hard_start_xmit() function, which then calls the specific ei_start_xmit() function on the device. The ei_start_xmit() function invokes ne2k_pci_block_output() to move the frame to the network interface. When the frame has been transmitted out, the ne2000 interface will notify the kernel with an interrupt, and the kernel will call the corresponding interrupt handler, ei_interrupt(). The ei_interrupt() function will first determine which type the interrupt is. When it finds out that the interrupt stands for frame transmission, it calls the ei_tx_intr() function, which in turn calls NS8390_trigger_send() to transmit the next frame on the interface (if any), and then calls netif_wake_queue() to let the kernel proceed to the next task.

Reception Process

Figure 3.48 presents the reception process of the previous example. When the network interface receives the frame, it will notify the kernel with an interrupt. The kernel then calls the corresponding handler, ei_interrupt(). The ei_interrupt() function determines which type the interrupt is, and calls the ei_receive() function because the interrupt stands for frame reception. The ei_receive() function will call ne2k_pci_block_input() to move the frame from the network interface to the system memory and fill the frame into the sk_buff structure. The netif_rx() function will pass the frame to the upper layer, and the kernel then proceeds to the next task.

Exercises

1. Explain how the frame on the network device is moved into the sk_buff structure (see ne2k_pci_block_input()).
2. Find out the data structure in which a device is registered.

Performance Matters: Interrupt and DMA Handling Within a Driver

Table 3.12 shows the interrupt handling time and DMA eclipse time spent in processing ICMP frames by the Realtek 8169 Ethernet adaptor on a PC with a 2.33 GHz CPU. The DMA eclipse time is *not* the consumed CPU time since the data transfer is offloaded to DMA. The results indicate that the processing time of interrupt handlers does *not* vary with frame size. The reason is that the major tasks of interrupt handlers, such as interaction with the underlying hardware by issuing commands to device registers, are independent of frames. On the other hand, the DMA time depends on the size of transferred frames. Another observation is that the RX time of the interrupt handler is *slightly* higher than the TX time, while the RX time of DMA is *much* higher than the TX time. The RX-interrupt handler needs to allocate and map the DMA buffer for transferring; thus it takes a bit more time than the TX-interrupt handler. Our measured RX DMA time includes the DMA transferring time as well as extra hardware processing time by the DMA controller, but the TX DMA time contains only DMA transferring, which results in the RX DMA time being much higher than the TX DMA time.

Finally, it is worth noting that the interrupt handling time depends on the CPU speed, and the DMA eclipse time mainly depends on the underlying *adaptor*. As we have shown in Subsection 1.5.3, the DMA time of the Intel Pro/100 Ethernet adaptor and a 1.1 GHz CPU is about 1 μs, and the processing time of the 64-byte packet in the link layer is about 8 μs (TX) and 11 μs (RX), which are different from the values here. The row for the packet of 100 bytes in Table 3.12 shows that the interrupt time is lower while the DMA time is higher. Although the values change, the observations made here are hardware-independent.

TABLE 3.12 Packet Processing Time by Interrupt and DMA

	Interrupt Handler		DMA	
Payload size of ICMP packet	TX	RX	TX	RX
1	2.43	2.43	7.92	9.27
100	2.24	2.71	9.44	12.49
1000	2.27	2.51	18.58	83.95

Time unit: μs

Historical Evolution: Standard Interfaces for Drivers

In the early x86-DOS years, operating systems did not provide any networking modules, so a driver was bound with applications directly and had to handle all networking functions itself. FTP Software, in 1986, developed the PC/TCP product, which is a TCP/IP library for DOS, and defined the Packet Driver interface, which regulates a programming interface between PC/TCP and the device drivers. With the help of the common interface, the driver developers would not need to modify too much in developing a driver for new hardware. Commercial operating systems standardized their interfaces, for example, the ODI (Open Data-link Interface) by Novell and Apple and the NDIS (Network Driver Interface Specification) by Microsoft and 3Com. Linux did not specify any name for its interface until kernel version 2.4. It used the interrupt-driven approach to handle the received frames. Since kernel version 2.5, a new interface, called NAPI (New API), is designed to support high-speed networking, but it is still an optional feature in kernel version 2.6 when implementing a driver. The idea behind the NAPI design is that too-frequent interrupts degrade the system performance. NAPI uses the interrupt handler interchangeably to keep latency short, and it uses round-robin polling to process *multiple* frames at one time instead of triggering the interrupt handler every time.

There is another interface that a device driver must support: the hardware specification. A specification, often called a *data sheet*, documents the interface between the driver and hardware. It provides detailed programming information, including the functions and widths of *I/O registers* and properties of *DMA controllers*. Device developers follow the specification to initialize the hardware, acquire the status, request DMA transfer, and transmit and receive frames. Novell NE2000 LAN cards were sold so successfully that its device driver became a de facto standard. Many manufacturers claimed their network chipsets be NE2000-compatible to simplify the driver development. To be compatible with NE2000, the functions of I/O registers and DMA controllers have to mimic the NE2000 data sheet completely. Due to its limited functionality, NE2000 is no longer popular. Following the data sheet of a hardware controller to program the controller has become a standard practice for driver developers.

3.7 SUMMARY

We started from the key concepts of the link layer, including framing, addressing, error control, flow control, and medium access control. These higher-level concepts provide the mechanisms above physical signal transmission for two or more nodes to communicate with each other. We then learned popular link technologies for both wired and wireless connections in terms of these concepts. Among the wired and wireless technologies, we paid special attention to Ethernet and IEEE 802.11 WLAN, as they have been the dominant technologies in their species. Generally, Ethernet is *faster* and more *reliable,* but 802.11 WLAN has *mobility* and its deployment is easier. We also introduced the bridging technology to interconnect multiple LANs. The main issues of bridging include frame forwarding, spanning-tree protocol to avoid a forwarding loop, and virtual LAN for easy LAN configuration. After all those technologies, we explained the implementation of device drivers for a network interface. You should know how the network interface operates in detail from these implementations.

Although the speed of both Ethernet and IEEE 802.11 WLAN have increased greatly over the years, the increase is mostly due to advances in *signal processing* technology in the physical layer. The link parts, such as framing, are left almost unchanged for backward compatibility. However, the link technology also has its own advances, such as better configurability, better medium access control (e.g., full-duplex operation), and better security. Mechanisms such as *link aggregation* also contribute the aggregate throughput between the nodes. Ongoing evolution includes higher speed, *link-level QoS,* and *power-saving* mechanisms. Speed is always a target to pursue. Currently, 40 Gbps and 100 Gbps Ethernet are emerging. The raw data rate is boosted to 600 Mbps in 802.11n. Link-level QoS is provided in wireless technologies such as WiMAX, and power-saving technology is always of great concern for mobile devices.

The link-layer protocols primarily deal with *connectivity* between two nodes that are *directly linked,* via either wired or wireless links. However, the connectivity between two arbitrary nodes in the Internet is more difficult because the packets from one node to the other may pass through multiple links in the huge Internet, which includes billions of hosts. First, there must be a *scalable addressing* mechanism to address so many hosts in the Internet, so that the nodes between the source and the destination hosts do not have to keep the route to each possible destination in the entire address space. Second, the route must be *updated regularly* to reflect the up-to-date connectivity status from the source to the destination. For example, if a link is broken in a route, there must be some way to be aware of this problem, and to pick a new route from the source to the destination. Those are issues to be addressed in the network layer in Chapter 4. Because the Internet Protocol is the dominant protocol in the network layer, the chapter shall cover how the Internet Protocol solves the issues of scalable addressing, packet forwarding, and scalable exchange of routing information.

COMMON PITFALLS

Ethernet Performance (Utilization in Half-Duplex and Full-Duplex Mode)

Researchers were once interested in the maximum channel utilization of Ethernet under extremely heavy load, despite the fact that the situation is unlikely to happen. Computer simulation, mathematical analysis, and real-world measurement are possible approaches to obtain the value. Unlike simple mechanisms such as ALOHA and slotted ALOHA, mathematically analyzing a full set of CSMA/CD mechanisms is difficult. When the experimental Ethernet was invented at the Xerox lab, Bob Metcalfe and David Boggs published a paper in 1976 that reported a maximum of about 37% channel utilization that Ethernet could reach with their simplified model. Unfortunately, this value has continued to be cited over years, even though the Ethernet technology has been utterly different from the experimental model since the DIX standard. Different FCS, different preamble, different address format, different PHY and so on—except that the spirit of CSMA/CD was preserved. Moreover, 256 stations are assumed in the same collision domain, which is unlikely to happen in the real world.

A later paper published by David Boggs et al. in 1988 tried to clarify the pitfalls. They performed real-world testing on a 10 Mbps Ethernet system with 24 stations by flooding frames constantly. It showed the utilization is more than 95% with the maximum frame and about 90% with the minimum frame under stress testing.[10] It showed Ethernet performance is rather satisfactory.

[10] Boggs' paper counts overheads in header, trailer, and IFG in utilization. Hence, 100% utilization is assumed if there is no collision despite those overheads in his paper.

As switches become more popular, multisegment networks are divided into many individual collision domains. The situation of many stations in the same collision domain is further reduced. Since the advent of full-duplex operation, no restriction is imposed by CSMA/CD at all, so both ends of a link can transmit as fast as it can. For a switch that affords the maximum frame rate and data capacity, it is called a *wire-speed* or *nonblocking* switch.

Another problem that might be of concern is that the data field in the Ethernet frame is not "long" enough. Unlike other technologies, say Token Ring, which has data fields of 4528 bytes at 4 Mbps and 18,173 bytes at 16 or 100 Mbps, the data field is only 1500 bytes out of 1518 bytes of a maximum untagged frame. One may suspect that the percentage of non-data overheads, including header information, trailer, and IFG, is larger than that in other technologies.

There is a historical reason why the Ethernet frame is not so long. Ethernet was invented more than 30 years ago, and memory was expensive at that time. The buffer memory for frames was quite limited in size in those days. It made sense to design a frame that was not too long, either was the data field. For large data transfer such as FTP traffic, which tends to transfer with long frames, the data field can occupy as high as 1500/(1518 + 8 + 12) = 97.5% of the channel bandwidth. The overheads are quite low! Significantly increasing the maximum frame size helps little to reduce the overheads.

Collision Domain, Broadcast Domain, and VLAN

The first two terms often seem confusing to students who first learn Ethernet. A collision domain is the range of network in which more than one transmission at the same time results in a collision. For example, a repeater hub and the stations attached to it form a collision domain. In contrast, a switch explicitly separates collision domains from one port to another. In other words, a transmission from a shared LAN attached to one port of the switch will not result in a collision with another transmission from the same LAN but through another port.

However, when a frame has a broadcast address as the destination, a switch will still forward to all ports but the source. The range of network that the broadcast traffic can reach is a broadcast domain, so we may confine the broadcast traffic's range for security reasons or to save bandwidth within a LAN.

A VLAN approach also separates broadcast domains from one another, but it is a logical separation from physical connectivity. In other words, no physical connection needs to be changed. It is the configuration of devices that performs the separation as if it were a physical change. A device providing high-layer connectivity, such as a router, is needed to connect two or more separate VLANs.

5-4-3 Rule and Multisegment Networks

It is said that Ethernet follows the 5-4-3 rule. It sounds easy to remember, but the rule is not as simple as it sounds. The rule is actually one of the conservative rules that validate the correctness of 10 Mbps multisegment Ethernet networks. It is not a law that every Ethernet deployment should follow.

As we mentioned, the round-trip propagation time in a collision domain should not be too long for proper operation. Different transmission media and the number of repeater hubs incur different delays, however. As a quick guide for network administrators, the IEEE 802.3 standard offers two *transmission system models*. Transmission system model 1 is a set of configurations that meet the above requirements. In other words, if you follow these configurations, your network will work properly. Occasionally, you may need to deploy your network in a way other than the configurations in transmission system model 1. You have to calculate yourself whether your network is qualified for the requirements. Transmission system model 2 offers a set of calculation aids to you. For example, it tells you the delay value of a segment of a certain medium type.

Clause 13, "System considerations for multi-segment 10 Mbps baseband networks," cites the following rule for transmission system model 1: *"When a transmission path consists of **four** repeater sets and **five** segments, up to **three** of the segments may be mixing and the remainder must be link segments."*

This is the well-known 5-4-3 rule. A mixing segment is a medium with more than two physical interfaces on it. A link segment is a full-duplex-capable medium between exactly two physical interfaces. One often refers to a link segment as a segment without PCs, but it is not a precise description. The rule means if you configure your network this way, it can work. As more and more segments operate in full-duplex mode, this rule has become outdated.

Big-Endian and Little-Endian

Those who are familiar with network programming may be confused by big-endian and little-endian. They know network byte order. For example, Internet Protocol (IP) uses big-endian for byte ordering. However, we mention that Ethernet transmits data in little-endian order. Is there a contradiction?

Consider a four-byte word, each byte denoted by $b_3b_2b_1b_0$ in decreasing order of significance. Here are two options for storing it in memory:

1. Store b_3 in the lowest byte address, b_2 in the second-lowest byte address, and so on.
2. Store b_3 in the highest byte address, b_2 in the second-highest byte address, and so on.

The former is known as the big-endian byte order, and the latter is known as the little-endian byte order. The ordering varies with the CPU and OS on a host. This results in inconsistency when transmitting some multi-byte data, say integers, over the network. A network byte ordering is enforced to maintain consistency. The most popular network layer protocol, Internet Protocol, uses big-endian ordering. Whatever the host's byte ordering is, the data should be converted into network byte ordering before transmission and then be converted back into the host's byte ordering upon reception, if there is an inconsistency.

That is the business of Internet Protocol. The link protocol receives data from the upper-layer protocols byte by byte. The byte ordering on the upper-layer protocols is of no consequence to the link protocol. The link protocol is concerned with *bit ordering* in transmission, not byte ordering.

Ethernet uses little-endian bit ordering. It transmits the least significant bit first and the most significant bit last in byte transmission. Conversely, Token Ring or FDDI transmits the most significant bit first and the least significant bit last in byte transmission. They are known to use big-endian bit ordering. They should not be confused with byte ordering.

FURTHER READINGS

PPP

PPP, PPPoE, and IPCP are defined in RFC 1661, RFC 2516, and RFC 1332, respectively. Sun's hands-on book introduces practical PPP operation on Unix.

- W. Simpson, "The Point-to-Point Protocol (PPP)," RFC 1661, July 1994.
- L. Mamakos, K. Lidl, J. Evarts, D. Carrel, D. Simone, and R. Wheeler, "A Method for Transmitting PPP over Ethernet," RFC 2516, Feb. 1999.
- G. McGregor, "The PPP Internet Protocol Control Protocol (IPCP)," RFC 1332, May 1992.
- A. Sun, *Using and Managing PPP,* O'Reilly, 1999.

Ethernet

Seifert is a coauthor of the IEEE 802.1 and 802.3 standard. His *Gigabit Ethernet* book characterizes technical accuracy and market insight, and it is a must if you hope to get into technical details of Gigabit Ethernet without being fed up with the detailed but boring wording in the standard. He also has a book with a full discussion on switches. You will find in his book great details on STP, VLAN, link aggregation, and other concepts. Spurgeon is an experienced network architect; his book introduces the Ethernet from an administrative point of view.

- Rich Seifert, *Gigabit Ethernet,* Addison Wesley, 1998.
- Rich Seifert, *The Switch Book,* Wiley, 2000.
- Charles E. Spurgeon, *Ethernet: The Definitive Guide,* O'Reilly, 2000.

Here is a list of standards documents. All of the IEEE 802 standards have been freely available on http://standards.ieee.org/getieee802/. A white paper is published by 10 Gigabit Alliance, a technical consortium promoting the next-generation 10-Gigabit Ethernet.

- ISO/IEC Standard 8802-3, "Carrier Sense Multiple Access with Collision Detection (CSMA/CD) Access Method and Physical Layer Specifications," 2000.
- 10 Gigabit Ethernet Alliance, "10 Gigabit Ethernet Technology Overview: White paper," http://www.10gea.org, Sept. 2001.

Following are the MAC Bridge Standard and the VLAN Bridge Standard, also available on the Web site mentioned above.

- ISO/IEC Standard 15802-3, "Media Access Control (MAC) Bridges," 1998 Edition.
- IEEE 802.1Q, "Virtual Bridged Local Area Networks," 1998 Edition.

Following are several well-cited papers about research on Ethernet. The first two are early performance analysis on Ethernet.

- R. M. Metcalfe and D. R. Boggs, "Ethernet: Distributed Packet Switching for Local Computer Networks," *Communications of the ACM,* Vol. 19, Issue 7, July 1976.
- D. R. Boggs, J. C. Mogul, and C. A. Kent, "Measured Capacity of an Ethernet: Myths and Reality," *ACM SIGCOMM Computer Communication Review,* Vol. 18, Issue 4, Aug. 1988.
- W. Willinger, M. S. Taqqu, R. Sherman, and D. V. Wilson, "Self-Similarity Through High Variability: Statistical Analysis of Ethernet LAN Traffic at the Source Level," *IEEE/ACM Trans. Networking,* Vol. 5, Issue 1, pp. 71–86, Feb. 1997.
- G. Kramer, B. Mukherjee, S. Dixit, Y. Ye, and R. Hirth, "Supporting Differentiated Classes of Service in Ethernet Passive Optical Networks," *Journal of Optical Networking,* Vol. 1, Issue 9, pp. 280–298, Aug. 2002.
- J. Zheng and H. T. Mouftah, "Media Access Control for Ethernet Passive Optical Networks: An Overview," *IEEE Communications Magazine,* Vol. 43, No. 2, pp. 145–150, Feb. 2005.

Wireless Protocols

Here we list the wireless LAN standards, also available on the Web site mentioned above. There is also a good book on IEEE 802.11, and three well-cited papers on QoS enhancements and network performance for IEEE 802.11 wireless LAN.

- ANSI/IEEE Standard 802.11, "Wireless LAN Medium Access Control (MAC) and Physical Layer (PHY) Specification," 1999 Edition.
- M. Gast, *802.11 Wireless Networks: The Definitive Guide,* 2nd Edition, O'Reilly, 2005.
- Q. Ni, L. Romdhani, and T. Turletti, "A Survey of QoS Enhancements for IEEE 802.11 Wireless LAN," *Journal of Wireless Communications and Mobile Computing,* Vol. 4, Issue 5, pp. 547–577, Aug. 2004.
- A. Balachandran, G. M. Voelker, P. Bahl, and P. V. Rangan, "Characterizing User Behavior and Network Performance in a Public Wireless LAN," *ACM SIGMETRICS Performance Evaluation Review,* Vol. 30, Issue 1, June 2002.
- D. Pilosof, R. Ramjee, D. Raz, Y. Shavitt, and P. Sinha, *Understanding TCP Fairness over Wireless LAN,* INFOCOM, 2003.

Following are the standards document, a good tutorial, and a well-cited paper on Bluetooth, followed by a well-cited paper and book on WiMAX.

- Bluetooth Specification Documents, http://www.bluetooth.com/English/Technology/Building/Pages/Specification.aspx.
- P. Bhagwat, "Bluetooth: Technology for Short-Range Wireless Apps," *IEEE Internet Computing,* Vol. 5, Issue 3, pp. 96–103, May/June 2001.
- A. Capone, M. Gerla, and R. Kapoor, "Efficient Polling Schemes for Bluetooth Picocells," IEEE International Conference on Communications, June 2001.
- Z. Abichar, Y. Peng, and J. M. Chang, "WiMAX: The Emergence of Wireless Broadband," *IT Professional,* Vol. 8, Issue 4, July 2006.
- Loutfi Nuaymi, *WiMAX: Technology for Broadband Wireless Access,* Wiley, 2007.

Device Drivers

This is an excellent book that teaches you how to write Linux device drivers.

- J. Corbet, A. Rubini, and G. Kroah-Hartman, *Linux Device Drivers,* 3rd Edition, O'Reilly, 2005.

FREQUENTLY ASKED QUESTIONS

1. What are the byte and bit orders in IP over Ethernet?
   Answer:
   Byte order: big-endian, i.e., high-order byte transmitted first.
   Bit order: little-endian, i.e., low-order bit transmitted first.
2. Why FCS at the tail? IP checksum in the header?
   Answer:
   FCS: computed by hardware, appended and examined on the fly.
   IP checksum: computed by software usually, stored and processed.

3. Why is big bandwidth delay product (BDP) bad for CSMA/CD?
   Answer:
   Big BDP means small frames, compared with long links. It implies low link efficiency when other stations keep idle, as a small frame propagates through a long link.
4. What is the problem in half-duplex Gigabit Ethernet?
   Answer:
   Time to transmit a minimum frame might be smaller than the round-trip propagation time. Then collision detection would fail to abort a collided transmission in time, i.e., the transmission ends before the sending station senses the collision.
5. What is the minimum frame length, in meters, when transmitted in Gigabit Ethernet?
   Answer: $64 \times 8 / 10^9 \times 2 \times 10^8 = 25.6$ meters.
6. Why not CSMA/CD for wireless LAN?
   Answer:
   The collision at the receiver, if due to a terminal hidden from the sender, would not be sensed by the sender. So, CD won't work here. In addition, the sender could not sense while transmitting.
7. What problem does the RTS/CTS mechanism solve for CSMA/CA in wireless LAN?
   Answer:
   It solves the hidden terminal problem by having the terminals around the receiver keep silent (after receiving the CTS) when the data frame is being received by the receiver.
8. What are the differences between collision domain, broadcast domain, and VLAN? (Describe what they are, their scopes and whether they can overlap.)
   Answer:
   Collision domain: No two stations in this domain can transmit successfully at the same time; also a broadcast domain in a hub but reduced to a port in a switch.
   Broadcast domain: A broadcast frame will be received by all stations in this domain; also a collision domain in a hub but a set of ports in a switch.
   VLAN: a broadcast domain artificially partitioned from a switch or a set of switches.
9. Layer-2 bridging vs. Layer-3 routing? (Compare their forward mechanisms, management, and scalability.)
   Answer:
   Bridging: by flooding or tables of self learning; plug-and-play; limited to thousands.
   Routing: by tables of global or local information; configuration required; scalable.
10. Layer-2 bridging on a large campus network? Why not?
    Answer:
    Each bridging switch on the campus needs to learn and memorize all hosts on the campus, which requires a large table. Meanwhile, frequent flooding would happen when not all hosts are learned.
11. Why do we say bridges are transparent to hosts while routers are not?
    Answer:
    In bridging, hosts transmit frames regardless of whether the destinations are on the same LAN or not. In routing, hosts explicitly send packets to the default routers if the destinations are not on the same subnet. Thus, hosts are aware of routers but unaware of bridges.
12. Why do we need a spanning tree in transparent bridging?
    Answer:
    To eliminate loops in the topology, which confuse bridges and result in frame looping.
13. How do we design a MAC in an IC? (Describe the general design flow and the variables used in programming.)
    Answer:
    Design flow: block diagram with input and output signals → state machine of each block/module → Verilog or VDHL parallel hardware programming → synthesized and simulated circuits → layout and tape-out.
    Variables: program output variables/signals as parallel functions of input variables/signals and local variables/signals.
14. How does a driver work to send and receive frames? (Describe the handling of outgoing and incoming packets, with hardware and interrupt handling.)
    Answer:
    Outgoing packet handling: invoke remote DMA to move frames to the interface card, write commands to the command register, register an interrupt handler that reads the status register, and send subsequent frames.
    Incoming packet handling: register an interrupt handler that reads the status register, and invoke remote DMA to move frames into main memory.
15. What does a network adaptor driver want when it probes the hardware? For what? What interrupts may lead a system to execute a network adaptor driver?
    Answer:

    1. IRQ number: to bind an interrupt handler to a hardware number.

2. I/O port numbers: to map hardware registers to a region of I/O port numbers used to read status and write commands.

3. Hardware interrupts due to frame arrivals, transmission completion, or abnormal transmissions.

EXERCISES

Hands-On Exercises

1. Read the following two documents and see how the IEEE standards come out. Write a summary of the standardization process.
    1. 10 Gigabit Ethernet Alliance,"10 Gigabit Ethernet Technology Overview: White paper," http://www.10gea.org, September 2001.
    2. http://www.ieee802.org/3/efm/public/sep01/agenda_1_0901.pdf
2. You may download IEEE 802 standards at http://standards.ieee.org/getieee802/
   Write down the development goals of the following projects: 802.1w, 802.3ac, 802.15, 802.16, and 802.17.
3. Find the MAC address of your network interface card. Check http://standards.ieee.org/regauth/oui/oui.txt to compare its OUI with what has been registered.
4. Use Sniffer or similar software to find out how many kinds of "protocol types" in the "Type" field of the Ethernet frames you capture. What transport/application layer protocols, if any, do they belong to?
5. Find out whether your network interface card is operating in half-duplex or full-duplex mode.
6. Trace the source code of the following protocols:

1. HDLC	2. PPPoE
3. Wireless LAN	4. Bluetooth

   Explain the purpose of each major function in the protocol implementation and draw a flowchart with the function names to show the execution flow.
7. After making the kernel and choosing some drivers to be modularized, how do we compile the driver, install the driver, and run these modules? Please also compose one small module to validate your answer. Show what commands are needed to compile and install your module. How do you verify whether your module has been installed successfully? (Hint: Read insmod(8), rmmod(8), and lsmod(8).)
8. A packet's life: Test how much time a packet spends on the driver, DMA, and CSMA/CD adaptor. (You can use "rdtscll" defined in <asm/msr.h> to get the past CPU clock cycle.)

Written Exercises

1. We know 32-bit IPv4 addresses may not be long enough. Are 48-bit MAC addresses long enough? Write down a short discussion to justify your answer.
2. Read RFC 1071 and RFC 1624 to see how IP checksum is computed. Then practice with the following trivial blocks of words by hand:

   0x36f7 0xf670 0x2148 0x8912 0x2345
   0x7863 0x0076

   What if the first word above is changed to 0x36f6? RFCs are available at http://www.ietf.org/rfc.html.
3. Compute the CRC code, given the message 1101010011 and the pattern 10011. Verify that the code is correct.
4. Why is the destination address field usually located in the head of a frame, and the FCS field located in the tail of a frame?
5. What are the advantages and disadvantages if we make the minimum Ethernet frame larger?
6. Suppose data payload in a frame is prepended with 40 bytes of IP and TCP headers. How many bits of data payload per second can be carried in the 100 Mbps Ethernet if each frame is a maximum untagged frame?
7. Should a switch recompute a new FCS of an incoming frame before it is forwarded?
8. There is an optional priority tag in the Ethernet frame, but it is not often employed. Why?
9. Why does not Ethernet implement a complicated flow control mechanism such as sliding-window?
10. What happens if your network interface card runs in full-duplex mode in a shared network?
11. Should each port in a switch have its own MAC address? Discuss it.
12. Suppose each entry in the address table of a switch needs to record the MAC address, 8-bit port number, and 2-bit aging information. What is the minimum memory size if the table can record 4096 entries?
13. Suppose bit stuffing with 0 is used after 5 consecutive 1's. Assuming the probabilities of 0's and 1's in the bit stream are equal and the occurrences are at random, what is the transmission overhead of the bit stuffing

scheme? (Hint: Formulate a recursive formula $f(n)$ to find the expected number of overhead bits in an n-bit string first.)

14. Write a simulation program to verify that the numerical answer to Problem 13 is correct.

15. In 1000BASE-X, a frame of 64 bytes is first block coded with 8B/10B before transmitting. Suppose the propagation speed is 2×10^8. What is the frame "length" in "meters"? (Suppose the cable is 500 m long.)

16. What is the probability of two stations taking five more trials to resolve collisions after they have the first collision? (Suppose only two stations are in the collision domain.)

17. What is the maximum number of frames a switch of 16 Fast Ethernet (100 Mbps) ports may deal with if each port operates in full-duplex mode?

18. A CPU executes instructions at 800 MIPS. Data can be copied 64 bits at a time, with each 64-bit word copied costing six instructions. If an incoming frame has to be copied twice, how much bit rate, at most, of a line can the system handle? (Assume that all instructions run at the full 800-MIPS rate.)

19. A frame of 1500 bytes travel through five switches along the path. Each link has a bandwidth of 100 Mbps, a length of 100 m, and a propagation speed of 2×10^8 m/sec. Assuming a queuing and processing delay of 5 ms at each switch, what is the approximate end-to-end delay for this packet?

20. What is the probability that one out of 100 frames of 1000 bytes suffers from an error on average if the bit error rate is 10^{-8}?

Chapter 4

Internet Protocol Layer

The Internet Protocol (IP) layer, also referred to as layer 3 or the network layer in the OSI model, provides a *host-to-host* transmission service. It is the *most* critical layer of the Internet Protocol stack and much more complicated than the link layer because it provides end-to-end connectivity between any two hosts, which may be separated by thousands of miles. The key challenge to the IP layer is how to provide scalable connectivity between any two hosts efficiently; specifically, it faces connectivity, scalability, and efficient resource sharing problems. First, the essential problem is how to connect any two hosts at arbitrary locations in the global network. Second, to connect billions of hosts spread all over the world requires very scalable *addressing, routing,* and packet *forwarding* mechanisms. Finally, the limited resources, such as processing power and bandwidth, of intermediary devices, such as routers, must be shared efficiently in order to provide satisfactory services to end users.

Both control-plane mechanisms and data-plane mechanisms are required to provide the host-to-host transmission service. The control plane deals with control protocols to determine how packets should be processed. For example, *routing,* as one of the most important functions of the IP layer, is mainly to find a routing path between any two hosts and *store* the routing information in a router's specially designed data structure, called the routing or forwarding table. On the other hand, the data plane deals with how to process data packets. For example, *forwarding,* another important function of the IP layer, transfers a packet from an incoming network interface to an outgoing network interface in a router based on the routing table. There are also other mechanisms required to support the connectivity function, such as *address configuration, address translation,* and *error reporting*. This chapter describes all the major mechanisms of the control plane and data plane used in the Internet to provide the host-to-host connection service.

The chapter is organized as follows: Design issues of the Internet Protocol layer are discussed in Section 4.1. Mechanisms of the data plane and control plane, along with their open source implementations, are described in the subsequent sections. For data-plane mechanisms, we present the Internet Protocol version 4 *(IPv4)* and show how it provides host-to-host service in a scalable and efficient way. At the end of Section 4.2, we illustrate the network address translation *(NAT)* mechanism, which was assumed to be a *transient* solution to the problem of IPv4 address shortage. In Section 4.3, the Internet Protocol version 6 *(IPv6),* proposed to solve several problems encountered by IPv4, is described.

The next four sections discuss mechanisms of the control plane. We examine mechanisms for *address management,* including address resolution protocol *(ARP)* and dynamic host IP configuration protocol *(DHCP),* in Section 4.4. The protocol for handling Internet *errors,* the Internet error control protocol *(ICMP),* is presented in Section 4.5. The most important control mechanism of the IP layer is *routing,* which finds a path between two hosts. These Internet routing protocols are detailed in Section 4.6 to show how routing is done in a scalable manner. Finally, in Section 4.7, we review the *multicast* routing protocols, an *extension* of point-to-point routing to multipoint-to-multipoint routing.

4.1 GENERAL ISSUES

The goal of the network layer, or the IP layer in the TCP/IP reference model, is to transport packets from a sending host to a receiving host. Unlike the services provided by the link layer where communication is achieved between two *adjacent* hosts, services provided by the network layer allow communication between *any* two hosts, no matter how far away they are. This connectivity requirement introduces three general issues, namely how to connect networks via link-layer technologies, how to identify a host globally, and how to find a path between two hosts and forward packets along the path. Solutions to these issues must be very scalable to accommodate the connections among billions of hosts. Finally, it also needs to address how to share limited resources, such as bandwidth, efficiently.

4.1.1 Connectivity Issues

Internetworking

Connectivity is certainly the essential requirement for transporting packets from one host to another. Many issues need to be resolved for such host-level connectivity. First, how are hosts connected? Hosts may connect to the network via different link-layer technologies such as Ethernet or wireless LAN. As we have seen in Chapter 3, a basic limitation on these link-layer technologies is *distance*. That is, the *coverage* of a LAN cannot exceed a certain distance. There is also a limit on the *number* of nodes that can share the bandwidth of a LAN. Therefore, it takes a large number of LANs and their *internetworking* devices to organize hosts scattered around the world. A set of connected networks is referred to as an *internetwork,* or *internet* for short. The global internetwork that is widely used today is called the *"Internet."* The internetworking devices that connect networks into an internetwork are usually called routers. Connectivity between any two hosts can be achieved by using routers to connect local area networks into a global internetwork. Figure 4.1 shows an example of an internetwork with routers and heterogeneous kinds of LANs.

Addressing

The second issue of connectivity at the network layer is how to *identify* a host in a global internetwork, which is the issue of *addressing*. Unlike addressing in the link layer, the address of a host at the network layer requires *global* identification of the network it

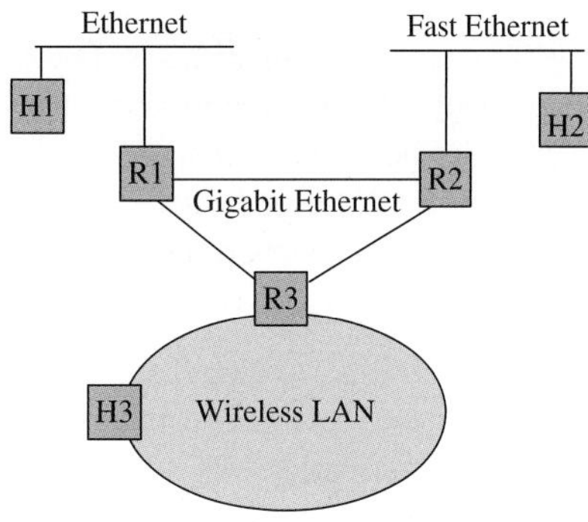

FIGURE 4.1 An example of internetworks.

resides in. In other words, the address of a host needs to identify the network the host belongs to and the host itself. This kind of address is called a hierarchical address. Assigning a host a network layer address also creates a new issue: A host will have a network address (or more) for each network interface card, in addition to its link addresses. Therefore, *address resolution* between these two layers becomes a new issue. Related to the addressing issue is how to assign a network layer address to a host. In reality, it can be done manually or automatically. If it is done automatically, the address can be assigned statically or dynamically. In most cases, a host would like to have its address configured automatically and dynamically, so a dynamic host configuration protocol is needed.

Routing and Forwarding

Given that a host can be identified, the next issue is how to find a path to transport packets from one host to another. A path consists of a *concatenation* of adjacent routers. The issues of finding a path and transporting packets along the path are called *routing* and *forwarding,* respectively. Routing protocols running at the control plane are responsible for *finding* a path between two hosts (or networks). Routing tables are built to record the results of routing. When a packet arrives at a router, it will be forwarded to the next hop on the routing path according to the routing table entry that matches the packet's destination address. Here we make the distinction between routing and forwarding clear: Routing is performed by routing protocols, which require exchange of routing messages and calculation of the shortest path, whereas forwarding is performed by hosts or routers by looking up the routing table and finding the most appropriate network interface to forward the packet.

4.1.2 Scalability Issues

Scalability is important to internetworking when we consider the number of hosts and networks that are connected in the Internet. Scalability is especially important for routing and forwarding—it is very challenging to find a path to a host within a set of billions of hosts efficiently. We shall see in this chapter how network *hierarchy* is used to solve the scalability problem. In the Internet, nodes are grouped into subnetworks, usually referred to as *subnets*. Each subnet represents a logical *broadcast*

Principle in Action: Bridging vs. Routing

There are some similarities between bridging and routing. For example, both can be used for connecting two or more LANs, and both look up a table for forwarding packets. However, they are quite different in other respects. In this sidebar, *bridge* is a general term for all kinds of bridges, two-port or multiple-port.

Layering: A bridge is a link-layer device, while a router is a network-layer device. A bridge forwards a frame based on the link-layer header information, e.g., destination MAC address, while a router forwards a packet based on the network layer header information, e.g., destination IP address.

Table: A bridge usually builds a forwarding table through *transparent* self-learning, while a router builds a routing table by running a routing protocol *explicitly*. A bridge also needs to run a spanning tree protocol to avoid *looping* when more than one bridge is connected.

Collision domain vs. broadcast domain: A bridge is used to separate a *collision,* domain, while a router is used to separate a *broadcast* domain. A collision domain refers to a network segment in which hosts share the same transmission medium and might have a collision if two or more packets are transmitted simultaneously. An *n*-port bridge could separate one collision domain into *n* collision domains by dividing the collision domain among *n* ports. However, all these collision domains are still under the *same* broadcast domain unless VLANs are created. A broadcast domain refers to a network in which all nodes can communicate with each other by broadcast at the link layer. From the perspective of Internet Protocol, a broadcast domain corresponds to an IP subnet. An *n*-port router could separate one broadcast domain into *n* broadcast domains. When VLANs are created on a backbone of bridges, the concept of broadcast domain becomes very important. All hosts within a VLAN, no matter how many bridges are among them, are in the *same* broadcast domain and shall be reached by broadcast at the link layer. On the other hand, two hosts in two different VLANs can only communicate through a router even if they are connected to the same bridge.

Scalability: Bridging is *less* scalable than routing due to the broadcast requirement. As was previously mentioned, hosts connected by one or more bridges are still within a broadcast domain and shall be reached by broadcast. Therefore, if millions of hosts are bridged together, it will be very difficult, if not impossible, to deliver a broadcast message to all hosts. Meanwhile, when a MAC address is *not* learned into the forwarding table, *flooding* will be used to forward a frame, which is extremely inefficient in a large internetwork.

domain, so hosts within a subnet can send packets to each other directly without assistance from routers. Several subnets are then grouped into *domains*. *Intra-domain* and *inter-domain* routing are done separately by different routing protocols, and the entries in a routing table may represent a subnet or a domain.

Several issues on routing need to be addressed, as discussed in Chapter 1. It should be clear now, by considering the scalability requirement, that the chosen solutions for Internet routing are *hop-by-hop, shortest path* routing done on *per-destination-network* granularity. How to compute a path and how to gather routing information also depends on scalability. For intra-domain routing, scalability is less of a problem, and *optimality* is often more important. Therefore, one of the objectives of routing within a domain is efficient resource sharing, which is achieved by finding the shortest path between each source-destination pair. Routing information can be gathered either by *exchanging* information between adjacent routers only or by *flooding* routing information to all routers within the same domain. Hence, intra-domain routing decisions (finding the shortest path) can be based on *partial* routing information or *global* routing information. On the other hand, for inter-domain routing, scalability is more important than optimality. Another issue that needs to be considered for inter-domain routing is administrative *policies* made by different domain administrators who may wish to prohibit some traffic traversing through certain domains. As a consequence, policy-based routing is more important than efficient resource sharing. For scalability and policy-based routing, inter-domain routing usually *exchanges* only *summarized* information between adjacent routers and makes routing decisions based on *partial* routing information. We shall discuss the routing issues raised in Section 4.6 in more detail.

4.1.3 Resource Sharing Issues

Stateless and Unreliable

Finally, let us address several resource sharing issues. In the Internet, resources are shared freely without any control at the network layer. The Internet Protocol provides a *connectionless* service model to upper layers. Under the connectionless service model, packets need to carry enough information in their headers to enable intermediate routers to route and forward packets to their destinations correctly. As a consequence, *no* setup mechanism is required before sending packets. This is the simplest way to share network resources. The connectionless service model also implies *best effort* service, although it need not be. When forwarding packets, routers just do their best to forward packets correctly to their destinations based on routing tables. If something goes wrong, such as a packet getting lost, failing to reach its destination, or being delivered out of order, the network does nothing to fix the problem. The network just makes its best effort to deliver packets. This also implies that the service provided by the network layer is *unreliable*.

Because the service at the network layer is unreliable, an *error reporting* mechanism is needed to inform the original source and/or the upper layer of the source host. Issues on error reporting include how to transmit error messages, how to identify the type of error, how to let the source know which packet caused the error, how to handle error messages at the source, and whether the bandwidth used by error messages should be limited.

The final issue in resource sharing is security. There are several aspects to the security issue. *Access control* deals with who has the rights to access network resources. *Data security* deals with encrypting packets to protect data against eavesdropping. Finally, there is the issue of *system security,* which protects a host from illegal intrusion or virus attacks. We shall defer the discussion of them to Chapter 8, though some of them, say access control and data security, could be resolved in the IP layer.

4.1.4 Overview of IP-Layer Protocols and Packet Flows

Figure 4.2 gives a roadmap of the protocols that we discuss in this chapter. When a host powers on, the DHCP protocol can be used to *configure* its IP address, subnet mask, default router, etc. After the host is properly configured, a packet sent from the upper layer, such as TCP or UDP, is then processed by the IP layer to determine how to *forward* the packet. Whether the packet is to be sent directly to the receiver located within the same subnet or to the router for packet forwarding, the ARP protocol is used to *translate* the IP address of the receiver to its link layer (MAC) address. If there is an error in IP processing, the ICMP protocol is used to send error messages to the source that generates the original IP packet. If the packet is sent to a router, usually the default router, the packet will be forwarded by the router according to the packet's destination address and the routing information in the routing table. The routing table is *maintained* by the routing protocol running at the router. When the packet arrives at the receiver, the packet is received and processed by the IP protocol, and if there are no errors, it is sent to the corresponding upper-layer protocol. If a private IP address is used for privacy or security reasons, the network address translation protocol (NAT) is used to *translate* the IP address and/or the transport layer identifier (TCP/UDP *port number*) of IP packets to achieve global Internet connectivity.

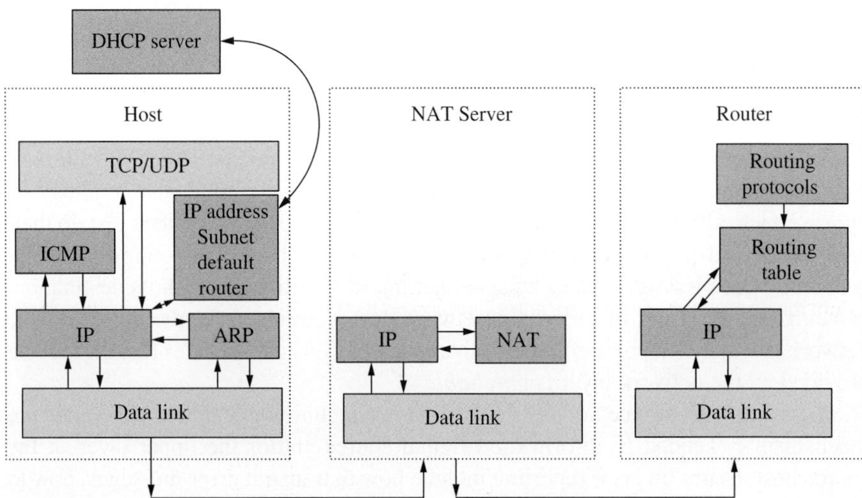

FIGURE 4.2 Protocols in shaded box discussed in this chapter.

Open Source Implementation 4.1: IP-Layer Packet Flows in Call Graphs

Overview

The IP layer sits upon the link layer and under the transport layer in the Internet Protocol stack. With the layering approach, interfaces shall be provided between two adjacent layers. Therefore, the interfaces of the IP layer include that with the link layer and that with the transport layer. As in Chapter 3, we examine these two interfaces through the packet reception path and the packet transmission path. In the reception path, a packet is received from the link layer and then passed to transport-layer protocols, including TCP, UDP, and raw IP socket interface. In the transmission path, a packet is received from one of the transport-layer protocols and then passed to the link layer.

The Reception Path

A frame received by the network interface card will trigger an interrupt, and the interrupt handler calls `net_rx_action()` to process the incoming frame. As described in Chapter 3, the actual function that invokes the network-layer protocol handler is `netif_receive_skb()`. Then the function registered to `backlog_dev.poll()` is invoked to process the following reception operations. As shown in Figure 4.3, when the network-layer protocol type registered in `sk_buff` is the IP protocol, `ip_rcv()` will be called as the protocol handler. The packet is then passed through several IP layer functions which will be discussed later in this chapter. If the packet is for the local host, `ip_local_deliver()` is called, and then it calls `ip_local_deliver_finish()` to deliver the packet to the transport-layer protocol handler. The handler is either `raw_v4_input()`, `udp_v4_rcv()`, or `tcp_v4_rcv()`, depending on whether the upper-layer protocol is raw IP socket interface, UDP, or TCP, respectively.

The Transmission Path

The transmission path is also shown in Figure 4.3. An upper-layer protocol pushes the packets to the IP layer into its queue. `ip_append_data()`, `ip_append_page()`, or `ip_queue_xmit()` is called to deliver a packet to the IP layer, depending on which transport layer protocol is used. To avoid sending too many small packets, the former two functions store data on a temporary buffer first, and later `ip_push_pending_frames()` is called on the temporary buffer to actually pack data into packets of an appropriate size. All these functions will call `dst_output()`, which subsequently calls the virtual function `skb->dst->output()` registered in the `sk_buff` to invoke the network layer handler `ip_output()` if the network layer protocol is IP. If no fragmentation is required, `ip_finish_output2()` will deliver the packet to the link layer via `net_tx_action()`, as described in Chapter 3.

Continued

Exercises

Trace the source code along the reception path and the transmission path to observe the details of function calls on these two paths.

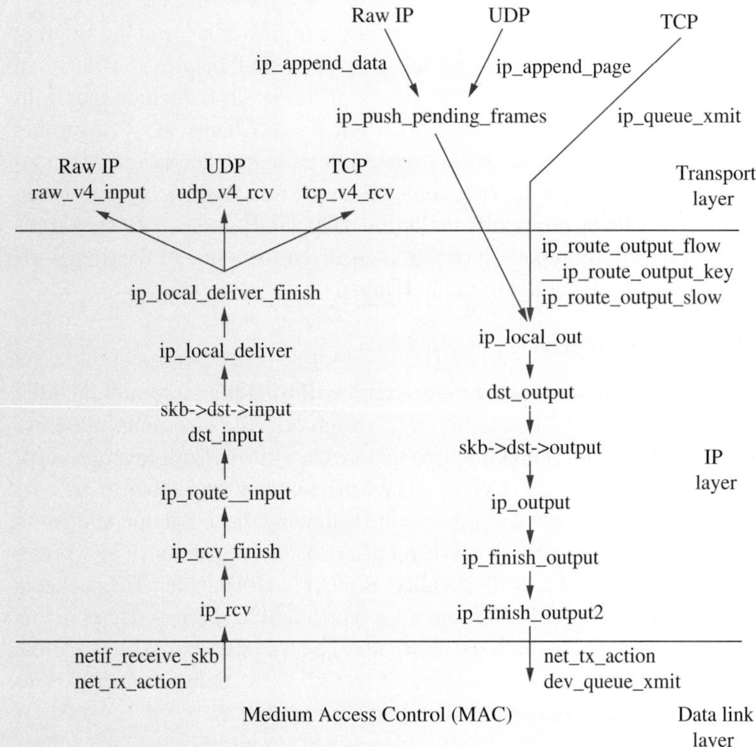

FIGURE 4.3 Packet flows in call graphs.

Performance Matters: Latency Within the IP Layer

Figure 4.4 shows the latency breakdown of important IP-layer functions to transmit 64-byte ICMP packets. The total latency is about 4.42 μs, and the bottleneck function `ip_finish_output2()` occupies more than 50% of total processing time. As mentioned in Open Source Implementation 4.1, `ip_finish_output2()` delivers packets to the link layer. Before calling `net_tx_action()`, it needs to prepend the Ethernet headers to packets. The prepending task invokes memory copying and therefore consumes more time than other functions.

Figure 4.5 profiles the latency of packet-receiving functions in the IP layer. The top four time-consuming functions are `ip_route_input()` (26%),

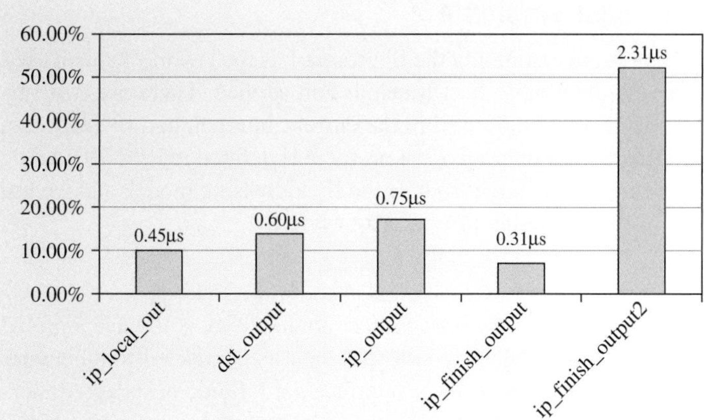

FIGURE 4.4 Latency in transmitting ICMP packets in the IP layer.

`ip_local_deliver_finish()` (24%), `ip_rcv()` (17%), and `ip_rcv_finish()` (16%). `ip_route_input()` consumes time on querying the routing tables. `ip_local_deliver_finish()` removes the IP header, finds out the correct transport layer protocol handler of the packet by a hash table lookup, and then passes it to the handler. `ip_rcv()` validates the header checksum field in IP packets. Finally, `ip_rcv_finish()` updates the statistics of the routing table.

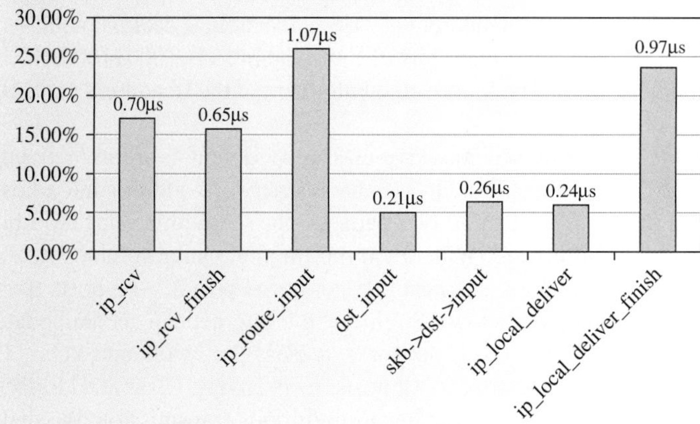

FIGURE 4.5 Latency in receiving ICMP packets in the IP layer.

4.2 DATA-PLANE PROTOCOLS: INTERNET PROTOCOL

In this section, we first examine the current version of Internet Protocol, IPv4. In IPv4, a special type of address, called a *private* IP address, is used for security and IP address depletion reasons. In the second subsection, we examine the network address translation (NAT) protocol, which enables hosts with private IP addresses to access the Internet.

4.2.1 Internet Protocol Version 4

The Internet Protocol, or more commonly the IP protocol, is the key mechanism used in the Internet to provide the host-to-host transmission service. There are two versions of the IP protocol: IP version 4, used in the current Internet, and IP version 6, to be used in the next-generation Internet. IPv4 protocol is defined in RFC 791, while IPv6 is defined in RFC 2460. We first introduce the IP addressing model, and we use this model to explain how the Internet provides connectivity.

IPv4 Addressing

The first thing required in building the host-to-host connectivity is to have a global and unique addressing scheme to identify a host. A host is connected to a network via an interface, such as an Ethernet network interface card. Some hosts and routers may be equipped with more than one network interface. For each network interface, an IP address is used to identify the interface for sending and receiving IP packets. To locate a network interface among billions of hosts, we need some kind of *hierarchical* structure to organize and locate an IP address *globally*. The hierarchical structure of the IP address is very similar to that of the postal address. The postal address of our home consists of the number, the road, the city, and the country so that the post office can easily identify where to deliver our mail. Similarly, the IP addressing scheme has a hierarchical structure so that intermediate routers can easily identify to which *networks* an IP packet should be delivered.

Each *IP address* is 32 bits (4 bytes) long and consists of two parts: a *network* address and a *host* id. Typically, an IP address is written in a dotted-decimal notation. For example, in Figure 4.6, the first eight bits of the IP address is 10001100, which is equivalent to 140 in decimals. The four decimal numbers of the IP address are then separated by dots.

IP uses a *classful* addressing scheme. Five classes of IP addresses are defined, as shown in Figure 4.7. All classes of addresses have a network address and a host id, but they differ in the lengths of these two parts. A class A address has an 8-bit network address and a 24-bit host id. With IPv4, the Internet can accommodate up to 2^7 class A networks, and each class A network can have up to $2^{24} - 2$ hosts (two special addresses are reserved; see below). Similarly, the Internet can accommodate up to 2^{14} class B networks and 2^{21} class C networks. A class B network and a class C network can have up to $2^{16} - 2$ hosts and $2^8 - 2$ hosts, respectively. Class D addresses are *multicast* addresses, which allow multipoint-to-multipoint transmission. We shall discuss IP multicast in Section 4.7. The fifth class, starting with the address prefix 11110, is reserved for future use.

Given the *starting bits* of the classful addresses as shown in Figure 4.7, the *range* of each class of addresses is also fixed. The class A addresses cover the range from 0.0.0.0 to 127.255.255.255. (Note that 0.0.0.0/8 is reserved for local identification

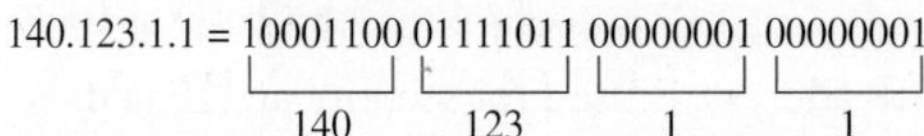

FIGURE 4.6 Dotted-decimal notation of an IP address.

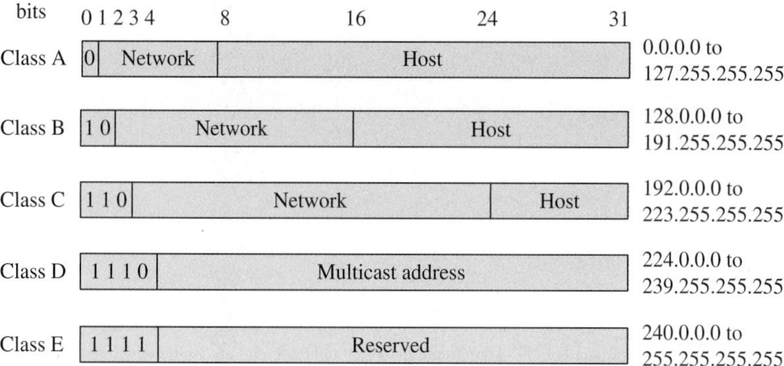

FIGURE 4.7 The classful IPv4 address formats.

and 127.0.0.0/8 is reserved for loopback test.) From 128.0.0.0 to 191.255.255.255 and from 192.0.0.0 to 223.255.255.255 are ranges for the class B and the class C addresses, respectively. The class D address ranges from 224.0.0.0 to 239.0.0.0. Finally, the addresses from 240.0.0.0 to 255.255.255.255 are reserved for future use. (Note that 255.255.255.255 is a *broadcast* address in a subnet.)

Some IP addresses in each class are reserved for special use. If the host id is zero, it is used to represent an IP subnet. For example, 140.123.101.0 is a class B subnet address. On the other hand, if bits of the host id are all 1, it is used for broadcast in that IP subnet. Finally, the IP address, 255.255.255.255, is used to broadcast packets in an IP subnet when the source host does not know its own IP address yet, as when a host needs to contact a DHCP server to obtain its IP address. We shall discuss the DHCP protocol in Section 4.4.

IP Subnetting

The network address of an IP address is supposed to uniquely identify a physical network. However, a physical network is usually constructed using LAN technologies, as described in Chapter 3. For a class A or B network, the number of host ids is much larger than any LAN technology can support. Therefore, it is not practical to expect there to be only one physical network, or LAN, in a class A or B network. As a consequence, an organization that owns a class A, class B, or even class C network address often divides its own network into several sub-networks (subnets). Logically, two hosts in the same IP subnet must be able to send packets to each other *directly* using link-layer technologies, without passing the packets through a router. To maintain the hierarchical structure of the IP address, all hosts in the same IP subnet must have the same *prefix* (leftmost bits) in their IP addresses. Therefore, part of the host id is used to denote the *subnet address* within a class A, B, or C network, as shown in Figure 4.8. The number of bits used to denote the subnet address depends on the number of subnets and the number of hosts within a subnet that the administrator of the organization desires. For example, a class B address with an 8-bit subnet address and an 8-bit host id will result in up to 2^8 subnets and $2^8 - 2$ hosts within each subnet.

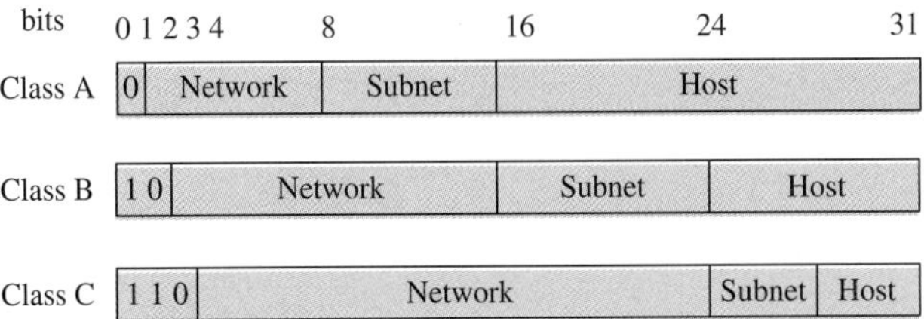

FIGURE 4.8 IP subnet addressing.

In order to determine whether two hosts are within the same IP subnet, the notation of *subnet mask* is applied to IP subnetting. The subnet mask indicates the length of the leftmost bits of an IP address, which are used as the subnet address. Continuing with the preceding subnetting example of a class B address, the subnet address is the 24 leftmost bits of the 32-bit IP address. Two notations are used to denote the subnet mask. First, we can use a 32-bit string in which the subnet-address part and the host-id part are filled with 1's and 0's accordingly to denote the subnet mask, e.g., 255.255.255.0 in our example. Alternately, we can denote an IP address as 140.123.101.0/24, where /24 indicates that the subnet mask is 24 bits long.

A typical network thus consists of several subnets, and hosts in the same subnet have the same subnet mask and subnet address. For example, in Figure 4.9, there are five hosts connecting to three subnets, namely 140.123.1.0, 140.123.2.0, 140.123.3.0. Hosts H1 and H2 are connected to the same subnet and thus have the same subnet address, namely 140.123.1.0. Subnets are connected with routers (R1~R3) to form an internetwork. The network interface of a router connected to a subnet also has the same subnet mask and subnet address as those of hosts in the same subnet. Notably, each router is usually equipped with several network interface cards. Some of them connect routers to subnets of hosts; however, some of them are used to connect routers to form a traffic exchange or distribution backbone, such as the 140.123.250.0 subnet in Figure 4.9.

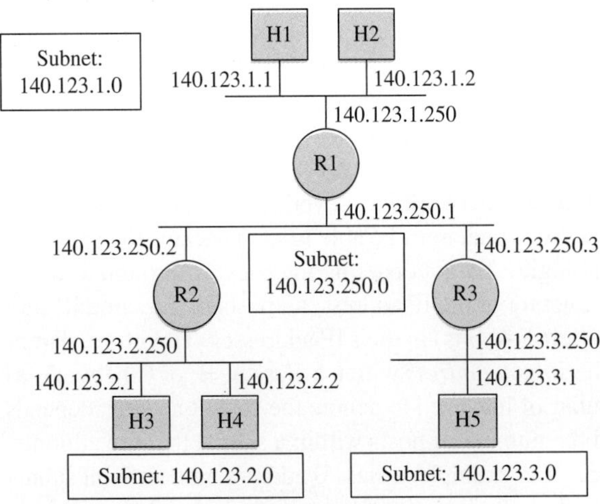

FIGURE 4.9 An example of IP subnetting.

CIDR Address

There are a couple of problems with the classful IP addressing. First, due to the fixed length of the network address, there is a dilemma when assigning IP addresses to a medium-sized organization, for instance, an organization that has up to 2000 hosts. A class C network address is too small for such an organization since it can support only up to 254 hosts, whereas a class B network address is too large as it would leave more than 63,000 addresses unused. A possible solution is to assign more than one class C network address to the organization, but with this solution, *scalability* for routing and forwarding now becomes a problem. With classful IP addressing, *each* class C network address occupies an entry in the routing table of a backbone router. However, for an organization with several class C addresses, the routing entries associated with these class C addresses all should point to the same routing path to the organization. This results in the problem that the size of the routing table at backbone routers would be very large, as there are many class C network addresses, but many of the entries in the routing table would carry the same routing information.

Classless Inter-Domain Routing (CIDR) is thus proposed to solve the problems. With CIDR, the *network* part of an IP address can have an arbitrary length. A medium-sized organization will be assigned a *block* of IP addresses, which are usually *consecutive* class C network addresses. For example, an organization with 2000 hosts can be assigned a block of IP addresses ranging from 194.24.0.0 to 194.24.7.255 with the subnet mask 255.255.248.0 or 194.24.0.0/21. That is, the first 21 bits are used to specify the organization's network address. A backbone router would need only *one* routing entry to record the network interface to the organization, as illustrated by Figure 4.10. IP subnetting within the organization can be done as mentioned before.

Packet Forwarding

Recall from Section 4.1 that forwarding is the process of receiving a packet from the upper layer or a network interface and sending it out on the appropriate network interface. Both hosts and routers need to forward packets. For a host, packets from the upper layer need to be sent on one of its outgoing network interfaces. For a router, packets from its network interfaces need to be forwarded on to other network interfaces. The key idea of the IP forwarding process is that if the destination of the packet

Destination	Next hop
194.24.0.0	19.1.1.250
194.24.1.0	19.1.1.250
194.24.2.0	19.1.1.250
194.24.3.0	19.1.1.250
194.24.4.0	19.1.1.250
194.24.5.0	19.1.1.250
194.24.6.0	19.1.1.250
194.24.7.0	19.1.1.250

Destination	Prefix length	Next hop
......	......	......
194.24.0.0	/21	19.1.1.250
......	......	......

FIGURE 4.10 Comparison of a routing table with and without CIDR.

to be forwarded is located in the *same* subnet as the forwarding node, the packet is sent *directly* to the destination. Otherwise, the forwarding node needs to look up the routing table to find the appropriate *next hop* router to forward the packet, and then sends the packet directly to the next hop router. A routing table entry consists of a *(Destination/SubnetMask, NextHop) pair,* but it may also contain additional information, depending on the type of routing protocols running underneath. The destination is usually expressed in the form of a network address, e.g., 194.24.0.0/21. NextHop is either a *router IP address* or a network *interface*. The next-hop router must be in the same subnet as one of its network interfaces such that it can be communicated with directly. Normally, there is an entry recording a *default router* with the destination address '0.0.0.0/0'. If the destination of a packet does not match any entries of the routing table, it will be forwarded to the default router.

We can describe the packet-forwarding algorithm from two aspects. First, for a host, we consider the case where there is a packet from the upper layer, say TCP, to be sent to the destination. In particular, we consider the most common case where the host has only one network interface card and one default router. In this case, the IP forwarding algorithm operates as follows:

```
If the packet is to be delivered to the same host
     Deliver the packet to an upper-layer protocol
Else If (NetworkAddress of the destination == My subnet
address)
     Transmit the packet directly to the destination
Else
     Look up the routing table
     Deliver the packet to the default router
End if
```

Now, let us consider the case where a router or a host with forwarding capability receives a packet from one of its network interfaces. In this case, the packet may be forwarded to the destination on the appropriate network interface, or delivered locally to an upper-layer protocol if the destination address is the host itself. The forwarding algorithm works as follows:

```
If the packet is to be delivered to the upper layer
     Deliver the packet to an upper-layer protocol
Else Look up the routing table
     If the packet is to be delivered to a directly
connected subnet
       Deliver the packet directly to the destination
     Else
       Deliver the packet to a next hop router
     End if
End if
```

Three operations in the previous two algorithms deserve further discussion. First, how does the forwarding host obtain the network address of the destination and determine whether the node itself and the destination are *directly* connected? This Boolean judgment can be easily implemented by using the following operation:

If ((HostIP ^ DestinationIP) & SubnetMask)==0)

where ^ is the *bitwise-exclusive-or* operation and & is the *bitwise-and* operation.

Second, delivering a packet to the destination within a subnet requires forming a Layer-2 frame with the MAC address of the destination. This involves the operation of *address resolution,* which we shall describe in Section 4.4. Finally, the procedure of *looking up the routing table* is described next.

Routing Table Lookup

As we have seen, routing table lookup is an essential operation to the IP forwarding algorithm. Due to the CIDR addressing, looking up the routing table is now known as the *longest prefix matching* problem. That is, the routing entry that matches the *longest* prefix of the destination address of the packet should be chosen for forwarding. Consider the case where there are two organizations: A and B. Organization A owns the IP addresses from 194.24.0.0 to 194.24.6.255. Since packets destined to any IP addresses in this range should be routed to the same network interface, it needs only *one* routing entry in the routing table to route packets to organization A. As a result of route summarization, the network address of the routing entry for organization A is denoted by 194.24.0.0/21. Organization B only owns a class C network address, from 194.24.7.0 to 194.24.7.255. Therefore, the routing entry for organization B records the network address 194.24.7.0/24. Now, suppose we want to look up the routing entry for the destination IP address 194.24.7.10. Clearly, the destination IP address matches *both* routing entries, that is, ((194.24.7.10^194.24.0.0) & 255.255.248.0) == 0 and ((194.24.7.10^194.24.7.0) & 255.255.255.0) == 0. We know 194.24.7.10 belongs to organization B, so the routing entry with the *longer* network address, 194.24.7.0/24, should be chosen. Examining both cases carefully, we find that 194.24.7.10 matches the first 24 bits of 194.24.7.0/24 but only 21 bits of 194.24.0.0/21. Now it should be clear why longest prefix matching is adopted.

Recently, fast algorithms for longest prefix matching have been proposed. In the literature, forwarding tables with cache, hash, and hardware-based implementation (parallel algorithm, CAM-based or DRAM-based) are some well-known solutions. In Linux, the lookup algorithm is mainly based on *two-level hashing*. The traditional BSD implementation uses the *trie* data structure. A trie, also called a prefix tree, is an ordered tree data structure. Since the IP address is a string of bits, the trie used for longest prefix matching is a binary trie, as shown in Figure 4.11. A router first builds a dictionary, which consists of all routing prefixes. A trie can then be built by adding prefixes one by one from the dictionary into the trie structure. A node, marked with * in Figure 4.11, on the trie carries next-hop information if it corresponds to a prefix in the dictionary. In a search of the longest prefix matching for a destination address, each edge on the trie represents a binary bit string which directs the search until it cannot proceed any further. The node where the search ends stores the next-hop information as the result of longest prefix matching. For example, using the trie

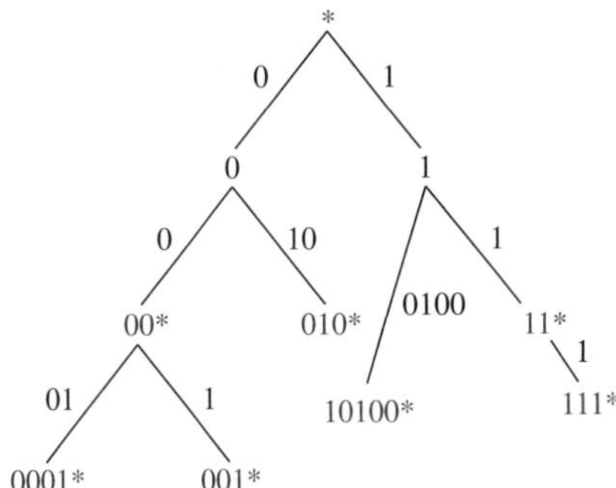

FIGURE 4.11 An example of trie with prefixes {00*,010*, 11*, 0001*, 001*, 10100*, 111*}.

in Figure 4.10 to search the longest prefix matching for address 00001111, we start from the root, move along the left branch twice and end up at the node 00* since the third and fourth bits of the address are 00, which do not match any child of node 00*. Therefore, the longest prefix matching is the prefix 00*.

Open Source Implementation 4.2: IPv4 Packet Forwarding

Overview

Now let us examine how packet forwarding is done in Linux 2.6 kernel. A packet is forwarded based on the routing table entry selected by the longest prefix matching algorithm. The chosen entry contains the next-hop information for packet forwarding. The first step of packet forwarding is to look up the routing table for the entry corresponding to the result of longest prefix matching. Looking up the routing table is time consuming, especially when doing longest prefix matching. Therefore, good data structures have been proposed to speed up the search in the routing table, for example, use of trie, or binary search based on prefix length. On the other hand, since the same destination is likely to be visited frequently, storing the search result of the first visit in a *routing cache* and then searching the routing cache for subsequent visits could save a lot of time on routing-table lookups. Therefore, in Linux 2.6 implementation, a routing cache is used to accelerate the destination address lookup process. With the assistance of the routing cache, a full search in the routing table is performed only in case of a cache miss.

Block Diagram

The call graph of Linux 2.6's IPv4 packet forwarding process is given in Figure 4.12. For packets that come from the upper layer, if the routing path is not known yet, the main function that determines the output device (interface) is `__ip_route_output_key()` (in `src/net/ipv4/route.c`). The `__ip_route_output_key()` tries to find the routing path (output

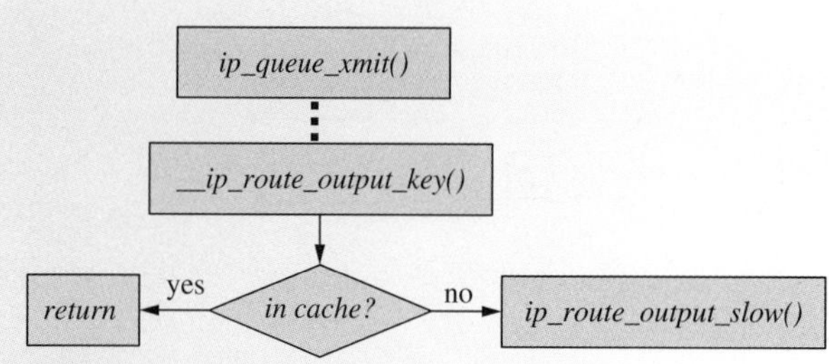

FIGURE 4.12 IP forwarding implementation: `__ip_route_output_key`.

device) in the *routing cache* using the *hash* function, `rt_hash()`, which eventually calls Bob Jenkins's hash function `jhash()` in `include/linux/jhash.h` (see also `http://burtleburtle.net/bob/hash/`). If the routing path is not in the routing cache, `ip_route_output_slow()` is then called to look up the destination in the *routing table* by calling `fib_lookup()`.

Algorithm Implementations

Upon receiving a packet from a network interface, the packet is first copied into kernel's `sk_buff`. Typically `skb->dst` is NULL, i.e., no virtual cache path for this packet, and `ip_rcv_finish()` calls `ip_route_input()` to determine how to forward the packet. As in the previous case, `ip_route_input()` tries to find the routing path in the routing cache first. If not found, `ip_route_input_slow()` is called, which in turn calls `fib_lookup()` to look up the routing table.

Data Structures

The routing cache is maintained with the `rt_hash_table` data structure, which is an array of `rt_hash_bucket`. Each entry of the `rt_hash_table` points to a list of `rtable`'s, as shown in Figure 4.13. The `rt_hash()` hashes on three parameters derived from the packet: source address, destination address, and type of service. When the hash entry is obtained by `rt_hash()`, linear search is performed on the list of `rtable`'s to which the entry points.

If the destination address cannot be found in the routing cache, the Forwarding Information dataBase (FIB) will be searched. The FIB data structure is rather complicated, as shown in Figure 4.14. Linux 2.6 kernel allows multiple IP routing tables, each described by an independent `fib_table` data structure. The last field of this data structure, `tb_data`, points to an `fn_hash` data structure, which consists of a hash table, `fn_zones`, and a hash list, `fn_zone_list`. The `fn_zones` is an array of 33 `fn_zone`'s, where `fn_zones[z]` points to a hash table for prefix length of `z`, 0 <= `z` <= 32. All non-empty entries of `fn_zones` are then linked by the `fn_zone_list`, headed with the entry with the longest prefix. The `fib_lookup()` calls each table's `tb_lookup()` function to search the routing table. The default `tb_lookup()` function is

Continued

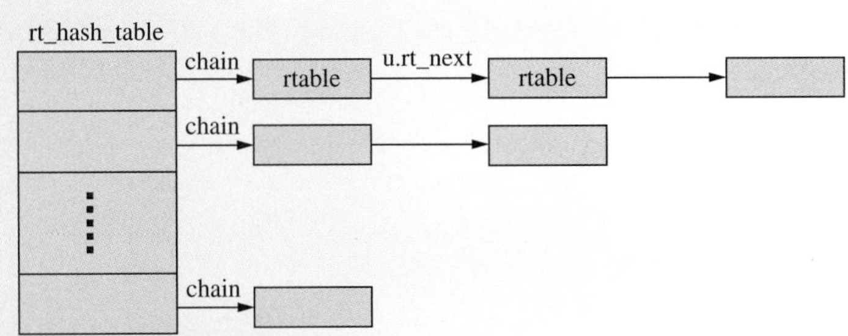

FIGURE 4.13 Routing cache.

`fn_hash_lookup()` (in `src/net/ipv4/fib_hash.c`), which sequentially searches the hash table of each prefix length by traversing through the `fn_zone_list`. This *sequential* search ends when a match is found. By searching from the *head* of `fn_zone_list`, longest prefix matching is guaranteed. That is, the *first* match is the *longest* match.

In the middle of Figure 4.14, each entry of `fn_zones` points to an `fn_zone` data structure. The `fn_zone` consists of one pointer to the `fn_zone_list`, and a hash table, `fz_hash`, which is an array of pointers to `fib_node`'s. A `fib_node` corresponds to a unique subnet. The hash key, `fn_key`, is the prefix of the subnet, e.g., if the subnet is 200.1.1.0/24, then the `fn_key` is 200.1.1. The hash function, `fn_hash()`, is defined as an inline function in `src/net/ipv4/fib_hash.c`. The `fn_alias` entry in each `fib_node` points to a `fib_alias` structure, which contains some basic information of the subnet such as `fa_tos`, `fa_type`, and `fa_scope`, and a pointer

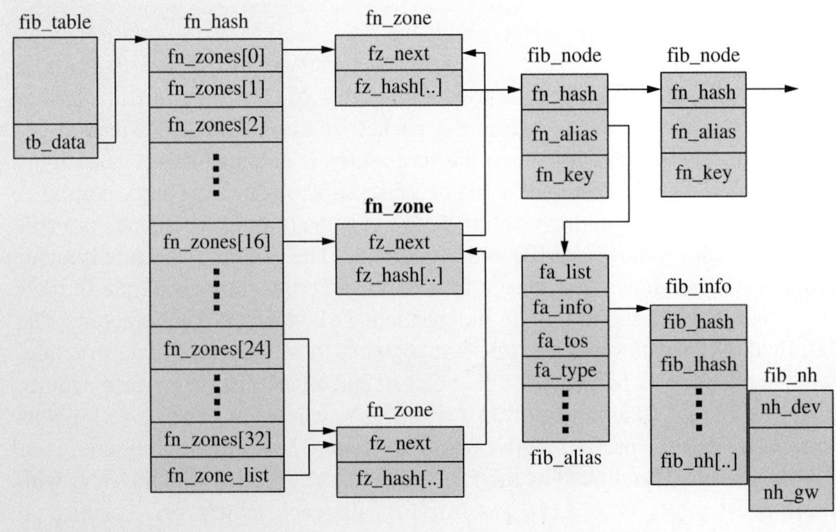

FIGURE 4.14 FIB data structure.

to a `fib_info` data structure. Finally, the `fib_info` contains the detailed information of a routing entry, including the *output device* and the *next-hop router*.

The default size of the hash table (the number of entries of `fz_hash`) is 16 for any nonzero prefix length. If the number of nodes stored in the hash table exceeds twice the table size, the table size is increased to 256 for the first occurrence, then to 1024 for the second occurrence, and after that the table size is doubled whenever the condition occurs.

Exercises

1. Use an example to trace `__ip_route_output_key()` and write down how the routing cache is searched.
2. Trace `fib_lookup()` to explore how FIB is searched.

Performance Matters: Lookup Time at Routing Cache and Table

For the *first* packet arrival in a packet flow, the routing mechanism is likely to incur two route lookup operations, one on the routing cache, which leads to a lookup miss, and then the other on the FIB routing table producing a hit. For each of the *subsequent* packet arrivals in the flow, the routing mechanism can find in the routing cache the lookup result for the first packet arrival, which means one lookup on the cache only. One interesting question is how fast we can perform route lookup in these two data structures. We need to measure the time spent on executing `ip_route_output_key()` and `ip_route_output_slow()`. On a lightly loaded Linux router handling 64-byte packets, our measurement yields 0.6 μs and 25 μs for `ip_route_output_key()` and `ip_route_output_slow()`, respectively, which indicates that these two differ by a factor of 42. Though both are hash tables, the FIB table is an *array* of hash tables, which would require *sequential* hashing from the table with the longest prefixes.

Packet Format

Next we look at IP packet format. An IP packet consists of a header field followed by a data field, and its length must be a multiple of 4-byte words. The format of the IP header is shown in Figure 4.15. We describe the semantics of each field in the following:

- *Version Number:* The version number specifies the version of the IP protocol. The current version of the IP protocol is 4 and the version for next generation IP is 6.
- *Header Length:* The IPv4 header has a variable length. This field specifies the length of the IP header in units of 4-byte words. Without the option field, the typical header length is five words, i.e., 20 bytes.

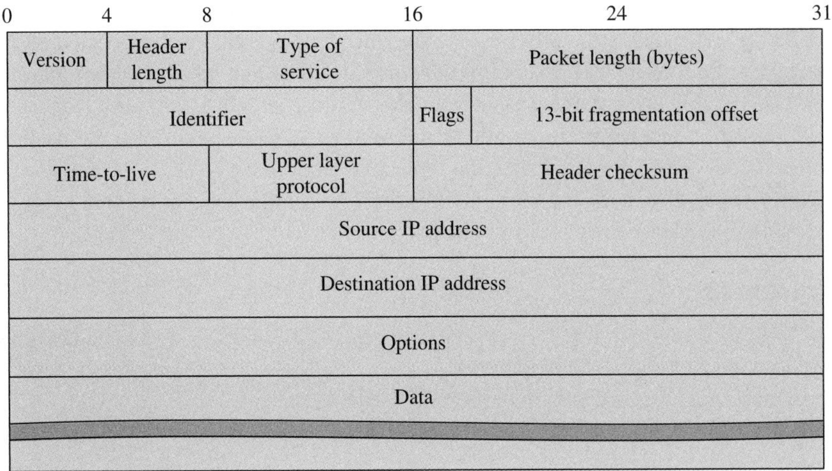

FIGURE 4.15 IPv4 packet format.

- *Type of Service (TOS):* TOS specifies the desired service of the IP packet. Ideally, routers will handle the packet according to the TOS of the packet. However, not all routers have implemented this capability. According to RFC 791 and 1349 (see Figure 4.16), the first three bits in TOS are used to define the precedence of the packet. The following four bits define the performance metrics to optimize when handling this packet. The performance metrics are delay, throughput, reliability, and cost. More recently, RFC 2474 defines the first six bits as the Differentiated Services (DS) field, which carries the DS codepoint of the packet.
- *Packet Length:* This field specifies the total IP packet length, including the header and data, in number of bytes. Since it is 16 bits long, the maximum length of an IP packet is 65,536 bytes, which is referred to as the *maximum transmission unit* (MTU).
- *Identifier:* The identifier uniquely identifies an IP packet. It is also called the *sequence number,* particularly useful in *IP fragmentation*. We shall discuss the topic of IP fragmentation in detail later.

Precedence	Type of Service	R

Precedence defined
In RFC 791:
111: network control
110: Internetwork control
101: CRITIC/ECP
100: Flash override
011: Flash
010: Intermediate
001: Priority
000: Routine

TOS defined in RFC 1349:
1000: minimize delay
0100: maximize throughput
0010: maximize reliability
0001: minimize cost
0000: normal service
1111: maximize security

R: Reserved

FIGURE 4.16 Definition of TOS.

- *Flags:* The low-order two bits of the flags field are used for fragmentation control. The first control bit is called the *do not fragment* bit. The IP packet should not be fragmented if this bit is set. The last bit is called the *more fragments* bit. If set to 1, it indicates that the current packet is in the middle of a large packet.
- *Fragmentation Offset:* This field indicates the position of the fragment in the original packet if the current packet is a fragment. The offset is measured in units of *8 bytes* because this field has only 13 bits after yielding 3 bits to the flags field.
- *Time-to-Live (TTL):* TTL specifies the maximum number of routers the packet is allowed to traverse through. It is called *hop limit* in the new version of the IP protocol. Each router *decreases* TTL by *one* before forwarding it to the next hop router. If TTL reaches zero, the packet is discarded and an error message, i.e., an ICMP message, is sent to the source.
- *Upper Layer Protocol:* This field indicates the upper-layer protocol to which this packet should be passed. For example, a value of 1, 6, 17 indicates that the upper-layer protocol is ICMP, TCP, and UDP, respectively. RFC 1700 defines possible numbers used for this field.
- *Header Checksum:* The checksum is used to detect bit errors in a received IP packet. Unlike CRC, this 16-bit checksum is computed and filled by treating the whole IP header as a sequence of *16-bit* words, *summing* these words using 1's complement arithmetic, and then *complementing* the result. We have described a similar process in Chapter 3. Though the protection of this 16-bit checksum is not as strong as CRC-16, it is faster to compute and can be easily done in software. At the destination, an error is detected if summing up all 16-bit words of the IP header does not yield a *zero*. An erroneous packet is usually discarded.
- *Source and Destination IP Address:* These two fields specify the IP address of the source and the destination. As discussed above, the *destination* address is the key to forwarding the packet to the final destination.
- *Options:* The options field is not required in every packet. It has a variable length, depending on the option type. Usually, the option field is used for testing or debugging. Therefore, it involves the cooperation of routers. For example, *source routing* is a commonly used option which specifies the routing path, i.e., a list of routers from the source to the final destination. The options field is rarely used and thus not included in the fixed part of the IP header.
- *Data:* The data field contains the protocol data unit (PDU) from the upper layer, which is to be delivered to the destination.

Packet Fragmentation and Reassembly

As the IP protocol has its MTU limit, each link-layer protocol also has an often *tighter* limit on the maximum frame size that can be transferred at a time. For example, recall that the Ethernet has an MTU limit of 1518 bytes, which include 18 bytes of protocol overhead and 1500 bytes of payload (upper-layer data). In other words, when transmitting an IP packet over an Ethernet interface, the maximum length of the IP packet is 1500 bytes. However, the packet from the upper layer could be larger than 1500 bytes, the hard limit of the Ethernet protocol, as we can see that

Open Source Implementation 4.3: IPv4 Checksum in Assembly

Overview

The checksum of an IP header is calculated by treating the whole IP header as a sequence of *16-bit* words, summing these words using 1's complement arithmetic, and then complementing the result.

Algorithm Implementations

The IP header checksum is computed using the `ip_fast_csum()` function (in `src/include/asm_i386/checksum.h`). Since the checksum will be computed for each IP packet, it requires a fast algorithm. Linux kernel optimizes the checksum computation by writing this function in machine-dependent assembly languages. For 80x86 machines, the `ip_fast_csum()` function does the summation in *32-bit* instead of 16-bit words. The code in C would look like:

```
for (sum=0;length>0;length--)
      sum += *buf++;
In ip_fast_csum(), the code is translated to:
"1: adcl 16(%1), %0 ;\n" /* the sum is put in %0; summation
is in 32-bit */
"lea 4(%1), %1 ;\n" /* advance the buf pointer by 4 (in
bytes) */
"decl %2 ;\n" /* decrease the length by 2 (in 16 bits) */
"jne 1b ;\n" /* continue the loop until length==0 */
```

The result is then *copied* to another register. These two registers are shifted to have 16 bits in their *low-order* bits and then added up. Taking the complement of the result gives the checksum.

Exercises

Write a program to compute IP checksum and verify the correctness of the program by comparing to a real IP packet captured by the Wireshark software.

the MTU of the IP protocol is 65,536 bytes. Fragmentation allows us to divide a large IP packet into two or more smaller IP packets that are small enough to pass through the link layer, as illustrated in Figure 4.17. These smaller IP packets are called IP *fragments*. Since the MTU varies depending on which link-layer protocol is being used underneath, fragmentation may be performed at the source node as well as at the intermediate routers. Reassembly is the work to rebuild the *original* IP packet using these IP fragments. In the IP protocol, reassembly is done at the *final destination* only to avoid prolonged buffering at routers.

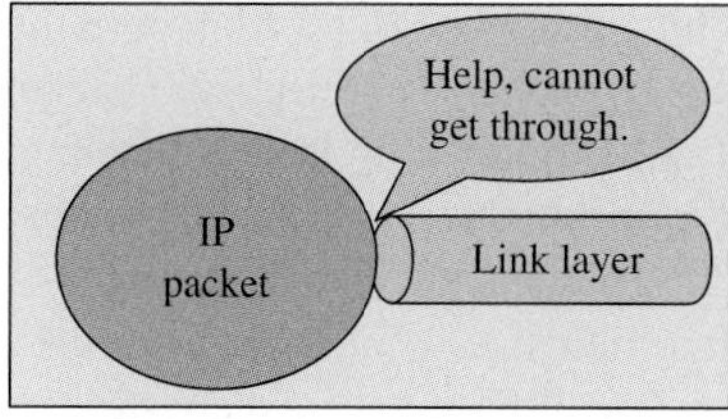

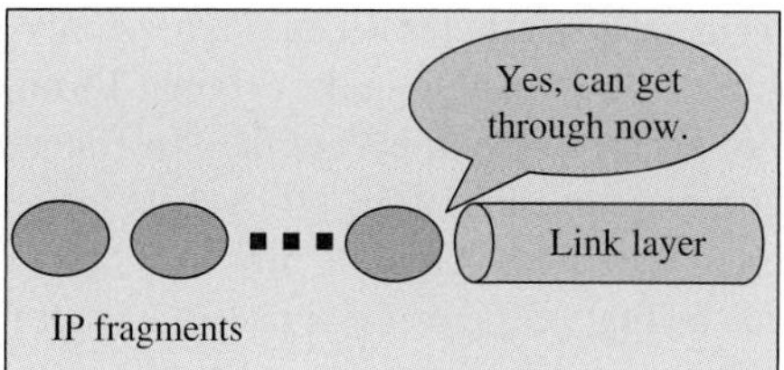

FIGURE 4.17 IP fragmentation.

How we reassemble an IP packet affects the design of the fragmentation procedure, so let us consider the IP reassembly process first. To reassemble an IP packet, we need to collect all the fragments of the same packet. Therefore, we need to have an identifier to differentiate these fragments from those of other packets, and we need to know whether we have collected *all* of the fragments yet. To do this, the IP fragmentation procedure gives all fragments from the same packet the same number in the *identifier* field (or the *sequence number* field) of the header. It uses the *more fragments* bit in the flags field to indicate whether this fragment is the last fragment. Given all of the fragments of an IP packet, a reassembler needs to determine the position of each fragment in the original packet. This is done by recording the offset in the *fragmentation offset* field of the IP header. Therefore, each fragment is actually a normal IP packet that carries fragmentation information in the header and a portion of the data of the original packet. Just like a normal IP packet, an IP fragment can be further fragmented at intermediate routers. The destination uses the *identifier, flags,* and *fragmentation offset* fields in the header to reassemble the original packet.

Figure 4.18 shows an example of fragmenting a 3200-byte packet into three fragments to pass an Ethernet interface. (Recall that the MTU of the Ethernet is 1518 bytes, with 18 bytes of the header and the trailer.) Note that the fragmentation

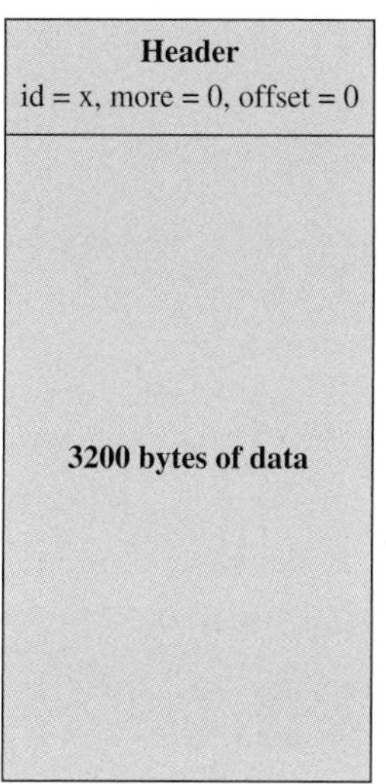

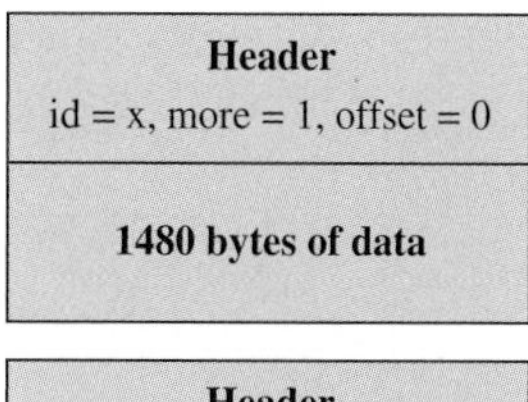

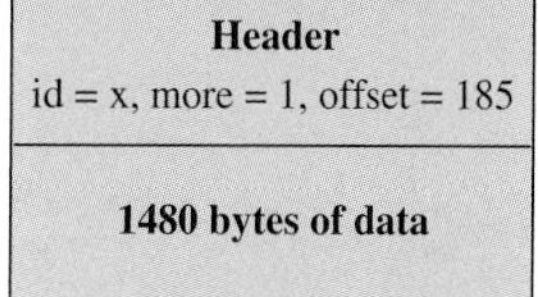

Header
id = x, more = 0, offset = 370
240 bytes of data

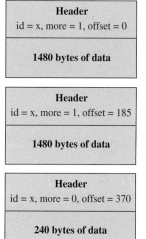

(a) Original packet

(b) Fragments

FIGURE 4.18 An example of IP fragmentation.

offset is in units of 8 bytes because it uses only 13 bits instead of 16 bits to record the fragment's offset position in the original 16-bit long IP packet. Therefore, the packet length of each fragment, except the last fragment, must be a multiple of 8 bytes. In of Figure 4.18, excluding the 20-byte IP header, the maximum number of bytes that can be put into a fragment is 1500 – 20, i.e., 1480. The header of each fragment is the same as that of the original packet except in two fields: *flags* and *fragmentation offset*. The *more* bit of the *flags* should be set to 1 for all fragments except the last one. The destination can distinguish fragments of the same packet by the *identifier* field, to identify the last fragment by the *more* bit, and reassemble the fragments into their right position using the *fragmentation offset*.

Open Source Implementation 4.4: IPv4 Fragmentation

Overview

Fragmentation is required when transmitting an IP packet with a size larger than the link layer's MTU. Therefore, size check is necessary before transmitting an IP packet. All fragments of an IP packet should have the same identifier. In addition, the *more* flag needs to be set for all fragments except the last one. The offset field also needs to be set properly such that the fragmentation offset is in units of 8 bytes, and all fragments except the last one should have a fragment size in *multiples* of 8 bytes. To successfully reassemble an IP packet from its fragments, the reassembly function relies on information from the *identifier, more* flag, and *offset* field in the header of these fragments. Besides, the implementation of reassembling fragments should be carefully designed to avoid buffer overflow attacks.

Data Structures

The data structure for the IP header is `iphdr`, defined in `src/include/linux/ip.h`.

```
struct iphdr {
     #if defined(_LITTLE_ENDIAN_BITFIELD)
          __u8 ihl:4,
               version:4;
#elif defined (__BIG_ENDIAN_BITFIELD)
          __u8 version:4,
               ihl:4;
#else
#error "Please fix <asm/byteorder.h>"
#endif
          __u8 tos;
          __be16 tot_len;
          __be16 id;
```

```
        __be16 frag_off;
        __u8 ttl;
        __u8 protocol;
        __sum16 check;
        __be32 saddr;
        __be32 daddr;
        /*The options start here. */
};
```

Algorithm Implementations

In the following, we focus on fragmentation and reassembly functions. Fragmentation could be done when an IP packet is to be delivered to a network interface. The upper-layer protocol calls `ip_queue_xmit()` to send the upper-layer data through the IP layer. After routing is determined in `ip_queue_xmit()`, `ip_queue_xmit2()` will be called to check whether the packet length is larger than the MTU of the next link. If yes, `ip_fragment()` is called to perform the fragmentation. A while loop in `ip_fragment()` is responsible for fragmenting the original packet. The size of a fragment, except the last one, is set to the largest multiplicative number of 8 bytes that is less than the MTU. Each fragment is then sent sequentially to the network interface after its header and data are set properly. (These functions are located in `src/net/ipv4/ip_output.c`.)

Figure 4.19 shows the call graph of the reassembly procedure. (Most of the functions are located in `src/net/ipv4/ip_fragment.c`.) When an IP packet is received from the link layer, the `ip_rcv()` function is called to process this packet. It calls `ip_route_input()` to determine whether to forward the packet or to deliver it to upper layers. In the latter case, `ip_local_deliver()` is called, which calls `ip_defrag()` if the *more* bit or the *fragmentation offset* in the header is not zero. IP fragments are maintained in a hash table called `ipq_hash`, which is an array of the `ipq` structure. The hash function, `ipqhashfn()`, is called to hash IP fragments into the `ipq_hash` hash table, based on four fields: identifier, source IP address, destination IP address, and upper-layer protocol id. The `ip_defrag()` function first calls `ip_find()`, which in turn calls `ipqhashfn()` to find the queue of the `ipq` structures that store the fragments of the same packet. If no such queue is found, it will call `ipq_frag_create()` to create a queue, which then calls `ipq_frag_intern()` to place the queue into the hash table. The `ip_defrag()` function then calls `ip_frag_queue()` to put the fragment into the queue. If all fragments have been received, `ip_frag_reasm()` is called to reassemble the packet.

Exercises

Use Wireshark to capture some IP fragments and observe the identifier, the more flag, and the offset field in their headers.

Continued

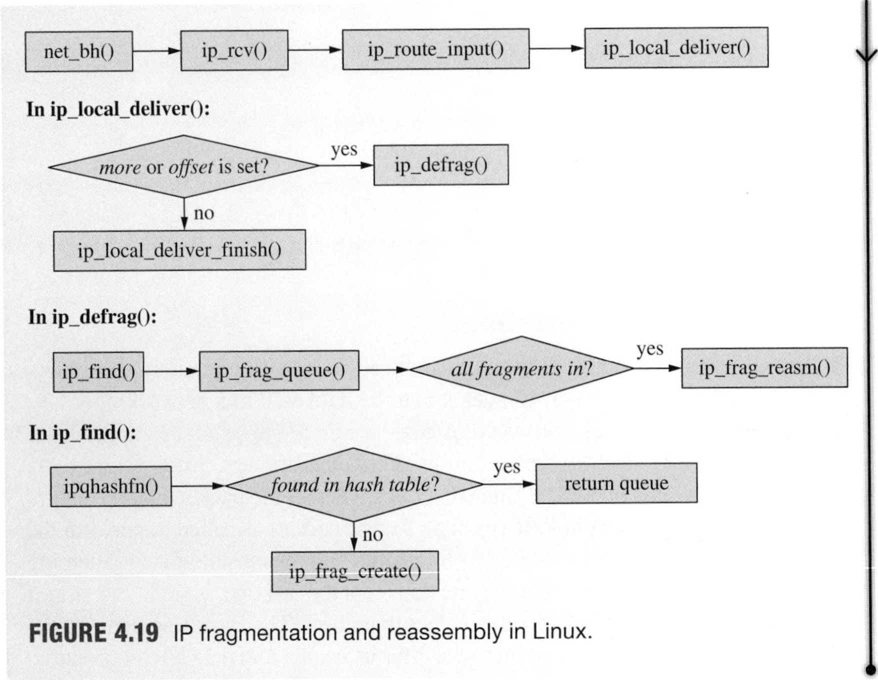

FIGURE 4.19 IP fragmentation and reassembly in Linux.

4.2.2 Network Address Translation (NAT)

For privacy and security reasons, there are some IP addresses that are reserved for sole private, intra-enterprise communications. These addresses, known as *private IP addresses,* are defined in RFC 1918. Three blocks of the IP address space reserved for private internets are:

10.0.0.0 – 10.255.255.255 (10.0.0.0/8),
172.16.0.0 – 172.31.255.255 (172.16.0.0/12),
192.168.0.0 – 192.168.255.255 (192.168.0.0/16).

As we can see, the first block is a *single* class A network number, the second block is a set of *16 contiguous* class B network numbers, and the third block is a set of *256 contiguous* class C network numbers.

Beside privacy and security concerns, there are some other reasons for using private addresses; for example, to avoid changing IP addresses as external network topology changes (such as change of ISP). Recently, a quite common reason is due to the IP address *depletion* problem. While we may solve this problem naturally by adopting the next-generation Internet Protocol, private IP addresses and *network address translation* (NAT) are used as a short-term solution.

Basic NAT and NAPT

NAT is a method used to map IP addresses from one group to another. More commonly, NAT is used to provide connectivity between the public Internet and

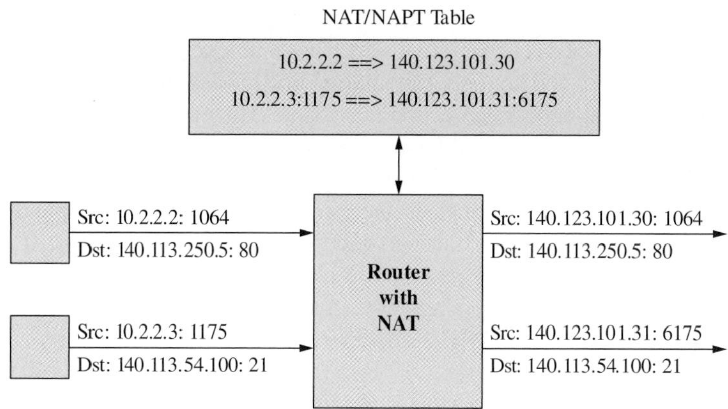

FIGURE 4.20 Examples of basic NAT and NAPT.

private internets in a way that is transparent to end users. There are two variations of NAT, *basic* NAT and Network Address *Port* Translation (NAPT). To allow a host with a private IP address to access the public Internet, basic NAT assigns a globally unique *public* IP address to each host in the private network, dynamically or statically. The source addresses of packets originated from the private network are replaced by their source's assigned global IP address. The same applies to the destination addresses of incoming packets destined for internal hosts in private internets.

Basic NAT requires one public IP address for each internal host that wants to access the public Internet. However, for small companies (Small Office, Home Office [SOHO]), many internal hosts need to share a small number of IP addresses. Therefore, an alternative approach, NAPT, extends the translation to include IP address and transport layer identifier. By NAPT, two internal hosts that share the same global IP address are differentiated by their transport layer identifier, such as TCP/UDP *port number* or ICMP *message identifier*. Figure 4.20 shows the basic NAT and NAPT translation. An NAT *translation table* is created and maintained for IP address and/or transport layer identifier translation. For basic NAT, each entry in the translation table contains a pair of addresses: (private address, global or public IP address). For example, in the NAT table of Figure 4.20, the private address 10.2.2.2 is mapped to 140.123.101.30. Therefore, all packets with source IP address 10.2.2.2 will be intercepted and their source IP address will be changed to 140.123.101.30 by the NAT server. On the other hand, each entry of an NAPT table contains IP address and transport layer identifier: (private address, private transport id, global IP address, global transport id). For example, in the NAPT table of Figure 4.20, all packets with source IP address 10.2.2.3 and port number 1175 will be intercepted and their source IP address and port number will be changed to 140.123.101.31 and 6175 accordingly by the NAT server.

Static or Dynamic Mapping

The NAT translation table can be configured and updated statically or dynamically. An organization that has plenty of global IP addresses and uses NAT for privacy and security reasons can manually set up a one-to-one mapping between global and private IP addresses. In this case, each internal host owns a unique global IP address that is transparent to the user, and not only can internal hosts access the public Internet, but also access from the opposite direction is possible. However, in most cases, the NAT table is updated on demand. NAT maintains a *pool* of global IP addresses. When an outgoing packet arrives, NAT looks up the table for the source address of the packet. If an entry is found, NAT translates the private address to the corresponding global IP address. (In NAPT, the transport layer identifier is also translated.) Otherwise, an *unassigned* entry is selected from the IP address pool and assigned to the internal host that owns the source address. (Similarly, a new transport layer identifier is selected in the case of NAPT.) A *timer* is associated with each entry so that inactive entries can be released.

Although in most cases, NAT is used for unidirectional access to the public Internet, creating a new NAT mapping at the arrival of an incoming packet is still possible. For example, when NAT receives a domain name lookup for an internal host with no corresponding entry in the NAT table yet, a new entry can be created and the newly assigned IP address can be used in the *reply* to the domain name lookup. A more complicated scenario, called *twice NAT,* is also possible where two end hosts in communication are both internal hosts in private networks (see RFC 2663).

Principle in Action: Different Types of NAT

Depending on how an external host can send a packet through a mapped public address and port, implementations of NAT can be classified into four types: *full cone, restricted cone, port restricted cone,* and *symmetric*. Among them, *full cone* is the most common implementation in the market, while *symmetric* provides the best security in the sense that it is most difficult to traverse. The operation details of these implementations are depicted in Figure 4.21 and briefly described here.

Full cone: Once an internal address (iAddr: iport) has been mapped to an external address (eAddr: eport), all packets from (iAddr: iport) will be sent through (eAddr: eport), and any external host can send packets to (iAddr: iport)

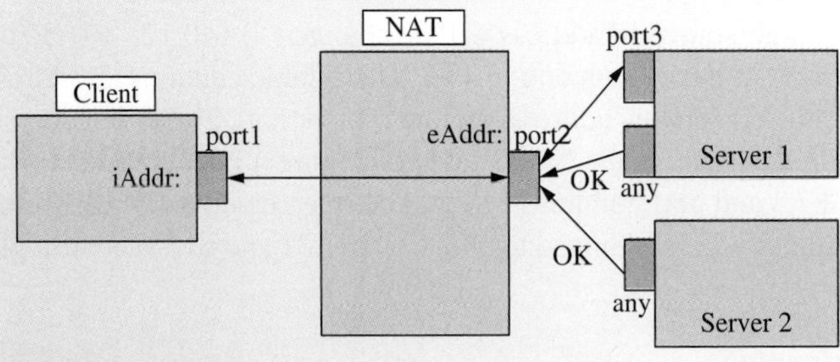

FIGURE 4.21(a) Full cone NAT.

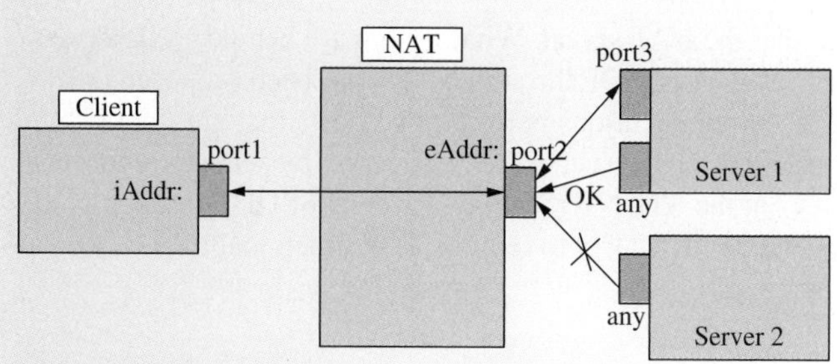

FIGURE 4.21(b) Restricted cone NAT.

through (eAddr: eport). That is, the NAT server will not check the *source* IP address and port number of *incoming* packets.

Restricted cone: Same as above, except that only external hosts that have received packets from (iAddr: iport) can send packets to (iAddr: iport) through (eAddr: eport). That is, the NAT server will memorize the *destination* IP address of *outgoing* packets and check the *source* IP address of *incoming* packets against the memorized destination IP addresses.

Port restricted cone: Same as above, except that external hosts must use the same port that has received packets from (iAddr: iport) to send packets to (iAddr: iport) through (eAddr: eport). That is, the NAT server will check both the source IP address and the port number of incoming packets.

Symmetric: Same as port restricted cone's operation for *incoming* packets. However, the mapping of (iAddr: iport) to (eAddr: eport) is *unique* for each *external* source IP address and port. That is, *outgoing* packets from the same (iAddr: iport) will be mapped to *different* (eAddr: eport) if the outgoing packets have different *destination* IP addresses *or* port numbers.

When two hosts communicate, if the initiator, often a client, is behind NAT while the responder, often a server, is not, one of the above address resolution processes will be invoked. The alternative would require basic NAT or port

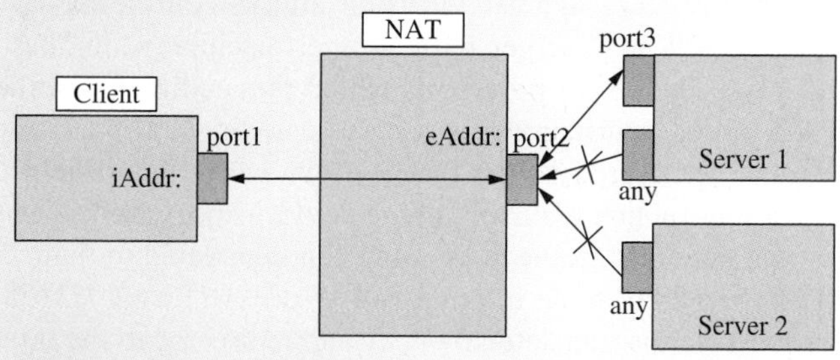

FIGURE 4.21(c) Port restricted cone NAT.

Continued

redirection configured at the NAT server. What if both are behind NAT servers? The STUN (Simple Traversal of UDP through NATs) has been proposed in RFC 3489 to provide UDP communications between two hosts that are *both* behind NAT servers. The basic idea is to traverse the NAT server by sending requests to a *STUN server*. Later on, the STUNT (Simple Traversal of UDP through NATs and TCP too) protocol extends STUN to include TCP functionality.

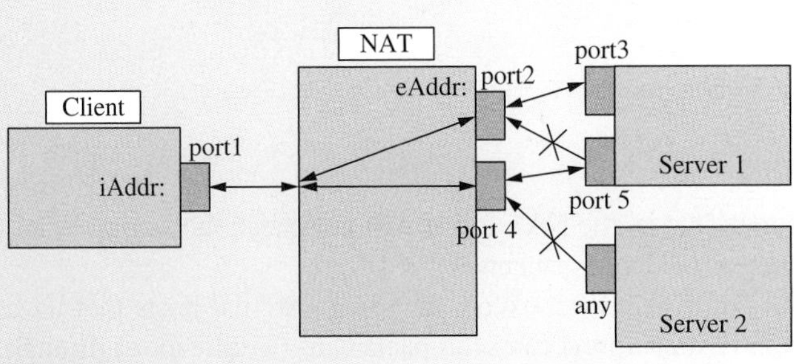

FIGURE 4.21(d) Symmetric NAT.

Port Redirection and Transparent Proxy

Besides providing Internet access, NAT can also be applied to more secured or efficient applications such as *port redirection* and *transparent proxy*. For example, a network administrator may want to redirect all WWW requests to a specific IP address and a private port number. The administrator can create a record in the database of the domain name server (DNS), such as a record that maps www.cs.ccu.edu.tw to 140.123.101.38. Then, an entry is created in the NAT table to redirect the mapping to the desired private address and port number—for example, mapping 140.123.101.38:80 to 10.2.2.2:8080 where ":80" and ":8080" represent port numbers (these shall be introduced formally in Chapter 5). Therefore, hosts in the public Internet know only that the WWW server is www.cs.ccu.edu.tw with IP address 140.123.101.38; with its private address unrevealed, the actual server could be more secure against intrusion attacks. Furthermore, it becomes easier to replace the WWW server with another machine which has a different private IP address. The above process is called port redirect. Another example of using NAT, called transparent proxy, is to redirect all outgoing WWW requests to a transparent proxy such that a *proxy cache* could help to accelerate request processing or that a *proxy server* could inspect the requests or responses. For example, an entry in the NAT table can be created to map the WWW service (140.123.101.38:80) to an internal WWW proxy (10.1.1.1:3128). An outgoing WWW request is thus translated by NAT and redirected to the internal WWW proxy server first. In the case of a caching proxy, the internal proxy may then prepare the response from its local cache directly or forward the request to the real server.

Principle in Action: Messy ALG in NAT

Since translations by NAT and NAPT change addresses in the IP header and transport layer header, checksums of these headers need to be *recomputed* after the translation. Furthermore, translations of IP addresses and/or transport identifiers may affect the functionality of some applications. In particular, any applications that encode source or destination IP addresses or ports in their protocol messages will be affected. Therefore, NAT is often accompanied by *application level gateways* (ALGs). Let us consider the NAT modification needed for ICMP and FTP.

ICMP is an error-reporting protocol for TCP/UDP/IP. We will detail ICMP in Section 4.5. An error message of ICMP, such as destination unreachable error, embeds the packet in error within the payload of the ICMP packet. Therefore, not only the address of the *ICMP packet* but also the source or the destination address of the original *erroneous packet* needs to be translated by NAT. However, any change in these addresses requires recomputing the checksum of the *ICMP header* as well as the checksum of the *embedded IP header*. For NAPT translation, the TCP/UDP port number of the embedded IP header also needs to be modified. In case of ICMP echo request/reply messages, which use a *query identifier* to identify echo messages, this query identifier is equivalent to the transport layer identifier and thus needs to be translated as well. Therefore, the checksum of the ICMP header also needs to be recomputed if the query identifier is modified.

File transfer protocol (FTP) is a popular Internet application, to be introduced in Chapter 6. FTP also requires an ALG to keep functioning correctly under NAT translation. The problem comes from the FTP *PORT command* and *PASV response* because these two commands contain an IP address/TCP port number pair *encoded in ASCII*. Therefore, FTP ALG needs to make sure the IP address and port number in PORT and PASV commands are translated accordingly. The problem becomes further complicated as the *length* of the *ASCII-encoded* IP address and port number may change *after* the translation, say from *13* octets in 10.1.1.1:3128 to *17* octets in 140.123.101.38:21. Thus, the packet length may be changed as well, which in turn may affect the sequence number of subsequent TCP packets. To make these changes transparent to the FTP application, the FTP ALG needs a special table to *correct* the TCP sequence and acknowledge numbers. The correction needs to be performed on all subsequent packets of the connection.

Open Source Implementation 4.5: NAT

Overview

Before Linux kernel version 2.2, NAT implementation was known as IP masquerade. Starting from Linux kernel version 2.4, NAT implementation has been integrated with `iptables`, an implementation of the packet filtering function. The implementation of NAT can be classified into two types: *source* NAT, for

Continued

outgoing packets, and *destination* NAT, for *incoming* packets from the Internet or the upper layer. Source NAT changes the source IP address and transport layer identifier, while destination NAT changes the destination address and transport id. Source NAT is done after packet filtering and before packets are sent to the output interface. The *hook* name in `iptables` for source NAT is called `NF_INET_POST_ROUTING` in Linux. Destination NAT is done *before* packet filtering is applied to packets from the network interface card or the upper-layer protocols. The hook for the former is called `NF_INET_PRE_REOUTING`, and for the latter it is called `NF_INET_LOCAL_OUT`.

Data Structures

Data structures for IP tables that set up source NAT and destination NAT hooks (see `/net/ipv4/netfilter/nf_nat_rule.c`):

```
static struct xt_target ipt_snat_reg _read_mostly = {
    .name = "SNAT",
    .target = ipt_snat_target,
    .targetsize = sizeof(struct nf_nat_multi_range_
    compat),
    .table = "nat",
    .hooks = 1 << NF_INET_POST_ROUTING,
    .checkentry = ipt_snat_checkentry,
    .family      = AF_INET,
};
static struct xt_target ipt_dnat_reg _read_mostly =
{
    .name = "DNAT",
    .target = ipt_dnat_target,
    .targetsize = sizeof(struct nf_nat_multi_range_
    compat),
    .table = "nat",
    .hooks = (1 << NF_INET_PRE_ROUTING) |
    (1 << NF_INET_LOCAL_OUT),
    .checkentry = ipt_dnat_checkentry,
    .family = AF_INET,
};
```

Data structures for NAT hook functions, such as `nf_nat_in`, `nf_nat_out`, `nf_nat_local_fn`, and `nf_nat_fn`, which we will trace later (see `/net/ipv4/netfilter/nf_nat_standalone.c`):

```
static struct nf_hook_ops nf_nat_ops[] _read_mostly
= {
    /* Before packet filtering, change destination */
{
            .hook              = nf_nat_in,
            .owner             = THIS_MODULE,
```

```
                .pf             = PF_INET,
                .hooknum        = NF_INET_PRE_ROUTING,
                .priority       = NF_IP_PRI_NAT _ DST,
        },
    /* After packet filtering, change source */
    {
                .hook           = nf_nat_out,
                .owner          = THIS_MODULE,
                .pf             = PF_INET,
                .hooknum        = NF_INET_POST_ROUTING,
                .priority       = NF_IP_PRI_NAT_SRC,
        },
    /* Before packet filtering, change destination */
    {
                .hook           = nf_nat_local_fn,
                .owner          = THIS_MODULE,
                .pf             = PF_INET,
                .hooknum        = NF_INET_LOCAL_OUT,
                .priority       = NF_IP_PRI_NAT_DST,
        },
    /* After packet filtering, change source */
    {
                .hook           = nf_nat_fn,
                .owner          = THIS_MODULE,
                .pf             = PF_INET,
                .hooknum        = NF_INET_LOCAL_IN,
                .priority       = NF_IP_PRI_NAT_SRC,
        },
};
```

Finally, the data structure for tracking connections:

```
struct nf_conn {
...
    struct nf_conntrack_tuple_hash tuplehash[IP_CT_DIR_
    MAX];
...
    struct nf_conn *master;
    /* Storage reserved for other modules: */
    union nf_conntrack_proto proto;
    /* Extensions */
    struct nf_ct_ext *ext;
...
};
struct nf_conn_nat
{
    struct hlist_node bysource;
    struct nf_nat_seq seq[IP_CT_DIR_MAX];
    struct nf_conn *ct;
```

Continued

```
    union nf_conntrack_nat_help help;
#if defined(CONFIG_IP_NF_TARGET_MASQUERADE) || \
    defined(CONFIG_IP_NF_TARGET_MASQUERADE_MODULE)
    int masq_index;
#endif
};
```

Figure 4.22 shows the relationship among these data structures.

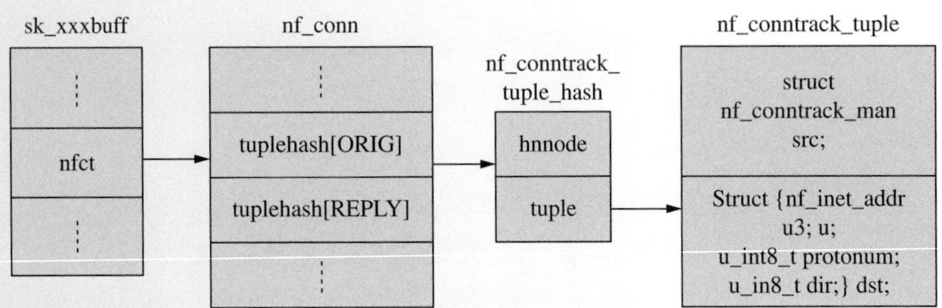

FIGURE 4.22 Data structures for NAT implementation.

Algorithm Implementations

The NAT module is initialized by calling `nf_nat_standalone_init()`, which calls `nf_nat_rule_init()` to register `iptables` and `nf_register_hooks()` to set up NAT hook functions. After the initialization, `iptables` and hook functions are set as shown in Figure 4.23.

As shown in Figure 4.23, functions that perform NAT for the hooks of `NF_INET_PRE_ROUTING`, `NF_INET_LOCAL_OUT`, and `NF_INET_POST_ROUTING` are `nf_nat_in()`, `nf_nat_local_fn()`, and `nf_nat_out()`, respectively. All of these three functions eventually call `nf_nat_fn()` to perform the NAT operations.

Figure 4.24 depicts the call graph of `nf_nat_fn()`. The `nf_nat_fn()` function obtains connection tracking information (`nfct` and `nfctinfo`) from `sk_buff`. If `nfctinfo` is `IP_CT_NEW` and NAT has not been initialized, `alloc_null_binding()` will be called in case `LOCAL_IN` does not have a chain, that is, the NAT rule has not been set yet; otherwisc, `nf_nat_rule_find()` will be called. Both of these functions call `nf_nat_setup_info()` to perform network address translation of the packet. In `nf_nat_setup_info()`, `get_unique_tuple()` is called to obtain the translation result as a tuple. It calls `find_appropriate_src()` to search the `ipv4.nat_bysource` hash table if it is a source NAT (SNAT). If not successful, it calls `find_best_ips_proto()` to get a new tuple for this translation.

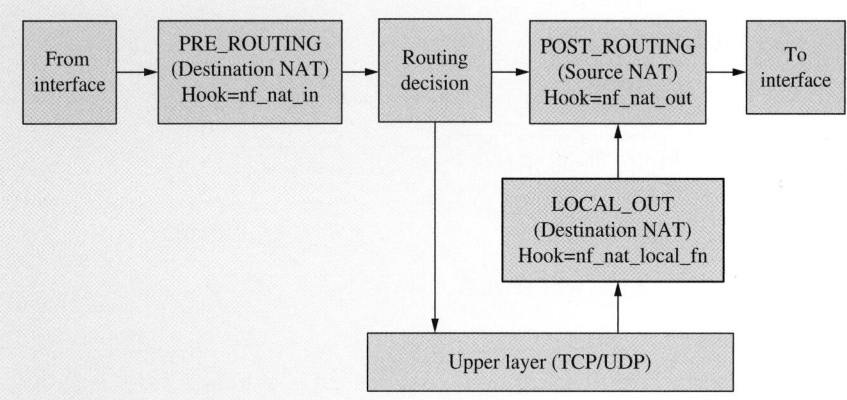

FIGURE 4.23 NAT packet flows.

After IP-level translation as stated above is done, *transport*-layer NAT function is called. ALG functions are called *helper* functions. For example, the helper function of FTP ALG is `nf_nat_ftp()`. Figure 4.25 shows the call graph of the FTP ALG implementation in Linux kernel version 2.6. Through the *mangle* array, `mangle_rfc959_packet()` is called if the packet contains the PORT or PASV command; `mangle_eprt_packet()` is called if the packet contains the EPRT command (PORT command for IPv6); and `mangle_epsv_packet()` is called if the packet contains the EPSV command. All of them call `nf_nat_mangle_tcp_packet()` to deal with the change required for TCP, such as sequence number and checksum recomputation.

Let us take the ICMP as an example of NAPT. The function `icmp_manip_pkt()` is used to change the checksum and query id of an ICMP message. A unique query id within the user-specified range is found by `icmp_unique_tuple()`, which searches the specified range linearly. The checksum of ICMP and IP is recomputed by `inet_proto_csum_replace4()`, which in turn calls `csum_partial()` for the actual checksum adjustment. `csum_partial()` is implemented in assembly language for faster execution.

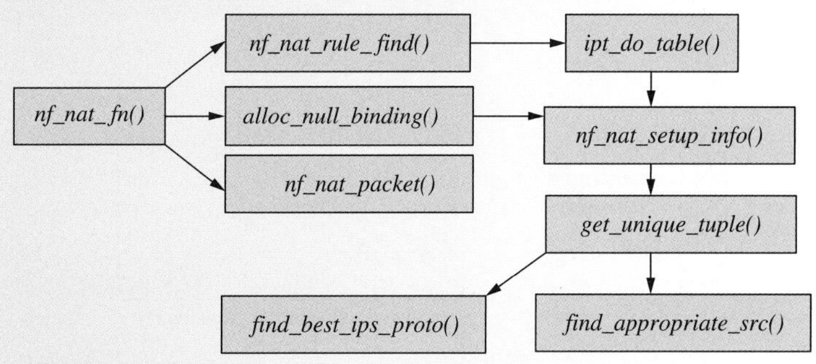

FIGURE 4.24 Call graph for Linux implementation of NAT.

Continued

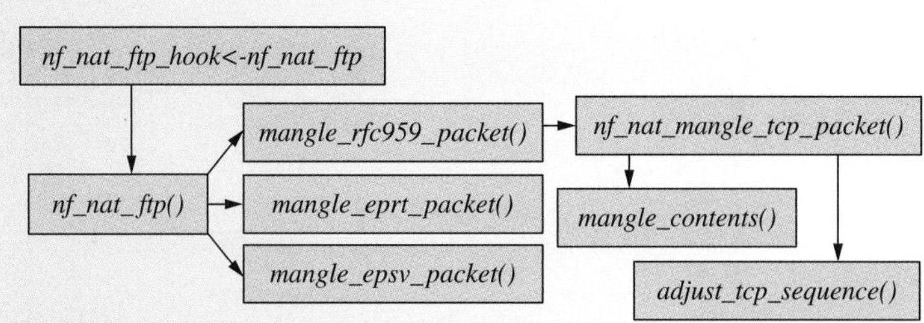

FIGURE 4.25 Call graph for FTP ALG.

Exercises

Trace `adjust_tcp_sequence()` and explain how to adjust the sequence number of TCP packets when packets are changed due to address translation.

Performance Matters: CPU Time of NAT Execution and Others

Though the NAT implementation in the Linux kernel also exercises hashing, its execution time is *higher* than that of the lookup functions for packet forwarding. There are two reasons for this. In Figure 4.23, a packet would go through destination NAT first and source NAT later, each invoking lookup into the hash table. Another reason is that extra ALG *helper* functions need to be called in addition to the translation of IP address and port number. Figure 4.26 plots the latency of an ICMP packet with 64 bytes payload on a 2.33 GHz CPU for forwarding (by cache and FIB, labeled “Routing cache” and “Routing FIB,” respectively), NAT, firewall, and VPN

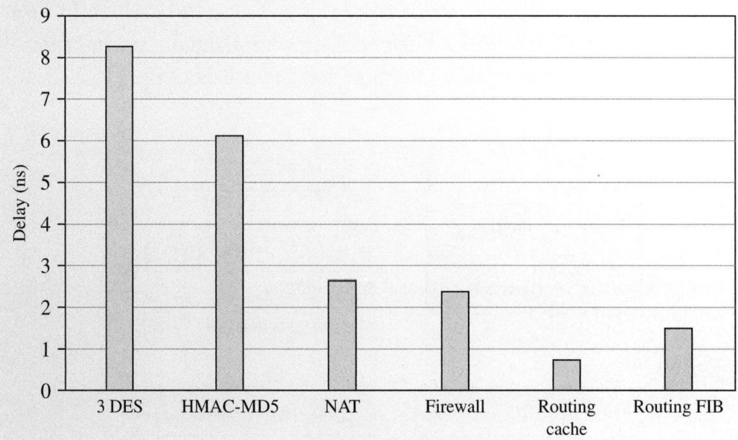

FIGURE 4.26 Latency for important network functions.

(by encryption and authentication, labeled "3DES" and "HMAC-MD5," respectively). The latter two shall be covered in Chapter 8. Though NAT consumes about the same amount of CPU time as firewall does and more than forwarding does, the NAT's latency is simply much smaller than those incurred by authentication and encryption. Apparently the rank by the urgency to call for hardware acceleration shall be: encryption, authentication, NAT, firewall, and then forwarding. For throughput below 100 Mbps, only encryption and authentication would definitely require hardware solutions. The throughputs of software implementation in Linux kernel achieve about 73 Mbps and 85 Mbps for 3DES and HMAC-MD5, respectively. But for multi-gigabit throughput, *all* of them would resort to hardware accelerators.

4.3 INTERNET PROTOCOL VERSION 6

The current version of Internet Protocol encounters several problems, and the most noticeable one is the shortage of the 32-bit IP address space. It is predicted that the world will run out of the IANA IPv4 unallocated addresses in 2011, considering current Internet growth trends and the inefficient use of the IP address space. In 1991, the IETF called for proposals for the new version of IP, known as IP Next Generation (IPng). Several proposals were received, and the one chosen was called Simple Internet Protocol Plus (SIPP). The original address size proposed was 64 bits, which was doubled to 128 bits by IETF IPng Directorate later. Since version number 5 was assigned to an experimental protocol already, the official version number assigned to this new Internet Protocol is version 6, known as IPv6. Migration to IPv6 is considered the long-term solution to the IPv4 address depletion problem.

Several new features are considered and intended to be supported in IPv6. First, the address size is extended to *128 bits*. Second, to speed up the packet processing at routers, *fixed*-length header format is adopted. Support for quality of service is also considered by including a *flow label* in the header. A new address type, called *anycast,* is proposed for sending packets to anyone in a group of hosts. (Usually, this

Historical Evolution: NAT vs. IPv6

Both NAT and IPv6 try to tackle the address shortage problem of IPv4. Clearly, as of 2010, NAT is the adopted solution due to its compatibility with the current Internet. The history of the Internet tells us that *evolution* is preferred over *revolution.* The change from IPv4 to IPv6 is like a revolution, which requires software change in all end-user devices and networking devices such as routers. On the other hand, the use of NAT is like evolution, which only requires deployment of NAT servers at some subnets that are short of IPv4 public addresses. However, as we approach the exhaustion of the IPv4 unallocated addresses, there seems no choice but to adopt the IPv6 revolution. To date, this is still a debatable pending issue.

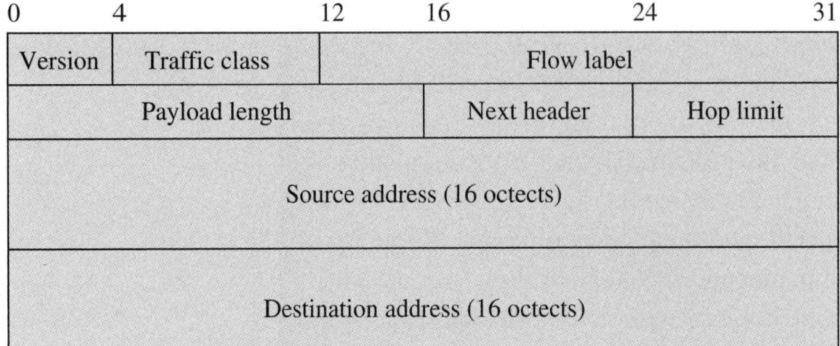

FIGURE 4.27 IPv6 header format.

is used for sending to one of the reachable routers within a subnet.) IPv6 also supports *autoconfiguration,* similar to the function of DHCP. Finally, IPv6 uses *extension headers* to support fragmentation, security, enhanced routing, and other features.

4.3.1 IPv6 Header Format

The format of the IPv6 header is shown in Figure 4.27. As its original name indicated, the design principle of IPv6 is simple. Several header fields that are not used in most in IPv4 packets have been removed from IPv6 to speed up packet processing and forwarding at routers. As a result, the IPv6 header has a fixed length of *40 bytes* with no option field. Additional functions are performed using *extension headers,* which we shall discuss later.

- *Version Number:* As in IPv4, the header starts with a *version* field, which is set to 6 for IPv6 as discussed above.
- *Traffic Class:* The *Traffic Class* field indicates the service desired by the packet, similar to TOS in IPv4. This field is used to differentiate service classes of different packets. For example, the first six bits are used as the DS codepoint in the Differentiated Services (DiffServ) framework [RFC 2472].
- *Flow Label:* The *Flow Label* field is used intentionally to identify packets of the same flow in order to provide differentiated quality of service. For example, packets of an audio stream, which certainly needs low transmission delay and jitter, can be treated as a flow. However, the exact way of defining a flow is not clearly stated yet. Therefore, a flow can be a TCP connection or a source-destination pair, but in common practice, a flow usually consists of packets with the same source IP address, destination IP address, source port number, destination port number, and transport layer protocol. Clearly, packets of the same TCP connection will form a flow according to this definition.
- *Payload Length:* The 16-bit *Payload Length* field indicates the length of the packet in bytes, *excluding* the 40-byte header. Therefore, the maximum payload length is 65535 bytes.
- *Next Header:* The *Next Header* field identifies the upper-layer protocol or the next extension header. It is used to replace the protocol field and the option field in IPv4. If there is no special option, the Next Header identifies the upper-layer protocol running over IPv6, e.g., TCP or UDP. If special options such as fragmentation, security, and enhanced routing are needed, the IPv6 header is

followed by one or more extension headers whose type is indicated by the Next Header field.

- *Hop Limit:* The *Hop Limit* field, which is called Time-to-Live (TTL) in IPv4, has its name corrected and is used in the same manner as TTL in IPv4.
- *Source and Destination Addresses:* Finally, the header ends with the source and the destination IP address, each of 128 bits. In IPv6, there are three types of addresses, namely, unicast, anycast, and multicast, which we will describe in detail later.

Careful readers may notice that several header fields in IPv4 have been removed from the IPv6 header. First, there is no *checksum* anymore. Two good reasons to remove checksum from the header are: First, reliability can be provided by a higher-layer protocol such as TCP, and we avoid recomputing checksum at intermediate routers. Second, *fragmentation* flags and offset no longer exist, as fragmentation is not allowed at intermediate routers. Again, this is to alleviate the processing load on routers. Fragmentation and other options such as source routing are now handled by extension headers, a more efficient and flexible mechanism than to IPv4. Since there is no Options field in the IPv6 header, the length of the IPv6 header is fixed, and a fixed-length header also improves the processing speed at routers.

4.3.2 IPv6 Extension Header

IPv6 uses extension headers to support fragmentation and other options. The Next Header field of the IPv6 header indicates the type of the extension header following the IPv6 header. Each extension header also has a Next Header field to indicate the type of the extension header or the upper-layer protocol header following it. Figure 4.28 gives three examples of the use of extension headers. Case (a) is the most common case where the IPv6 header is followed by the *TCP header*. In this case, the Next Header field of the the IPv6 header has value 6, which is the protocol id of TCP. If enhanced routing is desired, the *routing header* can be used as shown in Figure 4.28 (b). In this case, the Next Header field of the IPv6 header has value 43, where value 43 indicates the routing header following the IPv6 header, and the Next Header field of the routing extension header contains value 6. Similarly, if routing option and fragmentation are required, the

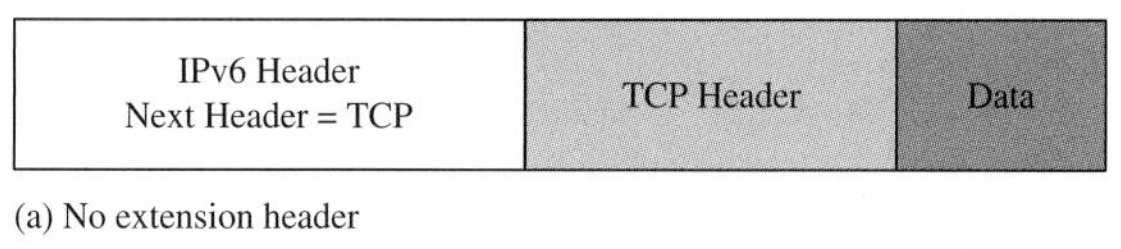

(a) No extension header

IPv6 Header Next Header = Routing	Routing Header Next Header = TCP	TCP Header	Data

(b) IPv6 header followed by a routing header

IPv6 Header Next Header = Routing	Routing Header Next Header = Frag.	Fragment Header Next Header = TCP	TCP Header	Data

(c) IPv6 header followed by a routing header and a fragment header

FIGURE 4.28 IPv6 extension headers.

TABLE 4.1 Order of IPv6 Extension Headers

Basic IPv6 header
Basic IPv6 header
Hop-by-Hop Options header (0)
Destination Options header (60)
Routing header (43)
Fragment header (44)
Authentication header (51)
Encapsulating Security Payload header (50)
Destination Options header (60)
Mobility header (135)
No Next header (59)
Upper-layer header: TCP(6), UDP(17), ICMPv6(58)

sequence of extension headers is shown in Figure 4.28 (c). The Next Header field of the routing header has value 44 to indicate the next header is a *fragment header*.

Several rules for processing extension headers are recommended in RFC 2460. First, the *order* of extension headers should follow Table 4.1. Although, as stated in RFC 2460, IPv6 nodes must accept and attempt to process extension headers in any order, it is strongly advised that sources of IPv6 packets adhere to the recommended order. In particular, the Hop-by-Hop Options header is restricted to appearing only immediately after an IPv6 header as it is processed by all intermediate routers along the routing path. Secondly, extension headers must be processed strictly in the order in which they appear in the packet since the contents and semantics of each extension header determine whether or not to proceed to the next header. Thirdly, intermediate routers (i.e., not the destination node) should *not* process extension headers except the Hop-by-Hop Option header. Finally, each extension header can occur at most *once* only, except for the Destination Options header, which occurs at most twice (once before a Routing header and once before the upper-layer header).

4.3.3 Fragmentation in IPv6

Fragmentation in IPv6 differs slightly from that in IPv4. First, to simplify packet processing at routers, fragmentation is not allowed at routers. That is, fragmentation is performed only by *sources*. Second, the fragment information, such as the "more fragment" bit and fragment offset, is carried by an extension header called *fragment header* instead of the IPv6 header. Figure 4.29 shows the format of the fragment

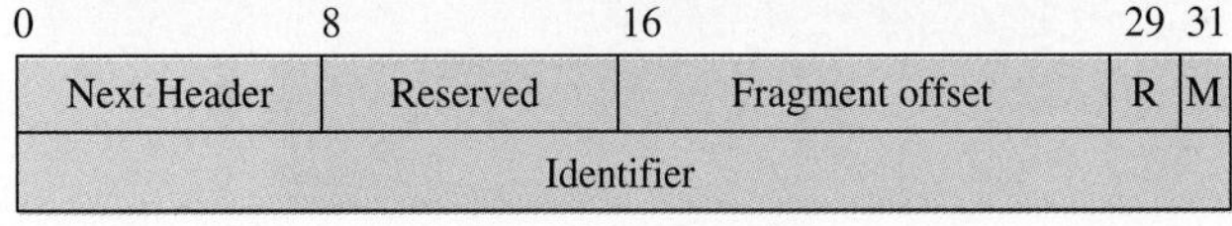

FIGURE 4.29 Fragment header

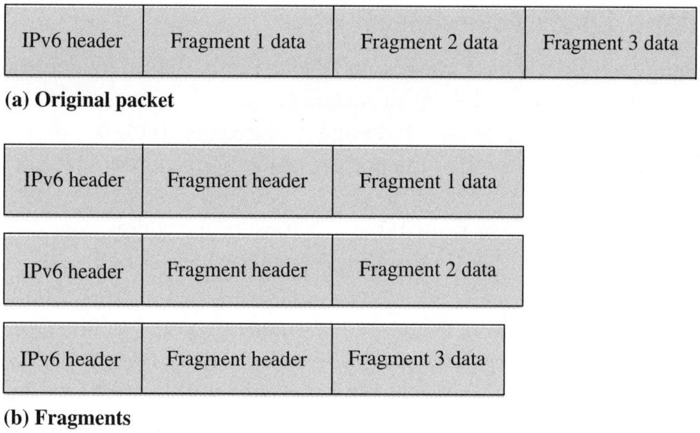

IPv6 header	Fragment 1 data	Fragment 2 data	Fragment 3 data

(a) Original packet

IPv6 header	Fragment header	Fragment 1 data
IPv6 header	Fragment header	Fragment 2 data
IPv6 header	Fragment header	Fragment 3 data

(b) Fragments

FIGURE 4.30 Example of IPv6 fragmentation.

header. The Next Header field indicates the type of the next header. The *fragment offset* and the *more fragment bit* (the *M* bit in the figure) are used the same way as in IPv4. Figure 4.30 shows an example of fragmenting a large packet into three fragments. The more fragment bit is set to 1 in the first two segments. The fragment offset is still measured in *8 octets*.

However, one issue remains unclarified: Since fragmentation is not allowed at immediate routers, how can a source know the MTU of a routing path and perform the fragmentation accordingly? There are two approaches to solving this problem. First, in IPv6 networks, each link is required to have an MTU of *1280 bytes* or greater. Therefore, a source can *always* assume the MTU of each routing path is 1280 bytes and fragment packets into fragments of 1280 bytes or shorter. Second, a source can run the Path MTU Discovery protocol (RFC 1981) to *discover* the path MTU. IPv6 hosts are strongly encouraged to implement the Path MTU Discovery protocol to take advantage of path MTUs greater than 1280 octets.

4.3.4 IPv6 Address Notation

Due to the length of the IPv6 address, the dotted decimal notation used for IPv4 is not suitable for representing an IPv6 address. Instead, the *colon hexadecimal* notation is used, which has the form X:X:X:X:X:X:X:X, where X is a hexadecimal code of a 16-bit piece of the IPv6 address. Following is an example of the colon hexadecimal representation:

3FFD:3600:0000:0000:0302:B3FF:FE3C: C0DB

The colon hexadecimal notation is still quite long and, in most cases, consists of a large number of contiguous zeros. Therefore zero compression is proposed, which replaces a sequence of contiguous zeros with a pair of colons. For example, the preceding address can be rewritten as:

3FFD:3600::0302:B3FF:FE3C: C0DB

4.3.5 IPv6 Address Space Assignment

Unlike IPv4, IPv6 addresses do *not* have classes. In IPv6, a prefix is used to identify different usages of the IPv6 address. The most recent definition on the use of the prefix in IPv6 is in RFC 4291: IP Version 6 Addressing Architecture. Table 4.2 shows the current IPv6 prefix allocation as well as the portion of the IPv6 address space allocated to a given prefix, which is the ratio of the prefix-occupied space to the whole IPv6 address space. As we can observe from Table 4.2, most of the address space is unassigned—currently, only 15% of the IPv6 address space has been assigned.

There are three types of IPv6 addresses: unicast, multicast, and anycast. Some noteworthy unicast addresses include *IPv4 compatible address* (prefix 00000000), *Global Unicast Address,* and *Link Local Unicast Address*. A multicast address begins with prefix 11111111. Finally, the anycast address has a *subnet prefix* followed by a number of *zeros,* similar to the *IPv4 subnet address* format. A group of nodes (routers) may share an anycast address. Packets destined for an anycast address should be delivered to exactly one member of the group, usually the *closest* one.

TABLE 4.2 Prefix Assignments of IPv6 Addresses

Prefix	Address Type	Portion
0000::/8	Reserved	1/256
0100::/8	Unassigned	1/256
0200::/7	Unassigned	1/128
0400::/6	Unassigned	1/64
0800::/5	Unassigned	1/32
1000::/4	Unassigned	1/16
2000::/3	Global Unicast Address	1/8
4000::/3	Unassigned	1/8
6000::/3	Unassigned	1/8
8000::/3	Unassigned	1/8
A000::/3	Unassigned	1/8
C000::/3	Unassigned	1/8
E000::/4	Unassigned	1/16
F000::/5	Unassigned	1/32
F800::/6	Unassigned	1/64
FC00::/7	Unique Local Unicast	1/128
FE00::/9	Unassigned	1/512
FE80::/10	Link Local Unicast Address	1/1024
FEC0::/10	Unassigned	1/1024
FF00::/8	Multicast Address	1/256

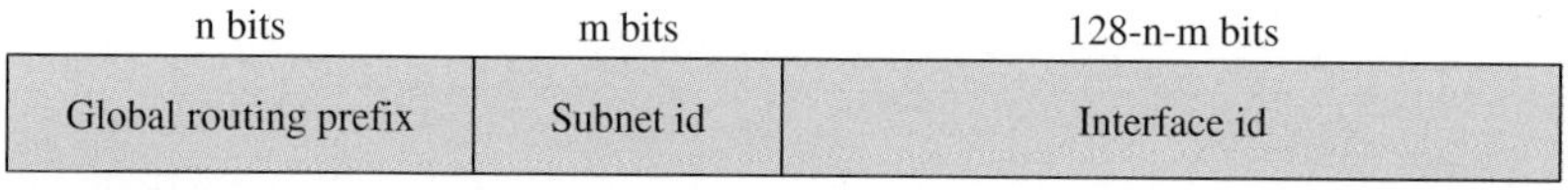

n bits	m bits	128-n-m bits
Global routing prefix	Subnet id	Interface id

FIGURE 4.31 IPv6 global unicast address format.

Addresses that begin with prefix 00000000 are reserved for IPv4 compatibility. There are two ways to encode IPv4 addresses into IPv6 addresses. A computer that runs IPv6 software may be assigned an IPv6 address that begins with *96 zero* bits followed by the 32-bit IPv4 address, referred to as the *IPv4-compatible IPv6 address*. For example, the IPv4-compatible IPv6 address of 140.123.101.160 is 0000:0000:0000:0000:0000:0000:8C7B:65A0, which can also be written as ::8C7B:65A0. A conventional IPv4 computer that does *not* understand IPv6 will be assigned an IPv6 address that begins with *80 zero* bits and then *16 one* bits followed by the 32-bit IPv4 address, referred to as the *IPv4-mapped IPv6 address*. For example, the *IPv6 non-compatible address* or IPv4-mapped IPv6 address of 140.123.101.160 is ::FFFF:8C7B:65A0.

Two special addresses also start with prefix 00000000. The address with all zeros is a *unicast unspecified address,* which is used by a host during the bootstrap procedure. The *loopback address,* used for local test, is ::1.

IPv6 allows multiple addresses to be assigned to an interface. Therefore, an interface may have more than one Global Unicast Address and Link Local Unicast Address simultaneously. The Link Local Address is *not* globally unique, and thus it is used for addressing on a single link for purposes such as automatic address configuration and neighbor discovery. The Link Local Address contains a prefix 1111111010 followed by *56 zero* bits and then a *64-bit interface id*. The interface id can be encoded from its hardware address, for example the EUI-64 format.

The general format for the IPv6 Global Unicast Address is shown in Figure 4.31. To support routing and address aggregation, the global routing prefix is typically hierarchically structured. Besides, all Global Unicast Addresses other than those starting with binary 000 have a 64-bit interface id field. As shown in Table 4.2, currently, assignable Global Unicast Addresses have a prefix of 2000::/3. Up to the date of writing (November 2009), there are 36 prefix assignments made by IANA to RIRs (RIPE NCC, APNIC, ARIN, LACNIC, and AfriNIC). Most recent IPv6 unicast address prefix assignments can be found at http://www.iana.org/assignments/ipv6-unicast-address-assignments.

IPv6 multicast addresses begin with prefix 11111111, as shown in Figure 4.32. Unlike IPv4, which relies on TTL to control the scope of multicast, the IPv6 multicast address contains a *scope* field to indicate the scope of multicast; five multicast scopes are supported: *node-local, link-local, site-local, organization-local,* and *global*. It also has a flag field with a T bit to indicate whether the multicast address is only a *transient* address (T = 1) or a *well-known* address (to provide persistent multicast service).

Some multicast addresses have been reserved for special purposes. For example, FF02:0:0:0:0:0:0:2 is used to reach *all routers* on the same physical network. Examples of reserved multicast addresses are shown in Table 4.3.

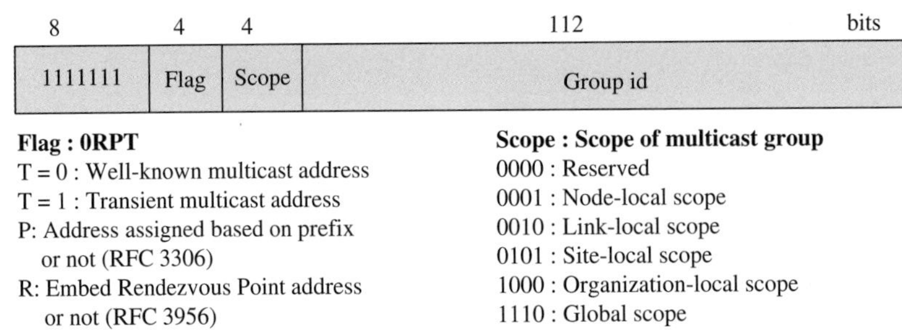

FIGURE 4.32 Format of IPv6 multicast address.

4.3.6 Autoconfiguration

One of the special features of IPv6 is support of autoconfiguration. Unlike DHCP, which requires a DHCP server or a relay agent in each network, IPv6 supports *serverless* autoconfiguration. A host first generates a unique *link local* address. The 64-bit interface id, which contains the lower bits of the link local address, can be encoded from its unique *hardware address,* as described above. The host then uses this address to send a *router solicitation* message (an ICMP message). Upon receiving the solicitation message, the router will reply with a *router advertisement* message which contains the subnet prefix information. The host can then use the subnet prefix to generate its global address.

4.3.7 Transition from IPv4 to IPv6

When and how will the current Internet transit to IPv6? The problem is quite difficult as a new version of IP means a new version of network software, and it is impossible to have a "flag day" to have all hosts in the Internet change their software to the new version at the same time. In this case, how could the Internet operate when both IPv4-compatible hosts and IPv6-compatible hosts coexist? Two approaches are proposed in RFC 1933: *dual-stack* and *tunneling*. Another approach, protocol translator, has also been proposed to address the IPv6 transition problem.

TABLE 4.3 Reserved IPv6 Multicast Addresses

Scope	Reserved Address	Purpose
Node-local	FF01:0:0:0:0:0:0:1	All nodes address
	FF01:0:0:0:0:0:0:2	All routers address
Link-local	FF02:0:0:0:0:0:0:1	All nodes address
	FF02:0:0:0:0:0:0:2	All routers address
	FF02:0:0:0:0:1:FFxx:xxxx	Solicited node address
Site-local	FF05:0:0:0:0:0:0:2	All routers address
	FF05:0:0:0:0:0:0:3	All DHCP servers address

The dual-stack approach is to have a host (or router) run both IPv6 and IPv4. Consider a case where a subnet consists of both IPv4-compatible hosts and IPv6-compatible hosts. An IPv6 host would run both IPv4 and IPv6 such that it can use IPv4 packets to communicate with IPv4-compatible hosts and IPv6 packets to communicate with IPv6-compatible hosts. Another example is to have the subnet router of a pure IPv6 network run both IPv4 and IPv6 protocols. IPv6 packets originated from the subnet are translated to IPv4 packets by the router when leaving the network. On the other hand, IPv4 packets received by the router are translated to IPv6 packets before being forwarded to the destination. Note that the translation may lose some information as the headers of two protocols are not fully compatible.

An alternate approach is IP tunneling, which refers to the process of encapsulating an IP packet in the payload field of another IP packet. A tunnel may be built between the sender and receiver or between two routers. In the first case, both sender and receiver are IPv6 compatible, but routers in between are not. The sender can *encapsulate* an IPv6 packet in an IPv4 packet with the destination as the receiver's address. This IPv4 packet is then forwarded as a normal IPv4 packet in the IPv4 network, and finally arrives at the receiver. For the sender that knows the receiver's IPv4 and IPv6 addresses, *IPv4-compatible IPv6 address* can be used. A tunnel can also be built between two routers. Consider a case where two pure IPv6 networks are connected by an IPv4 backbone network. IPv6 packets originated from the subnet will be encapsulated into an IPv4 packet with the destination as the receiver's router. When this IPv4 packet arrives at the receiver's router, the router will recognize it as an encapsulated packet, then extract and forward the embedded IPv6 packet to the receiver. Many proposals for tunneling, including configured tunneling and automatic tunneling, have been raised. Tunnel broker, proposed in RFC 3053, can help users to configure bidirectional tunnels. As described in RFC 3056, a special address prefix to help connections of IPv6 domains via IPv4 clouds is called *6to4*. A remedy for the *6to4* problem for hosts behind an IPv4 NAT to connect to IPv6 hosts is called *Teredo,* which is defined in RFC 4380. Another automatic tunneling mechanism that aims to connect IPv6 hosts and routers over an IPv4 network is called *Intra-Site Automatic Tunneling Addressing Protocol* (*ISATAP*), as defined in RFC 5214.

Another possible approach is *protocol translator,* which translates from one protocol to another when communicating pure IPv4 hosts and pure IPv6 hosts. Protocol translation requires that a gateway sit between IPv4 and IPv6 networks or a middleware in the protocol stack to translate IPv6 protocols and addresses to those of IPv4, and vice versa. Solutions proposed include SIIT (RFC 2765), NAT-PT(RFC 2766, 4966), BIS (RFC 2767), and BIA (RFC 3338). The translation mechanisms also require DNS extensions to support IPv6, which are defined in RFC 3596.

4.4 CONTROL-PLANE PROTOCOLS: ADDRESS MANAGEMENT

In this section, we address two mechanisms for IP address management. In the first subsection, we examine the Address Resolution Protocol (ARP) for translation between the Internet Protocol layer (Layer-3) address and the link layer (Layer-2) address. In the second subsection, we discuss the Dynamic Host Configuration Protocol (DHCP) for dynamic and automatic IP address configuration.

4.4.1 Address Resolution Protocol

Recall that when a host wants to send a packet to a destination, the host first determines whether the destination resides within the same IP subnet. If yes, the packet is delivered directly *via the link layer* to the destination; otherwise, the packet is sent, also via the link layer, to a router for forwarding. The question is that since the IP address is used at the IP layer while the hardware (MAC) address (e.g., the 48-bit Ethernet address) is used at the link layer, how can the host use the destination IP address in the packet header to obtain the MAC address of the destination or the router? Therefore, we need an address resolution protocol that *translates* an IP address to a MAC address.

In general, address resolution can be realized in two approaches: with or without a server. If there is an address resolution server, all hosts can send registration messages to the server so that the server knows the mapping of IP address to MAC address for all hosts. A host can then query the server when it needs to send a packet to another host (or router) within the subnet. To avoid manually configuring the address resolution server parameters at each host, the host can broadcast the registration message. The disadvantage of this approach is that we need an *address resolution server* within each IP subnet. The Address Resolution Protocol (ARP), adopted by the Internet, uses the other serverless approach. When a host needs to query the MAC address of the destination, it *broadcasts* an ARP request message. The destination will reply with an ARP reply message upon receiving the request. Since the ARP request contains the IP and MAC addresses of the sender, the destination can send the ARP reply using *unicast*. It would be too inefficient if ARP were run each time an IP packet was sent. Therefore, each host maintains a *cache table* of (IP address, MAC address) pairs so that there is no need to run ARP if the mapping can be found in the cache. On the other hand, ARP adopts the soft state approach, which allows a host to dynamically change its IP address or MAC address (e.g., change the network interface card). That is, a *timer* is associated with each entry in the cache table, and the timer-expired entries will be discarded. Since the ARP request message is a broadcast message, all hosts can receive it and see the IP and MAC address of the sender; as a "good" side effect, the cache entry for the sender can be *refreshed* by the broadcast message.

On some special occasions, we may need a reverse mapping from MAC address to IP address, called reversed ARP protocol. For example, a diskless workstation that knows its own MAC address may need to obtain its IP address from a server before it can use that IP address to access the network file system (NFS) or to retrieve the image of an operating system to boot. In the following, we will see that ARP also supports reverse ARP request and reply operations.

ARP Packet Format

The ARP protocol is a general protocol for translating addresses between the network layer and the link layer. The ARP packet format is shown in Figure 4.33. The address type and address length fields allow ARP to be used for various network- and link-layer protocols. The *hardware address type* and *protocol address type* indicate

0	8	16	24	31
Hardware Address Type		Protocol Address Type		
H. Addr Len	P. Addr Len	Operation Code		
Sender Hardware Address (0-3)				
Sender Hardware Addr (4-5)		Sender Protocol Addr (0-1)		
Sender Protocol Addr (2-3)		Target Hardware Addr (0-1)		
Target Hardware Address (2-5)				
Target Protocol Address				

FIGURE 4.33 ARP packet format.

which protocols are used for the link layer and the network layer, respectively. The most common hardware address type is Ethernet, which has the value of 1; the IP protocol type is 0x0800. Address type fields are followed by two length fields: the hardware address length and the protocol address length. Ethernet and IP have the value of 6 and 4, respectively. The *operation code* indicates the operation of the ARP message. There are four operation codes: *request* (1), *reply* (2), *RARP request* (3), and *RARP reply* (4). The next two fields are the *sender's* link layer address and IP address. The last two fields are the *receiver's* link layer address and IP address. In an ARP request message, the sender will fill in the *Target Hardware Address* field with zero bits, as it does not know the receiver's hardware address yet.

Since both ARP and IP (and other network-layer protocols) are carried in the payload of a link-layer frame, the control information for multiplexing and demultiplexing packets of different network-layer protocols are required at the link-layer header. For example, Ethernet has a 2-byte type field to indicate the upper-layer protocol. The protocol id for IP and ARP are different, *0x0800* and *0x0806,* respectively. In Ethernet, broadcasting an ARP request message can be done by filling in the destination address with 0xFFFFFFFFFFFF.

Open Source Implementation 4.6: ARP

Overview

Implementation of the ARP protocol requires an ARP cache table and functions to send and receive ARP packets. Most of the source codes of ARP can be found in `src/net/ipv4/arp.c`.

Data Structures

The most important data structure is `arp_tbl`, which keeps most the of important parameters used by ARP. The `arp_tbl`, defined as `struct neigh_table`, consists of a `hash_buckets` entry to hold the ARP cache of neighbor information. The following shows the data structure for `neigh_table`:

Continued

```
struct neigh_table
{
    struct neigh_table      *next;
    int                     family;
    int                     entry_size;
    int                     key_len;
    __u32   (*hash)(const void *pkey, const struct net_
device *);
    int                      (*constructor)(struct
neighbour *);
    int                      (*pconstructor)(struct
pneigh_entry *);
    void                     (*pdestructor)(struct
pneigh_entry *);
    void                        (*proxy_redo)(struct
sk_buff *skb);
    char                    *id;
    struct neigh_parms      parms;
    int                     gc_interval;
    int                     gc_thresh1;
    int                     gc_thresh2;
    int                     gc_thresh3;
    unsigned long             last_flush;
    struct timer_list         gc_timer;
    struct timer_list         proxy_timer;
    struct sk_buff_head       proxy_queue;
    atomic_t                entries;
    rwlock_t                lock;
    unsigned long            last_rand;
    struct kmem_cache                 *kmem_cachep;
    struct neigh_statistics *stats;
    struct neighbour       **hash_buckets;
    unsigned int           hash_mask;
    __u32                  hash_rnd;
    unsigned int           hash_chain_gc;
    struct pneigh_entry    **phash_buckets;
};
```

Block Diagram

Sending and receiving ARP packets are handled by `arp_send()` and `arp_rcv()`, respectively. Call graphs for `arp_send()` and `arp_rcv()` are shown in Figure 4.34. `arp_send()` calls `arp_create()` to create an ARP packet and `arp_xmit()`, which in turn calls `dev_queue_xmit()` to send out the ARP packet. When an ARP packet is received, `arp_process()` is called to process the packet accordingly. In `arp_process()`, `__niegh_lookp()` is called to search the `hash_buckets` with the source IP address as the hash key.

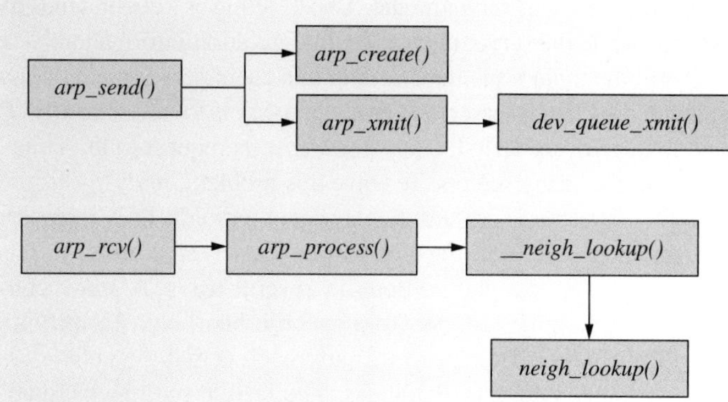

FIGURE 4.34 Call graphs for `arp_send()` and `arp_rcv()`.

Algorithm Implementations

The task of `arp_process()` is to send a reply if there is a request for the host or if there is a request for someone else the host holds a proxy for; or to process a reply from someone else the host sent a request to. For the latter case, the entry corresponding to the source of the reply message in the ARP table is updated. To implement this update, `arp_process()` first calls `__niegh_lookp()` to locate the corresponding entry in the ARP table. It then calls `neigh_update()` to update the status of this entry.

Exercises

The function `__neigh_lookup()` is a common function that implements hash buckets.

1. Use a free text search or cross reference tool to find out which functions call `__neigh_lookup()`.
2. Trace `__neigh_lookup()` and explain how to look up an entry from hash buckets.

4.4.2 Dynamic Host Configuration

From Section 4.2, we can observe that each host needs to be properly configured with an *IP address, subnet mask,* and *default router*. (We also need to configure at the host the parameters relevant to the *domain name server,* which we shall discuss in Chapter 6.) To a naïve user, such a configuration process does not make any sense, and it often becomes the burden of network managers. Misconfiguration of the network-layer parameters happens every day without surprise. Unfortunately, unlike the MAC address of an Ethernet card, these parameters *cannot* be configured during the manufacturing stage because the IP address has a hierarchical structure. Clearly, an automated configuration method is needed. IETF thus proposed the Dynamic Host Configuration Protocol (DHCP) to solve the automated configuration problem.

In general, DHCP follows the client-server model. A host, acting as a client, sends its request to the DHCP server, while the server replies the configuration information back to the host. *Scalability* is still the main issue in designing this client-server model. First of all, how does a host reach the DHCP server? An easy approach is to have *one* DHCP server per IP subnet and to have every DHCP client *broadcast* its request to its subnet. However, this would result in too many servers. To solve this problem, *relay agents* are used in subnets where no DHCP server is present. A relay agent forwards DHCP request messages to a DHCP server and then returns the replies from the server to hosts.

Assigning an IP address to a host can be done in several ways. A *static* configuration approach maps a specific IP address to a specific host, e.g., identifying each host by its MAC address. The advantage of this approach is that the network is better managed, as each host has a unique IP address. The DHCP only helps to automatically configure each host's IP address. To trace which host owns a specific IP address when there is a network security problem is as easy as manual configuration. However, when the number of hosts in a subnet is larger than the number of legal IP addresses owned by the subnet, we need another approach, the dynamic configuration approach, to adaptively assign IP addresses to *active* hosts. In this approach, the DHCP server is configured with a *pool* of IP addresses that are assigned to hosts on demand. When a host requests an IP address, the DHCP server selects an unassigned IP address from the pool and assigns it to the host. A more complicated use of this approach is that each host can send its preferred IP address, usually the IP address it was assigned last time, to the server and the server will assign the preferred address to the host if it is currently available. To prevent the IP address from being occupied by an inactive host, the server actually "loans" an IP address to a host for a limited time only. A host needs to request the IP address again before the lease *expires,* and of course, the currently assigned IP address will be the preferred address.

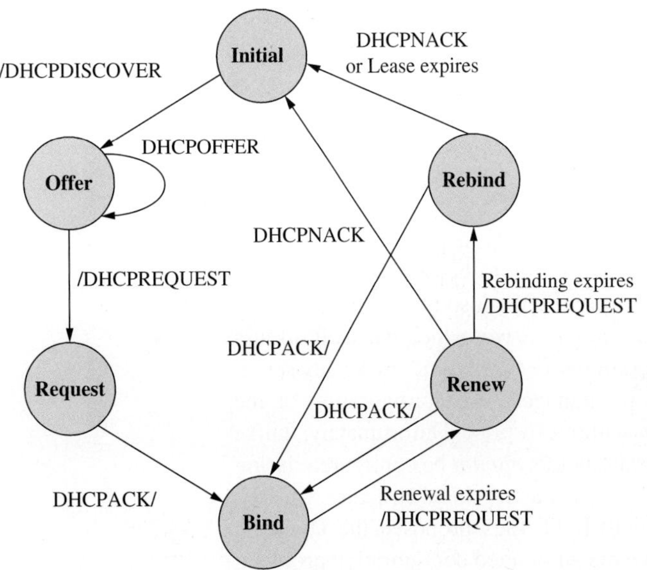

FIGURE 4.35 State diagram for DHCP.

FIGURE 4.36 DHCP packet format.

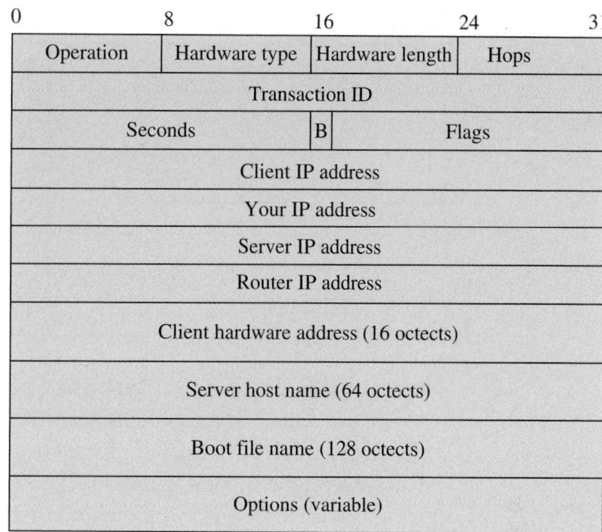

DHCP Operation

The detailed DHCP procedure is shown in Figure 4.35. When a host first boots, it *broadcasts* a DHCPDISCOVER message, which is packed in a *UDP* packet with port *67*. All DHCP servers that receive the message will send back a DHCPOFFER message on *UDP* port *68*. The client selects one offer if there is more than one available, and sends a DHCPREQUEST message to the server that gave the offer. If everything is all right, the server replies a DHCPACK message. At this time, the client is configured with an IP address as well as other information provided by the server. The client needs to send a DHCPREQUEST message *again* before the lease renewal timer expires (which is usually set to *one-half* of the lease expiration time). If no DHCPACK messages are received before lease rebinding time, the client sends a DHCPREQUEST message again. The client gives up its IP address when a DHCPNACK message is received or when the lease expiration timer expires.

The packet format of DHCP [RFC 2131] is shown in Figure 4.36, which is derived from BOOTP. (BOOTP was originally designed to enable automatic boot configuration for diskless workstations.) The *hardware type* indicates the link-layer protocol, and the *hardware length* is the length of the link-layer address in bytes. The *hops* field is set to zero by the client and *increased* by one when the packet passes a *relay agent*. The B bit in flags is set if the client wants to receive replies using the *broadcast* address instead of its hardware unicast address. Some of the fields are used in BOOTP but are not used by DHCP. The option field is used to carry additional information, such as subnet mask. More than one option can be packed into a message. The option field starts with a 4-byte magic cookie 0x63825363, followed by a list of options.

The format of each option, as shown in Figure 4.37, consists of a *3-octect header* followed by data in octets. The 3-octect header includes 1-octect code, 1-octect length, and

FIGURE 4.37 Header of the DHCP option field.

0	8	16	23
Code (53)	Length (1)	Type (1–7)	

TABLE 4.4 DHCP Message Types

Type	DHCP Message
1	DHCPDISCOVER
2	DHCPOFFER
3	DHCPREQUEST
4	DHCPDECLINE
5	DHCPACK
6	DHCPNACK
7	DHCPRELEASE

1-octect type fields. To convey different types of DHCP messages, the code value is set to 53 and the value of the type field, shown in Table 4.4, indicates which message is sent. For example, a DHCP DISCOVER message is encoded as code=53, length=1, type=1.

For each type of DHCP message, additional options packed in the code-length-type format are appended at the end. For example, the DHCP DISCOVER message may use code 50 to specify the desired IP address. In this case, the option has code=50, length=4, type=the desired IP address.

Following are some commonly used options [RFC 2132]:

Code: 0 Pad option
Code: 1 Subnet mask
Code: 3 Routers
Code: 6 Domain name servers
Code: 12 Host name
Code: 15 Domain name
Code: 17 Boot path
Code: 26 Interface MTU
Code: 40 NIS Domain name
Code: 50 Requested IP address (DHCPDISCOVER)
Code: 51 IP address lease time
Code: 53 Message type
Code: 54 Server identifier
Code: 55 Parameter request list
Code: 56 Error message
Code: 57 Maximum DHCP message size
Code: 58 Renewal (T1) time value
Code: 59 Rebinding (T2) time value
Code: 60 Vendor class identifier
Code: 61 Client-identifier
Code: 255 End option

FIGURE 4.38 shows an example of the option field of a DHCP OFFER message.

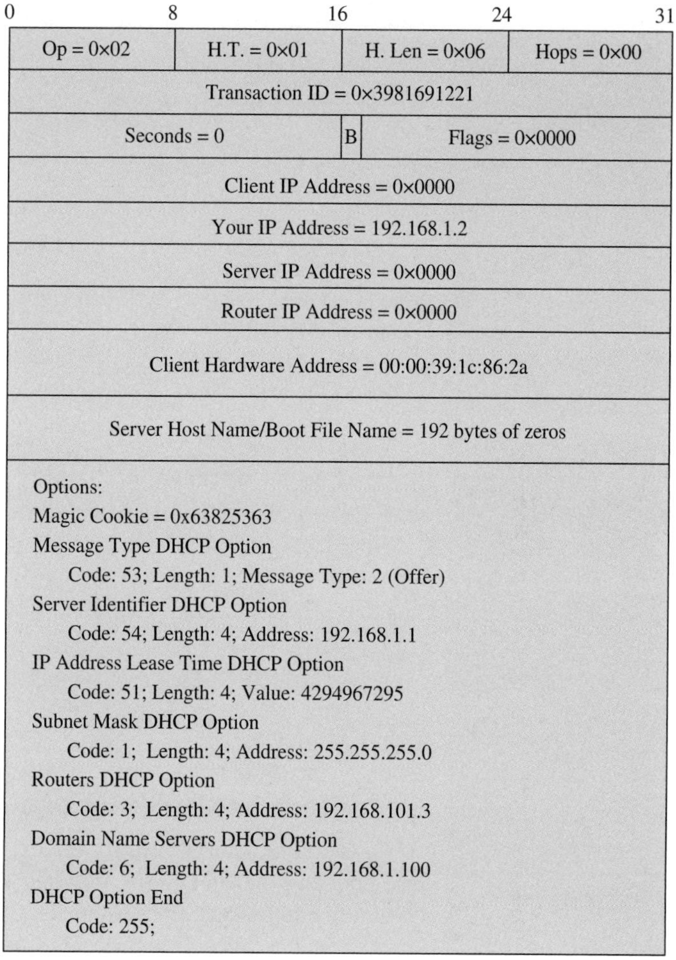

FIGURE 4.38 An example of DHCP OFFER message.

0	8	16	24	31
Op = 0×02	H.T. = 0×01	H. Len = 0×06	Hops = 0×00	
Transaction ID = 0×3981691221				
Seconds = 0		B	Flags = 0×0000	
Client IP Address = 0×0000				
Your IP Address = 192.168.1.2				
Server IP Address = 0×0000				
Router IP Address = 0×0000				
Client Hardware Address = 00:00:39:1c:86:2a				
Server Host Name/Boot File Name = 192 bytes of zeros				

Options:
Magic Cookie = 0x63825363
Message Type DHCP Option
    Code: 53; Length: 1; Message Type: 2 (Offer)
Server Identifier DHCP Option
    Code: 54; Length: 4; Address: 192.168.1.1
IP Address Lease Time DHCP Option
    Code: 51; Length: 4; Value: 4294967295
Subnet Mask DHCP Option
    Code: 1; Length: 4; Address: 255.255.255.0
Routers DHCP Option
    Code: 3; Length: 4; Address: 192.168.101.3
Domain Name Servers DHCP Option
    Code: 6; Length: 4; Address: 192.168.1.100
DHCP Option End
    Code: 255;

Open Source Implementation 4.7: DHCP

Overview

DHCP is implemented as a variation of the BOOTP protocol. Information is carried in the option field starting with a magic cookie 0x63825363. After verifying this magic cookie, DHCP messages are processed according to the option code defined in RFC 2132.

Data Structures

The data structure for the BOOTP/DHCP protocol is `struct bootp_pkt` in `src/net/ipv4/ipconfig.c`.

Continued

```
struct bootp_pkt {                    /* BOOTP packet format */
struct iphdr iph;                     /* IP header */
struct udphdr udph;                    /* UDP header */
u8 op;                               /* 1=request, 2=reply */
u8 htype;                            /* HW address type */
u8 hlen;                             /* HW address length */
u8 hops;                             /* Used only by gateways */
__be32 xid;                           /* Transaction ID */
__be16 secs;                          /* Seconds since we
started */
__be16 flags;                         /* Just what it says */
__be32 client_ip;                      /* Client's IP address
if known */
__be32 your_ip;                       /* Assigned IP address */
__be32 server_ip;                    /* (Next, e.g. NFS)
Server's IP address */
__be32 relay_ip;                           /* IP address of BOOTP
relay */
u8 hw_addr[16];                        /* Client's HW address */
u8 serv_name[64];                      /* Server host name */
u8 boot_file[128];                     /* Name of boot file */
u8 exten[312];                         /* DHCP options/BOOTP
vendor extensions */
};
```

Algorithm Implementations

If autoconfiguration is defined, the `ip_auto_config()` will be called and the defined protocol (RARP, BOOTP, or DHCP) will be used to configure the host's IP address and other parameters. As shown in Figure 4.39, `ic_bootp_send_if()`, called from `ip_auto_config()`, will send out the `DHCPREQUEST` message to the DHCP server if the IP address of the DHCP server is known, or broadcast the `DHCPDISCOVER` message otherwise. In particular, the options of these DHCP messages, such as requests for subnet mask and default gateway, are set up by the `ic_dhcp_init_options()` function. A DHCP client needs to wait for a `DHCPACK` before using the requested IP address; see `ic_dynamic()`.

A received DHCP message is processed by the `ic_bootp_recv()` function. Only `DHCPOFFER` and `DHCPACK` messages are processed in the current implementation. The additional configuration information is handled by `ic_do_bootp_ext()`, and currently, only code 1 (subnet mask), 3 (default gateway), 6 (DNS server), 12 (host name), 15 (domain name), 17 (root path), 26 (interface MTU), and 42 (NIS domain name) are processed. Note that additional configuration information is always the last part of the DHCP message and ends with the octet 0xFF (see the example in Figure 4.38).

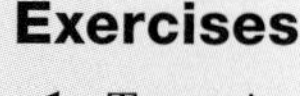

Exercises

1. Trace `ic_bootp_recv()` and explain how the option field of the DHCP message is processed.
2. There are many new DHCP options defined after RFC 2132. Taking RFC 5417 as an example, read the RFC and see what options have been defined.

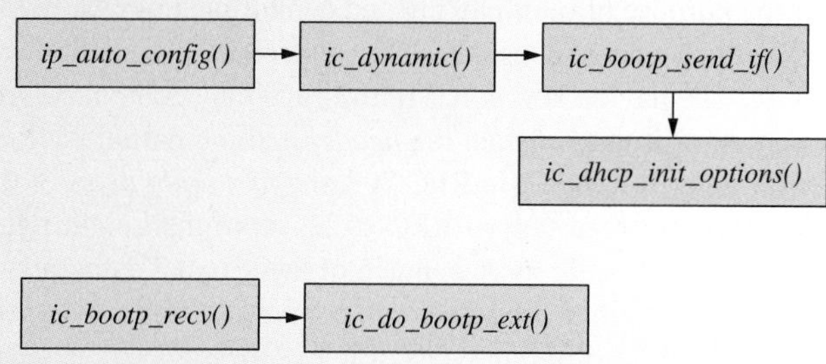

FIGURE 4.39 Call graph of DHCP open source implementation.

4.5 CONTROL PLANE PROTOCOLS: ERROR REPORTING

Errors occur in the Internet occasionally. For example, a packet cannot be forwarded any further due to a zero TTL or due to the unreachable destination. Recall that you often see an error message from your browser showing that the server may be down. The Internet could handle errors differently—for example, it could just ignore the errors and silently drop error packets. However, for debugging, managing, and tracing network status, *reporting errors* to the source node or the intermediate routers is a better solution. The Internet Control Message Protocol (ICMP) is mainly designed for reporting errors, found by routers or hosts, to the *source* node. It can also be used for informational reporting.

4.5.1 ICMP Protocol

ICMP can be used to report errors of TCP/IP protocols and the status of a host/router. In most cases, ICMP is implemented as part of IP. Although it is a control protocol at the IP layer, ICMP messages are *carried* by IP packets, that is, ICMP lies above IP, as shown in Figure 4.40. Therefore, ICMP is like an upper-layer protocol to IP. An ICMP message is carried in the payload of an IP packet, and the upper-layer protocol id in

FIGURE 4.40 ICMP over IP.

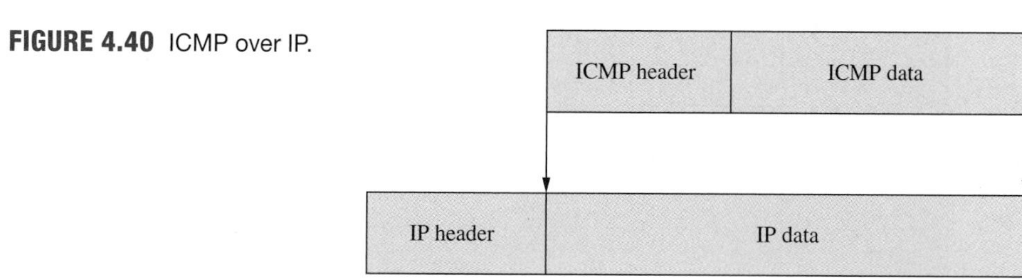

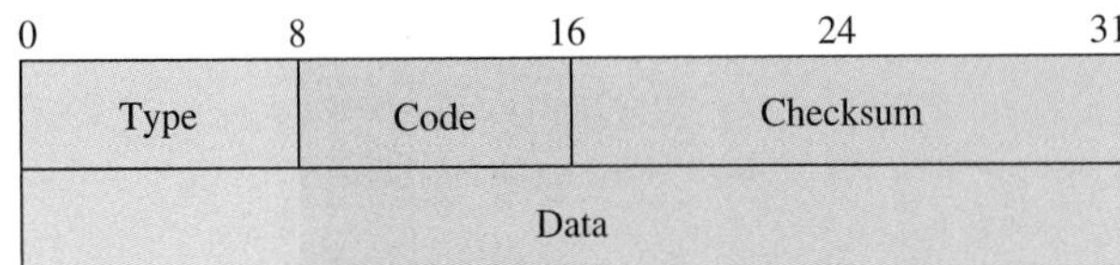

FIGURE 4.41 ICMP packet format.

the IP header is set to 1 for the purpose of multiplexing and demultiplexing. An ICMP message consists of two parts: the header and the data. The header has a *type* and a *code* field, as shown in Figure 4.41. The payload of an ICMP message may contain control data for an informational report, or it may contain the *header* and the partial payload of the erroneous IP packet for an error report. (In RFC 792, the *first eight bytes* of the datagram that triggered the error are reported; in RFC 1122, more than eight bytes may be sent; in RFC 1812, a router should report as much of the original datagram as possible in the payload without the length of the ICMP datagram exceeding 576 bytes.) Different syntax formats are defined for different types of ICMP messages.

The list of types and codes of commonly used ICMP messages for IPv4 is shown in Table 4.5. Four of them are informational messages, namely *echo reply* and *request, router advertisement,* and *discovery;* the rest are error messages. For a source to know whether a destination is alive, it can send an echo request message to the destination. Upon receiving the echo request, the destination responds with an echo reply message. The payload of these two messages contains a *16-bit identifier*

TABLE 4.5 Types and Codes of ICMP for IPv4

Type	Code	Description
0	0	Echo reply (ping)
3	0	Destination network unreachable
3	1	Destination host unreachable
3	2	Destination protocol unreachable
3	3	Destination port unreachable
3	4	Fragmentation needed and DF set
3	5	Source route failed
3	6	Destination network unknown
3	7	Destination host unknown
4	0	Source quench (congestion control)
5	0	Redirect (destination network)
5	1	Redirect (host)
8	0	Echo request (ping)
9	0	Route advertisement
10	0	Router discovery
11	0	TTL expired
12	0	Bad IP header

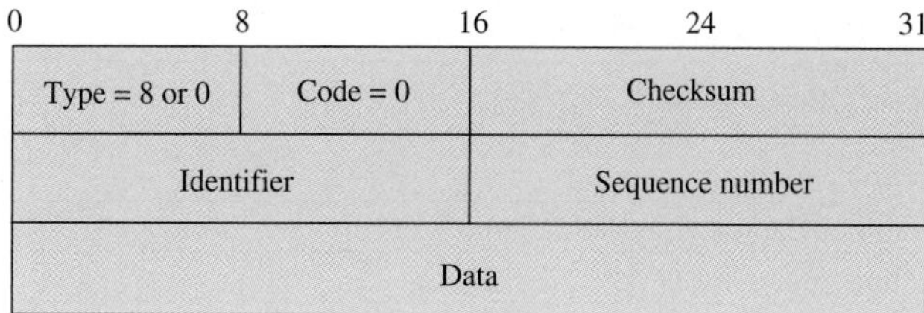

FIGURE 4.42 ICMP echo request and reply message format.

and a *16-bit sequence number* such that the source can match replies to the corresponding requests, as shown in Figure 4.42. The well-known debugging tool, *ping,* is implemented using ICMP echo request and echo reply messages.

Among the ICMP error messages, *destination unreachable* (type 3) is used to report various unreachable reasons, such as network, host, or port unreachable. However, code 4 of a type 3 message is used to report the error that fragmentation is needed at an intermediate router (due to MTU), but the *do not fragment* bit in the IP header is set. Type 4 and type 5 messages are seldom used in practice. The *source quench* message (type 4) is designed to allow a router to send an error message to the source when the packet causes buffer overflow (due to congestion). Upon receiving a source quench message, a source should reduce its transmission rate. For an IP subnet with more than two routers, the *redirect* message (type 5) is used to inform the host of a better alternative route to the destination. Usually, the better route is to send the packet to another router in the same subnet. Type 12 messages are used to report errors in the IP header, such as invalid IP header or wrong option field.

The *time exceeded* message, type 11, is sent to the source host when the TTL of the IP packet reaches zero after TTL decrement at a router. This type of message is particularly interesting as the traceroute program uses it to trace the route from a source host to a destination. The traceroute program sends a sequence of ICMP messages to the destination as follows: First, it sends an ICMP echo request with *TTL=1* to the target machine. When the first router on the route to the destination receives this message, it responds with a time exceeded ICMP error message, as the TTL reaches zero after decrement. The traceroute program, upon receiving the time exceeded message, then sends another echo request with *TTL=2* to the destination. This time, the message will pass the first router but will be discarded by the second router, and then the second router will send another time exceeded message back to the source. The traceroute program continues sending ICMP echo requests with incremental TTL values until it receives an echo reply from the destination. Each time the traceroute program receives a time exceeded message, it learns a new router on the route. (Note that actually, most traceroute programs send *three* echo request messages for a given TTL value and record the response time from each router.)

For the next-generation Internet Protocol, a new set of ICMP types and codes is defined, as shown in Table 4.6. The packet format of ICMPv6 is the same as that of ICMPv4, but the values of the ICMPv6 type field are defined in a more recognizable way such that error messages have a type less than 127 and informational messages have a type larger than 127 but less than 256.

TABLE 4.6 Types and Codes of ICMPv6

Type	Code	Description
1	0	No route to destination
1	1	Communication with destination administratively prohibited
1	3	Address unreachable
1	4	Port unreachable
2	0	Packet too big
3	0	Hop limit exceeded in transit
3	1	Fragment reassembly time exceeded
4	0	Erroneous header field encountered
4	1	Unrecognized Next Header type
4	2	Unrecognized IPv6 option encountered
128	0	Echo request
129	0	Echo reply
130	0	Multicast Listener Query
131	0	Multicast Listener Report
132	0	Multicast Listener Done
133	0	Router Solicitation
134	0	Router Advertisement
135	0	Neighbor Solicitation
136	0	Neighbor Advertisement
137	0	Redirect

Open Source Implementation 4.8: ICMP

Overview

An ICMP message is sent when a packet cannot be forwarded or when some ICMP service request, such as an ECHO request, is received. For the former case, an ICMP message is sent during the packet forwarding process, such as `ip_forward()` or `ip_route_input_slow()`. For the latter case, an ICMP message is received from the link layer, and `icmp_rcv()` is called to process the request.

Data Structures

To deal with different types of ICMP messages by different handlers, the table `icmp_pointers[]` is used to store ICMP handlers (see `src/net/ipv4/icmp.c`). For example, `icmp_unreach()` is used for type 3, 4, 11, and 12; `icmp_redirect()` for type 5; `icmp_echo()` for type 8; `icmp_timestamp()` for type 13; `icmp_address()` for type 17; `icmp_address_reply()` for type 18; and `icmp_discard()` for other types. The `icmp_pointers[]` table is set up as follows:

```
static const struct icmp_control icmp_pointers[NR_
ICMP_TYPES + 1] = {
...
     [ICMP_REDIRECT] = {
          .handler = icmp_redirect,
          .error = 1,
},
...
[ICMP_ECHO] = {
          .handler = icmp_echo,
},
...
[ICMP_TIMESTAMP] = {
          .handler = icmp_timestamp,
},
...
[ICMP_ADDRESS] = {
          .handler = icmp_address,
},
[ICMP_ADDRESSREPLY] = {
          .handler = icmp_address_reply,
},
};
```

Algorithm Implementations

Figure 4.43 shows the call graph for sending and receiving an ICMP message. When an IP packet is to be forwarded, `ip_forward()` is called to process the packet. If there is something wrong with the packet, `ip_forward()` will call `icmp_send()` to send an ICMP message back to the source host. The sequence of steps for checking the packet in `ip_forward()` is as follows: First, if the packet's TTL is less than or equal to 1, an ICMP time exceeded message is sent. Second, if strict source routing is requested and the next hop obtained from the routing table is not the router specified by the packet, an ICMP destination unreachable message is sent. Third, if route redirect is needed, `ip_rt_send_redirect()` is called to redirect the packet, which then calls `icmp_send()` to send an ICMP redirect message. Finally, if the length of the packet is larger than the interface's MTU and the do not fragment bit is set, then an ICMP destination unreachable (with code=4, `ICMP_FRAG_NEEDED`) message is sent.

Recall that a received IP packet that matches none of the routes stored in the cache will be processed by the `ip_route_input_slow()` function. If the resultant routing table lookup returns `RTN_UNREACHABLE`, `ip_error()` is called, which will invoke `icmp_send()` to send an ICMP destination unreachable message back to the source.

Continued

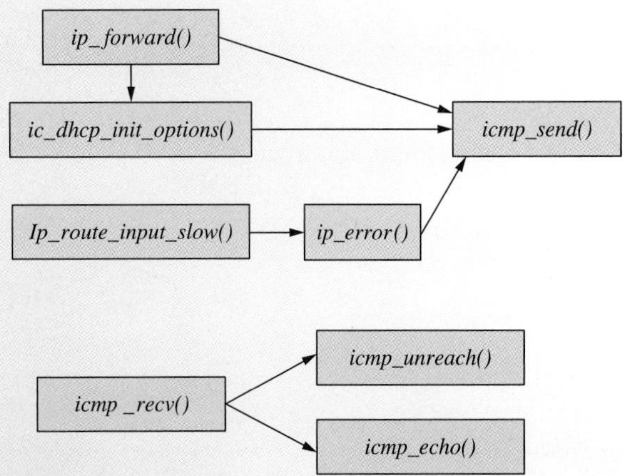

FIGURE 4.43 Call graph for sending and receiving an ICMP message.

Finally, let us examine how to process an incoming ICMP packet. When an ICMP message is received, the *bottom half* interrupt handler of the network interface card will call the `icmp_rcv()` function, which then calls an appropriate ICMP type handler according to the type field of the ICMP message. Most of the ICMP types are processed by the `icmp_unreach()` function. Besides checking the received ICMP message, the `icmp_unreach()` function will pass error packets to the appropriate upper-layer protocol if the error handler of that protocol has been defined. A received echo request is processed by the `icmp_echo()` function such that if the echo reply option is not disabled, an echo reply message will be returned to the source node.

As a final remark, ICMPv6 functions are implemented in similar ways (see `src/net/ipv6/icmp.c`). ICMP messages are sent by `icmpv6_send()`, and `icmpv6_rcv()` is called to receive ICMP messages. Echo request messages are replied by `icmpv6_echo_reply()`, and other error messages, such as packet too big, destination unreachable, time exceeded, and parameter problem, are processed by `icmpv6_notify()`, which will pass error packets to upper-layer protocols if error handlers have been defined. Neighbor discovery is a new feature of IPv6 that consists of five types of messages: router solicitation, router advertisement, neighbor solicitation, neighbor advertisement, and route redirect. The function `ndisc_rcv()` (see `src/net/ipv6/ndisc.c`) is called upon receiving these types of messages, and this function then switches to different functions based on the message type. For example, `ndisc_router_discovery()` is called to process router advertisements.

Exercises

Write a pseudocode for the traceroute program, given that you can call the ICMP functions in the kernel.

4.6 CONTROL PLANE PROTOCOLS: ROUTING

In the data plane, we have seen how a router forwards packets by looking up its routing table. Assuming that the routing table is built and maintained correctly, the *forwarding* process is quite simple and straightforward; nevertheless, it all depends on the task of *routing* to compute routes and maintain the routing table. In this section, we shall first discuss the underlying principles of routing and then address how routing is done in the Internet.

4.6.1 Routing Principles

The task of the IP layer is to provide host-to-host connectivity. This connectivity allows one host to send packets to another remote host. To achieve this task, a route (a sequence of adjacent routers) needs to be established for each source-destination pair so that packets can be transferred along the route. The task of finding the route from the source to the destination host is called routing.

Desirable properties of a routing mechanism include *efficient, stable, robust, fair,* and *scalable*. Since the Internet uses packet switching, resources are shared and packets are stored and forwarded by routers. Therefore, the major objective of routing is efficient resource sharing while maintaining good performance, such as low delay and low packet loss, and optimal routing shall maximize resource *utilization,* minimize packet *delay,* and/or minimize packet *loss*. (Note that these goals may conflict with each other.) Scalability is always important in the Internet. Scalable routing includes a scalable *data structure* for the use of a routing table, a scalable routing information *exchange* mechanism, and a scalable algorithm for route *computation*. Besides, it is also very important not to form any cycle within a route, since *packet looping* may waste a lot of bandwidth and cause the network to become unstable. Due to the large number of routers in the Internet, robust routing is necessary to prevent a failed link or router, that is, a single point of failure, from affecting the whole network. Finally, fairness is also desirable because nodes should be treated equally.

There are three broad categories of routing: point-to-point, point-to-multipoint, and multipoint-to-multipoint. The first one is referred to as unicast routing and the other two are referred to as multicast routing. For unicast transmission, packets are to be transferred from one source to one destination. For multicast transmission, there could be one or more source hosts, and packets are to be transferred from these source hosts to more than one destination host. Clearly, unicast routing would be very different from multicast routing. Unicast routing, as a more common case, is to find a route between a source host and a destination host. On the other hand, multicast routing is to find multiple routes from one or more sources to multiple destinations, which usually form a tree structure referred to as a *multicast tree*. In this section, we focus on unicast routing and leave multicast routing to the next section.

Global or Local Information

Unicast routing protocols are differentiated from other routing protocols by the type of routing information being used, how routing information is exchanged, and how routes are determined. A route can be computed based on *global* (complete) information or *local* (partial) information about the network. If global information is available, route computation can take the status of all routers and links in the network into consideration. Otherwise, route calculation considers only information from adjacent routers and links. Routing information needs to be exchanged among routers so that global or local information about the network can be obtained. Usually, global information is obtained via a reliable *broadcasting* mechanism, while local information can be obtained by *exchanging* information with *adjacent* neighbors.

The issue of how to determine a route can be examined from several aspects. First, a route can be determined dynamically or statically. Static routing tables can be configured manually by network administrators. However, they cannot adapt to dynamic network failures. Therefore, routing protocols are used to dynamically update routing tables in the Internet. Second, a route can be determined by a *centralized* or a *distributed* algorithm. Centralized algorithms require global information, and they can be run at a central site or *distributively* at each router. Some routing protocols in the Internet adopt the latter approach, called *quasi-centralized* algorithms, for better robustness. However, some Internet routing protocols determine the route distributively using distributed algorithms. Finally, a route can be determined hop-by-hop at each intermediate router or be computed at the source host. If routing is done at each hop (router) separately, either quasi-centralized or distributed algorithms are preferred. The Internet adopts *hop-by-hop* routing as the default routing mechanism while also supporting source routing as an option.

What is an optimal route? Different applications may have different criteria. Interactive applications such as telnet may want a route with minimum delay, while multimedia applications may want a route with sufficient bandwidth as well as low delay and jitter. Traditionally, a link is associated with a *cost* intended to characterize the desirability of routing through this link. For example, a link's cost may reflect the delay or available bandwidth on the link. The routing problem is then modeled as a graph theory problem where nodes are routers and edges are links. After transforming a network into a graph, the routing problem is equivalent to the *least-cost path* problem. Two types of routing algorithms are used in the Internet to solve the least-cost path problem: *link state routing* algorithms and *distance vector routing* algorithms. We shall examine these two types of algorithms in detail.

Optimality of Hop-by-Hop Routing

You may wonder if routing is done separately at each router, how can we be sure that packets will be forwarded on the optimal route? There is an *optimality principle* of Internet *hop-by-hop routing*. That is, if k is an intermediate node on the optimal route from the source host s to destination d, then the route from s to k on the optimal route from s to d is also the optimal route from s to k. Therefore, each router can simply trust its neighbor that if this neighbor is the *next hop* on the *optimal route* to a remote destination, this neighbor will indeed know how to forward packets to the destination along the optimal route. By the optimality principle, each router can construct a *shortest-path tree* with itself as the root spanning all other routers in the network.

Principle in Action: Optimal Routing

In the literature, a graph is used to formulate the routing problem. A graph *G=(N, E)* consists of a set of nodes, *N,* and a set of edges, *E.* Corresponding to the IP routing problem, a node in the graph represents a router in the Internet and an edge between two nodes represents the physical link between two adjacent routes. Figure 4.44 shows an example of such a graph model.

Recall that the routing problem is to find a path between a source node and a destination node. Apparently, there are many alternate paths between each pair of source-destination nodes. Optimal routing is to choose the *best* path for each source-destination pair. But what is the *best* path? How to define the quality of a path? In the graph shown in Figure 4.45, we can see that each edge is associated with a *cost.* In the graph model, the cost of a path is defined as the sum of all the edge costs along the path. By assuming the edge costs are given, the optimal routing problem becomes finding the *least-cost path.* Furthermore, if all edges in the graph have the same cost, the *least-cost path* becomes the *shortest path.* Several well-known algorithms were proposed in the graph theory literature in 1950s, e.g., the Kruskal algorithm and Dijkstra's algorithm. Most of these algorithms are actually finding the shortest path from a source node to all other nodes in the graph, called *shortest spanning tree* or *minimal spanning tree.*

Apparently, how to define the edge cost determines the quality and the meaning of the *least-cost path.* In some routing protocols, such as RIP, the edge cost is set to 1 for all edges such that the *least-cost path* is the *shortest path,* that is, the path with minimum hop count or the path that traverses the least number of routers. That seems a reasonable choice because passing a router introduces additional processing, transmission, and queuing delay. However, each router might have different processing capabilities, and each edge might have different bandwidth and traffic load from others, too. That is, their processing, transmission, and queuing delays may be different. Therefore, some other routing protocols, such as OSPF, allow multiple definitions of the edge cost, each related to a certain kind of quality-of-service metric, such as delay, bandwidth, reliability, or packet loss. It is possible to support multiple routing tables, one for each type of QoS. In summary, although edge costs are assumed to be given in the graph abstraction model, how to define the edge cost is very critical to determining the quality of the *optimal path,* i.e., the *least-cost path.*

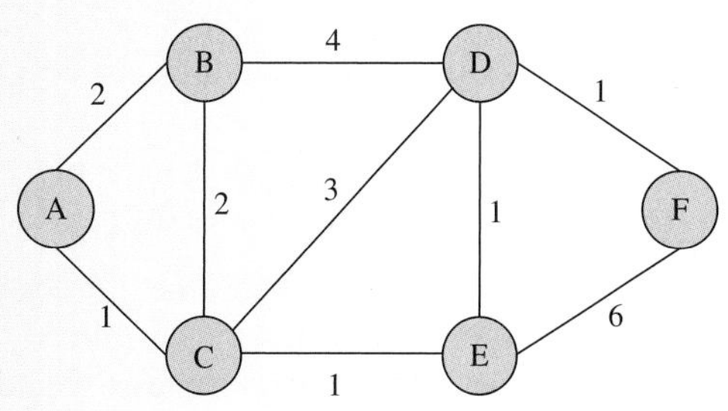

FIGURE 4.44 Graph model for route calculation.

```
For each v in V-{s} {
        If v is adjacent to s
                C(v)=lc(s,v)
                p(v) = s
Else
                C(v)=∞
}
T = {s}
While (T≠V) {
        find w not in T s.t. C(w) is the minimum for all w in (V-T)
        T = T ∪ {w}
        For each v in V-T {
                C(v) = MIN(C(v), C(w)+lc(w,v))
                If ((C(w)+lc(w,v)) > C(v)) p(v) = w
        }
}
```

FIGURE 4.45 Dijkstra's algorithm.

Link State Routing

Link state routing requires global information to compute least-cost paths. The global information means the network topology with all link costs, and it is obtained by having each router *broadcast* the costs of its adjacent outgoing links to *all other* routers in the network. As a result, all routers in the network will have a *consistent* view of the network topology and link costs. *Dijkstra's* algorithm is then used to compute the least-cost paths at each router. Because all routers use the same least-cost path algorithm and network topology to build their routing tables, packets will be forwarded on the least-cost path in a hop-by-hop manner (recall the optimality principle of Internet hop-by-hop routing).

Dijkstra's algorithm computes the least-cost path from a source node to all other nodes in the network, which forms a *least spanning tree*. A routing table is then built based on this *least spanning tree*. The basic idea of Dijkstra's algorithm is to find the least-cost path to all other nodes *iteratively*. During each iteration, a new least-cost path from the source node to one of the destination nodes is selected. That is, after the kth iteration, k least-cost paths to k destination nodes are known. Therefore, for an N-node network, the Dijkstra's algorithm will terminate after $N-1$ iterations. Figure 4.45 shows the pseudocode of Dijkstra's algorithm. The following notations are used in the pseudocode:

- *lc(s,v):* link cost from node s to node v. If s and v are not directly connected, the link cost from s to v is set to infinity.
- *C(v):* up to current iteration, the least cost of the path from the source node to node v.
- *p(v):* the immediately preceding node of v along the least-cost path.
- *T:* the set of nodes whose least-cost path is known

Initially, a node only needs to know the link costs of its *outgoing* links. The cost to an adjacent node is set to the cost of the link directly connected to it. The algorithm maintains a set of nodes, T, that are on the least spanning tree. Initially, T contains only the source node s. At each iteration, it selects the node w that has the minimum cost, $C(w)$,

FIGURE 4.46 An example network.

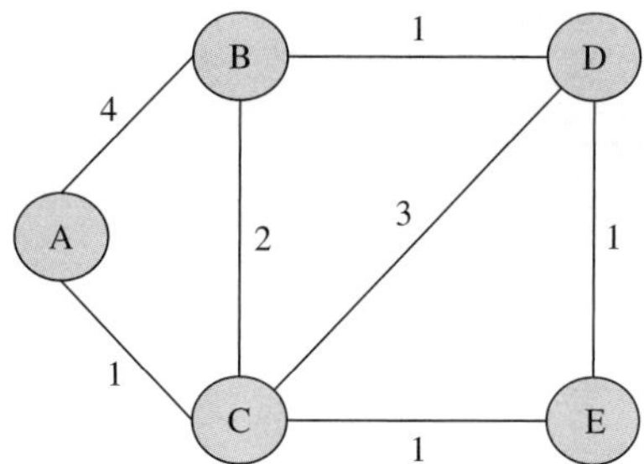

from the nodes that are not on the spanning tree yet. After node *w* is added to the tree, i.e., into the set *T*, the cost of a node *v* that is not on the tree is updated if the cost from the source to *v* could be reduced by going through this new added node *w*. The while loop is guaranteed to terminate after *N*–1 iterations, and *p(v)* records the parent of *v* on the *least spanning tree*. The routing table can then be built based on *p(v)*.

Let us further illustrate Dijkstra's algorithm by an example. Consider the network in Figure 4.46 with node *A* being the source node. The result at the end of each iteration is summarized in Figure 4.47. Initially, *A* knows only the costs to *B* and *C*, which are *4* and *1*, respectively. The costs to *D* and *E* are infinity, as they are not directly connected to *A*. During each iteration, a node with the minimum cost but not included in *T* yet is chosen. (A tie is broken by random selection if there is any.) Therefore, in the first iteration, node *C* is selected and added to the set *T*, which means that the least-cost path from *A* to *C* is determined now and the cost is *1*. With this information, all other nodes can now try to connect to *A* through *C*. (Again, recall the optimality principle of hop-by-hop routing.) For example, *D* and *E* can reach *A* through *C* now at the sum of the cost from *D* (or *E*) to *C* and the least cost from *C* to *A*. We can also observe that the cost to *B* can be reduced if the path traverses *C*, i.e., from *A* to *C* and then from *C* to *B*. At the end of the first iteration, *C* has been added to the set *T*. Besides, *B*, *D*, and *E* have updated their least costs from *A*. In the second iteration, *E* has the least cost and thus is added to *T*. The least cost from *A* to *D* is also updated because the path from *A* to *D* through *E* has a cost smaller than that of the path through *C*. The loop continues until all nodes are added in *T*, as shown in Figure 4.47. The least-cost path from A to all other nodes can be constructed by using the predecessor node information. Do not forget the task of a routing algorithm is to construct the routing table. After constructing the least-cost path from A to other nodes, the final routing table of A is shown in Figure 4.48. For example, the results of Figure 4.47 show that the least the cost path from *A* to *D* is *A->C->E->D*, and the path cost is 3. Therefore, the next hop from *A* to *D* in Figure 4.48 is *C* and the cost is 3.

FIGURE 4.47 Results of running Dijkstra's algorithm on the network in Figure 4.46.

Iteration	**T**	*C(B),p(B)*	*C(C),p(C)*	*C(D),p(D)*	*C(E),p(E)*
0	*A*	4,*A*	1,*A*	∞	∞
1	*AC*	3,*C*		4,*C*	2,*C*
2	*ACE*	3,*C*		3,*E*	
3	*ACEB*			3,*E*	
4	*ACEBD*				

Destination	Cost	NextHop
B	3	*C*
C	1	*C*
D	3	*C*
E	2	*C*

FIGURE 4.48 The routing table of node *A* in the network of Figure 4.46.

Distance Vector Routing

The distance vector algorithm is another major routing algorithm used in the Internet. While the link state algorithm is a quasi-centralized algorithm that uses global information, the distance vector algorithm is an *asynchronous, distributed* algorithm that uses *local* information. It uses only information *exchanged* from the directly connected *neighbors*. The distributed *Bellman-Ford* algorithm is used to calculate the least-cost path asynchronously. That is, unlike link state routing, it does *not* require all the routers to exchange link state information and compute a routing table *at the same time*. Instead, each router will perform the route computing when it receives new routing information from neighbors. After the computation, new routing information will be sent to its neighbors.

Figure 4.49 shows the pseudocode for the distance vector routing algorithm. Initially, each router knows the costs to its directly connected neighbors, as in Dijkstra's algorithm. Each router then asynchronously runs the algorithm shown in Figure 4.48. When a router has new routing information, such as a new least cost to a destination, it will send the routing information to its directly connected neighbors. When a router receives routing information from its neighbors, it will *update* its routing table if necessary. The routing information may contain the cost to a *destination* which is *new* to the router. In this case, a new routing entry is created, and the cost to that destination is computed as the *sum* of the cost to the neighbor plus the cost from the

```
While (1) {
   If node x received route update message from neighbor y {
       For each (Dest, Distance) pair in y's report {
          If (Dest is new) { /* Dest not in routing table */
              Add a new entry for destination Dest
              rt(Dest).distance = Distance+lc(x,y)
              rt(Dest).NextHop = y
          }
       else if ((Distance+lc(x,y))&rt(Dest).distance){
          /* y reports a shorter distance to Dest */
          rt(Dest).distance = Distance+lc(x,y)
          rt(Dest).NextHop = y
       }
   }
   Send update messages to all neighbors if route changes

   Also send update messages to all neighbors periodically
}
```

FIGURE 4.49 The distance vector routing algorithm.

neighbor to the destination. (The latter cost is known from the routing information.) If the routing cost to the destination already exists in the routing table, the router will check if the new cost results in a new least-cost path. That is, if the sum of the cost to the neighbor plus the cost from the neighbor to the destination is *less than* the cost recorded in the routing table, then the routing entry is *updated* with the new cost and the neighbor becomes the *new* next hop to that destination.

Let us consider Figure 4.46 again as an example and use this example to show how node *A* computes its routing table based on the distance vector algorithm. Since distance vector algorithm runs asynchronously, it is very difficult to give a clear picture of the whole network when the routing table at each router changes asynchronously. Therefore, we shall *pretend* the algorithm runs *synchronously* at each router in our illustration. That is, we assume that each router exchanges its new routing information with its neighbors simultaneously. After the routing information is exchanged, each router then computes its new routing table simultaneously. The procedure then repeats until the routing table at each router converges to a stable state. (We shall check if the final routing table at each router is the same as the one computed using Dijkstra's algorithm.)

Initially, node *A* knows only the cost to its neighbors, as shown in Figure 4.50. Then, node *A* informs its neighbors about this routing table. Similarly, nodes *B* and *C* also send their new routing table information to node *A*. For example, node *B* tells node *A* that its cost to node *C* and *D* is 2 and 1, respectively. Based on this information, node *A* creates a new routing entry for node *D* with a cost of 5 (4 + 1). Similarly, Node *C* also tells node *A* that its cost to node *B, D,* and *E* is 2, 3, and 1, respectively.

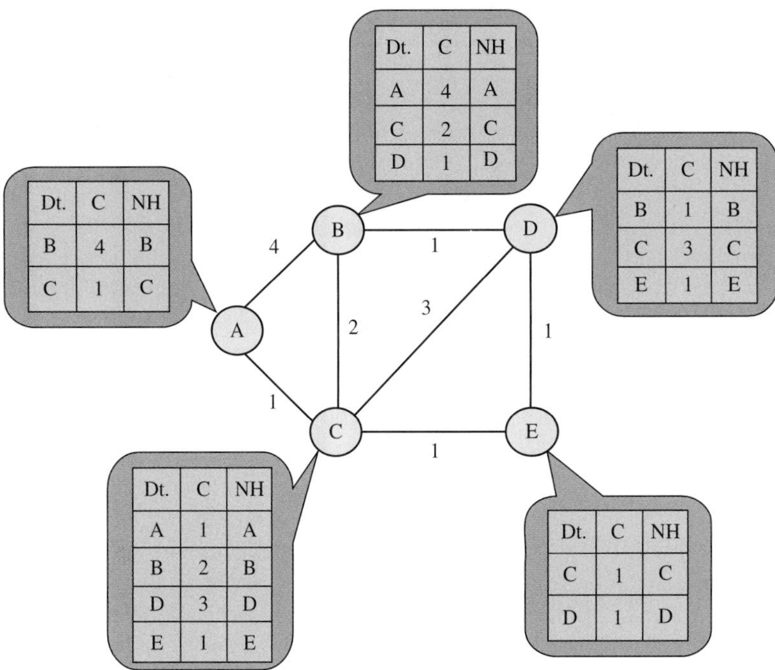

FIGURE 4.50 Initial routing tables for nodes in Figure 4.46.

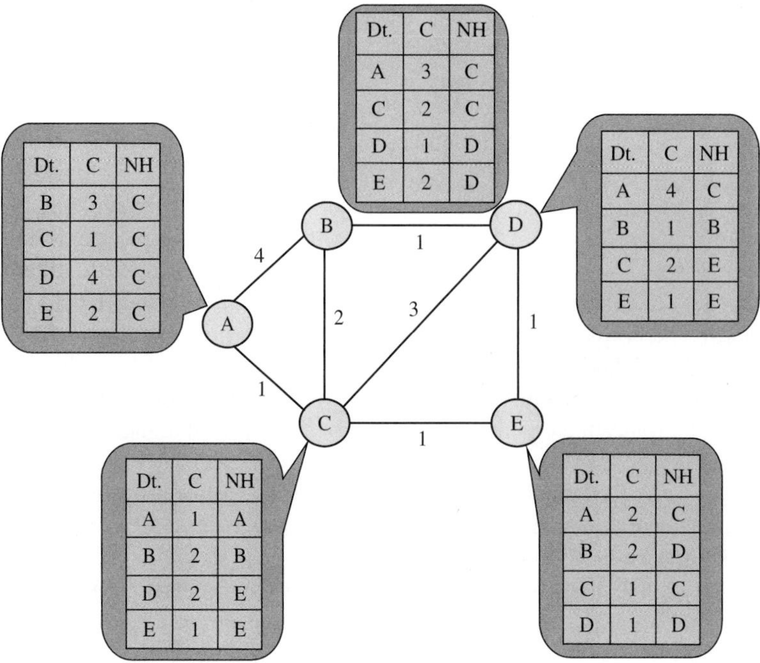

FIGURE 4.51 Intermediate routing tables (until the second step) for nodes in Figure 4.45.

With this information, node *A* updates its cost to *B* and *D* to 3 (1 + 2) and 4 (1 + 3). Since node *E* is new to node *A,* node *A* also creates a routing entry for node *E* with a cost of 2 (1 + 1). At this time, all nodes have their routing tables updated and shall inform their neighbors of the new routing table information again. (Note that node *C* knows its least cost to node *D* is 2 at this time, as shown in Figure 4.51.) When node *A* receives new routing information from node *B* and *C,* the last to be updated is the least cost to node *D,* and node *C* tells node *A* that its new cost is 2 instead of 3. Therefore, the new least cost from node *A* to node *D* becomes 3. The final routing table obtained by each node is shown in Figure 4.52, if no new cost updates are found. Readers shall notice that it is the same as the one calculated by Dijkstra's algorithm.

The Looping Problem of Distance Vector Routing

As we can observe from the preceding example, the distance vector routing algorithm requires several iterations of exchanging routing updates between neighbors before the routing table stabilizes. Will there be any problem using *unstable* routing tables to forward packets during the *transient* period? Or to be more specific, is it possible that packets can be forwarded around a loop due to *inconsistency* among nodes' routing tables? Unfortunately, the answer is yes. In particular, there is an interesting phenomenon called *"good news travels fast while bad news travels slowly."* That is, a router learns a better least-cost path very quickly but realizes a path with a large cost very slowly.

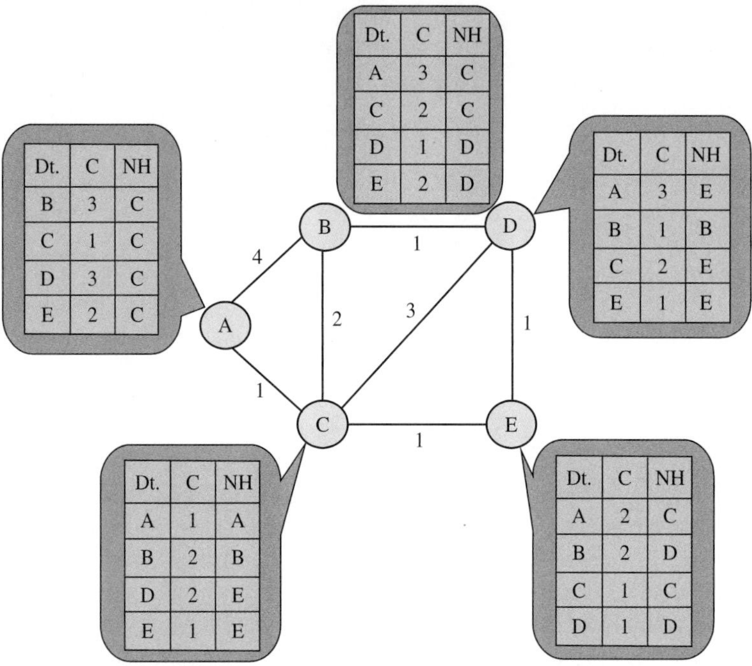

FIGURE 4.52 Routing table for node *A* in Figure 4.46 after convergence.

Let us use the network in Figure 4.53 as an example to explain how good news travels fast. Originally, the cost of the link between *A* and *C* is 7. If the cost changes to 1, node *A* and node *C* will inform their neighbors. With one routing update message, nodes *B, D,* and *E* will know that their least costs to *A* have changed to 3, 4, and 2, respectively. With another run of sending routing update messages, all routing tables will converge, and node *D* knows its least cost to *A* is 3 after the second run. Clearly, the good news that the cost of a link decreases dramatically travels fast to all nodes in the network.

On the other hand, let us consider the change of the link cost in Figure 4.54 to explain why bad news travels slowly. When the link between *A* and *C* goes down (i.e., cost becomes infinity), other nodes besides node *A* and *C* may not learn this quickly. When the link goes down, node *C* will inform its neighbors that its cost to

FIGURE 4.53 Good news travels fast in the distance vector algorithm.

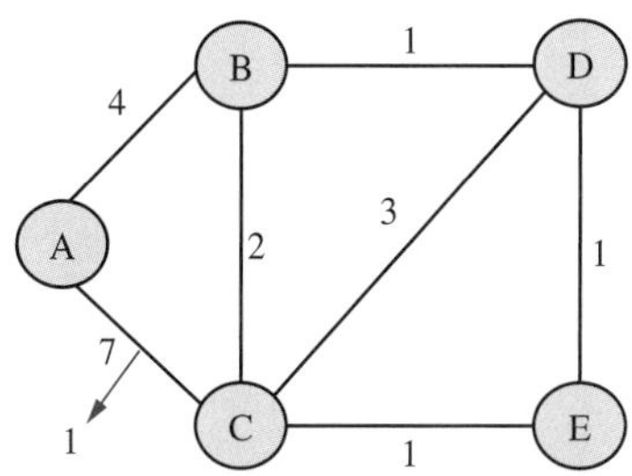

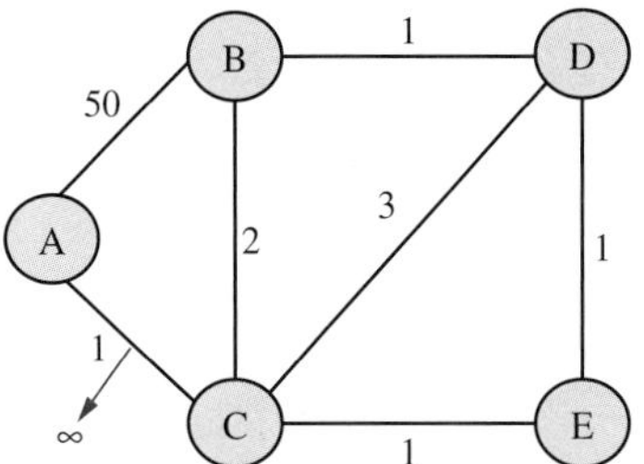

FIGURE 4.54 Bad news travels slowly in the distance vector algorithm.

node *A* is infinity now. However, depending on the *arrival times* of routing updates, node *E* may inform node *C* immediately that its cost to node *A* is 2. (Node *C* may also receive information from *B* and *D* that their least costs to *A* are 3 and 4, respectively.) Therefore, node *C* updates the entry for node *A* in its routing table with a cost of 3 and the new next hop *E*. As we can see, this updating is *wrong* because a routing loop is formed between *C* and *E*. That is, node *C* thinks that it should forward packets destined to *A* through node *E* while node *E* also thinks that these packets should be forwarded to node *C*. Packets will then be bounced back and forth between node *C* and *E* forever. The problem is that node *C* and node *E* will not learn the correct route in a short period of time. Let us continue with our example and see when all nodes can learn about the bad news. As node *C* updates its routing table, it then sends the route update message to its neighbors. Nodes *B, D,* and *E* will then update their least costs to *A* to 5, 3, and 4, respectively. After node *E* sends this new update message to *C,* node *C* then updates its cost to *A,* again, to 5. This procedure repeats until node *B, C, D,* and *E* all learn that their least-cost path to *A* is through *B* instead of *C*. Because the cost of the link between *A* and *B* is quite large, it will take more than 25 iterations of routing updates before routing tables converge. If there is no link between *A* and *B,* then the procedure will repeat until the cost to *A* is so huge that nodes *B, C, D,* and *E* believe their costs to *A* are infinity. Therefore, this bad news travels slowly principle is also known as the *"count to infinity"* problem.

Several partial solutions have been adopted in practice to cope with the looping problem. From the preceding example, we can observe that the looping problem occurs because node *C* does not know that the least-cost path from node *E* to node *A* passes itself. Therefore, the simplest solution, called *split horizon,* is to *prohibit* node *E* from telling node *C* its least cost to node *A*. In general, a router should not tell its neighbors those least-cost routes learned from them. For example, since node *E* learned its least-cost path to node *A* from node *C,* node *E* should not include its least cost to node *A* in the message for node *C*. In an even stronger approach, called *poison reverse,* node *E* should tell node *C* that its least cost to node *A* is infinity. Unfortunately, these two solutions only solve the looping problem involved with *two* nodes. For a larger routing loop, a more sophisticated mechanism is required, such as to add the *next hop* information in routing update messages. Another approach adopted by some commercial routers is to use a *hold down timer*. In this approach, a router will keep its least-cost path information for a time equal to the hold down timer before making routing updates. For example, continuing the preceding example, when node *E* receives the routing update from node *C* and knows its least cost to node *A* becomes infinity, node *E* should not update its routing table nor send new routing updates to node *C* until the hold down timer expires. This will prevent node *C* from receiving least-cost path information from all other nodes to node *A* and thus will grant node *A* and node *C* some time to let all other nodes know that the link between node *A* and node *C* has failed.

Hierarchical Routing

The number of routers in the Internet is huge. Therefore, for scalability, routers are not connected into a flat network. Otherwise, neither the link state algorithm nor the distance vector algorithm would be scalable enough for a network of hundreds of thousands of routers. Just image how large the size of the routing entries would be if all routers in the Internet were connected into a flat network. There is another reason why we prefer partitioning routers into groups: *administrative autonomy*. For example, there are many Internet Service Providers (ISPs), each of which has its own routers and backbone network. Naturally, each ISP would like to have total control of its routers and backbone bandwidth such that it may want to prohibit traffic from other ISPs passing through its backbone. As a consequence, Internet routers are organized into two levels of hierarchy. At the lower layer, routers are grouped into administrative domains, or *autonomous systems* (ASs). Routers within an AS are under the same administrative control and run the same routing protocol, called *intra-domain* routing protocol or *interior gateway protocol* (IGP). Selected routers, called *border routers,* from an AS will have physical links connected to border routers of other ASs. Border routers are responsible for forwarding packets to outside ASs. The routing protocol run among these border routers, referred to as the *inter-domain* routing protocol or *exterior gateway protocol* (EGP), may be different from the intra-domain routing protocol.

The Internet can therefore be viewed as a set of interconnected autonomous systems. There are three types of ASs: *Stub AS, multihomed AS,* and *transit AS*. Many users access the Internet through campus networks or enterprise networks, which are typical stub ASs. Since a stub AS has only one border router and connects to only one ISP, there is no transit traffic passing through stub ASs. Multihomed ASs may have more than one border router and connect to more than one ISP. However, multihomed ASs also do not allow transit traffic to pass through. Most ISPs need to allow transit traffic and have many border routers connecting to other ISPs. Therefore, they are called transit ASs.

In the following two subsections, we examine intra-domain routing and inter-domain routing separately. Figure 4.55 shows a simple network consisting of three domains (ASs): domain *A, B,* and *C*. Within each domain, there are several intra-domain routers, for example, intra-domain router *B.1, B.2, B.3,* and *B.4* within domain *B*. An interior gateway protocol will be run among these routers to establish and maintain their routing tables. *A.3, B.1, B.4,* and *C.1* are border routers and run an exterior gateway protocol to exchange routing information. Domains *A* and *C* are stub ASs because they do not allow transit traffic, while domain *B* is a transit AS. Let us explain how intra-domain routing and inter-domain routing are used to send packets from a host in domain *A* to a destination in domain *C*. First, based on the

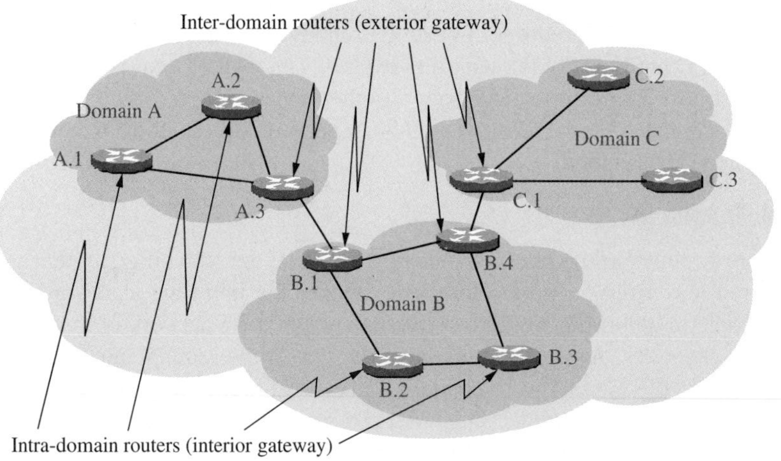

FIGURE 4.55 Inter-AS and intra-AS routing.

result of intra-domain routing, all packets originated from domain *A* and destined to *C* need to be passed to *A*'s border router, *A.3*. Router *A.3* will forward these packets to *B.1* based on the routing result of inter-domain routing. Router *B.1* knows to forward these packets to *B.4* based on inter-domain routing, but knows the actual path to route to *B.4* based on intra-domain routing. (That is, the route between *B.1* and *B.4* is found by intra-domain routing.) Finally, router *B.4* forwards these packets to the border router of domain *C*, i.e., *C.1*, based on the result of inter-domain routing. Router *C.1* then forwards these packets to appropriate routers based on the result of intra-domain routing.

As a final remark, let us reexamine the scalability problem of Internet routing. If all routers in Figure 4.55 are viewed as a flat network, then there are 10 routers, and each router needs to know the routing information of the other nine routers in the network. However, with the two-level hierarchical organization, each router only needs to communicate with two or three routers. Routing information of a domain is summarized and exchanged among border routers (or exterior gateways) first, and then the summarized information will be propagated to all the interior routers. Scalability is thus achieved by limiting the number of routers that need to communicate and exchange routing information.

4.6.2 Intra-Domain Routing

An AS comprises of several physical networks which are connected via routers. Providing connectivity among these networks is the task of routers. Recall that routers in an AS are under the same administrative control. Therefore, the network administrator of an AS has total control over all the routers, and decides how to configure these routers, what routing protocols to run on these routers, and how to set link costs. Given the homogeneous configuration and routing protocols, the optimal path, i.e., the least-cost path, found by the routing protocol reflects the administrator's concern for route quality. For example, if link cost is set according to delay, a path with a shorter delay is preferred by the administrator. Usually, the link cost is set such that the efficiency of resource sharing *within* an AS can be maximized.

A routing protocol called an intra-domain routing protocol or interior gateway protocol (IGP) is used to maintain the routing table at each router such that the connectivity among all routers in the AS is achieved. In practice, two commonly used intra-domain routing protocols are RIP (Routing Information Protocol) and OSPF (Open Shortest Path First). We examine these two protocols from the following aspects: what kind of path selection algorithm is used, how it operates, scalability and stability considerations, packet format, and open source implementation.

RIP

RIP, one of the most widely used intra-domain routing protocols, was originally designed for Xerox PARC Universal Protocol to be used in the Xerox Network Systems (XNS) architecture. Its wide use was due to its inclusion (the *routed* daemon) in the popular Berkeley Software Distribution (BSD) version of UNIX in 1982. The first version of RIP (RIPv1) was defined in RFC 1058, and the latest update of RIPv2 was defined in RFC 2453.

RIP is a canonical example of a *distance vector routing* protocol. It is a very simple routing protocol designed for small networks. The link cost metric used by RIP is *hop count,* i.e., all links have a cost of 1. In addition, RIP limits the maximum cost of a path to *15,* i.e., a path with a cost of 16 means unreachable. Therefore, it is only suitable for small networks with a *diameter* of less than 15 hops. The RIP protocol uses two types of messages: request and response. The response message is also known as the *RIP advertisements*. These messages are sent over *UDP* using port *52*. Because the distance vector algorithm is used to find the least-cost path, when there is a link cost change, adjacent routers will send RIP advertisements to their neighbors. Each advertisement may consist of up to *25 routing entries,* i.e., *distance vectors*. Each routing entry contains a *destination* network address, the *next hop,* and the *distance* to the destination network. RIP supports multiple address families. That is, the destination network address is specified by using a family field and a destination address field. In RIP, routers also send RIP advertisements to neighbors *periodically,* with a default period of 30 seconds. In addition, two timers are associated with each routing entry. The first one is a *route invalid timer,* called *timeout*. If no routing update for this route is received before the timeout timer expires, the routing entry is marked as an invalid (obsolete) entry. The default value for this timer is 180 seconds. Once an entry is marked as invalid, a deletion process begins which sets the second timer, called the *garbage-collection timer,* to *120* seconds and the cost for that route to *16* (*infinity*). When the *garbage-collection* timer expires, the route is deleted from the routing table.

Several mechanisms are adopted in RIP to cope with the stability problem of distance vector routing. First, limiting the path cost to 15 enables a failure link to be identified *quickly*. Three partial solutions to the looping problem are also adopted, namely split horizon, poison reverse, and stabilization (hold down) timer. As discussed above, split horizon suppresses updates on the *backward* route. Poison reverse explicitly sends updates to a neighbor, but for the routes learned from that neighbor,

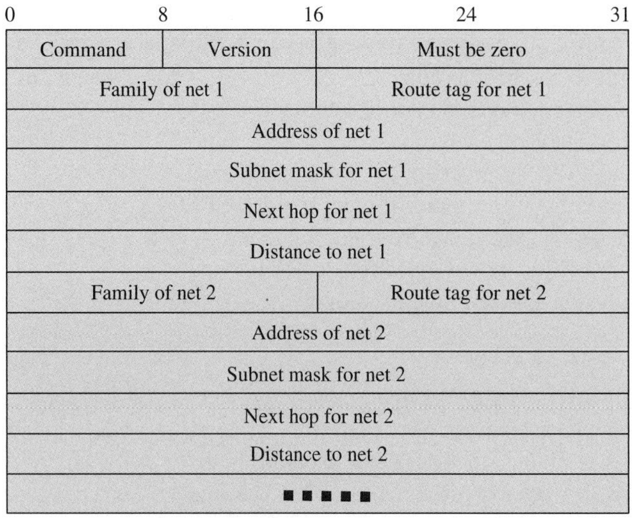

0–7	8–15	16–31
Command	Version	Must be zero
Family of net 1		Route tag for net 1
Address of net 1		
Subnet mask for net 1		
Next hop for net 1		
Distance to net 1		
Family of net 2		Route tag for net 2
Address of net 2		
Subnet mask for net 2		
Next hop for net 2		
Distance to net 2		
■■■■■		

FIGURE 4.56 RIPv2 packet format.

poison reverse sets their route metric in the update to *infinity*. Stabilization timer avoids sending route updates too quickly.

RIP Packet Format

The second version of RIP has better scalability than the first version. For example, RIPv2 supports CIDR, which allows aggregation of routes with arbitrary prefix length. The packet format of RIPv2 is shown in Figure 4.56. Each packet is filled with *routing entries*. Each routing entry consists of information such as address (protocol) family, destination address, subnet mask, next hop, and distance.

RIP Example

Let us look at an example of the RIP routing table. The routing table shown in Figure 4.57 is taken from the border router of a department of a university (only

Destination	Gateway	Distance/Hop	Update Timer	Flag	Interface
35.0.0.0/8	140.123.1.250	120/1	00:00:28	R	Vlan1
127.0.0.0/8	Directly connected			C	Vlan0
136.142.0.0/16	140.123.1.250	120/1	00:00:17	R	Vlan1
150.144.0.0/16	140.123.1.250	120/1	00:00:08	R	Vlan1
140.123.230.0/24	Directly connected			C	Vlan230
140.123.240.0/24	140.123.1.250	120/4	00:00:22	R	Vlan1
140.123.241.0/24	140.123.1.250	120/3	00:00:22	R	Vlan1
140.123.242.0/24	140.123.1.250	120/1	00:00:22	R	Vlan1
192.152.102.0/24	140.123.1.250	120/1	00:01:04	R	Vlan1
0.0.0.0/0	140.123.1.250	120/3	00:00:08	R	Vlan1

FIGURE 4.57 RIP routing table from cs.ccu.edu.tw.

part of the routing table is shown). This router has several ports. One of them is connected to the AS border gateway, 140.123.1.250. The rest of the interfaces are connected to local IP subnets. VLAN is enabled such that the whole department is partitioned into several VLANs. CIDR is supported, thus the destination network address is associated with a subnet mask length. Most of the routes are learned from RIP advertisements (flag *R*). Subnets that are directly connected have zero cost and are manually configured (flag *C*). The routing table also shows the update timer for each routing entry.

Open Source Implementation 4.9: RIP

Overview

Most of the open source implementations of routing protocols, such as *routed* and *gated,* operate in user space. Implemented as the application-layer user processes, routing protocols can send and receive messages over TCP or UDP (see Figure 4.58). Since 1996, the Zebra project (http://www.zebra.org), a free routing software distributed under the GNU General Public License, has become one of the major players in open source implementations of routing protocols.

Zebra

Zebra is targeted at providing reliable route servers with full function routing protocols. Several commonly used routing protocols are supported, such as RIPv1, RIPv2, OSPFv2, and BGP-4 (see Table 4.7). The modular design of Zebra software allows it to support multiple routing protocols; that is, Zebra has a *process* for each protocol. Modularity also makes Zebra flexible and reliable. Each routing protocol can be upgraded independently, and failure of one routing protocol does not affect the entire system. Another advanced feature of Zebra is that it uses *multithread* technology. These good features of Zebra make it a top-quality routing engine software. The current version of Zebra is beta 0.95a released in 2005. Platforms

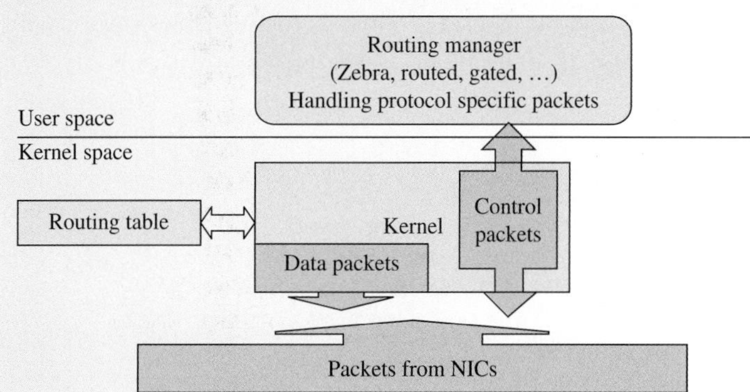

FIGURE 4.58 Implementation of routing protocols as user processes.

Continued

TABLE 4.7 RFCs Supported by Zebra

Daemons	RFC #	Function
ripd	2453	Manages RIPv1, v2 protocol
ripngd	2080	Manages RIPng protocol
ospfd	2328	Manages OSPFv2 protocol
ospf6d	2740	Manages OSPFv3 protocol
bgpd	1771	Manages BGP-4 and BGP-4+ protocol

supported by Zebra include Linux, FreeBSD, NetBSD, and OpenBSD. In 2003, a new project, called Quagga (http://www.quagga.net), was forked from the GNU Zebra, which aimed to build a more involved community than Zebra.

Block Diagram

In the following, we will use Zebra as our example for open source implementation of routing protocols. We examine the implementation of RIP, OSPF, and BGP in Zebra. Before we look at the implementation of each routing protocol, let us discuss the general software architecture of Zebra. Figure 4.59 shows the architecture of Zebra, where *routing daemons* communicate with the *Zebra daemon,* which in turn communicates with the kernel through varied APIs, such as `netlink` and `rtnetlink`.

The interaction between a routing daemon and the Zebra daemon follows a client/server model, as shown in Figure 4.60. It is possible to run multiple routing protocols on the same machine. In this case, each routing daemon (process) has its own routing table, but they need to communicate with the zebra daemon to change the kernel routing table.

Data Structures

The global routing table entrance in Zebra described in the data structure `vrf_vector`. `vrf_vector` consists of a set of dynamic routing tables and a set of static routing configurations, as shown in the following codes:

```
    struct vrf {
       u_int32_t id; /* Identifier (routing table
vector index). */
       char *name; /* Routing table name. */
       char *desc; /* Description. */
       u_char fib_id; /* FIB identifier. */
       struct route_table *table[AFI_MAX][SAFI_MAX];
          /* Routing table. */
       struct route_table *stable[AFI_MAX][SAFI_MAX];
          /* Static route configuration. */
}
```

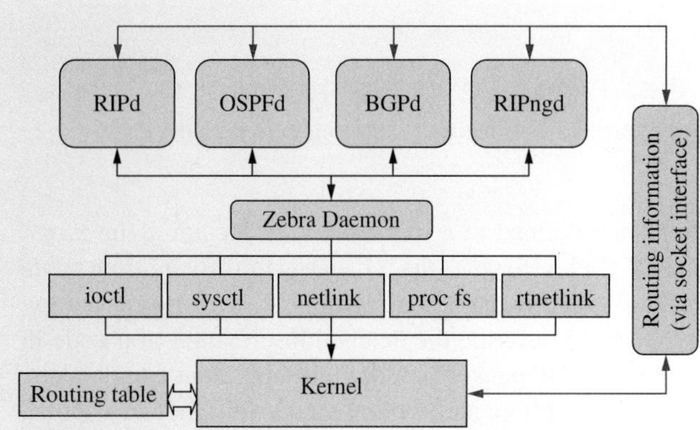

FIGURE 4.59 Architecture of Zebra.

Each `route_table` consists of a *tree* of routing entries. Each routing entry is described by the structure `route_node`. Two important variables in the `route_node` structure are `prefix` (`struct prefix p;`) and `info` (`void *info;`), which describe the actual prefix and route information of this route entry, respectively. Each routing process will define its own instances of these structures; for example, the RIP process casts the variable info to a pointer of `struct rip_info`.

Algorithm Implementation

A route process maintains its routing table and route nodes in the routing table through a set of functions, such as `vrf_create()`, `vrf_table()`, `vrf_lookup()`, `route_node_lookup()`, `route_node_get()`, and `route_node_delete()`. For example, the RIP process calls `route_node_get (rip->table, (struct prefix *) &p)` to get the route node for the prefix `p`.

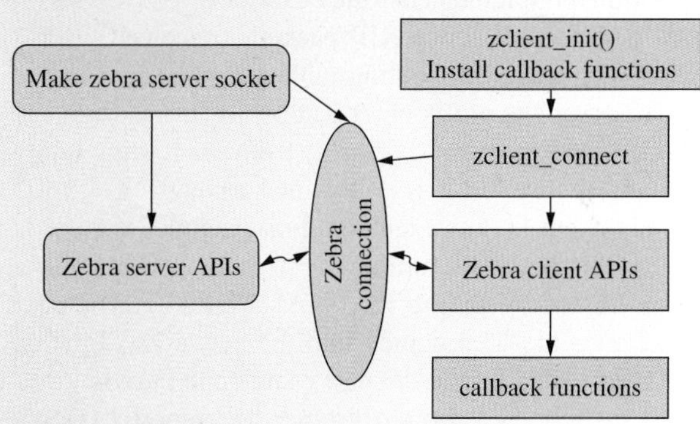

FIGURE 4.60 Client/server model of Zebra.

Continued

RIP Daemon

Overview

The RIP protocol is implemented as a routing daemon, called ripd.

Data Structures

The related data structures are defined in `ripd/ripd.h`, including the `rip_packet` structure for RIP packet format, the `rte` structure for *routing table entry* in a RIP packet, and structure `rip_info` for RIP routing information (pointed to by `route_node` to describe the detailed information of a node in the routing table). The `rte` in a RIP packet includes four important components: network prefix, subnet mask, next hop, and routing metric (distance), as shown below.

```
struct rte
{
 u_int16_t family;    /* Address family of this route.
*/
u_int16_t tag;        /* Route Tag which included in
RIP2 packet. */
struct in_addr prefix;    /* Prefix of rip route. */
struct in_addr mask;  /* Netmask of rip route. */
struct in_addr nexthop;  /* Next hop of rip route. */
u_int32_t metric;   /* Metric value of rip route. */
};
```

As mentioned, the maximum metric is 16 for RIP. A definition of this maximum value could also be found in `ripd/ripd.h` as follows.

```
#define RIP_METRIC_INFINITY       16
```

Algorithm Implementations

The call graph of ripd is shown in Figure 4.61.

The Bellman-Ford algorithm is implemented in the `rip_rte_process()` function defined in `ripd/ripd.c`. When a RIP packet is received, `rip_rte_process()` is called with the `rte` (routing table entry) carried in the RIP packet as a parameter. Based on the prefix of `rte`, `route_node_get()` is called to fetch the node information (`route_node`) from the routing table. Once the RIP route information (`rip_info`) is obtained through the "info" pointer, the Bellman-Ford algorithm is then executed. For example, if there is no RIP route information for this node, the prefix (Dest) must be new and a new `rip_info` structure is created by calling `rip_info_new()`. The next hop and distance (metric) of `rte` are then copied into the new entry. Finally, `rip_zebra_ipv4_add()` is called to add the new route node into the routing table. Otherwise, if the `rte` reports a shorter distance to the prefix (Dest), the code in `rip_rte_process()` performs the route update on the route node of this prefix in the routing table.

Exercises

Trace `route_node_get()` and explain how to find the `route_node` based on the prefix.

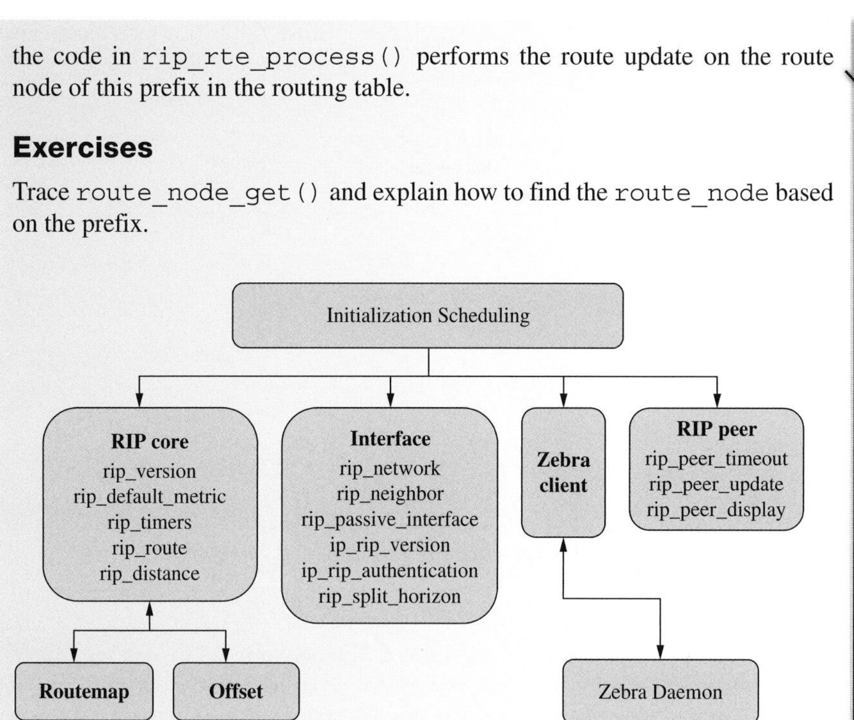

FIGURE 4.61 Call graph of ripd.

OSPF

Open Shortest Path First (OSPF), another commonly used intra-domain routing protocol, is considered the successor to RIP and the dominant intra-domain routing protocol. The second version of OSPF and its extension for IPv6 are defined in RFC 2328 and RFC 5340, respectively. Unlike RIP, OSPF is a *link-state routing* protocol. Link-state information is flooded to *all* routers in the domain. Each router uses Dijkstra's algorithm to calculate the least-cost path tree using itself as the root, and then builds the routing table based on this tree.

OSPF has several unique features that make it superior to RIP. First, for *load balancing,* OSPF supports equal-cost *multipath* routing. With this feature, traffic can be evenly distributed over equal-cost routes. Second, to support CIDR routing, each route is described by a prefix length. Third, multicast routing can be based on the results of unicast routing. The multicast routing protocol, Multicast OSPF (MOSPF), uses the *same* topology database as OSPF. Next, for stabilization and security reasons, a routing message is accompanied by an 8-byte password for *authentication.* Finally, for scalability, OSPF has two levels of hierarchy so that an OSPF autonomous system can be further partitioned into *areas*. An area is a group of contiguous

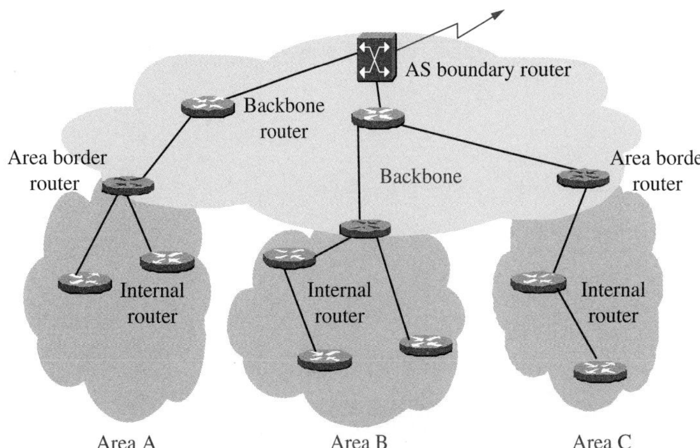

FIGURE 4.62 Two-level hierarchical structure of OSPF.

networks and hosts. The topology of an area is *invisible* from outside. Routing in an AS thus takes place at two levels: *intra-area routing* and *inter-area routing*.

Hierarchical OSPF Network

Figure 4.62 shows a hierarchically structured OSPF network. As we can see from the figure, routers are classified into four types: two types of boundary routers and two types of internal routers. An area consists of several internal routers and one or more *area border routers*. Internal routers only perform intra-area routing and learn routing information about the outside area from area border routers. An area border router participates in *both* inter-area and intra-area routing. It is responsible for summarizing the routing information of other areas inside and outside the AS and broadcasting the routing information throughout the area. The *AS boundary router* participates in intra-domain routing (at the *inter-area* level) and inter-domain routing. It runs OSPF to obtain the routing information in the AS and some exterior routing protocol, such as BGP, to learn the routing information outside the AS. External routing information is then advertised through the AS without modification. *Backbone routers* are intermediate routers that connect AS boundary routers and area border routers.

OSPF Example

Let us use the network of Figure 4.63 as an example to show how two levels of hierarchical routing are performed in OSPF.[1] The AS of Figure 4.63, which consists of five internal routers (*RT1, RT2, RT8, RT9,* and *RT12*), four area border routers (*RT3, RT4, RT10, RT11*), one backbone router (*RT6*), and two AS boundary routers (*RT5, RT7*), is configured into three areas. Area 2 is a special type of area called a *stub*. An area can be configured as a stub if there is only *one* single exit point from the area. The purpose of configuring an area as a stub is to avoid external routing information being broadcast into a stub area. The AS consists of 11 subnets (*N1* through *N11*), and is connected to four external networks (*N12* to *N15*). Note that a link cost in

[1] The example is taken from RFC 2328.

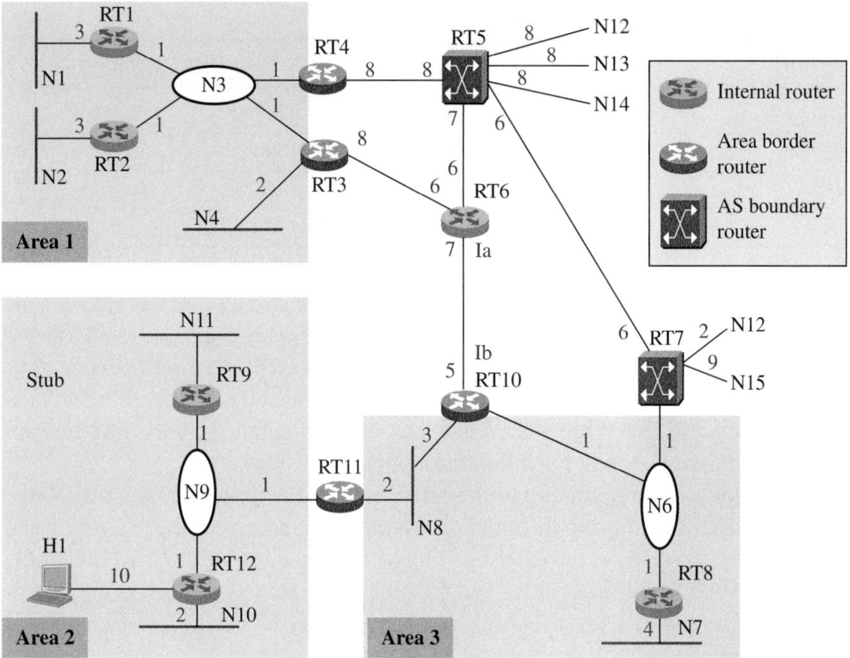

FIGURE 4.63 An example OSPF network.

Figure 4.63 is *directional*. That is, the two end points of a link may assign different costs to the link. For example, the link between *RT3* and *RT6* has a cost of 8 and 6 for *RT3-to-RT6* and *RT6-to-RT3,* respectively.

Let us first consider the intra-routing of area 1. After exchanging routing information via flooding, area border routers *RT3* and *RT4* calculate the shortest paths by using the Dijkstra algorithm. The *summarized* routing information is then advertised to the AS backbone via *inter-area routing*. Table 4.8 shows the routes advertised by *RT3* and *RT4*. For internal routers *RT1* and *RT2,* the routing table for intra-area networks is built similarly. Table 4.9 shows the intra-area routing table for *RT1*.

Area border routers then exchange the *intra-area route summaries* with each other on the AS backbone. Every area border router will hear the intra-area route summaries from all other area border routers. Based on these route summaries, each area border forms a graph of the distance to all networks outside of its area, again by

TABLE 4.8 Routes Advertised to the Backbone by RT3 and RT4

Network	Cost Advertised by RT3	Cost Advertised by RT4
N1	4	4
N2	4	4
N3	1	1
N4	2	3

TABLE 4.9 Intra-Area Routing Table for RT1

Network	Cost	Next Hop
N1	3	Direct
N2	4	RT2
N3	1	Direct
N4	3	RT3

the Dijkstra algorithm. Area border routers then summarize and flood routes of the whole AS throughout each area. Table 4.10 shows the *inter-area routes* advertised into area 1 by *RT3* and *RT4*. Note that area 2 is configured as a *stub* network, thus routing information of *N9, N10, N11* is condensed to one entry. Usually a network is configured as a stub area if there is a single exit point from this network. External AS routing information is not flooded into/throughout stub areas.

Besides the inter-area routing information, area border routers *RT3* and *RT4* will also hear *AS-external* routing information from AS boundary routers, i.e., *RT5* and *RT7*. There are two types of the external route cost. *Type 1 external cost* is compatible with costs of routing within the area, and the cost to an external network is the sum of the internal cost and the external cost. *Type 2 external cost* is an order of magnitude larger than the internal cost, so the cost to an external network is solely determined by the *external* cost. When *RT3* or *RT4* broadcasts external costs learned from *RT5* or *RT7* into area 1, internal routers of area 1, such as *RT1,* will build their routes to external networks based on the *type* of external costs advertised. Finally, Table 4.11 shows part of the routing table of *RT4* with *intra-area, inter-area,* and *external* routes.

OSPF Packet Format

There are five types of OSPF messages, all beginning with the same header as shown in Figure 4.64. The *Type* field indicates the type of message, and Table 4.12 shows the five OSPF message types. The *Type* field is followed by the IP address and the area ID of the *source router*. The entire message, except the authentication data, is protected by a 16-bit checksum to which various types of authentication mechanisms can be applied. The *Authentication Type* indicates the mechanism being used.

TABLE 4.10 Routes Advertised to Area 1 by RT3 and RT4

Destination	Cost Advertised by RT3	Cost Advertised by RT4
Ia, Ib	20	27
N6	16	15
N7	20	19
N8	18	18
N9–N11	29	36
RT5	14	8
RT7	20	14

TABLE 4.11 Routing Table of RT4

Destination	Path Type	Cost	Next Hop
N1	intra-area	4	RT1
N2	intra-area	4	RT2
N3	intra-area	1	Direct
N4	intra-area	3	RT3
N6	inter-area	15	RT5
N7	inter-area	19	RT5
N8	inter-area	25	RT5
N9–N11	inter-area	36	RT5
N12	Type 1 external	16	RT5
N13	Type 1 external	16	RT5
N14	Type 1 external	16	RT5
N15	Type 1 external	23	RT5

Except for the *hello* message, the other types of OSPF messages are used to request, send, and reply *link-state* information. An OSPF message may contain one or more *link-state advertisement* (LSA) messages, each describing the cost information of a link or a router. There are also five types of LSA messages, or LSAs, as shown in Table 4.13, and all types of LSAs share the same header, as shown in Figure 4.65. Each type of LSA is used by different routers to describe different routing information. For example, *AS-external* LSAs originating from AS boundary routers describe routes to destinations in other autonomous systems.

4.6.3 Inter-Domain Routing

The task of inter-domain routing is to achieve connectivity among autonomous systems in the Internet. While intra-domain routing takes place within an AS that is under the same administrative control, inter-domain routing is much harder to accomplish due to the large number of ASs and the complicated relationships between ASs. The most apparent feature of inter-domain routing is that among its concerns, *reachability* is more important than *resource utilization*. Since each AS may run a different routing protocol and assign link costs based on *different* criteria, finding the

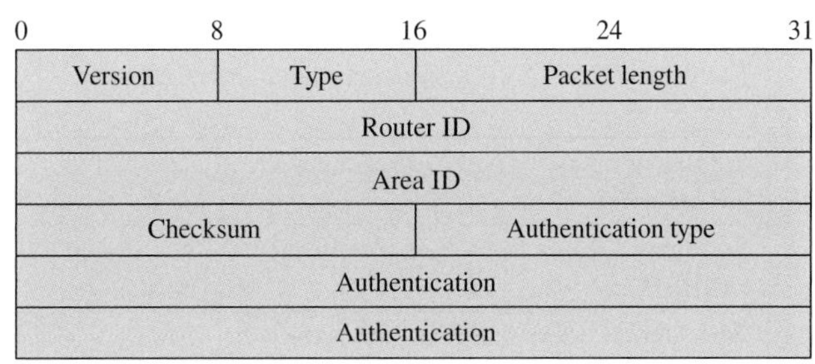

FIGURE 4.64 OSPF header format.

TABLE 4.12 Five Types of OSPF messages

Type	Description
1	Hello
2	Database Description
3	Link State Request
4	Link State Update
5	Link State Acknowledgment

least-cost path between a source-destination pair may be *meaningless*. For example, a cost of 15 is considered a large cost in one AS running RIP but a relatively small cost in another AS running OSPF. Therefore, link costs of different ASs may *not* be *compatible,* and thus *additive*. (Recall that OSPF has two types, Type 1 and Type 2, of external cost for the same reason.) On the other hand, finding a *loop-free* path to reach a destination network is more important in inter-domain routing. The complicated relationship between ASs makes the task of finding a loop-free path nontrivial. For example, consider a university that owns an AS number and runs BGP to connect to two Internet service providers (ISPs), AS number X and Y, respectively. Assume that the university purchases more bandwidth from the ISP with AS number X. In addition, the university certainly does not want transit traffic from AS X to AS Y or vice versa passing through its domain. Therefore, it may set up a policy: "route all traffic to AS X unless it is down; in that case, route traffic to AS Y" and "do not carry traffic from AS X to AS Y or vice versa." Such routing is referred to as *policy routing,* where a policy allows the administrator of a routing domain to set rules on how to route packets to destinations. A policy may specify preferred ASs or not-to-transit ASs. Policy routing also deals with security and trust issues. For example, we may have a policy stating that traffics destined for an AS may not be routed through certain domains, or that packets with prefix p should only be routed through AS X if prefix p is reachable from AS X. In summary, *scalability* and *stability* are more important in inter-domain routing than *optimization*.

TABLE 4.13 Five Types of LSAs

LS Type	LS Name	Originated by	Scope of Flood	Description
1	Router LSAs	All routers	Area	Describes the collected states of the router's interfaces to an area
2	Network LSAs	Designated router	Area	Contains the list of routers connected to the network
3	Summary LSAs (IP network)	Area border router	Associated areas	Describes routes to inter-area networks
4	Summary LSAs (ASBR)	Area border router	Associated areas	Describes routes to AS boundary routers
5	AS-external LSAs	AS boundary router	AS	Describes routes to other ASs

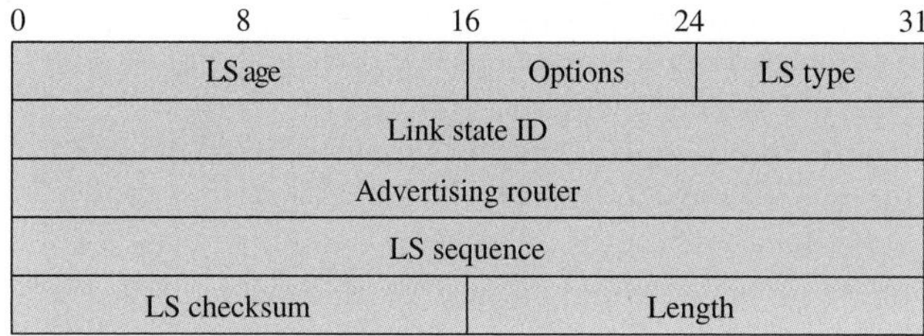

FIGURE 4.65 LSA header format.

Open Source Implementation 4.10: OSPF

Overview

The most interesting part of the OSPF source code is the implementation of Dijkstra's algorithm as shown in Figure 4.45. Dijkstra's algorithm is implemented in `ospf_spf_calculate()` (defined in `ospf_spf.c`), which is called by `ospf_spf_calculate_timer()` to calculate the shortest paths for each area when the scheduled timer expires (scheduled by `ospf_spf_calculate_schedule()`).

Data Structures

Related data structures include `vertex`, `route_table`, and `route_node` defined in `ospf_spf.h` and `table.h`. The root of the shortest path tree across an area is pointed to by the variable `area->spf`, and each node in the tree is described by a structure of `vertex`:

```
struct vertex
   {
    u_char flags;
    u_char type; /* router vertex or network vertex */
    struct in_addr id; /* network prefix */
    struct lsa_header *lsa;
    u_int32_t distance;
    list child; /* list of child nodes */
    list nexthop; /* next hop information for routing
table */
};
```

Algorithm Implementations

The `ospf_spf_calculate()` is scheduled to run when various types of LSAs (Network LSA, Router LSA, Summary LSA) are *received* or when the

Continued

virtual link or the status of the area border router has been changed. Figure 4.66 shows the call graph of `ospfd` of Zebra.

The *while* loop of Figure 4.45 is implemented by a *for* loop in `ospf_spf_calculate()`. The list of nodes (candidates) not included in T (i.e., `V-T` in Figure 4.45) is obtained by the `ospf_spf_next()` function first. The node which has the minimum cost is obtained from the head of the candidate list. The `ospf_vertex_add_parent()` is called to set up the next hop information (i.e., `p(v)=w` in Figure 4.45), and then the node is added to the SPF tree by `ospf_spf_register()`. The operation on updating the cost of nodes (`C(v)=MIN(C(v), C(w)+c(w,v))`) is also performed in `ospf_spf_next()` by the following statement:

```
w->distance = v->distance + ntohs (l->m[0].metric);
```

Exercises

Trace the source code of Zebra and explain how the shortest path tree of each area is maintained.

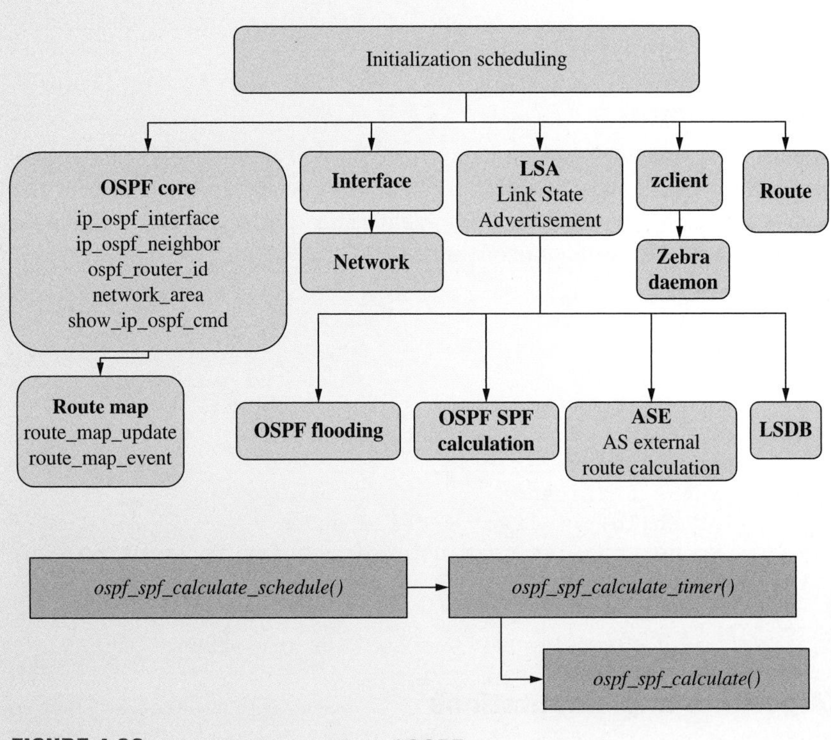

FIGURE 4.66 Zebra implementation of OSPF.

Performance Matters: Computation Overhead of Routing Daemons

Figure 4.67 compares the execution time of the core function in RIP and OSPF routing daemons, i.e., `rip_rte_process()` and `ospf_spf_calculate()` for RIP and OSPF, respectively. RIP scales well even under a 1500-router network. However, the execution time of OSPF exceeds 10 ms in a 250-router network and surpasses 100 ms in a 1500-router network. Computational complexity of the routing algorithm is the key impact factor on the execution time. RIP adopts the Bellman-Ford algorithm, whose time complexity is less than the Dijkstra algorithm used by OSPF.

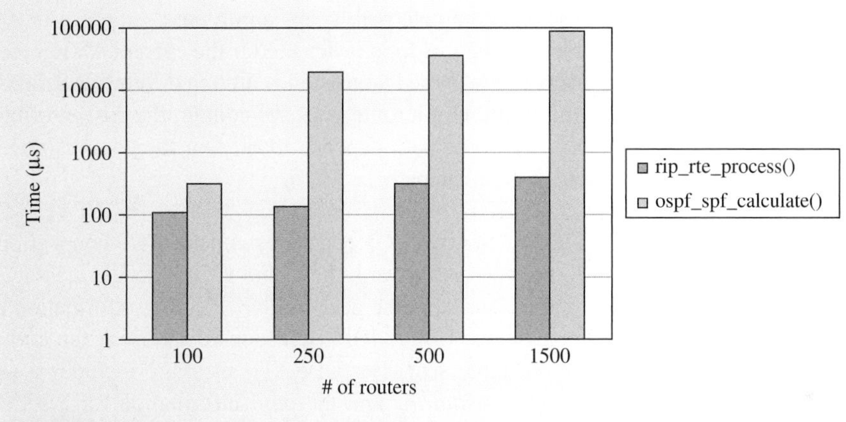

FIGURE 4.67 Execution time of RIP and OSPF.

BGP

The Border Gateway Protocol version 4 (BGP-4) is the current de facto standard for inter-domain routing. The most recent RFC for BGP-4 is RFC 4271. Since the backbone of a large ISP (an AS by itself) that hosts many enterprise or campus ASs is very likely to have more than one border router connected to other ASs, there are two types of BGP: *interior* BGP (IBGP) and *exterior* BGP (EBGP). An IBGP session is established for communication between two BGP routers within the same AS, say an ISP, while an EBGP session is established for two BGP routers in different ASs. The purpose of IBGP is to make sure that if there are multiple routers running BGP in the same AS, the routing information between them is kept synchronized. At least one of the routers in an AS is selected as the representative of the AS, called a *BGP speaker*. A BGP speaker uses an EBGP session to exchange routing information with *peer* BGP speakers in other ASs. Furthermore, as stability and reliability are very important to inter-domain routing, BGP runs over *TCP* on port *179,* and authentication can be used to further secure the TCP connection. For routers *within* the same

AS, a *logical fully connected* mesh is constructed based on TCP and the underlying IBGP sessions. (Again, among the interior BGP routers, one of them is designated as the BGP speaker which represents and speaks for the AS.) Finally, CIDR is also supported by BGP.

Path Vector Routing

The large number of AS routers in the Internet makes *distance vector* algorithm more suitable for BGP than link state algorithm. However, since reachability and loop-free operation are more important concerns than route optimization, BGP adopts *path vector* algorithm, a *variant* of distance vector algorithm, for finding the routing path between two networks. The path vector algorithm also exchanges routing information with *neighbors only,* but in order to prevent looping, the *complete path* information is advertised when exchanging a route entry. Since each AS has a unique AS number (a 16-bit identifier), a complete path keeps an ordered sequence of AS numbers the path has traversed through. A loop is detected if the current AS number is found in the path. Furthermore, due to the inconsistency among different ASs' cost definitions, the exchanged information of a route does *not* contain the cost information. Therefore, the selection of a route path depends mostly on the administrative preference and the number of ASs on the path.

There are four types of BGP packets, including OPEN, KEEPALIVE, UPDATE, and NOTIFICATION. After two BGP routers establish a TCP connection, an OPEN message is sent to the peer. Afterward, they send KEEPALIVE messages to each other periodically to make sure that the peer is alive. Routing information is exchanged using UPDATE messages. Unlike RIP, BGP does *not* refresh the entire table periodically due to its big table size. The UPDATE message includes a set of routes that the sender wants to *withdraw* and the *path* information for a set of destination networks. The format of UPDATE messages is shown in Figure 4.68. The *path attributes* are applied to all destinations listed in the destination networks (called Network Layer Reachability Information, NLRI). Information carried in path attributes may include the *origin* of the path information (from IGP, EGP, or incomplete), the list of ASs on the *path* to the destination, the *next hop* to the destination, the discriminator used for multiple AS *exit points* (Multi_Exit_Disc, MED), the

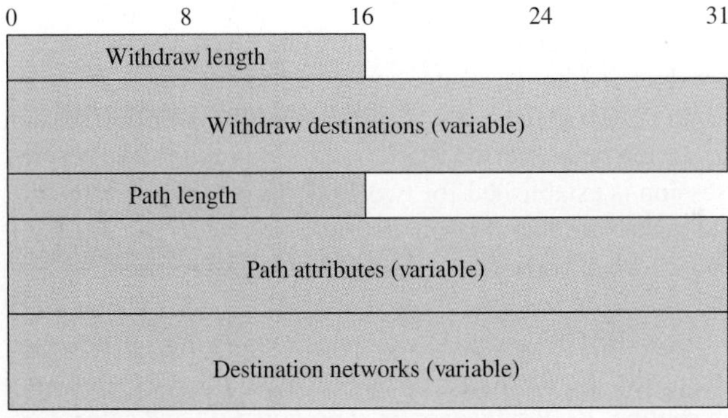

FIGURE 4.68 Packet format for a BGP UPDATE message.

local preference (LOCAL_PREF) to indicate the preference of routers within an AS, routes that have been *aggregated,* and the identifier of the AS that aggregates routes. Finally, a NOTIFICATION message is sent to the peer when an error is encountered.

Each BGP router keeps *all* feasible paths to a destination, but advertises only the *"best"* path to its neighbors. Selecting the "best" route depends on the policies of the AS. However, in general, preference goes to *larger LOCAL_REF, shorter path, lower origin code* (IGP is preferred to EGP), *lower MED, closer* IGP neighbor, and BGP router with lower IP address. After the "best" route is determined for a destination,[2] the *BGP speaker* then advertises the highest degree of preference of each destination to *neighbor BGP speakers* via EBGP. A BGP speaker will also propagate its learned routing information to BGP routers (non BGP speakers) via IBGP.

BGP Example

Finally, let us look at an example of a BGP routing table. Table 4.14 shows part of the BGP table taken from the border router of a university. (The full BGP table of an Internet backbone router has more than 300,000 routing entries; see http://bgp.potaroo.net/ for the current BGP table size.) The AS number of the university is 17712. The first routing entry indicates that the BGP router had received UPDATE messages, regarding the destination network of 61.13.0.0/16, from three neighbors, 139.175.56.165, 140.123.231.103, and 140.123.231.100. The best AS path to 61.13.0.0/16 is through 140.123.231.100 (maybe just because it is the shortest path). The origin code indicates that the router's neighbor 140.123.231.100 learned the AS PATH via an IGP protocol.

TABLE 4.14 A BGP Routing Table Example

Network	Next Hop	LOCAL_ PREF	Weight	Best?	PATH	Origin
61.13.0.0/16	139.175.56.165		0	N	4780,9739	IGP
	140.123.231.103		0	N	9918,4780,9739	IGP
	140.123.231.100	0	0	Y	9739	IGP
61.251.128.0/20	139.175.56.165		0	Y	4780,9277,17577	IGP
	140.123.231.103		0	N	9918,4780,9277,17577	IGP
211.73.128.0/19	210.241.222.62		0	Y	9674	IGP
218.32.0.0/17	139.175.56.165		0	N	4780,9919	IGP
	140.123.231.103		0	N	9918,4780,9919	IGP
	140.123.231.106		0	Y	9919	IGP
218.32.128.0/17	139.175.56.165		0	N	4780,9919	IGP
	140.123.231.103		0	N	9918,4780,9919	IGP
	140.123.231.106		0	Y	9919	IGP

[2] Actually, it can be a set of destination networks.

Open Source Implementation 4.11: BGP

Overview

BGP adopts distance vector routing but includes routing path information in its messages to avoid looping. It emphasizes *policy* routing instead of path cost optimization. Therefore, in its implementation, we shall look for how it chooses its *preferred* route according to some policies.

Data Structures

The BGP routing table is a structure of `bgp_table`, which consists of BGP nodes (structure of `bgp_node`) (see `bgpd/bpg_table.h`). Each `bgp_node` has a pointer to BGP route information, `struct bgp_info`, which is defined in `bgpd/bg_route.h`. The `bgp_info` consists of a pointer to `struct peer`, which stores neighbor routers' information.

Algorithm Implementations

Figure 4.69 shows the call graph of bgpd for processing a BGP packet. When a BGP UPDATE packet is received, the `bgp_update()` function is invoked with path attribute `attr` as one of its parameters. `bgp_update()` then calls `bgp_process()` to process updates on routing information, which in turn calls `bgp_info_cmp()` to compare the priority of two routes according to the following priority rule:

0. Null check: prefer non-null route
1. Weight check: prefer larger weight
2. Local preference check: if local preference is set, prefer larger local preference
3. Local route check: prefer static route, redistributed route, or aggregated route
4. AS path length check: prefer shorter AS path length
5. Origin check: prefer origin of the route learned in following order: IGP, EGP, incomplete
6. MED check: prefer lower MED (MULTI_EXIT_DISC)
7. Peer type check: prefer EBGP peer than IBGP peer
8. IGP metric check: prefer closer IGP
9. Cost community check: prefer low cost
10. Maximum path check: not implemented
11. If both paths are external, prefer the path that was received first (the oldest one)
12. Router-id comparison: prefer lower id
13. Cluster length comparison: prefer lower length
14. Neighbor address comparison: prefer lower IP address

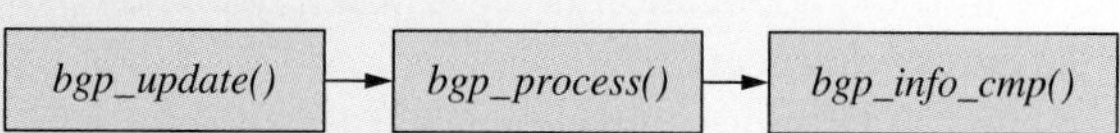

FIGURE 4.69 Call graph of bgpd in Zebra.

Exercises

In this exercise, you are asked to explore the prefix length distribution of the current BGP routing table. First, browsing at http://thyme.apnic.net/current/, you will find some interesting analysis of BGP routing tables seen by APNIC routers. In particular, "number of prefixes announced per prefix length" will let you know the number of routing entries of a backbone router and the distribution of prefix length of these routing entries.

1. How many routing entries does a backbone router own on the day you visit the URL?
2. Draw a graph to show the distribution of prefix length (length varies from 1 to 32) in a logarithmic scale because the number of prefixes announced varies from 0 to tens of thousands.

4.7 MULTICAST ROUTING

So far we have seen the complete Internet solution for host-to-host packet delivery from a single source to a single destination. However, many emerging applications require packet delivery from one or more sources to a group of destinations. For example, video conferencing and streaming, distance learning, WWW cache updating, shared whiteboard, and network games are popular applications of multiparty communications. Sending a packet to multiple receivers is called multicast. A multicast session consists of one or more senders, and usually several receivers that send or receive packets on the same multicast address.

4.7.1 Shifting Complexity to Routers

Scalability is still the major concern in implementing the Internet multicast service. We first address several issues from the aspects of senders, receivers, and routers while keeping scalability in mind. A sender may face the following questions: How does the sender send a packet to a group of receivers? Does the sender need to know *where* and *who* the receivers are? Does the sender have control over the *group membership?* Can more than one sender send packets to a group simultaneously? Keeping the sender's work as simple as possible can make the task of sending a packet to a *multicast group* highly scalable, so the solution provided by the Internet multicast is to remove the burden of multicast from the sender and leave it to Internet *routers*. This, however, shifts the complexity back to the core networks, the routers, and away from the hosts at the edge. It turns the core network from *stateless* to *stateful,* as we shall see later, which has a large impact on the infrastructure. Thus, whether to put multicast at the IP layer or leave it to the application layer is still a debatable issue. We shall turn to this issue at the end of this section.

As shown in Figure 4.7, a class D IP address space is reserved for multicast. A multicast group is assigned with a class D IP address. A sender intending to send packets to the multicast group just puts the group's class D IP address in the destination field of the IP header. A sender does *not* need to know *where* the receivers are and *how* packets are delivered to the group members. In other words, the sender is *off duty* on maintaining the list of group members and putting receivers' IP addresses in the IP header. Scalability is thus achieved since from a sender's perspective, sending a multicast packet is as simple as sending a unicast packet. Multiple senders can send packets to a multicast group simultaneously. The drawback is that the sender has no control on the group membership at the Internet layer (but could at the application layer).

From a receiver's aspect, one might ask the following questions: How does one *join* a multicast group? How does one know about ongoing multicast groups on the Internet? Can anyone join a group? Can a receiver *dynamically* join or leave a group? Can a receiver know other receivers in the group? Again, the solution of the Internet is to make the task of receiving a multicast packet as simple as receiving a unicast packet. A receiver sends a *join* message to the *nearest router* to indicate which multicast group (a class D IP address) it wants to join. A receiver can then receive multicast packets in the same way as receiving unicast packets. A receiver can join and leave a multicast group whenever it wishes. There is no specific mechanism other than manual configuration for assigning a class D IP address to a group. However, there are protocols and tools for *advertising* addresses of multicast sessions on the Internet. Furthermore, the IP layer does not provide mechanisms for knowing all receivers in a multicast group. It leaves the job to application protocols.

Finally, a router may ask how to deliver multicast packets. Does a router need to know all senders and receivers in a multicast group? As multicast senders and receivers shake off the burden of multicast, routers need to take on the burden of this work. There are two tasks for multicast routers: *group membership management* and multicast packet *delivery*. First, a router needs to know whether any host in its *directly connected subnets* have joined a multicast group. The protocol used to manage multicast group membership information is called Internet Group Management Protocol (IGMP). Next, a router needs to know how to deliver multicast packets to all members. One might think of establishing many one-to-one connections to deliver multicast packets. However, this is certainly not an efficient approach, as the Internet would be filled with *duplicated* packets. A more efficient approach is to establish a *multicast tree,* rooted at *each* sender or *shared* by the whole group. Multicast packets can then be delivered on the multicast tree where a packet is duplicated only at *branches* of the tree. The task of establishing a multicast tree is done by the multicast routing protocol, such as DVMRP, MOSPF, and PIM.

It should be clear now that the IP layer solution for multicast is to make the task of sender and receiver as simple as possible while leaving the burden on routers. In the following, we thus focus on the tasks of routers. Specifically, we first examine the group membership management protocol, which runs between *hosts* and the *designated router* of an IP subnet. It allows the designated router to know whether *at least one* host has joined a specific multicast group. We then discuss the multicast routing protocols. Multicast routing protocols, running among multicast-capable routers, are used to establish the multicast tree(s) for each multicast group. Finally, since most of the multicast routing protocols are designed for *intra-domain* multicast, we shall introduce some new developments for *inter-domain* multicast routing.

4.7.2 Group Membership Management

A router that is responsible for delivering multicast packets to its *directly connected IP subnet* is called a *designated router*. A designated router needs to maintain group membership information of all hosts in the subnet such that it knows whether packets destined for a specific multicast group should be forwarded into the subnet. The group membership management protocol used in the Internet is called Internet Group Management Protocol (IGMP).

Internet Group Management Protocol (IGMP)

The current version of IGMP is IGMPv3, defined in RFC 3376. IGMP allows a router to query hosts in its directly connected subnet to see whether any of them has joined a specific multicast group. It also allows a host to respond to the query with a report or to inform the router that the host will leave a multicast group.

Basically, there are three types of IGMP messages: *query, report,* and *leave*. The IGMP packet format is shown in Figure 4.70. The query message has a type value of 0x11. A query message could be a *general* query or a *group-specific* query. The multicast group address is filled with zeros when it is a general query message. An IGMPv3 membership report message has a type value of 0x22. For backward compatibility, the IGMPv1 membership report, IGMPv2 membership report, and IGMPv2 leave group message use type 0x12, 0x16, 0x17, respectively. IGMP messages are carried within an IP packet with protocol identifier *2* and sent to specific multicast addresses such as *all-systems* multicast address and *all-routers* multicast address.

Let us briefly view the operation of IGMP. A multicast router plays one of two roles: *querier* or *nonquerier*. A querier is responsible for maintaining membership information. If there is more than one router in an IP subnet, the router with the *smallest* IP address becomes the querier, and the other routers are nonquerier. Routers determine their roles by hearing the query messages sent by other routers. A querier will periodically send general query messages to solicit membership information. A general query message is sent to 224.0.0.1 (ALL-SYSTEMS multicast group).

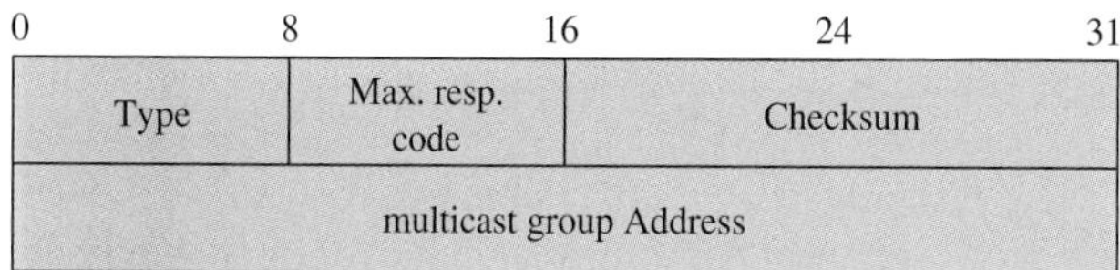

FIGURE 4.70 IGMP packet format.

At Least One Member or None

When a host receives a general query message, it waits a random amount of time between zero and the maximum response time, which is given in the general query message. The host then sends a report message with *TTL=1* when the timer expires. However, if the host sees report messages of the same multicast group sent by other hosts, the host will stop the timer and *cancel* the report message. The use of a random timer is to suppress *further* report messages from other group members as the router only cares whether *at least one* host joined the multicast group. Similar actions are taken when a host receives a group-specific query message if the host is a member of the multicast group specified by the query message.

When a router receives a report message, it adds the group reported in the message to the list of multicast groups in its database. It also sets a timer for the membership to the "Group Membership Interval," and the membership entry will be deleted if no reports are received before the timer expires. (Recall that query messages are sent periodically. So a router is expected to see reports back before the timer expires.) Besides responding to query messages, a host can send an *unsolicited report* immediately when it wants to join a multicast group.

When a host leaves a multicast group, it should send a leave group message to the all-routers multicast address (224.0.0.2) if it is *the* last host that replies to a query message to that group. When a queries router receives a leave message, for every "Last Member Query Interval" it sends group-specific queries to the associated group on the attached subnet for "Last Member Query Count" times. If no report is received before the end of "Last Member Query Interval," the router assumes that the associated group has no local member and that there is no need to forward the multicasts for that group onto the attached subnet. By this assumption, the router does not need to count how many hosts are members of the associated group when a host leaves the group; it simply asks "anybody still in this group?"

From the overview of IGMP operations, we can see that there is no control on who can join a multicast group or who can send packets to a multicast group. There is also no IP-layer mechanism for knowing the receivers in a multicast group. IGMPv3 adds support for *"source filtering"*: that is, a receiver may request to receive packets only from specific source addresses. A receiver may join a multicast group by invoking a function like IPMulticastListen (socket, interface, multicast-address, filter-mode, source-list), where the filter-mode is either INCLUDE or EXCLUDE. If the filter-mode is INCLUDE, the receiver expects to receive packets only from the senders in the source-list. On the other hand, if the filter-mode is EXCLUDE, no packets are to be received from senders in the source-list.

4.7.3 Multicast Routing Protocols

The second component of multicast is the multicast routing protocol, which builds multicast trees for multicast packet delivery. What should a multicast tree look like? From a *sender's* point of view, it should be a *unidirectional* tree rooted at the sender that can reach all receivers. However, what happens to a multicast group with more than one sender? In the Internet, two approaches have been adopted for building multicast trees; they differ in whether a *single* tree is used by *all* senders to deliver packets or whether each sender has a *source-specific* multicast tree to deliver packets. How scalable are these two approaches? The first approach, a *group shared tree,* is more scalable since a multicast router only maintains *per-group* state information, while the latter source-based approach requires *per-source per-group* state information. However, the source-based approach renders a shorter path because packets traverse along the tree. Multicast routing protocols that build source-based trees include Distance Vector Multicast Routing Protocol (DVMRP), Multicast extension of OSPF (MOSPF), and dense mode of Protocol Independent Multicast (PIM-DM). On the other hand, PIM sparse mode (PIM-SM) and Core-Based Trees (CBT) build group-shared trees. It appears that on a sparse group where members are distributed sparsely over a network topology, the shared tree approach is preferred for its scalability, which shall be clarified later.

Steiner Tree vs. Least-Cost-Path Tree

Before we describe the details of multicast routing protocols, let us examine two issues involved in building a multicast tree. We have discussed optimal point-to-point routing; what is optimal multicast routing? In the literature, the multicast problem is modeled as a graph theory problem in which each link is assigned a cost. Optimal multicast routing involves finding a multicast tree with minimum cost, where the cost of a multicast tree is the sum of the costs of all links on the tree. Certainly, the multicast tree must be rooted at the source and span to all receivers. The optimal multicast tree, or the tree with the least total cost, is called a *Steiner tree*. Unfortunately, the problem of finding a Steiner tree is known to be NP-complete, even if all the links have unit cost. Thus, most previous researchers have focused on developing *heuristic* algorithms that take *polynomial* time and produce near-optimal results. Furthermore, these heuristic algorithms often guarantee that their solutions are within twice the cost of the optimal solution. However, even though heuristic algorithms show good performance, none of the Internet multicast routing protocols try to solve the Steiner tree problem. Why? There are three obvious reasons that make these heuristic algorithms unpractical. First, most of these algorithms are *centralized* and require global information—that is, the information about all links and nodes in the network. However, a centralized solution is not suitable for the distributed Internet environment. Second, the Steiner tree problem is formulated for multicast with *static* membership, where the source node and all receivers are fixed and known a priori. This is certainly not the case in the Internet. Finally, the computational *complexity* of most heuristic algorithms is not acceptable for online computation. After all, minimizing the cost of a multicast tree is not as important as scalability. Furthermore, without a clear definition of the link cost, how can we interpret the cost of a multicast tree and how important is it to minimize the cost?

Another issue on building a multicast tree is whether the multicast routing protocol relies on some specific unicast routing protocol. Instead of solving the Steiner tree problem, most current Internet multicast routing protocols build the multicast tree based on *least-cost path* algorithms. For source-based trees, the path from the source to each destination is the least-cost path found by *unicast* routing.

The combination of least-cost paths from the source to each receiver thus forms a *least-cost-path tree* rooted at the source. For group-shared trees, least-cost-path trees are built from a center node (called a *rendezvous point* or core) to all receivers. Furthermore, the least-cost paths are used to send packets from sources to the center node. Since both types of trees are built based on the least-cost paths, the results of unicast routing certainly can be utilized. The question is then whether a multicast routing protocol needs the *cooperation* of certain specific unicast routing protocols, or whether it is *independent* of the underlying unicast routing protocol. For current Internet solutions, DVMRP is an example of the former approach while PIM, as its name indicates, is independent of unicast routing protocol. In the following, we introduce the two most commonly used multicast routing protocols: DVMRP and PIM.

Principle in Action: When the Steiner Tree Differs From the Least-Cost-Path Tree

Figure 4.71 shows a simple example where the least-cost-path tree is not the Steiner tree. In this example, *A* is the source node and *C, D* are two receivers. The least-cost path from *A* to *C* is the direct link from *A* to *C* with cost of 3. The same is true of least-cost path from *A* to *D*. Therefore, the least-cost path tree rooted from *A* and spanning to *C* and *D* has cost of 6. However, the optimal solution, the Steiner tree, is rooted from *A,* connects to *B* first, and then spans to *C* and *D*. The Steiner tree has a cost of 5, which is less than the least-cost-path tree.

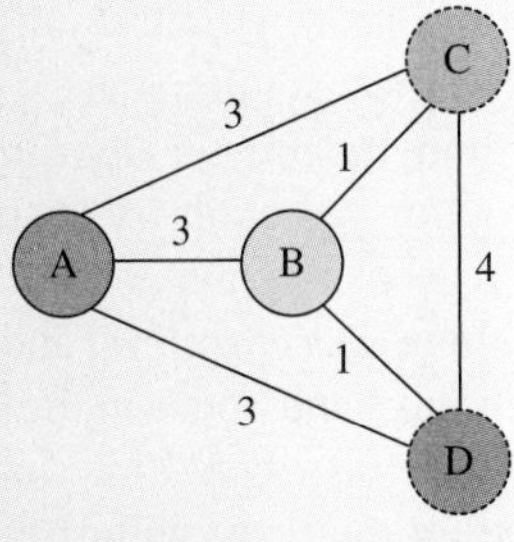

FIGURE 4.71 Example where Steiner tree differs from least-cost-path tree.

Distance Vector Multicast Routing Protocol (DVMRP)

DVMRP, proposed in RFC 1075, is the first and most widely used multicast routing protocol in the Internet. DVMRP has RIP as its built-in unicast routing protocol. When Internet multicast was initiated, DVMRP was the multicast routing protocol that ran on an experimental backbone called MBone. DVMRP constructs a *source-based* tree for each multicast sender. A multicast tree is constructed in two steps. In the first step, *Reverse Path Broadcast* (RPB) is used to broadcast multicast packets to all routers. *Prune* messages are then used to prune the RPB tree into a Reverse Path *Multicast* (RPM) *tree*.

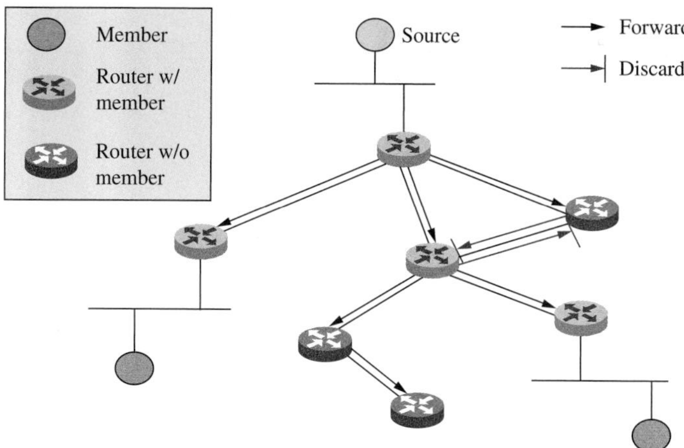

FIGURE 4.72 Reverse Path Broadcast (RPB).

Reverse Path Broadcast (RPB)

Traditionally, broadcast in a mesh network is implemented by *flooding,* i.e., forwarding a broadcast packet to all outbound links except the interface on which the packet was received. However, a router will receive the same packet more than once due to flooding. How do we avoid a router forwarding the same packet more than once? RPB is a brilliant idea that is illustrated in Figure 4.72. When a broadcast packet is received by a router, the packet is flooded (forwarded) only if the packet *arrived* on the link that is on the shortest (least-cost) path from the router *back* to the sender. Otherwise, the packet is simply discarded. A broadcast packet is guaranteed to be flooded by a router only *once,* and the flooding procedure stops when all routers have done the flooding once. A router may still receive the same packet more than once, but there is no looping or infinite flooding problem.

Clearly, RPB requires that each router has already built its unicast routing table. That is, DVMRP needs an underlying unicast routing algorithm. RPB is called "reverse path" because though the shortest-path tree should be rooted at the *sender* and toward the receivers, each router decides whether to flood the packets based on the information of the "reverse shortest path," i.e., from the *router* to the *sender.* As a consequence, packets arrive at each destination through the shortest path from the *receiver* to the *sender.* Why not just use the forward shortest path? Recall that the distance vector algorithm finds the next hop from a router to destinations. Therefore, a router that receives a broadcast packet does not know the shortest path from the sender to itself, but knows the shortest path from itself to the sender.

Reverse Path Multicast (RPM)

When a source broadcasts a multicast packet to all routers (and subnets), many routers and subnets that do not want to receive this packet cannot avoid receiving it. To overcome this problem, a router not leading to any receivers would send a prune to its *upstream* router, as shown in Figure 4.73. (Recall that a router knows

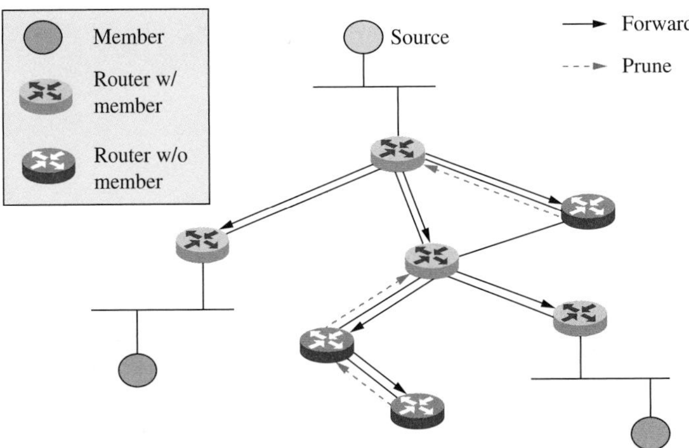

FIGURE 4.73 Pruning an RPB tree.

membership information via IGMP.) An intermediate router maintains a list of dependent *downstream* routers for each multicast group. When a prune message is received, an intermediate router then checks to see that none of its downstream routers have members that joined the multicast group—that is, that all of them have sent prune messages to it. If yes, it then sends another prune message to its upstream router. No packet will be sent to the router after it has been pruned from the RPB tree. As shown in Figure 4.74, a Reverse Path Multicast (RPM) tree will then be formed after pruning the RPB tree.

The next question is what happens if a host under a pruned branch wants to join the multicast group. There are two possible solutions. First, a prune message consists of a *prune lifetime,* which indicates how long a pruned branch will remain pruned. Therefore, after the prune lifetime times out, a pruned branch will be added back to

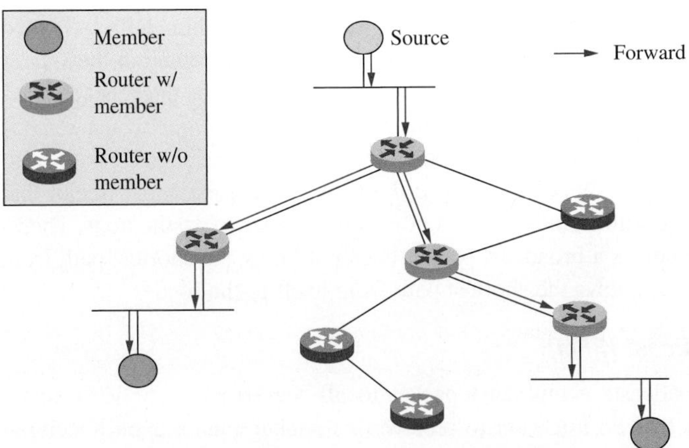

FIGURE 4.74 The RPM tree of Figure 4.73 after pruning.

the tree. In other words, a multicast packet will be flooded periodically when the prune lifetime expires. On the other hand, a router can also send a *graft* message explicitly to its upstream router to force a pruned branch to be added back to the multicast tree again.

DVMRP has several drawbacks. For example, the first few multicast packets have to be flooded to all routers. This makes it only work well for groups with *dense* members. The lifetime feature of a prune message also requires a router to periodically refresh its prune state. Finally, since DVMRP builds source-based trees, each router needs to maintain *per-source per-group* state information. For a multicast group with two senders, an intermediate router needs to maintain two states for this group because the multicast trees for different senders would be different. That is, how to forward packets depends on who the sender is. As a consequence, with DVMRP a large amount of state information needs to be stored at each router. In summary, even though DVMRP is not very scalable, DVMRP is still the most widely used protocol for its simplicity.

Protocol Independent Multicast (PIM)

As we have seen, DVRMP is not scalable for multicast groups with sparsely distributed members. The reasons are twofold: First, source-oriented tree construction, the way an RPB tree is pruned to an RPM tree, is not scalable; second, building a source-based multicast tree is not scalable as it requires too much state information. The state overhead grows quickly as the *path* gets longer and as the number of *groups* and *senders per group* gets larger. For *sparsely* distributed group members, a *shared* tree with *receiver*-oriented tree construction would be more scalable, so a new multicast routing protocol has been proposed for the Internet, called Protocol Independent Multicast (PIM) protocol. PIM explicitly supports two ways of constructing a multicast tree by using two modes. PIM *dense* mode (PIM-DM) constructs a *source-based* multicast tree in a manner very similar to DVMRP and is suitable for multicast groups with densely distributed members. On the other hand, PIM *sparse* mode (PIM-SM) constructs only a group *shared* tree for each multicast group and, thus, is suitable for groups with members that are widely dispersed. Since PIM-DM is very similar to DVMRP, we will only discuss PIM-SM in this section. A recent version of PIM-SM is described in RFC 4601. We also note that the scalability problem of multicast also results from a large number of multicast groups globally that are neither tackled by DVMRP nor PIM.

PIM-SM is designed with the principle that a router should not be involved in multicast routing of a multicast session if it does not lead to any *receiver*. Therefore, in PIM-SM, the tree is constructed in a *receiver-driven* manner: That is, a router that leads to the subnets where the receivers are located needs to send a join message *explicitly*. The center node of a shared tree is called a rendezvous point (RP). The RP of each multicast group is uniquely determined by a *hash* function which we shall describe later. The shared tree is thus called an *RP-based* tree (RPT). The router responsible for forwarding multicast packets and sending join messages for a subnet is called the *designated router* (DR). The routing table called the Multicast Routing Information Base (MRIB) is used by a DR to determine the next-hop neighbor to

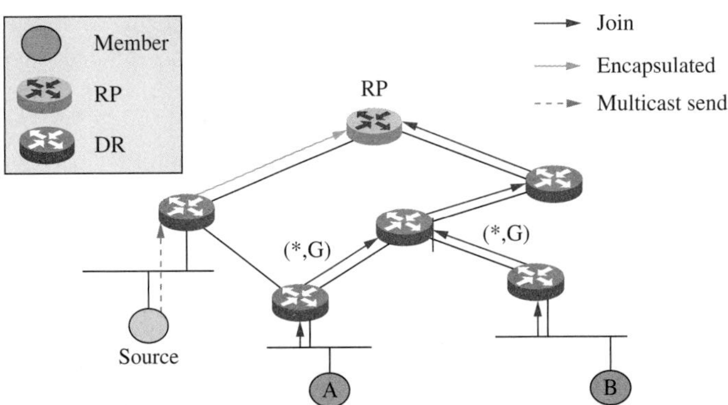

FIGURE 4.75 Operations of PIM-SM phase one.

which any join/prune message is sent. MRIB is either taken directly from the unicast routing table or derived by a separate routing protocol. Let us examine the *three phases* of PIM-SM that construct an RPT in a receiver-oriented manner.

Phase One: RP Tree

In phase one, an RP tree is constructed as shown in Figure 4.75. We describe the procedure from two aspects: receivers and senders. When a receiver wants to join a multicast group, it sends a join message to its DR using IGMP. Upon receiving the join message, the DR sends a general group join message to the *RP*. A general group join message is denoted by (*,G), which indicates that the receiver wants to receive multicast packets from *all* sources. As the PIM join message travels toward RP on the shortest path from DR to RP, it may finally reach RP (e.g., the join message from A in Figure 4.75), or may reach a router already on the RPT (e.g., the message from B in Figure 4.75). In both cases, routers on RPT will know that the DR wants to join the multicast group and will forward multicast packets along the reverse shortest path from RP to DR. A particular feature of PIM-SM is that no acknowledge message in response to a join message will be sent back to the DR. Therefore, a DR needs to send join message *periodically* to maintain the RPT; otherwise, it will be pruned after time out.

On the other hand, a sender that wants to send a multicast packet can just send it to the address of the multicast group. Upon receiving a multicast packet, the sender's DR *encapsulates* it into a PIM Register packet and then forwards it to the RP. When RP receives the PIM Register packet, it *decapsulates* it and forwards it to RPT. You may wonder why the sender's DR needs to encapsulate a multicast packet. Remember that any host can become a sender, so how does an RP know where the potential senders are? Even if the RP knows where the senders are, how does an RP receive packets from a sender? In the first phase, an RP receives multicast packets from a sender with the help of the sender's DR because this DR is able to identify a multicast packet and knows where the RP for the multicast group is located.

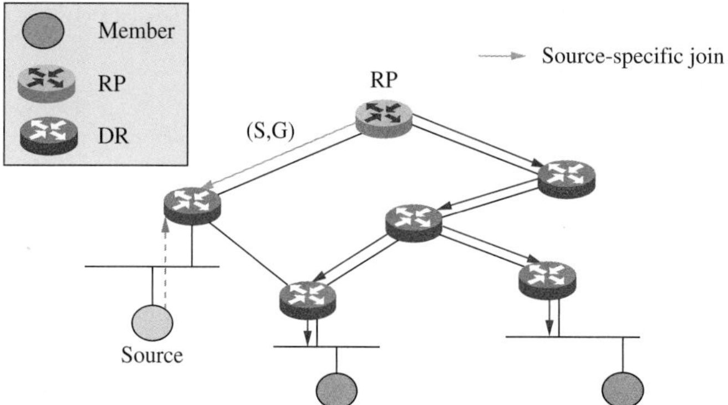

FIGURE 4.76 Operations of PIM-SM phase two.

Phase Two: Register-Stop

While the encapsulation mechanism allows an RP to receive multicast packets from a sender's DR, the operations of encapsulation and decapsulation are too expensive. Therefore, in phase two (shown in Figure 4.76), the RP would like to receive the multicast packets *directly* from the sender without encapsulation. To do so, the RP initiates a PIM *source-specific* join message to the sender. A source-specific *Join* message is denoted by (S,G), which indicates that the receiver wants to receive multicast packets only from the specific source S. When the source-specific join message traverses the shortest path from RP to the source, all routers on the path *record* the join information in their multicast state information. After the join message reaches the DR of the source, multicast packets start to flow following the *source-specific tree* (SPT), the (S,G) tree, to the RP. As a consequence, the RP may now receive duplicate packets, one in native multicast format and the other encapsulated. The RP discards the encapsulated packet and sends a PIM *Register-Stop* message to the DR of the sender. At the same time, RP should continue to forward multicast packets onto the RPT. Afterward, the DR of the sender will not encapsulate and forward multicast packets to the RP, so RP can receive native multicast packets directly from the sender.

An interesting scenario of this phase is: What if a router is on the source-specific tree as well as the RPT? Clearly, it is possible to make a *shortcut* by sending the multicast packets received from the source-specific tree directly to the downstream routers of the RPT.

Phase Three: Shortest-Path Tree

One of the disadvantages of delivering multicast packets on a shared tree is that the path from the sender to the RP and then from the RP to receivers may be quite long. A novel feature of PIM-SM is to allow a receiver's DR to optionally initiate a switch from an RPT to a *source-specific tree.* Figure 4.77 shows the steps performed to switch from an RPT to an SPT. A receiver's DR first issues a source-specific join message, (S,G), to the source S. The join message may either reach the source or converge at some router on the SPT. The DR then starts to receive two copies of multicast packets from both trees. It will drop the one received from RPT. The DR then sends a

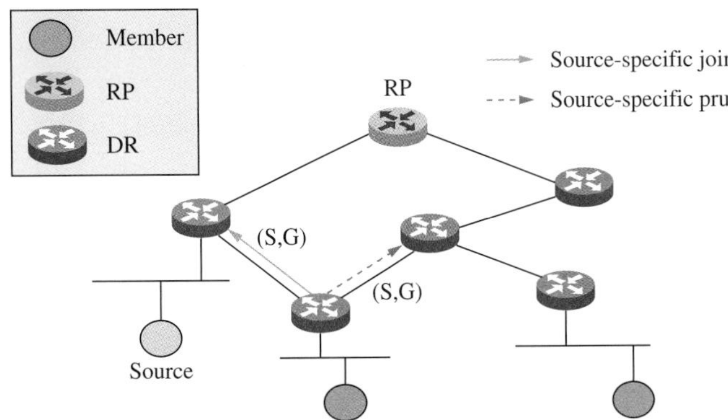

FIGURE 4.77 Operations of PIM-SM phase three.

source-specific prune message, (S,G), to the RP. The prune message either reaches the RP or is converged at some router on the RPT. The DR will then not receive packets from the RPT. Note that the prune message is a source-specific message because the DR still wants to receive packets from other senders via the RPT.

PIM-SM can also cooperate with some new features of IGMPv3, in particular the source-specific join feature. If a receiver sends a source-specific join using IGMPv3, the receiver's DR may omit performing a general group join, (*,G). Instead, it should issue a source-specific (S,G) join message. The multicast addresses reserved for source-specific multicast are in the range from 232.0.0.0 to 232.255.255.255. In addition, *source-specific multicast* (SSM) defined in RFC 4607 introduces a new one-to-many multicasting model. It describes how multicasting with a source address and a group address, particularly well-suited to dissemination-style applications, can be achieved using PIM-SM.

PIM Packet Format

Figure 4.78 shows the header of a PIM packet. The first field describes its PIM version; the current PIM version is 2. The second field is the type field. There are nine types of PIM packets, as shown in Figure 4.78. The third field is reserved for future use, and the last field is the checksum of the PIM packet, which is the 16-bit 1's complement of the 1's complement sum of the entire PIM packet.

0	8	16	24	31
Ver	Type	Reversed	Checksum	

Type	Description
0	Hello
1	Register
2	Register-Stop
3	Join/Prune
4	Bootstrap
5	Assert
6	Graft (used in PIM-SM)
7	Graft (used in PIM-DM)
8	Candidate-RP-Advertisement

FIGURE 4.78 PIM packet format.

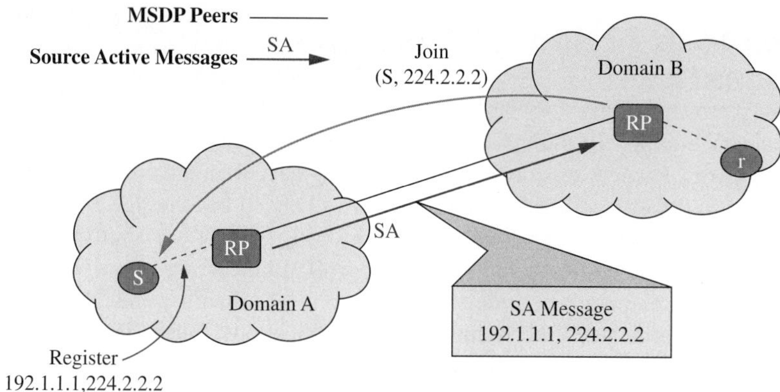

FIGURE 4.79 Operation flow of MSDP.

4.7.4 Inter-Domain Multicast

The idea of sharing a single RP with a group makes PIM-SM against the autonomous nature of a domain and thus hard to apply for the purpose of inter-domain multicast. For example, if a sender and a bunch of receivers within a domain form a multicast group but the RP for the group is located in an other domain, then all the packets need to go to the RP, which is in the other domain, before they can be received by those receivers. As a consequence, PIM-SM usually is not used across domains. Each group will have an RP within each domain.

If PIM-SM is used in a single domain, then each RP knows all of the sources and receivers of all groups under its management. However, it has no mechanism to know sources *outside* its domain. The Multicast Source Discovery Protocol (MSDP) is proposed for RPs to learn about multicast sources in remote domains. Specifically, the RP in each domain establishes an MSDP *peering* relation with RPs in remote domains. When the RP learns of a new multicast source within its own domain, it informs its MSDP peers using the Source Active message. Specifically, the RP *encapsulates* the *first* data packet received from the source into a Source Active message, and then sends the SA to *all* peers, as shown in Figure 4.79. If the receiving RP has a (*,G) entry for the group in the SA, the RP sends a (S,G) join message toward the original RP so that the packet can be forwarded to the RP. The RP also *decapsulates* the data and forwards it down its shared tree if there are receivers in its domain. A shorter path from the source could be established by sending a source-specific (S,G) join message. Each RP also periodically sends SAs, which include all sources within its domain, to its peers. RFC 3446 also proposes the Anycast RP protocol to provide fault tolerance and load sharing within a PIM-SM domain for MSDP applications.

On the other hand, multiprotocol extensions to BGP (MBGP), defined in RFC 2858, also allow routers to exchange multicast routing information. Therefore, if MBGP is adopted to provide MRIB, DRs of PIM-SM would also have inter-domain routes.

Principle in Action: IP Multicast or Application Multicast?

In the current Internet, IP multicasting still cannot be widely deployed due to several concerns. Routers supporting IP multicasting have to maintain the *states* of all active multicast sessions and therefore are likely to become the system bottleneck as these sessions grow in number, resulting in poor scalability. Additionally, transport layer functionalities to support IP multicasting are still open issues. For instance, there is no optimal solution to meet reliability and congestion control requirements for all IP multicasting applications. Furthermore, few Internet service providers (ISPs) are willing to support IP multicasting due to the lack of proper billing mechanisms, making IP multicasting difficult to deploy widely.

Several researchers have proposed the concept of application-level multicasting (ALM) to solve these problems. The basic idea of ALM is that the multicast service is provided by the application layer instead of the network layer. The user space deployment makes ALM compatible with current IP networks; that is, no change or special support is needed for routers and ISPs. In addition, ALM allows more flexible control in customizing application-specific aspects, making transport layer functionalities easy to deploy. Participants in an ALM session form an *overlay* that consists of *unicast* connections between participants. The participants can be either dedicated machines or end hosts. An *infrastructure-based* ALM approach refers to an approach in which the overlay is formed by *dedicated* machines, while the overlay of a *peer-to-peer-based* ALM approach is shaped by *end hosts*. More recently, ALM has become one of the special applications of the peer-to-peer model which we shall describe further in Chapter 6.

Open Source Implementation 4.12: Mrouted

Overview

The open source implementation of multicast routing we will look at is the mrouted, which implements the DVMRP protocol.

Data Structures

In mrouted, the multicast routing table is stored as a *doubly linked list* of routing entries represented by the structure "`rtentry`" (in `mrouted/route.h`). There is one routing entry for each *subnet* if its multicast capability is enabled. The list of active multicast groups in a subnet, referred to as group *table,* is pointed to by the `rt_groups` pointer, as shown in Figure 4.80. The group table consists of two doubly linked lists of group entries which are represented by the structure `gtable` (defined in `mrouted/prune.h`). The first linked list is a

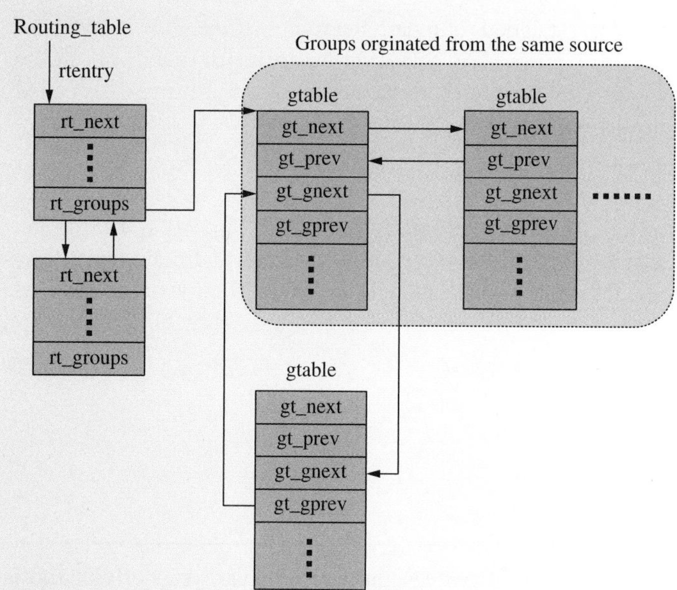

FIGURE 4.80 Data structures of mrouted.

list of active groups of the same source sorted by the group address under the routing entry pointed to by pointer `gt_next` and `gt_prev`. The second linked list (linked by `gt_gprev`, `gt_gnext`) is a list of active groups of *all* sources and groups and is pointed to by `kernel_table`.

Algorithm Implementations

Figure 4.81 shows the call graph of functions related to multicast routing in mrouted. When an IGMP packet is received, the `accept_igmp()` function is called to process the packet. Depending on the type and code of this packet, different functions are invoked accordingly. If the type is related to IGMP protocol, for example, membership query or report (version 1 or version 2), then `accept_membership_query()` or `accept_group_report()` is called, respectively. On the other hand, if the type of the packet is `IGMP_DVMRP`, then the code of the packet is checked to determine the corresponding operation. For example, if the code is `DVMRP_REPORT`, then the `accept_report()` is invoked. In `accept_report()`, routes reported in the packet are processed

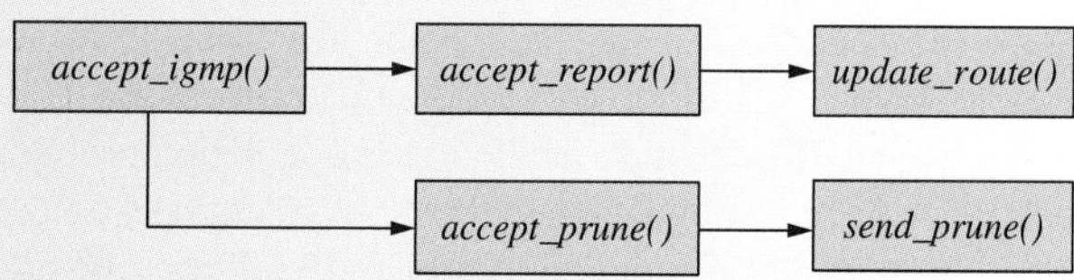

FIGURE 4.81 Mrouted open source implementation.

Continued

and update_route() is called to update the routes. If the code is DVMRP_PRUNE, then accept_prune() is called. In accept_prune(), if all the child routers have expressed no interest in the group, send_prune() is called to send a prune message to the upstream router.

Exercises

Trace the following three functions: accept_report(), update_route(), and accept_prune(), in the source code of mrouted and draw their flowcharts. Compare the flowcharts you draw with the DVMRP protocol introduced in this section.

4.8 SUMMARY

In this chapter, we have learned about the Internet Protocol (IP) layer, or the network layer, of the Internet Protocol stack. It is the most important layer for achieving global connectivity. We have discussed several mechanisms of the control plane and data plane used in the Internet to provide host-to-host connection service. Among these mechanisms we have discussed, routing and forwarding are the two most important in this layer. Routing, a control-plane mechanism, determines the route or path taken by packets from source router to destination router. Forwarding is a data-plane operation that transfers a packet from an incoming network interface to an outgoing network interface in a router based on the routing table computed by the control plane.

Given that a router may need to process millions of packets per second, scalability is very important to these two mechanisms. For routing, we have learned that the Internet adopts a *two-level* routing hierarchy, namely, intra-domain routing and inter-domain routing. At the lower layer, routers are grouped into autonomous systems (ASs). Routers within an AS are under the same administrative control and run the *same* intra-domain routing protocol, such as RIP or OSPF. Selected routers, called border routers, are connected to each other and are responsible for forwarding packets among ASs using the inter-domain routing protocol, such as BGP. We also have examined two underlying routing algorithms, namely, distance vector routing and link state routing. Current Internet routing protocols are designed based on one of these two basic routing algorithms. The distance vector routing algorithm adopts a *distributed* approach that only exchanges routing information with neighbors, while link state routing algorithm is a *centralized* approach that floods routing information to all routers within the same domain; thus each router can build a *global* topology database of all routers. For forwarding, we have learned that the data structure of the routing table and the lookup and update algorithms for this data structure are very critical to scalability. The routing table consists of more than 300,000 entries in the current Internet backbone, making forwarding even more challenging. In some circumstances, specific ASIC might be needed to offload routing table lookup from the CPU to achieve a forwarding speed of millions of packets per second.

Two versions of the Internet Protocol (IP) have been addressed in this chapter, IPv4 and IPv6. We assume that IPv6 will predominate in the next few years. To cope with the IP address depletion problem, we have also introduced the network address translation (NAT) protocol and private IP address. Besides the IP protocol, we have also studied several control-plane protocols, such as ARP, DHCP, and ICMP.

In this chapter, we also have described three types of communication, namely, unicast, multicast, and broadcast. In addition, we have seen a new type of communication, *anycast,* supported in IPv6. Unicast, i.e., point-to-point communication, has been the major focus of our discussion. Broadcast and multicast are also supported by IPv4/IPv6. An IP subnet is defined as a broadcast domain with an IP address called a subnet address, which can be obtained by an AND operation of an IP address and its subnet mask. Packets with an IP subnet address as their destination address are delivered to all hosts within the subnet, which usually corresponds to a LAN consisting of several Layer-2 devices. We have learned that several protocols rely on the broadcast service, such as ARP and DHCP. In the last part of this chapter, we also have seen several multicast routing protocols and membership management protocols.

Having completed the study of host-to-host connectivity, it is time for us to learn about *process-to-process* connectivity, the next upper layer in the Internet Protocol stack. We shall see how packets from different processes on the *same* host are multiplexed together to send through the IP protocol. We shall also learn how to build *reliable* communication over the best-effort service provided by the IP protocol. Finally, we shall see how to write network application programs through the *socket* programming interface.

COMMON PITFALLS

MAC Address, IP Address, and Domain Name

Each network interface is associated with at least one MAC address, one IP address, and one domain name. They are used by different layers of the protocol stack for addressing. The MAC address comes along with a network card; it is used by the link-layer protocols, and is a universal unique address assigned and "hard-coded" during the production of each network card. Thus, it is a *hardware address*. Usually, the MAC address does *not* have a hierarchical structure and can be used only for addressing in a *broadcast* environment. The IP address is used by the network-layer protocols as described in this chapter. Unlike the MAC address, the IP address has a hierarchical structure and can be used for routing. It is configured manually or automatically; thus, it is a *software address*. The domain name is a string of characters that is human readable. Although in most cases the domain name is a string of letters from the English alphabet, it could be in any language now. The purpose of the domain name is to enable people to easily remember the address of a host, especially for applications like WWW where the domain name is expressed in the URL format. When sending a packet, address translation is required for the protocol of each layer to fetch the correct address. Therefore, the Domain Name System (DNS) is used to translate the domain name to the IP address, and ARP is used to translate the IP address to the MAC address. Both DNS and ARP also support the *reversed* translation.

Forwarding and Routing

Again, it is very important to understand the differences between forwarding and routing. Forwarding is a data plane function, while routing is a control plane function. The task of forwarding is to transfer a packet from an incoming network interface to an outgoing network interface in a router, while that of routing is to find a routing path between any two hosts.

Classful IP and CIDR

Classful IP addressing refers to the original design of IP addresses in the Internet Protocol. With the classful IP address, the length of the network prefix is *fixed* for each class of IP addresses, and addresses can be easily differentiated by the first several bits. In addition, the maximum number of hosts that can be accommodated for a network prefix is also fixed. However, this design causes *inflexibility* in IP address allocation and increases the number of class C address *entries* in the routing table. Classless Inter Domain Routing (CIDR) is thus proposed to allow variable network prefix length. CIDR is most effective in aggregating several *consecutive* class C addresses. Currently, CIDR is supported by most routers.

DHCP and IPv6 Auto-Configuration

In IPv4, DHCP is used to automatically configure a host's IP address. However, in IPv6, autoconfiguration is supported via ICMPv6 protocol using router *advertisement* and router *solicitation* messages. Are they different and do we still need DHCP in an all-IPv6 network? The answer to both questions is yes. DHCP is based on BOOTP. As a consequence, a lot of fields in the packet header are unused, while option fields are used to carry information that we really need. The autoconfiguration process in IPv6 is a new design, not based on DHCP or BOOTP. However, for security or network management concerns, a network administrator may choose to use a DHCP server to control IP address assignment.

Multicast Tree and Steiner Tree

A Steiner tree, named after Jakob Steiner, is a tree rooted at a source node and spanning a set of destination nodes with the minimum cost. It differs from the minimum spanning tree by the fact that the set of destination nodes does not necessarily include all nodes (vertices) in the graph. Therefore, a Steiner tree could be viewed as one of the optimal solutions to a multicast routing. However, in all the multicast routing protocols we studied, none of them tried to construct a Steiner tree. Instead, most of them construct *reverse shortest-path trees,* either rooted at the source or the rendezvous point (RP). The rationale is that finding a Steiner tree is an NP-complete problem, and most heuristic algorithms require *global* information. Therefore, the reverse shortest-path tree becomes a more practical solution for building multicast trees in the Internet.

FURTHER READINGS

IPv4

For a historical view of the development of the Internet Protocol, the following papers are old but important pioneering works. Their key ideas have been reviewed in this chapter and Chapter 1.

- V. Cerf and R. Kahn, "A Protocol for Packet Network Intercommunication," *IEEE Transactions on Communications,* Vol. 22, pp. 637–648, May 1974.
- J. B. Postel, "Internetwork Protocol Approaches," *IEEE Transactions on Communications,* Vol. 28, pp. 604–611, Apr. 1980.
- J. Saltzer, D. Reed, and D. Clark, "End-to-End Arguments in System Design," *ACM Transactions on Computer Systems (TOCS),* Vol. 2, No. 4, pp. 195–206, 1984.
- D. Clark, "The Design Philosophy of the Internet Protocols," *Proceedings of ACM SIGCOMM,* Sept. 1988.

Related RFCs for IPv4, ICMP, and NAT are:

- J. Postel, "Internet Protocol," RFC 0791, Sept. 1981. (Also STD 0005.)
- K. Nichols, S. Blake, F. Baker, and D. Black, "Definition of the Differentiated Services Field (DS Field) in the IPv4 and IPv6 Headers," RFC 2472, Dec. 1998.
- J. Postel, "Internet Control Message Protocol," RFC 792, Sept. 1981. (Also STD 0005)
- P. Srisuresh and K. Egevang, "Traditional IP Network Address Translator (Traditional NAT)," RFC 3022, Jan. 2001.
- J. Rosenberg, R. Mahy, P. Matthews, and D. Wing, "Session Traversal Utilities for NAT (STUN)," RFC 5389, Oct. 2008.

Fast Table Lookup

One interesting topic for data plane packet processing is fast table lookup for packet forwarding and packet classification. The former is longest prefix matching on a single field (destination IP address), while the latter is multi-field matching on, say, 5-tuple (source/destination IP address, source/destination port number, protocol id). The first paper listed below is on packet forwarding with a software algorithm, which requires only a small table size, while the next two are hardware solutions. The last two papers are on packet classification with hardware solutions.

- M. Degermark, A. Brodnik, S. Carlsson, and S. Pink, "Small Forwarding Tables for Fast Routing Lookups," *ACM SIGCOMM'97,* pp. 3–14, Oct. 1997.
- M. Waldvogel, G. Varghese, J. Turner, and B. Plattner, "Scalable High Speed Routing Lookups," *ACM SIGCOMM'97,* pp. 25–36, Oct. 1997.

- P. Gupta, S. Lin, and N. McKeown, "Routing Lookups in Hardware at Memory Access Speeds," *IEEE INFOCOM,* Apr. 1998.
- P. Gupta and N. McKeown, "Packet Classification on Multiple Fields," *ACM SIGCOMM,* Sept. 1999.
- V. Srinivasan, G. Varghese, and S. Suri, "Packet Classification Using Tuple Space Search," *ACM SIGCOMM,* Sept. 1999.

IPv6

The RFC by Bradner and Mankin is the starter for the next-generation IP. They also published a book on IPng. The current version of IPv6, ICMPv6, and DNS can be found in RFC 2460, 4443, and 3596, respectively.

- S. Bradner and A. Mankin, "The Recommendation for the Next Generation IP Protocol," RFC 1752, Jan. 1995.
- S. Bradner and A. Mankin, *IPng: Internet Protocol Next Generation,* Addison-Wesley, 1996.
- S. Deering and R. Hinden, "Internet Protocol, Version 6 (IPv6) Specification," RFC 2460, Dec. 1998.
- A. Conta, S. Deering, and M. Gupta, "Internet Control Message Protocol (ICMPv6) for the Internet Protocol Version 6 (IPv6) Specification," RFC 4443, Mar. 2006.
- S. Thomson, C. Huitema, V. Ksinant, and M. Souissi, "DNS Extensions to Support IP Version 6," RFC 3596, Oct. 2003.

The basic IPv4 to IPv6 transition mechanisms for hosts and routers is described in RFC 4213. In addition, application aspects of transition mechanisms can be found in RFC 4038. For the three transition approaches, namely, dual stack, tunneling, and protocol translation, there have been many proposals. For example, tunnel broker is proposed in RFC 3053 to help users to configure bidirectional tunnels. The *6to4* and its remedy, *Teredo,* are described in RFC 3056 and 4380, respectively. A new IPv6 rapid deployment mechanism on IPv4 infrastructures (6rd) that builds upon 6to4 is proposed in RFC 5569. *ISATAP* is defined in RFC 5214. Solutions of protocol translation, such as SIIT and NAT-PT, are defined in RFC 2765 and 4966, respectively. Finally, Geoff Huston wrote several interesting articles about the IPv4 address depletion problem and transition process to IPv6.

- E. Nordmark and R. Gilligan, "Basic Transition Mechanisms for IPv6 Hosts and Routers," RFC 4213, Oct. 2005.
- M-K. Shin, Ed., Y-G. Hong, J. Hagino, P. Savola, and E. M. Castro, "Application Aspects of IPv6 Transition," RFC 4038, Mar. 2005.
- A. Durand, P. Fasano, I. Guardini, and D. Lento, "IPv6 Tunnel Broker," RFC 3053, Jan. 2001.
- B. Carpenter and K. Moore, "Connection of IPv6 Domains via IPv4 Clouds," RFC 3056, Feb. 2001.
- C. Huitema, "Teredo: Tunneling IPv6 over UDP through Network Address Translations (NATs)," RFC 4380, Feb. 2006.
- E. Exist and R. Despres, "IPv6 Rapid Deployment on IPv4 Infrastructures (6rd)," RFC 5569, Jan. 2010.
- F. Templin, T. Gleeson, and D. Thaler, "Intra-Site Automatic Tunnel Addressing Protocol (ISATAP)," RFC 5214, Mar. 2008.
- E. Nordmark, "Stateless IP/ICMP Translation Algorithm (SIIT)," RFC 2765, Feb. 2000.
- C. Aoun and E. Davies, "Reasons to Move the Network Address Translator–Protocol Translator (NAT-PT) to Historic Status," RFC 4966, July 2007.
- Geoff Huston, "IPv4 Address Report," retrieved April 24, 2010, from http://www.potaroo.net/tools/ipv4/index.html
- Geoff Huston, "Is the Transition to IPv6 a "Market Failure?'," The ISP Column, Apr. 2010, retrieved April 24, 2010, from http://cidr-report.org/ispcol/ 2009-09/v6trans.html.

Routing

The most recent RFCs for RIP, OSPF, and BGP are:

- G. Malkin, "RIP Version 2," RFC 2453, Nov. 1998.
- J. Moy, "OSPF Version 2," RFC 2328, Apr. 1998. (Also STD0054.)
- R. Coltun, D. Ferguson, J. Moy, and A. Lindem, "OSPF for IPv6," RFC 5340, July 2008.
- Y. Rekhter, T. Li, and S. Hares, "A Border Gateway Protocol 4 (BGP-4)," RFC 4271, Jan. 2006.

Optimal routing has been formulated as a network flow problem in the literature where traffics are modeled as flows between sources and destinations in the network. The textbook by Bertsekas and Gallagher gives a good tutorial on this treatment.

- D. Bertsekas and R. Gallagher, *Data Networks,* 2nd edition, Prentice Hall, Englewood Cliffs, NJ, 1991.

For more detailed study of Internet routing, OSPF, and BGP, the following books may be useful.

- C. Huitema, *Routing in the Internet,* 2nd edition, Prentice Hall, 1999.

- S. Halabi and D. McPherson, *Internet Routing Architectures,* 2nd edition, Cisco Press, 2000.
- J. T. Moy, *OSPF: Anatomy of an Internet Routing Protocol,* Addison-Wesley Professional, 1998.
- I. V. Beijnum, *BGP,* O'Reilly Media, 2002.

The dynamics of inter-domain routing have received attention through measurement and modeling. Many interesting results could be found in a special issue of *IEEE Network Magazine* on inter-domain routing, which was published in Nov-Dec 2005. Recently, the fault tolerance of BGP has also received much attention, especially the solution based on multipath routing. Papers by Xu et al. and Wang et al. are good examples.

- M. Caesar and J. Rexford, "BGP Routing Policies in ISP Networks," *IEEE Network,* Vol. 19, Issue 6, Nov/Dec 2005.
- R. Musunuri and J. A. Cobb, "An Overview of Solutions to Avoid Persistent BGP Divergence," *IEEE Network,* Vol. 19, Issue 6, Nov/Dec 2005.
- A. D. Jaggard and V. Ramachandran, "Toward the Design of Robust Interdomain Routing Protocols," *IEEE Network,* Vol. 19, Issue 6, Nov/Dec 2005.
- W. Xu and J. Rexford, "Miro: Multi-Path Interdomain Routing," *ACM SIGCOMM,* Sept. 2006.
- F. Wang and L. Gao, "Path Diversity Aware Interdomain Routing," *IEEE IEEE INFOCOM,* Apr. 2009.

Multicast

Although not very successful in Internet deployment, many protocols have been proposed for intra- and inter-domain multcast. A quite complete survey is done in a tutorial paper by Ramalho. For the original work on multicast, Deering and Cheriton's paper is a must read. For comparison of IPv4 multicast with IPv6 multicast, readers can refer to Metz and Tatipamula's paper.

- M. Ramalho, "Intra- and Inter-Domain Multicast Routing Protocols: A Survey and Taxonomy," *IEEE Communications Surveys and Tutorials,* Vol. 3, No. 1, 1st quarter, 2000.
- S. Deering and D. Cheriton, "Multicast Routing in Datagram Internetworks and Extended LANs," *ACM Transactions on Computer Systems,* Vol. 8, pp. 85–110, May 1990.
- C. Metz, and M. Tatipamula, "A Look at Native IPv6 Multicast," *IEEE Internet Computing,* Vol. 8, pp. 48–53, July/Aug 2004.

The most recent RFCs for multicast membership management and routing are:

- B. Cain, S. Deering, I. Kouvelas, B. Fenner, and A. Thyagarajan, "Internet Group Management Protocol, Version 3," RFC 3376, Oct. 2002.
- D. Waitzman, C. Partridge, and S.E. Deering, "Distance Vector Multicast Routing Protocol," RFC 1075, Nov. 1998.
- B. Fenner, M. Handley, H. Holbrook, and I. Kouvelas, "Protocol Independent Multicast–Sparse Mode (PIM-SM): Protocol Specification (Revised)," RFC 4601, Aug. 2006.
- N. Bhaskar, A. Gall, J. Lingard, and S. Venaas, "Bootstrap Router (BSR) Mechanism for Protocol Independent Multicast (PIM)," RFC 5059, Jan. 2008.
- D. Kim, D. Meyer, H. Kilmer, and D. Farinacci, "Anycast Rendevous Point (RP) Mechanism Using Protocol Independent Multicast (PIM) and Multicast Source Discovery Protocol (MSDP)," RFC 3446, Jan. 2003.

FREQUENTLY ASKED QUESTIONS

1. Why do we need both MAC address and IP address for a network interface? Why not just one address?
   Answer:
   If only IP address: no link layer operations, no bridging, no broadcast links.
   If only MAC address: no hierarchical Internet architecture, no subnet operations, no routing.
2. Why are MAC addresses flat but IP addresses hierarchical?
   Answer:
   MAC address: manufactured globally unique without location implication, thus flat.
   IP address: configured globally unique with location implication, thus hierarchical.
3. Why is netmask used inside a router and a host?
   Answer:
   Router: to select the longest one among the matched prefixes

Host: to determine whether the destination IP address is within my subnet

4. Routing vs. forwarding? (Compare their type of work and the algorithm used.)
Answer:
Forwarding: data-plane; longest prefix matching by table lookup.
Routing: control-plane; shortest path computation by Dijkstra or Bellman-Ford algorithm.

5. Why could there be multiple matched IP prefixes in a router's table lookup? (Explain what network configurations could result in this.)
Answer:
If an organization that is allocated a prefix, say 140.113/16, has created remote branches, say 140.113.0/18 and 140.113.192/18, it would have multiple prefixes, say 3 in this example, in all routers. If a packet is destined to 140.113.221.86, it would match both 140.113/16 and 140.113.192/18, with the latter being the longest match.

6. How is longest-prefix matching done in the Linux kernel? Why is the matched prefix guaranteed to be the longest?
Answer:
The forwarding table is organized into an array of hash tables of the same prefix length. The array is ordered according to the length of prefixes. Starting from the non-empty hash table with the longest prefixes, the first match is thus guaranteed to be the longest.

7. How is the forwarding table organized in the Linux kernel?
Answer:
It consists of a forwarding cache and a FIB (Forwarding Information Base), where the former is a hash table that stores the recently looked up entries and the latter is an array of hash tables of the same prefix length (and is looked up after a miss in the forwarding cache).

8. What header fields are needed in IP reassembly at destination hosts?
Answer:
Identifier, the more bit, and fragmentation offset.

9. What packet modifications are needed for FTP through NAT?
Answer:
Non-ALG modifications: source (destination) IP address and source port number for outgoing (incoming) packets, IP header checksum, and TCP checksum.
ALG modifications: IP address and port number in FTP messages, TCP sequence number, and TCP acknowledgement number.

10. What packet modifications are needed for ICMP through NAT?
Answer:
Non-ALG modifications: source (destination) IP address and source port number for outgoing (incoming) packets, and IP header checksum.
ALG modifications: ICMP checksum and IP address in ICMP messages.

11. How is the NAT table implemented in the Linux kernel?
Answer: A hash table

12. What header fields in IPv4 are removed from or added into the header of IPv6? Why?
Answer:
Removed from: header checksum, fragmentation (identifier, more bit, don't fragment bit, fragmentation offset), protocol, and options.
Moved into: flow label and next header.

13. How can IPv4 and IPv6 coexist?
Answer:
Dual stack: both IPv4 and IPv6 stacks in routers and hosts
Tunneling: v6-v4-v6 tunneling between IPv6 islands or v4-v6-v4 tunneling between IPv4 islands

14. How does a host translate IP addresses to MAC addresses through ARP?
Answer:
Broadcast an ARP request, with a specified IP address, on the local subnet and get a unicast ARP response from the host with the specified IP address.

15. How does a host obtain its IP address through DHCP or ARP?
Answer:
DHCP: broadcast DHCPDISCOVER to find a DHCP server and then get configurations.
ARP: broadcast an RARP request, with its own MAC address, and get unicast RARP response from the RARP server.

16. How are ping and tracepath implemented?
Answer:
Ping: ICMP echo request and reply
Tracepath: repeatedly send UDP or ICMP echo requests with TTL=1, 2, etc. until an ICMP port unreachable (for UDP) or ICMP echo reply (for ICMP echo request) is received from the target machine.

17. How does the count-to-infinity problem occur in RIP?
Answer:
A router detecting a link failure updates and exchanges distance vectors with its neighbor routers. If the router also receives and accepts a distance vector from its neighbor without checking whether the path is through itself, the routers might end up updating the distance vector of each other incrementally until information of an available path is propagated here. During this period, packet looping is possible between these two peer routers.
18. RIP vs. OSPF? (Compare their network state information and route computation.)
Answer:
RIP: exchanged distance vector with neighbors; distance vector updated by the Bellman-Ford algorithm.
OSPF: broadcast link state to all routers; routing table computed by the Dijkstra algorithm based on the whole topology.
19. Distance vector routing vs. link state routing? (Compare their routing message complexity, computation complexity, speed of convergence, and scalability.)
Answer:
Routing message complexity: DV > LS
Computation complexity: LS > DV
Speed of convergence: LS > DV
Scalability: DV > LS
20. RIP vs. BGP? (Summarize their similarities and differences.)
Answer:
Similarities: exchanged neighbor information, Bellman-Ford algorithm
Differences: distance vector vs. path vector (for loop-free routing), RIP-over-UDP vs. BGP-over-TCP, shortest-path routing vs. shortest-path and policy routing, single path vs. multiple path
21. Why do RIP, OSPF, and BGP run over UDP, IP, and TCP, respectively?
Answer:
RIP: one connectionless UDP socket, on UDP port 52, that can receive requests from and send responses (advertisements) to all neighbor routers.
OSPF: one raw IP socket used to broadcast link states to all routers in the domain.
BGP: connection-oriented TCP sockets for reliable transfer with remote peer routers.
22. Can you estimate the number of routing table entries in intra-AS and inter-AS routers? (Estimate the range or order of magnitude.)
Answer:
Intra-AS: tens to hundreds, depending on how large a domain is.
Inter-AS: tens of thousands world-wide, depending on the number of prefixes
23. How do routing protocols in zebra exchange messages with other routers and update routing tables in the kernel?
Answer:
Routing message exchange: through various sockets (IP, UDP, TCP) to other routers
Routing table update: through ioctl, sysctl, netlink, rtnetlink, etc. to access kernel
24. How does a router know through IGMP whether hosts in its subnet have joined a multicast group?
Answer:
The router broadcasts a general query or group-specific query (addressed to 224.0.0.1 all-system multicast group) on its subnet to solicit membership information. A host joins by responding/broadcasting an IGMP report with TTL=1 if no one on the subnet responds before its random timer expires. The router knows whether there are any hosts in a specific multicast group but does not know who and how many.
25. Does a router know exactly which hosts have joined a multicast group?
Answer:
No. It only knows whether there are any hosts of a subnet in a specific multicast group.
26. Source-based vs. core-based multicast tree? (Compare their number of states and scalability.)
Answer:
Number of states: source-based > core-based
Scalability: core-based > source-based
27. How many pieces of state information are kept in routers for source-based and core-based multicast routers, respectively? (Consider the numbers of multicast groups and sources.) What kinds of state information might be kept?
Answer:
Source-based: per-group x per-source, i.e., (group, source) pairs
Core-based: per-group
State information: membership state of a subnet, prune state, or join state.

28. Do multicast packets really flow on the shortest path in the reverse path multicasting in DVMRP?
Answer:
Not necessarily. The shortest path is from a downstream router to the source router. Its reverse path might not be the shortest from the source router to the downstream router.
29. What state information is kept in routers for the reverse path multicasting in DVMRP?
Answer:
Per-(group, source) prune state
30. How is the RP of a multicast group determined in PIM-SM?
Answer:
The same hash function, on class-D multicast IP addresses, is used by all multicast routers in the domain. The hashed value is transformed to select a multicast router from a list of candidate routers.

EXERCISES

Hands-On Exercises

1. Use Wireshark or similar software to observe fragments of a large IP packet.
2. Use Wireshark or similar software to capture packets for couple of seconds. Find an ARP packet and an IP packet from the data you have captured. Compare the difference between the MAC header of these two packets. Can you find the protocol ID for ARP and IP? Is the destination address of the ARP packet a broadcast address or a unicast address? Is this ARP packet a request or reply packet? Examine the payload of this ARP packet.
3. Use Wireshark or similar software to capture an IP packet and analyze the header and payload of this packet. Are you able to identify the transport layer protocol and the application layer protocol?
4. Use Wireshark or similar software to find out how ping is implemented using ICMP messages. Show the packets captured to verify your answer. Note that the ping command may be implemented differently on different operating systems. (Hint: Start capturing using Wireshark first, then use the command line to issue a ping command.)
5. Use Wireshark or similar software to find out how traceroute is implemented using ICMP messages.
6. Use visualroute or traceroute to find out the infrastructure of your domain and the routes to foreign countries. (Hint: traceroute will give you a list of routers; try to identify different types of routers by their subnet addresses and round trip delays.)
7. Build a NAT server using a Linux-based PC. (Hint: Linux implements NAT by IP TABLES.)
8. Build a DHCP server using a Linux-based PC.
9. Write a program to implement the ping command. (Hint: Use the raw socket interface to send ICMP packets. Refer to Chapter 5 for socket interfaces.)
10. Trace `ip_route_input()` and `ip_route_output_key()` in the Linux source codes. Describe how IP packets are forwarded to the upper layer and the next hop, respectively. (Hint: Both functions can be found in net/ipv4/route.c.)

Written Exercises

1. What would be the problems when two hosts use the same IP address and ignore each others' existence?
2. Compare the addressing hierarchy in the telephone system with that in the Internet. (Hint: The telephone system uses geographical addressing.)
3. Why is fragmentation needed in IP? Which fields in an IP header are needed for fragmentation and reassembly?
4. What is the purpose of the identifier field in the IPv4 header? Will wraparound be a problem? Give an example to show the wraparound problem.
5. How does the IP protocol differentiate the upper layer protocol of an IP packet? For example, how does it know whether the packet is an ICMP, TCP, or UDP packet?
6. How does an Ethernet driver determine whether a frame is an ARP packet?
7. Consider an IP packet traversing a router:
Which fields in the IP header must be changed by a router when an IP packet traverses the router?
Which fields in the IP header may be changed by a router?

Design an efficient algorithm for recalculating the checksum field. (Hint: think about how these fields are changed.)

8. Consider a company assigned an IP prefix of 163.168.80.0/22. This company owns three branches; these have 440, 70, and 25 computers, respectively. A router with two WAN interfaces is allocated at each branch to provide internetworking such that three routers are fully connected. If you are asked to plan subnet addresses for these three branches as well as addresses for router interfaces, what would you do? (Hint: a subnet is also required for each link between two routers.)
9. If a host has an IP address of 168.168.168.168 and a subnet mask of 255.255.255.240, what is its subnet address? What is the broadcast address of this subnet? How many legal IP addresses are available in this subnet? This IP address is a class B address. Suppose it belongs to a company. How many subnets can be created in this company if the subnet mask is fixed to 255.255.255.240 for all subnets?
10. Consider a host X with IP address 163.168.2.81 and subnet mask 255.255.255.248. Now, assume X sends a packet to the following IPs (hosts): 163.168.2.76, 163.168.2.86, 163.168.168.168, 140.123.101.1, respectively. How is routing different for each IP? How are different ARP packets sent to find out MAC addresses? (For each IP address, routing and ARP packets sent may be the same or different; explain your answer.)
11. When an IP packet is fragmented into fragments, a single fragment loss will cause the whole packet to be discarded. Consider an IP packet that contains 4800 bytes of data (from the upper layer) that is to be delivered to a directly connected destination. Consider two types of link layers with different MTUs. Type A technology uses 5 bytes of header and has an MTU of 53 bytes (you may think of it as the ATM technology). On the other hand, type B technology uses 18 bytes of header and has an MTU of 1518 bytes (say it is Ethernet). Assume the frame loss rate of type A is 0.001 while that of type B is 0.01. Compare the packet loss rate under these two types of link layer technology.
12. What is the minimum number of IP fragments required to send a 1 MB mp3 file over a fast Ethernet connection? (Hint: Ignore headers above the IP layer; a maximum IP fragment consists of a 20-byte header and a 1480-byte payload.)
13. When reassembling fragments, how does the receiver know whether two fragments belong to the same IP packet? How does it know whether the size of each fragment is correct?
14. In your opinion, how is quality of service better supported in IPv6?
15. Why is the order of IPv6 extension headers important and not to be altered?
16. Describe the path MTU discovery procedure defined in RFC 1981.
17. Compare the differences between IPv4 and IPv6 header formats. Discover the changes and explain why these changes were made.
18. Compare the differences between ICMPv4 and ICMPv6. Do we still need DHCP, ARP, and IGMP in IPv6?
19. In the IPv4 header, there is a protocol id field. What is the functionality of this field? Is there a corresponding field in the IPv6 header?
20. Given an IP packet of 6000 bytes, assume the packet is to be transmitted over Ethernet. Explain how it will be fragmented under IPv4 and IPv6, respectively. (You should clearly explain how many fragments will be produced, the size of each frame, and how related fields in each IP header will be set accordingly.)
21. Discuss the difficulties of building connectionless service over a virtual circuit subnet, e.g., IP over ATM.
22. How would the time out value of an ARP cache affect its performance?
23. An ARP request is broadcast in a subnet to obtain the MAC address of a host within the same subnet. Does it make sense to use an ARP request to obtain the MAC address of a remote host outside the subnet?
24. What would happen if an intruder usesd a DHCP spoofing device to send replies to DHCP requests ahead of replies from the real DHCP server?
25. Is it possible for an attacking device to continually request IP addresses from a real DHCP server with continually changing MAC addresses? (Hint: This is called the DHCP starvation problem.)
26. What are the differences between BOOTP and DHCP? Why is DHCP designed based on BOOTP?
27. Let A be a host with private IP that connects to the Internet through a NAT server. Can a host outside A's subnet telnet to A?
28. Why does NAT become a problem for P2P applications? Will we need different solutions for symmetric NAT and cone NAT?

29. Consider the following LAN with one Ether switch S, one intra-domain router R, and two hosts X and Y. Assume switch S has been just powered on.
    1. Describe the routing and address resolution steps performed at X, Y, and S when X sends an IP packet to Y.
    2. Describe the routing and address resolution steps performed at X, Y, and S when Y replies an IP packet to X.
    3. Describe the routing and address resolution steps performed at X, S, and R when X sends an IP packet to a host that is outside the domain. (Hint: Do not forget to explain how X knows of the router R.)

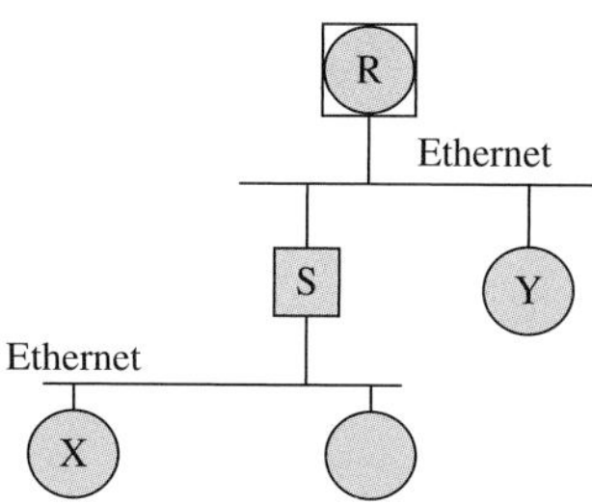

30. Consider the following network topology. Show how node *A* constructs its routing table using link state routing and distance vector routing, respectively.

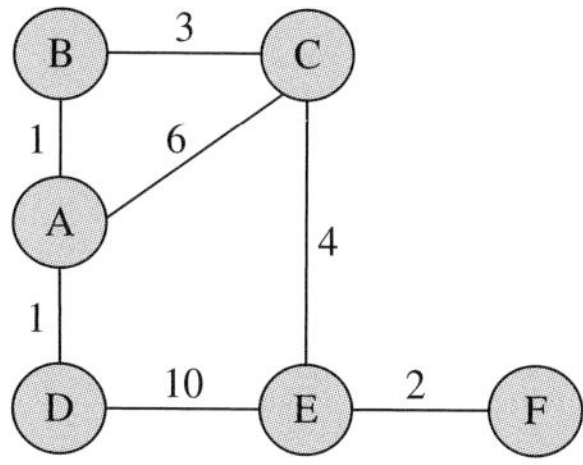

31. Continue from Question 30: Now suppose link *A-B* fails. How will the LS and DV routing react to this change?
32. Compare the message complexity and convergence speed of LS and DV routing.
33. Suppose that a positive lower bound is known for all link costs. Design a new link state algorithm which can add more than one node into the set N at each iteration.
34. Distance vector routing algorithm is adopted in intra-domain routing (e.g., RIP) as well as inter-domain routing (e.g., BGP), but it is implemented with different concerns and additional features. Compare the differences between intra-domain routing and inter-domain routing when both of them use the distance vector algorithm.
35. Route looping is a problem in RIP. Why is it not a problem in BGP?
36. What are the major differences between link state routing and distance vector routing? What are the stability problems of distance vector algorithms, and what are the possible solutions to these problems?
37. If the objective of routing is to find the path with the largest available bandwidth (called widest path), how do we define the link cost? What needs to be changed when computing the path cost? (Not just adding link costs into the path cost!)
38. What is longest prefix matching? Why should the router use longest prefix matching? Will this still be a problem for IPv6? (Why and why not, justify your answer.)
39. In order to provide QoS to some multimedia applications, QoS routing has been studied for a while (but without success). Consider a streaming video application that requires constant bit rate transmission. How do we perform QoS routing for this kind of application? Explain how to define the link cost function, how to compute a path cost from link costs, the granularity of routing decision, the interaction between application protocols and QoS routing.
40. Consider the tunneling technique between two mrouters. Describe how a multicast packet is encapsulated in a unicast packet. How does the mrouter at the other side of the tunnel know it is an encapsulated packet?
41. Since there are no centralized controls on IP multicast address assignment, what is the probability that two groups of users choose the same multicast address if they choose the address randomly?
42. Consider the operation of the IGMP protocol; when a router (querier) sends a group-specific query message to one of its subnets, how is the ACK (report message) explosion problem suppressed if there are many subscribers to the multicast group?
43. In IGMPv3, how do we subscribe multicast packets from a specific source?
44. Does DVMRP minimize the use of network bandwidth or end-to-end delay to each destination? Will a node receive multiple copies of the same packet? If yes, propose a new protocol such that all nodes will receive only one copy.

45. PIM consists of two modes: dense mode and sparse mode. What are the differences between these two modes? Why define two modes?
46. In PIM-SM, how does a router know where to find the RP for a newly joined member of a multicast group?
47. When a host sends a packet to a multicast group, how is the packet handled differently by the designated router under DVMRP and PIM-SM?
48. A multicast tree with the minimized cost is called a Steiner tree. Why do none of the protocols proposed in IETF RFCs try to construct a Steiner multicast tree?
49. In general, we may think that the cost of a source-based tree shall be less than that of a shared-based tree. Do you agree or not? Why? Construct a counter example to show that the cost of a source-based tree is actually larger than that of a shared-based tree.
50. Show the multicast tree built by DVMRP in the following network topology:

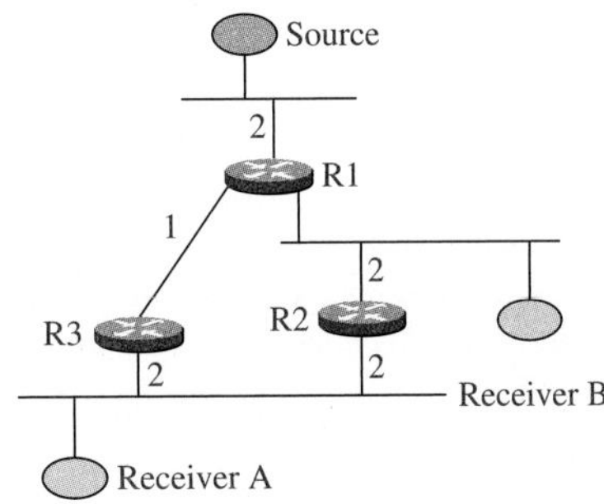

Chapter 5

Transport Layer

The transport layer, also known as the end-to-end protocol layer, is like the *interface* of the whole Internet Protocol suite, providing end-to-end services to application programs. Chapter 3 focuses on the link layer, which provides *node-to-node single-hop* communication channels between directly linked nodes. Issues such as "how fast to send the data" and "does the data correctly reach the receiver attached on the same wired or wireless link?" arise and are answered in Chapter 3. The IP layer provides *host-to-host multi-hop* communication channels across the Internet; similar issues arise for the IP layer and are answered in Chapter 4. Next, since there may be multiple application processes running on a host, the transport layer provides *process-to-process* communication channels between application processes on different Internet hosts. The services provided by the transport layer include (1) *addressing,* (2) *error control,* (3) *reliability,* and (4) *rate control*. The addressing service determines to which application process a packet belongs; error control detects if the received data is valid; the reliability service guarantees the transferred data will reach its destination; rate control adjusts how fast the sender should transmit the data to the receiver for the purpose of *flow control* and to the network for *congestion control*.

In the presence of different demands from a vast variety of application programs, exactly what services to offer in a transport protocol is a big issue. The transport protocols have evolved over time into two dominant ones: the sophisticated *Transmission Control Protocol* (TCP) and the primitive *User Datagram Protocol* (UDP). While TCP and UDP exercise the same addressing scheme and similar error-control methods, they differ much in their design for reliability and rate control: TCP elaborates all the services mentioned above, but UDP completely omits the reliability and rate control services. Due to its sophisticated services, TCP has to establish an end-to-end logical connection between communicating hosts first (i.e., it is *connection-oriented*) and keep necessary *per-connection* or *per-flow* state information at the end hosts (i.e., it is *stateful*). This connection-oriented and stateful design is intended to realize per-flow reliability and rate control for a specific process-to-process channel. On the other hand, UDP is *stateless* and *connectionless,* without having to establish a connection to exercise its addressing and error-control schemes.

To hosts running real-time transfer applications, the services provided by either TCP or UDP are limited and inadequate due to their lack of timing and synchronization information between communicating hosts. Therefore, real-time applications most often incorporate an extra protocol layer on top of the primitive UDP to enhance the service quality. One pair of standard protocols for this purpose is *Real-Time Transport Protocol* (RTP)/*Real-Time Control Protocol* (RTCP). This pair provides services such as synchronization between audio and video streams, data compression and decompression information, and path quality statistics (packet loss rate, end-to-end latency and its variations).

Since the transport layer is directly coupled with the application layer, the Internet socket, often simply called socket, serves as an important *application programming interface* (API) for programmers to access the underlying services of the Internet Protocol suite. Nevertheless, the TCP and UDP socket interfaces are not only accessible by the application layer. Applications can bypass the transport layer and directly use the services provided by the IP or link layer. Later we will discuss how Linux programmers access the services from the transport layer down to the IP layer or even to the link layer through various socket interfaces.

This chapter is organized as follows: Section 5.1 identifies the end-to-end issues of the transport layer, and compares them with those issues of the link layer. Sections 5.2 and 5.3 then describe how the Internet resolves the issues of the transport layer. Section 5.2 illustrates the *primitive* transport protocol UDP, which provides basic process-to-process communication channels and error control. Section 5.3 focuses on the widely used transport protocol TCP, which equips applications with not only process-to-process communication channels and error control but also reliability and rate control. The services of the Internet Protocol suite discussed so far, including those in Chapters 3, 4, and 5, can be directly accessed by application programmers through various socket interfaces. Section 5.4 explains the Linux approach of realizing the socket interfaces. However, because of the extra software layer for real-time applications, RTP/RTCP is often embedded as *library functions* in the applications. Section 5.5 describes how the application layer employs RTP/RTCP.

At the end of this chapter, you should be able to answer (1) *why* the transport layer of the Internet Protocol suite was designed into the way it is today, and (2) *how* Linux realizes the transport-layer protocols.

5.1 GENERAL ISSUES

The transport or end-to-end protocol, as its name suggests, defines the protocol responsible for data transfer between the *end points* of a communication channel. Let us first define some terminology used throughout this chapter: An application running over an operating system is a process, the data transfer unit in the transport layer is referred to as a *segment,* and the traffic flowing in a process-to-process channel is a *flow*. The most apparent service of the transport layer is to provide process-to-process communication channels to application processes. Since there may be multiple processes running on a single host simultaneously, with the aid of process-to-process channels, any processes running on any hosts in the Internet can communicate with one another. The issues concerning the process-to-process channel are very similar to those concerning the node-to-node channel in Chapter 3. In general, the transport

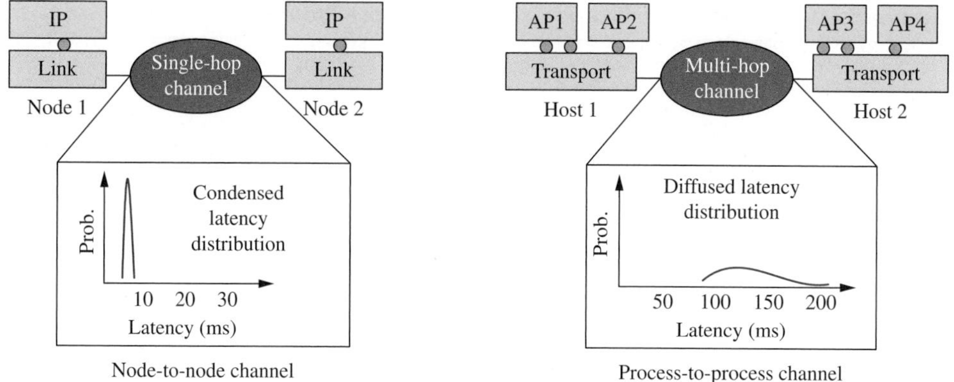

FIGURE 5.1 Differences between single-hop and multi-hop channels.

layer addresses the *connectivity* requirement by *process-to-process communication* plus *error control* on a per-segment basis and *reliability* control on a per-flow basis; it addresses the *resource sharing* requirement by imposing *rate control* on each flow.

5.1.1 Node-to-Node vs. End-to-End

For communication over the process-to-process channel, classical issues that had appeared in Chapter 3 arise again, but the solutions applicable there might not be applicable here. As shown in Figure 5.1, the major difference between the *single-hop node-to-node* and the *multi-hop process-to-process* channels lies in the *latency distribution;* latency is the time delay of transmission from one end host to the other over the channel. In Chapter 3, reliability and rate control issues are easier to resolve because the distribution of the latency between directly linked hosts is very condensed around a certain value that depends on the chosen link-layer technology. In contrast, the latency in the process-to-process channel is large and may vary dramatically, so reliability and rate control algorithms in the transport layer should accommodate large latency and dramatic variation in latency (often called jitter).

Table 5.1 presents a detailed comparison between link protocols on single-hop channels and transport protocols on multi-hop channels. Transport protocols provide services on top of the IP layer, whereas link protocols provide services upon the physical layer. Because there may be multiple nodes attached on the link, the link layer defines the node address (MAC address) to identify node-to-node communication channels over a direct link. Similarly, there may be multiple processes running on the host of each end, thus the transport layer defines the *port number* to address a process on a host.

Addressing

Addressing at the transport layer is rather simple—we just need to label each process running on the local host with a unique identification number. Therefore, the length

TABLE 5.1 Comparison Between Link Protocols and Transport Protocols

		Link Protocol	Transport Protocol
Base on what services?		Physical link	IP layer
Services	Addressing	Node-to-node channel within a link (by MAC address)	Process-to-process channel between hosts (by port number)
	Error control	Per-frame	Per-segment
	Reliability	Per-link	Per-flow
	Rate control	Per-link	Per-flow
Channel latency		Condensed distribution	Diffused distribution

of the process address should be short as compared to the link-layer or network-layer address, and the operating system of the local host could assign the address of a process locally. As we shall see in this chapter, the Internet solution uses a 16-bit port number as the address of a process. A port number for a particular application could be either a well-known number used by all hosts globally or any available number dynamically assigned by the local host.

5.1.2 Error Control and Reliability

Error control and reliability are important to end-to-end communication because the Internet occasionally loses, reorders, or duplicates packets. Error control focuses on detecting or recovering bit errors within a transferred data unit, be it a frame or a segment, while reliability further provides retransmission mechanisms to recover from what appears to be a missing or incorrectly received data unit. Table 5.1 indicates that the link protocols adopt error-control methods that operate on a per-frame basis, while the transport protocols adopt per-segment-based error control. The error detection code used in the link protocols and in the transport protocols are usually cyclic redundancy check (CRC) and checksum, respectively. As stated in Subsection 3.1.3, CRC is more robust in detecting multiple bit errors and easier to implement in hardware, while checksum in the transport protocols acts only as a double-check against nodal errors that occur in data processed at nodes.

For reliable transmission, end-to-end protocols provide per-flow reliability control, but most link protocols, such as Ethernet and PPP, do *not* incorporate retransmission in their mechanisms. They leave the burden of retransmission to their upper-layer protocols. However, some link protocols such as WLAN operate in environments where severe frame losses could occur, so these link protocols have built-in reliability mechanisms to improve the inefficiency resulting from *frequent* retransmissions by upper-layer protocols. For example, after a huge outgoing segment from the transport layer is split into 10 packets in the IP layer and then 10 frames in the WLAN, the WLAN can reliably transmit each of the 10 frames without appealing to end-to-end retransmission of the entire huge segment. The entire frame thus has a lower probability of being retransmitted end-to-end in comparison with the case if WLAN had no built-in reliability mechanism.

The latency distribution also is important to reliable transmission because it affects the design of the *retransmission timer*. As shown in Figure 5.1, the latency distribution of the link channel is condensed around a certain value, so it would be appropriate for us to set the retransmission timer of the link channel to timeout after a fixed period, say 10 ms. However, it is problematic to apply this technique to the transport layer due to the *diffused* latency distribution of the end-to-end channel. In Figure 5.1, for example, if we set the timeout value to 150 ms for an end-to-end channel, some segments would be falsely retransmitted and the network would contain many duplicate segments, but if we set the timeout value to 200 ms, lost segments would not be retransmitted until this long-waiting timer expires, resulting in poor performance. All these trade-offs influence the design choices of the link and end-to-end channels.

5.1.3 Rate Control: Flow Control and Congestion Control

Rate control, including flow control and congestion control, plays a more important role in transport protocols than in link protocols because the environment of wide area networks where the transport protocol operates is much more complex than that of local area networks where the link protocol runs. Flow control runs solely between the source and the destination, while congestion control runs between the source and the network. That is, congestion in the network could be alleviated by congestion control but not by flow control. There is no congestion control in link protocols because transmitters are only one hop away from the receivers.

Congestion control can be accomplished by the sender or by the network. Network-based congestion control employs various queuing disciplines and scheduling algorithms at intermediate routers to avoid network congestion. Sender-based congestion control relies on each sender's self-control to avoid sending too much data into the network too fast. Network-based congestion control, however, is beyond the scope of this chapter and shall be addressed in Chapter 7.

In literature, flow control or congestion control mechanisms can be classified into *window-based* and *rate-based*. Window-based control regulates the sending rate by controlling the number of *outstanding* packets that can be simultaneously in transit. An outstanding packet represents a packet that has been sent but its acknowledgment has not returned yet. On the other hand, a rate-based controlled sender directly adjusts its sending rate when receiving an explicit notification of how fast it should send.

Real-Time Requirements

Since real-time applications require extra information to construct the play-out, extra supports other than those just described should be available. They might include synchronization between audio and video streams, data compression and decompression information, and path quality statistics (packet loss rate, end-to-end latency, and its variations). To support these extra requirements, all required extra information, such as timestamp, codec type, and loss rate must be carried in the protocol message header. Since TCP and UDP do not have these fields in their headers, other transport protocols are needed to meet the real-time requirements.

5.1.4 Standard Programming Interfaces

Networking applications often access the underlying services through the *socket programming interfaces*. Most applications run over TCP or UDP, depending on whether they need reliability and rate control, and access them through the TCP sockets or UDP sockets, respectively. However, there are other applications that need to bypass the transport protocols to access the IP layer if they need to read or write the IP header, and some even need to access the link layer directly to read or write the link-layer header. Applications can access the IP layer and the link layer through the datagram sockets and raw sockets, respectively.

The BSD socket interface semantics has become the most widely used template in most operating systems, compared to the transport layer interface (TLI) socket and its standardized version X/Open TI (XTI), both of which were developed for AT&T Unix systems. With standardization of the socket programming interfaces, application programs are able to run on various operating systems that support the standard. However, developers often find porting efforts are still required for socket applications, for example, even for an application that has been running successfully on Linux to run over BSD, which differs from Linux only in error-handling functions.

5.1.5 Transport-Layer Packet Flows

During packet transmission, the transport layer receives data from the application layer through the socket interface, encapsulates the data with a TCP or UDP header, and passes the resultant segment on to the IP layer. Upon packet reception, the transport layer receives a segment from the IP layer, removes the TCP or UDP header, and passes the data to the application layer. The detailed packet flows are illustrated in Open Source Implementation 5.1.

Open Source Implementation 5.1: Transport-Layer Packet Flows in Call Graphs

Overview

The transport layer includes one interface with the IP layer and another with the application layer. As in Chapters 3 and 4, we examine these two interfaces through the reception path and the transmission path. In the reception path, a packet is received from the IP layer and then passed to an application layer protocol. In the transmission path, a packet is received from the application layer and then passed to the IP layer.

Data Structures

There are two data structures, `sk_buff` and `sock`, involved in almost every function call through the flows of packet processing. The former one, as defined in `include/linux/skbuff.h`, has been introduced in Chapter 1, while the definition of the latter one can be found in `include/linux/net/sock.h`. The `sock` structure for a TCP flow, for example, includes mainly a pointer to the structure `tcp_sock`, which maintains most necessary variables to run TCP, such as `srtt` for RTT estimation or `snd_wnd` for window congestion control. The `sock` also includes two queue structures, `sk_receive_queue` and `sk_write_queue`, to queue the packets received from the IP layer and the packets to be sent out, respectively. Moreover, the `sock` keeps the pointers to several callback functions to inform the application layer about new data available to be received or new memory space available to be filled.

Call Graphs

As shown in Figure 5.2, when the transport layer receives a packet from the IP layer, the packet is saved in an `skb` and passed to one of the three functions: `raw_v4_input()`, `udp_rcv()`, or `tcp_v4_rcv()`, based on its protocol id in the IP header. Then, each protocol has its associated lookup function, `_raw_v4_lookup()`, `udp_v4_lookup()`, and `inet_lookup()`, retrieve the `sock` structure corresponding to the packet. By the information in the `sock` structure, the transport layer can identify which flow an incoming packet belongs to. Then, the received packet is inserted into the queue of the flow by `skb_queue_tail()`.

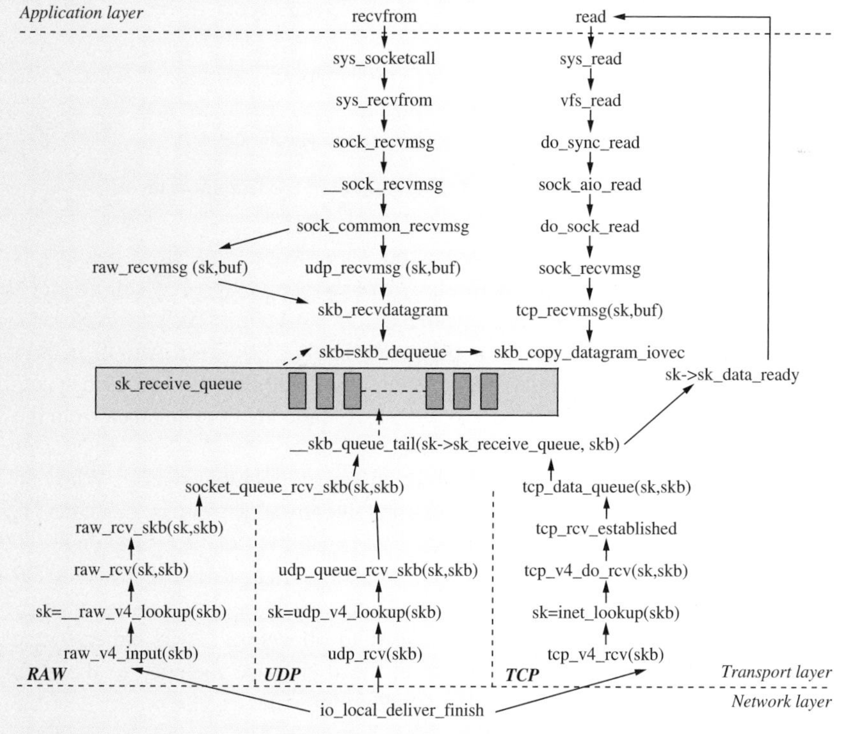

FIGURE 5.2 The call graph for an incoming packet in the transport layer.

Continued

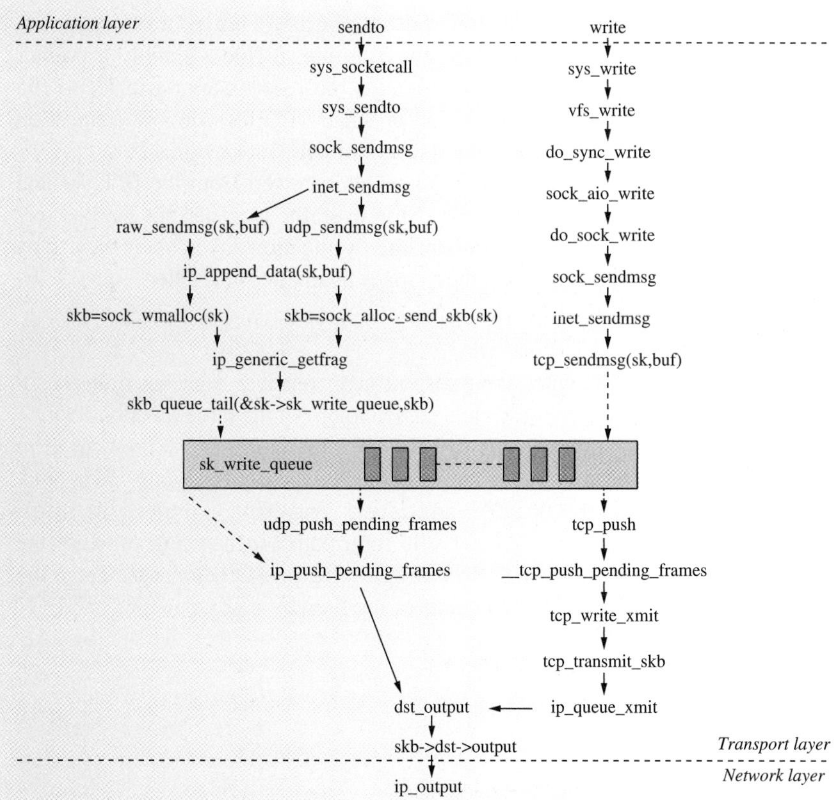

FIGURE 5.3 The call graph for an outgoing packet in the transport layer.

By `sk->sk_data_ready()`, the application where this flow belongs is notified of data being available for receipt. Next, the application may call `read()` or `recvfrom()` to obtain the data from the `sock` structure. The `recvfrom()` function triggers a series of function calls, and finally `skb_dequeue()` is used to remove the data from the queue corresponding to the flow into an `skb` space, and then `skb_copy_datagram_iovec()` is called to copy the data from the kernel-space memory to the user-space one.

Next, Figure 5.3 displays the call graph for an outgoing packet. When an application plans to send data into the Internet, it calls `write()` or `sendto()`, which then calls `raw_sendmsg()`, `udp_sendmsg()`, or `tcp_sendmsg()` based on the protocol specified when the socket is created. For a raw or UDP socket, `ip_append_data()` is called. Then, `sock_alloc_send_skb()` and `ip_generic_getfrag()` are called to allocate an `skb` buffer in the kernel-space memory and copy data from the user-space memory to the `skb` buffer, respectively. Finally, the `skb` is inserted into `sk_write_queue` of the `sock` structure. On the other hand, `ip_push_pending_frame()` repeatedly removes data from the queue and then forwards them to the IP layer. Similarly, for a TCP socket, `tcp_sendmsg()` and `skb_add_data()` are used to remove the tail `skb` from the queue and copy data into the kernel-space memory, respectively. If the amount of written data is more than the space available to the tail `skb`, a new skb buffer can be allocated in the kernel-space memory by `sk_stream_alloc_page()`. Finally, `ip_queue_xmit()` is called to forward data from the `sk_write_queue` into the IP layer via the `ip_output()` function.

Exercises

1. With the call graph shown in Figure 5.3, you can trace `udp_sendmsg()` and `tcp_sendmsg()` to figure out how exactly these functions are implemented.
2. Explain what the two big "while" loops in `tcp_sendmsg()` are intended for. Why are such loop structures not shown in `udp_sendmsg()`?

5.2 UNRELIABLE CONNECTIONLESS TRANSFER: UDP

User Datagram Protocol (UDP) is an *unreliable connectionless* transport protocol that does not provide reliability and rate control. It is a stateless protocol in that the sending or receiving of a segment is independent of that of any other segments. Although error control is also provided by UDP, it is optional. Due to its simplicity and nonretransmission design, many real-time applications where reliability is less of an issue adopt RTP over UDP to transmit real-time or streaming data. In recent years, peer-to-peer applications use UDP to send a large volume of queries to peers and then use TCP to exchange data with selected peers.

UDP provides the simplest transport services: (1) process-to-process communication channel and (2) *per-segment* error control.

5.2.1 Header Format

The UDP header serves only two functions: addressing and error detection. It consists of four fields: source and destination port number, UDP length, and UDP checksum, as shown in Figure 5.4. To provide a communication channel between two application processes that reside on different hosts in the Internet, each process should bind to a locally unique *port number* on its local host. Though each host handles the binding of ports to its processes independently, it proves useful to bind frequently used

FIGURE 5.4 UDP datagram format.

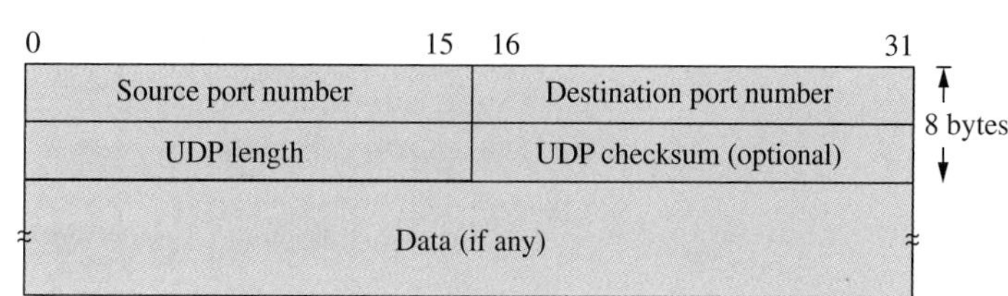

server processes (e.g., WWW) to *fixed* port numbers that are made well known to the public. Their services can then be accessed through the *well-known ports*. The port numbers of the client processes, however, are randomly selected for binding and are not necessary to be well known.

The source/destination port numbers, concatenated with the source and destination IP addresses and protocol ID (indicating TCP or UDP) in the IP header, form a *socket pair* of *5-tuple* with a total length of $32 \times 2 + 16 \times 2 + 8 = 104$ bits. Since the IP address is globally unique and the port number is locally unique, the 5-tuple thus uniquely identifies a *flow* of the process-to-process communication channel. In other words, packets of the same flow would have the same 5-tuple values. For IPv6 packets, the field "flow id" in the IP header is specifically designed for flow identification. Note that a socket pair is *full-duplex,* which means data can be transmitted through the socket connection in both directions simultaneously. In Figure 5.1, outgoing packets from application process AP1 flow from its source port to the destination port bound to application process AP3. Any data encapsulated with the same 5-tuple fields by application process AP1 on host 1 can be accurately transported to application process AP3 on host 2 without ambiguity.

UDP allows applications on different hosts to send data segments directly to one another without having to establish a connection first. A UDP port accepts segments from a local application process, packs them into units called datagrams of no more than 64K bytes, and fills the 16-bit source and destination port numbers and other UDP header fields of the datagrams. Each datagram is sent as a separate IP packet that is forwarded hop-by-hop to the destination as illustrated in Chapter 4. When the IP packets containing UDP data reach their destination, they are directed to the UDP port bound to the receiving application process.

5.2.2 Error Control: Per-Segment Checksum

Besides port numbers, the UDP header also provides a 16-bit checksum field for checking on the integrity of each datagram, as shown in Figure 5.4. Since the checksum computation for a UDP datagram is optional, it can be disabled by setting the checksum field to zero. The sender generates the checksum value and fills in the checksum field, which is to be verified by the receiver. To ensure that each received datagram is exactly the same as the one sent by the sender, the receiver recalculates the checksum with the received datagram and verifies if the result matches the value stored in the UDP checksum field. UDP receivers will *drop* the datagrams whose checksum field does not match the result they have calculated. This mechanism ensures per-segment data integrity but not per-segment data *reliability*.

The UDP checksum field stores the 1's complement of the sum of all 16-bit words in the header *and* payload. Its calculation is similar to IP checksum calculation discussed in Chapter 4. If a UDP datagram contains an odd number of octets to be check-summed, the last octet is *padded* at the end with zero bits to form a 16-bit word for checksum computation. Note that the pad is not transmitted as part of the datagram because the checksum verification at the receiver follows the same padding procedure. The checksum also covers a 96-bit *pseudo header,* consisting of four fields in the IP header: the source IP address, the destination IP address, protocol, and length. Checksum covering the pseudo header enables the receiver to detect the datagrams with incorrect delivery, protocol, or length information. For the case that the checksum computation results in zero, 0xFFFF is filled into the field. Open Source Implementation 5.2 details the checksum calculation process.

UDP checksum, though optional, is highly recommended because some link protocols do not perform error control. When implementing UDP over IPv6, checksum becomes mandatory as IPv6 does not provide checksum at all. UDP checksum is omitted only for some real-time applications where latency and jitter between the application processes are more critical than error control.

Open Source Implementation 5.2: UDP and TCP Checksum

Overview

The flowchart of checksum calculation along with IP checksum in Linux 2.6 can be learned by tracing source code from the function `tcp_v4_send_check()` in `tcp_ipv4.c`. The flowchart of UDP checksum is exactly the same as that of TCP.

Data Structures

A field called `csum` in the `skb` structure is to store the checksum of the application data carried by an `sk_buff`. The definition of `csum` can be found in `include/linux/skbuff.h`. When a packet is to be sent out, the value in `skb->csum` would be passed with *the packet header* to the checksum function to calculate the final checksum of the packet.

Algorithm Implementation

Figure 5.5 lists the partial code in `tcp_v4_send_check()`. The application data is first check-summed into `skb->csum`, and then by the functional call `csum_partial()`, `skb->csum` is check-summed again with the transport layer header referenced by pointer `th`. The calculated result is again check-summed with the source and destination IP addresses in the IP header by `tcp_v4_check()`, which wraps `csum_tcpudp_magic()`. The final result is stored in the TCP/UDP checksum field. On the other hand, the IP checksum is computed from the IP header independently, which could be found in `net/ipv4/af_inet.c` by searching the term "`iph->check`".

```
th->check = tcp_v4_check(len, inet->saddr, inet->daddr,
     csum_partial((char *)th,
     th->doff << 2,
     skb->csum));
```

FIGURE 5.5 The partial code for the checksum procedure of TCP/IP.

Continued

Block Diagram

The flowchart of checksum calculation is plotted in Figure 5.6 according to the preceding description. We can summarize several findings from the figure: (1) The transport-layer checksum is calculated from the checksum of application data; (2) the IP checksum does not cover the IP payload. In Figure 5.6, `D` stands for the pointer to the application data, `lenD` for the length of the application data, `T` for the pointer to the transport layer header (TCP or UDP), `lenT` for the length of the transport layer header, `lenS` for the length of the segment (including the segment header), `iph` for the pointer to the IP header, `SA` for the source IP address, and `DA` for the destination IP address.

Exercises

If you look at the definition of `csum` in the `sk_buff`, you may find its 4-byte memory space is shared with another two variables: `csum_start` and `csum_offset`. Explain the usages of these two variables and why both variables share with `csum` the same memory space.

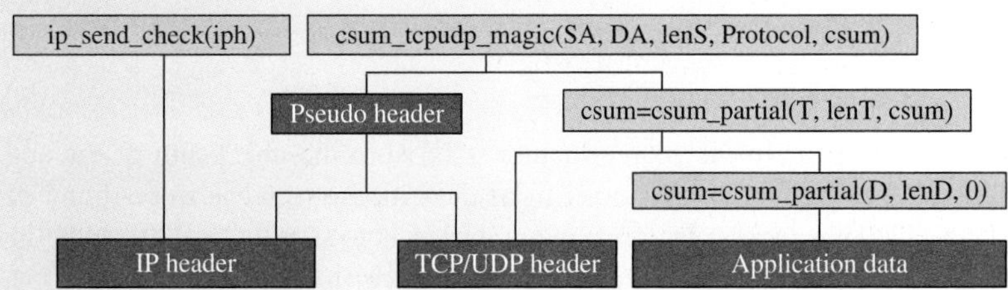

FIGURE 5.6 Checksum calculations of TCP/IP headers in Linux 2.6.

5.2.3 Carrying Unicast/Multicast Real-Time Traffic

Due to its simplicity, UDP is a suitable carrier for unicast or multicast real-time traffic. This is because real-time traffic has the following properties: (1) it does *not* need per-flow reliability (retransmitting a lost real-time packet could be meaningless because the packet might not arrive in time), and (2) its bit rate (bandwidth) depends mainly on the selected codec and is unlikely to be flow controllable. These two properties simplify the transport layer for real-time traffic to offering the addressing service only.

However, besides the basic process-to-process communication service, real-time applications also require additional services, which include synchronization between audio and video streams, data compression and decompression information, and path quality statistics. These services are mostly provided by the RTP, and therefore, in Section 5.5 we shall investigate the design of the RTP, which is built on top of UDP.

5.3 RELIABLE CONNECTION-ORIENTED TRANSFER: TCP

The majority of networking applications today use Transmission Control Protocol (TCP) to communicate because it provides reliable, in-order data delivery. Furthermore, TCP automatically adapts its sending rate to network congestion or changes in the receiving capability of the receiver.

TCP aims to provide (1) addressing of process-to-process communication channels, (2) per-segment error control, (3) per-flow reliability, and (4) per-flow flow control and congestion control. Addressing of channels and per-segment error control in TCP are the same as those in UDP. Since the latter two objectives are on a per-flow basis, we first discuss how a TCP flow is established and released in Subsection 5.3.1, and then illustrate TCP's reliability control in Subsection 5.3.2. Flow control and congestion control of TCP are presented in Subsection 5.3.3 and Subsection 5.3.4, respectively. The TCP header format is then elaborated in Subsection 5.3.5. Timer management issues of TCP are discussed in Subsection 5.3.6. Finally, TCP's performance problems and enhancements are addressed in Subsection 5.3.7.

5.3.1 Connection Management

Connection management deals with the process of end-to-end connection establishment and termination. As in UDP, a TCP connection is uniquely identified by the 5-tuple: source/destination IP addresses, source/destination port numbers, and the protocol ID. Establishing and terminating a TCP connection is similar to talking to someone over the phone in daily life. To talk to someone over the phone, we pick up the phone and then choose the callee's phone number (IP address) and extension number (port number) to dial. Next, we dial to the callee (issuing a connection request), wait for the response (connection establishment), and begin to speak (transferring data). Finally, we say goodbye and hand up the phone (disconnection).

Establishing a connection over the Internet is not as easy as it sounds due to the fact that the Internet occasionally loses, stores, and duplicates packets. In the Internet, packets are sent to their destination in the "store-and-forward" manner; that is, intermediate routers first store the received packets and then forward them to their destination or to the next hop. Storing packets in the Internet introduces packet delay and duplication that could confuse a sender or a receiver, and it is especially complicated to resolve the ambiguities if packets could live forever in the network. TCP chose to restrict the maximum lifetime of a packet to 120 seconds. Under this choice, TCP employs the three-way handshake protocol proposed by Tomlinson in 1975 to resolve the ambiguities caused by *delayed duplicate* packets.

Connection Establishment/Termination: Three-Way Handshake Protocol

At connection startup, both client and server processes randomly choose their initial sequence number (ISN) to reduce the ambiguous effects introduced by the delayed duplicate packets. When a client process wants to establish a connection with a server process, as shown in Figure 5.7(a), it sends a SYN segment specifying (1) the

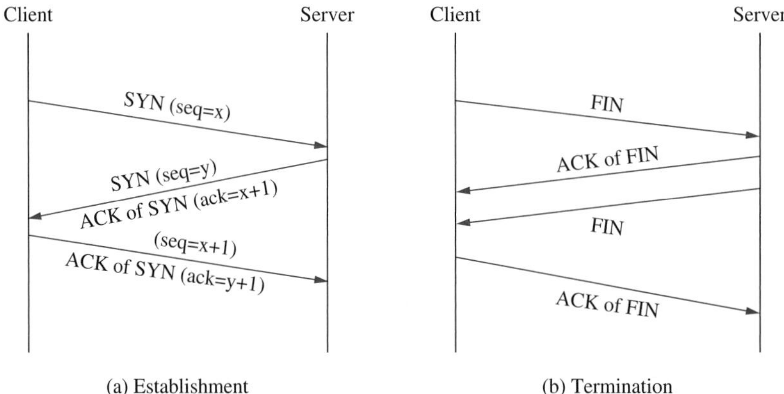

FIGURE 5.7 Handshake protocols for TCP connection establishment and termination.

port number of the server that the client wants to connect to and (2) the ISN of the data segments sent from the client. The server process responds to the SYN segment with an (ACK+SYN) segment to (1) acknowledge the request and also to (2) declare the ISN of the data segments sent from the server process. Finally, the client process must also acknowledge the SYN from the server process to confirm the connection establishment. Note that to notify the ISN of each direction, the sequence numbers and acknowledgment numbers must follow the semantics depicted in Figure 5.7(a). This protocol is known as the *three-way handshake protocol.*

The TCP connection termination takes four segments rather than three. As shown in Figure 5.7(b), it is a two-way handshaking for each direction, which consists of a FIN segment followed by an ACK of FIN segment. A TCP connection is *full-duplex*—data flowing from client to server or from server to client are independent of each other. Since closing one direction with a FIN segment does not affect the other direction, the other direction should also be closed with another FIN segment. Note that it is possible to close a connection by a 3-way handshake. That is, the client sends a FIN, the server replies with a FIN+ACK (just combines two segments into one), and finally the client replies with an ACK.

The party that sends the first SYN to initiate a TCP connection is said to perform an *active open,* while its peer that listens on the port to accept the incoming connection request is said to perform a *passive open*. Similarly, the party that sends the first FIN to terminate a TCP connection is said to perform an *active close,* and its peer performs a *passive close*. The details of their differences can be illustrated by the TCP state transition diagram described next.

TCP State Transition

A TCP connection progresses through a series of states during its lifetime. There are 11 possible states for a TCP connection, which are: LISTEN, SYN-SENT, SYN-RECEIVED, ESTABLISHED, FIN-WAIT-1, FIN-WAIT-2, CLOSE-WAIT, CLOSING, LAST-ACK, TIME-WAIT, and the fictional state CLOSED. CLOSED is fictional because it represents the state where the TCP connection is terminated. The meanings of TCP states are:

- LISTEN—waiting for a connection request from any remote TCP client.
- SYN-SENT—waiting for a matching connection request after having sent a connection request.
- SYN-RECEIVED—waiting for an acknowledgment of a connection request after having both received and sent a connection request.
- ESTABLISHED—an open connection; data can be sent in both directions. The normal state for the data transfer phase of the connection.
- FIN-WAIT-1—waiting for a connection termination request from the remote TCP, or an acknowledgment of the connection termination request previously sent.
- FIN-WAIT-2—waiting for a connection termination request from the remote TCP.
- CLOSE-WAIT—waiting for a connection termination request from the local user.
- CLOSING—waiting for an acknowledgment of a connection termination request from the remote TCP.
- LAST-ACK—waiting for an acknowledgment of the connection termination request previously sent to the remote TCP.
- TIME_WAIT—waiting for enough time before transitioning to the CLOSED state to ensure the remote TCP receives its last ACK.

As defined in RFC 793, TCP works by running a state machine as shown in Figure 5.8. Both client and server processes behave following this state transition diagram. Bold arrows and dashed arrows in the figure correspond to *normal* state transitions of the client and the server process, respectively. The entire state transition in Figure 5.8 can be divided into three phases: *connection establishment, data transfer,* and *connection termination*. A TCP connection enters the *data transfer* phase when both the client and the server transit to the ESTABLISHED state. In the *data transfer* phase, the client can send a request for service to the server; once the request has been granted, both parties can send data to each other over the TCP connection. In case of data service, most often the server process acts as a TCP sender transferring requested data files to the client process.

The state transitions of normal *connection establishment* and *connection termination* are shown in Figure 5.9, with labels indicating the states entered by the client and the server. Since it is possible for two sides to send a SYN to each other at the same time to establish a TCP connection, even though the possibility is small, the state transitions are also considered for this "simultaneous open" in Figure 5.8. Figure 5.10(a) shows the state transitions in simultaneous open. Similarly, it is permitted in TCP for both sides to do close, which is called "simultaneous close." The state transitions in this case are shown in Figure 5.10(b).

On the other hand, the state transitions in some abnormal cases, including lost SYN, lost SYN/ACK, and lost ACK during the connection establishment, are exhibited in Figure 5.11(a), (b), and (c), respectively. Lost segments trigger connection timeout at the client, which then returns to the CLOSED state, as seen in Figure 5.11(a) and (b). Connection timeout at the server in Figure 5.11(b) and (c),

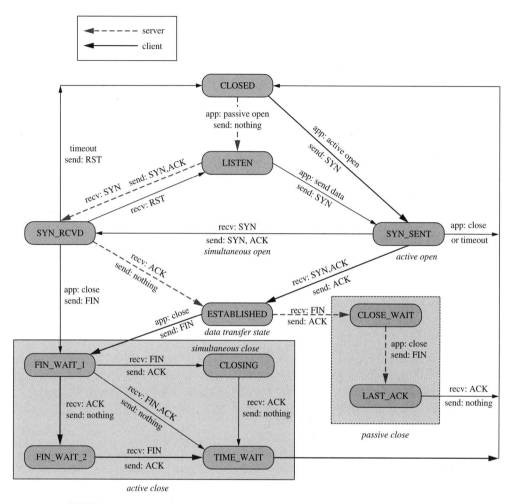

FIGURE 5.8 TCP state transition diagram.

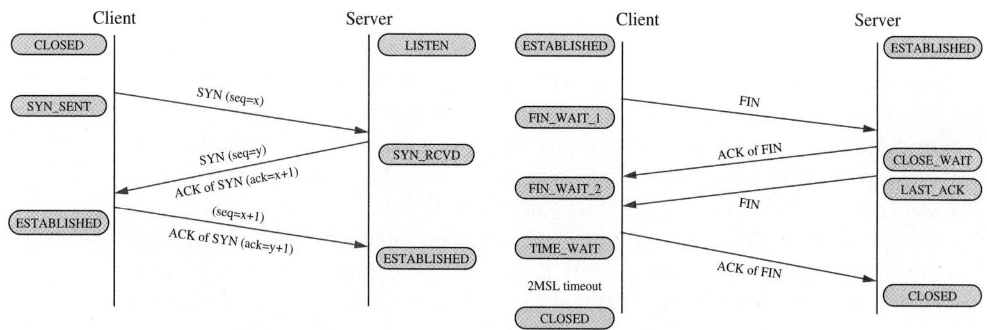

FIGURE 5.9 State transitions in connection establishment and termination.

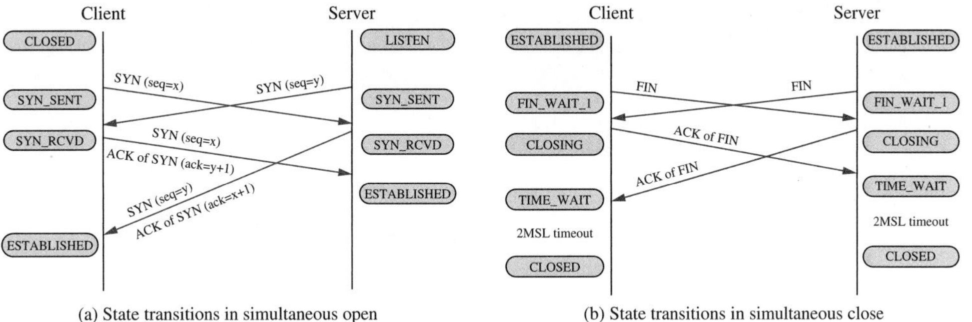

(a) State transitions in simultaneous open (b) State transitions in simultaneous close

FIGURE 5.10 State transitions in simultaneous open and simultaneous close.

however, results in returning to the CLOSED state and an RST segment being sent to reset the client's state.

There are also some other abnormal cases, for example, half-open connections, during the connection termination. A TCP connection is referred to as *half-open* when the host at one end of that TCP connection has crashed. If the remaining end is idle,

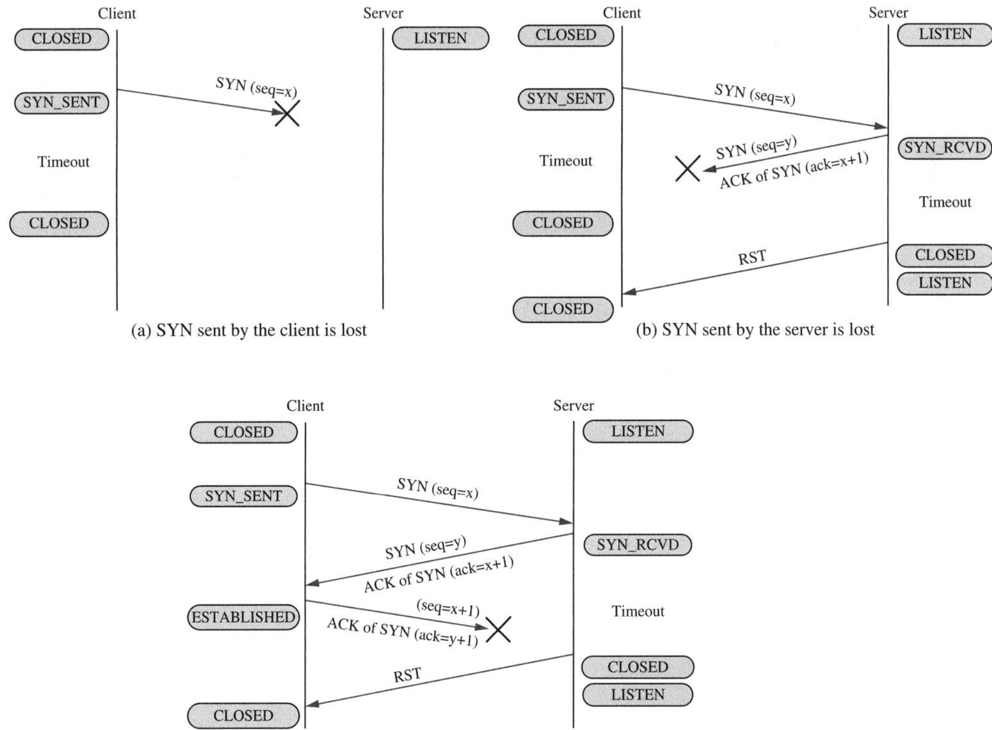

FIGURE 5.11 State transitions with packet loss in connection establishment.

the connection may remain in the half-open state for an unbounded period of time. The keepalive timer, which shall be introduced in Subsection 5.3.6, can solve this problem.

5.3.2 Reliability of Data Transfers

TCP uses checksum for per-segment error control and uses acknowledged sequence numbers for per-flow reliability control. The differences in their objectives and solutions are described here.

Per-Segment Error Control: Checksum

As mentioned in Section 5.2, TCP checksum calculation is exactly the same as that of UDP. It also covers some fields in the IP header to ensure that the packet has arrived at the correct destination. While UDP checksum is optional, TCP checksum is *mandatory*. Although both protocols provide a checksum field for data integrity, the checksum is a relatively weak check, as discussed in Section 3.1, compared to the 32-bit cyclic redundancy check used in Ethernet.

Per-Flow Reliability: Sequence Number and Acknowledgment

Per-segment checksum is inadequate to guarantee *reliable* and *in-order* delivery of a *whole* flow of packetized data that are transferred sequentially to the destination over a process-to-process channel. Since the packetized data may get lost occasionally in the Internet, there must be a mechanism to *retransmit* the lost ones. Moreover, because packets sent in sequence might be received out of order due to the stateless routing nature of the Internet, another mechanism must be presented to *resequence* the out-of-order packets. These two mechanisms rely on *acknowledgments* (ACKs) and *sequence number,* respectively, to provide per-flow reliability.

Conceptually, each octet of data is assigned a sequence number. Then, the sequence number of a segment represents the sequence number of its *first* data octet, which is stored in the 32-bit sequence number field of its TCP header. The TCP sender numbers and tracks its data octets that have been sent already and waits for their acknowledgments. On receiving a data segment, the TCP receiver replies with an ACK segment, which carries an *acknowledgment number* indicating (1) the expected sequence number of the *next* data segment and (2) that all data octets preceding the specified ACK number have been successfully received. For example, the TCP receiver may acknowledge a successfully received segment by replying an ACK=x, where x indicates: "All data octets preceding x have been received. The next expected segment's sequence number is x. Send it to me."

There are two possible types of ACKs: *selective ACK* and *cumulative ACK*. The selective ACK indicates that the receiver has received a segment whose sequence number is equal to the specified ACK number. The cumulative ACK indicates that all previous data octets preceding the specified ACK number have been received. Since asymmetric links are popular, such that the congestion might happen in the reverse path from client (the receiver end) to server (the sender end), ACKs could be lost more often than data. Therefore, TCP uses the cumulative ACK to compensate for the lost ACK with the subsequent ACKs.

Abnormal Cases: Data Loss, ACK Loss, Delay, and Out-of-Sequence

Figure 5.12 illustrates four abnormal cases that could occur during a TCP transmission. In the case of data loss, the sender will perceive this loss after the retransmission timeout, and then will retransmit the missing segment, as illustrated in Figure 5.12(a). On the other hand, a long propagation delay may cause a premature timeout, resulting in unnecessary retransmissions. As we can see in Figure 5.12(b), the receiver would regard the retransmitted packet as duplicate data and just drop it. In this case, the reliability is still guaranteed, but the bandwidth would be significantly wasted if this happened frequently. Thus, how to estimate a proper retransmission timeout is very important, and this estimation is explained in Subsection 5.3.6.

Figure 5.12(c) shows the benefit of using cumulative ACK in TCP. Here the ACK loss does not cause any unnecessary data retransmission because the subsequent ACK repeats the acknowledgment information in the lost ACK, i.e., ACK=180 repeats the information in the lost ACK=150. Using cumulative ACK also leads to an interesting situation when data segments are received *out-of-sequence*.

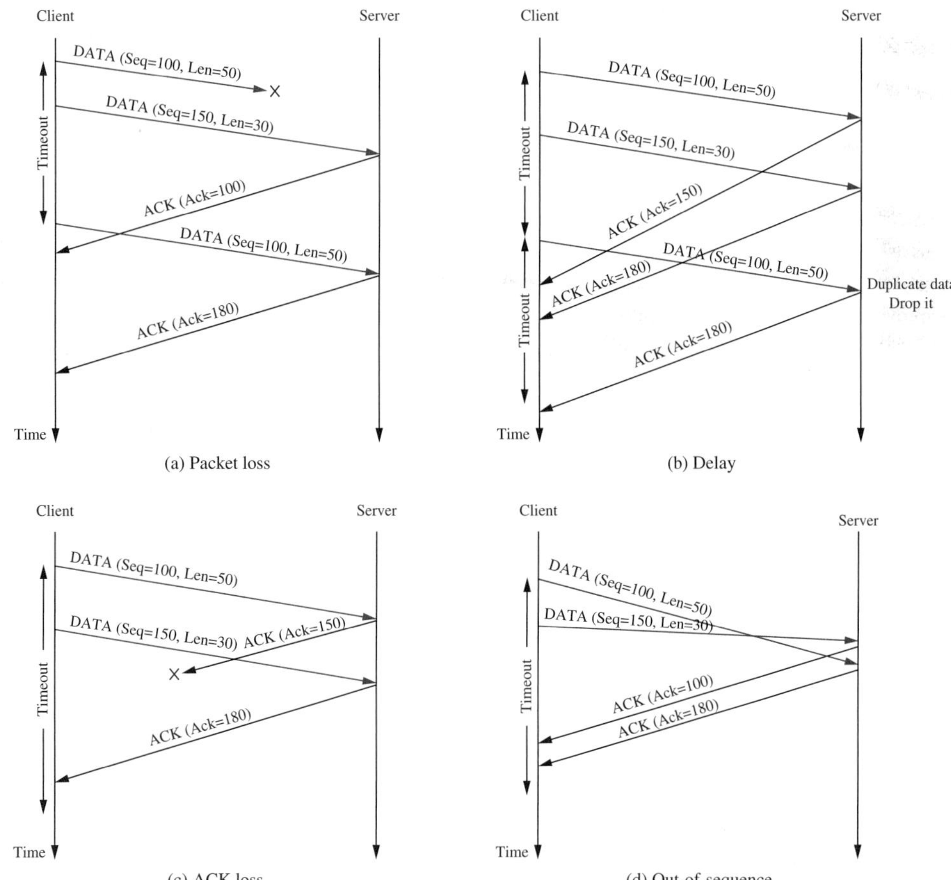

FIGURE 5.12 TCP reliability.

The receiver replies *duplicate ACKs* upon receiving next data segments, as shown in Figure 5.12(d), as if there were missing segments at the receiver. From Figure 5.12, we can understand that TCP can achieve the reliable transfer, with cumulative ACK and retransmission timeouts for acknowledgments.

5.3.3 TCP Flow Control

The latency distribution in the Internet is so diffused that the TCP sender needs to be intelligent and adaptive enough to maximize the performance while being polite to its receiver's buffer space and other senders' share of the network resources. TCP employs *window-based* flow control and congestion control mechanisms to determine how fast it should send in various conditions. By flow control the TCP sender can know how much bandwidth it can consume without overflowing its receiver's buffer. Similarly, by congestion control the TCP sender avoids overburdening the globally shared network resources. This subsection describes TCP flow control and leaves TCP congestion control to the next subsection.

Sliding-Window Flow Control

The window-based flow control exercises the sliding-window mechanism for the purpose of increasing the data transmission throughput. The sender maintains a window of sequence numbers, called *sending window,* which is described by a starting sequence number and an end sequence number. Only data segments with sequence numbers within this sending window can be sent. Data segments sent but not acknowledged are kept in a retransmission buffer. When the data segment with the starting sequence number has been acknowledged, this sending window will *slide*.

Figure 5.13 shows the pseudocode of sliding window in the sender. Also Figure 5.14 shows an example of sliding window. For clarity, we assume all segments have the same size. In Figure 5.14, in order to send a flow of segmented byte-stream data in sequence, the window only slides from left to right. In order to control the amount of *outstanding* segments in transit, the window augments and shrinks dynamically, as we shall see later. As the data segments flow toward the destination, the corresponding ACK

```
SWS: send window size.
n: current sequence number, i.e., the next packet to be transmitted.

LAR: last acknowledgment received.

if the sender has data to send
    Transmit up to SWS packets ahead of the latest acknowledgment LAR,
    i.e., it may transmit packet number n as long as n < LAR+SWS.
endif

if an ACK arrives,
    Set LAR as ack num if its ack num > LAR.
endif
```

FIGURE 5.13 Pseudocode of sliding window in the sender.

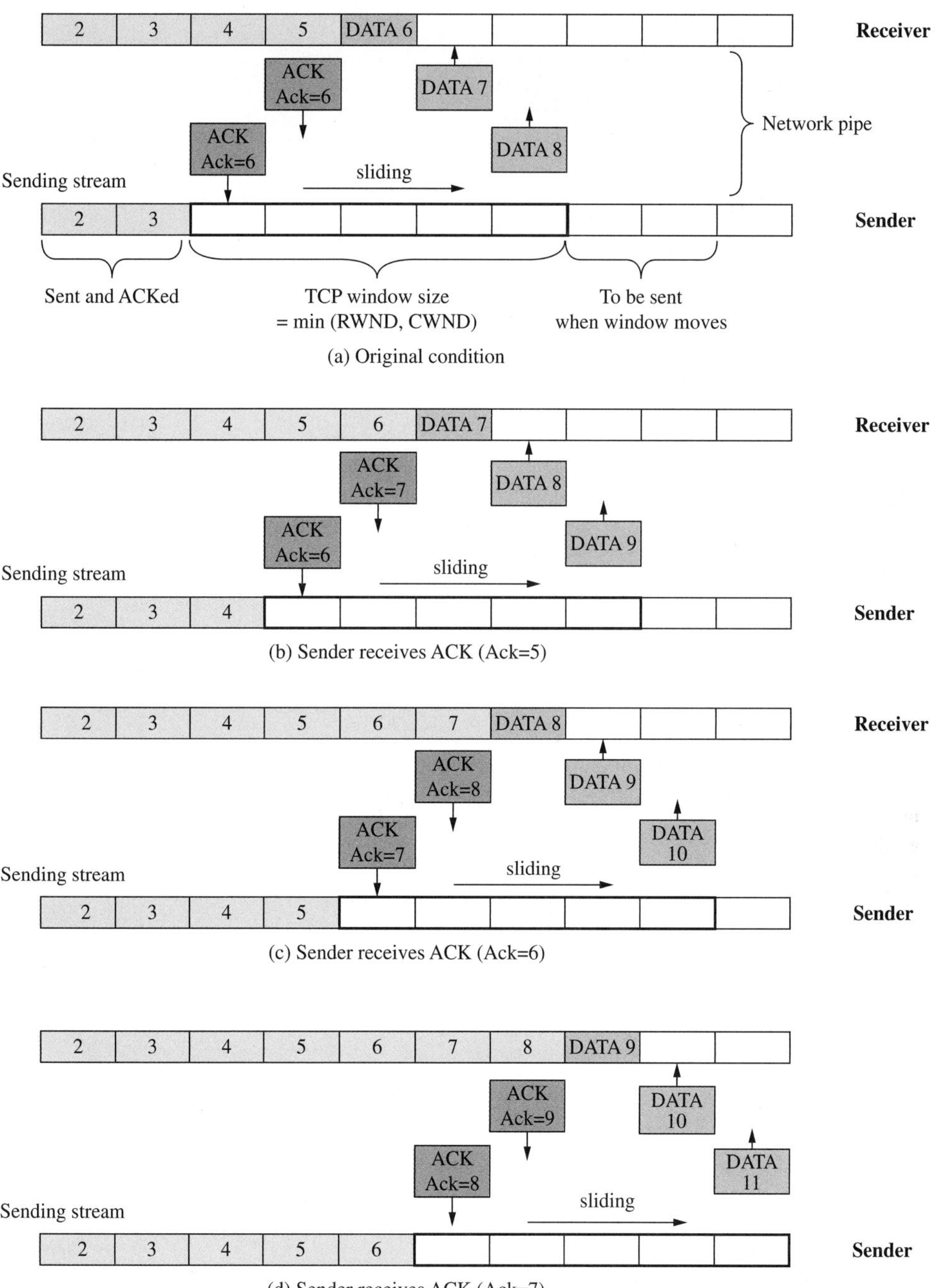

FIGURE 5.14 Visualization of a TCP sliding window.

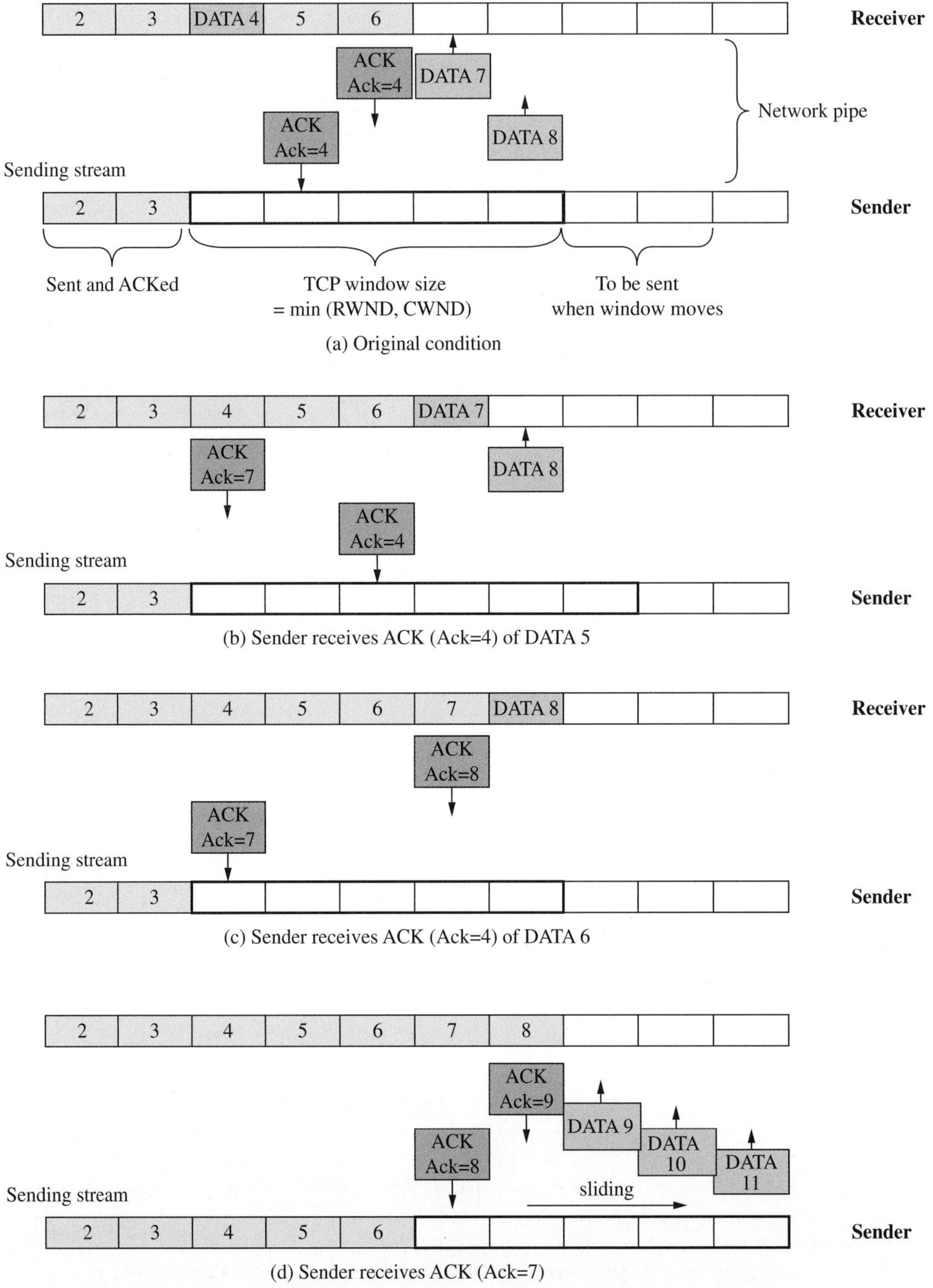

FIGURE 5.15 An example of TCP sliding window when data packets are out of sequence.

segments flow backward to the sender to trigger the sliding of the window. Whenever the window covers the segments that have not been transmitted, the segments are sent to the network pipe. In the original case, as shown in Figure 5.14(a), the range of the sliding window is segment 4 to segment 8, i.e., these segments have been sent. The sender receives the ACK (Ack=5), representing that the receiver has successfully received segment 4, the first segment of the sliding window. Therefore, the sender slides the window by one segment, as Figure 5.14(b) shows. Similarly, Figure 5.14(c) and (d) illustrate the sliding of the window when the sender receives ACK (Ack=6) and ACK (Ack=7), respectively. In the normal case, the sender slides the window by one segment when it receives an in-sequence ACK.

Now we observe the other condition where the packets arrive at the receiver out of sequence, as shown in Figure 5.15. In this case, the receiver first receives DATA 5, DATA 6, and then DATA 4. Since TCP uses cumulative acknowledgment, the sender will receive the first duplicate ACK (Ack=4) from the receiver upon receiving DATA 5, as seen in Figure 5.15(b). Now the window cannot slide. When the sender receives the second duplicate ACK (Ack=4) from the receiver upon receiving DATA 6, the window still cannot slide, as shown Figure 5.15(c). When the sender receives the ACK (Ack=7) from the receiver upon receiving delayed DATA 4, it slides the window by three segments.

Augmenting and Shrinking of Window Size

Another important issue in sliding-window flow control is the window size. The window size is determined by the minimum of two window values: *receiver window* (RWND) and *congestion window* (CWND), as illustrated in Figure 5.16. A TCP sender tries to simultaneously consider its receiver's capability (RWND) and network capacity (CWND) by constraining its sending rate to *min*(RWND,CWND). The RWND is *advertised* by the receiver, while CWND is *computed* by the sender as will be explored in Subsection 5.3.4. Note that the window size is actually counted in *bytes* rather than in *segments*. A TCP receiver advertises the amount of bytes available in its buffer into the 16-bit window size in the TCP header. The advertisement is used only when the segment has an acknowledgment, that is, when the ACK control bit is set. On the other hand, a TCP sender infers the amount of bytes allowed in the network in units of maximum segment size (MSS).

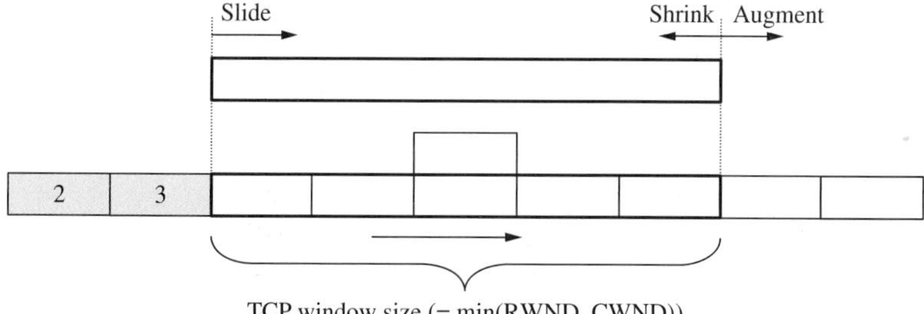

FIGURE 5.16 Window sizing and sliding.

Open Source Implementation 5.3: TCP Sliding-Window Flow Control

Overview

Linux 2.6 kernel implements the `tcp_write_xmit()` function in `tcp_output.c` to write packets onto the network. The function checks whether anything can be sent out by consulting the `tcp_snd_test()` function, where the kernel does several tests based on the concept of sliding window.

Algorithm Implementations

Three check functions are called in `tcp_snd_test()`: `tcp_cwnd_test()`, `tcp_snd_wnd_test()`, and `tcp_nagle_test()`. In `tcp_cwnd_test()`, by evaluating the condition `tcp_packets_in_flight() < tp->snd_cwnd`, the kernel judges whether the number of outstanding segments, including normal and retransmitted segments, is more than the current network capacity (`cwnd`). Secondly, in `tcp_snd_wnd_test()`, the kernel determines whether the latest sent segment has exceeded the limit of the receiver's buffer by the function call `after(TCP_SKBCB(skb))->end_seq, tp->snd_una + tp->snd_wnd)`. The `after(x,y)` function is a Boolean function corresponding to "x>y". If the latest sent segment (`end_seq`) has already been beyond the boundary of the unacknowledged octet (`snd_una`) plus the window size (`snd_wnd`), the sender should stop sending. Thirdly, in `tcp_nagle_test()`, the kernel performs the Nagle's test by `tcp_nagle_check()` which will be addressed in Subsection 5.3.7. Only if the segment passes these checks can the kernel call the `tcp_transmit_skb()` function to send out one more segment within the window.

Another interesting behavior we can observe from this implementation is that the Linux 2.6 kernel uses the finest granularity in sending out the segments within the window size. That is, it emits only *one* segment upon passing all the preceding tests and repeats all the tests for the *next* segment to be sent. If any window augmenting or shrinking happens during the process of sending out segments, the kernel can immediately change the number of allowable segments on the network. However, doing so introduces large overhead because it sends only one segment at a time.

Exercises

In `tcp_snd_test()`, there is another function `tcp_init_tso_segs()` called before the three check functions mentioned above. Explain what this function is for.

5.3.4 TCP Congestion Control

A TCP sender is designed to infer network congestion by detecting loss events of data segments. After a loss event, the sender politely slows down its transmission rate to keep the data flow below the rate that would trigger loss events. This process is called *congestion control,* which aims at achieving efficient resource utilization while avoiding network congestion. Generally speaking, the idea of TCP congestion control is for each TCP sender to determine the available bandwidth of the routing path from the sender to the receiver, so it knows how many segments can be in transit safely.

From Basic TCP, Tahoe, Reno to NewReno, SACK/FACK, and Vegas

The TCP protocol has evolved for over two decades, and many versions of TCP have been proposed to elevate transmission performance. The first version standardized in RFC 793 in 1981 defines the basic structure of TCP: i.e., the window-based flow control and a coarse-grain retransmission timer. Note that RFC 793 does *not* define congestion control mechanisms because in those days, the teletype network devices in use had per-link flow control and the Internet traffic was much less than it is today. TCP congestion control was introduced into the Internet in the late 1980s by Van Jacobson, roughly eight years after the TCP/IP protocol suite had become operational. At that time, the Internet had begun suffering from *congestion collapse*—hosts would send their packets into the Internet as fast as the receiver's advertised window would allow, then congestion would occur at some routers, causing packets to be dropped, and the hosts would timeout and retransmit the lost packets, resulting in even more serious congestion. Thus, TCP Tahoe, the second version released in BSD 4.2 in 1988, added the *congestion avoidance* and the *fast retransmit* scheme proposed by Van Jacobson. The third version, TCP Reno, extended the congestion control by including *fast recovery*. TCP Reno was standardized in RFC 2001 and generalized in RFC 2581. TCP Reno had become the most popular version by the year 2000, but in a recent report, TCP NewReno has now become more popular.

Several shortcomings exist in TCP Reno. The most noticeable is the *multiple-packet-loss* (MPL) problem that Reno often causes a timeout and results in low utilization when multiple segments are lost in a *short* interval. NewReno, SACK (Selective ACKnowledgment, defined in RFC 1072), and Vegas (proposed by L. Brakmo and L. Peterson in 1995) seek to resolve this problem with three different approaches. The TCP FACK (Forward ACKnowledgment) version then further improved the TCP SACK version. We first examine the basic versions of TCP congestion control, namely TCP Tahoe and TCP Reno. Further improvements through NewReno, SACK, FACK, and Vegas are left to Subsection 5.3.7.

TCP Tahoe Congestion Control

Tahoe uses a congestion window (`cwnd`) to control the amount of transmitted data in one round-trip time (RTT) and a maximum window (`mwnd`) to constrain the maximum value of `cwnd`. Tahoe estimates the amount of outstanding data, `awnd`, as `snd.nxt - snd.una`, where snd.nxt and snd.una are the sequence numbers

Historical Evolution: Statistics of TCP Versions

TCP NewReno has gradually become the major version of TCP in the Internet. According to a report from the International Computer Science Institute (ICSI), among all the 35,242 Web servers successfully identified in the report, the percentage of servers using TCP NewReno increased from 35% in 2001 to 76% in 2004. The percentage of servers supporting TCP SACK also increased from 40% in 2001 to 68% in 2004. Furthermore, TCP NewReno and SACK are enabled in several popular operating systems, including Linux, Windows XP, and Solaris. In contrast to the increasing usage of NewReno and SACK, the percentage of TCP Reno and Tahoe decreased to 5% and 2%, respectively. Among the reasons why TCP NewReno and SACK have been adopted quickly are that they provide higher throughput, a desirable property to users, and do not worsen network congestion, a primary concern of network administrators.

of the next unsent data and unacknowledged data, respectively. Whenever `awnd` is less than `cwnd`, the sender continues sending new packets. Otherwise, the sender stops. The control scheme of Tahoe can be divided into four states, whose transition diagram is depicted in Figure 5.17 and interpreted as follows:

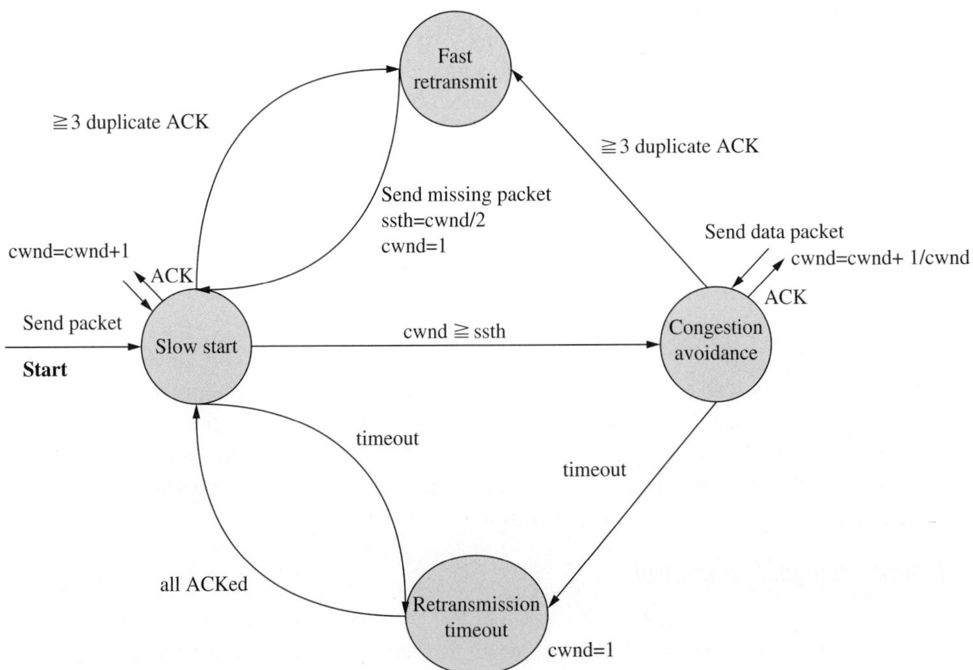

FIGURE 5.17 TCP Tahoe congestion control algorithm.

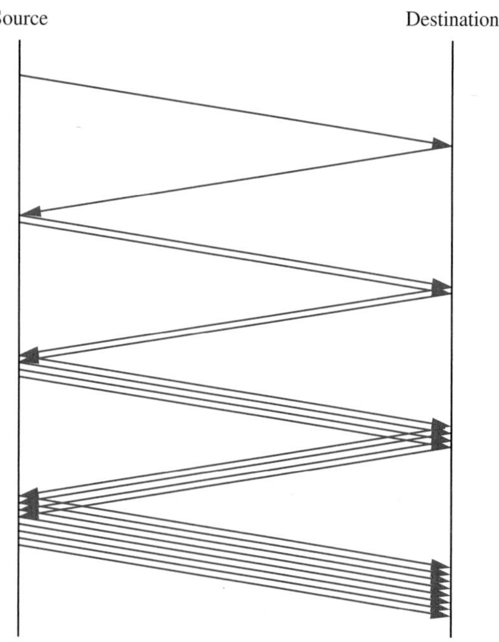

FIGURE 5.18 Visualization of packets in transit during slow start.

1. **Slow start:** Slow start aims at quickly probing available bandwidth within a few rounds of RTTs. When a connection starts or after a retransmission timeout occurs, the slow-start state begins by setting the initial value of `cwnd` to one packet, that is, MSS. The sender increases `cwnd` *exponentially* by adding one packet to `cwnd` each time it receives an ACK. So the `cwnd` is *doubled* (1, 2, 4, 8, etc.) after each RTT if all ACKs are received correctly in time, as shown in Figure 5.18. Thus, slow start is *not* slow at all. A TCP sender stays in the slow-start state until its `cwnd` reaches the slow-start threshold `ssthresh` (or `ssth` in Figure 5.17); after that, it enters the congestion-avoidance state. Note that when a connection starts, the `ssthresh` is set to the maximum value of the `ssthresh` (which depends on the data type to store `ssthresh`) so as not to limit the bandwidth probing of the slow-start. If triple duplicate ACKs are received, the TCP sender enters the fast-transmit state and the `cwnd` is reset to 1. If no ACK is received before retransmission timeout, the `cwnd` is reset to 1 and the TCP sender enters the retransmission-timeout state.
2. **Congestion avoidance:** Congestion avoidance aims at *slowly* probing available bandwidth but *rapidly* responding to congestion events. It follows the *Additive Increase Multiplicative Decrease* (AIMD) principle. Since the window size in the slow-start state expands exponentially, sending packets at this increasing speed would quickly lead to network congestion. To avoid this, the congestion-avoidance state begins when `cwnd` exceeds `ssthresh.` In this state, `cwnd` is added by `1/cwnd` packet upon receiving an ACK to make the window size grow *linearly*. As such, the `cwnd` is normally incremented by one after each RTT (by `1/cwnd` with each received ACK), but is reset to 1 if triple duplicate ACKs are received to trigger the fast-transmit state. Similarly, retransmission timeout

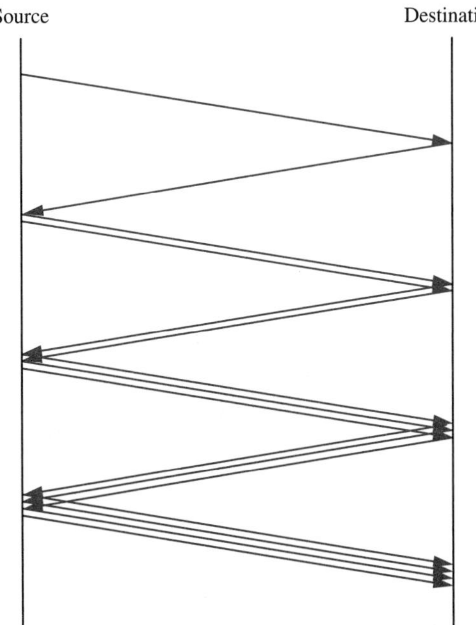

FIGURE 5.19 Visualization of packets in transit during congestion avoidance.

triggers the reset of the cwnd and the switch to the retransmission-timeout state. Figure 5.19 depicts the behavior of additive increase.

3. **Fast retransmit:** Fast retransmit targets transmitting the lost packet immediately without waiting for the retransmission timer to expire. As shown in Subsection 5.3.2, the duplicate ACK is caused by a lost data packet (in Figure 5.12[a]), or a duplicate data packet (in Figure 5.12[b]) or an out-of-order data packet received at the receiver (in Figure 5.12[c]). In case of a data packet loss, the sender should retransmit. Since the sender cannot tell what caused the duplicate ACK for sure, fast retransmit exercises a heuristic: If three or more duplicate ACKs are received in a row—*triple duplicate ACK* (TDA)—the TCP sender assumes packet loss has occurred. The sender then performs retransmission of what appears to be the missing packet, without waiting for a coarse-grain retransmission timer to expire. After the sender transmits the missing packet, it sets its ssthresh to *half* of the current value of cwnd according to AIMD and begins again in the slow-start state with the cwnd reset to 1.
4. **Retransmission timeout:** Retransmission timeout provides the last and slowest resort to retransmit the lost packet. The sender maintains a retransmission timer, which is used to check for timeout of an acknowledgment that can advance the left edge of the sending window. If a timeout occurs, as in the treatments in the fast-retransmit state, the sender reduces ssthresh to cwnd/2, resets the cwnd to 1, and restarts from the slow-start state. The timeout value highly depends on the RTT and the variance of the RTT. The more fluctuating the RTT measured, the larger should the timeout value be kept so as not to retransmit an already arrived-segment; the more stable the RTT measured, the closer to the RTT the timeout value can be set to quickly retransmit the lost segment. TCP

Open Source Implementation 5.4: TCP Slow Start and Congestion Avoidance

Overview

The slow start and congestion avoidance in `tcp_cong.c` of Linux 2.6 kernel are implemented by three functions, named `tcp_slow_start()`, `tcp_reno_cong_avoid()`, and `tcp_cong_avoid_ai()`.

Data Structures

Within the three functions, `tp` is the pointer to the socket structure `tcp_sock` whose definition can be found in `linux/include/linux/tcp.h`. The `tcp_sock` contains `snd_cwnd`, `snd_ssthresh` for storing congestion window and slow-start threshold, `snd_cwnd_cnt` for simplifying the congestion avoidance's implementation of adding `1/cwnd` packet on receiving each ACK, and `snd_cwnd_clamp` for limiting the congestion window (nonstandard).

Algorithm Implementations

The slow start and the congestion avoidance in `tcp_cong.c` of the Linux 2.6 kernel are summarized in Figure 5.20. Note that in the congestion avoidance, the adding of `1/cwnd` on receipt of each ACK is simplified to adding a full-size segment (MSS bytes) upon receiving all ACKs of `cwnd` segments, as shown in Line 5~11.

Exercises

The current implementation in `tcp_cong.c` provides a flexible architecture that allows replacing the Reno's slow-start and congestion-avoidance with others.

1. Explain how this allowance is achieved.
2. Find an example from the kernel source code that changes the Reno algorithm through this architecture.

```
1:  if (tp->snd_cwnd <= tp->snd_ssthresh) {          /* Slow start*/
2:      if (tp->snd_cwnd < tp->snd_cwnd_clamp)
3:          tp->snd_cwnd++;
4:  } else {
5:      if (tp->snd_cwnd_cnt >= tp->snd_cwnd) { /* Congestion
Avoidance*/
6:      if (tp->snd_cwnd < tp->snd_cwnd_clamp)
7:          tp->snd_cwnd++;
8:      tp->snd_cwnd_cnt=0;
9:      } else {
10:         tp->snd_cwnd_cnt++;
11:     }
12: }
```

FIGURE 5.20 TCP slow start and congestion avoidance in Linux 2.6.

adopts a highly dynamic algorithm proposed by Van Jacobson in 1988 that constantly adjusts the timeout interval based on continuous measurements of RTT, which will be discussed in Subsection 5.3.6.

TCP Reno Congestion Control

TCP Reno extended the Tahoe congestion control scheme by introducing the *fast-recovery* state to the subsequent recovery phase following a packet loss. The control scheme of Reno is depicted in Figure 5.21. Fast recovery concentrates on preserving enough outstanding packets in the network pipe to retain TCP's *self-clocking* behavior. The network-pipe concept and TCP's self-clocking behavior shall be detailed in Section 5.3.7. When fast retransmit is performed, `ssthresh` is set to half of `cwnd`, and then `cwnd` is set to `ssthresh` plus 3 because of the three duplicate ACKs. Every received duplicate ACK represents that another data packet has exited the network pipe, so for three duplicate ACKs that trigger the fast retransmit, a more correct thought is `awnd` minus 3 instead of `cwnd` plus 3, where `awnd` is the number of outstanding packets in the network pipe. However, in Reno, the calculation of `awnd` is `snd.nxt - snd.una`, which is fixed in this state. Hence Reno increases `cwnd`, rather than reducing `awnd`, to achieve the same purpose. When the ACK of the retransmitted packet is received, `cwnd` is set to `ssthresh` and the sender re-enters the congestion-avoidance state. In other words, `cwnd` is reset to half of the old value of `cwnd` after fast recovery.

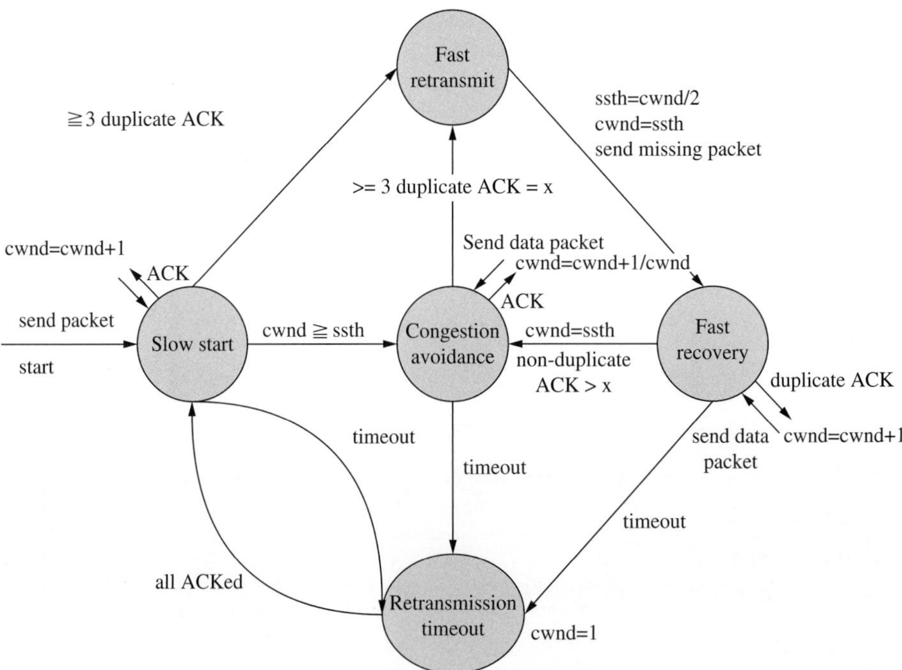

FIGURE 5.21 TCP Reno congestion control algorithm.

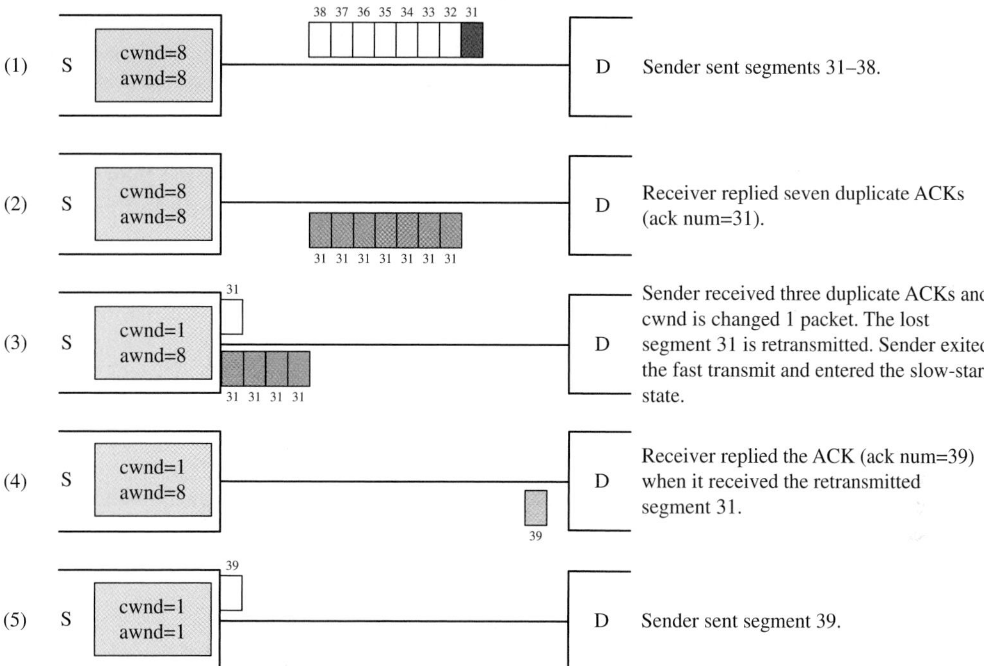

FIGURE 5.22 An example of TCP Tahoe congestion control.

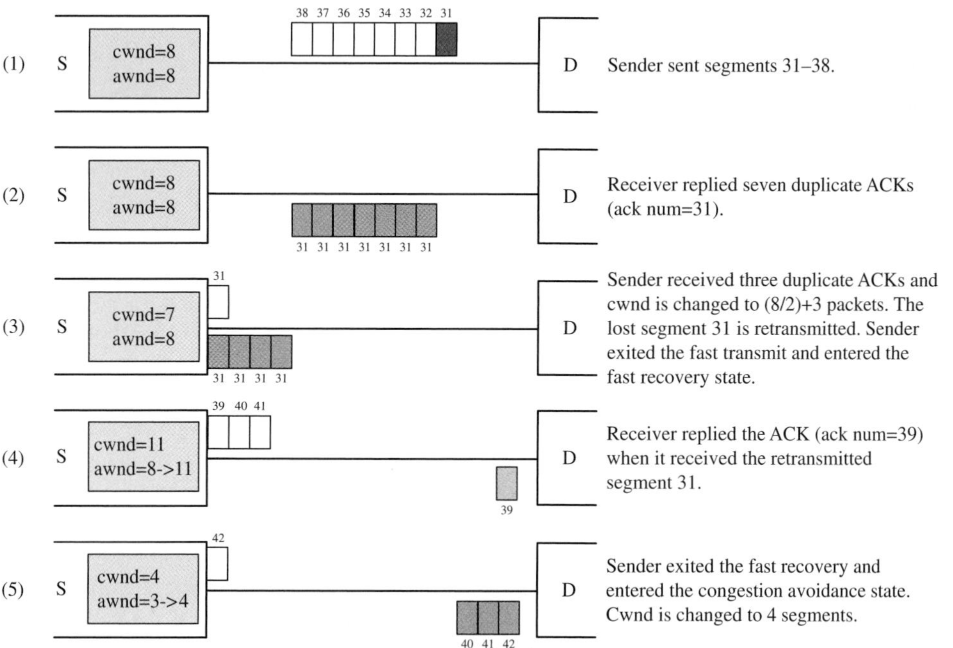

FIGURE 5.23 An example of TCP Reno congestion control.

We use an example to highlight the difference between Tahoe and Reno, which are shown in Figures 5.22 and 5.23, respectively. In these figures, the *ACK* of packet 30 was received and the sender transmitted packets 31 to 38. Assume that cwnd is equal to 8 packets and packet 31 was lost during transmission. Since packets 32, 33, 34, 35, 36, 37, and 38 were received, the receiver sent seven duplicate *ACK*s. The Tahoe sender discerns that packet 31 was lost when it receives the third duplicate *ACK,* and then immediately sets cwnd to one packet, retransmits the lost packet, and returns to the slow-start state. After receiving four more duplicate *ACK*s, the sender maintains cwnd as 1 and awnd as 8 (39–31). After receiving the *ACK* of packet 38, the sender can send the new packet 39.

On the other hand, when the Reno sender discerns that packet 31 was lost, it immediately sets cwnd to [8/2]+3 packets, retransmits the lost packet, and enters the fast-recovery state. After receiving four more duplicate *ACK*s, the sender continues to increase cwnd by 4 and can forward new packets 39, 40, and 41. After receiving the *ACK* of packet 38, the sender exits fast recovery, enters congestion avoidance, and sets cwnd to four packets, which is half of the old cwnd value. Since now awnd equals 3 (42–39), the sender can send the new packet 42.

Comparing Step (4) in Figures 5.22 and 5.23, Tahoe cannot send any new packets, but Reno can. Thus it is obvious that TCP Reno utilizes fast recovery to generate a more efficient transfer after a packet loss.

Although Reno had been the most popular TCP version, it suffers from the *multiple-packet-loss* problem that degrades its performance. We shall further investigate this problem and its solutions in Subsection 5.3.7.

Principle in Action: TCP Congestion Control Behaviors

Linux 2.6 is a joint implementation of various TCP versions, including NewReno, SACK, and FACK that will be studied in Subsection 5.3.7. However, their basic behavior under the one-packet-loss scenario is pretty much the same as that of Reno. Figure 5.24 displays an example snapshot of TCP congestion control of Linux 2.6. It is generated by processing the kernel logging of the sending window size and the sniffed packet headers.

In Figure 5.24(a) the cwnd grows rapidly beyond the figure's boundary in the slow-start state before congestion occurs at 1.45 second. However, note that the rwnd almost remains at 21 packets all the time so that the sending rate is bounded by 21 packets/RTT between 0.75 and 1.45 second, as shown in Figure 5.24(b). This is because the actual sending window size is determined by the minimum of the cwnd and rwnd. As such, the cwnd from 0.75 to 1.45 second grows with a somewhat less aggressive behavior than that from 0 to 0.75 second, since the rate of incoming ACKs is fixed during the 0.75 to 1.45 second period. From 0.75 to 1.45 second, the full-duplex network pipe is constantly filled up with 21 packets where about half of them are ACKs if the network's forward path and reverse path are symmetric.

When the congestion occurs at 1.5 second, the triple duplicate ACKs trigger the fast retransmit to retransmit the lost segment. The TCP source hereby enters the fast-recovery state, resetting the `ssthresh` to `cwnd/2=10` and `cwnd` to `ssthresh+3`. During the fast recovery, the TCP sender increments the `cwnd` by one MSS whenever receiving one more duplicate ACK to keep enough segments in transit. The fast-recovery state ends at 1.7 second when the lost segment is recovered. At this moment, `cwnd` is reset to `ssthresh` (previously set to 10) and changes to the congestion-avoidance state. After that, the `cwnd` is incremented by one MSS when all ACKs of the sliding window are received.

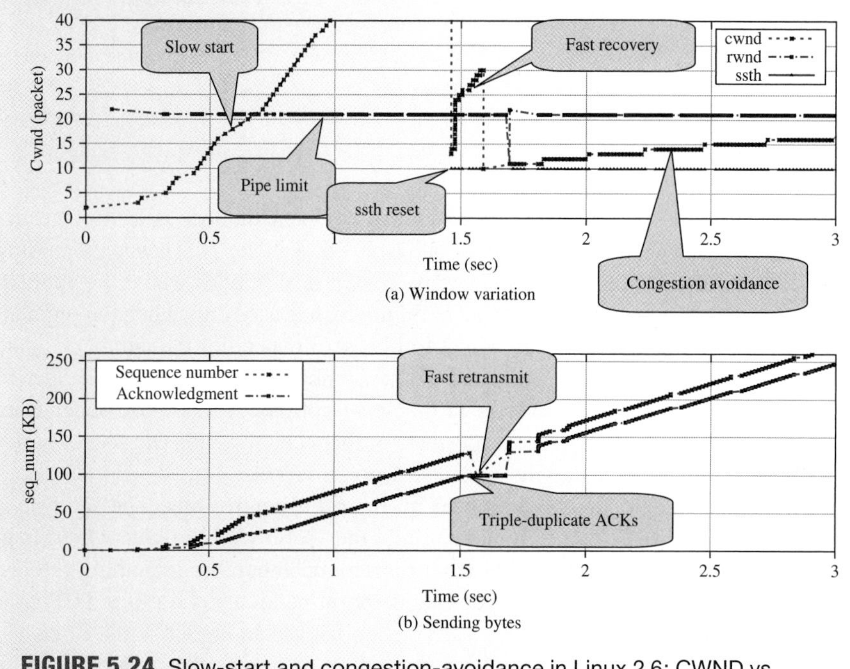

FIGURE 5.24 Slow-start and congestion-avoidance in Linux 2.6: CWND vs. sequence number.

5.3.5 TCP Header Format

In this subsection we examine other fields of the TCP header in Figure 5.25 that have not been mentioned so far. As indicated in Subsection 5.3.2, a TCP segment contains a 16-bit source port number, a 16-bit destination port number, a 32-bit sequence number, and a 32-bit acknowledgment number. These fields are carried in the TCP segment header to transmit over the network. The sequence number corresponds to the *first* data octet in this segment when the SYN bit is not set. If the SYN bit is set, the sequence number is the initial sequence number (ISN) and the first data octet is numbered ISN+1. If the ACK control bit is set, the acknowledgment number field contains the value of the *next* sequence number that the sender of the ACK segment

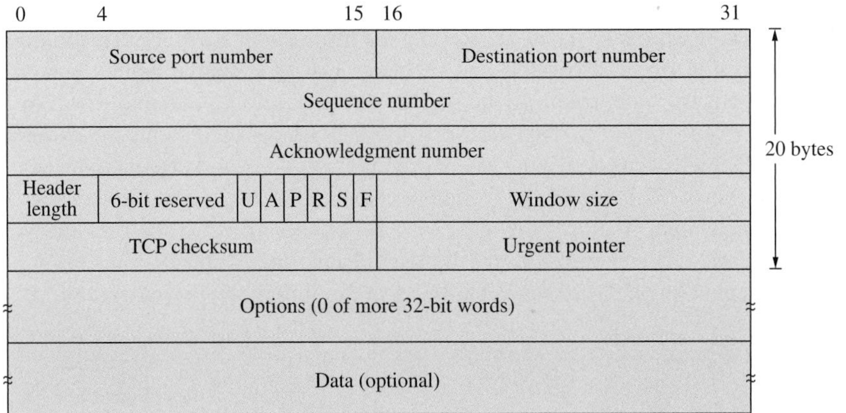

FIGURE 5.25 TCP header format.

is expecting to receive. Following the acknowledgment number is a 4-bit header length field, which indicates the number of 32-bit words in the TCP header, including the TCP options. From the technical perspective, it also implies where the application data begin. The 16-bit window size in Figure 5.25 is used only when the segment is an acknowledgment with the ACK control bit set. It specifies the number of data octets beginning with the one indicated in the acknowledgment field the sender of this segment, i.e., the TCP receiver, is willing to accept. The window size depends on the socket buffer size and the receiving speed of the receiving end. The socket buffer size can be programmed using the socket API `setsockopt()`.

The header length field is followed by the 6-bit control bits. The first bit is the URG bit, which is set to 1 to indicate that the 16-bit *Urgent pointer* field is in use. The Urgent pointer is an offset from the sequence number indicating the last urgent data byte. This mechanism facilitates the in-band signaling of a TCP connection. For example, users can use `Ctrl+C` to trigger an urgent signal to cancel an operation being performed on the peer end. Next comes the ACK bit, which specifies that the acknowledgment number field is valid. If the ACK bit is not set, the acknowledgment number field is ignored. The following is the PSH bit, whose job is to notify the receiver of the PSH-set packet to deliver all the data in its buffer to the receiving application immediately without waiting for sufficient application data to fill the buffer. The next bit is RST, which is used to *reset* a connection. Any host with an RST-set packet received should immediately close the socket pair associated with the packet. The next bit, SYN bit, is employed to initialize a connection, as shown in Subsection 5.3.1. The last bit, FIN, as illustrated in Subsection 5.3.1, is to indicate that no more data will be sent from the sender and both sides can close the connection.

The TCP header, along with options that will be discussed next, must be a multiple of 32-bit words. Variable padding bits are appended to the TCP header to ensure that the TCP header ends and the TCP payload begin on a 32-bit boundary. The padding is composed of zero bits.

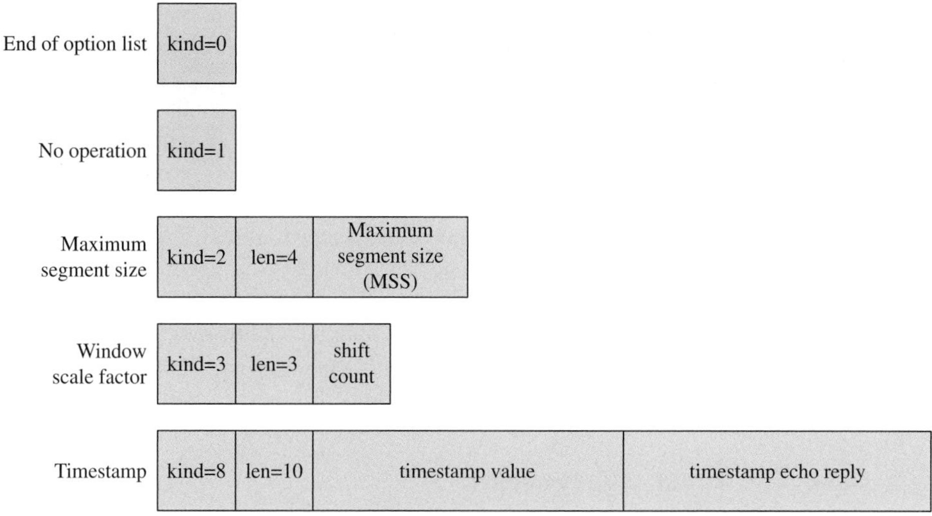

FIGURE 5.26 TCP options.

TCP Options

Options may occupy space at the end of the TCP header. An option is a multiple of octets and may begin on any octet boundary. Currently defined options include the End of Option List, No Operation, Maximum Segment Size, Window Scale Factor, and Timestamp. Note that all options are covered in the checksum computation. Figure 5.26 depicts the formats of TCP options. End of Option List and No Operation have only one octet of the option-kind field; the remaining options each contain 3-tuple fields: one octet of option-kind, one octet of option-length, and option-data. The option-length counts the two octets of option-kind and option-length as well as the octets of option-data. Note that the list of options may be shorter than what the data offset field might imply because the content of the header beyond the End-of-Option-List option must be a pad of zero bits.

End of Option List indicates the end of *all* options, not the end of *each* option. End of Option List is used only if it would not otherwise coincide with the end of the TCP header according to the Data Offset field. No Operation may be used between options, for example, to align the beginning of a subsequent option on a word boundary. There is no guarantee that senders will use this option, so receivers must be prepared to process options even if they do not begin on a word boundary.

If the Maximum Segment Size (MSS) option is present, then it communicates the maximum receive segment size at the TCP end that sends this segment. This field must be sent only in the initial connection request (in segments with the SYN control bit set). If this option is not used, any segment size is allowed.

The 32-bit sequence number would be run out if the transferring size exceeded 2^{32} bytes. Normally this would not be a problem because the sequence number can wrap around. However, in high-speed networks the sequence number may wrap around very quickly, so the wrapped-around sequence numbers may be confusing. Thus, the Protection Against Wrapped Sequence number (PAWS) is required to avoid the side effect. With the TCP Window Scaling Factor option, a TCP receiver can advertise a very large window size by negotiating a shift count with the sender to interpret the scale of window size. In this way, the sender can send at a very high speed. In order to enforce PAWS, the TCP Timestamp option is used to attach a timestamp to each segment sent. The receiver will copy the timestamp value to its corresponding ACK so that the segments with wrapped-around sequence numbers can be recognized without confusing the RTT estimator.

The additional TCP SACK option is used to improve the performance in the fast recovery stage of TCP congestion control. The option contains two fields indicating the start and the end of the sequence numbers of consecutively received segments. TCP SACK will be studied in detail in Subsection 5.3.7.

5.3.6 TCP Timer Management

Each TCP connection keeps a set of timers to drive its state machine, shown in Figure 5.8, even when there is no incoming packet to trigger the transitions of states. Table 5.2 summarizes the functions of these timers. In this subsection, we study two mandatory timers, the retransmission and persist timers, and one optional timer, the keepalive timer, in detail. These timers are implemented in different ways among operating systems due to concern about performance.

TABLE 5.2 Functions of All Timers

Name	Function
Connection timer	To establish a new TCP connection, a SYN segment is sent. If no response to the SYN segment is received within connection timeout, the connection is aborted.
Retransmission timer	TCP retransmits the data if data is not acknowledged and this timer expires.
Delayed ACK timer	The receiver must wait until delayed ACK timeout to send the ACK. If during this period there is data to send, it sends the ACK with piggybacking.
Persist timer	A deadlock problem is solved by the sender sending periodic probes after the persist timer expires.
Keepalive timer	If the connection is idle for a few hours, the keepalive timeout expires and TCP sends probes. If no response is received, TCP thinks that the other end has crashed.
FIN_WAIT_2 timer	This timer avoids leaving a connection in the FIN_WAIT_2 state forever, if the other end has crashed.
TIME_WAIT timer	The timer is used in the TIME_WAIT state to enter the CLOSED state.

(1) TCP Retransmission Timer

The role of the TCP retransmission timer has been introduced in Subsections 5.3.2 and 5.3.4, and this subsection studies the internal design of the RTT estimator. To measure RTTs, the sender places a timestamp in each data segment using TCP options, and the receiver reflects these timestamps back in ACK segments. Then the sender can measure an accurate RTT for every ACK with a single subtraction. The RTT estimator adopts the exponential weighted moving average (EWMA), proposed by Van Jacobson in 1988, which takes 1/8 of the new RTT measure plus 7/8 of the old smoothed RTT value to form the new estimate of the RTT. The 8 is the exponential value of 2, so this operation can be done simply with a 3-bit shift instruction. The "moving average" indicates that this calculation is based on a recursive form of average. Similarly, the new mean deviation is calculated from 1/4 of the new measure and 3/4 of the previous mean deviation. The 4 can be implemented with just a 2-bit shift instruction. The Retransmission TimeOut (RTO) is calculated as a linear function of measured mean RTT and mean RTT deviation, and is often formulated as RTO = RTT + 4 × deviation (RTT). In a path with high variance of latency, the RTO would increase significantly.

One problem encountered by the dynamic estimation of RTT is what to do when a segment times out and is sent again. When an acknowledgment comes in, it is unclear whether the acknowledgment refers to the first transmission or a later one. A wrong guess could seriously contaminate the estimation of RTT. Phil Karn discovered this problem in 1987 and proposed *not* to update RTT on any segments that have been retransmitted. Instead, RTO is doubled on each retransmission timeout until a segment gets through on the first time. This fix is known as Karn's algorithm.

Open Source Implementation 5.5: TCP Retransmission Timer

Overview

In the literature, the default value of the clock used for the round-trip ticks is 500 ms, i.e., the sender checks for a timeout every 500 ms. Since no packet will be retransmitted before the timeout, a TCP connection may take a long time to recover from such a situation, and TCP performance would be severely degraded, particularly when the Retransmission TimeOut (RTO) value is far smaller than 500 ms, which is quite possible under the current Internet. Now Linux 2.6 keeps a fine-grained timer to avoid such degradation.

Algorithm Implementations

When there is an incoming ACK from the IP layer, it is passed to the `tcp_ack()` function in `tcp_input.c`. There it updates the sending window by the `tcp_ack_update_window()` function, seeing if anything can be taken off the retransmission queue by the `tcp_clean_rtx_queue()` function and whether or not to adjust the `cwnd` accordingly by the `tcp_cong_avoid()`

Continued

function. The `tcp_clean_rtx_queue()` function updates several variables and invokes `tcp_ack_update_rtt()` to update the RTT measurements. If the Timestamp option is used, the function always calls `tcp_rtt_estimator()` to calculate the smoothed RTT, as shown in Figure 5.27. It uses the smoothed RTT to update the RTO value by the `tcp_set_rto()` function. If no Timestamp option is present, the updates will not be executed when the incoming ACK is acknowledging a retransmitted segment (according to Karn's algorithm).

The contents of the `tcp_rtt_estimator()`, as shown in Figure 5.27, follow Van Jacobson's suggestion in 1988 (and his further refinement in 1990) to compute a smoothed RTT estimate. Note that `srtt` and `mdev` are scaled versions of RTT and mean deviation so as to calculate the result as fast as possible. RTO is initialized to 3 seconds as defined in RFC 1122 and will vary from 20 ms to 120 seconds during the connection. These values are defined in `net/tcp.h`.

In Figure 5.27, `m` stands for the current measured RTT measurement, `tp` is the pointer to the `tcp_sock` data structure, as seen in Open Source Implementation 5.4, `mdev` refers to mean deviation, and `srtt` represents the smoothed RTT estimate. The operation >>3 is equivalent to division by 8 while >>2 is division by 4.

Exercises

Figure 5.27 shows how to update `srtt` and `mdev` based on `m` and their previous values. Do you know where and how the initial values of `srtt` and `mdev` are given?

```
m -= (tp->srtt >> 3);        /* m is now error in rtt est */
tp->srtt += m;        /* rtt = 7/8 rtt + 1/8 new */
if (m < 0) {
    m = -m; /* m is now abs(error) */
    m -= (tp->mdev >> 2); /* similar update on mdev */
if (m > 0)
        m >>= 3;
} else {
    m -= (tp->mdev >> 2); /* similar update on mdev */
}
```

FIGURE 5.27 RTT estimator in Linux 2.6.

(2) TCP Persist Timer

The TCP persist timer is designed simply to prevent the following deadlock: The receiver sends an acknowledgment with a receiver window size of 0, telling the sender to wait. Later, the receiver updates and advertises its window size, but the packet with the update is lost. Now both the sender and the receiver are waiting for each other to do something, which is a deadlock. Thus, when the persist timer goes off, the sender transmits a probe to the receiver, and the response to the probe gives the window size. If it is still zero, the persist timer is set again and the cycle repeats. If it is nonzero, data can now be sent.

(3) TCP Keepalive Timer (nonstandard)

Detecting crashed systems over TCP/IP is difficult. TCP does not require any transmission over a connection if the application is not sending anything, and many of the media over which TCP/IP is used (e.g., Ethernet) do not provide a reliable way to determine whether a particular host is up. If a server does not hear from a client, it could be because it has nothing to say, the network between the server and client may be down, the server's or client's network interface may be disconnected, or the client may have crashed. Network failures are often temporary (for example, it often takes a few minutes for new routes to stabilize when a router goes down), and TCP connections should not be dropped as a result.

Keepalive is a feature of the socket APIs in which an empty packet is sent periodically over an idle connection, which should invoke an acknowledgment from the remote system if it is still up, a reset by RST if it has rebooted, or a timeout if it is down. These are not normally sent until the connection has been idle for a few hours. The purpose is not to detect a crash immediately, but to keep unnecessary resources from being allocated forever.

If more rapid detection of remote failures is required, this should be implemented in the application protocol. Currently most daemon programs of applications such as FTP and telnet detect whether the user has been idle for a period. If yes, the daemon closes the connection.

Open Source Implementation 5.6: TCP Persist Timer and Keepalive Timer

Overview

In the Linux 2.6 kernel, the persist timer is called the probe timer. It is maintained by the `tcp_probe_timer()` function in `tcp_timer.c`, while the keepalive timer is maintained by the `tcp_keepalive_timer()` in `tcp_timer.c`.

Data Structures

To call both functions on time, they should be hooked on a time list. For example, `tcp_keepalive_timer()` is hooked on `sk->sk_timer` by `inet_csk_init_xmit_timers()`. The `sk_timer` is a `timer_list` structure whose definition can be found in `include/linux/timer.h`. The structure includes a function pointer to indicate which function would be called when the time is up. Also, a variable `data` is used to keep the parameter to be passed into the function. Herein `data` keeps a pointer to the corresponding socket to let `tcp_keepalive_timer()` know which socket to check.

Algorithm Implementations

The `tcp_probe_timer()` calls `tcp_send_probe0()` to send out a probe packet. The 0 in the function name means window size of 0 updated by

Continued

the receiver. If the receiver has a retransmission timeout, the sender will send a zero-window-probe segment that contains an old sequence number to trigger the receiver to reply a new window update.

The default calling period of the keepalive timer is 75 seconds. When it fires, it checks every established connection for idle ones and emits new probes for them. The number of probes for each connection is limited to 5 by default. So if the other end crashes but does not reboot, the probe-sender clears the TCP state by the `tcp_keepopen_proc()` function; if the other end crashes and reboots within the 5 probes, it will reply an RST when receiving a probing packet. The sender of the probe can then clear the TCP state.

Exercises

Read `net/ipv4/tcp_timer.c` to figure out where and how the `tcp_probe_timer()` is hooked. Is it directly hooked on a `time_list` structure just as `tcp_keepalive_timer()`?

5.3.7 TCP Performance Problems and Enhancements

Transmission styles of TCP-based applications can be categorized into (1) interactive connections and (2) bulk-data transfers. Interactive applications, such as telnet and WWW, perform *transactions* that consist of successive request/response pairs. In contrast, some applications have bulk-data transfers, such as downloading/uploading files using FTP or P2P. These two styles of data transmission have their own performance problems, as shown in Table 5.3, if the previously mentioned TCP versions are used. This subsection introduces the problems and presents their solutions.

(1) Performance Problem of Interactive TCP: Silly Window Syndrome

The performance of window-based flow control in TCP for interactive transactions suffers under a well-known condition called *silly window syndrome (SWS)*. When it occurs, small packets are exchanged across the connection, instead of full-sized segments, which implies more packets are sent for the same amount of data. Since each packet has a fixed size of header overhead, transmitting in small packets

TABLE 5.3 TCP Performance Problems and Solutions

Transmission Style	Problem	Solution
Interactive connection	Silly window syndrome	Nagle, Clark
Bulk-data transfer	ACK compression	Zhang
	Reno's MPL* problem	NewReno, SACK, FACK

*MPL stands for Multiple-Packet-Loss

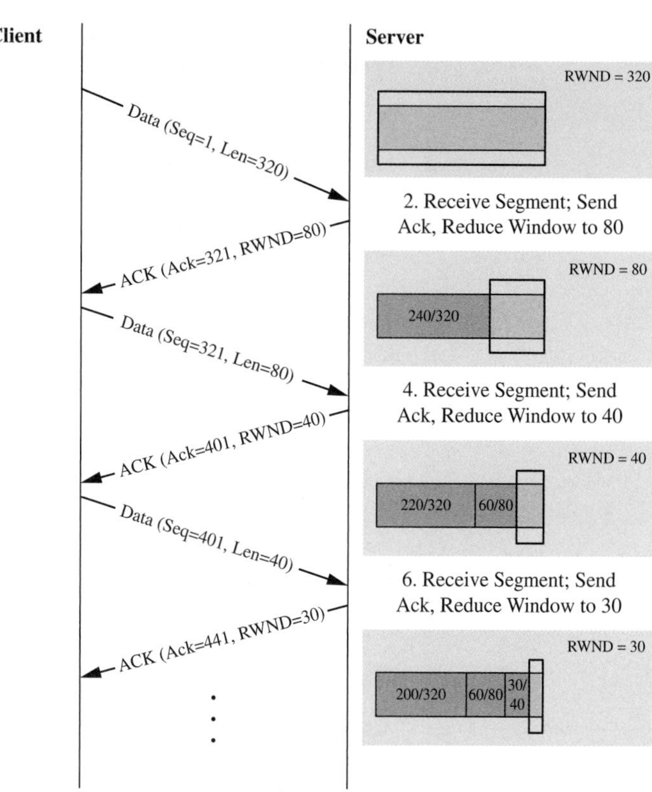

FIGURE 5.28 Silly window syndrome caused by the receiver.

means bandwidth wastage, which is particularly severe in a WAN though insignificant in a LAN.

The SWS condition could be caused by either end. The sender can transmit a small packet without waiting for more data from the sending application to send a full-sized packet. Take telnet, for example: Because in telnet each keystroke generates a packet and an ACK, telneting across a large-RTT WAN wastes the globally shared WAN bandwidth. Readers might argue that packets of interactive applications should be sent right away regardless of how small they are. However, bounded delay, say tens to one hundred milliseconds, of such packets would not affect the perceived interactivity.

The receiver also could cause the SWS condition. The receiver, without waiting for more data to be removed from the buffer to the receiving application, can therefore advertise a receiver window smaller than a full-sized packet, which eventually leads to the SWS condition. Let us consider an example shown in Figure 5.28. Suppose that MSS=320 and the server's initial RWND is set to this same value, 320. Also assume that the client always has data to send and the server is so busy that it removes only 1 byte of data from the buffer for every 4 bytes it receives. The example goes like this:

1. The client's window size is 320, so it immediately sends a 320-byte segment to the server.

2. When the server receives this segment, it acknowledges this segment. Since only 80 bytes are removed, the server reduces the window size from 320 to 80 and advertises RWND as 80 in the ACK.
3. The client receives this ACK, and knows that the window size has been reduced to 80, so it sends out an 80-byte segment.
4. When the 80-byte segment arrives, the buffer now contains 220 bytes (240 left from the first segment and assuming 20 extra bytes removed during the propagation delay). Then the server immediately processes one-fourth of those 80 bytes so that 60 bytes are added to the 220 bytes that already remain in the buffer. The server then sends an ACK with RWND=40.
5. The client receives this ACK, and knows that the window size has been reduced to 40, so it sends out a 40-byte segment.
6. The server removes 20 bytes during the propagation delay, which yields 260 bytes left in the buffer. It receives 40 bytes from the client, removes one-fourth, so 30 bytes are added to the buffer, which becomes 290 bytes. Thus the server reduces the window size to 320 – 290 = 30 bytes.

Solution to Silly Window Syndrome

To prevent the sender from initiating SWS, John Nagle in 1984 proposed a simple but elegant algorithm known as *Nagle's algorithm,* which reduces the number of packets being sent when the bandwidth is saturated: *Don't send a small new segment unless there is no outstanding data.* Instead, small segments are gathered together by TCP and sent in a single segment when the ACK arrives. The gathering would be bounded by RTT and thus would not affect the interactivity. Nagle's algorithm is elegant due to its *self-clocking* behavior: If the ACK comes back fast, the bandwidth is likely to be large so that the data packets are sent fast; if the ACKs come back with a long RTT, which might mean a narrowband path, Nagle's algorithm reduces the number of tiny segments by sending full-size segments. The pseudocode of Nagle's algorithm is shown in Figure 5.29.

On the other hand, to prevent the receiver from initiating SWS, the solution proposed by David D. Clark in 1982 is used. The advertisement would be delayed until the receiver buffer is half empty or available to a full-size segment, which thus guarantees a large window advertisement to the sender. Again, the delay is also bounded.

```
if there is new data to send
  if window size >= MSS and available data >= MSS
    send complete MSS segment
  else
    if there is outstanding data and queued data live time <threshold
     enqueue data in the buffer until an ACK is received
    else
      send data immediately
    endif
  endif
endif
```

FIGURE 5.29 Nagle's algorithm.

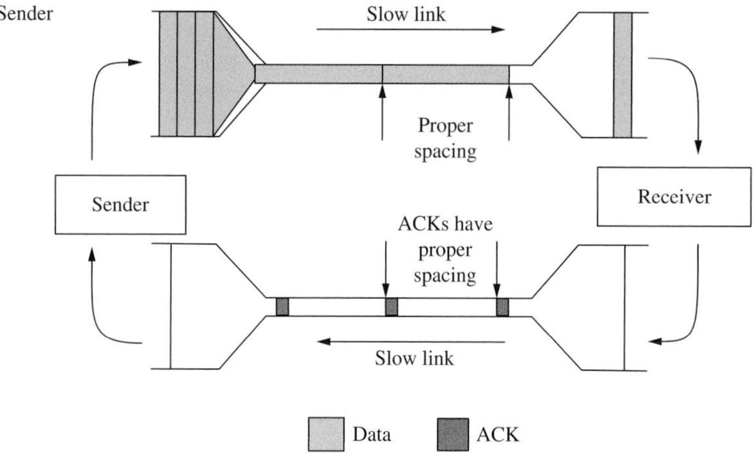

FIGURE 5.30 Visualization of end-to-end full-duplex network pipes.

(2) Performance Problem of Bulk-Data Transfers

The performance of window-based flow control for bulk-data transfers is best understood by the *Bandwidth delay product (BDP)* or the *pipe size*. In Figure 5.30, we can visualize a full-duplex end-to-end TCP network pipe consisting of a forward data channel and a reverse ACK channel. You can imagine a network pipe functioning as a water tube whose width and length correspond to the bandwidth and the RTT, respectively. Using this analogy, the pipe size then corresponds to the amount of water that can go into the water tube. If the full-duplex channel is always full, we can easily derive the performance of such connections as

$$\text{Throughput} = \frac{\text{Pipe Size}}{\text{RTT}}. \tag{5.1}$$

Intuitively speaking, Equation (5.1) means the amount of the data in the pipe deliverable in an RTT. The throughput, of course, is equal to the bandwidth of the pipe. However, the pipe might not always be full. When a TCP connection starts and encounters packet losses, TCP senders will adapt their windows to the network congestion. Before a TCP can fill up the pipe, its performance should be derived as

$$\text{Throughput} = \frac{\text{outstanding bytes}}{\text{RTT}} = \frac{\min(\text{CWND}, \text{RWND})}{\text{RTT}}. \tag{5.2}$$

Equations (5.1) and (5.2) imply that if the RTT of a TCP connection is fixed, the connection throughput is then bounded by the maximum of the network capacity (pipe size), the receiver's buffer (RWND), and the network condition (CWND). That is, Equation (5.1) is the upper bound on the throughput of the connection.

Because better performance implies better *effective* utilization of the network pipe, the process of *filling the pipe* significantly affects the performance. Figure 5.31 illustrates the steps of filling a network pipe using TCP.

Figure 5.31(1) to (6) demonstrates the first packet sent from the left party to the right party and an ACK replied from the receiver to the sender. After receiving the

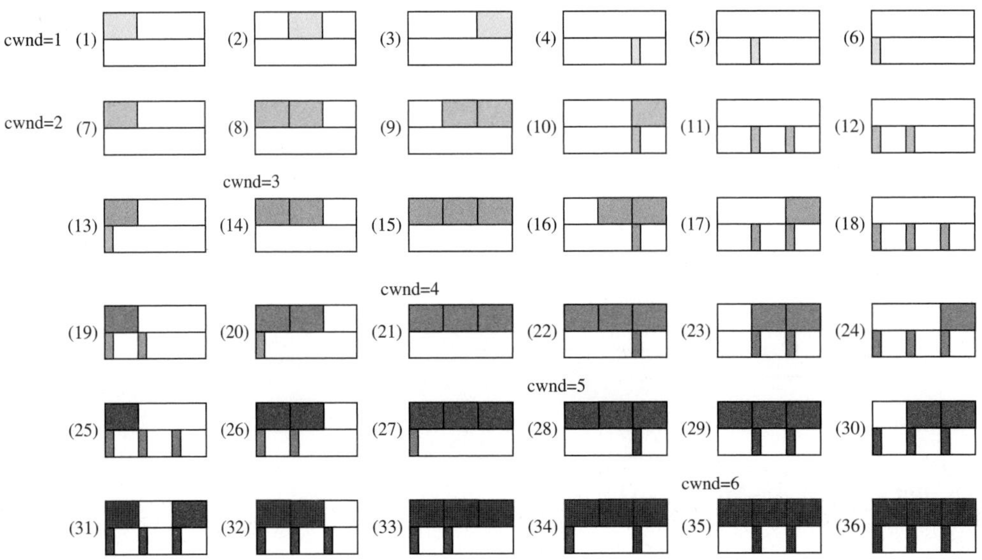

FIGURE 5.31 Steps of filling the pipe using TCP.

ACK, the sender raises its congestion window to 2 in Figure 5.31(7). This process continues as shown in the following subfigures in Figure 5.31. After the congestion window reaches 6 in Figure 5.31(35), the network pipe becomes full.

Note that the throughput of bulk data transfer using TCP can be modeled as a function of several parameters such as RTT and packet loss rate. Advances in this field target accurate prediction of a TCP source's throughput. The major challenge lies in how we interpret previously sampled packet loss events to predict future performance of a TCP connection. The intervals between packet losses can be independent or correlated. An easy-to-understand model appears in Padhye's work, which considers not only the packet loss recovered by the fast retransmit algorithm but also that recovered by RTO.

Next we shall study two major performance problems encountered by bulk-data transfers: the ACK-compression problem and the TCP Reno's multiple-packet-loss problem. Suggestions or solutions are discussed therein.

The ACK-Compression Problem

In Figure 5.32, the full-duplex pipe contains only the data stream from the sender on the left side, so the spacing between the ACKs can define a fixed clock rate which triggers new data packets from the sender. However, when there is also traffic generated from the right side, as indicated in Figure 5.32 and compared with Figure 5.30, consecutive ACKs could have improper spacing because the ACKs in the reverse channel could be mixed with data traffic in the same queue. Since the transmission time of a large data packet is far larger than that of a 64-byte ACK, the ACKs could be periodically compressed into clusters and could cause the sender to emit bursty data traffic, resulting in rapid fluctuations in the queue length at intermediate routers.

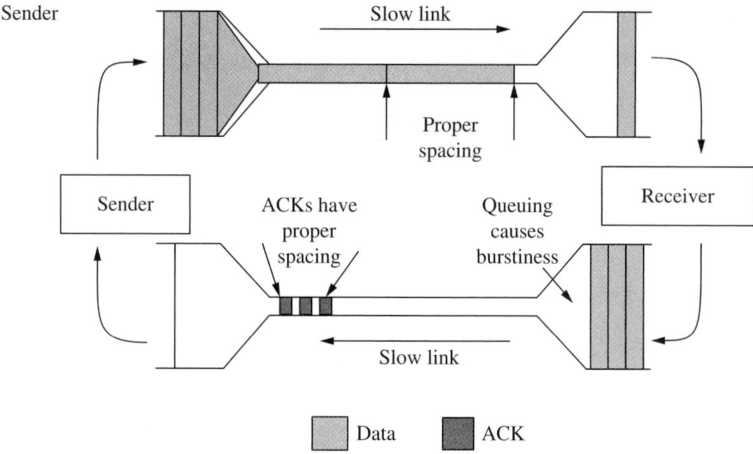

FIGURE 5.32 ACK-compression phenomenon.

The ACK piggybacked in the data packets may alleviate this ACK-compression problem. However, since the end-to-end channel is essentially a concatenation of hop-by-hop systems, cross traffic in the intermediate Internet routers can also cause this phenomenon.

Currently there is no obvious way to cope with the ACK-compression problem. Zhang, Shenker, and Clark in 1991 suggested using pacing of data packets by the TCP sender rather than solely relying on the ACK-clocking to alleviate the phenomenon. The clocking of ACKs has proven to be ineffective, as shown in Figure 5.32.

TCP Reno's Multiple-Packet-Loss (MPL) Problem

In Reno, when multiple packet losses occur within one window, since the receiver always responds with the same duplicate *ACK,* the sender assumes at most one new loss per RTT. Thus, in such a case, the sender must spend numerous RTTs to handle all of these losses. Meanwhile, the retransmission timeout occurs more often because only a few packets, which are limited due to reduction in `cwnd` triggered by fast recovery, can be sent even though there are many unacknowledged packets to be retransmitted. Let us go through the example depicted in Figure 5.33, where the *ACK* of packet 30 was received and the sender transmitted packets 31 to 38. Again, for clarity, the acknowledgment number in the *ACK* packet is the sequence number of the received packet, rather than the sequence number of the next packet the receiver expects to receive.

Assume that `cwnd` is equal to 8 packets and packets 31, 33, and 34 were lost during transmission. Since packets 32, 35, 36, 37, and 38 were received, the receiver sent five duplicate *ACK*s for lost packet 31. The sender discerns that packet 31 was lost when it receives the third duplicate *ACK* (ack num=31), and then immediately sets `cwnd` to [8/2]+3 packets and retransmits the lost packet. After receiving two more duplicate ACKs, the sender continues to increase `cwnd` by 2 and can forward a new packet 39. After receiving the *ACK* (ack num=33), the sender transits from fast recovery to congestion avoidance, and sets `cwnd` to 4 packets. Then, the sender receives

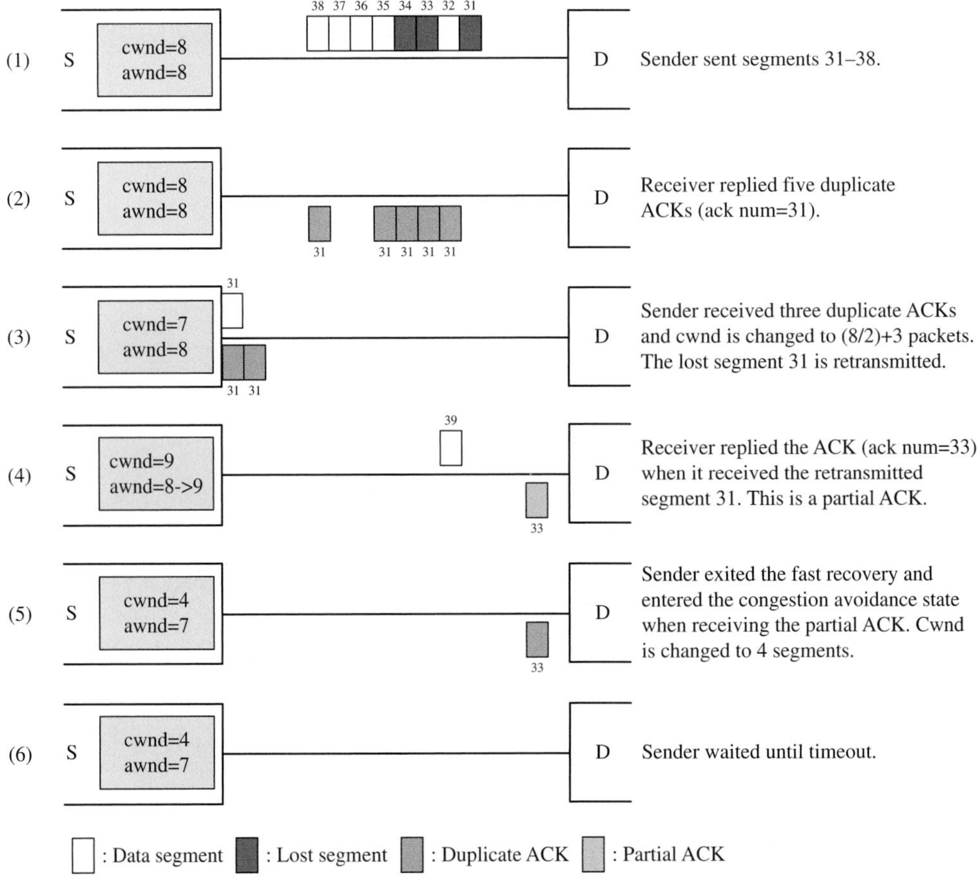

FIGURE 5.33 Reno's multiple-packet-loss problem.

one duplicate *ACK* (ack num=33). When `cwnd` equals 4 and `awnd` equals 7 (40-33), then the sender stops sending any packet, which results in a retransmission timeout!

Note that Reno does not always timeout when losing more than one segment within a window of data. When the multiple-loss event happens in the situation when `cwnd` is very large, any partial ACKs may not only bring Reno out of fast recovery, but may also trigger another fast retransmit because of another batch of triple duplicate ACKs. This is fine so far, though it will slow loss recovery. But if too many packets lost within the RTT cause the `cwnd` to be halved too many times in the following RTTs so that too few segments are outstanding in the pipe to trigger another fast retransmit, Reno will timeout, which prolongs the loss recovery further.

To alleviate the multiple-packet-loss problem, the NewReno and the SACK (Selective ACKnowledgment, defined in RFC 1072) versions seek to resolve this problem by two quite different approaches. In the former, on receiving partial acknowledgment, the sender continues operating in fast recovery rather than returning to congestion avoidance. On the other hand, SACK modifies the receiver behavior to report to the sender the noncontiguous sets of data that have been received and queued, with additional SACK options attached in the duplicated acknowledgments. With the information in SACK options, the sender can retransmit the lost packets correctly and quickly. Mathis and Mahdavi then proposed Forward ACKnowledment (FACK) to improve the fast recovery scheme in SACK. Compared to NewReno/SACK/FACK, which keep on polishing the fast retransmit and fast recovery mechanisms, TCP Vegas, proposed in 1995, uses the fine-grain RTT to assist in the detection of packet losses and congestion, which thus decreases the probability of the occurrence of timeout in Reno.

Historical Evolution: Multiple-Packet-Loss Recovery in NewReno, SACK, FACK, and Vegas

Here we detail further how the Reno's MPL problem is alleviated in NewReno, SACK, FACK, and Vegas, by using the same example as in Figure 5.33.

Solution 1 to TCP Reno's Problem: TCP NewReno

NewReno, standardized in RFC 2582, modifies the fast-recovery phase of Reno to alleviate the multiple-packet-loss problem. It departs from the original fast recovery scheme only when the sender receives the *ACK* that acknowledges the *latest* transmitted packet before detecting the *first* lost packet. Within NewReno, this exited time is defined as "the end point of fast recovery" and any nonduplicate *ACK* prior to that time is deemed a partial *ACK*.

Reno considers a partial *ACK* as a successful retransmission of the lost packet, so the sender returns to congestion avoidance to transmit new packets. In contrast, NewReno considers it as a signal of further packet losses, and thus the sender retransmits the lost packet immediately. When a partial *ACK* is received, the sender adjusts `cwnd` by deflating the amount of new data acknowledged and adding one packet for the retransmitted data. The sender remains in fast recovery until the end point of fast recovery. Thus, when multiple packets are lost within one window of data, NewReno may recover them without a retransmission timeout.

For the same example illustrated in Figure 5.33, the partial *ACK* (ack num=33) is transmitted when the retransmitted packet 31 in step 4 is received. Figure 5.34 illustrates the NewReno modification. When the sender receives the partial *ACK* (ack num=33), it immediately retransmits the lost packet 33 and sets `cwnd` to (9–2+1) where 2 is the amount of new data acknowledged (packets 31 and 32) and 1 represents the retransmitted packet that has exited the pipe. Similarly, when the sender receives the partial *ACK* (ack num=34), it immediately retransmits the lost packet 34. The sender exits fast recovery successfully until the *ACK* of packet 40 is received, without any timeout occurring.

Solution 2 to TCP Reno's Problem: TCP SACK

Although NewReno alleviates the multiple-packet-loss problem, the sender only learns of one new loss within one RTT. However, the SACK option, proposed in

Continued

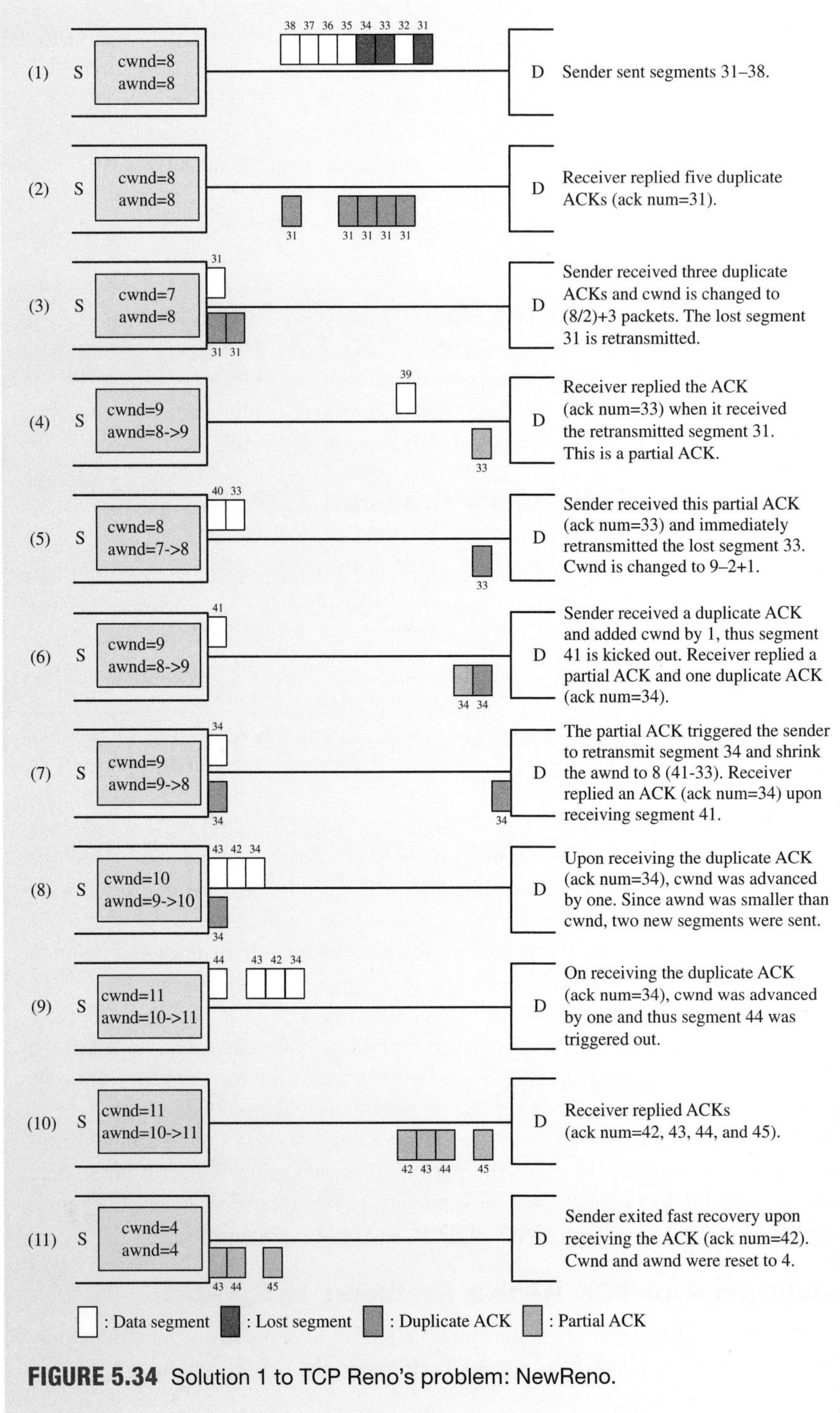

FIGURE 5.34 Solution 1 to TCP Reno's problem: NewReno.

RFC 1072, resolves this drawback. The receiver responds to the out-of-order packets by delivering the duplicate *ACK*s coupled with SACK options. RFC 2018 refines the SACK option and describes the behaviors of both the sender and receiver exactly.

One SACK option is applied to reporting one noncontiguous block of data, which the receiver successfully receives, via the two sequence numbers of the first and last packets in each block. Owing to the length limitation of the TCP option, there are a maximum number of SACK options allowed within one duplicate *ACK*. The first SACK option must report the latest block received, which contains the packet that triggers this *ACK*.

SACK adjusts `awnd` directly rather than `cwnd`. Thus, upon entering fast recovery, `cwnd` is halved and fixed during this period. When the sender either sends a new packet or retransmits an old one, `awnd` is incremented by 1. However, when the sender receives a duplicate ACK with a SACK option indicating that new data has been received, `awnd` is decreased by 1. Also, the SACK sender treats partial ACKs in a particular manner. That is, the sender decreases `awnd` by 2 rather than 1 because a partial ACK represents two packets that have left the network pipe: the original packet (assumed to have been lost) and the retransmitted packet.

Figure 5.35 illustrates an example of the SACK algorithm. Each duplicate *ACK* contains the information of the data blocks that were successfully received. When the sender received three duplicate *ACK*s, it knew that packets 31, 33, and 34 were lost. Therefore, if allowed, the sender could retransmit the lost packets immediately.

Solution 3 to TCP Reno's Problem: TCP FACK

FACK was proposed to be an auxiliary for SACK. In FACK, the sender uses the SACK options to determine the forwardmost packet that was received, where the forwardmost packet means the correctly received packet with the highest sequence number. FACK, for improved accuracy, estimates `awnd` as (`snd.nxt - snd.fack + retran_data`), where `snd.fack` is the forwardmost packet reported in the SACK options plus 1 and `retran_data` is the number of retransmitted packets after the previous partial *ACK*. Since the sender may have a long wait for three duplicate *ACK*s, FACK enters fast-retransmit earlier. That is, when `(snd.fack - snd.una)` is larger than 3, the sender enters fast retransmit without waiting for three duplicate *ACK*s.

Figure 5.36 depicts the FACK modification. The sender initiates retransmission after receiving the second duplicate ACK because `(snd.fack - snd.una)`, (36 – 31), is larger than 3. The lost packets can be retransmitted in FACK sooner than they can be in SACK since the former calculates `awnd` correctly. Thus, in Figure 5.36, it is evident that the number of outstanding packets stabilizes at four.

Solution 4 to TCP Reno's Problem: TCP Vegas

Vegas first revises Reno in its opportunity to trigger fast retransmit. Once a duplicate ACK is received, Vegas determines whether to trigger fast retransmit by

Continued

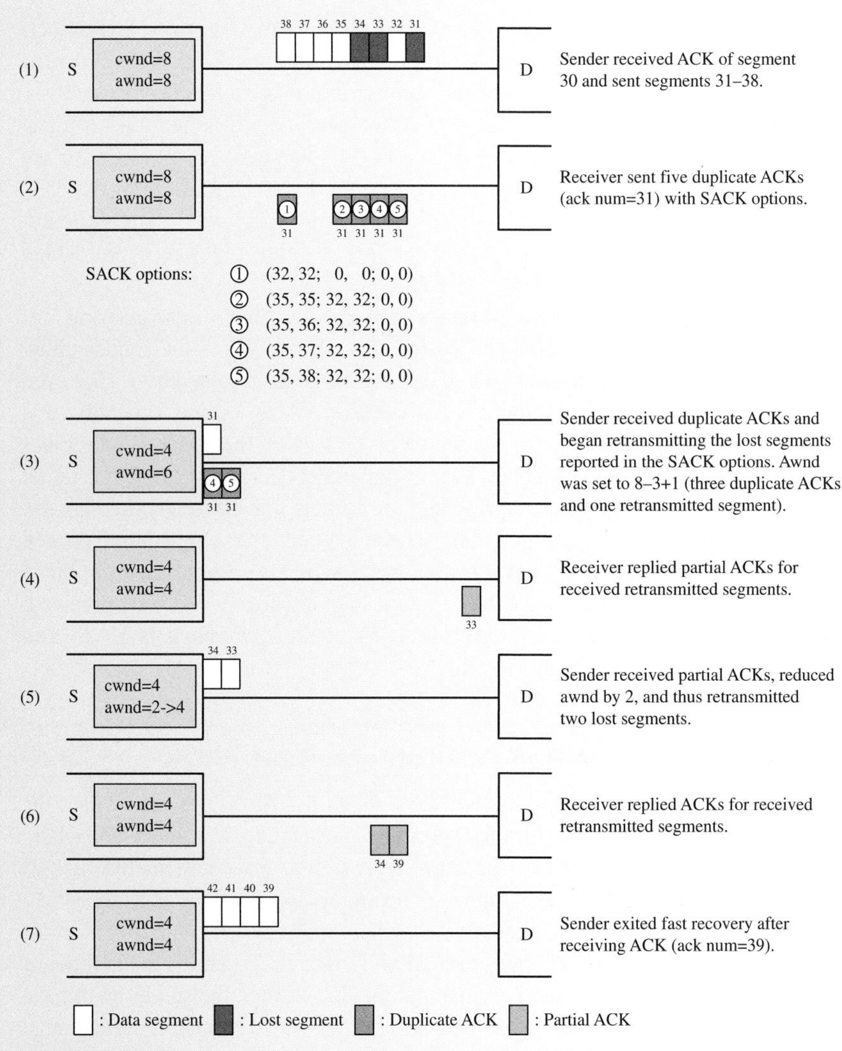

FIGURE 5.35 Solution 2 to TCP Reno's problem: TCP SACK option.

examining whether the difference between the current time and the sending time of the relevant packet plus the minimum RTT is greater than the timeout value. If yes, Vegas triggers fast retransmit without waiting for more duplicate ACKs. This modification can avert a situation in which the sender never receives triple duplicate ACKs, and therefore must rely on the coarse-grain retransmission timeout.

After a retransmission, the sender determines whether there is a multiple packet loss by checking the fine-grain timeout of unacknowledged packets. If any timeout occurs, the sender immediately retransmits the packet without waiting for any duplicate ACK.

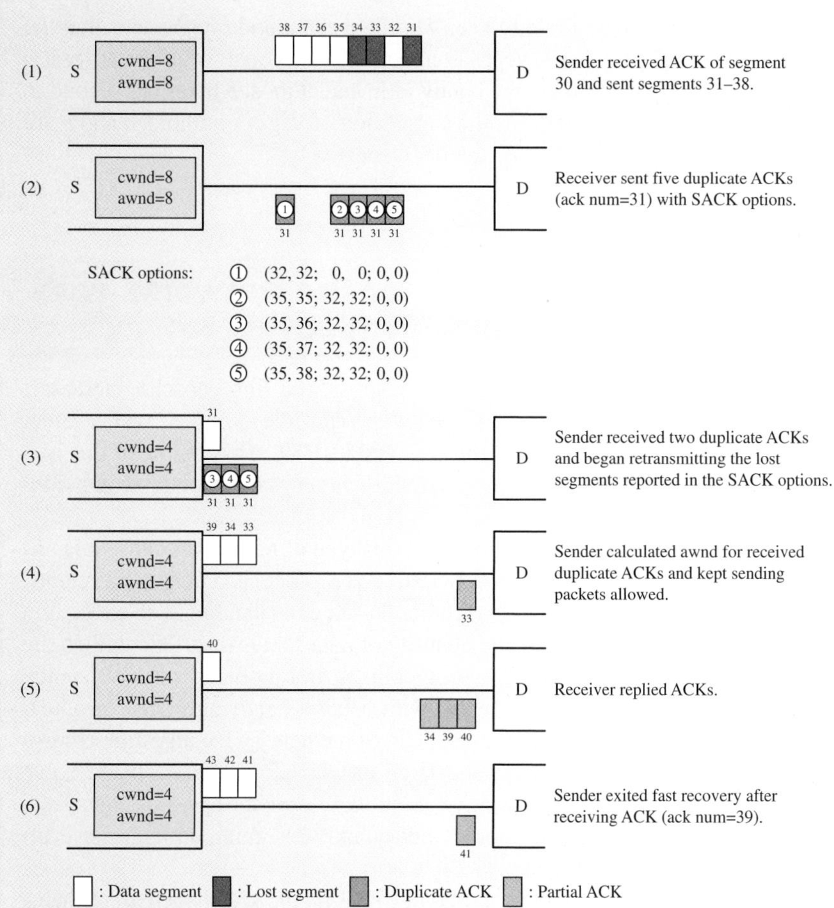

FIGURE 5.36 Solution 3 to TCP Reno's problem: TCP FACK modification.

Actually, TCP Vegas also uses the fine-grain RTT to improve the congestion control mechanisms. Compared to Reno, which reacts to packet losses and then decreases the sending rate to alleviate the congestion, Vegas tries to anticipate the congestion and then decrease the sending rate early to avoid congestion and packet losses. To anticipate the congestion, during the connection Vegas tracks the minimum RTT and saves it in a variable named *BaseRTT*. Then, by dividing `cwnd` by *BaseRTT,* Vegas learns the expected sending rate, denoted as *Expected,* which the connection can use without causing any packets queued in the path. Next, Vegas compares *Expected* with the current actual sending rate, denoted as *Actual,* and adjusts `cwnd` accordingly. Let $Diff = Expected - Actual$ and give two thresholds, $a<b$, defined in terms of KB/s. Then, `cwnd` in Vegas is increased by 1 per RTT when $Diff<a$, decreased by 1 if $Diff>b$, and fixed if *Diff* is between a and b.

Continued

Adjusting the sending rate to keep *Diff* between *a* and *b* represents that the network buffer occupied by a Vegas connection on average would be at least *a* bytes per second to well utilize the bandwidth, and at most *b* bytes per second to avoid overloading the network. At the suggestion of Vegas's authors, *a* and *b* are assigned to 1 and 3 times MSS/*BaseRTT*, respectively.

Principle in Action: TCP for the Networks with Large Bandwidth-Delay Product

As the network techniques continue to progress, the link capacity increases, resulting in a network path with a large *bandwidth-delay product,* which refers to the product of the bandwidth of the path and its RTT. An example of this network is that of satellite connections, where RTT is very large and link bandwidth may also be high.

Conventional TCP performs poorly in this type of network because it is unable to fully utilize the available bandwidth. The protocol can only achieve optimum throughput if a sender sends sufficiently large outstanding data exceeding the bandwidth-delay product. If the quantity of data sent is insufficient, then the path is not being kept busy, and the protocol is operating below peak efficiency for the path. However, in the network with a large bandwidth-delay product, this insufficient condition is likely to appear. Some new TCP congestion control schemes, BIC, CUBIC, FastTCP, and HighSpeed TCP (HSTCP), try to solve this problem. They are more *aggressive* about *increasing* the transmission speed, backing off when encountering losses but quickly resuming an aggressive increase in the transmission speed.

The most important component used in BIC is *binary* search increase. When a packet loss event happens, BIC reduces its window. The window size just before the reduction is set to the maximum and just after the reduction is set to the minimum. Then, BIC performs a binary search by jumping to the target, that is, the *"midpoint"* between the maximum and the minimum. The minimum or the maximum is undated according to whether a packet loss occurs. Binary search increase allows BIC to be aggressive when the difference between the current window size and the target window size is large. When the difference between the two window sizes shrinks, it forces the protocol to be less aggressive for TCP *fairness.*

CUBIC uses a simpler function, a *cubic* function whose shape is similar to the BIC window curve, to achieve the same goal. This function grows much more slowly than binary search increase near the target window size. Fast TCP measures *queuing delay,* instead of loss probability, to determine congestion in the network. By measuring this factor, it can increase the congestion window more quickly than TCP. HS-TCP is aggressive about increasing the congestion window after it reaches a window *threshold,* therefore more quickly responding to changes in available bandwidth. It uses a *table* to determine by what factor to increase the congestion window.

5.4 SOCKET PROGRAMMING INTERFACES

Networking applications use services provided by underlying protocols to perform special-purpose networking jobs. For example, applications such as `telnet` and `ftp` use services provided by the transport protocol; `ping`, `traceroute`, and `arp` directly use services provided by the IP layer; packet capturing applications running directly on link protocols may be configured to capture the entire packet, including the link protocol header. In this section, we shall see how Linux implements the socket interfaces for programming the preceding applications.

5.4.1 Socket

A *socket* is an abstraction of the end point of a communication channel. As its name suggests, the "end-to-end" protocol layer controls the data communications between the two end points of a channel. The end points are created by networking applications using socket APIs of an appropriate type. Networking applications can then perform a series of operations on that socket. The operations that can be performed on a socket include *control* operations (such as associating a port number with the socket, initiating or accepting a connection on the socket, or releasing the socket), *data transfer* operations (such as writing data through the socket to some peer application, or reading data from some peer application through the socket), and *status* operations (such as finding the IP address associated with the socket). The complete set of operations that can be performed on a socket constitutes the socket APIs.

To open a socket, an application program first calls the `socket()` function to initialize an end-to-end channel. The standard socket call, `sk=socket(domain, type, protocol)`, requires three parameters. The first parameter specifies the domain or address family. Commonly used families are `AF_UNIX` for communications bounded on the local machine, and `AF_INET` for communications based on IPv4 protocols. The second parameter specifies the type of socket. Common values for socket type, when dealing with the `AF_INET` family, include `SOCK_STREAM` (typically associated with TCP) and `SOCK_DGRAM` (associated with UDP). Socket type influences how packets are handled by the kernel before being passed up to the application. The last parameter specifies the *protocol* that handles the packets flowing through the socket. The `socket` function returns a file descriptor through which operations on the socket can be applied.

The values of the socket parameters depend on what underlying protocols are used. In the next two subsections we investigate three types of socket APIs. They correspond to accessing the transport layer, the IP layer, and the link layer, respectively, as we can see in their open source implementations.

5.4.2 Binding Applications through UDP and TCP

The services most widely used by networking applications are those provided by transport protocols such as UDP and TCP. A socket file descriptor is returned from the `socket(AF_INET, SOCK_DGRAM, IPPROTO_UDP)` function and

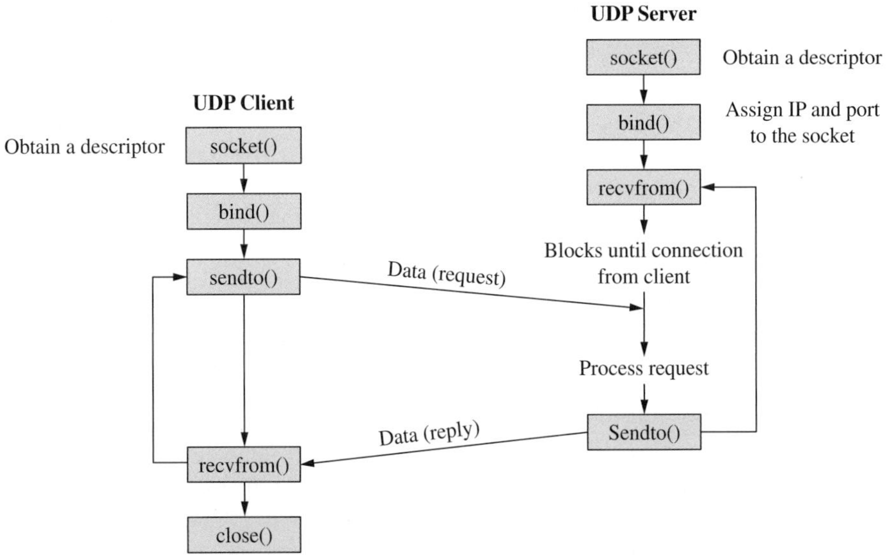

FIGURE 5.37 Socket functions for simple UDP client-server programs.

initialized as a UDP socket, where `AF_INET` indicates Internet address family, `SOCK_DGRAM` stands for datagram service, and `IPPROTO_UDP` indicates the UDP protocol. A series of operations can be performed on the descriptor, such as those functions in Figure 5.37.

In Figure 5.37, before the connection is established, the UDP server as well as the client creates a socket and uses the `bind()` system call to assign an IP address and a port number to the socket. Note that `bind()` is optional and is usually not called at the client. When `bind()` is not called, the kernel selects the default IP address and a port number for the client. Then, after a UDP server binds to a port, it is ready to receive requests from the UDP client. The UDP client may loop through the `sendto()` and `recvfrom()` functions to do some useful work until it finishes its job. The UDP server continues accepting requests, processing the requests, and feedbacking the results using `sendto()` and `recvfrom()`. Normally, a UDP client does not need to call `bind()` as it does not need to use well-known ports. The kernel dynamically assigns an unused port to the client when it calls `sendto()`.

Similarly, a socket file descriptor returned from `socket(AF_INET, SOCK_STREAM, IPPROTO_TCP)` is initialized as a TCP socket, where `AF_INET` indicates Internet address family, `SOCK_STREAM` stands for the reliable byte-stream service, and `IPPROTO_TCP` means the TCP protocol. The functions to be performed on the descriptor are depicted in Figure 5.38. Here by default `bind()` is not called at the client.

The flowchart of the simple TCP client-server programs is a little bit complex due to the connection-oriented property of TCP. It contains connection establishment, data transfer, and connection termination stages. Besides `bind()`, the server calls `listen()` to allocate the connection queue to the socket and waits for connection requests from clients. The `listen()` system call expresses the willingness of the server to start accepting incoming connection requests. Each listening socket contains two queues: (1)

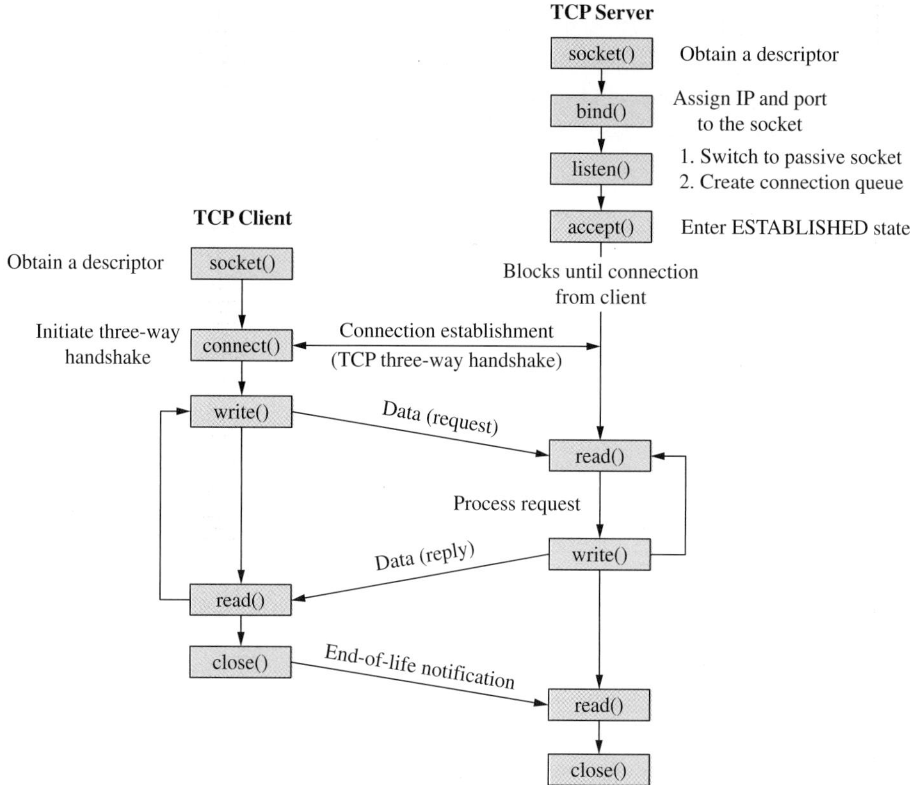

FIGURE 5.38 Socket functions for simple TCP client-server programs.

partially established request queue and (2) fully established request queue. A request would first stay in the partially established queue during the three-way handshake. After the connection is established with the three-way handshake finished, the request would be moved to the fully established request queue.

The partially established request queue in most operating systems has a maximum queue length, e.g., 5, even if the user specifies a value larger than that. Thus, the partially established request queue could be the target of a denial of service (DoS) attack. If a hacker continuously sends SYN requests without finishing the three-way handshake, the request queue will be saturated and cannot accept new connection requests from well-behaving clients.

The `listen()` system call is commonly followed by the `accept()` system call, whose job is to de-queue the first request from the fully-established request queue, initialize a new socket pair and return the file descriptor of the new socket created for the client. That is, the `accept()` system call provided by the BSD socket results in the automatic creation of a new socket, largely different from that in the TLI sockets where an application must explicitly create a new socket for the new connection. Note that the original listening socket is still listening on the well-known port for new connection requests. Of course the new socket pair contains the IP

Principle in Action: SYN Flooding and Cookies

Using the three-way handshake protocol might cause a *SYN flooding attack,* in which an attacker sends many successive SYN requests to a victim's system. It works as a server allocates resources after receiving a SYN but never receives an ACK. When these *half-open* connections exhaust all resources on the server, no new legitimate connections can be established, causing denial of service (DoS). There are two main methods to operate a SYN flooding attack: purposely not sending the last ACK, or spoofing the source IP address in the SYN, which causes the server to send the SYN+ACK to the falsified IP address, and thus never receive the ACK.

SYN cookies can be used to guard against SYN flooding attacks. SYN cookies are defined as "particular choices of initial TCP sequence numbers by TCP servers." A server using SYN cookies does not have to drop connections when its SYN queue, which stores the arriving SYNs, is full. Instead, it sends back a SYN+ACK with a particularly designed initial sequence number, that is, a SYN cookie. When the server receives a subsequent ACK from the client, it first checks this sequence number and then reconstructs the *pseudo* SYN queue entry, as if a SYN were stored in its SYN queue, using information *encoded* in this sequence number. That is, when SYN cookies are issued, the server does not rely on the SYN queue to keep track of the three-way handshake. Instead, it relies on the encoded SYN cookies. Thus, even if its SYN queue is full, the server is still capable of accepting real connections that finish the three-way handshake. As we shall see in Chapter 6, a similar cookie idea is also used for the stateless HyperText Transfer Protocol (HTTP) to keep track of long-term session states.

address and port number of the client. The server program can then decide whether or not to accept the client's connection request.

The TCP client uses `connect()` to invoke the three-way handshaking process to establish the connection. After that, the client and the server can perform byte-stream transfers between them.

Open Source Implementation 5.7: Socket Read/Write Inside Out

Overview

Figure 5.39 displays the relative location of each mentioned part of the Linux 2.6 kernel. General socket APIs and their subsequent function calls reside in the `net` directory. IPv4-specific source codes are put separately in the `ipv4` directory, as is the case for IPv6. The BSD socket is just an interface to its underlying protocols such as IPX and INET. The currently widely used IPv4

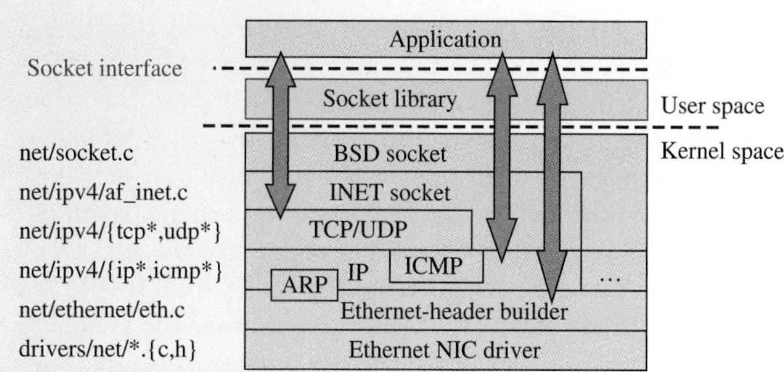

FIGURE 5.39 Protocol stack and programming interfaces in Linux 2.6.

protocol corresponds to the INET socket if the socket address family is specified as `AF_INET`. The dominant link-level technology, Ethernet, has its header built within the `net/ethernet/eth.c`. After that, the Ethernet frame is moved from the main memory to the network interface card by the Ethernet driver that resides in the `drivers/net/` directory. Drivers in this directory are hardware dependent, as many vendors have Ethernet card products with different internal designs. Similar structures also apply to WLAN and other links.

Algorithm Implementations

The internals of the socket APIs used by simple TCP client-server programs in Linux are illustrated in Figure 5.40. Programming APIs invoked from the

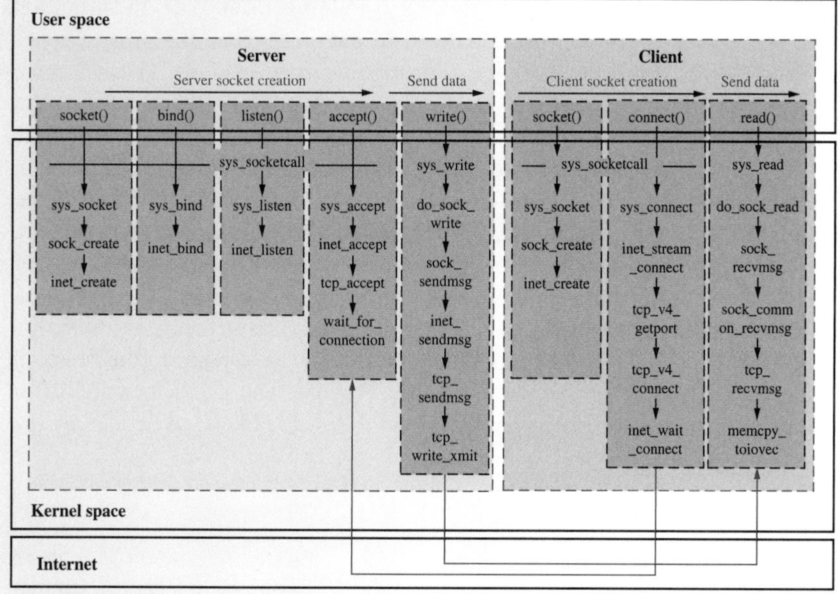

FIGURE 5.40 Socket read/write in Linux: Kernel space vs. user space.

Continued

user-space programs are translated into the sys_socketcall() kernel call and are then dispatched to their corresponding sys_*() calls. The sys_socket() (in net/socket.c) calls sock_create() to allocate the socket and then calls inet_create() to initialize the sock structure according to the given parameters. The other sys_*() functions call their corresponding inet_*() functions because the sock structure is initialized to Internet address family (AF_INET). Since read() and write() in Figure 5.40 are not socket-specific APIs but are commonly used by file I/O operations, their call flows follow their inode operations in the file system to find that the given file descriptor is actually related to a sock structure. Subsequently they are translated into the corresponding do_sock_read() and do_sock_write() functions, and so on, which are socket-aware.

In most UNIX systems the read()/write() functions are integrated into the Virtual File System (VFS). VFS is the software layer in the kernel that provides the file system interface to user space programs. It also provides an abstraction within the kernel which allows different file system implementations to coexist.

Data Structures

In Linux 2.6, the kernel data structures, used by the functions of a TCP connection as displayed in Figure 5.40, are illustrated in Figure 5.41. After the sender initializes the socket and gets the file descriptor (assumed to be in fd[1] in the open file table), when the user-space program operates on that descriptor, it follows the arrow link to point to the file structure, where it contains a directory entry f_dentry pointing to an inode structure. The inode structure can be initialized to one of various file system types supported by Linux, including the socket structure type. The socket structure contains a sock structure, which keeps network-related information and data structures from the transport layer down to the link layer. When the socket is initialized as a byte-stream, reliable, connection-oriented TCP socket, the transport layer protocol information tp_pinfo is then initialized as the tcp_opt structure, where many TCP-related variables and data structures, such as congestion window snd_cwnd, are stored. The proto pointer of the sock structure links to the proto structure that contains the operation primitives of the protocol. Each member of the proto structure is a function pointer. For TCP, the function pointers are initialized to point to the function list contained in the tcp_func structure. Anyone who wants to write his or her own transport protocol in Linux should follow the interface defined by the proto structure.

Exercises

As shown in Figure 5.41, the structure proto in the structure sock provides a list of function pointers that link to the necessary operations of a socket, such as connect, sendmsg, and recvmsg. By linking different sets of functions to the list, a socket can send or receive data over different protocols. Find out and read the function sets of other protocols such as UDP.

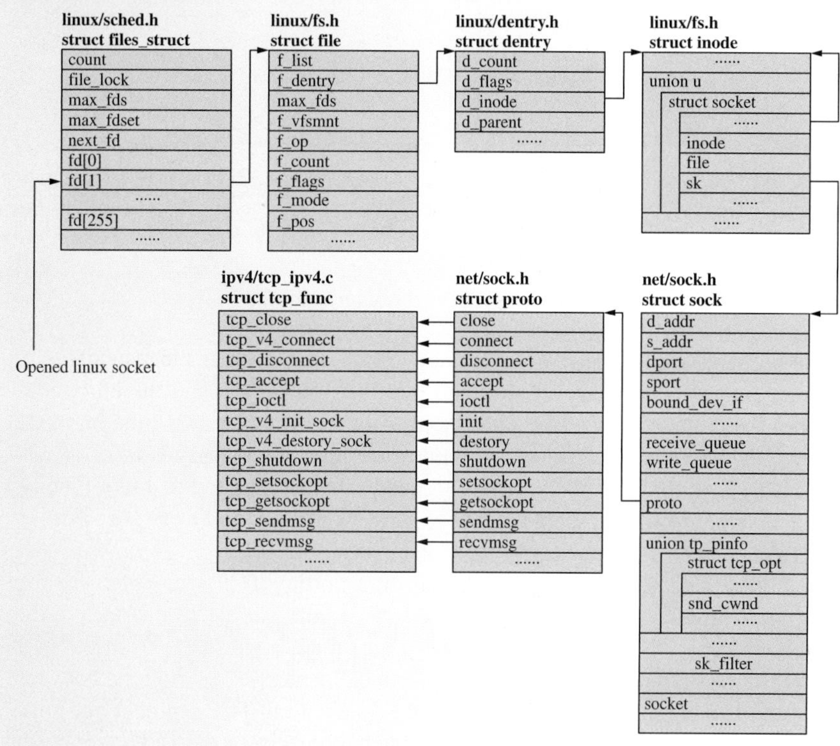

FIGURE 5.41 Kernel data structures used by the socket APIs.

Performance Matters: Interrupt and Memory Copy at Socket

Receiving segments at a socket actually invokes two processing flows, as shown in the call graph of Figure 5.42. The first flow starts from the system call, `read()`, later waits on the `tcp_recvmsg()` (for the case of TCP), which needs to be triggered by `sk_data_ready()`, and ends at the return to the user space. Thus, the time spent on this flow presents the user-perceived latency. The second flow starts from `tcp_v4_rcv()` (for the case of TCP) called by the IP layer with an incoming packet and ends at calling `sk_data_ready()` to trigger the resumption of first flow. Figure 5.42 shows the time spent on receiving

Continued

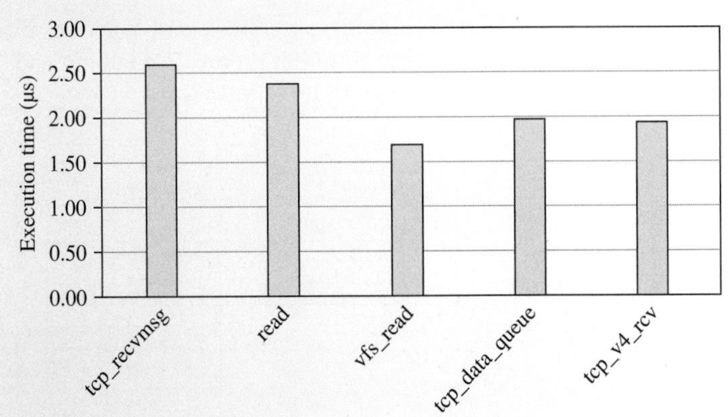

FIGURE 5.42 Latency in receiving TCP segments in the TCP layer.

TCP segments in the transport layer. `tcp_recvmsg()` takes the responsibility to copy data from the kernel structure into the user buffer, and therefore consumes the most time (2.6 μs). The system call, `read()`, spends time on mode switching between user and kernel modes. Besides, it also spends time on system table lookup. Therefore, `read()` spends significant time (2.4 μs). Finally, in the second flow, time spent on `tcp_data_queue()` and `tcp_v4_rcv()` are to queue and validate segments, respectively.

Figure 5.43 shows the time spent in transmitting TCP segments. The top two most time-consuming functions are functionally similar to the ones in the receiving case. They are `tcp_sendmsg()`, which copies data from the user buffer to the kernel structure, and the system call `write()`, switching between user and kernel modes. After examining the time of both TCP segment transmission and reception, we can conclude that the bottlenecks of the TCP layer occur at two places: memory copy between the user buffer and the kernel structure, and switching between user and kernel modes.

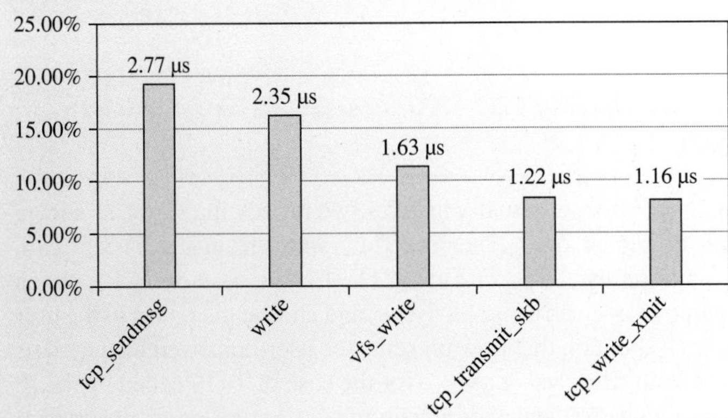

FIGURE 5.43 Latency in transmitting TCP segments in the TCP layer.

5.4.3 Bypassing UDP and TCP

Sometimes applications do not want to use the services provided by the transport layer. Tools such as `ping` and `traceroute` send packets directly without opening a UDP or TCP socket; they just use the services provided by the IP layer. Some applications even bypass the IP services and directly communicate over the link channel. For example, packet-sniffing applications, such as `tcpdump` and `wireshark`, capture raw packets directly on the wire. Such applications need to open a completely different socket compared with those of UDP or TCP. This subsection aims at exploring the programming method in Linux that can achieve these objectives. Next we go through three open source implementations that do the trick.

Open Source Implementation 5.8: Bypassing the Transport Layer

Overview

Since the arrival of Linux 2.0, a new protocol family called Linux packet socket (`AF_PACKET`) has been introduced to allow an application to send and receive packets that deal directly with the network card driver rather than the usual TCP/IP or UDP/IP protocol stack handling. Any packet sent through the socket can be passed directly to the Ethernet interface, and any packet received through the interface will be passed directly to the application.

Algorithm Implementations

The `AF_PACKET` family supports two slightly different socket types, `SOCK_DGRAM` and `SOCK_RAW`. The former leaves the burden of adding and removing Ethernet level headers to the kernel, while the latter gives the application complete control over the Ethernet header. Their implementations are in `net/packet/af_packet.c`. By checking the structure variable `packet_ops`, you can locate the main operation functions corresponding to the family, such as `packet_bind()`, `packet_sendmsg()`, and `packet_recvmsg()`.

The code in `packet_recvmsg()` is easy to understand. First, `skb_recv_datagram()` is called to get a packet via the `skb` buffer. Then, the packet data is copied by `skb_copy_datagram_iovec()` into the user space, which later will be passed to the user-space program. Finally, the `skb` is released by `skb_free_datagram()`.

Compared with `packet_recvmsg()`, `packet_sendmsg()` has a more complicated procedure. It first checks whether the link-layer source address has been assigned by the upper-space program. If not, it will set the address based on the information kept in the data structure of the output device. Then a `skb` buffer is allocated by `sock_alloc_send_skb()`, and user-space data will be copied into the `skb` buffer by `memcpy_fromiovec()`.

Continued

If the socket is opened in the SOCK_DGRAM type, dev_hard_header() is called to handle the Ethernet-level header. Finally, the packet will be sent out by dev_queue_xmit() and the skb buffer will be released by kfree_skb().

Usage Example

To open a socket the of AF_PACKET family, the protocol field given in the socket() call must match one of the Ethernet protocol identifiers defined in /usr/include/linux/if_ether.h, which represents the registered protocols that can be shipped in an Ethernet frame. Unless dealing with very specific protocols, you typically use ETH_P_IP, which encompasses all of the IP-suite protocols (TCP, UDP, ICMP, raw IP, and so on). However, if you want to capture all packets, ETH_P_ALL instead of ETH_P_IP will be used, as shown in the following example:

```
#include "stdio.h"
#include "unistd.h"
#include "sys/socket.h"
#include "sys/types.h"
#include "sys/ioctl.h"
#include "net/if.h"
#include "arpa/inet.h"
#include "netdb.h"
#include "netinet/in.h"
#include "linux/if_ether.h"

int main()
{
    int n;
    int fd;
    char buf[2048];
    if((fd = socket(PF_PACKET, SOCK_RAW, htons(ETH_P_
ALL))) == -1)
    {
        printf("fail to open socket\n");
        return(1);
}
while(1)
{
   n = recvfrom(fd, buf, sizeof(buf),0,0,0);
   if(n>0)
      printf("recv %d bytes\n", n);
}
return 0;
}
```

Since the sockets of the AF_PACKET family suffer from serious security vulnerabilities—for example, you can forge an Ethernet frame with a spoofed MAC address, they can be used only by users with the *root* privilege for the machine.

Exercises

Modify and compile the preceding example to dump the fields of the MAC header into a file and identify the transport protocol for each received packet. Note that you need to have the root privilege for the machine to run this.

Packet Capturing: Promiscuous Mode vs. Non-Promiscuous Mode

Packets in wired or wireless media can be captured by anyone who can directly access the transmission media. Applications that do such things are called *packet sniffers,* which are usually used for debugging network applications to check whether a packet is sent out with correct header and payload. The AF_PACKET family allows an application to retrieve data packets as they are received at the network-card level, but it still does not allow an application to read packets that are not addressed to its host. As we have seen before, this is because the network card discards all the packets that do not contain its own MAC address—an operation mode called non-promiscuous, where each network interface card minds its own business and reads only the frames directed to it. There are three exceptions to this rule:

1. A frame whose destination MAC address is the special broadcast address (FF:FF:FF:FF:FF:FF) will be picked up by any card.
2. A frame whose destination MAC address is a multicast address will be picked up by the cards that have multicast reception enabled.
3. A card that has been set in the promiscuous mode will pick up all the frames it senses.

Open Source Implementation 5.9: Making Myself Promiscuous

Overview

The last of the above three exceptions is, of course, the most interesting one for our purposes. To set a network card to the promiscuous mode, all we have to do is issue a particular ioctl() call to an open socket on that card. Since this is a potentially security-threatening operation, the call is only allowed for users with root privilege. If the "sock" contains an already-open socket, the following instructions will do the trick:

```
strncpy(ethreq.ifr_name,"eth0",IFNAMSIZ);
ioctl(sock, SIOCGIFFLAGS, &ethreq);
```

Continued

```
ethreq.ifr_flags |= IFF_PROMISC;
ioctl(sock, SIOCSIFFLAGS, &ethreq);
```

The `ethreq` is an `ifreq` structure defined in `/usr/include/net/if.h`. The first `ioctl` reads the current value of the Ethernet card flags; the flags are then ORed with `IFF_PROMISC`, which enables the promiscuous mode and are written back to the card with the second `ioctl`. You can easily check it out by executing the `ifconfig` command and observing the third line in the output.

Algorithm Implementations

Then, what happens to make your network card promiscuous after you invoke the system call `ioctl()`? Whenever an application-level program calls an `ioctl()`, the kernel calls `dev_ioctl()` to handle all network-type I/O control requests. Then, depending on the passing-in parameter, different functions will be called to handle the corresponding tasks. For example, `dev_ifsioc` would be called to set the interface flag corresponding to the sock when `SIOCSIFFLAGS` is given. Next, `_dev_set_promiscuity()` will be called to change the flag of the device via `ndo_change_rx_flags()` and `ndo_set_rx_mode()`, which are callback functions provided by the network device driver. The former function allows a device receiver to make changes to configuration when multicast or promiscuous is enabled, while the latter one informs the device receiver about the change of address list filtering.

Exercises

Read about network device drivers to figure out how `ndo_change_rx_flags()` and `ndo_set_rx_mode()` are implemented. If you cannot find out their implementations, then where is the related code in the driver to enable the promiscuous mode?

In-Kernel Packet Capturing and Filtering

Being an application and running as a process in the user space, a packet sniffer process may not be scheduled immediately by the kernel when a packet comes; thus the kernel should *buffer* it in the kernel socket buffer until the packet sniffer process is scheduled. Besides, users may specify *packet filters* to the sniffer for capturing only the packets of interest. The performance of packet capturing may degrade when packets are filtered at the user space because a huge amount of uninterested packets have to be transferred across the kernel-user space boundary. If sniffing at a busy network, such sniffers may not capture the packets in time before the packets overflow the socket buffer. Shifting the packet filters to the kernel would efficiently improve the performance.

Open Source Implementation 5.10: Linux Socket Filter

Overview

The `tcpdump` program accepts its user's filter request through the command line parameters to capture an interesting set of packets. Then `tcpdump` calls the `libpcap` (portable packet capturing library) to access the appropriate kernel-level packet filters. In the BSD systems, the Berkeley Packet Filter (BPF) performs the packet filtering in the kernel. Linux was not equipped with kernel packet filtering until the Linux Socket Filter (LSF) appeared in Linux 2.0.36. BPF and LSF are very much the same except for some minor differences such as user privilege to access the service.

Block Diagram

Figure 5.44 presents a layered model for packet capturing and filtering. The incoming packets are cloned from the normal protocol stack to the BPF, which then filters packets within the kernel level according the BPF instructions installed by the corresponding applications. Since only the packets passing through BPF will be directed to the user-space programs, the overhead of the data exchange between user and kernel spaces can be significantly reduced.

To employ a Linux socket filter with a socket, the BPF instruction can be passed to the kernel by using the `setsockopt()` function implemented in `socket.c`, and setting the parameter `optname` to `SO_ATTACH_FILTER`. The function will assign the BPF instruction to the `sock->sk_filter` illustrated in Figure 5.41. The BPF packet-filtering engine was written in a specific pseudo-machine code language inspired by Steve McCanne and Van Jacobson. BPF actually looks like a real assembly language with a couple of registers and a few instructions to load and store values and perform arithmetic operations and conditionally branch.

The filter code examines each packet on the attached socket. The result of the filter processing is an integer that indicates how many bytes of the packet (if any) the socket should pass to the application level. This contributes to a further advantage that since often for the purpose of packet capturing and filtering we are interested in just the first few bytes of a packet, we can save processing time by not copying the excess bytes.

Exercises

If you read the main page of `tcpdump`, you will find that `tcpdump` can generate the BPF code in the style of a human readable or C program fragment, according to your given filtering conditions: e.g., `tcpdump -d host 192.168.1.1`. Figure out the generated BPF code first. Then, write a program to open a raw socket (see Open Source Implementation 5.8), turn on the promiscuous mode (see Open Source Implementation 5.9), use `setsockopt`

Continued

to inject the BPF code into BPF, and then observe whether you indeed receive from the socket only the packets matching the given filter.

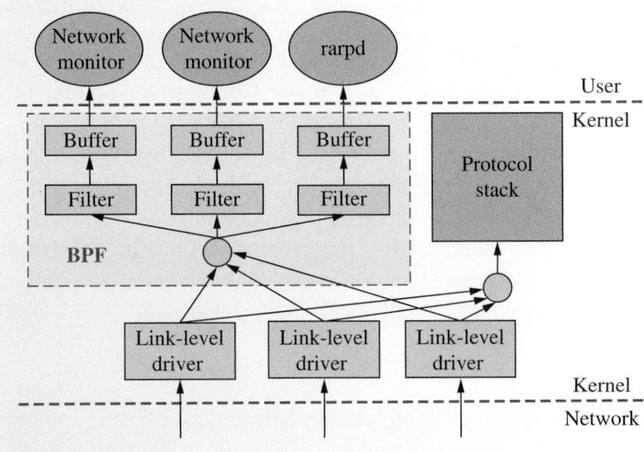

FIGURE 5.44 Toward efficient packet filtering: layered model.

5.5 TRANSPORT PROTOCOLS FOR REAL-TIME TRAFFIC

The transport protocols mentioned so far are not designed to accommodate the requirements of real-time traffic. Some other fine mechanisms are necessary to carry real-time traffic over the Internet. This section first highlights the requirements imposed by real-time traffic.

So far TCP can satisfy all requirements imposed by the non-real-time data traffic, including error control, reliability, flow control, and congestion control. Nevertheless, real-time traffic cannot be satisfied by either TCP or UDP, so several other transport protocols were developed for this very reason. The most popular one is RTP with its companion protocol RTCP. Since these transport protocols might not be mature enough for wide deployment, they are not implemented in the kernel but are often implemented as a library of functions to be called by application programs. Many real-time applications, such as Skype and Internet Radio, thus call these library functions, which then transmit their data over UDP. Since the resolved requirements are actually transport-layer issues, we addressed them in this chapter instead of in Chapter 6.

5.5.1 Real-Time Requirements

Real-time traffic often has multiple streams, such as video, audio, and text, to transfer within a *session,* which is a group of connections to transmit these streams. Thus, the first new requirement is the need to *synchronize* multiple streams within a session. Synchronization is also needed between the sender and the receiver in transferring and playing out the streams. Both kinds of synchronization require *timing* information passed between the sender and the receiver. Also, real-time traffic is more sensitive to the interrupt that may result from the *mobility* across different networks. Thus, supporting *service continuity* under mobility becomes the second new requirement.

Real-time traffic is continuous, and thus requires a stable, or smooth, available rate for transmission without lag. But it still needs to be smoothly congestion controlled to keep the Internet healthy and friendly to the self-regulating TCP traffic. This puts *smoothness* and *TCP-friendliness* as the third requirement. Some real-time traffic is so adaptive that it even changes the media coding rate, i.e., the average number of bits needed to encode one second of content, when the available rate fluctuates. This of course imposes the fourth requirement of gathering data for a *path quality* report for the sender.

Unfortunately, none of the popular transport protocols meet all of these four real-time requirements. As we shall see next, each of them meets some of the requirements. RTP and RTCP meet the first and the fourth ones and appear to be the most popular real-time transport protocols.

Multi-Streaming and Multi-Homing

Another transport protocol, Stream Control Transmission Protocol (SCTP), was introduced by R. Stewart and C. Metz in RFC 3286 and defined in RFC 4960. Like TCP, it provides a reliable channel for data transmission and uses the same congestion control algorithms. However, as the term "stream" appears in SCTP, SCTP provides two additional properties favorable to the streaming applications, which are the supports for multi-homing and multi-streaming.

The support for multi-streaming means that multiple streams, such as audio and video, can be transmitted concurrently through a session. That is, SCTP can support ordered reception individually for each stream and avoid the head-of-line (HOL) blocking that can occur with TCP. In TCP, control or some critical messages are often blocked because of a cloud of data packets queued ahead in the sender or receiver buffer.

The support for multi-homing means that even when a mobile user moves from one network to another, the user would not perceive any interrupt on its received stream. To support the multi-homing property, a session of the SCTP can be constructed concurrently by multiple connections through different network adapters, e.g., one from Ethernet and one from wireless LAN. Also, there is a heartbeat message for each connection to ensure its connectivity. Therefore, when one of the connections fails, SCTP can transmit the traffic through other connections immediately.

SCTP also revises the establishment and close procedures of a TCP connection. For example, a four-way handshake mechanism was proposed for connection establishment to overcome the security problem of TCP.

Smooth Rate Control and TCP-Friendliness

While TCP traffic still dominates the Internet, research indicates that the congestion control mechanism used in most versions of TCP may cause the transmission rate to oscillate too much to carry real-time traffic with low jitter requirements. Since TCP might not be suitable for real-time applications, developers tend to underdesign their congestion control or even to avoid using congestion control. Such an approach causes concern in the Internet community because the bandwidth in the Internet is publicly shared, and there is no control mechanism to decide how much bandwidth a flow should use in the Internet, which in the past has been self-controlled by TCP.

In 1998, a concept called TCP-friendly was proposed in RFC 2309. The concept held that a flow should respond to the congestion at the transit state and use no more bandwidth than a TCP flow at the steady state when both confront the same network conditions, such as packet loss ratio and RTT. Such a concept asks any Internet flow to use congestion control and use no more bandwidth than other TCP connections. Unfortunately, there is no answer to what is the best congestion control in this regard. Thus, a new transport protocol named Datagram Congestion Control Protocol (DCCP) was proposed in RFC 4340 by E. Kohler *et al.* DCCP allows free selection of a congestion control scheme. The protocol currently includes only two schemes, TCP-like and TCP-friendly rate control (TFRC). TFRC was first proposed in 2000 and defined as a protocol in RFC 3448 to detail what information should be exchanged between two end hosts to adjust the rate of a connection to meet TCP-friendliness.

Playback Reconstruction and Path Quality Report

As the Internet is a shared datagram network, packets sent on the Internet have unpredictable latency and jitter. However, real-time applications, such as Voice over IP

Principle in Action: Streaming: TCP or UDP?

Why is TCP not suitable for streaming? First, the loss retransmission mechanism is tightly embedded in TCP, which may not be necessary for streaming and even increases the latency and jitter for the received data. Next, continuous rate fluctuation may not be favored for streaming. That is, although the estimation on available bandwidth may be necessary for streaming to select a coding rate, streaming would not favor an oscillatory transmission rate, particularly the drastic response to packet losses, which was originally designed to avoid potential successive losses. Streaming applications may *accept* and *give up* losses. Since some mechanisms in TCP are not suitable for streaming, people turn to streaming over UDP. Unfortunately, UDP is too simple, providing no mechanism to estimate the current available rate. Besides, for security reasons UDP packets are sometimes dropped by the current intermediate network devices.

Although TCP and UDP are not suitable for streaming, they are still the only two mature transport protocols in today's Internet. Thus, most streaming data are indeed carried by the two protocols. UDP is used to carry pure *audio* streaming, like audio and VoIP. These streaming transmissions can simply be sent at a constant bit rate without much congestion control, because their required bandwidth is usually lower than the available bandwidth. On the other hand, TCP is used for streaming transmissions that require a bandwidth that is not always satisfied by the Internet—for example, the mix of video and audio. Then, to alleviate the oscillatory rate of TCP (the side effect of its bandwidth detection mechanism), a large buffer is used at the *receiver,* which *prolongs* the latency. Although the latency is tolerable for a one-way application, like watching clips from YouTube, it is *not* for an interactive application like a video conference. That is why researchers need to develop the smooth rate control introduced above.

(VoIP) and video conferencing, require appropriate timing information to reconstruct the playback at the receiver. The reconstruction at the receiver requires the *codec type* to choose the right decoder to decompress the payload, the *timestamp* to reconstruct the original timing in order to play out the data at the correct rate, and *sequence numbers* to place the incoming data packets in the correct order and to be used for packet loss detection. On the other hand, the senders of real-time applications also require *path quality feedbacks* from the receivers to react to network congestion. Additionally, in a multicast environment, the *membership* information needs to be managed. These control-plane mechanisms should be built into the standard protocol.

In summary, the data plane of real-time applications needs to address the codec, sequence number, and timestamp; in the control plane the focus is on the feedback report of the end-to-end latency/jitter/loss and membership management. To satisfy these requirements, RTP and RTCP have been proposed, as introduced in the next two subsections. Note that RTP and RTCP are often implemented by the applications themselves instead of by the operating system. Thus the applications can have full control over each RTP packet in such areas as defining the RTP header options.

5.5.2 Standard Data-Plane Protocol: RTP

RFC 1889 outlines a standard data-plane protocol: Real-time Transport Protocol (RTP). It is the protocol used to carry the voice/video traffic back and forth across a network. RTP does not have a well-known port because it operates with different applications that are themselves identified with ports. Therefore it operates on a UDP port, with 5004 designated as the default port. RTP is designed to work in conjunction with the auxiliary control protocol RTCP to get feedback on quality of data transmission and information about participants in the ongoing session.

How RTP Works

RTP messages consist of the header and payload. Figure 5.45 shows the RTP header format. The real-time traffic is carried in the payload of the RTP packet. Note that RTP itself does not address resource management and reservation and does not guarantee quality-of-service for real-time services. RTP assumes that these properties, if available, are provided by the underlying network. Since the Internet occasionally loses and reorders packets or delays them by a variable amount of time, to cope with these impairments, the RTP header contains *timestamp* information and a *sequence number* that allow the receivers to reconstruct the timing produced by the source. With these two fields the RTP can ensure that the packets are in sequence, determine if any packets are lost, and synchronize the traffic flows. The sequence number increments by 1 for each RTP data packet sent. The timestamp reflects the sampling instant of the first octet in the RTP data packet. The sampling instant must be derived from the clock that increments monotonically and linearly in time to allow synchronization and jitter calculations. Notably, when a video frame is split into multiple RTP packets, all of them have the same timestamp, which is why the timestamp is inadequate to resequence the packets.

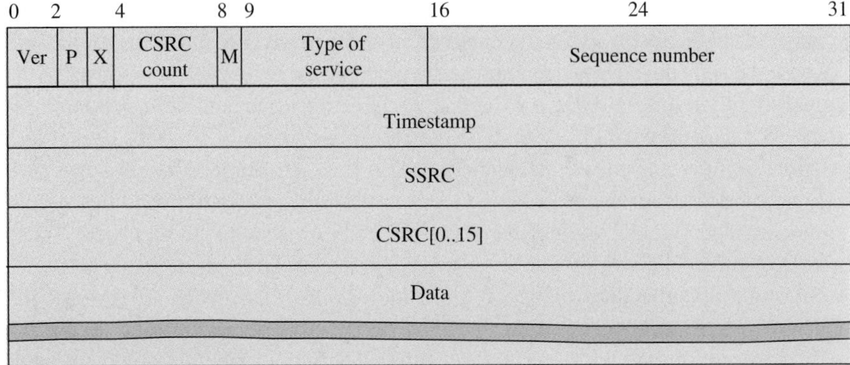

FIGURE 5.45 RTP header format.

One of the fields included in the RTP header is the 32-bit *Synchronization Source Identifier (SSRC),* which is able to distinguish synchronization sources within the same RTP session. Since multiple voice/video flows can use the same RTP session, the SSRC field identifies the transmitter of the message for synchronization purposes at the receiving application. It is a randomly chosen number to ensure that no two synchronization sources use the same number within an RTP session. For example, branch offices may use a VoIP gateway to establish an RTP session between them. However, many phones are installed on each side, so the RTP session may simultaneously contain many call connections. These call connections can be multiplexed by the SSRC field.

Codec Encapsulation

To reconstruct the real-time traffic at the receiver, the receiver must know how to interpret the received packets. The payload type identifier specifies the payload format as well as the encoding/compression schemes. Payload types include, among others, PCM, MPEG1/MPEG2 audio and video, JPEG video, and H.261 video streams. At any given time of transmission, an RTP sender can send only one type of payload, although the payload type may change during transmission, for example, to adjust to network congestion.

5.5.3 Standard Control-Plane Protocol: RTCP

RTCP is the control protocol designed to work in conjunction with RTP. It is standardized in RFC 1889 and 1890. In an RTP session, participants periodically emit RTCP packets to convey feedback on quality of data delivery and information about membership. RFC 1889 defines five RTCP packet types:

1. **RR:** Receiver report. Receiver reports are sent by participants that are not active senders within the RTP session. They contain reception quality feedback about data delivery, including the *highest packet number received,* the *number of packets lost, inter-arrival jitter,* and *timestamps* to calculate the round-trip delay between the sender and the receiver. The information can be useful for adaptive encodings. For example, if the quality of the RTP session is found to worsen as time goes by,

the sender may decide to switch to a low-bitrate encoding so that users may get a smoother feeling about the real-time transport. On the other hand, network administrators can evaluate the network performance by monitoring RTCP packets.

2. **SR:** Sender report. Sender reports are generated by active senders. Besides the reception quality feedback as in RR, SR contains a sender information section, providing information on inter-media synchronization, cumulative packet counters, and number of bytes sent.
3. **SDES:** Source description items to describe the sources. In RTP data packets, sources are identified by randomly generated 32-bit identifiers. These identifiers are not convenient for human users. RTCP SDESs contain globally unique identifiers of the session participants. They may include user's name, e-mail address, or other information.
4. **BYE:** Indicates the end of participation.
5. **APP:** Application-specific functions. APP is intended for experimental use when new applications or features are developed.

Since a participant may join or leave a session at any time, it is important to know who is participating and how good their received quality is. For this, the nonactive participants should periodically send the RR packets and send BYE when they plan to leave. On the other hand, the active sender should send the SR packets, which not only provide the same function as the RR packets but also ensure that each participant knows how to replay the received media data. Finally, to help the participants to get more information about others, the participants should periodically send the SDES packets with their identifier numbers to introduce their contact information.

Historical Evolution: RTP Implementation Resources

RTP is an open protocol that does not provide preimplemented system calls. Implementation is tightly coupled to the application itself. Application developers have to add the complete functionality in the application layer by themselves. However, it is always more efficient to share and reuse code rather than starting from scratch. The RFC 1889 specification itself contains numerous code segments that can be borrowed directly for the applications. Here we provide some implementations with source code available. Many modules in the source code can be usable with minor modifications. The following is a list of useful resources:

- **self-contained sample code in RFC1889.**
- **vat** (http://www-nrg.ee.lbl.gov/vat/)
- **tptools** (ftp://ftp.cs.columbia.edu/pub/schulzrinne/rtptools/)
- **NeVoT** (http://www.cs.columbia.edu/~hgs/rtp/nevot.html)
- **RTP Library** (http://www.iasi.rm.cnr.it/iasi/netlab/gettingSoftware.html) by E.A. Mastromartino offers convenient ways to incorporate RTP functionality into C++ Internet applications.

5.6 SUMMARY

In this chapter we first learned three key features considered in the transport layer to provide a process-to-process channel across the Internet: (1) port-level addressing, (2) reliable packet delivery, and (3) flow rate control. Then we learned about the unreliable connectionless transport protocol UDP and the widely used transport protocol TCP. Compared to UDP, which only adds the feature of port-level addressing on top of the IP layer, TCP is like a *total solution* with several well-proven techniques, including (1) the three-way handshake protocol for connection establishment/termination, (2) the acknowledgment and retransmission mechanism to ensure the receiver error-free reception of data from the source, which might be located thousands of miles away from the receiver, (3) the sliding-window flow control and evolving congestion control algorithm to elevate the transmission throughput and decrease the packet loss ratio. We illustrated various TCP versions and compared their behaviors in retransmitting *potentially* lost packets. Finally, we looked at the requirements and issues of a transport layer protocol for real-time streaming traffic, including multi-streaming, multi-homing, smooth rate control, TCP-friendliness, playback reconstruction, and path quality reporting.

Besides protocols, this chapter also explained the Linux approach to realizing the socket interfaces and described their function calls. The socket interfaces are the boundary between the kernel-space network protocols and the user-space applications. Therefore, with the socket interfaces, the application developers simply focus on what they want to send or receive over the Internet without dealing with the complicated four layers of network protocols and kernel issues, which greatly lowers the development barrier. In Chapter 6 we shall see various kinds of interesting and daily used applications, including e-mail, file transfer, WWW, instant text/voice communication, online audio/video streaming, and peer-to-peer applications. They ride on top of UDP, TCP, or both.

COMMON PITFALLS

Window Size: Packet-Count Mode vs. Byte-Count Mode

Different implementations could have different interpretations of the TCP standard. Readers may get confused about window size in packet-count mode and byte-count mode. Although `rwnd` reported by the receiver is in bytes, previous illustrations about `cwnd` have been in units of packets and then have been translated into bytes by multiplying the MSS in order to select the window size from `min(cwnd, rwnd)`. Some operating systems may directly use the byte-count mode `cwnd`, so the algorithm should be adjusted as follows:

```
if (cwnd < ssthresh){
      cwnd = cwnd + MSS;
else {
      cwnd = cwnd + (MSS*MSS)/cwnd
}
```

That is, in the slow start phase, rather than incrementing `cwnd` by 1 in the packet-count mode, we increment it by `MSS` in the byte-count mode every time an ACK is received. In the congestion-avoidance phase, rather than incrementing `cwnd` by `1/cwnd` in the packet-count mode, we increment it by a fraction of `MSS`, i.e., `MSS/cwnd`, every time an ACK is received.

RSVP, RTP, RTCP, and RTSP

This chapter discusses the RTP and RTCP protocols for real-time traffic in the Internet. However, their differences from other related protocols, such as RSVP and RTSP, need to be clarified:

- RSVP is the signaling protocol that notifies the network element along the path to reserve adequate resources, such as bandwidth, computing power, or queuing space, for real-time applications. It does not deliver the data. RSVP shall be studied in Chapter 6.

- RTP is the transport protocol for real-time data. It provides timestamp, sequence number, and other means to handle the timing issues in real-time data transport. It relies on RSVP, if supported, for resource reservation to provide quality of service.
- RTCP is the control protocol with RTP that helps with quality of service and membership management.
- RTSP is a control protocol that initiates and directs delivery of streaming multimedia data from media servers. It is the "Internet VCR remote control protocol." Its role is to provide the remote control. The actual data delivery is done separately, most likely by RTP.

FURTHER READINGS

TCP Standard

The headers and state diagram of TCP were first defined by Postel in RFC 793, but its congestion control technique was later proposed and revised by Jacobson because congestion was not an issue in the beginning of the Internet. Observations on the congestion control of TCP were given in the work by Zhang, Shenker, and Clark, while requirements for host system implementations and some corrections for TCP were given in RFC 1122. Stevens and Paxson standardized the four key behaviors of the congestion control in TCP. SACK and FACK were defined in RFC 2018 and the SIGCOMM'96 paper by Mathis and Mahdavi, respectively. Nagle's algorithm and Clark's approach to solve the silly window syndrome were described in Nagle's SIGCOMM'84 paper and RFC 813, respectively.

- J. Postel, "Transmission Control Protocol," RFC 793, Sept. 1981.
- V. Jacobson, "Congestion Avoidance and Control," *ACM SIGCOMM,* pp. 273–288, Stanford, CA, Aug. 1988.
- V. Jacobson, "Modified TCP Congestion Avoidance Algorithm," mailing list, end2end-interest, 30 Apr. 1990.
- L. Zhang, S. Shenker, and D.D. Clark, "Observations on the Dynamics of a Congestion Control Algorithm: The Effects of Two-Way Traffic," *ACM SIGCOMM,* Sept. 1991.
- R. Braden, "Requirements for Internet Hosts—Communication Layers," STD3, RFC 1122, Oct. 1989.
- W. Stevens, "TCP Slow Start, Congestion Avoidance, Fast Retransmit, and Fast Recovery Algorithms," RFC 2001, Jan. 1997.
- V. Paxson, "TCP Congestion Control," RFC 2581, Apr. 1999.
- M. Mathis, J. Mahdavi, S. Floyd, and A. Romanow, "TCP Selective Acknowledgment Options," RFC 2018, Oct. 1996.
- M. Mathis and J. Mahdavi, "Forward Acknowledgment: Refining TCP Congestion Control," *ACM SIGCOMM,* pp. 281–291, Stanford, CA, Aug. 1996.
- J. Nagle, "Congestion Control in IP/TCP Internetworks," *ACM SIGCOMM,* pp. 11–17, Oct. 1984.
- D. D. Clark, "Window and Acknowledgment Strategy in TCP," RFC 813, July 1982.

On TCP Versions

The first two papers compare different versions of TCP. The third paper introduces TCP Vegas, while the final two papers study and provide the solution to the application of congestion control in networks of high bandwidth-delay product.

- K. Fall and S. Floyd, "Simulation-Based Comparisons of Tahoe, Reno, and SACK TCP," *ACM Computer Communication Review,* Vol. 26, No. 3, pp. 5–21, Jul. 1996.
- J. Padhye and S. Floyd, "On Inferring TCP Behavior," in *Proceedings of ACM SIGCOMM,* pp. 287–298, San Diego, CA, Aug. 2001.
- L. Brakmo and L. Peterson, "TCP Vegas: End to End Congestion Avoidance on a Global Internet," *IEEE Journal on Selected Areas in Communications,* Vol. 13, No. 8, pp. 1465–1480, Oct. 1995.
- D. Wei, C. Jin, S. H. Low, and S. Hegde, "FAST TCP: Motivation, Architecture, Algorithms, Performance," *IEEE/ACM Transactions on Networking,* Vol. 14, No. 6, pp. 1246–1259, Dec. 2006.
- D. Katabi, M. Handley, and C. Rohrs, "Congestion Control for High Bandwidth-Delay Product Networks," in *Proceedings of ACM SIGCOMM,* pp. 89–102, Aug. 2002.

Modeling TCP Throughput

Two widely referred TCP throughput formulas were proposed in the following two papers. By giving packet loss ratio, RTT, and RTO, these formulas will return the mean throughput of a TCP connection.

- J. Padhye, V. Firoiu, D. Towsley, and J. Kurose, "Modeling TCP Throughput: A Simple Model and its Empirical Validation," *ACM SIGCOMM,* Vancouver, British Columbia, Sept. 1998.
- E. Altman, K. Avrachenkov, and C. Barakat, "A Stochastic Model of TCP/IP with Stationary Random Losses," *IEEE/ACM Transactions on Networking,* Vol. 13, No. 2, pp. 356–369, April 2005.

Berkeley Packet Filter

Here is the origin of the BSD packet filter.

- S. McCanne and V. Jacobson, "The BSD Packet Filter: A New Architecture for User-Level Packet Capture," *Proceedings of the Winter 1993 USENIX Conference,* pp. 259–269, Jan. 1993.

Transport Protocol for Real-time Traffic

The first two references present protocols for streaming traffic while the last two are classical TCP-friendly congestion control algorithms to control the throughput of streaming traffic over the Internet.

- R. Stewart and C. Metz, "SCTP: New Transport Protocol for TCP/IP," *IEEE Internet Computing,* Vol. 5, No. 6, pp. 64–69, Nov/Dec 2001.
- S. Floyd, M. Handley, J. Padhye, and J. Widmer, "Equation-Based Congestion Control for Unicast Applications," *ACM SIGCOMM,* Aug. 2000.
- Y. Yang and S. Lam, "General AIMD Congestion Control," *Proceedings of the IEEE ICNP 2000,* pp. 187–98, Nov. 2000.
- E. Kohler, M. Handley, and S. Floyd, "Designing DCCP: Congestion Control Without Reliability," *ACM SIGCOMM Computer Communication Review,* Vol. 36, No. 4, Sept. 2006.

NS2 Simulator

NS2 is a network simulator widely used by the Internet research community.

- K. Fall and S. Floyd, ns–Network Simulator, http://www.isi.edu/nsnam/ns/.
- M. Greis, "Tutorial for the Network Simulator ns," http://www.isi.edu/nsnam/ns/tutorial/index.html.

FREQUENTLY ASKED QUESTIONS

1. Layer-2 channel vs. Layer-4 channel? (Compare their channel length, error, and latency distribution.)
   Answer:
   Channel length: link vs. path
   Channel error: link vs. link and node
   Channel latency distribution: condensed vs. dispersed
2. TCP vs. UDP? (Compare their connection management, error control, and flow control.)
   Answer:
   Connection management: yes on TCP but no on UDP
   Error control:
   - UDP: optional checksum, no ack, no retransmission
   - TCP: checksum, ack, sequence number, retransmission

   Flow control:
   - UDP: none
   - TCP: dynamic window size to control outstanding bytes in transit, subject to network condition and receiver buffer occupancy.
3. Why does most real-time traffic run over UDP?
   Answer:
   Most real-time traffic can tolerate some loss but does not need delayed retransmissions. Its bit rate depends on the codec at the sender and should not be affected by the flow control mechanism.
4. What mechanisms are needed to support error control in TCP?
   Answer:
   Checksum, ack, sequence number, and retransmission.
5. Why does TCP need three-way handshake, instead of two-way, in connection setup?
   Answer:
   Both sides need to notify and ack the starting sequence number from each side. The first ack has been combined with the second notification. Thus, we still have three segments: first notification, first ack (second notification), and second ack.
6. When is a lost TCP segment retransmitted?
   Answer:
   Triple duplicate ack (quick) or RTO (retransmission timeout) (slow)
7. What factors are considered in deciding the TCP window size?
   Answer:
   Minimum (congestion window size, receiver window size) where the congestion window size runs AIMD (additive increase and multiplicative decrease) and the receiver window size is the advertised available buffer space of the receiver. The former is about the

network condition, while the latter is about the receiver condition.

8. How does the window grow in slow start and congestion avoidance?
Answer:
Slow start: exponential growth from 1 to 2, 4, 8, 16, etc.
Congestion avoidance: linear growth from, say, 32 to 33, 34, 35, etc.
9. Why are fast retransmit and fast recovery added to TCP? What major change does New Reno make?
Answer:
Fast retransmission: Retransmit if triple duplicate ack, i.e., earlier than RTO.
Fast recovery: Maintain the self-clocking behavior (by having enough window size to send new segment) during the loss recovery.
NewReno: Extend the fast recovery phase (which has large enough window size) until all segments sent before detecting triple duplicate ack are acked, which speed up the recovery of multiple packet losses.
10. How is the socket implemented in Linux? (Briefly describe the processing flow of socket functions and the data structures of sockets.)
Answer:
Processing flow: Socket functions called in a client or a server are system calls that generate software interrupts, which force the system to enter into the kernel mode and execute registered kernel functions to handle the interrupts. These kernel functions move data between kernel space buffer, i.e., `sk_buff`, and user space buffer.
Data structures: Special inode structure in the file system.
11. What are the available kernel-space and the user-space programs of Linux to filter and capture packets?
Answer:
Kernel space: Linux socket filter
User space library: libpcap
User space tool: tcpdump, wireshark, etc.
12. What extra support can be done over RTP and RTCP that cannot be done over UDP?
Answer:
RTP: codec encapsulation, timestamp for delay measurement, sequence number for loss detection, and synchronization.
RTCP: report delay, jitter, loss to the sender for codec bit rate adjustment.

EXERCISES

Hands-On Exercises

1. Ns-2 is the most popular simulator for TCP research. It includes a package called NAM that can visually replay the whole simulation in all timescales. Many Web sites that introduce ns-2 can be found on the Internet. Use NAM to observe a TCP running from a source to its destination, with and without buffer overflow at one intermediate router.

   - Step 1: Search the ns-2 Web site and download a suitable version for your target platform.
   - Step 2: Follow the installation instructions to install all the packages.
   - Step 3: Build a scenario consisting of three cascaded nodes, one for the Reno TCP source, one for an intermediate gateway, and one for the destination. The links to connect them are full-duplex 1 Mbps.
   - Step 4: Configure the gateway to have a large buffer. Run a TCP source toward the destination.
   - Step 5: Configure the gateway as to have a small buffer. Run a TCP source towards the destination.

   For all the Reno TCP states that the Reno TCP source in the preceding two tests enters, screen dump them and indicate which state the TCP source is in. The figures should be *correlated*. For example, to represent the slow start behavior you may display it with two figures: (1) an ACK is coming back; (2) the ACK triggers out two new data segments. Carefully organize the figures so that the result of this exercise is no more than one A4 page. Only display necessary information in the screen dumps. Pre-process the figures so that no window decorations (window border, NAM buttons) are displayed.
2. Exponential Weighted Moving Average (EWMA) is commonly used when the control needs to smooth out rapidly fluctuating values. Typical applications are smoothing the measured round-trip time, or

computing the average queue length in Random Early Detection (RED) queues. In this exercise, you are expected to run and observe the result of an EWMA program. Tune the network delay parameter to observe how the EWMA value evolves.

3. Reproduce Figure 5.24.
   - Step 1: Patching kernel: Logging time-stamped CWND/SeqNum
   - Step 2: Recompiling
   - Step 3: Installing new kernel and reboot
4. Linux Packet Socket is a useful tool when you want to generate arbitrary types of packets. Find and modify an example program to generate a packet and sniff the packet with the same program.
5. Dig out the retransmit timer management in FreeBSD 8.X Stable. How does it manage the timer? Use a compact table to compare it with that of Linux 2.6. Hint: You can begin the exercise by reading and tracking the calling path of the function `tcp_timer_rexmt()` in `netinet/tcp_timer.c` of FreeBSD and `tcp_retransmit_timer()` in `net/ipv4/tcp_timer.c` of Linux.
6. How does Linux integrate NewReno, SACK, and FACK in one box? Identify the key differences in variables mentioned in Subsection 5.3.8 and find out how Linux resolves the conflict.
7. What transport protocols are used in Skype, MSN, or other communication software? Please use wireshark to observe their traffic and find out the answer.
8. What transport protocols are used in MS Media Player or RealMedia? Please use wireshark to observe and find out the answer.
9. Write a client/server program with the socket interface. The client program may send out the words to the server once the user presses Enter, and the server will respond to these words with any meaningless terms. However, the server will close the connection once it receives the word bye. Also, once someone keys in "GiveMeYourVideo," the server will immediately send out a 50 MB data file with message size of 500 bytes.
10. Write a client/server program or modify the client program in Problem 9 to calculate and record the data transmission rate every 0.1 second for a 50 MB data transmission with message size of 500 bytes. Use xgraph or gnuplot to display the results.
11. Continue the work done in Problem 9. Modify the client program to use a socket embedded with a socket filter to filter out all packets that include the term "the_packet_is_infected". Then, compare the average transmission rate provided by the sockets for the data transmission of 50 MB with that done by a client program that simply discards these messages at the user layer. Hint: Open Source Implementation 5.10 provides information about how to embed a socket filter into your socket.
12. Modify the programs written in Problem 9 to create a socket based on SCTP to demonstrate that the voice talk can continue without any blocking due to the transmission of the large file, i.e., to demonstrate the benefit of multi-streaming from SCTP. Hint: You can find a demo code from the Internet by typing the keywords "SCTP multi-streaming demo code" into a search engine.

Written Exercises

1. Compare the role of error control between the data link layer, IP layer, and end-to-end layer. Of the link-layer technologies, choose Ethernet as the topic to discuss. Use a table with *keywords* to compare the objective, covered fields, algorithm, field length, and any other same/different properties. Why should there be so many error controls throughout a packet's life? List your reasons.
2. Compare the role of addressing between the data link layer, IP layer, end-to-end layer, and real-time transport layer. Of the link-layer technologies, choose Ethernet to discuss. Among the real-time transport protocols, choose RTP to discuss. Compare the objective, uniqueness, distribution/hierarchy, and other properties using a table filled with keywords.
3. Compare the role of flow control between the data link layer and end-to-end layer. Of the link-layer technologies, choose Fast Ethernet to discuss. Compare the objective, flow control algorithms, congestion control algorithms, retransmission timer/algorithms, and other important properties using a table filled with keywords. Further explanations should also be given to nontrivial table entries.
4. A mobile TCP receiver is receiving data from its TCP sender. What will the RTT and the RTO evolve when the receiver gets farther away and then nearer? Assume the moving speed is very fast so that the propagation delay ranges from 100 ms to 300 ms within 1 second.
5. A connection running TCP transmits packets across a path with 500 ms propagation delay without being bottlenecked by any intermediate gateways. What is

the maximum throughput when the window scaling option is not used? What is the maximum throughput when the window scaling option is used?

6. Given that the throughput of a TCP connection is inversely proportional to its RTT, connections with heterogeneous RTTs sharing the same queue will get different bandwidth shares. What will be the eventual proportion of the bandwidth sharing among three connections if their propagation delays are 10 ms, 100 ms, and 150 ms, and the service rate of the shared queue is 200 kbps? Assume that the queue size is infinite without buffer overflow (no packet loss), and the maximum window of the TCP sender is 20 packets, with each packet having 1500 bytes.
7. What is the answer in Question 6 if the service rate of the shared queue is 300 kbps?
8. If the smoothed RTT kept by the TCP sender is currently 30 ms and the following measured RTTs are 26, 32, and 24 ms, respectively, what is the new RTT estimate?
9. TCP provides a reliable byte stream, but it is up to the application developer to "frame" the data sent between client and server. The maximum payload of a TCP segment is 65,495 bytes if it is carried over an IP datagram. Why would such a strange number be chosen? Also, why do most TCP senders emit only packets with packet size smaller than 1460 bytes? For example, even though a client might send 3000 bytes via write( ), the server might read only 1460 bytes.
10. In most UNIX systems it is essential to have root privilege to execute programs that have direct access to the internetworking layer or link layer. However, some common tools, such as `ping` and `traceroute`, can access the internetworking layer using a normal user account. What is the implication behind this paradox? How do you make your own programs that can access the internetworking layer similar to such tools? Briefly propose two solutions.
11. Use a table to compare and explain all socket domains, types, and protocols that are supported by Linux 2.6.
12. The RTP incorporates a sequence number field in addition to the timestamp field. Can RTP be designed to eliminate the sequence number field and use the timestamp field to resequence the out-of-order received packets? (Yes/No, why?)
13. Suppose you are going to design a real-time streaming application over the Internet that employs RTP on top of TCP instead of UDP. What situations will the sender and the receiver encounter in each TCP congestion control state shown in Figure 5.21? Compare your expected situations with those designed on top of UDP in a table format.
14. Recall from Figure 5.1 that it is the delay distribution that requires different solutions to the same issues in single-hop and multi-hop environments. How will the delay distribution evolve if the transmission channel is of one-hop, two-hop, and 10-hop? Draw three *co-related* delay distribution figures as in Figure 5.1 to best illustrate the outstanding steps of increasing the hop count (e.g., 1-, 2-, and 10-hop).
15. When adding a per-segment checksum to a segment, TCP and UDP all include some fields in the IP layer before the segment has been passed to its underlying layer, the IP layer. How could TCP and UDP know the values in the IP header?
16. The text goes into some detail introducing the different versions of TCP. Find *three* more TCP versions. Itemize them and highlight their contributions within three lines of words for each TCP version.
17. As shown in Figure 5.41, many parts in Linux 2.6 are not specific for TCP/IP, such as read/write functions and socket structure. From the viewpoint of a C programmer, analyze how Linux 2.6 organizes its *functions* and *data structures* to be easily initialized into different protocols. Briefly indicate the basic C programming mechanisms to achieve the goals.
18. As described in Section 5.5, many protocols and algorithms are proposed to handle the challenges to carrying streaming through the Internet. Please find open solutions that support the transmission of media streaming over the Internet. Then, observe these solutions to see whether and how they handle the issues addressed in Section 5.5. Do these solutions implement the protocols and algorithms introduced herein?
19. Compared with loss-driven congestion controls like that used in NewReno and SACK, TCP Vegas is an RTT-driven congestion control, which actually is a novel idea. However, is TCP Vegas popularly used in the Internet? Are there any problems when the flows of TCP Vegas compete with those of the loss-driven controls against a network bottleneck?
20. Are there any other RTT-driven congestion controls besides TCP Vegas? Or, can you find any congestion controls that concurrently consider packet losses and RTT to avoid the congestion and control the rate? Are they robust and safe to deploy in the Internet?

21. As introduced in Subsection 5.4.1, when you intend to open a socket for a connection between processes or hosts, you need to assign the *domain* argument as AF_UNIX and AF_INET, respectively. Below the socket layer, how are different data flows and function calls implemented for sockets with different domain arguments? Are there other widely used options for the domain argument? In what kind of condition will you need to add a new option to the argument?
22. Besides AF_UNIX and AF_INET, are there other widely used options for the domain argument? What are their functions?

Chapter 6

Application Layer

With the underlying TCP/IP protocol stack, what useful and interesting *application services* can we offer on the Internet? Starting from the early 1970s, several Internet applications were developed to enable users to transfer information over the Internet. In 1971, RFC 172 unveiled the *File Transfer Protocol (FTP),* which allowed users to list files on *remote* servers and transfer files back and forth between the local host and the remote server. In 1972, the first *electronic mail (e-mail)* software (SNDMSG and READMAIL) was developed, with its protocol later being standardized as *Simple Mail Transfer Protocol (SMTP)* in RFC 821 in 1982. SMTP allows e-mails to be sent between computers, and it gradually became the most popular network application. The first *Telnet* specification, RFC 318, was published in the same year. Telnet allowed users to log onto *remote* server machines as if they were sitting in front of those computers. In 1979, *USENET,* a consortium of UNIX companies and users, was established. USENET users formed thousands of newsgroups that operated on bulletin board-like systems where users could read and post messages. The messages transferring between news servers were later standardized as *Network News Transfer Protocol (NNTP)* in RFC 977 in 1986.

In the 1980s, a new type of Internet service began to emerge. Different from the preceding systems, which were typically accessible only to authorized users, many of the new Internet services were *open* to virtually anyone having appropriate client software. *Archie* was the first Internet search engine that allowed users to search in the database of selected anonymous FTP sites for files. *Gopher* servers provided a menu-driven interface to search the Internet for keywords in the title or abstract of files. The Gopher protocol was later standardized in RFC 1436 in 1993. The *Wide-Area Information Server (WAIS),* defined in RFC 1625 in 1994, harnessed multiple gophers to search the Internet and had the search results ranked by relevance. The *World Wide Web (WWW)* originated in 1989 at the European Laboratory for Particle Physics (CERN). Later specified as *HyperText Transfer Protocol (HTTP)* in RFC 1945 in 1996, it allowed access to documents in the format of Hypertext Markup Language (HTML) that integrated text, graphics, sounds, video, and animation.

As new Internet applications keep emerging, one interesting question arises: What are the driving forces to create new applications? Alongside the above-mentioned evolution of Internet services, it is easy to conclude that *human-machine* and *human-human* communications have been two major driving forces that push forward the development of new Internet applications. Generally speaking, the human-machine communication is for accessing data and computing resources on the Internet. For example, telnet provides a way to use resources on remote machines; FTP facilitates data sharing; Gopher, WAIS, and WWW are capable of searching and fetching documents; and the list continues. *Domain Name System (DNS),* specified in RFC 1035 in 1987, solves the problems of host addressing and naming by abstracting a host's IP address as an understandable host name. *Simple Network Management Protocol (SNMP),* specified in RFC 1157 in 1990, can be used by administrators for remote network management and monitoring. On the other hand, human-human communication is for message exchange. To name a few examples, e-mail provides an *asynchronous* way to exchange messages between users; *voice over IP (VoIP),* with a protocol defined as *Session Initiation Protocol (SIP)* in RFC 2543 in 1999, is a *synchronous* method of human-human communication. VoIP enables people to use the Internet as the transmission medium for telephone calls. Meanwhile, *machine-machine* communications such as peer-to-peer *(P2P)* applications are emerging. P2P is considered the future of message and data exchange because it allows users to exchange files with peers without going through centralized servers. BitTorrent (BT) is an example of P2P applications. Though IETF does *not* have protocols standardized for P2P, JXTA (Juxtapose), a P2P protocol specification begun by Sun Microsystems in 2001, aims to improve the interoperability of P2P applications.

Before designing a new Internet application, one needs to resolve some general and application-specific issues first. The general issues range from how to design the protocol messages for client requests and server responses—whether these messages should be presented as *fixed-length binary* strings as the lower-layer protocols or as *variable-length ASCII* codes—to how clients locate servers or how servers make themselves accessible to the clients, whether the client/server should run over TCP or UDP, and whether servers should serve clients *concurrently* or *iteratively.* The application-specific issues, however, depend on the functions and characteristics of the application. In Section 6.1, we discuss these general issues. The application-specific issues are left to sections on individual applications.

First, DNS, a *hierarchical naming* service, is presented in Section 6.2. We introduce key concepts of DNS, such as domain hierarchy, name servers, and name resolution, as well as its classic open source package, *Berkeley Internet Name Domain (BIND).* Next, e-mail is addressed in Section 6.3. We focus on message formats and three e-mail protocols, with *qmail* explained as the example open source implementation. WWW is introduced in Section 6.4, which covers Web naming and addressing. Also discussed are Web data formats, HTTP, its proxy mechanism, and the well-known *Apache* as its open source example. Section 6.5 examines FTP with its file transfer services, operation models, and open source example *Wu-ftp.* Network management is explained in Section 6.6. We examine SNMP, including its architecture framework, data structures for information management, and *net-snmp* as its open source implementation. Then we discuss two Internet multimedia applications, VoIP and streaming, in Section 6.7 and Section 6.8, respectively, where *Asterisk* and *Darwin* are their open source examples. Finally, Section 6.9 addresses peer-to-peer applications with *BitTorrent (BT)* as the example implementation.

Historical Evolution: Mobile Applications

In contrast to desktop applications, mobile applications are designed to run on handheld devices with high *mobility,* such as smart phones and cellular phones. These devices are usually pocket-sized computing devices equipped with some degree of computing and Internet-connection capabilities and limited storage and battery power. On smart phones with large screen display, multi-touch interface, accelerated graphics, accelerometer, and location-based technology, mobile applications help users stay organized, find nearby resources, work outside workplaces, and synchronize data with their online accounts or personal computers. There are several mobile device platforms and many applications developed for them. Table 6.1 lists six mobile application marketplace providers. Application Marketplace is a popular online service that allows users to browse and download all kinds of applications, ranging from business to game and from entertainment to educational.

As desktop applications are mature but still evolving, a new spectrum of mobile applications is on the horizon. Let us look at four popular mobile applications for the iPhone. With *Evernote,* users can keep captured notes, photos, and audio files *synchronized* across multiple platforms with an online account accessible from any browser. As a GPS/3G-enabled location-based service, *AroundMe* lists *by proximity* services such as restaurants and parking lots around users. *Associated Press Mobile News Network* is a location-based personalized news service that delivers local and interesting news to users. *Wikipanion* is the Wikipedia browsing application that searches and renders the Web pages automatically while users type in keywords.

TABLE 6.1 Six Mobile Application Marketplace Providers

Name	Provider	Available Applications	Operating System	Development Environment
Android Market	Google	15,000	Android	Android SDK
App Catalog	Palm	250	webOS	Mojo SDK
App Store	Apple	100,000	iPhone OS	iPhone SDK
App World	RIM	2000	BlackBerry OS	BlackBerry SDK
Ovi Store	Nokia	2500	Symbian	Symbian SDK
Marketplace for Mobile	Microsoft	376	Windows Mobile	Windows Mobile SDK

6.1 GENERAL ISSUES

Since a variety of applications need to coexist on the Internet, how clients and servers identify each other is the first technical issue. We address this by revisiting the concept of *port* introduced in Chapter 5. Before providing a service on the Internet, a server must start its *daemon* process first; a daemon refers to a software program running in the background to provide services. Thus the second issue is how servers get started. The way to start a daemon process can be *direct* or *indirect;* that is, a daemon can run either standalone or under the control of a super daemon. Internet applications can be categorized as *interactive, file transfer,* or *real-time,* each placing different requirements on *latency, jitter, throughput,* or *loss.* Some applications pumping real-time traffic are strict to low-latency requirements but could tolerate some data loss. Other applications generate *short interactive* or *long file transfer* traffic; the former demands low latency and the latter usually could accommodate longer latency, but both prioritize reliable transfer without loss. These requirements need to be handled by the servers, thus making classification of Internet servers our third issue. Finally, though all lower-layer protocol messages are fixed-length binary strings, the same style could not be applied to application-level protocols because their request and response messages are so *diverse* and often contain *variable* and *long* parameters. Thus, this is our fourth general issue.

6.1.1 How Ports Work

Every server machine on the Internet offers its service through TCP or UDP port(s), as explained in Section 5.1. Ports are used to name the end points of logical connections that carry long-term or short-term conversations. According to the port number assignment by the Internet Assigned Numbers Authority (IANA), the port numbers are divided into three categories as follows:

1. The Well Known Ports from 0 to 1023.
2. The Registered Ports from 1024 to 49151.
3. The Dynamic and/or Private Ports from 49152 through 65535.

The Well Known Ports can only be used by system (or root) processes or by programs executed by privileged users. The Registered Ports can be used by ordinary user processes. The Dynamic Ports are free for anyone to use.

To show how ports work, we illustrate a practical example in Figure 6.1. The server machine is running four daemons to provide different services. Each daemon is listening to inbound client arrivals and client requests on its own unique port. In Figure 6.1, the FTP daemon, for example, is listening to port 21 and waiting for client requests to arrive. When an FTP client originates an outbound connection, it is assigned by the kernel an unused port above 1023 as its source port, which is 2880 in our example. The FTP client specifies in the connection request its own IP address and source port as well as the server machine's IP address and server port, i.e., 21. Then the connection request is sent to the server machine. Immediately upon receiving the client's connection request, the FTP daemon creates a copy of itself, called

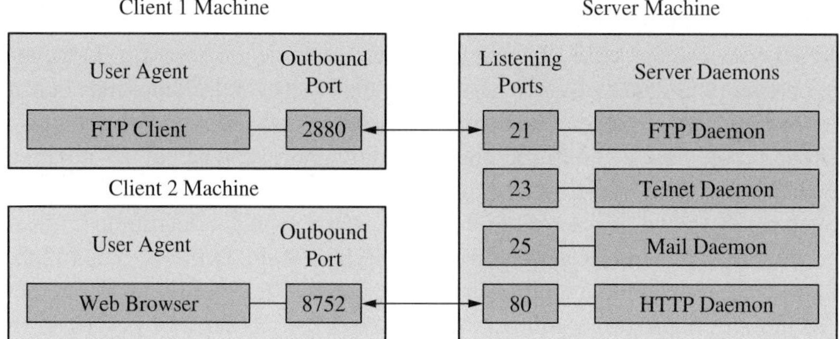

FIGURE 6.1 An example of how ports work.

forking a child process. The child process then has the connection established with the FTP client and handles subsequent requests from that client while the parent process goes back to listen to other client arrivals.

6.1.2 How Servers Start

On most UNIX/Linux platforms, server processes can run either standalone or under the control of a super daemon called `(x)inetd`. When running, the `(x)inetd` listens on all service ports by binding sockets to the ports, for the services listed in its configuration file. When a client arrival is found on one of its ports, the `(x)inetd` looks up what service the port corresponds to, invokes the corresponding server program to serve the client, and continues to listen on the ports.

Getting server programs started by the `(x)inetd` has some advantages. First, when the configuration file of a server program is changed, the change can take effect immediately since the `(x)inetd` restarts the server program to read the configuration file *every time* when a client arrives. On the other hand, standalone servers require an explicit restart before changes in the configuration can take effect. Second, when a server crashes, the `(x)inetd` spawns a new server process, whereas a crashed standalone server may stay unnoticed so that the service becomes unavailable. Although the `(x)inetd` has the aforementioned advantages, it has two shortcomings leading to performance degradation. One is that it must fork and execute a server program for each client arrival. The other is that the server program must build its executable image and read the configuration file for each client. In general, using the standalone scheme is recommended for heavily loaded servers.

6.1.3 Classification of Servers

Internet servers can be classified from two perspectives. One is how a server handles requests, either *concurrently* or *iteratively*. The other way of classification depends on the underlying transport protocol. A *connection-oriented* server can be implemented with TCP, while a *connectionless* server can be implemented with UDP. The combination of these perspectives yields four types of Internet servers.

Concurrent Server vs. Iterative Server

Most Internet services are based on the client-server model, whose aim is to enable user processes to share network resources; that is, several clients may reach one server concurrently. Servers respond to this design principle with two schemes: A concurrent server handles multiple clients simultaneously, whereas an iterative server handles clients one by one.

A concurrent server processes multiple clients at a time with concurrency. When the server accepts a client, it creates a copy of itself, be it a *child process* or a *thread.* For simplicity, here we assume a child process is created. Each child process is an instance of the server program, and it inherits the socket *descriptors,* described in Subsection 5.4.2, and other variables from the parent process. The child process serves the client and frees the parent process so it can accept new clients. Since the parent process simply handles new client arrivals, it would not be *blocked* by heavy workload from clients. Similarly, since each client is handled by a child process and all processes can be scheduled to run by the processor, concurrency between children, and hence between existing clients, can be achieved.

In contrast to the concurrent server, an iterative server processes only one client at a time. When multiple clients arrive, instead of forking any child processes, the server *queues* clients and handles them in a sequential order. If too many clients are present or some clients have requests with long service times, iterative processing may cause blocking, which prolongs the response time to clients. Therefore, an iterative server is only suitable in the scenarios where clients have *few* requests with *short* service times.

Connection-Oriented Server vs. Connectionless Server

Another way of classifying servers is by whether they are connection-oriented or connectionless. A connection-oriented server uses TCP as its underlying transport protocol, whereas a connectionless server adopts UDP. Here we discuss differences between these two.

First, for each packet sent, a connection-oriented server has 20 bytes of TCP header overhead, while a connectionless server has only 8 bytes of UDP header overhead. Second, a connection-oriented server must establish a connection with the client before sending data, and must terminate the connection afterward. The connectionless server, however, simply transmits the data to the client without a connection setup. Because a connectionless server does not maintain any connection state, it can dynamically support more *short-lived* clients. Finally, when one or more links between the client and the server become congested, the connection-oriented server throttles the client by TCP's congestion control, as illustrated in Subsection 5.3.4. On the other hand, the connectionless client and server have an unregulated data sending rate, which is constrained only by the application itself or the bandwidth limit of the access links. Thus, excessive loss due to persistent congestion could happen to the connectionless Internet service, and it costs the client or server extra efforts to retransmit the lost data if needed.

We list popular Internet applications and their corresponding application protocols and transport protocols in Table 6.2. The table shows that e-mail, remote terminal access, file transfer, and Web applications use TCP as the underlying

TABLE 6.2 Application Layer Protocols and Underlying Protocols

Application	Application Layer Protocol	Underlying Protocol
Electronic mail	SMTP, POP3, IMAP4	TCP
Remote terminal access	Telnet	TCP
File transfer	FTP	TCP
Web	HTTP	TCP
Web caching	ICP	Typically UDP
Name resolution	DNS	Typically UDP
Network file system	NFS	Typically UDP
Network management	SNMP	Typically UDP
Routing protocol	RIP, BGP, OSPF	UDP (RIP), TCP (BGP), IP (OSPF)
Internet telephony	SIP, RTP, RTCP, or proprietary (e.g., Skype)	Typically UDP
Streaming multimedia	RTSP or proprietary (e.g., RealNetworks)	Typically UDP, sometimes TCP
P2P	Proprietary (e.g., BitTorrent, eDonkey)	UDP for queries and TCP for data transfer

transport protocol to convey the application-level data because the proper operation of these applications depends on reliable data delivery. On the other hand, name resolution applications like DNS run over UDP rather than TCP to avoid connection establishment delay. Network management applications employ UDP to carry management messages across the Internet since they are transaction-based and must run even under a bad network condition. UDP is preferred to TCP in RIP because updates on the RIP routing table are periodically exchanged between neighboring routers so that lost updates can be recuperated by more recent updates. However, TCP is used in BGP for BGP routers to maintain a keepalive mechanism with *remote* peer BGP routers. Internet telephony and audio/video streaming applications typically run over UDP. These applications could tolerate a small fraction of packet loss, so reliable data transfer is not critical to their operation. In addition, most multicast applications run over UDP simply because TCP cannot work with multicasting. One interesting thing about P2P applications is that they run over UDP to send voluminous search queries to peers and then use TCP to do the actual data transfer with selected peers.

Four Types of Servers

Servers introduced so far can be categorized into the following four combinations:

1. Iterative connectionless servers
2. Iterative connection-oriented servers
3. Concurrent connectionless servers
4. Concurrent connection-oriented servers

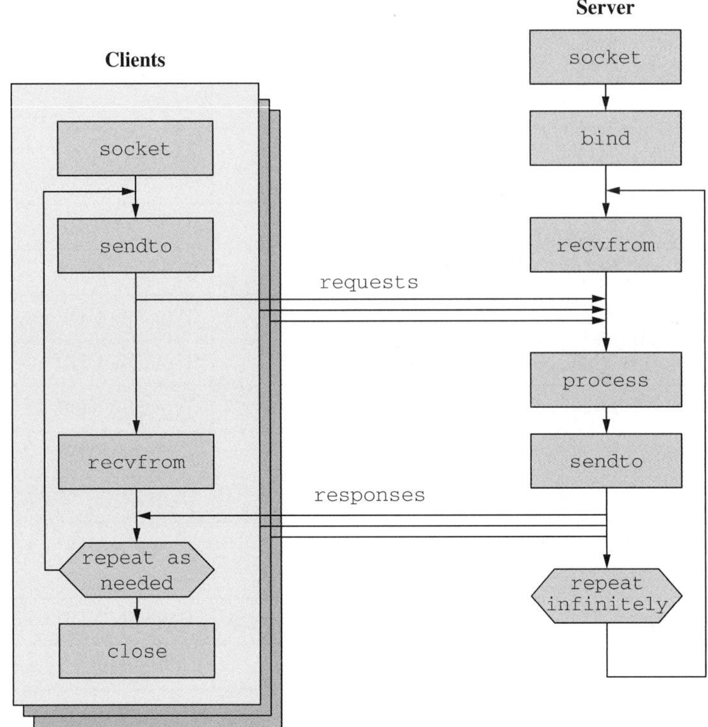

FIGURE 6.2 Iterative connectionless clients and server.

Iterative connectionless servers are common and trivial to implement. Figure 6.2 shows the corresponding work flow between the iterative connectionless client and server. First, a server creates a socket bound to the well-known port for the offered service. Afterward, the server simply repeatedly calls the `readfrom()` function to read client requests from the socket, where client requests are served one after another from the request *queue*. The server sends the responses by calling `sendto()`. Due to the simplicity of this architecture, iterative connectionless servers are good enough for *short-lived* or *non-critical* services.

An iterative connection-oriented server is a single process that handles client connections one at a time. As before, the server first creates a socket bound to a port. Then the server puts the socket in the passive mode to listen for the first connection arrival. Once accepting a client connection, it repeatedly receives requests from the client and formulates the responses. When the client finishes, the server closes the connection and returns to the wait-to-accept stage for the next connection arrival. New connection arrivals during the service time, if any, are *queued*. For short-lived connections, the iterative connection-oriented mode works well, but the server could have less overhead if running in the iterative connectionless mode instead. For long-lived connections, this mode would result in poor concurrency and latency. Thus, it is seldom used.

Concurrent connectionless servers are suitable for services which have a high request volume but yet still need a quick turnaround time. DNS and Network File System (NFS) are two examples. A concurrent connectionless server first creates a socket bound to a port but leaves the socket *unconnected,* i.e., usable to talk to any clients. The server then begins to receive requests from clients and handles them by forking child processes (or threads), which exit immediately upon completion.

Concurrent connection-oriented servers, whose processing flow is depicted in Figure 6.3, are embraced widely. Basically they work similarly to the concurrent connectionless servers but differ in the connection setup, which involves an

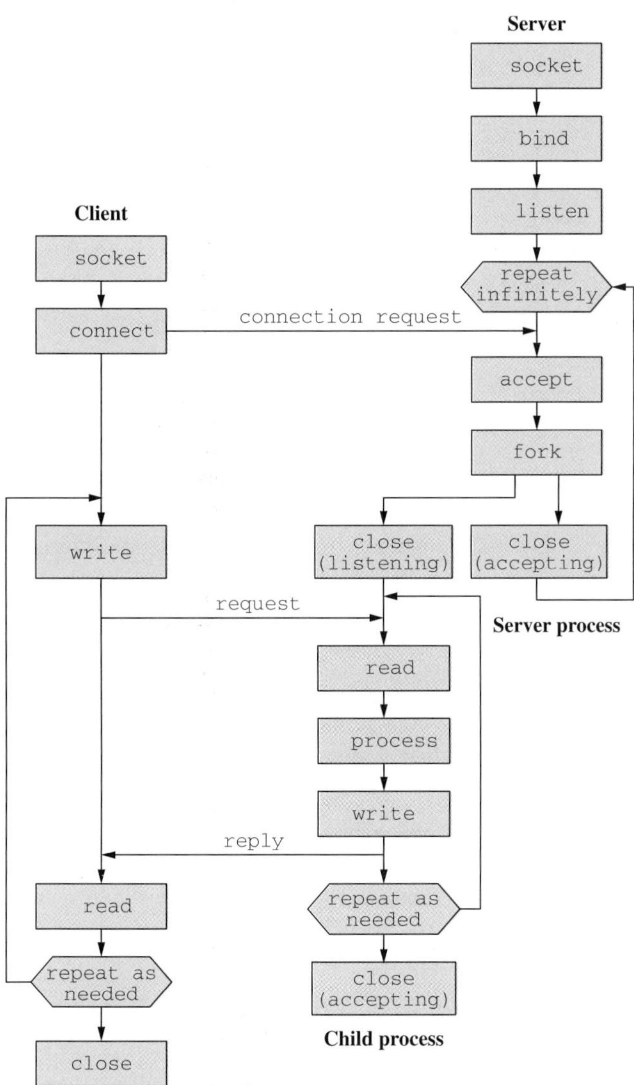

FIGURE 6.3 Concurrent connection-oriented client and server.

Historical Evolution: Cloud Computing

Traditionally an organization tends to own the network infrastructure, server platform, and application software and operate its own computing environment. Another paradigm, called *cloud computing,* is to outsource the computing environment to a *centralized* service provider whose infrastructure might be distributed or centralized. The National Institute of Standards and Technology (NIST) defines cloud computing as a model for enabling convenient on-demand access to a shared pool of configurable computing resources that can be rapidly provisioned and released with minimal management efforts. Evolved from *network computing* with the simple *thin-client heavy-server* concept, cloud computing goes one step further to outsource those heavy servers to service providers with three service provisioning models—software as a service (SaaS), platform as a service (PaaS), and infrastructure as a service (IaaS).

Google Apps (http://google.com/a/) and Apps.Gov (http://apps.gov) are two early cloud service providers. Eventually there may be a very limited number of public B2C (business-to-consumer) clouds operated by companies like Google, Microsoft, and Amazon, but many public B2B (business-to-business) clouds by, say, IBM, and even more private clouds by vendors and manufacturers. Here "public" or "private" means whether or not the cloud offers services to the public.

additional TCP three-way handshake. There are two kinds of sockets used by the server program: the *listening* socket used by the parent process and the *connected* or *accepting* sockets used by the child processes. After the server creates a socket bound to a port and puts it into the listening mode, the server process blocks on the `accept()` function until a client connection request arrives. Upon returning from `accept()` with a new file descriptor for the connected socket, it forks a child process that inherits both sockets. The child process closes the listening socket and communicates with the client through the connected socket. The parent process then closes the connected socket and comes back to block on `accept()`.

6.1.4 Characteristics of Application Layer Protocols

Internet servers and clients run on end hosts and communicate via application-layer protocols. An application-layer protocol specifies both the syntax and semantics of the messages exchanged between the client and the server. The syntax defines the format of the messages, whereas the semantics specify how clients and servers should interpret the messages and respond to the peers. In comparison with the underlying transport protocols and Internet Protocol, application-layer protocols have many different characteristics, as described below.

Variable Message Format and Length

Unlike Layer-2 to Layer-4 protocols, whose messages have fixed format and length, either request commands or response replies of application-layer protocols can have variable format and length. This is due to various options, parameters, or contents of different sizes to be carried in the commands or replies. For example, while sending an HTTP request, a client can add some fields to the request to indicate what browser and language the client is using. Similarly, an HTTP response varies its format and length according to different types of contents.

Various Data Types

Application-layer protocols have various data types, by which we mean both commands and replies can be transmitted in textual or nontextual format. For example, telnet clients and servers send commands in binary format starting with a special octet (111111), while SMTP clients and servers communicate in U.S. 7-bit ASCII code. An FTP server transfers data in ASCII or binary form. A Web server replies textual Web pages and binary images.

Statefulness

Most application layer protocols are *stateful.* That is, the server retains information about the session with the client. For instance, an FTP server remembers the client's current working directory and current transfer type (ASCII or binary). An SMTP server remembers information about the sender and the recipients of an e-mail message while waiting for the DATA command to transmit the message's content. However, for efficiency and scalability, HTTP is designed to be a stateless protocol, though some *add-on* states beyond the original protocol design could be maintained by clients and servers. Another stateless example is SNMP, which also has to deal with efficiency and scalability issues. DNS could be stateless or stateful, depending on how it operates, as we shall see next.

6.2 DOMAIN NAME SYSTEM (DNS)

The Domain Name System (DNS) is a hierarchical, distributed database system used to map between host names and IP addresses for various Internet applications. It is designed to provide practical and scalable name-to-address (sometimes address-to-name) translation service. In this section, we address three aspects about DNS: (1) the name space's architecture under which DNS works, (2) the structure of *resource records* (RR) that define the name-to-address mappings, and (3) operation models between name servers and resolvers. Lastly, we shall introduce an open source implementation, `BIND`, in hope of offering readers a practical view of DNS.

6.2.1 Introduction

Computer hosts connected to the network need a way to recognize each other. In addition to the binary IP address, each host may also register an ASCII string as its host name. Just like the address in the postal system, which contains a series of letters specifying the country, province, city, and street information, the ASCII string uniquely identifies the location of the host and is also easier to remember than the IP address.

Years back, in the age of ARPANET, a file `HOST.TXT` was used by the authoritative organization called the *Network Information Center (NIC)* to store ASCII names and corresponding IP addresses of all hosts in a region. Administrators of hosts under ARPANET periodically fetched from the NIC the latest `HOST.TXT`, and sent their changes to the NIC. Whenever a host wanted to connect to another, it translated the destination host's name into the IP address according to the `HOST.TXT`. This approach works just fine for a small network. However, when it comes to a large-scale network, scalability and management problems arise.

RFC 882 and 883, later obsoleted by RFC 1034 and 1035, proposed the concept and specifications of a hierarchically distributed DNS that provides scalable Internet host addressing and mail forwarding support as well as protocols and servers used to implement domain name facilities. Hosts under the DNS have a unique *domain name.* Each DNS *name server* of a *domain* maintains its own database of name-to-address mappings so that other systems (clients) across the Internet can query the name server through the DNS protocol messages. But how can we divide the domain name space into domains? The next subsection answers this question.

6.2.2 Domain Name Space

Top-Level Domains

For better regulation and scalability of domain name translation in a large network, the domain name space is divided into several categories of top-level domains, as shown in Table 6.3. Each domain represents a particular service or meaning, and can extend down to various sub-domains and again to sub-sub-domains to form a hierarchical domain tree. A host in a domain tree inherits the purposes of successive domains on the backward path to the root. For example, the host www.w3.org is intended to serve as the official site of the WWW consortium, which is a nonprofit organization as indicated by its top level domain org.

With hierarchical division of the domain name space, the location of a host (or domain) in a domain tree can be easily identified and therefore allows us to infer the structure of DNS. Figure 6.4 gives us an example of how the cs.nctu.edu.tw domain is recognized. Note that domain names are case insensitive, which means the uppercase "CS" is the same as the lowercase "cs."

Except for the top-level domains, which are already standardized, a domain has full authority on its successive domains. The administrator of a domain can arbitrarily divide it into sub-domains and assign them to other organizations, either by following the form of the top-level ones (such as com under tw) or by creating new domain names (such as co under uk). This process is called *domain delegation,* which greatly reduces the management burden on upper-level domains.

Zones and Name Servers

It is important to have clear differentiation between domain and *zone* before getting into this section. A domain is usually a superset of zones. Taking Figure 6.4, for example, the tw domain contains four zones: org, com, edu, and tw itself (you may want to try http://www.tw). To be specific, the tw zone contains domain names of

TABLE 6.3 Top-Level domains

Domain	Description
com	Commercial organizations such as Intel (intel.com).
org	Nonprofit organizations such as WWW consortium (w3.org).
gov	U.S. government organizations such as National Science Foundation (nsf.gov).
edu	Educational organizations such as UCLA (ucla.edu).
net	Networking organizations such as Internet Assigned Numbers Authority, which maintains the DNS root servers (gtld-servers.net).
int	Organizations established by international treaties between governments. For example, International Telecommunication Union (itu.int).
mil	Reserved exclusively for the United States Military. For example, Networking Information Center, Department of Defense (nic.mil).
Two-letter country code	The two-letter country code top level domains (ccTLDs) are based on the ISO 3166-1 two-letter country codes. Examples are tw (Taiwan) and uk (United Kingdom).
arpa	Mostly unused now, except for the in-addr.arpa domain, which is used to maintain a database for reverse DNS queries.
Others	Such as .bi (business), .idv (for individuals), and .info (similar to .com).

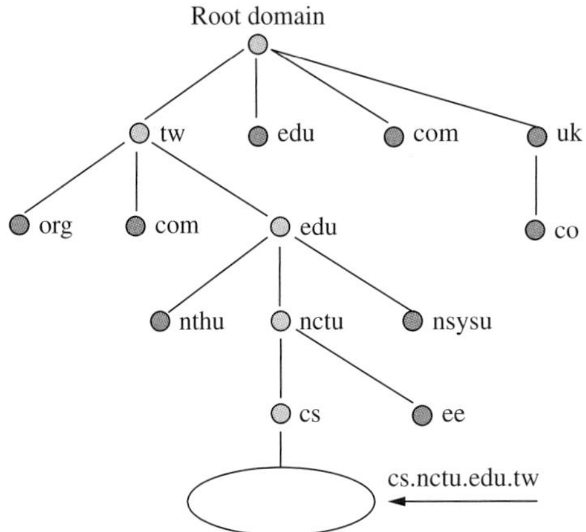

FIGURE 6.4 Locating the cs.nctu.edu.tw domain in the name space.

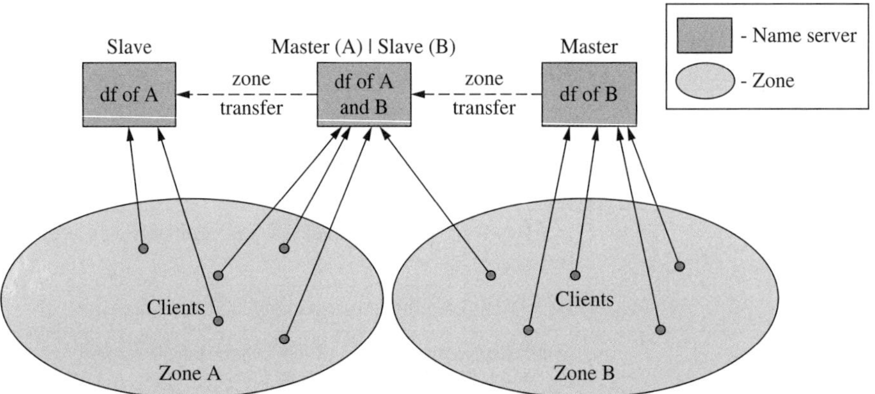

FIGURE 6.5 Relation between master-slave name servers. (df: zone data file)

the form *.tw, excluding *.org.tw, *.com.tw and *.edu.tw. Hosts of the .tw zone are usually for the purpose of administering the delegated sub-domains.

Name servers, usually running on port 53, are hosts that contain a database built with zone data files and a resolution program to answer DNS queries. In a name server, a zone is a basic management unit whose information is stored in a *zone data file*. Upon receiving a DNS query, which gives a domain name and requests its corresponding IP address, the name server looks up its database for the answer. The server replies to the client if there is a lookup match; otherwise, it performs further lookups in other name servers. A name server may be authoritative for multiple zones, which means its database may cover more than one zone and hence more than one zone data file, as depicted in Figure 6.5. In the figure, squares and ellipses represent name servers and zones, respectively; the name server in the middle covers both zone A and zone B.

For availability and load balancing concerns, a zone may also be supervised by multiple name servers to avoid possible breakdown caused by a high request rate overwhelming a single server. Servers that serve the same zone can be divided into a single master and many slaves. A master name server has authority to insert/delete hosts into/from a zone, whereas the slaves can only obtain the zone information from their master through a process referred to as *zone transfer.* Figure 6.5 illustrates that the master name server of zone A could be a slave name server of zone B.

6.2.3 Resource Records

A zone data file comprises several *resource records (RRs)* describing DNS settings of the zone. An RR typically contains a five tuple: the owner (the domain name that indexes the RR), TTL (Time-To-Live, a limit on the time period for which resolvers can cache this RR), class (IN is usually adopted, standing for the Internet system), type, and RDATA (a variable-length string of octets that describes the resource). Six types of RRs are commonly used in describing various aspects of a domain name:

Start of Authority (SOA): An SOA marks the beginning of a DNS zone data file and identifies the authority of that zone. That is, when we want to know the authoritative name server of a zone, we issue a query for its SOA. An example is given below:

```
cs.nctu.edu.tw. 86400 IN SOA csserv.cs.nctu.edu.tw.
  help.cs.nctu.edu.tw.

 (
    2009112101 ; Serial number
    86400      ; Refresh after 1 day (86400 seconds)
    3600       ; If no response from master, retry after
                  1 hour
    1728000    ; If still no update, the data expires
                  after 20 days
    86400      ; TTL of RRs if cached in other name servers
 )
```

It would be more readable with a forward interpretation that "the cs.nctu.edu.tw domain has an authoritative name server csserv.cs.nctu.edu.tw." This interpretation is applicable to the rest of the RRs. The domain name help.cs.nctu.edu.tw following the authoritative server specifies the mailbox of the administrator responsible for the zone, as defined in RFC 1035. However, help.cs.nctu.edu.tw will be translated to help@cs.nctu.edu.tw automatically by DNS applications. The serial number is used by a slave name server to trigger updates on the zone data file that occur only when the slave's copy has a serial number smaller than the master's copy. For this reason, the serial number is usually set as the date of modification.

Address (A): This is the most important and the most frequently used RR for matching domain names to IP addresses as requested by the *forward query.* Since multi-homed hosts have multiple network interface cards and therefore multiple IP addresses, it is allowed to have multiple A RRs pertaining to the same domain name. An example for a multi-homed host would be:

```
linux.cs.nctu.edu.tw    86400  IN  A  140.113.168.127
                        86400  IN  A  140.113.207.127
```

It means queries for linux.cs.nctu.edu.tw will be returned with these two IP addresses.

Canonical Name (CNAME): A CNAME creates an alias with a domain name that points to the canonical domain name of an IP address, which is especially useful for running multiple services from a single IP address. In the following example, cache.cs.nctu.edu.tw is originally used for Web caching service at IP address 140.113.166.122 and is thus the *canonical name* of this IP address. However, at the same time, it also acts as a Web server, so an alias of www.cs.nctu.edu.tw is created:

```
www.cs.nctu.edu.tw.   86400 IN CNAME cache.cs.nctu.edu.tw.
cache.cs.nctu.edu.tw. 86400 IN A     140.113.166.122
```

In this way, when an alias name is queried, the name server first looks for the corresponding canonical name and then the IP address of the canonical name, and finally returns both results.

Pointer (PTR): The PTR RRs, as opposed to the A RRs, point to domain names from their corresponding IP addresses. The so-called *reverse query,* querying with an IP address for the domain name, adopts this scheme. For example, the RR

```
10.23.113.140.in-addr.arpa. 86400 IN PTR laser0.cs.nctu.edu.tw.
```

provides the reverse mapping from the IP address 140.113.23.10 to the domain name laser0.cs.nctu.edu.tw, where the IP address is represented as a sub-domain under the in-addr.arpa domain for reverse DNS lookup. Note that the PTR stores an IP address as a sequence of bytes in reverse order, since a domain name gets less specific from left to right. In other words, the IP address 140.113.23.10 is stored as the domain name 10.23.113.140.in-addr.arpa pointing back to its canonical name.

Name Server (NS): An NS RR marks the beginning of a DNS zone data file and supplies the domain name of a name server for that zone. It often appears as following an SOA RR to provide additional name servers for *request referral* described in the next subsection. For example, an NS entry for the CS name server in the NCTU's name server mDNS.nctu.edu.tw can be:

```
cs.nctu.edu.tw. 86400 IN NS csserv.cs.nctu.edu.tw.
```

which enables the name server to refer queries for hosts under the cs.nctu.edu.tw domain to the authoritative host, cisserv.cs.nctu.edu.tw. Notice that the name server defined in the SOA RR always has an NS RR and that the corresponding A-type RR must accompany the NS RR for an in-zone name server in the zone data file.

Mail Exchanger (MX): An MX RR publishes the name of the mail server for a domain name. This is used to implement mail forwarding. For example, a mailer trying to send e-mails to help@cs.nctu.edu.tw might ask the name server for mailing information about cs.nctu.edu.tw. With the following MX RRs,

```
cs.nctu.edu.tw  86400  IN  MX  0 mail.cs.nctu.edu.tw.
cs.nctu.edu.tw  86400  IN  MX  10 mail1.cs.nctu.edu.tw.
```

the mailer knows to forward the e-mail to the mail exchanger, mail.cs.nctu.edu.tw. The number before the mail-exchanger field represents its preference value when there are multiple exchangers to choose from. In this example, the mailer would choose the first one, which has a better (lower) preference value for mail forwarding. The second one would not be selected unless the first goes down.

6.2.4 Name Resolution

Another important component in DNS is the resolver program. It usually consists of library routines used by applications such as Web browsers to translate ASCII strings of URLs into valid IP addresses. A resolver generates DNS queries to name servers listening on either UDP or TCP port 53, and interprets the responses from the servers. The name resolution involves a querying resolver and a queried local name server, sometimes including name servers of other zones as well.

Multiple Iterative Queries

In the best scenario, a query from a resolver would be answered right away by the local name server if the server finds an answer in its database. If not, the server conducts *multiple iterative queries* rather than simply bouncing the unanswered query back to the resolver. As depicted in Figure 6.6, after the local name server receives a query for "www.dti.gov.uk", it starts multiple iterative queries by asking a name server in the root domain instead of name server(s) just one level above because they probably do not know the answer or whom to refer to. If the answer is not found, the root server responds by referring to the name server in the domain name hierarchy that is closest to the one containing the destination host. There might be multiple candidates suitable for referrals, but only one of them is chosen, in a round-robin manner. The local server then repeats its query to the referred name server, say the "uk" name server, which may again reply with another referral, say "gov.uk" name server, and so on, until the query reaches a name server for the domain where the destination host resides. In our example, the query ends at "dti.gov.uk" name server. This name server then provides the IP address of the host to the local name server, which then relays the answer back to the resolver and completes the name resolution process.

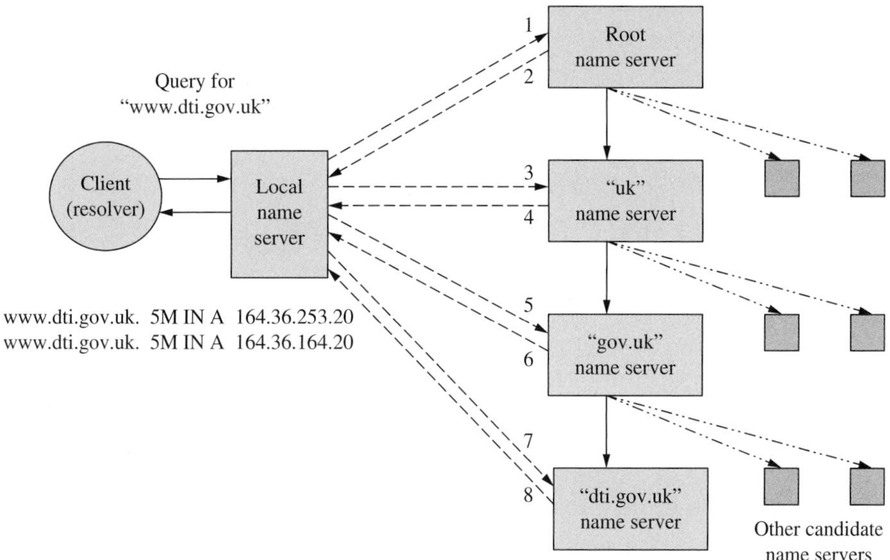

FIGURE 6.6 Multiple iterative resolution for www.dti.gov.uk.

Notably the resolver here is said to undergo a *recursive query,* whereas a *recursion-capable* local name server keeps states to resolve the recursive query by *multiple iterative queries.* If the local name server is not recursion-capable, the resolver has to send *iterative* queries to other known name servers. Fortunately, most local name servers are recursion-capable.

Let us take the reverse DNS lookup as another example, where a recursive query for the domain name corresponding to IP address 164.36.164.20 is resolved by multiple iterative queries. That is, we are looking for the RR:

```
20.164.36.164.in-addr.arpa. 86400  IN   PTR www.dti.gov.uk.
```

Whenever the local name server cannot find the corresponding RR in its database, it asks the root name server that is authoritative for the .arpa domain. The root name server, though probably not having the required RR either, may provide some RRs as referral information, for example:

```
164.in-addr.arpa.      86400  IN  NS  ARROWROOT.ARIN.NET.
ARROWROOT.ARIN.NET.    86400  IN  A   198.133.199.110
```

which states that the 164.*.*.* domain is under the authority of the name server ARROWROOT.ARIN.NET. with IP address 198.133.199.110, which again may refer the query to a better name server according to its local RRs:

```
36.164.in-addr.arpa.   86400   IN   NS    NS2.JA.NET.
NS2.JA.NET.            86400   IN   A     193.63.105.17
```

Finally, the required RR is found in the name server NS2.JA.NET.

As we can see in these two examples, all name servers except the local one only provide *referrals* when they do not have the desired RR, instead of issuing queries on behalf of the local name server. The latter approach would not be scalable for the nonlocal name servers keeping the states of all queries in process. Thus, only the recursion-capable local name servers are *stateful,* while other nonlocal name servers run in a *stateless* mode.

Historical Evolution: Root DNS Servers Worldwide

A root DNS server answers queries for the DNS *root zone* in the hierarchical domain name space. The root zone means the top-level domains (TLDs) that are the highest level of domain names of the Internet, including *generic* top-level domains (gTLDs) like .com, and *country code* top-level domains (ccTLDs) such as .tw. As of the early 2010s, there are 20 generic TLDs and 248 ccTLDs in the root zone. The root DNS servers are very important to the Internet because they are the very *first* line in translating domain names into IP addresses worldwide.

There are 13 root name servers (see http://www.root-servers.org/) that implement the root DNS zone. Each of the 13 root name servers is labeled with an identifier letter from A to M. While only 13 identifier letters are used, each identifier's operator can use *redundant* physical server machines to provide high-performance DNS lookup and great fault tolerance. Table 6.4 shows root

TABLE 6.4 Root DNS Servers

Letter	IP Addresses	Operator	Location	Sites
A	IPv4:198.41.0.4 IPv6:2001:503:BA3E::2:30	VeriSign, Inc.	Los Angeles, CA, US; New York, NY, US; Palo Alto, CA, US; Ashburn, VA, US	Global: 4
B	IPv4:192.228.79.201 IPv6:2001:478:65::53	USC-ISI	Marina del Rey, California, US	Local: 1
C	IPv4:192.33.4.12	Cogent Communications	Herndon, VA, US; Los Angeles, CA, US; New York, NY, US; Chicago, IL, US; Frankfurt, DE; Madrid, ES	Local: 6
D	IPv4:128.8.10.90	University of Maryland	College Park, MD, US	Global: 1
E	IPv4:192.203.230.10	NASA Ames Research Center	Mountain View, CA, US	Global: 1
F	IPv4:192.5.5.241 IPv6:2001:500:2f::f	Internet Systems Consortium, Inc.	**Global:** Palo Alto, CA, US; San Francisco, CA, US **Local:** 47 worldwide	Global: 2 Local: 47
G	IPv4:192.112.36.4	U.S. DOD Network Information Center	Columbus, OH, US; San Antonio, TX, US; Honolulu, HI, US; Fussa, JP; Stuttgart-Vaihingen, DE; Naples, IT	Global: 6
H	IPv4:128.63.2.53 IPv6:2001:500:1::803f:235	U.S. Army Research Lab	Aberdeen Proving Ground, MD, US	Global: 1
I	IPv4:192.36.148.17	Autonomica	34 worldwide	Local: 34
J	IPv4:192.58.128.30 IPv6:2001:503:C27::2:30	VeriSign, Inc.	**Global:** 55 worldwide **Local:** Dulles, VA, US; Seattle, WA, US; Chicago, IL, US; Mountain View, CA, US; Beijing, CN; Nairobi, KE; Cairo, EG	Global: 55 Local: 5
K	IPv4:193.0.14.129 IPv6:2001:7fd::1	RIPE NCC	**Global:** London, UK; Amsterdam, NL; Frankfurt, DE; Tokyo, JP; Miami, FL, US; Delhi, IN **Local:** 12 worldwide	Global: 6 Local: 12
L	IPv4:199.7.83.42 IPv6:2001:500:3::42	ICANN	Los Angeles, CA, US; Miami, FL, US; Prague, CZ	Global: 3
M	IPv4:202.12.27.33 IPv6:2001:dc3::35	WIDE Project	**Global**: Tokyo, JP (3 sites); Paris, FR; San Francisco, CA, US; **Local:** Seoul, KR	Global: 5 Local: 1

Continued

DNS server information with the IP address of the *representative* servers shown in the second column. In the name resolution process, a query that cannot be answered by a local name server is first forwarded to one out of the 13 *preconfigured* representative root name servers, in a random or round-robin fashion. The representative server then *redirects* the local name server to one of its redundant servers, which then replies with the address of the next-level authoritative name server. In Table 6.4, the difference between global and local sites lies in the concern of load balancing for global or local queries.

Protocol Message Format

The message used in the DNS protocol contains the following five sections, as shown in Figure 6.7.

Header section: This includes the control information about the query. The ID is a unique number identifying a message, and is used to match replies to outstanding queries. The second row contains some flags indicating the type (query or response specified in QR), operation (forward or reverse query specified in OPCODE), recursive query desired (RD) or available (RA), and error codes (RCODE) of the message. Other fields give the number of entries in the sections after Header.

Question section: This is used to carry the question in a query. The QDCOUNT in the Header section specifies the number of entries in this section (usually 1).

Answer, Authority, and *Additional* sections: Each of these contains a number of RRs where the *owner* information stored in ASCII format is of *variable* length, with the count of the RRs specified in ANCOUNT, NSCOUNT, and ARCOUNT in the Header section. The first two sections tell the answer to the query and the corresponding authoritative name server, while the Additional section provides useful information related to the query but not

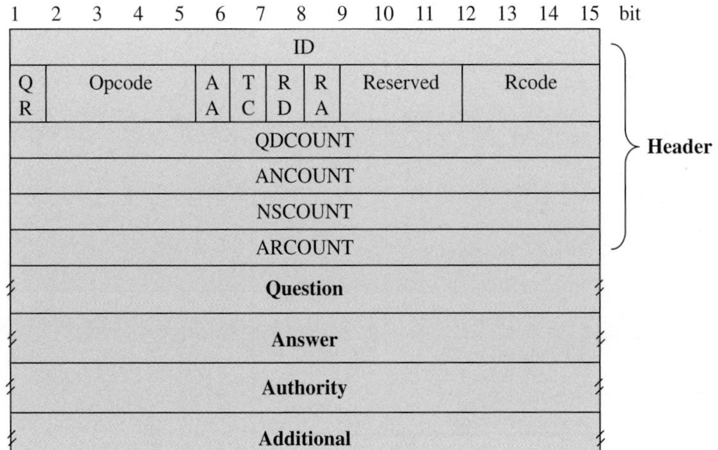

FIGURE 6.7 Inside a DNS message.

the exact answer. For example, if there is one entry like "nctu.edu.tw. 259200 IN NS ns.nctu.edu.tw." in the Authority section, there probably will be an entry like "ns.nctu.edu.tw. 259200 IN A 140.113.250.135" in the Additional section to provide the Address RR of that authoritative name server.

Open Source Implementation 6.1: BIND

Overview

The Berkeley Internet Name Domain (BIND), maintained by Internet Software Consortium (ISC), implements a domain name server for BSD-derived operating systems. The BIND consists of a multithreaded (OS dependent) daemon called `named` and a resolver library. The resolver is a set of routines in a system library that provides the interface through which applications access the domain name services. Some advanced features and security add-ons are also included in BIND. BIND is by far the most common software used to provide the DNS service on the Internet today. It runs on most UNIX-like operating systems including FreeBSD and Linux.

We can summarize BIND as a concurrent multithreaded implementation of DNS. BIND supports both connection-oriented and connectionless services on port 53, though the latter is frequently preferred for fast response. The default query resolution is recursive to the resolver, but is carried out by multiple iterative queries. Recall that all DNS servers except the local DNS server remain stateless.

Block Diagram

The `named` daemon by default runs as the root. For security concerns, `named` can also run as non-root by the `chroot()` system call (called the "least privilege" mechanism). Normally it listens for requests on port 53 over TCP or UDP. Conventionally we choose UDP to transport ordinary messages for reasons of performance, but TCP must be used for zone transfers to avoid the possible dropping of zone data files.

With the multithread support, three main manager threads are created: the *task manager, timer manager,* and *socket manager,* which are shown in Figure 6.8 and described in the paragraphs that follow. In Figure 6.8, each task is associated with a timer from the timer manager. Among all tasks, four of them are run-able, and the socket manager is issuing an I/O completion event into Task1.

Since BIND 9 supports multi-processor platforms, each CPU is associated with a worker thread created by the task manager to handle various tasks. A task has a series of events (for example, resolution requests, timer interrupts) ordered in a queue. When a task's event queue is non-empty, the task is run-able. When the task manager assigns a run-able task to a worker thread, the worker thread executes the task by handling the events in the task's event queues.

A timer is attached to a task for various purposes such as timeout of a client request, request scheduling, and cache invalidation. The timer manager is used to create and regulate timers which themselves are sources of events. The socket

Continued

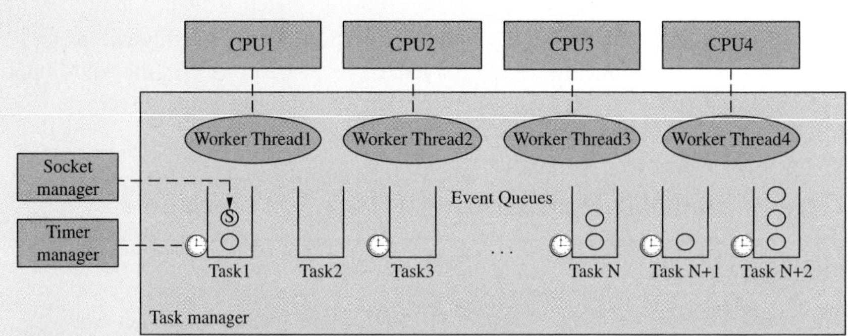

FIGURE 6.8 Relationship among task manager, timer manager, and socket manager in BIND.

manager provides TCP and UDP sockets which are also sources of events. When a network I/O completes, a completion event for the socket is posted to the event queue of the task that requested the I/O service.

Many other sub-managers are created to support the managers just described—for example, the zone manager for zone transfer, and the client manager for processing incoming requests and generating the corresponding replies.

Data Structures

BIND's database stores the zone information based on the `view` data structure, which has a set of zones. It divides the users into groups with different privileges to access the DNS server. In other words, a user is permitted only to access those `views` he is authorized to see.

A practical example of user partitioning with `views` may be the so-called *split DNS*. An enterprise or a service provider typically contains two kinds of hosts: ordinary hosts and servers. Since the DNS information of the servers needs to be published to the outside world, to a degree the enterprise should allow queries from external users to access some of its name servers. However, the enterprise's network topology may thus be exposed to the outside world if external users can query other hosts in its domain. This can be solved by split DNS, in which two types of DNS servers, external and internal, are adopted. The former provides information about the servers for external queries, while the latter serves only internal hosts. Though this scheme does solve the potential risk of private information exposure, the use of additional DNS servers causes extra financial expense. Fortunately, with the help of the `view` structure, only one server is needed to support the split DNS by categorizing users into external and internal groups.

Figure 6.9 shows the data structure used by `named`. If there is no explicit `view` statement in the configuration file, a default `view` that matches any user is formed by all zone data files. When more than two `views` are created, they are concatenated as a link list. The server matches the incoming query with

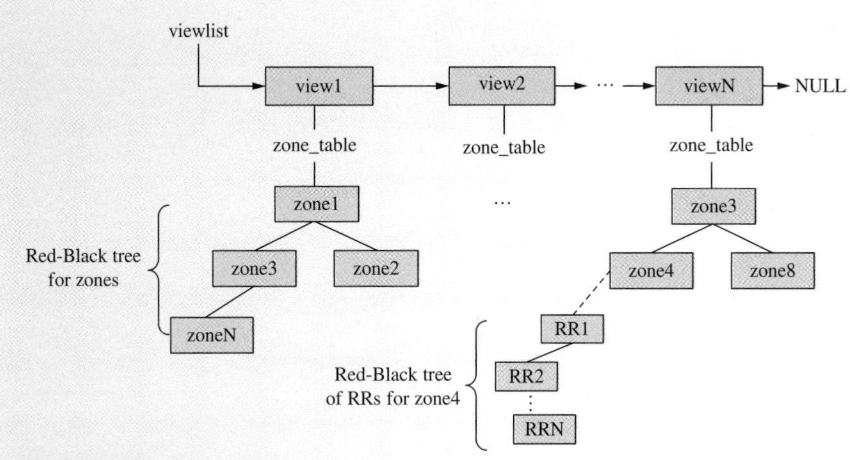

FIGURE 6.9 Data structure inside `named`.

`views` according to its source address and access control lists of the `views`. Afterwards, the first match is selected.

Algorithm Implementations

Within a `view` are those authoritative zones organized as a Red-Black Tree (RBT). RBT is a *balanced* tree that avoids the worst-case search but also provides a fairly good search time in log(N), where N denotes the number of nodes in the tree. The RRs in a zone data file are also implemented as an RBT to exploit the existing code and facilities for zones. In this stage, the best zone for the requested RR is chosen and the matching process continues in the RBT of that zone until the desired RR is found. If no match is found, the server resorts to external name servers to carry on the query process for the client.

`Dig`—A Small Resolver Program

Along with `named` in the BIND suite is a powerful resolver tool called domain information groper (`dig`). As shown in Figure 6.10, it performs DNS lookups and displays richer information, as compared with another popular tool `nslookup`, from the queried name server. In addition to the simple query, users may even use `dig` with the "`+trace`" option to *trace* the queried name servers along the iterative path.

Exercises

1. Find the .c file and the lines of code that implement the iterative resolution.
2. Find which RRs are looked up in forward query and reverse query, respectively, on one of your local hosts.
3. Retrieve all RRs in your local name server with `dig`.

Continued

```
; <<>> DiG 9.2.0 <<>> www.nctu.edu.tw
;; global options: printcmd
;; Got answer:
;; ->>HEADER<<- opcode: QUERY, status: NOERROR, id: 26027
;; flags: qraa rd ra; QUERY: 1, ANSWER: 1, AUTHORITY: 3, ADDITIONAL: 3

;; QUESTION SECTION:
;www.nctu.edu.tw.    IN    A

;; ANSWER SECTION:
www.nctu.edu.tw.    259200    IN    A    140.113.250.5

;; AUTHORITY SECTION:
nctu.edu.tw.    259200    IN    NS    ns.nctu.edu.tw.
nctu.edu.tw.    259200    IN    NS    ns2.nctu.edu.tw.
nctu.edu.tw.    259200    IN    NS    ns3.nctu.edu.tw.

;; ADDITIONAL SECTION:
ns.nctu.edu.tw.    259200    IN    A    140.113.250.135
ns2.nctu.edu.tw.   259200    IN    A    140.113.6.2
ns3.nctu.edu.tw.   259200    IN    A    163.28.64.11
```

FIGURE 6.10 Example query with `dig` for www.nctu.edu.tw.

6.3 ELECTRONIC MAIL (E-MAIL)

E-mail, FTP, and telnet were the *three* earliest Internet applications from the 1970s. However, e-mail retains much more popularity than the other two. Though *instant messaging* is catching up, e-mail is still the essential Internet application in daily life. This section first introduces the components and processing flows of an e-mail delivery system. We then describe the basic and the advanced e-mail message formats: Internet Message Format and Multipurpose Internet Mail Extensions (MIME). Next we illustrate the protocol for *sending* and *receiving* e-mails, Simple Mail Transfer Protocol (SMTP); and the protocols for *retrieving* e-mails from mailboxes, Post Office Protocol (POP) and Internet Message Access Protocol (IMAP). Finally, we pick `qmail` as an example of e-mail's open source implementation.

6.3.1 Introduction

Today's e-mail service can be tracked back to the early ARPANET period when standards for encoding of e-mail messages were first proposed in 1973 (RFC 561). An e-mail sent in the early 1970s would closely resemble one sent on the Internet today. Further evolution in the early 1980s set the foundation for the current e-mail service.

E-mail is a method of sending messages from one user to another via computer networks. Traditionally, a letter is composed by a sender, dropped into a post-box, temporarily stored in a post office and then delivered to a recipient's mailbox, and finally retrieved from the mailbox by the recipient. The way to send, receive, and retrieve an e-mail is analogous to the mail delivery process. A sender composes his e-mail message with a computer and sends the message to a mail server. After that, the mail server transfers the mail to the recipient's mailbox at the destination mail server. Finally the recipient retrieves the message from his mailbox with account and password information. In this way, an e-mail can be delivered to any recipient within seconds rather than the days needed by regular mails.

Internet Mail Addressing

Just like names and addresses on envelopes, a mechanism is required to express the sender and recipient information of an e-mail for transfer purposes. Each e-mail user can be reached by his own e-mail address, with a format defined as

user@{host.}network.

An e-mail address consists of three parts. The first part and the second part identify the username and the mail server of the recipient, respectively. There is always an @ (at) symbol separating the first part from the second part, suggesting that "this user dwells in that mail server." The third part tells the network or domain where the mail server is located. Note that the second part is often omitted for simplicity because the mail server of a domain can be looked up from DNS's mail exchanger (MX) resource records, as explained in Section 6.2. An e-mail address example is

ydlin@cs.nctu.edu.tw

where the mail server resides in the network of the Department of Computer Science ("*cs*") of National Chiao Tung University ("*nctu*") under the Ministry of Education ("*edu*") of Taiwan ("*tw*").

Components of Internet Mail System

The next question is what components compose an e-mail system. An e-mail system consists of four critical logical elements: Mail User Agent (MUA), Mail Transfer Agent (MTA), Mail Delivery Agent (MDA), and Mail Retrieval Agent (MRA), as shown in Figure 6.11. The following briefly describes each of them.

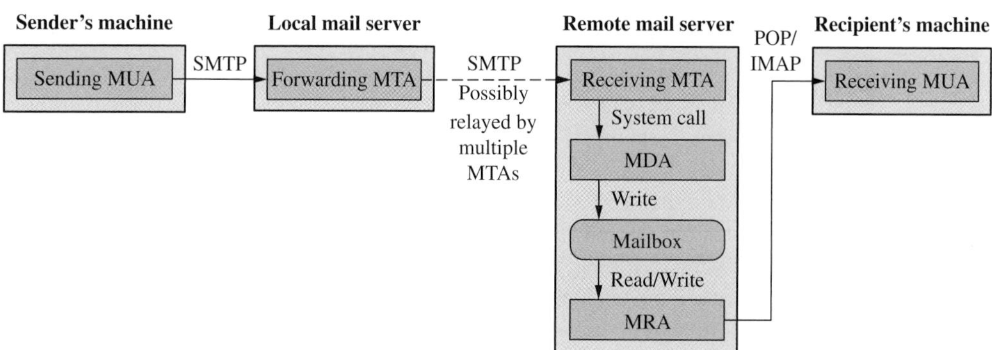

FIGURE 6.11 Logical elements of e-mail systems.

Mail User Agent (MUA)

An MUA is an e-mail client program through which users send and receive messages. An MUA often employs an editor software for users to display and edit messages. In addition to reading and writing messages, MUAs also enable users to attach files to the e-mail. Popular MUA applications include `elm`, `mutt`, and `pine` in the UNIX-based systems, and `Outlook Express` and `Thunderbird` in the Microsoft Windows series. Automated scripts or programs that send and receive messages for users can also be considered MUAs.

Mail Transfer Agent (MTA) and Mail Delivery Agent (MDA)

MTAs such as `sendmail`, `qmail`, and `postfix` for the UNIX platforms are used to accept messages from MUAs through Simple Mail Transfer Protocol (SMTP) and pass them directly to the MTA at the remote mail server or to the intermediate MTA for relaying. The MDA at the remote mail server then obtains messages from the receiving MTA and writes them into the recipient's mailbox for later retrieval.

Mail Retrieval Agent (MRA)

An MRA is used to fetch messages from a mailbox on a server and then passes them to an MUA through Post Office Protocol (POP) or Internet Message Access Protocol (IMAP).

From Figure 6.11, we can see that a message, from the composition by the sender to the final stage of being fetched by a recipient's machine, traverses several components of the e-mail system. These components need some protocols to transport messages. Typically, a sender MUA sends messages to an MTA using SMTP. Thus, MTAs are also known as SMTP servers. A recipient can fetch his messages from a mail server via POP or IMAP. Therefore, the mail servers that store messages and handle retrieval requests from users are called POP servers or IMAP servers. We shall discuss these protocols in detail in Subsection 6.3.3.

6.3.2 Internet Message Standards

An e-mail message normally consists of two parts, one being the special data, the other being the message body. The special data can be categorized according to their intended administrative purposes. The first category is information specific to the transport medium, such as the address of the sender and recipient. Thus, this type of data is called the *envelope.* It may be passed alone by MTAs as the message to the recipient. The second category is the *message header,* including the subject and the recipients' names, followed by a blank line and the *message body.*

The base standard for e-mail messages is defined in RFC 822, later obsoleted by RFC 2822 and then RFC 5322. RFC 822 specifies considerable details about the message header format and leaves the message body as flat ASCII text. However, it could cope with various growing demands such as supporting binary characters, international character sets, and multimedia mail extensions. Thus, an enhancement known as *Multipurpose Internet Mail Extensions (MIME)* was proposed in RFC 1341, later obsoleted by RFC 2045~2049, to deal with these new demands. In the rest of this section, we shall introduce these two standards.

RFC 822—Internet Message Format

RFC 822 specifies the syntax of e-mail messages. In its definition, a message consists of an envelope and contents that include message header and body. Table 6.5 summarizes common message header fields defined in RFC 822. Each field consists of a field name, a colon, and, for most fields, a value. These fields can be classified into different types according to their purposes.

The originator fields specify the sender information of a message. The `From:` field tells who wrote and sent the message. The `Reply-To:` field specifies the address the sender wants the recipient's reply to be directed to. This is useful when the sender has several e-mail addresses, but wants to receive the responses from the mailbox that is used most frequently.

The receiver fields indicate the recipients of the message. A common syntax is that any two adjacent recipient addresses in a receiver field are separated by a comma. The `To:` field gives the primary recipients of the message. The `Cc:` field gives a list of recipient addresses that will receive *carbon copies* of the message. In fact, there is no difference between the primary and secondary recipients in message delivery. Usually, the recipients in the `To:` field might be expected to act on the message while the `Cc:` recipients just receive a copy for reference. The `Bcc:` field

TABLE 6.5 Common Message Header Fields

Type	Field	Description
Originator	`From:`	The person(s) who sent this message.
	`Reply-To:`	Provides a general mechanism to indicate any mailbox(es) to which responses are to be sent.
Receiver	`To:`	The primary recipients of the message.
	`Cc:`	Carbon copy to secondary recipients.
	`Bcc:`	Blind carbon copy to recipients who receive the message without others, including the To: and Cc: recipients, seeing who else received it.
Trace	`Received:`	A copy of this field is added by each transport service that relays the message.
	`Return-Path:`	Added by the final transport system that delivers the message to its recipient.
Reference	`Message-ID:`	Contains a unique identifier generated by the mail transport on the originating system.
	`In-Reply-To:`	Previous correspondence that this message answers.
Other	`Subject:`	Provides a summary, or indicates the nature, of the message.
Date	`Date:`	Supplies the date and time the mail was sent.
Extension	`X-anything:`	Used to implement additional features that have not yet made it into an RFC, or never will.

contains a list of additional recipient addresses that will receive *blind* carbon copies. The difference is that the `Bcc:` recipients are concealed from other users who receive the message.

The trace fields provide an audit trail of the message-handling history and indicate a route back to the sender of the message. Each machine that processes the message will be inserted into the `Received:` field with its machine name, a message ID, time and date it receives the message, which machine it is from, and which transport software is used. The `Return-Path:` field is added by the final transport system that delivers the message. This field tells how to route the response back to the message's source.

The `Message-ID:` field contains a unique identifier generated by the mail transport on the originating system. It also indicates the version of the message. The `In-Reply-To:` field identifies previous correspondence that the message answers. The `Subject:` field describes the content of the message in a few words. The `Date:` field supplies the date and time the message was sent. The extension field is used to implement additional features that have not yet been defined in the standard. All user-defined fields should have names that begin with the string "`X-`".

Figure 6.12 is an example of a message of a header, which says ydlin@cs.nctu.edu.tw sent a message to rhhwang@exodus.cs.ccu.edu.tw with a subject entitled "book." The message was processed by mail.cs.nctu.edu.tw, virus-scanned by the csmailgate.cs.nctu.edu.tw, and finally delivered to the mail server at exodus.cs.ccu.edu.tw.

```
Return-Path: <ydlin@cs.nctu.edu.tw>
Delivered-To: rhhwang@exodus.cs.ccu.edu.tw
Received: from csmailgate.cs.nctu.edu.tw (csmailgate2.cs.nctu.edu.tw [140.113.235.117])
by exodus.cs.ccu.edu.tw (Postfix) with ESMTPS id 431B212B01D
for <rhhwang@exodus.cs.ccu.edu.tw>; Tue, 23 Jun 2009 00:25:52 +0000 (UTC)
Received: from mail.cs.nctu.edu.tw (csmail2 [140.113.235.72])
by csmailgate.cs.nctu.edu.tw (Postfix) with ESMTP id 119193F65F
for <rhhwang@exodus.cs.ccu.edu.tw>; Tue, 23 Jun 2009 00:22:57 +0800 (CST)
Received: from nctuclcc065391 (f5hc76.RAS.NCTU.edu.tw [140.113.5.76])
by mail.cs.nctu.edu.tw (Postfix) with ESMTPSA id 0577762148
for <rhhwang@exodus.cs.ccu.edu.tw>; Tue, 23 Jun 2009 00:22:57 +0800 (CST)
Message-ID: <6CF49E76B3C6488AAB184E4A82FFDF66@nctuclcc065391>
Reply-To: “Dr Ying-Dar Lin” <ydlin@cs.nctu.edu.tw>
From: “Dr Ying-Dar Lin” <ydlin@cs.nctu.edu.tw>
To: <rhhwang@exodus.cs.ccu.edu.tw>
Subject: book
Date: Tue, 23 Jun 2009 00:22:59 +0800
MIME-Version: 1.0
Content-Type: multipart/alternative;
boundary=”—=_NextPart_000_04F2_01C9F398.C3392310”
X-Priority: 3
X-MSMail-Priority: Normal
X-Mailer: Microsoft Outlook Express 6.00.2900.5512
X-MimeOLE: Produced By Microsoft MimeOLE V6.00.2900.5579
X-UIDL: mcA”!Ak,”!-Xn!!:pg”!
```

FIGURE 6.12 An example message header.

TABLE 6.6 MIME Header Fields

Field	Description
`MIME-Version:`	Describes the version of the MIME message format.
`Content-Type:`	Describes the MIME content type and subtype.
`Content-Transfer-Encoding:`	Indicates the encoding method for transmission.
`Content-ID:`	Allows one body of information to refer to another.
`Content-Description:`	Possible description for a body of information.

Multipurpose Internet Mail Extensions (MIME)

Multipurpose Internet Mail Extensions (MIME) is a specification for enhancing the conventional Internet message format. MIME enables e-mail messages to have

1. textual headers and message bodies in character sets other than 7-bit ASCII,
2. multiple objects being carried within a single message,
3. binary or application-specific file attachments, and
4. multimedia files such as images, audio, and video files.

MIME defines new header fields, as shown in Table 6.6. Although RFC 822 has been the only format standard for Internet messages, there are still circumstances when a mail-processing agent needs to know whether a message was composed with the new standard. Thus, the `MIME-Version:` field is used to declare the version of the Internet message format in use. The `Content-Type:` field describes the data contained in the message body so that the MUA can pick an appropriate mechanism to present the data to the user. It specifies the nature of data in the body or body parts by giving type and subtype identifiers and providing parameters needed for certain types. In general, the top-level media type declares the general type of data, while the subtype specifies a specific format for that type of data. The syntax of the `Content-Type:` field is

```
Content-Type := type "/" subtype [";" parameter]...
```

There are seven predefined content types, and their essential characteristics are summarized in Table 6.7. The *text* type is for sending materials principally in textual form. The *multipart* indicates data consisting of multiple body parts, each having its own data type. The *message* type indicates an encapsulated message. The *application* type indicates data that do not fit into any other category, such as uninterpreted binary data or information to be processed by a mail application. The *image* and *audio* types indicate image and audio data, respectively. The *video* type indicates that the body contains a time-varying picture image, possibly accompanied by color and coordinated sound.

Many content types are represented in their natural format such as 8-bit character or binary data. These types of messages may be sent through all kinds of networks; however, some transfer protocols cannot transmit such data. For example, SMTP restricts mail messages to 7-bit US-ASCII data with lines no longer than

TABLE 6.7 The MIME Content Type Set

Type	Subtype(s)	Important Parameters
`text`	plain, html	Charset
`multipart`	mixed, alternative, parallel, digest	Boundary
`message`	RFC 822, partial, external-body	Id, number, total, access-type, expiration, size, permission
`application`	octet-stream, postscript, rtf, pdf, msword	type, padding
`image`	jpg, gif, tiff, x-xbitmap	None
`audio`	basic, wav	None
`video`	Mpeg	None

1000 characters, including any trailing CRLF line separator. Thus, MIME encodes messages that have non-ASCII parts. The `Content-Transfer-Encoding:` field tells the recipient the way a message body was encoded and how to decode it. The possible values for this field are:

- **Quoted-Printable:** This is intended to present data that consists of octets corresponding to printable characters in the US-ASCII character set. Here the lines are no longer than 76 characters. After the 75th character, the rest are cut off and replaced with an "=" sign, which serves as an escape character.
- **Base64:** This is used for data and other text that was meant for people with MIME mail programs. The Base64 uses a 65-character subset of the US-ASCII character set to encode and decode character strings. Here the lines are no longer than 76 characters as with the Quoted-Printable encoding.
- **7bit:** This is the default value, which means the message contents are plain ASCII text.
- **8bit:** This is data made of 8-bit characters with short lines that end in CRLF.
- **Binary:** This is like 8-bit encoding but without CRLF line boundaries.
- **X-Encoding:** This represents any nonstandard Content-Transfer-Encoding. Therefore, any additional values must have a name beginning with "`X-`".

In constructing a high-level user agent, it may be desirable to allow a message body to refer to another one. Message bodies may be labeled accordingly with the `Content-ID:` field, which is syntactically identical to the RFC 822 `Message-ID:` field. `Content-ID` values should be as unique as possible. The `Content-Description:` field is used to place some descriptive information for a given message body. For example, it may be useful to mark an "image" message body as "The front cover of the book," by which the recipients of the message can know the meaning of this image.

Figure 6.13 shows an example of a MIME message. This image is encoded using the base64 encoding.

From: 'Yi-Neng Lin' <ynlin@cs.nctu.edu.tw>
To: ydlin@cs.nctu.edu.tw
Subject: Cover
MIME-Version: 1.0
Content-Type: image/jpg;
    name=cover.jpg
Content-Transfer-Encoding: base64
Content-Description: The front cover of the book

<.....base64 encoded jpg image of cover...>

FIGURE 6.13 An example of a MIME message.

6.3.3 Internet Mail Protocols

An e-mail system relies on mail protocols to transport messages among clients and servers. Here we introduce three common mail protocols—SMTP, POP3, and IMAP4. As described in Subsection 6.3.1, SMTP is used to send messages from a mail client to a mail server, i.e., MUA to MTA, and also between mail servers, i.e., MTA to MTA. POP3 is used for clients to retrieve messages from a mail server, i.e., MRA to MUA. IMAP4 is similar to POP3 but supports some additional features such as storing and manipulating messages on the mail server. We shall now describe these protocols.

Simple Mail Transfer Protocol (SMTP)

Simple Mail Transfer Protocol (SMTP), first defined in RFC 821 and later obsoleted by RFC 2821 and 5321, is a standard host-to-host mail transport protocol traditionally operating over TCP on port 25. A daemon that listens to port 25 and speaks SMTP is called an SMTP server, i.e., MTA. The SMTP server deals with messages from senders and other mail servers. It accepts incoming connections and then delivers messages to appropriate recipients or to the next SMTP server. If an SMTP server is unable to deliver a message to a particular address and the errors are not due to permanent rejections, the message is put in a message queue for later delivery. Retries of delivery continue until the delivery succeeds or the SMTP server gives up; the give-up time is generally at least four to five days. If the SMTP server gives up the delivery, it returns the undeliverable message with an error report to the sender.

After an SMTP client (MUA or MTA) establishes a two-way transmission channel to an SMTP server (MTA), the client can generate and send SMTP commands to the server. SMTP replies are sent from the server to the client in response to the commands. Table 6.8 lists some important SMTP commands. `HELO` is used to identify the SMTP client to the SMTP server at the beginning of the session. `MAIL FROM:` informs the SMTP server who the originator is. It is used before specifying recipients for each message, or after a `RSET`. `RCPT TO:` announces to the SMTP server to whom the message has been sent. Multiple recipients are allowed, but each must have its own mailbox listed in `RCPT TO:`, which immediately follows the `MAIL FROM:`. `DATA` indicates the mail data. Everything entered following `DATA` is treated as the message body, and is sent to the recipients. The mail data is terminated by the

TABLE 6.8 Important SMTP Commands

Command	Description
HELO	Greet the receiver with the sender's domain name.
MAIL FROM:	Indicates the sender, but could be spoofed, too.
RCPT TO:	Indicates the recipient.
DATA	Indicates the mail data, terminated by a "." in a single line.
RSET	Reset the session.
QUIT	Close the session.

character sequence "<CRLF>.<CRLF>" which is a new line containing only a "." (period) followed by another new line. When the period is entered, the message may be queued or sent immediately. RSET resets the state of the current session; both the MAIL FROM: and RCPT TO: for the current transaction will be cleared. Finally, QUIT is used to close the session.

Whenever the SMTP server receives a command from a client, the server responds with a three-digit numerical code that indicates the success or failure of the command. Table 6.9 summarizes the response codes. The 200 or 2xx response means the previous command has been handled successfully.

After seeing the syntax and semantics of SMTP commands and replies, let us follow the interactions between the client and the server in an example session in Figure 6.14, in which ynlin sends an e-mail to ydlin. Note that "R" is the response from the receiving server, while "S" is the input by the sending client.

Post Office Protocol Version 3 (POP3)

Post Office Protocol version 3 (POP3), first defined in RFC 1081 and later obsoleted by RFC 1225, 1460, 1725, and 1939, is designed for user-to-mailbox access. A daemon that listens to port 110 and speaks POP3 is called a POP3 server. The POP3 server accepts connections from clients and retrieves messages for them. When a TCP connection is established between a client and the server, the server sends a greeting to the client and then exchanges commands and responses with the client.

TABLE 6.9 SMTP Replies

Response	Description
2xx	Command accepted and processed.
3xx	General flow control.
4xx	Critical system or transfer failure.
5xx	Errors with the SMTP command.

```
R: 220 mail.cs.nctu.edu.tw Simple Mail Transfer Service Ready
S: HELO CS.NCTU.EDU.TW
R: 250 MAIL.CS.NCTU.EDU.TW Hello [140.113.235.72]
S: MAIL FROM:<ynlin@CS.NCTU.EDU.TW>
R: 250 OK
S: RCPT TO:<ydlin@CS.NCTU.EDU.TW>
R: 250 2.1.5 <ydlin@CS.NCTU.EDU.TW>
S: DATA
R: 354 Start mail input; end with <CRLF>.<CRLF>
S: ...mail content...
S: .
R: 250 2.6.0 <SK3MoY3AYg00000001@CS.NCTU.EDU.TW> Queued mail for delivery
S: QUIT
R: 221 mail.cs.nctu.edu.tw Service closing transmission channel
```

FIGURE 6.14 An SMTP session.

A POP3 session progresses through a number of states during its lifetime. These states include AUTHORIZATION, TRANSACTION, and UPDATE. Once the client connects to the POP3 server and receives a greeting from the server, the session enters the AUTHORIZATION state. Then, to prove its identity, the client must tell the POP3 server its username and password. After the client has passed the identification check, the session enters the TRANSACTION state. At this time, the client can issue commands to the server and request the server to act on commands, for example, listing the messages on the maildrop. When the client has issued the QUIT command, the session enters the UPDATE state. In this state, the POP3 server releases any resources allocated to the client during the AUTHORIZATION state, says goodbye to the client, and finally closes the connection with the client.

Table 6.10 summarizes some essential POP3 commands. The third column indicates what session state a command belongs to. USER and PASS are used to identify the client in the AUTHORIZATION state. STAT gets the number of messages in and the octet size of the maildrop. LIST gets the size of one or all messages. If a message's name follows LIST as an argument, the information for that message will be reported. RETR is used to retrieve a message from the maildrop. DELE marks a message as deleted, and any future reference to the marked messages in a POP3 command generates an error. Note that the marked messages do not actually get deleted until the POP3 session enters the UPDATE state. NOOP stands for no operation, for which the POP3 server does nothing but replies with a positive response. RSET resets all messages that are marked as deleted to unmarked. Finally, QUIT turns the POP3 session into the UPDATE state and then terminates the session.

All POP3 replies begin with a status line. The status line comprises a status indicator and a keyword, possibly followed by additional information. There are currently two status indicators: positive ("+OK") and negative ("-ERR"). Additional information follows the status indicator on a single line of command results.

Figure 6.15 shows a POP3 session. Note that "S" is the response from the server while "C" is the input by the client. In this example, a user logs in on the POP3 server. First, he lists all messages in his maildrop. He then retrieves one message and terminates the session.

TABLE 6.10 Minimal POP3 Commands

Command	Description	Session State
USER *name*	Identifies the user to the server.	AUTHORIZATION
PASS *string*	Enters user password.	AUTHORIZATION
STAT	Gets the number of messages in and octet size of maildrop.	TRANSACTION
LIST [*msg*]	Gets the size of one or all messages.	TRANSACTION
RETR *msg*	Retrieves a message from the maildrop.	TRANSACTION
DELE *msg*	Marks the *msg* as deleted from the maildrop.	TRANSACTION
NOOP	No operation.	TRANSACTION
RSET	Resets all messages that are marked as deleted to unmarked.	TRANSACTION
QUIT	Terminates the session.	AUTHORIZATION, UPDATE

Internet Message Access Protocol Version 4 (IMAP4)

IMAP4, first defined in RFC 1730 and later obsoleted by RFC 2060 and 3501, is proposed as a replacement for the POP3 protocol. It comes from the need to use Web browsers anywhere to access e-mails on the server without actually downloading them. The main difference between IMAP4 and POP3 is that IMAP4 allows messages to be *stored* and *manipulated* on the mail system while POP3 only allows users to *download* their messages and store and manipulate messages on the users' machines. A daemon that listens to port 143 and speaks IMAP4 is called an IMAP4 server. IMAP4 lets users use an IMAP4 mail client on any PC to read, reply to, and

```
S: +OK POP3 Server mail.cs.nctu.edu.tw
C: USER ydlin
S: +OK send your password
C: PASS *******
S: +OK maildrop locked and ready
C: ejqwe
S: -ERR illegal command
C: STAT
S: +OK 1 296
C: LIST
S: +OK 1 messages (296 octets)
C: RETR 1
S: +OK 296 octets
… <server start to send the mail content> …
C: QUIT
S: +OK ydlin POP3 server signing off (maildrop empty)
```

FIGURE 6.15 A POP3 session.

store messages in hierarchical folders on IMAP4 servers, and synchronize client messages with the IMAP4 server.

An IMAP4 session progresses through three stages: the establishment of a client/server connection, an initial greeting from the server, and client/server interactions. An interaction consists of a client command, server data, and a server completion response. An IMAP4 server can be in one of four states. Most commands are valid only in certain states. These four states are described as follows:

1. **Non-authenticated:** When a connection is established between the IMAP4 server and the client, the server enters the `non-authenticated` state. The client must supply authentication credentials before most commands can be permitted.
2. **Authenticated:** When a pre-authenticated connection starts, the server enters the `authenticated` state when acceptable authentication credentials have been provided or after an error in mailbox selection. In the `authenticated` state, the client must select a mailbox to access before commands that affect messages can be permitted.
3. **Selected:** When a mailbox has been successfully selected, the server enters the `selected` state. In this state, a mailbox has been selected to access.
4. **Logout:** When the client asks to exit the server, the server enters the `logout` state. At this time, the server will close the connection.

Table 6.11 lists a summary of IMAP4 commands. We do not explain each command here. In short, IMAP4 includes operations for creating, deleting, and renaming mailboxes; checking for new messages; permanently removing messages; setting and clearing flags; RFC 822 and MIME message parsing and searching; and selective fetching of message attributes, texts, and portions thereof. Messages on IMAP4 servers are accessed with message sequence numbers or unique identifiers.

Each IMAP4 command starts with an identifier called a "tag" (typically a short alphanumeric string, e.g., A001, A002, etc.). Every command being sent must use a unique tag. There are two cases in which the client command is not sent completely. In either case, the client sends the second part of the command without any tag and the server then responds to this command with a line beginning with the token "+". The client must finish sending the whole command before sending another command.

TABLE 6.11 IMAP4 Command Summary

Session State	Commands
Any	`CAPABILITY, NOOP, LOGOUT`
`Non-authenticated`	`AUTHENTICATE, LOGIN`
`Authenticated`	`SELECT, EXAMINE, CREATE, DELETE, RENAME, SUBSCRIBE, UNSUBSCRIBE, LIST, LSUB, STATUS, APPDNED`
`Selected`	`CHECK, CLOSE, EXPUNCGE, SEARCH, FETCH, STORE, COPY UID`

```
S: * OK Dovecot ready.
C: a001 login user passwd
S: a001 OK Logged in.
C: a002 select inbox
S: * FLAGS (\Answered \Flagged \Deleted \Seen \Draft unknown-3 unknown-4 unknown-0 NonJunk
$MDNSent Junk $Forwarded)
S: * OK [PERMANENTFLAGS (\Answered \Flagged \Deleted \Seen \Draft unknown-3
unknown-4 unknown-0 NonJunk $MDNSent Junk $Forwarded \*)] Flags permitted.
S: * 885 EXISTS
S: * 0 RECENT
S: * OK [UNSEEN 869] First unseen.
S: * OK [UIDVALIDITY 1243861681] UIDs valid
S: * OK [UIDNEXT 5146] Predicted next UID
S: a002 OK [READ-WRITE] Select completed.
C: a003 fetch 2 full
S: * 2 FETCH (FLAGS (\Seen) INTERNALDATE “05-Apr-2009 17:50:01 +0800”
  RFC822.SIZE 2104 ENVELOPE (“Sat, 5 Apr 2009 17:50:01 +0800”

  “=?big5?B? Rnc6IFJlOiC4Z7ZPsMqk5KTOusOrScV2ss6tcKrt?=”
  ((“rhhuang” NIL “ rhhuang” “ rhhwang@exodue.cs.ccu.edu.tw”)) ((“rhhuang” NIL “ rhhuang”
  “rhhwang@exodue.cs.ccu.edu.tw”)) ((“rhhuang” NIL “ rhhuang” “ rhhwang@exodue.cs.ccu.edu.tw”))
  BODY (“text” “html” (“charset” “big5”) NIL NIL “base64”1720 22))

S: a003 OK Fetch completed.
C: a004 fetch 2 body[header]
S: * 2 FETCH (BODY[HEADER] {384}
S: From: “rhhuang” <rhhwang@exodue.cs.ccu.edu.tw>
S: To: “ydlin” ydlin@cs.nctu.edu.tw>
S: Subject: =?big5?B?Rnc6IFJlOiC4Z7ZPsMqk5KTOusOrScV2ss6tcKrt?=
S: Date: Sat, 5 Apr 2009 17:50:01 +0800
S: MIME-Version: 1.0
S: Content-Type: text/html; charset=”big5”; Content-Transfer-Encoding: base64
S: X-Priority: 3; X-MSMail-Priority: Normal; X-MimeOLE: Produced By Microsoft MimeOLE
S: a004 OK Fetch completed.
C: a005 store 2 +flags \deleted
S: * 2 FETCH (FLAGS (\Deleted \Seen))
S: a005 OK Store completed.
C: a006 logout
S: * BYE Logging out
S: a006 OK Logout completed.
S: Connection closed by foreign host.
```

FIGURE 6.16 An IMAP4 session.

The responses in IMAP4 can be tagged or untagged. A tagged status response indicates the completion of a client command with a matched tag. Untagged status responses indicate server greeting or server status other than the completion of a command. The sever status responses can take three forms: status response, server data, and command continuation request. A client must be prepared to accept the following responses at any time:

1. **Status response:** The status responses can indicate either the result (`OK`, `NO`, or `BAD`) of the completed client command or the server's greetings and alerts (`PREAUTH` and `BYE`).

2. **Server data:** The client must record certain server data when it is received, as noted in the description of that data. The data conveys critical information that affects the interpretation of all subsequent commands and responses. Data transmitted from the server to the client and status responses that do not indicate command completion are called untagged responses. Each untagged response is prefixed with the character "*".
3. **Command continuation request:** Theses responses indicate that the server is ready to accept the continuation of a command from the client. The remainder of this response is a line of text.

Figure 6.16 shows an example IMAP4 session. A user logs onto an IMAP4 server with his username and password. After being authenticated, the user manipulates the "inbox" mailbox. The user fetches a message, marks the message to be deleted, and finally terminates the session.

Historical Evolution: Web-Based Mail vs. Desktop Mail

Webmail is an e-mail service accessed by a Web browser, as opposed to a desktop e-mail program such as Microsoft Outlook or Mozilla's Thunderbird. A survey by *USA Today* in 2008 reported that the top four Webmail service providers were Microsoft Windows Live Hotmail, Yahoo! Mail, Google Gmail, and AOL Mail. These providers also provided desktop e-mail services for users to retrieve e-mails. Two advantages of Webmail over desktop e-mail service are *ubiquitous* accessibility and negligible maintenance overhead. With Webmail, e-mails are maintained and manipulated on a remote e-mail server through IMAP4 commands. In contrast, a desktop e-mail service requires clients to retrieve e-mails from e-mail servers through POP3 or IMAP4 commands and to store them locally in users' computers. Desktop e-mail still has two benefits: possessing *total control* over e-mails, and being able to efficiently access e-mails stored locally. It is interesting to note that engineers and scientists tend to prefer desktop e-mail over Webmail due to the need for total control.

Two interfaces exist in Webmail services: (1) a Web interface using `GET` and `POST` HTTP commands between clients and the frontend Webmail server and (2) an e-mail interface using POP3/IMAP4 commands between the frontend Webmail server and backend e-mail servers. The frontend Webmail server and backend e-mail server could be separated or integrated as shown in Figure 6.17(a) and 6.17(b), respectively. In Figure 6.17(b), both the first and the second interfaces are integrated on the machine.

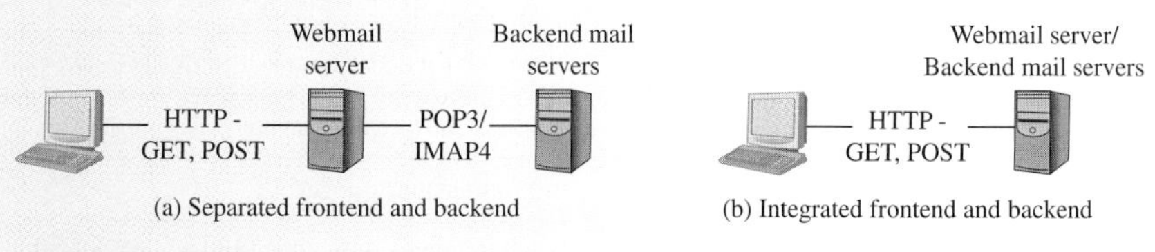

FIGURE 6.17 Webmail service architectures.

Open Source Implementation 6.2: qmail

Overview

qmail is a secure, reliable, efficient, and simple MTA designed for UNIX-like operating systems. It is targeted to be a replacement for sendmail, the most popular MTA on the Internet. Up to now, qmail has been the second most popular SMTP server and has had the fastest growth among all SMTP servers on the Internet. The reason we do not introduce sendmail here is that its program and configuration files are difficult to understand. We first introduce the qmail system structure, control files, and data flows. Then we go into details about qmail queue structure.

In summary, qmail is a concurrent implementation of the connection-oriented stateful SMTP (port 25), POP3 (port 110), and IMAP4 (port 143) protocols. It also supports MIME messages.

Block Diagram

An e-mail system performs a variety of tasks, such as handling incoming messages, managing the queue, and delivering messages to users. From the perspective of program structure, sendmail is *monolithic,* which means it puts all functions into a large, complex program. This causes more security bugs and difficulties in maintaining the program. qmail, however, is *modular,* which means a complete qmail system is composed of several modular programs. Each program of qmail is small and simple, and thus performs its specific tasks efficiently. The modular design makes each program run with as little privilege as possible, and therefore enhances the security. Due to its good design, qmail is also easy to set up and manage. The core modules of qmail and their functions are listed in Table 6.12. Figure 6.18

TABLE 6.12 Core Modules of qmail

Module	Description
qmail-smtpd	Receive a message via SMTP.
qmail-inject	Preprocess and send a message.
qmail-queue	Queue a message for delivery.
qmail-send	Deliver messages from the queue.
qmail-clean	Clean up the queue directory.
qmail-lspawn	Schedule local deliveries.
qmail-local	Deliver or forward a message.
qmail-rspawn	Schedule remote deliveries.
qmail-remote	Send a message via SMTP.
qmail-pop3d	Distribute messages via POP3.

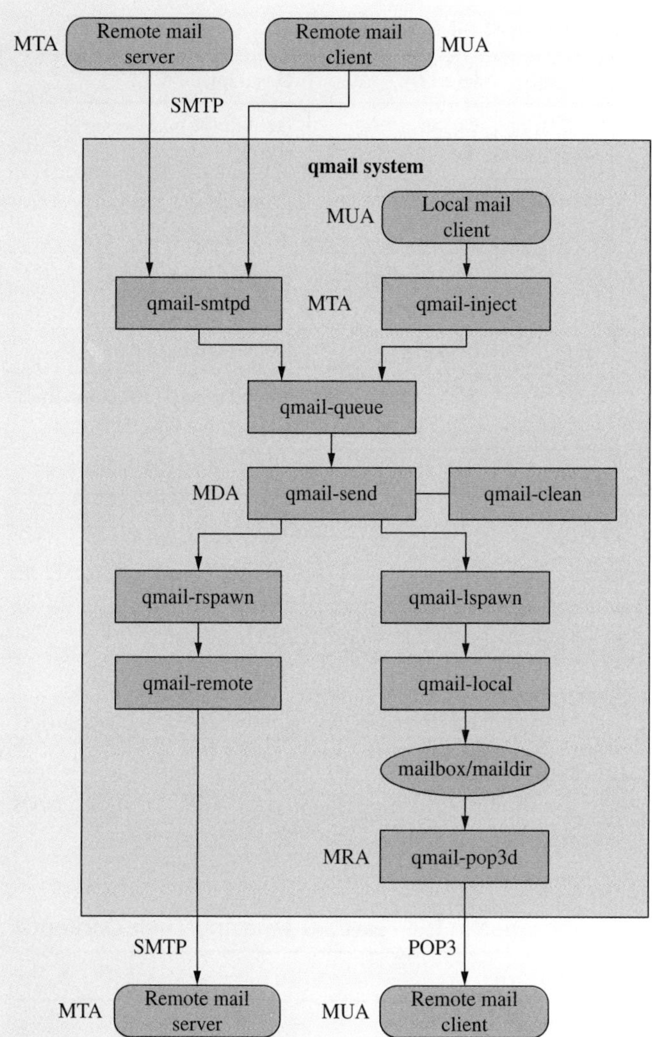

FIGURE 6.18 The data flows in the `qmail` suite.

shows the block diagram of these core modules. The data flows indicated in this block diagram shall be illustrated in the subsection on algorithm implementations.

Data Structures

`qmail` uses many configuration files to change the behavior of the system. These files are located under the `/var/qmail/control` directory. Before starting the `qmail` system, we need to modify some files for desired configurations. Table 6.13 lists some control files. Here we introduce the three most important files. The `me` file stores the full qualified domain name (FQDN) of the local host.

Continued

TABLE 6.13 Some Control Files of `qmail`

Control	Default	Used by	Description
`me`	FQDN of system	various	Default for many control files
`rcpthosts`	(none)	`qmail-smtpd`	Domains that `qmail` accepts messages for
`locals`	me	`qmail-send`	Domains that `qmail` delivers locally
`defaultdomain`	me	`qmail-inject`	Default domain name
`plusdomain`	me	`qmail-inject`	Added to any host name that ends with a plus sign
`virtualdomains`	(none)	`qmail-send`	Virtual domains and users

`rcpthosts` records all of the hosts that `qmail` shall receive messages for. Note that all of the local domains must be in this file. `locals` contains local hosts; that is, messages sent to these hosts shall be delivered to local users.

`qmail` Queue Structure

`qmail` temporarily stores received messages in a central queue directory for later delivery. This directory is located at `/var/qmail/queue`, and has several subdirectories to store different information and data. Table 6.14 describes these subdirectories and what they contain.

TABLE 6.14 Subdirectories in the `qmail` Queue and Their Contents

Subdirectory	Contents
`Bounce`	Permanent delivery errors
`Info`	Envelope sender addresses
`Intd`	Envelopes under construction by `qmail-queue`
`Local`	Local envelope recipient addresses
`Lock`	Lock files
`Mess`	Message files
`Pid`	Used by `qmail-queue` to acquire an i-node number
`Remote`	Remote envelope recipient addresses
`Todo`	Complete envelopes

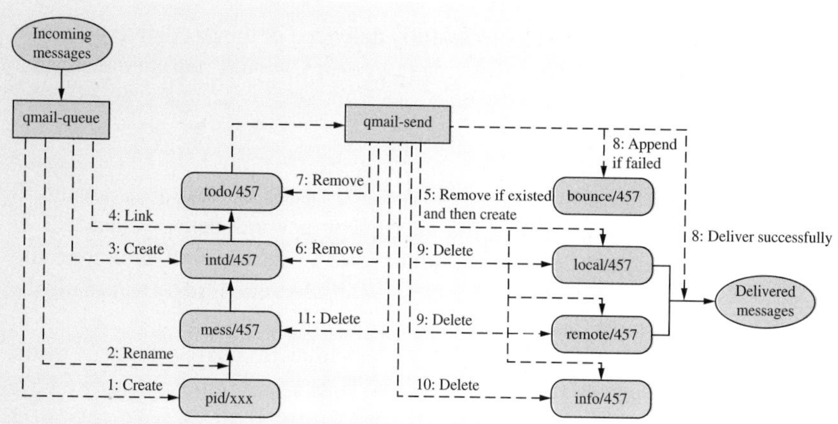

FIGURE 6.19 How messages pass through the `qmail` queue.

Messages, from entering to leaving the `qmail` queue, may pass through several subdirectories, as depicted in Figure 6.19. This comprises three phases: (1) messages enter the queue, (2) queued messages are preprocessed, and (3) preprocessed messages are delivered.

Entering the Queue

For an incoming message, `qmail-queue` first creates a file with a unique file name under the "`pid`" directory. The file system assigns a unique "`inode`" number, 457 for example, to the file. The unique `inode` number is used by `qmail-queue` to identify the message. `qmail-queue` renames the newly created file, `pid`/whatever, as `mess/457`, and writes the message to `mess/457`. Then, `qmail-queue` creates another new file, `intd/457`, and writes the envelope information to it. Next, `qmail-queue` links `intd/457` to `todo/457`. After this step, the message has been successfully queued and is to be preprocessed.

Message Preprocessing

The purpose of message preprocessing is for `qmail-send` to decide which recipients are local and which recipients are remote. When `qmail-send` finds `todo/457`, it first removes `info/457`, `local/457`, and `remote/457` if they exist. Then it reads `todo/457`, and creates `info/457` and possibly `local/457` and `remote/457`. After that, it removes `intd/457` and `todo/457`. The preprocessing for the message is finished at this time. The `local/457` or `remote/457` now contains the recipients' addresses. Each address is marked either `NOT DONE` or `DONE`. The definitions of `NOT DONE` and `DONE` are as follows:

NOT DONE: If there have been any delivery attempts, they have all met temporary failure. `qmail-send` should try to deliver to this address in the future.

Continued

DONE: The message was successfully delivered or the last delivery attempt met permanent failure. Either way, qmail-send should not attempt further delivery to this address.

Message Delivering

qmail-send delivers the message to a NOT DONE address at its leisure. It will mark the address as DONE if the subsequent message delivery succeeds. If encountering a permanent delivery failure, qmail-send will first append a note to bounce/457, creating bounce/457 if needed, and then mark the address as DONE. Note that qmail-send may inject a new bounce message to bounce/457 and delete bounce/457 at any time. Iteratively, qmail-send delivers the message to the addresses in local/457 and remote/457. After delivering to all the addresses, qmail-send deletes local/457 and remote/457. Then qmail-send eliminates the message. First, qmail-send checks for the existence of bounce/457. If bounce/457 exists, qmail-send handles it as described above. Once bounce/457 is deleted, qmail-send then deletes info/457 and finally mess/457.

Algorithm Implementations

After qmail has been set and is running properly, it is ready to receive messages from senders. A message, being received, queued, and finally delivered to the recipients by qmail, might pass through several modules. The block diagram in Figure 6.18 also shows the data flows in the qmail suite. First, a program receives a message from a sender. This program may be qmail-smtpd for the message sent via SMTP or qmail-inject for messages generated locally. Then qmail-queue is invoked by qmail-smtpd or qmail-inject to put the message into a central queue directory. The message is then delivered by qmail-send in cooperation with qmail-lspawn or qmail-rspawn, and cleaned by qmail-clean. If the message is for local users, qmail-lspawn invokes qmail-local to store it into the recipient's mailbox or mail directory. If the recipient of the message is not in the local system, qmail-rspawn invokes qmail-remote to send the message to the recipient's mail server. The recipients belonging to the local system can retrieve their messages through qmail-pop3d. Note that qmail-send, qmail-clean, qmail-lspawn, and qmail-rspawn are long-running daemons, while the others are invoked when needed.

Exercises

1. Find the .c files and the lines of code that implement qmail-smtpd, qmail-remote, and qmail-pop3d.
2. Find the exact structure definition of the qmail queue in an object of the qmail structure.
3. Find how e-mails are stored in the mailbox and mail directory.

6.4 WORLD WIDE WEB (WWW)

Simple yet powerful, the World Wide Web (WWW) has contributed to the phenomenal growth of the Internet and has changed the world in information sharing. Evolved from *anonymous* information sharing services including anonymous FTP, Archie, Gopher, and WAIS, WWW goes one step further to standardize and simplify the addressing methods into Universal Resource Locator (URL), multimedia content formats into HyperText Markup Language (HTML) and later eXtensible Markup Language (XML), and access protocols into HyperText Transfer Protocol (HTTP). This section first introduces Web naming and addressing with URL and other similar schemes. We then describe HTML, XML, and HTTP. Web caching and proxying mechanisms are also reviewed. Finally, Apache serves as our example of open source implementation, with its performance profiled.

6.4.1 Introduction

WWW provides a cyber space for universal access to knowledge, and it allows collaborators from different locations to share their ideas and all aspects of a common project. Unless two projects are developed collaboratively rather than independently, results from two parties might not be integrated into one cohesive piece of work. Started by Tim Berners-Lee as a project at the European Organization for Nuclear Research (CERN), WWW has been the most popular medium for information retrieval of all sorts since 1989.

By using a Web browser such as the commercially available Microsoft Internet Explorer (IE) or other emerging browsers like FireFox, Chrome, and Opera, users can access any online Web pages by an underlying procedure illustrated in Figure 6.20. First, the server name in the Universal Resource Locator (URL), which will be discussed shortly, is resolved into an IP address through DNS. The browser then connects, by TCP three-way handshake, to the Web server listening on a TCP port, usually port 80, at that particular IP address. Once the TCP connection is set, the browser issues a HTTP request for the resource to the Web server. The first requested resource is a Web page in HTML. The Web browser parses the requested Web page

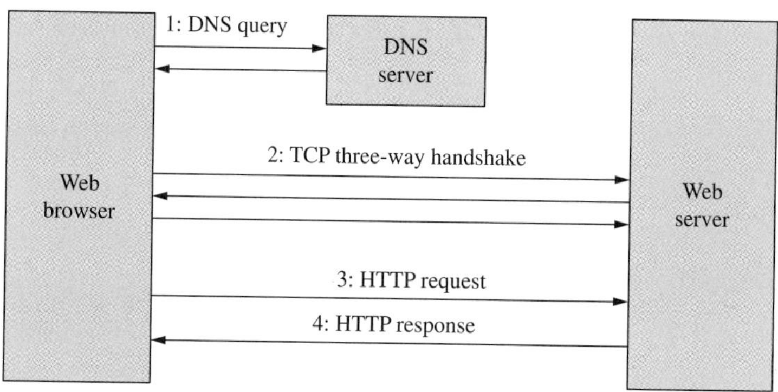

FIGURE 6.20 How a Web client interacts with a Web server.

immediately and might issue additional requests for images and any other files in the Web page.

HTTP 1.0 was standardized in RFC 1945 in 1996, while HTTP 1.1 was standardized in RFC 2068 in 1997 and later obsoleted by RFC 2616 in 1999. RFC 1866 defined HTML in 1995 and was obsoleted by RFC 2854 in 2000. Uniform Resource Identifier (URI) was defined in RFC 1808 in 1995 and obsoleted by RFC 3986 in 2005.

6.4.2 Web Naming and Addressing

The Web is an information space formed with a great quantity of Web pages and documents. The unit of information on the Web is known as a *resource.* How to find and manipulate resources in the space is an important issue. Web naming is a mechanism for naming resources on the Web, while Web addressing provides ways to access the resources. URIs are short strings that identify resources in the Web. URIs make resources available through a variety of naming schemes and access methods. Uniform Resource Locators (URLs) are a subset of URIs to describe the addresses of resources accessible on the Web. Another kind of URI is the Uniform Resource Name (URN). A URN is a name of global scope which does not imply a *location.* Figure 6.21 shows the relationship among URI, URL, and URN. Note that URLs are used for *locating* or finding resources, whereas URNs are used for *identification.*

Uniform Resource Identifier (URI)

A URI is a compact string of characters for identifying an abstract or physical resource. Any resource, whether a page of text, an image, a video or sound clip, or a program, has a name encoded in a URI. A URI typically consists of three pieces:

1. The naming scheme used to access the resource.
2. The name of the machine where the resource is housed.
3. The name of the resource itself, given as a path or a file name.

The generic syntax of URI includes both *absolute* and *relative* forms. An absolute identifier refers to a resource independent of the current context, while a relative identifier refers to a resource by how it differs from the current context's URI. The syntax of the absolute URI is:

```
<scheme>:<scheme-specific-part>#<fragment>
```

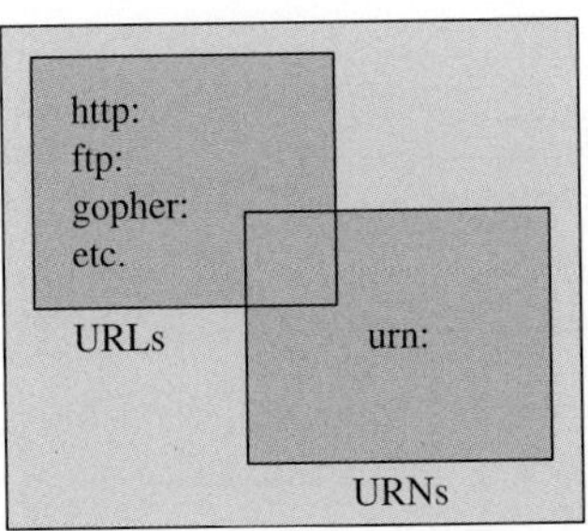

FIGURE 6.21 The relationship among URI, URL, and URN.

which consists of three parts: the name of the scheme being used (<scheme>), a string (<scheme-specific-part>) whose interpretation depends on the scheme, and an optional fragment identifier (<fragment>), which conveys additional reference information.

A subset of URI shares a common syntax to represent the hierarchical relationship within the name space. This yields a "generic URI" as

<scheme>:<authority><path>?<query>#<fragment>

where the scheme-specific-part is further broken down into <authority>, <path>, and <query> components. Many URI schemes include a top hierarchical element for a naming authority; thus the <authority> is used to govern the name space defined by the rest of the URI. The <path> component contains data specific to the authority, identifying the resource within the scope of the specified scheme and authority. The <query> component is a string of information to be interpreted by the resource.

Sometimes a URI can also take the form of a relative URI, where the scheme and usually also the authority component are missing. Its path generally refers to a resource on the same machine where the current context resides. The syntax of the relative URI is

<path>?<query>#<fragment>.

Figure 6.22 shows some URI examples. The first example URI may be interpreted as follows: Some book information residing on the server speed.cs.nctu.edu.tw are accessible via the path ~/ydlin/index.html through HTTP protocol. The last example is a relative URI. Assume we have the base URI http://www.cs.nctu.edu.tw/. The relative URI in the last example would be expanded to the full URI http://www.cs.nctu.edu.tw/icons/logo.gif.

Uniform Resource Locator (URL)

A URL is a compact string representation of a resource's location on the Internet. It is a form of URI. URLs make it possible to direct both people and software applications to a variety of information, available through a number of different Internet protocols. The common syntax of the URL is as:

<service>//<user>:<password>@<host>:<port>/<url-path>

where some or all of <user>:<password>@, ":<password>, ":<port>, and /<url-path> might be omitted. In the preceding syntax, the <service> refers to the specific schemes by which the resource is served. The schemes covered here are listed in Table 6.15. After the specific scheme comes the data starting with a double slash //. The <user> and <password> are options for the user name and

http://speed.cs.nctu.edu.tw/~ydlin/index.html#Books
http://www.google.com/search?q=linux
ftp://ftp.cs.nctu.edu.tw/Documents/IETF/rfc2300~2399/rfc2396.txt
mailto: ydlin@cs.nctu.edu.tw
news: comp.os.linux
telnet://bbs.cs.nctu.edu.tw/
../icons/logo.gif

FIGURE 6.22 Some URI examples.

TABLE 6.15 Specific Schemes in URLs

Service	Description
ftp	File Transfer Protocol
http	Hypertext Transfer Protocol
gopher	The Gopher protocol
mailto	Electronic mail address
news	USENET news
nntp	USENET news using NNTP access
telnet	Reference to interactive sessions
wais	Wide Area Information Servers
file	Host-specific file names
prospero	Prospero Directory Service

password. If present, the user name and password are separated by a colon (:) and followed by an at-sign (@). The <host> indicates the domain name or IP address of a network host. The <port>, separated from the host by a colon, is the host's port number to connect to. The <url-path> specifies the details of how the specified resource can be addressed. Note that the slash (/) between the host (or port) and the url-path is not part of the url-path.

Figure 6.23 shows some URL examples. The first URL indicates the location of an image file on the Web site www.cs.nctu.edu.tw, while the second is the Webmail site of the CS department accessible through SSL (Secure Socket Layer) protocol (specified by the "https" service scheme). The third URL indicates a text file available on the ftp server ftp.cs.nctu.edu.tw. In this example, the user logs onto the ftp server with his user name "john" and password "secret". The fourth example refers to a news article numbered 5238 in the newsgroup cs.course.computer-networks on the news server news.cs.nctu.edu.tw. The final URL shows an interactive service that may be accessed through port 110 by the telnet protocol.

Uniform Resource Name (URN)

A URL provides the location of a given resource on the Web. If the resource is moved to another location, its URL changes. URNs are intended to overcome this problem by providing a persistent identifier for resources. A URN is a location-independent

http://www.cs.nctu.edu.tw/chinese/ccg/titleMain.gif
https://mail.cs.nctu.edu.tw/
ftp://john:secret@ftp.cs.nctu.edu.tw/projects/book.txt
nntp://news.cs.nctu.edu.tw/cis.course.computer-networks/5238
telnet://mail.cs.nctu.edu.tw:110/

FIGURE 6.23 Some URL examples.

urn:path:/home/ydlin/courses/index.html
urn:www-cs-nctu-edu-tw:student
urn:isbn:0-201-56317-7

FIGURE 6.24 Some URN examples.

name that identifies a resource on the Web. The URN syntax, which consists of four parts, is:

```
<URN> ::= "urn:" <NID> ":" <NSS>
```

where the <URN> is only a label identifying the name being a URN, the "urn:" is a name space identifier used to determine how to handle the URN, the <NID> refers to a name space identifier, which designates the authority for this URN scheme, and the <NSS> is the name-specific string whose syntax and meaning are defined within the context of the <NID>. In other words, the meaning of the <NSS> is assigned and determined by the <NID> that owns that particular URN name space.

Figure 6.24 gives some URN examples. The "path", "www-cs-nctu-edu-tw", and "isbn" are name space identifiers. The first example consists of a naming authority or path "/home/ydlin/courses/index.html" and a unique string "index.html". The second example illustrates a student in the domain www-cs-nctu-edu-tw. The last example is a URN for a book. This URN uses the ISBN number of the book to name it. If a service wants to use a URL to refer to the book, it might look like

```
http://www.isbn.com/0-201-56317-7
```

which contains a specific protocol and a domain name that might be changed over time. The URN contains neither of these, so it is more stable. However, it is much more useful if there is a system that can map the name onto the corresponding resource. This process is called resolution and is similar to the way DNS takes a domain name and resolves it into the IP address. RFC 1737 concentrates on the case of a URN resolved to a URL, though a URN could be resolved to any network resource or services.

6.4.3 HTML and XML

HyperText Markup Language (HTML) is the predominant markup language for Web pages. As a descendent from Standard Generalized Markup Language (SGML) specified by the World Wide Web Consortium (W3C), HTML provides a means to describe the structure of text-based information in a document by denoting text as links, headings, paragraphs, lists, etc., and to supplement text with interactive *forms,* embedded *images,* and other *objects.* HTML is written in the form of "tags" surrounded by angle brackets.

Nevertheless, pure formatting has been considered insufficient to help readers digest information. It is hoped that one can define his own tags in the markup language to *describe* data rather than simply formatting them. This is where eXtensible Markup Language (XML) originates. XML was defined in RFC 4826 in 2007. It allows the user to define the markup elements, and helps information systems to share structured data. Unlike HTML, which supports only limited styles, XML provides a standard style specification called eXtensible Style Language (XSL).

Arbitrary levels of nested structure are allowed, compared to HTML, which accepts only a few levels. It supports a formal grammar that standardizes parsing and makes parsing easier. In addition to HTML-like simple links, XML is capable of *extended links,* in which the target includes multiple objects of the same or different types of resources. This enables flexible provisioning of content and can be implemented in XML Linking Language (XLink) and XML Pointer Language (XPointer).

6.4.4 HTTP

The HTTP messages consist of requests and responses between clients and servers. A request message consists of (1) the *request line,* which includes the *method* to be applied to the resource, the *identifier* of the resource, and the protocol *version* in use; (2) the *header,* which defines various *features* of the *data* that is requested or being provided; (3) an *empty line,* which is used to separate the header from the message body; and (4) an optional *message body.*

Table 6.16 lists request methods used in request messages. Many of them deserve further explanation. `CONNECT` is used to dynamically switch from a connection into a tunnel, e.g., SSL-encrypted tunneling, to *secure* the communication. `GET` is the most widely used method to retrieve a specified resource. `HEAD` is the pseudo version of `GET` and is often used to test hypertext links for validity, accessibility, and recent modification. A client can use `OPTIONS` to request information about the communication options available for the specified URL without initiating a resource action or a resource retrieval.

`POST` submits data as a new subordinate of the specified resource. `PUT` requests data to be stored exactly at the specified resource. If the specified resource already exists, the data should be considered a modified version of that which resides on the origin server. Though similar, POST and PUT have some differences. `PUT` is a limited operation and does nothing more than *putting* data at a specified URL. However, depending on the server logic, `POST` would allow the server to do whatever it wants with the data, including storing it in the *specified* page, a *new* page, or a *database,* or simply throwing it away. The method `TRACE` is used to invoke a remote application-layer *loop-back* of the request. `TRACE` allows the client to see

TABLE 6.16 Request Methods of the HTTP Protocol

Request Method	Description
`CONNECT`	Dynamically switch the request connection to a tunnel, e.g., SSL tunneling.
`DELETE`	Delete the specified resource at the server, if possible.
`GET`	Request a representation of the specified resource.
`HEAD`	Ask for the response as GET, but without the response body.
`OPTIONS`	Request for information about available options and/or requirements associated with the specified URL.
`POST`	Submit data to be a new subordinate of the specified resource.
`PUT`	Request data to be stored under the specified resource.
`TRACE`	Invoke a remote application-layer loop-back of the request.

TABLE 6.17 Response Status Codes of the HTTP Protocol

Response Status Code	Description
1xx	Informational—Request received, continuing process.
2xx	Success—The action was successfully received, understood, and accepted.
3xx	Redirection—Further action must be taken in order to complete the request.
4xx	Client Error—The request contains bad syntax or cannot be fulfilled.
5xx	Server Error—The server failed to fulfill an apparently valid request.

what is being received at the receiver end of the request and to use that data for testing or diagnostic information.

After receiving and interpreting a request message, a server responds with an HTTP response message. The first line of a response message includes the protocol *version* followed by a numeric *status* code and its associated *textual* phrase. Table 6.17 summarizes the response status codes. The status code is a three-digit integer code reporting the result of the attempt to satisfy the request. The `2xx` status code means the request has been handled successfully.

Figure 6.25 gives an example HTTP session in which the client downloads some image files and then uploads several documents to a remote server.

```
C: GET / HTTP/1.1\r\n
S: HTTP/1.1 200 OK\r\n
C: GET /images/doclist/icon_5_spread.gif HTTP/1.1\r\n
S: HTTP/1.1 200 OK\r\n
C: GET /images/doclist/icon_5_chrome_folder.gif HTTP/1.1\r\n
S: HTTP/1.1 200 OK\r\n
C: GET /doclist/client/js/3857076368-doclist_modularized-webkit_app__zh_tw.js HTTP/1.1\r\n
S: HTTP/1.1 200 OK\r\n
C: POST /ir HTTP/1.1\r\n
S: HTTP/1.1 200 OK\r\n
C: GET /DocAction?action=updoc&hl=zh_TW HTTP/1.1\r\n
S: HTTP/1.1 200 OK\r\n
C: GET /doclist/client/js/2829347588-doclist_upload__zh_tw.js HTTP/1.1\r\n
S: HTTP/1.1 200 OK\r\n
C: GET /images/doclist/icon_5_folder.gif HTTP/1.1\r\n
S: HTTP/1.1 200 OK\r\n
C: POST /upload/resumableupload HTTP/1.1\r\n
S: HTTP/1.1 201 Created\r\n
C: POST
/upload/resumableupload/AEnB2Uqc0vh4TlTW3Kblk5ayKtlptLcH-mVAd2cvLdSFD1jSIQd1nNdJeZ
bVhOsKliVO4VeR9MP_gleoUDwU24rO07vUHUYvsQ/0 HTTP/1.1\r\n
S: HTTP/1.1 200 OK\r\n
C: GET / HTTP/1.1\r\n
S: HTTP/1.1 200 OK\r\n
C: POST /ir HTTP/1.1\r\n
S: HTTP/1.1 200 OK\r\n
```

FIGURE 6.25 An example HTTP session.

From Stateless to Stateful

HTTP is basically a *stateless* protocol, that is, the server does not have any state kept during transactions with clients. A server fetches the page requested by the client and completes a transaction, so each transaction is independent of the other. However, an HTTP server can be made to act as if it were stateful, with help from the client.

Two ways exist to realize stateful HTTP transactions for applications that require statefulness. The first is to use the concept of *session,* in which all parameters pertaining to a potential session are kept in the server without client awareness. However, this method lacks scalability due to the server's limited memory space, resulting in session states that soon expire. To fix this drawback, relatively small *cookies* are employed as an alternative, in which states are sent in HTTP headers to the clients and then stored in the form of a cookie. Clients embed the cookie in the subsequent HTTP requests of the same session. Though scalability is greatly extended, this requires cooperation from clients, usually through manual settings by users to enable the use of cookies, and brings security risks to the clients.

In addition to the transaction-level statefulness, additional *connection-level* statefulness is provided in terms of *HTTP1.1 persistency.* That is, only one single TCP connection is enough for a client to carry on all transactions with a server, of course with configurable timeout timers in use. This significantly reduces the amount of time and memory space being consumed, compared to the ordinary HTTP1.0 which establishes one connection per transaction.

Principle in Action: Non-WWW Traffic Over Port 80 or HTTP

Usually an Internet application is associated with a well-known server port number. For example, port 53 for the DNS service, ports 20 and 21 for the FTP service, ports 25, 110, and 143 for the SMTP, POP3, and IMAP4 services, respectively, and port 80 for the HTTP service. Nowadays, networks carry more complex traffic such as P2P traffic that uses dynamically allocated port numbers. However, traffic on these non-well-known ports is often blocked by enterprise firewalls for various reasons. Thus, many such applications *disguise* their traffic over TCP port 80 or within HTTP messages in order to pass through firewalls. For example, Skype can be configured to run over port 80. Windows Live Messenger uses the Microsoft Notification Protocol (MSNP) over TCP port 1863 to transmit messages, but optionally, it can *encapsulate* MSNP messages within HTTP messages.

Transmitting over port 80 is different from transmitting over HTTP. The former is easily done by building connections with port 80, while the latter encapsulates the original traffic in HTTP messages. In either case, the goal is to evade firewalls that bypass traffic over port 80 or HTTP messages. Consequently, firewalls or network administrators cannot rely on port numbers or HTTP messages to identify the message type because the traffic recognized as Web traffic could be something else.

Historical Evolution: Google Applications

In the era of cloud computing, software would be leased to the client as a service instead of being sold and owned. Although well known for providing Internet search service, Google has released several Web-based products, including *Gmail, Google Maps, Google Calendar, Google Talk, Google Docs, Google Sites, Google Notebook,* and *Google Chrome,* and Picasaweb/Picasa. Techniques such as replica servers, data backup, and cloud computing are used by Google to distribute the workload among servers and raise the entire performance. In the beginning, Google applications just supported *online* versions, where all operations were transformed into sequential commands, transmitted over the Internet to and completed by Google servers, but now they also support *offline* versions where users operate locally and transmit the final results when connected to Google servers.

Table 6.18 summarizes the features of different categories of Google applications. *Google Docs* is a Web-based online application suite similar to Microsoft Office, with more support for online collaborative works. *Google*

TABLE 6.18 Categories of Google Applications

Categories	Application Name	Comments
Office suites	Google Docs	• Support text editing for documents, spreadsheets, and presentations • Collaborative editing of documents • Support online use
Web	Google Sites, Google Notebook	• Collaborative content editing of Web sites • Support online use
Photo editing	Picasaweb, Picasa	• Organize/edit digital photos • Support online/offline use
Instant messaging/ voice	Google Talk	• Use XMPP/Jingle protocol • Support online use
Web browser	Google Chrome	• Webkit layout engine • V8 Javascript engine • Support online/offline use
Time management	Google Calendar	• Agenda management, scheduling, shared online calendars and mobile calendar sync • Support online/offline use
Maps	Google Maps, Google Earth	• Online mapping service • Support online use
Communication/ collaboration	Google Wave	• Designed to integrate e-mail, instant messaging, Wiki, and social network services
Mail	Gmail	• Web-based interface • Support POP3, IMAP4, and SMTP • Support online/offline use

Notebook is a Web-based online notebook. *Google Chrome* is a Web browser that uses the Webkit layout engine and the V8 Javascript engine. *Google Earth* is a geographic information system that displays detailed satellite map and even street views. *Google Wave* is a Web-based service designed to integrate e-mail, instant messaging, and social networking for personal and collaborative communication. The participants can send, reply, and edit the message documents called *waves,* add participants, and be notified of changes and replies to the waves in real time as they are typed by other collaborators.

6.4.5 Web Caching and Proxying

Web caching is a mechanism to expedite document downloading on the World Wide Web. Just like the ordinary caching concept in computer systems, a copy of remote content previously retrieved by users is kept locally in the cache server for future access to improve bandwidth efficiency and, most importantly, the responsiveness of the surfing experience. This is especially helpful for frequently requested Web pages.

Upon receiving a request, the cache server checks whether a valid copy is present. If yes (cache hit), then the server returns the cached page immediately to the client; otherwise the client (browser) will receive the message Page Unfound. The client browser then continues the quest of retrieval by sending a request directly to the Web server, bypassing the cache server. To achieve maximum satisfaction from Web caching, some aspects need to be considered.

Candidates to be cached: Though disk manufacturing technology has been advancing in recent years, size limits still require users not to abuse the disk quota. The same applies to the caching mechanism, which relies mainly on the disk storage. Therefore, a screening process is necessary to identify the caching targets, which often means frequently fetched *static* pages, rather than CGI/PHP/ASP–based *dynamic* content.

Content replacement: To further deal with possible shortage in disk storage, some replacement techniques such as *removal* and *threshold* are usually adopted. The former, exercised under limited storage, simply removes old pages in order to make new accommodations, though a selection procedure may be applied based on pages' popularity and freshness. Under a relatively relaxed storage requirement, a threshold may be set on the content, above which the content replacement is executed.

Cache coherence: In addition to ordinary replacement to identify and remove old content, each cached item is also associated with an expiration time to prevent its becoming outdated. Expiration times can be calculated from the last time the document was requested or from the last validation date, which is thought to be more appropriate. The trade-off for the latter is, however, the increased computation and communication overhead, especially at peak times.

Transparent Proxy

A cache server can also act as a proxy server, which helps forward queries to proper destinations if a cache miss occurs. The forwarding destination could be other cache servers or the corresponding Web server. This feature is beneficial in two respects. First, the overhead of resending the request from the client to the Web server is eliminated. Second and most importantly, the utmost control of the network can be achieved by *concentrating* all the accesses to the proxy server and monitoring them.

Normally the Web caching feature requires that the client preconfigure the browser to make sure it checks with the cache server in the first place; in other words, the browser must know the address of the cache server. Nonetheless, the complex manual configuration usually prevents users from activating Web caching. Fortunately, this can be dealt with by *transparent proxy,* which involves a gateway-level technique called *port redirection.* Take the popular open-source package `Squid` that supports both caching and proxying as an example. The gateway server of a network collects all the Web accesses destined for port 80 and redirects them, for example, using `iptables` in Linux, to the `Squid` server, which oftentimes is integrated in the same gateway. In this way, the server is virtually transparent to general users, and manual configuration becomes unnecessary. Scenario (1) in Figure 6.26 depicts the concept of transparent proxy integrated within a gateway.

Nonetheless, not all system administrators prefer the integrated proxy/cache server deployment, either due to performance concerns or to the fact that no gateway is present in their network topology. In this situation, a standalone server box can be applied in collaboration with a separate router via policy routing, or with a Layer-4 switch via switch rules based on destination port number, as shown in scenario (2) in Figure 6.26.

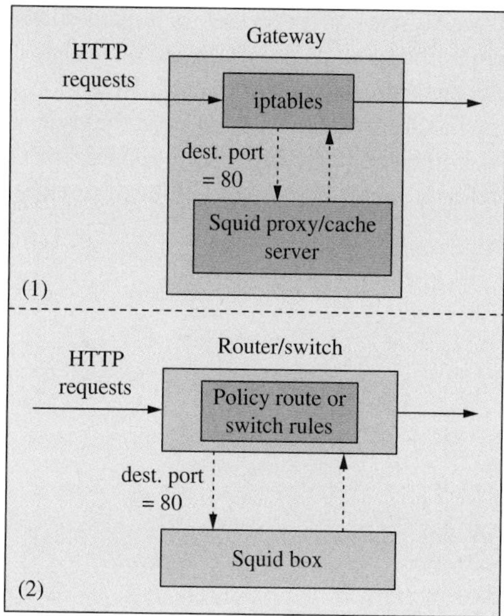

FIGURE 6.26 Two types of configuration for transparent proxy.

Open Source Implementation 6.3: Apache

Overview

Undoubtedly Apache stands out as the state of the art when it comes to open source Web servers. With its full-featured capability such as dynamic pages with database (ex: PHP+Mysql or the built-in `mod_dbd` module), SSL (Secure Socket Layer) support, IPv6 support, XML support, and scalable multithread architecture, Apache continues to dominate the Web server market with a share of 47% as of 2010.

As the demands on various Web-related services increases, the Apache Web server has also become one of the most complex servers in the open source community. However, thanks to its modular design, the internal design of the Apache program still can be outlined here. Generally speaking, Apache is a concurrent *preforked* implementation of the connection-oriented stateless HTTP protocol with binding to port 80. Apache also supports long-term statefulness by embedding *cookies* in HTTP messages.

Block Diagram

The main components of the Apache server program are hierarchical in nature, and can be categorized into three parts: (1) server process initialization, (2) master server, and (3) worker process or worker thread depending on the implementation, as shown in Figure 6.27. We shall describe them in accordance with the processing flow in Figure 6.29. Next, let us go through the concept of "pool," which is significant in the design of this software.

Data Structures

Like the common impression of pool as a group of processes or threads, in Apache memory resources are also manipulated as pools, each of which manages a linked list of resource blocks as basic elements of a pool. However, when allocating blocks on a pool, it is necessary to clean up the pool at the right time in case the program forgets to free the memory. To ensure appropriate deallocation of blocks, a number of built-in hierarchical pools with different

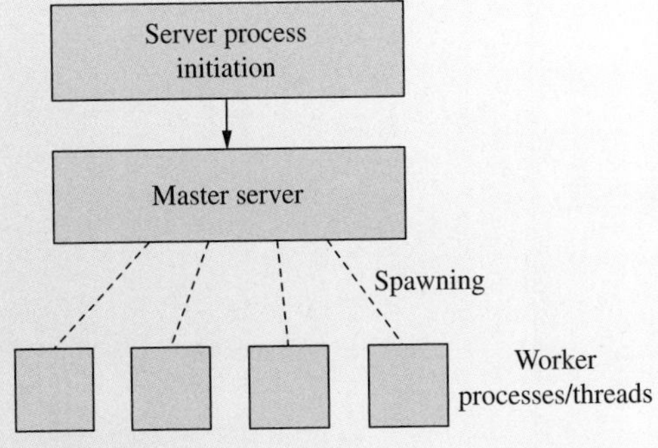

FIGURE 6.27 Internal architecture of Apache.

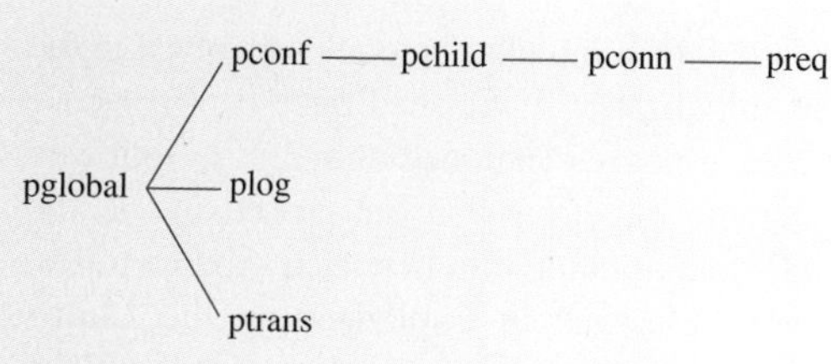

FIGURE 6.28 Hierarchy of pools in Apache.

lifetimes are supported, as shown in Figure 6.28. A pool further comprises a linked list of sub-pools. While the pool `pglobal` exists for the entire runtime of the server, the `pconf`, `plog`, and `ptrans` pools exist only until the server is restarted. Similar lifetime rules apply to `pchild` (child/worker process/thread), `pconn` (connection), and `preq` (request). A pool can be created by `apr_pool_create()` in Figure 6.29, where `parent` is designated as the parent pool of the `newpool`. The root parent, `pglobal`, is automatically created during server startup so that sub-pools can be initiated whenever needed (i.e., when new connections are to be established, when new requests arrive, etc).

Algorithm Implementations

Now let us discuss Apache's processing flow in Figure 6.29. The server startup is done by `init_process()`, which creates a pool of processes for initial use. The

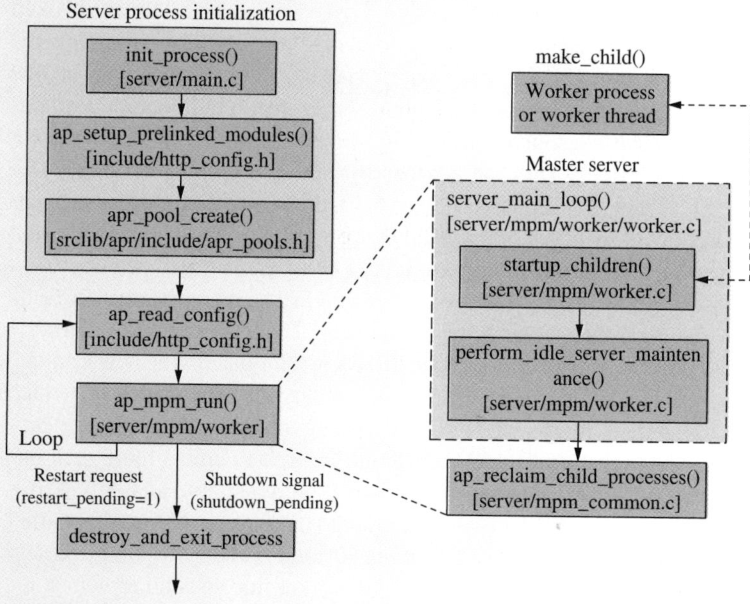

FIGURE 6.29 Inside Apache Web server.

Continued

ap_setup_prelinked_modules() then initializes modules involved in the initial operation. The server process initialization is finished once apr_pool_create() has created various resource pools mentioned above. It is followed by ap_read_config() processing the directives that are passed in via the command line, and recursively reading configuration files in related subdirectories.

The ap_mpm_run(), a major milestone in implementing the Multi-Processing Module (MPM), is invoked to start a process as a master server. Two types of MPMs, *prefork* and *worker,* are supported. The prefork mechanism implements a nonthreaded, preforking Web server, in which a preconfigured number of processes will be forked to responsively serve incoming requests. It is also the best MPM for isolating each request so that a problem with a single request will not affect any other. However, this MPM lacks scalability and is preferably used in old operating systems where a threading library is not well supported. Modern operating systems such as Linux and FreeBSD are well equipped with threading libraries, and thus do not have this issue.

To complement the weakness of the prefork MPM, the worker MPM implements a hybrid multithreaded, multi-process server. Similar to the prefork mechanism, a number of processes are preforked, but multiple threads are further pre-invoked within each process. Using threads can serve a large number of requests with fewer system resources, as compared with a purely process-based server. Yet the worker MPM still retains much of the stability of a process-based server by running multiple processes, each with many threads. Therefore, we shall use the worker MPM for the rest of the explanation, though similar procedures in the server/mpm/prefork/ directory can be expected for the prefork MPM.

Within the ap_mpm_run(), the server_main_loop() is invoked to spawn a preconfigured number of child server processes by repeating the make_child() function in startup_children(). Depending on the chosen multi-processing strategy, each child server may require another initialization phase to access resources needed for proper operation, for example, for connecting to a database. This can be done by calling the child_main() in the make_child(). As shown in Figure 6.30, it initiates the environment settings such as critical sections for the child by apr_run_child_init(), and then spawns a preconfigured number of threads by apr_thread_create(), which subsequently invokes start_threads(). The start_threads() deals with the creation of two types of threads: The create_listener_thread() function creates the listener thread, which listens for new connection requests, and the worker_thread() creates the worker thread, which processes the socket by process_socket() and ap_process_connection(). Note that no listener thread will be created unless more than one worker thread exists. The idea can be explained with a simple analogy: A restaurant needs to be sure the chefs (worker threads) are ready before the waiter/waitress (listener threads) can start accepting customer orders. So it is necessary to check from time to time the availability of worker threads, and replenish the thread pool whenever needed.

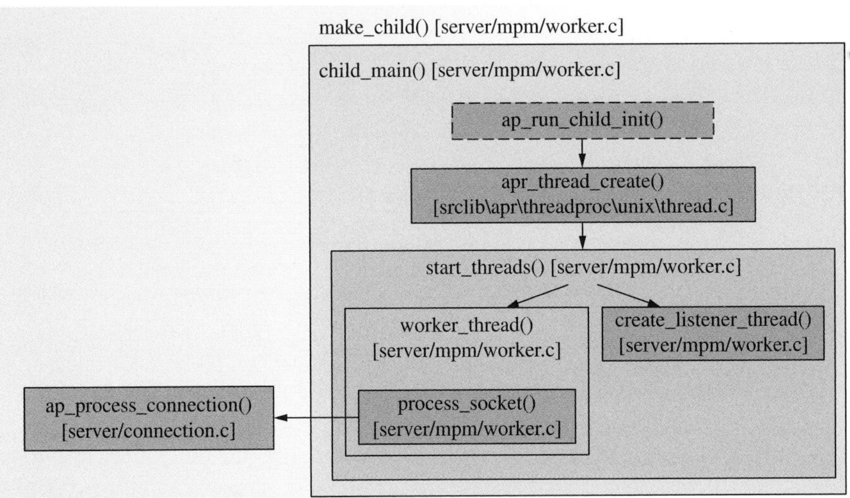

FIGURE 6.30 Inside the `make _ child()` procedure.

While the child servers are busy processing requests, the master server that executes `server_main_loop()` in Figure 6.29 enters the `perform_idle_server_maintenance()` after the spawning, looking for dying (with SERVER_GRACEFUL status, meaning graceful shutdown) and dead (with SERVER_DEAD status) child servers. By monitoring the dying and dead servers, Apache can know whether or not to spawn more servers. Finally, if a shutdown signal is caught by `ap_mpm_run()`, the master server starts to reclaim all child servers with `ap_reclaim_child_processes()`.

Exercises

1. Find which .c file and lines of code implement prefork. When is prefork invoked?
2. Find which .c file and lines of code implement cookie persistence.
3. Find which .c files and lines of code implement HTTP request handling and response preparation.

Performance Matters: Throughput and Latency of a Web Server

Figure 6.31 shows the call graph of HTTP request processing within the Apache Web server. `ap_run_create_connection()` allocates and initializes data structures for an incoming request, `ap_read_request()` parses the request, and then `ap_process_request_internal()` checks the authorization. To reply to a request, `ap_invoke_handler()` invokes the content generator to prepare the response data, `check_pipeline_flush()` completes any

Continued

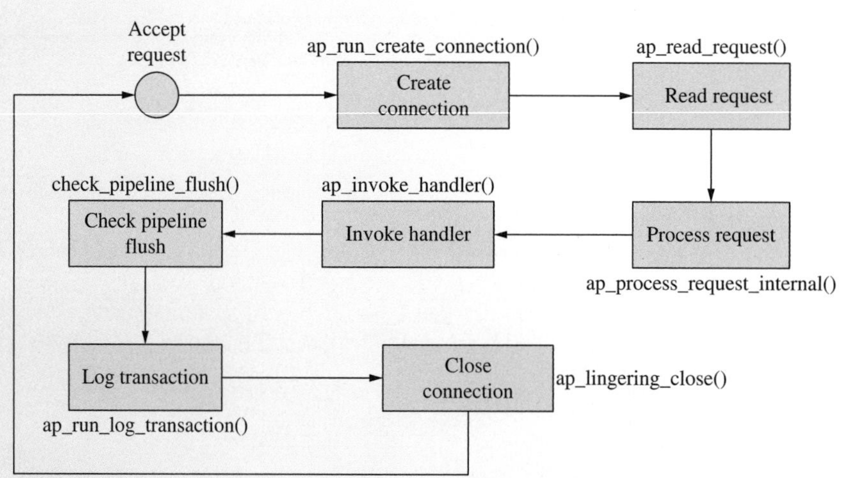

FIGURE 6.31 HTTP request handling in the Apache Web server.

deferred responses, and `ap_run_log_transaction()` logs the data about the connection. Finally, `ap_lingering_close()` closes the connection and cleans up data structures.

Figure 6.32 illustrates the time each function spent on processing HTTP requests. The most noticeable observation is that the time spent on `ap_invoke_handler()` increases with file size. In the experiment, an HTTP response was configured as replying a static, i.e., on-disk, Web page, so the task of content generator invoked by `ap_invoke_handler()` is to read the Web page from disk and then to transmit the file content to the client. It is a time-consuming task if all files need to be read from the disk to the user-space memory before transmission.

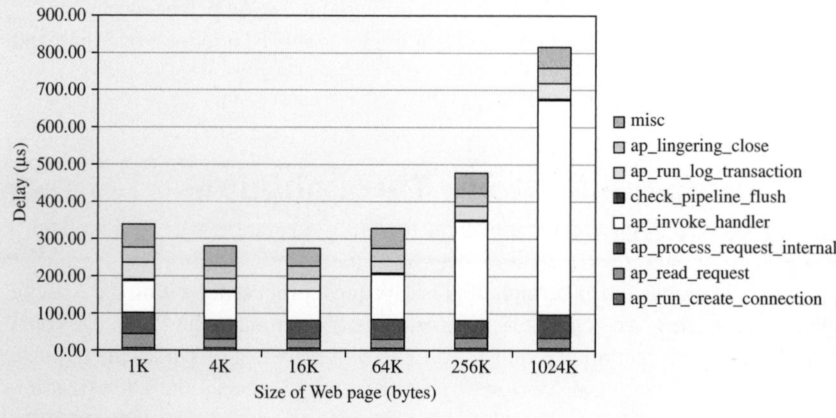

FIGURE 6.32 Latency of major functions in HTTP request handling.

Linux provides the `sendfile()` system call to accelerate the data-copying task, and `ap_invoke_handler()` utilizes the system call to generate HTTP responses. The prototype of `sendfile()` is `ssize_t sendfile(int out_fd, int in_fd, off_t *offset, size_t count)`, by which the Linux kernel copies directly from one file descriptor, e.g., a file on disk, to the other file descriptor, e.g., socket, without frequent context switches between user space and kernel space. This feature is called *zero-copy.* Each time it is called, `sendfile()` copies a file fraction whose size depends on the file system structure, so `sendfile()` has to be called multiple times before completing the file copy. Table 6.19 lists the time for which `sendfile()` is called to send Web pages. When the size of Web page increases, the proportion of `ap_invoke_handler()`'s execution time consumed by `sendfile()` grows. Only 35% of `ap_invoke_handler()`'s executing time is spent on `sendfile()` to send a 1 kB Web page back to a client, while it becomes 87% when the size of the Web page is 1024 kB.

TABLE 6.19 **Ratio of `sendfile()` to `ap_invoke_handler()`**

File size	1 kb	4 kb	16 kb	64 kb	256 kb	1024 kb
# of calling `sendfile()`	1	1	1	2	7	15
Total execution time (μs) of `sendfile()`	37	37	42	78	215	527
Time ratio of `sendfile()` to `ap_invoke_handler()`	35%	38%	40%	53%	77%	87%

6.5 FILE TRANSFER PROTOCOL (FTP)

As one of the earliest Internet applications, the file transfer protocol (FTP) is not as simple as it sounds. In fact, it has a unique *two-connection operation* model that exercises *out-of-band signaling,* by which commands/replies and user data are transferred on separate *control* and *data* connections, respectively. Most other applications run *in-band* signaling, where control and data go through the same connection. Probably the only similar one is P2P, which often sends voluminous UDP segments as queries/responses and establishes TCP connections for real data transfer. This section illustrates this tricky two-connection operation model and how an FTP server changes from *active* to *passive* mode to connect behind a firewall or NAT. FTP protocol messages are also introduced. We pick `wu-ftp` as the example open source implementation.

6.5.1 Introduction

Decades ago, people wrote programs and saved them on tapes or disks. To run the programs on a remote machine, all the tapes and disks had to be shipped to and loaded into that machine, which was often inconvenient and time-consuming. To solve the inefficiency of shipping files on tapes and disks, the File Transfer Protocol (FTP) was designed to allow users to efficiently and reliably transfer files from one host to another over the Internet. Another benefit that comes with FTP is the data replication, which enables a larger scale of data backup. FTP was first proposed in RFC 172 in 1971, later obsoleted by RFC 265, 354, 542, 765, and finally standardized in RFC 959 in 1985. RFC 3659 in 2007 is the latest update on FTP extensions.

Like many other network applications, FTP operates in the client-server model and runs over TCP, and therefore guarantees a point-to-point reliable connection. FTP offers two kinds of accesses: *authenticated* and *anonymous*. The former requires an account/password pair for user authentication, while the latter is usually unrestricted, though some source IP addresses might be banned for administrative concerns. All an anonymous user has to do is log in as "anonymous" or "ftp" and enter the user's e-mail address as a password, which is not strictly checked in many cases.

For example, if you want to download a file via FTP from another university, you would need to log in onto a local computer first. You also need a login name and password to access your account on the remote FTP server you will FTP from, unless you use anonymous FTP. There are five major steps in an FTP session:

1. Connect to or log in onto the computer the target files are to be downloaded to (or uploaded from).
2. Invoke the FTP client program.
3. Connect to the remote FTP server the files are to be downloaded from (or uploaded to).
4. Provide user name and password for login on the remote server.
5. Issue to the FTP server a sequence of commands to view and transfer the target files.

An FTP client application can run in UNIX-like or Windows systems. Basic commands are generally supported on FTP server sites, as described in Table 6.20.

One may even use a Web browser to initiate an FTP session. For example, in the anonymous mode, if you type

```
ftp://ftp.cs.nctu.edu.tw
```

TABLE 6.20 Some FTP User Commands

Command	Description
OPEN	Connect to a remote host
CAT	View a file in a remote host
GET	Retrieve files in a remote host
RENAME	Change the name of a file in a remote host
RM	Delete a file in a remote host
QUIT	Terminate an FTP session

in the URL field of the browser, the browser automatically logs you onto the FTP site as an anonymous user if that site permits anonymous login. In the authenticated mode, the login format in the URL field is as

```
ftp://user1@ftp.cs.nctu.edu.tw
```

which means the user wants to login on ftp.cis.nctu.edu.tw as "user1". An input window will then appear for password input.

6.5.2 The Two-Connection Operation Model: Out-of-Band Signaling

The FTP communication between client and server employs two separate connections, the *control* connection with the server listening on TCP port 21 and the *data* connection with the server listening on TCP port 20. As implied by the words themselves, the control connection deals with the exchange of commands, parameters, replies, and some marks for error recovery, while the data connection is dedicated to the transfer of files. The former lasts for the entire FTP session, while the latter is created and deleted as needed. Unlike most other applications, where control and data messages are mixed and carried through the same connection, that is, in-band signaling, this two-connection mechanism is often called out-of-band signaling. As shown in Figure 6.33, the procedure of an FTP session is detailed below.

After establishing the *control* connection and finishing the authentication process, the client issues an FTP request, `PORT h1, h2, h3, h4, p1, p2`, to the server saying, "Can you connect a *data* connection to me on port number p1p2 at the IP address h1.h2.h3.h4?" and listens on the specified port of that address. Note that h1~h4 and p1, p2 are hexadecimal. The server then replies with an appropriate status code to the client for acknowledgment. Next the client can issue commands for listing, downloading, appending, or uploading files in the file

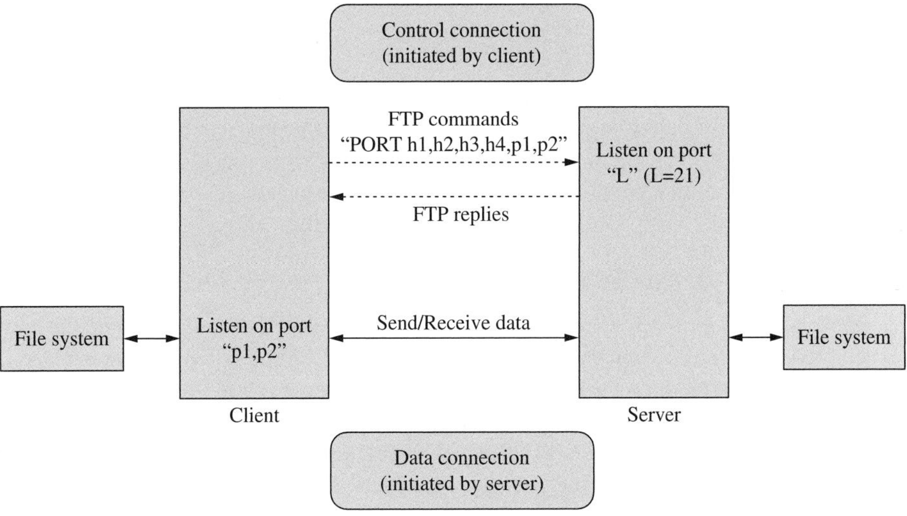

FIGURE 6.33 Basic operation model of FTP.

Historical Evolution: Why Out-of-Band Signaling in FTP?

Since FTP, predated by telnet by just a few days, is the second-oldest application protocol in Internet history, the exact reasons why FTP adopted out-of-band signaling may no longer be recognized now. However, there is a common consensus on it, though a bit historical.

The original design of file transfer service used Data Transfer Protocol (DTP) as the data plane protocol, while the FTP was responsible only for the control connection. After IP was created, the DTP was replaced by TCP. Rather than merging both control and data connections into one TCP connection, FTP continues to use the two-connection mechanism to minimize the impact on existing implementations.

What comes as a surprise is that this out-of-band signaling also improves FTP's performance. It avoids extra efforts to distinguish the control and data segments as would occur in the single-connection scenario. That is, transferring the file over the dedicated data connection avoids the extra overhead of processing headers or control information. Another advantage is that during a prolonged file transfer on a data connection, the control connection is still available for directory lookup or initiating another file transfer over yet another data connection. In addition, the two-connection model also enables the use of a middle control host as described above.

system of the server. The server will initiate a *data* connection for file transfer. Note that since each of these commands involves an independent data connection, a `PORT` command should always be issued before any of them. After all operations are finished, the client sends "`QUIT`" over the control connection to the server to terminate the FTP session.

Sometimes the host issuing FTP commands does not need to be the client or the server; that is, it could be just a broker between clients and servers, arranging data connections between them through FTP commands. This model may be used, for example, in a mutual backup system where file servers listen on ports specified by a central controller, and wait for the order of data transfer.

Active Mode vs. Passive Mode

In the preceding model, the control connection is initiated by the client while the data connection is initiated by the server. This kind of initiation is called *active mode* from the perspective of the *server*. Yet there is another scheme called *passive mode* where both connections are initiated by the client.

As depicted in Figure 6.34, a server in the active mode connects back to the client when receiving an FTP request. However, if the client is behind an NAT or firewall, the data connection from the server will probably be blocked. When detecting this blocking problem, either manually by the user or automatically by the client

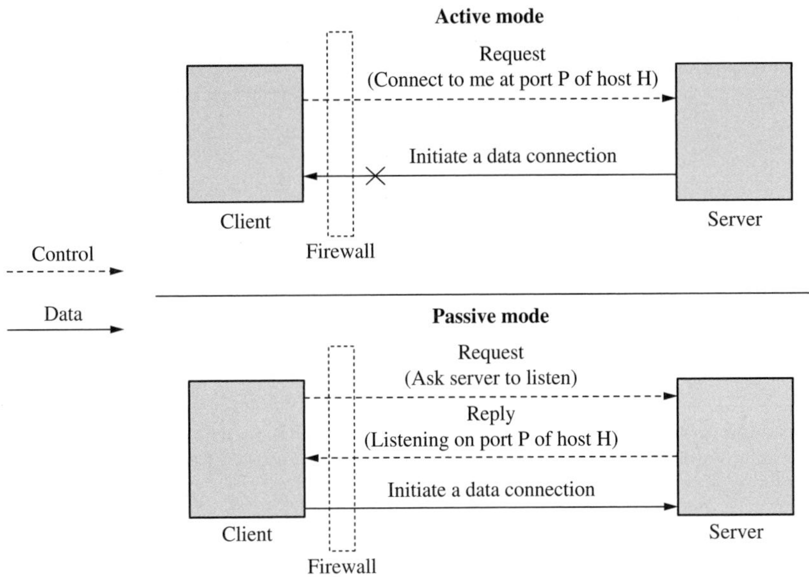

FIGURE 6.34 Active mode vs. passive mode.

application, the client asks the server again for passive FTP by issuing the `PASV` command, which asks the server to *listen* on a specific port for the data connection. If the request is granted by the server, the server acknowledges the client back by issuing `PORT` with the IP address and port number, other than 20, that it currently listens on. Now both sides enter the passive mode. The client then initiates the data connection to the server and starts file transfer.

6.5.3 FTP Protocol Messages

Table 6.21 lists major FTP commands. Note that the commands here are different from the ones in Table 6.20, which are site-supported commands for end users; these are FTP protocol messages defined in the RFC. The server maps a user command to one or more FTP commands, which perform the actual operations. For example, when we type the user command

```
rename path_of_source_file path_of_dest_file,
```

the server maps it to the following two operations:

```
RNFR path_of_source_file    (ReNameFRom)
RNTO path_of_dest_file      (ReNameTO)
```

to complete the renaming of the file.

The FTP server always sends a reply to acknowledge to the client the execution status of the previously issued command. There are five functional groups of reply

TABLE 6.21 Major FTP Commands

Command	Description	Type
USER	Send the user name	Access control
PASS	Send the password	Access control
PORT	Send the IP and port of the client to which the data is retrieved	Transfer parameter
PASV	Tell the server to listen on a data port rather than initiate a data connection	Transfer parameter
RETR	Ask server to transfer a copy of the requested file to the client	File service
STOR	Cause the server to accept and receive the data and store it as a file	File service
RNFR	Specify the path of a source file to rename from	File service
RNTO	Specify the path of a destination file to rename to	File service
ABOR	Tell the server to abort the previous command and the corresponding data transfer	File service

codes, as shown in Table 6.22, with their second digit indicating the syntax error, status of control and data connections, etc., and the third digit representing the fine-grained degradation of the conditions within the scope of the second digit.

Figure 6.35 is an example FTP session. We log in as user "www" and retrieve a file named "test." The client asks the server to connect to it at 140.113.189.29 on two

TABLE 6.22 Five Categories of FTP Replies

Reply	Description	Type
1yz	The requested action is being initiated; expect another reply before proceeding with a new command.	Positive preliminary reply
2yz	The requested action has been successfully completed.	Positive complete reply
3yz	The command has been accepted, but the requested action is being held, waiting for further information from another command.	Positive intermediate reply
4yz	The command is not accepted and the requested action did not take place. The action can be requested again.	Transient negative completion reply
5yz	Similar to 4yz, except that the error condition is permanent, so the action cannot be requested again.	Permanent negative completion reply

```
STATUS:> Connecting to www.cis.nctu.edu.tw (ip = 140.113.166.122)
STATUS:> Socket connected. Waiting for welcome message... 220
         www.cis.nctu.edu.tw FTP server (Version wu-2.6.0(1) Mon Feb 28 10:30:36 EST
         2000) ready.
COMMANDS:>              USER www
           331 Password required for www.
COMMANDS:>              PASS ********
           230 User www logged in.
COMMANDS:>              TYPE I
           200 Type set to I.
COMMANDS:>              REST 100
           350 Restarting at 100. Send STORE or RETRIEVE to initiate transfer.
COMMANDS:>              REST 0
           350 Restarting at 0. Send STORE or RETRIEVE to initiate transfer.
COMMANDS:>              pwd
           257 "/home/www" is current directory.
COMMANDS:>              TYPE A
           200 Type set to A.
COMMANDS:>              PORT 140,113,189,29,10,27 ← tell the server where to connect to
           200 PORT command successful.
COMMANDS:>              LIST                      ← retrieve directory listing
           150 Opening ASCII mode data connection for /bin/ls. ← File status okay;
           about to open data connection
.......list of files....
COMMANDS:>              TYPE I
           200 Type set to I.
COMMANDS:>              PORT 140,113,189,29,10,31
           200 PORT command successful.
COMMANDS:>              RETRtest                  ← retrieve the file "test"
           150 Opening BINARY mode data connection for test (5112 bytes).
```

FIGURE 6.35 An example FTP session.

different ports, 4135 (i.e., 1027 in hexadecimal) and 4145 (i.e., 1031 in hexadecimal), for retrieving the directory listing and the file "test," respectively.

Restarted Transfer With the Checkpoint

So far we have introduced the initialization, commands, and replies of an FTP session. FTP also implements a restart mechanism for recovery from errors such as encountering a broken path and a dead host or process. The main idea lies in the use of the "marker," which consists of the *bit count* of the file being transferred.

During the transmission of a file, the sender inserts a marker at a convenient place within the data stream. Upon receiving a marker, the receiver writes all prior data to the disk, marks the corresponding position of the marker in the local file system, and replies to the user, i.e., the control host, which might or might not co-locate with the sender at the same machine, with the latest marker position of both the sender and the receiver. Whenever a service failure occurs, a user can issue the *restart* command with the preceding marker information to restart the sender at the *checkpoint* of the previous transmission.

Open Source Implementation 6.4: wu-ftpd

Overview

`Wu-ftpd` is one of the most popular FTP daemons. Originally developed at Washington University, it is now maintained by the WU-FTPD Development Group (http://www.wu-ftpd.org/).

In addition to the basic file transfer functions described previously, `wu-ftpd` also provides useful utilities, such as virtual FTP servers and on-the-fly (created when needed) compression. These utilities are *not* defined in the RFC, but indeed facilitate the administrative work and improve the efficiency of file transfer. In summary, `wu-ftpd` is a concurrent implementation of connection-oriented stateful FTP protocol with binding to port 20 and 21.

Algorithm Implementations

There are two major phases in the execution of `wu-ftpd`, service initialization phase and command acceptance/execution phase. As illustrated in Figure 6.36, `wu-ftpd` exercises a typical concurrent-server model that forks child processes to serve clients.

In the service initialization phase, we first execute the "`ftpd`" command, either from the shell (command-line interpreter) or from `(x) inetd`, to start the server with some options to characterize its behavior. For example, the option "`-t`" is to specify the timeout limit of idle connections to avoid the waste of system resources; "`-p`" is to specify the data port number when the owner of the

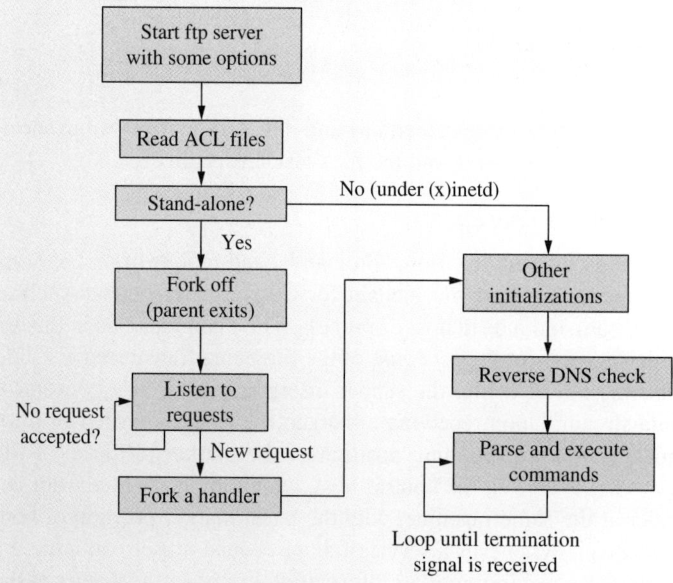

FIGURE 6.36 Execution flow inside `wu-ftpd`.

server process does not have super-user privilege, which means the owner can use only a port number larger than 1024 instead of the default port 20. The server then reads the access control list in the `ftpaccess` file into the memory, which informs the server about the settings of its access capabilities.

After reading the main configurations, the initial server process forks a new process as a standalone server listening for new requests and then exits to let the newly created server process run alone. Upon the acceptance of a request, the server forks a handler process to deal with the subsequent procedures in that FTP session. If the server is not running as a standalone server, it means the server was invoked by `(x)inetd`. In the end of the service initialization phase are other initialization work for reverse DNS to check the client, file conversion check, and virtual host allocation to map the request of different destination site names to the corresponding configurations, and so on.

In the second phase, the main tasks of parsing and execution of FTP commands are done through the use of `Yacc` (Yet Another Compiler-Compiler). The `Yacc` user specifies the structures of FTP input, together with the code segment to be invoked when the structure is recognized. `Yacc` exploits the structural input of FTP commands by turning such specification into subroutines at the compile time to handle the inputs.

Virtual FTP Server

Virtual FTP servers are usually adopted when servicing more than one domain on a single machine. They allow an administrator to configure the system so that a user connecting to ftp.site1.com.tw and another user connecting to ftp.site2.com.tw each gets his own FTP banner and directory even though they are on the same port on the same machine. As shown in Figure 6.37, this can be achieved

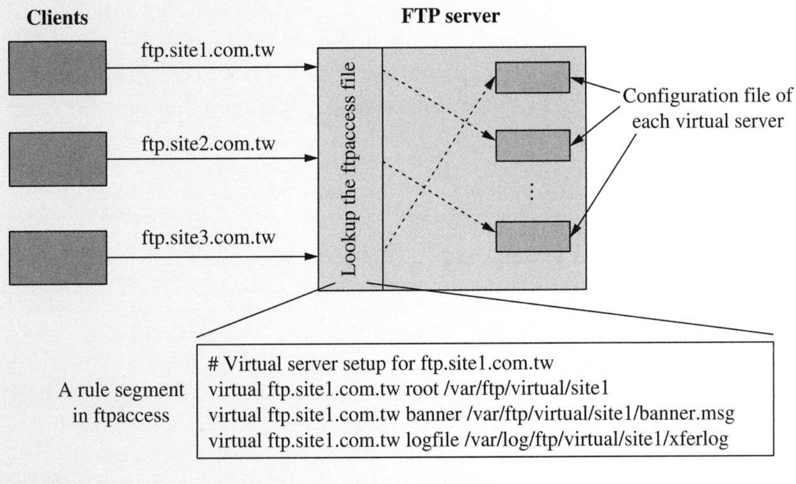

FIGURE 6.37 Concept of the virtual FTP servers.

Continued

```
Userynlin logged in.
Logged in to wwwpc.cis.nctu.edu.tw.
ncftp /home/ynlin > Is
Ltar.gz          Desktop/          ucd-snmp-4.2.1/
ncftp /home/ynlin > get ucd-snmp-4.2.Ltar.gz
ucd-snmp-4.2.ltar.gz:          7393280 bytes 552.83 kB/s
ncftp /home/ynlin >lls -I
drwxr-xr-x 24 gis88559 gis88      3584 Oct 8 12:18 .
drwxr-xr-x 88 root gis88          2048 Sep 10 17:48 ..
-rw-r---- 1 gis88559 gis88     7393280 Oct 8 12:18 ucd-snmp-4.2.ltar.gz
```

FIGURE 6.38 Download of a file with on-the-fly compression.

through the use of a configuration file named "ftpaccess." There are four basic parameters needed to set up a virtual FTP server: the server name (or IP), root directory, welcome message banner, and transfer log. Upon receiving a request, the FTP daemon matches the destination site name in the request with rules specified in ftpaccess. The matched request is accepted and then processed as in an ordinary FTP server.

On-The Fly Compression

Since FTP needs at least two protocol messages (PORT and RETR) to download a file, we can easily imagine how it would affect the network when downloading lots of small files—they will be full of messages for connection setup and teardown. To complement this drawback, wu-ftpd provides another great utility called "on-the-fly compression," i.e., the server compresses files (directories) right before they are sent to users. Figure 6.38 is an example.

As we can see in the example, the client gets a file "ucd-snmp-4.2.1.tar.gz" when there is no such "tar-ball" (the compressed tar archive file) but only a directory "ucd-snmp-4.2.1" in the server. The trick is that the server extracts the postfix of the file name and executes proper actions according to the postfix by rules specified in a configuration file named "ftpconversions." In this case, the invoked action is to execute the "tar -zcf" command with the given file name. Table 6.23 lists some important configuration files of wu-ftpd.

TABLE 6.23 Four Important Configuration Files of wu-ftpd

File Name	Description
ftpaccess	Used to configure the operations of the ftp daemon.
ftpconversions	Specify the postfix of a retrieved file and its corresponding operations.
ftphosts	Used to deny/allow some hosts to log in as certain accounts.
ftpservers	List the virtual servers and the corresponding directories containing their own configuration files.

Exercises

1. How and where are the control and data connections of an FTP session handled concurrently? Are they handled by the same process or by two processes?
2. Find which .c file and lines of code implement active mode and passive mode. When is the passive mode invoked?

6.6 SIMPLE NETWORK MANAGEMENT PROTOCOL (SNMP)

Among all applications presented in this chapter, network management is the only one *not* designed for common users. In fact, it is for network *administrators* to remotely manage the network. We first introduce the concepts and framework of network management. Then we present the standardized Management Information Base (MIB) used to represent the *states* of the managed devices and Simple Network Management Protocol (SNMP) used to access MIB. An open source implementation called `Net-SNMP` is brought in to allow us to trace its operation for a better understanding of the whole architecture.

6.6.1 Introduction

People have longed for monitoring and controlling networks since the birth of the Internet. Many small tools have been used for years to achieve this goal; for example, `ping`, `traceroute`, and `netstat` (refer to Appendix D for details), where the former two are based on ICMP and the latter is through system calls such as `ioctl`. Even though they do meet the basic requirements for a small-scale network environment of a few hosts and network devices, information provided by these tools no longer satisfies network administrators when it comes to a large-scale network. What they want is a more generic and systematic *infrastructure* to facilitate the network management work.

This is where Simple Network Management Protocol (SNMP) comes into play. The idea is to install an *agent* program on all devices to be managed so that a *manager* program can collect and update management information for a device by querying the agent through a standard protocol. The management information is maintained in the *management objects* of a standardized Management Information Base (MIB). These provide several benefits. First, the use of standardized MIB and SNMP enables *interoperability* between multi-vendor managers and devices. Second, the development cost for the *agent* is mainly due to program porting and hence is greatly reduced. Similarly, the management functions could be clearly defined for the network administrators and hence the developers of the *manager* programs, so the architecture is more *scalable,* in terms of the number of managed devices.

MIB and its enhanced version MIB-II were first defined in RFC 1066 and RFC 1158 in 1988 and 1990, respectively. SNMP was first proposed in RFC 1098 in 1989, known as SNMPv1, and received positive responses for the integration of many categories of management objects and the interoperability among multi-vendor products. In 1993, the second version of SNMP, known as SNMPv2, was presented in RFC 1441 to enhance the functionality of the first version. Finally, in 1998, SNMPv3 was published in RFC 2261, addressing some security add-on functionalities discussed in the first version. All three versions of SNMP share the same basic structure and components.

The evolution of network management continued and contributed the highest percentage of RFCs produced by all application-layer protocols. There are many other supplementary protocols and MIBs proposed for network management—for example, Remote network MONitoring (RMON) MIB with extensive traffic measurements as defined in RFC 1271 in 1991, and its enhanced RMON2, defined in RFC 2021 in 1997, and the more recent MIB for IPv6-based OSPFv3, defined in RFC 5643 in 2009. However, they are beyond the scope of this text and will not be discussed.

6.6.2 Architectural Framework

An SNMP environment typically contains five basic components: management station, agent, managed object, managed device, and management protocol. Relationships between these components are depicted in Figure 6.39 and described below.

Management station: Also called *manager,* it is responsible for coordinating all agents under its authority. It checks the status of each agent regularly, and queries or sets the values of managed objects as needed.

Agent: As a middleman running on a managed device between the management station and the managed objects, an agent is responsible for performing the network management functions requested by management stations.

Managed object and MIB: A managed object characterizes one aspect of the managed device. Examples include the system uptime, number of the packets that have been received, and number of active TCP connections in the system. An MIB is a collection of managed objects that form a virtual information store.

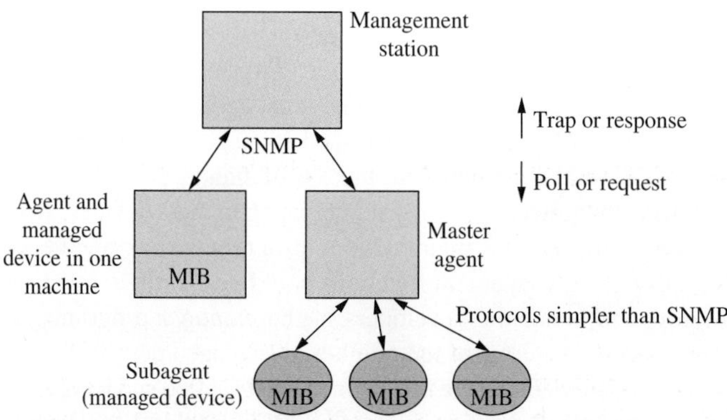

FIGURE 6.39 Architectural framework of SNMP.

Managed device: This could be a router, switch, host, or any device in which an agent and an MIB are installed.

Management protocol: This is used as a common method to convey information between management stations and agents.

Poll-Based and Trap-Based Detection

There are three basic activities in operating an SNMP environment: *get, set* and *trap.* The first two are used by a management station to get/set the values of objects at the agent, while the last is used by an agent to notify the management station of certain events.

Because SNMP is based on UDP, there are no persistent TCP connections, but there are transactions for the management station to know the healthiness of the agents. Two schemes are usually seen in the detection of agent status: *poll-based* and *trap-based.* In poll-based detection, a management station periodically sends inquiry messages to the agent and receives the agent status in response. Though the poll-based detection is intuitive and simple, with this scheme the management station becomes a bottleneck when there are a large number of agents to monitor.

Trap-based detection is proposed to avoid this drawback. Instead of being passively asked, the agents actively *trap* the management station when events happen to the managed objects. The event-driven trap reduces unnecessary messages as we would see in the poll-based detection. For the most part, when rebooting, a management station merely checks the agent to have a basic picture of all its agents.

Proxying

Proxying is considered another useful operating scheme in SNMP in addition to the ordinary relationship between a management station and the agent. For simple and inexpensive devices like modems, hubs, and bridges, it might not be practical to implement the whole TCP/IP suite (including UDP) just to be compatible with SNMP. To accommodate those without SNMP support, a concept of *proxying* is proposed: a mechanism whereby one system "fronts" for another system in responding to protocol requests. The former system is called the master agent and the latter is the subagent. As shown in Figure 6.39, the master agent, not implemented with any MIBs, handles the SNMP requests from the management station on behalf of the subagent. All a master agent does is to translate SNMP requests into some non-SNMP messages understandable to the subagent. Although subagents are supposed to be very simple, some protocols such as Agent eXtensibility (AgentX) and SNMP Multiplexing (SMUX) were developed to enhance the subagent.

6.6.3 Management Information Base (MIB)

An MIB can be viewed as a tree-like virtual information store, though it is not used as a database to store the information. Actually it is merely a specification that lists the managed objects, with each object in an *MIB tree* being uniquely identified by an object identifier (*OID*). For example, in Figure 6.40, which shows the

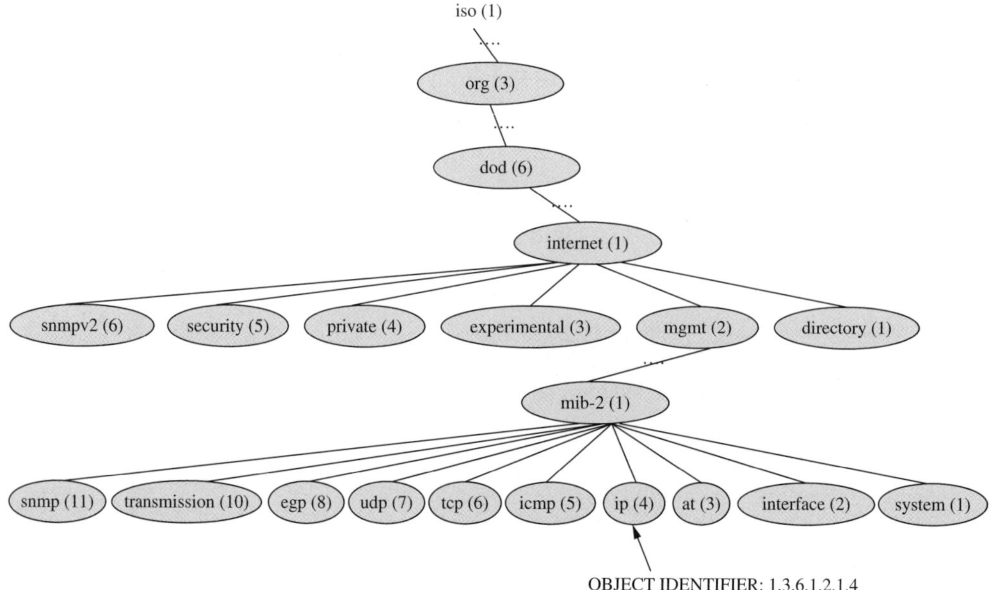

FIGURE 6.40 The Internet-standard MIB: MIB-II.

structure of the Internet-standard MIB—*MIB-II*—the `ip` object group is identified by OID 1.3.6.1.2.1.4. With the associated OID an object has better accessibility. Only *leaf* objects in an MIB tree are accessible with OID values; for example, the `sysUpTime`, which is a leaf node under the `system` group. Therefore, a typical scenario of accessing MIB objects could be like this:

1. The management station sends messages to the agent with OIDs of particular objects it queries for.
2. Upon receiving the requests, the agent first checks if the object really exists, and then verifies the accessibility. If the action fails, the agent responds to the management station with appropriate error messages. Otherwise, it looks for the corresponding value of the *object instance* in files, registers, or counters of the local system.

Object and Object Instance

One may get confused about the meanings of "object" and "object instance." For example, people think they want to get objects for management information, while in fact they are getting *object instances.* An object has two attributes, *type* and *instance.* An object type gives us the syntactic description and properties of the object, whereas the object instance is a particular instance of an object type with a specific value bound to it. Take the object `sysUpTime` as an example. The object type says that the system uptime is measured in terms of `TimeTicks` and read-only for all accesses; the object instance, on the other hand, tells us the time elapsed since the system's last reboot. In addition to simple objects, there are two types of *compound* objects: *scalar* and *tabular.* Scalar objects define a single but *structured* object instance, whereas tabular objects define *multiple* scalar object instances grouped in a table. To differentiate from the expression of the scalar objects under a tabular object, an ordinary scalar object is expressed using the OID of the object with an additional 0 concatenated to its OID.

Nowadays, almost all MIB activities occur in the portion of the ISO branch and are dedicated to the Internet community under object identifier 1.3.6.1. The adoption of MIB in SNMP also provides the extensibility such that one can build one's own MIB under the *experimental* and *private* branches. The former is used to identify objects being designed by IETF working groups, and once those objects become standard, they are moved under the `mgmt(2)` subtree. Right beneath the private branch resides an MIB subtree called *enterprise,* which is reserved for networking device vendors to use. Nevertheless, in order to guarantee the interoperability and avoid collisions of OIDs between devices from different vendors, a registration of MIB objects to *Internet Assigned Numbers Authority (IANA)* is always recommended.

The major contribution of MIB-II is the definition of the object group "*mib-2,*" which describes the management of TCP/IP-based internets more precisely. We summarize each of the object groups of MIB-II in the following list.

1. `system`: Provides general information about the managed system. For example, the name, up time, and location of the system.
2. `interface`: Supplies the configuration information and statistics of each physical interface. For example, type, physical address, and status of the interfaces.
3. `at`: Address translation between network addresses and physical addresses. However, it is deprecated in the RFC and only tobork-level addresses may be associated with each physical address.
4. `ip`: Information about implementation and operation of IP in a local system. For example, routing table and default TTL.
5. `icmp`: Information about the implementation and operation of ICMP. For example, the number of ICMP messages sent and received.
6. `tcp`: Information about the implementation and operation of TCP. For example, the number of maximum and active connections in the system.
7. `udp`: Information about the implementation and operation of UDP. For example, the number of datagrams sent.
8. `egp`: Information about the implementation and operation of EGP (External Gateway Protocol).
9. `transmission`: Related information and statistics about different transmission schemes.
10. `snmp`: Information about the accesses (get, set and trap) and errors of SNMP operations.

Example—TCP Connection Table in MIB-II

The TCP connection table under the `tcp` group in MIB-II is presented in Figure 6.41. It provides us a good example of how Structure of Management Information (SMI), first defined in RFC 1442, is used to implement an MIB.

```
-- the TCP Connection table
      -- The TCP connection table contains information about this
      -- entity's existing TCP connections.

      tcpConnTable OBJECT-TYPE
        SYNTAX  SEQUENCE OF TcpConnEntry
        ACCESS  not-accessible
        STATUS  mandatory
        DESCRIPTION
            "A table containing TCP connection-specific information."
        ::= { tcp 13 }
      tcpConnEntry OBJECT-TYPE
        SYNTAX  TcpConnEntry
        ACCESS  not-accessible
        STATUS  mandatory
        DESCRIPTION
            "Information about a particular current TCP connection.  An
object of this type is transient, in that it ceases to exist when (or soon after)
the connection makes the transition to the CLOSED state."
        INDEX  { tcpConnLocalAddress,
                 tcpConnLocalPort,
                 tcpConnRemAddress,
                 tcpConnRemPort }
        ::= { tcpConnTable 1 }
      TcpConnEntry ::=
        SEQUENCE {
          tcpConnState  INTEGER,
          tcpConnLocalAddress  IpAddress,
          tcpConnLocalPort  INTEGER (0..65535),
          tcpConnRemAddress  IpAddress,
          tcpConnRemPort  INTEGER (0..65535)
        }
       tcpConnState   OBJECT-TYPE
        SYNTAX  INTEGER {
         closed(1), listen(2), synSent(3), synReceived(4)
         established(5), finWait1(6), finWait2(7), closeWait(8),
         lastAck(9), closing(10), timeWait(11), deleteTCB(12) }
        ACCESS  read-write
        STATUS  mandatory
        DESCRIPTION
            "The state of this TCP connection.."
        ::= { tcpConnEntry 1 }
      tcpConnLocalAddress    OBJECT-TYPE
        SYNTAX  IpAddress
        ACCESS  read-only
        STATUS  mandatory
        DESCRIPTION
            "The local IP address for this TCP connection.  In the case of a
connection in the listen state which is willing to accept connections for any IP
interface associated with the node, the value 0.0.0.0 is used."
        ::= { tcpConnEntry 2 }
      tcpConnLocalPort   OBJECT-TYPE
        SYNTAX  INTEGER (0..65535)
        ACCESS  read-only
        STATUS  mandatory
        DESCRIPTION
            "The local port number for this TCP connection."
        ::= { tcpConnEntry 3 }
      tcpConnRemAddress    OBJECT-TYPE
        SYNTAX  IpAddress
        ACCESS  read-only
        STATUS  mandatory
        DESCRIPTION
            "The remote IP address for this TCP connection."
        ::= { tcpConnEntry 4 }
      tcpConnRemPort   OBJECT-TYPE
        SYNTAX  INTEGER (0..65535)
        ACCESS  read-only
        STATUS  mandatory
        DESCRIPTION
            "The remote port number for this TCP connection."
        ::= { tcpConnEntry 5 }
```

FIGURE 6.41 The TCP connection table in the MIB-II specification.

The TCP connection table in Figure 6.41 is a two-dimensional table where each row representing a connection (`TcpConnEntry`) contains the five properties of a TCP connection as its columns: connection state, local/remote IP address, and local/remote port number. Each column in a row is a *scalar element* and has its attribute fields defined in SMI. The table is constructed by using two Abstract Syntax Notation One (ASN.1): "SEQUENCE OF" and "SEQUENCE". The former is to group one or more objects of the same type, `TcpConnEntry` in this case, while the latter is to group scalar elements possibly of different types, `tcpConnState`, `tcpConnLocalAddress`, `tcpConnLocalPort`, `tcpConnRemAddress`, and `tcpConnRemPort` in this case. In addition, it takes four elements in a row, as indicated in the INDEX clause in the left-middle part of Figure 6.41, to identify a connection. Table 6.24 is an example TCP connection table, which gives us a clear view.

From the table we can see that four connections are currently present in the system, and each one can be uniquely identified (indexed) by its local/remote IP addresses and local/remote port numbers (also known as a "socket pair"). Note that each scalar object in the table also has its own OID so that modification on its value is possible. For example, OID of the "established state" in the fourth entry is assigned "x.1.1.*140.113.88.164.23.140.113.88.174.3082*", with its postfix chosen in light of

TABLE 6.24 TCP Connection Table in a Tabular View

tcpConnTable (1.3.6.1.2.1.6.13) tcpConnEntry = (x.1)					
	tcpConnState (x.1.1)	tcpConnLocalAddress (x.1.2)	tcpConnLocalPort (x.1.3)	tcpConnRemAddress (x.1.4)	tcpConnRemPort (x.1.5)
x.1	Listen	0.0.0.0	23	0.0.0.0	0
x.1	Listen	0.0.0.0	161	0.0.0.0	0
x.1	close Wait	127.0.0.1	161	127.0.0.1	1029
x.1	established	140.113.88.164	23	140.113.88.174	3082

INDEX

the connection it belongs to, and its value can be modified accordingly whenever the state is changed.

6.6.4 Basic Operations in SNMP

We mentioned that there are three kinds of activities in SNMP: get, set and trap. Actually, they can be further specified with operations shown in Table 6.25, where each operation is encapsulated in a Protocol Data Unit (PDU) as the basic unit in SNMP operations. Note that the version field in the table means the SNMP version at the time the PDUs were proposed. The PDUs proposed in version 1 are still being widely used with some functional enhancements in version 2.

TABLE 6.25 Basic Operations in SNMP

PDU	Descriptions	Version
GetRequest	Retrieve the value of a leaf object	V1
GetNextRequest	Get the object lexicographically next to the one specified	V1
SetRequest	Set (update) a leaf object with a value	V1
GetResponse	Response for GetRequest (value) or SetRequest (ACK)	V1
Trap	Issued by agent to notify the management station of some significant event asynchronously	V1
GetBulkRequest	Retrieve large blocks of data, such as multiple rows in a table.	V2
InformRequest	Allows one MS to send trap information to another MS and receive a response	V2

PDU: Basic data unit in SNMP operations
MS: Management Station
Variable-binding list: A list of variables and corresponding values in a PDU

Each SNMP message, encapsulated in a UDP datagram, is made up of three major parts: the *common SNMP header, operation header,* and *variable-binding list.* The common SNMP header consists of the SNMP version, the *community* (a *cleartext* password for access control), and the PDU type. The first column of Table 6.25 lists the possible PDU types. The operation header provides information on the operation, including request-id (assigned to match outstanding requests) and error status. The variable-binding list, consisting of a sequence of *variable-value pairs,* is used to assist the information exchange. Normal operations perform a *single* retrieval and set on an object by `GetRequest` and `SetRequest`, respectively. However, it is also possible to access *multiple* objects at a time. The management station puts the OIDs of the objects in the "variable" fields of the variable-binding list, and sends the PDU to an agent which in turn fills up the corresponding value fields and replies the management station as a `GetResponse` PDU.

Traversing an MIB Tree

The `GetNextRequest` is used to get the object *lexicographically* next to the specified OID. Though much about it resembles `GetRequest`, it is helpful in exploring the structure of an MIB tree. To clarify the idea of this PDU, let's use again the TCP connection table of Table 6.24 but show it in a tree structure in Figure 6.42.

There exist hierarchical relationships and thus a lexicographical order in the tree of OIDs that is traversable using DFS (Depth First Search). Consider a management station using only the `GetRequest` PDU. Because the OIDs in an MIB tree are not consecutive, the management station has no way to know the MIB structure if it does

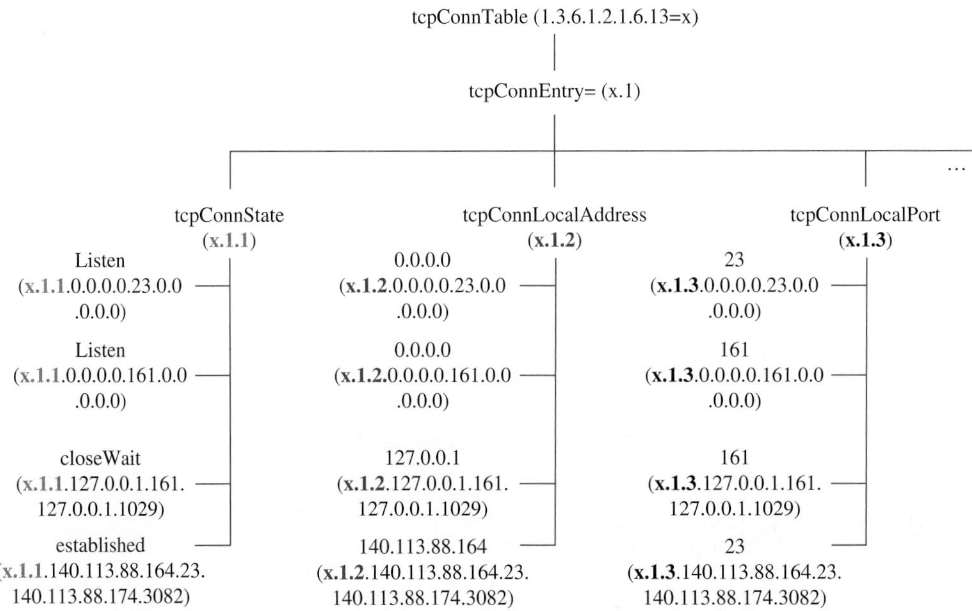

FIGURE 6.42 TCP connection table in a lexicographical view.

not have a complete table of OIDs. However, once equipped with `GetNextRequest`, the management station can traverse the tree completely.

Bulk Transfer of MIB Objects

The `GetBulkRequest` PDU is adopted in SNMPv2 for efficiency. Compared to `GetNextRequest`, `GetBulkRequest` supports a more powerful retrieving scheme, the *range* retrieval for *multiple* objects, rather than several consecutive retrievals. The management station just specifies in the PDU the starting OID and the range to retrieve. The agent receiving the PDU sends back to the management station a `GetResponse` whose variable-binding list is embedded with those requested variable-value pairs. For the example in Figure 6.42, `GetBulkRequest [2,4] (system, interface tcpConnState, tcpConnLocalAddress, tcpConnLocalPort)` will return four variable-value pairs.

Open Source Implementation 6.5: `Net-SNMP`

Overview

Originally developed at Carnegie Mellon University (around 1995) and the University of California at Davis (between 1995 and 2000), this package is now maintained by the `Net-SNMP` development team (since 2000) hosted at http://sourceforge.net/projects/net-snmp. It provides (1) an extensible agent with the MIB compiler by which one could develop his or her own MIB, (2) SNMP libraries for further development, (3) tools to get or set information from an SNMP agent, and (4) tools to generate and handle SNMP traps. It also supports SNMPv1, v2, v3 and other SNMP-related protocols. Different from most other open source implementations in this chapter, `Net-snmp` is an *iterative* implementation supporting both connectionless (on UDP port 161) and connection-oriented (on TCP port 1161) models of the *stateless* SNMP protocol.

Basic Commands and Examples

Table 6.26 shows the descriptions of some commands in Net-SNMP and the corresponding PDUs being used. Basically they are pure implementations of the PDUs of different versions. In Figure 6.43, we use `snmpget`, `snmpset` and `snmpwalk` for demonstration. `snmpwalk` traverses all objects under a subtree with the `GetNextRequest` PDU. We use a preconfigured user "ynlin" with its password "ynlinpasswd" to retrieve the *object instance* system.sysContact.*0*. The security level is set to "`authNoPriv`" (which means authentication only, no data privacy, i.e., data encryption, is needed), and the authentication method is set to MD5.

Algorithm Implementations

Figure 6.44 shows how `Net-SNMP` runs internally. The server is started up by executing the `snmpd` with some options such as logging in `syslog` and

Continued

TABLE 6.26 Some Commands for Query, Set and Trap in `Net-SNMP`

Name	Description and Example	PDU Used
SNMPGET	Retrieve the value of a leaf object using get.	GetRequest
SNMPSET	Set (update) a leaf object with a value.	SetRequest
SNMPBULKGET	Get multiple objects at a time. Possibly under different subtrees.	GetBulkRequest
SNMPWALK	Explore all the objects under a subtree of the MIB.	GetNextRequest
SNMPTRAP	Uses the TRAP request to send information to a network manager. More than one object identifier can be applied as arguments.	Trap
SNMPSTATUS	Used to retrieve several important statistics from a network entity. Errors will also be reported, if any.	
SNMPNETSTAT	Displays the values of various network-related information retrieved from a remote system using the SNMP protocol.	

starting with certain modules. The `init_agent()` is then called to read the configuration files, set up the needed data structures (e.g. object tree), and possibly initialize other subagents such as `AgentX`. Further loading of the

```
$ snmpget -v 3 -u ynlin -l authNoPriv -a MD5 -A ynlinsnmp localhost system.sysContact.0
system.sysContact.0 = ynlin@cis.nctu.edu.tw

$ snmpset -v 3 -u ynlin -l authNoPriv -a MD5 -A ynlinsnmp localhost system.sysContact.0
s gis88559 system.sysContact.0 = gis88559

$ snmpget -v 3 -u ynlin -l authNoPriv -a MD5 -A ynlinsnmp localhost system.sysContact.0
system.sysContact.0 = gis88559

$ /usr/local/bin/snmpbulkwalk -v 3 -u ynlin -l authNoPriv -a MD5 -A ynlinpasswd localhost
system system.sysDescr.0 = Linux ynlin2.cis.nctu.edu.tw 2.4.14 #5 SMP Thursday
November 22 23:6 system.sysObjectID.0 = OID: enterprises.ucdavis.ucdSnmpAgent.linux
system.sysllpTime.0 = Timeticks: (30411450) 3 days, 12:28:34.50 system.sysContact.0 =
gis88559 system.sysName.0 = ynlin2.cis.nctu.edu.tw system.sysLocation.0 = ynlin2
system.sysORLastChange.0 = Timeticks: (0) 0:00:00.00 system.sysORTable.sysOREntry.
sysORID.1 = OID: ifMIB
system.sysORTable.sysOREntry.sysORID.2 = OID: .iso.org.dod.internet.snmpV2.snmpB
system.sysORTable.sysOREntry.sysORID.3 = OID: tcpMIB system.sysORTable.sysOREntry.
sysORID.4 = OID: ip system.sysORTable.sysOREntry.sysORID.5 = OID: udpMIB
```

FIGURE 6.43 Example of snmpget, snmpset, and snmpwalk in SNMPv3.

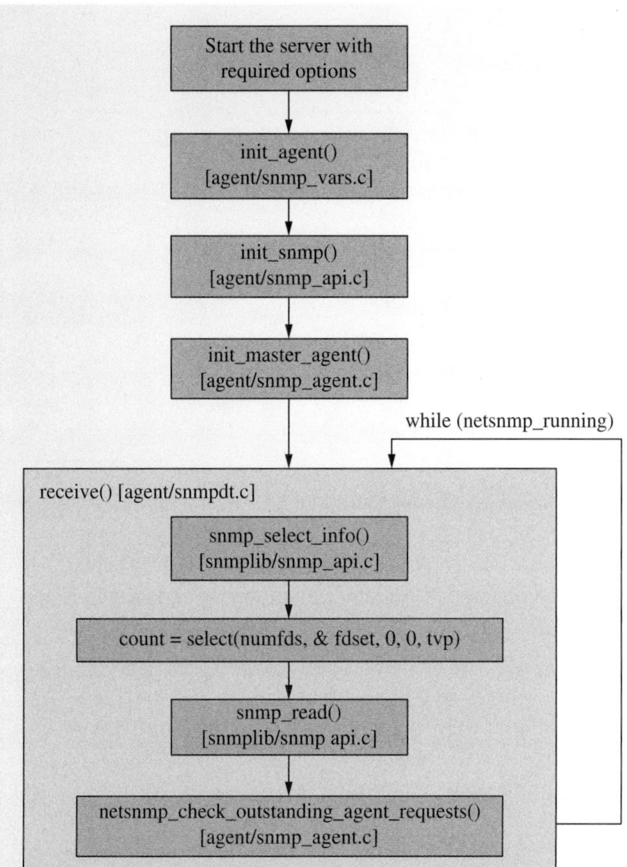

FIGURE 6.44 Processing flow inside Net-SNMP.

configurations is done by `init_snmp()`, which also parses the MIB modules. A master agent is then started. It declares required sessions whose structure is depicted in Figure 6.45, and registers callbacks for the corresponding session. For example, the `handle_master_agentx_packet()` function is registered for the session named `sess` for `AgentX`-specific packet processing. Finally, the program enters a receiving loop dealing with various sessions.

Sessions are served with the `select()` function by I/O multiplexing with other daemons. However, the `snmp_select_info()` function has nothing to do with this technique. Instead, it performs the housekeeping work on (1) the active sessions for the forthcoming `select()` and (2) sessions to be closed, and active sessions are recorded in the `fd_set` and `numfd` structure. The `snmp_read()` function reads requests of selected sessions. It checks whether those in the `fd_set` belong to SNMP packets using the `snmp_parse()` function, and then strips off the unnecessary portion from the request to form

Continued

```
/** snmp version */
long        version;
/** Number of retries before timeout. */
int         retries;
struct snmp_session *subsession;
struct snmp_session *next;
/** UDP port number of peer. (NO LONGER USED - USE peername INSTEAD) */
u_short         remote_port;
/** My Domain name or dotted IP address, 0 for default */
char        *localname;
/** My UDP port number, 0 for default, picked randomly */
u_short         local_port;
/** Function to interpret incoming data */
netsnmp_callback callback;
/** Session id - AgentX only */
long        sessid;
* SNMPv1, SNMPv2c and SNMPv3 fields
```

FIGURE 6.45 Structure of a session (partial).

an SNMP PDU. The resulting PDU is passed to the callback routine registered previously for the session, and demanded information is sent back to the inquirer once the routine returns successfully.

Finally, the `netsnmp_check_outstanding_agent_requests()` checks whether there are any outstanding delegated requests. If positive, it verifies with the access control module (ACM), and processes the requests once the verification is passed.

When a module needs more time to complete an incoming request, it can mark the request as *delegated* and return, allowing the agent to process other requests. For example, the agent marks any request that must be processed by an `AgentX` subagent as delegated, so as to free itself up to process other requests while waiting for the subagent to respond. `Net-SNMP` requires that all pending delegated requests are completed before the `set` request can be processed. If there are still pending requests, the `set` and all other incoming requests are queued until they are finished.

Exercises

1. Find which .c files and lines of code implement the set operation.
2. Find out the exact structure definition of an SNMP session.

6.7 VOICE OVER IP (VoIP)

Among the two real-time applications presented in this chapter, Voice over IP (VoIP) is considered *hard* real-time while streaming is *soft* real-time. The former has a round-trip time (RTT) constraint of around 250 ms as the threshold for users' delay perception, but the latter could accommodate an RTT up to seconds with its delayed playback. Thanks to the over-provisioned optical backbone,

VoIP took off after the early 2000s. Along the evolution, two standards have been developed: H.323 from ITU-T and SIP from IETF. SIP won but hasn't dominated the market because there are several other *proprietary* VoIP protocols. This section introduces and compares H.323 and SIP, and illustrates Asterisk as the open source implementation of SIP.

6.7.1 Introduction

The telephone service and the equipment that makes it possible are taken for granted in most parts of the world. Availability of a telephone, fixed or mobile, and access to low-cost, high-quality worldwide networks are considered essential in a modern society. However, the world of voice communication is no longer dominated by the traditional Public Switched Telephone Network (PSTN). A paradigm shift has occurred since more voice communications are packetized and transported over the Internet. Voice communications using the Internet Protocol, called VoIP or IP Telephony, has become especially attractive given the following virtues:

Inexpensive cost: There could be real savings on long distance telephone calls, especially for companies with international branches and markets. The flat-rate charging model on the Internet means you only pay the *fixed* access fee, regardless of how much and how long you send the data, which is quite different from the charging model of the PSTN.

Simplicity: An integrated voice/data network could simplify network operations and management. Managing one network should be more cost-effective than managing two.

Less bandwidth consumption: The voice channels within a telephone company circuit are chopped into a standard 64 kbps using *pulse code modulation* (PCM). Under an IP network, on the other hand, with a powerful codec, the bandwidth of a single voice channel can be further reduced to 6.3 kbps using G.723.1.

Extensibility: New types of services exploiting the real-time voice communications and data processing could be supported. New features could be extended to, for example, whiteboard, call center, teleworking, and distance learning.

Though VoIP has many advantages, issues such as quality of service (QoS) need to be addressed to reduce the impact of loss, latency, and jitter inherited from the IP network. Thanks to the huge investment in the optical network infrastructure around the year 2000, VoIP applications nowadays run satisfactorily in most areas, which was not the case a decade ago.

This section covers two kinds of VoIP protocols, H.323 and SIP, and their extension architectures. H.323, defined by the International Telecommunications Union (ITU-T), was developed earlier but has been replaced by SIP from IETF. Its simplicity makes SIP a favorable solution over H.323. SIP was defined in RFC 2543 in 1999 and later obsoleted by RFC 3261 in 2002.

Historical Evolution: Proprietary VoIP Services—Skype and MSN

A number of applications, either public domain or proprietary, have been developed in the history of VoIP. However, prevalence has only been gained by some of them, such as Skype (proprietary), MSN (proprietary), and Asterisk (open source). Surprisingly enough, among the three of them only Asterisk follows the SIP protocol, while the other two cultivate their own, i.e., the *encrypted* Skype protocol and the MSNMS (MSN Messenger Service) protocol. Even though MSN had provided the SIP option in its 2005 version, interoperability has been abandoned.

It is believed that they resorted to similar approaches, namely an SIP-like protocol as they have been widely discussed and analyzed. However, due to business concerns, a private community is maintained by using a transport protocol other than RTP/RTCP and different codecs. This trend pretty much resembles the traditional telecom market, in which bare interoperability exists among products of different vendors. The number of users for Skype is 443 million (42.2 million active users per day) as of early 2010, while that of MSN is not disclosed. Asterisk is supposed to attain many fewer users than the other two due to complexity of installation and operation. It is adopted more by enterprises than by end users.

6.7.2 H.323

The H.323 protocol suite was the dominant VoIP protocol adopted by many commercial products. This recommendation, first released in 1996, originally targeted multimedia conferencing over LANs but was later extended to cover VoIP. Further enhancements include the ability for end points to configure QoS through ReSerVation Protocol (RSVP), URL-style addresses, call setup, bandwidth management, and security features.

Elements in an H.323 Network

An H.323 environment, called a *zone,* typically comprises four kinds of elements: one or more terminals, gateways, multipoint control units (MCU), and an administrative gatekeeper, as defined below.

1. *Terminal:* An H.323 terminal, usually a client-side software, is used for initializing two-way communication with another H.323 terminal, MCU, or gateway.
2. *Gateway:* This acts as a middleman between a VoIP zone and another type of network, usually a PSTN network, providing the translation services for the two-way communication.
3. *Multipoint control unit:* An MCU is an H.323 end point that manipulates three or more terminals or gateways participating in a multipoint conference. It can be either standalone or integrated into a terminal, a gateway, or a gatekeeper.
4. *Gatekeeper:* This provides various services for other entities in the network such as address translation, admissions control, and bandwidth control. Supplementary

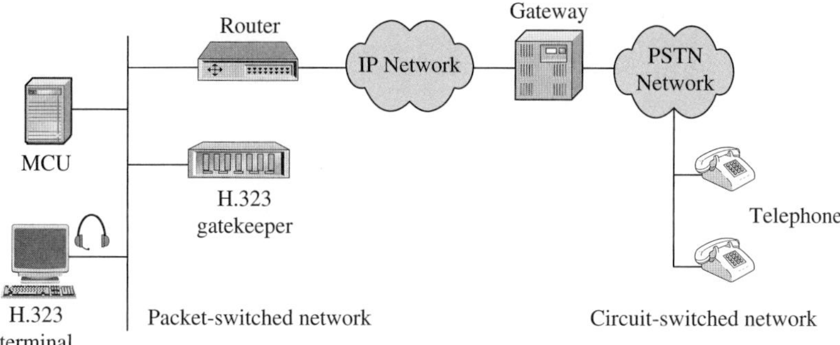

FIGURE 6.46 An H.323 environment.

services like location service, i.e., locating a gateway for a registered terminal, and call management may also be included. However, it is optional because two terminals could still contact each other without additional service support.

Figure 6.46 shows the relationships between the four elements in an H.323 zone. A normal VoIP transaction can be described as follows: Every entity in the H.323 network has a unique network address. Whenever a terminal wants to connect to another for a voice conversation, it first issues a request to the gatekeeper, if required, for call admission. If admitted, the caller sends a connection request specifying destination address and port, like ras://host@domain:port, to the remote terminal. After some capability negotiations, a communication channel is built for the two terminals. MCU and gateway would be involved only in a three-way call and internetwork call, respectively.

Protocol Stack of H.323

Figure 6.47 shows the H.323 protocol family, which can be divided into two planes: control plane and data plane. The control plane coordinates the setup and teardown process of a VoIP session, while the data plane deals with the encoding and transmission of the voice or multimedia data. We describe the function of each protocol in the paragraphs that follow.

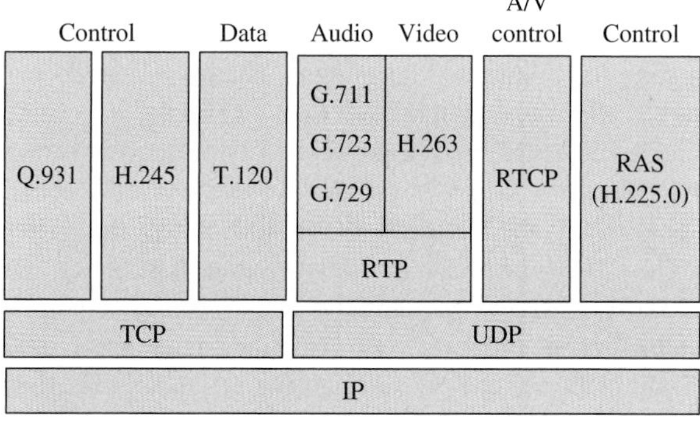

FIGURE 6.47 Protocol stack of H.323.

Registration Admission and Status (RAS) is a signaling method between a gatekeeper and the end points that it controls. Defined in H.225.0, it supports the registration/deregistration, admission, bandwidth change, and disengagement of a call for a terminal. Q.931 is a signaling method for call setup and teardown between two terminals. Since it is a variation of the Q.931 protocol defined for PSTN, the design for internetworking H.323 and PSTN is also simplified. H.245 is used for capability negotiation, such as the types of audio (G.711, G.723, G.729) or video (H.263) codec, between two terminals, and determines the master-slave relationships of terminals. The master-slave distinction is necessary since there needs to be an arbiter (the master) to describe logical channel characteristics and determine the multicast group addresses for all the RTP/RTCP sessions. A number of logical channels can be built by H.245 after those initializations are completed. T.120 comprises a set of data protocols for multimedia conferencing, for example, application sharing, whiteboard, and file transfer during a VoIP session.

As presented in Section 5.5, Real-time Transport Protocol (RTP) is a simple protocol designed to transport and synchronize real-time traffic by exploiting the sequence numbers not presented in existing transport protocols like UDP. Real-Time Control Protocol (RTCP), defined also by IETF as a companion of RTP, is based on the periodic transmission of control packets to all participants in the session. It is mainly responsible for providing feedback for all participants about the quality of the data transmission, which helps suggest proper codec adoption. The underlying transport protocol must provide multiplexing of the RTP and RTCP packets, by using, for example, separate port numbers with UDP. RTP and RTCP were covered comprehensively in Section 5.5. In addition to their use in H.323 and SIP for VoIP, we see them again in Section 6.8 in connection with streaming.

Setup Procedure of an H.323 Call

There are two cases of the setup procedure for an H.323 call: one with a gatekeeper and one without. Typically a quality, fully controllable call involves an administrative gatekeeper in the local zone cooperating with a remote gatekeeper. This model is known as "gatekeeper-routed call signaling."

Figure 6.48 shows the general setup procedure of a gatekeeper-routed H.323 call. In the presence of a gatekeeper, all control messages, including call requests, are sent or routed to it. A call request is handled by RAS implemented in a gatekeeper for registration admission and other services such as address translation and bandwidth allocation required by VoIP service providers for billing and accounting. The local gatekeeper then issues a setup message to the callee, who then asks its own gatekeeper if it wants to handle this session. If permitted, the callee sends a positive reply to the originating gatekeeper and all future *control* messages will be routed through these two gatekeepers.

After a call request is granted by the gatekeepers of both sides, the caller proceeds with Q.931 setup. The Q.931 protocol is used to essentially "ring the phone" and return the dynamically allocated port for the H.245 control channel. After the H.245 channel establishment process with capability negotiation and master-slave determination, logic channels are opened and the two terminals start conversation based on RTP and monitored by RTCP. The closing of channels and teardown of calls are done in a similar manner.

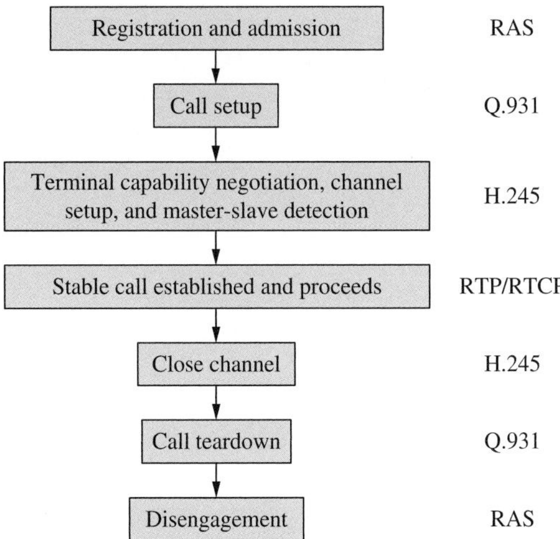

FIGURE 6.48 Setup procedure of an H.323 call.

It is not hard to see that the overhead of message exchanges in H.323 is huge, especially when the gatekeeper-routed model is used. To overcome this drawback, a procedure named *fast connect* is introduced. In the fast connect procedure, H.245 information is carried within the Q.931 messages, and there is no separate H.245 control channel. Therefore bringing a call to a conclusion is also faster. The call is released simply by sending the Q.931 Release Complete message that also has the effect of closing all of the logical channels associated with the call as H.245 does.

6.7.3 Session Initialization Protocol (SIP)

The Session Initialization Protocol (SIP) is an alternative signaling protocol for VoIP. Proposed by IETF, it was targeted to replace H.323 from ITU-T for its simplicity and compatibility with existing protocols in the IP networks, where most of the protocols are also defined by IETF, anyway. With session description and multicast capability provided by other supplementary protocols, it is easy to handle the setup, modification, and teardown of multimedia sessions. Due to the real-time nature, it also relies on the RTP as its transport protocol.

Like HTTP, which is a text-based protocol, SIP borrows its message types and header fields, and the client-server scheme as well. However, unlike HTTP which is over TCP, SIP may use UDP or TCP. Multiple SIP transactions can be carried in a single TCP connection or a UDP flow. In addition, user mobility is satisfied by proxying and redirecting, which provides the current location of a user.

Elements in a SIP Network

Since SIP is client-server based, there must be at least a caller, referred to as User Agent Client (UAC) and a callee, referred to as User Agent Server (UAS), plus some assistant servers, as shown in Figure 6.49 and described below.

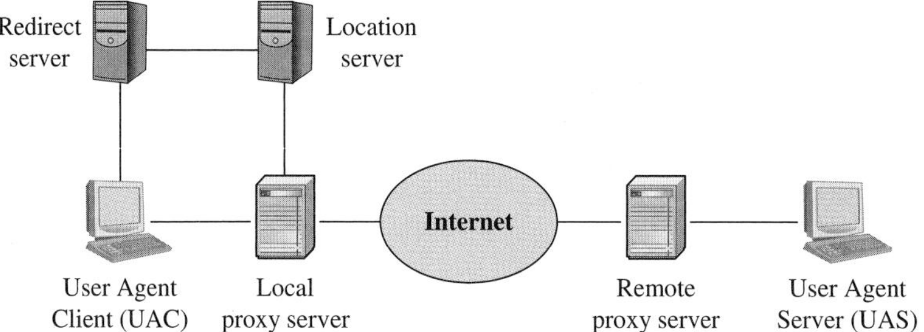

FIGURE 6.49 A SIP environment.

1. *Proxy* servers: A SIP proxy server, like the one in HTTP, acts on behalf of a client, and forwards requests to the other servers, possibly after translating the requests. It could be used to store information for billing and accounting purposes.
2. *Redirect* server: The redirect server responds to a client's requests by *informing* it of the requested server's address. It does not initiate a SIP request as the proxy server does, nor does it accept calls like a UAS.
3. *Location* server: The location server is used to handle requests from the proxy server or the redirect server for the callee's possible location. Typically it is an external server that uses non-SIP protocol or routing policies to locate the user. A user may *register* its current location to the server. Co-location with other SIP servers is possible.

A UAC issues a calling request, also known as an `INVITE` request, either directly to the UAS or through the proxy. In the former case, if the UAC only knows the URL of the UAS but has no idea about the location of the UAS, the `invite` request is sent to the redirect server, which asks the location server for location information for the UAS, assuming the UAS has registered in the location server, and then replies to the UAC. If a proxy is used, the UAC simply sends the request to the proxy without worrying about the location of the UAS. The proxy will contact the location server. Oftentimes a proxy server is implemented with the redirect capability. A UAC just specifies what service, redirection or proxy, it wants when contacting that proxy server.

Protocol Stack of SIP

Several protocols, as shown in Figure 6.50, are required to build up the basis of SIP operations. The real-time transport by RTP, monitored by RTCP, is the same as H.323. We detail SIP and its supplementary protocols, Session Announcement Protocol (SAP) and Session Description Protocol (SDP).

SIP clients are identified by a SIP URL which follows the "user@host" format. Note that this type of addressing looks similar to an e-mail address. The user part may be the name of the user or a telephone number. The host part may be a domain name, a host name, or a numeric network address. For example,

```
callee@cs.nctu.edu.tw and
+56667@nctu.edu.tw.
```

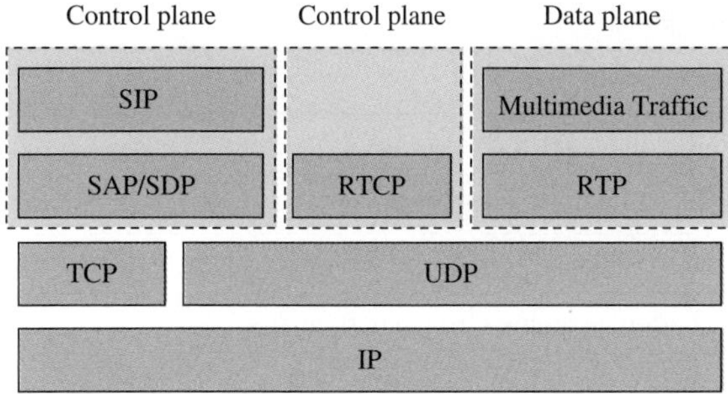

FIGURE 6.50 Protocol stack of SIP.

Setup Procedure of a SIP Call

Once the callee's address is known, a caller may issue a series of commands or operators to initiate a call. Table 6.27 lists the operators or commands in SIP. The first four operators are used in call setup and teardown. A general scenario would be like this: A caller issues `INVITE`, which typically contains a session description written in SDP, to the callee specified in a URL for a new VoIP session, and waits for the response. If the destination IP address is known, the request is sent directly to the callee. Otherwise it is sent to the local proxy server with a built-in location server, in either *redirection* mode or *proxy* mode. For the latter case, the proxy forwards the `INVITE` message according to address information from the location server, possibly through other proxies, to the destination.

Now the callee's telephone is rung. If the callee agrees with the session requirements, checked by the local machine, and wants to participate the session, i.e., pick up the phone, it replies to the caller with an appropriate reply code such as `200 OK`, as shown in Table 6.28. The caller then acknowledges the callee's response by sending an `ACK` message. The handshake is thus completed and a conversation starts. However, chances are that the callee is so busy that the `INVITE` request is not handled for a long period. In this event, the caller may give up and send a `CANCEL` message for this invitation.

TABLE 6.27 Some SIP Commands

Operators	Description
INVITE	Invite a user to a call
ACK	Confirmation for the final response
BYE	Terminate a call between end points
CANCEL	Terminate the search for a user or request for a call
OPTIONS	Features supported for a call
REGISTER	Register current location of the client with location server
INFO	Use for mid-session signaling

TABLE 6.28 SIP Reply Codes

Reply Code	Description
1xx (Informational)	Trying, ringing and queued
2xx (Successful)	The request was successful
3 xx (Redirection)	Give information about the receiver's new location
4xx (Request Failures)	Failure responses from a particular server
5xx (Server Failures)	Failure responses given when a server itself has erred
6xx (Global Failures)	Busy, decline, requests not acceptable

When the conversation is to be closed, one of the participants hangs up and causes a `BYE` message to be sent. The receiving host then responds with `200 OK` to confirm the receipt of the message, and at the same time the call is terminated.

While SIP acts as a command generator in a session, SDP, which is also a text-based protocol, is used to *describe* the characteristics of the session to session participants. A session consists of a number of *media streams.* Therefore, the description of a session involves the specification of a number of parameters related to *each* of the media streams,

Historical Evolution: H.323 vs. SIP

Though the H.323 protocol has been defined since 1996, it has failed to capture the market in the way it was supposed to. Analysts have suggested various reasons for the failure of H.323, including the complex signaling, scalability issues, and security issues in H.323. This is why SIP was developed—to have a lightweight and easy-to-implement alternative. Among other advantages, SIP is a *proposed standard,* defined in RFC 2543 and obsoleted by RFC 3261, that has approval and backing from the IETF. Nevertheless, H.323 still has its advantageous features. Following are some other differences between these two protocols.

1. Message encoding: H.323 encodes messages in the binary format, rather than the ASCII text format, so that it is more compact for transmission. However, it is easier for developers to debug and decode with ASCII strings. Methods for ASCII compression are also provided in SIP.
2. Channel types: H.323 can exchange and negotiate on channel types such as video, audio, and data channels. An SIP UAC can only propose a set of channel types within which other UASs are limited. If not supported, the UAS responds to the INVITE message with error codes such as 488 (not acceptable here) and 606 (not acceptable), or warning codes such as 304 (media type not available).
3. Data conferencing: H.323 supports video, audio, and data conferencing (with T.120). It also has defined procedures to control the conference, while SIP supports only video and audio conferencing and is not capable of controlling the conference.

such as transport protocol and media type (audio, video or application), as well as the session itself, such as protocol version, origin, session name, and session start/stop time.

Although SDP describes the characteristics of a session, it does *not* provide a means for session advertisement at the beginning of a session setup. For this, SAP is used for *advertising* multimedia conferences and other multicast sessions, as well as sending the relevant session setup information, to the participants during a SIP session. A SAP announcer *periodically* sends an announcement packet to a well-known multicast address and port (9875) so that receivers, i.e., potential session participants, can use the session description to start the tools required to participate in the session. Note that the payload of the packet containing the description of the multicast session must be written in the SDP format for interoperability among all participants, since there is *no* capability negotiation in a SAP announcement.

Open Source Implementation 6.6: Asterisk

Overview

Rather than looking at simple point-to-point VoIP software, we examine an integrated PBX (Private Branch eXchange) system, Asterisk, which bridges between softphones or between softphones and traditional phones in PSTN via a PSTN gateway. As Figure 6.51 shows, an Asterisk server acts as a communicator between PSTN and a VoIP network. A VoIP network may comprise a PC-based phone with VoIP software installed or a SIP-capable phone. A traditional phone can even be applied when coupled with an Analog Telephony Adaptor (ATA adaptor), which translates analog signals into a VoIP data stream. Technically speaking, Asterisk is a *concurrent* implementation of the *connection-oriented stateful* SIP protocol and the *connectionless stateless* RTCP/RTP protocols. The port it binds is *not* specific.

Block Diagram

Asterisk provides a framework to build a *customized* VoIP system. As shown in Figure 6.52, the inherent flexibility comes from the addition and removal of

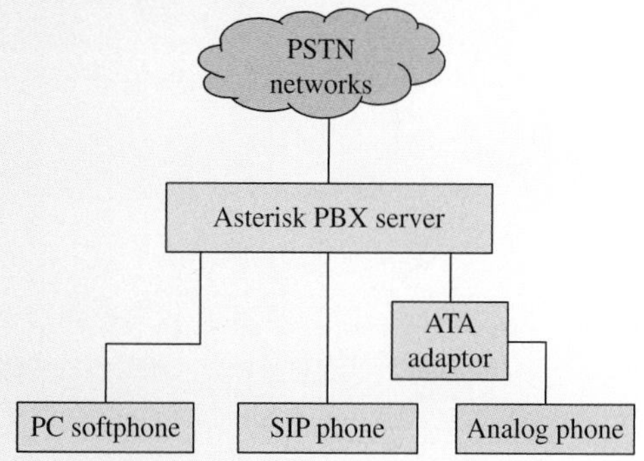

FIGURE 6.51 An Asterisk-based VoIP environment.

Continued

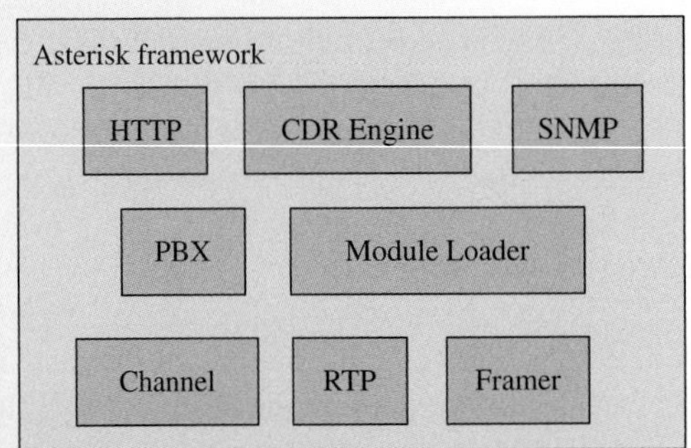

FIGURE 6.52 Framework of Asterisk.

modules such as channel, RTP, and framer used to establish the basic transport service. The core functionality of Asterisk is to serve as a PBX that *exchanges* calls locally in, say, an office or a building. Yet additional utilities such as HTTP server, SNMP agent, and Call Detail Record (CDR) engine for ease of high-level management can also be equipped.

Data Structures

A PBX switches calls to their corresponding destinations. However, at the destination a number of *extension numbers* may be present, and thus another level of switching is required locally. To implement this scheme, within an Asterisk PBX, two concepts named *context* and *extension* are introduced, in which the latter enlarges the *callee group* while the former further extends the number of groups supported. As shown in Figure 6.53, by incorporating the contexts *multiple* companies or organizations can each have their own extension space while sharing just one single PBX.

It is further designed so that each extension can have multiple *steps*—called *priorities* here—in order to organize a *dial plan* that allows users to pre-setup their

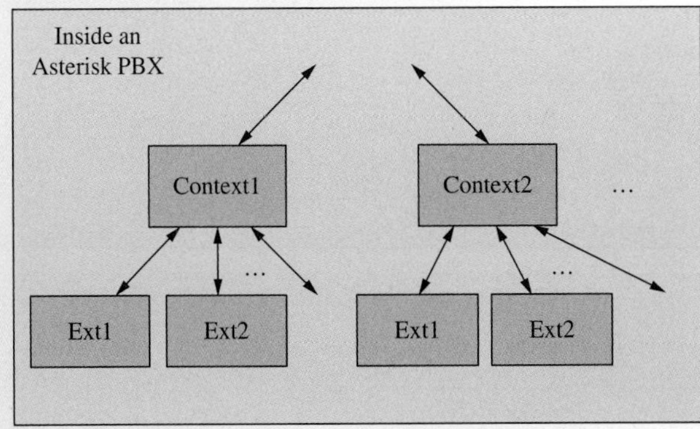

FIGURE 6.53 Contexts for multiple groups and their extensions.

own calls for automation purposes. A priority is associated with an application that performs a specific action. For example, a call could be composed of (1) a call action to connect to the callee by an application *"Call"* at priority 1, (2) an answer action that involves the playback of a prerecorded sound file by an application *"Answer"* at priority 2, and finally (3) a hand-up action to close a channel by an application *"HangUp"* at priority 3.

Algorithm Implementations

The internal execution of Asterisk can be divided into four steps: (1) initialization of management interface, (2) call origination with required parameters such as priority and application, (3) channel setup for data transportation, and (4) forking of a serving thread that establishes the `pbx` structure and carries out the call.

Initialization of Management Interface

The detailed processing flow is shown in Figure 6.54 and elaborated as follows: At the very beginning `init_manager()` is called to load configurations

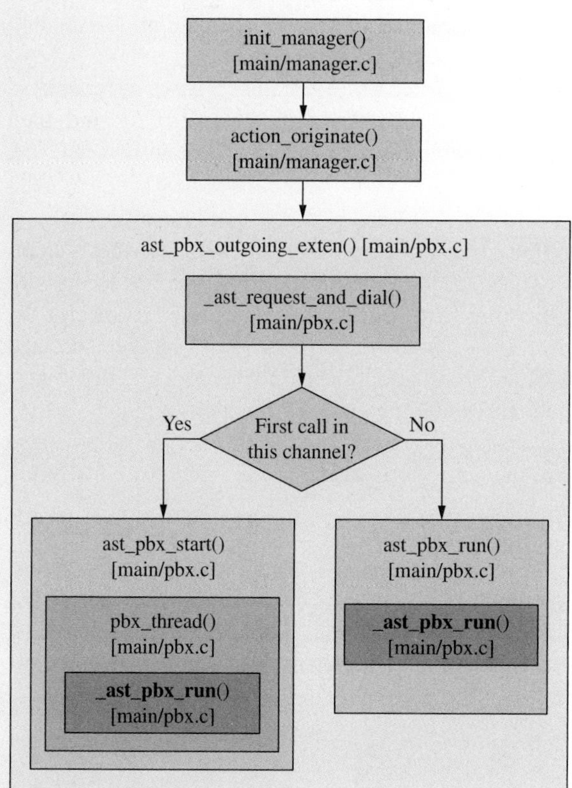

FIGURE 6.54 Call flow within the Asterisk.

Continued

and register important callback functions, namely the "actions." Example actions, in addition to those mentioned above, include (1) `Ping` for testing both endpoints and keeping the connection alive, (2) `Originate` for initiating a call, and (3) `Status` for listing channel status. After the initialization is completed, it starts to listen to connection requests. Note that a "manager" session in Asterisk typically means an HTTP session with a management interface for a user to perform demanded actions. Therefore, multiple manager sessions are possible by creating the corresponding threads on a *nonblocking* socket, and an *event queue* is employed for actions triggered in those sessions.

Call Origination

When the user of a manager session places a call, the `action_originate()` is called with a message containing various parameters describing the call such as caller ID, action ID, channel name, extension/context/priority, account of the user, and application. The originating action is actually placed into a *caller queue,* rather than executed immediately, in case of simultaneous call events with insufficient resources. The `ast_pbx_outgoing_exten()`, which contains a series of important procedures carrying out the calling, is executed after verifying the authentication status of the user account.

The `ast_pbx_outgoing_exten()` calls `_ast_request_and_dial()`, which subsequently calls the `ast_request()` and then `chan->tech->requester()`, which asks for a channel for transport of voice.

Channel Setup

The `chan` is an instance of the `ast_channel` structure that describes a channel. Among the attributes of the structure the most critical one has to do with `tech`, an instance of the structure `ast_channel_tech` used to specify the transport technology. Since `chan->tech->requester()` has been defined as a function pointer, here we intend to adopt the case where `sip_request_call()` is registered as the corresponding callback function to request a SIP-based channel. Eventually a channel is granted and the channel identifier is also returned all the way back to the `ast_pbx_outgoing_exten()` for future use of other upper-layer procedures.

The `sip_request_call()`, which resides in `channels/chan_sip.c`, checks whether the specified codec is supported and, if positive, invokes `sip_alloc()` to build a SIP private data record, `sip_pvt`. The `sip_pvt` structure consists of dozens of elements describing the private dialog of the SIP session during session registration and call placement—for example, CallerID, IP address, capability, SDP session ID, and RTP socket descriptor.

Thread Forking

The `ast_pbx_outgoing_exten()` continues the dialing by invoking either `ast_pbx_start()` or `ast_pbx_run()`, depending on whether this is the

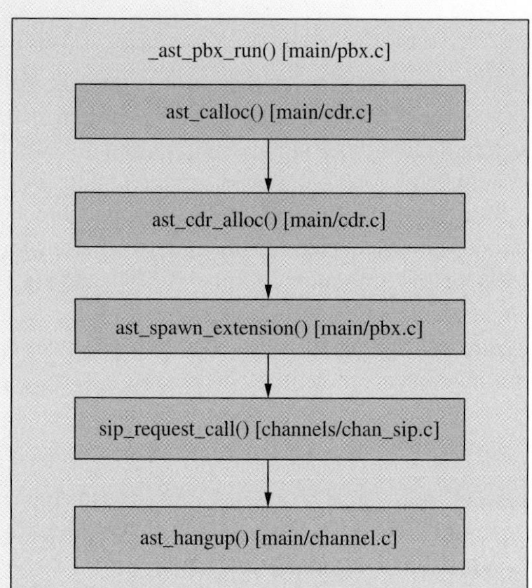

FIGURE 6.55 Inside the `__ast_pbx_run()` function.

first call to the *same* destination. If it is indeed the first call, a serving thread is created to execute `pbx_thread()`, which subsequently invokes the `_ast_pbx_run()`, and to increment the call count.

In Figure 6.55, `_ast_pbx_run()`, as the main serving procedure of the call, establishes the private `pbx` structure for the channel using `ast_calloc()` and the CDR structure for recording the calling activities using `ast_cdr_alloc()`. It then loops on all priorities of this context/extension executing the designated applications with `ast_spawn_extension()` until a hang-up event is triggered and handled by `ast_handup()`, i.e., the previously registered hand-up action. Within the `ast_spawn_extension()`, the preregistered callback function, `sip_request_call()` as mentioned previously, is called to build a `PVT` structure describing the SIP session. Afterwards an RTP/RTCP transport is also initiated and assigned to the `PVT` structure by executing `ast_rtp_new_with_bindaddr()` (not shown in this figure) during `sip_request_call()`.

Exercises

1. Find the .c file and lines where `sip_request_call()` is registered as a callback function.
2. Describe the `sip_pvt` structure and explain important variables in that structure.
3. Find the .c file and lines where the RTP/RTCP transport is establish for the SIP session.

6.8 STREAMING

As a *soft* real-time application, streaming achieved its popularity sooner than VoIP in the late 1990s before the huge investment in the optical backbone around 2000. It could *absorb* and thus *accommodate* much higher latency and jitter than VoIP. In this section, we first introduce the architecture and components of streaming clients and servers. Then we describe the common *compression/decompression* techniques that significantly reduce the video/audio bit rate, which facilitates network transport. Next, two streaming mechanisms, Real-Time Streaming Protocol (RTSP) and HTTP streaming, are introduced and compared. Advanced issues, including *QoS control* and *synchronization* during streaming, are addressed. Last, the Darwin Streaming Server (DSS) is presented as the example open source implementation.

6.8.1 Introduction

Traditional multimedia entertainment was mostly carried out by storing or downloading a media file to a client PC before it was played. However, this download-and-play manner cannot support *live* programs, and requires, for *recorded* programs, long latency in starting the playback and large storage on the client side. Streaming, which was designed to overcome these drawbacks, is used to distribute live or recorded media streams to audiences *on-the-fly.* Unlike the download-and-play model, a movie can be played once its *initial* piece arrives at the client. Then, transfer and playback are done *concurrently,* or are *interleaved.* A streamed movie is never actually downloaded since the packets are discarded right after they are played out. In this way, it saves both startup latency and storage overhead at the client side, and supports live programs.

It takes many functions to form a streaming system. For example, a *compression* mechanism is needed to convert the video and audio data from digital camera into a proper format. We also need special-purpose *transport protocols* for real-time data transmission. QoS control must be provided to ensure *smoothness* in streaming the session. The client needs a decompressor or *decoder,* in hardware or software, and a *playback* mechanism adaptive to latency, jitter, and loss. Some *synchronization* is needed to coordinate the video and audio playback.

A streaming architecture is given in Figure 6.56. There are typically two kinds of participants: a streaming server that distributes the media content, and a number of clients joining the multimedia session. A general streaming processing is summarized as follows: Raw video and audio data from the recording device are *compressed,* i.e., *encoded,* and *stored* in a storage device. When receiving a client's request, the streaming server retrieves the stored content to be sent via a transport protocol. Before sending the content, some application-level QoS control modules are invoked to *adapt* bit streams to the network status and QoS requirements.

After being successfully received at the client, packets are processed through the transport layer and then the receiver QoS module, and finally *decoded* at the video/audio decoder. Before the packets are played out, media *synchronization* mechanisms are performed to synchronize the video and audio presentations. We elaborate on these components in the next three subsections.

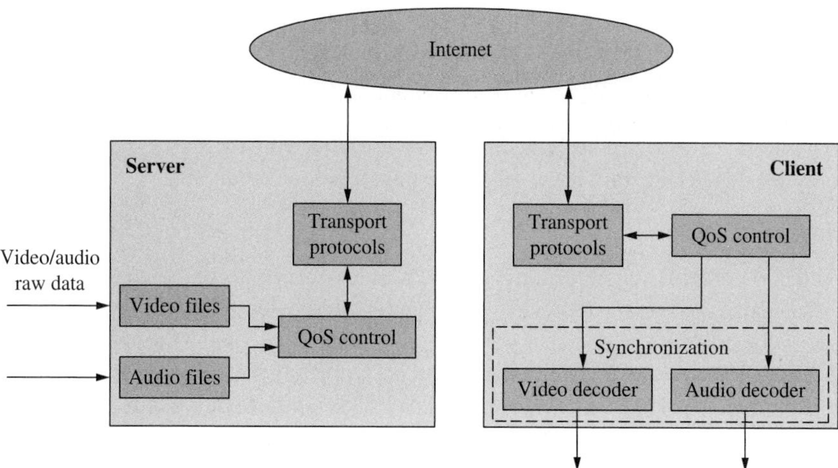

FIGURE 6.56 Architecture and components for streaming.

6.8.2 Compression Algorithms

The truth is that raw video/audio data is huge. Ten seconds of raw, uncompressed NTSC (National Television System Committee), a standard of television, will fill as much as 300 MB of storage space. That is why compression is much needed, especially for creating video files small enough to play over the Web.

A compression algorithm analyzes the data and removes or changes bits so that the *integrity* of the original content is retained as much as possible while reducing the file size and bit rate. Three characteristics of compressing algorithms are commonly examined: *temporal* and/or *spatial, lossy* or *lossless,* and *symmetrical* or *asymmetrical.*

Spatial and/or Temporal

Spatial compression looks for similar patterns or repetitions within a still *frame.* For example, in a picture that includes a blue sky, spatial compression would notice a particular area, i.e., sky, that contains similar pixels, and reduce the file size by recording much shorter bit streams to denote "the specified area is light blue" without the burden of describing thousands of repeated pixels. *Almost all* video compression methods/format recognized by ITU-T or ISO adopt a discrete cosine transform (DCT) for spatial redundancy reduction.

Temporal compression, on the other hand, looks for changes during *a sequence of frames.* For example, in a video clip of a talk, since it is often the case that only the speaker moves, temporal compression would only notice those changed pixels around the speaker. It compares the first frame, which is fully described and known as a *key* frame, with the next, called a *delta* frame, to find anything that changes. After the key frame, it only keeps the *changed* information in the subsequent frames. If there is a *scene change* where most of the content is different from the previous frame, it tags the *first* frame of the new scene as the next key frame and continues comparing the subsequent frames with this new key frame. The resulting file size is thus quite sensitive to the number of key frames. The MPEG (Motion Picture Exert Group) standard, one of the most popular video codecs, employs temporal compression.

Note that these two techniques are *not exclusive* to each other. For example, almost all QuickTime movies involve both compression techniques.

Lossless or Lossy

Whether a compression algorithm is lossless or lossy depends on whether or not all original data can be *recovered* when the file is uncompressed. With lossless compression, every single bit of data that was originally in the file remains the same after the file is uncompressed. All of the information is completely restored. This is generally the technique of choice for text or spreadsheet files, where losing words or financial numbers certainly poses a problem. For multimedia data, the Graphics Interchange File (GIF) is an image format used on the Web that provides lossless compression. Other formats include PNG and TIFF.

On the other hand, lossy compression reduces a file by permanently *eliminating* certain information, especially *redundant* information. When the file is uncompressed, only a part of the original information is still there, although the user might not notice it. Lossy compression is generally used for video and audio, where a certain amount of information loss would not be detected by most users. The JPEG image file, commonly used for photographs and other complex still images on the Web, has lossy compression. Using JPEG compression, an editor could decide how much loss to introduce and *trade off* between file size and image quality. Video compression standards such as MPEG-4 and H.264 also adopt lossy compression for a relatively larger *compression ratio* compared to the lossless scheme.

Symmetrical or Asymmetrical

The major difference between symmetrical and asymmetrical lies in the time taken for compression and decompression. The times for compression and decompression with a symmetrical method are the same, while they are different when an asymmetrical one is adopted. More specifically, asymmetrical means it takes more time to compress the multimedia data and, in a sense, the resulting quality is higher. Therefore a streaming server usually carries files compressed asymmetrically (such as MPEG and AVI videos) so as to alleviate the decompression load and provide satisfactory quality to its clients. Nonetheless, for real-time video conferencing over cellphones, symmetrical codecs such as H.264 are frequently used. The encoder hardware is simply not powerful enough to afford the asymmetrical scheme.

6.8.3 Streaming Protocols

Figure 6.57 is the protocol stack for streaming. Though there are other proprietary streaming protocols, here we introduce two streaming mechanisms that are frequently used in the public domain: RTSP and HTTP.

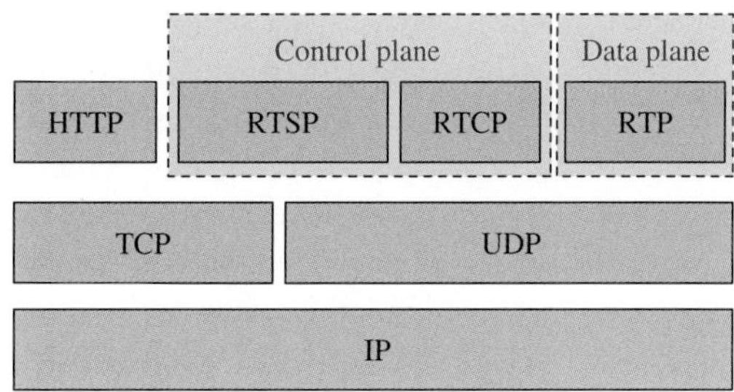

FIGURE 6.57 Protocol stack for streaming.

Real-Time Streaming Protocol (RTSP)

Real-Time Streaming Protocol (RTSP) is a client-server multimedia session control protocol that works well for both large audiences (multicast) and media-on-demand single-viewer (unicast). One of the main functions is to establish and control streams of video and audio media between media server and client. The way a stream is controlled is defined in a server-side *presentation description file,* which can be obtained by the client using e-mail. It states the encodings, language to use, transport capabilities, and other parameters that enable the client to choose the most appropriate combination of media. It also supports VCR-like control operations such as stop, pause/resume, fast forward, and fast backward. Similar to SIP, RTSP may also invite others to participate in an existing streaming session. As a whole, it has the following properties:

1. HTTP-friendly and extensible: Since RTSP has syntax and message format in ASCII strings similar to HTTP, an RTSP message can be parsed by a standard HTTP parser, while at the same time more methods can be added easily. URLs and status codes can be reused, too.
2. Transport-independent: Both UDP and TCP can be used to deliver the RTSP control messages through transport negotiation between client and server. However, TCP is not well suited for transmitting multimedia presentations, which relies on time-based operation, or for large-scale broadcasting. HTTP streaming over TCP is examined later. The default port for both transport protocols is 554.
3. Capability negotiation: For example, if seeking is not implemented in the server, the client has to disallow moving a sliding position indicator in the user interface.

RTSP Methods

There are several methods to be performed on the resource indicated by the URL in the request. Unlike HTTP, where requests can be initiated only by clients, an RTSP-enabled streaming server can communicate with the clients to update the presentation description file by `ANNOUNCE` and can check the health of the clients with `GET_PARAMETER` as "ping". Following are some methods that must be supported in an RTSP implementation to perform basic RTSP sessions.

1. `OPTIONS`: An `OPTIONS` request may be issued whenever a client is going to try a nonstandard request. If the request is granted by the server, a 200 OK response is returned.

2. `SETUP`: This is used to specify the transport mechanism when retrieving streaming data at a URL.
3. `PLAY`: The `PLAY` method informs the server to start sending data using the transport mechanism specified in `SETUP`. Some parameters within the header of the request can be set for extra functionalities. For example, having "Scale" set to 2 means doubled viewing rate, i.e., fast forward.
4. `TEARDOWN`: This is to stop the stream delivery of a particular URL. The corresponding session is closed until another `SETUP` request is issued.

HTTP Streaming

In addition to RTSP, it is possible to stream video and audio content over HTTP, which is also called *pseudo-streaming*. The trick is that a client has to buffer current media content, which is sent via TCP at a bandwidth possibly higher than required by the player, and play out from the buffer. However, it is much more likely to cause major packet drop-outs, low performance, and high delay jitter due to the *retransmission* nature of TCP when it keeps resending the lost packet before sending anything further. The result is that it could not deliver as much content as UDP and RTSP do. The sidebar in Subsection 5.5.1 has addressed these issues. While this method is not robust and efficient, it nevertheless serves as a reasonable and convenient alternative, without the RTSP support, for delivering streaming content at a small scale.

Historical Evolution: Streaming with Real Player, Media Player, QuickTime, and YouTube

With the introduction of streaming by RealNetworks in 1995, vendors of multimedia players started to complement their product lines with streaming capability. This produced three major camps: Microsoft (Media Player), Apple (QuickTime), and the pioneering RealNetworks (RealPlayer), in addition to other players of much smaller scale. Nonetheless, to form a complete solution for streaming, a player also needs to incorporate with a content provider, namely a server. For this Microsoft has the Windows Media Services (proprietary), while Apple has the QuickTime Streaming Server (proprietary) and Darwin Streaming Server (open source), and RealNetworks is equipped with the Helix DNA Server (supporting both private and open source versions).

Though based on common transport architecture, RTSP/RTCP/RTP, interoperability is not supported among those servers and players due to different streaming container formats (e.g., AVI, RM, WMV) and license restrictions. Nonetheless, standard formats such as MPEG are frequently supported.

Another rapidly emerging streaming technology is via Flash Media Server from Adobe Systems. Using a proprietary content type (FLV) and transport method (Real Time Messaging Protocol, RTMP, over TCP), it has become the major approach for on-demand video streaming over HTTP, called pseudo-streaming in this section. The well-known video sharing portal, YouTube, adopts this technology.

6.8.4 QoS and Synchronization Mechanisms

The question of how users feel has always been important in networking services. In streaming, there are two factors that directly affect the user-perceived quality: the *QoS control* on data transmission and the *synchronization* between the video and audio content.

QoS Control Mechanisms

Imagine a streaming session with poor QoS control. The quality is usually satisfiable under a normally loaded network. However, when the network is heavily loaded, the increasing packet *loss* rate will lead to broken or delayed frames and thus a rough play-out. Moreover, since the session coordinator is unaware of the network condition, it may even admit extra streams that worsen the quality of all involved sessions.

The objective of QoS control is therefore to maximize the streaming quality in the presence of packet loss. QoS control in streaming typically takes the form of *rate control,* which attempts to achieve the goal by matching the rate of the stream to the *available bandwidth.* Here we briefly introduce two approaches for rate control.

1. Source-based rate control: As the name suggests, the sender is responsible for adapting the video transmission rate through *feedback* about the network condition, or according to some modeling formulas. The feedback is usually the available bandwidth obtained from probing. The rate adaptation could keep the packet loss below a certain threshold. Adaptation may also be performed according to some TCP-like models so that packet loss can be alleviated as with TCP.
2. Receiver-based rate control: Under receiver-based rate control, regulation is done by the receiver by adding or dropping channels with the sender. Since a video can be decomposed into *layers* of different importance, with each layer transmitted in the corresponding channel, the network can be further relieved by deleting layers, and thus channels, that are less important.

There is another hybrid version that is based on the preceding two approaches. In this version the receiver regulates the receiving rate by adding or dropping channels while the sender adjusts the sending rate according to the feedback from the receiver. In addition to rate control, buffer management mechanisms, which prevent *overflow* or *underflow* to achieve smooth playback, are often applied to the receiver for better tolerance to possible network changes.

Synchronization Mechanisms

The second factor in user-perceived quality in streaming is whether the video and audio content is well synchronized. While the network as well as the operating systems may pose delays for the media streams, media synchronization is required to ensure proper rendering of the multimedia presentation at the client.

There are three levels of synchronization: *intra-stream* synchronization, *inter-stream* synchronization, and *inter-object* synchronization. They are briefly described here.

1. Intra-stream synchronization: A stream consists of a sequence of time-dependent data units that need to be strictly *ordered* and well *spaced.* Without the intra-stream synchronization, the presentation of the stream might be disturbed by pauses, gaps, or temporary fast-forwards.
2. Inter-stream synchronization: Since a multimedia session is mainly made up of video and audio streams, inappropriate synchronization between streams would lead to mismatch between, for example, the lips and the voice of the speaker.
3. Inter-object synchronization: The streaming content can be further abstracted to the object level and divided into two categories, the *time-dependent* objects used in the preceding two schemes, and *time-independent* objects. A good example of the time-independent objects would be the commercial banner or image that appears at the edge of a screen regardless of video and audio streams. As a result of poor inter-object synchronization, a commercial banner might be incorrectly displayed in, say, a news report where it is not supposed to appear.

Open Source Implementation 6.7: Darwin Streaming Server

Overview

The Darwin Streaming Server (DSS) is the open source version of Apple's QuickTime Streaming Server (QTSS). The DSS allows users to deliver streaming media over the Internet with RTP and RTSP. Users can tune in to the broadcast of live or prerecorded programs, or they can view prerecorded programs on demand. The DSS provides a high degree of customizability where developers can extend and modify the existing modules to fit their needs. The DSS runs on a variety of operating systems and supports a range of multimedia formats, including H.264/MPEG-4 AVC, MPEG-4 Part 2, 3GP, and MP3. In addition, the DSS provides an easy-to-use Web-based administration, authentication, server-side playlists, relay support, and integrated broadcaster administration.

Block Diagram

The DSS can be divided into two parts: *core server* and *modules.* Figure 6.58 shows the DSS block diagram. The core server is like an interface between clients and modules to provide *task scheduling,* while modules are called by task objects to provide specific functions. Objects are defined later in the data structures. Under such a framework, DSS can support *asynchronous* operations ranging from accepting client requests, allocating resources, scheduling requests, suspending requests, streaming programs, and interacting with clients, to recycling resources.

To explain the relationship between two kinds of objects: *socket event* and *task,* we illustrate how a client connection is handled. When the DSS accepts a connection from a client, a socket event will be *caught* and the `RTSPListenerSocket` task object is *signaled.* If everything goes well, the

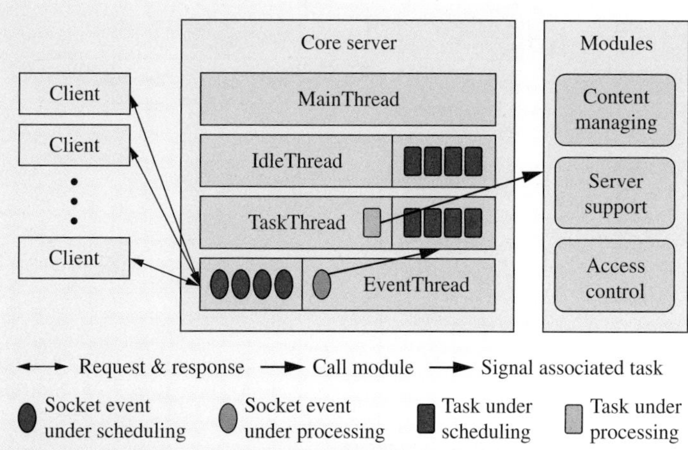

FIGURE 6.58 The DSS block diagram.

`RTSPListenerSocket` task object will create a new `RTSPSession` task object to handle this RTSP session. Next, the client can send a `PLAY` command to request media content. After handling this command, the `RTSPSession` task object may create a new `RTPSession` task object and then put it into scheduling to *continuously* stream media content back to the client. Both task objects would last until the client sends a `TEARDOWN` command to close this RTSP session.

Modules can be statically compiled-in or dynamically linked. There are three types of modules: (1) *content managing* modules, which manage the RTSP requests and responses related to media sources such as a stored file or live broadcast, (2) *server support* modules, which perform server data gathering and logging functions, and (3) *access control* modules, which provide authentication and authorization functions as well as URL path manipulation. The core server loads and initializes these modules when the stream server starts running.

Data Structures

To know how the core server works, first we should know what a task is. Figure 6.59 shows the important object classes of the DSS. Class `Task` is the base class of all classes that can be scheduled. A task is an object instance, which is the type of class directly or indirectly inheriting from class `Task`, and which therefore can be scheduled in the `fHeap` and `fTaskQueue` of a `TaskThread`. While `fTaskQueue` is a FIFO queue, tasks inside `fHeap` are popped out according to their expected wakeup time.

The `Signal()` is used to schedule task objects into the `fTaskQueue` of `TaskThread` with specific events marked in the `fEvents` variable. `Run()`, a virtual function, provides a general interface to be invoked when it is time for the task object to operate. In general, `Run()` operates according to the events marked in the `fEvents` variable.

Continued

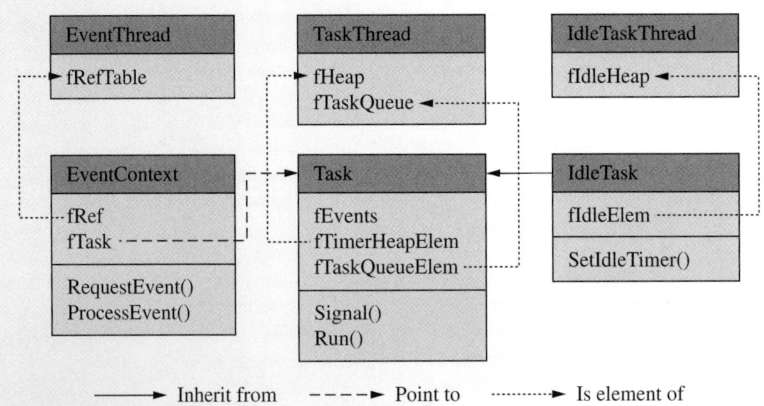

FIGURE 6.59 Relationships of important classes.

Algorithm Implementations

Task Handling

The DSS uses a set of preforked threads to support the operations mentioned here. It is different from other servers such as Apache and `wu-ftpd`, which *dedicate* a single thread to serve a client throughout the entire session. Tasks of DSS can be *scheduled* and *switched* between different threads. The reason for this OS-like design results from the *long session life* of stream applications. In this case, a large number of overlapping sessions could be handled by just a few threads.

As shown in Figure 6.60, in addition to `MainThread`, there are three types of threads in the core server : (1) `EventThread`, (2) `TaskThread`, and (3)

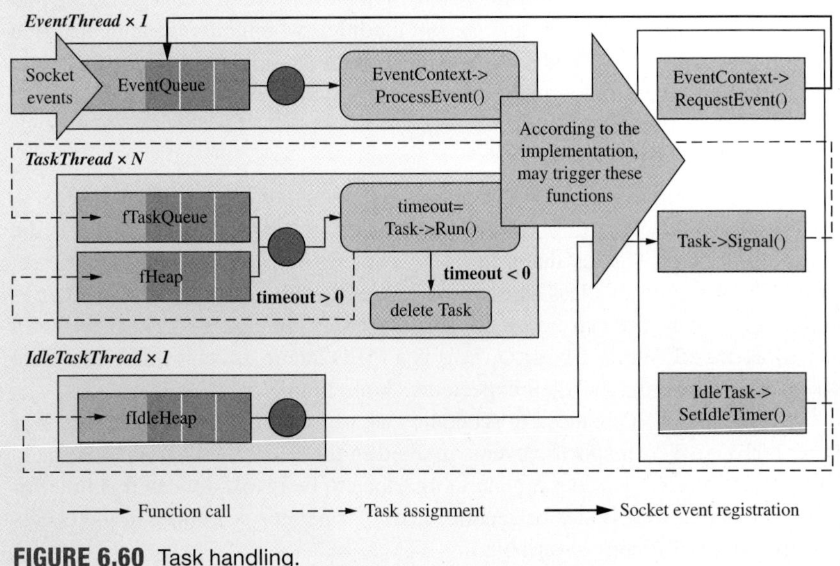

FIGURE 6.60 Task handling.

IdleTaskThread. Objects inheriting from the EventContext class register their fRef into the fRefTable of EventThread. Once a client connects or sends a command to the DSS, EventThread will get socket events and then find the associated EventContext from fRefTable, executing its ProcessEvent() to signal the related task object pointed to by fTask to react to the client.

When a task object is signaled, it will be assigned to one of the N TaskThreads in a round-robin fashion and will be put into the fTaskQueue. TaskThread will first check to see if there is any task in the fHeap whose sleeping time has elapsed. If there is not, it will check the fTaskQueue instead. Once the TaskThread gets a task, it invokes the Run() implementation of that task to deal with events marked in the fEvents variable. According to the return value of Run(), the task will be deleted or put into fHeap to be processed again after a while.

Once the SetIdleTimer() of an IdleTask object, also a task object, is invoked, the task object will be put into fIdleHeap to wait for the sleeping time to elapse. This is similar to putting a task object into the fHeap of a TaskThread, but the difference is that after popping the task object out of the IdleHeap, IdleTaskThread does nothing but signal it to let the task object get scheduled again.

According to the different implementations of Run() and ProcessEvent(), functions such as RequestEvent(), Signal(), and SetIdleTimer() could be invoked for tasks to be scheduled. How to design a task suitable for a system like the DSS is another lesson for programmers.

RTSP Session Handling

When the RTSPListenerSocket object accepts a connection, it creates an RTSPSession object and makes this object schedulable. Inside the Run() implementation of RTSPSession class, there is a well-defined state machine, which is used to track the process state of RTSP handling. Because the real state transition diagram is too complex to describe here, we simplify it as shown in Figure 6.61. Starting from Reading First Request, if the first request

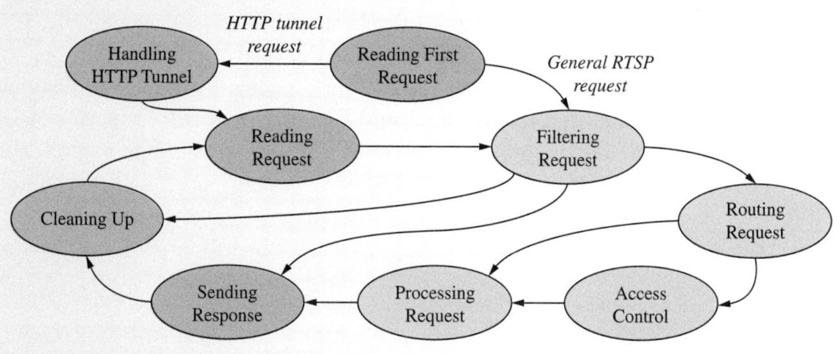

FIGURE 6.61 RTSP handling state transition diagram.

Continued

of the RTSP session is for HTTP tunneling, the state switches to `Handling HTTP Tunnel` to handle HTTP tunneling.

If it is a general RTSP request, the state goes through `Filtering Request` to parse the request, `Routing Request` to route the request to a content directory, `Access Control` for authentication and authorization, and `Processing Request` for RTP session setup and accounting. All these four states use functionalities provided by related modules. After sending a response back to the client and cleaning up the data structure for handling the request, the state goes back to `Reading Request` for the next RTSP request.

Exercises

1. Find out under what situation the DSS core server will put the `RTSPListenerSocket` object into the `fIdleHeap` of `IdleTaskThread` for waiting.
2. Refer to the function `Task::Signal()`. Explain the procedure of assigning a `Task` object to a `TaskThread`.

6.9 PEER-TO-PEER APPLICATIONS (P2P)

In the 1990s, the client-server model was believed to be a scalable solution for Internet applications for a number of reasons. For example, users' computers were dumb in terms of computing power and storage; the 80–20 rule indicated that most network traffic is devoted to retrieving only the most popular Web pages. It might have been true in the past that a powerful server could serve the purpose of storing information and sharing it in an efficient, stable, and scalable manner. However, with the rapid increase in computing power, network bandwidth, and hard disk storage of personal computers, users' computers are not dumb any more. Furthermore, as broadband access from home prevails, more computers, acting like servers, *always* stay on the Internet. Therefore, in recent years, more Internet applications were developed based on Peer-to-Peer (P2P) architecture. These applications introduce not only a new communication model but also new creative ideas and business models into the Internet. Noticeably, P2P already accounts for 60% of Internet traffic according to CacheLogic's report!

Here we introduce P2P applications from four aspects: (1) a general overview of the operations of P2P, (2) a review of several P2P architectures, (3) performance issues of P2P, and (4) a case study on a popular P2P file sharing application, BitTorrent (BT) and its open source implementation. Readers are advised that this section is heavier than the other sections in this chapter, mostly due to the more complicated behaviors of P2P.

6.9.1 Introduction

Unlike the client-server model, P2P is a distributed network architecture in which participants act as both clients and servers. Participants in a P2P network are usually normal users' computers. Based on some P2P protocols, they are able to construct a *virtual overlay network* at the *application layer* on top of the underlying IP network, as shown in Figure 6.62. Nodes in an overlay network are participants, while an overlay link is usually a TCP connection between two participants. For example, the virtual link between P1 and P2 in Figure 6.62 is a TCP connection passing through routers R1, R2, and R3 in the underlying IP network. Participants in P2P networks are called peers as they are assumed to play equivalent roles as both resource consumers and resource producers. Peers share a part of their own resources, such as processing power, data files, storage capacity, and network link capacity, through *direct* communication without going through intermediary nodes.

In general, operations in P2P systems consist of three phases: joining the P2P overlay network, resource discovery, and resource retrieval. Firstly, a peer joins the P2P overlay network by some join procedure. For example, a peer can send a join request to a well-known bootstrap server to obtain a list of existing peers on the overlay or through manual configuration. After joining the P2P overlay network, a peer often tries to search the network for an object shared by other peers. How to search an object in the distributed network is the most challenging problem for P2P applications. The search algorithm could be based on a central directory server, request flooding, or distributed hash table (DHT), depending on the underlying P2P architecture. We shall describe different P2P architectures next. If the search succeeds, the peer will obtain the information of the resource holders, such as their IP addresses. Retrieving the shared object is rather simple as direct TCP connections can be built between the seeking peer and the resource holders. However, complicated downloading mechanisms could be needed in light of factors such as holder's upload bandwidth, concurrent downloading, unexpected disconnection of holders, how to resume downloading after a disconnected peer reconnects to the Internet, and so on.

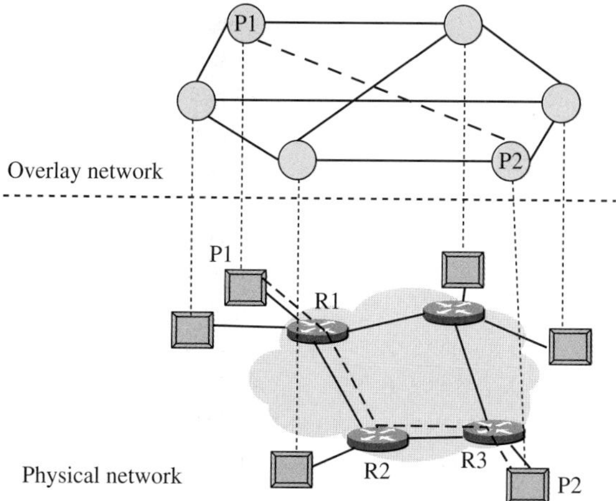

FIGURE 6.62 P2P overlay network on top of the underlying IP network.

Historical Evolution: Popular P2P Applications

There are other P2P applications beyond file sharing. P2P communications through messages, voice, and video are popular. Streaming through P2P is gaining momentum; so is P2P computing for collaboration and research. Table 6.29 categorizes popular P2P applications. Generally speaking, the whole operation of a P2P application can be divided into P2P and non-P2P parts. At the initialization stage, participants in a P2P application usually connect to some preconfigured servers to retrieve updates or messages, which is the traditional client/server relationship. Afterward, the participants start to build their own overlay connections with each other to exchange information, which is the P2P relationship.

TABLE 6.29 Categories of Peer-to-Peer Applications

Categories	Application Name	Features
File sharing	Napster, Limewire, Gnutella, BitTorrent, eMule, Kazaa	• Search and download shared files from others • Large files could be broken into chunks • The largest portion of P2P traffic
IP telephony	Skype	• Call anywhere in the Internet for free • P2P file-sharing built on top of Kazaa • Servers for presence information and skype-out billing
Streaming media	Freecast, Peercast, Coolstreaming, PPLive, PPStream	• Built on top of the underlying P2P file-sharing network of Kazaa • On-demand content delivery • Search and relay streams through peers
Instant messaging	MSN Messenger, Yahoo Messenger, AOL Instant Messenger, ICQ	• Messages/audio/file exchange
Collaborative community	Microsoft GROOVE	• Document sharing and collaboration • Keep data shared among users up-to-date • Integrate messaging and video conferencing
Grid computing	SETI@HOME	• For scientific computation • Aggregate millions of computers to search for extraterrestrial intelligence

Historical Evolution: Web 2.0 Social Networking: Facebook, Plurk, and Twitter

Compared to the traditional Web 1.0, where content and services are provided solely by servers and the visibility of this information is on servers only, Web 2.0 allows clients to *contribute* contents and services and to interact with peers. Examples include Wikipedia, Web Services, blogs, micro-blog, and online communities. A typical Web 2.0 application allows clients to interact with others by e-mail or instant messaging, update personal profiles to notify others, or modify contents of Web sites collaboratively. Facebook, Plurk, and Twitter belong to the type of Web 2.0 social networking services that build online communities to connect with friends, and a recommendation system linked to trust. In addition, Plurk and Twitter provide the services of micro-blog, which are similar to a traditional blog but limited in the size of contents. Entries in micro-blog could consist of a single sentence, an image, or a short 10-second video. Table 6.30 summarizes their features. Facebook is popular because of its rich features and applications that make it easier to interact with friends. Plurk and Twitter catch up due to its sharing comments with friends in real time.

TABLE 6.30 Features of Facebook, Plurk, and Twitter

Application	Service Type	Features
Facebook	Social networking	• Hundreds of millions of active users • Over 200 groups of different interests or expertise • A markup language, Facebook Markup Language, for developers to customize their applications • Wall: a user's space for friends to post messages • Pokes: a virtual nudge to attract the attention of others • Photos: upload photos • Status: inform friends of their whereabouts and actions • Gifts: send virtual gifts to friends • Marketplace: post free classified ads • Events: inform friends about upcoming events • Video: share homemade videos • Asynchronous games: a user's moves are saved on the site and the next move could be made at any time
Plurk	Social networking, micro-blogging	• Short messages (up to 140 characters) • Updates (called plurks) listed in chronological order • Respond updates by messaging • Group conversation between friends • Emoticons with text
Twitter	Social networking, micro-blogging	• Short messages (up to 140 characters) • Messages (called tweets) on the author's page delivered to the subscribers (known as followers) • Support SMS messages

6.9.2 P2P Architectures

The way of forming a P2P overlay network could be classified into three categories: centralized, decentralized and unstructured, and decentralized but structured. It is also related to the evolution of P2P applications that the centralized P2P is the first generation, and decentralized and unstructured P2P is the third generation. The way that a P2P overlay is organized, referred to as the infrastructure, affects its search operation and the overlay maintenance overhead.

Centralized

The centralized approach utilizes a central directory server for locating objects in the P2P network, as shown in Figure 6.63. The central directory server is a stable, always-on server just like a WWW or FTP server. Peers can join the P2P network by registering themselves to the directory server first. Peers also inform the directory server of objects to be shared, e.g., a list of music files with metadata. To search an object, a peer just sends the query message to the central directory server. The search could take the form of keyword search or metadata search, such as a keyword in the song title or name of singer. Since all objects to be shared have been registered to the server, the search could be done at the server alone. If the search succeeds, a reply consisting of a list of the content holders' information is sent back to the inquirer. The inquirer in turn selects one or more peers in the list to download the object directly from.

This approach is adopted by Napster, which is considered the pioneer of recent P2P development. Napster, created by Shawn Fanning, is a program that allowed users to share and swap music files through a centralized directory server. It became very popular quickly right after its first release. However, it was sued by the Recording Industry Association of America (RIAA) for copyright infringement in December 1999. In July 2000, the court ordered Napster to shut down. Napster was acquired by Bertelsmann later in 2002.

The centralized approach is very simple, easy to implement, and can support various kinds of search such as keyword, full-text, and metadata search. Ironically, it is not a true P2P system as it relies on a central directory server. Without this server, the system will not work anymore. As a consequence, it suffers the problems of the

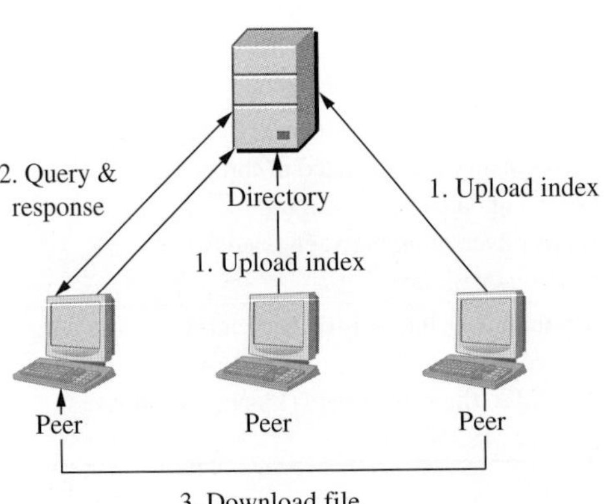

FIGURE 6.63 Centralized P2P.

client-server model, such as the server being the performance bottleneck, unreliability due to a single point of failure, and not scalable and vulnerable to DoS attacks. Most importantly, it holds the responsibility for copyright infringement.

Decentralized and Unstructured

To get rid of the directory server of the centralized approach, the decentralized and unstructured approach floods query messages to peers within an overlay network to search for shared objects, as shown in Figure 6.64. To reduce the overhead traffic incurred by flooding, limited-scope flooding is adopted such that a query message will not be forwarded after a certain hop-count. Upon receiving a query message, if a neighboring peer holds resources that matched the query, the current hop will respond with a query hit message to the previous sender instead of to the original inquirer in Figure 6.64; if the query is not a duplicate and its scope-limit is not reached, forward the query message to all the neighboring peers; discard the message otherwise. A query hit message is returned along the reverse path back to the inquirer. The inquirer in turn can download the object directly from the object holder.

To join the P2P network, a peer needs some kind of out-of-band mechanism to know at least one of the peers already on the overlay network. The peer then sends a join message (or ping message) to the peer already on the overlay. The existing peer then replies its identity as well as a list of its neighbors. It may also forward the join message to one or all of its neighbors. Upon receiving join reply messages, the newcomer knows more peers on the overlay and begins establishing TCP connections with selected peers that will become its neighbors.

The advantage of this approach is that it is fully decentralized, robust to peer failures, and difficult to shut down. However, the flooding approach is apparently not scalable because of excessive query traffic. In the case of limited-scope flooding, another critical problem emerges that it might occasionally fail to find a shared object that actually exists in the system. The first version of Gnutella is an example of this approach. To solve the scalability problem, FastTrack, a proprietary protocol of Kazaa, and later versions of Gnutella adopt a hierarchical overlay, as shown in Figure 6.65.

FIGURE 6.64 Limited-scope query flooding in decentralized and unstructured P2P system.

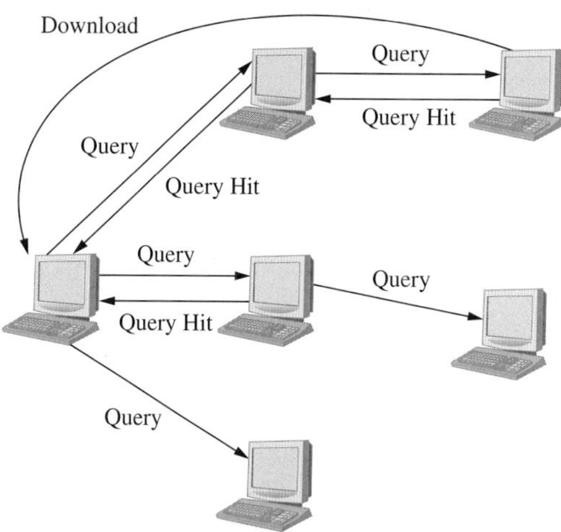

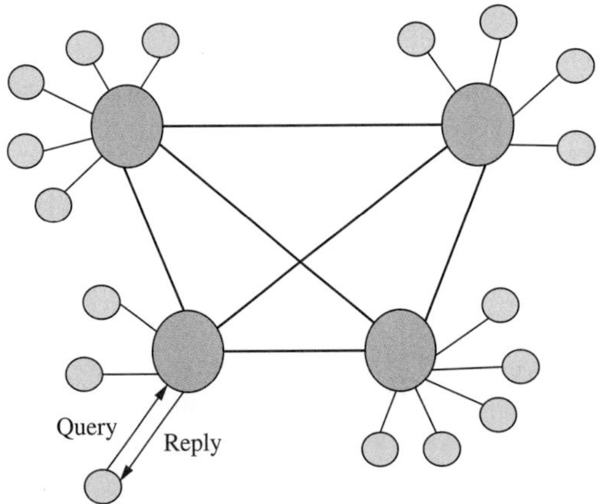

FIGURE 6.65 Hierarchical overlay with super peers.

The hierarchical overlay divides peers into ordinary peers and super peers. When a peer first joins the overlay, it acts as an ordinary peer and connects to at least one super peer. Later on, it may be elected as a super peer if it stays on for a long time and/or has high upload bandwidth. A super peer acts as a local directory database that stores the indexes of objects shared by ordinary peers. To search for a data object, an ordinary peer sends a query message to its super-peer neighbor. The super peer may reply to the query if the shared object can be found in its local directory; otherwise, it broadcasts the query to neighboring super peers using limited-scope flooding. Therefore, this approach builds a two-level hierarchical overlay where the lower level adopts the central directory server approach while the upper level adopts the decentralized and unstructured approach.

Decentralized but Structured

Neither Napster nor Gnutella organizes their peers into a structured overlay. The centralized directory in Napster is not scalable, while the way queries are propagated in Gnutella is rather random and thus not very efficient. Therefore, a better approach is to combine the distributed directory service with an efficient query routing scheme, which leads to the development of the decentralized and structured P2P systems, such as Chord, CAN, and Pastry.

The key ideas of this approach are as follows: For distributed directory service, a hash function maps peers and objects into the same address space so that objects can be deterministically assigned to peers in a distributive manner. For efficient query routing, peers are organized into a structured overlay based on their positions in the address space. The hash function should hash the set of peers and objects uniformly across the address space, known as consistent hashing. The hash function runs distributedly on each peer; therefore, this approach is also called Distributed Hash Tables (DHT). The following presents an overview on the operations of a DHT system and uses Chord as an example.

As mentioned, all peers and objects are hashed into the same address space. To avoid collision, the address space shall be large enough, e.g., 128 bits. A peer may use its IP address or other identity as the input to the hash function and obtain the hash result as its node ID. Similarly, a peer may obtain the object ID of an object by supplying the object's filename or some form of URI as the input to the hash function. As the node ID and object ID share the same address space, the key idea is to have each peer host the directory service for the object that has the object ID the same as its node ID.

Based on this idea, each peer first generates its own node ID by a predefined hash function. Then for each object being held and to be shared, it generates the object ID by the same or another hash function. For each object, the peer will send a register message to the node that has the node ID the same as the object's ID. If a peer wants to query an object, it uses the hash function to generate the object ID and sends the query message to the node that hosts the object's ID. We shall assume that an efficient routing mechanism is available to route the query message. If the address space is full of peers and objects, then some node would have the same node ID as the object's ID. Unfortunately, we expect the address space to be sparsely occupied by peers and objects, so a peer with that object's ID may not exist. To get around this problem, the registration message for an object ID is routed to the peer with the node ID closest to the object's ID, and so is the query message. In this way, a peer is able to provide directory service for objects that have IDs close to its node ID.

The problem is then how to route a message to a peer with node ID closest to the destination ID, which is the ID of an object or a peer, in a structured overlay. The key is to have each peer maintain a specially designed routing table such that every peer could forward the arriving message to a neighboring peer with a node ID that is closer to the destination. Let us use Chord as an example to explain how the routing table is set up to achieve efficient routing. Chord views its address space as a one-dimensional circular space so that peers in the space form a ring overlay.

Figure 6.66 shows an example of a 10-node Chord overlay in a 6-bit address space. The routing table in Chord is called a finger table. For an m-bit address space, the finger table of a node with ID = x consists of at most m entries and the i-th entry points to the first node with ID following the ID of $x + 2i^{-1}$ modulo 2^m, for $1 \leq i \leq m$. Let us consider the finger table of node *N8* in Figure 6.66, where $m = 6$. In this example, node ID ranges from *N0* to *N63,* but only 10 nodes really exist on the ring.

Each node is responsible for providing directory service for objects with ID larger than the ID of its previous node but less than or equal to its ID. For example, node *N15* will keep information about objects with ID from 9 to 15. With this in mind, let us examine the entries of *N8*'s finger table. The first entry, $i = 1$, keeps the next-hop information that leads to the node hosting *N9.* This entry points to the first node whose ID is *greater than or equal to* 9, which is node *N15.* That is, if there is a query message regarding object ID 9, the message will be forwarded to *N15,* which actually does provide directory service for this object. Let us use the last entry, $i = 6$, as another example. The last entry shall point to the node providing directory service for object ID 8 + 32 = 40. The entry points to *N42,* which is responsible for objects with ID from 31 to 42.

Now, let us consider the case of routing a query message for object 54 from *N8,* as shown in Figure 6.67. To route a message, a node looks up its finger table for the last entry with ID less than the object ID. Therefore, *N8* looks up the last entry

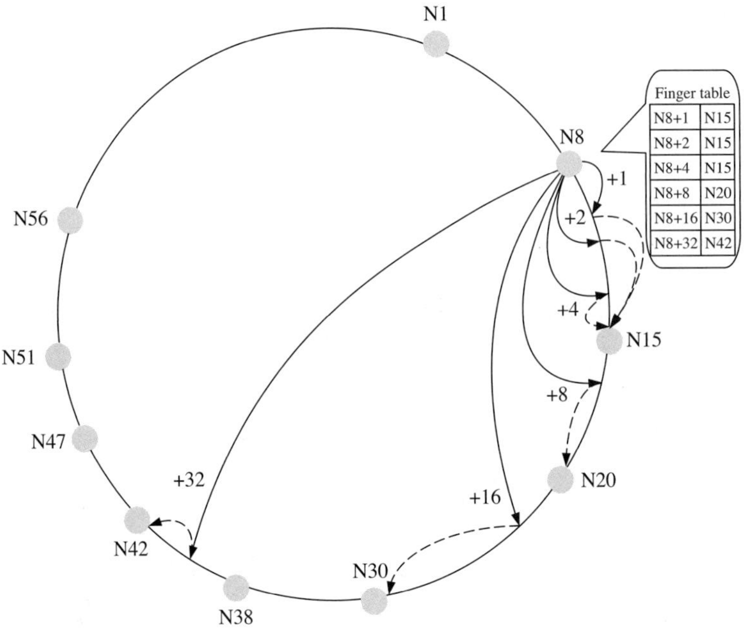

FIGURE 6.66 Finger table of Chord.

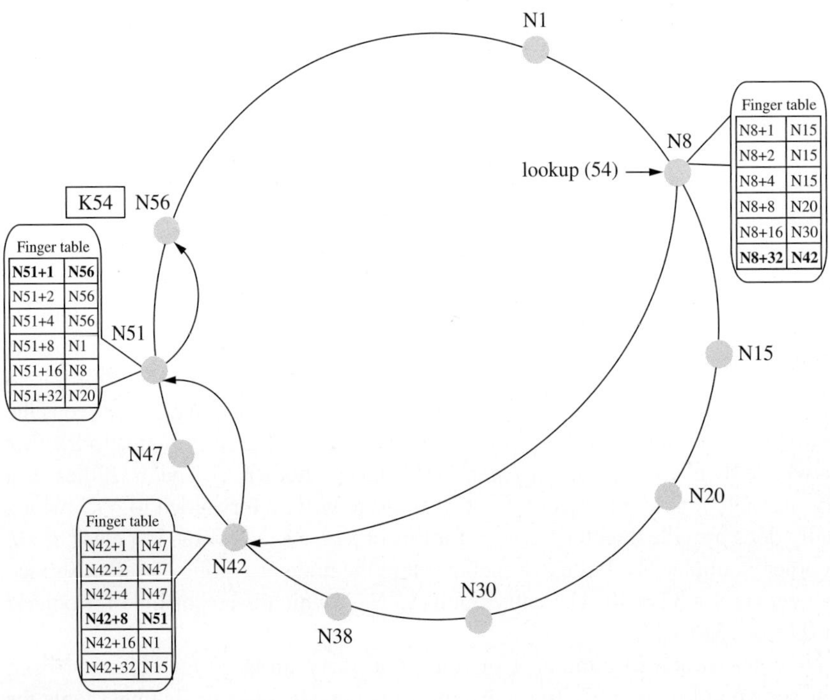

FIGURE 6.67 Routing in Chord.

(ID = 40 < 54) and forwards the message to *N42*. The distance from 42 to 54 is $12 < 2^4$, therefore, *N42* looks up the fourth entry (ID = 50 < 54) and forwards the message to *N51*. Finally, the distance from 51 to 54 is $3 < 2^2$, so *N51* looks up the second entry (ID = 53 < 54) and forwards the message to *N56*. Since *N56* is responsible for the directory service of object 54, it will reply the query message upon receiving the query. An interesting question is how many hops are required to forward the message. The answer is, it is bounded by $log(n)$. An intuitive rationale is that each routing hop will reduce the distance to the destination ID by a factor of 2. For example, the distance from 8 to 54 is 46, which is 101110 when represented in binary. As a consequence, when the entry of 2^5 is selected at *N8*, the message is forwarded to a node with ID larger or equal to 40 (8 + 32) which has a distance less than 23 (46/2) to node 54. In other words, with the finger table, Chord is able to reduce the searching space by a factor of 2 at each routing step.

Many DHT-based P2P systems with clever designs have been proposed. However, they are built upon the same ideas of distributed directory service and efficient routing based on a structured overlay. Although they are decentralized and efficient, a major drawback of DHT is that search is limited to exact match. Recall that an object ID is obtained by hashing its name. A slight difference in the name will result in a wild difference in the hash result. Therefore, it becomes difficult to search in a DHT by keywords, semantic search, or full-text search. Another disadvantage of DHTs is the overhead of overlay construction and maintenance.

Others

As different infrastructures have their own advantages and disadvantages, several hybrid as well as hierarchical infrastructures have been proposed in the literature.

6.9.3 Performance Issues of P2P Applications

There are several performance issues of P2P applications that draw much attention from researchers. The following discusses some major issues.

Free Riding

The scalability of P2P systems relies on contributions from peers. If a peer only consumes but contributes little or no resources, it becomes a free rider of the system. If there are many free riders in the system, the system will degrade to a client-server model where most free-rider peers act as clients while a small number of non-free-rider peers act as servers contributing most of the resources. This will become a serious problem if a P2P system does not support some mechanisms to prevent it. Results from Hughes, Coulson, and Walkerdine in 2005 indicate that 85% of peers share no files in Gnutella, which does not have any anti-free-riding mechanism. A common solution to the free-riding problem is to implement some incentive mechanisms. For example, tit-for-tat in BitTorrent, which we examine next, gives upload priority to those peers that have higher download rates. Other solutions, such as reward-based and credit-based mechanisms, have also been proposed in the literature.

Flash Crowd

The flash crowd phenomenon refers to a sudden, unanticipated growth in the demand for a particular object, e.g., a new release of a DVD video or mp3 file. Issues related to this phenomenon include how to deal with a sudden large volume of query messages and how long it takes to find and download the object within a short time period. Though different types of P2P infrastructure require different solutions, in general, caching the object's index on peers that have forwarded the reply message could reduce the query traffic as well as the latency of query messages. On the other hand, duplicating the object to as many peers as possible could increase the download speed. For example, a peer will become a seed, i.e., a resource provider, when it has completely downloaded the file.

Topology Awareness

DHT-based P2P systems can guarantee an upper bound on the routing path's length. However, a link on the path corresponds to a transport-layer connection in the underlying physical network, as shown in Figure 6.62. Such a virtual link could be a long end-to-end connection across continents or a short one within a local area network. In other words, if peers choose their overlay neighbors without considering the underlying physical topology, the resultant P2P overlay network may have a serious topology mismatch to the underlying physical network. Therefore, how to perform topology-aware overlay construction and overlay routing significantly affects the performance of P2P systems. Many route-proximity and neighbor-proximity enhancements for P2P overlay systems have been proposed based on RTT measurement, preference of routing domain or ISP, or geographical information.

NAT Traversal

A peer can establish a transport-layer connection to another peer directly only if the destination peer has a public IP address. However, many broadband access users are connected to the Internet through NAT devices. If both peers are behind NAT devices, they cannot connect to each other without help from other peers or STUN servers, as we discussed in Chapter 4. Therefore, the basic requirement for a P2P system is to provide peers with NAT traversal mechanisms. In most cases, NAT traversal is solved by relay peers or super peers that have public IP addresses.

Churn

Churn refers to the phenomenon that peers dynamically join and leave the system at will. Intuitively, a high churn rate seriously affects the stability and scalability of a P2P system. For example, a high churn rate may cause a tremendous overlay maintenance overhead and dramatic degradation in routing performance (including correctness of routing) in DHT-based systems. To cope with churn, a P2P system should avoid a rigid structure or relation among peers, such as a tree structure in P2P video streaming, and peers shall maintain a list of potential neighbors for quick and dynamic neighbor replacement when needed.

Security

There are several security issues in P2P systems. Examples include P2P programs with back hole (Trojan Horse), spurious content, or leaking of files not to be shared. Spurious content or the content pollution problem in a P2P system could reduce content availability and increase redundant traffic. For example, a malicious user may share a popular mp3 file with part of the content modified (polluted). Users that downloaded this polluted file will usually try to download the file from other sources again. If polluted content (objects) is spread all over the P2P system, users may lose interest in participating in this P2P system as most downloaded objects are useless. Solutions to the content pollution problem include protecting the content with message digest such as MD5, peer reputation system, and object reputation system. For example, in BitTorrent, the MD5 digest of each piece of a shared file is stored in the metadata file, i.e., the .torrent file. In FastTrack, the UUHash mechanism prevents file pollution by hashing selected blocks of a file using MD5.

Copyright Infringement

Finally, it should be noted that sharing copyrighted objects through P2P systems is a serious problem that hinders the promotion and usage of P2P systems. Many universities and organizations prohibit their users from running P2P applications. In addition, it is not only P2P users who are responsible for copyright infringement; so are the companies that host P2P applications, especially in cases where P2P systems will not be able to exist without their servers, as was the case with Napster.

6.9.4 Case Study: BitTorrent

BitTorrent (BT), originally designed by Bram Cohen in 2001, has become a very popular file sharing software nowadays. In 2004, it contributed about 30% of Internet traffic. Although there are several competitors now, such as eDonkey and eMule, it is still a very popular file sharing software. BT is a well-thought-out protocol with several unique features: (1) use of tit-for-tat as an incentive mechanism to cope with free riders; (2) use out-of-band search to avoid copyright infringement issue; (3) use of pull-based swarming for load balancing; (4) use of hash check to prevent propagation of spurious pieces; (5) after a peer has successfully downloaded a file, it becomes a seeder to distribute the file.

Before we describe the protocol, we first introduce some terminologies used in BT. A file to be shared is cut into *pieces* of a fixed size. A piece is further divided into *chunks,* the basic data unit for a peer to request for content. The integrity of a piece is protected by an SHA-1 hash code so that a polluted piece will not be propagated. A peer becomes a seeder if it has successfully downloaded the file. There is a tracker for each file or group of files to be shared. The tracker tracks the downloading peers and seeds, and coordinates the file distribution among peers. Although the tracker-less BT system where every peer acts as a tracker has become available since 2005, it is still more common to use centralized trackers. Therefore, we will review the BT protocol with centralized trackers.

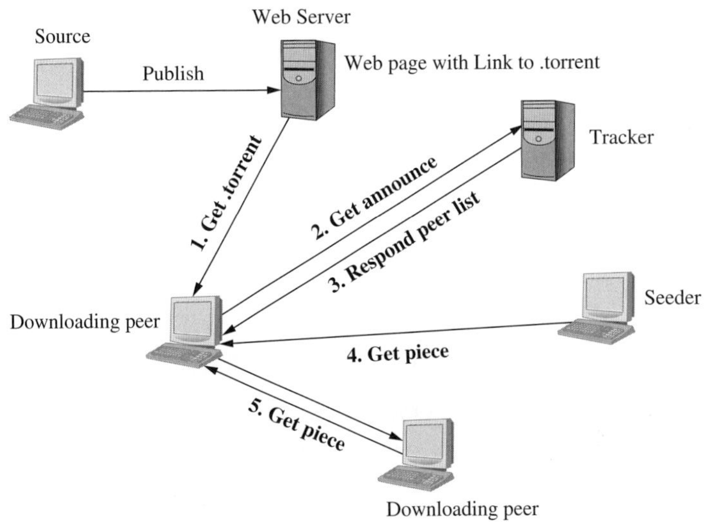

FIGURE 6.68 Operation steps of BitTorrent.

Operation Overview

Figure 6.68 is a brief overview of the operations of BT. To share a file, a peer first creates a ".torrent" file, which contains metadata about the file to be shared, including the file name, file length, the piece length being used, SHA-1 hash code for each piece, state information of each piece, and URL of the tracker. The torrent file is usually published to some well-known Web site. To find and download a file, users browse the Web to find a torrent of the file first. The torrent file is then opened with a BT client program. The client connects to the tracker and gets a list of peers currently downloading the file. After that, the client connects to those peers to obtain the various pieces of the file according to a piece selection algorithm.

Piece Selection

For the first few pieces (usually around four), the client just randomly selects a piece to download, referred to as random first piece selection. After the initial phase, the rarest first policy kicks in. The rarest first policy selects the most scarce piece to download first because the most scarce piece may not be available later on due to some peers' departure. It also ensures that a large variety of pieces are downloaded from the seeder. Finally, to speed up the completion of a file download at the end, a peer with only a few pieces missing will enter an end-game mode and send requests for all missing pieces to all the peers.

Peer Selection

A peer may receive requests for pieces from other peers. BT uses a built-in incentive algorithm, known as tit-for-tat, to select the peers to upload their interested pieces. Tit-for-tat is the most prevalent strategy for the prisoner's dilemma in game theory. The basic idea is that an agent will cooperate if the opponent was cooperative;

otherwise, if the opponent provoked, the agent will retaliate. The peer selection algorithm consists of three components: choking/unchoking, optimistic unchoking, and anti-snubbing.

Tit-for-tat is adopted in the choking/unchoking algorithm. Choking refers to a temporal refusal to upload to a peer. At the beginning, all peers are choked. The peer then unchokes a fixed number (usually 4) of peers; some of them (usually 3) are based on the tit-for-tat while the rest (usually 1) are based on optimistic unchoking. From those interested in the peer's pieces, the tit-for-tat algorithm selects a fixed number of peers (usually 3) from which the peer downloaded most. Specifically, the selection is based solely on the download rate of each peer. The tit-for-tat algorithm is down every 10 seconds and the download rate is evaluated based on a 20-second moving window. However, the new peer needs to move its first step when it initially joins the system; it is also desirable to move the first step to explore better peers that are currently not cooperating. Therefore, the idea of optimistic unchoking is to select one peer at random from those interested in the peer's piece, regardless of their download rate. Optimistic unchoking is performed every 30 seconds to select peers in a circular order. Finally, the anti-snubbing algorithm is run whenever the peer is choked by all of its peers, referred to as snubbed, e.g., it does not receive any data in 60 seconds. A snubbed peer does better to run optimistic unchoking more often to explore more peers that are willing to cooperate. Therefore, the anti-snubbing algorithm stops uploading to peers selected by tit-for-tat so that optimistic unchoking can be performed more often.

Open Source Implementation 6.8: BitTorrent

Overview

There are several free client software programs for file sharing networks, such as Limewire of Gnutella, eMule of eDonkey, and uTorrent and Azureus of BitTorrent. With different design philosophy and infrastructure, they address performance issues of P2P systems differently. For example, Gnutella adopted the decentralized and unstructured topology, and later the super-peer hierarchy. DHT technology is adopted by eMule and BT to avoid the centralized tracker (server). As a result, Gnutella, known for its decentralized, serverless topology, is extremely resilient to random node failure; eMule, known for its distributed tracker, is based on a DHT solution Kademlia; BT is known for dividing a large file into pieces, adopting tit-for-tat to cope with free riders, and integrity check to prevent propagation of spurious pieces. Since BT has so many unique features, it remains one of the most popular P2P file sharing software programs. Recall that solutions adopted by BT to cope with performance issues are:

1. Tit-for-tat to avoid free riders: BT implements tit-for-tat based on the download rate between two peers. The advantage of using the download rate as the criterion for reciprocation is that it can be easily implemented with local information at each peer. Alternative solutions, such as the reputation-based

Continued

approach and the download rate to all peers, require information from other peers, and whether the information is correct remains a question. On the other hand, BT's approach is unfair to the newcomers.

2. Out-of-band search to avoid copyright infringement: BT assumes a peer is able to find the .torrent file first without specifying how. This approach is a simple and effective way to decline the responsibility for copyright infringement. The disadvantage is that the distribution of .torrent files relies on third-party servers.
3. Pull-based swarming for load balancing: Based on tit-for-tat, peers upload pieces to other peers in order to download pieces they need. This approach is quite effective to force peers to contribute pieces they already downloaded. Therefore, peers can speed up the download process as more peers join the system. A potential problem of this approach is that a peer may leave the system as soon as it completes its download, which is called the leech problem. Clearly, the longer a seeder stays, the better the swarming performance.
4. Message digest to protect integrity of each piece: BT adopts SHA-1 to protect the integrity of each piece. Though this approach can effectively prevent propagation of spurious pieces, it requires SHA-1 computation on every piece retrieved. In FastTrack (KaZaa), message digest is only applied to partial blocks of a file. Doing so would save some computation overhead, but it would also allow an attacker to pollute a file without being caught.

Since the protocol specification of BitTorrent is free to use, many BT client programs are open-source. Among them, uTorrent, Vuze, and BitComet are some of the most popular client programs. In this section, we trace Vuze version 4.2.0.2, which is implemented in Java.

Files and Data Structures

Most of Vuze's core packages are located under the .\com\aelitis\azureus\core directory. Packages that can be found in this directory are shown in Table 6.31.

Most codes for peer selection and piece selection are under the directory.\com\aelitis\azureus\core\peermanager. Under this directory, the piece selection and peer selection algorithm can be found in the directory of \piecepicker and \unchoker, respectively; codes for the status information of connected peers can be found in the \peerdb directory.

Another important directory is the \org\gudy\azureus2\core3 directory. The main program for controlling the piece and peer selection is `PEPeerControlImpl.java`, which is located under \peer\impl\control of this directory. The classes for the peer and piece objects are `PEPeer` and `PEPiece`, which are defined in \org\gudy\azureus2\core3\peer.

Figure 6.69 shows the class hierarchy of `PEPeer`, `PEPiece`, and `PEPeerManager`.

TABLE 6.31 Packages in com.aelitis.azureus.core

Packages	
package	clientmessageservice
package	cnetwork
package	content
package	crypto
package	custom
package	devices
package	dht
package	diskmanager
package	download
package	drm
package	helpers
package	impl
package	instancemanager
package	Iws
package	messenger
package	metasearch
package	monitoring
package	nat
package	networkmanager
package	neuronal
package	peer
package	peermanager
package	proxy
package	security
package	speedmanager
package	stats
package	subs
package	torrent
package	update
package	util
package	versioncheck
package	vuzefile

Algorithm Implementations

Main Program

The main program for controlling the piece and peer selection is the `PEPeerControlImpl` class, which inherits from two classes, `PEPeerManager` and `PEPeerControl`. A detailed inheritance diagram

Continued

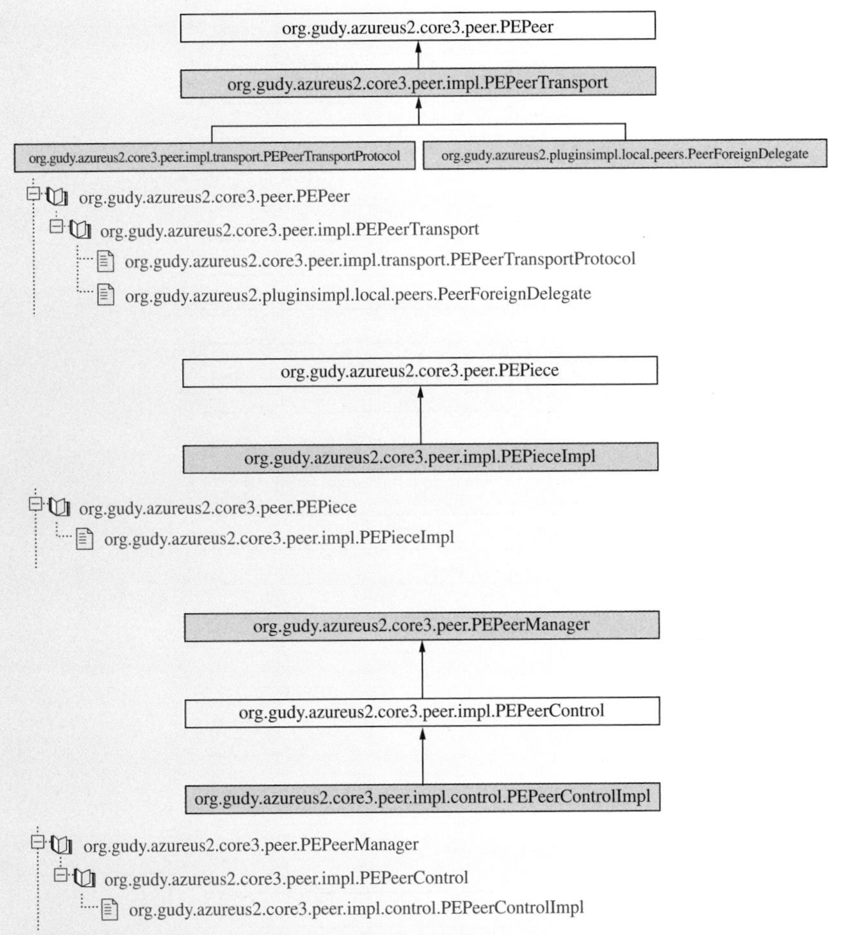

FIGURE 6.69 Class hierarchy of `PEPeer`, `PEPiece`, and `PEPeerManager`.

for `PEPeerControlImpl` is shown in Figure 6.70. The constructor of this class creates the object `piecePicker`. The function is also defined in this class; schedule() calls `checkRequests()` and `piecePicker.allocateRequests()` to schedule piece requests if the peer is not in the seeding mode. It then calls `doUnchokes()` to handle peer choking and unchoking. In `doUnchokes()`, `unchoker.calculateUnchokes()` is called to determine which peers to unchoke.

Implementation of Peer Selection

The unchoking algorithms for downloading peer and seeding peer are implemented in DownloadingUnchocker.java and SeedingUnchocker.java under the .\com\aelitis\azureus\core\peermanager\unchoker directory. Let us trace the codes for tit-for-tat and optimistic unchoking. The main function of tit-for-tat

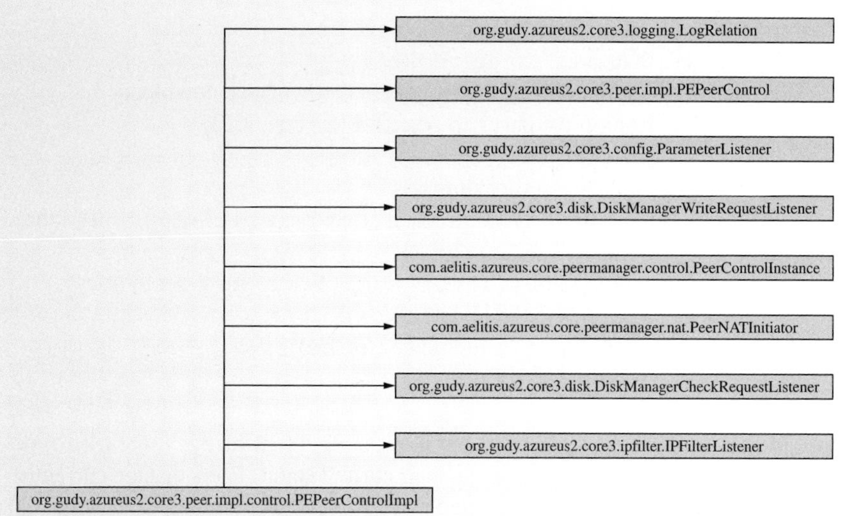

FIGURE 6.70 Detailed inheritance diagram for `PEPeerControlImpl`.

is implemented in `calculateUnchokes()`. Four peer lists are used in this function: `chokes`, `unchokes`, `optimistic_unchokes`, and `best_peer`. They are used to bookkeep peers to be choked, unchoked, optimistic unchoked, and best peers to be unchoked based on the downloading rate. The pseudocode for `calculateUnchokes()` is given as follows:

```
    calculateUnchokes()
BEGIN
    get all the currently unchoked peers;
    IF the peer is not previously choked by me {
        IF the peer is unchokable {
            add it to the unchokes list;
            IF the peer is previously optimistic unchoked
                add it to the optimistic_unchokes list;
        }
        ELSE
            add the peer to the chokes list
    }
    IF not forced to refresh the optimistic unchoke peers {
        Move the peers in the optimistic_unchokes list to the
best_peers
            list until the number of peers exceeds max_optimistic
    Add peers to the best_peers list if its download rate is higher than 256
    Call UnchokerUtil.updateLargestValueFirstSort to sort
the best_peers
          list according to the download rate
```

Continued

```
IF we still have not enough peers in the best_peers list
    (less than max_to_unchoke) {
    fill the remaining slots with peers that we have downloaded
        from in the past (uploaded_ratio < 3);
}
IF we still have remaining slots
  Call UnchokerUtil.getNextOptimisticPeer to get more
optimistic
        unchoke peers. (factor_reciprocated is set to true)
Call chokes.add() to update chokes
Call unchokes.add() to update unchokes
END
```

In this function, peers are first put into the list of chokes, unchokes, or optimistic_unchokes based on their current status. Peers that are currently optimistic unchoked will remain unchoked unless the number of optimistic unchokes exceeds the max_optimistic threshold. Then, for peers that are interested in our pieces (peer.isInteresting()) and are unchokable (UnchokerUtil.isUnchokable), the method peer.getStats().getSmoothDataReceiveRate() is called to obtain their download rate. These peers are sorted a into the best_peers list according to the rate by calling UnchokerUtil.updateLargestValueFirstSort(). If the number of peers in the best_peers list is less than max_to_unchoke, the maximum number of peers to be unchoked, peers that have uploaded_ratio less than 3 are added to the best_peers list where uploaded_ratio is the ratio of total data bytes sent over total data bytes received (plus BLOCK_SIZE-1). If the size of best_peers is still less than max_to_unchoke, then UnchokerUtil.getNextOptimisticPeer() is called to find more peers for optimistic unchokes. The UnchokerUtil.getNextOptimisticPeer() function either takes into account the peer reciprocation ratio when picking optimistic peers or just randomly select peers from the optimistic_unchokes list, depending on whether the factor_reciprocated parameter is true. The reciprocation score is defined as the difference between total data bytes sent and total data bytes received, and a lower score is preferred.

Implementation of Piece Selection

The getRequestCandidate() method, defined in PiecePickerImpl.java under the .\com\aelitis\azureus\core\peermanager\piecepicker\impl directory, is the core method for deciding which block to download. Two parameters are important to know first: priority and avail. Priority is the aggregate priority of the piece under inspection, while avail is the swarm-wide availability level of the piece under inspection. There are three stages in this method. First, if there is a FORCED_PIECE or a reserved piece, it will be started/resumed if possible. Second, find the rarest piece with the highest priority which has already been loaded and can possibly be continued by scanning all the active pieces. Availability of a piece is represented by `availability[i]`. Third, if there is no piece to resume, find a list of the rarest pieces with the highest priority as candidates for starting the download of a new piece. The method returns `int[] pieceNumber` and `blockNumber` if a request to be made is found.

Exercises

1. Explore the locality by considering the round-trip delay and changing the random selection code in the `getNextOptimisticPeer()` function accordingly. For example, you may give preference to peers with lower round-trip delay.
2. Discuss why it is important to consider locality in choosing optimistic unchoked peers. Note that optimistic unchoke plays an initiation role in finding potential tit-for-tat peers.

6.10 SUMMARY

Unlike other chapters in this text, it is more difficult but still necessary to capture the *common* themes for the Internet applications. This chapter started from the general issues concerning the design of *all* Internet applications. We learned how well-known ports work, how servers run as daemon processes, the differences between the combinations of concurrent connection-oriented servers and iterative connectionless servers, and why application protocols have variable-length ASCII messages and statefulness/statelessness. Then we covered major application protocols, from the fundamental DNS, to the classic SMTP, POP3, IMAP4, HTTP, FTP, and SNMP, and well into the real-time SIP, RTP, RTCP, RTSP, and various P2P protocols. For each application protocol, we described design concepts, protocol messages and behaviors, example sessions when needed, and one popular open source package. We do not plan to summarize the design concepts of individual applications here. Instead, we re-examine their common characteristics: well-known ports, variable-length ASCII, statefulness, and concurrency. Through this, we can better appreciate these characteristics and the possibilities beyond the current practices.

First, the practice that classifies application traffic according to port numbers no longer works very well. Many applications run themselves over port 80 or encapsulate their messages in the HTTP messages in order to pass through firewalls that allow only Web traffic. Additionally, P2P applications often select their port numbers dynamically well beyond the range of well-known ports. Thus, *deep packet inspection* (DPI) into the application headers or even payloads is needed for accurate classification. Secondly, unlike the binary fixed-length protocol headers in lower layers, application protocols have variable-length ASCII formats. Table lookup algorithms used in single-field (destination IP address) packet forwarding and multi-field (5-tuple) packet classification cannot be applied here. Instead, DPI with regular expression *parsing* or signature-based *string matching* is needed for classification or security purposes. This fixed-to-variable gap has an analogy in the area of database systems, where traditional *relational* databases are fixed-length tables and *semistructured* data formatted in XML or *unstructured* data indexed by search engines are variable-length strings. Just like the increased percentage of semistructured or unstructured data in the world of databases, variable-length protocol message handling is gaining more attention in the world of networking.

Thirdly and fourthly, being stateful is a *design* choice of a protocol while being concurrent is an *implementation* decision of a protocol server. Most application protocols chose to be stateful to keep track of client connections, except HTTP and SNMP for efficiency and scalability reasons. DNS is something in between. Local DNS servers are mostly stateful and recursive to be *fully responsible* for a DNS query, while all other DNS servers are stateless and iterative for the same reasons of efficiency and scalability. Though stateless in their nature, HTTP servers could turn stateful for long sessions by the mechanism of *cookies*. For concurrency, the decision depends on the *time* required to serve a session or a request. If the service time is short, the server could remain iterative. SNMP belongs to this, and thus the server in net-snmp is implemented as an iterative server. All other open source packages in this chapter have concurrent server implementations due to their prolonged service time.

From Chapter 2 to Chapter 6, we have learned all the protocol layers. There are two advanced issues that deserve special treatment: quality of service (QoS) and network security. Once we achieve connectivity, we expect the connectivity to be *fast* enough and *secure* enough. QoS or performance issues are central in the design of all network systems or components. In Chapter 7, QoS is treated formally with two *total* solutions, IntServ and DiffServ, and six important *building blocks*. Although these two total solutions did not succeed, technologies for some building blocks have prevailed in our daily Internet life. In Chapter 8, we shall classify the security issues into *access* security, *data* security, and *system* security, addressing who can access what, private data on the public Internet, and system vulnerabilities to intruders, respectively. State-of-the-art solutions to these issues shall be presented.

COMMON PITFALLS

Alternatives to Server Concurrency

The simplest way to program a concurrent connection-oriented server is to fork a child process on demand to serve a newly accepted client connection. This is exercised in wu-ftp introduced in Open Source Implementation 6.4. But there are many other alternatives to achieve this concurrency considering the issues of *overhead, latency,* and *scalability.* Forking a process is expensive since it involves *creating* a new entry in the process table, *allocating* memory space for the process body, and *copying* from the parent process body to the child process body. A low-overhead alternative is *threading,* where a thread is created with its body shared with its parent thread, thus no memory allocation or copy. Asterisk in Open Source Implementation 6.6 belongs to this category. On the other hand, forking or threading *on demand* introduces startup latency in serving the incoming clients. Preforking or prethreading with a *pool* of *idle* processes or threads to dispatch surely would reduce this startup latency. This pool could be monitored periodically to keep its size between a high threshold and a low threshold. Apache introduced in Open Source Implementation 6.3 runs this approach.

Finally, an even tougher issue is the scalability when a server has to handle thousands of concurrent connections. This happens often to a *proxy* server, which stands between clients and servers. It would not be feasible to maintain thousands of processes or threads in a single server. There are two common solutions: a single process with *I/O multiplexing* or a *larger* number of connections served and *switched* between a *smaller* number of processes or threads, i.e., no *per-connection* process or thread. The former does I/O multiplexing, by the `select()` function in the single process, to listen on an array of per-connection sockets and handle those sockets with new arrivals. Squid is an open source proxy that runs this. The latter schedules and switches the connections between a pool of processes and threads throughout the lifetime of the connections. BIND, qmail, and Darwin introduced in Open Source Implementation 6.1, 6.2, and 6.7 run this solution.

DNS Queries: Recursive or Iterative

When we say a DNS query resolution process is recursive, it does not imply *all* DNS servers are recursive and stateful. In fact, only the *local* DNS servers are recursive and stateful. All the other DNS servers in the DNS hierarchy are iterative and stateless. That is, they only *reply* or *redirect* a query from local DNS servers, but do not *forward* the query to other DNS servers. The reason is the scalability concern on heavily loaded servers, especially those near the root of the hierarchy. On the other hand, the local DNS servers would not be heavily loaded since they are far away from the root of the hierarchy and could handle the recursive resolution. Though less likely, it is possible that the local DNS servers run iteratively. Then it is the business of the resolver (the DNS client) to handle the recursion.

ALM vs. P2P

Due to the lack of wide-scale deployment of network-layer IP multicast, application-layer multicast (ALM) gained a lot of attention in the early 2000s. As its name implies, ALM supports group applications through TCP or UDP sockets among participating nodes. That is, ALM implements the multicast service at the application layer without the need for a network-layer multicast protocol. It can be seen as a special type of peer-to-peer (P2P) application as it builds a *multicast tree* at the application layer and intermediate nodes of the tree are required to relay packets from parents to children. Therefore, these nodes behave like data consumers as well as data providers, just like peers in P2P systems. How to build the *multicast overlay* is the main focus of ALM research. On the other hand, P2P refers to a much wider range of applications which may or may not need multicast support. For example, the most popular application, file sharing, does not need multicast support. Even for the video streaming application, most P2P systems developed recently adopted the concept of data-driven overlay network, or *mesh overlay,* instead of *tree overlay,* mainly for robustness. Coolstreaming is a typical example.

FURTHER READINGS

DNS

A number of RFCs have been proposed regarding DNS ever since its debut in 1987. Here we list some classic RFCs that pioneered the standardization. Albitz and Liu have also published a popular book on this. The BIND project homepage is also added for your own examination.

- P. Mockapetri, "Domain Names—Concept and Facilities," RFC 1034, Nov. 1987.
- P. Mockapetri, "Domain Names—Implementation and Specification," RFC1035 Nov. 1987.
- M. Crawford, "Binary Labels in the Domain Name System," RFC 2673, Aug. 1999.
- P. Albitz and C. Liu, *DNS and BIND,* 5th edition, O'Reilly, 2006.
- BIND: a DNS server by Internet Systems Consortium, available at https://www.isc.org/products/BIND/

MAIL

Below we list some of the latest batch of RFC updates on e-mail. It is obvious that the design of e-mail systems has never stopped evolving. The qmail project site is also given for your initial trial on building an e-mail system.

- J. Yao and W. Mao, "SMTP Extension for Internationalized E-mail Addresses," RFC 5336, Sept. 2008.
- J. Klensin, "Simple Mail Transfer Protocol," RFC 5321, October 2008.
- P. Resnick, "Internet Message Format," RFC 5322, October 2008.
- The qmail project, http://www.qmail.org/top.html.

WWW

Following are some classical works on WWW, including one of the pioneering articles on searching the Web and the RFC for HTTP 1.1, which updated HTTP 1.0 in 1999 and has been widely adopted ever since. Also read what Tim Berners-Lee said about the future architecture of the WWW.

- S. Lawrence and C. L. Giles, "Searching the World Wide Web," *Science*, Apr. 1998.
- R. Fielding et al., "Hypertext Transfer Protocol—http/1.1," RFC 2616, June 1999.
- World Wide Web Consortium (W3C), "Architecture of the World Wide Web, Volume One," W3C Recommendation, Dec. 2004.
- The Apache project, http://www.apache.org/

FTP

It seems that development of FTP is still progressing, though at a relatively slower pace. You might be curious about how the latest FTP extensions look. Check them out at RFC 3659.

- J. Postel and J. Reynolds, "File Transfer Protocol (FTP)," RFC 959, Oct. 1985.
- S. Bellovin, "Firewall-Friendly FTP," RFC 1579, Feb. 1994.
- M. Horowitz et al., "FTP Security Extensions," RFC 2228, Oct. 1997.
- P. Hethmon, "Extensions to FTP," RFC 3659, Mar. 2007.
- The wu-ftp project, available at http://www.wu-ftpd.org/

SNMP

The number of RFCs on SNMP would surprise you. Following are some important ones for your reference. But we suggest you buy a book before you get lost in the SNMP jungle.

- M. Rose and K. McCloghrie, "Structure and Identification of Management Information for TCP/IP-based Internets," RFC 1155, May 1990.
- J. Case et al., "A Simple Network Management Protocol (SNMP)," RFC 1157, May 1990.
- J. Case et al., "Textual Conventions for Version 2 of the Simple Network Management Protocol (SNMPv2)," RFC 1903, Jan. 1996.
- J. Case et al., "Protocol Operations for Version 2 of the Simple Network Management Protocol (SNMPv2)," RFC 1905, Jan. 1996.
- J. Case et al., "Management Information Base for Version 2 of the Simple Network Management Protocol (SNMPv2)," RFC 1907, Jan. 1996.
- J. Case et al., "Introduction to Version 3 of the Internet-Standard Network Management Framework," RFC 2570, Apr. 1999.
- D. Harrington, "An Architecture for Describing SNMP Management Frameworks," RFC 2571, Apr. 1999.
- The Net-SNMP project, available at http://www.net-snmp.org/.
- Douglas Mauro and Kevin Schmidt, *Essential SNMP,* 2nd edition, O'Reilly 2005.

VoIP

Here are the RFCs for the major building blocks of VoIP. RTCP is part of RFC 3550. Play around with Asterisk and immerse yourself in the VoIP world.

- M. Handley et al., "Session Announcement Protocol," RFC 2974, Oct. 2000.
- J. Rosenburg et al., "SIP: Session Initiation Protocol," RFC 3261, June 2002.
- H. Schulzrinne et al., "RTP: A Transport Protocol for Real-Time Applications," RFC 3550, July 2003.
- Asterisk, the Open-Source PBX and Telephony Platform, available at www.asterisk.org/

Streaming

Though the transport protocol for streaming applications may vary, from ordinary RTP to the proprietary RDT (Real Data Transport) from RealNetworks as an example, the control protocol is basically RTSP. Experience it with the Darwin and the Helix packages. Additionally, you do not want to miss the hottest RTMP protocol that empowers Flash video portals like YouTube.

- H. Schulzrinne et al., "Real Time Streaming Protocol (RTSP)," RFC 2326, Apr. 1998.
- M. Kaufmann, "QuickTime Toolkit Volume One: Basic Movie Playback and Media Types," Apple Computer, Inc., 2004.
- The Darwin Project, available at http://developer.apple.com/opensource/server/streaming/index.html
- The Helix Project, available at http://en.wikipedia.org/wiki/Helix_(project).
- The RTMP protocol specification, available at http://www.adobe.com/ devnet/rtmp/

P2P

Tired of the superficial P2P clients? The following research works surely will take you to the underground realm of the P2P kingdom.

- Q. Lv, P. Cao, E. Cohen, K. Li, and S. Shenker, "Search and Replication in Unstructured Peer-to-Peer Networks," in *Proceedings of ACM Supercomputing,* 2002.
- S. Androutsellis-Theotokis and D. Spinellis, "A Survey of Peer-to-Peer Content Distribution Technologies," *ACM Computing Surveys,* Vol. 36, No. 4, pp. 335–371, Dec. 2004.
- Daniel Hughes, Geoff Coulson, and James Walkerdine, "Free Riding on Gnutella Revisited: The Bell Tolls?," *IEEE Distributed Systems,* Vol. 6, No. 6, June 2005.
- Javed I. Khan and Adam Wierzbicki (eds.), "Foundation of Peer-to-Peer Computing," Special Issue, *Computer Communications,* Volume 31, Issue 2, Feb. 2008.

FREQUENTLY ASKED QUESTIONS

1. Why are protocol messages of most Internet applications ASCII and variable length?
   Answer:
   ASCII: easy to decode and flexible to extend
   Variable length: a wide range of parameter values and length
2. Why do servers running over TCP and UDP have concurrent and iterative implementations, respectively?
   Answer:
   Concurrent: if overlapped service times (usually long)
   Iterative: if non-overlapped service times (usually short)
   TCP: reliable connection-oriented services
   UDP: unreliable connectionless services
   The most common combinations are concurrent TCP (long and reliable) and iterative UDP (short and unreliable).
3. How do DNS servers resolve a domain name into an IP address?
   Answer:
   The local name server first checks its own cache. If this results in a miss, it queries one of the root name servers, which redirects the local name server to a second-level name server. The second-level name server redirects to a third-level name server, and so on, until a name server responds with an RR record (A record) for this domain name. This process is iterative, which is more common than recursive (all involved name servers needed to keep states during the query process).
4. How do DNS servers resolve an IP address into a domain name?
   Answer:
   Same as answer to Question 3 except PTR records, instead of A records, are looked up.
5. What resource records are used in forward-DNS and reverse-DNS, respectively?
   Answer:
   Forward-DNS: A records
   Reverse-DNS: PTR records
6. What entities and protocols are involved if you send an e-mail for your friend to read?
   Answer:
   SMTP: MUA (mail user agent) → MTA (mail transfer agent) of local mail server
   SMTP: MDA (mail delivery agent) of local mail server → MTA of remote mail server
   MDA → mailbox in remote mail server
   POP3 or IMAP4: MRA (mail retrieval agent) of remote mail server → MUA
7. POP3 vs. IMAP4? (Compare their number of commands, flexibility, and usage.)
   Answer:
   Number of commands: IMAP4 > POP3
   Flexibility: IMAP4 > POP3
   Usage: Web mail (IMAP4) vs. download (e.g., Outlook) (POP3)
8. What POP3 messages are exchanged when you download mail from the server?
   Answer:
   STAT, LIST, RETR, DELE, QUIT, +OK, -ERR, etc.
9. What HTTP messages are exchanged in downloading, filling, and uploading a Web form?
   Answer:
   GET, POST or PUT, HTTP/1.1 200 OK, etc.
10. What does connection persistence mean in HTTP 1.1?
    Answer:
    Multiple HTTP requests can be sent in a TCP connection.
11. Forward-caching vs. reverse-caching? (Compare their location and cache content.)
    Answer:
    Forward-caching: at the content consumer side (clients); heterogeneous from many sites
    Reverse-caching: at the content provider side (large Web site); homogeneous from this site
12. How does an HTTP proxy intercept HTTP requests destined for HTTP servers?
    Answer:
    It does a TCP three-way handshake with the client, accepts the HTTP request, handles the request (say caching, filtering, logging), and sends the HTTP response to the client if OK. If needed, it establishes a TCP connection with the HTTP server, forwards the HTTP request to the server, gets the response, handles the response (say filtering and logging), and sends the response back to the client.
13. What does an HTTP caching proxy do if it has a cache miss? How many TCP connections does it establish for a specific client?
    Answer:
    It establishes a TCP connection to the server and forwards the request to the server. The response is then passed back to the client. It has two TCP connections: one TCP connection with the client and another TCP connection with the server.

14. Active mode vs. passive mode in FTP? (Describe from whose perspective is the mode and how the data connection is established.)
    Answer:
    It's from the server's perspective.
    Active mode: The client issues "PORT IP-address port-number" through the control connection to the server. The server replies 200 and then connects to the client to establish the data connection.
    Passive mode: The client issues "PASV" through the control connection to the server. The server replies with the IP address and port number on which it would listen. The client then connects to the specified port to establish the data connection.
15. Control and data connections in FTP? (Explain why we need two connections.)
    Answer:
    This out-of-band signaling is to exchange control messages even when a long data transfer is ongoing.
16. What protocol messages on the control connection are exchanged in downloading and uploading a file in FTP, using active mode and passive mode, respectively?
    Answer:
    Active download: PORT, 200, RETR, 200
    Passive download: PASV, 200 IP-address port-number, RETR, 200
    Active upload: PORT, 200, STOR, 200
    Passive upload: PASV, 200 IP-address port-number, STOR, 200
17. Why is streaming quite robust to Internet delay, jitter, and loss?
    Answer:
    Many streaming sources exercise a scalable layered coding scheme, and they adjust their codec bit rate according to the measured network condition. Most streaming receivers have a jitter buffer to delay the playout time of audio/video to absorb the jitter and play out smoothly. Since the traffic is one-way without interaction, the increased delay is OK for users.

EXERCISES

Hands-On Exercises

1. Read first the "dig" manual of BIND9 (including the later versions), especially the "+trace" and "+recursive" options, and answer the following questions.
   a. A query generated by dig is by default a recursive query (so that a local name server continues the query on behalf of the client). Why is it used by dig (or resolver routines in other applications)? Also, issue a recursive query to www.ucla.edu, and explain each RR in all five sections of the reply.
   b. Describe each consulted name server in an iterative query for www.ucla.edu using dig.
2. Build an e-mail system on your Linux PC using qmail. The system should provide SMTP, POP3, and IMAP4 services. Write down your operations step by step. Please refer to the documents in http://www.qmail.org/.
3. Read the SMTP and POP3 commands. Then telnet to your SMTP server (port 25) and send a message to yourself. After that, telnet to your POP3 server (port 110) and retrieve the message. Record everything that happens in the sessions.
4. Build a Web server on your Linux PC using Apache. Modify the configuration file to set up two virtual hosts. In addition, write some HTML pages and put them in the document root directory of Apache. Write down your virtual host's setting and capture a browser screen showing your HTML files.
5. Telnet to your Web server (port 80) and get a document using HTTP 1.0. Observe the HTTP response headers. Record everything that happens in the session.
6. Build a caching proxy server on your Linux PC using Squid and configure your Web browser to use it. Browse your Web site several times and trace the log files of Apache and Squid to observe which server services the requests. Explain the contents of the log files.
7. Read the descriptions of HTTP request and response headers. Use Sniffer or similar software to observe the HTTP requests and responses generated in Exercise 6. Capture some screens and explain.
8. Install and run wu-ftpd or any other ftp server. Configure it to support both virtual ftp server and on-the-fly compression. Write down your operations step by step and your configuration files.
9. Install and run Net-SNMP. Use snmpbulkget to retrieve `tcpConnTable` in the local host. Write down your operations step by step and record your results.

10. Explore the locality by changing the random selection code in the `getNextOptimisticPeer()` function to consider the round-trip delay. For example, you may give preference to peers with lower round-trip delay. Discuss why it is important to consider locality in choosing optimistic unchoke peers. Note that optimistic unchoke plays an initiation role for finding potential tit-for-tat peers.

Written Exercises

1. Which port(s) and starting mode ((x)inetd or stand-alone) do the Internet applications covered in this chapter use? List your answers in a table.
2. What are the major differences between the interactive connectionless server and concurrent connection-oriented server when dealing with concurrent requests?
3. How many zones are in the nctu domain in Figure 6.4?
4. How many root name servers are there? Please list them.
5. What RRs may be used in the following situations? Explain each of them using an example.
   a. In the process of a forward query.
   b. In the process of a reverse query.
   c. Resolve the domain name B, which is an alias of domain name A.
   d. In mail forwarding.
6. When sending e-mail messages, we can put the recipients' e-mail addresses in the Cc: and Bcc: fields. What are the differences between the two fields?
7. Webmail is Web browser based and includes support for POP3 and IMAP4. Describe the differences between POP3-based Webmail and IMAP4-based Webmail.
8. Spam is flooding the Internet with many copies of the same e-mail message, in an attempt to force the message on people who would not otherwise choose to receive it. Propose some strategies for fighting spam.
9. What is the relationship among URI, URL, and URN? Write two examples for each scheme and explain their meanings.
10. What are the similarities and differences between HTML and XML?
11. What are HTTP 1.1 pipelining and persistent connection? What are their benefits?
12. Describe how HTTP and HTML redirect an HTTP connection to a different destination.
13. When does a caching proxy not cache an object?
14. What are the major differences between strong cache consistency and weak cache consistency? Which consistency scheme is suitable for a news site? Why?
15. Without setting up your browser to use a caching proxy manually, how do you force HTTP requests passing through a caching proxy?
16. Describe the processes of setting up an active and a passive connection for FTP, respectively (including the command and parameters used). Assume that the control connection has already been established on port 21.
17. Explain the reply codes in the example FTP session in Figure 6.34.
18. What is the relationship between ASN.1, SMI, and MIB?
19. How does a management station *efficiently* get the objects in the MIB tree in Figure 6.39 using GetNextRequest PDU? Please illustrate this. (Hint: multiple objects in variable-binding list.)
20. What applications does an agent have? How does an SNMP agent process a query request with its engine and applications?
21. Compare the pros and cons of voice transmission over IP and frame relay. Please compare them in terms of their performance and topologies/costs for deployment.
22. What is the relationship between SIP, SDP, and SAP?
23. What are the differences between H.323 and SIP? Explain it in terms of their components and functionalities.
24. What are the advantages and disadvantages between RTSP and HTTP streaming?
25. How is QoS control implemented in the streaming server as well as the client? What can a client do if the delay/jitter of the packets is high?
26. How do audio and video messages get synchronized in streaming?

7

Chapter

Internet QoS

The Internet has grown in a healthy manner for decades. Its healthiness has been greatly dependent on TCP, which exercises end-to-end congestion control to refrain from overloading the Internet. However, real-time applications such as streaming, VoIP, and parts of P2P running over UDP are not *TCP-friendly,* as discussed in Section 5.5. Some of them also demand a specific quality of service (QoS). A path that reserves enough bandwidth to guarantee QoS in terms of low or bounded delay, low loss rate, and low jitter is often necessary for these applications.

Unfortunately, it is hard for the current Internet to provide such a path because the Internet has been built on a freely competitive network architecture whose core is stateless, with complex control functions pushed to the end hosts. Thus, it is much easier to modify protocols at the end hosts than in the middle at the routers and switches. Most IP routers support the best-effort service only. Routers forward the arriving packets of any applications as fast as possible without caring whether or when end hosts could receive them. More specifically, the best-effort service means all packets arriving to a router are inserted into a queue until the queue overflows, while the router sends out packets from the queue in a sequential order at its maximal rate. When the network loading is light, the best-effort service is enough for most applications. The loading, however, depends on how fast the Internet bandwidth grows versus how fast new applications and users consume the Internet bandwidth.

What should we do to turn the Internet into a QoS-enabled network? The answer can be found by referring to the faded Asynchronous Transfer Mode (ATM) networking since it was capable of supporting QoS. Inspired by the QoS design in the ATM networks, researchers proposed a similar architecture, called *Integrated Services (IntServ),* to provide two end hosts a path with guaranteed bandwidth and delay. Similar to ATM, end hosts of a flow in IntServ have to negotiate with routers to establish a *flow* path and reserve the resources along the path before sending their data packets. Besides, for all routers on the reserved path, they have to know not only *where* a packet should be forwarded as they always do, but also *when* is the right time to send the packet to meet its QoS requirement. To achieve this objective, the single-queue architecture in a router is replaced by multiple *per-flow* queues where packets are no longer served in the first-in-first-out (FIFO) fashion. As a packet arrives at a router, it is dispatched to a dedicated queue and might be served sooner than another packet that arrived earlier but was dispatched to a low-priority queue.

Unfortunately, the *per-flow* handling of IntServ is simply *not scalable* in a large network like the global Internet or even a regional network belonging to a single service provider. Therefore, another architecture named *Differentiated Services (DiffServ)* was proposed. Instead of per-flow handling, the basic objective of DiffServ is to perform *per-class* handling to provide hosts with differentiated service *classes.* Hosts first negotiate with the service provider to identify their desired classes of service before using the network, while the service provider allocates the agreed-on amount of resources for the service classes. Then, each hop of the DiffServ network would treat packets with different *forward behaviors* according to their service classes. Since dynamic path establishment and on-demand resources reservation are not necessary in DiffServ, DiffServ indeed is simpler and more scalable than IntServ. Thus, it has a higher probability of being implemented on the Internet.

Aside from IntServ or DiffServ, what basic components are needed to provide a *total solution* to QoS at the control plane and the data plane? Section 7.1 answers this question in a general manner and provides a QoS framework. It also describes the traffic control (TC) modules of Linux systems as a *reference design* for the

Historical Evolution: The QoS Hype around 2000s

In the 1990s, the Internet became a phenomenon due to the introduction of WWW. The WWW not only boosted the number of Internet users, but also changed the content of the Internet from text to multimedia and from static to dynamic. Contents originally carried by TV and phone were transmitted over the Internet. These unexpected changes exhausted the bandwidth of the Internet and triggered the demand for *resource reservation.*

For this problem, due to the high cost of the Internet bandwidth at that time, researchers studied how to divide the traffic into different *classes* and then provide high-quality service to the paying users and best-effort service to the public, under the assumption that all traffic is physically carried over the same network. Meantime, other researchers sought to increase the link bandwidth at a low cost. Finally, because of breakthroughs in *optical* technology, the Internet bandwidth became cheap, abundant, and *overprovisioned.* Internet service providers simply invested more in building high-bandwidth optical links when more bandwidth was needed. Therefore, the number of published research papers on Internet QoS diminished after the early 2000s.

Now, have QoS issues and requirements disappeard from the Internet? No. Its playground has just moved from the wired to the *wireless* environment since wireless bandwidth is still scarce today, and also from networks to *servers* since servers become the bottleneck when the network bandwidth is large enough. In fact, it is easy to find QoS in new wireless standards, e.g., WiMAX. Nevertheless, the scope of QoS issues is now limited to *links* and *nodes,* instead of the global Internet.

QoS framework. Section 7.2 then goes into more detail about the preceding two QoS architectures, per-flow IntServ and per-class DiffServ, and makes a comparison to differentiate them.

Although no large-scale QoS-enabled IP network exists so far, most IP traffic control components have been provided in operating systems. In fact, some components are already used everywhere in routers, gateways, or servers, although a total solution to QoS is not deployed. Thus, it pays to study these components further. What alternative algorithms have been developed for them? This is answered in Section 7.3. Along with the algorithmic discussion of each component, the open source implementation of TC in Linux is presented to show the adopted algorithm in TC and how exactly it is implemented for a router.

7.1 GENERAL ISSUES

In order to provide QoS in the IP network, IP routers need to be equipped with many additional functions. First, a host needs to request resource reservation at the routers along the path to its destination, through a *signaling protocol.* The request might be routed through a path where the routers have a better chance to offer the requested resources, which is called *QoS routing* in contrast to ordinary routing without concern for resource availability. The routers along the path then do *admission control* to accept or decline the request. If a host's reservation request is accepted by all routers on the path, the routers reserve the resource and are ready to serve the flow from the host. The routers need to enforce the QoS provisioning by first *classifying* all incoming packets into per-flow or per-class queues, *policing* the queues to see if they consume more than the requested resources, and then *scheduling* these queues to make sure they get their nominal share of bandwidth. These data plane operations are called *classification, policing,* and *scheduling,* respectively.

In the most generic form, there could be six components in a QoS framework, as shown in Figure 7.1. In this section, we introduce their concepts and capabilities. From the discussion, you can see the difficulties in designing them. Discussions on algorithmic designs for each component are left to Section 7.3. At the end, we give an overview of the open source Traffic Control (TC) module in Linux.

Requirements for the QoS Network			
Control Plane	Signaling Protocol	QoS Routing	Admission Control
Data Plane	Classification	Policing	Scheduling

FIGURE 7.1 Six components for building a QoS-aware network element.

7.1.1 Signaling Protocol

A signaling protocol is a common language used to negotiate with a router for resource reservation. It is the first requirement in a QoS-enabled network because QoS is provided through cooperation between hosts and all routers in a network. Several signaling protocols are proposed for various purposes. Among them, the most famous is *Resource ReserVation Protocol* (RSVP), which is used by applications to reserve resources in the network. Another example is *Common Open Policy Service* (COPS) protocol, a simple query-response protocol used in the policy management system that is a part of the QoS management architecture. A new working group named Next Steps in Signaling (NSIS) was formed in IETF to investigate more flexible IP signaling architecture and protocols (see RFC 4080).

7.1.2 QoS Routing

If *routing* is regarded as static road signs guiding vehicles at the fork of the road, *QoS routing* could be viewed as an advanced road sign system that provides not only the distance to the destination but also the vehicles' expected arrival time at the destination through various alternative roads. It provides this based on the congestion condition of these alternative roads. In the current IP network, routers make decisions based on some basic information, such as selection of the smallest hop-count path based on the destination IP address, which is like the distance information on the road signs. However, a QoS router needs to consider also whether the bandwidth, delay, and loss ratio of the path meet the requested QoS. Since this information is much more dynamic than the hop-count, it is more difficult to collect and exchange it in a large network.

7.1.3 Admission Control

The QoS routing, like the advanced road sign system in the preceding example, can guide packets to the best path, but the chosen path later may still be congested. To prevent packets from suffering congestion, we need to further control the number and the type of allowed packets on the path. *Admission control* is responsible for this job. It is deployed at the entries of a network, or gateway routers, to decide whether to allow the packets of a flow into the network by comparing the amount of *required* resources with the amount of currently *available* resources. Such a comparison is difficult because the amounts of both resources *vary* with time. Figure 7.2 shows an example. A bandwidth request for 3 Mbps arrives at router A. Then, router A decides whether to accept the request based on its time-varying available bandwidth. The difficulty in router A's decision is how to correctly estimate the bandwidth usage to ensure there will be enough bandwidth to successfully transmit the admitted flow while keeping the bandwidth highly utilized.

7.1.4 Packet Classification

After a suitable path is negotiated, selected, and admitted through the signaling protocol, QoS routing, and admission control, respectively, data packets are on their

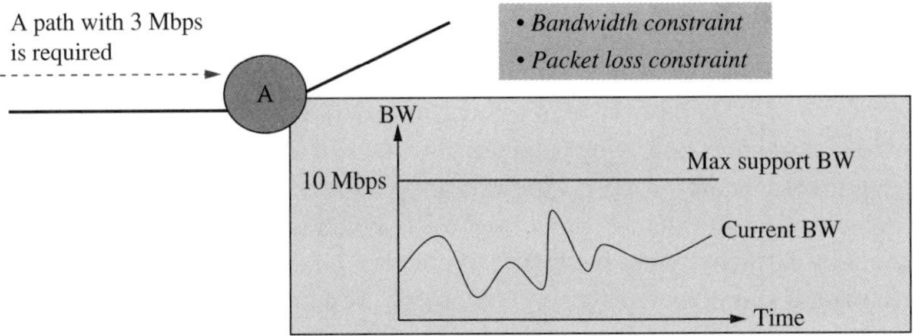

FIGURE 7.2 An operating example of admission control.

way now toward the destination. However, the network still needs a component to identify packets in order to enforce QoS. For example, we need to know which flow a packet belongs to in order to provide QoS accordingly. Since there are various rules to classify packets, it might cost several comparisons to classify one packet into a particular *flow* or *class.* While the job of packet classification is heavy, doing it *fast* in obedience to many classification rules is necessary. Thus, how to classify packets quickly becomes the major issue of the component.

In IntServ, the classification component is to identify which *flow* a packet belongs to according to the values of five fields in the packet header. In DiffServ, it performs range matching on multiple fields at the network edge and simple matching on single fields at the network core to classify packets into *classes* instead of flows.

7.1.5 Policing

There will always be some vehicles exceeding the speed limit on the road, which brings danger to other vehicle drivers. A similar scenario also happens in a network, so we need a *policing* component to monitor the traffic. If the arrival rate of a traffic source exceeds its allocated rate, the policing component needs to mark, drop, or delay some of its packets. However, in most cases the policing threshold is not an exact value, and a minor variation in the threshold value is tolerable. Therefore, source traffic is usually described by a traffic model, and policing is performed according to the traffic model. The most popular policing mechanism is called *token bucket,* which grants the policed traffic a limit on the *mean rate* while permitting it to send at a *maximum rate* during a time period of a *burst.*

7.1.6 Scheduling

Scheduling is the major component of QoS-enabled networks. Its general goal is to enforce resource sharing between different flows or classes subject to some predefined rules or ratios. There are various scheduling algorithms that have been proposed to achieve specific purposes. Some methods are simple, and some are complex and ingenious enough to provide an exact guarantee of fair sharing.

As illustrated in Figure 7.3, a *scheduler* should offer two basic external functions, *enqueue* and *dequeue,* to receive a new packet arrival and to decide the next packet to

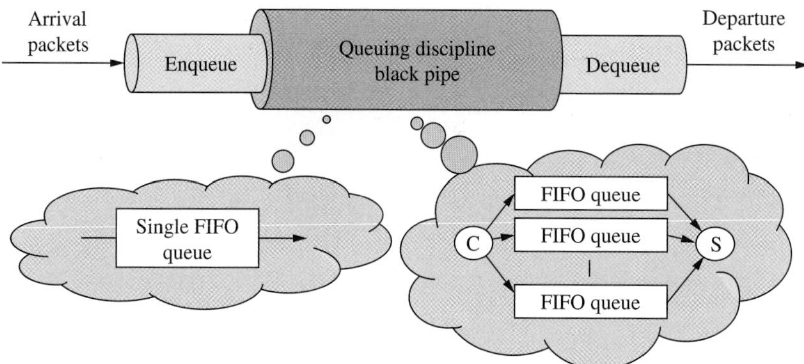

FIGURE 7.3 The concept and possible architectures of scheduling.

forward, respectively. Then, there should be an internal algorithm to schedule packets in the "scheduling black pipe," which can be divided into (1) buffer management within a queue and (2) resource sharing among multiple queues. Buffer management within a queue is also called *queuing discipline,* as we can see in the open source implementation of TC.

Open Source Implementation 7.1: Traffic Control Elements in Linux

Overview

The Linux kernel provides a wide variety of traffic control functions. One could use these functions to construct an IntServ router, a DiffServ router, or any other QoS-aware router. The relationship between TC and other router functions are given in Figure 7.4. Here TC is used to replace the role of `Output Queuing` in the original Linux kernel. It consists of the following three types of elements:

- filters
- queuing disciplines (`qdisc`)
- classes

Block Diagram

In Figure 7.4, the filters are responsible for classifying packets based on some particular rules or fields in the packet header. Their source-code files are named with the `cls_` prefix and put in the directory `/usr/src/linux/sched/`. For example, the file `cls_rsvp.c` implements flow identification required in an IntServ router.

The queuing disciplines support two basic functions, enqueue and dequeue. The former function decides whether to drop or queue the packets, while

Continued

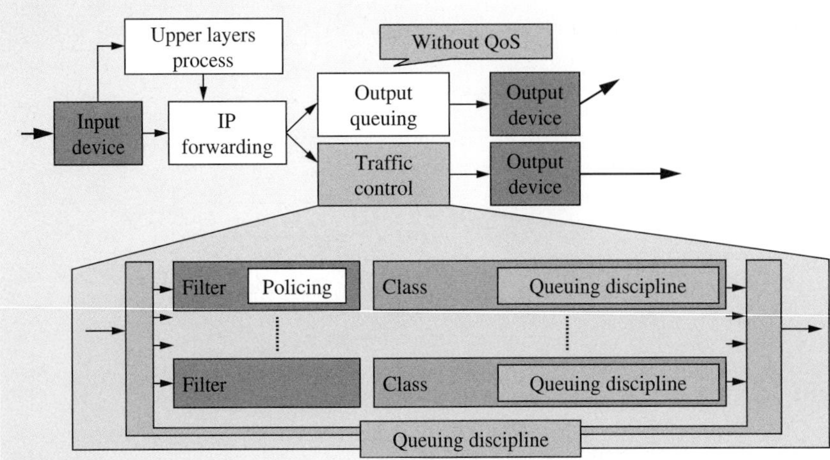

FIGURE 7.4 A simple combination of TC elements in Linux.

the latter function determines the transmitted order of the queued packets or simply delays the transmission of some queued packets. The simplest queuing discipline is FIFO, which queues the arriving packets until the queue is full and sends out the packets in the queue in the order in which they arrive. However, some queuing disciplines are more complex, such as CBQ implemented in `sch_cbq.c`, which queues packets into different classes, each subject to its own queuing discipline, like FIFO or RED. The source codes of queuing disciplines and classes are located in `/usr/src/linux/sched/` too, but their file names begin with `sch_`. As for the low level of the packet queuing structure, `sk_buff` is used to link packets whose structure has been described in Section 1.5.

Algorithm Implementations

The bottom half of Figure 7.4 shows a possible combination of the control elements mentioned above. There could be various combinations where a queuing discipline might consist of multiple classes and multiple filters might classify packets into the same class. TC users can design the structure of the traffic control elements at the data plane by the Perl script according to their needs.

Figure 7.5 further illustrates the flowchart of an even simpler combination in TC, where only one `qdisc` is deployed. When a packet arrives TC from the upper layer, the packet is inserted into the corresponding queue by `qdisc_enqueue()`. Then, if it is the right time to send out the packet, the timer will trigger `qdisk_wakeup()` to select and send out packets by `qdisk_dequeue()` and `hard_start_xmit()`, respectively. Once a packet is sent out, the `net_bh()` may also ask `qdisk_run_queues()` to activate the transmission of the next packet.

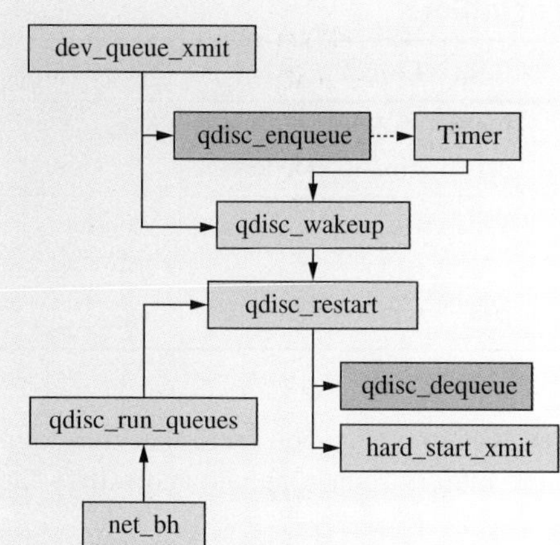

FIGURE 7.5 The flowchart of the qdisc element.

Exercises

Could you reconfigure your Linux kernel to install the TC modules and then figure out how to set up these modules? In the open source implementations in this chapter, we shall detail several TC elements related to the text. Thus, it is a good time to prepare yourself with this exercise. You can find useful references in the Further Readings section for this chapter.

7.2 QoS ARCHITECTURES

Herein we introduce two QoS architectures that were proposed to IETF in the 1990s and provide a guide to how to turn the Internet from a best-effort network into a QoS-enabled one. *Integrated Services (IntServ)* is a complete architecture, able to satisfy any QoS requirements raised from critical network applications. It can provide these applications with a virtual private path with bandwidth reservation and a guaranteed worst-case delay bound. This, however, would be an expensive solution. Thus, a simplified and more practical architecture was proposed: the *Differential Services (DiffServ)* architecture. As implied by its name, DiffServ aims to provide differential service for different levels of users, instead of service with bandwidth and delay guarantees. Unfortunately, even though DiffServ is more practical than IntServ, it is also not widely deployed in the global Internet yet. Many service providers, however, do provide priority services to, for example, VoIP applications, through service level agreements (SLAs) signed with their customers.

7.2.1 Integrated Services (IntServ)

This subsection describes the general operating process of IntServ. We first introduce three service types an application can get in an IntServ network. Then we

TABLE 7.1 Service Types Provided in IntServ

Service Types	Guaranteed	Control Load	Best Effort
Provided QoS	- Guaranteed bandwidth - End-to-end delay bound	Emulate a lightly loaded network for applications	None
Application examples	VoIP and video conference	Video streaming	Website browsing
RFC	RFC 2212	RFC 2211	None

talk about the reservation request, i.e., the signaling protocol, from the viewpoint of an application. Then we describe how the IntServ routers handle and satisfy the reservation request.

Service Types

Besides the best-effort service the current Internet provides for a flow, two additional service types are defined in the IntServ specifications: guaranteed service and control-load service, as listed in Table 7.1.

Once an application subscribes to the guaranteed service, it can deliver its traffic on a path with the guaranteed available bandwidth and end-to-end worst-case delay bound. The guarantee on the end-to-end worst-case delay bound means that for all packets transmitting on this path, the delay for any packet must be smaller than the required bound on the packet delay. Such a service would be subscribed to by interactive real-time applications, such as VoIP and video conferencing, since any additional packet delay could significantly affect the user perception and would hardly be tolerated by users.

The control-load service in IntServ provides the subscribed flow with a path where the packet transmission is likely going through a low-utilization link. That is, when the service is subscribed, the quality required by a flow will be satisfied most times. Although the control-load service is not as good as the guaranteed service, it is cheaper and suitable for some noninteractive real-time applications. For example, online movies can subscribe the control-load service to ensure that most packets can be received at the expected time, especially when the bandwidth provided by the free best-effort service is far below the codec rate. Then, before playing the video stream, the player program can buffer a period of media data to cover the period of quality degradation caused by possible short-term congestion during streaming. Since the users of the control-load service can tolerate such short-time quality degradation, the network resources can be shared by more users, and thus the control-load service would be cheaper than the guaranteed service.

The Trip of a Resource Reservation Request

After an application, such as an on-line movie player, decides which service type to subscribe to and how much bandwidth and how much delay are required by its flow, it needs to send a QoS request with the subscription information and the source traffic description to reserve the resources in the IntServ domain. The request will be

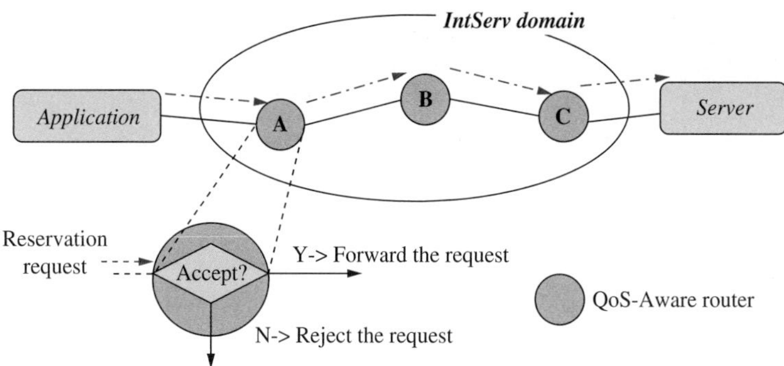

FIGURE 7.6 The RSVP process from the viewpoint of an application.

received by the nearest IntServ router, as shown in Figure 7.6. The router will decide whether to accept the request based on its status and, if it accepts, will then forward the request to the next router. After all routers on the path accept the request, the resource reservation process is finished, and the application can begin to receive packets with a guaranteed QoS. RSVP is the protocol for such a reservation communication in IntServ.

Request Handling by IntServ Routers

Once an RSVP request is received, the IntServ router passes it to the *signaling processing* component, which corresponds to the *signaling protocol* component shown in Figure 7.1. According to the result of its negotiation with the *admission control* component, the router would update the signaling packet and forward it to the next router. That is, the *signaling processing* component only plays as a "transcriber" to transcribe the decision made by the admission control component. In fact, admission control is the actual component in charge of resource management of the output link. The functions of admission control can be divided into two parts. One is to gather and maintain the current usage of the output link and the other is to decide whether the residual resources are enough to satisfy the requirement of the new request.

Besides the two aforementioned components, another one in the control plane of the IntServ router is *QoS routing*. Because IntServ employs admission control to manage bandwidth allocation, the QoS routing component is not emphasized here. However, it can be used to find a path that can provide the desired QoS guarantee. That is, the existence of QoS routing, though optional, is helpful in increasing the chance of successful resource reservation along the found path.

Request Enforcement in IntServ Routers

After the path is created successfully, data packets start being transmitted on it. The routers on the path should guarantee that the way the packets of the application are treated conforms to their subscribed service. Such promises are enforced by three basic components in the data plane of the router: *flow identifier or classifier, policer,* and *scheduler,* as illustrated in Figure 7.7. For data packets, the entrance of the

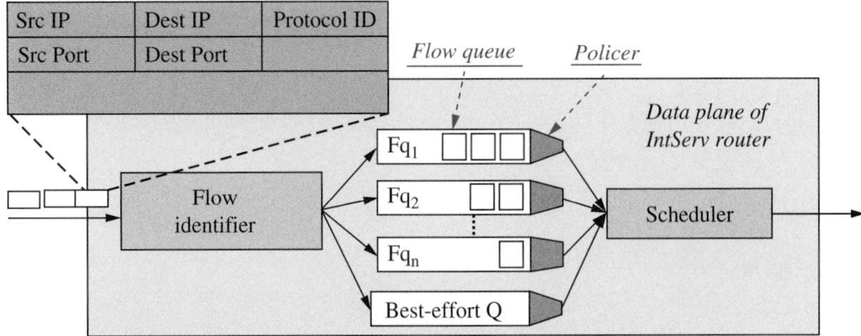

FIGURE 7.7 The data plane in an IntServ router.

router is the *flow identifier* component, which identifies whether a packet belongs to a reserved flow according to the five fields of the packet header (source IP address, destination IP address, source port number, destination port number, and protocol ID). Those packets belonging to a particular reserved flow are inserted into the corresponding flow queue. Basically, in the IntServ architecture, each reserved flow has an individual queue. Packets not belonging to any reserved flow are classified into the best-effort FIFO queue. Notably, it is necessary to reserve a portion of resources for the best-effort traffic to avoid starvation.

After a packet enters its corresponding flow queue, the next component to handle the packet is the *policer*. It monitors the incoming traffic of the flow to determine whether the traffic conforms to the behavior as claimed in its request for resource reservation. Those "out-of-profile" packets might be dropped or delayed until the traffic conforms to the claimed behavior. Next, the scheduler selects one packet from the head packets of the policed flow queues. The packet selected by the scheduler is sent to the output link. In most cases, the output link does not have to queue packets anymore because the output rate must be smaller than or equal to the physical link rate.

The role of the scheduler is important to IntServ because it is the key to providing the characteristics of flow isolation and the guaranteed service with a critical end-to-end delay bound. It aims to reduce the worst-case latency of a flow and provide fair treatment among all reserved flows. Notably, fair might not mean equal, and more explanation shall be given in Subsection 7.3.4.

7.2.2 Differentiated Services (DiffServ)

Although IntServ supplies an accurate QoS, the IntServ architecture is not scalable for an ISP to deploy. Besides, its enforcement mechanisms might consume too much computing resources, especially for core routers, which have to handle a huge number of flows. Its highly complex design would cause a bad utilization of network resources and a high deployment expense. Obviously, the Internet needs a simple, scalable, and manageable solution. The Differentiated Services (DiffServ) is designed for this goal. Figure 7.8 shows the basic element tree of DiffServ. The first level shows the necessary functions for DiffServ, while the following levels list the specific protocols or components to achieve these functions.

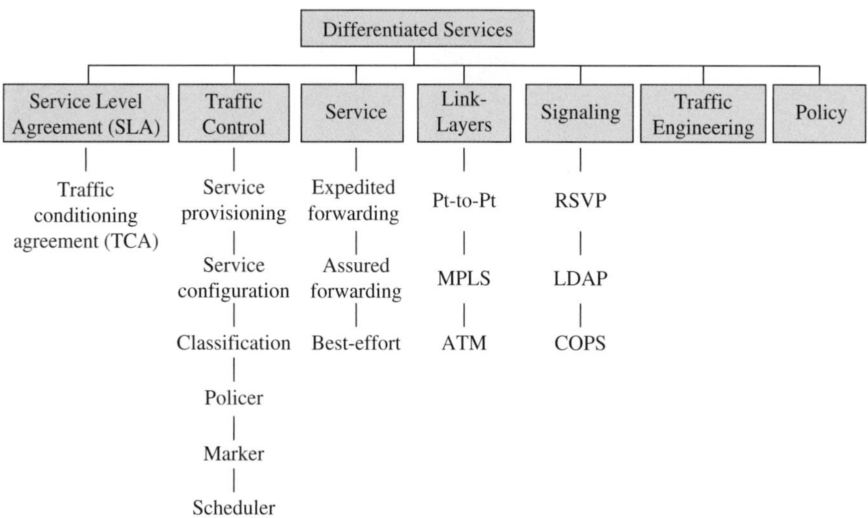

FIGURE 7.8 The basic element tree of DiffServ.

General Model

A DiffServ network consists of one or many DiffServ domains, and one DiffServ domain consists of several routers. There are two types of routers in a DiffServ domain, as plotted in Figure 7.9. A router at the boundary of a domain is called an *edge router*, be it *ingress* or *egress*, while that at the interior is called a *core router*. An ingress router is an entrance to a domain. It handles packets in two steps before forwarding them to core routers. The first step is to *identify* and *mark* packets based on some predefined policies. The mark on the packet affects the forwarding treatment received by the packet in the domain. The second step is to *police* and *shape* packets based on the traffic profile as negotiated between the customer and service provider before the beginning of the service. The second step assures that the traffic injected into the domain is within the service ability of the domain because no further

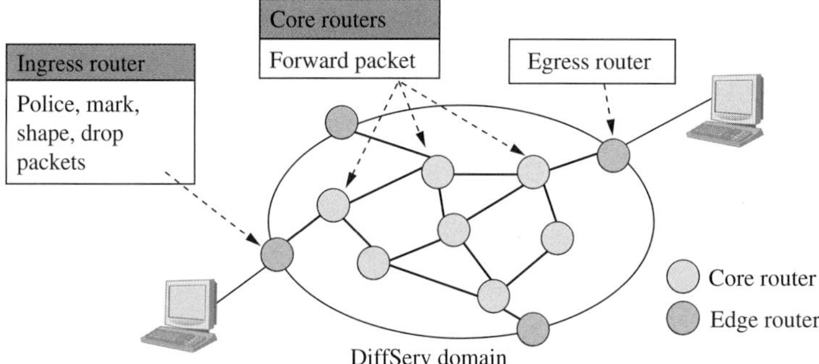

FIGURE 7.9 The architecture of a DiffServ domain.

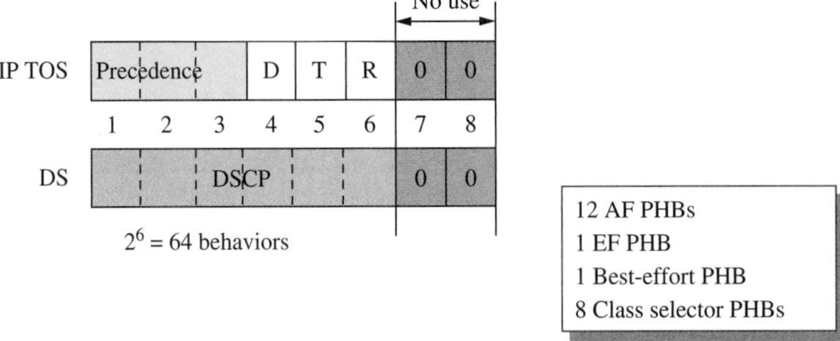

FIGURE 7.10 The DS field redefined from the TOS field of IPv4 header.

control shall be performed at the interior of the domain. The task of the core router simply is to forward packets with the particular behavior according to the mark on the packets. Packet remarking and traffic reshaping could be performed at the egress router according to the service agreement negotiated between the current domain and the next domain.

DS Field

The edge DiffServ router marks packets entering the DiffServ domain. The mark on a packet tells the core router how to treat the packet. Since DiffServ is directly built on the IP network without introducing additional layers, the mark must be saved in the IP header. Thus, DiffServ reclaims the 8-bit Type of Service (TOS) field in the IPv4 header to indicate forwarding behaviors. The replacement field is called the DiffServ (DS) field, and only six bits are used as a DS Code Point (DSCP) to encode the per-hop-behavior (PHB), as shown in Figure 7.10. The 6-bit DSCP field can represent 64 distinct values. These values are divided into three pools as shown in Table 7.2. The code points defined in pool 1 correspond to the major standard PHBs. The code points in the other two pools are reserved for experimental and local uses.

Per-Hop Forward Behaviors

Here we introduce four groups of forwarding behaviors and their corresponding recommended code points defined in the standard. The first two groups, Default PHB and Class Selector PHB, provide a limited backward compatibility since the DS field is redefined from the original IP TOS field. The other two PHB groups, *Assured*

TABLE 7.2 Allocated Space of Code Points

Pool	Code Point Space	Assignment Policy
1	xxxxx0	Standard action
2	xxxx11	Experimental and local use
3	xxxx01	Similar to above but may be subject to standard action

Forwarding (AF) PHBs and *Expedited Forwarding* (EF) PHB, are standardized by the IETF to provide DiffServ.

Default PHB Group

For most packets in the IP network, the TOS field is useless and its value is set to zero. In order to let these DiffServ-unaware packets pass through the DiffServ network, DiffServ defines the default DSCP value as 000000, simply equal to the value of the TOS field in most DiffServ-unaware packets. For these packets, DiffServ inserts them into the best-effort queue and reserves a minimal bandwidth for them.

Class Selector PHB Group

Though the TOS field is not used in most cases, some vendors actually use the first three bits of the TOS field to identify some IP functionalities. To allow these IP functionalities to coexist with the DiffServ implementations, a DSCP field that contains xxx000 is mapped to a group of PHBs that forward packets with different priorities. The packet with a large DSCP is expected to be forwarded with a higher priority than one with a small DSCP value.

AF PHB Group

The PHB of the AF group guarantees to forward every packet of a traffic source if these arriving packets conform to the traffic profile of their source; the profile is called the traffic conditioning agreement (TCA). Then, for the packets exceeding its TCA, the AF PHB forwards them if possible.

There are four forwarding classes in the AF PHB group, and each class is allocated a certain amount of bandwidth and buffer space. For each class, traffics are divided into three levels of drop precedence. That is, there are a total of 12 individual PHBs in the AF group. As soon as the buffer of a class is nearly full, which implies the amount of the arriving traffic exceeds the allocated bandwidth of the class, the packet with a high drop precedence level would be discarded with a higher probability than the packet with a low drop level.

In order to avoid congestion in a class, the amount of traffic arriving to the class needs to be controlled. Moreover, because the class of a packet is not changed in the same DiffServ domain, the edge router needs to admit, shape, and even drop packets to keep the DiffServ domain from being overloaded. As mentioned earlier, DiffServ relies on the provision and monitoring at the edge routers to provide QoS.

In fact, to detect whether the congestion happens is an interesting research issue. There are many algorithms about buffer management proposed to detect the congestion and reduce its side effects in advance, such as random early detection (RED) proposed by S. Floyd and V. Jacobson in 1993. We shall look at these buffer management algorithms in Subsection 7.3.5.

EF PHB Group

The EF PHB is supposed to provide a performance similar to the traditional point-to-point leased-line service, forwarding packets with low loss, low latency, and low jitter. To offer these three characteristics, the core router in DiffServ must be able to

TABLE 7.3 AF PHB and EF PHB, and Their Relative Features

PHB Group	AF (Assured Forwarding)					EF (Expedited Forwarding)	Best-Effort
Features	Olympic service (an example) four delay priority classes, each with three drop precedence subclasses					Premium/virtual leased line service	none
Recommended DSCP in DS-field		AF1	AF2	AF3	AF4	101110	000000
	Low	010000	011000	100000	101000		
	Middle	010010	011010	100010	101010		
	High	010100	011100	100100	101100		
Traffic control	Static SLA policing, classification, marking, RIO/WRED scheduling					Dynamic SLA policing, classification, marking, priority/WFQ scheduling	FIFO scheduling
Nonconforming traffic	Re-mark as best-effort					Drop	Forward

reserve bandwidth at any time at least an amount enough to transmit the EF traffic at the rate specified in the source's traffic profile.

In the core router, EF traffic can preempt other traffic types to get the guarantee on their three "low" characteristics. The simplest way to implement such a guarantee in a core router is to classify different types of traffic into individual queues, and then always forward packets from the queue of the EF traffic until the queue becomes empty. However, to avoid starving other traffics or forwarding the EF traffic itself in burst, a strict constraint on the rate of sending the EF traffic into the network is necessary. Usually, a shaper implemented by a token bucket would be deployed at the edge router to meet such a constraint. Then, all out-of-profile nonconforming traffic would be forwarded with the default PHB or simply be discarded at the edge router.

Compared to the AF PHB, the EF PHB has a higher quality of service and a lower burst tolerance. Obviously, the EF PHB is a good choice for traffic with a constant bit rate and high quality requirement. On the other hand, the AF PHB is more suitable for traffics that are bursty but tolerant of packet loss. Their relative features are listed in Table 7.3.

A Packet's Life in a DiffServ Domain

A packet's life in a DiffServ domain can be divided into three stages: ingress, interior, and egress. The first and the third stages are handled by edge routers, while the second is handled by core routers. Here we detail each stage by describing the operations in the corresponding routers.

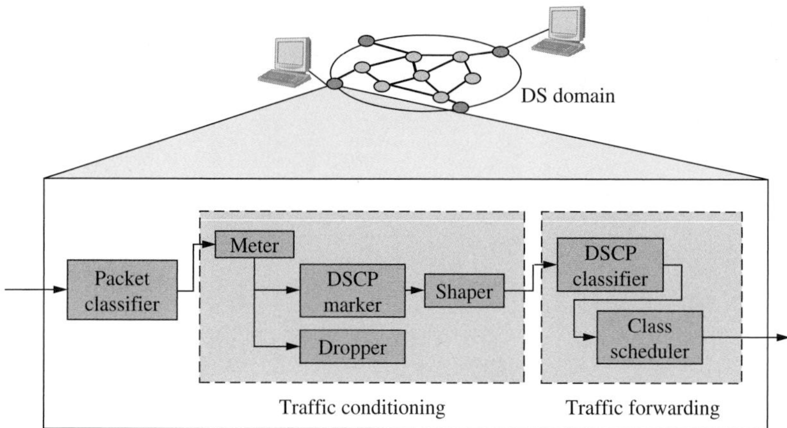

FIGURE 7.11 The ingress stage of a packet in the edge router.

Ingress Stage

As illustrated in Figure 7.11, in the ingress stage, each packet passes through three blocks: traffic classification, traffic conditioning, and traffic forwarding. In the first block, the classifier identifies the arrival traffic based on the predefined policies, and tells the components that follow which traffic profile they should take to manage the behavior of the traffic. The classified packets are then passed to the second block, traffic conditioning.

In the second block, according to the definition in the traffic profile, the meter measures the traffic and categorizes the packets as either *in-profile* or *out-of-profile.* For the in-profile packets, the marker gives them the suitable code point to let them successfully pass through the domain. For the out-of-profile packets, they might be dropped or marked with a code point corresponding to the forward behavior with a high drop probability. Alternatively, they are just passed into the shaper as the in-profile packets. However, unlike the in-profile packets, which pass through the shaper almost without any delay, the out-of-profile packets would be *delayed* until they conformed to their traffic profile.

In the traffic forwarding block, the marked packets would be inserted into the corresponding class queues. The implementation of the DSCP classifier is far simpler than the packet classifier mentioned in the first block, which simply looks at the DS field of the packet marked in the traffic conditioning block and then dispatches it to the corresponding class queue. Meanwhile, the class scheduler forwards the packets from each class queue at a particular forwarding rate that is configured according to the volume of admitted traffic.

Interior Stage

Unlike the ingress stage, which has multiple processing blocks, the interior stage has only one block, as shown in Figure 7.12. The simple architecture of the interior stage reduces the implementation cost of core routers and increases the forwarding speed. The core router is only responsible for triggering per-hop behaviors based on

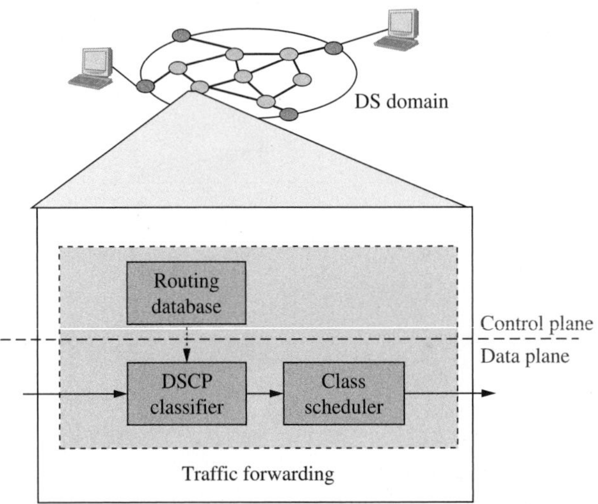

FIGURE 7.12 The interior stage of a packet in the core router.

the DSCP of the packets, which is similar to the operation of the third block of the ingress stage.

Egress Router

Compared to the ingress router in charge of the normal operation of a DS domain, the egress router only has to collect some statistics on the packets leaving the domain. The statistics may include the actual throughput and delay perceived by users when their packets pass through the DS domain. These statistics are useful to verify whether the agreed levels of QoS are satisfied.

Comparison with IntServ

Compared with IntServ, the implementation of the DiffServ architecture is simpler but rough. First, DiffServ does not provide the on-demand reservation of resources offered by IntServ. Under DiffServ, the users have to sign a contract with the service provider statically or dynamically to define how much traffic will be injected into the network or what kind of QoS behavior is desired. Then, based on the contract, the service providers can build a network with enough resources to meet the user requirements. Second, the arrival traffic in DiffServ is divided into groups, called *forwarding classes.* Since the number of groups is limited, the traffic from multiple users might be aggregated into one class, hence one queue, implying that the transmission quality perceived by a user might be affected by other users of the same class. Thirdly, the five-tuple packet classification is handled at the boundary of the DiffServ domain. That is, only the edge routers need to classify and mark packets. The core routers forward the packets with different behaviors simply based on the mark on the packet header.

Table 7.4 shows the major differences between the architectures of DiffServ and IntServ. The design of DiffServ avoids the difficulty of classifying and scheduling a huge number of packets in core routers, which in fact is the major problem in IntServ.

TABLE 7.4 Differences between DiffServ and IntServ

Compared Items	DiffServ	IntServ
Manageable unit	Class	Flow
Router capability	Edge and core	All-in-one
Defined in the standard	Forwarding behavior	Service type
Guarantee required	Provisioning	Reservation
Work region	Domain	End-to-end

Principle in Action: Why Both DiffServ and IntServ Failed

Though DiffServ is more scalable than IntServ, it still failed to become widely deployed. One would argue that the bandwidth *over-provisioning* that resulted from advances in optical technology and investment in high-speed links has eliminated the need to exercise complicated QoS architecture and mechanisms to make the Internet QoS-enabled. Another argument is that both IntServ and DiffServ would turn the stateless IP network to *stateful* and *semi-stateful,* respectively. For IntServ, *all* routers would become stateful to keep track of all reservation states. For DiffServ, at least all *edge* routers would have to keep those states to classify and mark packets.

These of course violate the original design philosophy of the Internet, though whether this statelessness property of the Internet should be kept is a debatable issue. Multi-Protocol Label Switching (MPLS) in a sense breaks that statelessness in a *local* domain by allowing stateful but *faster switching* to substitute stateless but slower routing. MPLS succeeds in scaling to some extent. Scaling MPLS to the *global* Internet, however, would face the same problem both IntServ and DiffServ encounter. Nevertheless, QoS is an end-to-end issue spanning multiple domains or service providers, but MPLS can improve the performance in just a domain without resorting to an end-to-end solution.

Principle in Action: QoS in Wireless Links

Although QoS architectures DiffServ and IntServ failed to be deployed in the Internet, we can find the QoS-related specifications in the recent wireless standards, such as IEEE 802.11e and 802.16. QoS still gets much attention in wireless networks because the wireless networks today have *not* provided sufficient bandwidth for users. Thus, QoS-related mechanisms and algorithms are required to ensure the transmission quality of real-time traffic when this traffic is mixed with other background traffic.

For users in WLAN, IEEE 802.11e defines two access modes, Enhanced Distributed Channel Access (EDCA) and Hybrid coordination function

Continued

Controlled Channel Access (HCCA), in the MAC layer to satisfy the requirement of QoS. EDCA provides high-*priority* traffic a higher chance of being sent than low-priority traffic. The former traffic in EDCA would be sent after a *shorter* waiting time and for a *longer* time interval, named Transmit Opportunity (TXOP), than the latter traffic. On the other hand, HCCA is a *polling-based* mode just like PCF, an access mode defined in IEEE 802.11, where an access point actively schedules the order and frequency of stations to be polled and thus determines the QoS received by each station. The key difference is that a polled station in PCF sends only *one* packet in one polling round, but the station in HCCA is free to send packets during the given TXOP of the polling round. Thus, HCCA has lower overhead for each packet transmission than PCF.

For users in WMAN, IEEE 802.16 introduces four classes of services: UGS Unsolicited Grant Service (UGS), real-time Polling Service (rtPS), non-real-time Polling Service (nrtPS), and Best Effort (BE). UGS is supposed to emulate a T1/E1 link to *periodically* transmit fixed-length packets, while rtPS and nrtPS guarantee a *minimum* throughput for real-time and non-real-time traffic of variable-length packets, respectively. By contrast with 802.11e, which is based on CSMA/CA, 802.16 uses TDMA to manage the wireless media. A base station (BS) in 802.16 has to schedule the media for each subscriber station, which thus is a *central control* mode naturally and a convenient architecture for the deployment of QoS.

7.3 ALGORITHMS FOR QoS COMPONENTS

After presenting the architectures of QoS-enabled IP networks, we then focus on the techniques for constructing the components of a QoS-enabled network, which have more research issues than the architecture. There are many algorithms related to these QoS components. We first describe the algorithms for admission control and flow identification. Then we introduce shaping and policing mechanisms, such as token bucket and its variations. Next, the scheduling algorithms are described, which are usually more complicated than other components. Finally, we discuss several packet discard mechanisms, which can be deployed at core routers or the current Internet routers to alleviate the congestion problem due to bursty traffic. Five open source implementations of TC are picked to illustrate the implementations of classical QoS-related algorithms.

7.3.1 Admission Control

After an application sends a QoS request to a router to establish a flow, the admission control component needs to decide whether to accept the new flow passing through the router. The admission of a new flow is based on the current resource usage of the output link and the requirement described in the request. A good admission control design should admit as many requests as possible to exhaust the resources of the router while ensuring that the QoS requirements of all admitted flows are satisfied. The approaches can be classified into two types: statistics-based and measurement-based.

Statistics-Based Control

For statistics-based admission control, a traffic source should describe its behavior, e.g., mean rate or peak rate, in the request, and the router should simply calculate an accumulated traffic function to estimate the total usage of resources and decide whether to accept the flow. However, it is hard to define the accumulated traffic function under the trade-off between bandwidth utilization and loss probability.

For example, we can describe the traffic source by two parameters, peak rate and average rate, and assume it conforms to an on-off model, which means the source either transmits at its peak rate or is idle. Then, the accumulated traffic function could simply be the summation of the *peak* rate of all flows. If the calculated result is under the maximum constraint after adding the peak rate asked by the new request, the request is accepted. Otherwise, it is rejected. Such a function guarantees the bandwidth allocation for the traffic without any packet loss, but results in low bandwidth utilization. What happens if we use the summation of *average* rate as the accumulated traffic function? Then, although the link will have a higher utilization, the accepted flows might suffer congestion and experience packet losses frequently.

For such a trade-off, the term *equivalent capacity* was introduced in 1991 and was commonly used in the literature of admission control. Equivalent capacity represents the minimum bandwidth required by a set of multiplexed flows over a link with a *bound* on the probability of encountering *queue overflow.* Thus, when given the overflow probability and the statistical characteristics of the flows, one can calculate the equivalent capacity and design a mechanism to admit new flows when the required total mean bandwidth of admitted flows is smaller than the equivalent capacity, while guaranteeing the packet losses encountered by the admitted flows will be lower than the given threshold.

Measurement-Based Control

Since it is hard to have a suitable accumulated traffic function, some researchers suggest measuring the current bandwidth usage directly. In order to obtain a representative measured value and avoid a sudden burst value, one could calculate the new usage estimation with exponentially weighted moving-average (EWMA); that is, averaging the new measurement with the last estimation by

$$Estimation_{new} = (1 - w) \times Estimation_{old} + w \times Measured_{new},$$

where w is the weight ratio of the new measurement. Large w makes the history expire quickly, which means that the algorithm is more aggressive and the resources have a higher probability of being highly utilized, but the flows might not get their desired treatment as described in their QoS requirement. For example, the admission control might accept a request if the current estimation is right below some maximum constraint, but it is possible that the estimation turns to the high value next time. Then, the acceptance might cause the resources to become overloaded and to affect the treatment of all accepted flows, including the new one.

The other measurement approach is time window. The estimation is drawn from several consecutive measurement intervals, as calculated by

$$Estimation = f(C_1, C_2, C_3, \ldots, C_n),$$

where C_i is the average rate measured on a sample interval and f could be a maximum function. Again, when a smaller n is given, the estimated bandwidth usage is usually lower and thus has more room to accept new flows, and high utilization thus may be achieved. On the other hand, when a larger n is given, the algorithm becomes conservative in estimating the bandwidth usage, hence accepting fewer new flows. Then flows can receive better treatment in most cases, but at the cost of low resource utilization.

Open Source Implementation 7.2: Traffic Estimator

Overview

TC provides a simple module to estimate the current transmission rate in bytes and in packets. You can find the module in the file net/core/gen_estimator.c. As mentioned, there are two approaches to measuring the transmission rate: EWMA and time window. Since EWMA takes less memory than the time window approach and is easier to implement, Linux uses EWMA to implement its traffic estimator.

Data Structures

The data structure used to keep the measured results of a flow is called `gen_estimator`, as shown below.

```
struct gen_estimator
{
   struct list_head          list;
   struct gnet_stats_basic   *bstats;
   struct gnet_stats_rate_est *rate_est;
   spinlock_t               *stats_lock;
   int                      ewma_log;
   u64                      last_bytes;
   u64                      avbps;
   u32                      last_packets;
   u32                      avpps;
   struct rcu_head           e_rcu;
   struct rb_node            node;
};
```

Because the rate estimator provides rate estimation in bytes and in packets, you can find paired names of variables in the estimator, e.g., `last_bytes/last_packets` and `avbps/avpps`, whose usages are explained later. In fact, even the substructure `rate_est` as well as `bstats` also consists of two variables: one for the estimation in bytes and the other in packets. The `rate_est` saves the rate-estimation results while `bstats` records the amount of data counted by the estimator so far.

```
1: struct gen_estimator *e;
...
2: nbytes = e->bstat->bytes;
3: npackets = e->bstat->packets;

4: brate = (nbytes - e->last_bytes)<<(7 - idx);
5: e->last_bytes = nbytes;
6: e->avbps += ((s64)brate - e->avbps) >> e->ewma_log;
7: e->rate_est->bps = (e->avbps+0xF)>>5;

8: rate = (npackets - e->last_packets)<<(12 - idx);
9: e->last_packets = npackets;
10: e->avpps += ((long)rate - (long)e->avpps) >> e->ewma_log;
11: e->rate_est->pps = (e->avpps+0x1FF)>>10;
```

FIGURE 7.13 A code segment in the function `est _ timer()` of `estimator.c`.

Algorithm Implementations

The traffic estimator includes three major functions. Function `gen_new_estimator()` handles the creation of a new estimator and function `gen_kill_estimator()` deletes the idle estimator. Function `est_timer()` is invoked by the Linux kernel once the setting time is up where the time interval is set to (1 << `interval`), i.e., 2^{interval}, seconds. In `est_timer()`, a sending rate is calculated and EWMA is implemented by the code listed in Figure 7.13.

For the paired names of variables, you can find the paired codes in Figure 7.13 (lines 4 through 7 versus lines 8 through 11). The code is performed for a flow every $2^{(\text{idx}-2)}$ seconds. Each flow can have its desired idx, which is set in `gen_new_estimator()`. Also, to avoid floating-point computing, the values in `avbps` and `avpps` are scaled by 2^5 and 2^{10}, respectively, compared to their actual values. Next, to estimate the rate in bytes, as written in line 4, the estimator first gets the amount of data counted during the 2^{idx} seconds by subtracting `e->last_bytes` from `e->bstat->bytes`.

Then, in order to get the mean rate `avbps` during the past $2^{(\text{idx}-2)}$ seconds, the difference is supposed to be divided by $2^{(\text{idx}-2)}$, i.e., right shifting it by (idx–2) bits. However, to have the 5-bit binary fraction as `avbps` does, the operation in line 4 is a left shift by (7–`idx`) bits, that is, >> (`idx`–2) << 5. Then, after getting the new mean rate, Line 6 performs the EWMA operation to get the smooth rate estimation in bytes, and finally saves the estimated rate in `rate_est->bps`. Similarly, we can get the smooth rate estimation in packets by running lines 8 through 11.

Exercises

1. Explain how line 6 or 10 performs the EWMA operation. What is the value of the historical parameter w used in the EWMA equation?
2. Read `gen_estimator.c` to find out how the `gen_estimator` of all flows are grouped. Do you know why the parameter `idx` is counted from 2?

7.3.2 Flow Identification

In IntServ, since individual resources are reserved for each flow, *flow identification* or *classification* is necessary to decide which flow a packet belongs to. Besides, it is necessary to have a table with per-flow entries to store the flow identifier and QoS parameters. The flow identifier in IntServ is composed of five header fields of a packet, which are the source IP address and port, destination IP address and port, and protocol ID as mentioned in Subsection 7.2.1. The length of the identifier is 32 + 16 + 32 + 16 + 8 = 104 bits, which takes 13 bytes. We need an effective data structure to store the table and execute flow identification.

Identification or classification is a classical data search problem. Many data structures are capable of storing the flow table, but there is a trade-off between time and space. A simple data structure is the binary tree; its space requirement is small, but multiple memory access operations are necessary to identify a packet. The other extreme is direct memory mapping, but it does not meet the space requirement. To balance between the time and space requirements, using a hash structure is a common and popular approach. However, if we further study the hash structure, we can find there are many uncertain reasons that affect the performance of flow identification in the hash table, e.g., hash function and collision resolution.

Open Source Implementation 7.3: Flow Identification

Overview

There are many algorithms and data structures proposed to implement flow identification. Their common issue is how to classify packets within the shortest time while using the smallest memory space. As you proceed, a *double-level hash* structure is used in the TC of Linux. Obviously, compared with direct memory mapping and tree structure, the hash structure has a better trade-off between time and space. You can find the structure and code in `net/sched/cls_rsvp.h`.

Data Structures

According to the definition of IntServ, a flow is identified by five fields. A double-level hash structure is illustrated in Figure 7.14. The first-level hash is keyed by the *destination* IP address, port number, and protocol ID. Its hash result indicates which list of RSVP sessions the packet belongs to. Based on the definition in the RFC of RSVP, an RSVP session represents a unidirectional flow and is identified by the combination of the destination IP address, destination port number, and protocol ID. Next, by using the second-level hash with the source IP address and source port number as the hash key, we can further identify which flow the packet belongs to.

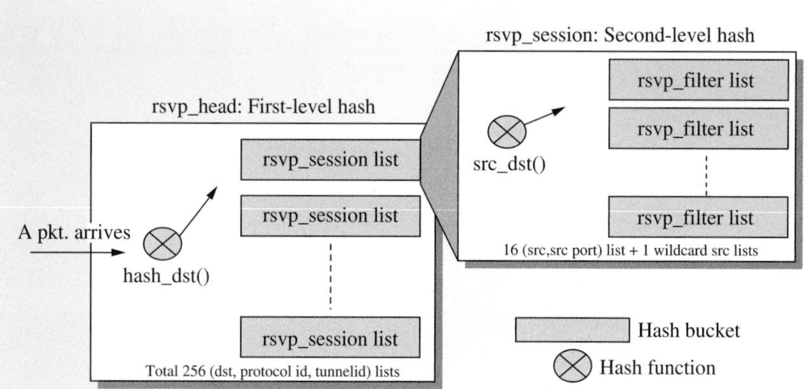

FIGURE 7.14 The double-level hash structure in `CLS _ RSVP.C`.

Algorithm Implementations

The major function to support flow identification is `rsvp_classify()`, and its flowchart is in the left part of Figure 7.15. The right part of Figure 7.15 shows the flowchart of the function `rsvp_change()`, which adds a new flow identification filter or modifies the existing one. Both flowcharts are easy to follow and are self-explanatory.

Exercises

1. Is there any reason that the destination IP address and port number are used in hashing before the source IP address and port number?
2. Could you find what hash function is used for the identification by reading the code in `net/sched/cls_rsvp.h`?

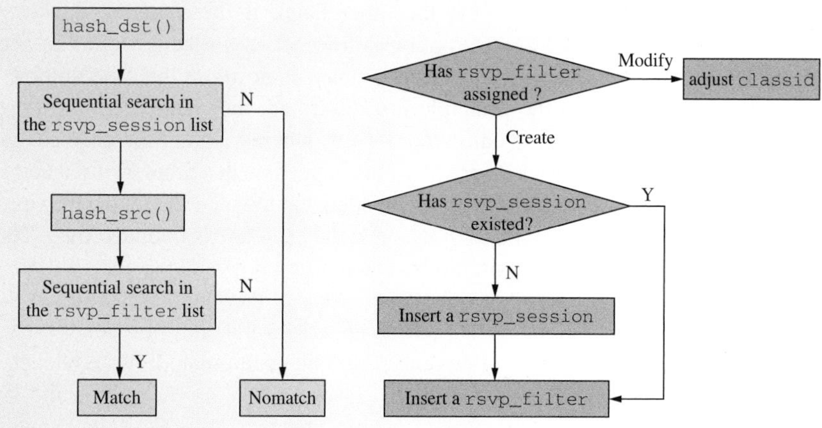

FIGURE 7.15 The flowchart of two functions in `CLS_RSVP.c`.

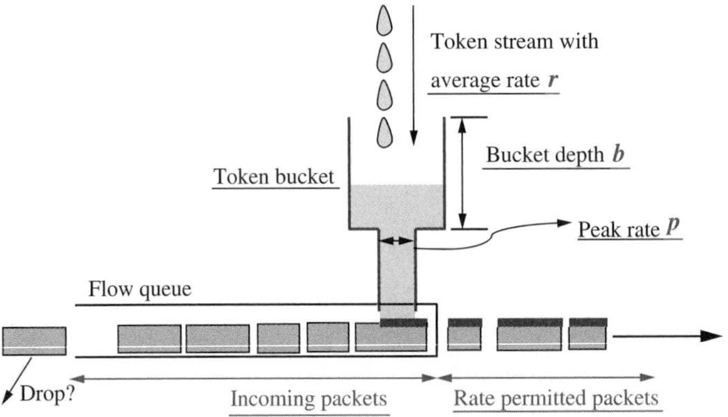

FIGURE 7.16 The operation architecture of a leaky bucket.

7.3.3 Token Bucket

A token bucket mechanism can *police* a flow's arrival rate and *bound* the rate in a region. In DiffServ, it can be deployed at an edge router to regulate the arrival rate of a flow to ensure that the rate conforms to that in the contract the with the ISP. As illustrated in Figure 7.16, the mechanism consists of a *token bucket* and a *token stream.*

The stream fills the bucket with tokens at a *fixed* rate r while the bucket can accumulate tokens up to a maximum volume b, which is the bucket depth. The basic principle is that a certain number of tokens are needed to permit a packet to pass through. The amount of tokens required for passing a packet is the same as the packet's length in bytes. As packets are permitted to leave the queue, tokens begin to *leak* from the bucket until the bucket is empty. Then, when the bucket is empty, packets are blocked in the queue, and newly arriving packets are even dropped when the queue is full. On the other hand, if there are no packets in the queue or the rate of token consumption is lower than r, tokens would be accumulated in the bucket, but the accumulated amount is no more than the volume of the bucket, b. According to the principle just described, the *maximum burst length* permitted by the token bucket is equal to $r \times t + b$, where t is the time elapsed since the beginning of a burst of packet arrivals. This happens when a burst of packets arrive to an empty queue with the bucket fully loaded. On the other hand, the maximum burst length can also be expressed as $p \times t$ since the peak rate is bounded by p. Thus, we get the time period of the maximum burst length $t = b/(p - r)$.

Figure 7.17 shows a possible operating case of token bucket during 24 seconds. Assume that $r = 1$ unit/s, $p = 2$ units/s, $b = 15$ units, and no packet arrivals for the first 10 seconds. That is, 10 tokens would be accumulated in the bucket, as shown in Figure 7.17(a). Then, suppose that three packets arrive right at the 10th second, with length equal to 10, 9, and 5 units, respectively. Next, as shown in Figure 7.17(b), because the peak rate $p = 2$, the first packet is released at $t = 15$s, even though there are 10 units of tokens, enough to release the packet, in the bucket at $t = 10$ s. After the first packet is released, 5 units of tokens accumulated during

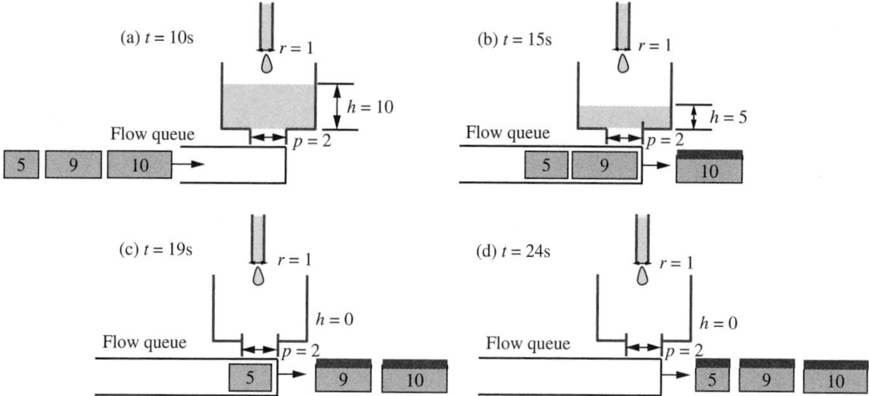

FIGURE 7.17 An operating case of leaky bucket.

seconds 10 through 15 are left in the bucket. By adding another 4 units of tokens during seconds 15 through 19, the second packet can be released at 19 s, as seen in Figure 7.17(c). Finally, since there are no tokens left in the bucket at t = 19 s, the last packet has to wait for another 5 seconds to get enough tokens to be released, as seen in Figure 7.17(d).

Open Source Implementation 7.4: Token Bucket

Overview

The idea of the token bucket mechanism is simple, but a straightforward implementation might impose a heavy load to the kernel. In a naïve implementation, the mechanism is supposed to have a token generator that periodically fills tokens into the bucket. Moreover, to support fine-grained rate regulation, the generator has to add a small token in a short period, instead of a large token in a long period. Obviously, such an implementation becomes a nightmare for the kernel, particularly when there are many token buckets for many traffic classes and each generator has to add small tokens at a high frequency to regulate a high-rate flow. Fortunately, it is not implemented that way in Linux. It adds tokens only when checking the eligibility of a packet to leave the queue.

Data Structures

The token bucket mechanism is used widely for policing or shaping the network traffic. You can find its implementations in `act_police.c` or `sch_tbf.c` in the Linux kernel. Below we introduce the code in `sch_tbf.c`. Parameters and variables used in the implementation of token bucket are defined as

Continued

```
struct tbf_sched_data
{
/* Parameters */
   u32        limit;  /* Maximal length of backlog: bytes */
   u32        buffer; /* Token bucket depth/rate: MUST BE >= MTU/B */
   u32        mtu;
   u32        max_size;
   struct qdisc_rate_table *R_tab;
   struct qdisc_rate_table *P_tab;
/* Variables */
   long tokens;                    /* Current number of B tokens */
   long ptokens;                   /* Current number of P tokens */
   psched_time_t t_c;          /* Time checkpoint */
   struct timer_list wd_timer;          /* Watchdog timer */
}
```

R_tab and buffer in tbf_sched_data are corresponding to the *r* and *b* of the token bucket shown in Figure 7.17, respectively, while tokens represents the number of tokens already accumulated in the bucket. Notably, in the structure tbf_sched_data, the unit of the token bucket size is time in μs. That is, given the transmitted rate R_tab, buffer represents the maximum time permitted to transmit packets. Also, token represents the actual period permitted to transmit packets.

Algorithm Implementations

In the original design of token bucket, when the amount of accumulated tokens is larger than the packet size in the head of the queue, packets are permitted to be sent at a *peak rate,* where the peak rate is usually equal to the link speed. However, since some applications might need to limit the peak rate to a specific value, TC provides a second set of token buckets (P_tab, mtu, ptokens) to support this requirement. These two token bucket mechanisms ensure that the traffic will conform to the requirement with mean rate = *R* and maximum burst period = buffer with peak rate = *P*, where *R* and *P* are indicated in structure R_tab and P_tab, respectively.

Figure 7.18 shows the flowchart of enqueue() in sch_tbf.c. First, the function checks whether the packet length is smaller than the maximum allowed size of the queue. Then, the packet will be inserted into the queue if the queue is not full. Compared to enqueue(), dequeue() is more complicated because it has to maintain the variables of the token bucket, as shown in Figure 7.19.

The function first calculates the amount of tokens accumulated after the last checking time t_c and saves the amount in toks. Surely, the accumulation is limited to the maximum value of the buffer. Then, if the peak rate

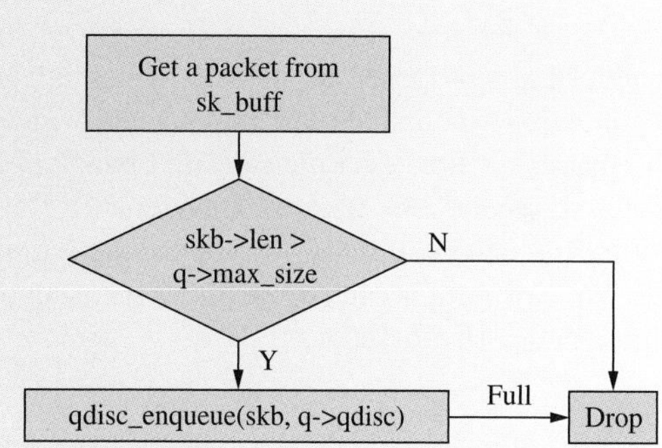

FIGURE 7.18 The flowchart of the function `enqueue()` in `scf _ tbf.c`.

is given, it estimates the residual time permitted to transmit packets if the current packet is sent out at the peak rate *P* and saves the estimation in `ptoks`. Similarly, it estimates the residual time if the packet is sent out at the mean rate *R* and saves it back to `toks`. Next, if both residual times estimated are larger than 0, the packet is allowed to be sent out. Otherwise, the packet will be inserted back to the head of its corresponding queue to wait for its next opportunity for transmission.

Exercises

As mentioned in the beginning of the data structure, you can find another implementation of token bucket in `act_police.c`. Explain how the token bucket is implemented for that policer.

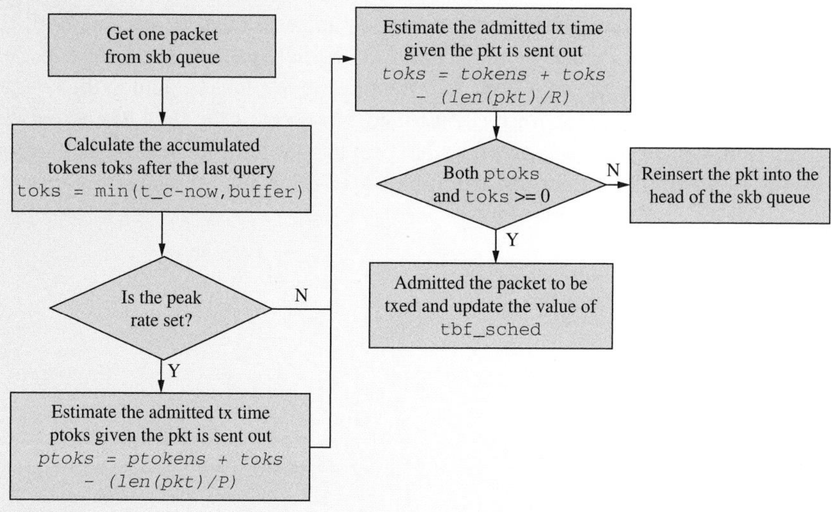

FIGURE 7.19 The flowchart of the function `dequeue()` of `sch _ tbf.c`.

7.3.4 Packet Scheduling

There are many types of scheduling algorithms proposed to allocate bandwidth in different styles. Among them, the *fair-queuing* type is the most famous and widely studied one for packet scheduling. It ensures all flows get their desired bandwidth and guarantees the *worst-case delay bound* received by packets. Besides, if a flow does not use up its allocated bandwidth, the bandwidth can be proportionally and *fairly* shared among other busy flows. We can further categorize this type of algorithm into two classes: *round robin* based and *sorted* based.

Round Robin Based

The algorithms in this class are heuristic. The most famous one is the *weighted round robin (WRR)* scheduler. In WRR, each active flow can send out a particular number of packets in one round. The number of packets sent by one flow corresponds to the value of its weight. For example, if the weights for two flows are 1 and 2, then the number of packets sent by the two flows in one round could be 100 and 200, respectively. WRR is simple, but it performs well *only* in a network where all packets are *equal in length* because WRR does not consider the size of packets in scheduling. A flow with a small weight may get more data sent if the size of all its packets is larger than that of a flow with a large weight.

An improved version, *deficit round robin (DRR),* was proposed by M. Shreedhar and G. Varghese in 1996 for the network with packets of different sizes, e.g., the Internet. Instead of the number of packets allowed to be sent in one round, DRR limits each flow by the number of bytes sent in one round. As illustrated in Figure 7.20, a deficit counter is maintained for each flow to keep track of the allowed amount of data in this round. Whenever a flow gets its turn, the counter is added by a fixed *quantum* proportional to the weight of the flow. Then, packets can be sent out from the flow queue as the counter is decremented by the size of these packets until the residual amount in the counter is not enough for the next packet. Then, the schedule would proceed to serve the next flow. In principle, the residual amount in the counter of a flow would be preserved for its next round. However, if the flow has no packets pending in the queue, its counter would be reset to zero until its next packet arrival. Also, the flow would be removed from the round-robin list temporarily. Since the

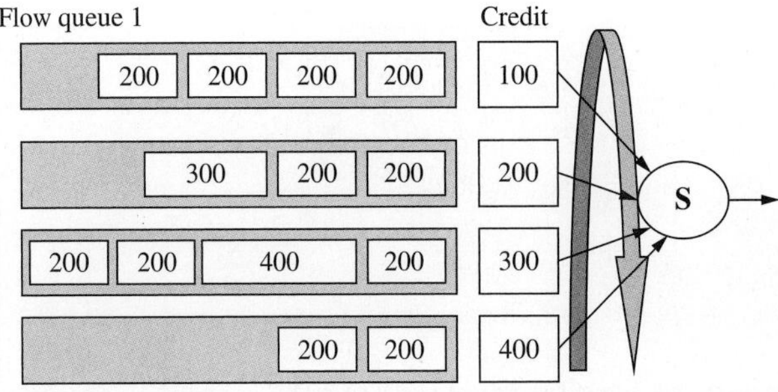

FIGURE 7.20 An illustration of the DRR algorithm.

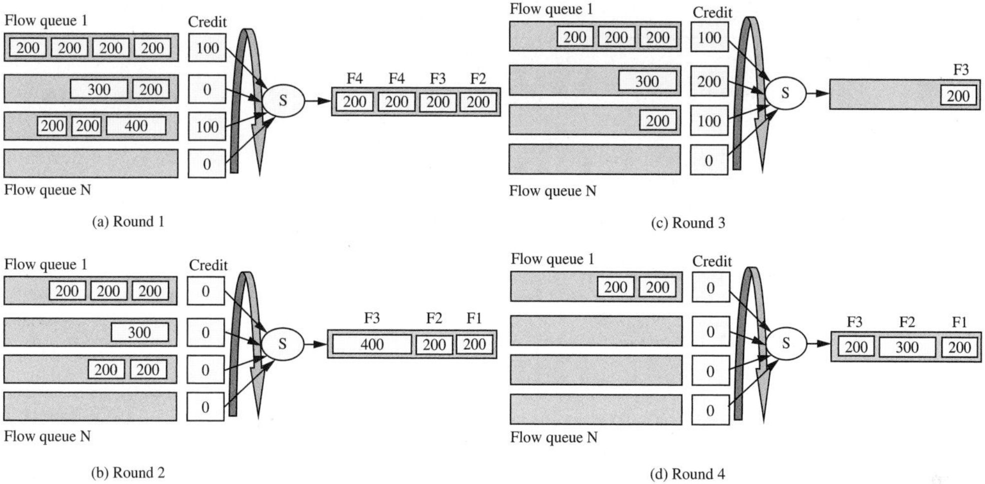

FIGURE 7.21 An operating case of DRR.

round robin list becomes short due to the removal, active flows can be served more frequently and can send out more packets within a cycle to share the unused bandwidth of inactive flows.

The four parts of Figure 7.21 show the changes from Figure 7.20 in the next four rounds. As shown in Figure 7.21(a), after the operation of the first round at least one packet is released from each flow queue except Flow 1 since the value in the counter of Flow 1 is not enough to release its first packet (100 < 200). On the other hand, 100 credits (300 – 200) are left in the counter of Flow 3, which is reserved for the next round since the third flow queue is non-empty. Next, in the second round, the four counters are added by 100, 200, 300, and 400, whose values thus become 200, 200, 400, and 400, respectively, and now are enough to release the first packet of Flows 1, 2, and 3. This results in Figure 7.21(b). Note that the counter value of Flow 4, 400, is reset to 0 because the fourth flow queue is empty. Then, in the third round shown in Figure 7.21(c), while the counter of the fourth flow is kept at 0 due to the empty queue, the counters of the first three flows are added again, but only one packet is released from Flow 3. The left credits for the non-empty flow queues would be reserved for the fourth round. Finally, after the credit update of the fourth round, the counters of Flows 1 and 2 turn to 200 and 400, respectively, which are thus enough for each flow to release one packet, as shown Figure 7.21(d). Besides, since no packets are queued in Flows 2 and 3, the residual credits of Flows 2 and 3 would be discarded, just like Flow 4.

This type of scheduler is simple in its concept and implementation, but it only ensures each flow getting the desired bandwidth *over a long timescale.* As the number of flows becomes large, a flow might wait a long time for its turn to send out packets. If packets of the flow arrive at a constant bit rate, long waiting time might cause the flow a large delay *jitter,* which means that some packets might be sent out quickly and others might be served slowly, depending on their arrival time to the queue.

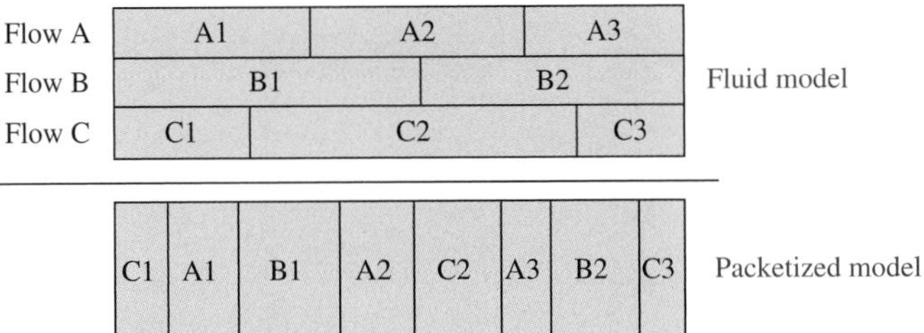

FIGURE 7.22 Packet transmission order in the fluid and packetized models.

Sorted Based

The concept of the sorted-based scheduler is very different from that of the round-robin-based scheduler. Before describing it, we first introduce a conceptual scheduler that is applied only to the *fluid-model* network architecture. Assume there are three flows fairly sharing a 3 Mbps link. In the fluid-model architecture, the scheduler is able to divide the link into three *virtual* links. Each flow can send out packets at 1 Mbps continuously over its virtual link without any delay caused by other flows. In addition, when one flow has no packets to send, the residual bandwidth can be proportionally shared by other flows. In other words, the other two flows could each use 1.5 Mbps. Such ideal scheduling is called *generalized processor sharing (GPS),* and it is impossible to implement because an output link can transmit only one packet at a time. The reality belongs to the packetized model. Figure 7.22 illustrates the difference between the fluid model and the packetized model. Packet transmissions from different flows proceed *simultaneously* in the fluid model but are *interleaved* in the packetized model.

Although the optimal scheduler cannot be realized, we can calculate the order in which the packets are sent out in the fluid model based on the size and arrival time of packets. Then, a scheduler of the packetized model is considered ideal if it can send out packets in the same order of *transmission completion* as the optimal scheduler of the fluid model. The idea is easy, but it is nontrivial to achieve the transmission completion order as in the fluid model. There are many proposed algorithms, but their design can be boiled down to a trade-off between exact bandwidth sharing and implementation complexity. Below we detail one version of sorted-based schedulers, *packetized GPS (PGPS),* proposed by A.K. Parekh and R.G. Gallager in 1993, to illustrate the operation of such schedulers.

Packetized GPS

PGPS is also called *weighted fair queuing (WFQ).* The default operation is that each packet gets a *virtual finish timestamp (VFT)* as it arrives at the flow queue, and the scheduler selects the packet with the *smallest* VFT among all flow queues to send out. The computation of VFT is related to the arrival *virtual system time (VST),* the size of the packet, and the reserved bandwidth of the flow the packet belongs to. Since the VFT of packets determine their transmission order, the VFT computation is the key to determining whether the packetized model scheduler effectively emulates the fluid model scheduler.

According to the algorithm, if the flow is active, which means there are packets pending in its flow queue, the VFT of the next arrival packet is equal to

$$F_i^k = F_i^{k-1} + \frac{L_i^k}{\phi_i}$$

where F_i^k is the VFT of the kth packet of flow *i,* L_i^k is the length of the kth packet of flow *i,* and ϕ_i is the allocated bandwidth. Theoretically, if the first packet of each flow arrives at the same time and all flows are backlogged forever, according to the preceding equation, it is easy to get the same transmission completion order of packets as in the fluid model scheduler. Unfortunately, it is a rare case. In the real case, a flow might become idle and later busy again. Thus, it is necessary to consider how to set the VFT for the first packet of an active flow. In general, the VFT of the first packet arrival is calculated by

$$F_i^k = V(t) + \frac{L_i^k}{\phi_i}$$

where *V(t)* is the VST which is a linear function of real time *t* in each of the time intervals split by the events of packets arriving to or departing from any empty queue. Assume the whole time is split into *n* intervals. T_i and S_i denote the starting actual time and virtual time of the ith interval, respectively, where $i = 1\ldots n$. Then, $V(t)$ in the ith interval can be expressed as

$$V(t) = S_i + (t - T_i)K_i, \text{ where}$$

$$S_i = S_{i-1} + (T_i - T_{i-1})K_{i-1},\ S_0 = 0,\ T_0 = T,\ K_i = \left(\sum_{i \in A} \phi_i\right)^{-1},$$

and *A* is the set of the active flows during the ith interval.

Again, based on the case shown in Figure 7.20, Figure 7.23 shows the packet scheduling results when WFQ is used, where the weights of the four flows are 0.1, 0.2, 0.3, and 0.4, respectively, whose proportions are just like that of their quantum given in Figure 7.20. Assume all packets arrive at the same time, meaning their *V(t)* = 0. Also, besides displaying the length of packets, each packet is tagged with an id in Figure 7.23(a). Then, Figure 7.23(b) shows the VFT of each packet, calculated based on the formula given above. For example, the VFT of the first packet in Flow queue 2 can be obtained by adding *V*(0) to the quotient of its length 200 and its flow weight 0.2, which thus is equal to 1000. Then, the VFT of its next packet, the packet of id 6, would be equal to *V*(0) + (200/0.2) + (200/0.2), or 2000. Finally, after getting the VFTs of all packets, it is easy to get the releasing order of packets under the WFQ scheduler, as shown in Figure 7.23(c).

Actually, the definition of *V*(*t*) is the key issue to designing such a sorted-based scheduler. While it takes too much effort to compute a *V*(*t*) that can ensure the transmission completion order of packets in PGPS exactly equal to that in GPS, an easy-to-compute *V*(*t*) might cause a newly active flow to get a small or large VFT and thus to share more or less bandwidth than other active flows, which not only degrades the fairness of bandwidth allocation but also affects the scheduler's guarantee on the worst-case delay.

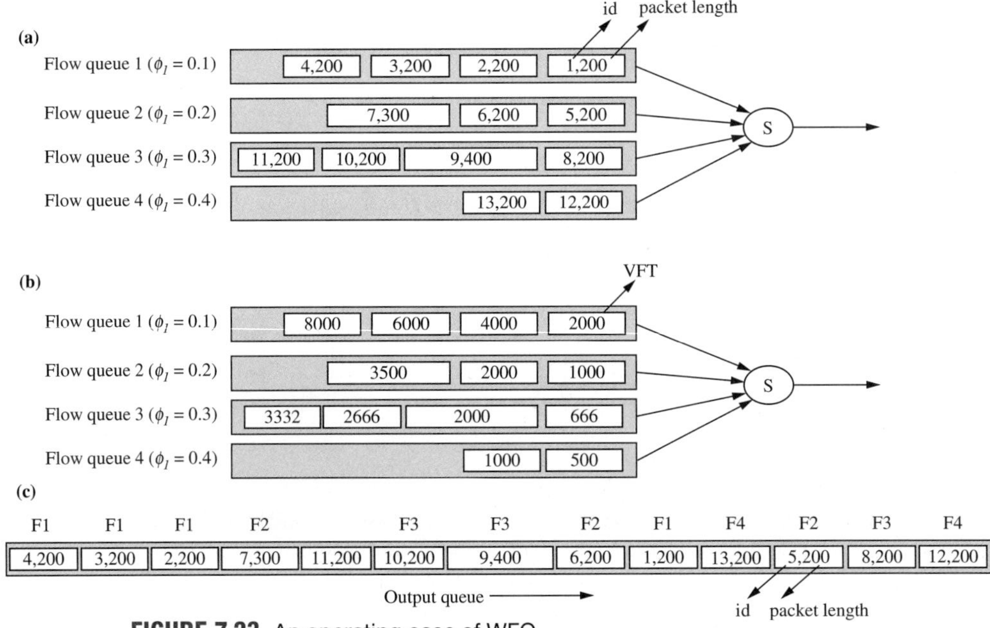

FIGURE 7.23 An operating case of WFQ.

Open Source Implementation 7.5: Packet Scheduling

Overview

Many algorithms have been proposed to handle the scheduling issue. In fact, it is a long list even if we consider only the fair-queuing schedulers. The reason for so many algorithms is the difficulty of scheduling packets accurately and efficiently. Explained below is the implementation of the sorted-based PGPS algorithm, which is the ancestor of many existing algorithms but the most difficult one to implement.

Data Structures

The PGPS algorithm is implemented in the `csz_qdisc_ops` module of `net/sched/sch_csz.c`. The module allocates a structure `csz_flow` for each flow to keep its information. There are two variables, *`start`* and *`finish`*, keeping the minimal and maximal finish timestamp of packets in its flow queue. In principle, the head packet of a flow queue has the smallest finish timestamp and the tail packet has the largest timestamp. Besides the structure `csz_flow`, the `csz_qdisc_ops` module maintains two lists, `s` and `f`, to implement the

PGPS scheduler. The item in the lists is the address that points to the structure `csz_flow`. Although both lists are used to link the active flows, the list `s` is ordered based on the variable `start` in the structure `csz_flow`, where the `start` of each flow keeps the virtual finish timestamp (VFT) of the head packet in the flow queue. The list `s` thus helps `csz_dequeue()` to quickly pick up the next transmission packet from the proper flow queue since the head packet of the first flow queue in the list `s` must have the smallest VFT. On the other hand, the list `f` is ordered based on the variable `finish`, where the `finish` of each flow keeps the VFT of the tail packet in its queue. The list `f` is involved in the calculation of the virtual system time of PGPS, as introduced later along with the function `csz_update()`.

Algorithm Implementations

Next we introduce the three major functions in the `csz_qdisc_ops` module and show their flowcharts. The function `csz_enqueue()` is the entry of the module and a flowchart is illustrated in Figure 7.24. For a packet arrival, the `csz_enqueue()` first calculates its VFT. To calculate the VFT of the first packet of an active flow, a current virtual system time (VST) is necessary. Thus, the function `csz_update()` is invoked before the calculation. For the flow turning active, the `csz_enqueue()` needs to wake it up by inserting it into the list *s*, which gives the flow a chance to send packets again.

As illustrated in Figure 7.25, the function `csz_dequeue()` keeps on sending out the head packet of the flow queue pointed to by the first entry in the list *s*. Whenever the packet of a flow is sent out, `csz_dequeue()` shall

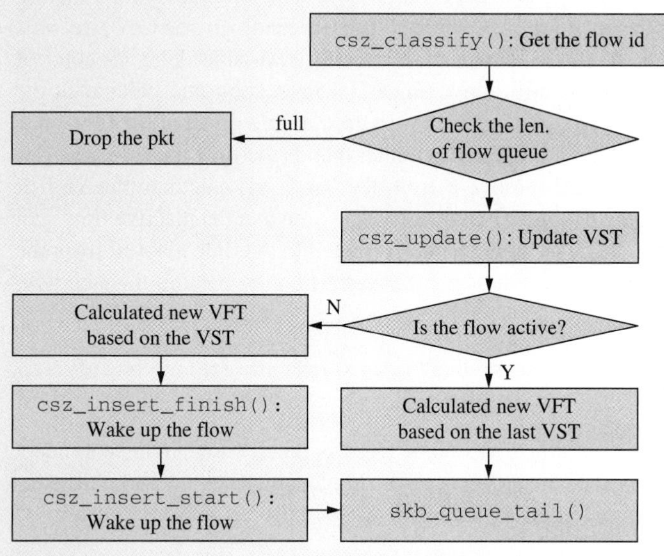

FIGURE 7.24 The flowchart of the function `csz _ enque()`.

Continued

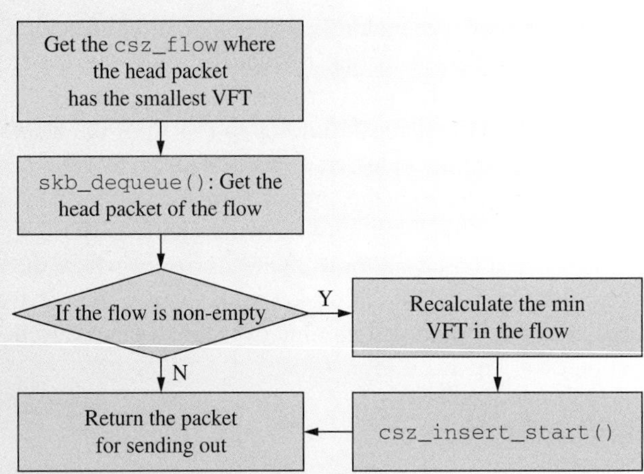

FIGURE 7.25 The flowchart of the function `csz_deque()`.

call `csz_insert_start()` to re-insert the flow into the list `s` again to keep its chance in the next round if the flow queue is not empty. For the flow whose queue is empty, it would be removed from the list *s* to avoid wasting system resources.

The third function, `csz_update()`, plays a key role in the `csz_qdisc_ops` module, as plotted in Figure 7.23. It is in charge of calculating the VST. Based on the description in PGPS, a VST is calculated whenever a packet arrives and departs. However, by the maintenance of list `f`, the `csz_qdisc_ops` recalculates the VST only when a packet arrives. It is maintained by the function `csz_update()`, as mentioned previously. First, the `csz_update()` records the time elapsed from the last invocation time to a variable delay. Second, it assumes that all flows are still active since last invocation and calculates the current VST. Then the VST is compared with the variable finish of the first entry in the list `f`, denoted as F. If the VST is smaller than F, the flow must be inactive. The `csz_update()` will remove it from the list `f` and calculate the VST at the time when the flow becomes inactive, i.e., the time that the inactive flow sent out the last packet. The delay will also be corrected to the time elapsed from the flow becoming inactive. Next, the `csz_update()` goes back to the step with double-borders in Figure 7.26 until the correct VST is obtained and all inactive flows are removed from the list `f`.

Exercises

1. Compared to the complicated PGPS, DRR is much easier both in concept and implementation. You can find its implementation in `sch_drr.c`. Please read the code and explain how this simple yet useful algorithm is implemented.

2. There are several implementations of scheduling algorithms in the folder `sched`. For each implementation, can you find how it differs from others? Do all of them belong to the fair-queuing scheduling?

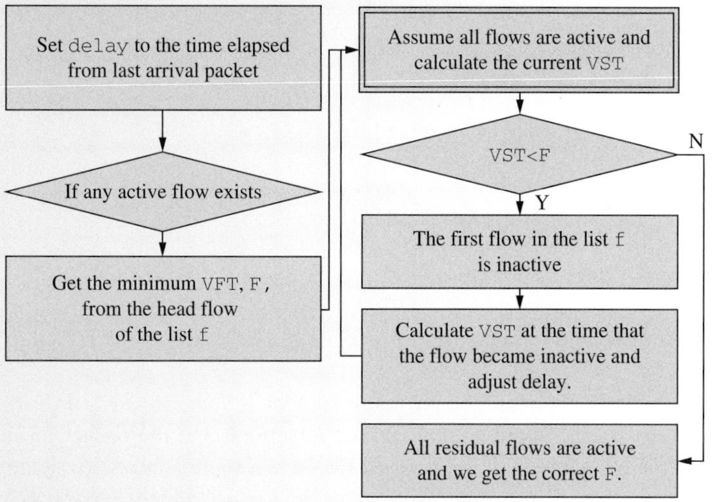

Set `delay` to the time elapsed from last arrival packet

If any active flow exists

Get the minimum `VFT`, `F`, from the head flow of the list `f`

Assume all flows are active and calculate the current `VST`

`VST<F`

Y

N

The first flow in the list `f` is inactive

Calculate `VST` at the time that the flow became inactive and adjust delay.

All residual flows are active and we get the correct `F`.

FIGURE 7.26 The flowchart of the function `csz _ update()`.

7.3.5 Packet Discarding

Besides the scheduling algorithms handling multiple queues, the packet discarding mechanism for a *single* queue is necessary in the QoS architecture, where multiple flows might pump packets into one single-class queue to share allocated bandwidth for the queue. Such a discarding mechanism might stop the misbehaving flows from pumping more packets into a queue to overuse its bandwidth. Two types of packet discarding mechanisms are introduced as follows.

Tail Drop

Tail drop is the simplest packet discard policy and is normally used with FIFO queuing. This policy drops new packet arrivals when there is no more space left in the queue, as shown in Figure 7.27(a). Packet arrivals will be dropped until the queue space becomes available. Because tail drop is the default policy of FIFO queuing, some problems that often appear in FIFO queuing would also occur in tail drop. For example, as a bursty source shares a FIFO queue with other sources having a smooth rate, the bursty one might occupy all available queue space for a short period, which forces new packet arrivals of other sources to be dropped. The problem could be avoided if we divide the single queue into multiple queues. That is, each traffic source owns its length-limited queue.

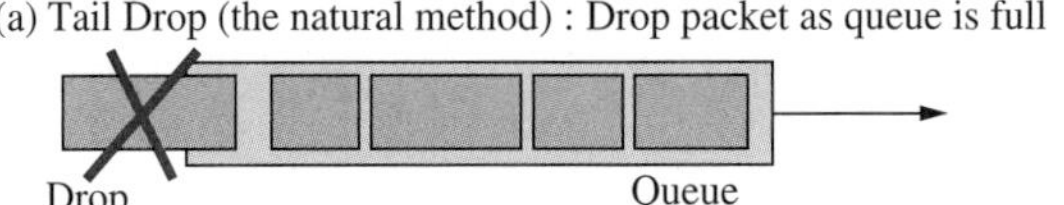

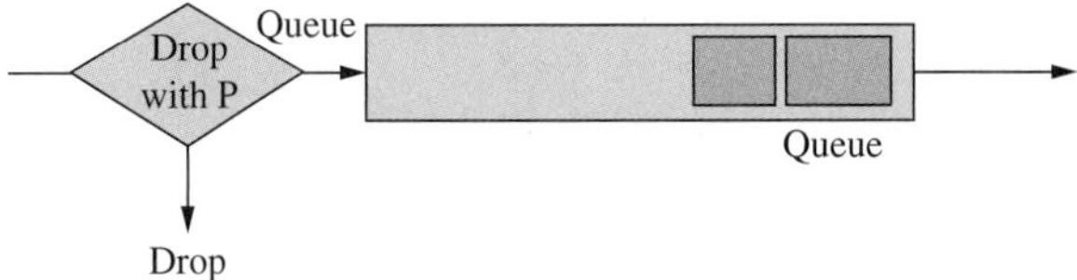

FIGURE 7.27 Illustrations for (a) Tail Drop and (b) Early Drop.

However, this means some packets might be dropped even when the router still has queue space.

Thus, the current implementation in many routers is *longest queue tail drop (LQTD)*. All service queues share a *common* memory pool, and the packet located at the tail of the *longest* queue will be dropped first when there is no more space to queue a new packet arrival. This refinement makes the service classes whose arrival rate exceeds their allocated service rate have a high dropping probability, while the service classes operating within their allocated rate would experience a low dropping probability since they usually have a shorter queue.

Early Drop

Although LQTD can efficiently prevent any flow from over-occupying the queue space, it needs packet classification to identify which flow a packet belongs to, which is burdensome if there are many flows passing the router. Thus, if using one queue for all flows is preferred, a possible way of preventing resource abuse is to drop new packet arrivals with some *probability* that the queue is going to be full, as shown in Figure 7.27(b). Such an idea is called *early drop*. The policy is expected to warn traffic sources early that the queue size would be insufficient so that these sources might reduce their rate to prevent packet loss. Such a policy can avoid dropping *consecutive* packets in a short time, as can occur with the tail drop policy. Consecutive dropping often heavily degrades the throughput of TCP flows.

The key issue in designing such a policy is to decide whether the queue space is going to be full. A *threshold* on the queue length might be the most heuristic way. Once the queue length is longer than the threshold, new packet arrivals will be discarded with a probability. However, due to the large variation of queue length, a suddenly accumulated long queue might not always imply an upcoming event of full queue. The consequence of early drop might result in a total of more dropped packets than in the tail drop policy under the same packet arrivals, though consecutive dropping is avoided by early drop.

Open Source Implementation 7.6: Random Early Detection (RED)

Overview

Just like the situation of the scheduling algorithms, there are many queuing management (QM) algorithms proposed to determine how to drop packets in order to avoid the congestion of a queue and the degradation in TCP throughput. Among them, we introduce an early-drop style of the QM algorithms, *random early detection* (RED). We introduce RED here because it is the most well known early-drop QM algorithm.

Data Structures

The implementation of the RED algorithm can be found in `net/sched/sch_red.c`. The structure `red_sched_data` keeps the necessary parameters to operate the algorithm, e.g., `qave`, `qth_max`, and `qth_min`. RED relies on the average queue length `qave` to predict the upcoming of a full queue and avoid unnecessary packet dropping. When `qave` is smaller than the minimum threshold `qth_min`, all arrivals can be inserted into the queue. Then, when `qave` is larger than `qth_min`, the arrival is dropped based on a probability Pb calculated as

$$Pb = \max\_P \cdot \frac{(\min\{qave, qth\_max\} - qth\_min)}{(qth\_max - qth\_min)},$$

where `max_P` is the maximum probability of dropping packets when `qave` >= `qth_max`, whose value, however, is suggested to be 0.1 or 0.2, instead of 1. Setting `max_P` to 1 would drop all arrival packets, which is unnecessary since there is still space to queue packets even when `qave` is longer than `qth_max`.

Algorithm Implementations

Here we examine the code segment that determines whether to enqueue or drop (mark) a packet.

```
1 if (++q->qcount) {
2 if (((q->qave - q->qth_min)>>q->Wlog)*q->qcount < q->qR)
3 goto enqueue;
4 q->qcount = 0;
5 q->qR = net_random()&q->Rmask;
6 sch->stats.overlimits++;
7 goto mark;
```

In the code segment, line 2 judges whether to enqueue an arrival or not. And `qR` is an integer random variable between 0 and `Rmask`, where `Rmask` = 2^{Plog}. In the implementation, to ensure that all arithmetic uses only shift operations, `qave`, `qth_max`, and `qth_min` are fixed floating-point numbers with the fixed floating

Continued

point stored at `Wlog`, i.e., their actual values are equal to their present value divided by 2^{Wlog}. Obviously, line 2 is much different from the probabilistic equation shown above. To figure out how line 2 implements the equation, we first ignore the variable `qcount`. Next, since `max_P` in the implementation is carefully chosen as

$$\frac{qth\_max - qth\_min}{2^{Wlog+Plog}},$$

we can rewrite the equation for `Pb` as

$$Pb = \frac{(qave - qth\_min)}{2^{Wlog+Plog}}$$

Then, the packet would be enqueued if $Pb < \frac{q->qR}{2^{Plog}}$, where the right side of the inequality is a random variable between 0 and 1 based on the definition of `qR` written in line 5. Finally, by multiplying both sides of the inequality by 2^{Plog}, we get the implementation of line 2. Here we come back to explain the purpose of `qcount`. The value of `qcount` at line 2 is 0 when `qave` first falls in the range between the two thresholds and is kept at 1 until `qave` leaves the range. Thus, it ensures that the first packet to arrive after the `qave` falls into the range can be inserted.

Another key design in RED is the calculation of the average queue length `qave`, which is an *exponential* average of the real queue length, i.e.,

$$qave = qave * (1 - w) + sch-> stats.back\ log * w,$$

where `sch->stats.backlog` is the current queue length. The `w` is a weight of the old `qave` in calculating the new one and is set to $1/(2^{Wlog})$. Then, since `sch->stats.backlog` is an integer, by transferring it into a number with a fixed floating point at `Wlog` as `qave`, the preceding equation is implemented as `q->qave = q->qave - (q->qave >> q->Wlog) + sch->stats.backlog.`

Example

Next, Figure 7.28 gives an example to illustrate the operation of RED. Let *`qth_min`* = 1, *`qth_max`* = 4, *`max_P`* = 0.1 and *`w`* = 1. Such a *`w`* implies that *`qave`* is always equal to the present queue length. Then, as shown in Figure 7.28(a), since no packets are in the queue, *`qave`* = 0 and the dropping probability *`Pb`* is set at 0. However, after packets 1 and 2 are inserted as shown in Figure 7.28(b), *`qave`* is increased to 2, leading *`Pb`* to be adjusted to 0.033. In this situation some packets may be discarded, e.g., packet 3. Finally, as shown in Figure 7.28(c), more packets are inserted, increasing *`qave`* over the bound of *`qth_max`* of 4, and thus a higher *`Pb`*, 0.1, is applied. That is, more packets would be discarded, e.g., packets 8 and 10.

Exercises

From `/net/sched/` you can find a variant of RED, named generic RED (GRED), implemented in `sch_gred.c`. Figure out how it works and how it differs from RED.

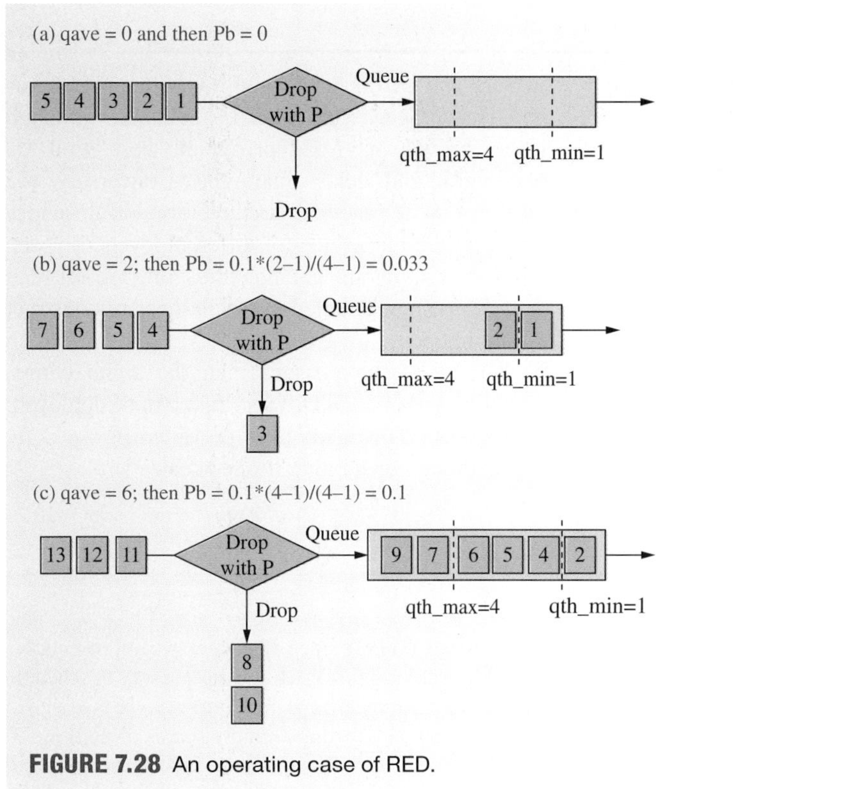

FIGURE 7.28 An operating case of RED.

Principle in Action: QoS Components in Daily Usage Today

Though IntServ and DiffServ were never deployed on a global scale to achieve the QoS-enabled Internet, some QoS components have a daily presence in our Internet on a *local* scale. None of them are *control-plane* components, which would require the RSVP protocol that tends to change the stateless nature of the Internet.

Here let us review real examples. Flow identification or classification is heavily used in firewalls for access control, for security rather than QoS purposes, where certain IP subnets or port numbers are banned. Token bucket is used in Ethernet switches to limit the rate well below the link capacity on certain switch ports. Packet scheduling is commonly applied to access links to enforce bandwidth management on some applications, especially P2P, which consumes a lot of bandwidth. Packet discarding or queue management is exercised in many backbone routers to alleviate congestion and avoid consecutive packet loss. In conclusion, though IntServ and DiffServ might be history, many of their technology components have prevailed.

7.4 SUMMARY

This chapter began by introducing six key components involved in building a QoS network. The three control-plane components, *signal protocol, QoS routing,* and *admission control,* take charge of the negotiation of resources among routers, the determination of a QoS-guaranteed path, and the control of a network loading, respectively. The two data-plane components, *policer* and *scheduler,* control the forwarding time and order of received packets, according to the third data-plane component, *classifier,* which classifies packets into different queues.

With these complements as building blocks, IETF proposed two Internet QoS architectures, IntServ and DiffServ, to build a QoS-enabled Internet. The *IntServ* is an expensive solution, although it can provide a virtual private network with the bandwidth and delay guarantee. Conversely, the DiffServ is a practical architecture but provides only differential service for different levels of users. After presenting the architectures of QoS-enabled IP networks, we detailed the techniques to construct the components of a QoS-enabled network, which have more research issues than the architectures. Although IntServ and DiffServ failed to be deployed, many QoS components have prevailed in our daily usage, though on a rather limited scale.

COMMON PITFALLS

Shaping and Scheduling

Although both operations would regulate the throughput of a flow, their purposes are different. The goal of shaping is to *change* or *limit* the throughput of a flow on its mean or variance to make sure the throughput from the shaper conforms to the profile of the flow. Its operation is on one flow only. However, scheduling is usually for a group of flows competing for a link with limited bandwidth. Scheduling is in charge of allocating the bandwidth for these flows based on a predefined policy, e.g., equally or proportionally sharing. How about using a bunch of shapers to replace a scheduler? It is really a bad idea. First, operating a bunch of shapers costs more in hardware resources than a scheduler. Second, since there is no communication between these shapers, it is hard to allocate the *unused* bandwidth in real time to those flows that need more.

WRR and WFQ

It is important to re-emphasize the difference between weighted round robin (WRR) and weighted fair queuing (WFQ) since they are two representative scheduling algorithms. WRR is a simple way to schedule packets for a group of flows. Each flow queue is assigned a weight, and the scheduler simply serves these flows in *round-robin* fashion. Then, whenever a flow is served, the number of packets permitted to be sent out would be a multiple of its weight. Although the WRR concept and implementation are simple, each flow might wait a long time to get served when the number of flows increases, particularly if packets of the flow happen to miss their turn. WFQ is designed to avoid just this problem. It serves flow queues in a *dynamic* order, sorted by the timestamp of the head packet of each flow. Therefore, at the moment that a packet should be sent out, WFQ would serve it and then change to another flow. Since no missing case would happen under WFQ, WFQ can guarantee shorter *worst-case delay bound* and better *fairness* than DRR.

FURTHER READINGS

QoS Architectures and Protocols

Among the readings cited here, the first is a specialized book to introduce QoS and the second is a good tutorial paper on IP QoS topics. The third describes the general idea and architecture of IntServ, while the following two define its guaranteed and control-load services, respectively. The sixth paper is a useful tutorial paper for RSVP. The seventh defines the architecture of DiffServ, and from the seventh you can learn how the ToS field of the IPv4 header is reclaimed in DiffServ. The following two RFCs describe two types of forwarding behaviors in DiffServ. Finally, the last two are related to the QoS deployment in wireless and Web services, respectively.

- Z. Wang, *Internet QoS: Architectures and Mechanisms for Quality of Service,* Morgan Kaufmann Publishers, 2001.
- X. Xiao L.M. Ni, "Internet QoS: A Big Picture," *IEEE Network,* Vol. 13, Issue 2, pp. 8–18, Mar. 1999.
- R. Braden, D. Clark, and S. Shenker, "Integrated Services in the Internet Architecture: An Overview," RFC 1633, June 1994.
- S. Shenker, C. Partridge, and R. Guerin, "Specification of Guaranteed Quality of Service," RFC 2212, Sept. 1997.
- J. Wroclawski, "Specification of the Controlled-Load Network Element Service," RFC 2211, Sept. 1997.
- L. Zhang, S. Deering, D. Estrin, S. Shenker, and D. Zappala, "RSVP: A New Resource Reservation Protocol," *IEEE Network,* Vol. 7, Issue 5, Sept. 1993.
- S. Blake, D. Black, M. Carlson, E. Davies, Z. Wang, and W. Weiss, "An Architecture for Differentiated Services," RFC 2475, Dec. 1998.
- K. Nichols, S. Blake, F. Baker, and D. Black, "Definition of the Differentiated Services Field (DS Field) in the IPv4 and IPv6 Headers," RFC 2474, Dec. 1998.
- J. Heinanen, F. Baker, W. Weiss, and J. Wroclawski, "Assured Forwarding PHB Group," RFC 2597, June 1999.
- B. Davie et al., "An Expedited Forwarding PHB," RFC 3246, Mar. 2002.
- H. Zhu, M. Li, I. Chlamtac, and B. Prabhakaran, "A Survey of Quality of Service in IEEE 802.11 Networks," *IEEE Wireless Communications,* Vol. 11, No. 4, pp. 6–14, Aug. 2004.
- R. Pandey, J. Fritz Barnes, and R. Fritz Barnes, "Supporting Quality of Service in HTTP Servers," *Proceedings of ACM Symposium on Principles of Distributed Computing,* pp. 247–256, 1998.

QOS COMPONENTS

Following is a list of classic papers about the QoS components. The first three are for admission control, and the fourth is for packet classification. The next five papers are on scheduling and the final two are on RED and another AQM algorithm.

- R. Guerin, H. Ahmadi, and M. Naghshineh, "Equivalent Capacity and Its Application to Bandwidth Allocation in High-Speed Networks," *IEEE Journal on Selected Areas in Communications,* Vol. 9, No. 7, pp. 968–981, Sept. 1991.
- S. Jamin, P. B. Danzig, S. J. Shenker, and L. Zhang, "A Measurement-Based Admission Control Algorithm for Integrated Service Packet Networks," *IEEE Transactions on Networking,* Vol. 5, Issue 1, pp. 56–70, Feb. 1997.
- J. Qiu and E. W. Knightly, "Measurement-Based Admission Control with Aggregate Traffic," *IEEE/ACM Transactions on Networking,* Vol. 9, Issue 2, pp. 199–210, Apr. 2001.
- T. V. Lakshman and D. Stiliadis, "High-Speed Policy-Based Packet Forwarding Using Efficient Multi-Dimensional Range Matching," *ACM SIGCOMM,* pp. 203–214, Oct. 1998.
- A. K. Parekh and R.G. Gallager, "A Generalized Processor Sharing Approach to Flow Control in Integrated Services Networks: The Single Node Case," *IEEE/ACM Transactions on Networking,* Vol. 1, Issue 3, pp. 344–357, June 1993.
- M. Shreedhar and G. Varghese, "Efficient Fair Queueing Using Deficit Round Robin," *IEEE/ACM Transactions on Networking,* Vol. 4, Issue 3, pp. 375–385, June 1996.
- D. Stiliadis and A. Varma, "Latency-Rate Servers: A General Model for Analysis of Traffic Scheduling Algorithms," *IEEE/ACM Transactions on Networking,* Vol. 6, Issue 5, pp. 611–624, Oct. 1998.
- J. C. R. Bennett and H. Zhang, "WF2Q: Worst-Case Fair Weighted Fair Queueing," in *Proceedings of the IEEE INFOCOM,* Mar. 1996.
- J. Golestani, "A Self-Clocked Fair Queueing Scheme for Broadband Applications," in *Proceedings of the IEEE INFOCOM,* June 1994.
- S. Floyd and V. Jacobson, "Random Early Detection Gateways for Congestion Avoidance," *IEEE/ACM Transactions on Networking,* Vol. 1, Issue 4, pp. 397–413, Aug. 1993.
- S. Athuraliya, V. H. Li, S. H. Low, and Q. Yin, "REM: Active Queue Management," *IEEE Network,* Vol. 5, Issue 3, pp. 48–53, May/June 2001.

Linux Traffic Control Modules

Here are two Web pages on how to set up and configure the traffic control modules in Linux.

- Jason Boxman, "A Practical Guide to Linux Traffic Control," URL: http://blog.edseek.com/~jasonb/articles/traffic_shaping/.
- Martin A. Brown, "Traffic Control HOWTO," URL: http://tldp.org/HOWTO/Traffic-Control-HOWTO/index.html.

FREQUENTLY ASKED QUESTIONS

1. What control-plane and data-plane mechanisms are needed to provide a QoS guarantee in the Internet?
   Answer:
   Control plane: signaling protocol, admission control, QoS routing
   Data plane: classification, policing, scheduling
2. WFQ (weighted fair queuing) vs. WRR (weighted round robin)? (Compare their complexity and scalability.)
   Answer:
   Complexity: WFQ (O(log n)) > WRR (O(1))
   Scalability: WRR > WFQ
3. Why is RED (Random Early Discard) better than FIFO (First-In First-Out), especially for real-time traffic?
   Answer:
   RED avoids bursty dropping, i.e., contiguous packet losses, that would happen to FIFO. Real-time traffic usually has redundant and layered coding where data can be recovered as long as the loss is scattered, i.e., noncontiguous.
4. IntServ vs. DiffServ? (Compare their QoS granularity, complexity at edge routers, complexity at core routers, and scalability.)
   Answer:
   QoS granularity: IntServ (per-flow) > DiffServ (per-class)
   Complexity at edge routers: DiffServ > = IntServ
   Complexity at core routers: IntServ > DiffServ
   Scalability: DiffServ > IntServ
5. What are the barriers to deploying IntServ? (List at least two barriers.)
   Answer:
   Scalability (per-flow QoS), stateful routers, QoS signaling by applications
6. What are the barriers to deploying DiffServ? (List at least two barriers.)
   Answer:
   Stateful edge routers, QoS signaling by applications, or bandwidth brokers

EXERCISES

Hands-On Exercises

1. RSVP is a signaling protocol designed for end hosts to negotiate resource reservation with routers. Send RSVP requests from your Linux-based PC running the TC (Traffic Control) module, and use *Wireshark* to capture them. Then see whether you can understand the meaning of the value in each field of the request.
2. Assume there is a router connecting two links, A and B. Set up the router to measure the average throughput (bytes/s) of the traffic passing from A to B. The measurement should be reported on a per-minute basis. You are encouraged to show in real time the measurement in a chart to let the network administrators remotely check it via the Web browser.
3. Follow up on Exercise 2 by setting up an admission controller at the router to monitor the establishment of TCP connections with TCP SYN requests passing from B to A. Then let the controller begin to filter out such requests when the average throughput from A to B, or B to A, approaches 80% of the bandwidth of link B.
4. As a follow-up to Exercise 3, instead of only filtering out the requests, could you emulate a TCP reject message at the router to inform the requester about the failure?
5. Set up the token bucket in your Linux system to regulate the maximum output rate of your network adaptor to a smaller value. Then observe the regulation effect by measuring the throughput of an FTP connection.
6. Assume you are an ISP and plan to provide a bandwidth management service for your business customers on their access links. One of your customers hopes to reserve 50% of the downlink bandwidth for the R&D group. Set up a QoS-aware ISP-side edge gateway to meet the goal. The classifier in the gateway should classify inbound packets into two classes. The first class is for packets sent to the PCs in the R&D group, while the other class is for other packets. You can demonstrate

that the service is workable by showing that the quality of watching an online streaming at a PC in the R&D group is totally unaffected by the overloaded download traffic to the PCs in the other groups.

7. First install RED for the queuing management of your outgoing link. Then, establish multiple long-live TCP flows over the link and compare their total throughput with that of a link managed with FIFO. Also, try to observe the difference between `qave`, mentioned in Open Source Implementation 7.6, and the real queue length.

Written Exercises

1. As mentioned in Section 7.1, there are six basic components required by a QoS-aware router. Draw a block diagram to illustrate an IntServ router with the six components and the operating relationship among them. Of course, adding extra components is allowed.
2. Assume the traffic is regulated by a token bucket with parameters (r, p, B). Discuss the effect caused by the token bucket. For example, what is the behavior of the traffic after the regulation? Or, if we tune any one parameter, how does the behavior change?
3. There are two common traffic estimation methods introduced in measured-based admission control. One is EWMA and the other is time window. Further compare the difference in estimation between them.
4. There is a 10^7 bits/sec link and WRR is used to schedule. Suppose that the link is shared by N flows whose packet size is 125 bytes. Assume we plan to *equally* allocate $8*10^6$ bits/sec bandwidth for half of the flows and the residual bandwidth for the other half. Then, if N−1 flows are active and *backlogged,* what is the possible worst delay suffered by the first packet of the only nonactive flow?
5. Generally speaking, WRR is suitable for the network whose packet size is of a fixed length, and DRR is an improved version that can handle packets of variant lengths. In fact, due to its simple implementation, DRR is more popular, but it cannot guarantee a small worst-case delay. Study their abilities about the worst-case delay guarantee. Is it possible to improve DRR to provide a smaller worst-case delay than WRR?
6. A trace on queue length and calculation on average queue length periodically are required in the original algorithm of RED, which poses a big load in the implementation. In TC, a better technique is provided to reduce the load. You should observe the source code in the file `sch_red.c` and try to picture a flowchart and describe how the problem is solved in the implementation.
7. In an access link, the bandwidth management for the downlink traffic is performed at the ISP-side edge router. However, if the ISP does not provide such a service, then is it possible or meaningful to do it at the customer-side edge gateway? Justify your answer.
8. Find a business case that successfully deployed QoS-aware routers on their network to provide QoS for their customers.
9. The queuing management algorithm RED was proposed to alleviate the congestion in a router. There are lots of research papers analyzing and improving the RED algorithm. What are the issues addressed by these papers? Why is it so interesting to the research community? Also, has RED been widely deployed in the routers of the Internet?
10. List the typical traffic classes required by an enterprise and then identify the QoS requirement of each class in term of packet loss, bandwidth, delay, and jitter.
11. There have been numerous and mature scheduling algorithms proposed in the past two decades, but most of them are designed for wired networks. Identify the new requirements or difficulties in applying these algorithms on the wireless network to provide users with QoS.
12. Describe the pros and cons of using WFQ to implement bandwidth management.
13. Figure 7.17 illustrates how a token bucket is operated. Assume that $r = 1$ unit/s, $p = 4$ units/s, $b = 20$ units and no packet arrivals for the first 15 seconds. Then, suppose that 4 packets arrive right at the 15th second, with length equal to 2, 10, and 4 units, respectively. Take the assumption described above and calculate the releasing time of the 4 packets.

8 Chapter

Network Security

Network security has become a very important issue since many security failures have occurred on the Internet, particularly in recent years. Computer scientists are not the only ones interested in these incidents; the general public also frequently learns about them from the news. Naïve Internet users may become the victims in these incidents, as when their personal data are compromised for malicious purposes.

Security concerns began with data security, then focused on access security, and more recently on system security. The first of these issues is related to protecting *private* data transmitted on the *public* Internet so that the data will not be eavesdropped or faked. The second issue is associated with controlling *access* to the internal and external networks based on the *policy* of an organization or an Internet service provider. That is, it decides *who* can access *what*. Finally, the third issue is about protecting networks and systems so that they are not *vulnerable* to attacks from the Internet. In this chapter we discuss the major problems and the design issues involved in solving them.

Data transmitted on the Internet are insecure as they could be easily captured en route for analysis. The content may be revealed to a third party, stealthily modified in the middle, or faked from a malicious source. Therefore, the essential problem of data security is how to protect the data from being peeped, modified, or faked. First, the data should be *encrypted* into scrambled *ciphertext* so that only the receiver can *decrypt* them back to the original data. The encryption and decryption mechanisms must be very difficult and time-consuming for a third party to crack but efficient enough for the sender and receiver to execute. Second, the transmitted data must be authenticated to prove the content's integrity.

An organization or an Internet service provider may want proper control over its access to network resources and systems on the Internet based on its own policy. The key problem of access security is therefore who can access what. The information to identify "who" can access may be located in the network layer and transport layer headers in the packets, such as IP addresses, port numbers, and protocols, or in the packet payload, such as URLs. The administration can deploy a *firewall* or a filtering device between the internal and the external network and enforce the control policy as a set of rules. These devices examine the information in the incoming or outgoing packets, which may be in the network, transport, or application layer, to determine whether to pass or drop them.

Finally, let us look at system security. An attacker may try to find and exploit vulnerabilities of a system to intrude into that system for various purposes, such as stealing critical information, controlling that system to launch another attack, disabling an important service, and so on. The key problem in system security is how to identify the various types of intrusions and defend the systems against them. Identification includes checking for attacking signatures or discovering anomalous behaviors. Checking signatures may miss unknown attacks (i.e., false negatives) but anomaly analysis may lead to false positives if normal traffic behaves unusually, so there is a trade-off between *false positives* and *false negatives.* Therefore, the identification approach must be designed precisely in order to minimize false positives and false negatives.

We cover data security, access security, and system security in Sections 8.2, 8.3, and 8.4, respectively. In Section 8.2, we present several cryptographic algorithms to show how they are designed for protecting data, and how they are realized in the Internet protocols and architectures, such as *Secure Socket Layer* (SSL) and *Virtual Private Network* (VPN). We interleave into the text the open source implementations of the 3DES encryption algorithm (in the VHDL hardware language), the MD5 authentication algorithm (in the Linux kernel), and the IPsec VPN (in the Linux kernel).

In Section 8.3, we introduce the types of firewalls and filtering devices that realize the access control. Netfilter/iptables and Firewall Toolkit (FWTK) are given as the open source implementations for network/transport-layer firewalls and application-layer firewalls, respectively. In Section 8.4, we examine common attack techniques and malicious programs, and then elaborate on how to identify them, while also considering the design issues and trade-offs. The well-known ClamAV and Snort serve as the open source implementations for antivirus and intrusion detection, respectively. Another open source package for anti-spam, SpamAssassin, is also examined due to its similarity to ClamAV and Snort, which heavily rely on checking signatures.

8.1 GENERAL ISSUES

As explained above, the security topics include data security, access security, and system security. The foundation of data security is cryptography. We first cover the cryptography algorithms and their applications in protecting private data transmitted on the public network. For access security, firewall systems are the most popular devices. The types of firewalls and how they work are then introduced. Today's Internet is vulnerable to various network attacks. Thus, we examine the issues about various attacks and how to protect systems from attacks.

8.1.1 Data Security

As e-transactions via networks grow in popularity, the security issues of sending sensitive data such as banking data, passwords, and credit card numbers become critical. Such sensitive data may be intercepted for recording, analyzing, reproducing, or spoofing purposes. It is challenging to solve this problem. If the network security is not guaranteed, fewer people will use the network for these purposes.

In this chapter, we explain cryptography operations and examples through three virtual characters: Alice (represented as sender A), Bob (represented as receiver B), and Trudy (represented as intruder T). For example, when Alice sends plaintext data to Bob without protection, the middle person Trudy can easily read and collect the plaintext between them, and may reproduce, modify, or spoof these data. When the fake data reach Bob, Bob will think they are from Alice. The plaintext data should be encrypted before being sent. We first discuss the techniques of encryption and decryption.

We begin with the traditional theory of cryptography. The *symmetric encryption* or *single-key encryption* system was proposed first. This uses a common key to encrypt and decrypt data. Since the common key must be exchanged, efficiently distributing this key in a secure manner is essential. Diffie and Hellman proposed the asymmetric encryption method in 1976. This method uses different keys to encrypt and decrypt data, thus the name *asymmetric* encryption. Therefore, the key distribution in networks becomes simple and secure. Several representative systems are developed according to these two encryption systems. For instance, Data Encryption Standard (DES) and International Data Encryption Algorithm (IDEA) are based on symmetric encryption, while RSA (from the initials of the three inventors' last names) is based on asymmetric encryption.

Let us assume that the sender Alice and receiver Bob are located at different sites. Since they are unable to recognize each other in person, they have to authenticate each other to ensure the identity of the person in communication. They also need to ensure that the received data are identical to the original copy, and were not modified, spoofed, or maliciously forged during the network transaction. We have a detailed description of *digital authentication* and the techniques of ensuring *data integrity* in this chapter.

After introducing the algorithms in cryptography, we introduce how network protocols of the link layer, the network layer, and the transport layer realize network security based on cryptography. Besides the tunneling protocols in the link layer, the Internet Security Protocol (IPSec) operates in the network layer. Operating security protocol in the network layer has a few advantages. First, not only applications on top of TCP but also other applications can have security provided by IPSec. Second, it is not susceptible to common attacks on TCP, such as forging RSTs to disconnect a connection. IPSec supports two types of security protocols in the IP network layer: *Authentication Header* (AH) protocol and *Encapsulation Security Payload* (ESP) protocol. The former provides the authentication of source node and data integrity. The latter supports complete authentication, data integrity, and security mechanisms, so it is more complicated than the AH. The description of the IPSec protocol and its application, Virtual Private Network (VPN), shall be explained in detail in this chapter.

The Secure Socket Layer (SSL) protocol serves as a security mechanism for transferring encrypted data. The protocol is widely used in applications such as secure Web browsing and secure mail delivery. Although SSL is secure for data communication, it is still insufficient to provide a complete secure environment for online payment via credit cards in electronic commerce. The receiver has a chance to abuse the credit card information elsewhere. Therefore, we introduce the Secure Electronic Transaction (SET) standard and explain its operations.

8.1.2 Access Security

Imposing access control on the border between the external and the internal networks is important to network security. The access control is generally bidirectional. Restricting access from the external to the internal can protect hosts in the internal network from illegal access, and restricting access from the internal to the external is usually based on policy considerations. For example, an organization may not want its employees to access any external FTP sites during working hours, and so traffic destined for the common FTP port, i.e., port 21, are simply dropped by the organization's filtering devices.

The firewall systems enforce access control by filtering incoming and outgoing packets according to a set of rules in the security policy. They either permit or deny the packets by matching the information in the packets against the rules. Therefore, fast rule matching is essential to the firewall's performance. If the matching is not fast enough, the firewall itself becomes a bottleneck.

Firewall systems generally come in two types: *packet filter-based firewall* and *application gateway-based firewall*. The former filters packets by referring to the fields in the network layer (referred to as L3) and transport layer (referred to as L4) headers, and thus it operates at the network layer and the transport layer. The filtering is fast since those fields are usually only a few bytes at fixed positions. However, access control by looking at only L3 and L4 information may not be sufficient, as it is possible to hide services on ports other than well-known ports. For example, if an FTP service is located on port 1234, then blocking accessing to port 21 simply does not work. Therefore, looking for signatures of applications is sometimes necessary if the filtering is meant to be precise, and this is referred to as gateway-based firewall. Moreover, if the policy is associated with the packet contents, examining the application information is also a must. For example, both allowed and banned URL requests may be destined to port 80. Neither restricting nor opening port 80 can work. The solution is to match the requests against a set of blacklist or whitelist URLs.

Examining application content is no free lunch. First, the packets may need to be assembled to restore the application content for examination. Second, the firewalls may need to keep the connection states to reflect the status of each connection. Third, scanning the packet content for application signatures is more complicated than matching fixed fields in the packet headers, so the performance issues are even more critical. Section 8.3 introduces two examples of open source implementation: a packet filter–based firewall, NetFilter, and an application gateway–based firewall, Firewall Toolkits (FWTK).

8.1.3 System Security

Defects in protocol, software, and system design result in vulnerabilities that hackers can exploit. The hackers may intrude into a vulnerable system to steal secret information, make a system's service crash, gain the administrator authority of that system, and propagate malicious programs. These malicious behaviors must be detected and curbed for system security. Given the huge amount of network traffic every day, it is impossible for network administrators to manually examine what is going on from the traffic log file. An intrusion detection (or prevention) system is therefore deployed to analyze the traffic to *detect* attacks. It may either generate *alerts* that indicate the attack type and related information (e.g., source of the attacker), or *prevent* the attacks by blocking them upon detection. The detection may be based on a set of rules that describe the attacking scenario or signatures for *known* attacks, or look for anomalies in the traffic. The former may ignore unknown attacks (so-called *false negatives*) since no rules describe them. The latter could find out unknown attacks, but may also generate *false positives* more easily since normal traffic may behave like anomalous traffic. There is a trade-off between the two techniques. Moreover, intrusion detection is usually for purpose of forensics since it only monitors the traffic and does not *block* an attack. If the system is too slow to catch up with the amount of traffic, it just drops some packets and perhaps loses the alerts of a few possible attacks, but does not harm normal communications. An intrusion prevention system, on the other hand, is deployed at the gateway of incoming and outgoing traffic. It has the ability to *block* a detected attack but if it is unable to catch up with the amount of traffic, it becomes a bottleneck to system performance, and the bidirectional communications might be slowed down.

Wild propagation of malicious programs, also known as *malware,* has become a major threat on the Internet. Those programs may do harm on an infected system, such as making a service crash or stealing confidential information. They may look indistinguishable from other normal programs, or even run stealthily without a user's awareness. A common approach to detecting them is scanning the code for signatures of these malicious programs, but detection is getting difficult as they tend to hide themselves in various ways. For example, they may encrypt the code with various keys, and decrypt the code only when they are executed. Therefore, scanning the executables for signature matching becomes ineffective. A possible solution is actually running the malware and watching its behavior. However, the malware may be equipped with several *antidetection* mechanisms, such as detecting the existence of the analysis program and pretending to behave well if it discovers that someone is analyzing it. We also cover these issues in Section 8.4.

8.2 DATA SECURITY

Section 8.1 discussed the evolution of cryptography and its applications. This section first dives into the principles of cryptography. For the symmetric key systems, we cover Data Encryption Standard (DES), Triple-DES (3DES), and Advanced Encryption Standard (AES). For the asymmetric key systems, we examine RSA (Rivest, Shamir, and Adleman). Next we introduce Message Digest algorithm 5 (MD5) for authentication. Finally, the applications of cryptography to virtual private networks (VPNs) are presented, including Point-to-Point Tunneling Protocol (PPTP) and Layer 2 Tunneling Protocol (L2TP) at the link layer, IP Security (IPsec) at the network layer, and Secure Socket Layer (SSL) and Secure Electronic Transaction (SET) at the transport layer. The example open source implementations are on 3DES, MD5, and IPSec.

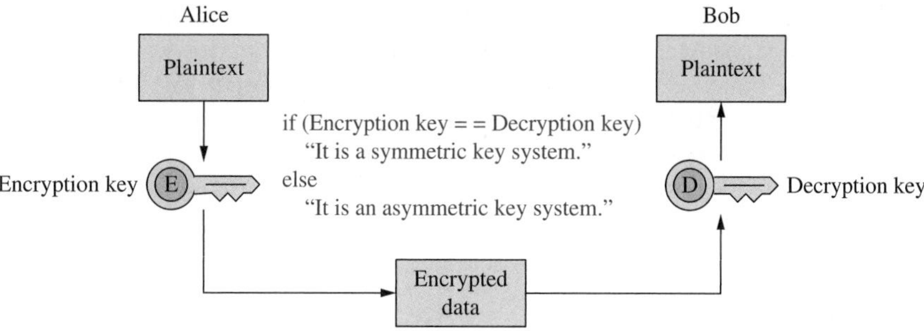

FIGURE 8.1 Data encryption and decryption.

8.2.1 Principles of Cryptography

Figure 8.1 shows the procedure of data encryption and decryption. To achieve data security, Alice could encrypt important data before transmitting. Even though Trudy intercepts the encrypted data, she cannot get the original plaintext. As a result, data encryption protects the confidentiality of the original text. After Bob receives the encrypted data, Bob can understand the plaintext from Alice by decrypting it with the decryption key.

Symmetric key systems adopt a common key to encrypt and decrypt the plaintext, while the keys are different for encryption and decryption in the asymmetric key system. Since Alice and Bob share a common key, the key value must be distributed from one to the other in a secure manner, or the encrypted data would be revealed to unauthorized people. Simply encrypting the key and then transmitting it faces the same problem as encrypting the data. A *key distribution center* (KDC) can provide the service for the users to register and share their secret keys. A well-known example that uses a KDC is the Kerberos protocol, in which two entities in the work can identify each other. However, the KDC itself must be trusted, and it could become a single point of failure. Therefore, the asymmetric key system is the solution. The keys for encryption and decryption are paired. Alice uses a key in the pair to encrypt the data such that only Bob owns the other key to decrypt. As a result, there is no need to distribute Bob's key to Alice. Although this system looks ideal, a critical problem with it is that the computation of encryption and decryption is slow. In practice, the asymmetric key system is therefore used to distribute only the common key in the symmetric key system. After both peers own the symmetric key, they can use the key to transmit a large volume of data. The security and efficiency are thus balanced.

Symmetric Key System

A well-known example of the symmetric key system is the Data Encryption Standard (DES) adopted by the U.S. government to secure data in 1977. DES uses a 56-bit symmetric key for encryption and decryption. The International Data Encryption Algorithm (IDEA) also uses the symmetric key system. At present, the 56-bit DES algorithm is still popular, although a more secure system, the 112-bit DES algorithm, can be used, but only in the United States.

The 56-bit DES encrypts each 64-bit data block unit via a 56-bit key, and produces the monoalphabetic result; therefore, the DES will obtain the same encrypted data of the same plaintext if it uses the same key for the encryption. The operations of DES include the permutation ciphers, substitution ciphers that are repeated for 16 iterations in the computation. Figure 8.2 shows the principle of DES operation, which is also described as follows: First, the plaintext is partitioned into 64-bit data blocks. Each block, $T = t_1 t_2 \ldots t_{64}$, performs the initial transposition to obtain T_0, where T_0 is $t_{58} t_{50} t_{42} \ldots t_{23} t_{15} t_7$, which forms two 32-bit blocks, R_0 and L_0, as

$$T_0 = L_0 R_0,$$

where

$$L_0 = t_{58} t_{50} t_{42} \ldots t_{16} t_8$$
$$R_0 = t_{57} t_{49} t_{41} \ldots t_{15} t_7.$$

The data blocks of L_0 and R_0 are the inputs of the next iteration as

$$L_1 = R_0$$
$$R_1 = L_0 \oplus f(R_0, K_1),$$

where K_1 is derived from the 56-bit key.

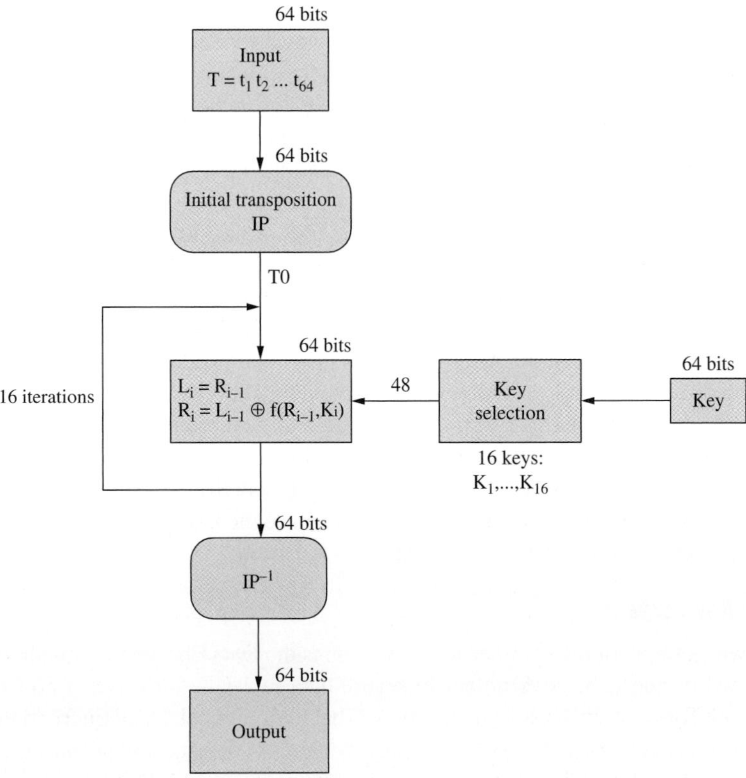

FIGURE 8.2 Encryption procedure of DES.

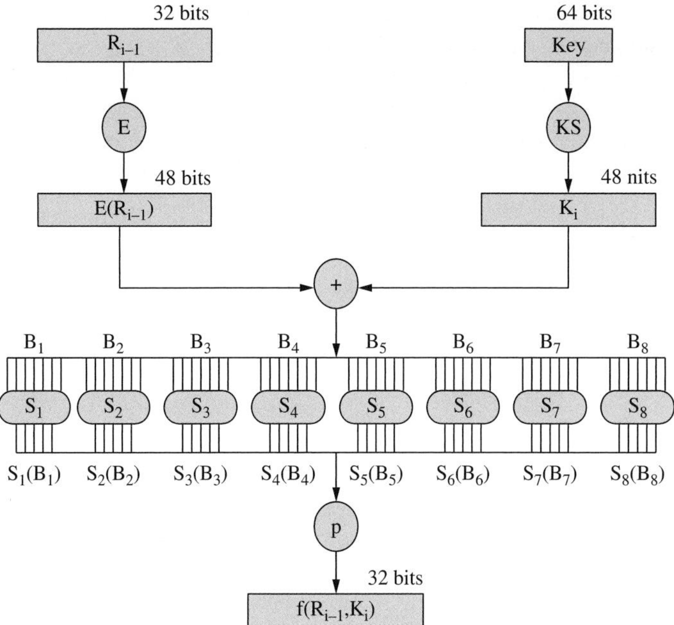

FIGURE 8.3 Computation process of $f(R_{i\text{-}1}, K_i)$.

After that, the result becomes $T_1 = L_1R_1$. The 56-bit key is pre-computed as sixteen 48-bit keys: $K_1, K_2, \ldots, K_{16}$. Figure 8.3 shows the process of $f(R_0, K_1)$, where the 32-bit R_0 and the 48-bit K_1 are the encryption inputs. First, the 32-bit R_0 is expanded to get a 48-bit result by the operation of $E(R_0)$. Second, both the 48-bit $E(R_0)$ and 48-bit K_1 perform an XOR operation to obtain a 48-bit result, which will be partitioned into eight 6-bit inputs, $B_1, B_2 \ldots B_8$, for the following substitution.

After substitution of S_i, eight 4-bit blocks, $S_i(B_i)$, are obtained. The computation then performs a 32-bit permutation to get $f(R_0, k_1)$, and finally R_1 can also be obtained by the operation $L_0 \oplus f(R_0, k_1)$.

Repeating the same iteration 16 times, i.e., $L_{i+1}R_{i+1} \leftarrow L_iR_i$, $i = 0, \ldots, 15$, can obtain $T_{16} = L_{16}R_{16}$. The computation then performs the inverse initial transposition to get 64-bit encrypted data. Reversing the procedure of encryption can decrypt the plaintext from the encrypted data.

RSA Data Security once offered $10,000 to whomever could decrypt the plaintext from the text encrypted by the 56-bit DES algorithm. A team decrypted the encrypted data in fewer than four months. Another person decrypted the latest round of the DES challenge in 22 hours in 1999. Therefore, DES is not secure enough if the data is vitally important. For ordinary applications, it could be considered secure enough, as preceding decryption attempts relied on heavy computation by a large set of computers. Repeating the DES algorithm several times could be more secure than the single DES system since the attackers may need to find out more keys in the iterations. For instance, the U.S. government recommends the triple-DES (3DES) and 128-bit DES algorithms as the standard for encryption and decryption in the United

States. Suppose K1, K2, and K3 are the three keys in the three iterations. The encryption and decryption procedures are

$$\text{Encryption: } E_{K3}(D_{K2}(E_{K1}(P))) = C, \text{ and}$$

$$\text{Decryption: } D_{K1}(E_{K2}(D_{K3}(C))) = P,$$

where P is the plaintext, C is the ciphertext, E is the DES encryption, and D is the DES decryption. The procedures are all composed of the DES computation, and can reuse the existing DES functional blocks in implementation. Open Source Implementation 8.1 describes an implementation of 3DES.

Open Source Implementation 8.1: Hardware 3DES

Overview

Here we introduce a *hardware* implementation of 3DES, as it is a common approach for accelerating 3DES computation. The 3DES computation involves a large number of bit-level operations, such as substitution and permutation (see the introduction to the DES computation). If the 3DES computation is implemented in software, each operation will take several instructions to complete, as the inherent operands are usually a word consisting of multiple bytes. Moreover, hardware implementation allows operations on the data blocks in parallel. It is therefore more natural to implement the 3DES computation in hardware.

An open source project on the opencores Web site (*www.opencores.org*) is dedicated to 3DES implementation in VHDL. We use this project as an example to explain the open source implementation, which supports three 64-bit DES keys, and is compliant with the NIST FIPS 46-3 standard. Since 3DES computes DES three times, the components in each stage of the hardware design are mapped to the functional blocks in the DES computation, such as S-box for substitution and P-box for permutation. The design is straightforward, realizing the aforementioned operations with a large number of signal assignments in turn.

Block Diagram

Figure 8.4 illustrates the major functional blocks. Three blocks of the DES computation are cascaded in sequence to perform the computation with three

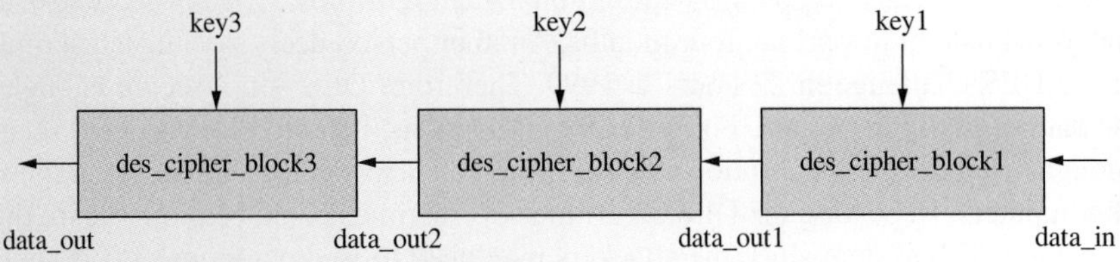

FIGURE 8.4 Functional blocks in the 3DES module.

TABLE 8.1 Signals in the Interface of the Main Functional Block

Signal	Direction	Description
KEY1_IN[0:63]	IN	The first 64-bit key
KEY2_IN[0:63]	IN	The second 64-bit key
KEY3_IN[0:63]	IN	The third 64-bit key
FUNCTION_SELECT	IN	Encryption or decryption
LDKEY	IN	Indicates the keys are ready
LDDATA	IN	Indicates the data are ready
RESET	IN	Reset to the initial state
CLOCK	IN	Synchronous clock input
DATA_OUT[0:63]	OUT	64-bit encrypted/decrypted data
OUT_READY	OUT	Output data are ready

different keys. The data output of each block is the input of the next block. Inside each block are the functional blocks of key expansion, substitution, permutation, and so on. Their relationship is mapped from the computation illustrated in Figures 8.2 and 8.3.

Data Structures

The signals in the interface of the main functional blocks are listed in Table 8.1.

Note that even though each key length is 64 bits long, eight of the bits are for parity check and will be discarded before the encryption/decryption computation. Each key has indeed only 56 bits.

Algorithm Implementations

Upon initialization, the main functional block (in `tdes_top.vhd`) sets the next state to `WaitKeyState`, and reads `FUNCTION_SELECT` to determine whether to execute encryption or decryption. The block then waits for the keys until they are available (`LDKEY` == 1), and enters `WaitDataState`, in which the block waits for data until they are available (`LDDATA` == 1). The code segment for the initialization is as follows:

```
if reset = '1' then
        nextstate           <= WaitKeyState;
        lddata_internal     <= '0';
        out_ready           <= '0';
        fsel_internal       <= function_select;
        fsel_internal_inv   <= not function_select;
```

Continued

```
else
     data_out                    <= data_out_internal;
     out_ready                   <= des_out_rdy_internal;
     case nextstate is
         when WaitKeyState =>
          if ldkey = '0' then
             nextstate        <= WaitKeyState;
          else
          // read keys here; the codes not shown;
          nextstate    <= WaitDataState;
          end if;
       when WaitDataState =>
         if lddata = '0' then
            nextstate           <= WaitDataState;
            ld_data_internal   <= '0';
         else
         // read data here; the codes not shown;
         end if;
end if;
```

Three DES blocks (in the block named `des_cipher_top`) are in the design, each of which reads the three keys, respectively. The operations of the DES are in `e_expansion_function.vhd`, `p_box.vhd`, `s_box.vhd`, and so on. For example, the substitution operation is further divided into eight modules, from `s1_box.vhd` to `s8_box.vhd`, as there are eight such substitutions (See Figure 8.3). The code segment for substitution in `s1_box.vhd` is as follows:

```
begin
SPO        <= "1110" when A = x"0" else
              "0000" when A = x"1" else
              "0100" when A = x"2" else
              "1111" when A = x"3" else
              "1101" when A = x"4" else
              "0111" when A = x"5" else
              "0001" when A = x"6" else
              …. // all combinations of 6-bit A's
end
```

For brevity, we do not look deeply into each block, and leave the details to the reader.

Exercises

1. Point out which components in the design are likely to be inefficient if it were implemented in software.
2. Find out in the code how the initial 56-bit key is transformed into the 48-bit keys in each of the 16 iterations.

Although DES and 3DES can be easily implemented in hardware, they are slow in software implementation due to their bit-level operations. The AES (Advanced Encryption Standard) algorithm can be better implemented in software. The substitutions and permutations in its encryption/decryption procedure are all in the *byte* level. The operations are much more suitable to software implementation because it is trivial to swap two bytes or replace the content of a byte in software. The AES algorithm comes with keys of 128 bits, 192 bits, and 256 bits. Besides the efficiency of AES, it is much more secure than DES for its vast key space. Even a 128-bit key takes a great deal of effort to crack. Therefore, AES is secure enough for the purpose of data security.

Asymmetric Key System

The symmetric key system uses the same key for both encryption and decryption, but the key should be distributed in a secure approach first. The asymmetric key system (or public key system) uses a pair of keys to encrypt and decrypt data, respectively. One key can be well-known, the *public key,* and the other key must be private, the *private key.* In Figure 8.5, for example, Alice uses Bob's public key for encryption, and Bob uses his private key to decrypt the encrypted data. Because only Bob has the private key, nobody else could decrypt the encrypted information, even though the public key is well-known. Moreover, Alice can also be uniquely identified by encrypting the data with her private key because nobody else has her private key (see Subsection 8.2.2).

RSA is the most famous asymmetric key algorithm, named after three MIT professors, Ronald Rivest, Adi Shamir, and Leonard Adleman. Although RSA can solve the problem of key distribution, its computation complexity is high and thus inappropriate for encrypting/decrypting normal data. Therefore, RSA is often used for key distribution or authentication, while a symmetric key system encrypts and decrypts a vast amount of data. Figure 8.6 describes the procedure of selecting public and private keys in RSA:

1. Select two very large primes, p and q. The larger the primes are, the harder the crack is, but the computation time will also be increased significantly. RSA Labs suggests the selected primes be larger than 10^{100}.

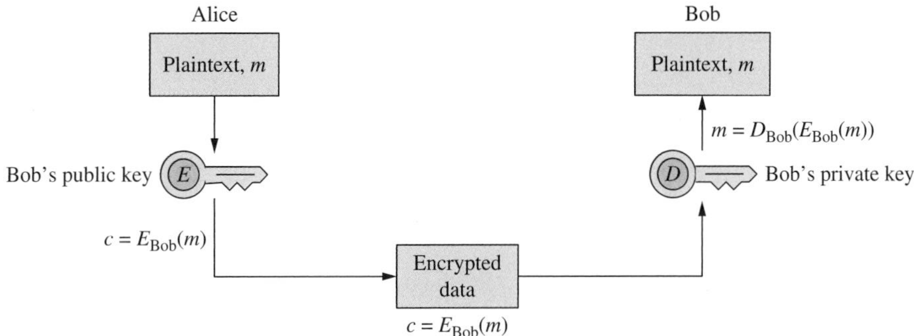

FIGURE 8.5 Asymmetric key cryptography.

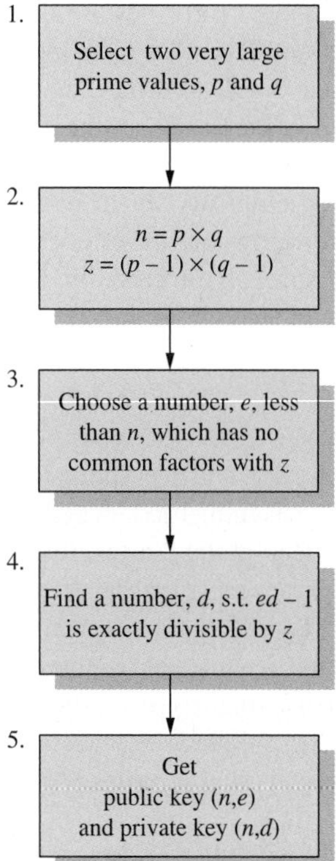

FIGURE 8.6 Procedures of public key and private key selection by RSA.

2. Compute n by $p*q$ and z by $(p\text{-}1)*(q\text{-}1)$, i.e., $n=p*q$ and $z=(p\text{-}1)*(q\text{-}1)$.
3. Choose a value e as the public key, which is less than n and a relative prime to z.
4. Compute a value d as the private key, where $e*d$-1 should be divisible by z.

Therefore, Bob can distribute the public key (n,e) to anyone, and then Alice can use this key to encrypt data and Bob can use his private key (n,d) to decrypt data. For instance, Alice wants to transmit a bit stream m to Bob, where $m < n$. Alice first computes m^e and divides it by n to get the remainder c, where c is the cipher or encrypted data. Once Bob receives the encrypted data c, he computes c^d and divides it by n to get the remainder m, where m is the original plaintext. The following equations summarize the process:

$c = m^e \bmod n$ // use the (n,e) public key to encrypt plaintext into encrypted data c.

$m = c^d \bmod n$ // use the (n,d) private key to decrypt the encrypted data, and then get plaintext m.

Next, we give a trivial example to describe the procedure. First, Bob selects $p = 11$ and $q = 17$, and then computes n by $p*q$ ($n = 187$) and z by $(p\text{-}1)*(q\text{-}1)$ (i.e., 160). Second, Bob selects 23 as e, where e is a relative prime to z. Finally, Bob computes $(z + 1)/e$ to obtain $d = 7$. Therefore, Bob distributes the public key ($n = 187$, $e = 23$) to Alice.

Plaintext	m	m^e	$c = m^e \bmod n$
'c'	3	94143178827	181
'l'	12	6.6247E+24	177
'a'	1	1	1
'p'	16	4.9517E+27	169

FIGURE 8.7(a) Procedure of Alice encrypting plaintext "clap" by using public key (n = 187, e = 23).

She uses the public key to encrypt the plaintext m and gets the encrypted data c. After Bob receives the encrypted data c, he decrypts it with his private key (n = 187, d = 7).

Assume that Alice sends the plaintext of "clap" to Bob. She first maps characters a~z to numbers 1~26 and obtains 'c' = 3, 'l' = 12, 'a' = 1 and 'p' = 16. Figure 8.7(a) shows the encryption procedure with public key (n = 187, e = 23), and Figure 8.7(b) shows the decryption procedure with private key (n = 187, d = 7).

Both the encryption and decryption procedures have exponential operation, which results in high computation complexity. The efficiency of DES is about 100 times faster than that of RSA in software computation and 10^3~10^4 times faster in hardware computation. Therefore, most applications combine the symmetric and asymmetric key systems. The sender Alice randomly generates a session (symmetric) key to encrypt the plaintext into the ciphertext c. She then uses Bob's public key (asymmetric) to encrypt the session key, and sends c to Bob. After Bob receives c, he first uses his private key (asymmetric) to decrypt the encrypted session key, and then derives the session key for future encryption and decryption. Hence, the key distribution procedure is safe and leads to efficient data transmission.

In practice, the public key of a user can be derived from the *Certificate Authority* (CA), an organization that maintains the credibility of these public keys as well as the user's identity. In this mechanism, a user must register his/her public key first, and the CA must carefully verify the identity of the user, or it can be easily subverted. The public key as well as the information of the user's identity will be included in a digitally signed certificate issued from the CA. Therefore, the other users can verify the user's identity from the digital certificate and make sure the public key is really from that user.

Encrypted text, c	c^d	$m = c^d \bmod n$	Plaintext
181	6.3642E+15	3	'c'
177	5.4426E+15	12	'l'
1	1	1	'a'
169	3.9373E+15	16	'p'

FIGURE 8.7(b) Procedure of Bob decrypting by using secret key (n = 187, d = 7).

Principle in Action: Secure Wireless Channels

Wireless networks broadcast frames in essence. Securing wireless transmission channels is critical, otherwise anyone could easily sniff the traffic. In the wireless LAN technology, IEEE 802.11 comes with a Wired Equivalent Privacy (WEP) standard, which protects data in the wireless medium. In this standard, a data stream is encrypted with the RC4 algorithm. RC4 is pretty simple. At the transmitting station, RC4 *XOR*s the data stream with a key stream to generate the cipher stream. At the receiving station, RC4 XORs the cipher stream with exactly the same key stream to recover the original data. Both the transmitting and receiving stations can synchronize the key stream because both use the same seed to generate the key stream with a pseudorandom number generator.

WEP is not very secure, due to its design flaw. In August 2001, a paper titled "Weakness in the Key Scheduling Algorithm of RC4" by Fluhrer et. al. was published to attack the WEP. Simply put, it is possible to deduce the content of the key stream from the weak initialization vector (IV) that is part of the WEP key. The IV value is transmitted in clear text, and by collecting a sufficiently large number of frames, the key stream can be recovered from the weak IV values present in the frames. A program called AirSnort (airsnort.shmoo.com) is available publicly for this attack.

To address the severe flaw, the Wi-Fi Alliance introduced the Wi-Fi Protected Access (WPA) specification, which was later extended to be the IEEE 802.11,i ratified in 2004. In 802.11i, the Advanced Encryption Standard (AES) becomes the approach for encrypting wireless data, and the IEEE 802.1X serves as the authentication mechanism. This new standard is available in many new products, making the wireless LAN a more secure environment.

8.2.2 Digital Signature and Message Authentication

Besides data encryption, Bob needs to ensure the data are really from Alice because the intruder Trudy may pretend to be Alice to send the data. In the asymmetric key system, *digital signature* is the most popular authentication method. There are three advantages of applying digital signature to transmission data: (1) the receiver can ensure the data are really from the sender, (2) the sender cannot deny the transmission, and (3) nobody can modify the received data, producing data integrity.

An asymmetric key system and a hash function can realize digital signature. In Figures 8.8 and 8.9, Alice uses a digital signature to authenticate herself when sending the plaintext to Bob. In Figure 8.8, Alice first computes the plaintext via a hash function to derive a unique hash value of "12340782", then encrypts the hash value with her private key, and sends the encrypted text "??!!??!!", i.e., Alice's digital signature, with the plaintext to Bob. After Bob receives the plaintext Alice's with digital signature, he decrypts the digital signature of "??!!??!!" with Alice's public key to get the hash value of "12340782", and computes the plaintext with the same hash function to obtain the hash value of "12340782". If both hash values are equal, Bob

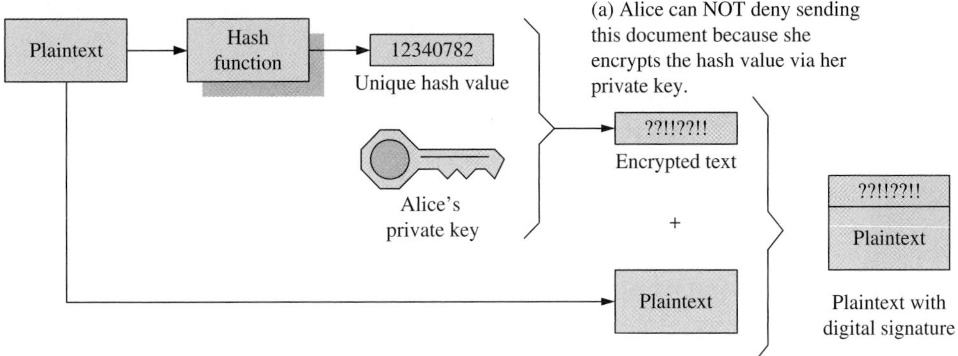

FIGURE 8.8 Alice sends the document with digital signature.

can be sure that the plaintext is sent by Alice. In other words, digital signatures can realize the following three functions:

Alice cannot deny she has sent this document because she encrypts the hash value via her private key.

Bob cannot modify the received document; otherwise both hash values will be distinct.

The document has not been modified because it contains the same hash value of "12340782".

If the sender uses a secret key to encrypt the hash value of the plaintext, and the receiver also uses the same secret key to decrypt the encrypted hash value for verification, the encrypted hash value is called message authentication code (MAC). The concept is similar to digital signature, but the secret key to encrypt and decrypt the hash value is *symmetric.* Therefore, the receiver must share the secret key beforehand. The MAC mechanism can provide *data integrity* and *authentication,* but not *nonrepudiation,* since anyone who owns the secret key can generate the MAC of other messages.

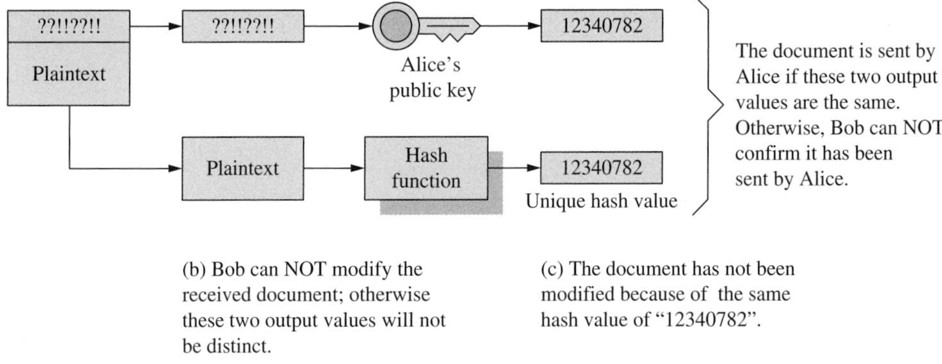

FIGURE 8.9 Bob identifies whether the received document with digital signature is from Alice or not.

We have mentioned that Alice should generate a hash value for the corresponding plaintext. The hash value is called the message digest (MD). The function of message digest is to keep data integrity. Popular hash functions include MD4, MD5, and Secure Hash Algorithm (SHA), etc. MD4 and MD5 were proposed by Ron Rivest in 1992, and MD5 is the most commonly adopted algorithm to generate a 128-bit message digest. The U.S. government uses SHA-1, which generates a 160-bit message digest and is more robust than MD5.

Open Source Implementation 8.2: MD5

Overview

MD5 is common in many security applications that verify whether the data has been stealthily modified. The computation goes through the data to derive the MD5 value. An open source implementation of MD5 is available in the `md5.c` file under the `crypto` directory of the widely available Linux 2.6.x kernel source. The MD5 algorithm keeps updating a 128-bit state (i.e., four 32-bit words) after reading each batch of 512 bits from the source message during the computation. In the final iteration, the last batch of data is padded up to 512 bits if it is shorter than 512 bits.

Block Diagram

The main three functions in md5.c are `md5_init()`, `md_update()`, and `md_final()`. The first initializes the 128-bit state, the second keeps updating the state in each iteration, and the last computes the final MD5 value from the last batch of data. Figure 8.10 illustrates the execution flow of the MD5 computation.

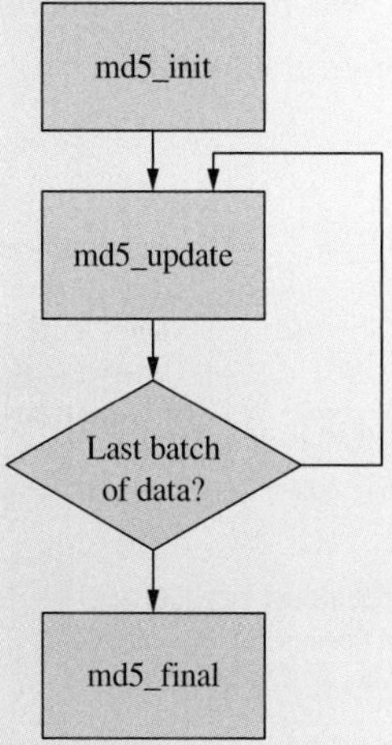

FIGURE 8.10 Main functional blocks in md5.c and the execution flow.

Data Structures

The 128-bit state is initialized in the `md5_init()` function as follows, where the `mctx` structure also includes auxiliary variables such as the `block` array and the `byte_count` variable for computation:

```
mctx->hash[0] = 0x67452301;
mctx->hash[1] = 0xefcdab89;
mctx->hash[2] = 0x98badcfe;
mctx->hash[3] = 0x10325476;
```

Algorithm Implementations

After initialization, the `md5_update()` function grabs the source message in batches of 64 bytes (equivalent to 512 bits), and proceeds with the MD5 computation with the following code segment:

```
     const u32 avail = sizeof(mctx->block) - (mctx->byte_
count & 0x3f);
     mctx->byte_count += len;
     if (avail > len) {
             memcpy((char *)mctx->block +
(sizeof(mctx->block) - avail), data, len);
             return 0;
     }
     memcpy((char *)mctx->block +
(sizeof(mctx->block) - avail),data, avail);
     md5_transform_helper(mctx);
     data += avail;
     len -= avail;

     while (len >= sizeof(mctx->block)) {
             memcpy(mctx->block, data,
sizeof(mctx->block));
             md5_transform_helper(mctx);
             data += sizeof(mctx->block);
             len -= sizeof(mctx->block);
     }
     memcpy(mctx->block, data, len);
     return 0;
```

Here the `data` array is the source message to be transformed into the MD5 value, and the message length is `len`. The `md5_update()` function attempts to read from `data` until the `block` array (64 bytes) is filled up. Once the array is filled up, the `md5_transform_helper()` function is invoked, in which the `md5_transform()` function is invoked in turn.

The `md5_tranform()` function is the main part of the MD5 computation (see RFC 1321 for details). The function performs four similar *rounds* of 16 operations in order. For example, the 16 operations in the first round are as follows:

Continued

```
MD5STEP(F1, a, b, c, d, in[0] + 0xd76aa478, 7);
MD5STEP(F1, d, a, b, c, in[1] + 0xe8c7b756, 12);
MD5STEP(F1, c, d, a, b, in[2] + 0x242070db, 17);
MD5STEP(F1, b, c, d, a, in[3] + 0xc1bdceee, 22);
MD5STEP(F1, a, b, c, d, in[4] + 0xf57c0faf, 7);
MD5STEP(F1, d, a, b, c, in[5] + 0x4787c62a, 12);
MD5STEP(F1, c, d, a, b, in[6] + 0xa8304613, 17);
MD5STEP(F1, b, c, d, a, in[7] + 0xfd469501, 22);
MD5STEP(F1, a, b, c, d, in[8] + 0x698098d8, 7);
MD5STEP(F1, d, a, b, c, in[9] + 0x8b44f7af, 12);
MD5STEP(F1, c, d, a, b, in[10] + 0xffff5bb1, 17);
MD5STEP(F1, b, c, d, a, in[11] + 0x895cd7be, 22);
MD5STEP(F1, a, b, c, d, in[12] + 0x6b901122, 7);
MD5STEP(F1, d, a, b, c, in[13] + 0xfd987193, 12);
MD5STEP(F1, c, d, a, b, in[14] + 0xa679438e, 17);
MD5STEP(F1, b, c, d, a, in[15] + 0x49b40821, 22);
```

Here a, b, c, and d are the states of four 32-bit words from the hash array, and MD5STEP is a macro defined as follows:

```
#define MD5STEP(f, w, x, y, z, in, s) \
(w += f(x, y, z) + in, w = (w<<s | w>>(32-s)) + x)
```

The nonlinear functions from *F1* to *F4* applied in the four rounds are defined as follows:

```
#define F1(x, y, z) (z ^ (x & (y ^ z)))
#define F2(x, y, z) F1(z, x, y)
#define F3(x, y, z) (x ^ y ^ z)
#define F4(x, y, z) (y ^ (x | ~z))
```

If the message length is not a multiple of 64 bytes, the last part will be padded until the total length is a multiple of 64 bytes. Simply put, the padding is a bit 1 followed by a number of zeros, and finally the original message length represented in bits. The md5_final() function does the padding and computes the final output by calling the md5_tranform() function on the last block array. The md5 value will be finally stored in the hash field of mctx structure.

Exercises

1. Numerical values in a CPU may be represented in little endian or big endian. Explain how the md5.c program handles this disparity in representation for the computation.
2. Compared with sha1_generic.c in the same directory, find where and how the sha_tranform() function is implemented. What is the major difference between the implementations of md5_transform() and sha_tranform()?

8.2.3 Link Layer Tunneling

A popular security mechanism in the link layer is *tunneling,* which is based on packet encapsulation. Tunneling builds a private communication tunnel over public networks. If a user wants to access the corporate network, he/she just dials to the local network access server (NAS) of that company and uses the NAS to establish a tunnel to the corporate network. The Layer-2 tunneling can support IP, IPX, NetBEUI, and AppleTalk at the same time.

A well-known example of Layer-2 tunneling is PPTP (abbreviation of Point-to-Point Tunneling Protocol) defined in RFC 2637, which is developed to be used on VPN. PPTP encapsulates encrypted PPP frames in IP datagrams in the tunnel. PPTP tunnels have two modes: the client-initiated mode, in which the client initiates a direct connection to the PPP server, and the ISP-initiated mode, in which the client establishes a PPP session with the ISP access server first and then establishes tunnels with a remote PPTP server. Several connections can share the established tunnel by means of call identifier.

L2TP (Layer-2 Tunneling Protocol) combines the merits of Cisco's Layer-2 Forwarding (L2F) and Microsoft's PPTP. L2TP has several advantages over its predecessors. For example, PPTP supports only one tunnel at a time per user, while L2TP can support multiple simultaneous tunnels. Note that an L2TP packet is carried within a UDP datagram, even though L2TP usually carries PPP sessions within its tunnel and has "Layer-2" in its name.

Each end of the L2TP tunnel acts as an L2TP access concentrator (LAC) on the client side and L2TP network server (LNS) on the server side. The L2TP has two message types: control and data. The control message for establishing and managing tunnels is sent over a lower-level reliable transport service. The data message carries the actual data over unreliable transfer modes such as UDP. The tunnel establishment, like that in PPTP, can also be shared by many connections by means of call ID. L2TP can also be implemented along with IPSec to be introduced in Subsection 8.24. After negotiation and establishment of the L2TP tunnel, L2TP packets are then encapsulated by IPSec to provide confidentiality.

8.2.4 IP Security (IPSec)

The IETF establishes an open standard of network security protocol in the network layer, i.e., Internet Protocol Security (IPSec). We first introduce the concept of IPSec, and then describe its mechanism by defining the IP Authentication Header, IP Encapsulation Security Payload, and the key management to achieve data integrity, authentication and privacy in secure communication.

Many commercial services were built to run over the Internet, so private communication over the Internet is of concern. Several standards for network security in the session layer and application layer have been proposed. For example, SET and SSL can achieve secure HTTP. Since the Internet is Internet Protocol (IP)-based, a secure mechanism in the IP layer is necessary to integrate various security mechanisms in the upper layer. Therefore, the IETF established IP Security (IPSec) for

IPv4/v6 to achieve the following goals: authentication, integrity, confidentiality, and access control.

The first version of IPSec (RFC 1825 to RFC 1829) was proposed in 1995. It has two primary modes: IP Authentication Header (AH) and IP Encapsulation Security Payload (ESP). The former provides the integrity and authentication of data, while the latter provides secure data transfer. The AH and the ESP header include two optional headers for using IPSec in IPv6. The first version of IPSec has no description of key exchange and management. It defines only the packet format. In 1998, the second version (RFC 2401, RFC 2402, RFC 2406) was proposed to include Security Association (SA) and key management, IKE (Internet Key Management). Consequently, the IPSec became complete.

Security Association

For private communication in IPSec, Security Association (SA) is designed to establish a unidirectional connection of secure transfer, and it is also the most important concept in the IPSec. Several important parameters are defined: the authentication algorithm and its keys, the encryption/decryption algorithms and the keys, a valid period of keys, etc. A unique SA can be defined by the IP address of a host, a security identification code (represents AH or ESP), and a 32-bit Security Parameter Index (SPI). Since SA is unidirectional, it requires two SAs to build a bidirectional point-to-point connection. An SA can use either AH or ESP as the security protocol.

Authentication Header

RFC 1828 suggests IPSec use the MD5 algorithm for authentication. The sender computes a message from the transmitted IP packet and a secret key with the MD5 algorithm, and then adds the message into the packet. After receiving this packet, the receiver performs the same MD5 calculation to obtain the message value. The receiver compares the value with that in the packet. If both are equal, the authentication is successful. Because the MD5 calculation is applied to the entire IP packet, this method not only performs authentication but also certifies the data integrity.

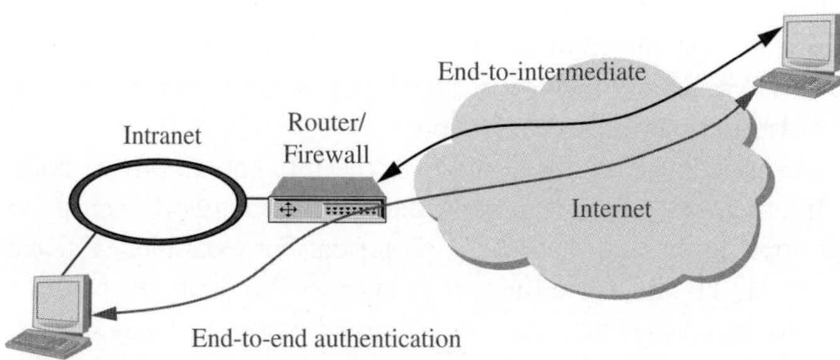

FIGURE 8.11 Authentication types.

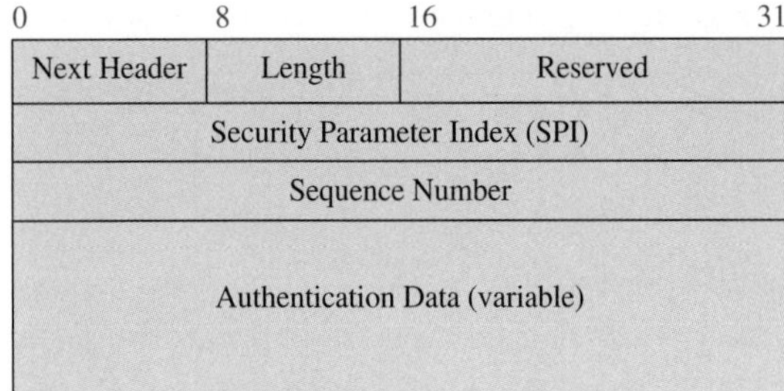

FIGURE 8.12 The Authentication header.

For authentication, IPSec defines two modes: the end-to-end mode and the end-to-intermediate mode. Figure 8.11 shows the main difference. In the former mode, both parties of the communication perform the authentication. This mode is used when both parties do not have confidence in the security of network facilities but still expect to ensure the transmission security. In the latter, the authentication is performed at one party and at the router or firewall in the local area network of the other party. In this way, the router or firewall plays the role of a "security gateway." In other words, the gateway should guarantee the security of the local area network.

Figure 8.12 shows the format of the authentication header. The first field, Next Header, represents the protocol type of the next payload after the authentication header. Following is the 8-bit Length field. The 16-bit Reserved field is reserved for future use and is set to 0 at present. The SPI field represents a unique SA. The Sequence Number represents the sequence number of packets to prevent the replay attack.

Encapsulation Security Payload

Encapsulation Security Payload (ESP) adopts DES or 3DES to provide secure IP packet transmission. ESP not only guarantees data security, but also achieves authentication and data integrity. ESP can run in two modes: the *transport mode* that encrypts the block in the transport layer and the *tunnel mode* that encrypts the entire IP packet.

Figures 8.13 and 8.14 show the two modes. In the transport mode, the ESP header is located before the data block. This mode has a shorter encrypted part than the tunnel mode, so the required bandwidth is also less. In the tunnel mode, the ESP header is located before the encrypted IP packet. The mode produces a new IP header. It is suitable in an environment protected by a security gateway. During

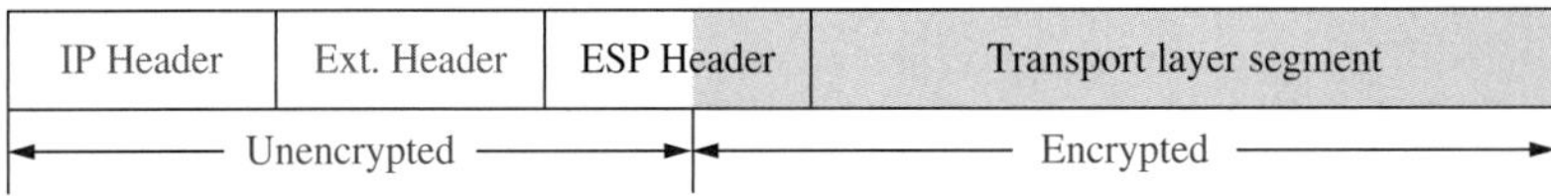

FIGURE 8.13 Transport mode ESP.

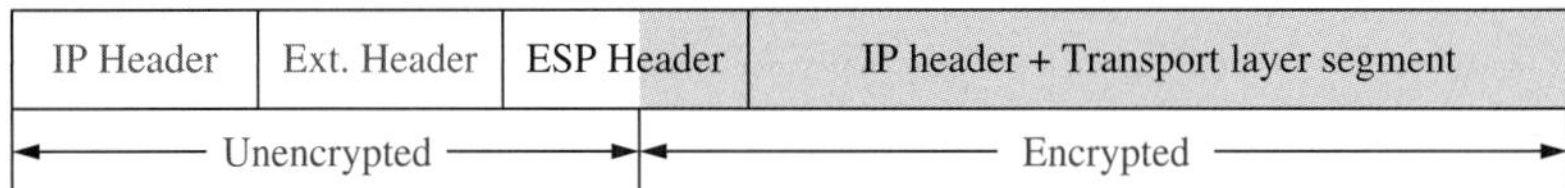

FIGURE 8.14 Tunnel mode ESP.

transmission, the sender or the gateway encrypt an IP packet, and then the encrypted packet is sent to the receiver's gateway, which then decrypts the IP packet and sends the original plaintext data to the receiver.

Key Management

Because AH authentication and ESP encryption need both encryption and decryption keys, key management is important in the IPSec standard. The main key management protocol includes SKIP (Simple Key management for IP) and ISAKMP/Oakley (Internet Key Exchange, IKE). SKIP, proposed by Sun Microsystems, adopts the Diffie Hellman's key exchange algorithm to transmit the secret key based on the public key system.

The ISAKMP consists of two major steps. In the first step, both ends of ISAKMP set up a secure and authenticated channel, the first ISAKMP SA, via negotiation. In the second step, it uses the first SA to build the AH or ESP SA. The primary difference between ISAKMP SA and IPSec SA is that ISAKMP SA is bidirectional, but IPSec SA is unidirectional.

Open Source Implementation 8.3: AH and ESP in IPSec

Overview

The implementation of IPSec is available in both open source packages and the Linux kernel. The former includes Openswan (http://www.openswan.org) and strongSwan (http://www.strongswan.org); the latter is Linux kernel 2.6. Integrating IPSec into the Linux kernel is an independent work from scratch. Since the Linux kernel is very popular among Linux users, we introduce the IPSec implementation in the Linux kernel herein.

IPSec has two primary modes: AH and ESP. The source code of the AH implementation for IPv4 is in `net/ipv4/ah4.c` (or `ipv6/ah6.c` for IPv6), while that of the ESP implementation for IPv6 is in `net/ipv4/esp4.c` (or `ipv6/esp6.c` for IPv6).

Block Diagram

Figure 8.15 presents the block diagrams of the implementation. Both `ah4_init()` and `esp4_init()` register the pointers to related handlers, and the states in both are also initialized. When packets are received or to be delivered, the `xfrm_input()` and `xfrm_output()` functions invoke the corresponding function according to which mode is used: AH or ESP.

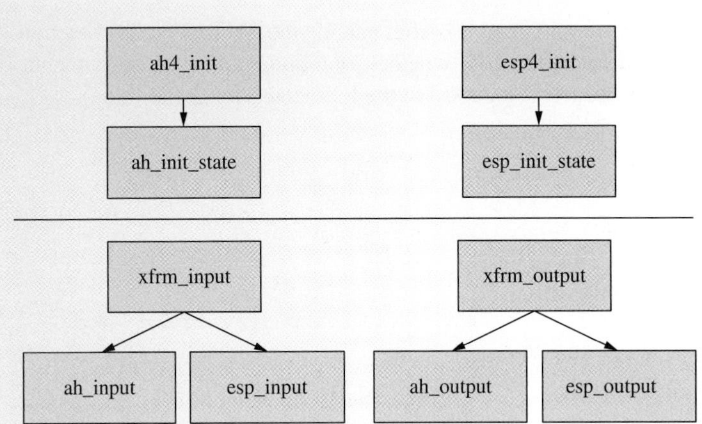

FIGURE 8.15 Main functions in the AH and ESP implementation in the Linux kernel.

Data Structures

In both modes, the authentication header and the ESP header are both defined in `include/linux/ip.h` as follows:

```
struct ip_auth_hdr {
        __u8 nexthdr;
        __u8 hdrlen;
        __be16 reserved;
        __be32 spi;
        __be32 seq_no;
        __u8 auth_data[0];
};
struct ip_esp_hdr {
        __be32 spi;
        __be32 seq_no;
        __u8 enc_data[0];
};
```

Algorithm Implementations

In the beginning of the AH implementation, the `ah4_init()` function calls `inet_add_protocol(&ah4_protocol, IPPROTO_AH)` to register the structure of the AH handler, i.e., `ah4_protocol`. The handler field of this structure is the `xfrm4_rcv()` function, which will receive and handle the IPSec packets. Note that the structure of the ESP handler also points to `xfrm4_rcv()` (see `esp4.c`), meaning which protocol to parse is left to later work. The `xfrm4_rcv()` function will eventually call the function to decode the packet and get the input state (see the `xfrm_input()` function in the `net/xfrm/xfrm_input.c`), which will in turn call the `ah4_input()` function (hooked to the

Continued

ah_type structure as seen in ah4.c). After parsing the AH header, this function performs the following code to verify whether *ah->auth_data* (i.e., the authentication data in the AH header) is identical to the ICV (integrity check value).

```
u8 auth_data[MAX_AH_AUTH_LEN];
memcpy(auth_data, ah->auth_data, ahp->icv_trunc_len);
skb_push(skb, ihl);
err = ah_mac_digest(ahp, skb, ah->auth_data);
if (err)
        goto unlock;
if (memcmp(ahp->work_icv, auth_data, ahp->icv_trunc_len))
        err = -EBADMSG;
```

In the code, the original ah->auth_data is first backed up in auth_data, and then the ah_mac_digest() function computes the ICV (in the ahp structure) just like the ah_output() function does (see below). Both values are compared to check whether the packet is valid. If it is valid, the packet is accepted; otherwise, the packet is discarded.

The ah_output() function also calls ah_mac_digest() to generate the ICV for verification on the receiver side, and then copies this value to ah->auth_data in the AH header with the following code:

```
err = ah_mac_digest(ahp, skb, ah->auth_data);
memcpy(ah->auth_data, ahp->work_icv, ahp->icv_trunc_len);
```

For simplicity, we introduce only the AH implementation herein. The ESP implementation is left to the reader for further study.

Exercises

1. Find in xfrm_input.c how the xfrm_input function determines the protocol type and calls either the ah_input() or the esp_input() function.
2. Briefly describe how a specific open source implementation of hash algorithm, e.g., MD5, which consists of md5_init, md5_update and md5_final, is executed in the *ah_mac_digest* function.

8.2.5 Transport Layer Security

In network security, an important approach for offering secure and reliable transactions between client and server hosts is to combine cryptography and authentication in the transport layer. A good solution to transport layer security is the Secure Socket Layer (SSL). Nevertheless, e-commerce needs more protection for transactions as well as integration with credit card systems, so Security Electronic Transaction (SET) was proposed for this purpose.

Secure Socket Layer (SSL)

NetScape proposed SSL to support encryption and authentication of data exchange between a Web client and the server. It was later standardized as the Transport Layer Security protocol (TLS) in RFC 2246. SSL/TLS operates between the transport and application layers. Before performing SSL, the client and server should negotiate the data encryption algorithm such as DES or IDEA. After the negotiation, the encryption and decryption processes follow in the data transmission. Figure 8.16 shows the SSL transaction flow:

- Client sends "SSL Client Hello" message to start the encryption mechanism with Server.
- Server replies with "SSL Server Hello" message to Client, and then sends its certification back to Client to request Client's certification.
- Client sends its certification to Server. (Client's certification should be optional as most clients do not have certification.)
- After that, Server and Client negotiate the key exchange, in which the session key is encrypted with Server's public key. Finally, Client and Server both share the session key and perform secure data exchange with it.

SSL supports data encryption between Client and Server, but it lacks an integrated secure payment mechanism at the backend, e.g., secure payment with credit card. Assume that Alice orders something from Bob and pays for it by credit card. The credit card information should be securely sent to Bob. Since Bob has the key to decrypt the encrypted information of Alice's credit card, Bob may abuse Alice's credit card information. SSL also lacks a certification mechanism to certify Client's credit card transactions. Once a hacker has somebody's credit card number, he may abuse it.

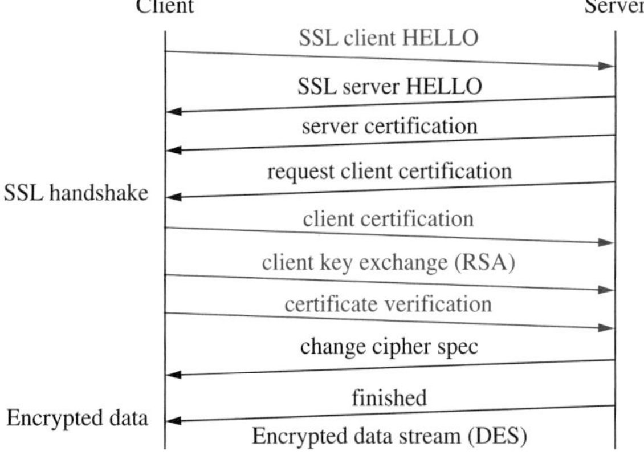

FIGURE 8.16 SSL transaction flow.

Historical Evolution: HTTP Secure (HTTPS) and Secure Shell (SSH)

HTTP Secure (HTTPS) uses the SSL/TLS protocol to provide data encryption and secure identification to HTTP. Therefore, an outsider is unable to view the real content in the payloads, even though the packets might be *eavesdropped.* The Web *server* must be provided with a public-key certificate signed by a certificate authority (CA). The certificate contains a public key and the owner's identity. The CA is an organization that issues such a certicate, and guarantees that the certificate can be trusted. The *browser* will *verify* the truth of the certificate when the user browses a Web site providing HTTPS access, and will warn the user if the certificate is susceptible. The user therefore will not be easily cheated by a *fake* Web site. However, it is still the user that defines the security of HTTPS. If a user simply ignores the warning and goes on viewing the Web site, the security will be void. As opposed to HTTP, HTTPS runs on port 443 by default, and is accessed with the URL beginning with "https."

Like HTTPS, SSH (standing for Secure Shell), running on port 22, can provide similar security. As opposed to telnet, the data transmitted in SSH is encrypted, so it is a good replacement for the insecure telnet. The usage of SSH is versatile, including SSH FTP (known as SFTP) or Secure Copy (known as SCP) for secure file transmission. Also similar to HTTPS, SSH supports key exchange and server authentification. It also supports a public-key mechanism for user authentication, in addition to the password mechanism. For example, a user can generate a public key and store it on the server. The user keeps its own private key, and the key pairs can be verified when the user logs into the server. Due to its security, SSH is very popular for execution in a remote shell and secure file transmission.

Secure Electronic Transactions (SET)

Visa, MasterCard, IBM, Microsoft, and HP cooperatively proposed Secure Electronic Transactions (SET) in February 1996. The Secure Electronic Transaction LLC (also called the SETC) organization was established in July 1997 to manage and promote the SET protocol. The characteristics of SET are:

- SET provides only the encryption of related information in payment, while SSL encrypts information between the client and server.
- SET encrypts highly sensitive data transferred among the buyer, selling party, and selling party bank, all required to have the digital certification.
- The main difference between SET and SSL is that SET will not give the credit card number to the seller, so the seller cannot abuse the number.

Figure 8.17 illustrates the operation of SET, which involves four main roles: buyer Bob, e-shop seller Alice, cardholder's bank, and e-shop's bank. Bob's public key (E_B) and private key (D_B), Alice's public key (E_A) and private key (D_A), and certifications of four parties are involved in the operations of SET. The flow of the transaction is as follows:

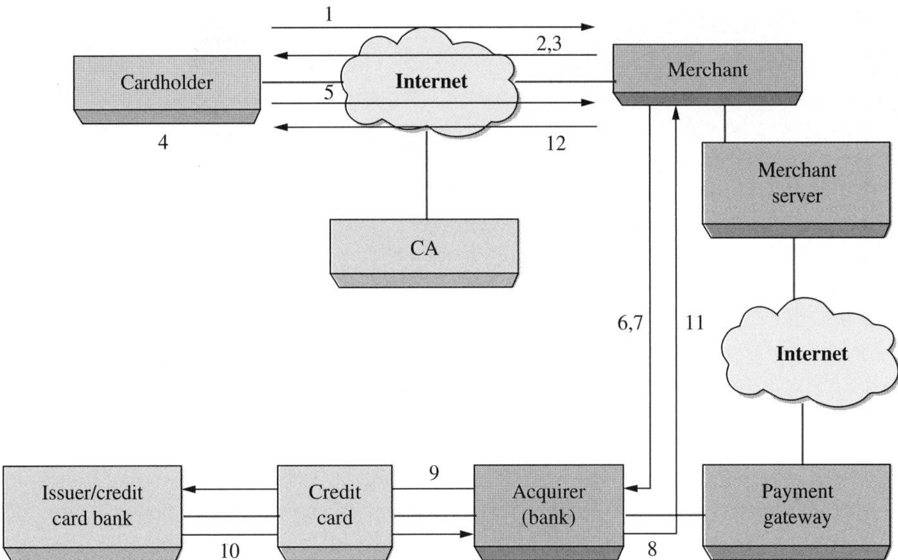

FIGURE 8.17 The flow of SET operation.

1. Bob selects a product from Alice's e-shop and informs Alice that he will pay by credit card.
2. Alice returns the transaction ID of this order to Bob.
3. Alice sends her certification and public key and the public key of her bank to Bob.
4. Bob receives the messages at Step 3.
5. Bob makes the order through the network and has order information (OI) and purchase information (PI). He encrypts OI with Alice's public key and sends it to her. At the same time, Bob encrypts PI with the public key of Alice's bank and sends it to the bank.
6. Alice sends "Request to Certificate" message to Bob's credit card bank with the order ID.
7. Alice uses the public key of her bank to encrypt the following messages: Bob's encrypted PI, her certification, and "Request to Certificate" message, and sends them to her bank.
8. Alice's bank decrypts these encrypted messages and checks whether they have been modified.
9. Alice's bank uses the original exchange mechanism of credit card to process the related operation.
10. Bob's bank replies the certification result to Alice's bank.
11. If Alice's bank receives "successful certificated," then it replies the message to Alice.

If everything is fine, Alice sends the reply of the order message to Bob to ensure that the transaction has been done. Each pair of request and response needs two parties to protect any third party from modifying or gathering secure information. Furthermore, Alice cannot obtain Bob's credit card number. As a result, SET can ensure a secure transaction environment through networks.

8.2.6 Comparison on VPNs

It is a good time to compare the VPN technologies presented in the preceding three subsections. According to the protocols on which the VPN is based, the VPN technology can be classified into L2TP/PPTP (at the link layer), IPSec (at the network layer), and SSL (above the transport layer) VPNs. Generally, the *higher* the layer within which the VPN operates, the *easier* the setup and configurations can be; however, operating at a *lower* layer could support a *wider* range of upper-layer protocols.

L2TP VPN supports authentication and privacy derived from PPP. The authentication protocols that L2TP supports include PAP, CHAP, MS-CHAP v1 and v2, etc., while the data can be encrypted with algorithms such as 3DES. Its best advantages are the ability to transport a wide range of L2 protocols: Ethernet, Frame Relay, PPP, ATM, etc., and non-IP protocols, such as IPX or Appletalk. However, L2TP is *not* secure enough, and may be subject to several attacks. Simply put, L2TP provides authentication between the LAC and the LNS in the tunnel level, but the authentication is still not on a per-packet basis. For example, the attacker has a chance of *hijacking* an L2TP tunnel *prior* to the tunnel establishment. Moreover, L2TP does not provide key management services. Due to the dominance of Internet Protocol, the need for non-IP support is also *decreasing*. L2TP also requires the installation of L2TP client software before using it.

In the tunnel mode of IPSec, the entire IP packet is encrypted, and the packet is encapsulated with a new IP header. Therefore, IPSec can serve the purpose of creating VPN. We will not repeat the details of IPSec but will summarize the advantages and disadvantages of IPSec VPN here. Like L2TP VPN, IPSec can support all upper-layer protocols besides TCP. Moreover, it is *immune* to TCP-related attacks such as *denial of service* and forged RST to terminate a connection. Its primary disadvantage is that it is harder to *deploy*. First, the system must support IPSec and have related client software. This drawback has negative effects on deployment at a large scale. Second, traffics in IPSec VPN must be *explicitly* permitted by the corporate firewalls, and thus using IPSec VPN requires extra work in firewall configuration.

SSL VPN has become popular recently because it is very user friendly. A user can simply use an ordinary browser to set up the VPN. The operation of SSL VPN is simple. In the beginning, the user contacts the VPN gateway through a browser. After the user logs in, the gateway will authenticate itself to the user and send an encrypted *session cookie* to the browser. Both of them then start to communicate and exchange the session key. Since so many devices can now browse Web, this feature is quite advantageous and is the main reason for the popularity of SSL VPN.

8.3 ACCESS SECURITY

Controlling access between the private and the public networks is an essential solution to network security. In this section, we cover the network devices for access control—the firewalls. Firewalls can filter network traffic according to the information in the network/transport layers, such as IP addresses and port numbers, or application-layer information, such as URLs. After a brief overview of firewall systems, we introduce each type of firewall. `Netfilter/iptables` and `FWTK` are two example open source implementations.

8.3.1 Introduction

A firewall is a common product to protect enterprise networks by providing access control between the private and the public network. The packets can pass through the firewall if they are permitted by access rules; otherwise they will be blocked. The blocking action may be also audited. Since the hosts in the private network are hidden behind the firewall, accessing them must be explicitly permitted by the firewall. Unauthorized outside users are not aware of the servers or hosts in the private network behind the firewall.

Firewall filtering is bidirectional. An organization can also restrict its users' access to the Internet from its private network based on some access policies. For example, the employees may not be allowed to access external FTP sites during working hours.

Since packets from either direction must pass through a firewall, the efficiency with which the firewall classifies a large number of packets is critical, or the firewall could become a bottleneck. Although the examined packet information is generally L3 and L4 information, such as IP addresses and port numbers, examining only the L3 and L4 information becomes insufficient as (1) a given service may not run on a standard well-known port, making it easy to evade the control policy, and (2) finer-grained control based on application-layer information is needed. For example, a Web filter can examine whether the URL request points to a permitted site.

Therefore, two types of firewalls are needed: network/transport layer firewalls and application layer firewalls, in terms of the checked fields of a packet. Detailed descriptions are given in the next two subsections.

8.3.2 Network/Transport Layer Firewall

A network/transport layer firewall is also called a packet filter; i.e., it filters the packets based on fields in the network layer and the rules configured by the administrators. The fields can be protocol ID, source/destination IP address, source/destination port number of TCP or UDP, etc. Such firewalls can be further separated into screened host firewall and screened subnet firewall. Figure 8.18 shows the framework of screened host firewall. In a screened host firewall, both incoming and

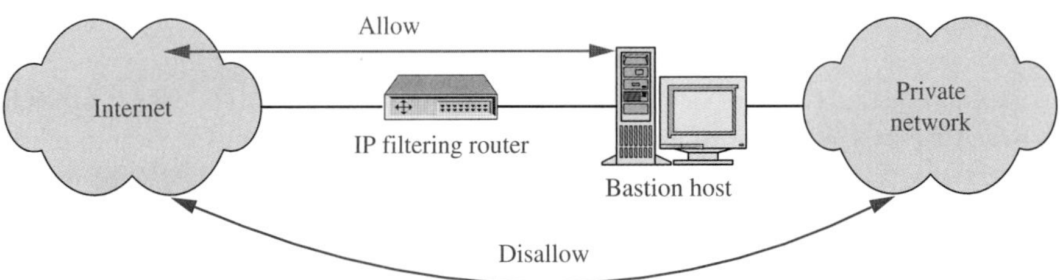

FIGURE 8.18 Screened host firewall.

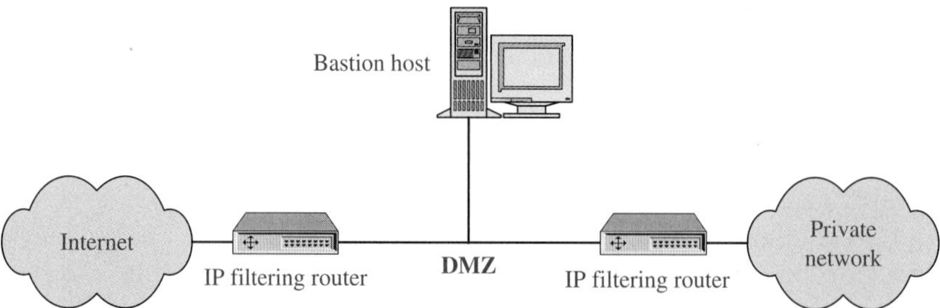

FIGURE 8.19 Screened subnet firewall.

outgoing packets must pass through the bastion host. In other words, the IP filtering router can permit or prohibit packets across the bastion host according to the rules that specify the IP addresses to be allowed or disallowed.

In this framework, the bastion host is outside the private network and must resist any attack. This framework has the advantage that setting packet filtering in the IP filtering router is simple because packets in both directions must pass through the bastion host. Its drawback is that if the administrator permits a particular service in the private network, the entire private network will be exposed to the public network. The security would decrease dramatically if packets could access the private network via these services.

Figure 8.19 shows the framework of a screened subnet firewall, which utilizes two IP filtering routers in the private network and DMZ (Demilitarized Zone). In practice, this framework can also be implemented with a single router with multiple interfaces (to the Internet, private network, and DMZ). Because an IP filtering router is built near the private network, the hosts in the private network do not expose themselves to the public network even though the IP filtering router near the Internet opens some services in the private network without passing through the bastion host. This can avoid the drawback of screened host firewall. Setting the IP filtering router is similar to screened host firewall. The IP filtering router next to the public network sets the access rules to confirm the destination IP address to the private network, and the source IP address from private network to public network must be that of the bastion host. The IP filtering router next to the private network sets the access rules to confirm that the destination IP address of the packets from the private network and the source IP address of packets to the private network must be the bastion host.

If an organization provides some services to the Internet, such as e-mail, Web, and DNS, these servers should not be located inside the private network. If these servers are compromised, an attacker then can reach all the hosts in the private network via the compromised servers as if there were no firewalls. The DMZ, an area between the external firewall and the internal firewall, is the right location to place the servers. Even if an attacker has compromised the servers in the DMZ, he or she is still unable to access the hosts in the private network behind the internal firewall. Note that the servers in the DMZ should not be allowed to actively access the private network, or the attacker still has a chance to reach the private network if the servers in the DMZ are compromised.

Open Source Implementation 8.4: Netfilter and iptables

Overview

Netfilter is a set of checkpoints in the system kernel that monitor the packets passing through individual communication protocols. These checkpoints are called *hooks.* With these hooks, it becomes possible to manipulate the packets on the packet path in the kernel. Each hook has a unique hook number so Netfilter can check whether the current communication protocol has a registered hook for the packets being processed via Netfilter. If a registered hook exists, these packets must be checked and must follow the definitive rules to be processed with the following five actions:

- NF_ACCEPT*: Accept the packet.*
- NF_DROP*: Drop the packet without processing it.*
- NF_STOLEN*: Netfilter processes packet, but not the following communication protocol.*
- NF_QUEUE*: Save packet into the queue.*
- NF_REPEAT*: Call this hook to process packet again.*

Block Diagram

In Netfilter, IP tables perform packet checking against five registered hooks:

1. NF_INET_PRE_ROUTING
2. NF_INET_LOCAL_IN
3. NF_INET_FORWARD
4. NF_INET_POST_ROUTING
5. NF_INET_LOCAL_OUT

Figure 8.20 shows the relation between five hooks.

`NF_INET_PRE_ROUTING` represents the hook before the host receives the packet and before it has processed the routing function. `NF_INET_LOCAL_IN` is the hook to find which destination address is the host after processing the routing function. `NF__INET_FORWARD` is the hook for the packets that must be transferred to another host after processing the routing function. `NF_INET_POST_ROUTING` is the hook after completing the routing function. `NF_INET_LOCAL_OUT` represents the hook before processing the routing function.

When the hooks proceed to examine packets, the packet-filtering rules from *iptables,* which is a user-space program that specifies the conditions to accept, drop, or queue the packets, must be applied.

Data Structures

The following three data structures represent an iptables rule:

1. `struct ipt_entry`, includes the following fields.
   - `strcut ipt_ip` : the IP header to be matched.

Continued

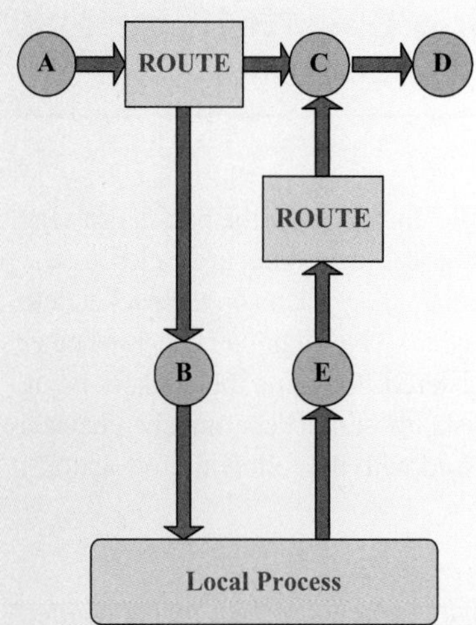

FIGURE 8.20 Hooks registered with Netfilter.

- nf_cache: the bit sequence representing which fields in the IP header must be checked.
- target_offset: represents the initial location of struct ipt_entry_target.
- next_offset: the offset from the beginning of a rule at which the ipt_entry_target structure is.
- comefrom: a field for the kernel to track the packet transmission.
- struct ipt_counters: records the number of packets and the packets themselves that match a rule.

2. struct ipt_entry_match: records the compared packet content.
3. struct ipt_entry_target: records actions (i.e., the targets) after comparison.

Algorithm Implementations

The source codes of iptables are located in the net/ipv4/netfilter directory (relative to the kernel source tree). The ipt_do_table() function in ip_tables.c handles a packet examined by a rule specified in the iptables program. The prototype of the hook is as follows:

```
ipt_do_table(struct sk_buff *skb, unsigned int hook,
const struct net_device *in, const struct net_device
*out, struct xt_table *table);
```

Here skb points to the packet, hook is the hook number that identifies a hook, in and out are the input and output network devices, and table is the rule table. In the beginning, the `ipt_do_table()` function attempts to locate the list of rules indexed from `hook` in the following statements:

```
private = table->private;
table_base = (void *)private->entries[smp_processor_id()];
e = get_entry(table_base, private->hook_entry[hook]);
```

Here `e` is a pointer to the `ipt_entry` structure of the rule. After the list of rules indexed from `hook` is found, the code starts to match the IP header information, e.g., the source and destination IP addresses, of each rule with that of the incoming packet. If the header information is matched, then the code continues to match the packet content specified in the `ipt_entry_match` structure. The following code corresponds to the matching process.

```
if    (ip_packet_match(ip,     indev,     outdev,     &e->ip,
mtpar.fragoff)) {
    struct ipt_entry_target *t;
    if (IPT_MATCH_ITERATE(e, do_match, skb, &mtpar) != 0)
           goto no_match;
```

Here the `ip_packet_match()` function matches the header information, and the `IPT_MATCH_ITERATE` macro matches the packet content. The following statement is then called to get the target (i.e., action) of the rule if the packet is matched.

```
t = ipt_get_target(e);
```

Otherwise the execution just continues matching the next rule (from the `no_match` label).

Exercises

1. Indicate which function is eventually called to match the packet content in the `IPT_MATCH_ITERATE` macro.
2. Find out where the `ipt_do_table()` function is called from the hooks.

8.3.3 Application Layer Firewall

An application layer firewall filters the packets in the application layer against a set of application signatures such as URLs. This type of firewall can provide finer access control than those examining only the L3 and L4 information. For example, the destination port number of HTTP requests is usually 80. If a network administrator wants to block access to only a blacklist of Web sites, it will be insufficient for a firewall to examine only the port number, as all HTTP requests are targeted at port 80. Therefore, it is necessary to examine the packet content.

Since the application content is not available until a TCP connection has been established, a common type of application layer firewall is the proxy server. For example, a host that accesses a Web resource first establishes a connection with the local proxy, and then it sends out the URL request, which is examined by the firewall. If the URL is permitted, the proxy forwards the URL request via another connection to the Web server; otherwise, the request is simply not forwarded. Not only HTTP but also other protocols such as FTP, SMTP, POP3, and so on can be filtered in a similar manner. Open Source Implementation 8.5 shows the example of FireWall Toolkit (FWTK), which is an application-layer firewall that supports filtering these application protocols.

Open Source Implementation 8.5: FireWall Toolkit (FWTK)

Overview

FireWall Toolkit (FWTK) is a set of proxy programs for building an application-layer firewall. In the set are the firewalls for major application protocols such as SMTP, FTP, and HTTP proxy servers. Development of the original FWTK package stopped more than 10 years ago, but it was later resurrected as a package named `openfwtk` in SourceForge to resume the development.

When a program in this package is executed, the file `netperm-table` is loaded for the settings and rules of packet filtering. The file is common for the applications in FWTK, and contains two rule types: generic proxy rules and application-specific rules. The `cfg_append()` function in `cfg.c` calls the `read_config_line()` function to read and parse each line in `netperm-table`.

The primary entry in `netperm-table` has three fields: application name, parameter name, and parameter content. We use the configuration for the `squid-gw` HTTP application proxy as an example. For example, the following two rules forbid all accesses that give an IP address as the host name and allow accesses to the .edu domain in plain HTTP URLs.

```
squid-gw: deny-destinations http*://*.*.*.*
squid-gw: destinations http://www.*.edu
```

Block Diagram

We use the `squid-gw` proxy as the example to introduce the execution flow of application-layer firewalls. Figure 8.21 presents the major blocks invoked in the `main()` function of the `squid-gw` proxy. In the execution flow, the configuration is first read in `config_global()`. When the HTTP request arrives, it is processed and matched against the rules within `http_process_request()`. If the access is granted, `http_send_request()` sends the request and `http_response()` processes the response.

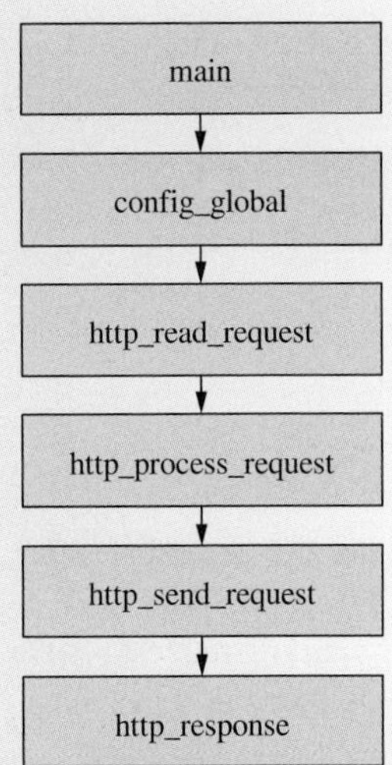

FIGURE 8.21 Block diagram of the `squid-gw` execution flow.

Data Structures

The most important data structure in this package is the *`Cfg`* structure, which stores the configuration and the rules. Its definition is presented below.

```
typedef struct cfgrec {
      int      flags;          /* see below */
      int        ln;             /* line# in config file */
      char       *op;            /* facility name */
      int        argc;           /* number of arguments */
      char       **argv;         /* vector */
      struct  cfgrec    *next;
} Cfg;
```

From the `next` field, it can be found that the structure is a node in a list. After reading each line in `netperm-table`, the `cfg_append()` function stores each line of the configuration into a node, which is appended to the list. The `flags` field is `PERM_ALLOW`, `PERM_DENY` or 0 (if the configuration line is related to neither permission nor denial). The `op` field is the object, such as `connect` and `href`, that the action refers to. The associated arguments and their number are stored in `argv` and `argc`.

Algorithm Implementations

The primary functions executing such rules are in `squid-gw.c`. When receiving a forwarding request from a client, *`squid-gw`* iteratively compares the request with each stored rule. The rule-matching code segment in `static int match_destination (Cfg *cf, const char *s, const struct url`

Continued

*u, const char *method) called from http_process_request() indirectly (two other functions in between) is presented as follows:

```
if (cf->argc > 0 && (strcmp (cf->argv[0], "GET") == 0
                  || strcmp (cf->argv[0], "HEAD") == 0
                  || strcmp (cf->argv[0], "POST") == 0))
{
  if (strcmp (cf->argv[0], method) != 0)
    return -1; /* Skip the complete rule */
  ++i; /* Skip the request method */
}
```

In this piece of code, the configuration is stored in the cf structure after netperm-table is parsed. If the request method, i.e., GET, HEAD, or POST, is specified in a rule (cf->argv[0]), the method of the forwarding request is first checked. The complete rule is simply ignored if the two methods do not match. After comparing the request method, the following code segment is executed:

```
while (i < cf->argc && cf->argv[i][0] != '-')
  {
    if (strcmp (cf->argv[i], "*") == 0)
      cmp = 0;
    else
      {
        if (url_parse (&pattern, (octet*) cf->argv[i],
strlen (cf->argv[i]), UPF_WILDCARD | UPF_NODEFPORT) != 0)
          url_error ("destinations", cf->ln);
        cmp = url_compare ((octet*) cf->argv[i],
&pattern, (octet*) s, u, UCF_IGNORE_CASE | UCF_WILDCARD);
      }
    if (cmp == 0)
    // A URL match is found. Details skipped here.
  }
```

The URLs specified in that rule are matched against those in the forwarding request in turn. If the URL in comparison is a wildcard character, a match is asserted (cmp == 0); otherwise, the URL is parsed and compared with that in the forwarding request. The comparison continues until a match is found. The access will be granted if a match is not found (not shown in the above code segment). The two functions for URL parsing and URL comparison are url_parse() and url_compare(). They are implemented in url.c. We leave the details of URL parsing and comparison to readers.

Exercises

1. Find out how the url_parse() and url_compare() functions are implemented in this package.
2. Do you think the rule-matching approach is efficient? What are possible ways to improve the efficiency?

Principle in Action: Wireless Access Control

A trivial approach to wireless access control is allowing access only from wireless interfaces whose MAC addresses are on the *white* list. However, this approach can be easily compromised because the source MAC address can be easily *spoofed.* A stronger access control is mandatory.

The access control mechanism can be implemented in the link layer or even in a higher layer. In the link layer, the pre-shared key mode in the Wi-Fi Protected Access (WPA) specification provides passphrase protection *without* the need of an authentication server. The Extended Authentication Protocol (EAP) mode in IEEE 802.1X defines the whole procedure to identify and authenticate the user before granting the network access. In higher layers, deploying Virtual Private Network (VPN) is a good choice for securing wireless networks. The VPN technology, which provides authentication, privacy, and confidentiality, is an *additional* protection on top of WPA.

Compared with firewalls that examine the network layer and the transport layer header information, an application-layer firewall is more complicated. The fields in the network-layer header or transport-layer header are fixed in position and length. The complexity of packet filtering in the former firewall, which matches these fixed fields against the policy rules, is moderate. In comparison, an application-layer firewall needs to examine the packet content in the same view as the destination application, parse the application protocol to restore its semantics, and search the packet content (within the related application fields) for a set of signatures. The position in which a signature may occur is not fixed, and the lengths of the signatures may vary a lot. The signature may be represented in a complex form, such as regular expressions, making signature matching even more complicated.

In addition to the complexity of signature matching, if the application-layer firewall is implemented as a proxy like FWTK, it can leverage the protocol stack in the operating system to perform all the work to restore the packet content, such as packet reassembly, but the firewall is not *transparent* to the users. The users must configure their application to use the proxy. An application-layer firewall can be made transparent by silently eavesdropping the packets and reassembling the packets to restore the content, but the program should deal with the complexities that the TCP protocol stack handles. This overhead is nontrivial. All of these issues make the efficiency of an application-layer firewall a great challenge.

8.4 SYSTEM SECURITY

Methods of attacking a system involve three tasks: gathering information, exploiting vulnerabilities, and then attacking with malicious codes. Gathering information means obtaining critical or private information by means of monitoring, scanning, and social engineering. Knowing the system information, an attacker then attempts to find and leverage the vulnerabilities on that system. Finally, the attacker launches an attack by infiltrating malicious programs into the system or directly attacking the system. We cover the techniques in each of these tasks. After introducing the techniques from an attacker's perspective, we present various defense techniques. We pick ClamAV, Snort, and Spamassassin as the example open source implementations.

8.4.1 Information Gathering

An attacker usually scans a target system to gather information such as service-providing programs, open ports, or even exploits before launching the subsequent attacks. The gathering techniques involve *scanning* and *monitoring*. Two typical types of scanning are *remote scanning* and *local scanning*. Monitoring gathers information about network or computer systems, such as passwords. Two typical types of monitoring are *sniffing* and *snooping*. Jung et. al in 2004 discussed how to detect port scanning with a statistical approach.

Remote Scanning

Remote scanning means to scan a remote target system to gather information such as host name, open-service, service-providing program, and possible remote exploits. An example of remote scanning software is Nessus (www.nessus.org), which adopts a client/server framework and provides a GUI for easy operation.

Local Scanning

Local scanning means to scan a local target system to gather information such as significant system files, privileged programs, and possible exploits within the host. Its representative is COPS in UNIX. TIGER is another local scanning program and also works under UNIX.

Sniffing

Sniffing suggests intercepting packets to access the information via local area networks. A host normally accepts only packets destined to itself, but it can eavesdrop all the packets through it by configuring its network interface in the "promiscuous mode." A well-known program for this type of monitoring is Sniffer.

A sniffing program called a distributed network sniffer can be hidden at the server and client ends. An attacker can invade a host and install a "client" program to monitor all the packets, analyze user identifiers and passwords, and send those data to the "server."

Snooping

This type of system monitoring means monitoring memory, disks, and/or other stored data to gain information inside the host: e.g., monitoring and recording which key is struck on the keyboard. Based on the gathered information, an attacker can intrude into other hosts later.

Snooper usually uses a pack of backdoor programs. We will describe the backdoor programs in malicious code as well as the functions of system monitoring.

Social Engineering

Social engineering tries to manipulate human weakness rather than attack through systems or the Internet. An example is that the attacker sends an e-mail or makes a call to the user, claiming he is the system operator and asking the user for his private information. Social engineering also includes peeking for the password while the hacker stands behind the user.

8.4.2 Vulnerability Exploiting

Vulnerabilities are design errors in programs or software that an intrusion can exploit to obtain important system information or administrator authority or to disable the system. There are numerous programs in the world, and many may have errors. Even when programs have no errors in their design, their users may still make mistakes in operation that create vulnerabilities.

Buffer overflow is the most well-known design error. Input data may overflow the buffer space without careful checking on the buffer's capacity. If the user stores 101 bytes in a 100-byte array, the extra one byte may overwrite other variables and lead to unexpected execution results. Figure 8.22 shows an example in which the user uses the vulnerability of buffer overflow to run his program. When the `called()` function is called, the operating system will set up a stack for the function. In this example, the user just needs to store data containing attacking codes in the buffer. If the program does not check the input size, the data could be arbitrarily long and hence overwrite the returning address in the stack with the starting address of the piece of attacking code. When the function finishes, the control will return to the caller by referring to the fake returning address, and the program flow will go to the attacking code.

Remote Vulnerabilities

A hacker may intrude into remote systems to get unauthorized data, user's ID and password, or system administrator authority by remote exploits. Since the target is a remote system, such exploits usually take place in online service, e.g., the mail

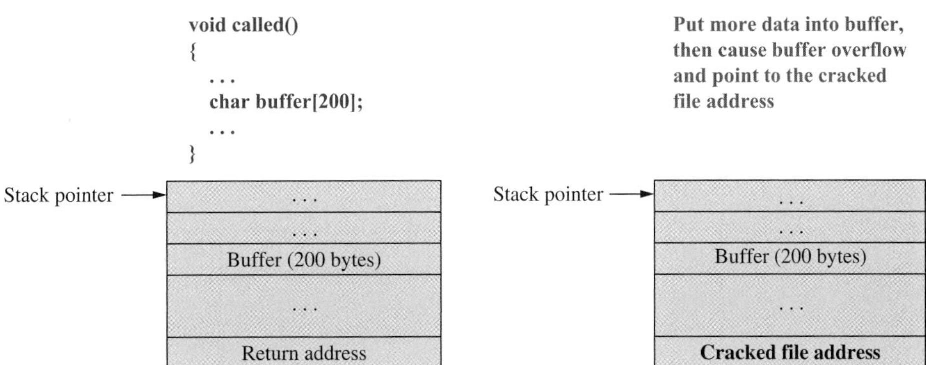

FIGURE 8.22 An example of buffer overflow.

service provided by *sendmail,* which was reported to have exploits several times. Most of these exploits are buffer overflows.

Another example is `wu-ftpd`, whose 2.6 version has the buffer overflow problem. It occurs in the function `*printf()` in the command *`site exec`*. A hacker may use a formatted string to overwrite the return address to get the buffer overflow.

A package of Web clustering named Piranha comes with a default user ID *piranha* with the password *q* after installation. If the system operator installs the package without changing the default account, the hacker may apply this user ID to access the program, resulting in a remote exploit. Table 8.2 lists several remote exploits that can provide access to the operator's password.

One more example of remote vulnerability is the protocol-based attack. The protocol-based attack tries to attack a remote host by exploiting errors, poor design, or ambiguous definition in TCP/IP. For example, IP spoofing can attack an address-based authentication system, in which a hacker intrudes into a system by spoofing the destination IP address as acceptable by the system.

Local Vulnerabilities

In an attack on local vulnerabilities, a hacker acquires unauthorized data or higher-priority authority, such as an administrator's password, from a normal user identity on a system. This vulnerability usually occurs in the design of a privileged program or an implementation error.

TABLE 8.2 A List of Remote Vulnerabilities to Obtain the Administrator's Rights

Vulnerabilities	Application	Version	Reason
phf remote command execution vulnerability	Apache Group Apache	1.0.3	Input validation error
Multiple vendor BIND (NXT oveflow) vulnerabilities	ISC BIND	8.2.1	Buffer overflow
MS IIS FrontPage 98 extensions buffer overflow vulnerability	Microsoft IIS	4.0	Buffer overflow
Univ. of Washington imapd buffer overflow vulnerability	University of Washington imapd	12.264	Buffer overflow
ProFTPD remote buffer overflow	Professional FTP proftpd	1.2pre5	Buffer overflow
Berkeley Sendmail daemon mode vulnerability	Eric Allman Sendmail	8.8.2	Input validation error
RedHat Piranha Virtual Server package default account and password vulnerability	RedHat Linux	6.2	Configuration error
Wu-ftpd remote format string stack overwrite vulnerability	Washington University wu-ftpd	2.6	Input validation error

For example, Xterm is a terminal emulator in the X Window system. In its early version, it was vulnerable to a buffer overflow exploit: If the system replaces Xterm with SUID root, i.e., Xterm is executed with the identity of root, the attacker might get the administrator authority.

Password Cracking

Password cracking is an attempt to find out the passwords on a system by trying possible passwords, which may be directly derived from a dictionary file, and from a number of combinations and mutations of the words in the dictionary. A password-cracking program requires a system file in which the accounts and encrypted passwords on a system are stored, say `/etc/shadow` in UNIX systems. Password cracking proceeds as follows:

1. Pick up a possible password from the dictionary file. The password may be a combination of or mutations from one or multiple words from the file.
2. Encrypt the password in exactly the same way as that in the system password file, say using SHA1.
3. Compare the encrypted password with that to be cracked. If both are the same, the cracking succeeds. Otherwise, go back to step (1) and try another password until the cracking program guesses correctly.

The password file is normally well protected, and only the administrator can read that file. Password cracking is nontrivial in practice. Common approaches are exploiting vulnerabilities (e.g., using buffer overflow attacks) of a system, executing a program in the context of administrator's rights to get the file, or finding that the administrator has stored a copy of the password file in an unsafe manner. If the password file is unavailable, it is still possible to guess the passwords by attempting to log in. However, it is quite possible that the host will record the attacker's attempts and allow only a few password errors. The efficiency of cracking depends on the system speed and the complexity of passwords. It would take less time if the system is very fast and the password is easy to guess (e.g., the password is an ordinary English word).

Denial of Service (DoS)

The denial-of-service (DoS) attack can block services on a server so that others are unable to access them. Its trick is to exhaust the limited resources so the service cannot be carried on. For example, the TCP SYN flood attack fills up the waiting queues of the target host, and the ICMP echo reply flood attack exhausts the bandwidth of the host. In the case of the TCP SYN flood attack, since TCP sets up a connection with three-way handshaking, the attacker stages continuous SYN packets with fake addresses, but never supplies the ACK packets in the third step of the handshaking, resulting in full waiting queues. The host cannot accept any more connections when the queue is full. In the ICMP echo reply flood attack, the hacker simultaneously produces a huge number of ICMP echo requests to the target system. Since the target system will reply the same number of replies back to the requesters, the huge number of ICMP packets will completely exhaust the network bandwidth. Schuba et. al in 1997 analyzed how the DoS works in depth.

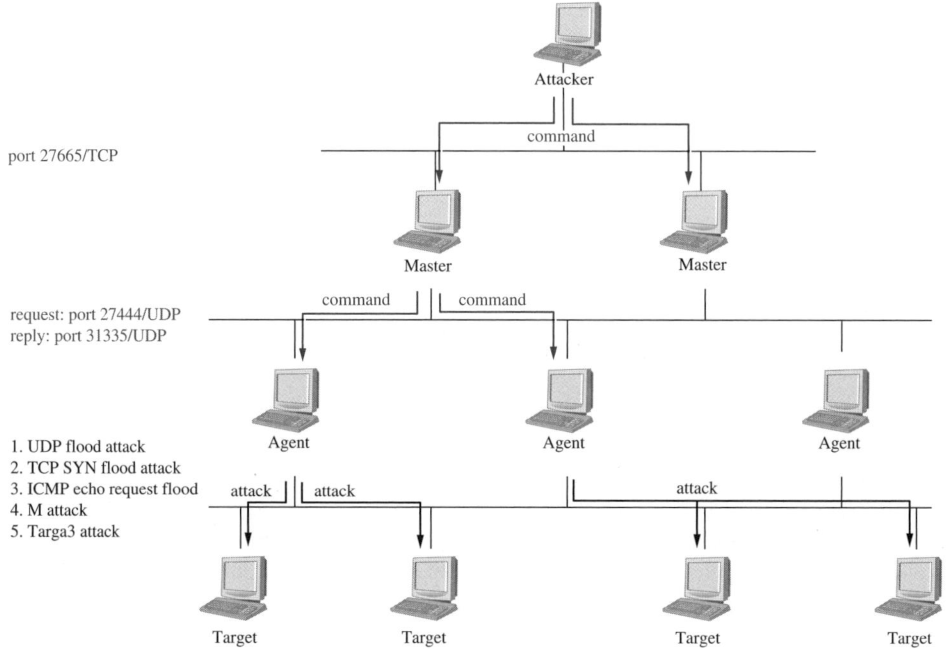

FIGURE 8.23 Distributed denial of service (DDoS).

Launching the DoS attack on a large scale is called distributed DoS (DDoS). Figure 8.23 shows an example of the DDoS attack. The hacker controls a number of agents on the victim hosts. Once the hacker sends the attack command to all the agents, they can generate a large number of attacks at the same time.

Trinoo is a client/server denial-of-service attacking program based on the UDP flood attack. The attacker sends out a large number of UDP packets (which probably have spoof addresses to avoid being tracked) to the victim system, which will result in a traffic jam or even stop the service. A Trinoo program includes several masters and numerous daemons. The attacker first connects to the master and issues an attacking command with several important parameters such as IP addresses of targets and when to start the attack. After receiving an attack order, the master will connect to all the daemons, which then start the attack to all predefined victim systems. The attack proceeds as follows:

1. The attacker connects to the master using port 27665/TCP.
2. The master connects to the daemons using port 27444/UDP.
3. The daemons respond to the master using 31335/UDP.
4. The daemons start the attack to the victim systems using UDP flood attacks.

8.4.3 Malicious Code

The attack with malicious code, also known as malware, involves the hacker attacking a target system via an external device or network. Several types of malicious code are introduced here.

Virus

Viruses demonstrate self-replication and destruction in their behaviors. Originally, a virus referred to a program that modified other programs to include a copy of itself. The usual infection path in early days was copying a file from a disk. The term *virus* has become a generic name for malware to the ordinary public.

Worm

Due to its popularity, the Internet has become the major path of malware propagation. A worm is a self-propagating program on the Internet. An attack implants a worm into a target system, attacks the target, and then propagates the worm to other systems. It begins with scanning from an infected host for other vulnerable hosts and then replicating itself to them. The network may be choked with the large number of worms propagating on the network. Staniford et. al in 2002 studied several ways to propagate worms efficiently.

Two well-known examples are Code Red and Nimda. These use distributed denial-of-service (DDoS) to attack Microsoft IIS systems. The propagation occupies a large amount of network bandwidth, and prevents the servers from accepting normal requests. The DDoS attack quickly spreads all over the world, and results in serious traffic jams in networks.

Trojan

A Trojan disguises itself as an innocent program or file. This term comes from the ancient Greek tale in which an attacking force penetrates a walled city by hiding inside a huge horse figure that is pulled through the gates. Since the Trojan looks benign, a user will be tricked into executing or opening it. After the user acts on the program or file, the Trojan can do something harmful, such as installing another malware or crashing a program.

Backdoor

For easy access to the victim system next time after a successful intrusion, the hacker can implant a hidden backdoor program in it. For example, Back Orifice 2000 (BO2K) is a backdoor program in the Windows environment for fully controlling the system via a TCP or UDP connection. It also supports file transfer, monitoring, and recording user operations. Furthermore, it can be enhanced with additional plug-ins, such as the code to send an e-mail to the attacker while the host is connected to the Internet.

Bot

A bot is short for "robot," meaning that the infected systems can be controlled by a "botmaster" through a command & control (C&C) channel. The infected systems and the botmaster are referred to as "botnet." After a botmaster takes over these systems, it can order the infected systems to launch a distributed denial-of-service, steal valuable information from these systems, and send a huge number of spam e-mails. Rajab et. al in 2006 had studied botnet behaviors in depth.

Based on differences between C&C channels, a botnet can be classified as an IRC botnet, a P2P botnet, or a hybrid. A botmaster in an IRC botnet controls the bots using the IRC protocol. Since the botmaster controls the bots in a centralized manner, it is subject to a single point of failure. Therefore, P2P botnets, which transmit the commands through P2P networks such as Overnet, are getting popular as they are more robust.

Open Source Implementation 8.6: ClamAV

Overview

ClamAV is an open source package for virus scanning. Due to the rapid propagation of malicious codes and their variants, ClamAV claims have detected over 570,000 malicious codes (viruses, worms and trojans, etc.) with the release of the 0.95.2 version. The signatures exist in several forms, including MD5 for the entire executable, MD5 for a certain PE section (part of an executable file), basic signatures of fixed strings (to be scanned in the entire file), extended signatures (in a simplified form of regular expressions containing multiple parts, plus the specification of target file types, offset of a signature, and so on), logical signatures (multiple signatures combined with logical operators), and signature based on archive metadata. Please read the *signatures.pdf* in the ClamAV documents for details.

Block Diagram

We present the block diagrams in two major execution flows. The first flow is loading the signature database, and the second is scanning a file for viruses. Figure 8.24 presents the block diagram for signature loading. The `cl_load()` function does a few initial checks and then calls `cli_load()` to read the signature file. Accorinding to the file's extension name (i.e., the type of signature file), `cli_load()` calls different functions for loading and parsing signatures.

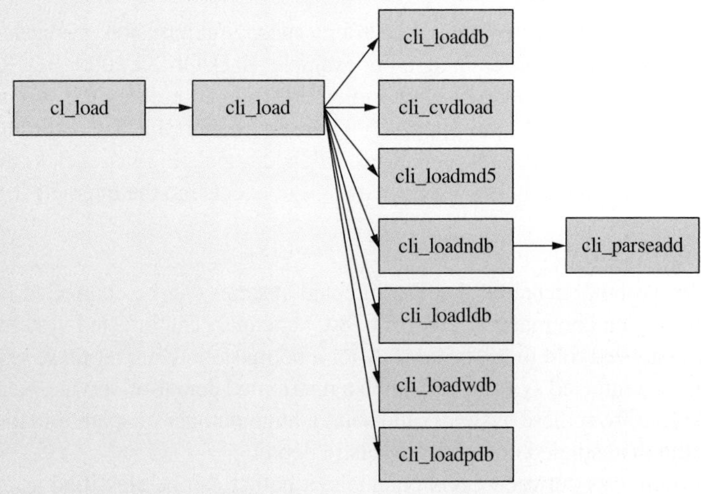

FIGURE 8.24 The block diagram for signature loading.

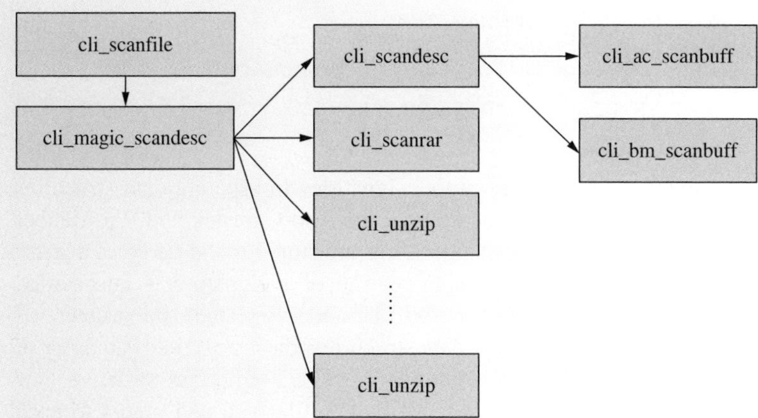

FIGURE 8.25 The block diagram for signature matching.

Take the ndb file, for example. The `cli_loadndb()` function is called, and each line in the ndb file is parsed and added into the data structure representing the signatures.

Figure 8.25 presents the block diagram for signature matching. The `cli_scanfile()` opens the file and calls `cli_magic_scandesc()` to scan the file. The `cli_magic_scandesc()` attempts to identify the file type, and calls the corresponding routines to handle the file. For example, if the file is compressed in an RAR format, `cli_magic_scandesc()` calls `cli_scanrar()` to uncompress the file. Note that the file may pack several files in a compressed file. Therefore, `cli_scanrar()` may again recursively call `cli_magic_scandesc()` to handle these files. In the last level of recursion (if any), `cli_scandesc()` will be called to read the file into a buffer batch by batch. Then the scanning routines, `cli_ac_scanbuff()` and `cli_bm_scanbuff()`, are called to scan the buffer for viruses. The former scans the buffer with the Aho-Corasick (AC) algorithm, and the latter scans the same buffer with the Wu-Manber algorithm (incorrectly called the Boyer-Moore [BM] algorithm in ClamAV).

Data Structures

The types of target files allowed in ClamAV are specified in `matcher.h`. The code of the specification is as follows:

```
static const struct cli_mtarget cli_mtargets[CLI_MTARGETS]
= {
   { 0, "GENERIC", 0, 0 },
   { CL_TYPE_MSEXE, "PE", 1, 0 },
   { CL_TYPE_MSOLE2, "OLE2", 2, 1 },
   { CL_TYPE_HTML, "HTML", 3, 1 },
   { CL_TYPE_MAIL, "MAIL", 4, 1 },
```

Continued

```
    { CL_TYPE_GRAPHICS, "GRAPHICS", 5, 1 },
    { CL_TYPE_ELF, "ELF", 6, 1 },
    { CL_TYPE_TEXT_ASCII,"ASCII", 7, 1 },
    { CL_TYPE_PE_DISASM, "DISASM", 8, 1 }
};
```

As we have mentioned, ClamAV stores signatures in separate data structures also according to target files by using both the Aho-Corasick and Wu-Manber algorithms. The signatures of both algorithms are stored in the `cli_matcher` structure (see `matcher.h`). If the target file of a signature is unspecified (e.g., a basic signature), the signature will be added into the data structure as the "generic" type. To access these data structures, the `root` field (an array of pointers to the `cli_matcher` structure) in the `cl_engine` structure (see `others.h`) serves as the array indexed by the file type and points to each separate data structure. Therefore, ClamAV scans a file for only the signatures of the "generic" type and those associated with the specific file type. For example, when scanning a file of the PE format (the Microsoft executable), ClamAV will not load the signatures associated with other types (such as HTML). This approach can reduce false positives and speed up the scanning process because of fewer signatures to be scanned.

Algorithm Implementations

The driving engine of ClamAV is the `libclamav` library, which contains the codes to handle archives, compressed files, and executable packers (programs to pack the executables to obfuscate code analysis and scanning), as well as the signature-matching engines. When ClamAV is launched, the `cl_load()` function in `readdb.c` loads signatures from the database and stores the signatures in separate data structures according to the target file types and the matching algorithms (Aho-Corasick and the Wu-Manber). The matchers of both algorithms are in `matcher-ac.c` and `matcher-bm.c`, respectively. The former is responsible for extended signatures of multiple parts, as the automation in the Aho-Corasick algorithm can better represent those signatures. The latter is responsible for basic and MD5 signatures, plus extended signatures of a single part (i.e., without special characters such as wildcards), as the Wu-Manber algorithm can handle fixed (usually long) strings easily.

The `scanners.c` file contains the major functions to drive virus scanning. As we mentioned under "Block Diagram," these functions are called starting from `cl_scanfile()`. After several function calls, the `cli_magic_scandesc()` function determines the type of the archive or compressed file (or a raw file) by calling the `cli_filetype2()` function. For each file type, the `cli_magic_scandesc()` calls a specific function, say `cli_scanrar()`, for decoding and scanning the file. No matter what type the file is, after decoding or decompressing until a raw file is derived, the `cli_scandesc()` function will eventually be called to start virus scanning. It calls the signature matchers (in `matcher-ac.c` and `matcher-bm.c`), which then scan the file for the signatures of the corresponding target type.

Exercises

1. Find out how `cli_filetype2()` called by `cli_magic_scandesc()` identifies the file types.
2. Find out the number of signatures associated with each file type (or the generic type) in both scanning algorithms in your current version of ClamAV. (Hint: Use sigtool to decompress the ClamAV virus databases files [*.cvd] and examine the resulted extended signature format files [*.ndb].)

8.4.4 Typical Defenses

Having described the attack methods, we introduce several defense methods in this section. The defenses include data encryption, authentication, access control, auditing, monitoring, and scanning. Table 8.3 lists popular packages categorized into four types, i.e., prevention, control, detection, and record. Prevention means keeping away from the attacker, e.g., data encryption. Control adopts authentication and access control to prevent unauthorized users from accessing unauthorized password/IDs. Detection means detecting any attacks, such as monitoring and scanning. Record means recording messages to track attackers, such as auditing. These techniques shall be described in the following subsections.

TABLE 8.3 Protection Packages

Types of Defense	Software	URL
Data encryption	PGP	http://www.pgpi.org/
	SSH	http://www.openssh.com/
Access control	Firewall-1	http://www.checkpoint.com
	Ipchains	http://people.netfilter.org/~rusty/ipchains/
	TCP Wrappers	ftp://ftp.porcupine.org/pub/security/index.html
	Portmap	http://neil.brown.name/portmap
	Xinetd	http://www.xinetd.org/
Monitoring	Tripwire	http://www.tripwire.com
	RealSecure	http://www.iss.net
Scanning	Pc-cillin	http://www.trend.com.tw

Auditing

Auditing records security-related events in log files, such as logging numbers of failure logins or some important activities. The log files are useful for tracking and analyzing who or which system was attacked, so the administrator can protect the system to avoid the same attack again. Existing operating systems have auditing functions, such as the system file wtmp of UNIX. The wtmp file records all login and logout states of all users. In Microsoft Windows systems, Event Viewer performs the same function of auditing.

Monitoring

This mechanism monitors the system for any abnormal activities, such as continuous logging failures. When it detects an attack, the system will (1) call the system operator by sending an e-mail, pager, or alarm, (2) stop system or related services to reduce possible damages, and (3) try to track the attacker. The system may use attack signatures as a clue to identify the attack type.

There are two types of monitoring: network-based and host-based. The former monitors for any abnormal Internet activities in network hosts. It intercepts packets from the network interface card, then analyzes any unusual influence on hosts, and reacts appropriately. Network-based monitoring can detect denial-of-service attacks, such as TCP SYN flooding. Once it finds that the source of the SYN packet is illegal, the monitoring will send an RST packet to the host under attack and stop it from indefinite waiting for impossible feedback. Host-based monitors can monitor for any abnormal behaviors on a host, such as user logging and activities of system operators and file systems. If abnormal activities are detected, the monitor will respond properly. An example is Tripwire, which regularly examines significant files and compares these important files with those in the database for any illegal modification.

Intrusion Detection and Prevention

Intrusion detection systems (IDS) detect intrusions based on known signatures or anomalous traffic. The former approach scans the packets for known intrusion signatures, but may have *false negatives* for unknown intrusions. The latter method looks for anomaly with the traffic, usually in a statistical approach, so that even unknown intrusions could be detected. But it may generate false positives if the normal Internet activities behave abnormally. It is a trade-off between the two approaches. Whatever the approach is, the IDS will generate an alert and may log the packet that triggers the alert when an intrusion is detected.

The limitation of IDSs is that they generate an alert only upon detecting an intrusion; they are unable to *prevent* the intrusion. An IDS just passively taps a wire and thus is unable to stop intrusions from entering the internal network. An approach to resolving this problem is sending a TCP RST packet to either the source or the destination of the connection so that a connection containing malicious traffic can be terminated. This approach, however, is not reliable. First, this approach is effective only for TCP connections. Second, the sequence number of the RST packet should match the expected sequence number of the receiver (i.e., the acknowledgment number that the receiver gives the sender). If the latency of the RST packet transmission is long due to heavy network traffic, there is a race condition where the sender may have sent more traffic to the receiver, making the sequence number of the RST incorrect. Thus the RST packet may be simply rejected. The IDS can work *inline,* by occupying the wire on which packets are transmitted, or it may work with a firewall, e.g., netfilter on Linux. Therefore, the IDS can actively *block* the traffic if an intrusion is found. This type of system is called an intrusion *prevention* system (IPS).

Although an IPS can block intrusions, it has some disadvantages. First, if the alert is a false positive, then innocent traffic will be blocked. An IDS does not have that problem. It just generates an alert of false positives, and the administrator can simply ignore the alert message. Second, if the IPS is inline but is not fast enough to catch up with the speed of network transmission, then the IPS becomes a bottleneck. This is not a problem to an IDS; the IDS just drops some packets and may have false negatives, but the traffic transmission will not be slowed down by the IDS.

Principle in Action: Bottleneck in IDS

It was reported around the year 2000 that pattern matching is a bottleneck in network intrusion detection systems, particularly *Snort.* Since then, a number of research efforts, many focused on hardware acceleration, have led to accelerated string matching of Snort up to multi-gigabits per second. Therefore, the performance problems seem to have been well solved.

Things are not as simple as they look, however. First, many researchers assume signatures can be scanned in a large byte stream. However, packets must be *reassembled* before becoming a byte stream, and an attacker may *split* packets into small IP fragments or TCP segments, making packet reassembly an effort. Second, to avoid false positives due to short signatures, the signatures are usually associated with certain contexts, meaning that they are significant only if the *contextual* conditions are also met. Here is an example of Snort rules.

```
web-client.rules:alert tcp $EXTERNAL_NET $HTTP_PORTS ->
$HOME_NET any (msg:"WEB-CLIENT Portable Executable binary
file transfer"; flow:to_client,established; content:"MZ|90
00|"; byte_jump:4,56,relative,little; content:"PE|00
00|"; within:4; distance:-64; flowbits:set,exe.download;
flowbits:noalert; metadata:service http; classtype:misc-
activity; sid:15306; rev:1;)
```

The options such as `byte_jump`, `distance` and `within` stand for a given position (actually, certain protocol fields) at which the following signature (in `content`) is effective. Generally, *protocol parsing* becomes even more important in signature matching, since an increasing number of signatures depend on context derived from protocol parsing.

Third, an attacker may *obfuscate* the packet content by various types of character encoding, making *normalization* needed before signature matching. Fourth, some detection techniques, such as detecting port scanning, may *correlate* information from multiple connections, so signature matching may involve byte streams from multiple connections.

Continued

Given these complexities, it is hardly expected that the performance of the *entire* intrusion detection system will be as fast as the throughput of signature matching alone, which is claimed to be up to multi-gigabits per second due to Amdahl's law. The actual performance of the system and its robustness when facing adversaries such as *evasion* should be watched and studied carefully to reach the target performance.

Principle in Action: Wireless Intrusions

Unlike ordinary intrusion detection systems that monitor network traffic for signatures of intrusions, a wireless intrusion detection system monitors the radio spectrum for wireless intrusions, which involve the presence of *unauthorized* access points. The detection is important, since if a careless employee uses such a rogue access point, the entire internal network may be exposed to external access. A wireless prevention system can automatically prevent this threat from occurring. Another function of a wireless intrusion detection system is detecting wireless attacks, including *unauthorized association, man in the middle attack, MAC address spoofing,* and *denial-of service-attack.*

A wireless intrusion/prevention system consists of three major components: (1) sensors, (2) server, and (3) console. The sensor can capture frames on the wireless channel throughout its coverage area. The server then analyzes these frames for intrusion detection, and the console is for the administrator to configure the system and for reporting possible intrusions. The administrator can look into the report just like that in an ordinary intrusion detection system.

Open Source Implementation 8.7: Snort

Overview

Snort is a popular open source detection tool that monitors the network and detects possible intrusions. It can capture the packets on the network interface with the `libpcap` library and also read packet trace in PCAP format for off-line analysis. After acquiring the packets to be analyzed, Snort examines the packets to see whether they match any of the *detection rules,* which consider certain values in the packet headers and certain *signatures* in the packet content that may indicate the occurrence of an intrusion. If a match is found, Snort will generate an *alert* to notify the administrator of a possible intrusion occurrence. Following is an example of a detection rule.

```
alert tcp any any -> 10.1.1.0/24 80 (content: "/cgi-bin/
phf"; msg: "PHF probe!";)
```

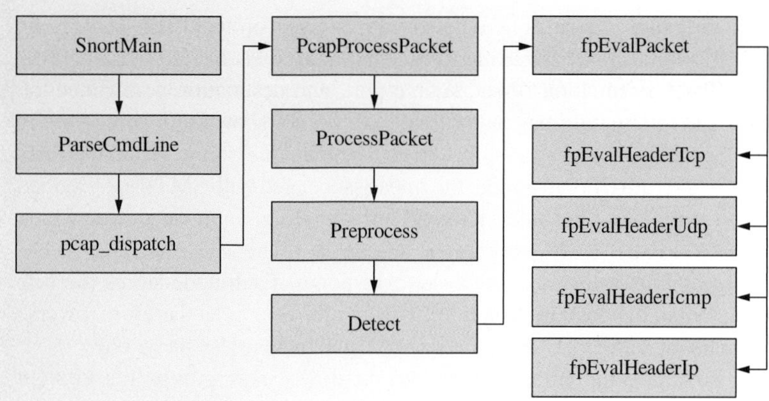

FIGURE 8.26 Block diagram of Snort.

Block Diagram

Figure 8.26 presents the main block diagram in Snort. `SnortMain()` is the main function that reads command-line arguments with `ParseCmdLine()`. It then calls `pcap_dispatch()`, which is a function in `libpcap` as Snort captures packets through the `libpcap` library. The `pcap_dispatch()` function registers a callback function, `PcapProcessPacket()`, which is called when each captured packet is ready for processing. The `PcapProcessPacket()` will call `Preprocess()`, which will call each preprocessor (see the section on "Algorithm Implementations") hooked in a list in sequence. After preprocessing, the `Detect()` function is called to parse the protocol header and match the rules associated with the unique port of the packet (see "Rule Detecting," below). When an intrusion is found, an alert is generated to an output plug-in, which may record the alert in a file, dump it to the control, and so on.

Data Structures

Besides the `PV` structure that contains the global information, the most important data structure in Snort is the rule tree that stores the Snort rules. There are three main structures for the rule tree: `ListHead`, `RuleTreeNode`, and `OptTreeNode`. The `ListHead` structure is defined as follows:

```
typedef struct _ListHead
{
    RuleTreeNode *IpList;
    RuleTreeNode *TcpList;
    RuleTreeNode *UdpList;
    RuleTreeNode *IcmpList;
    struct _OutputFuncNode *LogList;
    struct _OutputFuncNode *AlertList;
    struct _RuleListNode *ruleListNode;
} ListHead;
```

Continued

In the data structure, the rules associated with a given protocol (IP, TCP, UDP, or ICMP) are stored in separate rule trees. The main fields in `RuleTreeNode` are source IP set, destination IP set, source port, and destination port. Since the `RuleTreeNode` structure has many fields, we do not show them here. Among the fields, the *destination port* usually serves as the *unique* port to group the rules in the `OptTreeNode`. For example, the rules assocciated with SMTP are grouped together, and port 25 implies rules in the group. Therefore, Snort can decide which group of rules to match by looking up the unique port. The `RuleTreeNode` has a field that points to a list of `OptTreeNode` nodes. Each node stores the rule options (including the content signature) in each rule. Snort can therefore traverse through the list of `OptTreeNode` nodes, and match the rules one by one.

Since matching the rules one by one is slow, Snort groups the content signatures in the same list into a set and matches them together, known as *set-wise matching*. If a signature is found, the remaining rule options in the associated `OptTreeNode` node will be checked next. If all the rule options in that node are matched, the rule is matched and the corresponding alert is generated. Due to set-wise matching, Snort does not traverse the list of nodes one by one, and the matching efficiency is improved.

Algorithm Implementations

Preprocessing

The packets may be IP fragments or TCP segments (particularly small ones). They may preclude the correct detection of signatures in the packets. For example, a packet containing a signature "bad" may be fragmented into several pieces containing "b," "a," and "d" separately. If Snort examines packets one by one, it will not find the signature. Therefore, the IP fragments or TCP segments should be *reassembled* first to restore the original semantics before further examination.

Furthermore, HTTP requests may be *encoded* in several ways and may complicate the analysis. The requests should be *normalized* before the analysis. Note that the fragments/segments in the previous example or different encodings may be created intentionally by an attacker to escape the detection of Snort. This technique is called *evasion* and should be handled in a modern NIDS. Moreover, the diversity of IP addresses and port numbers can also be audited to determine whether *portscanning* occurs. Simply put, the packets should be *preprocessed* in several stages before the detection.

Snort implements preprocessing with a number of *preprocessor plug-ins* for extensibility. These plug-ins can hook their functions to a list, and Snort will traverse the list to call them one by one before detection in the `Preprocess` function (in `detect.c`). The following code presents how the preprocessors are invoked.

```
int Preprocess(Packet * p)
{
  ...
          PreprocessFuncNode *idx = PreprocessList;
```

```
        /*
        ** Turn on all preprocessors
        */
        boSetAllBits(p->preprocessor_bits);
        for (; (idx != NULL) && !(p->packet_flags &
PKT_PASS_RULE); idx = idx->next)
        {
            if (((p->proto_bits & idx->proto_mask) ||
(idx->proto_mask == PROTO_BIT__ALL)) &&
                 IsPreprocBitSet(p, idx->preproc_bit))
        {
                 idx->func(p, idx->context);
        }
    }
...
}
```

Packet Decoding

After preprocessing, the packet decoder decodes packet headers in each layer of the protocol stack. The following is a sample code in the `fpEvalPacket()` function (in `fpdetect.c`).

```
int fpEvalPacket(Packet *p)
{
    ...
    int ip_proto = GET_IPH_PROTO(p);
    switch(ip_proto)
    {
        case IPPROTO_TCP:
            DEBUG_WRAP(DebugMessage(DEBUG_DETECT,
                        "Detecting on TcpList\n"););

            if(p->tcph == NULL)
            {
                ip_proto = -1;
                break;
            }
            return fpEvalHeaderTcp(p);

          case IPPROTO_UDP:
              DEBUG_WRAP(DebugMessage(DEBUG_DETECT,
                          "Detecting on UdpList\n"););

              if(p->udph == NULL)
              {
                  ip_proto = -1;
                  break;
              }
```

Continued

```
            return fpEvalHeaderUdp(p);
        .....
    }
}
```

From the sample code, you can see the packet header is parsed for the upper-layer protocol (TCP, UDP or others) and then the corresponding function will follow for further decoding.

Rule Detecting

The detection engine checks for a number of *options* in the detection rules. These are also implemented in plug-ins for extensibility (under the `detection-plugins` directory). Among the options, `content` and `pcre` are the most critical as they specify the malicious signatures in *fixed strings* and *regular expressions* for pattern matching (performed in `sp_pattern_match.c` and `sp_pcre.c`, respectively). However, specifying only the signatures is insufficient since they may be significant only within certain contexts (e.g., in a certain field or position of the application content). Without restricting the signatures within the contexts, you may receive many *false positives.* Some of the options can help to precisely specify the contexts. For example, the `distance` option specifies how far into the packet Snort should search for a signature. The `byte_test` and `byte_jump` options can parse the application fields and *skip* certain fields if a signature should not appear in those fields. Besides the options that specify the contexts, some options can specify the message that appears in an alert or the identifier of the rule. Interested readers are referred to the Snort manual.

Logging and Alerting

Logging and Alerting includes several recording and alerting modes. They are implemented in plug-ins for extensibility. Since they are less relevant to network security, we do not go into detail here.

Exercises

1. List five preprocessors in Snort and study the execution flow of each one of them.
2. Find out what multiple-string matching algorithm is used for signature matching in Snort and where the algorithm is implemented.

Anti-Spam

Like intrusion detection, recognizing and filtering spam also involves scanning the mail messages (reassembled from the packet content) for signatures of spam. Unlike intrusion detection, the match with the signature in a spam-filtering rule only implies that the mail is more likely to be spam; it is also possible for normal mail to have one of the characteristics described in a rule. Judging a mail message solely by a rule may lead to a high false-positive rate. The determination is usually based on an adequate amount of evidence accumulated from rule matching. We take a look at how spam is filtered by examining the open source implementation of a popular spam-filtering package, SpamAssassin.

Open Source Implementation 8.8: SpamAssassin

Overview

SpamAssassin is an open source package that can identify and filter spam, i.e., unsolicited e-mails. It is implemented in Perl and can work with a mail server to filter spam messages before the users receive them. The filtering mechanisms include methods such as analysis on mail header and text, Bayesian filtering, and DNS blocklists. These analysis steps are implemented as plug-ins for flexibility.

Block Diagram

`Mail::SpamAssassin` (implemented in `SpamAssassin.pm`) is a Perl object that uses a set of rules tested on mail headers and bodies to identify spam. Figure 8.27 presents the main execution flow to analyze mail and determine whether it is spam or not. The `check_message_text` method calls `parse` and `check` in turn for spam analysis. The former will parse the raw mail content (e.g., decoded from the MIME structure) into the `Mail::SpamAssassin::Message` object, which will be checked for spam later.

The latter `check` method in `Mail::SpamAssassin::PerMsgStatus` will run the SpamAssassin rules to check the mail message. The process invokes a number of plug-ins for various analysis approaches, such `HeaderEval.pm` and `BodyEval.pm` for parsing mail headers and bodies. There are also some interesting plug-ins, such as `ImageInfo.pm` for counting number of images in the mail, finding image sizes, and so on. The check accumulates a score that represents the likelihood of spam. In other words, the higher the score is, the more likely the mail is spam. If spam is found and Bayesian learning is enabled, SpamAssassin may call the `learn` method to learn from the spam report.

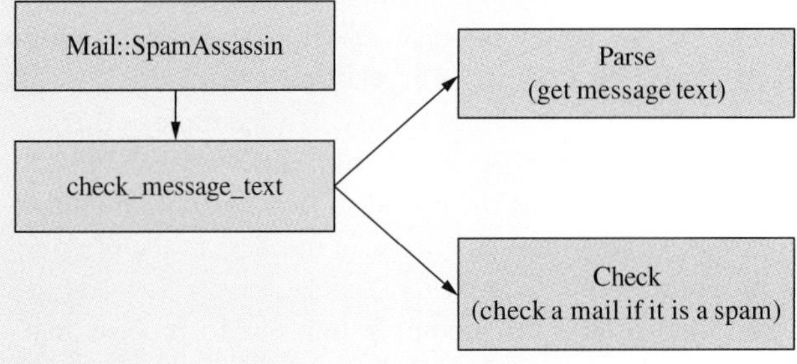

FIGURE 8.27 Main functions in *`Mail::SpamAssassin`* for spam analysis.

Continued

Data Structures

The `Mail::SpamAssassin` object has a few important attributes in SpamAssassin. They are `Conf` for the configuration information, `plugins` for plug-in handlers, and several path variables such as the rule paths. The plug-in handlers, as we have mentioned, are invoked during spam analysis. The mail message is encapsulated in the `Mail::SpamAssassin::Message` object after parsing the mail, and the score is stored in the `Mail::SpamAssassin::PerMsgStatus` object during the spam analysis.

Algorithm Implementations

SpamAssasin filters e-mails by a large set of *rules,* documented in the *.cf files under the *rules* directory. Note that SpamAssassin reads **.cf* in a lexical order so that rules in later files can override earlier files. A rule characterizes a possible feature of a spam message by specifying a signature in Perl Compatible Regular Expression (PCRE). If the feature is found, the score that indicates spam is accumulated. For example, a sample rule in the rule file `20_head_tests.cf` for analyzing the mail headers is as follows:

```
header FROM_BLANK_NAME      From =~ /(?:\s|^)"" <\S+>/i
describe FROM_BLANK_NAME    From: contains empty name
```

The rule checks whether the characters in the sender's name are white space or empty. If a blank name is found, SpamAssassin adds 1.0 (if the score is not explicitly specified) to the score, which helps determine whether the mail is spam. Each rule file contains rules like this for spam analysis. If the accumulated score finally reaches a threshold (5.0 by default) specified in the `user_prefs` file, the mail under analysis will be considered spam. SpamAssassin can also determine spam from Bayesian learning (see the `sa-learn.raw` file for the source code). We do not go into this part in detail here. SpamAssassin can also adjust the score according to a black or white list. For example, assume a sender has sent a mail message with the score of 20, which was considered spam. If it later sends another mail message with the score 2.0 based on the rules, the score will be automatically adjusted by adding a `delta` value of `(mean-2.0)*factor`, where mean = (20 + 2.0)/2 = 11. Therefore, the black or white list can be automatically adjusted in addition to manual configuration.

Functions to evaluate certain complex rules are implemented as plug-ins, such as `HeaderEval.pm` and `BodyEval.pm`, under the `lib/Mail/SpamAssassin/Plugin` directory for extensibility. For example, `check_illegal_chars` in the `20_head_tests.cf` file checks for 8-bit and other illegal characters that should be MIME encoded. The evaluation cannot be expressed simply in PCRE, so it is implemented as a function in the plug-in.

The `spamd.raw` program is the daemon for SpamAssassin. It loads the SpamAssassin filters, and then listens for incoming requests to process mail messages. It listens on port 783 by default, but the port number is configurable on the command line. When receiving a connection, it spawns a child to handle in SpamAssassin a new mail message from the network and dump the processed message back to the socket before closing the connection. The following is the code for spawning a child from `spamd.raw`.

```
sub spawn {
......
  $pid = fork();
  die "spamd: fork: $!" unless defined $pid;
  if ($pid) {
    ## PARENT
    $children{$pid} = 1;
    info("spamd: server successfully spawned child
process, pid $pid");
   ...
else {
    ## CHILD
   ......
    $spamtest->call_plugins("spamd_child_init");
......
}
```

`spamd` relies on `SpamAssassin.pm`, which is the main component of SpamAssassin. It handles the parsing and checking (through rule evaluation, learning, black/white listing, etc.) of mail messages, and uses the aforementioned mechanisms to evaluate whether the mail is spam. If the mail is spam, `SpamAssassin.pm` will call the `report_as_spam` function to return the report.

Exercises

1. Why is SpamAssassin implemented in Perl rather than in C or C++?
2. Discuss the pros and cons of using Bayesian filtering compared with rule-based approaches.

Performance Matters: Comparing Intrusion Detection, Antivirus, Anti-Spam, Content Filtering, and P2P Classification

Many network security packages utilize string matching algorithms to match signatures. Figure 8.28 draws the average execution time of string matching functions for each program to process one byte of packet data, i.e., application header and payload. Notably, the total execution time of a program grows as the time consumed by string matching functions increases. IDS, i.e., Snort, which is the most efficient program in the comparison, spends less than 10 ns on

Continued

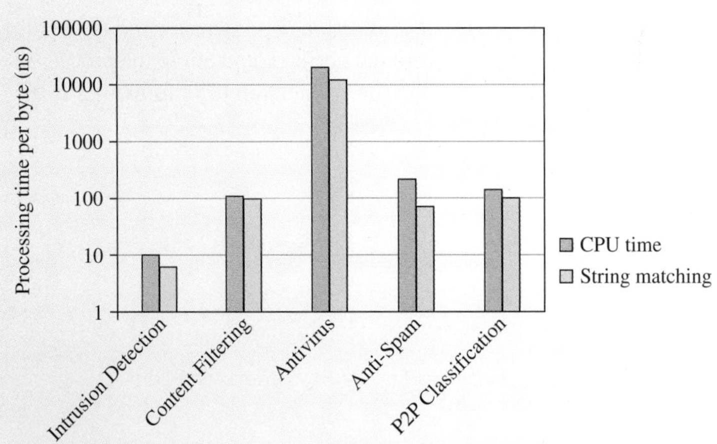

FIGURE 8.28 Execution time and string matching time of various applications.

processing each byte, while an antivirus program, i.e., ClamAV, consumes 1000 times, i.e., 10 μs, more than IDS. Other programs—including content filtering, i.e., DansGuardian, anti-spam, i.e., SpamAssassin, and P2P classification i.e., L7-filter—spend about 100 ns to process one byte.

The performance of these programs is highly related to *where* and *how* string matching works. Therefore, Table 8.4 compares the five packages in terms of the percentage of time spent on string matching and where string matching is applied. The overall performance of Snort is efficient because it employs *byte-jump* string matching, i.e., only examining the content of *specific offset* in a packet, to accelerate the matching task. This is because attacks are mostly embedded in specific application headers instead of payloads. DansGuardian authorizes an HTTP packet by using its blacklist database, which documents hundreds of denied URLs, file types, and keywords. The DansGuardian database is *simpler* and *smaller* than the one used in antivirus programs, which usually contain at least tens of thousands of signatures. Therefore, although the percentage of string-matching time in DansGuardian is higher than the one in ClamAV, each round of string-matching consumes much less time than ClamAV. Finally, SpamAssassin reduces the string-matching cost by *skipping* the attachments in e-mails, and L7-filtering eases the string-matching overhead by checking only the *first few* packets of a connection.

TABLE 8.4 String Matching Exercised by Applications

	Snort	DansGuardian	ClamAV	SpamAssassin	L7-filter
Percentage of string matching	62%	86%	57%	31%	70%
Inspection depth	Byte jump	Http request/ response	All attachment content	Mail header/ body	First 10 packets

8.5 SUMMARY

We classified the issues of network security into *data security, access security,* and *system security.* Data security involves *protecting* and *authenticating* data transmitted over the Internet by virtue of *cryptography.* The key for encryption and decryption could be *symmetric* or *asymmetric.* The former is faster in computation, but reliable distribution of the key could be a problem. The latter does not have to distribute the symmetric key, but the computation time is long for a large volume of data. Security protocols such as Secure Socket Layer (SSL) realize those cryptography mechanisms in practical network protocols. Besides data protection, *digital signature* and *message authentication* can ensure the originality of data.

Access security controls the access between the internal and external networks, so that the traffic between the two networks must obey the policies specified by the network administrators. Network devices such as firewalls can enforce the access policies. Those devices can filter network traffic based on information in IP headers, TCP/UDP port numbers, or application headers and payloads.

System security aims to protect the system from external attacks. An attacker (perhaps an automatic program such as a worm) may try to find the *vulnerabilities* of a system, and then *exploit* the vulnerabilities to control or disable the system. A defense system should find vulnerabilities before an attacker and patch them, find out possible attacks, and stop the attacks from entering the system. That is why we have vulnerability scanners, intrusion detection systems, virus scanners, and spam filters.

The struggles between attackers and defenders are endless. As our daily life has come to rely heavily on the Internet, network security has become an important topic. Nowadays, protecting the data with cryptography alone is insufficient. An attacker will try to exploit potential vulnerabilities and access the systems in a *stealthy* approach, so a defender has to (1) eliminate the vulnerabilities as much as possible and (2) effectively detect the attacks. The former is nontrivial because software is getting much larger and more complicated, so finding possible vulnerabilities is also getting difficult. The users should frequently apply new patches to eliminate vulnerabilities. The latter is also a challenge as an attacker will find every possible way to evade the detection. Worse yet, an attacker may leverage cryptography to *protect* the attacks, e.g., encrypting a malicious program or encrypting malicious content transmitted over the Internet, making effective detection a bigger challenge than ever. Even though we can design a clever and complicated approach for intrusion detection, we should also care about speeding up the intrusion detection simultaneously as the volume of Internet traffic increases rapidly. Therefore, speeding up intrusion detection or virus scanning with hardware acceleration or multicore processors is also a trend.

COMMON PITFALLS

When to Use Which: DES, 3DES, and AES

Given several symmetric encryption algorithms, such as DES, 3DES, and AES, it may be hard to choose when to use which. As discussed in this chapter, the DES key is only 56 bits, and it is possible to crack the key with brute force. That is why 3DES came into existence, but 3DES is three times more expensive in computation. Both algorithms are designed with hardware implementation in mind, so they are sluggish in software implementation for their bit operations, such as substitution and permutation. As AES came out in around 2001, it is getting popular, and can be found in well-known software, such as SSH clients or Skype. AES intends to eventually replace 3DES in *software* for its advantages in implementation.

Stateless and Stateful Firewalls

Firewalls can be stateless or stateful. A stateless firewall inspects the packets individually, and is *unaware* of the existence of connections. This stateless nature may be insufficient in some applications. For example, when an FTP client connects to a server in the active mode, it tells the server its listening port for the server to connect back. If the client-side firewall is unaware of the FTP command informing the listening port, the server will fail to connect back due to the *blocking* of the firewall. Another situation is that an attacker may make the traffic look like the response to a request by selecting a *source* port in the set of well-known ports. Since a firewall usually allows a client from the internal network to connect to an external network, the firewall normally does not block the traffic in response. If a firewall does not record that there has been a request in a connection, it has no way to *distinguish* whether the response is a fake or not. Then the attacker has a chance to penetrate the firewall by faking a response. In these cases, a stateful firewall can solve this problem by keeping the information about a connection, despite the more complicated design.

Malware: Virus, Worm, Trojan, Backdoor, Bot and More

Malware is the abbreviation for "malicious softwar," which is designed to do something harmful to a computer system. Malware comes in a variety of forms: viruses, worms, Trojans, backdoors, bots, and so on. These terms are dubbed according to their propagation strategies or malicious behaviors. However, they are also known as "viruses" by the public. So many terms look confusing and misleading, and they may be easily misused.

Note that a computer virus was originally defined as: "a program that can infect other programs by modifying them to *include* a possibly evolved copy of itself." This definition is no longer sufficient to describe the diversity of malware. Although it is not incorrect to use the term "virus" to refer to all the types of malware, (e.g., the open source virus scanner actually scans viruses, Trojans, backdoors, and so forth), a professional in network security knows the difference between terms.

Caution: Malware Analysis on a Sandbox

Signature matching is a common technique for malware detection. However, many malware programs can easily evade the detection by *polymorphic* code, which is scrambled code with identical semantics, or by *packing,* which compresses or encrypts the code, making signature matching or static analysis of the code difficult.

Another common approach is running a suspicious program on a sandbox, which is basically a *virtual machine.* Since the execution environment is virtual, any harm performed on the environment can be easily recovered without hurting a real system, and the running condition is easily controllable. The dynamic analysis can watch the invoked *system calls,* the changes of *files* and *registry,* and the *network activities* of the program in execution.

Although dynamic analysis seems workable, there are still some tricks by the malware writers to make the analysis unreliable. First, malware may attempt to *detect* the existence of a virtual machine. If a virtual machine exists, the malware will pretend to behave well and exit normally. To the best of our knowledge, existing virtual machines are *all* detectable in some way, even with the latest virtualization technology such as *Intel VT* (Virtualization Technology). Second, the malicious behaviors of malware may be triggered by some values or conditions. For example, malware might be activated only on a special *date* or with the existence of a given *file.* Therefore, a single run is hardly conclusive about malicious behaviors. Although some research works attempt to analyze possible branches during execution to find out the *hidden* behaviors and trigger values, their approaches might not work in general cases due to the variety of triggering conditions. Therefore, the output of malware analysis should be carefully interpreted, or there will be false negatives.

FURTHER READINGS

General Issues

The following are textbooks and magazines for a general introduction to computer and network security. For students who would like to pursue this area, these references provide materials for quickly grasping basic concepts.

- W. Stallings, *Cryptography and Network Security,* 4th edition, Prentice Hall, 2005.
- C. Kaufman, R. Perlman, and M. Speciner, *Network Security: Private Communication in a Public World,* Prentice Hall, 2002.
- W. Stallings, *Network Security Essentials: Applications and Standards,* 3rd edition, Prentice Hall, 2006.
- *IEEE Security & Privacy Magazine.*

Cryptography and Security Protocols

The following selected book and documents are related to cryptography and security protocols. Cryptography is itself a broad domain of research, and it is impossible to cover it in just in a few sections. The first is a good introduction to this domain. We also provide some references for security protocols below.

- J. Katz and Y. Lindell, *Introduction to Modern Cryptography: Principles and Protocols,* Chapman & Hall, 2007.
- R. Rivest, "The MD5 Message-Digest Algorithm," Apr. 1992, http://sunsite.auc.dk/RFC/rfc/rfc1321.html
- MIT distribution site for PGP (Pretty Good Privacy), http://web.mit.edu/network/pgp.html
- The OpenSSH Project, http://www.openssh.com
- S. R. Fluhrer, I. Mantin, and A. Shamir, "Weakness in the Key Scheduling Algorithm of RC4," *Lecture Notes in Computer Science (LNCS),* Vol. 2259, pp. 1–24, Aug. 2001.

Network Security Equipment and Monitoring

Common network security equipment includes firewalls, VPNs, intrusion detection systems, antivirus systems, content filters, and others. The first three books cover firewalls, VPN facilities, and a well-known intrusion detection system, Snort. The fourth book introduces a number of tools and techniques for network security monitoring. The last two are well-cited papers about intrusion detection other than Snort and detecting portscanning.

- E. D. Zwicky, S. Cooper, and D. B. Chapman, *Building Internet Firewalls,* 2nd edition, O'Reilly Media, 2000.
- R. Yuan, T. Strayer, and W. T. Strayer, *Virtual Private Networks: Technologies and Solutions,* Addison-Wesley, 2001.
- B. Caswell, J. Beale, and A. R. Backer, *Snort IDS and IPS Toolkit,* Syngress, 2007.
- R. Bejtlich, *The Tao of Network Security Monitoring: Beyond Intrusion Detection,* Addison-Wesley, 2004.
- V. Paxson, "Bro: A System for Detecting Network Intruders in Real-Time," *USENIX Security Symp.*, Jan. 1998.
- J. Jung, V. Paxson, A. Berger, and H. Balakrishnan, "Fast Portscan Detection Using Sequential Hypothesis Testing," IEEE Symp. On Security and Privacy, May 2004.

Hacking Techniques

The following books introduce techniques to hack software, system, and network vulnerabilities. The readers can know what hackers do from the materials in these books. The last four are well-cited papers about attack techniques and events on the Internet.

- J. Scambray, S. McClure, and G. Kurtz, *Hacking Exposed: Network Security Secrets & Solutions,* 6th edition, McGraw-Hill, 2009.
- J. Erickson, *Hacking: The Art of Exploitation,* 2nd edition, No Starch Press, 2008.
- S. Harris, A. Harper, C. Eagle, and J. Ness, *Gray Hat Hacking: The Ethical Hacker's Handbook,* 2nd edition, McGraw-Hill, 2007.
- G. Hoglund and G. McGraw, *Exploiting Software: How to Break Code,* Addison-Wesley, 2004.
- C. L. Schuba, I. V. Krsul, M. G. Kuhn, E. H. Spafford, A. Sundaram, and D. Zamboni, "Analysis of a Denial of Service Attack on TCP," *IEEE Symp. Security &* Privacy, May 1997.
- S. Staniford, V. Paxson, and N. Weaver, "How to 0wn the Internet in Your Spare Time," USENIX Security Symposium, Aug. 2002.
- M. Handley and V. Paxson, "Network Intrusion Detection: Evasion, Traffic Normalization and End-to-End Protocol Semantics," USENIX Security Symposium, Aug. 2001.
- M. A. Rajab, J. Zarfoss, F. Monrose, and A. Terzis, "A Multifaceted Approach to Understanding the Botnet Phenomenon," ACM Internet Measurement Conference (IMC), Oct. 2006.

Malware Detection and Analysis

The first book introduces building a honeypot for capturing attacks and malware. The latter two offer a solid view of virus research and practices in implementation and detection of rootkits. The last three items are well-cited papers for malware analysis.

- N. Provos and T. Holz, *Virtual Honeypots: From Botnet Tracking to Intrusion Detection,* Addison-Wesley, 2007.
- P. Szor, *The Art of Computer Virus Research and Defense,* Addison-Wesley, 2005.
- B. Blunden, *The Rootkit Arsenal: Escape and Evasion in the Dark Corners of the System,* Jones & Barlett, 2009.
- C. Willems, T. Holz, and F. Freiling, "Toward Automated Dynamic Malware Analysis Using CWSandbox," *IEEE Security & Privacy,* Vol. 5, Issue 2, pp. 32–39, Mar. 2007.

- G. Gu, P. Porras, V. Yegneswaran, M. Fong, and W. Lee, "BotHunter: Detecting Malware Infection Through IDS-driven Dialog Correlation," USENIX Security Symposium, June 2007.
- N. Provos, D. McNamee, P. Mavrommatis, K. Wang, and N. Modadugu, "The Ghost in the Browser: Analysis of Web-based Malware," USENIX Workshop on Hot Topics in Botnets (HotBots), Apr. 2007.

FREQUENTLY ASKED QUESTIONS

1. Private key algorithm vs. public key algorithm? (Compare their computation complexity, security, and usage.)
   Answer:
   Computation complexity: public key algorithm > private key algorithm
   Security: public key algorithm > private key algorithm
   Usage: public key algorithm for small data, private key algorithm for high-volume data
2. How can we combine the private key algorithm and the public key algorithm?
   Answer:
   Use a public key algorithm, say RSA, to transfer the key used in the private key algorithm, say 3DES. Once done, use the private key algorithm for data encryption and decryption.
3. Where do we use transport-mode IPSec and tunnel-mode IPSec, respectively? What parts of the packets do they encrypt?
   Answer:
   Transport mode: between remote clients and offices; TCP or UDP segments only
   Tunnel mode: between branch offices; entire IP packets
4. In tunnel-mode IPSec, if authentication is done before encryption, what sequence of headers would we have in the packets? (The headers include AH (Authentication Header), ESP (Encapsulation Security Payload), IP, TCP or UDP.)
   Answer:
   IP, ESP, IP, AH, TCP, or UDP.
5. Packet-filter vs. application-proxy firewalls? (Compare their purpose and where they are implemented in Linux systems.)
   Answer:
   Packet-filter firewall: access control based on 5-tuple fields; in kernel (iptables)
   Application-proxy firewall: access control based on application requests and responses; in a proxy daemon (FWTK or squid)
6. Virus vs. worm? (Compare their characteristics and model of replication.)
   Answer:
   Virus: a program attached to a file; through e-mail attachment or Web page
   Worm: a standalone program; through security hole attacks
7. DoS (denial of service) vs. buffer overflow attack? (Compare their purpose and operations.)
   Answer:
   DoS: to exhaust or block the service resources; send a large number of requests to exhaust the server or send only one malicious request to run the server into a blocking or deadlock mode
   Buffer overflow attack: to impose a backdoor program on the victim; overflow the victim's stacked program counter and its program code by passing an oversized parameter
8. In what situation will an IDS (intrusion detection system) such as Snort have a false positive or false negative?
   Answer:
   False positive: The signatures are too short and the normal text happens to have the signatures.
   False negative: The signatures are not generic enough to match the intrusion in the text.

EXERCISES

Hands-On Exercises

1. The *crypt* function is for password encryption based on the DES algorithm with variations. Please write a program to find out the password encrypted into "xyNev0eazF87U" using the *crypt* function (see the man page for its usage). You may use the brute-force method or any other *smarter* approaches (preferred) to guess. The password is not a random string, so you have a chance to crack it.

2. Set up *iptables* to block the outgoing connection to a certain IP address, and try to see whether the blocking works.
3. In a public key system using RSA, Bob owns the private keys d=5, n=35 and gets the ciphertext c=10 to him. What is the plaintext M?
4. Use *Nessus* (*http://www.nessus.org/nessus*) to find the services running on the hosts in your subnet, and indicate what they are. Are there any services not running on well-known ports, e.g., a Web service not on port 80?
5. Run Snort to listen to the traffic on the interface you specify. The more traffic the better. What alerts are raised by Snort? Do you think they are false positives? You may capture the traffic in a file and let Snort read the file off-line. Therefore, you have a chance to manually analyze the packets or connections that cause an alert later.
6. Trace the source code in *portscan.c* and *spp_portscan.c* in the preprocessors directory of the Snort source code. Describe briefly how Snort detects portscannning in the traffic traces.
7. Find out how many rules are in your current Snort rule set.
8. Trace the source code in *matcher-ac.c* and *matcher-bm.c,* and describe how ClamAV scans for virus signatures.
9. Use the UPX packer (http://upx.sourceforge.net) to pack a Windows binary executable in PE format. After that, use a PE viewer, say Anywhere PE viewer (http://upx.sourceforge.net/), to point out what has been changed.

Written Exercises

1. What is the primary encryption function in each iteration of the DES system?
2. Figure out the breaking time of key size 32, 56, 128, and 168 bits, if single decryption time is 1 μs and 10^{-6} μs, respectively.
3. In a public key system using RSA with the public keys e=5, n=35, Trudy intercepts the ciphertext C=10. What is the plaintext M?
4. Is it efficient to implement the DES (or 3DES) algorithm in software? Why is the implementation a target for hardware acceleration?
5. What are the requirements of digital signature?
6. What is the difference between network- and application-layer firewall?
7. What is the procedure of a DDoS attack? What was the attack procedure of the Nimda worm in October 2001?
8. How do we achieve authentication and privacy simultaneously by using authentication header (AH) and encapsulation security payload (ESP) in IPSec?
9. How does an attack own a large number of hosts to launch a distributed denial-of-service (DDoS) attack? Please discuss possible approaches.
10. A NIDS has the ability to "see" packets on the network, so it also has a chance to scan for viruses inside the packet payload. But this is not the case in practice. What are the difficulties in trying to do that?
11. What are possible reasons for *false positives* from NIDS alerts?
12. Please enumerate an example of an attack that cannot be detected by a Snort rule, even though you try to write a new rule. Why can it not be detected by a rule?
13. What are possible techniques to evade the analysis of NIDS? Please enumerate a few of them.
14. ClamAV claims a very large signature set (larger than 500,000). Are there really so many viruses in the wild, i.e., on the Internet? What are possible reasons that so many signatures are needed?

A Appendix

Who's Who

Many organizations and people have made significant contributions to the evolution of data communications. However, it is impossible to cover all of them here. Since the main theme of this text is the Internet architecture and its open source implementations, we focus on two groups, the Internet Engineering Task Force (IETF) and several open source communities; the former defines the Internet architecture while the latter implements it in an open source manner. Other standards bodies and the network research community have also played important roles in the evolution. So have the faded technologies that helped to shape the Internet today but did not survive the evolution. Though the materials presented in this appendix are nontechnical, they provide a review of the path to what we have today. Understanding this evolution and the driving forces behind it will enable you to appreciate these efforts and will also encourage you to participate in the ongoing evolution.

Unlike many other standards organizations, IETF does not have a clear membership, and it runs in a *bottom-up,* instead of *top-down,* manner. Anyone is welcome to participate, and those who are active lead the works. You do not have to pay to play. Besides, you *implement as you go,* compared to *"specify first and implement later"* in many organizations. "We reject kings, presidents, and voting. We believe in rough consensus and running code," said David Clark, a key contributor to the Internet architecture. The process to define a standard Request for Comments (RFC) document looks quite loose, but renders at least one (preferably two) solid and publicly available implementations once the standard is agreed upon. We could say that the standardization process of the Internet architecture has the open source spirit, as a way to confirm that the proposed solution works fine.

Although the open source movement started in 1984, 15 years later after the first Internet node was established in 1969, it works hand-in-hand with the Internet as they leverage each other. The Internet provides the guiding standards to ensure the interoperability of various open source implementations, and it serves as the platform to coordinate the efforts distributed worldwide. The open source movement facilitates the Internet's "implement-as-you-go" standardization process, and it helps to attract worldwide contributors and users. It would be difficult to distribute these running codes for worldwide users to adopt or to coordinate the distributed efforts to get the codes fixed and running if they were not open source.

In addition to IETF, several institutes and standards bodies helped to design protocols or implement the designed protocols. The Information Science Institute (ISI) at the University of Southern California (USC) designed and implemented several key protocols. The International Computer Science Institute (ICSI) in Berkeley developed some important algorithms and tools. The Computer Emergency Response Team (CERT) at Carnegie Mellon University coordinated security threat management. The European Telecommunications Standards Institute (ETSI) produced mobile communications standards. Most popular link-layer protocol standards, including Ethernet and WLAN, were produced by the Institute of Electrical and Electronics Engineers (IEEE). Meanwhile, many researchers have made key contributions to the architectures, protocols, or algorithms used in the Internet. All these contributions should be recognized.

While we review who's who, we should look not only at the survivors but also at the faded technologies. They may be "dinosaurs" who prevailed for some time before they became obsolete, or they may have produced "bubbles" that attracted huge investments but were eventually burst. The reasons for their failure might have been the technology or the market. A superior technology that requires tremendous overhead to interoperate with or replace the existing technologies might end up being a part of history. An inferior but simpler solution may outlast many more sophisticated competitors. A consensus is that "IP everywhere, or anything over IP and IP over anything." Similarly, "Ethernet everywhere" (into offices as well as homes) has become another consensus. IP and Ethernet did not appear to be superior in all aspects, but they have prevailed and will survive well into the future.

In Section A.1, we first review IETF history and how it produces RFCs. The statistics of over 6000 RFCs are presented. Then we introduce in Section A.2 several open source communities that produce running codes of kernels, over 10,000 packages, and even ASIC hardware designs. They open up the system from the top (i.e., applications), the middle (i.e., kernel and drivers), down to the bottom hardware (i.e., ASIC designs). These open source resources are all accessible at your fingertips. Network research community and other standards bodies are reviewed in Section A.3. Finally, in Section A.4, we examine the dated technologies of the past, and try to explain why they did not endure.

A.1 IETF: DEFINING RFCs

We intend to answer many questions here: How did the standardization body of the Internet evolve? Who played the major role? How does the IETF operate to define an RFC? Why are there so many RFCs? How are these RFCs distributed in defining the various layers in the protocol stack? The answers should open the door for understanding and participating in IETF activities.

A.1.1 IETF History

In the late 1970s, recognizing that the growth of the Internet was accompanied by a growth in the size of the interested research community and therefore an increased need for coordination mechanisms, Vint Cerf, the manager of the Internet program at DARPA, formed several coordination bodies. In 1983, one of these bodies turned into the Internet Activities Board (IAB), which governs many task forces. The Internet Engineering task force (IETF) at the time was just one of many IAB task forces. Later, the more practical and engineering side of the Internet grew significantly. This growth resulted in an explosion in attendance at IETF meetings in 1985, and Phil Gross, chair of IETF, was compelled to create substructures to the IETF in the form of working groups (WGs).

The growth continued. The IETF combined WGs into areas, and designated area directors for each area, and an Internet Engineering Steering Group (IESG) was then formed from the area directors. The IAB recognized the increasing importance of the IETF, and restructured the standards process to explicitly recognize the IESG as the major standards review body. The IAB was also restructured so that the rest of the task forces (other than the IETF) were combined into an Internet Research Task Force (IRTF). In 1992, the IAB was reorganized and renamed the Internet Architecture Board, operating under the auspices of the Internet Society. A more "peer"-like relationship was defined between the new IAB and IESG, with the IETF and IESG taking a greater responsibility for the standards approval.

Members of IETF WGs cooperate mainly through mailing lists and meetings held three times a year. Internet users are free to join IETF, and can do so simply by subscribing to mailing lists of specific WGs, through which they can communicate with other members in the WGs. The regular meetings aim to allow active WGs to present and discuss their working results. IETF had held 76 meetings as of March 2010. Each meeting lasts for five to seven days, and the meeting location is chosen by the host organization.

Historical Evolution: Who's Who in IETF

In 40 years, over 6000 RFCs have been produced. The most famous contributor is Jonathan Postel, who was the RFC editor from 1969 until his death in 1998. He was involved in over 200 RFCs, most of which are the fundamental protocols of the Internet, like IP and TCP. Behind Jonathan Postel, Keith McCloghrie is the person with the second highest number of RFCs. Keith has 94 RFCs, most of which are about SNMP and MIB. Table A.1 lists the top 10 contributors and their key contributions based on the number of their published RFCs.

TABLE A.1 Top Contributors of RFCs by Number

Name	# of RFCs	Key Contributions
Jonathan B. Postel	202	IP, TCP, UDP, ICMP, FTP
Keith McCloghrie	94	SNMP, MIB, COPS
Marshall T. Rose	67	POP3, SNMP
Yakov Rekhter	62	BGP4, MPLS
Henning Schulzrinne	62	SIP, RTP
Bob Braden	59	FTP, RSVP
Jonathan Rosenberg	52	SIP, STUN
Bernard Aboba	48	RADIUS, EAP

A.1.2 The RFC Process

IETF groups WGs into eight areas, each containing one or two area directors. Most RFCs are published after internal working of a specific WG. Figure A.1 shows the RFC process. Various stages need to be gone through in publishing an RFC, and each stage is reviewed by the IESG. To publish an RFC, an *Internet Draft* (ID) is first published, and will be put in an ID directory of the IETF for review. Sometime after the publication of the ID (at least two weeks), the author of the ID can send an e-mail to an RFC editor, to request that the ID be made into an Informational or Experimental RFC, and the RFC editor will then ask IESG to review the ID. Before it becomes an RFC, the authors of the ID can modify its contents. If the ID is not modified or turned into an RFC in six months, it will be removed from the ID directory of the IETF, and the authors will be informed. Meanwhile, if the ID is reviewed and ready to become an RFC, its authors will have 48 hours to check the document for mistakes such as incorrect spelling or erroneous references. Once it becomes an RFC, the content can no longer be modified.

As shown in Figure A.1, every RFC has a *status,* including Unknown, Standard (STD), Historic, Best Current Practice (BCP), and general (Informational and Experimental). The Unknown status was assigned to most RFCs published in the early years of IETF, and has not appeared since October 1989. The STD status denotes an Internet standard, the BCP status indicates the best way to achieve something, and the general status shows that the RFC is not yet ready to, or may not be intended to, be standardized. An RFC must progress through three stages to become an STD: Proposed-STD, Draft-STD, and STD. These stages are termed *maturity levels,* meaning that an RFC in the STD status should go through all these stages. Steps to different stages have different limitations. For example, if an RFC is stable, has resolved known design

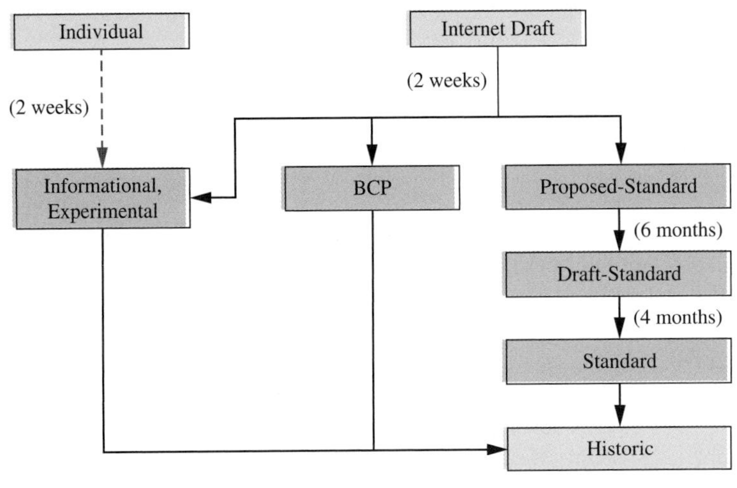

FIGURE A.1 The RFC Process.

issues, is believed to be well understood, has received significant community reviews, and appears to enjoy sufficient community interest to be considered valuable, it can be granted the Proposed-STD status. To gain the Draft-STD status, a Proposed-STD RFC must have at least two independent and interoperable *implementations* and stay in the processing queue for at least six months. To progress from Draft-STD to STD status, the RFC must have significant implementation and successful *operation experience,* and must also have spent at least four months in the processing queue. A specification that has been suppressed by a more recent specification or that is considered obsolete for any reason is assigned the Historic status.

The BCP process resembles the Proposed-STD process. The RFC is submitted to IESG for review; once it is approved by IESG, the process ends. The Informational and Experimental processes differ from STD's and BCP's. Documents intended to be published under these nonstandard statuses can be either submitted to IESG by IETF WGs or directly submitted to an RFC editor by individuals. For the first case, IESG still takes responsibility for reviewing and approving the document as in the STD process. For the second case, however, the RFC editor has the final decision, and the IESG only reviews and provides feedback. The RFC editor will first publish such a document as an Internet Draft, wait two weeks for comments from the community, judge its suitability to be an Informational or Experimental RFC in his or her expert opinion, and then accept or reject it. IESG reviews the document and suggests whether or not to standardize it. If the document is recommended for standardization and the authors agree, it will enter the STD process. Otherwise, it will be published as an Informational or Experimental RFC. Figure A.1 illustrates the RFC process for the STD, BCP, and general status.

RFC serial numbers are assigned according to the order of approval. Some serial numbers have special meanings. For example, RFC serial numbers ending with 99 represent the RFCs that make a short introduction to the following 99 RFCs, while serial numbers ending with 00 represent the IAB Official Protocol Standards, which provide short status reports of current RFC standards. Interested readers are further referred to RFC 2026: The Internet Standards Process.

A.1.3 The RFC Statistics

As of November 2010, RFC serial numbers had been assigned up to 6082. Among them, 205 serial numbers are unused, so there are only 5877 RFCs. To understand how RFCs are distributed, we compiled the statistics for these RFCs. Figure A.2 presents the statistics and indicates that the top three RFC statuses are Informational, Proposed Standard, and Unknown, respectively. Not surprisingly, RFC 1796 has stated: "Not all RFCs are Standards." Publishing as an Informational RFC is easier than passing through the STD process. Becoming a Standard needs to be widely proven, so many RFCs stay in the Proposed Standard level. Finally, the Unknown status is ranked third, because IETF did not develop the maturity levels and review process until RFC 1310.

Table A.2 counts the RFCs related to well-known protocols in four layers. The statistics include Point-to-Point Protocol (RFC 1661) for the data link layer, Internet Protocol (RFC 791) for the network layer, Transmission Control Protocol (RFC 793) for the transport layer, and Telnet Protocol Specification (RFC 854) for the application layer. In fact, only about 30% of over 6000 RFCs are commonly used

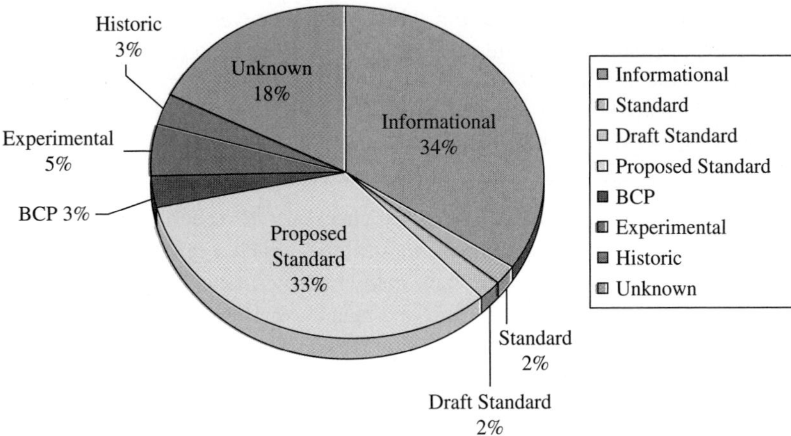

FIGURE A.2 Statistics for RFC Status.

in the Internet, which raises the question: Why are there so many RFCs? There are several reasons. First, once an RFC is generated, nobody can modify it. Thus many RFCs are *obsolete* or *updated* by new RFCs. Second, a single protocol might be defined by *several* RFCs. A single protocol with abundant functionalities might not be completed in its first version, and thus new *features* or *options* are added individually as demands emerge. Finally, numerous RFCs define emerging technologies which might not be deployed because of various difficulties or newer alternatives.

Take the TELNET protocol as an example. About 108 RFCs describe this protocol. Among these 108 RFCs, 60 define *options* for TELNET, only eight RFCs describe the main protocol, and the remaining documents are protocol-related discussions, comments, encryption methods, or experiences. These options were defined as the new demands for the TELNET protocol emerged, and they made the protocol more functionally complete. Among the eight RFCs, RFC 854 is the most

TABLE A.2 Well-Known Protocols Defined by 1561 RFCs

Layer	Protocol	Count	Layer	Protocol	Count
Data link	ATM	46	Transport	TCP	111
	PPP	87		UDP	21
Network	ARP/RARP	24	Application	DNS	105
	BOOTP/DHCP	69		FTP/TFTP	51
	ICMP/ICMPv6	16		HTTP/HTML	37
	IP/IPv6	259		MIME	99
	Multicast	95		SMTP	41
	RIP/BGP/OSPF	154		SNMP/MIB	238
				TELNET	108

up-to-date protocol definition of TELNET, while the other seven have become obsolete or have been updated.

A.2 OPEN SOURCE COMMUNITIES

As previously mentioned, implementation is necessary for each standard RFC and should be open to the public to prove its usability. Such a guideline promotes the development of the open source. In fact, many open source communities devote themselves to implementing these new Internet standards. Before introducing these communities, we intend to answer the following questions: How and why did the whole game of open source begin? What are the rules of the game in releasing, using, modifying, and distributing an open source package? What running codes have been produced so far, in applications, kernels, and ASIC designs? This overview shall lead readers to enter the open source game.

A.2.1 Beginning and Rules of the Game

Free Software Foundation

In 1984, Richard Stallman (RMS, www.stallman.org) founded the Free Software Foundation (www.fsf.org), which is a tax-exempt charity that raises funds for work on the GNU Project (www.gnu.org). GNU, a *recursive* acronym for "GNU's Not Unix" and a homophone for "new," aims to develop Unix-compatible software and advocates software freedom. The *copyleft* and *GPL* were proposed to guarantee this freedom. Copylefts, in essence, are copyrights with GPL regulations. RMS himself is not only a "preacher," but also a major open source software contributor. He is the principal author of GNU C Compiler (GCC), GNU symbolic debugger (GDB), GNU Emacs, and so forth. All these packages are essential tools in GNU/Linux, and there are about 55 GNU packages in the Fedora 8.0 distribution, which includes a total of 1491 packages.

License Models

How to handle the intellectual property of an open source package is an interesting and sometimes controversial issue. It is important to select an appropriate license model to release an open source package to the public. Generally speaking, there are three natures of a license model to be aware of: (1) Is it *free* software? (2) Is it *copyleft?* (3) Is it *GPL-compatible?* Free software means the program can be freely modified and redistributed. Copyleft usually means giving up intellectual property and private licensing. GPL-compatible packages are legal to *link* GPL software. Nevertheless, there are too many license models out there. We only describe three major ones: GPL, LGPL, and BSD.

General Public License (GPL) is a free software license and a copyleft license. It is self perpetuating and infectious in that it *strictly* ensures that derivative works will be distributed under the same license model, i.e., GPL. The Linux kernel itself is GPL. In addition to derivative works, programs *statically linked* with Linux should be GPL, too. However, programs *dynamically linked* to Linux do not have to be GPL. Lesser GPL (LGPL), once known as library GPL, permits *linking* with non-free (proprietary) modules.

For example, since there are plenty of other C libraries, the GNU C library, if under GPL, would have driven proprietary software developers away to use other alternatives. Thus there are cases in which LGPL can help free software to attract more users and programmers. The GNU C library is thus LGPL. The Berkeley Software Distribution (BSD), on the other extreme, states that the code is free as distributed and allows derivative works to be covered under *different* terms, as long as necessary *credit* is given. Apache, BSD-related OS, and the free version of Sendmail are all licensed under BSD. In short, GPL means it is a public property which you cannot own privately, while BSD implies a gift that anyone can take away. All other licensing models are between these two extremes.

A.2.2 Open Source Resources

Linux

People seldom emphasize Linux as *GNU/Linux*. Indeed, the Linux kernel is the magician and GNU packages perform all the tricks. In 1991, Linus Torvalds, a graduate student at the Helsinki University in Finland, wrote a real Unix-compatible operating system and posted it on the newsgroup comp.os.minix. He handed on the kernel maintenance to Allan Cox after 1994, while still monitoring kernel versions and what's in and out, and letting others deal with "user space" issues (libraries, compilers, and all kinds of utilities and applications that go into any Linux distributions). GNU/Linux has proven to be a successful combination. Eric Raymond (www.tuxedo.org/~esr), another "preacher," described this change in software development as the "open source movement" in 1998.

Taxonomy of Packages

The number of open source packages has reached over 10,000. This huge library can be divided into three major categories: (1) the operating environments with console or GUI interfaces, (2) daemons that provide various services, and (3) programming toolkits and libraries for programmers. We dug into this huge library to summarize the statistics shown in Figure A.3. For example, there are 97 daemons for HTTP; Apache is just one of them and happens to be the most popular one.

Linux Distributions

If the kernel is the foundation of a building and every open source *package* is a brick on top of it, a Linux distribution from a vendor is then the appearance of a building with the foundations, all kinds of bricks, and the furnishings. These vendors test, integrate, and put the open source software together. Next we introduce a few well-known Linux distributions.

Slackware (www.slackware.com) is a distribution that has a long history, is widespread, and is mostly noncommercial. It is stable and easy to use. Debian (www.debian.org) is formed and maintained by nearly 1000 volunteers. Many advanced users have found flexibility and satisfaction in the Debian distributions. Red Hat Linux (www.redhat.com), distributed by the S&P 500 company Red Hat, Inc., began as a Linus distribution packaged with Red Hat Packaging Manager *(RPM)*, which provided easier installing, uninstalling, and upgrading than the primitive ".tar.gz."

Console/GNOME/KDE/X11

[247] Administration
[019] AfterStep Applets
[019] Anti-Spam
[119] Applications
[048] Backup
[008] Browser Addons
[023] CAE
[034] CD Writing Software
[196] Communication
[030] Compression
[009] Core
[130] Database
[063] Desktop
[027] Development
[006] Dialup Networking
[055] Documentation
[108] Drivers
[088] Editors
[062] Education
[165] eMail
[008] Embedded
[088] Emulators
[068] Encryption
[028] Enlightenment Applets
[023] FTP Clients
[044] File Managers
[052] File Systems
[051] Financial
[179] Firewall and Security
[026] Fonts and Utilities
[593] Games
[277] Graphics
[008] Home Automation
[103] IRC
[053] Java
[074] Log Analyzers
[208] MP3
[010] Mail Clients
[051] Mini Distributions
[021] Mirroring
[351] Misc
[028] Modeling
[007] Modem Gettys
[184] Monitoring
[003] Motif
[032] Multimedia
[480] Networking
[048] News
[053] OS
[048] Office Applications
[042] Packaging
[053] Printing
[189] Scientific Applications
[007] Screensavers
[031] Shells
[265] Sound
[136] System
[041] TV and Video
[011] Terminals
[190] Text Utilities
[665] Utilities
[004] VRML
[033] Video
[038] Viewers
[684] Web Applications
[038] Web Browsers
[121] Window Maker Applets
[039] Window Managers

Daemons

[007] Anti-Virus
[005] Batch Processing
[030] BBS
[010] Chat
[032] Database
[026] DNS
[015] Filesharing
[009] Finger
[022] FTP
[006] Hardware
[097] HTTP
[013] Ident
[013] IMAP
[050] IRC
[015] Mailinglist Managers
[231] Misc
[027] MUD
[009] Network Directory Service
[013] NNTP
[023] POP3
[071] Proxy
[031] SMTP
[005] SNMP
[002] Time

Development

[010] Bug Tracking
[068] Compilers
[014] CORBA
[073] Database
[038] Debugging
[084] Environments
[028] Game SDK
[048] Interfaces
[173] Java Packages
[028] Kernel
[001] Kernel Patches
[121] Languages
[485] Libraries
[100] Perl Modules
[008] PHP Classes
[001] Pike Modules
[057] Python Modules
[031] Revision Control
[019] Tcl Extensions
[017] Test Suites
[558] Tools
[178] Web
[055] Widget Sets

FIGURE A.3 Taxonomy of open source packages.

RPM makes *software dependency* transparent, not troublesome. Red Hat, Inc., took Red Hat Linux as their commercial product, Red Hat Enterprise Linux (RHEL), until 2004, and thereafter stopped maintaining Red Hat Linux, probably due to copyright and patent problems. At present, RHEL has evolved from a community-supported distribution named Fedora, sponsored by Red Hat. CentOS (Community ENTerprise Operating System, www.centos.org), is another community-supported distribution.

It provides a free enterprise-class computing platform that maintains 100% binary compatibility with RHEL. Like the relation between RHEL and Fedora, SuSE Linux (www.novell.com/linux/) and openSUSE (www.opensuse.org) are the enterprise product and community-supported distribution sponsored by Novell, respectively. SuSE is known for good documentation and abundant package resources. Mandriva Linux (http://www.mandriva.com/), formerly Mandrake Linux, began with simply combining the Red Hat distribution with KDE (K Desktop Environment) and many other unique, feature-rich tools. This combination turned out to be so popular that a company called Mandriva was then founded. Ubuntu (http://www.ubuntu.com), named from the Bantu words for "humanity toward others," is a distribution based on Debian and uses GNOME (the GNU Network Object Model Environment) as its graphical desktop environment. It is famous for its ease of installation and user-friendly interface. Since 2006, Ubuntu is reported to be the most popular distribution.

A.2.3 Web Sites for Open Source

Freshmeat.net and SourceForge.net

The Web sites *Freshmeat.net* was set up to provide a platform for Linux users to find and download the software packages released under open source licenses. For each package, besides the brief description, homepage URL, release focus, recent changes, and dependent libraries, three interesting indexes are given in Freshmeat.net, which are *rating, vitality,* and *popularity*. A user vote mechanism provides the rating, while the other two indexes are calculated based on the age of project, number of announcements, date of last announcement, number of subscriptions, URL hits, and record hits. Besides the packages, Freshmeat.net includes many original articles to introduce the software and programming.

Freshmeat.net is supported and maintained by Geeknet, Inc. According to the statistics given on the Web sites, Freshmeat.net introduces more than 40,000 projects. The statistics also report the top 10 projects, sorted by popularity and vitality. For example, two famous projects in the top 10 lists are GCC and MySQL, where GCC is the well-known GNU compiler mentioned previously and MySQL is one of the most popular open source databases on the Internet.

Unlike Freshmeat.net, which provides the information for users to look up, compare, and download packages, *SourceForge.net* provides a free platform for package developers to manage projects, issues, communications, and codes. It hosts over 230,000 projects! The most active project in SourceForge.net is Notepad++, while the most downloaded one is eMule. The former is a text editor used in Windows, while the latter is a P2P file sharing program.

OpenCores.org

Not only software packages can be open source; so can hardware designs. The OpenCores.org community collects people who are interested in developing hardware and like to share their designs with others, just like open source software. The only difference here is that the codes are in *hardware* description languages like Verilog and VHDL. The community and its Web portal were founded by Damjan Lampret in 1999. As of December 2009, there were 701 projects hosted on its Web site and 500,000 Web hits/month. These projects are classified into 15 categories, such as arithmetic core, communication core, cypto core, and DSP core.

As with Freshmeat.net, OpenCores.org also maintains several interesting indexes for each project, such as popularity, downloads, activity, and rating. For example, the top six by popularity are OpenRISC 1000, Ethernet MAC 10/100Mbps, ZPU, I2C core, VGA/LCD controller, and Plasma.

A.2.4 Events and People

Table A.3 lists major events in the open source movement. Lots of contributors spend their time developing open source software. Here we mention only some well-known people, while credit should also go to people who receive less public attention.

TABLE A.3 Open Source Timeline

1969	Internet started as ARPAnet. Unix.
1979	Berkeley Software Distribution (BSD).
1983	Sendmail by Eric Allman.
1984	Richard Stallman started the GNU project.
1986	Berkeley Internet Name Domain (BIND).
1987	Perl by Elaine Ashton.
1991	Linus Thorvald wrote Linux.
1994	Allan Cox carried on the Linux kernel maintenance. PHP by Rasmus Lerdorf.
2/1995	Apache HTTP Server Project with 8 team members.
3/1998	Navigator went Open Source.
8/1998	"Sure, we're worried."— Microsoft president Steve Ballmer.
3/1999	Macintosh released Darwin (kernel of MacOSX) under APS license.
7/2000	No. of Apache Web servers exceeded 11 million (62.8% of the whole market).
10/2000	Sun Microsystems made the StarOffice code available.
10/2003	UK government announced a deal with IBM on open-source software.
10/2004	IBM offered 500 patents for open source developers.
1/2005	Sun Microsystems opened the Solaris operation system.
5/2007	Microsoft claimed Linux infringed its patents.
11/2007	Google announced an open mobile device platform named Android.
9/2008	Microsoft CEO confessed that 40% of Web servers run Windows but 60% run Linux.
7/2009	Google introduced its open-source OS, Google Chrome OS.

A.3 RESEARCH AND OTHER STANDARDS COMMUNITIES

Besides IETF and open source communities, there are several important research institutes and standard bodies that have also contributed much to the evolution of the Internet. We introduce them here.

ISI: Information Sciences Institute at University of Southern California

ISI is a research and development center for advanced computer and communication technologies, founded in 1972. ISI now has eight divisions and hosts more than 300 researchers and engineers. Its computer network division is one of the birthplaces of the ARPANET, the Internet's predecessor. The division is also involved in the development of many daily-used Internet protocols and packages, such as TCP/IP, DNS, SMTP, and Kerberos.

ICSI: International Computer Science Institute in Berkeley

ICSI is an independent nonprofit institute for research in computer science, which was established in 1988 and includes four major research groups: Internet research, theoretical computer science, artificial intelligence, and natural speech processing. The scientists in the Internet research group have been involved in many well-known and widely-deployed network algorithms and tools, such as RED, TCP SACK, TFRC, and network simulator 2. The group also presented a series of measurements and observations on the current status of Internet traffic and security, which are highly useful to the design and testing of new network protocols and algorithms.

CERT: Computer Emergency Response Team at Carnegie Mellon University

The CERT Coordination Center was founded in the Software Engineering Institute when the Morris worm caused 10% of Internet systems to halt in 1988. The major works in the center include software assurance, secure systems, organizational security, coordinated response, and education/training. CERT is also the birthplace of the World Wide Web.

ETSI: European Telecommunications Standards Institute

ETSI was created in 1988 and is a standardization organization of the telecommunications industry in Europe. Its produced standards include fixed, mobile, radio, and Internet technologies. The most significant successful standard pushed by ETSI is GSM (Global System for Mobile Communications).

IEEE: Institute of Electrical and Electronics Engineers

IEEE is the largest professional association in electrical engineering, computer science, and electronics with more than 365,000 members in over 150 countries (as of 2008). The association publishes about 130 journals or magazines, hosts over 400 conferences per year, and produces many textbooks. It is also one of the most important developers of international standards in communications. Many PHY and MAC protocols are standardized in the series of IEEE 802 standards, including 802.3 (Ethernet), 802.11 (Wireless LAN), and 802.16 (WiMAX). The contents of these standards are introduced in Chapter 3.

ISO: International Organization for Standardization

ISO, as the largest developer and publisher of international standards, is involved in almost all domains—technology, business, government, and society. Many famous telecommunication systems are standardized by ISO. For example, the telephone network is based on its Public Switched Telephone Networks (PSTN) standard. ISO also made many standards in data networks, although not all of these standards are used in today's Internet, e.g., the OSI 7-layer network architecture.

Individual Contributions

Finally, we honor some individuals whose efforts established the fundamental architecture of the Internet. J.C.R. Licklider and Lawrence Roberts led the ARPA project in the 1960s to create the ARPANET. Paul Baran, Donald Davies, and Leonard Kleinrock are often acclaimed as the "fathers" of the Internet for building the initial packet-switched ARPANET back in 1969. Bob Kahn and Vint Cerf developed TCP and IP in the early 1970s. Robert M. Metcalfe and David R. Boggs co-invented the first Ethernet technology in 1973. Jon Postel subsequently wrote many RFCs for TCP/IP, DNS, SMTP, FTP, etc. David D. Clark acted as a chief protocol architect in the development of the Internet architecture in the 1980s. Van Jacobson contributed to TCP congestion control in the late 1980s. Sally Floyd developed RED and CBQ and improved TCP in the 1990s. Tim Berners-Lee invented the World Wide Web in 1989, which led to an explosive growth of the Internet in the 1990s.

A.4 HISTORY

This subsection describes the short-lived or failed technologies in the Internet and the reasons for their failure. Figure A.4 shows a timeline for these technologies. The hollow bar means the technology was studied for many years but did not get deployed or accepted by the market, while the solid bar means it has been deployed, but was replaced by a later technology or failed to replace the existing one. Their brief histories follow.

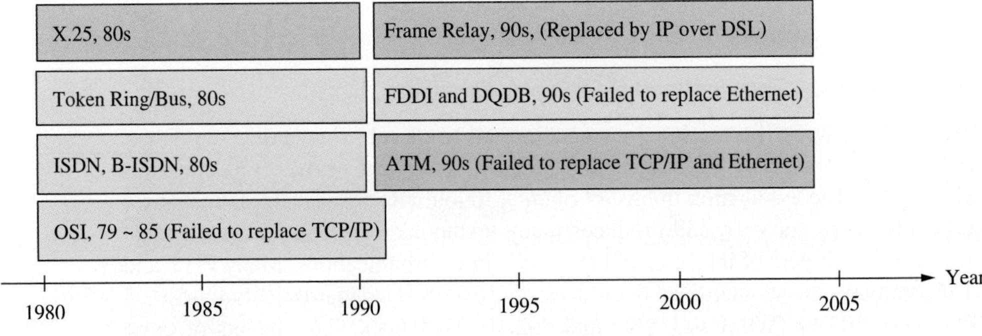

FIGURE A.4 Timeline with some short-lived and failed technologies.

Architecture Standards: OSI

The seven-layer Open System Interconnection (OSI) architecture was proposed in 1980 by Zimmerman and later adopted by the International Organization for Standardization (ISO) in 1994. It aimed to replace the emerging four-layer TCP/IP stack defined in 1981. It had two extra layers—presentation and session layers—which were thought to be more *complete* and structured than TCP/IP. But why did OSI fail? There are two main reasons. First, TCP/IP was already prevailing on the UNIX operating system that most computers run. That is, it had a strong *vehicle* to penetrate the world. Second is that the claimed structural completeness was *not* critical as long as all sorts of applications could run on TCP/IP smoothly. The result proved that on the Internet there is no absolute authority. Even a technology approved and supported by an international standards body could fail. OSI is just one of the *many* examples.

Integrated Services: ISDN, B-ISDN with ATM

Carrying voice and data on the same network had been a long-term effort in the telecom industry. As far back as the mid-1980s, the industry had only POTS for voice services and launched its connection-oriented X.25 for limited data services mostly for financial applications and enterprise networking. X.25 was a successful service, and was later gradually replaced by Frame Relay in the 1990s and then IP over Digital Subscriber Line (DSL) in the 2000s as the data services evolved toward the Internet. But the data services remained separate from the voice services until Integrated Services Digital Network (ISDN) emerged in the late 1980s as the *first* try to combine these two public services. ISDN *integrated* the user interfaces to access data and voice services, but still had two *separate* backbone networks, one circuit-switched to carry voices and another packet-switched but connection-oriented to carry data. ISDN was a moderate, but brief, success in the late 1980s to the mid-1990s with service providers in many countries.

To eliminate ISDN limitations on the *fixed* user interfaces, *narrow* bandwidth, and *separate* backbones, broadband-ISDN (B-ISDN) was proposed to ITU in the early 1990s to provide *flexible* interfaces, *broadband* services, and a *unified* backbone which relied on cell-switching Asynchronous Transfer Mode (ATM) technologies where a cell was a fixed-size, 53-byte packet to facilitate *hardware* switching. Similar to the fate of OSI, ATM was a complete, sophisticated technology, but it needed to coexist with TCP/IP which already dominated public data networks. This coexistence was *painful* because of the conflicting natures of connection-oriented, cell-switching ATM and connectionless, packet-switching IP, either through Internetworking (ATM-IP-ATM or IP-ATM-IP) or hybrid stacking (IP-over-ATM). The effort was abandoned in the late 1990s after *billions* in investments and "*tons*" of research. B-ISDN was never deployed commercially. TCP/IP won the second major war and continued to extend its services from data to voice and video.

WAN Services: X.25 and Frame Relay

If TCP/IP was the data service solution proposed by the datacom camp, X.25 was the *first* data service solution presented by the telecom camp. X.25 had three layers of protocols and was connection oriented, but it was slow due to the high protocol processing overhead. Thus it was redesigned to compress its protocol stack into the two-layer Frame Relay, which remained connection oriented. The transition to Frame Relay was evolutionary and seldom noticed. Today there are still financial systems using either X.25 or Frame Relay, as most enterprise customers have switched to IP over DSL.

One interesting observation is that almost all data services rolled out from the telecom camp were *connection oriented* and eventually failed or were replaced. The same might happen in wireless data services, including GSM/GPRS and 3G with circuit-switched voice services and packet-switched but connection-oriented data services. On the other hand, WiMAX pushed by the datacom camp and some telecom players does *not* differentiate data and voice *explicitly,* and positions itself as a pure layer-2 technology to carry IP and above. If history repeats itself, the end result should be clear.

LAN Technologies: Token Ring, Token Bus, FDDI, DQDB, and ATM

Similar to IP, Ethernet has been a long-term winner since the early 1980s. It won mainly because it remained simple and it evolved through many generations. Its first competitors in the 1980s were Token Ring and Token Bus, which had *bounded* transmission latency for a station attached to the ring or bus due to the nature of round-robin token passing. But this advantage did not win them a market share because of the higher hardware complexity in the interface cards and the concentrators. The theoretical unbounded latency did not hurt Ethernet, since in reality the latency was acceptable. The second competitors in the early 1990s were Fiber Distributed Dual Interface (FDDI) and Dual Queue Dual Bus (DQDB), which operated at 100 Mbps, compared to 10 Mbps Ethernet at that time, and provided QoS, i.e., bounded latency. FDDI enhanced the token passing protocol similar to Token Ring, while DQDB ran a sophisticated mechanism of "requesting in upstream minislots for downstream data slots." In response, Ethernet evolved to 10/100 Mbps versions and protected its market dominance by its hardware simplicity again.

The third competitor in the mid-1990s, ATM, was an effort branched from a grand effort of B-ISDN. In the 1990s, ATM aimed to span not only last-mile interfaces but also WAN, (the backbone) and LAN. ATM LAN provided an impressive capacity of a gigabit per second and comprehensive integration from LAN to WAN. It failed because its B-ISDN umbrella was abandoned and Ethernet evolved into its 10/100/1000 Mbps versions. Chapter 3 has complete coverage on the evolution of Ethernet.

FURTHER READINGS

IETF

Almost all IETF-related documents are online accessible. No specific books are on IETF or RFCs alone. Thus readers are referred to the official site of IETF at www.ietf.org.

Open Source Development

The first entry is the first open source *project*. The next two are the famous article on open source and the book derived from it. The fourth one is an overview of open source development.

- R. Stallman, The GNU project, http://www.gnu.org
- E. S. Raymond, "The Cathedral and the Bazaar," May 1997, http://www.tuxedo.org/~esr/writings/cathedral-bazaar/cathedral-bazaar
- E. S. Raymond, *The Cathedral and the Bazaar: Musings on Linux and Open Source by an Accidental Revolutionary,* O'Reilly & Associates, Jan. 2001.
- M. W. Wu and Y. D. Lin, "Open Source Software Development: An Overview," *IEEE Computer,* June 2001.

Appendix B

Linux Kernel Overview

One question arises when teaching protocol designs interleaved with their Linux open source implementations. Students might not be familiar with the Linux environment for *users, administrators,* and *developers;* nor do they have enough experience in *tracing* complicated source codes. Regarding the Linux environment for users and administrators, there are plenty of easy-to-read references available. For developers, there are several good references, but they are too thick for students taking a computer networks course to read quickly. Learning to trace complicated source codes is another barrier to overcome. Thus, we provide exposure to source code in this appendix, while the Linux tools for development and utility are introduced in Appendix C and Appendix D, respectively.

This appendix gives a simple guide for tracing the Linux kernel. The same practices could be applied to trace Linux application programs. We first review the *Linux source tree* with emphasis on *networking,* which is the focus of this text, followed by an introduction to a couple of useful tools for tracing the Linux source code. Section B.1 reviews the kernel source tree, under the directory with the default name /usr/src/linux, by classifying twenty directories into seven categories, describing the coverage of these categories, and listing their important example modules.

Section B.2 summarizes the open source implementations covered in Chapters 3, 4, and 5 in a table. This directs readers to focus on source codes of networking and narrow down which program *functions* to trace. Note that the open source implementations in Chapter 6 are user-space programs which are not in the Linux kernel. The summary table does not include the open source implementations of advanced QoS and security features discussed in Chapters 7 and 8, though some of them are within the Linux kernel.

To trace complicated source codes, efficient tools are essential. Section B.3 introduces several popular tracing tools and physically walks through a sample open source implementation, IP reassembly covered in Chapter 4, with the tool `LXR` *(Linux Cross Reference).* Readers could apply the same practice to all other open source implementations covered in this text.

Distributions and Versions

Linux was written by Linus Torvalds in 1991, while he was a graduate student at Helsinki University in Finland. The development was done on Minix for PC with an 80386 processor. However, the kernel cannot work by itself without system software such as shell, compilers, libraries, text editors, and so forth. Therefore, Linux version 0.99 was published using the GNU General Public License in December 1992. Torvalds later handed on the kernel maintenance to Allan Cox after 1994.

There are many Linux distributions, such as Red Hat, SuSE, Debian, Fedora, CentOS, and Ubuntu. However, it does not matter which distribution you install; they share the *same* Linux kernel. They differ in their add-ons. You may choose a distribution that has a graphical installer, easy server configuration tools, high security, and good online support.

There are also many versions of the Linux kernel. Each version is denoted by *x.y.z* where *x* is the major version number, *y* is the minor version number, and *z* is the release number. After version 2.6.8, a fourth number may be added to indicate a trivial version number. As a convention, the Linux kernel uses odd minor version numbers to denote *development releases* and even minor version numbers to denote *stable releases*. As of June 2009, the most up-to-date version is v2.6.30.

B.1 KERNEL SOURCE TREE

The Linux source code of version 2.6.30 consists of the following 20 first-level directories: `Documentation`, `arch`, `block`, `crypto`, `drivers`, `firmware`, `fs`, `include`, `init`, `ipc`, `kernel`, `lib`, `mm`, `net`, `samples`, `scripts`, `security`, `sound`, `usr`, `virt`. Each directory contains files for a specific propose. For example, the files under `Document/` are written to illustrate the design concept or implementation details of the Linux kernel. Due to the highly evolving nature of Linux, the name and location of a directory might be changed, e.g., firmware image files were extracted from `drivers/` to the `firmware/` directory since version 2.6.27. Or new directories are created for new frameworks, e.g., the sound architecture and its first-level directory, `sound/`, were proposed in version 2.5.5, or driven by new features, e.g., the support of virtualization platforms results in the `virt/` directory in 2.6.25.

From a high-level view, we can still classify those directories into seven categories as summarized in Table B.1: creation, architecture-specific, kernel core, file system, networking, drivers, and helper. The remainder of this section introduces each of the categories in order to provide on overview of the Linux kernel.

- Creation
  The files in this category help in the making of the kernel and kernel-related systems. Two directories belong to this category: the `scripts/` and the `usr/` directories. The `scripts/` directory contains command-line scripts, and C source codes to build the kernel. For example, when you type `'make menuconfig'` under the top-level directory of the kernel source, it actually executes the procedures defined in the `scripts/kconfig/Makefile`. Then the source codes under the `usr/` directory can be used to build a cpio-archieved[1] initial ramdisk, `initrd`, which can be mounted by the kernel in the booting stage before loading the actual file system.[2]

[1]Before Linux 2.6, the `initrd` was generated from the image of a file system, i.e., dumping the layout of a file system byte by byte. To do that, you needed the administrative privilege, which might be inconvenient to a developer. Linux 2.6 adds a new `initrd` format that directly utilizes the

Continued

TABLE B.1 Summary of Linux Kernel Source

Category	Directories	Description
Creation	`usr/, scripts/`	Help in the making of the kernel
Architecture-specific	`arch/, virt/`	Architecture-specific source and header files
Kernel core	`init/, kernel/, include/, lib/, block/, ipc/, mm/, security/, crypto/`	Core functions and frameworks used in kernel
File system	`fs/`	File system-related source codes
Networking	`net/`	Networking-related source codes
Drivers	`drivers/, sound/, firmware/`	Device drivers
Helper	`Documentation/, samples/`	Document and sample codes that help you get involved in the kernel development

- Architecture-specific
  Platform-dependent codes are placed under the `arch/` directory. To reduce porting efforts, the design of the Linux kernel separates the low-level, architecture-specific functions, such as memory copy (`memcpy`), from the generic routines. In the early versions, the architecture-specific header files, i.e., `*.h` files, were located under the `include/asm-<arch>` subdirectory. Since the release of version 2.6.23, those files were progressively moved to the `arch/` directory. For example, codes specific to the x86 PC architecture are under the `arch/x86` subdirectory. Now all architecture-specific header files have been put under the `arch/` directory.

  Linux also plans to support kernel-based, hardware-assisted *virtualization*. The related code is located under the `virt/` directory. At present, only one module that utilizes the Intel VT-x extensions is available.
- Kernel core
  This category contains the code that provides the core functions of the kernel. It includes the kernel start-up procedures and management routines. Specifically, the `init/main.c` calls many initialization functions, brings

user-space archiver, `cpio`, to create the `initrd`, so that all users can play the kernel compilation without bothering the administrators.

[2]The kernel needs the `initrd` to bring out the actual file system if the actual file system is unrecognized by the kernel, e.g., it is stored on an encrypted disk.

up the ramdisk, executes user-space system-initialization programs, and then starts scheduling. The implementations of the initialization, scheduling, and synchronization and process management functions are actually under the `kernel/` directory, while the memory management routines are under the `mm/` directory and the inter-process communication (IPC) functions, e.g., shared memory management, are under the `ipc/` directory.

This category also covers kernel-space shared functions, e.g., the string comparison function (`strcmp`), implemented under the `lib/` directory. The cryptographic application programming interface (API) is isolated to a first-level directory, `crypto/`. Their header files (`*.h`) as well as other common header files, such as the TCP header, shared by all kernel modules are located in the `include/` directory.

Finally, the generic frameworks defined by Linux also belong to this category. These include the block-device interface, which is under the `block/` directory, and the security framework and its implementation, e.g., the Security Enhanced Linux *(SELinux),* placed under the `security/` directory. Although the sound architecture, called Advanced Linux Sound Architecture *(ALSA),* is also a *common* architecture in Linux, we like to place such files in the drivers category. This is because most of the files under the `sound/` directory are actually device drivers.

- File system
  Linux supports dozens of file systems implemented under the `fs/` directory. The core of all file systems is called the virtual file system (VFS), which is an abstract layer providing the file system interface to user space. Briefly, a new file system complying with the VFS will call `register_filesystem()` and `unregister_filesystem()` to register and disassociate itself from the kernel, respectively.

  Among those file systems, the most common one at present might be the third extended file system *(ext3)*. The source code of *ext3* and its successor, *ext4,* is located in the `fs/ext3` and `fs/ext4` subdirectories, respectively. Similarly, source code for the famous Network File System *(NFS)* is under the `fs/nfs` subdirectory.
- Networking
  The networking architecture and the protocol-stack implementation under the `net/` directory might be the most active part in the kernel development. For example, since the release of version 2.6.29, Linux has supported WiMAX, and its source code is under the `net/wimax/` subdirectory. Section B.2 elaborates on the `net/` directory.
- Drivers
  This category includes the kernel source code of device drivers within three first-level directories: `drivers/`, `sound/`, and `firmware/`. All kinds of drivers except the sound card drivers are put under the `drivers/` directory. Due to the presence of a uniform sound architecture mentioned above, i.e., ALSA, the sound card drivers were moved to the first-level directory, `sound/`. The `firmware/` directory contains firmware image files extracted from device

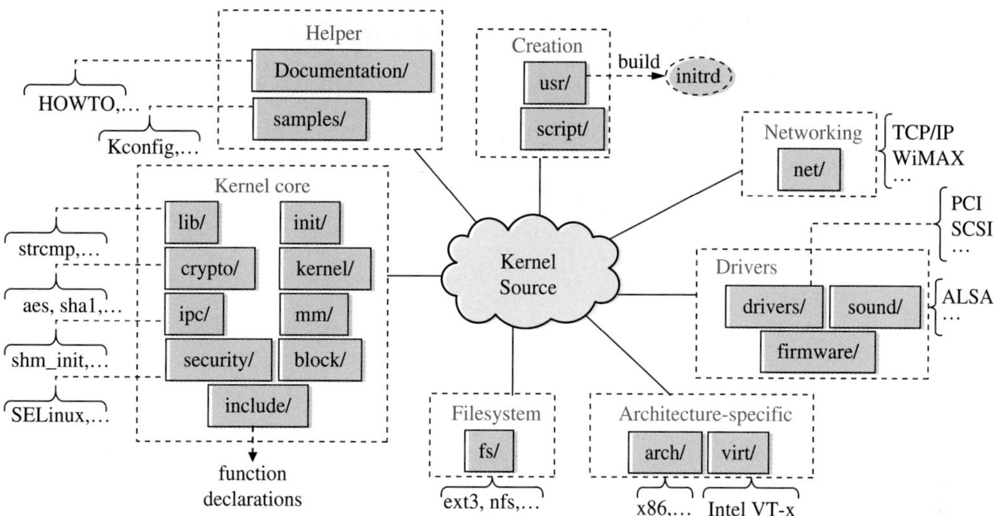

FIGURE B.1 Kernel source tree.

drivers. The licenses of those firmware images are documented in `firmware/WHENCE`.[3]

- Helper

  Plenty of documents are left in the kernel source code under the `Documentation/` directory to help a kernel newbie become a guru. The `HOWTO` file might be the first document you should read. It teaches you how to become a Linux kernel developer. The `kernel-docs.txt` file lists hundreds of online documents illustrating developments from the kernel to drivers. If you are planning to participate in the kernel development, the `CodingStyle`, `SubmittingDrivers`, `SubmittingPatches`, and the files under the `development-process/` subdirectory are worth a read. Under this directory, you can also find a particular driver or subsystem design documents; e.g., file system-related documents are under the `filesystems/` subdirectory. Finally, to know the big picture of the `Documentation/` directory `00-INDEX` would be your first choice.

  With the release of version 2.6.24, came the first-level directory `samples/`. Just as its name implies, sample codes are put under this directory. For example, you can learn how to add your customized options for the "make menuconfig" interface by referring to the `Kconfig` file. Currently, few examples are in this directory, but we believe the number should increase in later releases.

Finally, we summarize in Figure B.1 the twenty first-level directories of the kernel source tree, its corresponding seven categories, and the examples given above.

[3]Firmware is machine code or binary configurations that aim at optimizing the functionality of hardware. It can be saved as image files, i.e., the firmware image files, and either compiled with the drivers or loaded during runtime. Moreover, it is provided by the vendor, and therefore requires license from the vendor.

B.2 SOURCE CODE FOR NETWORKING

Among these directories, three directories, include/, net/, and drivers/, are the most relevant to the protocols we present in this text. The include/ directory contains declaration files (*.h). Declarations that are related to kernel and network are defined under the include/linux directory and the include/net directory, respectively. For example, the IP header, struct iphdr, is declared in include/linux/ip.h, and IP-related flags, constants, and functions are declared in include/net/ip.h.

On the other hand, the net/ directory has most of the codes that are related to networking. Specifically, common core functions are defined in the .c files under net/core, such as dev.c and skbuff.c. Implementation of the socket interface is done in net/socket.c; codes for TCP/IPv4 protocols are under net/ipv4, such as ip_input.c, ip_output.c, tcp_cong.c, tcp_ipv4.c, and tcp_output.c; codes for the IPv6 protocol are under net/ipv6, such as ip6_input.c, ip6_output.c, and ip6_tunnel.c.

Finally, drivers, the interfaces between hardware devices and the operating system, are implemented in the drivers/ directory. There are many subdirectories under this directory. The drivers for Ethernet network interface cards can be found in the drivers/net directory, e.g., 3c501.c, 3c501.h as 3Com 3c501 Ethernet driver. Codes for the PPP protocol discussed in Chapter 3 are also under this directory, such as ppp_generic.c.

Table B.2 summarizes directories, files, and functions of the open source implementations traced in Chapters 3, 4, and 5. When tracing them, you can first find the file for the specific source code and then trace major functions listed in this table to understand the main flow of program execution. Section B.3 introduces tools for efficient source code tracing.

TABLE B.2 Summary of Directories and Files Related to Networking

Layer	Topics	Directory	Files	Functions	Descriptions
Data Link	Receiving frames	net/core/	dev.c	net_rx_action()-> netif_receive_skb()	Upon NET_RX_SOFTIRQ interrupt, kernel calls net_rx_action() which in turn calls netif_receive_skb() to process the frame
Data Link	Sending frames	net/core/	dev.c	net_tx_action()-> dev_queue_xmit()	Upon NET_TX_SOFTIRQ interrupt, kernel calls net_tx_action() which in turn calls dev_queue_xmit() to send the frame
Data Link	Netcard drivers	drivers/ net/	3c501.c, etc.	el_interrupt(), el_open(), el_close(), etc.	network interface drivers, include interrupt handlers
Data Link	PPP outgoing flow	drivers/ net/	ppp_generic.c	ppp_start_xmit(), ppp_send_frame(), start_xmit()	PPP daemon calls ppp_write while kernel calls ppp_start_xmit()

Layer	Topics	Directory	Files	Functions	Descriptions
Data Link	PPP outgoing flow	`drivers/net/`	ppp_generic.c	ppp_start_xmit(), ppp_input(), ppp_receive_frame(), netif_rx()	ppp_sync_receive() takes out the tty->disc_data, frame received through netif_rx() or skb_queue_tail()
Data Link	Bridging	`net/bridge/`	br_fdb.c	__br_fdb_get(), fdb_insert()	Self-Learning Bridging, MAC table lookup
Data Link	Bridging	`net/bridge/`	br_stp_bpdu.c	br_stp_rcv(), br_received_config_bpdu() br_record_config_information(), br_configuration_update()	Spanning Tree protocol
Network	Packet forwarding	`net/ipv4/`	route.c	ip_queue_xmit(), __ip_route_output_key(), ip_route_output_slow() fib_lookup() ip_rcv_finish(), ip_route_input(), ip_route_input_slow()	Forward packets based on routing cache; if cache miss, forward based on routing table
Network	IPv4 checksum	`include/asm _ i386/`	checksum.h	ip_fast_csum()	Speed up checksum computation with codes in machine-dependent assembly language
Network	IPv4 fragmentation	`net/ipv4/`	ip_output.c ip_input.c ip_fragment.c	ip_fragment(), ip_local_deliver(), ip_defrag(), ip_find(), ipqhashfn(), inet_frag_find(), ipq_frag_create()	IP packet fragmentation and reassembly procedure; hash is used to identify fragments of a packet
Network	NAT	`net/ipv4/netfilter/`	nf_conntrack_core.c nf_nat_standalone.c nf_nat_ftp.c nf_nat_proto_icmp.c ip_nat_helper.c	nf_conntrack_in(), resolve_normal_ct(), nf_conntrack_find_get(), nf_nat_in(), nf_nat_out(), nf_nat_local_fn(), nf_nat_fn(), nf_nat_ftp(), nf_nat_mangle_tcp_packet(), mangle_contents(), adjust_tcp_sequence() icmp_manip_pkt()	Perform source NAT after packet filtering and before sending to the output interface; perform destination NAT before packet filtering for packets from network interface card or upper layer protocols. NAT ALG (helper function) for FTP and ICMP
Network	IPv6	`net/ipv6/`	ip6_fib.c	fib6_lookup(), fib6_lookup_1(), ipv6_prefix_equal()	Look up the IPv6 routing table (FIB), which is stored in a binary radix tree
Network	ARP	`net/ipv4/`	arp.c	arp_send(), arp_rcv(), arp_process()	Implementation of the ARP protocol, including send, receive, and process ARP packets
Network	DHCP	`net/ipv4/`	ipconfig.c	ic_bootp_send_if(), ic_dhcp_init_options(), ic_bootp_recv(), ic_do_bootp_ext()	Implementation of the DHCP/BOOTP/RARP protocol; we trace the send and receive procedure of a DHCP message

Layer	Topics	Directory	Files	Functions	Descriptions
Network	ICMP	net/ipv4/	icmp.c	icmp_send(), icmp_unreach(), icmp_redirect(), icmp_echo(), icmp_timestamp, icmp_address(), icmp_address_reply(), icmp_discard(), icmp_rcv()	Implementation of ICMPv4; different types of ICMP messages are processed by corresponding functions
Network	ICMPv6	net/ipv6/	icmp.c ndisc.c	icmpv6_send(), icmpv6_rcv(), icmpv6_echo_reply(), icmpv6_notify(), ndisc_rcv(), ndisc_router_discovery()	Implementation of ICMPv6, including five new types of ICMPv6 messages, i.e., router solicitation, router advertisement, neighbor solicitation, neighbor advertisement, and route redirect messages
Transport	UDP and TCP checksum	net/ipv4/	tcp_ipv4.c	tcp_v4_send_check(), csum_partial(), csum_tcpudp_magic()	Computation of the checksum of a TCP/UDP segment, including pseudo header
Transport	TCP sliding window flow control	net/ipv4/	tcp_output.c	tcp_snd_test(), tcp_packets_in_flight(), tcp_nagle_check()	Check following three conditions before sending out a TCP segment: (1) outstanding segments is less than cwnd; (2) number of sent segments plus the one to be sent is less than rwnd; (3) perform Nagle's test
Transport	TCP slow start and congestion avoidance	net/ipv4/	tcp_cong.c	tcp_slow_start(), tcp_reno_cong_avoid(), tcp_cong_avoid_ai()	TCP slow start and congestion avoidance
Transport	TCP retransmit timer	net/ipv4/	tcp_input.c	tcp_ack_update_rtt(), tcp_rtt_estimator(), tcp_set_rto()	Measure RTT, calculate the smoothed RTT, and update the Retransmission TimeOut (RTO)
Transport	TCP persistence timer and keepalive timer	net/ipv4/	tcp_timer.c	tcp_probe_timer(), tcp_send_probe0(), tcp_keepalive(), tcp_keepopen_proc()	Codes for managing the persistent timer (probe timer) and keepalive timer
Transport	TCP FACK implementation	net/ipv4/	tcp_output.c	tcp_adjust_fackets_out(), tcp_adjust_pcount(), tcp_xmit_retransmit_queue()	Compute packets in flight using FACK information
Transport	Socket Read/ Write Inside out	net/	socket.c	sys_socketcall(), sys_socket(), sock_create(), inet_create(), sock_read(), sock_write()	Explain how the user space's socket interfaces are implemented in the kernel space
Transport	Socket Filter	net/	socket.c	SYSCALL_DEFINE5 (setsockopt,...) sock_setsockopt()	Implementation of the Berkeley Packet Filter (BPF)

B.3 TOOLS FOR SOURCE CODE TRACING

There are several ways to browse the Linux source code in order to search the declaration of a variable/function or usage (reference) of a variable/function. The easiest way is to browse the source code on a Web site. For example, `LXR` (http://lxr.linux.no/), the Linux Cross-Reference, provides Web-based Linux source code indexing, cross referencing, and navigation. The search function of `LXR` allows you to search for where a variable or function is declared and referenced. It also provides full text search.

Another common tool for hackers is `cscope`. `Cscope` is an interactive, screen-oriented tool that allows users to locate specified elements of code in C, *`lex`*, or *`yacc`* source files. It uses a symbol cross-reference to locate functions, function calls, macros, variables, and preprocessor symbols in the source files. As an example, `cscope` can be used in two steps to trace the Linux source code. First, under the directory of the source code, you can get the list of file names under this directory and subdirectories in a file called `cscope.files` by "`find. -name '*.[chly]' -print | sort > cscope.files`". You can then build the symbol cross-reference database, `cscope.out` by default, by "`cscope -b -q -k`". Now you can search a variable or function using the command `cscope -d`. A more detailed description of `cscope` is in Subsection C.3.1.

Finally, there are several source code documentation generator tools that are quite handy to use. For example, Doxygen (http://www.stack.nl/~dimitri/doxygen/), a freeware program released under the GNU General Public License, can cross-reference documentation and code to generate documents in various formats, including HTML, Latex, RTF (MS-Word), PostScript, hyperlinked PDF, compressed HTML, and Unix man pages. It can also extract the code structure from undocumented source files. The code structure can be visualized by many means, including dependency graphs, inheritance diagrams, and collaboration diagrams.

Example: Trace of Reassembly of IPv4 Fragments

Let us use Figure 4.19 in Chapter 4 as the example of using the `LXR` web site to trace the source code. Figure 4.19 shows the call graph of the reassembly procedure for fragmented IP packets. For ease of explanation, we redraw the figure here as Figure B.2.

Now, let us start by locating the `ip_local_deliver()` function. To do that, we use the search toolbar of the `LXR` Web site and type in `ip_local_deliver` to search the function, as shown in Figure B.3.

`LXR` returns a Web page indicating two kinds of information: where the function is implemented and where the function is declared. In our example, illustrated in Figure B.4, codes for `ip_local_deliver()` start from *line 257* in the `net/ipv4/ip_input.c` file, and the declaration for

Continued

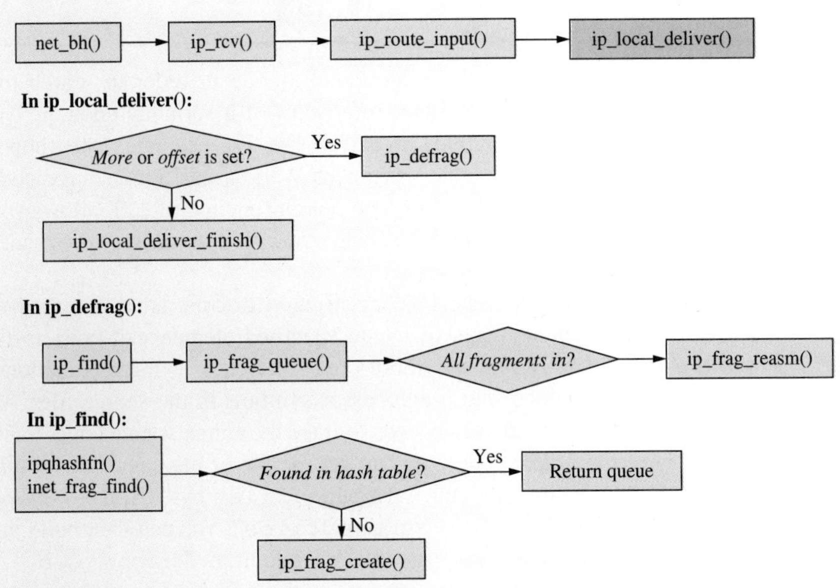

FIGURE B.2 Call graph of reassembly procedure.

`ip_local_deliver()` is at *line 98* of `include/net/ip.h`. To trace the source code of `ip_local_deliver()`, we can click on the hyperlink of `net/ipv4/ip_input.c`.

In addition to locating the code and declaration of the function, we can also check the usage of this function, i.e., where the function is referenced (called), by clicking on the `[usage...]` link. For example, when clicking on the usage link of the declaration, LXR returns reference information as listed in Figure B.5. From this page, we can see that `ip_local_deliver()` is referenced six times by functions defined in two files: `net/ipv4/ipmr.c` and `net/ipv4/route.c`.

If we click on `net/ipv4/ip_input.c`, LXR will return the codes for `ip_local_deliver()` implemented in `net/ipv4/ip_input.c`, as shown in Figure B.6. By referring to the call graph of Figure 4.19, it can be clearly understood that if the offset has value and the `more` bit or `offset` is set, `ip_defrag()` will be called. So let us continue tracing the code for `ip_defrag()` by clicking the hyperlink (`ip_defrag`).

LXR will show the search results for `ip_defrag`, as we can see in Figure B.7. This page tells us it is implemented in `/net/ipv4/ip_fragment.c`. Let us continue tracing by clicking on the link.

FIGURE B.3 LXR search bar.

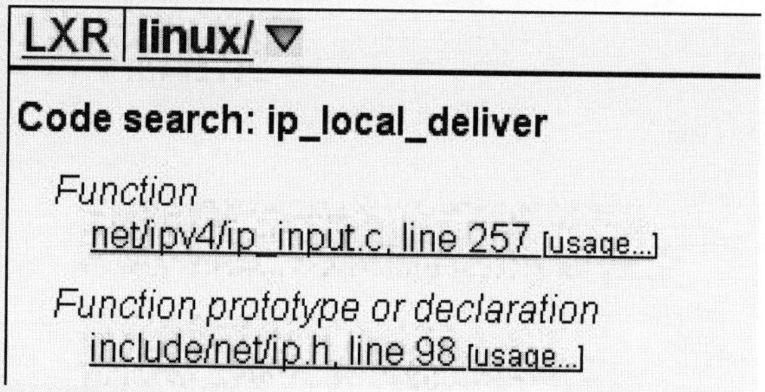

LXR | linux/ ▽

Code search: ip_local_deliver

Function
net/ipv4/ip_input.c, line 257 [usage...]

Function prototype or declaration
include/net/ip.h, line 98 [usage...]

FIGURE B.4 Search results from `LXR`.

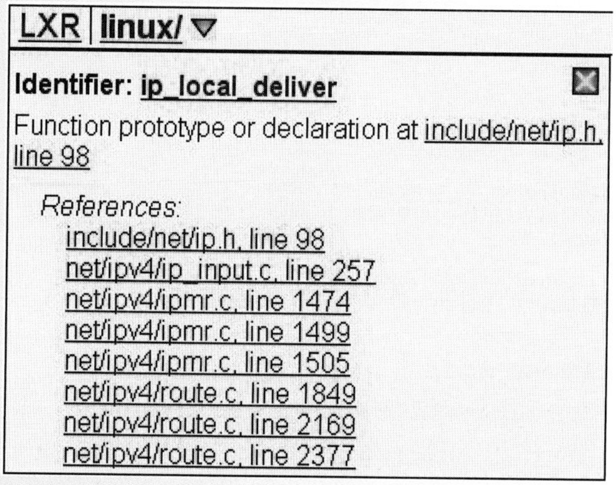

LXR | linux/ ▽

Identifier: ip_local_deliver

Function prototype or declaration at include/net/ip.h, line 98

References:
include/net/ip.h, line 98
net/ipv4/ip_input.c, line 257
net/ipv4/ipmr.c, line 1474
net/ipv4/ipmr.c, line 1499
net/ipv4/ipmr.c, line 1505
net/ipv4/route.c, line 1849
net/ipv4/route.c, line 2169
net/ipv4/route.c, line 2377

FIGURE B.5 Usage of `ip_local_deliver()`.

```
int ip_local_deliver(struct sk_buff *skb)
{
        /*
         *      Reassemble IP fragments.
         */

        if (ip_hdr(skb)->frag_off & htons(IP_MF | IP_OFFSET)) {
                if (ip_defrag(skb, IP_DEFRAG_LOCAL_DELIVER))
                        return 0;
        }

        return NF_HOOK(PF_INET, NF_INET_LOCAL_IN, skb, skb->dev, NULL,
                       ip_local_deliver_finish);
}
```

FIGURE B.6 Source of `ip_local_deliver()`.

Continued

LXR | linux/ ▽

Code search: ip_defrag

Function
net/ipv4/ip_fragment.c, line 571 [usage...]

Function prototype or declaration
include/net/ip.h, line 347 [usage...]

FIGURE B.7 Search results of `ip _ defrag()`.

```
/* Process an incoming IP datagram fragment. */
int ip_defrag(struct sk_buff *skb, u32 user)
{
        struct ipq *qp;
        struct net *net;

        net = skb->dev ? dev_net(skb->dev) : dev_net(skb->dst->dev);
        IP_INC_STATS_BH(net, IPSTATS_MIB_REASMREQDS);

        /* Start by cleaning up the memory. */
        if (atomic_read(&net->ipv4.frags.mem) > net->ipv4.frags.high_thresh)
                ip_evictor(net);

        /* Lookup (or create) queue header */
        if ((qp = ip_find(net, ip_hdr(skb), user)) != NULL) {
                int ret;

                spin_lock(&qp->q.lock);

                ret = ip_frag_queue(qp, skb);

                spin_unlock(&qp->q.lock);
                ipq_put(qp);
                return ret;
        }

        IP_INC_STATS_BH(net, IPSTATS_MIB_REASMFAILS);
        kfree_skb(skb);
        return -ENOMEM;
}
```

FIGURE B.8 Source of `ip _ defrag()`.

Code search: ip_find

Function
net/ipv4/ip_fragment.c, line 222 [usage...]

FIGURE B.9 Search result of `ip _ find()`.

Figure B.8 shows the codes for `ip_defrag()`. Referring to the call graph again, after some housekeeping work, `ip_defrag()` first calls `ip_find()` to look up or create the queue header for fragments of this packet. It then calls `ip_frag_queue()` to process the fragment. If all fragments are received, `ip_frag_queue()` will call `ip_frag_reasm()` to reassemble the packet.

By clicking the hyperlink of `ip_find`, we will be able to locate the function and get access to its source codes, as shown in Figure B.9 and Figure B.10, respectively. Again, referring to the call graph, `ip_find` first calls `ipqhashfn()` to get a hash value and uses it to find the queue header by calling `inet_frag_find()`.

In `inet_frag_find()`, if no queue header is found, it will create one by calling inet_frag_create(). The source code for inet_frag_find() is shown in Figure B.11.

```
static inline struct ipq *ip_find(struct net *net, struct iphdr *iph, u32 user)
{
        struct inet_frag_queue *q;
        struct ip4_create_arg arg;
        unsigned int hash;

        arg.iph = iph;
        arg.user = user;

        read_lock(&ip4_frags.lock);
        hash = ipqhashfn(iph->id, iph->saddr, iph->daddr, iph->protocol);

        q = inet_frag_find(&net->ipv4.frags, &ip4_frags, &arg, hash);
        if (q == NULL)
                goto out_nomem;

        return container_of(q, struct ipq, q);

out_nomem:
        LIMIT_NETDEBUG(KERN_ERR "ip_frag_create: no memory left !\n");
        return NULL;
}
```

FIGURE B.10 Source of `ip_find()`.

```
struct inet_frag_queue *inet_frag_find(struct netns_frags *nf,
                struct inet_frags *f, void *key, unsigned int hash)
        __releases(&f->lock)
{
        struct inet_frag_queue *q;
        struct hlist_node *n;

        hlist_for_each_entry(q, n, &f->hash[hash], list) {
                if (q->net == nf && f->match(q, key)) {
                        atomic_inc(&q->refcnt);
                        read_unlock(&f->lock);
                        return q;
                }
        }
        read_unlock(&f->lock);

        return inet_frag_create(nf, f, key);
}
```

FIGURE B.11 Source of `ip_frag_find()`.

FURTHER READINGS

Related Books

The following two books published by O'Reilly are the guide books and also the reference books of many kernel developers. The first one covers the fundamentals of the Linux kernel, such as memory management, process management, scheduling routines, and file systems. The second book details the development of Linux device drivers.

- M. Cesati and D. P. Bovet, *Understanding the Linux Kernel*, 3rd edition, O'Reilly Media, 2005.
- J. Corbet, A. Rubini, and G. Kroah-Hartman, *Linux Device Drivers*, 3rd edition, O'Reilly Media, 2005.

Online Links

Here we list three Web sites highly related to this appendix. These classic sites are likely to exist and prosper for years to come.

1. Linux kernel archives, http://kernel.org/
2. Linux foundation, http://www.linuxfoundation.org/
3. Linux cross reference (LXR), http://lxr.linux.no/

Appendix C

Development Tools

In Section B.3, we introduce several tools for source code tracing and walk through an example with `LXR` (Linux Cross Reference). Tracing, however, is just a step toward *understanding* a program. Other steps are required to complete the development process. This appendix presents a comprehensive set of development tools for Linux developers. A Linux developer might write a program on a Linux *host* but run it on a non-Linux *target* machine, or vice versa. It is also possible that both host and target are Linux-based. Here we focus on the Linux host, i.e., development environment, regardless of the platform of the target machine. We introduce essential and popular tools used in various stages of the development process, from programming, debugging, and maintaining to profiling and embedding.

Section C.1 guides readers to begin the development journey with programming tools. A good first step would be writing the first piece of code using a powerful text editor, such as *Visual Improved* (`vim`) or *GNOME editor* (`gedit`). Then compile it to binary executables with *GNU C compiler* (`gcc`), and furthermore automate some repetitive compiling steps with the `make` utility.

The old 80/20 rule still applies to programming where 80% of your codes come from 20% of your efforts, leaving 80% of your efforts to debug 20% of your program. Therefore you would need some debugging tools discussed in Section C.2, including the source-level debugger, *GNU Debugger* (`gdb`), one with a graphical user interface, such as *Data Display Debugger* (`ddd`), and the remote kernel debugger, *Kernel GNU Debugger* (`kgdb`). As the dependency between software components is more sophisticated and the sources of contribution become more scattered, Section C.3 illustrates how a developer manages dozens of source files with `cscope`, and co-developers should agree on a version control system, such as *Global Information Tracker (Git),* to avoid development chaos and to ease collaboration.

To find the bottleneck of a program, Section C.4 describes how developers could utilize the profiling tools, *GNU Profiler* (`gprof`) and *Kernel Profiler* (`kernprof`). Section C.5 introduces how to accelerate the porting effort on embedded systems using the space-optimized utilities, `busybox`, the lightweight toolchain, `uClibc`, and the embedded image builder of the root file system, `buildroot`.

For each tool, we introduce its purposes and functions, followed by its how-to with examples. At the end, some tips are provided to help familiarize you with the tool. This appendix is not meant to be a complete user guide, but should serve as a start.

C.1 PROGRAMMING

This section covers the essential tools for programming, from `vim` and `gedit` for program editing to `gcc` and `make` for program compilation. The essence of programming languages is not discussed here.

C.1.1 Text Editor – `vim` and `gedit`

Irrespective of your choice of programming language, you would need an editor, which is a program used to create and modify text files. It plays an essential role in a programmer's working hours, since a clumsy text editor will waste time while an efficient one will offload chores and leave more time for thinking.

What Are `vim` and `gedit`?

Among the many text editors available, such as `pico`, `joe`, and `emacs`, *Visual Improved* (`vim`), an improved version of `vi`, is currently one of the most popular text editors. Its balance between ease of use and power makes it more user-friendly than `emacs` yet more feature-rich than `pico`. `Vim` has an extensible syntax dictionary which highlights the syntax with different colors for documents it recognizes, including c codes and html files. Advanced users use `vim` to compile their codes, to write macros, to browse a file, and even to write a game, such as TicTacToe.

As a command-line editor, `vim` is widely used by administrators. However, as a desktop utility, it can become a bit complicated for end users. The built-in GUI editor, *GNOME editor* (`gedit`), is commonly used in the desktop environment in Linux. `Gedit` allows users to edit multiple files with a tab bar, highlighting the syntax as `vim` does, spellchecking the text, and printing a file.

How to `vim` and `gedit`

Before getting started with `vim`, one should be aware that `vim` operates in two phases (or modes) instead of one phase like `pico` or other ordinary text editors. Try this: Start vim (type `vim` to edit a new file or `vim filename` to open an existing file) and edit for a minute. If you do not type any special character, you find nothing on the screen. When you try to move around by pressing the arrow keys you find the cursor does not move. Things get even worse as you cannot find your way out. These initial barriers frustrate quite a few newbies. However, the world will begin to shine as you get to know when to insert text and when to issue a command.

In the *Normal mode* (command mode), characters are treated as commands, meaning they trigger special actions, e.g., pressing `h`, `j`, `k`, and `l` would move the cursor to the left, up, down, and right, respectively. However, characters are simply inserted as text in the *Insert mode*. Most commands can be concatenated in a more sophisticated operation,

```
[#1] commands [#2] target,
```

where anything enclosed within brackets is optional; `#1` is an optional number, e.g., 3, specifying `commands` are to be done 3 times; `commands` are any valid vim operations, e.g., `y` for yank (copy) the text; `#2` is another optional number, similar to `#1`, specifying the number (or range) of targets being affected by the `commands`;

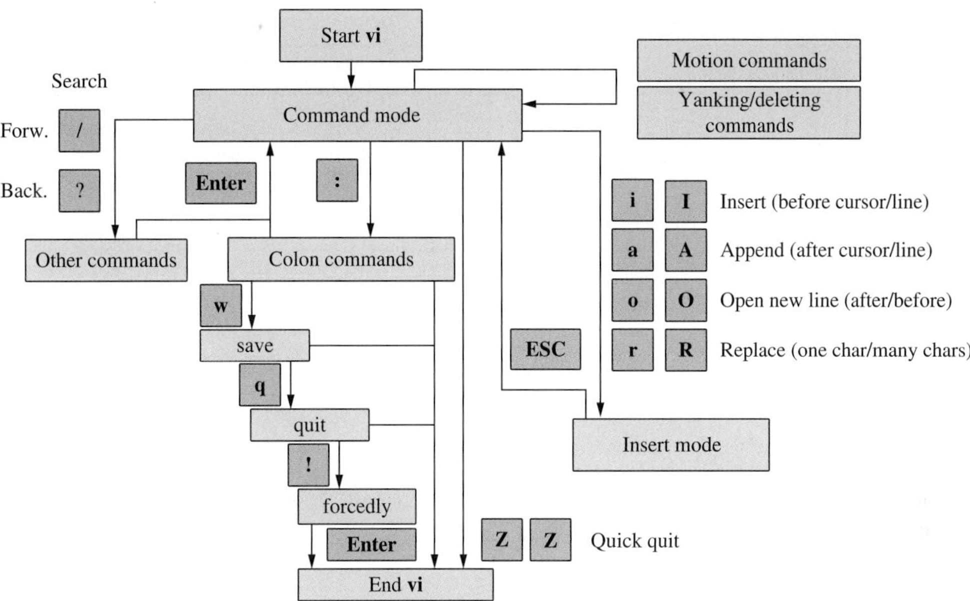

FIGURE C.1 Operating modes of the `vim` text editor.

and `target` is the text to which you want to apply the `commands`, e.g., `G` for end of file. Although most of the commands are played on the main screen, some colon commands (commands that start with a colon) are keyed at the very bottom of the screen. When dealing with these colon commands, you need to type a colon, which moves the cursor to the last line of the screen, then issue your command string and terminate it by pressing the `<Enter>` key. For example, `:wq` would save your current file and quit. The overall operating modes of the vim text editor are illustrated in Figure C.1. Important editing comands are listed in Table C.1.

The use of `gedit` is much simpler than `vim`. A file being edited is shown in the edit area, where you can use your mouse to position and highlight text. The tab bar lists all files being edited. An asterisk is marked if a file is modified but not saved. The tool bar provides the easy way to create, open, save, and print a file. A screenshot of `gedit` is in Figure C.2.

Tip

- `Vim` operates in two modes: Insert mode and Command mode. If you become confused about the Insert mode commands, you can always press the `ESC` key to get back to the Command mode.

C.1.2 Compiler – `gcc`

With a text editor at hand, one could begin to write a program. Then you would need a compiler to convert source code written in a high-level language to binary object code. Since it is common to incorporate existing routines already compiled, a second-stage process using a utility called *linker* is often used to link the compiled

TABLE C.1 Important Commands for Cursor Movement and Text Editing

Command Mode		Effects
Motion	`h, j, k, l`	left, down, up, right
	`w, W`	forward next word, blank delimited word
	`e, E`	forward end of word, of blank delimited word
	`b, B`	backward beginning of word, of blank delimited word
	`(,)`	sentence back, forward
	`{, }`	paragraph back, forward
	`0, $`	beginning, end of line
	`1G, G`	beginning, end of file
	`nG or :n`	line n
	`fc, Fc`	forward, back to char c
	`H, M, L`	top, middle, bottom of screen
Yanking	`yy`	Copy current line
	`:y`	Copy current line
	`Y`	Copy until end of line
Deleting	`dd`	Delete current line
	`:d`	Delete current line
	`D`	Delete until end of line

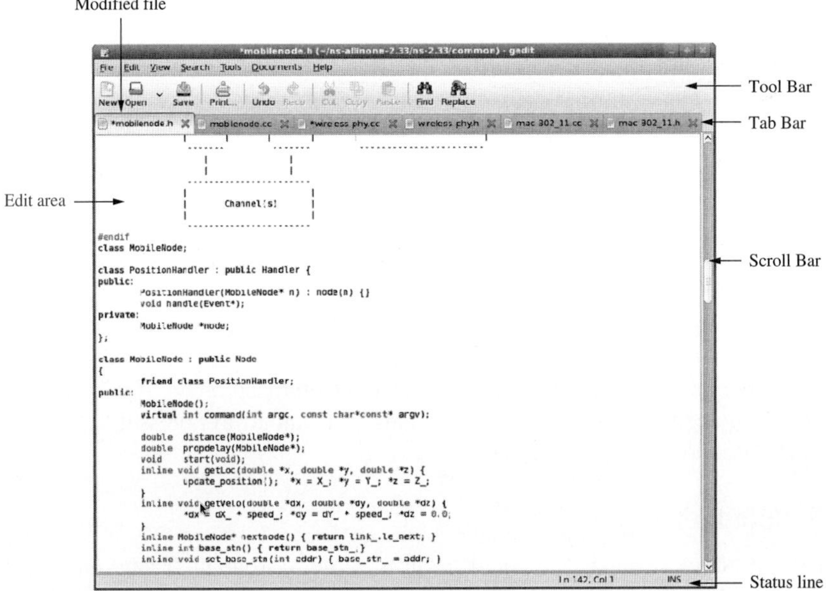

FIGURE C.2 Screenshot: the main window of `gedit`.

code with existing routines to create the final executable application. This multiple-stage process of the gcc compiler is shown in Figure C.3.

What Is gcc?

The *GNU C compiler* (gcc), which by default expects ANSI C,[1] is a well-known C compiler on most Unix systems. It was primarily written by Richard Stallman, who founded a charity, Free Software Foundation (FSF), to raise funds for works on the GNU Project. With the efforts of other gcc advocates, gcc has integrated several compilers (C/C++, Fortran, Java) and is now called the *GCC Compiler Collection.*

How to gcc

Suppose you are writing a program and have decided to split it into two source files. The main file is called main.c and the other one is sub.c. To compile the program, you may simply type

```
gcc main.c sub.c
```

which creates an executable program named a.out by default. If you prefer, you may specify the name of the executable, e.g., prog, by

```
gcc -o prog main.c sub.c
```

As you can see, it is very simple. However, this method could be very inefficient, especially if you are making changes to only one source file at a time, when you recompile it frequently. Instead, you should compile the program as follows:

```
gcc -c main.c
gcc -c sub.c
gcc -o prog main.o sub.o
```

The first two lines create object files, main.o and sub.o, and the third line links the objects together into an executable. If you are then to make a change to sub.c only, you can recompile your program by just typing the last two lines.

This all might seem a little silly for the example above, but if you have ten source files instead of two, the latter method would save you a lot of time. Actually, the entire compilation process could be automated as you can see in the next subsection.

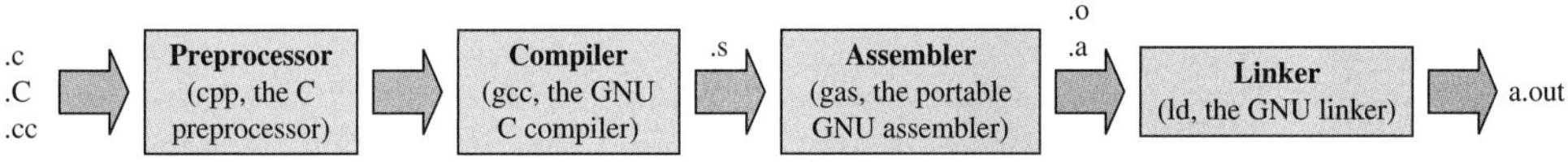

FIGURE C.3 The work flow[2] of gcc.

[1]ANSI C is more strongly-typed than the original C, and is likely to help you catch some bugs earlier during coding.

[2]The output of the preprocessor usually directly feeds into the compiler.

Tips

There are two common errors when using `gcc`. One error indicates the syntax errors in the source, and the other is the unresolved symbols when linking object files. `Gcc` shows a syntax error as follows:

- `sourcefile: In function 'function_name': error messages`
- `sourcefile:#num: error: error messages`

It says that there might be some errors near the line `#num` in the file `sourcefile`. Notably, the error is not always close to line `#num`. For example, when the error is caused by missing brackets or unwanted brackets, the reported `#num` would be far away from the actual error spot.

The format of an unresolved linking symbol is as follows:

- `objectfile: In function 'function_caller':`
- `sourcefile: undefined reference to 'function_callee'`

It tells the developers that the function `function_callee` cannot be resolved when linking. That unresolved function is used by the function `function_caller` in the file `sourcefile`. To solve the problem, you can check whether a necessary object file or library that contains `function_callee` is unlinked.

C.1.3 Auto-Compile – `make`

While a successful, error-free compilation is certainly a great joy, a repetitive compilation process during the development of programs would be a chore for programmers. An executable program may be built from tens or hundreds of `.c` files, requiring all the `.c` files to be compiled with `gcc` to `.o` files, and then linked together, possibly with additional library routines. This process is tedious and likely to introduce mistakes. It is why `make` matters.

What Is `make`

`Make` is a program that provides a relatively high-level way to specify necessary source files to build a derived object and steps to automate the building process. `Make` reduces the likelihood of error and simplifies a programmer's life. Notably, `make` provides implicit rules or shortcuts for many common actions such as turning `.c` files into `.o` files.

How to `make`

`Make` processes a file, called a `Makefile`. The basic syntax in a `Makefile` is

```
target: dependencies
<command list>
```

which tells `make` to produce the `target` from `dependencies` by executing a list of commands. The dependencies need to be resolved before generating the current target, which brings the chance of building some big applications by dividing and conquering.

Example

In the example in Figure C.4, the content of a `Makefile` is listed first by the command `cat`. This `Makefile` says that `prog` depends on two files `main.o` and `sub.o`, and that they in turn depend on their corresponding source files (`main.c`

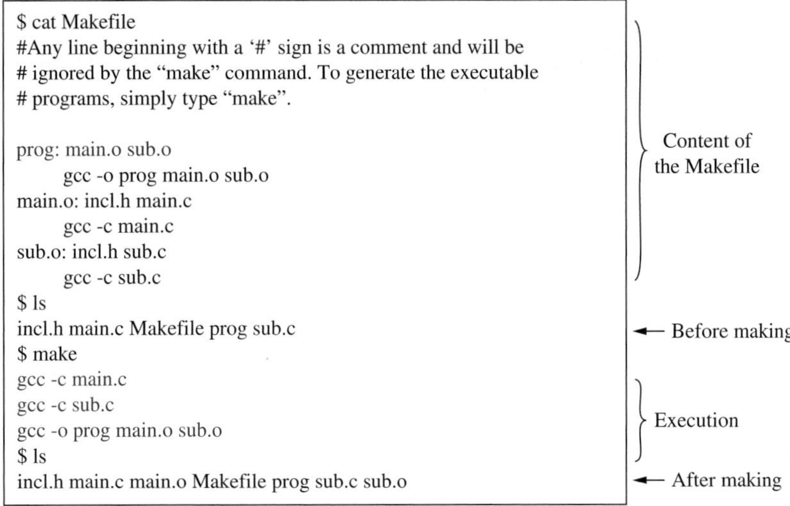

```
$ cat Makefile
#Any line beginning with a '#' sign is a comment and will be
# ignored by the "make" command. To generate the executable
# programs, simply type "make".

prog: main.o sub.o
	gcc -o prog main.o sub.o
main.o: incl.h main.c
	gcc -c main.c
sub.o: incl.h sub.c
	gcc -c sub.c
$ ls
incl.h main.c Makefile prog sub.c
$ make
gcc -c main.c
gcc -c sub.c
gcc -o prog main.o sub.o
$ ls
incl.h main.c main.o Makefile prog sub.c sub.o
```


FIGURE C.4 An example of `make`.

and `sub.c`), in addition to the common header file, `incl.h`. By executing the command, `gcc`, the dependencies, `main.o` and `sub.o`, are compiled and linked into the target, `prog`, automatically.

Tip

- In writing the `Makefile`, a `TAB` character has to be placed at the beginning of each command statement.[3]

C.2 DEBUGGING

When writing a program, unless it is way too trivial, one must have struggled hard enough to locate and remove bugs from a program. This digging-for-bugs process is known as debugging, and the tool being used is a debugger. Generally speaking, the purpose of a debugger is to let you investigate what is going on inside a program while it is running or what a program was doing at the moment it crashed. Here we introduce three debuggers: a general one, `gdb`, a graphical version, `ddd`, and a remote kernel debugger, `kgdb`.

C.2.1 Debugger - `gdb`

The traditional debugger used in Linux/FreeBSD is `gdb`, the *GNU Project debugger*. It is designed to work with a variety of languages, but is primarily targeted at C and C++ developers. While `gdb` is a command line interface, it has a few graphical

[3] It is a historical artifact, but no one wants to change it.

interfaces to it, such as ddd. In addition, gdb can also be run over serial links for remote debugging, such as kgdb.

What Is gdb?

gdb can do mainly four kinds of things, plus other things in support of these, to help you catch bugs in the act:

1. Start your program, specifying anything that might affect its behavior.
2. Make your program stop on specified conditions.
3. Examine what has happened, when your program has stopped.
4. Change things in your program, so you can experiment with the effects of correcting one bug.

How to gdb

You can read the official gdb manual to learn all about gdb. However, a handful of commands are enough to get started using the debugger. Before loading the executable into gdb, the target program, say prog, should be compiled with the -g flag, e.g., gcc -g -o prog prog.c.

Then, start gdb with the command gdb prog. You should see a gdb prompt following it. Then, browse the source code by issuing the command list, which by default shows the first 10 lines of the source code for the current function, and subsequent calls to list display the next 10 lines, and so on.

When trying to locate a bug, you could run the program once upon entering gdb and ensure the bug is reproduced. Then you can backtrace to see a stack trace, which usually reveals the troublemaker. Now you can use list again to identify the location of the problem, use next to step the execution, and carefully make use of setting a breakpoint with the command break and printing the variables with the command print. You should be able to locate the bug and finally quit gdb. By the way, gdb has a set of information pages and also has built-in help accessible via the help command.

Example

The example in Figure C.5 demonstrates a common programming fault caused by memory allocation. When the program is first run in gdb, it causes a segment fault. We examine the current stack frames and find out that it might be a fault in the function Hello. A breakpoint is hence set there, and the program is run again. When reaching the breakpoint, gdb suspends. We browse the source code, and step the execution. After we examine the variable, str, we find the bug: The pointer does not have a valid memory address.

C.2.2 GUI Debugger - ddd

What Is ddd?

Since gdb and many others are all command-line debuggers, which are not very friendly to use, the *Data Display Debugger* (DDD) provides a convenient front-end to all of these debuggers. Besides existing `gdb` capabilities, `DDD` has become popular because of its interactive graphical data display, where data structures are displayed as graphs.

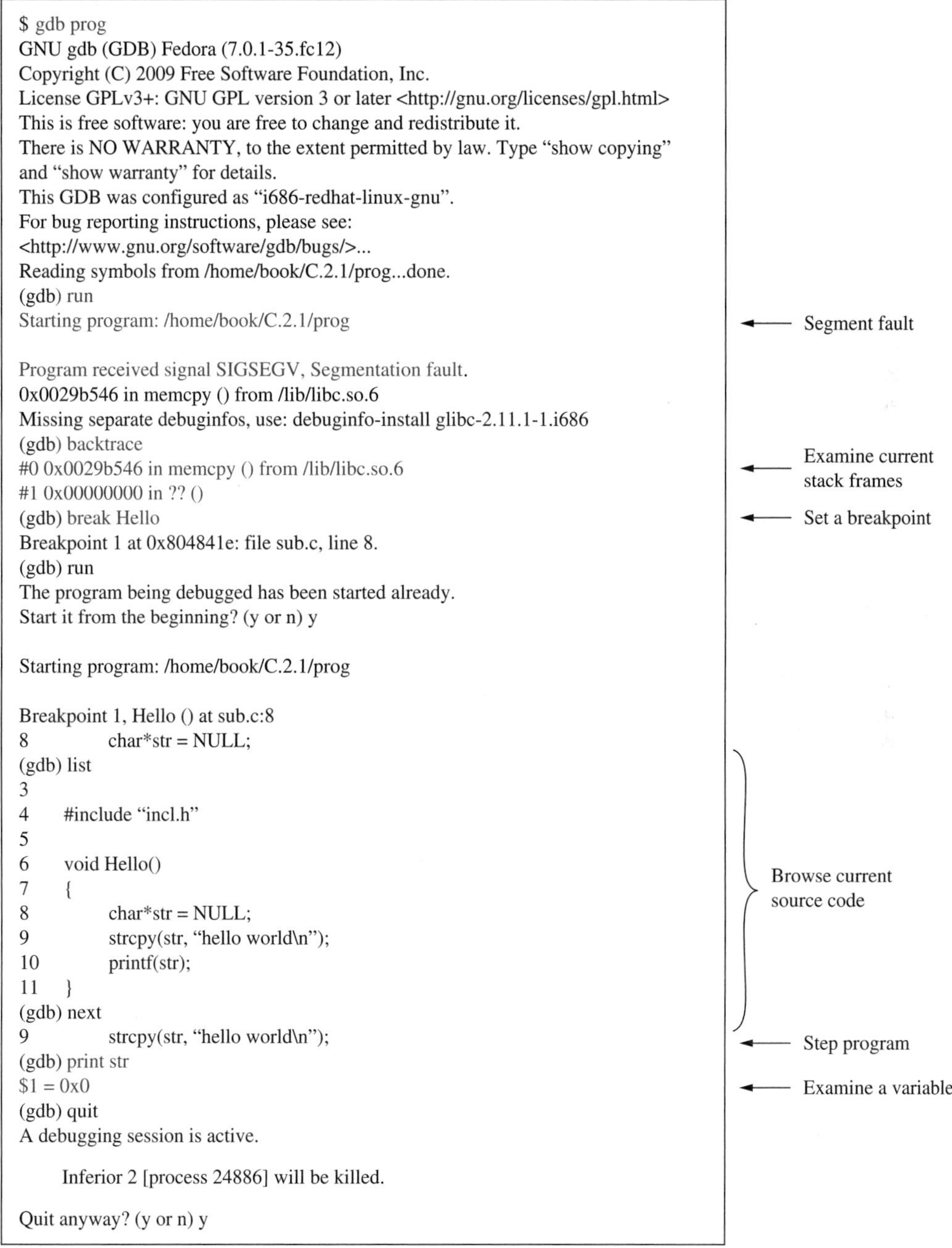

```
$ gdb prog
GNU gdb (GDB) Fedora (7.0.1-35.fc12)
Copyright (C) 2009 Free Software Foundation, Inc.
License GPLv3+: GNU GPL version 3 or later <http://gnu.org/licenses/gpl.html>
This is free software: you are free to change and redistribute it.
There is NO WARRANTY, to the extent permitted by law. Type "show copying"
and "show warranty" for details.
This GDB was configured as "i686-redhat-linux-gnu".
For bug reporting instructions, please see:
<http://www.gnu.org/software/gdb/bugs/>...
Reading symbols from /home/book/C.2.1/prog...done.
(gdb) run
Starting program: /home/book/C.2.1/prog

Program received signal SIGSEGV, Segmentation fault.
0x0029b546 in memcpy () from /lib/libc.so.6
Missing separate debuginfos, use: debuginfo-install glibc-2.11.1-1.i686
(gdb) backtrace
#0 0x0029b546 in memcpy () from /lib/libc.so.6
#1 0x00000000 in ?? ()
(gdb) break Hello
Breakpoint 1 at 0x804841e: file sub.c, line 8.
(gdb) run
The program being debugged has been started already.
Start it from the beginning? (y or n) y

Starting program: /home/book/C.2.1/prog

Breakpoint 1, Hello () at sub.c:8
8           char*str = NULL;
(gdb) list
3
4     #include "incl.h"
5
6     void Hello()
7     {
8           char*str = NULL;
9           strcpy(str, "hello world\n");
10          printf(str);
11    }
(gdb) next
9           strcpy(str, "hello world\n");
(gdb) print str
$1 = 0x0
(gdb) quit
A debugging session is active.

      Inferior 2 [process 24886] will be killed.

Quit anyway? (y or n) y
```


FIGURE C.5 An example of debugging with `gdb`.

How to ddd

To use DDD you also have to compile your code with debug information included. In Unix that means you should include the -g option in the gcc compile command. If you have never run DDD before, you may have to tell DDD to use the gdb debugger by typing "ddd --gdb" at the command-line prompt. You only have to do this once. Subsequently, to run DDD you type "ddd prog" where prog is the name of your program, and a window like the one in Figure C.6 pops up.

The center of all things in Figure C.6 is the source code. The current execution position is indicated by a green arrow; breakpoints are shown as stop signs. You can navigate around the code using the Lookup button on the tool bar or the Open Source button from the File menu. Double-clicking on a function name leads you to its definition. Using the Undo and Redo buttons of the Command Tools, you can navigate to previous and later positions—similar to your Web browser.

You can set and edit breakpoints by right-clicking the mouse in the white space left to a statement in the source window; to step through your program or to continue execution, use the floating Command Tools on the right. Command-line aficionados still can find a debugger console at the bottom. If you need anything else, try the Help menu for detailed instructions.

Moving the mouse pointer on an active variable shows its value in a little pop-up screen. Snapshots of more complex values can be "printed" in the debug console. To view a variable permanently, use the Display button. This creates a permanent data

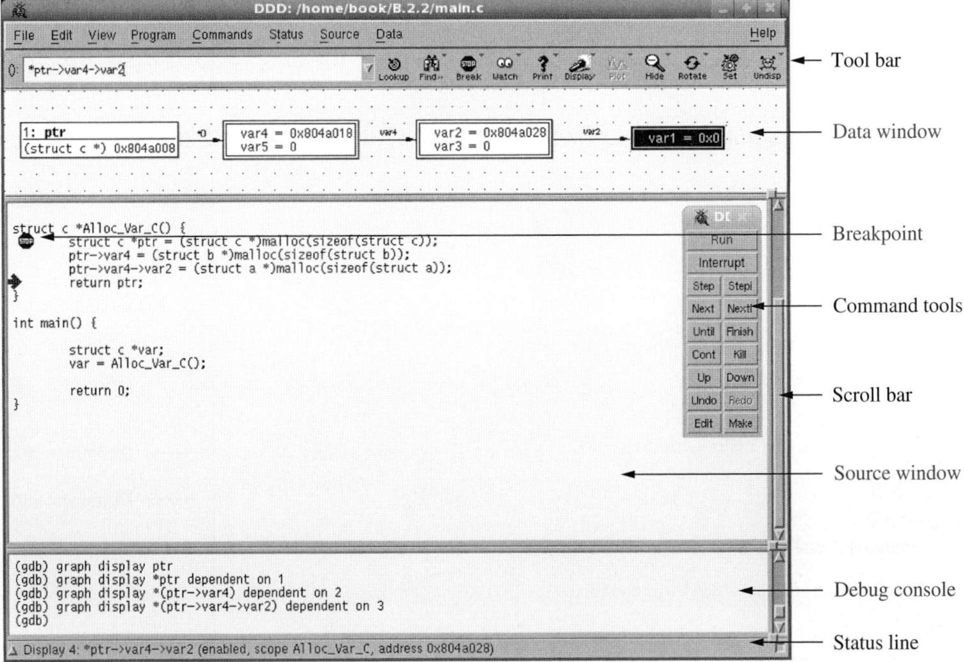

FIGURE C.6 Screenshot: the main window of ddd.

window which shows the variable name and its value. These displays are updated every time the program changes its state.

To access a variable value, you must bring the program to a state where the variable is actually alive; that is, within the scope of the current execution position. Typically, you set a breakpoint within the function of interest, run the program, and display the function's variables.

To actually visualize data structures (that is, data as well as relationships), `DDD` lets you create new displays out of existing displays by simply double-clicking on the pointer variable. For instance, if you have displayed a pointer variable list, you can dereference it and view the value it points to. Each new display is automatically laid out in a fashion to support simple visualization of lists and trees. For instance, if an element already has a predecessor, its successor will be laid out in line with these two. You can always move elements around manually by simply dragging and dropping the displays. Also, DDD lets you scroll around, lay out the structure, change values manually, or see them change while the program runs. An Undo/Redo capability even lets you redisplay previous and later states of the program, so that you can see how your data structure evolves.

C.2.3 Kernel Debugger – `kgdb`

What Is `kgdb`?

`kGDB` is a source-level debugger for the Linux kernel, which provides a mechanism to debug the Linux kernel using the debugger, `gdb`, introduced earlier. `kGDB` is a patch to the kernel, and you need to recompile the kernel once it is patched. It allows a user running `gdb` on a development host to connect to a target (over a serial RS-232 line) running the `kGDB`-patched kernel. Kernel developers can then "break" into the kernel of the target, set breakpoints, examine data, and other relevant debugging functions one would expect. In fact, it is pretty much similar to what one would do with `gdb` on a user-space program.

Since `kGDB` is a kernel patch, it adds the following components to a kernel on the target machine:

1. `gdb` stub—The `gdb` stub is the heart of the debugger. It handles requests coming from `gdb` on the development (or host) machine and controls the execution flows of all processors on the target machine.
2. Modifications to fault handlers—Kernel gives control to debugger when an unexpected fault occurs. A kernel that does not contain `gdb` panics on unexpected faults. Modifications to fault handlers allow kernel developers to analyze unexpected faults.
3. Serial communication—This component uses a serial driver in the kernel and offers an interface to the `gdb` stub in the kernel. It is responsible for sending and receiving data on a serial line. This component is also responsible for handling control break requests sent from `gdb`.

How to `kgdb`

Since Linux kernel 2.6.26, `kGDB` has been integrated with the mainstream of the kernel source tree. What you have to do is enable the `kGDB` option in the kernel configuration, then compile and install the `kgdb`-patched kernel. To force the kernel to pause the boot process and wait for a connection from `gdb`, the parameter "`gdb`" should be passed to the kernel. This can be done by typing "`gdb`" after the name of the kernel on the `LILO` command line. The default serial device and baud rate are set to `ttyS1` at a baud rate of 38400. These parameters can be changed by using "`gdbttyS=`" and "`gdbbaud=`" on the command line.

After the kernel has booted up to the point where it is waiting for a connection from the `gdb` client, there are three things to be done on the development machine: Set the baud rate acceptable to the target machine, set the serial port used by it, and resume the execution of booting on the target. These can be done by the following three commands in `gdb`:

- `set remotebaud <your baud rate>`
- `target remote <the local serial port name>`
- `continue`

To trigger the debug mode on the target, you can either press `Ctrl-C` on the target machine or issue the `gdb` command, `interrupt`, from the development machine. Then you can use all `gdb` commands to trace or debug the target Linux.

Tip

- A successful setting in the target machine will prompt a message like "waiting for remote debug…" during the kernel booting. `kgdb` will wait for commands from the development machine to instruct its next step. Usually it will be the `gdb` command, `continue`. Without any input command, the target will freeze.

C.3 MAINTAINING

When a software project is small, it is easy to remember most locations of data structure definitions and function implementations. However, when it grows, it becomes hard to memorize everything. You need a tool to help you in managing hundreds of variable and function declarations. By the same token, a good project comes from the teamwork of brilliant developers. Codevelopers have to use a version control system to synchronize the modifications from each other. This section introduces `cscope,` which handles the code-browsing task for a single developer, and `Git,` which controls the source code for codevelopers.

C.3.1. Source Code Browser – `cscope`

What Is `cscope`?

`Cscope` is a source code browsing tool originally developed at Bell Labs. In 2000, it was open-sourced. `Cscope` enables you to search a variable, macro, or function declaration, called functions, and a callee of functions, as well as replace text and even call an external text editor to modify source code. It is so powerful that AT&T used it to manage projects involving 5 million lines of C/C++ codes.

How to cscope

The first step in using cscope is to build the cross-reference table from the source (.c) and header (.h) files. Cscope by default assumes the list of those files is written in a file named cscope.files. Therefore, you can issue the following Unix command to prepare the cscope.files:

- find . -name '*.[chly]' -print | sort > cscope.files

Now you can tell cscope to construct the cross-reference table with the following command:

- cscope -b -q [-k]

where the flag -b builds the cross-reference table, the flag -q enables the construction of invert index tables, and the flag -k is an optional flag used only when your project is part of the kernel source. After executing the command, three files are created:

cscope.out: the cross-reference table
cscope.in.out and cscope.po.out: the invert index tables.

It is time to launch cscope. Try the following command, which will execute cscope with a text-mode user interface:

- cscope -d

where the flag, -d, indicates using the existing cross-reference tables without updating them. In addition, cscope can be combined with emacs or vim, for example, integrated with vim by adding "cs add cscope.out" into .vimrc.

Example

Figure C.7 shows a screenshot of cscope. There are two areas displayed on the cscope interface. One is the command area where the cscope functions are listed. The other is the result area where the query results are shown. You can switch between the two areas by pressing the TAB key. In addition, you can switch commands on the command area or select a result on the result area by using the UP and DOWN keys on that area. Try to specify a function name in the command area, "Find this C symbol," and the result is shown in the result area. You can now switch to the result area, pick an entry, and press the Enter key calling the external text editor to modify it. Finally, pressing the ? key brings you the help manual, and pressing Ctrl-D quits cscope.

Tips

- The cscope command, "Find this egrep pattern," could help you find out what you want to search, when you forget the full name of a symbol.
- Use the cscope command, "Change this text string," when you need to change the name of a symbol widely separated in many files at one time.

```
C symbol:  Alloc_Var_C

  File       Function       Line
0 incl.h     <global>        18    extern struct c*Alloc_Var_C();
1 main.c     main            7     var = Alloc_Var_C();
2 sub.c      Alloc_Var_C     13    struct c *Alloc_Var_C() {
```
(Result area)

```
Find this C symbol:
Find this global definition:
Find functions called by this function:
Find functions calling this function:
Find this text string:
Change this text string:
Find this egrep pattern:
Find this file:
Find files #including this file:
Find all function definitions:
Find all symbol assignments:
```
(Command area)

FIGURE C.7 An example run of `cscope`.

C.3.2. Version Control – `Git`

What Is `Git`?

`Git` *(Global Information Tracker)*[4] is a source code control system originally developed by Linus Torvalds. Two well-known features of `Git` are high performance and distributed architecture. Because of its efficiency, currently hundreds of open source projects, including the Linux kernel and Google Android OS, are controlled by `Git`. `Git` provides a distributed control architecture. Each developer can decide when and how to branch a project by using `Git`.

How to `Git`

The first thing is to create a repository. A repository is a directory containing a source-controlled project. You can have a repository by either initializing a directory that holds the working project or cloning from an existing `Git`-controlled project. This can be done by the following commands:

- `git init project_directory`

or,

- `git clone git_controlled_url`

[4]Actually, the word Git is a British slang for "pig headed, think they are always correct, argumentative." Torvalds quipped: "I'm an egotistical bastard, and I name all my projects after myself. First Linux, now Git."

TABLE C.2 Important `git_controlled_url` Available in `Git`

Format	Description	Example of Git Checkout
local_path	The `Git` repository is on the `local _ path`.	Git clone /home/Bob/ project
https://host/path	The `Git` repository is controlled by a `Git`-aware web server.[5]	Git clone https://1.2.3.4/ project.git
https://host/path	Same as above, but with SSL encryption.	Git clone git://1.2.3.4/ project.git
ssh://user@host/remote_ path	The `Git` repository is stored on `host/ remote _ path`, and it can be accessed through a secure tunnel using the SSH protocol.[6]	Git clone ssh:// Bob@1.2.3.4/home/Bob/ project
git://host/remote_path	The `Git` repository is stored on the remote host via the Git protocol.[7]	Git clone https://1.2.3.4/ project.git

where the `git_controlled_url` is the location of a `Git` repository hosted by other developers. Some important formats of `git_controlled_url` are listed in Table C.2.

After creating a repository, you can create new files or modify existing files under the repository. Before committing changes, you may want to examine the differences between the last version and the current working project. This can be done by the following command:

- `git diff`

To commit your changes, you can execute the following commands:

- `git add.; git commit -m "your log messages"`

Typically, a project leaves several branches during development. Some branches implement experimental ideas, some satisfy different requirements for different

[5]Read the `Git User's Manual` on the `Git` homepage to learn how to integrate your Web server with `Git`.
[6]`SSH` *(Secure Shell)* is a network protocol that provides an authenticated and encrypted channel between two networking devices. It is built-in on the most common Linux distributions like Fedora. To enable it, you might need to reconfigure your firewall settings, allowing the incoming traffic access to port 22, and start up its daemon, `sshd`.
[7]The easiest way to support the `Git` protocol is to run a Git daemon by the command: "Git daemon."

customers, and some are milestones. Creating a new branch in `Git` is done by the command:

- `git branch new_branch_name`

Listing existing branches can be done by the command:

- `git branch`

Note that the current active branch is marked with an asterisk and the default branch name is `master`. Switching between branches can be done by

- `git checkout branch_name`

Merging a branch with the current active branch is the following command:

- `git merge branch_name`

If your project was cloned from an existing open source project, it is time to contribute your changes to the open source community. `Git` provides several ways for codevelopers to merge their repositories. The simplest way is to send back source-code patches by e-mail. Each patch represents the differences between one version and its successive version. `Git` uses the following command to generate a series of patches starting from the cloning time to the latest version you committed.

- `git format-patch origin`

In fact, the patch files are formatted as e-mail files, so they can be sent directly to other developers by e-mail client. The receiver uses the command to import patches:

- `git am *.patch`

Example

Although `Git` can automatically merge the source codes of two branches, it is still not smart enough to merge a conflict caused by different modifications over the same code segment. Unfortunately, this is a common case, especially in a hotly developing project. Luckily, the manual merge procedure is simple enough to be learned by everyone.

Consider this case: Two branches modify the same function with different means. One branch, say bonjour_version, specifies the string "`Bonjour!\n`" to the variable, `str`. The second branch, say goodday_version, modifies the same variable, but associates it with the string "`Good day!\n`." When one wants to merge the two branches, a conflict arises.

To help resolve such conflicts, `Git` encloses the conflict code segment with three lines: <<<<<<<, =======, and >>>>>>>. The code segment within the less-than symbols and the equals is the source belonging to the current branch, and the code segment within the equals and the greater-than symbols is the source of the other branch. You can easily find out the differences, resolve the conflict by editing the source code, and then successfully commit the correct version. This example is illustrated in Figure C.8.

```
$ git branch                                                        } Current branch is
  bonjour_version                                                   } "goodday_version"
*goodday_version
  master
$ git merge bonjour_version                                         } Failed to merge two branches
Auto-merging sub.c                                                  } at the first time
CONFLICT (content): Merge conflict in sub.c
Automatic merge failed; fix conflicts and then commit the result.
$ head -13 sub.c
#include <stdio.h>
#include <string.h>
#include <stdlib.h>

#include "incl.h"

void printHello()
{
<<<<<<< HEAD                                                        }
        char *str = "Good day!\n";                                  }
=======                                                             } Here is the conflict
        char *str = "Bonjour!\n";                                   }
>>>>>>> bonjour_version                                             }
$ vi sub.c                                                          <-- Resolve the conflict manually
$ git add . ; git commit-m "a merged version"                       <-- Successfully merge
[goodday_version 626937e] a merged version
```

FIGURE C.8 An example of `Git` conflict requiring manual merge.

Tips

- `CVS (Concurrent Versions System)` is another source code control system, much like the once-popular `RCS (Revision Control System)`. Unlike `Git`, `CVS` is centralized; that is, there is a central database storing the whole project. Every developer can check out his own copy of the tree into his home directory. Under `CVS`, multiple developers work on the same project at the same time.
- `SVN` *(Subversion)* is a successor to `CVS`, so its syntax looks like that in the original `CVS`. The major advantage of `SVN` compared to `CVS` is that it supports the transactions. Thus, when committing multiple files, by the principle of "all or nothing" `SVN` assures that either all files are successfully committed or none of them are changed.

C.4 PROFILING

After coding and debugging, your program may now start doing its duty. How do you know whether the program runs efficiently? Without profiling, you probably need a stopwatch to evaluate it. Profiling records the statistics of a running program. A developer can therefore measure the performance of his implementation by analyzing the profiling report. In this section, two profiling tools, one for the user-space applications and the other for the kernel, are introduced.

C.4.1 Profiler – gprof

What Is gprof?

GNU profiler, gprof, allows you to profile a running program. It reports the profiling results into two tables, the *flat profile* and the *call graph*. The flat profile reports the invoked count and the time spent on each function. The call graph further details the time spent and the relation of a function to its descendants. Examining the gprof results enables you to find bottlenecks and bad design in programs.

How to gprof

To use gprof, your program must be recompiled with a special gcc flag, -pg so that gcc can instrument the monitoring and recording routines into the program. For example, to enable the profiling feature of a program named prog, the command would be

```
gcc -pg -o prog main.c
```

Then your program is run as usual to collect the profiling results. The results will be stored in the file gmon.out. After the program terminates, you can read the results by executing the command

- gprof -b program_name

where the flag -b tells gprof not to show the verbose explanations.

Example

The example shown in Figure C.9 demonstrates the results reported by gprof. There are three functions, funcA, funcB, and funcC used by the main routine. As reported in the flat profile, funcA takes the most time, about 3.38 seconds, and funcB is repeatedly called 101 times. Among the 101 calls, the call graph further shows that 100 of those calls are from funcC.

Tips

- To profile a daemon program, you have to turn off its daemon feature, because the profiling results are only available when a program is terminated. In most cases you can do it by finding the function call, daemon, and then commenting it out.
- Two other well-known profilers in Linux are LTTng (lttng.org) and OProfile (oprofile.sourceforge.net). LTTng needs to instrument the source code of a target program with a profiling API provided by LTTng or callback functions written by testers. OProfile can profile a program without modifying its source code. Unlike the compiler-assistance technique used by gprof, OProfile benefits from a kernel driver. The driver that comes with OProfile collects the statistics periodically. The advantage of OProfile is that it can profile across multiple programs without any source code—it is called a system-wide profiler—whereas the disadvantages are its system overhead and its need for super-user privileges.

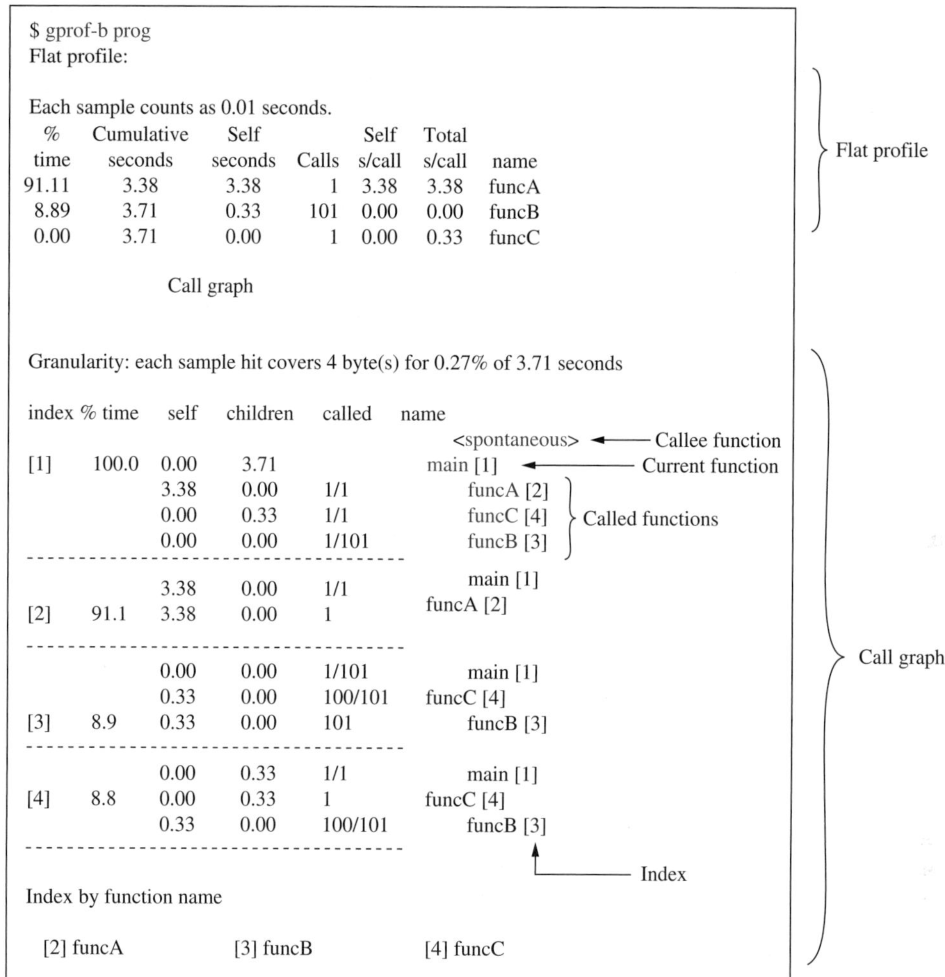

```
$ gprof-b prog
Flat profile:

Each sample counts as 0.01 seconds.
  %    Cumulative    Self            Self    Total
 time    seconds    seconds  Calls  s/call  s/call   name
91.11      3.38       3.38       1   3.38    3.38    funcA
 8.89      3.71       0.33     101   0.00    0.00    funcB
 0.00      3.71       0.00       1   0.00    0.33    funcC

                Call graph


Granularity: each sample hit covers 4 byte(s) for 0.27% of 3.71 seconds

index % time   self   children   called    name
                                               <spontaneous>
[1]    100.0   0.00     3.71                 main [1]
               3.38     0.00      1/1            funcA [2]
               0.00     0.33      1/1            funcC [4]
               0.00     0.00      1/101          funcB [3]
-----------------------------------------------
               3.38     0.00      1/1            main [1]
[2]     91.1   3.38     0.00      1          funcA [2]

-----------------------------------------------
               0.00     0.00      1/101          main [1]
               0.33     0.00      100/101    funcC [4]
[3]      8.9   0.33     0.00      101            funcB [3]
-----------------------------------------------
               0.00     0.33      1/1            main [1]
[4]      8.8   0.00     0.33      1          funcC [4]
               0.33     0.00      100/101        funcB [3]
-----------------------------------------------

Index by function name

  [2] funcA               [3] funcB               [4] funcC
```


FIGURE C.9 Screenshot of `gprof`.

C.4.2 Kernel Profiler – `kernprof`

What Is `kernprof`?

`Kernprof` is a set of Linux kernel patches and tools, provided as open source by SGI (Silicon Graphics International). With `kernprof`, system analysts can see the time spent on each kernel function and find bottlenecks in the kernel, similar to what `gprof` does for user-space applications.

How to `kernprof`

To enable `kernprof`, your kernel source has to be patched. Therefore, you have to download the patch matching your kernel version on the Webpage of `kernprof` first. After patching the kernel, you can now recompile and install the `kernprof`-patched kernel. Next, a character device, which provides the communication channel between its user-space control program (named `kernprof`) and the patched kernel, has to be created manually. This can be done by the following command:

- `mknod /dev/profile c 190 0`

where the value 0 represents the first CPU of your system. Similarly, you can create a character device for each of the remaining CPUs.

There are several profiling modes provided by `kernprof`. The PC (Program Counter) sampling mode periodically collects the information of executing functions, and its results are like the flat profile generated by `gprof`. The call graph mode constructs a call graph, which is useful for kernel tracing. The annotated call graph mode mixes the above two modes, so the results are matched to the default output in `gprof`.

Unlike `gprof`, which collects information during the life of a program, you have to explicitly start up and turn off `kernprof` yourself by issuing commands. For example, to start up `kernprof` in the annotated call graph mode, you can specify the command

- `kernprof -b -t acg`

where the flag, `-t acg`, represents the annotated call graph mode. To stop `kernprof` and generate a `gprof`-readable result, i.e., `gnome.out`, the following commands are used:

- `kernprof -e`
- `kernprof -g`

Finally, you can use `gprof` to read the results by issuing,

- `gprof file_of_vmlinux`

Tips

- A `kernprof`-enabled kernel would slow down your Linux. According to the FAQ of `kernprof`, it might decrease system performance by over 15%. So one may prepare two kernels, a `kernprof`-enabled one and the normal one, and switch among them using the boot loader.
- Besides `LTTng` and `OProfile` motioned previously, `Kernel Function Tracer` (`KFT`, elinux.org/Kernel_Function_Trace) is another alternative famous for Linux kernel profiling. `LTTng` and `KFT` need a kernel patch, as `kernprof` does, before profiling, while `OProfile` is presented as a kernel driver and a user-space daemon. Therefore, it can be loaded and executed dynamically without tainting the kernel source.

C.5 EMBEDDING

Porting your project to an embedded system could be much harder than developing it on the desktop. The first and perhaps the most important design goal is trimming the code size because embedded systems have limited resources. Besides, you probably need a toolchain, i.e., the cross-compiler and libraries, to compile and link programs for specific target architectures, and `to` prepare the root file system. The file system contains the "`/`" root directory and all required files and directories for booting, such as the `/bin`, `/etc`, and `/dev` directories. There are open source projects to help you to build a tiny enough embedded Linux. This section discusses how to accelerate the porting effort using the space-optimized common programs (so-called utilities), the lightweight toolchain, and the embedded root file system.

C.5.1 Tiny Utilities – `busybox`

What Is `busybox`?

Dozens of essential utilities are required for a running Linux application. However, many of them have the common routines like string copy, rarely used functions like on-demand help, and unnecessary documents like operating manuals. It is good to reduce the program size by removing them. `Busybox` integrates many common and essential utilities into one single space-optimized program.

How to `busybox`

Because `busybox` is highly configurable, compiling a customized version is very easy. First, you can use the command

- `make menuconfig`

to select the utilities you need and disable the unwanted ones. In particular, on the screen of `menuconfig`, you can use the `UP` and `DOWN` keys to move the cursor, the `Enter` key to select submenus, the `SPACE` key to select/de select an option, and choose the `Exit` option to save and quit a submenu or the configuration. Figure C.10 is the screenshot of `menuconfig`.

Next, type

- `make`

to compile the `busybox`, which will produce the executable program, named `busybox`, under the current directory. `Busybox` behaves as different utilities by first checking its program name while executing, so you have to construct a symbolic link of each utility name to the `busybox`. For example, if the utility `find` is replaced by `busybox`, the symbolic link

```
find->busybox
```

must exist. Thus, installing `busybox` involves copying the program to your embedded system and preparing the symbolic links.

Tip

- Although configuring and compiling `busybox` is easy, the hardest part is to select what is really essential in your embedded system. One shortcut is to observe the existing root file system of an embedded Linux system, e.g., the root file system built by `buildroot` in the next subsection.

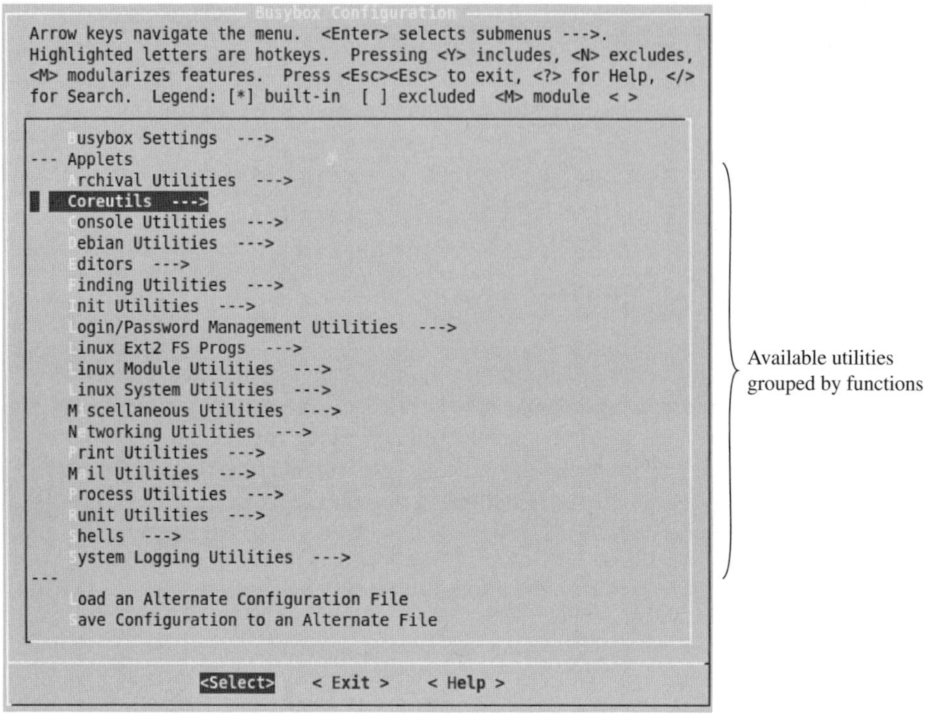

```
Busybox Configuration
Arrow keys navigate the menu.  <Enter> selects submenus --->.
Highlighted letters are hotkeys.  Pressing <Y> includes, <N> excludes,
<M> modularizes features.  Press <Esc><Esc> to exit, <?> for Help, </>
for Search.  Legend: [*] built-in  [ ] excluded  <M> module  < >

    usybox Settings  --->
--- Applets
    rchival Utilities  --->
    Coreutils  --->
    onsole Utilities  --->
    ebian Utilities  --->
    ditors  --->
    inding Utilities  --->
    nit Utilities  --->
    ogin/Password Management Utilities  --->
    inux Ext2 FS Progs  --->
    inux Module Utilities  --->
    inux System Utilities  --->
   M scellaneous Utilities  --->
   N tworking Utilities  --->
    rint Utilities  --->
   M il Utilities  --->
    rocess Utilities  --->
    unit Utilities  --->
    hells  --->
    ystem Logging Utilities  --->
---
    oad an Alternate Configuration File
    ave Configuration to an Alternate File

        <Select>    < Exit >    < Help >
```

Available utilities grouped by functions

FIGURE C.10 Configuring the `busybox`.

C.5.2 Embedding Development – `uClibc` and `buildroot`

What Is `uClibc` and What Is `buildroot`?

The GNU C library, `glibc`, is the most common C library used for a Linux desktop or server system. It is designed to be compatible with all kinds of C standards and legacy systems, although the compatibility increases its size. It also offers many ways to optimize execution speed, though some of them require more memory space. `uClibc` is the library completely redesigned for embedded systems. Therefore, the size of a program linked with `uClibc` can be much smaller than with `glibc`.

A C library needs a corresponding toolchain, i.e., cross compiler and system software utilities, to help a program linking with it. The `uClibc` development team states that the easiest way to prepare all of them at one time is to use the `buildroot` project. `Buildroot` is a set of `makefile`'s that can automatically download required packages from the Internet to build a customized root file system. By default, it compiles and links the program with `uClibc`. Moreover, it utilizes the `busybox` presented in Subsection C.5.1. As a result, the space requirement of the file system constructed by `buildroot` is small and suitable for embedded systems.

How to `buildroot`

`Buildroot` is as highly configurable as the `busybox` project. Their compiling procedures are the same. Thus, we issue the command `make  menuconfig` to

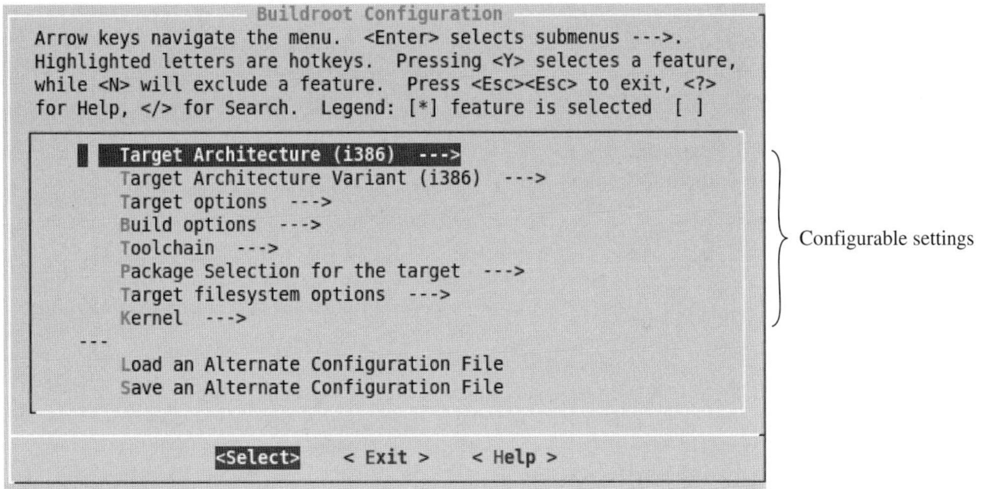

FIGURE C.11 Configuring the `buildroot`.

configure settings, and type `make` to compile `buildroot`. The resulting image of the file system built by the `buildroot` project resides in the directory `binaries/uclibc/`. Figure C.11 is the screenshot of its `menuconfig`.

Tip

- Here is a method to verify the functionality of a built root file system,[8] if the target machine has the same architecture as the development platform. The first step is to locate the directory of the compiled root file system. Near the end of `buildroot` compilation, a variable, `rootdir`, is the one we look for. Assume the directory is named `directory_root`, i.e., `rootdir=directory_root`. Then, type `chroot directory_root sh`, which changes the root directory to the compiled one. Then you can execute any program just as it is already installed on the target machine. At any time, you can use the command `exit` to change back to your original root.

FURTHER READINGS

Related Books

The following books cover most of the topics mentioned in this appendix. Unfortunately, no book written for profiling is good enough to suggest.

- R. Mecklenburg, *Managing Projects with GNU Make (Nutshell Handbooks)*, 3rd edition, O'Reilly Media, 2009.

[8]For example, you might want to check whether a shell script can correctly call your program, `/bin/your_prog`. One way is to put everything on the target machine and then really launch the script to verify its execution flow. The other way provided in this tip is to launch it on the development platform.

- R. M. Stallman, R. Pesch, and S. Shebs, *Debugging with GDB: The GNU Source-Level Debugger,* 9th edition, Free Software Foundation, 2002.
- M. Bar and K. Fogel, *Open Source Development with CVS,* 3rd edition, Paraglyph, 2003.
- C. Pilato, B. Collins-Sussman, and B. Fitzpatrick, *Version Control with Subversion,* 2nd edition, O'Reilly Media, 2008.
- C. Hallinan, *Embedded Linux Primer: A Practical Real-World Approach,* Prentice Hall, 2006.

Online Links

Here we summarize the Web sites of all development tools covered in this appendix. These classic sites are likely to exist for years to come.

1. VIM (Vi IMproved), http://www.vim.org/
2. gedit, http://projects.gnome.org/gedit/
3. GCC, http://gcc.gnu.org/
4. GNU Make, http://www.gnu.org/software/make/make.html
5. GDB, http://sources.redhat.com/gdb/
6. DDD, http://www.gnu.org/manual/ddd/
7. kGDB, http://kgdb.sourceforge.net/
8. cscope, http://cscope.sourceforge.net/
9. CVS, http://www.cvshome.org/
10. GNU gprof, http://www.cs.utah.edu/dept/old/texinfo/as/gprof.html
11. Kernprof, http://oss.sgi.com/projects/kernprof/
12. BusyBox, http://www.busybox.net/
13. uClibc, http://www.uclibc.org/
14. Buildroot, http://buildroot.uclibc.org/

Appendix D

Network Utilities

Both users and administrators of Linux systems often need tools to help them to *understand* their systems. For example, one may need to check the IP address of a host or examine the traffic statistics of a network interface. On the other hand, in addition to the development tools presented in Appendix C, developers may also need tools to *observe* the network to facilitate the debugging process. Before and after the development of a real system, one may need to simulate (or emulate) the system design and test the developed system. Collectively we call these tools network utilities. This appendix classifies these utilities into six categories: name-addressing, perimeter-probing, traffic-monitoring, benchmarking, simulating/emulating, and finally, hacking.

Section D.1 discusses how name-addressing helps in knowing who-is-who on the Internet using `host` to query through DNS, and acquiring local (e.g., LAN) who-is-who with the *Address Resolution Protocol* (`arp`) and the *Interface Configurator* (`ifconfig`). When a network does not work as expected, one should employ perimeter-probing discussed in Section D.2 to either `ping` for the availability of a remote host or `tracepath` for any network bottleneck. Once troubleshooting is done, packets should begin to flow. Section D.3 presents tools for traffic monitoring. Packets can be dumped for examining of header and payload in great details with `tcpdump` or `Wireshark`. Some useful network statistics and information can be collected using `netstat`.

As performance is a critical issue, a connected network is only considered workable when its performance has been measured. Hence, Section D.4 introduces the benchmarking tool, *Test TCP* (`ttcp`) for host-to-host throughput analysis. On the other hand, often it is too costly and risky to develop a system without evaluating the design first. In this case, either simulation by *Network Simulator* (`ns`) or emulation by `NIST Net`, discussed in Section D.5, should be used. Finally, in Section D.6, the hacking methodology using exploit-scanning with `Nessus` is briefly described; this might be controversial, but it is placed here as a complement to Chapter 8.

D.1 NAME-ADDRESSING

The first step in communication usually is to resolve the name of the peer into the IP address or the IP address of the peer into the MAC address. The former is the Internet's who-is-who which, as discussed in Chapter 6, can be done through Domain Name System

(DNS), while the latter is the local who-is-who which, as examined in Chapter 4, can be done through Address Resolution Protocol (ARP). This section discusses how name-addressing tools help in knowing who-is-who on the Internet and on LANs.

D.1.1 Internet's Who-Is-Who – `host`

What Is `host`?

`Host` is a program that enables users to query the IP addresses corresponding to a domain name, or vice versa. It implements the DNS protocol to communicate with a local DNS server, which in turn queries other DNS servers that have the mapping.

How to `host`

Using `host` is straightforward. To query the IP addresses of a domain name, just execute

- `host domain_name`

Similarly, looking up the domain name of an IP address can be done by

- `host ip_address`

Example

In the example shown in Figure D.1, we want to look up the IP addresses of www.google.com. `Host` tells us that www.google.com has an alias name, www.l.google.com, and the name is bound to six IP addresses.

Tip

- By default, `host` issues the queries to the system-configured local DNS server. You can also specify a domain name server, say `target_dns`, by
  - `host query_name target_dns`

D.1.2 LAN's Who-Is-Who – `arp`

What Is `arp`?

The communication of upper-layer applications is over the IP layer, while the actual packet delivery inside a LAN is based on the MAC addresses. `Arp` is the program that

```
$ host www.google.com
www.google.com is an alias for www.l.google.com.
www.l.google.com has address 74.125.153.103
www.l.google.com has address 74.125.153.104
www.l.google.com has address 74.125.153.105
www.l.google.com has address 74.125.153.106
www.l.google.com has address 74.125.153.147
www.l.google.com has address 74.125.153.99
```

FIGURE D.1 An example of using `host`.

helps users to look up the MAC address of an IP address or vice versa. Administrators can also use `arp` to manage the system-wide ARP table, such as adding a static ARP entry.

The inside of the `arp` program is through the ARP. Basically, `arp` broadcasts an ARP request message on the LAN to query the MAC address of a specific IP address. The device with the IP address sends a unicast ARP response to the querying host. The results could be dynamically cached in the system-wide ARP table of the querying host to accelerate the response time for future queries.

How to `arp`

Using `arp` is also straightforward. To query the MAC address of an IP address, you can specify the command

- `arp -a IP_address`

Adding an entry in the ARP table is done by

- `arp -s IP_address MAC_address`

And remove an entry with

- `arp -d IP_address`

Finally, you can browse the system-wide ARP table by just typing

- `arp`

Example

Figure D.2 demonstrates the browsing results of the system-wide ARP table. On the table, we can see that there are two entries, 88-router.cis.nctu.edu.tw and 140.113.88.140, bound for the network interface, `eth0`. The flag `C` indicates that this is a cached entry (not a static entry) on the system.

Tip

- When a host on your LAN changes its network adaptor, you might not be able to access it immediately due to the ARP cache table. To solve it, you can either wait for the cache timeout or use `arp -d` to remove the cached entry described above.

D.1.3 Who Am I – `ifconfig`

What Is `ifconfig`*?*

`Ifconfig` (InterFace CONFIGurator) is a program that allows users to query the IP address, MAC address, and statistics of network interfaces. Administrators can also use it to set the IP address and enable/disable a network interface.

```
$ arp
Address                  HWtype  HWaddress          Flags Mask    Iface
88-router.cs.nctu.edu.t  ether   00:19:06:e8:0e:4b  C             eth0
140.113.88.140           ether   00:16:35:ae:f5:6c  C             eth0
```

FIGURE D.2 An example of using `arp`.

```
$ ifconfig
eth0      Link encap:Ethernet  HWaddr 00:1D:92:F1:8A:E9
          inet addr:192.168.1.1  Bcast:192.168.88.255  Mask:255.255.255.0
          inet6 addr: fe80::21d:92ff:fef1:8ae9/64  Scope:Link
          UP BROADCAST RUNNING MULTICAST  MTU:1500  Metric:1
          RX packets: 1147154 errors:0 dropped:0 overruns:0 frame:0
          TX packets:296781 errors:0 dropped:0 overruns:0 carrier:0
          collisions:0 txqueuelen:100
          RX bytes:312608565 (298.1 MiB)  TX bytes: 110166934 (105.0 MiB)
          Memory:fe940000-fe960000
```

FIGURE D.3 An example of using `ifconfig`.

How to `ifconfig`

Using `ifconfig` is straightforward. To query the settings of network interfaces, you can specify the command

- `ifconfig [interface_name]`,

where the `interface_name` is an optional argument which can be used to specify a network interface. Without any argument, `ifconfig` will show the settings of current active interfaces. Administrators can use

- `ifconfig <interface_name> inet IP_address`

to set the IP address of a network interface, and use

- `ifconfig <interface_name> down/up`

to disable/enable an interface.

Example

Figure D.3 is an example of using `ifconfig`. The result shows that the system has one interface, named `eth0`. Its IP address is 192.168.1.1 and MAC address is 00:1D:92:F1:8A:E9. The interface is currently active—note the UP flag—and has transmitted 296781 packets (or about 105 MB). The detailed meaning of the remaining output can be found from the online manual.

Tip

- On the Microsoft Windows platform, there is a similar command line program, `ipconfig`.

D.2 PERIMETER-PROBING

When a network does not work as expected, one could employ perimeter-probing tools to check host availability or find network bottlenecks.

D.2.1 Ping for Living – `ping`

What Is `ping`?

`Ping` can examine the availability of the path from the host to a target machine. It uses two messages defined in the Internet Control Message Protocol (ICMP). The first message is the ICMP echo request, which is sent by the host to the target. When receiving the request, the target responds with an ICMP echo reply message to the host. The host can therefore know the availability and calculate the time interval between request and reply.

How to `ping`

Try the following command

- `ping target_machine`

to check the host availability between your system and the target. Press `Ctrl-C` to terminate the examination and obtain a summarized report.

Example

The example shown in Figure D.4 exhibits the `ping` results. By reading the results, we can know the packet loss rate and the response time, including minimum, average, and maximum response time, to the target 192.168.1.2.

Tip

- By default, `ping` sends a request every second. You can adjust it by specifying the flag, `-i`, e.g.,

  `ping -i 10 192.168.1.2,`

  which issues an ICMP echo request every 10 seconds.

D.2.2 Find the Way – `tracepath`

What Is `tracepath`?

Using `ping`, you might find that the packet loss rate to a target is abnormally high or the response time is slow. To find the bottleneck in the path between your host and the target, `tracepath` is the tool to use.

```
$ ping 192.168.1.2
PING 192.168.1.2 (192.168.1.2) 56(84) bytes of data.
64 bytes from 192.168.1.2: icmp_seq=1 ttl=128 time=2.01 ms
64 bytes from 192.168.1.2: icmp_seq=2 ttl=128 time=1.90 ms
64 bytes from 192.168.1.2: icmp_seq=3 ttl=128 time=1.96 ms
^C
--- 192.168.1.2 ping statistics ---
3 packets transmitted, 3 received, 0% packet loss, time 2990ms
rtt min/avg/max/mdev = 1.909/1.962/2.017/0.044 ms
```

Report for each iteration (the three "64 bytes from" lines)

Summarized report (the last two lines)

FIGURE D.4 An example of using `ping`.

`Tracepath` utilizes the time to live (TTL) field in the IP header well. It sends a UDP/IP query message in which TTL is set to 1, so the nearest router will immediately respond to the source with an ICMP time exceeded. The source can therefore calculate the round trip time (RTT) to the nearest router. Similarly, `tracepath` steps up the TTL in a query message to measure the RTTs of additional routers. With those RTTs, users can find the bottleneck on the path from the source to the target. `Tracepath` can also discover the maximum transmission unit (MTU) in a path.

How to `tracepath`

Using `tracepath` is easy. To examine the path to a target machine, you can simply use the command

- `tracepath target_machine`

You can add a flag, `-l pktlen`, to set the size of the initial query message. `Tracepath` adjusts the message length automatically when encountering message-too-long rejections bouncing back from intermediate routers. An optional /`port` argument can be appended after the `target_machine` to specify the target port number in the UDP query messages. In some versions of `tracepath`, it is by default 44444, and in others it is chosen randomly. Some routers, unfortunately, only respond to a query message with a target port ranging from 33434 to 33534, which are settings in the classic `traceroute` utility. Therefore we suggest that you explicitly specify a port number (33434 is a good magic number) when you use the utility.

Example

Figure D.5 shows the results coming from `tracepath` to www.google.com. The round trip time between the source and each intermediate router (and the target) is displayed as one line in the results. At the beginning, `tracepath` issued a 2000-byte query message. The first hop denied it and asked `tracepath` to use

```
$ tracepath -l 2000 www.google.com/33434
 1:  Stanley.cs.nctu.edu.tw (140.113.88.181)          0.048ms  pmtu 1500
 1:  88-router.cs.nctu.edu.tw (140.113.88.254)        1.904ms
 1:  88-router.cs.nctu.edu.tw (140.113.88.254)        2.589ms
 2:  140.113.0.198 (140.113.0.198)                    0.824ms
 3:  140.113.0.166 (140.113.0.166)                    0.753ms  asymm 4
 4:  140.113.0.74 (140.113.0.74)                      0.543ms  asymm 5
 5:  140.113.0.105 (140.113.0.105)                    1.096ms
 6:  Nctu-NonLegal-address (203.72.36.2)              5.227ms
 7:  TCNOC-R76-VLAN480-HSINCHU.IX.kbtelecom.net (203.187.9.233)  5.090ms
 8:  TPNOC3-C65-G2-1-TCNOC.IX.kbtelecom.net (203.187.3.77)  23.713ms
 9:  TPNOC3-P76-10G2-1-C65.IX.kbtelecom.net (203.187.23.98)  10.498ms
10:  72.14.219.65 (72.14.219.65)                      44.223ms  asymm 11
11:  209.85.243.30 (209.85.243.30)                    6.663ms  asymm 12
12:  209.85.243.23 (209.85.243.23)                    6.603ms  asymm 13
13:  72.14.233.130 (72.14.233.130)                    14.260ms
14:  ty-in-f99.1e100.net (74.125.153.99)              6.802ms  reached
     Resume: pmtu 1500 hops 14 back 51
```

FIGURE D.5 An example of using `tracepath`.

1500 bytes, i.e., the message "pmtu 1500" in the first line. The 1500-byte messages are acceptable to all remaining hops. Finally, the message "asymm #" represents a possible asymmetric routing path found by `tracepath`.

Tips

- `Traceroute` is an alternative well known in the Unix world. Due to security concerns, however, some Linux distributions, like Ubuntu, do not include it.
- `Tracert` is a similar utility in the Windows platform. Instead of UDP, `tracert` uses ICMP Echo Request as its query messages.

D.3 TRAFFIC-MONITORING

The implementation of a networking protocol needs to be verified on the real networks. This section introduces tools for traffic monitoring. Packets can be dumped to examine their headers and payloads in great detail, and some useful network statistics and information can be collected.

D.3.1 Dump Raw Data – `tcpdump`

What Is `tcpdump`?

`Tcpdump` is the most popular command-line sniffer for enabling privileged users to dump traffic received on a network interface. The dumped traffic can be printed on the console instantly or saved in files to be analyzed later. The power of `tcpdump` comes from using the `libpcap` library, which provides a programming interface for capturing traffic. A Windows-platform project, `WinDump`, is the porting of `tcpdump`.

How to `tcpdump`

To capture everything, you can just type the command

- `tcpdump`

and press `Ctrl-C` to terminate capturing. A more common way to use `tcpdump` is to assign filtering conditions so that only packets matching the conditions would be dumped. There are dozens of filter conditions that can be used by `tcpdump`. Here we introduce important conditions by using an example that might satisfy the most common capturing requirement for protocol analysis. The scenario is like this: You want to record the flows whose source or destination IP address is `target_machine` and TCP port number is `target_port`. Suppose the `target_machine` is on the network interface, `eth0`. The `tcpdump` command will be

- `tcpdump -i eth0 -X -s 0 host target_machine and port 80`

where the argument `-i eth0` tells `tcpdump` to trace packets passing `eth0`, the arguments `-X -s 0` ask `tcpdump` to print full packets including header and payload, the expression `host target_machine` indicates only to capture the packets whose source or destination is `target_machine`, and similarly, the expression `port 80` limits the port number.

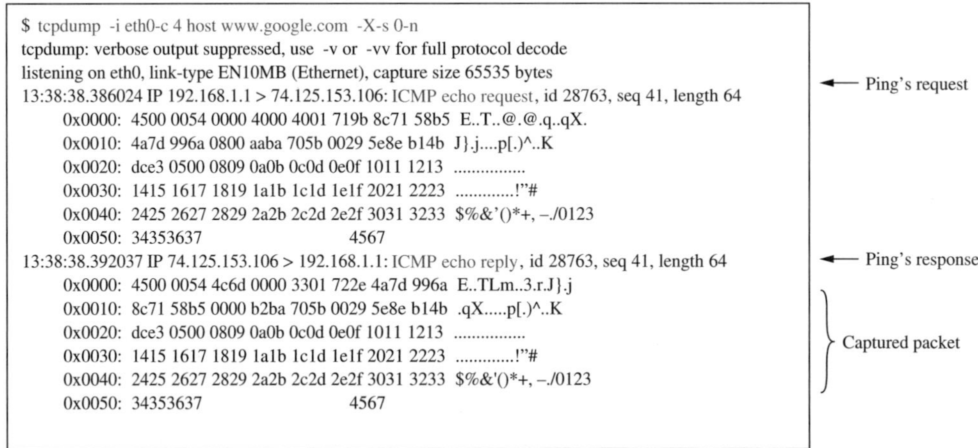

FIGURE D.6 An example of using `tcpdump`.

Example

Figure D.6 displays the results of tracing two `ping` iterations. To limit the capture to only four packets, you can specify the argument, `-c 4`. There are two columns in which to present a captured packet: The left is presented in hex characters, and the right is displayed as ASCII characters. Nonprintable characters will be replaced by dots.

D.3.2 GUI Sniffier – `Wireshark`

What Is `Wireshark`?

`Wireshark` is another sniffer featuring a GUI. `Ethereal` is its original name, and the project was renamed to `Wireshark` in 2006.

How to `Wireshark`

Starting capturing in `Wireshark` can be done by pressing the `Interfaces` button of the `Capture` submenu on the menu bar. You can also find the `Stop` button on that submenu.

The power of `Wireshark` comes from its friendly user interface. As shown in Figure D.7, there are four major areas in the main window of `Wireshark`. The first is the filter bar. You can set the filtering constraints by either typing the filtering rules directly or using the `Expression` button. The second area shows the captured packets. When the cursor points to an entry, its description, such as the MAC address, will be shown in the third area. Finally, the fourth area displays the full packet content.

D.3.3 Collect Network Statistics – `netstat`

What Is `netstat`?

`Netstat` is a command line tool that can show the connection status, statistics of protocol usage, and routing tables.

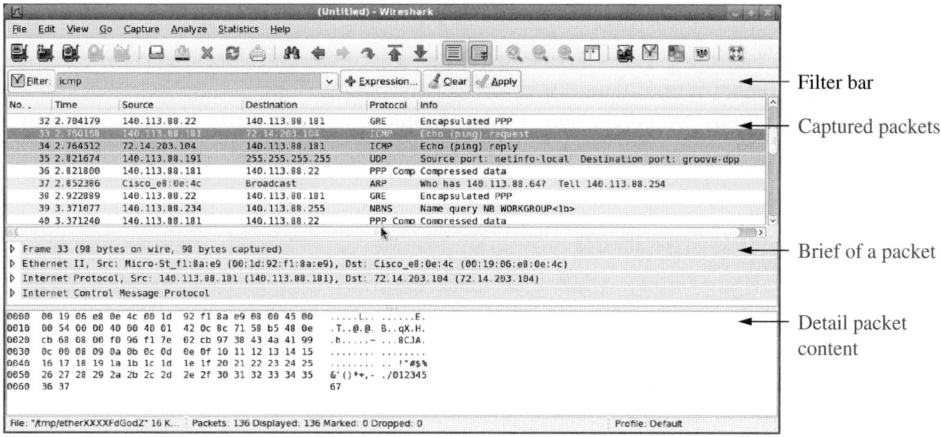

FIGURE D.7 Screenshot of `Wireshark`.

How to `netstat`

The first major function of `netstat` is to show the connection status. You can type the following command

- `netstat -an`

where the flag `-a` tells `netstat` to list the status of all protocols, and the flag `-n` shows the resulting address in numerical form, which is much faster than showing the domain name.

The second function of `netstat` is to display the statistics of protocol usage, which can be done by

- `netstat -s`

The final function is to present the routing tables by executing

- `netstat -rn`

Example

Figure D.8 shows the display of connection status. You can see that the machine is listening to many ports (with status `LISTEN`), such as 80 (the Apache Web service), and there is one connection from 192.168.1.2.

```
$ netstat -an
Active Internet connections (servers and established)
Proto Recv-Q Send-Q Local Address        Foreign Address        State
tcp        0      0 0.0.0.0:22           0.0.0.0:*              LISTEN
tcp        0      0 0.0.0.0:80           0.0.0.0:*              LISTEN
tcp        0      0 192.168.1.1:22       192.168.1.2:50910      ESTABLISHED
```

FIGURE D.8 Results of `netstat`.

Tip

- The connection status is also useful as a tool to detect hacking. For example, the signature of a denial of service (DoS) attack is thousands of non-`LISTEN` connections. You could also backtrace the source of attacks from the results of `netstat`.

D.4 BENCHMARKING

A connected network is only considered workable when it has been tested and measured. In this section, a common benchmarking tool for host-to-host throughput analysis is presented.

D.4.1 Host-to-Host Throughput – `ttcp`

What Is `ttcp`?

Test TCP, `ttcp`, is the benchmark program for testing the TCP and UDP throughput between two machines. Some routers now incorporate a version of this tool, enabling you to easily evaluate network performance.

How to `ttcp`

`Ttcp` has two modes, transmit mode and receive mode, which can be specified by the arguments `-t` and `-r`, respectively. The benchmarking process begins by launching `ttcp` at the receive mode on one machine, and then executing `ttcp` at the transmit mode on the other machine. You can feed a specific workload, which usually presents as a file, at the transmit-mode `ttcp`. The workload will be transmitted to the receive-mode `ttcp`. The statistics are shown in both at the end of the transmission. The results include the throughput and the number of I/O calls per second.

Example

In the example shown in Figure D.9, the sender reads the file, `test_file`, as the workload, and transmits it to the receiver at 192.168.1.1. The receiver does not save the received content but discards it directly, i.e., output to `/dev/null`. The results show that the sender requires 12,500 I/O calls to transmit 102,400,000 bytes, and the throughput measured by the receiver is 723,557.59 KB/sec.

Tips

- To generate a large demo file on the sender side, you can use the command `dd` as follows:
  - `dd if=/dev/zero of=demo_file size = <size_in_512_bytes>` where `if=/dev/zero` tells `dd` to create a file whose content is padding with zero, `of=demo_file` specifies the output file name, and `size_in_512_bytes` is a number indicating the size of the output file.
- To measure UDP throughput, you can specify the flag `-u` on calling `ttcp`.

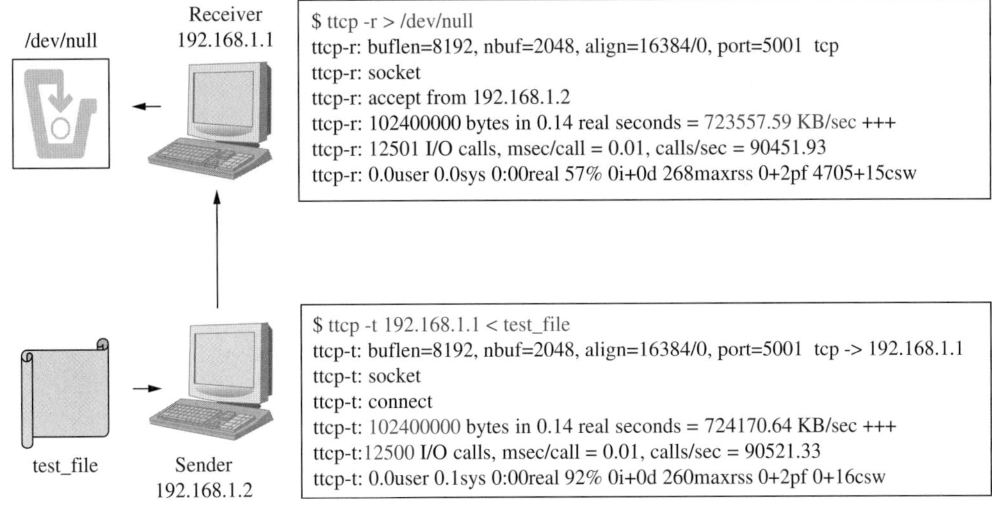

FIGURE D.9 An example of using `ttcp`.

D.5 SIMULATION AND EMULATION

Developing a real network could be costly. Before the development, a less-costly performance evaluation could be done. The simulation or emulation tools can be used to evaluate the design of a complete network or a network component.

D.5.1 Simulate the Network – `ns`

What Is `ns`?

`Ns`, which began in 1989 as a variant of the REAL (Realistic and Large) network simulator, is a collaborative simulation platform that provides common references and test suites to simulate packet-level discrete events from the link layer and up for both wired and wireless network conditions. A few of its powerful features include scenario generation, which creates a customized simulation environment, and visualization with the aid of `nam` (Network Animation). Notably, `ns` is implemented in two languages, C++ (for `ns` core) and `OTcl` (for `ns` configuration), to balance run-time efficiency and scenario-writing convenience. The project is well known as `ns-2`, because version 2 is its current stable release.

How to `ns`

Compiling `ns` is easy because the project has a script, `install`, that can automatically configure and compile it. Try the following commands to build `ns`:

- `cd ns-allinone-<version>;. /install`

where `<version>` is the version number of the `ns` project. As of June 2009, the most up-to-date version was 2.34. `Ns` simulates a network scenario, which is

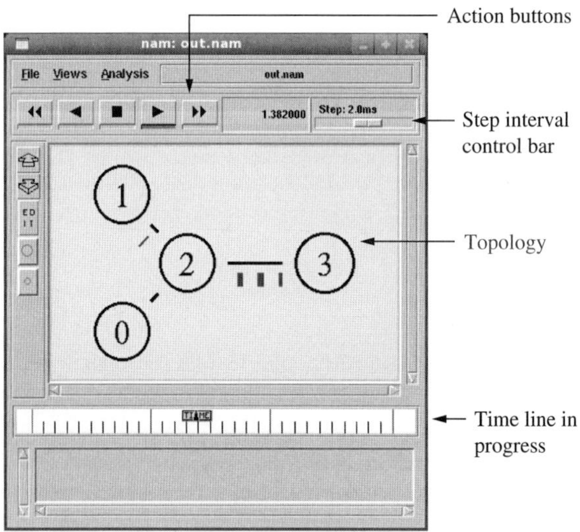

FIGURE D.10 Screenshot of `nam`.

written in the syntax of `OTcl` script. Assume you have written a scenario script, named `demo.tcl`. You can execute the following command to simulate it:

- `ns demo.tcl`

A scenario would contain network type, topology, nodes, traffic flows, and timing events. The simulation process could be recorded, so that it can be visualized animatedly by an `ns` utility, network animator (`nam`).

Example

Writing a network script with the `OTcl` script language is a bit complicated. Fortunately, there are dozens of example scripts with the `ns` project. You can read them in the directory:

- `ns-allinone-<version>/ ns-<version>/tcl/ex`

Figure D.10 demonstrates the simulation results of an example, `simple.tcl`. In this example, four nodes are wired, two traffic flows are scheduled, and the simulation process is recorded and visualized by `nam`.

D.5.2 Emulate the Network – `NIST Net`

What Is `NIST Net`?

A network emulator provides simple user entry of network parameters (e.g., delay, loss, jitter) for emulating a wide range of network types with a small lab setup. With `NIST Net`, you can observe quite a few network statistics, including packet delay, packet reordering (due to delay variance), packet loss, packet duplication, and bandwidth limitation. Figure D.11 illustrates the network architecture of `NIST Net`. The

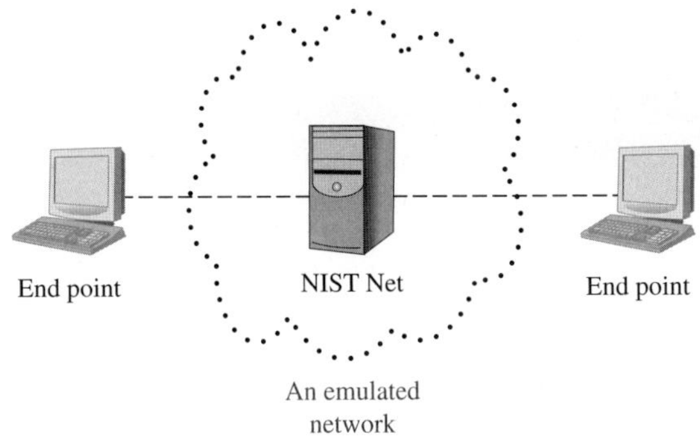

FIGURE D.11 The network architecture of `NIST Net`.

traffic flows of end points directly connecting to `NIST Net` could experience the impact of network parameters as if they were really passing through a large network.

How to `NIST Net`

`NIST Net` is composed of user-space tools and kernel modules. The kernel modules emulate the impact of network parameters on the data traffic. Although presented as kernel modules without the needs of kernel patch, the compilation of `NIST Net` still refers to the settings of the Linux kernel source, e.g., the content in `/usr/src/linux/.config`. Thus, a kernel source configuration is required before compiling the `NIST Net`. This can be done by typing the following command under the Linux kernel source directory:

- `make menuconfig`

After compiling and installing the `NIST Net` package, the kernel modules can be loaded with the command

- `Load.Nistnet`

Now you can use the command

- `xnistnet`

to configure and monitor the `NIST Net`.

Example

Figure D.12 demonstrates the screenshot of the `xnistnet` program. You can add a source/destination pair and modify its network parameters with the program. The traffic flow of the pair will experience the impact of network parameters, such as the delay, bandwidth, and drop rate, when passing through this machine.

Tip

- To relay data traffic, the `NIST Net` machine must be configured as routing-enabled. This can be done by setting the value to 1 on the file `/proc/sys/net/ipv4/ip_forward`. In other words, the command is
  - `echo 1 > /proc/sys/net/ipv4/ip_forward`

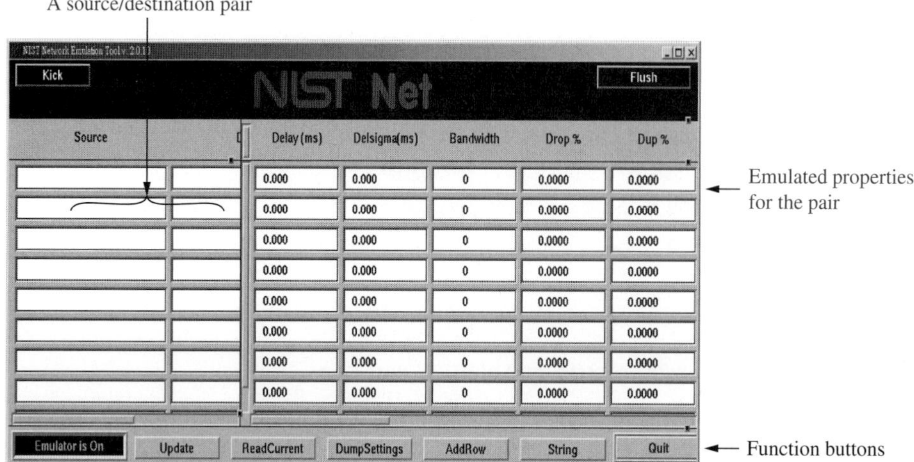

FIGURE D.12 Screenshot of `NIST Net`.

D.6 HACKING

Hacking methodology using exploit-scanning tools is presented in this section. A network administrator can use those tools to identify the vulnerabilities of the administered network.

D.6.1 Exploit Scanning – `Nessus`

What Is `Nessus`?

`Nessus` is one of the most popular exploit-scanning programs used in the Linux community. As shown in Figure D.13, `Nessus` is designed with a three-tiered architecture. The client is a GUI program that allows administrators to control and manage the `Nessus` daemon, `nessusd`. The exploiting methods and hacking database are

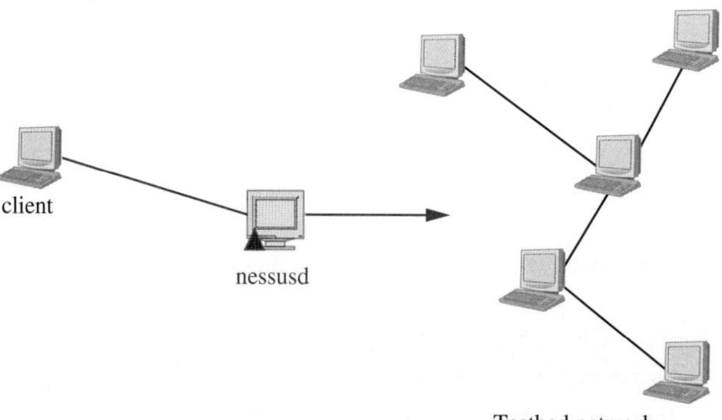

FIGURE D.13 The network architecture of `nessus`.

built into the Nessus daemon. The daemon also takes the responsibility of scanning the target network, collect scanning results, and reporting to the client.

How to Nessus

The source of Nessus is composed of four parts: nessus library, libnasl, nessus core, and the hacking database, called plugin in the Nessus world. To install Nessus, you have to download those parts from the homepage of Nessus, and compile and install them in turn. The next step is to execute the command

- nessus-mkcert

which prepares a certificate used in the communication between Nessus client and daemon.

After successful installation, you can start up the Nessus daemon, i.e., nessusd, and add the first valid Nessus administrator by executing the command

- nessus-adduser

Then you can execute the Nessus client, i.e., nessus, on the client machine, and connect the client to the daemon.

Example

To check the vulnerabilities of a target machine, a Nessus administrator first chooses some hacking methods using the Nessus client. He or she can press the Plugins button on the tab bar and select the available hacking methods on the tab window. A screenshot of the selection window is shown in Figure D.14. Next, he or

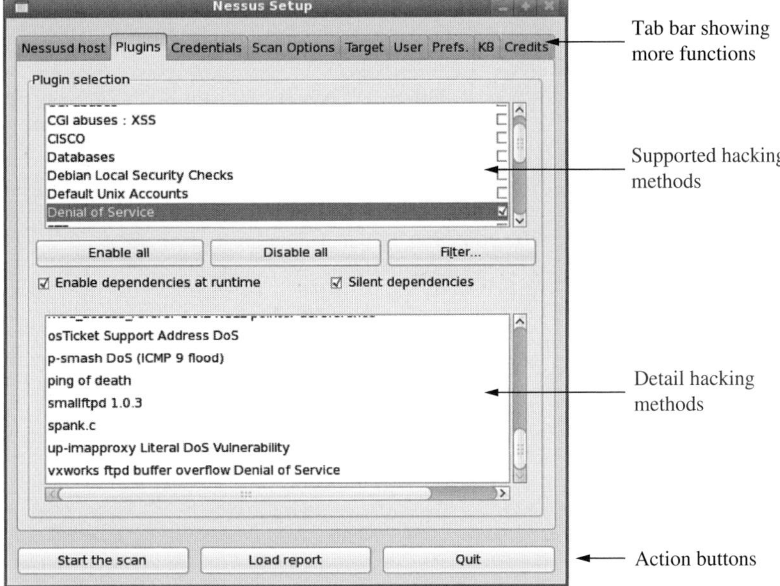

FIGURE D.14 Screenshot of Nessus 2.

she assigns the target machine on the `Target` tab window and presses the `Start the scan` button to start the scan. After scanning, a report window will pop up to report the scanning results.

Tips

- After installing the `Nessus's` dynamic link library, `libnasl`, you will need to refresh the system-wide library cache. This can be done by either rebooting or by using the following command:
  - `ldconfig /usr/local/lib`
- Be careful; some scanning methods might harm or crash the target system.
- Since the release of `Nessus 3`, Nessus was no longer open-sourced and was only released in binary executables. It is still free to use the latest version of `Nessus` in noncommercial organizations. A forked project called `OpenVAS` is open-sourced and under development.

FURTHER READINGS

Related Books

The following books cover most of the topics mentioned in this appendix. The first book tells you how to use GNU tools to manage networking. The second one provides hands-on instructions for Linux TCP/IP. The final book, though it was published in 1998, is still the classic book for learning network programming.

- Tobin Maginnis, *Sair Linux and GNU Certification, Level 1: Networking,* John Wiley & Sons, 2001.
- P. Eyler, *Networking Linux, a Practical Guide to TCP/IP,* New Riders, 2001.
- W. Richard Stevens, *UNIX Network Programming,* Prentice Hall, 1998.

Online Links

Here we summarize the Web sites of all network utilities covered in this appendix. Again, these classic sites are likely to exist for years to come.

1. arp and ifconfig, http://www.linuxfoundation.org/en/Net:Net-tools
2. host (a.k.a., bind9-host), https://www.isc.org/download
3. ping, http://directory.fsf.org/project/inetutils/
4. tracepath, http://www.skbuff.net/iputils
5. tcpdump, http://www.tcpdump.org/
6. Wireshark, http://www.wireshark.org/
7. ttcp, http://www.pcausa.com/Utilities/pcattcp.htm
8. WebBench 5.0, ftp://ftp.pcmag.com/benchmarks/webbench/
9. The Network Simulator - ns-2, http://www.isi.edu/nsnam/ns/
10. NIST Net, http://snad.ncsl.nist.gov/itg/nistnet/
11. Nessus, http://www.nessus.org/

Index

D

G

N

O

Q

U

V